The Colobines

Natural History, Behaviour and Ecological Diversity

The colobines are a group of Afroeurasian monkeys that exhibit extraordinary behavioural and ecological diversity. With long tails and diverse colourations, they are medium-sized primates, mostly arboreal, that are found in many different habitats, from rain forests and mountain forests to mangroves and savannah. Over the last two decades, our understanding of this group of primates has increased dramatically. This volume presents a comprehensive overview of the current research on colobine populations, including the range of biological, ecological, behavioural and societal traits they exhibit. It highlights areas where our knowledge is still lacking and outlines the current conservation status of colobine populations, exploring the threats to their survival. Bringing together international experts, this volume will aid future conservation efforts and encourage further empirical studies. It will be of interest to researchers and graduate students in primatology, biological anthropology and conservation science. Additional online resources can be found at www.cambridge.org/colobines.

Ikki Matsuda is Associate Professor at Chubu University Academy of Emerging Sciences, Adviser at the Japan Monkey Centre and specially appointed Associate Professor at the Wildlife Research Center of Kyoto University, Japan. His expertise in primate ecology, in particular of the proboscis monkey in Malaysia and black-and-white colobus in Uganda, is based on extensive fieldwork. He is the co-editor of *Primates in Flooded Habitats* (Cambridge University Press, 2019).

Cyril C. Grueter is a primatologist and biological anthropologist. He is Senior Lecturer at the University of Western Australia, Perth, and Adjunct Professor at the International Centre of Biodiversity and Primate Conservation, Dali University, China. He has been actively involved in research on snub-nosed monkeys in China since 2002, mountain gorillas in Rwanda since 2009 and chimpanzees and colobus monkeys in Rwanda since 2015.

Julie A. Teichroeb is a primate behavioural ecologist and Associate Professor at the University of Toronto Scarborough, Canada. She began studying wild white-thighed colobus in Ghana in 2000 and Rwenzori Angolan colobus in Uganda in 2013. She is the co-editor of *Primate Research and Conservation in the Anthropocene* (Cambridge University Press, 2019).

Cambridge Studies in Biological and Evolutionary Anthropology

Also available in the series

53. *Technique and Application in Dental Anthropology* Joel D. Irish and Greg C. Nelson (eds.) 978 0 521 87061 0
54. *Western Diseases: An Evolutionary Perspective* Tessa M. Pollard 978 0 521 61737 6
55. *Spider Monkeys: The Biology, Behavior and Ecology of the Genus Ateles* Christina J. Campbell (ed.) 978 0 521 86750 4
56. *Between Biology and Culture* Holger Schutkowski (ed.) 978 0 521 85936 3
57. *Primate Parasite Ecology: The Dynamics and Study of Host-Parasite Relationships* Michael A. Huffman and Colin A. Chapman (eds.) 978 0 521 87246 1
58. *The Evolutionary Biology of Human Body Fatness: Thrift and Control* Jonathan C. K. Wells 978 0 521 88420 4
59. *Reproduction and Adaptation: Topics in Human Reproductive Ecology* C. G. Nicholas Mascie-Taylor and Lyliane Rosetta (eds.) 978 0 521 50963 3
60. *Monkeys on the Edge: Ecology and Management of Long-Tailed Macaques and their Interface with Humans* Michael D. Gumert, Agustín Fuentes and Lisa Jones-Engel (eds.) 978 0 521 76433 9
61. *The Monkeys of Stormy Mountain: 60 Years of Primatological Research on the Japanese Macaques of Arashiyama* Jean-Baptiste Leca, Michael A. Huffman and Paul L. Vasey (eds.) 978 0 521 76185 7
62. *African Genesis: Perspectives on Hominin Evolution* Sally C. Reynolds and Andrew Gallagher (eds.) 978 1 107 01995 9
63. *Consanguinity in Context* Alan H. Bittles 978 0 521 78186 2
64. *Evolving Human Nutrition: Implications for Public Health* Stanley Ulijaszek, Neil Mann and Sarah Elton (eds.) 978 0 521 86916 4
65. *Evolutionary Biology and Conservation of Titis, Sakis and Uacaris* Liza M. Veiga, Adrian A. Barnett, Stephen F. Ferrari and Marilyn A. Norconk (eds.) 978 0 521 88158 6
66. *Anthropological Perspectives on Tooth Morphology: Genetics, Evolution, Variation* G. Richard Scott and Joel D. Irish (eds.) 978 1 107 01145 8
67. *Bioarchaeological and Forensic Perspectives on Violence: How Violent Death is Interpreted from Skeletal Remains* Debra L. Martin and Cheryl P. Anderson (eds.) 978 1 107 04544 6

68. *The Foragers of Point Hope: The Biology and Archaeology of Humans on the Edge of the Alaskan Arctic* Charles E. Hilton, Benjamin M. Auerbach and Libby W. Cowgill (eds.) 978 1 107 02250 8
69. *Bioarchaeology: Interpreting Behavior from the Human Skeleton, second Ed.* Clark Spencer Larsen 978 0 521 83869 6 & 978 0 521 54748 2
70. *Fossil Primates* Susan Cachel 978 1 107 00530 3
71. *Skeletal Biology of the Ancient Rapanui (Easter Islanders)* Vincent H. Stefan and George W. Gill (eds.) 978 1 107 02366 6
72. *Demography and Evolutionary Ecology of Hadza Hunter-Gatherers* Nicholas Blurton Jones 978 1 107 06982 4
73. *The Dwarf and Mouse Lemurs of Madagascar: Biology, Behavior and Conservation Biogeography of the Cheirogaleidae* Shawn M. Lehman, Ute Radespiel and Elke Zimmermann (eds.) 978 1 107 07559 7
74. *The Missing Lemur Link: An Ancestral Step in Human Evolution* Ivan Norscia and Elisabetta Palagi 978 1 107 01608 8
75. *Studies in Forensic Biohistory: Anthropological Perspectives* Christopher M. Stojanowski and William N. Duncan (eds.) 978 1 107 07354 8
76. *Ethnoprimatology: A Practical Guide to Research at the Human-Nonhuman Primate Interface* Kerry M. Dore, Erin P. Riley and Agustín Fuentes (eds.) 978 1 107 10996 4
77. *Building Bones: Bone Formation and Development in Anthropology* Christopher J. Percival and Joan T. Richtsmeier (eds.) 978 1 107 12278 9
78. *Models of Obesity: From Ecology to Complexity in Science and Policy* Stanley J. Ulijaszek 978 1 107 11751 8
79. *The Anthropology of Modern Human Teeth: Dental Morphology and Its Variation in Recent and Fossil Homo Sapiens, 2nd ed.* G. Richard Scott, Christy G. TurnerII, Grant C. Townsend and María Martinón-Torres 978 1 107 17441 2
80. *The Backbone of Europe: Health, Diet, Work, and Violence over Two Millennia* Richard H. Steckel, Clark Spencer Larsen, Charlotte A. Roberts and Joerg Baten (eds.) 978 1 108 42195 9
81. *Hunter-Gatherer Adaptation and Resilience: A Bioarchaeological Perspective* Daniel H. Temple and Christopher M. Stojanowski (eds.) 978 1 107 18735 1
82. *Primate Research and Conservation in the Anthropocene* Alison M. Behie, Julie A. Teichroeb and Nicholas M. Malone (eds.) 978 1 107 15748 4
83. *Evaluating Evidence in Biological Anthropology: The Strange and the Familiar* Cathy Willermet and Sang-Hee Lee (eds.) 978 1 108 47684 3
84. *The Genetics of African Populations in Health and Disease* Muntaser E. Ibrahim and Charles N. Rotimi (eds.) 978 1 107 07202 2
85. *The Evolutionary Biology of the Human Pelvis: An Integrative Approach* Cara M. Wall-Scheffler, Helen K. Kurki and Benjamin M. Auerbach 978 1 107 19957 6
86. *Evolution, Ecology and Conservation of Lorises and Pottos* K. A. I. Nekaris and Anne M. Burrows (eds.) 978 1 108 42902 3
87. *The Biodemography of Subsistence Farming: Population, Food and Family* James W. Wood 978 1 107 03341 2
88. *Patterns of Human Growth, 3rd Ed.* Barry Bogin 978 1 108 43448 5

The Colobines

Natural History, Behaviour and Ecological Diversity

Edited by

IKKI MATSUDA
Chubu University Academy of Emerging Sciences

CYRIL C. GRUETER
The University of Western Australia

JULIE A. TEICHROEB
University of Toronto Scarborough

CAMBRIDGE
UNIVERSITY PRESS

CAMBRIDGE
UNIVERSITY PRESS

University Printing House, Cambridge CB2 8BS, United Kingdom

One Liberty Plaza, 20th Floor, New York, NY 10006, USA

477 Williamstown Road, Port Melbourne, VIC 3207, Australia

314–321, 3rd Floor, Plot 3, Splendor Forum, Jasola District Centre, New Delhi – 110025, India

103 Penang Road, #05–06/07, Visioncrest Commercial, Singapore 238467

Cambridge University Press is part of the University of Cambridge.

It furthers the University's mission by disseminating knowledge in the pursuit of education, learning, and research at the highest international levels of excellence.

www.cambridge.org
Information on this title: www.cambridge.org/9781108421386
DOI: 10.1017/9781108347150

First published 2022

Printed in the United Kingdom by TJ Books Limited, Padstow Cornwall

A catalogue record for this publication is available from the British Library.

Library of Congress Cataloging-in-Publication Data
Names: Matsuda, Ikki, 1978- editor. | Grueter, Cyril C. editor. | Teichroeb, Julie A. editor.
Title: The colobines : natural history, behaviour and ecological diversity / edited by Ikki Matsuda, Cyril C. Grueter, Julie A. Teichroeb.
Description: Cambridge, United Kingdom ; New York, NY : Cambridge University Press, 2022. | Series: Cambridge studies in biological and evolutionary anthropology | Includes bibliographical references and index.
Identifiers: LCCN 2021019851 (print) | LCCN 2021019852 (ebook) | ISBN 9781108421386 (hardback) | ISBN 9781108411035 (paperback) | ISBN 9781108347150 (epub)
Subjects: LCSH: Colobine monkeys. | Colobine monkeys–Behavior. | Colobine monkeys–Ecology.
Classification: LCC QL737.P93 C574 2022 (print) | LCC QL737.P93 (ebook) | DDC 599.8/2–dc23
LC record available at https://lccn.loc.gov/2021019851
LC ebook record available at https://lccn.loc.gov/2021019852

ISBN 978-1-108-42138-6 Hardback

Additional resources for this publication at http://www.cambridge.org/colobines.

Contents

Contributors

Katherine R. Amato
Department of Anthropology, Northwestern University, Evanston, USA

Andie Ang
Raffles' Banded Langur Working Group, Mandai Nature, Singapore

Kirrily Apthorp
School of Archaeology and Anthropology, Australian National University, Canberra, Australia

Alison M. Behie
School of Archaeology and Anthropology, Australian National University, Canberra, Australia

Thomas M. Butynski
Eastern Africa Primate Diversity and Conservation Program and Lolldaiga Hills Research Programme, Nanyuki, Kenya

Colin A. Chapman
Department of Anthropology, Center for the Advanced Study of Human Paleobiology, George Washington University, Washington, DC, USA
School of Life Sciences, University of KwaZulu-Natal, Pietermaritzburg, South Africa
Shaanxi Key Laboratory for Animal Conservation, Northwest University, Xi'an, China

Marcus Clauss
Clinic for Zoo Animals, Exotic Pets and Wildlife, Vetsuisse Faculty, University of Zurich, Zurich, Switzerland

Jonathan B. Clayton
Department of Biology, University of Nebraska at Omaha, Omaha, NE, USA
Callitrichid Research Center, University of Nebraska at Omaha, Omaha, NE, USA
Department of Food Science and Technology, University of Nebraska-Lincoln, Lincoln, NE, USA

Amélie Corriveau
Research Institute for the Environment and Livelihoods, Charles Darwin University, Darwin, Australia

Yvonne A. de Jong
Eastern Africa Primate Diversity and Conservation Program and Lolldaiga Hills Research Programme, Nanyuki, Kenya

Allegra N. DePasquale
Department of Anthropology and Archaeology, University of Calgary, Calgary, Canada

Wendy M. Erb
K. Lisa Yang Center for Conservation Bioacoustics, Cornell Lab of Ornithology, Cornell University, Ithaca, New York, USA

Fabiola Espinosa-Gómez
Facultad de Medicina Veterinaria y Zootecnia, Universidad Popular Autónoma del Estado de Puebla, Puebla, México

Katarina D. Evans
Graduate Program in Anthropology, City University of New York, New York, USA

Peter J. Fashing
Department of Anthropology and Environmental Studies Program, California State University, Fullerton, Fullerton, USA
Centre for Ecological and Evolutionary Synthesis, Department of Biosciences, University of Oslo, Oslo, Norway

Stephen R. Frost
Department of Anthropology, University of Oregon, Eugene, USA

Christopher C. Gilbert
Department of Anthropology, Hunter College of the City University of New York, New York, USA
PhD Program in Anthropology, Graduate Center of the City University of New York, New York, USA
New York Consortium in Evolutionary Primatology, New York, USA

Cyril C. Grueter
School of Human Sciences and Centre for Evolutionary Biology (School of Biological Sciences), University of Western Australia, Perth, Australia
International Centre of Biodiversity and Primate Conservation, Dali University, Dali, China

Vanessa L. Hale
Department of Veterinary Preventive Medicine, Ohio State University College of Veterinary Medicine, Columbus, USA

Rebecca Hendershott
School of Archaeology and Anthropology, Australian National University, Canberra, Australia

Alison P. Hillyer
Department of Animal Science, Writtle University College, Essex, UK

Inza Koné
Centre Suisse de Recherches Scientifiques en Côte d'Ivoire, Abidjan, Côte d'Ivoire

Amanda H. Korstjens
Department of Life and Environmental Sciences, Bournemouth University, and Landscape Ecology and Primatology, Poole, UK

Ikki Matsuda
Chubu University Academy of Emerging Sciences, Aichi, Japan
Wildlife Research Center, Kyoto University, Kyoto, Japan
Japan Monkey Centre, Inuyama, Japan
Institute for Tropical Biology and Conservation, Universiti Malaysia Sabah, Kota Kinabalu, Malaysia

Tilo Nadler
Vietnam Primate Conservation Program, Three Monkeys Wildlife Conservancy, Cuc Phuong Commune, Vietnam

Masato Nakatsukasa
Laboratory of Physical Anthropology, Graduate School of Science, Kyoto University, Kyoto, Japan

Vincent Nijman
Anthropology and Geography, Oxford Brookes University, Oxford, UK

Dominique L. Raboin
Department of Anthropology, Rutgers University, New Brunswick, USA

Christian Roos
Gene Bank of Primates and Primate Genetics Laboratory, German Primate Center, Leibniz Institute for Primate Research, Göttingen, Germany

Tom S. Roth
Department of Biology, Utrecht University, Utrecht, the Netherlands
Cognitive Psychology Unit, Institute of Psychology, Leiden University, Leiden, the Netherlands

Jessica M. Rothman
Department of Anthropology, Hunter College of the City University of New York, New York, USA
Graduate Program in Anthropology, City University of New York, New York, USA

Kayla Ruskin
School of Archaeology and Anthropology, Australian National University, Canberra, Australia

Ken Sayers
Southwest National Primate Research Center, Texas Biomedical Research Institute, San Antonio, USA

Valérie A. M. Schoof
Bilingual Biology Program, Department of Multidisciplinary Studies, Glendon College, York University, Toronto, Canada

John Sha
National Parks Board, Singapore

Elisabeth H. M. Sterck
Department of Biology, Utrecht University, Utrecht, the Netherlands
Animal Science Department, Biomedical Primate Research Centre, Rijswijk, the Netherlands

Julie A. Teichroeb
Department of Anthropology, University of Toronto Scarborough, Toronto, Canada

Larry R. Ulibarri
Department of Anthropology, University of Oregon, Eugene, USA

Kim Valenta
Department of Anthropology, University of Florida, Gainesville, USA

Mary S. Willis
Department of Nutrition and Health Sciences, University of Nebraska Lincoln, Lincoln, USA

Barth W. Wright
Department of Anatomy, Kansas City University of Medicine and Biosciences, Kansas City, USA

Qihai Zhou
Key Laboratory of Ecology of Rare and Endangered Species and Environmental Protection, Ministry of Education, Guangxi Key Laboratory of Rare and Endangered Animal Ecology, Guangxi Normal University, Guilin, China

Dietmar Zinner
Cognitive Ethology Laboratory, German Primate Center, Leibniz Institute for Primate Research, Göttingen, Germany

Foreword

On the dust jacket of *Colobine Monkeys: Their Ecology, Behaviour and Evolution*, which John Oates and I author-edited in 1994, someone had written 'and will remain a significant and useful reference for many years to come'. Neither John nor I expected that this would apply for a quarter of a century, and we have been humbled by the continued reference to the work provided by a diverse group of inspiring colleagues who were interested in this remarkable radiation of African and Asian primates. It was a great pleasure, therefore, to be invited to provide a foreword to this new compilation of the latest research and thinking on colobine monkeys, and I thank the editors for the opportunity.

In the 40 years since I started researching colobine monkeys, many things have changed, and looking at this volume my first observation is that it is very good to see so many new names and research groups that have taken up colobine studies, especially from colobine range countries. It is also good to see in these pages acknowledgement of many colleagues, some no longer with us, whose insightful research has helped guide our understanding over the years.

The first detailed ecological studies in the 1970s and early 1980s did not involve laptops, or mobile phones, or GPS, or camera traps, and we recorded thousands of hours of field observations with the help of pencils (which didn't smudge in the rain), carbon copies, topo' maps and excellent local field assistants. New technologies have been developed with spectacular speed since then to bring new insights today, the most conspicuous of which are advances in genetic techniques. These have supported the proposal in this book that there are 10 genera, 78 species and 124 taxa of colobines, up from 'at least 30 species which can be grouped into 4–9 genera', as noted in *Colobine Monkeys*. Yet the lists of scientific name changes confirm that colobine taxonomy is 'one of the most disputed among primates', and research is still needed to iron out the taxonomic wrinkles. More scientific name changes can be expected.

This in turn raises the challenge of what common names to use for colobine species. For African species, 'colobus' has been widely accepted as the English language name and is used with an adjective – olive, red and black-and-white – for the three genera. For Asian colobines, it is more perplexing. Fortunately, the decision in this volume to include the Indian and Sri Lankan species in a single genus, *Semnopithecus*, gives an opportunity to use the term 'langur' for this group of species, which is used by millions of local people throughout South Asia – but not by those in Southeast Asia. The 'odd-nosed monkey' is another appropriate English common name for those species that do indeed have odd noses (referred to as 'snub-nosed' species in 1994). What is less clear is what to call *Trachypithecus* and *Presbytis* species, which are different from the langurs. The English term 'leaf monkey' was used in *Colobine Monkeys* as a collective term for the *Presbytis* species, given that they eat lots of leaves and live in very leafy rainforests. The Malay word *lutong* is the local name for *Trachypithecus* species at several places in Southeast Asia, although it is little used beyond that, so we will have to await the conclusions of further analysis to resolve this issue of suitable English common names.

In the field, many local names are onomatopoeic and reflect the diversity of languages and the rich cultural heritage in colobine range countries. Good examples include *chengkong* for *T. obscurus*, with its booming adult male loud call in West Malaysia, or *kelasi* for *P. rubicunda*, with its rather truncated and quieter alarm call in Sabah. In fact, the sounds of adult male loud calls are often the first and main feature used for species identification during field surveys, and the lack of a systematic assessment of all colobine adult male loud calls does seem to be a gap in our research knowledge. This would complement the findings of morphological and genetic studies, and could help resolve issues of taxonomy and nomenclature.

This new volume shows that innovative genetic techniques have given us more information on digestive physiology, and yet neither physiology nor dental morphology provides a simple framework with which to predict diet or nutritional strategies. Tooth wear patterns do not correspond with particular diets, and forestomach fermentation does not provide any simple model for resolving feeding strategies to increase the intake of protein, energy and micronutrients *versus* minimizing the intake of digestion inhibitors, toxins and indigestible fibre. A great variety of colobine species live in very varied habitats, confounding simple ecological models.

The early hypothesis that food supply limits colobine numbers probably does apply in many cases, but despite the careful work reported here, it has again been difficult to confirm any general model across all sites. Forest plant species composition, seasonality of plant part production and quality of foliage are all patchy and highly variable. Furthermore, human hunting can have devastating effects, especially for bushmeat in West Africa, and predation by chimpanzees has been shown to greatly reduce colobus numbers at some East African sites.

Protected area management and prohibitions on hunting will continue to be the cornerstones of conservation strategies, which clearly need to be made more effective. And as the tide of land-use change relentlessly rolls in, we need a stronger set of forest management interventions to improve degraded forests and reconnect forest fragments in agricultural landscapes. This will improve meta-population management between forest patches, and keep open options for adaptation to future climate change impacts. In fact, this is probably the most conspicuous change between the two volumes – climate change was not mentioned 25 years ago.

As we look at the evidence from the field and try to ensure that good science underpins future conservation and development strategies, we tend to focus on the direct threats, when the underlying drivers of deforestation also need to be addressed. Our challenge is to connect with and influence governments, businesses and communities to support forest and primate conservation, and this must flow from global policy dialogues, such as the Convention on Biological Diversity and the United Nations Framework Convention on Climate Change, to national strategies that need appropriate funding to well-equipped managers of forests and protected areas. And we need to build up and support great conservation leaders for the future.

To conclude, it is much appreciated that authors in this compendium have often referred to work in *Colobine Monkeys* and built our current understanding from those foundations. Looking ahead, it is intriguing to imagine what new technologies will deepen our understanding in the next 25 years and what new conservation challenges we will face. As these processes evolve, it is worth remembering that good work always stands out, and it is a pleasure to see the very substantial amount of new knowledge and thinking shared in this volume. It is essential reading on colobine natural history, and it will certainly be 'a significant and useful reference for many years to come'.

Glyn Davies
Professor (honorary), Durrell Institute of Conservation and Ecology (DICE),
University of Kent, UK

Acknowledgements

We first thank the contributing authors for their patience, dedication and cooperation. Most of the authors also provided constructive comments on other chapters in the book, helping us to integrate the various chapters. Our appreciation also goes to the following colleagues who reviewed submitted chapters as external reviewers, providing invaluable comments and suggestions: Alex Miller, Alexander Georgiev, Danica Stark, David Chivers, Eva Wikberg, Carel P. van Schaik, Goro Hanya, Iulia Bădescu, Liu Zhijin, Muhammad Abu Bakar Abdul-Latiff, Nelson Ting, Oliver Schülke, Peter Lucas, Serge A. Wich, Takashi Hayakawa, W. Scott McGraw and Yamato Tsuji. We are grateful to Glyn Davies and John Oates, not only for inspiring our work as young scholars with their original book on colobine monkeys, but also for valuable input on this book. We thank the staff of Cambridge University Press, especially Olivia Boult and Jenny van der Meijden, for helping shepherd this book through the various stages of production.

Ikki Matsuda thanks the staff of the Chubu University Academy of Emerging Sciences and the members of 'Tsuda CREST' (Japan Science and Technology Agency, Core Research for Evolutional Science and Technology 17941861/ #JPMJCR17A4) for their inspiration, support and assistance while he worked on this book. He is particularly grateful to the late Nishimura Akisato and to Seigo Higashi for their helpful mentoring, encouragement and humour from the time when he was their student and started working on colobine monkeys on the island of Borneo. Finally, he expresses his deepest thanks to his wife, Yuko.

Cyril Grueter is grateful to all those people who supported his endeavour to conduct his dissertation research on the enigmatic snub-nosed monkeys in the highlands of Yunnan. It was this extended stint in Yunnan that triggered Cyril's unwavering fascination with colobines and ultimately led to his participation in this book project. Of particular mention are Carel van Schaik, Gustl Anzenberger, Craig Kirkpatrick, Wei Fuwen, Long Yongcheng, Jutta Porr, Othmar Porr and Carol Jin.

Julie Teichroeb thanks the Natural Sciences and Engineering Research Council of Canada for funding her work on colobus in Ghana and Uganda. She is also grateful to Pascale Sicotte, Tania Saj, James Paterson and Colin Chapman for mentorship and support, aiding her in many years of fieldwork endeavours. Finally, work on this book would not have been possible without the ongoing encouragement of Greg, Annabel and Jasper Bridgett.

Finally, we acknowledge the non-human primates, especially colobines, that inspired and continue to inspire us.

1 General Introduction

Ikki Matsuda, Cyril C. Grueter and Julie A. Teichroeb

Colobinae, which includes more than 70 species grouped into 10 genera distributed throughout Asia and Africa, show a wide range of ecological and social traits. The colobines are generally forest-living and arboreal, which can make research on this often-elusive group difficult. Despite these challenges, our understanding of colobine behaviour, ecology and morphology has increased a great deal over the decades since the first research review on this primate subfamily was published by Davies and Oates (1994). While new research has demonstrated the incredible variation of colobine natural history, and the adaptability of this group, some colobine populations have declined and are now critically endangered. *The Colobines* brings together experts from around the world in an innovative volume that summarizes the current knowledge on colobine populations. It highlights areas where knowledge is lacking and stresses the importance of this information for conservation. The book is an edited volume with 22 chapters that examine the biological, ecological and societal traits of colobines.

The first section of the book overviews the taxonomy and phylogeny of extant and fossil colobines. The number of species has increased from the 24 that were recognized in the late 1960s to 80 at the present time, due to the elevation of various subspecies to the species level and additions of entirely new species, such as the black snub-nosed monkey (*Rhinopithecus strykeri*) discovered in north-eastern Myanmar in 2010 or the Popa langur (*Trachypithecus popa*) from central Myanmar in 2020 (Chapters 2 and 4). Recent developments in molecular genetics also contribute to expanded taxonomic and phylogenetic classifications. New species have been discovered not only in extant colobines but also in fossil colobines, with the greatest increase in the colobine fossil record in the Late Miocene of Africa (Chapter 3) since the previous 1994 review (Davies and Oates 1994).

The book's second part focuses on colobine anatomy and physiology. Chapter 5 discusses recent studies on the effect of food variability and food physical properties on dental function, especially in Asian colobines. The distinct digestive features of colobines (i.e. foregut fermentation) differ from other primate groups (i.e. hindgut fermentation). There are new developments in our understanding of colobine digestion, including a 'rumination' strategy in proboscis monkeys (*Nasalis larvatus*), the first documented among primate species (Chapter 6). Although there has not been much progress in terms of clarifying their anatomical and physiological attributes, there has been a dramatic increase in the number of colobus species whose diet and nutrient intake have been studied, as well as numerous advances in colobus nutrition research (Chapter 8). Notably, technological innovations in genetic analysis (e.g. next-generation sequencing) now allow us to collect detailed genetic information on gastrointestinal microbiota genomes (Chapter 7), which were not described in the previous colobine review in 1994.

The third section documents and summarizes the ecology and behaviour (distribution, habitat, climate, diet, activity patterns, range use, predation, social system and reproduction) of all colobine lineages (Chapters 9–15). Colobines have traditionally been believed to live without food competition or social stratification within or between groups; however, this presumption was largely based on the notion that these species exploit ubiquitous food sources, such as leaves. Recent studies have reported high levels of fruit and/or seed consumption in response to variation in local environmental conditions and have revealed that even leaves vary in their quality and distribution. Many colobines are subject to scramble and contest competition for food; thus, previous assumptions about food competition and its effects on social relationships in folivores are incorrect for most colobine populations. This indicates that an update of how colobines fit into socioecological models is necessary (Chapters 16 and 17). In addition, recent colobine socioecological studies have provided new findings on the complex spatio-temporal social dynamics (i.e. multilevel societies) seen in some species, such as snub-nosed monkeys (*Rhinopithecus* spp.), which were not discussed in the first colobine review (Chapter 18). Based on this accumulated information, competition for food resources, predation, disease and factors affecting population dynamics have been reviewed (Chapter 19).

The final section of the book discusses the fact that an increasing number of colobine species face extinction both in Asia (Chapter 20) and in Africa (Chapter 21) mainly through forest loss and hunting. The detailed information provided on colobine conservation may help prioritize and focus future conservation initiatives.

The aim of this work is to deliver a comprehensive overview of the current research on colobine populations, highlight areas where our knowledge is still lacking and present the current status of colobine populations, emphasizing their conservation importance and exploring the nature of threats to their future survival. We hope that this book will become a 'go-to' resource for primate researchers and students and believe that it will provide a departure point from which biological, ecological and societal studies and future conservation efforts can spring. *The Colobines* sets the stage for a new wave of research on colobines in areas where our understanding is just beginning.

2 Taxonomic Classification of Colobine Monkeys

Christian Roos

Introduction

Colobine or leaf-eating monkeys are a species-rich group of Old World primates with extant species mainly found in the tropical belt of Africa and throughout most of South and Southeast Asia. Today, 10 genera, 80 species and 125 taxa (species and subspecies) are recognized (following Mittermeier et al. 2013; Rowe & Myers 2016; Roos et al. 2020; for a full list of colobine taxa, see ESM, Appendix 2.1). However, the classification of colobine monkeys has changed considerably over the decades, mainly concerning the number of taxa recognized (genera, species), but also concerning the genus, species group and species affiliation of certain taxa. The number of genera has increased from 6 recognized in 1976 to 10 in 2013/2016. Part of this is due to a recent emphasis on the use of time since divergence to differentiate taxa above the species level, as opposed to the traditional method of using morphological differentiation. The number of species has increased even more drastically; from 24 recognized in 1967 (Napier and Napier 1967) to 80 in 2020 (Mittermeier et al. 2013; Rowe & Myers 2016; Roos et al. 2020). This is partially due to the description of new species, e.g. *Rhinopithecus strykeri* or *Trachypithecus popa*, but mainly due to the elevation of various subspecies to species level as a result of adopting the Phylogenetic Species Concept (PSC; Cracraft 1983; for a detailed discussion about species concepts, their pros and cons and their applicability, see Groves 2012; Groves et al. 2017) and by applying molecular genetics. Comprehensive genetic data from colobines, however, are still rare and exist only for a few taxa, but available information provides nonetheless important insights into colobine phylogeny (see Chapter 4) and for instance, led to the taxonomic reassignment of several taxa; e.g. Nilgiri and purple-faced langurs are today recognized as species of *Semnopithecus* instead of *Trachypithecus* (Karanth et al. 2008; Mittermeier et al. 2013; Osterholz et al. 2008; Rowe and Myers 2016; Zhang and Ryder 1998).

In this chapter, I give an overview of the taxonomic classification of colobine monkeys. I follow the taxonomy proposed by Mittermeier et al. (2013) and Rowe and Myers (2016) and discuss taxonomic changes mainly since the seminal work by Napier and Napier (1967) and studies thereafter. Generally, taxonomy is a dynamic science and species delimitations should be regarded as taxonomic hypotheses. The taxonomy of colobines is still under debate and no overall accepted taxonomy is available, which is also reflected by the diverging opinions among the contributors of

This chapter includes Electronic Supplementary Material (ESM) at: www.cambridge.org/colobines

this book. Part of this debate is due to a lack of ecological, behavioural and genetic data for many colobine species, which has led to classifications largely based on phenotypical differences determined from museum specimens. But an important component is also a general lack of agreement among systematists regarding taxonomic philosophy and how classifications should be generated. The Mittermeier et al. (2013) and Rowe and Myers (2016) classifications generally follow a time-based classification at the genus level and the PSC at the species level, although some exceptions exist where there is a lack of data and/or consensus. Consequently, more work is needed to increase knowledge about colobine diversity and to come to an agreement on taxonomic philosophy towards categorizing this diversity in order to establish a refined and broadly acceptable colobine taxonomy.

Colobine Monkeys

Colobine or leaf-eating monkeys constitute the primate subfamily Colobinae. Together with their sister clade, the cheek-pouched monkeys (subfamily Cercopithecinae), they form the Catarrhini family of Cercopithecidae (Old World monkeys) (Davies and Oates 1994; Groves 2001; Mittermeier et al. 2013; Rowe 1996; Rowe and Myers 2016). African and Asian colobines are traditionally regarded as reciprocally monophyletic clusters (Davies and Oates 1994; Groves 2001; Napier 1970) and sometimes classified as subtribes based on morphology, the African Colobina and the Asian Semnopithecina (Szalay and Delson 1979) or Presbytina (Delson 1975; note: Presbytina has priority), or as tribes based on temporal divergence (Colobini, Presbytini) (Mittermeier et al. 2013; Perelman et al. 2011; Rowe and Myers 2016). However, the reciprocal monophyly of African and Asian colobines was repeatedly questioned. Groves (1989) suggested *Nasalis* (with *Simias* as subgenus) as sister group to all other colobines and classified them as Nasalinae as opposite to Colobinae; both together formed the family of Colobidae. In contrast, Jablonski (1998a) suggested *Procolobus* as sister lineage to all other colobines, while Roos et al. (2011), based on retroposon integrations, found *Colobus* in this position. However, mitochondrial and nuclear sequence data support reciprocal monophyly of African and Asian clades (Finstermeier et al. 2013; Perelman et al. 2011; Pozzi et al. 2014; Roos et al. 2011; Sterner et al. 2006; Springer et al. 2012; Ting et al. 2008; Wang et al. 2012). Here, I recognize African and Asian colobine groups as reciprocal monophyletic clades and classify them as tribes, Colobini and Presbytini, as they separated roughly at the same time, ca. 12 million years ago, as did the two Cercopithecinae tribes, Papionini and Cercopithecini (Finstermeier et al. 2013; Perelman et al. 2011; Pozzi et al. 2014; Springer et al. 2012).

African Colobines

Following Mittermeier et al. (2013) and Rowe and Myers (2016), African colobines are grouped into three genera with a total of 23 species. The three genera refer to black-and-white colobus (genus *Colobus*), olive colobus (genus *Procolobus*), and red colobus (genus *Piliocolobus*) (Groves 2001; Mittermeier et al. 2013; Rowe and Myers 2016). However, in the past these three genera were combined into either a single genus (*Colobus*) with three subgenera (Napier and Napier 1967) or into two genera, *Colobus* and *Procolobus*, with either the former (Napier and Napier 1985) or the latter containing *Piliocolobus* as a subgenus (Brandon-Jones 1984a; Davies and Oates 1994; Groves 1989; Grubb et al. 2003; Kuhn 1967; Rowe 1996; Strasser and Delson 1987). Genetic data confirm a sister group relationship between *Procolobus* and *Piliocolobus*, and show that the three major lineages diverged 6–10 million years ago (Finstermeier et al. 2013; Perelman et al. 2011; Pozzi et al. 2014; Roos et al. 2011; Springer et al. 2012; Ting 2008a).

Black-and-white colobus, genus *Colobus*, are distributed across equatorial Africa. In earlier times, only one (*guereza*; e.g. Schwarz 1929) or two species (*guereza*, *polykomos*; e.g. Napier and Napier 1967) were recognized, but nowadays there is consensus that *Colobus* contains (four to) five species (Dandelot 1971; Davies and Oates 1994; Groves 2001; Groves et al. 1993; Mittermeier et al. 2013; Napier and Napier 1994; Oates and Trocco 1983; Rowe 1996; Rowe and Myers 2016). Two of them, the King colobus (*C. polykomos*) and the white-thighed colobus (*C. vellerosus*), are monotypic, while the black colobus (*C. satanas*) contains two subspecies, the Angolan colobus (*C. angolensis*) seven subspecies and the guereza (*C. guereza*) eight subspecies (Mittermeier et al. 2013; Rowe and Myers 2016). It should be noted that the PSC has not been fully applied to this group, and that at least some of the *Colobus* subspecies could be elevated to species status upon re-evaluation of their diversity.

The genus *Procolobus* is monotypic and contains only the olive colobus, *P. verus* (Davies and Oates 1994; Groves 2001; Grubb et al. 2003; Mittermeier et al. 2013; Napier 1985; Napier and Napier 1967, 1994; Rowe 1996; Rowe and Myers 2016). The species has a disjunct distribution in western Africa, but there is no evidence for any subspecific variation (Davies and Oates 1994).

Red colobus monkeys, genus *Piliocolobus*, have a wide, but patchy distribution from Senegal in West Africa across the continent to Zanzibar in the East. The taxonomy of red colobus monkeys is debated and various classifications with different numbers of species and varying taxon assemblies were proposed. While Rahm (1970), followed by Davies and Oates (1994), lumped all taxa in the single species *badius*, Napier (1985) and Napier and Napier (1967, 1994) recognized two species, *kirkii* and *badius*. Delson et al. (1982), Groves (1993) and Rowe (1996) listed four species (*badius, pennantii, preussi, rufomitratus*), Oates (1986, 1996a) five species (*badius, gordonorum, kirkii, pennantii, rufomitratus*), Dandelot (1971) split red colobus monkeys into eight species (*badius, ellioti, kirkii, pennantii, preussi, rufomitratus, tholloni, waldronae*), and Groves (2001) into nine species (*badius, foai, gordonorum, kirkii, pennantii, preussi, rufomitratus, tephrosceles, tholloni*). Recently, a total of 17 taxa, all recognized as monotypic species (Upper Guinea red colobus, *P. badius*; Bouvier's red colobus, *P. bouvieri*; Niger Delta red colobus, *P. epieni*; Foa's red colobus, *P. foai*; Udzungwa red colobus, *P. gordonorum*; Zanzibar red colobus, *P. kirkii*; Lang's red colobus, *P. langi*; Oustalet's red colobus, *P. oustaleti*; Lomami red colobus, *P. parmentieri*; Pennant's red colobus, *P. pennantii*;

Preuss's red colobus, *P. preussi*; Tana River red colobus, *P. rufomitratus*; Semliki red colobus, *P. semlikiensis*; Temminck's red colobus, *P. temminckii*; ashy red colobus, *P. tephrosceles*; Tshuapa red colobus, *P. tholloni*; Miss Waldron's red colobus, *P. waldronae*), have been suggested (Mittermeier et al. 2013; Rowe and Myers 2016). The current classification is mainly based on investigations of museum specimens and limited data from the field. Much more work, including ecological, phenotypical, acoustic and genetic studies, is needed to better describe and understand diversity in red colobus monkeys. So far, only a single genetic study on intra-generic diversity in *Piliocolobus* has been published (Ting 2008a), which however, allows first intriguing insights into *Piliocolobus* phylogeny and suggests relatively deep splits among various taxa; the most recent common ancestor of the genus has been dated back to ca. 3 million years (Ting 2008a; see also Chapter 4).

Asian Colobines

Incorporating the recently proposed changes in Trachypithecus taxonomy (Roos et al. 2020), Asian colobines contain 57 species in seven genera. However, the classification of Asian colobines is in ongoing debate and needs further clarification. Although Groves (1989) suggested *Nasalis* (with *Simias* as subgenus) as a sister clade to all other colobines, a common ancestry of Asian colobines is generally accepted and confirmed by genetic data (Perelman et al. 2011; Pozzi et al. 2014; Roos et al. 2011; Springer et al. 2012; Sterner et al. 2006; Ting et al. 2008; Wang et al. 1997, 2012; Zhang and Ryder 1998). In most classifications, Asian colobines are divided into two groups, a langur group subsuming the genera *Presybtis*, *Trachypithecus* and *Semnopithecus*, and an odd-nosed monkey group with the genera *Rhinopithecus*, *Pygathrix*, *Nasalis* and *Simias* (Groves 2001; Mittermeier et al. 2013; Rowe 1996; Rowe and Myers 2016). Genetic data clearly confirm the monophyly of the odd-nosed monkey group, but not of the langur group (Finstermeier et al. 2013; Liedigk et al. 2012; Perelman et al. 2011; Pozzi et al. 2014; Roos et al. 2011; Springer et al. 2012; Sterner et al. 2006; Ting et al. 2008; Wang et al. 2012). In fact, mitochondrial and nuclear data revealed contradicting branching patterns among the three langur genera and the odd-nosed monkeys, and have been suggested to be the result of ancient hybridization events among the three langur genera (e.g. Roos et al. 2011; Ting et al. 2008; Wang et al. 2012; see also Chapter 4).

The genus-level classification of members of the (probably paraphyletic) langur group was one of the most controversial discussed topics in colobine taxonomy, but seems to be settled now. Today, most authorities recognize three genera, surilis (genus *Presbytis*), lutungs (genus *Trachypithecus*), and Indian langurs (genus *Semnopithecus*) (Brandon-Jones et al. 2004; Davies and Oates 1994; Groves 1989, 2001; Mittermeier et al. 2013; Roos et al. 2014; Rowe 1996; Rowe and Myers 2016), but in the past one to four genera were proposed. While Napier (1985) and Napier and Napier (1967, 1994) combined all taxa of the langur group into the single genus *Presbytis*, Hill (1934) and Pocock (1935, 1939) divided them into four genera (*Presbytis, Semnopithecus, Trachypithecus, Kasi*). Already Reichenbach (1862) recognized these four groups, but classified them as subgenera of the genus *Semnopithecus*. Alternative classifications suggest two genera, *Presbytis* and *Semnopithecus*, with *Trachypithecus* as subgenus of the latter (Brandon-Jones 1984a, 1995a,b, 1996; Strasser and Delson 1987). Most recent classifications do not accept *Kasi* as a valid genus or subgenus, but Rowe (1996) maintained *Kasi* as a subgenus of *Trachypithecus*. In fact, genetic studies have shown that the two species of *Kasi*, the Nilgiri and purple-faced langur, are paraphyletic and nested within the *Semnopithecus* clade, and consequently should be assigned to this genus (Karanth et al. 2008; Osterholz et al. 2008; Zhang and Ryder 1998).

Compared to the langur group, the genus-level classification of the members of the odd-nosed monkey group was historically less problematic. Generally, it is accepted that the odd-nosed monkeys contain four clearly distinct lineages that are commonly recognized as distinct genera, snub-nosed monkeys (genus *Rhinopithecus*), doucs (genus *Pygathrix*), the proboscis monkey (genus *Nasalis*), and the simakobu (genus *Simias*) (Brandon-Jones et al. 2004; Groves 2001; Jablonski 1998a; Jablonski and Peng 1993; Mittermeier et al. 2013; Napier and Napier 1967, 1994; Rowe and Myers 2016). However, in the past *Rhinopithecus* was classified as a subgenus of *Pygathrix* (Brandon-Jones 1984a, 1996b; Davies and Oates 1994; Delson 1975; Groves 1970, 1989; Napier 1985; Rowe 1996). Likewise, *Simias* was proposed as subgenus of *Nasalis* (Brandon-Jones 1984a, 1996b; Delson 1975; Groves 1970, 1989; Rowe 1996). Genetic data suggest a close phylogenetic relationship between *Nasalis* and *Simias*, and a basal position of *Rhinopithecus* among odd-nosed monkeys (Liedigk et al. 2012; Roos et al. 2011; see also Chapter 4), thus rejecting a monophyletic *Rhinopithecus-Pygathrix* clade. Jablonski (1998a) and Jablonski and Peng (1993) further divided *Rhinopithecus* into two subgenera, *Presbyticus* with *R. avunculus* and *Rhinopithecus* subsuming all other snub-nosed monkey taxa, which, however, is not well accepted. Interestingly, *Simias* and *Nasalis* diverged relative recently, just 1–2 million years ago (Liedigk et al. 2012; Roos et al. 2011; see also Chapter 4). This is well in the range of temporal divergences typically found among species and consequently, both genera would need to be combined into a single genus when a time-based classification at the genus level is applied.

Langur Group

Surilis, genus *Presbytis* (*sensu stricto*), occur in the Sundaland region of Southeast Asia with main distributions on Sumatra, Borneo, Java, the Mentawai Islands and the Malay Peninsula. Napier and Napier (1967) divided surilis into five species, *aygula* (=*comata*), *frontata*, *melalophos*, *rubicunda* and *potenziani*, of which the former four were grouped into the *P. aygula* (=*comata*) group, referring to today's genus *Presbytis*, while *potenziani* was assigned to the *P. cristatus* group, which refers to today's genus *Trachypithecus*. Later on, Napier (1985) and Napier and Napier (1994) correctly assigned *potenziani* to what is now referred to as the *P. melalophos* group and recognized, following Groves (1970), a total of seven species, *melalophos*, *frontata*, *rubicunda*, *potenziani*, *comata*, *hosei* and *thomasi*. Davies and Oates

(1994) and Rowe (1996) followed this classification, but Rowe (1996) in addition separated *femoralis* from *melalophos*. Brandon-Jones (1984a, 1995a, 1996b) recognized also seven species, but he used a different species assembly. He also accepted *frontata*, *potenziani* and *rubicunda* as distinct species, however, he divided the *melalophos* complex into three species, *melalophos*, *femoralis* and *siamensis*, and separated *fredericae* from *comata*, while he followed Napier and Napier (1967) by integrating *thomasi* and *hosei* into *comata*. Although there is now general consensus concerning the distinct species status of *comata*, *hosei*, *frontata*, *thomasi* and *potenziani*, there is ongoing debate about the taxonomy of the *melalophos* complex. Traditionally all taxa were combined into the single species *melalophos* (Chasen 1940; Davies and Oates 1994; Napier 1985; Napier and Napier 1967, 1994), but it was proposed to split them into two (Aimi and Bakar 1992, 1996; Pocock 1935; Rowe 1996; Wilson and Wilson 1977), three (Brandon-Jones 1984a, 1996b; Brandon-Jones et al. 2004), five (Groves 2001), or even eight species (Mittermeier et al. 2013; Roos et al. 2014; Rowe and Myers 2016). Recently, also the two subspecies of *potenziani* and the three subspecies of *hosei* were elevated to species (Mittermeier et al. 2013; Roos et al. 2014; Rowe and Myers 2016). Following the most recent classification (Mittermeier et al. 2013; Roos et al. 2014; Rowe and Myers 2016), the genus *Presbytis* comprises a total of 17 species. Twelve of them, the black-and-white langur (*P. bicolor*), Miller's grizzled langur (*P. canicrus*), white-fronted langur (*P. frontata*), Hose's langur (*P. hosei*), black-crested Sumatran langur (*P. melalophos*), mitred langur (*P. mitrata*), Natuna Islands langur (*P. natunae*), Pagai langur (*P. potenziani*), Sabah grizzled langur (*P. sabana*), Siberut langur (*P. siberu*), black Sumatran langur (*P. sumatrana*), and Thomas's langur (*P. thomasi*), are monotypic, while the cross-marked langur (*P. chrysomelas*) and Javan langur (*P. comata*) contain two subspecies each, the banded langur (*P. femoralis*) three subspecies, the pale-thighed langur (*P. siamensis*) four subspecies, and the maroon langur (*P. rubicunda*) five subspecies. The herein adopted classification of *Presbytis* is highly disputed and should be treated as preliminary, but it reflects best phylogenetic relationships among taxa (Md-Zain 2001; Md-Zain et al. 2008; Meyer et al. 2011; Vun et al. 2011; see also Chapter 4).

With 20 species currently recognized, the genus *Trachypithecus* is the most speciose among all Asian colobines. The genus is widely distributed on the mainland and Sundaland region of Southeast Asia, from Bhutan and Assam in the West, to Vietnam and Southern China in the East, and South to Java. Napier and Napier (1967) classified taxa of today's genus *Trachypithecus* as members of the *Presbytis cristatus* group and recognized a total of seven species, *cristatus*, *francoisi*, *geei*, *pileatus*, *obscurus*, *phayrei* and *potenziani*. One of these species, *potenziani*, was later correctly reallocated to the *P. aygula* (=*comata*) group (i.e. genus *Presbytis*) (Napier 1985; Napier and Napier 1994). Davies and Oates (1994) in principle followed this classification, but included also the two species of the *Presbytis senex* (=*vetulus*) group (Napier 1985; Napier and Napier 1967, 1994), *vetulus* and *johnii*, in *Trachypithecus*, and separated *T. auratus* from *T. cristatus* according to Weitzel and Groves (1985). Rowe (1996) adopted the classification of Davies and Oates (1994), but additionally recognized *delacouri* as a full species. In contrast, Brandon-Jones (1984a, 1995b, 1996b) divided *Trachypithecus* (as subgenus of *Semnopithecus*) into 12 species, *vetulus, johnii, pileatus geei, cristatus, auratus, obscurus, barbei, francoisi, hatinhensis, laotum* and *delacouri*. Compared to other classification, he placed *phayrei* in *obscurus*, and recognized *barbei* as distinct species. Moreover, he separated the *francoisi* subspecies *delacouri, hatinhensis* and *laotum* from the nominate form, and reclassified *poliocephalus* as subspecies of the South Indian *johnii*. In 1992, he described a new taxon, *ebenus*, from northern Vietnam as subspecies of the Javan *auratus* (Brandon-Jones 1995b). Roos et al. (2007) subsequently reallocated *ebenus* to the *francoisi* complex and recognized four species within the group, *francoisi, poliocephalus* (including *leucocephalus*), *delacouri*, and *laotum* (with *hatinhensis* as subspecies and *ebenus* as synonym of *hatinhensis*). Brandon-Jones et al. (2004) eventually accepted *Trachypithecus* as a full genus and recognized the following nine species: *auratus, villosus* (=*cristatus*), *barbei, obscurus, francoisi* (including *ebenus* and *hatinhensis*), *laotum, poliocephalus* (including *leucocephalus*), *geei* and *pileatus*. In contrast, Groves (2001) proposed a classification of *Trachypithecus* into 17 species, arranged in five species groups. According to his arrangement, the *pileatus* group consists of *pileatus, geei* and *shortridgei*, the *cristatus* group of *cristatus, auratus, germaini* and *barbei*, the *obscurus* group of *obscurus* and *phayrei*, the *francoisi* group of *francoisi, hatinhensis, poliocephalus, laotum, delacouri* and *ebenus* and the *vetulus* group includes *vetulus* and *johnii*. The taxonomy of Groves (2001) was generally adopted by Mittermeier et al. (2013), Roos et al. (2014) and Rowe and Myers (2016), although with some minor changes. First, the two species of the *vetulus* group were reassigned to *Semnopithecus* (Karanth 2008; Karanth et al. 2008; Osterholz et al. 2008; Wang et al. 2012, 2015; Zhang and Ryder 1998). Second, *barbei* was reallocated to the *obscurus* group (Geissmann et al. 2004). Third, *leucocephalus* was separated from *poliocephalus* on species level (Liu Z et al. 2013a). Fourth, *phayrei crepusculus* was elevated to species level (Liedigk et al. 2009; Roos et al. 2019). Fifth, a new species as described from central Myanmar (*T. popa*) and phayrei shanicus was elevated to species level and renamed into melamera (Roos et al. 2020). Sixth, within the *T. cristatus* group, *mauritius* and *margarita* were elevated to full species and a new taxon, *selangorensis*, was described (Nadler et al. 2005; Roos et al. 2008). By incorporating these changes, the genus *Trachypithecus* contains four species groups and a total of 22 species: *T. pileatus* group with golden langur (*T. geei*), capped langur (*T. pileatus* with four subspecies) and Shortridge's langur (*T. shortridgei*), *T. cristatus* group with silvered langur (*T. cristatus* with two subspecies), Selangor silvery langur (*T. selangorensis*), East Javan langur (*T. auratus*), West Javan langur (*T. mauritius*), Germain's langur (*T. germaini*) and Annamese langur (*T. margarita*), *T. obscurus* group with dusky langur (*T. obscurus* with seven subspecies), Phayre's langur (*T. phayrei*), Shan States langur (*T. melamera*), Popa langur (*T. popa*), Indochinese grey langur (*T. crepusculus*) and Tenasserim langur (*T. barbei*), and the *T. francoisi* group with the François's langur (*T. francoisi*), white-headed langur (*T. leucocephalus*), Cat Ba langur (*T. poliocephalus*), Delacour's langur (*T. delacouri*), Hatinh langur (*T. hatinhensis*), Laos langur (*T. laotum*) and black langur (*T. ebenus*).

Similar to *Presbytis*, the classification of *Trachypithecus* is not fully clarified and needs additional work.

The genus *Semnopithecus* encompasses the langurs of the Indian subcontinent. Most commonly, the genus (or *Presbytis entellus* group) was considered to contain only a single species, the Hanuman langur, *entellus*, with 10–16 subspecies (Brandon-Jones et al. 2004; Davies and Oates 1994; Ellermann and Morrison-Scott 1951; Groves 1989; Napier 1985; Napier and Napier 1967, 1994; Pocock 1928, 1939; Roonwal 1981a; Roonwal and Mohnot 1977; Roonwal et al. 1984; Rowe 1996). However, Hanuman langurs have sometimes been divided into two (either *entellus* and *hypoleucos*; Brandon-Jones 1984a, 1996b, or *entellus* and *priam* Brandon-Jones 2004), four (*entellus, schistaceus, priam, hypoleucos*) (Hill 1939), or seven species (*schistaceus, ajax, hector, entellus, hypoleucos, dussumieri, priam*) (Groves 2001). Moreover, two species, *vetulus* and *johnii*, previously assigned to the genus *Kasi* or *Trachypithecus* have been recently integrated into *Semnopithecus* based on genetic evidence (Karanth 2008; Karanth et al. 2008; Osterholz et al. 2008; Wang et al. 2012, 2015; Zhang and Ryder 1998). In general, the current taxonomy of *Semnopithecus* follows Groves (2001) with the exception that *dussumieri* is not recognized as valid species (Ashalakshmi et al. 2015; Nag et al. 2011) and by including *vetulus* and *johnii*. Accordingly, *Semnopithecus* contains a total of eight species, Bengal sacred langur (*S. entellus*), Chamba sacred langur (*S. ajax*), Terai sacred langur (*S. hector*), Nepal sacred langur (*S. schistaceus*), Malabar sacred langur (*S. hypoleucos* with three subspecies), tufted grey langur (*S. priam* with three species), Nilgiri langur (*S. johnii*), and purple-faced langur (*S. vetulus* with four subspecies). As for the other two langur genera, also for *Semnopithecus* more work, particularly for the northern taxa is required.

Odd-Nosed Monkey Group

Snub-nosed monkeys, genus *Rhinopithecus*, occur only in China, Vietnam and Myanmar, with all species having relatively small geographical distributions (Groves 2001; Mittermeier et al. 2013; Roos et al. 2014; Rowe 1996; Rowe and Myers 2016). Originally, only two species, *avunculus* and *roxellana*, the latter with three subspecies, have been recognized (Ellermann and Morrison-Scott 1951; Napier and Napier 1967, 1994). However, Groves separated first *brelichi* as distinct species (Groves 1970), which was followed by Napier (1985). Later on, Groves (1989) also elevated *bieti* to full species, a classification that is now widely accepted (Brandon-Jones 1984a, 1996b; Brandon-Jones et al. 2004; Davies and Oates 1994; Jablonski 1998a; Jablonski and Peng 1993; Mittermeier et al. 2013; Roos et al. 2007, 2014; Rowe 1996; Rowe and Myers 2016). In contrast, a separation of *avunculus* in its own subgenus *Presbyticus* from its congenerics as proposed by Jablonski (1998a) and Jablonski and Peng (1993) has not been adopted and can also not be justified with available genetic data (Liedigk et al. 2012; Roos et al. 2007; Yu et al. 2016; see also Chapter 4). In 2011, a new species of snub-nosed monkey, *strykeri*, was described from the border region of Myanmar and China (Geissmann et al. 2011). Although closely related to *bieti*, its distinctiveness was confirmed by genetics (Liedigk et al. 2012; Zhou et al. 2014). By adding *strykeri*, the genus *Rhinopithecus* contains a total of five species. Four of them, the Tonkin snub-nosed monkey (*R. avunculus*), the Guizhou snub-nosed monkey (*R. brelichi*), the Yunnan snub-nosed monkey (*R. bieti*), and the Myanmar or black snub-nosed monkey (*R. strykeri*), are monotypic, while for the golden snub-nosed monkey (*R. roxellana*) three subspecies are listed.

Doucs, genus *Pygathrix*, are found in Vietnam, Laos and Cambodia, east of the Mekong River. Traditionally, only one species, *nemaeus*, with two subspecies has been recognized (Davies and Oates 1994; Groves 1970; Jablonski and Peng 1993; Napier 1985; Napier and Napier 1967, 1994), although sometimes both taxa have been classified as separate species (Brandon-Jones 1984a; Brandon-Jones et al. 2004; Rowe 1996). An additional taxon, *cinerea*, was described as a subspecies of *nemaeus* (Nadler 1997). Brandon-Jones et al. (2004) followed this subspecies arrangement, while most other authorities support a species level recognition for *cinerea* (Groves 2001; Mittermeier et al. 2013; Roos et al. 2014; Rowe and Myers 2016). The distinctiveness of all three douc taxa is supported by genetic data (Liedigk et al. 2012; Roos and Nadler 2001; Roos et al. 2007). Accordingly, the three taxa of *Pygathrix* are currently classified as separate species, the red-shanked douc (*P. nemaeus*), the black-shanked douc (*P. nigripes*), and the grey-shanked douc (*P. cinerea*).

The genus *Nasalis* contains the single species *N. larvatus*, the proboscis monkey from Borneo. The species is commonly regarded as monotypic (Davies and Oates 1994; Groves 1970, 2001; Mittermeier et al. 2013; Napier and Napier 1967, 1994; Roos et al. 2014; Rowe 1996; Rowe and Myers 2016), but sometimes two subspecies are listed (e.g. Brandon-Jones et al. 2004).

The genus *Simias* comprises the single species *S. concolor* (Davies and Oates 1994; Groves 2001; Grubb et al. 2003; Mittermeier et al. 2013; Napier and Napier 1967, 1994; Rowe 1996; Rowe and Myers 2016). The simakobu or pig-tailed langur is endemic to the Mentawai Islands and contains two subspecies.

Future Directions

The taxonomic classification of colobines is one of the most disputed among primates with different opinions concerning the number of genera and species to be recognized, and also concerning how to best group taxa, i.e. their assignment to species, species groups and genera. In recent years, our knowledge about colobines has expanded considerably and many taxonomic issues were settled. However, compared to the cercopithecines, colobines are still a neglected group of primates and we have to learn more about their taxonomic diversity and evolutionary history, particularly regarding geographically widespread and taxon-rich genera such as *Piliocolobus*, *Colobus*, *Presbytis*, *Trachypithecus* and *Semnopithecus*. Accordingly, much more work in the field and laboratory providing information on ecology, behaviour, morphology and genetics is needed. However, to establish a well-grounded and broadly acceptable colobine taxonomy, we need, besides additional biological data, also an agreement among systematists regarding taxonomic philosophy and how classifications should be generated.

Acknowledgements

I thank the editors for inviting me to contribute to this important book on one of the most fascinating and neglected groups of primates. Many thanks also to Cyril C. Grueter, Ikki Matsuda and three anonymous reviewers for their valuable comments on an earlier version of this book chapter. Dedicated to my friend and hero Colin P. Groves (1942–2017).

3 The Colobine Fossil Record

Stephen R. Frost, Christopher C. Gilbert and Masato Nakatsukasa

Introduction

Delson (1994) and Jablonski (2002) have provided the most recent, comprehensive reviews of the fossil record for colobine monkeys, and Takai and Maschenko (2009) and Jablonski and Frost (2010) have done so for the Asian and African records, respectively. The decade(s) since these reviews have seen a considerable expansion of the fossils known throughout the Old World. Here we present an update of these reports.

Perhaps the greatest increase in the colobine fossil record has been in the Late Miocene of Africa (Table 3.1; Figure 3.1). This part of the record has increased greatly in diversity of specimens, the number of sites where they occur, and pushed the first appearance datum of colobines back approximately 3 million years. Later African colobine fossils have added a few new species since those previous reports, but most have increased evidence for morphology, taxonomic and paleobiological information. Finally, in Asia, several new genera have become more commonly recognized, and new discoveries of the first fossil colobines in Myanmar and Taiwan have been made.

Colobines from the Miocene of Africa

The divergence age of the Colobinae and Cercopithecinae is estimated from ~21.5–14.5 Ma (full range with 95% confidence intervals = ca. 25~13 Ma) (Raaum et al. 2005; Sterner et al. 2006; Ting 2008a; Perelman et al. 2011; Reis et al. 2018). However, the currently recognized colobine fossil record barely extends to the Middle Miocene.

Victoriapithecids and other stem Old World monkeys range from latest Oligocene through Late Miocene (ca. 25–12.5 Ma) of eastern and northern Africa (Miller et al. 2009; Stevens et al. 2013; Rasmussen et al. 2019). The earliest true cercopithecid, however, is a small colobine (unnamed) from the Tugen Hills, Kenya represented by a lower premolar and molar from the Kabasero section (12.5 Ma) of the Ngorora Formation (Benefit and Pickford 1986; Rossie et al. 2013). While these teeth are tentatively assigned to the same taxon, they show a relatively large size ratio (Rossie et al. 2013). The molar exhibits derived colobine features (e.g. increased cusp height relative to the height of the lingual notch, cusps positioned closer to the margin of the tooth, longer shearing crest length) though to a lesser degree than extant colobines,

Table 3.1. Classification of Colobinae, emphasizing fossil forms

Family Cercopithecidae Gray 1821
Subfamily Colobinae Jerdon 1867
Subtribe Colobina Jerdon 1867
Genus *Colobus* Illiger 1811
†*C.* sp.
†?*C. freedmani* Jablonski and Leakey 2008
Genus *Procolobus* de Rochebrune 1887
Genus *Piliocolobus* de Rochebrune 1887
Genus †*Libypithecus* Stromer 1913
†*L. markgrafi* Stromer 1913
Genus †*Cercopithecoides* Mollett 1947
†*C. williamsi* Mollett 1947
†*C. coronatus* (Broom and Robinson 1950)
†*C. meaveae* Frost and Delson 2002
†?*C. kerioensis* Leakey et al. 2003
†*C. alemayehui* Gilbert and Frost 2008
†*C. haasgati* McKee et al. 2011
†?*C. bruneti* Pallas et al. 2019
Subtribe Presbytina Gray 1825
UNNAMED TAXON A – 'Langur Clade'
Genus *Presbytis* Eschscholtz 1821
†*P.* sp.
Genus *Tryachypithecus* Reichenbach 1862
†*T. auratus sangiranensis* Jablonski and Tyler 1999
Genus *Semnopithecus* Desmarest 1922
S. sp.
†*S. gwebinensis* Takai et al. 2016
UNNAMED TAXON B – 'Odd-nosed Clade'
Genus *Pygathrix* Geoffroy Saint-Hilaire 1812
Genus *Rhinopithecus* Milne-Edwards 1872
†*R. lantianensis* (Hu and Qi 1978)
†*R. roxellanae tingianus* Matthew and Granger 1923
Genus *Nasalis* Geoffroy Saint-Hilaire 1812
Genus *Simias* Miller 1903
Subtribe insertae sedis
Genus †*Mesopithecus* Wagner 1839
†*M. pentelicus* Wagner 1839
†*M. monspessalnus* Gervais 1849
†?*M. sivalensis* (Lydekker 1878)
Genus †*Dolichopithecus* Depéret 1889
†*D. ruscinensis* Depéret 1889
†*D. balcanicus* Spassov and Geraads 2007
Genus †*Parapresbytis* Borissoglebskaya 1981
†*P. eohanuman* Borissoglebskaya 1981
Genus †*Paracolobus* Leakey 1969
†*P. chemeroni* Leakey 1969

Table 3.1. (cont.)

†?*P. mutiwa* Leakey 1982
†*P. enkorikae* Hlusko 2007
Genus †*Rhinocolobus* Leakey 1982
†*R. turkanaensis* Leakey 1982
Genus †*Microcolobus* Benefit and Pickford 1986
†*M. tugenensis* Benefit and Pickford 1986
†*M.* sp.
Genus †*Kuseracolobus* Frost 2001
†*K. aramisi* Frost 2001
†*K. hafu* Hlusko 2006
†cf. K. sp.
Genus †*Kanagawapithecus* Iwamoto et al. 2005
†*K. leptopostorbitalis* Iwamoto et al. 2005
Genus †*Myanmarcolobus* Takai et al. 2015
†*M. yawensis* Takai et al. 2015

Note: Only species represented by fossils are listed. Dagger (†) indicates extinct taxa.

possibly indicating a lesser degree or incipient form of dedicated folivory (Rossie et al. 2013). It is small for a colobine, similar to the 2 Ma younger *Microcolobus tugenensis* (see below).

The second oldest colobine, *Microcolobus* is known from two localities in Kenya. The type species *M. tugenensis* is from Ngeringerowa (9.5–9 Ma) in the Tugen Hills (Benefit and Pickford 1986; Gilbert et al. 2010). The hypodigm includes only a single, well-preserved mandible, similar in size to that of *Procolobus verus*, the smallest extant colobine (Benefit and Pickford 1986). The mandibular body shows modern colobine affinities, such as absence of median symphyseal foramen and a robust corpus that deepens posteriorly. On the other hand, unlike extant colobines it lacks the inferior transverse torus below the genioglossal fossa. Molar cusps are moderately high relative to those of extant colobines (Benefit and Pickford 1986; Benefit 2000; Suwa et al. 2015).

Microcolobus is also known from Nakali (~9.9–9.8 Ma), Kenya, approximately 65 km northeast of Ngeringerowa (Kunimatsu et al. 2007). For the last 10 years, a great number of colobine fossils have been discovered from Nakali. The lower teeth and jaw show affinities with *M. tugenensis* (Y. Kunimatsu, pers. comm.; see also Nakatsukasa et al. 2010). However, since there is also some morphological variation among these specimens and as *M. tugenensis* is known from a single specimen, it is unclear whether they are conspecific with *M. tugenensis*, therefore the Nakali colobine has only been referred to genus as *Microcolobus* sp. (Nakatsukasa et al. 2010; Kunimatsu et al. 2007, 2016). In fact, Benefit and Pickford (1986) noted that a colobine lower molar discovered at Nakali in the 1970s is larger and mesiodistally elongated compared to those of the *M. tugenensis* type. This raised the possibility that another colobine taxon existed in Nakali.

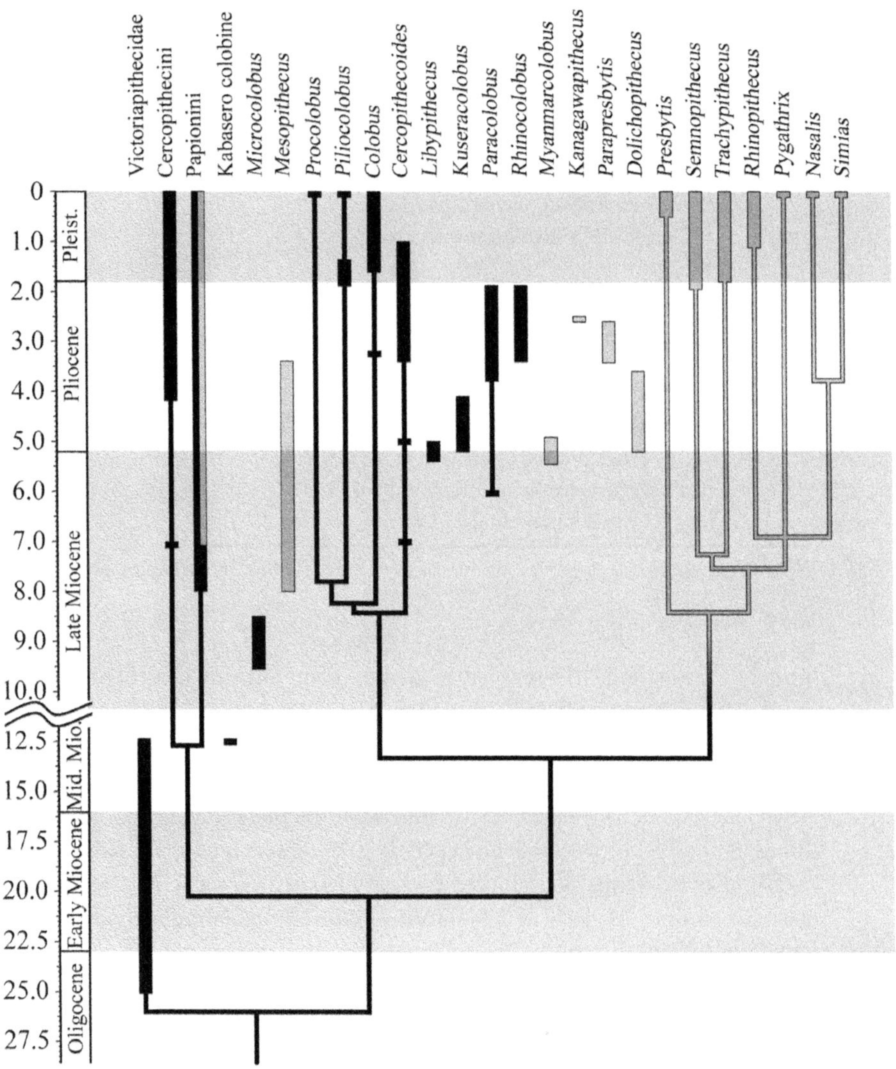

Figure 3.1 Phylogeny of Colobinae with time in Ma indicated on the vertical axis; wavy lines indicate a change in scale. Broader boxes indicate temporal range of fossils allocated to genus with some confidence. Narrower lines indicate the relationships among extant genera after Xing et al. (2007), Ting et al. (2008) and Perlman et al. (2011). Branch lengths based on molecular clock estimates from Raaum et al. (2005), Tosi et al. (2003, 2005), Sterner et al. (2006), Ting (2008) and Perelman et al. (2011). Black branches indicate Africa and grey Eurasia.

Similar to the early colobines from Kabasero, *Microcolobus* was probably not a committed folivore. Benefit and Pickford (1986) and Benefit (2000) noted that molar cusps of *M. tugenensis* had lower relief (thus shorter shearing crests) than those of extant colobines. The base of the lower molar lingual notch approximates mid-crown height, which is high relative to living colobines (Suwa et al. 2015). Based on the shearing crest length, Benefit (2000) concluded that *M. tugenensis* consumed fruits nearly twice as much as leaves. A 3D landmark-based geometric-morphometric study of the molar crown in *Microcolobus* specimens from Nakali also revealed that they fall within the cluster of living cercopithecins and not extant colobines (D. Shimizu, in prep.).

Microcolobus is the earliest colobine whose postcranial morphology has been studied. Nakatsukasa et al. (2010) described two colobine partial skeletons from Nakali, with one of them being associated with a lower molar similar to those of *M. tugenensis*. Body mass of one individual was estimated as ca. 5 kg from the femoral head size. The described postcranial bones of *Microcolobus* sp. exhibit a number of synapomorphies shared with extant colobines related to arboreal locomotion: a mediolaterally wide distal humeral joint, globular humeral capitulum, deeply angled zona conoidea, short medial trochlear keel, long and medially projecting medial epicondyle, tall and proximally projecting olecranon, posteriorly dislocated fovea on the radial head, low femoral greater trochanter, wide talar head with high axial rotation, and proximodistally short cuboid and ectocuneiform. However, one significant synapomorphy found in all extant colobines, namely thumb reduction, is not observed (Nakatsukasa et al. 2010). As discussed elsewhere, *Mesopithecus* (~8 Ma) from Eurasia also retained a longer thumb than is present in extant colobines (Gabis 1960; Delson 1975; Frost et al. 2015). It is therefore possible that thumb reduction in colobines has evolved independently in Africa and Asia. The earliest evidence of colobine thumb reduction does not appear in the fossil record until much more recently, ~1.9 Ma (Frost et al. 2015).

After approximately 9 Ma, colobine fossil localities are found across eastern, southern and northern Africa. Among them, the oldest with secure radiometric dating is Chorora, Ethiopia (Suwa et al. 2015; Katoh et al. 2016). Two lower molars (probably, m1 and m2) discovered from Beticha (8 Ma) are morphologically similar to *Microcolobus* in showing moderate occlusal relief development. However, they are larger than homologues of *M. tugenensis*. Coupled with its younger age, Suwa et al. (2015) placed the Beticha colobine as distinct from *M. tugenensis*. At Beticha, at least one cercopithecine (papionin) taxon is also known. Two colobine premolars (P3 and P4) discovered from Teso Tadecho (~7.5 Ma) are conservative in terms of their unreduced protocones (Suwa et al. 2015). Suwa et al. (2015) noted a similarity of this P4 to the one discovered at Lukeino (6 Ma) in size and shape (see below).

In southern Africa, the only known Miocene colobine locality is Harasib (ca. 9 Ma based on biochronology), Namibia, where Conroy et al. (1996) reported a lower molar reminiscent of *Microcolobus*. Like *Microcolobus*, the cusps are moderate in height and the mesial and distal shelves are approximately equally long (Conroy et al. 1996). Although several cercopithecid postcranial specimens have been collected from Harasib, their taxonomic status is uncertain (Conroy et al. 1996).

After 7.4 Ma, colobines are more abundant and diverse in the fossil record. Leakey et al. (2003) reported two species of colobines from the Lower Nawata Member (7.4–6.5 Ma; McDougall and Feibel 2003), Lothagam, Kenya. One taxon (Colobinae sp. A) is smaller than the extant *Colobus guereza* (male 9 kg, female 7.5 kg; Delson et al. 2000), but the mesiodistal length of its lower molar (LT 24107) is comparable to the Chorora (Beticha) colobine. Several isolated teeth and a mandibular fragment have been attributed to this species. The other species (Colobinae sp. 'B') clearly exceeds the guereza in size. Notable fossils attributed to this species consist of a relatively well-preserved juvenile mandible, a fragment of frontal bone and a calcaneus, in addition to isolated teeth and adult mandibular fragments. An unassociated proximal femur and humerus show typical colobine attributes (e.g. wide ranges of hip excursion and shoulder joint motion). However, the degree of arboreal functional signal is modest compared to modern colobines (Leakey et al. 2003).

From the Mpesida Beds of the Tugen Hills (~7.2–6.2 Ma; Kingston et al. 2002), lower molars with modern colobine affinity and dated to 6.4 Ma have been discovered. The size of these molars slightly exceeds that of their homologues in the guereza, and Gilbert et al. (2010) referred them to Colobinae sp. 'A'. Molars of Colobinae sp. 'A' exhibit well-developed cuspal relief, similar to modern colobines. A colobine with similarly modern dental morphology is also known from the nearly contemporaneous site of Lemudong'o, Kenya (see below). However, the Mpesida colobine is larger and probably represents a different taxon (Gilbert et al. 2010).

The Lukeino Formation of the Tugen Hills (6.2–5.7 Ma; Deino et al. 2002) has yielded a lower molar and talus of a small colobine. Gilbert et al. (2010) have referred to these specimens as Colobinae sp. B. The molar is smaller than Colobinae sp. A from the Mpesida Beds (inferred body size ~7 kg), but likewise exhibits a high capacity of shearing. The talus exhibits typical colobine characters and is similar to African colobines rather than Asian colobines (Gilbert et al. 2010). Additionally, there is a colobine-like premolar (its colobine status is indeterminate) equivalent in size to king colobus (male 10 kg, female 8 kg; Fleagle 2013) and too large to be attributed to Colobinae sp. B (Gilbert et al. 2010). Thus, multiple colobines existed in the Late Miocene of the Tugen Hills, as is the case for the Lower Nawata at Lothagam. Similar to Lothagam and Beticha, a cercopithecine (cf. *Parapapio lothagamensis*) is documented in the Lukeino Formation as well.

Multiple colobines (at least 3 species) are known from Lemudong'o (~6 Ma), Kenya (Hlusko 2007). Most abundant is *Paracolobus enkorikae*, which is comparable to the king colobus in size and much smaller than its Pliocene congeners (>30 kg). However, *P. enkorikae* is otherwise similar to its congeners morphologically. The mandible is deep and displays modern colobine-like symphyseal morphology with molars that exhibit a great amount of occlusal relief (Hlusko 2007). Hlusko (2007) proposed that *Paracolobus* may have closer evolutionary affinities to modern *Colobus* than other larger Plio-Pleistocene colobines (such as *Cercopithecoides*, *Rhinocolobus* and *Kuseracolobus*), but no shared derived features have been described. A second colobine close to *Microcolobus* in dental dimensions, but distinct in its more derived dental and symphyseal morphology, has also been described from Lemudong'o. It also differs from *P. enkorikae* in its shorter molar row and more convex maxillary cheek tooth row. A third colobine is represented by several dental specimens much bigger than those of *P. enkorikae*. They display typical colobine crown morphology. Most of the colobine postcrania discovered at Lemudong'o have been attributed to *P. enkorikae*, with the humerus, ulna and femur displaying features reminiscent of modern arboreal colobines.

From several Late Miocene localities in the Middle Awash, at least two colobine species are represented (Frost et al. 2009). These include a mandible and several isolated teeth of *Kuseracolobus aramisi* from the ~5.3 Ma Kuseralee Member of the Sagantole Formation, along with several isolated teeth similar in size and morphology to those of *K. aramisi* from ~5.7 Ma sediments of the Adu Asa Formation (Frost et al. 2009). In addition, several isolated colobine teeth that are significantly larger are also present from both the ~5.7 and ~5.3 Ma horizons. A distal humerus and astragalus consistent in size with *K. aramisi* show adaptations for mostly arboreal locomotion (Frost et al. 2009).

Senut (1994) reported two molars with modern colobine affinity from the Nkondo Formation, Nkondo-Kaiso area, Uganda, in the Albertine Rift. Senut (1994) assigned them to cf. *Paracolobus*. The fauna of the Nkondo Fm. suggests a similar age to the Lukeino Formation (Pickford et al. 1993). From Plio-Pleistocene sites in this area, mandibular and humeral fragments attributable to Colobinae have also been discovered (Senut 1994).

Miocene colobine localities in North (and North-central) Africa date to around ~8–6 Ma. Menacer (Marceau) is a Turolian locality in Algeria (ca. 8–7 Ma). Cercopithecid specimens collected from this locality were originally referred to *Macaca flandrini* (Arambourg 1959); however, Delson (1975) pointed out that part of the assemblage, including the type specimen, is colobine. Thus, Delson (1975) used the name of *?Colobus flandrini* to refer the colobine hypodigm to a 'form-genus'. This is a large colobine (as large as *Cecopithecoides williamsi*) with modern colobine dental features (Simons and Delson 1978).

A colobine is also documented from As Sahabi, Libya along with a papionin (Boaz and Meikle 1982; Meikle 1987). The age of As Sahabi is estimated at ~7 Ma based on the fauna (Boaz 2008), which shows some similarity with that of Toros-Menalla, Chad (Boaz 2008). Most Sahabi cercopithecid fossils are papionins, and colobines were probably rare (Benefit et al. 2008). Molar morphology and dental microwear suggest that the Sahabi colobine was still only moderately folivorous, a likely primitive retention (Benefit 2008). There are several distal humeri known from Sahabi, with one of them displaying features more consistent with extant colobines, such as a better-developed lateral trochlear keel and well-rounded capitulum (Boaz and Meikle 1982; Meikle 1987: Benefit et al. 2008).

Six colobine fossils were recently described from the *Sahelanthropus tchadensis*-bearing locality (TM 266) at Toros-Menalla, Chad as the type series of the new species *Cercopithecoides bruneti* (Pallas et al. 2019). Authigenic $^{10}Be/^{9}Be$ dating suggests an age between 6.8 and 7.2 Ma (Lebatard et al. 2008, 2010; see also Suwa et al. 2015). The species is similar in size to the largest extant colobines, but smaller than *Cercopithecoides williamsi*, *C. coronatus*,[1] and other large Plio-Pleistocene colobines

[1] *Cercopithecoides kimeui* known from eastern Africa is most likely conspecific with large fossils of *Cercopithecoides* from Kromdraai B, Swartkrans (e.g. SK 552), and Bolt's Farm Pit 6 (e.g. Anderson et al. 2014; 2015). As such, *Cercopithecoides coronatus* (Broom and Robinson 1950) has priority over *Cercopithecoides kimeui* (Leakey 1982).

(Pallas et al. 2019). While generally similar to other members of the genus in dental morphology, the mandibular corpus is relatively deep, which is a notable distinction from all other congeners except the slightly younger *C. kerioensis* from Lothagam. Given these morphological distinctions, it is quite possible that *C. bruneti* and *C. kerioensis* belong in a separate genus (see also below). However, as with other *Cercopithecoides* species, the postcrania suggest adaptations to terrestrial locomotion and substrate use, differing from other Late Miocene African colobines such as *Microcolobus, Paracolobus enkorikae*, and *Kuseracolobus* (Hlusko 2007; Frost et al. 2009; Nakatsukasa et al. 2010; Pallas et al. 2019).

Libypithecus markgrafi is known from an almost complete cranium of a male from the relatively young site Wadi Natrun (latest Miocene or earliest Pliocene), Egypt. It has a relatively long snout and well-developed sagittal crest (Szalay and Delson 1979). Well-developed shearing crests and high frequency of microwear scratches suggest that *Libypithecus* was a specialized leaf eater (Benefit 2008). It has a maxillary sinus unlike modern colobines, but similar to *Cercopithecoides* and *Kuseracolobus* (Rae et al. 2007; Frost et al. 2020a).

Plio-Pleistocene Colobines from Africa

During the Plio-Pleistocene, the colobine monkeys of Africa were considerably more diverse than the extant radiation in terms of body size, locomotor mode, and most probably diet and other aspects of their ecology as well (Jablonski 2002; Jablonski and Frost 2010; Anderson 2019). During this time, at least five distinct genera are known. The most common and widespread of these is *Cercopithecoides*, a genus that spans the continent, ranging from the Late Miocene (see above) through Middle Pleistocene (ca. 7–1 Ma), and including a half dozen species (Freedman 1957; Leakey 1982; Frost and Delson 2002; Leakey et al. 2003; Gilbert and Frost 2008; McKee et al. 2011; Pallas et al. 2019). The various species ranged in size from slightly larger than extant *Colobus* (e.g. *C. meaveae, C. alemayehui*) up to some of the largest colobines known (*C. coronatus*) with male masses approaching ~50 Kg (Delson et al. 2000; Frost et al. 2003; Jablonski et al. 2008; Pallas et al. 2019). *Cercopithecoides* is characterized by a shallow, but robust mandible, often with a median mental foramen, relatively broad upper molars that are sometimes low-crowned, and where known, postcranial adaptations for terrestrial locomotion (Birchette 1982; Leakey 1982; Frost and Delson 2002; Jablonski et al. 2008; Frost et al. 2015; Pallas et al. 2019).

Six Plio-Pleistocene species of *Cercopithecoides* are recognized here, in addition to *C. bruneti* from the Late Miocene of Chad (see above): *C. kerioensis, C. williamsi, C. coronatus, C. haasgati, C. meaveae* and *C. alemayehui*. From sediments equivalent to the Apak member of the Nachakui Formation, *C. kerioensis* is recognized at Lothagam, but its preserved morphologies, including a deep mandible and the presence of a sagittal crest, are distinct from all other members of the genus (except *C. bruneti*, see above) and suggest that it may require a new genus.

Cercopithecoides williamsi is perhaps the best known *Cercopithecoides* taxon, from eastern and southern African sites between ~2.8–1.6 Ma (Figure 3.2). It was a large monkey (males estimated ~25–30 kg; Delson et al. 2000), with associated postcrania showing clear adaptations for terrestrial locomotion. Furthermore, a partial skeleton of *C. williamsi* from the Koobi Fora Fm., Upper Burgi Member (1.9 Ma) has a small pollical metacarpal indicating a reduced thumb comparable to extant Colobina, a significant synapomorphy making it one of the few fossils showing any clear phylogenetic link with a modern colobine subtribe (Frost et al. 2015).

Cercopithecoides coronatus (including previously recognized *C. kimeui*, see footnote above) is the largest known species of *Cercopithecoides* (males up to ~50 kg; Delson et al. 2000), and similar to *C. williamsi*, is found across eastern and southern African Plio-Plesitocene sites between ~2.6–1.5 Ma (and possibly even 3.4–1.2 Ma; Leakey and Leakey 1973; Leakey 1982; Frost and Delson 2002; Frost et al. 2003; Jablonski et al. 2008; Jablonski and Frost 2010). Limited postcrania suggest that *C. coronatus* was also terrestrial, similar to *C. williamsi* (Jablonski et al. 2008; Jablonski and Frost 2010).

Cercopithecoides meaveae is known from Leadu (possibly ca. 2.8) and the Sidi Hakoma Member of the Hadar Formation (~3.4–3.3 Ma), and is thus slightly older and smaller (~20 kg in males) than *C. williamsi* and *C. coronatus* (Frost and Delson 2002; Jablonski and Frost 2010). The holotype (A.L. 2–34) is a partial skeleton, which is notable because it appears more semi-terrestrial than *C. williamsi* and *C. coronatus* (Frost and Delson 2002; Jablonski and Frost 2010).

Cercopithecoides haasgati is known only from Haasgat, South Africa (~2.3–1.8 Ma; McKee et al. 2011; Herries et al. 2014). Cranially, it smaller than *C. williamsi*, but it is distinctive in its megadontia so that it overlaps *C. williamsi* in dental size (McKee et al. 2011; Frost and Gilbert, pers. obs.).

Finally, *C. alemayehui*, known from the Daka Member (~1.0 Ma), Bouri Formation of the Middle Awash, is similar in cranial and dental size to *C. meaveae* (Gilbert and Frost 2008). While the mandible is not preserved, the male type (and only) specimen displays relatively long nasal bones, a more prominent supraorbital torus, and relatively large and square upper molars compared to similarly sized *Cercopithecoides* species (Gilbert and Frost 2008).

Given the modern-looking dentition and cusp height observed in unworn *Cercopithecoides* molars, the diets of *Cercopithecoides* species are generally assumed to be folivorous. However, unlike extant colobines, *Cercopithecoides* has a distinctive pattern of dental wear, unusual among colobines, with all of the teeth subject to extreme wear. The molar wear is particularly unusual; as the cusps and cross-lophs are often worn completely flat (Freedman 1957; Szalay and Delson 1979; Leakey 1982; Jablonski and Frost 2010). This is in contrast to the pattern among extant colobines where even in advanced stages of wear the cross-lophs remain sharp and prominent (Delson 1973). This extensive wear may suggest an unusually high degree of dietary grit, and hint at distinctive dietary adaptations as well. Based on molar morphology Benefit (1999) estimated *C. williamsi* was a folivore, but used the pattern of wear to argue it was a grazer. She estimated *C. coronatus* to be far less folivorous,

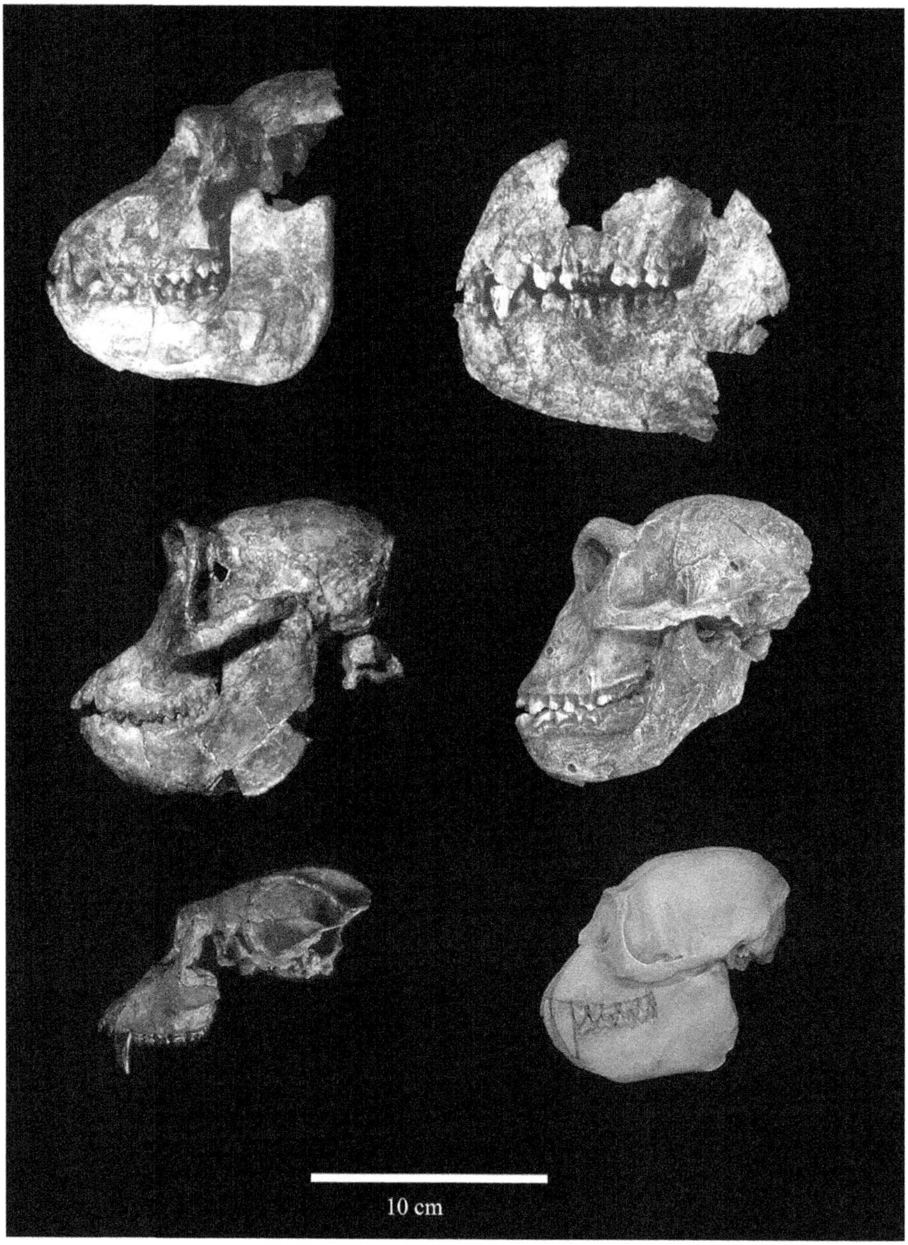

Figure 3.2 Lateral views of skulls of representative African fossil colobines. Top row: *Paracolobus chemeroni* male (KNM-BC 3, holotype) left, and *?Paracolobus mutiwa* male (KNM-WT 16827) right. Middle row: *Rhinocolobus turkanaensis* female (KNM-ER 1485) left, and *Cercopithecoides williamsi* female (BF 42) right. Bottom row: *Libypithecus markgrafi* male (BSM 1914 II 1), and *Colobus guereza* male (Cast) right.

however. Microwear based on molars from Koobi Fora, Makapansgat, Sterkfontein and Swartkrans, was consistent with grazing or folivory but material from Makapansgat and Koobi Fora showed increased pitting, and therefore may indicate more hard objects (El-Zaatari et al. 2005; Teaford et al. 2008). Isotopic analysis of the South African material shows a bimodal distribution with some individuals at the C^3 end of the spectrum and others at the C^4 end (though not as far as contemporary *Theropithecus*), with no overlap (Codron et al. 2005; Fourie et al. 2008).

Paracolobus is known from the latest Miocene *P. enkorikae* from Lemmudong'o (see above), as well as two very large, divergent and distinctive Plio-Pleistocene forms. The type species, *P. chemeroni* is best represented by a partial skeleton of a large male individual from the Chemeron Formation, Tugen Hills, Kenya dated to 3.2 Ma (Leakey 1969; Hill et al. 2002). A mandible of a male individual from the Middle Awash (dated to 2.5 Ma) may also be attributed to this species (Frost 2001b). Among the largest known colobines (males ca. 35–45 kg), *P. chemeroni* is characterized by a moderately long face with short nasal bones, deep mandible that lacks expansion of the gonial region (Figure 3.2), relatively long limbs, a very large foot and other postcranial adaptations that suggest a moderate degree of terrestriality, but less so than in *Cercopithecoides* (Leakey 1969; Leakey and Leakey 1973; Birchette 1982; Delson 1994; Delson et al. 2000; Frost 2001b; Anderson 2019). Dentally, it is a modern colobine, but the P^3 has a well-developed protocone, unlike extant colobinans (Strasser and Delson 1987). The ankle, however suggests African colobine affinity in that the ectocuneiform lacks a proximal cuboid facet (Strasser and Delson 1987).

Although currently recognized as congeneric with *P. chemeroni, P. mutiwa* is a very distinctive species (Figure 3.2), currently known from the Turkana Basin between about 2.7 and 2 Ma, including a large male partial skeleton (KNM-WT 16827) from Lomekwi, West Turkana, dated to just under 2.6 Ma (Leakey, 1982, 1987; Harris et al. 1988). While similar in dental and estimated body size to *P. chemeroni* (Delson et al. 2000; Anderson 2019), the face and mandible of *P. mutiwa* are considerably larger than those of *P. chemeroni* (Leakey 1987; Harris et al. 1988; Figure 3.2). The rostrum is prognathic with maxillary fossae and ridges more typical of papionins than colobines, and the mandibular corpus is extremely deep with the gonial region broadly expanded (Leakey 1982, 1987; Harris et al. 1988; Jablonski et al. 2008). The limb bones of *P. mutiwa* are similar in their epiphyseal diameters to those of *P. chemeroni,* but significantly shorter in length (Delson 2000; Anderson 2019). Functional morphology of the limb bones, especially the hip, also suggests that it was more terrestrially adapted than *P. chemeroni* (Ting 2001; Frost and Delson 2002; Anderson 2019). Differences are large enough among these two species, especially in terms of rostral morphology, limb lengths and robusticity, to warrant generic separation.

Another highly distinctive Plio-Pleistocene colobine is *Rhinocolobus turkanaensis*, best known from the Koobi Fora and Shungura Formations, but also possibly Hadar, dated to 3.4 – 1.6 Ma (Leakey 1982, 1987; Delson 1984; Frost and Delson 2002). Among the three middle Pliocene large colobines (*Cercopithecoides, Paracolobus,*

Rhinocolobus) it is the most clearly adapted to arboreal locomotion (Delson 1994; Frost and Delson 2002; Jablonski et al. 2008; Anderson 2019). Facially, it is among the more distinctive cercopithecids, being highly prognathic at the level of the alveolar plane, but with among the shortest nasal bones of any colobine so that the piriform aperture opens superiorly rather than anteriorly (Leakey and Leakey 1973; Leakey 1982, 1987; Jablonski et al. 2008). This is different from the prognathism of *Nasalis* where the nasal bones are among the longest of any colobine (Groves 1989; Ravosa and Profant 2000). Furthermore, the nasals of the holotype male cranium (Omo 75 '69 1012) are flanked by small bilateral pits adjacent to rhinion, and instead of the clear border typical of most primates, the superior half of the piriform aperture has a flattened, roughened surface that could be a muscle attachment or other similar marking (Figure 3.3; Frost 2001b; pers. obs.). This latter feature is also visible on the male maxilla Omo 323 '76 905. The mandibular corpus is relatively deep and narrow, deepens posteriorly, the gonial region is expanded and the ramus is tall and vertically oriented (Leakey 1982, 1987).

Dentally, *R. turkanaensis* has the reduced P^3 protocone typical of Colobinans (Strasser and Delson 1987). Molar morphology is consistent with a derived folivore

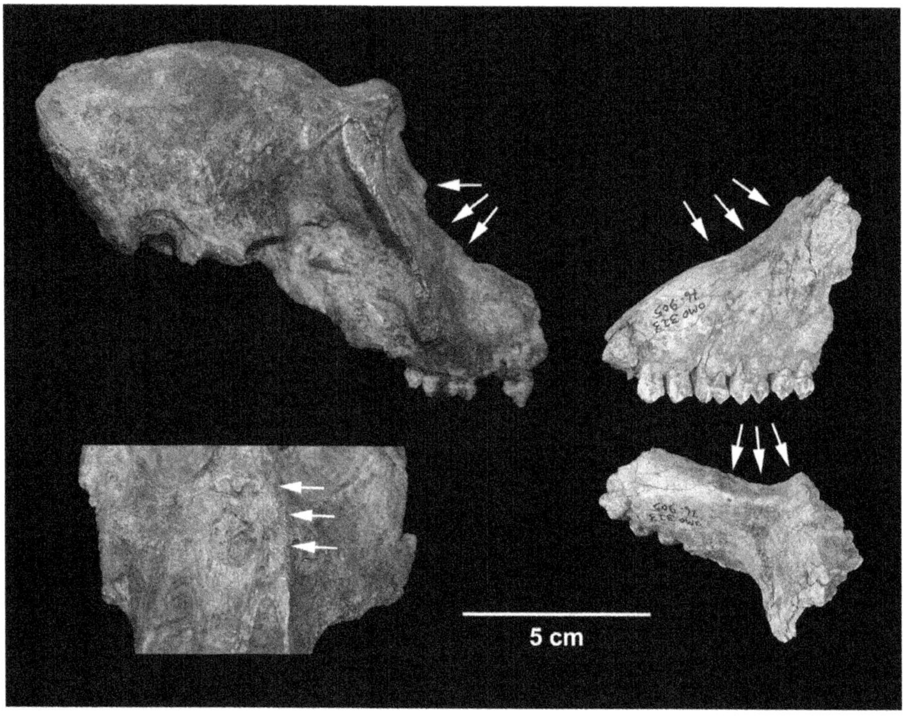

Figure 3.3 *Rhinopithecus turkanaensis* specimens. Top left: lateral view of holotype male OMO 75 '69 1012. Bottom left: oblige anterio-superior view of piriform aperture of the same specimen. Top right: male maxilla OMO 323 '76 905 lateral view. Bottom right: dorsal view of the same specimen. White arrows indicate unusual roughened and excavated surface of the superior half of the piriform aperture and small bilateral pits adjacent to rhinion.

(Benefit 1999), and microwear is similar to that of *Colobus guereza, Theropithecus gelada*, and *Cercopithecoides williamsi* (Teaford et al. 2008).

Kuseracolobus is a genus from the latest Miocene and early Pliocene (5.7–4.1 Ma) of Ethiopia, Kenya and possibly Tanzania, represented by two or more species. *Kuseracolobus aramisi* is best known from Aramis and its stratigraphic equivalents in the Middle Awash along with similarly aged deposits at Gona (Frost 2001a; Semaw et al. 2005; White et al. 2009; Levin et al. 2008, in press; Frost et al., 2021a). It is similar in size to *Cercopithecoides meaveae* and *Nasalis larvatus* and characterized by short face, maxillary sinus, deep and robust mandibular corpus that deepens posteriorly, with at least some gonial expansion (Frost 2001a; Frost et al. 2020a). Analysis of carbon isotopes from tooth enamel indicate *K. aramisi* had a C^3 dominated diet (Levin et al. 2008; White et al. 2009).

A second larger species, *K. hafu* comes from somewhat younger deposits (4.1 Ma) at Asa Issie in the Middle Awash (Hlusko 2006; White et al. 2006). Both species are potentially associated with postcrania consistent with arboreal locomotion and substrate use (Hlusko 2006; Frost et al. 2009, 2020a; White et al. 2009). A potential third species, somewhat smaller than *K. aramisi*, is represented by fragmentary colobine fossils from Kanapoi, Kenya dated to 4.2 Ma, which had been tentatively allocated to *Cercopithecoides* (Harris et al. 2003; Frost et al. 2020b). The mandibular material shows the deeper, more robust corpus of *Kuseracolobus* rather than *Cercopithecoides* (Frost et al. 2020b).

While too fragmentary to be certain, fossil colobines from the Upper Laetolil Beds at Laetoli, Tanzania (3.6–3.8 Ma) seem most consistent with *Kuseracolobus*. Previously identified as cf. *Paracolobus* sp. and cf. *Rhinocolobus* sp. (Leakey and Delson 1987; Harrison 2011a), these highly fragmented elements are close in size to those of *K. hafu*. Morphologically, they display a clear maxillary sinus, a rostrum that is shorter than that of *R. turkanaensis*, but perhaps longer than that of *C. williamsi*, and a robust and apparently deep mandibular corpus with clear *prominentia laterales* (Leakey and Delson 1987; Harrison 2011a; pers. obs.).

Molecular clock estimates suggest the extant colobinan genera *Colobus, Piliocolobus* and *Procolobus* had already diverged by the latest Miocene (Ting 2008a). Nonetheless, the earliest appearance of any of them is in the Pleistocene approximately 1.6 Ma in the Turkana Basin (Leakey 1987; Jablonski and Leakey 2008). While there are a few specimens from Kanam East that may be Pliocene, they are of uncertain provenience (Harrison and Harris 1996). Middle Pleistocene fossils clearly allocated to *Colobus* are known from the Afar region of Ethiopia and Sudan (Simons 1967; Kalb et al. 1982; Frost 2001b; Frost and Alemseged 2007). Fossil colobines consistent in size with *Colobus* and *Piliocolobus* are known from throughout eastern Africa back to approximately 2.5 Ma (Frost 2001b; Jablonski and Frost 2010).

Fossil Colobines from Eurasia

The earliest, most widespread and longest lasting colobine from Eurasia, *Mesopithecus*, comes from sites throughout Europe, Iran, Afghanistan, Pakistan, and China ranging from somewhat before 8 Ma until ~2.5 Ma; with one possible occurrence 11–10 Ma (Delson 1973; Szalay and Delson 1979; Zapfe 1991; Andrews et al. 1996; Harrison and Delson 2007; Jablonski et al. 2011; Alba et al. 2015; Lazaridis et al. 2018; Koufos 2019; Khan et al. 2020). Two European species are recognized: the larger Late Miocene (~8–6 Ma) *M. pentelicus*, best known from Pikermi, Greece and the smaller Pliocene (~5–2.6 Ma) *M. monspessulanus*. Sometimes *M. delsoni* from Ravin des Zouaves-5, Greece (ca. 8.2 Ma), is recognized as distinct from *M. pentelicus* by dental proportions (Alba et al. 2015; Koufos 2019). Additionally, several fragmentary specimens from the Dhok Pathan interval (~7.5 – 5.3 Ma) of the Siwalik Hills assemblage have been allocated to *M. sivalensis* (Harrison and Delson 2007), and more tentatively some dento-gnathic fragments from Hasnot, Pakistan have been allocated to *Mesopithecus* sp. (Khan et al. 2020). Terminal Miocene specimens from Shuitangba, Yunan, China may represent *M. pentelicus*, and if so, indicate the species had one of the widest distributions among all known primates (Jablonski et al. 2011, 2014).

By far the best known in terms of morphology and paleobiology is *M. pentelicus* (Figure 3.4), whereas the others are generally distinguished on size and detailed dental morphological grounds. *Mesopithecus pentelicus* was similar in size to the larger extant langurs (~10–13 Kg) and *M. monsspessulanus* somewhat smaller (8–10 Kg; Delson et al. 2000). Compared to extant colobines, *M. pentelicus* was probably more semi-terrestrial based on elbow and ankle morphology (Delson 1973; Youlatos and Koufos 2009), whereas *M. monspessalanus* may have been arboreal (Youlatos and Koufos 2009). Dental functional morphology suggests *Mesopithecus* was not as adapted to folivory as most extant colobines, and microwear texture analysis supports greater frugivory and seed-eating (Benefit 2000; Merceron et al. 2009).

Phylogenetically, *Mesopithecus* may be a stem colobine (Delson 1973, 1975; Szalay and Delson 1979; Strasser and Delson 1987; Jablonski 2002; Alba et al. 2014, 2015; Frost et al. 2015), a stem presbytinan (Delson 1973, 1994; Szalay and Delson 1979), or member of the odd-nosed colobines (Jablonski 1998b, 2002; Groves 2000; Pan et al. 2004). The thumb of *M. pentelicus* relative to the other digits is similar in proportion to those of cercopithecines and *Microcolobus* (Jouffroy et al. 1991; Zapfe 1991; Nakatsukasa et al. 2010; Frost et al. 2015) favouring its position as a stem colobine, or possibly a stem presbytinan if thumb reduction occurred in parallel in the two subtribes (Frost et al. 2015). The tarsus, however, lacks a proximal ectocuneiform-cuboid facet, a condition more typical of African colobines, although one that shows significant individual variation (Strasser and Delson 1987).

A significantly larger colobine from the early Pliocene of Europe is *Dolichopithecus*, best known by the type species *D. ruscinensis* from the approximately 4 Ma site of Perpignan, France (Szalay and Delson 1979; Delson 1994; Figure 3.4). Additional fragmentary remains come from throughout Europe, and may include a second, smaller species, *D. balcanicus*, from Bulgaria (Spassov and Geraads 2007). It is larger than all extant colobines, except for the largest Himalayan populations of *Semnopithecus*, but smaller than some of the very large African

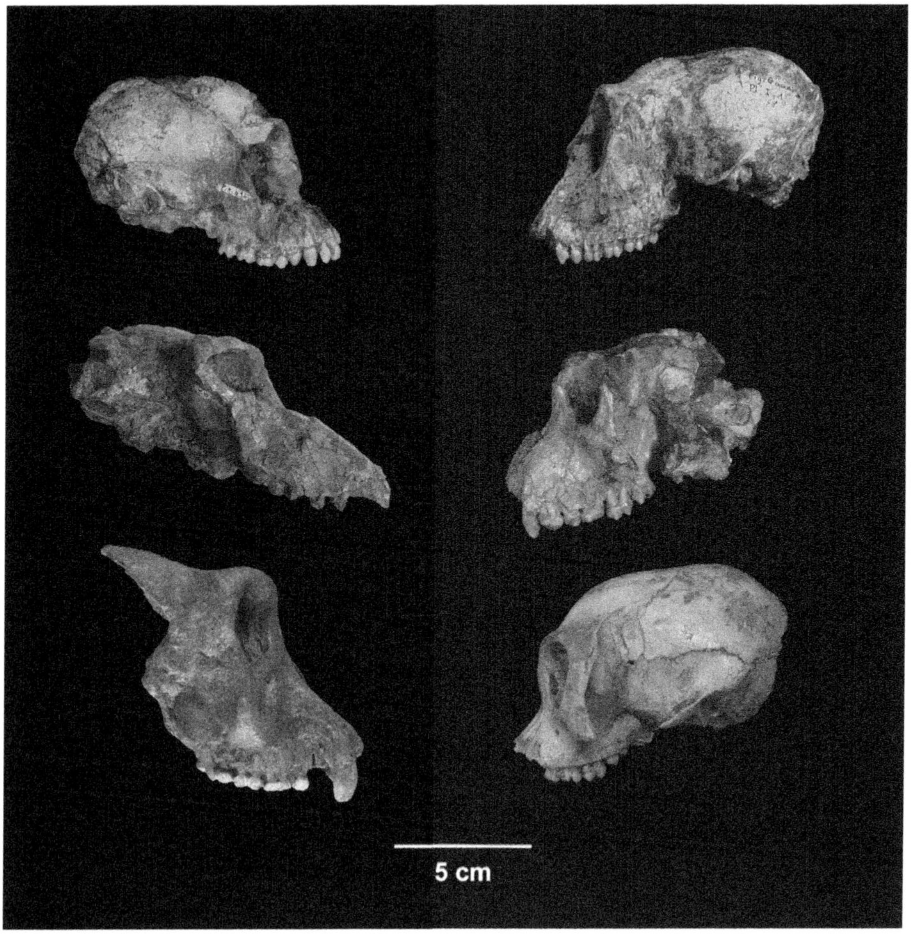

Figure 3.4 Lateral views of skulls of representative Eurasian fossil colobines. Top row: *Mesopithecus pentelicus* female (Pik 016) left, *M. pentelicus* male (Pik 035) right. Middle row: *Dolichopithecus ruscinensis* male (Per 002) left (photo courtesy of Takeshi Nishimura), *P. ruscinensis* female (Per 001, Lectotype) right. Bottom row: *Kanagawapithecus leptopostorbitalis* male (KPM-NNC005802, holotype) left (photo courtesy of Takeshi Nishimura), *Rhinopithecus roxellana tingianus* subadult (AMNH 18466, holotype) right (photo courtesy of Julia Arenson).

colobines (e.g. *Rhinocolobus, Paracolobus* and *Cercopithecoides coronatus*; Delson 1994; Delson et al. 2000).

Morphologically, *Dolichopithecus* has a long rostrum (especially in males) and narrow interorbital region for a colobine (Szalay and Delson 1979; Jablonski 2002; Figure 3.4). The humerus and ulna show adaptations of the elbow for terrestrial locomotion, and the phalanges are short and robust (Delson 1973; Szalay and Delson 1979; Jablonski 2002). Nonetheless, *Dolichopithecus* seems to occur in relatively wooded habitats and is sometimes associated with *Mesopithecus monspessulanus* and *Macaca* (Delson 1973; Andrews et al. 1996). The proximal ectocuneiform-cuboid facet is present, perhaps suggesting affinity with extant Asian colobines, but this is a variable feature within species (Strasser and Delson 1987).

Several colobines similar in size to *D. ruscinensis* that come from eastern Eurasia may be close relatives of *Dolichopithecus*. Surprisingly, Pliocene (MN 16a, 3.4–2.6 Ma) colobine fossils have been discovered from Mongolia and Russia near Lake Baikal, the highest latitude cercopithecids known from Asia, and were named *Parapresbytis eohanuman* (Borissoglebskaya 1981; Kalmykov and Maschenko 1992; Takai and Maschenko 2009). Distinction from *Dolichopithecus* has been supported based on relatively large and robust incisor and canine teeth that frequently show heavy wear, a shorter rostrum, and broader interorbital pillar more typical of colobines in general (Kalmykov and Maschenko 1992; Jablonski 2002; Takai and Maschenko 2009). However, several researchers have suggested these differences may indicate specific or even subgeneric status, but do not warrant generic separation (Delson 1994; Iwamoto et al. 2005; Spassov and Geraads 2007). A distal humerus and proximal ulna from Shamar, Mongolia, have been argued to suggest relatively terrestrial adaptation (Delson 1994), however metric analysis supported more arboreal adaptation (Egi et al. 2007).

Another striking find is a well-preserved male face of a large colobine from the late Pliocene (ca. 2.5 Ma) of central Japan, initially described as a new subgenus *Dolichopithecus (Kanagawapithecus)* (Iwamoto et al. 2005; Figure 3.4). Its dental morphology is quite similar to that of *D. ruscinensis*, but the face appears shorter and the interorbital region broader than is the case for *D. ruscinensis*, although this may in part be due to distortion in the fossils from Perpignan (Iwamoto et al. 2005; Spassov and Geraads 2007). The single individual is also larger than males of *D. ruscinensis* in estimated body mass based on molar dimensions (Nishimura et al. 2012). The presence of a maxillary sinus in the Japanese specimen also favours generic distinction (Nishimura et al. 2012).

The relationships among these three Pliocene larger colobines of Eurasia to one another and to extant and other fossil colobines are poorly resolved (Delson 1994; Jablonski 2002; Iwamoto et al. 2005; Spassov and Geraads 2007; Takai et al. 2009; Nishimura et al. 2012).

Recently described *Myanmarcolobus yawensis* is a medium to large colobine from the latest Miocene or early Pliocene of Myanmar (Takai et al. 2015). The only specimen is a mandibular corpus fragment preserving the molar teeth, but little of the bone inferior to the roots. Two isolated colobine molars were recovered from a nearby locality, but their taxonomic affinity is unclear (Takai et al. 2015).

Other than the new species *Semnopithecus gawensis* from late Pliocene Myanmar, no extant Asian colobine genera are present in the fossil record until the late early or Middle Pleistocene (Szalay and Delson 1979; Delson 1994; Jablonski 2002; Takai and Maschenko 2009; Takai et al. 2015). Specimens attributable to *Rhinopithecus* have been described from northern and southern China, and possibly Taiwan (Delson 1994; Jablonski 2002; Takai and Maschenko 2009; Chang et al. 2012). *Presbytis* and *Trachypithecus* have been found at several middle to late Pleistocene localities throughout mainland and island southeast Asia (Szalay and Delson 1979; Delson

1994; Jablonski 2002; Takai and Maschenko 2009), and *Semnopithecus* from the late Pleistocene of India (Jablonski 2002; Roberts et al. 2014).

Discussion

In the 1994 *Colobine Monkeys* volume by Glyn Davies and John Oates, only *M. tugenensis* from Ngeringerowa, two isolated cheek teeth from Nakali, and *?Colobus flandrini* from Menacer were discussed by Delson (1994) in the section covering the African Miocene, with the Plio-Pleistocene diversification of the colobines being the major focus of the paper. However, the enriched fossil record from the Miocene of Africa in the last two decades is remarkable, and early colobine evolution is becoming better documented. Currently, fossil colobines predating 8 Ma number 3 or 4 taxa. They exhibit molar morphology which is distinguished from cercopithecines by a greater amount of occlusal relief and sharper, more oblique lophs/lophids, but they are still conservative relative to extant colobines (Benefit 2000; Rossie et al. 2013; Suwa et al., in press). The majority are diminutive, although the Beticha colobine might have been guereza-sized (at least dentally).

Suwa et al. (2017) suggested that these early colobines (including the Eurasian *Mesopithecus*) might be part of a poorly represented radiation of stem colobines. In fact, recent discoveries of fossil cercopithecoids extending back to the latest Oligocene (*Nsungwepithecus gunnelli*; Stevens et al. 2013) and earliest Miocene (*Alophe metios*; Rasmussen et al. 2019) make molecular clock estimates suggesting an early Miocene divergence for Cercopithecinae and Colobinae more likely. If true, the first 5–7 million years of colobine evolution is still undocumented. Furthermore, if the split between extant Colobina and Presbytina occurred between ~13.5–9.0 Ma (Ting 2008a; Perelman et al. 2011; Reis et al. 2018), at least some of the earliest known fossil colobines could potentially be attributable to one of these extant subtribes.

Future research into colobine phylogenetic relationships will be crucial moving forward, and as alluded to above, is needed to document diagnostic craniodental characters separating the extant African and Asian clades. Despite being well documented with numerous taxa represented by numerous partial crania and skeletons, the phylogenetic relationships among fossil colobines are virtually unknown. This is largely because there are few craniodental features known to distinguish extant African and Asian clades from each other as well as from stem colobines. Understanding fossil colobine phylogenetic relationships is crucial to understanding many aspects of colobine evolution, such as the evolution of substrate use (e.g. how many times did terrestriality evolve?), the evolution of thumb reduction (e.g. did the common ancestor of crown colobines possess a reduced pollex or did this happen independently in Colobina and Presbytina?), and the number of biogeographic dispersal events into Eurasia (e.g. one or multiple?), just to name a few outstanding issues. While we view the conservative morphology of early fossil colobines such as *Microcolobus* as indicative of their likely stem position in colobine phylogeny, a better understanding and documentation of craniodental features separating the

Colobina and Presbytina will be necessary to confirm any current phylogenetic hypotheses. The level of thumb reduction in *C. williamsi* is strongly suggestive of affinities with the extant Colobina and, by extension, perhaps most other *Cercopithecoides* species as well (Frost et al. 2015). The isolated talus from the Lukeino Formation displaying a restricted groove for flexor tibialis may also be indicative of the presence of true colobinans in the fossil record by ~6 Ma (Gilbert et al. 2010), but additional diagnostic material is needed to be certain.

In any case, more dentally derived colobines appear after 7.5 Ma (e.g. Teso Tadecha, Mpesida, Toros-Menalla, Lukeino, Lemudong'o, Middle Awash), coupled with more committed folivorous dietary adaptations. By approximately 6 Ma a minimum of 3 genera and probably 6–10 species are represented. They are generally large-sized with some significantly larger than extant colobines, although smaller colobines were also present (e.g. Colobinae sp. B from Lukeino).

African Miocene colobines with postcranial information include *Microcolobus* (ca. 10 Ma), *C. bruneti* (7 Ma), *P. enkorikae* (6 Ma), and *K. aramisi* (5.7 Ma). All except for *C. bruneti* were largely arboreal (Hlusko 2007; Frost et al. 2009; Nakatsukasa et al. 2010; Pallas et al. 2019). Colobine postcranial fossils from the Lower Nawata also display modern arboreal colobine features (Leakey et al. 2003). Thus, if many of these Miocene taxa are indeed stem colobines (as is often assumed, see above), it is strongly suggested that the colobine last common ancestor was arboreal (see also Hlusko 2006). Some terrestrial locomotor signal observed in the Lower Nawata fossils (Leakey et al. 2003) would be better interpreted as an early case of terrestrial shift within colobines, rather than a retention of ancestral condition.

Reduction of the thumb is an extraordinary feature in extant colobines, with partial reduction in Asian colobines and more complete loss of the external thumb in African colobines (Strasser and Delson 1987). Only three fossil colobines allow diagnosis of this feature: *Microcolobus* sp., *Mesopithecus pentelicus*, and *Cercopithecoides williamsi*. Among these taxa, the Miocene forms have unreduced thumbs, while the pollex in *C. williamsi* appears fully reduced (Zapfe 1991; Nakatsukasa et al. 2010; Frost et al. 2015). Information from additional fossil colobines and a clearer picture of fossil colobine phylogenetic relationships are necessary to fully interpret these observations for colobine evolution (see above; Frost et al. 2015). However, an evolutionary a trade-off sacrificing precision grip for might be postulated improved efficiency of rapid arboreal movements (such as running, bouncing or leaping) on and between branches (see Tuttle 1975). Perhaps retention of precision grip was more important in Miocene colobines that had not committed to folivory (see Benefit 2000; Merceron et al. 2009), as precision grip would be important in foraging on smaller more scattered items such as seeds.

As discussed by Frost et al. (2015), the apparent lack of any significant thumb reduction in *Mesopithecus* could imply that either *Mesopithecus* is a stem colobine or that extant Asian colobines evolved thumb reduction independently from crown African colobines. The former scenario would imply multiple colobine dispersal events out of Africa, while the latter scenario would only necessitate a single dispersal event. Deciding between these two hypotheses will again depend on a better understanding of fossil colobine phylogeny.

Regardless of the number of dispersals by colobines between continents, the evolutionary history of colobines on both landmasses was likely affected by major climatic changes over the last 15 million years (e.g. Cerling et al. 1998; Zachos et al. 2001). These included increased aridity, seasonality and vegetative change in Africa (e.g. de Menocal 2004; Levin 2015) and increased uplift of the Himalaya-Tibetan Plateau and the establishment of the monsoon system by approximately 8 Ma in South Asia (e.g. Zisheng et al. 2001). Exactly how, these changes impacted colobines is not currently known, but they seem to have ultimately led to their extinction in Europe and temperate parts of Africa. It may also have played a role in the fact that colobines spread to Eurasia (ca. 8.5 Ma) prior to cercopithecines (ca. 6 Ma) (Jablonski 2002; Alba et al. 2014).

Finally, in modern habitats, colobines are usually sympatric with cercopithecines (Fleagle 2013). Colobine-cercopithecine sympatry is documented in many post-7.5 Ma Miocene localities, including Chorora (Beticha), Lothagam, Tugen Hills (Lukeino), Middle Awash, Gona, Menacer and Sahabi (Delson 1975; Meikle 1987; Leakey et al. 2003; Frost et al. 2009; Gilbert et al. 2010; Suwa et al. 2015; Levin et al. in press). This phenomenon superficially appears to indicate that committed folivory in colobines enabled niche partitioning with sympatric cercopithecines. However, the currently known earliest cercopithecine does not predate 7.5 Ma (Beticha). Therefore, this might simply be a result of poor sampling of cercopithecines at earlier localities (Ngorora, Ngeringerowa, Nakali). Coexistence and niche partitioning with cercopithecines are important issues to understand in colobine evolution. However, as with many of the issues discussed here, further exploration of the fossil record is necessary to conclude whether the under-representation of early cercopithecines is a real evolutionary phenomenon reflecting their delayed diversification and/or paleobiogeography or merely fossil sampling bias.

Acknowledgements

We sincerely thank Ikki Matsuda for inviting us to contribute this chapter to this important book, and we appreciate his great patience in waiting for its completion. We thank the editor and an anonymous reviewer for their helpful comments on a previous version of this manuscript. We thank Takeshi Nishimura for allowing us to reproduce the images of *Dolichopithecus* and *Kanagawapithecus* and Julia Arenson for the image of *Rhinopithecus roxellanae tingianus*.

4 Molecular Phylogeny and Phylogeography of Colobines

Christian Roos and Dietmar Zinner

Introduction

Colobine monkeys constitute a diverse subfamily within the Old World monkey family Cercopithecidae, but they have attracted relatively little scientific attention compared to their sister group, the Cercopithecinae. For instance, when searching PubMed (www.ncbi.nlm.nih.gov/pubmed/) for keywords 'phylogeny, evolution, DNA', a total of 870 publications are revealed for cercopithecines, but only 57 for colobines (22 March 2019). Likewise, when searching the GenBank Nucleotide database (www.ncbi.nlm.nih.gov/nucleotide/), 2,725,189 DNA sequences are obtained for Cercopithecinae, but only 530,100 for Colobinae. Although more work on colobine phylogeny was published in recent years, colobine monkeys continue to be one of the most understudied primate groups in terms of phylogeny and phylogeography, and much of their evolutionary history is still poorly understood. Nevertheless, available genetic studies have revealed interesting and unexpected insights into colobine evolution. In this chapter, we provide an overview of the current knowledge about Colobinae phylogeny and phylogeography. Moreover, we present and discuss phylogenetic relationships among all 10 colobine genera and 68 of the 80 recognized species based on published and unpublished mitochondrial sequence data. How certain clades/lineages should be ranked taxonomically is a matter of debate, in particular of the applied species concept. We follow here the taxonomy of Mittermeier et al. (2013) and Rowe and Myers (2016) (see also Chapter 2).

Colobine Monkeys

Extant colobine monkeys are mainly found in the tropical belt of Africa and throughout most of South and Southeast Asia, with a larger diversity in Asia (7 genera, 57 species) than in Africa (3 genera, 23 species) (Mittermeier et al. 2013; Rowe and Myers 2016; see also Chapter 2). Based on geographical distribution and morphological features, colobines have been divided into African (Colobini) and Asian (Semnopithecini or Presbytini) groups (Davies and Oates 1994; Delson 1975; Groves 2001; Napier 1970; Szalay and Delson 1979). Both groups have been suggested to form reciprocally monophyletic groups (Napier and Napier 1967; Davies and Oates 1994; Groves 2001), which is supported by mitochondrial and nuclear DNA sequence data (Figures 4.1a and 4.1b; Finstermeier et al. 2013; Perelman et al.

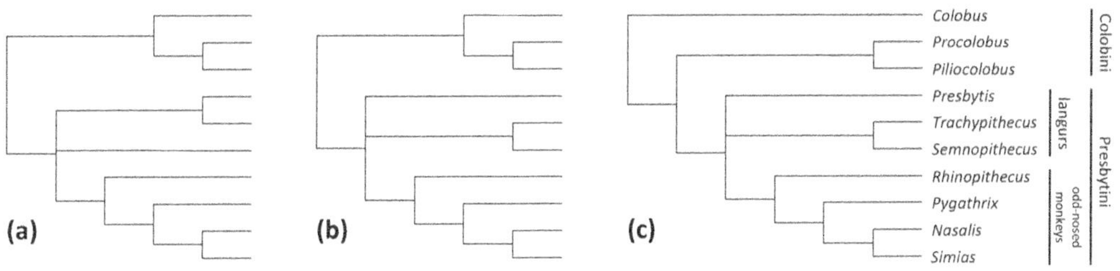

Figure 4.1 Contradicting phylogenetic relationships among colobine genera based on (a) mitochondrial DNA, (b) nuclear sequence data and (c) retroposon integrations.

2011; Pozzi et al. 2014; Roos et al. 2011; Springer et al. 2012; Sterner et al. 2006; Ting et al. 2008; Wang et al. 2012). However, retroposon integrations, a kind of repetitive element in the nuclear genome that can be used as molecular-cladistic markers, suggest the genus *Colobus* as sister lineage to all other colobines, making African colobines a paraphyletic group (Figure 4.1c; Roos et al. 2011). As mitochondrial and nuclear DNA sequences support reciprocal monophyly of African and Asian colobines, the branching pattern as obtained from retroposon integrations could be the result of incomplete lineage sorting or of a rare introgression event in African colobines that is difficult to trace with available data. Assuming that the basal position of *Colobus* as displayed by retroposon integrations is correct, Roos et al. (2011) suggested hybridization as the reason for the observed gene tree discordances. Accordingly, *Colobus* would indeed be the sister group to all other colobines but later obtained its mitochondrial genome from a *Piliocolobus*/*Procolobus* ancestor via female introgression. However, as currently only three retroposon integrations support this scenario, additional work is needed to fully uncover the phylogenetic relationships among African colobine genera.

Asian colobines are traditionally divided into the langur (genera *Semnopithecus*, *Trachypithecus*, *Presbytis*) and odd-nosed monkey groups (*Simias*, *Nasalis*, *Pygathrix*, *Rhinopithecus*) (Davies and Oates 1994; Groves 2001; Mittermeier et al. 2013; Napier and Napier 1967; Rowe and Myers 2016). While genetic data strongly support monophyly of the odd-nosed monkey group, the langur group appears to be paraphyletic (Figure 4.1; Liedigk et al. 2012; Perelman et al. 2011; Roos et al. 2011; Springer et al. 2012; Sterner et al. 2006; Ting et al. 2008; Wang et al. 2012; Zhang and Ryder 1998). Specifically, mitochondrial DNA suggests a *Trachypithecus*/*Presbytis* clade and an early separation of *Semnopithecus* among Asian colobines (Figures 4.1a, 4.2 and 4.3), while nuclear sequence data support a *Semnopithecus*/*Trachypithecus* clade and an early separation of *Presbytis* (Figures 4.1b and 4.1c; Liedigk et al. 2012; Perelman et al. 2011; Roos et al. 2011; Sterner et al. 2006; Ting et al. 2008; Wang et al. 2012). Again, various explanations for these gene tree discordances are discussed, but hybridization is generally favoured as the causal mechanism (Roos et al. 2011; Ting et al. 2008; Wang et al. 2012).

Combining all available information from molecular studies and the fossil record, the data suggest that colobine monkeys most likely evolved in Africa in the Early

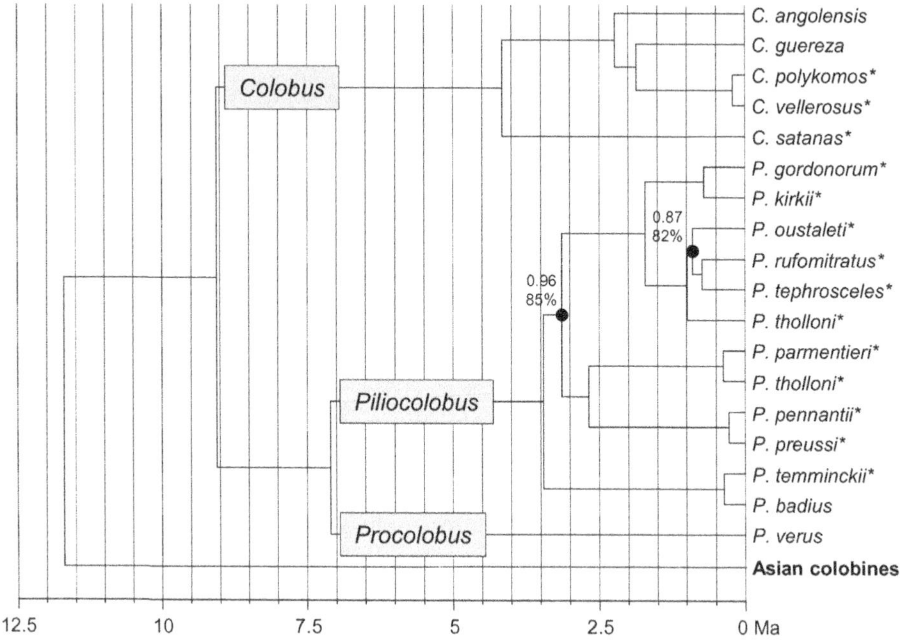

Figure 4.2 Ultrametric tree showing phylogenetic relationships among the African colobines based on mitochondrial DNA. For species labelled with an asterisk, only ~4000 bp of mitochondrial sequence information was available, while for all other species, the complete mitochondrial genome (~16,500 bp) was used. Nodes labelled with black dots exhibit posterior probabilities <1.0 and bootstrap values <95%. Bootstrap values and posterior probabilities were obtained from maximum-likelihood analysis with 10,000 ultrafast bootstrap replicates in IQ-TREE 1.5.2 (Nguyen et al. 2015) and Bayesian analysis with 10 million generations (25% burn-in) in MrBayes 3.2.6 (Ronquist et al. 2012), respectively. Molecular dating was performed with the BEAST 2.4.8 package (Bouckaert et al. 2014) using a relaxed clock model and a Yule speciation prior. To calibrate the molecular clock, we constrained the split between African and Asian colobines at 12.28–9.42 Ma (see Perelman et al. 2011). Ninety-five per cent highest posterior densities are not shown.

Miocene, 18–16 million years ago (Ma) (Davies and Oates 1994; Perelman et al. 2011; Roos et al. 2011; Stewart and Disotell 1998). Following the scenario proposed by Roos et al. (2011), on the African continent, *Colobus* split off first from the colobine stem, ~11 Ma, followed shortly afterwards by the ancestor of *Piliocolobus* and *Procolobus*. After this initial separation, hybridization between both *Colobus* and the *Piliocolobus*/*Procolobus* ancestors might have occurred, until they finally diverged 9–7.5 Ma. Presumably, respective splitting and hybridization events took place in western Africa, because all three African colobine genera occur there in sympatry (Davies and Oates 1994; Mittermeier et al. 2013; Rowe and Myers 2016), and the most ancient intra-generic splits in *Piliocolobus* and *Colobus* are found there as well (Figure 4.2; Ting 2008a). The ancestor of Asian colobines diverged from African colobines 12–10 Ma and subsequently invaded Eurasia (Goodman et al.

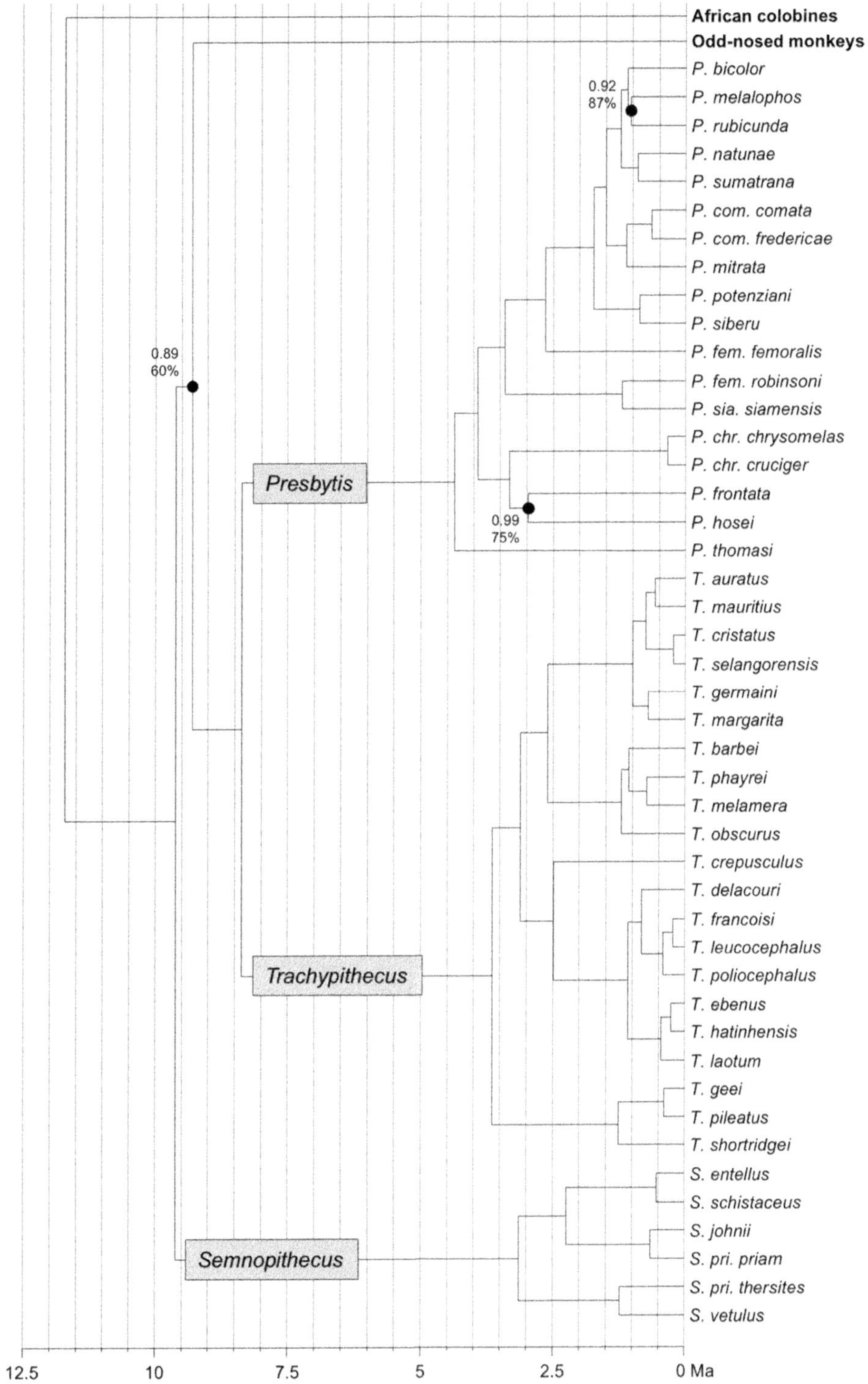

Figure 4.3 Ultrametric tree showing phylogenetic relationships among the Asian langur genera based on complete mitochondrial genomes (~16,500 bp). Nodes labelled with black dots

1998; Liedigk et al. 2012; Raaum et al. 2005; Roos et al. 2011; Sterner et al. 2006), probably via an emerging land bridge connecting Africa and the Arabian Peninsula (Stewart and Disotell 1998; Whybrow 1992).

After their arrival in Asia, colobine monkeys diverged 10–8 Ma into three lineages: *Semnopithecus*, *Trachypithecus/Presbytis* and the odd-nosed monkey group (Liedigk et al. 2012; Roos et al. 2011, 2019). This splitting event most likely occurred in southwestern China, probably in the Hengduan mountain range in the border region of today's Myanmar, India and China (Jablonski 1998a; Peng et al. 1993; Roos et al. 2011). During the Miocene, this region was affected by major geological and topographical changes, for instance, regional tectonic uplift and subsidence related to the orogeny of the Himalayan mountain range (An et al. 2001) and the emergence of the large Southeast Asian rivers (Mekong, Salween, Yangtze) (Hallet and Molnar 2001). These changes might have resulted in a series of vicariance events that have promoted the diversification of the lineages of Asian colobines and other primates (e.g. gibbons; Thinh et al. 2010) during the Late Miocene. Further support for this region as the 'cradle' of extant Asian colobines is provided by the discovery of a fossil colobine belonging to the genus *Mesopithecus* in northeastern Yunnan Province, near Zhaotong, that was classified as a stem colobine (Jablonski et al. 2011). After the initial split, *Semnopithecus* invaded the Indian subcontinent, while the ancestor of *Trachypithecus/Presbytis* colonized the Southeast Asian mainland, and the progenitor of the odd-nosed monkeys invaded the region of today's China.

After the separation from *Presbytis*, *Trachypithecus* came into secondary contact with *Semnopithecus*, providing opportunities for gene flow. However, in contrast to the mitochondrial capture event proposed for African colobines, for *Semnopithecus* and *Trachypithecus*, male introgression followed by nuclear swamping seems to be the more likely process (Roos et al. 2011). As a result of this unidirectional introgression, the original nuclear genome of *Trachypithecus* might have been largely replaced by that of *Semnopithecus*, while the original mitochondrial genome of *Trachypithecus* was retained. In contrast, there is no indication for hybridization among genera of the odd-nosed monkey group. This group shows a north–south diverging pattern, with *Rhinopithecus* splitting first, followed by *Pygathrix*, and with *Nasalis* and *Simias* separating at last (Liedigk et al. 2012; Roos et al. 2011, 2019).

Figure 4.3 (*cont.*) exhibit posterior probabilities <1.0 and bootstrap values <95%. Bootstrap values and posterior probabilities were obtained from maximum-likelihood analysis with 10,000 ultrafast bootstrap replicates in IQ-TREE 1.5.2 (Nguyen et al. 2015) and Bayesian analysis with 10 million generations (25% burn-in) in MrBayes 3.2.6 (Ronquist et al. 2012), respectively. Molecular dating was performed with the BEAST 2.4.8 package (Bouckaert et al. 2014) using a relaxed clock model and a Yule speciation prior. To calibrate the molecular clock, we constrained the split between African and Asian colobines at 12.28–9.42 Ma (see Perelman et al. 2011). Ninety-five per cent highest posterior densities are not shown.

African Colobines: Colobus Monkeys

According to molecular genetic studies (Roos et al. 2011; Ting 2008a; but see retroposon data in Roos et al. 2011), olive colobus (genus *Procolobus*) and red colobus (genus *Piliocolobus*) cluster together, and black-and-white colobus (genus *Colobus*) constitute their sister lineage. *Colobus* diverged 9–7.5 Ma from the *Procolobus/Piliocolobus* clade, and the latter two separated 7–6 Ma (Figure 4.2; Finstermeier et al. 2013; Perelman et al. 2011; Roos et al. 2011; Sterner et al. 2006; Ting 2008a).

Although the branching pattern among African colobine genera is generally well settled, phylogenetic relationships within the polytypic genera *Colobus* and *Piliocolobus* are only partially resolved, and so far only a single molecular genetic study investigating several of the African colobine species has been published (Ting 2008a). For *Colobus*, Ting (2008a), using a ~4000-bp-long fragment of the mitochondrial genome, found strong support for an early separation of *C. satanas* from the main stem ~4 Ma, followed successively by *C. angolensis* and *C. guereza* ~2 Ma, before finally *C. polykomos* and *C. vellerosus* diverged ~0.2 Ma (Figure 4.2). For *Piliocolobus*, Ting (2008a) investigated 11 of the 17 species (Mittermeier et al. 2013; Rowe and Myers 2016; see also Chapter 2) and found four major lineages that were established during initial differentiation events 3.5–2.5 Ma, which follow largely a West to East African pattern. The first contains *P. badius* and *P. temminckii*; the second *P. pennantii* and *P. preussi*; the third *P. parmentieri* and *P. tholloni*; and the fourth *P. gordonorum*, *P. kirkii*, *P. oustaleti*, *P. rufomitratus*, *P. tephrosceles* and again *P. tholloni* (Figure 4.2; Ting 2008a). In the latter clade, *P. gordonorum* and *P. kirkii* form a sister clade to the other four species and diverged from them ~1.5 Ma. Speciation events in these two sub-clades occurred 1.0–0.6 Ma, while in the other three clades, differentiation into species occurred ~0.3 Ma.

Interestingly, *P. tholloni* is mitochondrially paraphyletic, with one lineage clustering with *P. parmentieri* and the other with *P. oustaleti*, *P. rufomitratus* and *P. tephrosceles*. This mitochondrial phenomenon is most likely the result of hybridization and/or the retention of ancestral lineages (Ting 2008a), but further investigations are necessary to clarify the reasons for these findings.

Asian Colobines, Langur Group

As already mentioned, the langur group is probably paraphyletic, and similarities in phenotypical and anatomical appearance are likely the result of a mixture of common ancestry (*Presbytis* and *Trachypithecus*) and ancient hybridization (*Trachypithecus* and *Semnopithecus*). Surilis (genus *Presbytis*) are mainly found in the Sundaland region and comprise 17 species (Mittermeier et al. 2013; Roos et al. 2014; Rowe and Myers 2016; see also Chapter 2). Only a few molecular genetic studies are available for *Presbytis* (Abdul-Latiff et al. 2019; Md-Zain 2001; Meyer et al. 2011; Vun et al. 2011); all used only short fragments of the mitochondrial genome and thus were not able to solve the branching pattern among taxa significantly. In contrast, our complete mitochondrial genome data provide a well-resolved phylogeny (Figure 4.3). Accordingly, *P. thomasi* was the first species to split from the common lineage, ~4.4 Ma, while the remaining taxa diverged ~3.9 Ma into a pure Borneo clade and a mixed clade containing taxa from Borneo, Sumatra, Java, Malay Peninsula and the Mentawai Islands. Within the pure Borneo clade, speciation events leading to *P. chrysomelas*, *P. frontata* and *P. hosei* occurred 3.3–3.0 Ma. Unfortunately, data for *P. sabana* and *P. canicrus* are not yet available. The two subspecies of *P. chrysomelas*, *P. c. chrysomelas* and *P. c. cruciger*, separated ~0.3 Ma. In the mixed clade, the taxa from the northern part of the Malay Peninsula, *P. femoralis robinsoni* and *P. siamensis siamensis*, diverged from the remaining taxa ~3.4 Ma, while the taxon from the southern part of the Malay Peninsula, *P. femoralis femoralis*, clusters with the latter and separated from them ~2.6 Ma. Accordingly, *P. femoralis* appears as a paraphyletic group. Unfortunately, no data from additional subspecies of *P. femoralis* and *P. simanensis* are available to trace their phylogenetic relationships.

Among the remaining taxa, the species from the Mentawai Islands, *P. siberu* and *P. potenziani*, diverged first, ~1.7 Ma, and further separated into species ~0.9 Ma. *P. mitrata* from southern Sumatra clusters with *P. comata* from Java, while the more northern Sumatran species, *P. bicolor*, *P. melalophos* and *P. sumatrana*, cluster with *P. natunae* from the Natuna Islands and *P. rubucinda* from Borneo. The split between these two major clades occurred ~1.5 Ma, with subsequent speciation events lasting until ~0.9 Ma. In general, nuclear sequence data (Roos, unpublished data) provide a highly similar tree topology with similar divergence times; however, in contrast to the mitochondrial gene tree, nuclear DNA supports a common ancestry of *P. femoralis*, *P. siamensis*, *P. chrysomelas* and *P. natunae*. These findings reveal some interesting hypotheses: (1) *P. rubicunda* from Borneo, *P. natunae* from the Natuna Islands and *P. comata* from Java originated on Sumatra and left the island relatively recently, 1.0–0.9 Ma; (2) the recent migration of *P. rubicunda* to Borneo could be an explanation for its sympatry with other Bornean species; (3) secondary gene flow among *Presbytis* species seems to be rare and probably occurred only between *P. femoralis*, *P. siamensis*, *P. chrysomelas* and *P. natunae*; (4) the current classification of *Presbytis* into 17 species (Mittermeier et al. 2013; Roos et al. 2014; Rowe and Myers 2016; see also Chapter 2) reflects phylogenetic relationships better than previous classifications.

Lutungs (genus *Trachypithecus*) represent the most speciose (22 species) and the most widely distributed genus among all Asian colobines. They occur from Bhutan and Assam in the west to Vietnam and southern China in the east and south to Java (Mittermeier et al. 2013; Roos et al. 2014; Rowe and Myers 2016; see also Chapter 2). Lutungs can be phenotypically and genetically divided into four species groups. Mitochondrial genome and nuclear sequence data provide almost congruent phylogenies and suggest that the *T. pileatus* group diverged first (~3.6 Ma), followed by the *T. francoisi* group (~3.1 Ma), while the *T. obscurus* group and the *T. cristatus* group separated later (~2.6 Ma) (Figure 4.3; Roos et al. 2019). Interestingly, in earlier molecular studies, in which only a fragment of the mitochondrial genome, the cytochrome *b* gene, was analysed, the *T. pileatus* group clustered with

Semnopithecus and not with *Trachypithecus* (Karanth 2008, 2010; Karanth et al. 2008; Osterholz et al. 2008). Since nuclear DNA data suggested that the *T. pileatus* group actually clusters with other *Trachypithecus*, the observed gene tree discordance was regarded as an indication of a hybrid origin for the *T. pileatus* group (Karanth 2008, 2010; Karanth et al. 2008; Osterholz et al. 2008). However, the investigated cytochrome *b* gene sequences did not represent original mitochondrial sequence information but consisted of nuclear copies of the mitochondrial DNA (numts), which led to questioning the hybrid origin hypothesis. Wang et al. (2015), however, found an almost complete numt in the nuclear genome of members of the *T. pileatus* group. This numt is phylogenetically related to the mitochondrial genome of *Semnopithecus* but absent in other *Trachypithecus* species, suggesting that the group obtained this numt from a *Semnopithecus* ancestor via unidirectional introgression and that the *T. pileatus* group is indeed of hybrid origin.

Within the *T. pileatus* group, three species are recognized, of which *T. shortridgei* is sister to a *T. pileatus*/*T. geei* clade (Figure 4.3). *T. shortridgei* separated from *T. pileatus*/*T. geei* ~1.3 Ma, and the latter two split ~0.4 Ma. The *T. francoisi* group contains seven species, which radiated into a northern (*T. francoisi, T. poliocephalus, T. leucocephalus*), a central (*T. delacouri*) and a southern (*T. hatinhensis, T. laotum, T. ebenus*) lineage/clade (Roos 2004; Roos et al. 2007, 2019). The southern species represent a sister clade to the central and northern lineage/clade and separated from them ~1.1 Ma, while the central lineage and northern clade diverged ~0.8 Ma (Figure 4.3; Roos 2004; Roos et al. 2019).

Within the southern clade, *T. laotum* separated from *T. hatinhensis*/*T. ebenus* ~0.4 Ma. As Figure 4.3 depicts, *T. hatinhensis* and *T. ebenus* diverged ~0.2 Ma, but there is strong evidence that *T. ebenus* is nested within the *T. hatinhensis* clade (Roos 2004). Likewise, in the northern clade, *T. poliocephalus* is depicted as a sister lineage to a *T. leucocephalus*/*T. francoisi* clade (Figure 4.3), but *T. francoisi* seems to be polyphyletic with *T. leucocephalus* and *T. poliocephalus*, forming monophyletic clades nested within the polyphyletic *T. francoisi* cluster (Liu Z et al. 2013a). However, when considering nuclear sequence data, *T. francoisi* individuals cluster together and do not indicate polyphyly (Roos, unpublished data). Within the *T. cristatus* group, six species are recognized and group into mainland (*T. germaini, T. margarita*), Javan (*T. auratus, T. mauritius*) and central Sundaland (*T. cristatus, T. selangorensis*) clades (Figure 4.3; Nadler et al. 2005; Roos et al. 2008, 2019). The mainland clade branched off first (~1.0 Ma), and Javan and central Sundaland clades diverged ~0.8 Ma. Speciation events within these clades commenced ~0.7 Ma with the split between *T. germaini* and *T. margarita* and ended with the divergence of *T. cristatus* and *T. selangorensis* ~0.2 Ma. *T. cristatus* from Sumatra, Borneo and the Natuna Islands cluster together without any geographical structuring (Roos et al. 2008). The *T. obscurus* group consists of six species, *T. obscurus, T. barbei, T. phayrei, T. melamera, T. popa* and *T. crepusculus*. Mitochondrial DNA analyses surprisingly revealed that *T. crepusculus* is not closely related to other members of the *T. obscurus* group but instead represents a distant relative of the *T. francoisi* group; both diverged ~2.5 Ma (Figure 4.3; Geissmann et al. 2004; He et al. 2012; Karanth 2008; Karanth et al. 2008; Liedigk et al. 2009; Roos 2004; Roos et al. 2007, 2019, 2020). In contrast, nuclear data clearly link *T. crepusculus* with the *T. obscurus* group (Liedigk et al. 2009) and specifically with *T. barbei* (Roos et al. 2019). Roos et al. (2019) explains these findings with male introgression followed by nuclear swamping from *T. barbei* into a now extinct taxon, distantly related to the *T. francoisi* group, of which only the mitochondrial genome survived. Among the remaining members of the *T. obscurus* group, *T. obscurus* diverged ~1.2 Ma, followed shortly afterwards by the split between *T. barbei* and *T. phayrei/T. melamera* ~1.1 Ma (Figure 4.3; Roos et al. 2019, 2020). The latter two separated ~0.7 Ma. Overall, it seems, in contrast to other Asian colobines, that diversification events in different species groups of *Trachypithecus* occurred on similar time scales, suggesting that a unique large-scale range expansion contributed to simultaneous diversification.

The South Asian langurs, genus *Semnopithecus*, are predominately found on the Indian subcontinent and comprise eight species (Mittermeier et al. 2013; Roos et al. 2014; Rowe and Myers 2016; see also Chapter 2). Originally, the genus referred only to Hanuman langurs, but genetic data consistently showed that two phenotypically different species, *S. vetulus* and *S. johnii*, previously assigned to *Trachypithecus*, belong to the genus as well (Figure 4.3; Karanth 2008, 2010; Karanth et al. 2008; Osterholz et al. 2008; Wangchuk et al. 2008; Zhang and Ryder 1998). Molecular data have further shown that Hanuman langurs, traditionally lumped into a single species, *S. entellus*, contain various deep lineages which are paraphyletic in respect to *S. johnii* and *S. vetulus* (Karanth 2008, 2010; Karanth et al. 2008, 2010; Osterholz et al. 2008; Wangchuk et al. 2008). In fact, mitochondrial DNA data suggest that South Asian langurs diversified into three major clades, a Sri Lankan clade with *S. vetulus* and the Sri Lankan Hanuman langurs (*S. priam thersites*), a South Indian clade with *S. johnii* and the South Indian Hanuman langurs (*S. priam priam, S. p. anchises, S. hypoleucos*) and a pure North Indian Hanuman langur clade with *S. entellus, S. hector, S. schistaceus* and *S. ajax* (Figure 4.3; Karanth 2008, 2010; Karanth et al. 2008, 2010; Osterholz et al. 2008). Population genetic data confirmed the differentiation of South Indian taxa into four lineages (Ashalakshmi et al. 2015), but currently, no such data are available for the Sri Lankan and North Indian clades. According to mitochondrial sequence data, the Sri Lankan clade diverged first (~3.2 Ma), while the two mainland clades separated ~2.2 Ma (Figure 4.3).

Asian Colobines, Odd-Nosed Monkey Group

Genetic data provide strong evidence for monophyly of the odd-nosed monkeys (Figures 4.1 and 4.4; Liedigk et al. 2012; Perelman et al. 2011; Roos et al. 2011; Springer et al. 2012; Sterner et al. 2006; Ting et al. 2008; Wang et al. 2012; Zhang and Ryder 1998). However, in contrast to previous classifications in which *Rhinopithecus* was regarded as a sister lineage to *Pygathrix* (Brandon-Jones 1984a, 1996b; Davies and Oates 1994; Delson 1975; Groves 1970, 1989; Napier 1985; Rowe 1996), genetic data support a basal position of *Rhinopithecus* among odd-nosed monkeys, while *Pygathrix* is distantly related to the *Nasalis/Simias* clade (Liedigk

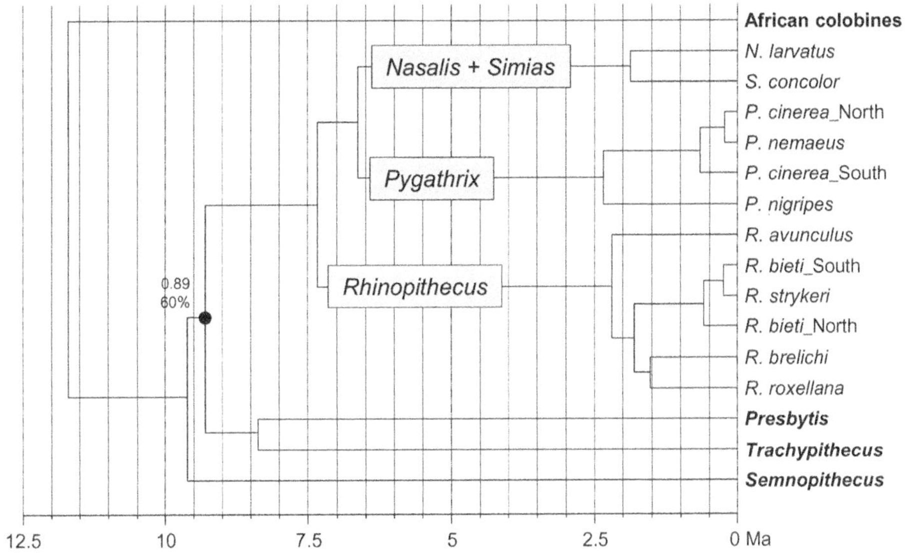

Figure 4.4 Ultrametric tree showing phylogenetic relationships among the odd-nosed monkeys based on complete mitochondrial genomes (~16,500 bp). Nodes labelled with black dots exhibit posterior probabilities <1.0 and bootstrap values <95%. Bootstrap values and posterior probabilities were obtained from maximum-likelihood analysis with 10,000 ultrafast bootstrap replicates in IQ-TREE 1.5.2 (Nguyen et al. 2015) and Bayesian analysis with 10 million generations (25% burn-in) in MrBayes 3.2.6 (Ronquist et al. 2012), respectively. Molecular dating was performed with the BEAST 2.4.8 package (Bouckaert et al. 2014) using a relaxed clock model and a Yule speciation prior. To calibrate the molecular clock, we constrained the split between African and Asian colobines at 12.28–9.42 Ma (see Perelman et al. 2011). Ninety-five per cent highest posterior densities are not shown.

et al. 2012; Perelman et al. 2011; Roos et al. 2011). According to molecular dating, *Rhinopithecus* diverged from the main stem ~7 Ma, followed by *Pygathrix* ~6 Ma, while *Nasalis* and *Simias* separated as recently as 2–1 Ma (Liedigk et al. 2012; Perelman et al. 2011; Roos et al. 2011, 2019).

Snub-nosed monkeys (genus *Rhinopithecus*) occur in China, Vietnam and Myanmar. In terms of genetics, they are by far the most studied colobines, because mitochondrial and nuclear sequence data and even whole-genome data are available for all five species. With these data, particularly with whole-genome data, it became obvious that snub-nosed monkeys exhibit a complex evolutionary history with various events of secondary gene flow among populations and species (Liedigk et al. 2012; Yu et al. 2016; Zhou et al. 2014, 2016). Based on mitochondrial data (Figure 4.4; Liedigk et al. 2012), *R. avunculus* diverged ~2.4 Ma, followed by the divergence of the ancestors of the Himalayan species (*R. bieti*, *R. strykeri*) and the northern species (*R. roxellana*, *R. brelichi*) ~2 Ma. Mitochondrial and nuclear data further suggest that the northern species diverged 1.8–1.1 Ma and remained separated thereafter, with only limited gene flow among them (Liedigk et al. 2012; Yang et al. 2012; Yu et al. 2016; Zhou et al. 2014, 2016). In contrast, *R. avunculus* most likely came into secondary contact with the ancestor of the Himalayan species, and gene flow among them occurred until ~0.7 Ma. Between 0.6 and 0.2 Ma, the ancestor of the Himalayan species originally split into three lineages (*R. bieti* haplogroup South, *R. bieti* haplogroup North, *R. strykeri*). The *R. bieti* haplogroup South occurs mainly in the southern part of the species' range (Liu et al. 2007) and is more closely related to *R. strykeri* than to *R. bieti* haplogroup North (Liedigk et al. 2012). After the separation of *R. strykeri* ~0.2 Ma, both *R. bieti* haplogroups came into contact again and homogenized their nuclear gene pools (Liu et al. 2009). Today, both mitochondrial haplogroups of *R. bieti* intergrade, but there is still a trend of a northern and a southern clade (Liu et al. 2007).

Douc langurs (genus *Pygathrix*) occur east of the Mekong River, in Vietnam, Laos and Cambodia. Three species of douc langurs replace each other from north to south. According to mitochondrial and nuclear sequence data, the southernmost species, *P. nigripes*, is clearly separated from its congenerics and diverged from them 2.5–1.6 Ma, while *P. cinerea* and *P. nemaeus* appear as closely related sister species that diverged from each other only recently (~0.2 Ma) (Figure 4.4; Liedigk et al. 2012; Perelman et al. 2011; Roos and Nadler 2001). Interestingly, when considering mitochondrial sequence data, *P. cinerea* is paraphyletic, with the *P. cinerea* haplogroup North being more closely related to *P. nemaeus* than to the *P. cinerea* haplogroup South, while nuclear sequence data suggest monophyly of *P. cinerea* (Liedigk et al. 2012). Liedigk et al. (2012) suggested secondary gene flow among *P. cinerea* populations as a potential cause for these findings.

The proboscis monkey, *Nasalis larvatus*, from Borneo and the simakobu, *Simias concolor*, from the Mentawai Islands are closely related and separated 1.9–1.1 Ma. This relatively recent split is surprising, because both taxa exhibit prominent morphological differences and thus suggest that autapomorphic morphological traits can emerge in relatively short time periods.

Conclusions and Future Directions

In recent years, tremendous advances have been made in understanding the evolutionary history of colobine monkeys. However, compared to the cercopithecines, colobine monkeys are still a neglected group of primates, and much more work is needed to fully uncover and understand their evolutionary history. Molecular genetic studies provided interesting and unexpected insights into colobine evolution and often changed traditional thinking. For instance, in the past, langurs were regarded as a monophyletic group and thus lumped into a single genus, *Presbytis* (Napier 1985; Napier and Napier 1967, 1994), while today, three, most likely paraphyletic langur genera are accepted (Brandon-Jones et al. 2004; Davies and Oates 1994; Groves 1989, 2001; Mittermeier et al. 2013; Roos et al. 2014; Rowe and Myers 2016). Also based on molecular data, Nilgiri and purple-faced langurs have been reassigned from *Trachypithecus* to *Semnopithecus* (Mittermeier et al. 2013; Karanth 2008; Karanth et al. 2008; Osterholz et al. 2008; Roos et al. 2014; Rowe and Myers

2016; Zhang and Ryder 1998). However, most molecular studies on colobines conducted so far used only mitochondrial sequence data. As the mitochondrial genome is only maternally inherited, it provides insight only into a particular, but important, part of the evolutionary history of a taxon, whereas its complete evolutionary history remains obscure. With an increasing number of studies using multi-locus data, discordances among gene trees and secondary gene flow, that is, hybridization or introgression, are regularly observed (for a review, see Zinner et al. 2011). Thus, to fully uncover the evolutionary history of taxa mitochondrial and nuclear sequences, in best case, whole genomes should be investigated. However, the major problem with colobines is the difficulty of getting hands on material for genetic studies, because colobines are rare in zoos, and sample collection in the field is likewise difficult for practical and administrative reasons. In this respect, museum specimens are of great value, as large numbers with mostly well-documented geographic origin are housed in the world's museum collections. With the advances in molecular genetics, particularly high-throughput sequencing technologies, it is possible to genetically investigate small amounts of highly degraded DNA as typically extracted from museum samples (or from non-invasively collected faecal material). With these new methods, a mass of genetic information, up to complete genomes, from many individuals can be generated in a time- and cost-efficient way. Although such data are almost absent for colobines so far, first attempts are under way, and soon comprehensive sequence data of colobines will be available.

Acknowledgements

We thank the editors for inviting us to contribute to this important book. Many thanks also to an anonymous reviewer for helpful comments on an earlier version of the manuscript and to numerous colleagues for providing valuable sample material.

5 Relationships between the Diet and Dentition of Asian Leaf Monkeys

Barth W. Wright and Mary S. Willis

Introduction

Some of the first colobine species were identified in the late eighteenth century and yet, a comprehensive taxonomic and ecological analysis of what was later to become a subfamily of Old World monkeys was not completed until the mid-twentieth century (Davies and Oates 1994). It was in this first synthesis of colobine monkey research, combining everything from ecology to social behaviour, anatomy and physiology to evolutionary history, that the dentition of colobines was described as 'generally quite homogenous' (Delson 1994). At the time the compilation was published, 1994, the most prominent dental studies had been conducted at the family level, and morphometric comparisons were made relative to the teeth of cercopithecines. Colobines were thus described, compared to other Old World species of similar body sizes, as leaf-eating monkeys with high, pointed molar cusps linked by ridges, and relatively deep lingual notches (Delson 1973; Kay, 1975, 1978, 1981; Kay and Hylander 1978; Benefit 1987). Moreover, colobine incisor rows were said to be narrow mesio-distally and 'sheathed' in enamel (Hylander 1975; Shellis and Hiiemae 1986). An assessment of the shape and size of colobine teeth compared to those of other anthropoids suggested that these dental features in colobines would enhance the extraction of required nutrients from the non-reproductive parts of trees and other plants. Furthermore, the observed exploitation of a high percentage of leaves, by a small number of taxa, was hypothesized as the primary selective agent for these characteristic morphological traits or features, e.g. a narrow incisor row with labial and lingual surface enamel, high molar cusps, long slicing crests, relatively thin molar enamel, and a relatively high molar surface area (Shultz 1958; Swindler et al. 1967; Zingeser 1970; Delson 1973; Swindler and Orlosky 1974; Kay 1975, 1978, 1981; Hylander 1975; Swindler 1976, 1979; Kay and Hylander 1978; Weitzel 1978; Teaford 1983; Napier and Napier 1985; Benefit 1987; Lucas and Teaford 1994).

Essentially, colobines have been described as primates that make minimal use of the anterior teeth compared to the posterior ones because that is how leaves and related food items are processed. For example, in three separate studies of a total of 57 primate species which included 17 colobines, the relative length of the incisor row was assumed to represent the relative amount of use of the anterior teeth for processing based on the food type most commonly consumed. However, there were few published data on food processing behaviour by primates in the wild. (Jolly 1970;

This chapter includes Electronic Supplementary Material (ESM) at: www.cambridge.org/colobines

Hylander 1975; Kay and Hylander 1978). Large, tough-skinned fruits were linked to extensive incisal preparation, while heavier molar mastication was described as critical for processing foods common in colobine diets, i.e. leaves, stems, berries, grasses, seeds, buds or flowers (Kay and Hylander 1978). Longer rows were hypothesized to permit more extensive use of the incisors as the more the dental surface area available, the longer they would withstand 'increased amounts of attrition and abrasion' (Kay and Hylander 1978: 178). Thus, relatively short incisal rows, such as those possessed by colobines, correlate with leaf consumption because they require less processing time, while longer rows indicated more emphasis on fruit (Jolly 1970; Hylander 1975; Kay and Hylander 1978).

The relationship between incisor row length and diet was suggested as applying to individual colobine species. Where sympatric species consume different food types, 'the more frugivorous of the two' would possess longer incisal tooth rows (Hylander, 1975: 1097). Thus, *Semnopithecus entellus* with relatively long rows was described as more frugivorous than closely related *S. senex* or *S. johnii*, who were thought to be more folivorous and hence with shorter rows (Hylander 1975; Kay and Hylander 1978). Among those species for whom diets were not well known, it was predicted that those with relatively short incisal occlusal surfaces would be consuming leaves, with extensive molar processing. *Presbytis potenziani* was predicted to be more frugivorous than sympatric *Simias concolor*, for example, while *Presbytis frontata* would consume more fruit than the 'highly folivorous' *Nasalis larvatus* (Hylander 1975; Kay and Hylander 1978).

Ideally, predictions about incisor row length, molar morphology, tooth use and dietary emphasis could be tested in long-term ecological studies measuring dental wear in each colobine species. From the results of such longitudinal studies, detailed ecological data and life-history variables could be correlated to specific dental patterns. However, among colobine taxa, and most especially Southeast Asian ones, longitudinal studies are rare; hence, few life-history variables for any species are available (Borries et al. 2001; Wich et al. 2007). But also, among those few species for whom longitudinal data have been collected, e.g, Thomas' langur (*Presbytis thomasi*) for 12.5 years at Ketambe Research Station, Sumatra, Indonesia and Hanuman langurs (*Semnopithecus entellus*) for 6 years at Ramnagar, Southern Nepal, site conditions were not ideal; individual animals were not tagged, long-term food acquisition and processing data not collected, and have not been made dental casts (Borries et al. 2001; Wich et al. 2007).

However, since the 1970s, many more Asian colobine species have been studied in the wild for one or two years. From these studies, we now know that there is signficant dietary diversity. Still after more than 50 years of primate dental research, it remains unclear why the Asian colobine radiation has been so successful, resulting in more than 40 species, many of whom are sympatric. Is there true dental uniformity, and if so, what has allowed colobines to exploit such an array of food types and textures? Perhaps as Davies and Oates (1994) suggested, 'The relative lack of interest in and knowledge of colobines, together with the concentration of field studies on a few species, has tended to obscure the fact that the colobines are an anatomically, ecologically and socially varied group of primates' (Davies and Oates 1994: 1). Both long-term and recently conducted field studies have resulted in dietary reclassifications for some species. For example, some colobine taxa have been reclassified in terms of dietary focus, described as primarily frugivorous or as fruit/seed specialists (Davies, 1984, 1991; Bennett and Davies 1994; Kirkpatrick 1998). In the present study, we turn to additional dental analyses to test a number of hypotheses concerning dental morphology and diet among primates generally, and colobines more specifically. Our variables are selected given previous comparative analyses of colobine and cercopithecine dental morphology (Lucas and Teaford 1994) and recently proposed models of dental attrition (Lucas et al. 2008) and enamel adaptation to fallback food use (Constantino et al. 2009). Lucas and Teaford (1994) hypothesized that colobine molars, which appear to be constructed of both wedges formed between cusps and mesio-distal crests, are adapted for leaf fracture, particularly young leaf fracture, and the fracture of the tough seeds of unripe fruits. They further suggested that ripe fruit seed swallowers should have the relatively largest/widest incisor rows, while seed destroyers (colobines relative to cercopithecines) should have the relatively smallest/narrowest incisor rows. More recently it was argued by Constantino et al. (2009) that relatively thick enamel protects molars from a diet rich in grit and phytoliths, which can lead to surface yielding (i.e. wear), or the consumption of large hard foods, which produces longitudinal cracks, beginning at the enamel-dentine junction, that are incurred before any surface yielding can take place. In turn, low, blunt dental surfaces, due to their greater radius of curvature, particularly when coupled with relatively large molar area, also were argued by Constantino et al. (2009) to prevent enamel cracking.

We first compare the relative size of the incisors to one another, the relative width of the upper versus the lower incisor row, and then the width of the incisor rows relative to the length of the molar rows in order to test the hypothesis of relative incisor size proposed by Lucas and Teaford (1994). We predict that those taxa that prey upon seeds (i.e. seed destroyers), such as *Presbytis*, will exhibit wider incisor rows than other species, which less frequently exploit fruits and fruit parts, such as *Pygathrix* (See ESM Table 5.1 for a full list of study species and their associated diets). Our focus then turns to an analysis of relative molar area, distance between molar cusps (referred to here as 'cuspal splay') relative to crown area, cusp height relative to crown area, and finally degree of crestedness[1] (average crest length) relative to molar area. Thus cusp height when coupled with degree of molar cresting and relative molar area, are used to indirectly assess enamel thickness, and the degree of bunodonty. The latter is a general term indicative of molars with rounded cusps, thereby suggesting the degree to which foods other than tough leafy tissues are consumed.

Methods

Metric and morphological data were collected from 647 wild-caught Asian colobine specimens housed at 20 museum collections worldwide (see Willis and Swindler

[1] We opt for the term 'cresting' or 'relative cresting' as opposed to 'shear' given the explanations put forward by Lucas (2004) for the slicing as opposed to shearing function of molar crests.

2004 for collections used and sample details). For our anterior dental and molar comparisons, we have representatives of the two major groups of Asian colobine: the *Semnopithecus-Trachypithecus-Presbytis* group and the odd-nosed monkeys (Roos and Nadler 2001; Bigoni et al. 2003; Roos 2004; Roos et al. 2007; Karanth et al. 2008; Roos et al. 2008; Zain et al. 2008). Although Asian colobine taxonomy had not been resolved prior to the genetic studies of the twenty-first century, data were collected using genus and species designations following multiple sources (Hill 1934; Pocock 1935; Tilson 1976; Brandon-Jones, 1984b, 1993; Aimi and Bakar 1992; Groves 1993; Zhang and Ryder 1998; Morales et al. 1999; Brandon-Jones et al. 2004); thus a conservative approach was employed that included eight genera: *Presbytis, Trachypithecus, Semnopithecus, Kasi, Nasalis, Simias, Pygathrix* and *Rhinopithecus*. In assessing how well our samples encompass the range of Asian colobine phylogenetic diversity, we refer to the mitochondrial gene trees of Roos et al. (2008) and Zain et al. (2008). Recent taxonomic resolution, using results of multiple studies, have affirmed the need for a conservative approach and allowed analysis of genus and species relationships not previously possible (Bigoni et al. 2003, 2006; Sterner et al. 2006; Karanth et al. 2008; Osterholz et al. 2008; Ting et al. 2008). Original records of capture, general morphology and measurements were examined for each individual specimen to increase placement accuracy within a particular taxon. Based on recent genetic resolution of South Asian colobine taxonomy, in this study we assessed seven genera – collapsing the genus *Kasi* into *Semnopithecus* – and 24 species (Karanth et al. 2008). We include species of four odd-nosed genera (*Nasalis* [1], *Pygathrix* [1], *Simias* [1], and *Rhinopithecus* [2]) and representatives of *Presbytis* (7), *Semnopithecus* (4) and *Trachypithecus* (6) (ESM Table 5.1). The majority of our species designations follow those recognized by the International Union for the Conservation of Nature (IUCN), with the exception that we refer to *Semnopithecus priam* as *S. thersites* and place *Trachypithecus vetulus* within the genus *Semnopithecus*. The latter change is supported by molecular data (Osterholz et al. 2008).

Only adult specimens, as determined by M_3 eruption, with relatively unworn teeth were examined. Specifically, specimens were excluded from the sample if the dentine exposed on each cusp exceeded pinpoint size. Measurements were made with digital calipers (*Mitutoyo 'Digimatic Caliper' Series 500*, Mitutoyo Corporation, Kanagawa, Japan) with tips ground to a fine point. A repeatability study, described in Willis and Swindler (2004), preceded data collection to ensure accurate measurement of each dental feature. During data collection, individual body weights were noted for each specimen weighed at the time of capture or collection. However, because few individuals had associated body weight data, the distance from glabella to inion was used as a size surrogate in regression analyses. Dental measurements were taken from the teeth of the left side to assess the maximum mesio-distal length and width of the maxillary and mandibular incisors and to assess all molar features of interest (Figure 5.1). In a subsequent data collection, notations of lingual incisor surface features were made for *Nasalis* specimens (15 females and 26 males) from the cast collection compiled by D.R. Swindler and obtained from the American Museum of

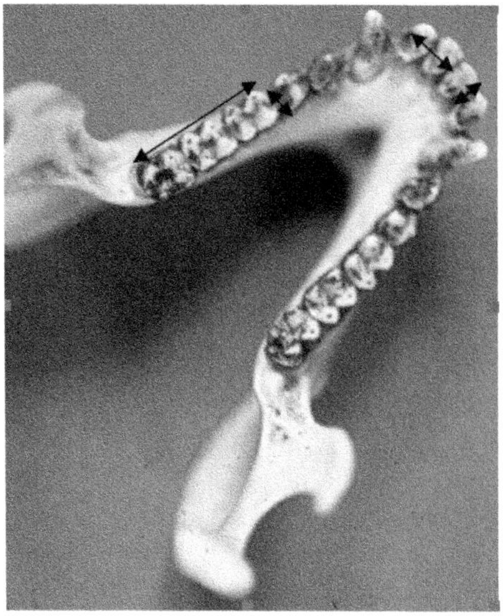

Figure 5.1 Mandible with arrows covering measured tooth areas.

Natural History, the Chicago Field Museum, and the National Museum of Natural History (Swindler 2002).

Incisor Morphology

Mean length and width measures and standard deviations were calculated for each maxillary and mandibular incisor for males and females of each Asian colobine species (ESM Tables 5.2–5.5). To determine whether relative differences in individual incisor lengths and widths exist among the seven genera, the mean lengths and widths of the mandibular and maxillary incisors were regressed against both body mass and glabella-inion length using least-squares regression (ESM Table 5.6). Data were analysed with Statistica (StatSoft, Tulsa, Oklahoma) and assessments were conducted separately for females and males of each species. Residuals were obtained from each least-squares analysis and incisor lengths and widths, as well as incisor row lengths, were compared between the genera with the largest sample sizes, *Presbytis*, *Trachypithecus* and *Nasalis*, using t-tests ($p \leq 0.05$) (ESM Table 5.7). Because multiple comparisons were performed, a Bonferroni adjusted alpha was also employed (Thorndike and Dinnel 2001). Row lengths were calculated by adding the mean mesio-distal lengths of the central and lateral incisor crowns and multiplying the resulting value by two. The mesio-distal length of the mandibular row was subtracted from the mesio-distal length of the maxillary row to determine the difference in row lengths for each species (ESM Table 5.8). Finally, to assess the proportional size of the mandibular incisor row on the mandibular molar row, mean molar row length values for each genus and species were obtained from a previous analysis of the same sample (ESM Table 5.9; Willis and Swindler 2004) and the proportional length of the lower incisal row over the lower molar row length was calculated.

Molar Morphology

Before further analysis of the molar data, average crestedness, average cusp height and average splay of molar cusps were calculated for the upper second molar and lower second molar. Average cresting was calculated from eight crest measurements on both the upper and lower left molars of all individuals including the lengths of the postmetacrista, premetacrista, postparacrista, preparacrista, preprotocrista, postprotocrista, prehypocrista and posthypocrista. Average splay was calculated with four measures including distance between lingual and buccal cusps and between mesial and distal cusps. Mesio and distolingual cusp heights and mesio and distobuccal cusp heights were used in the calculation of average cusp height. Means and standard deviations for individual lengths and widths of upper and lower molars, M1-M3, were published previously (see Willis and Swindler 2004). Gross molar area was calculated by taking the average of the mesial and distal buccolingual widths and multiplying this number by mesio-distal length. After calculating these variables, as with the incisors, we ran regression analyses for males and females separately, regressing molar area on skull length, and regressing average cusp splay, cusp height, and crestedness on molar area (ESM Table 5.10). Finally, we calculated a total of eight indices, four for the upper molar and four for the lower. These included an index of relative molar area (molar area/skull length), a splay index (average splay/molar area), height index (average cusp height/molar area), and a crest index (crest average/molar area) (Figures 5.4–5.7). We compared variation among the species in molar indices using the Kruskal-Wallis statistic and visualized differences among taxa using box and whisker plots. We interpret our morphological findings in light of the literature on diet as presented in ESM Table 5.1.

Results

Maxillary and Mandibular Incisor Size Sequence Patterns

Among all 24 species of Asian colobines in this study, the maxillary central incisor is longer mesio-distally than the lateral one (ESM Tables 5.2 and 5.3). For both male and female Asian colobines, that difference is greatest in the larger-bodied species and genera, e.g. *Nasalis, Rhinopithecus, Semnopithecus entellus schistaceus* and *Trachypithecus*, but less so in some of the smallest Asian colobines, e.g. species of *Presbytis* (ESM Tables 5.2 and 5.3). By contrast, size differences between the lower incisors are much smaller, and for most species of *Presbytis*, the lower central and lateral incisors are nearly the same mesio-distal length or the lateral incisor is just slightly longer than the central one (ESM Tables 5.4 and 5.5). Both females and males of the 24 Asian colobine species in this study have a mean difference between the mesio-distal length of the lower central and lateral incisors of 0.20 mm. In sum, among all 24 Asian colobine species, the maxillary central incisor is mesio-distally longer than the lateral incisor and these differences are significant (ESM Table 5.6; $P < 0.05$).

Compared to maxillary values, the differences between lower incisors in mesio-distal length are smaller than values obtained for the maxillary teeth, and in most species, the lower incisors of males and females are nearly equal in length, and/or the lateral incisor is slightly longer mesio-distally than the central one (ESM Tables 5.4 and 5.5). One species, *Presbytis hosei*, possesses a mesio-distally longer lateral incisor compared to the central one, while five species possess no significant mesio-distal length differences in the lower central and lateral incisors, i.e. *Presbytis comata, P. frontata, P. melalophus, P. rubicunda* and *Semnopithecus entellus thersites* (ESM Table 5.6; $P < 0.05$).

For most Asian taxa, the upper central incisors are nearly the same as the lateral incisors in bucco-lingual width; however, six of seven species of *Presbytis* for whom we have data, exhibit significant differences in width for females and/or males, as do three species of *Trachypithecus*; *T. cristata, T. obscura* and *T. pileatus* (ESM Table 5.6; $P < 0.05$). Within the mandible, results are much more consistent; the lateral incisor is wider, bucco-lingually, than the central one.

Relative Incisor Dimensions

Body weight was significantly correlated with the proposed size surrogate, glabella-inion ($r^2 = 0.71$ and 0.84 for females and males respectively; $P < 0.05$; ESM Table 5.7). In addition, glabella-inion length as a size surrogate explains as much as 75% of the maxillary central and lateral incisor variation observed in Asian colobines ($r^2 = 0.76$ for both females and males and $r^2 = 0.77$ and 0.74 for females and males respectively; $P < 0.05$; ESM Table 5.7). Similarly, as much as 65% of the lower central incisor and 50% of the lower lateral incisor variation is explained by glabella-inion as a size surrogate ($r^2 = 0.71$ and 0.66 for females and males respectively and $r^2 = 0.52$ and 0.50 for females and males respectively; $P < 0.05$; ESM Table 5.7). As might be expected, glabella-inion as a size surrogate explains less of the width difference in incisors for Asian colobines; 30–50% of the variation in width dimensions of the maxillary and mandibular central incisors obtained is explained by glabella-inion length ($r^2 = 0.46$ for both females and males in the width of the upper first incisor and $r^2 = 0.30$ and 0.40 for females and males respectively in the width of lower first incisor; $P < 0.05$; ESM Table 5.7). Finally, glabella-inion as a size surrogate explains as much as 45% of the variation in widths of the upper and lower lateral incisors in Asian colobines ($r^2 = 0.46$ and 0.49 for females and males respectively in the width of the upper second incisor, and $r^2 = 0.45$ and 0.59 for females and males respectively in the width of lower second or lateral incisor; $P < 0.05$; ESM Table 5.6).

Size-corrected residuals were examined using least-squares. Females and males of four species, *Presbytis frontata, Trachypithecus obscura, Rhinopithecus roxellana,* and *Semnopithecus entellus*, possess relatively longer upper and lower incisor rows than would be expected for head length. Females, but not males, of *Presbytis femoralis, P. thomasi*, and *Semnopithecus vetulus*, and males, but not females, of *Presbytis potenziana, Nasalis larvatus* and *Simias concolor* also exhibit longer maxillary and mandibular incisor rows for their head length. Both females and males of five species, *Presbytis rubicunda, Semnopithecus johnii, S. thersites, Trachypithecus francois*, and *T. geei*, have shorter incisal rows than might be expected for a given head length. Females of another four species, *Presbytis potenziani, P. hosei, Pygathrix nemaeus* and *Simias concolor*, have shorter upper and lower incisor rows than might be expected for head length, while males of three additional species possess relatively longer incisal rows, including *Presbytis comata, Rhinopithecus avunculus* and *Trachypithecus pileatus*. The remaining species and sexes exhibit a mixed pattern for size of the upper and lower row, where one row is longer than expected while the other is shorter.

Independent *t*-tests, as well as the Bonferroni method, were used to examine residual maxillary and mandibular incisor lengths and widths between those genera for which sample sizes were largest, i.e. *Presbytis, Trachypithecus* and *Nasalis* (ESM Table 5.8). Because some species of *Presbytis* and *Trachypithecus* had small sample sizes, values for all specimens examined within these genera were pooled. Males and females were analysed separately. There were no significant differences found in the lengths and widths of the maxillary first and second incisors ($P < 0.05$), I^1 and I^2, between females or males of *Presbytis, Trachypithecus* and *Nasalis* (ESM Table 5.8). Similarly, no significant differences in the length and width of the lower first incisor were obtained between females or males of *Presbytis, Trachypithecus* and *Nasalis* ($P < 0.05$; ESM Table 5.8). There were, however, significant differences in *t*-test results, as well as the Bonferroni method, in the length and width of the mandibular lateral incisor, I_1, between females, and males, of *Presbytis* and *Trachypithecus*. For their size, both females and males of *Presbytis* possess mesio-distally longer and bucco-lingually wider lower lateral incisors compared with females and males of *Trachypithecus* ($P < 0.05$; ESM Table 5.7). When row lengths are compared, the same results are obtained for males, but not females. Specifically, *Presbytis* males have longer mandibular incisor rows when compared to *Trachypithecus*, but not *Nasalis* ($P < 0.05$; ESM Table 5.8).

Incisor Row Length Differences by Species

Among all Asian colobine species, and in both sexes, the maxillary incisor row is longer than the mandibular one (ESM Table 5.9). However, for many species, the size difference of rows between males and females is minimal, e.g. *Presbytis comata, P. femoralis, P. frontata, Rhinopithecus avunculus, R. roxellana, Trachypithecus francoisi, T. geei, T. obscura* (ESM Table 5.9). In general, among species of *Presbytis*, the difference between the mesio-distal lengths of the upper and lower incisor row is nearly equal or larger for females than males (ESM Table 5.9). The opposite is true for *Trachypithecus*, where males have the largest difference between

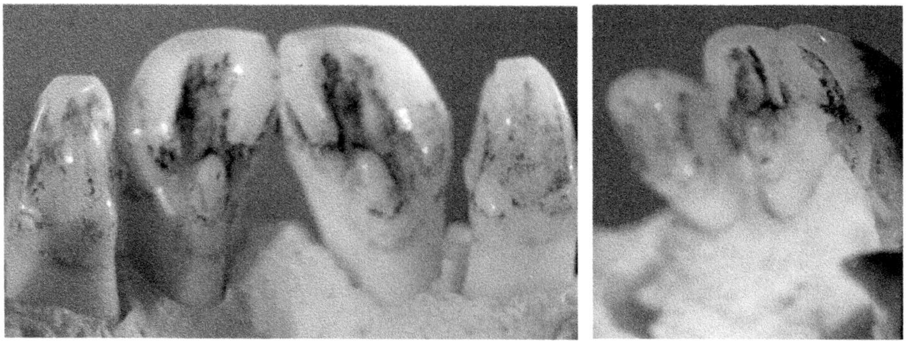

Figure 5.2 Lingual view of maxillary incisors of *Nasalis larvatus* with lingual tubercles (left) and side lingual view of maxillary incisors of *N. larvatus* with lingual tubercles (right).

the lengths of the incisal rows. Nearly all of the species within the larger-bodied genera have similar differences in the lengths of the upper and lower rows for males and females, except *Nasalis larvatus* and *Trachypithecus pileatus* (ESM Table 5.8).

Lingual Tubercles in *Nasalis larvatus*

We assessed *Nasalis larvatus* to determine whether the lingual tubercle was indeed present on most, if not all specimens, given that this had been identified as a unique feature of *Nasalis'* upper central incisors. First, among 41 *Nasalis* specimens, 15 females and 26 males, a lingual sulcus was present in the centre of the maxillary central incisor (Figure 5.2). Moreover, in all specimens, a lingual tubercle or worn elevation was present on the central maxillary incisors (Figure 5.3). For young specimens, the tubercle extended from the lower lingual sulcus, projecting outward and away from the tooth crown. In addition, all specimens possessed lingual tubercles on the lateral maxillary incisors, but these were not detached at one end as were those found in the upper central incisors.

Proportional Difference of Mandibular Incisor Row Width over Molar Row Length

Mandibular incisor width/molar row length proportions, for all species and sexes, are no less than 0.5 and no greater than 0.9 (ESM Table 5.10). Also, for 24 individual species, the proportion of the lower incisor row width over the mandibular molar row length is smaller for females than males of the same species, with a mean of 0.6 versus 0.8 for females and males respectively. In other words females have a narrower incisor row, compared to the molar row, than do conspecific males. Females and males of each species vary by a proportional difference of 0.1–0.3 (ESM Table 5.10). Males of some species have an incisor row that is nearly as wide as the molar row is long with a 0.9 proportional value of incisor over molar row length e.g. males of *Presbytis femoralis*, *P. frontata*, *P. hosei*, *P. rubicunda*, *P. thomasi*, *Trachypithecus obscura* and *T. pileatus*. None of the species who have the largest

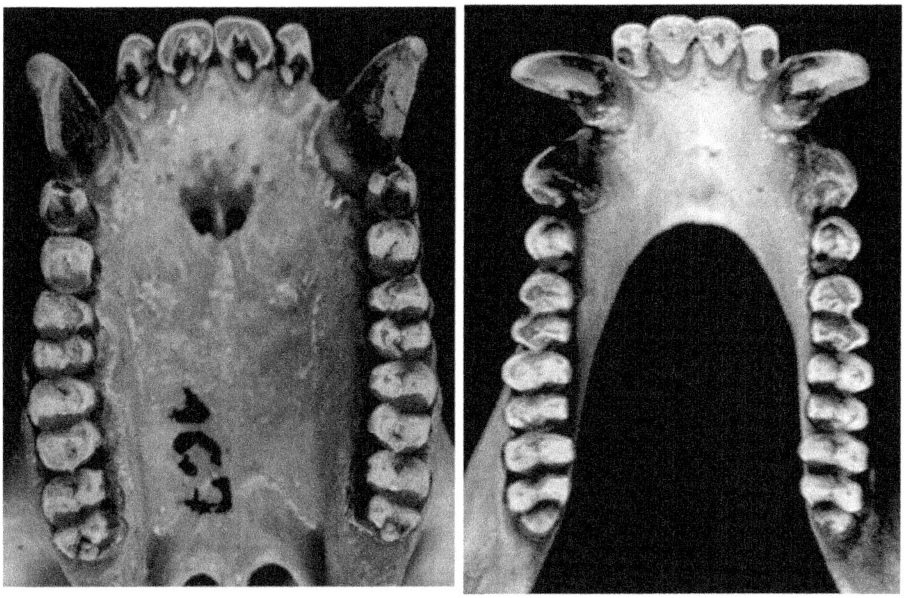

Figure 5.3 *Nasalis larvatus* maxilla exhibiting lingual tubercles on the central and lateral incisors and extensive incisal wear of occlusal edges and minimal molar wear (left), and *N. larvatus* mandible exhibiting extensive wear of incisor occlusal surface and minimal molar wear (right).

body sizes, e.g. *Nasalis larvatus, Pygathrix nemaeus, Rhinopithecus avunculus, R. roxellana* and *Semnopithecus*, have a proportional difference larger than 0.8 (ESM Table 5.10).

Molar Area

The largest genera (*Nasalis* and *Rhinopithecus*) exhibit the greatest molar areas relative to skull length, followed in descending order by *Semnopithecus*, *Pygathrix* and *Simias*, *Trachypithecus* and distantly by *Presbytis* (Figure 5.4). Molar size may be positively allometric, however, smaller teeth may also be associated with higher consumption of tough seeds as demonstrated by the small size of *Presbytis* molars.

Regression Analysis of Molar Variables

It is apparent from our regression analysis of molar variables among genera (ESM Table 5.11) that body size accounts for a large proportion of the variation in molar area, with this patterning holding for both the upper (♀ = 79%, ♂ = 80%) and lower (♀ = 80%, ♂ = 81%) molars. The high molar area indices for such genera as *Nasalis*, represented by the single species *N. larvatus*, and *Rhinopithecus*, represented by *R. roxellana* and *R. avunculus* further support this finding (Figure 5.4). Molar size, in

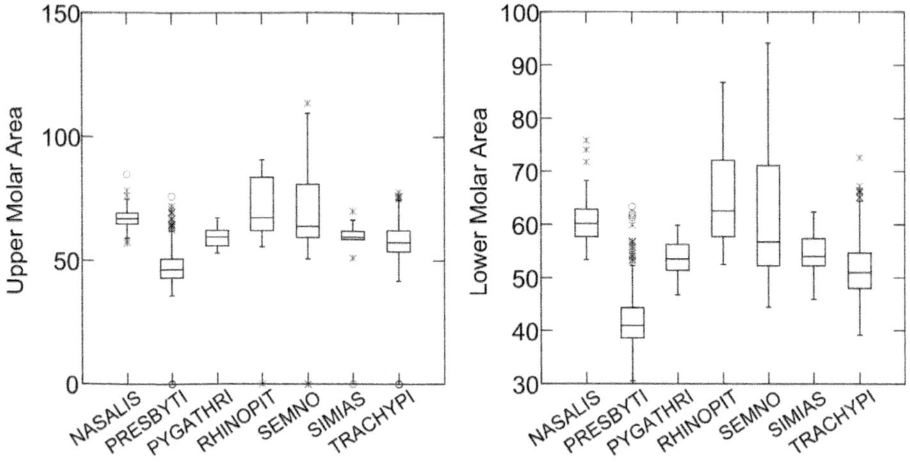

Figure 5.4 Box plots comparing upper and lower molar areas (see text for calculation) for the upper (left) and lower (right) M2 for all study genera.

turn, accounts for an even higher proportion of the variation in average cusp height (M^2 ♀ = 92%, ♂ = 95%; M_2♀ = 96%, ♂ = 95%, ESM Table 5.11). However, molar area accounts for considerably less of the variation in cusp splay (an indirect measure of the ability of teeth to slice foods) (M^2 ♀ = 57%, ♂ = 80%; M_2♀ = 47%, ♂ = 53%, ESM Table 5.11) and crestedness on the upper molars (M^2 ♀ = 56%, ♂ = 89%, ESM Table 5.11). It is notable that size accounts for more of the crestedness on lower dentition in females (M_2♀ = 93%, ♂ = 88%, ESM Table 5.11). However, if both splay and crestedness are indicative of the ability to slice leafy tissues, it appears that diet may be accounting for some of this variation as opposed to size alone. This is further emphasized in box plots of splay (Figure 5.5) and crestedness (Figure 5.7) which show the high average values for the relatively smaller-bodied *Presbytis* and *Trachypithecus*. It is notable that at least the median value for splay and crestedness in *Trachypithecus* exceeds that for *Pygathrix*, supporting the notion of ingestive folivory (Wright et al. 2008a,b) in the former, although it must be noted that *Pygathrix* is represented by the single species (*P. nemaeus*).

Molar Splay and Molar Cusp Height

As with all comparisons, there are significant differences among all the taxa in degree of cusp splay. The pattern for splay is essentially the inverse of that for molar area, with *Presbytis* having the highest index, followed in order by *Simias*, *Trachypithecus*, *Semnopithecus*, *Nasalis*, *Pygathrix* and *Rhinopithecus* (Figure 5.5). That the cusps are relatively far apart compared to molar area suggests longer blades for fracturing sheets of material like leaves, as opposed to creating wedges for the fracture of tough seeds, as Lucas and Teaford (1994) hypothesized. However, the angle of the wedge between the cusps is also dependent on the height of the cusps, and relative to molar area the pattern for cusp height among the taxa is essentially

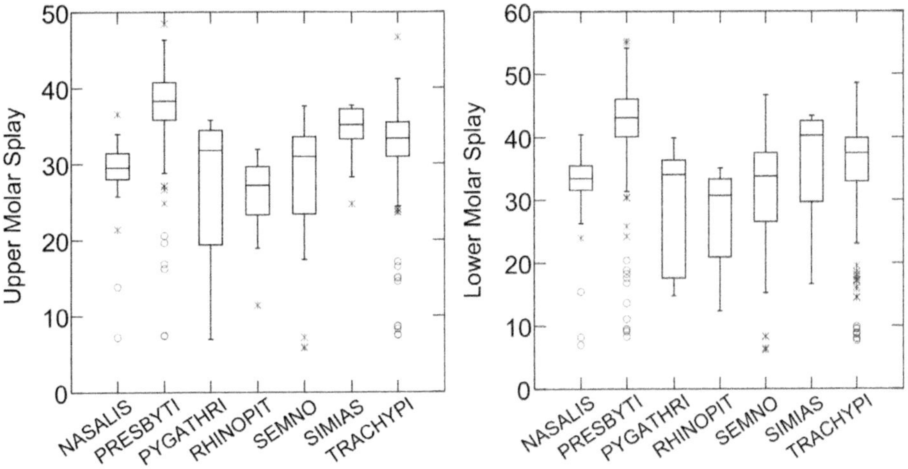

Figure 5.5 Box plots comparing indices of the distance between cusps (i.e. splay) (see text for calculation) for the upper (left) and lower (right) M2 for all study genera.

the same as that for splay with only *Nasalis* and *Pygathrix* switching positions slightly (Figure 5.6). *Presbytis* is found to have relatively small molars with relatively tall cusps that are relatively far apart. The smaller size may increase the force applied to a food per unit area, while the wedged cusps enhance fracture of the tough seeds of unripe fruit. The intermediate species in molar area, splay and height exhibit various levels of leaf and seed consumption, while *Rhinopithecus* exhibits molars that appear to be best suited for the processing of relatively hard, stiff foods, given that large teeth with low cusps help to protect the tooth crown from fracture when ingesting such foods.

Molar Cresting

The pattern for molar cresting is essentially identical to that for cusp height (Figure 5.7). It is notable that the genus that appears to consume the most seeds (*Presbytis*) exhibits the highest cresting index. This may be analogous to the crenulated surface of neotropical sclerocarps (foragers on fruits with hard pericarps) such as *Cacajao* and *Chiropotes* (Kinzey 1992). Again, *Nasalis* and *Rhinopithecus* exhibit the least cresting. *Rhinopithecus* appears to consume the fewest leaves relative to the other species, while *Nasalis* is notably folivorous. However, the bulk of the leaves consumed by *Nasalis* appear to be immature (ESM Table 5.1) and likely do not require enhanced cresting for fracture.

Discussion

The dentition of the colobines has been described as relatively homogeneous; however many species have not been thoroughly assessed while others have not been studied at all. This is especially true for the Asian colobines who might be expected to

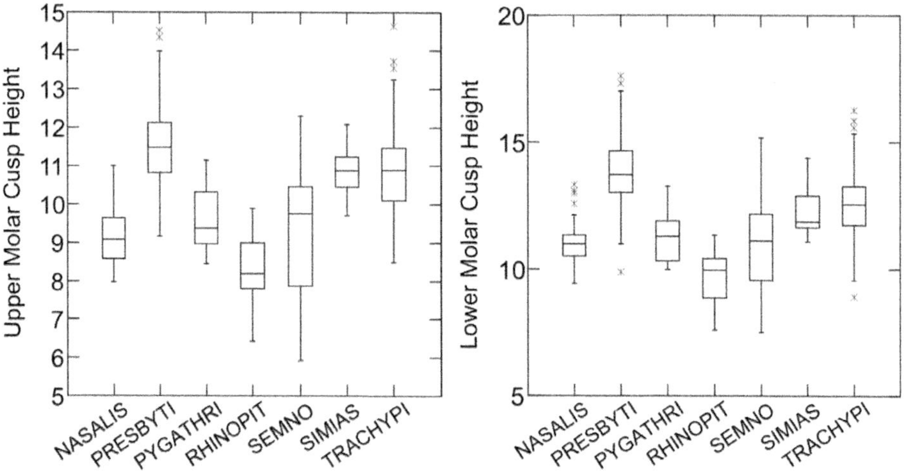

Figure 5.6 Box plots comparing indices for cusp height (see text for calculation) for the upper (left) and lower (right) M2 for all study genera.

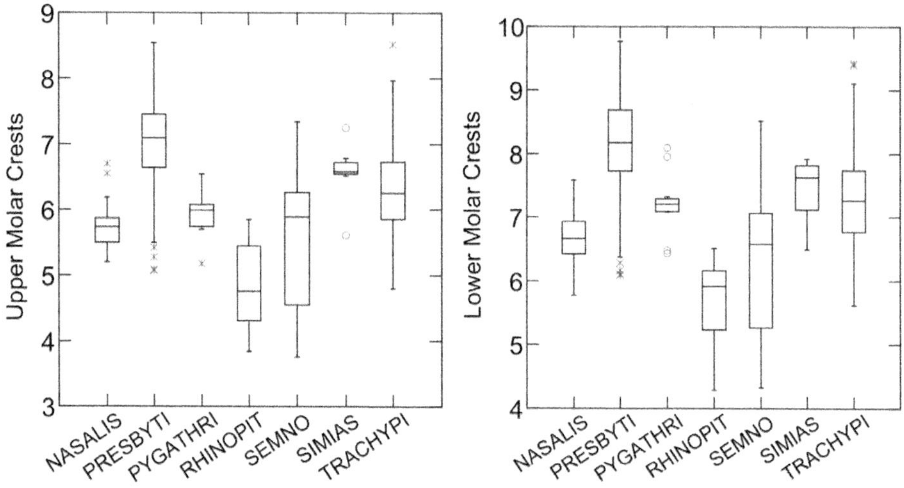

Figure 5.7 Box plots comparing indices of crestedness (see text for calculation) for the upper (left) and lower (right) M2 for all study genera.

show dental diversity; they are more diverse ecologically and taxonomically than their African counterparts. More than one third of the Asian taxa have not been comparatively assessed, e.g. *Presbytis femoralis, P. frontata, P. hosei, P. thomasi, Rhinopithecus* species, *Trachypithecus aurata, T. francoisi, T. geei and T. pileatus* (Willis and Hildebolt 1991). Consequently, there are few dental traits which can distinguish one taxon from another. More importantly, few data are available to explain and interpret the primate fossil record (Jablonski and Gu 1991). The present study includes data for 24 Asian colobine taxa, representing seven genera. Despite small sample sizes for nearly half of the species within this study, 10 of the 24 Asian colobines, results demonstrate diversity in both size and shape of the anterior and posterior dentition.

Members of the subfamily Colobinae have been associated with heteromorphic incisors, a maxillary central incisor that is mesio-distally longer than the lateral one, and relatively narrow incisal rows (Vogel 1966; Delson 1973, 1994; Hylander 1975; Swindler 1976, 2002; Lucas and Teaford 1994). Indeed the upper central incisor is significantly longer than the lateral one for each of the 24 taxa examined in this study. Thus we agree that maxillary incisors are likely different in mesio-distal length among the Asian colobines (Vogel 1966; Swindler 1976, 2002; Lucas and Teaford 1994). By contrast, more size variation is present in the lower jaw; the lower central incisor is significantly longer than the lateral one in just over half of the species examined (13 of 24). All of the *Trachypithecus* species, for example, have longer mandibular central incisors, while at least three *Presbytis species* have lower incisors of approximately equal length. So while Asian colobines generally appear to possess longer lower central incisors and more narrow lateral ones, species of the genus *Presbytis* may be the exception. Perhaps this is the reason for suggesting that colobines have lower incisors that are 'more or less' similar in size (Delson 1994).

Presbytis species often possess wider lateral incisors, in both the mandible and the maxilla. By contrast other Asian taxa, for which we have sufficient sample sizes, possess a wider mandibular lateral incisor, but not a wider maxillary one. Thus overall, Asian colobines possess upper and lower incisors that are not uniformly sized; the maxillary and mandibular lateral incisors are wider *or* broader labio-lingually than the central ones. This width difference reinforces the idea that Asian colobines also possess mandibular incisors that are heteromorphic, in one or more features and/or dimensions, as opposed to incisors which are more or less similar in size and shape.

The most frequently cited literature on incisor size in primates suggests that among cercopithecines, food size and type are reflected in the mesio-distal lengths of the incisor row. Relatively long incisor rows, such as that found in cercopithecines, equal an ability to process large fruits, while shorter row lengths provide limited ability to process large items, but enhance efficiency in processing small food items such as leaves and seeds (Hylander 1975; Hylander and Kay 1977). In this study, we found no significant differences in the lengths or widths of the maxillary incisors between *Presbytis, Trachypithecus* and *Nasalis*, but also no significant differences in the lengths of the mandibular incisors between these genera. There were significant differences found, however, in the relative lengths and widths of the mandibular lateral incisors for *Presbytis* compared to *Trachypithecus. Presbytis* possesses mesio-distally longer, and bucco-lingually wider, lower lateral incisors compared to *Trachypithecus*. These results hold for *Presbytis* males when row lengths are compared; *Presbytis* males have relatively longer, but also wider, mandibular incisor rows than *Trachypithecus*, but not than *Nasalis*. If diet was correlated with incisor breadth, then one would expect a subfamily with wide variation in habitat and diet to possess significant differences in the mesio-distal lengths of the incisor row. In this study of 24 Asian colobines, we did not find significant differences in row length, with the exception of a generic comparison of *Presbytis* versus *Trachypithecus*. The interpretation of this single result, however, becomes difficult when one considers that there are differences within and between genera, in terms of dietary emphasis, processing strategies, and gut morphology (Davies et al. 1988; Davies 1991; Ungar 1995, 1996; Caton 1999; Wright et al. 2008a,b). For example, among sympatric Asian anthropoids, including *Presbytis thomasi*, the incisors were used as often, if not more often, by folivorous species as compared to frugivorous ones (Ungar 1996). Heavy incisor use might be possible in species which possess a wide incisal row, regardless of length and food type. Similarly, it has been demonstrated that colobine incisors possess an enamel layer on both the labial, as well as the lingual sides, which results in a blunt edge (Shellis and Hiiemae 1986; Strasser and Delson 1987). One explanation for this design is that colobine incisors are better adapted for gripping and tearing leaves (Shellis and Hiiemae 1986; Strasser and Delson 1987). But perhaps it is the overall labio-lingual thickness or width of the incisors for all Asian taxa, but most notably for *Presbytis*, which also provides a strong platform for gripping *and* incising all food types.

Studies of African apes have indicated that mesio-distally longer incisal crowns do not slow wear, raising questions about the significance of incisor row length in primates (McCollum 2007). In one study of food processing among Asian colobine taxa, *Trachypithecus* processed leaves with the molars while *Pygathrix* was more reliant upon the incisors for reducing food particles (Babcock et al. 2009). Moreover, in some cases, the incisal row is nearly as long as the molar row, hence this occlusal surface is important in food processing. Among Asian colobines in this study, the smaller-bodied taxa possess an incisor row which is nearly as long as the molar row. Males of *Presbytis* have an incisor row which is 80%–90% of the molar row length, while females have an incisor row which is 70%–80% of the molar row. Larger-bodied taxa such as *Nasalis larvatus* have an incisor row which is 60% and 70% the length of the molar row for females and males respectively.

Although *Nasalis larvatus* has been assessed in more dental studies than any other Asian colobine species, and has often been used to represent all Asian taxa, it appears to be dentally distinctive. For example, *Nasalis is* the only taxon that was said to possess a unique lingual trait on the maxillary central incisors (Swindler, 1976, 2002; Willis and Hildebolt 1991). In this study, we were able to determine that indeed, a lingual tubercle is present at the base of the maxillary central incisor (Figure 5.2). But we also noted that such a tubercle is present in the maxillary lateral incisor as well (Figure 5.2). The tubercles are distinctive in that they are spur-like in shape, attached at the base but not at the top where there is an enamel extension (Figure 5.2). The discovery of this distinctive tubercle allowed reassignment in at least one museum during data collection. Subsequent examination of the collector's field notes verified the mistake in taxonomic designation and allowed the specimen to be properly labelled as *Nasalis*. *Nasalis* is also the only Asian colobine that appears to have distinctive dental development; the incisors erupt before the molars (Harvati 2000).

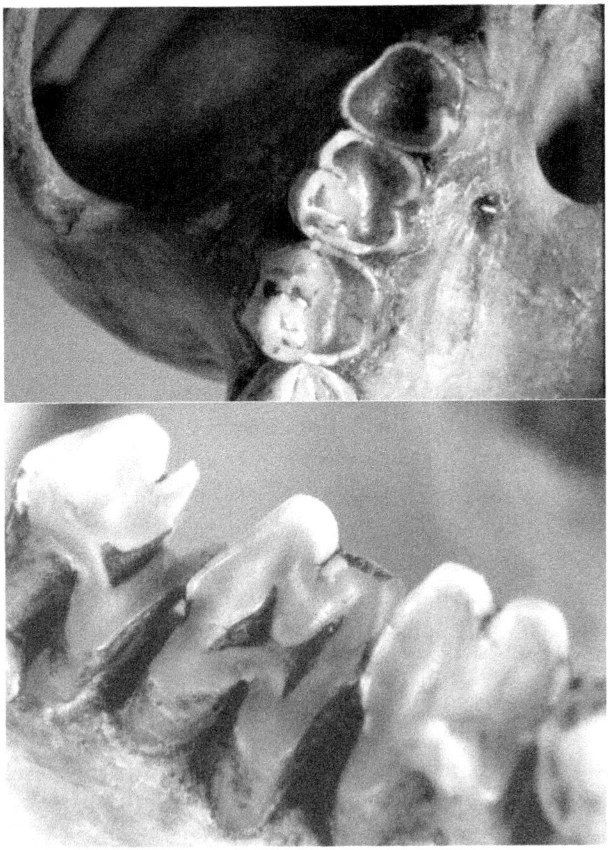

Figure 5.8 *Presbytis* maxilla exhibiting extensive wear of molar occlusal surface areas (left), and *Trachypithecus* mandible exhibiting extensive wear of molar occlusal surface areas (right).

Thus features which extend the life of the tooth might be important, particularly if the incisors experience heavy use. This is clearly the case for *Nasalis* males and females in this study as all subadult specimens showed dentine exposure of the upper and lower incisal row both before the canines had erupted and any wear was visible on the second and third molars. As in Figure 5.8, this dentine exposure of the entire incisor row was extensive even before any other wear was visible in the posterior tooth row.

Lucas and Teaford (1994) have suggested that seed destroyers have the relatively shortest incisor rows. We would thus expect *Presbytis* species to have the smallest row among colobines, but this is not the case. This generalization indeed appears to apply across more inclusive taxa within the order, but not among more exclusive taxa. The incisors may take on an array of different roles such as scrapers for those that exhibit geophageous behaviours (e.g. *P. rubicunda*; ESM Table 5.1). Greater mesio-distal length, as in *Nasalis* and *Semnopithecus*, may help to counteract bending in a sagittal plane, but understanding how and when this occurs demands the collection of detailed data on ingestive behaviour. Differential dental eruption patterns, such as those exhibited by *Nasalis* species, may also account for heavy wear in the incisal row (Figure 5.3). As noted above, unlike all other colobines, *Nasalis* erupts the incisors before the molars (Harvati 2000), hence the incisors may become worn early in life, before all other teeth have erupted and are in full occlusion.

Although colobines have been defined as folivorous species who minimize incisal use, feeding data and wear patterns suggest otherwise. Some Asian colobine taxa differ in the frequency of incisor use, yet all Asian colobines use the incisors in a variety of feeding contexts – from extensive incisal processing, to scraping with lower incisors, to open-mouthed scraping during geophagy, to separation of food particles from a variety of food types using the incisors to nip or break an initial piece or bite (Krishnamani and Mahaney 2000; Babcock et al. 2009). Consequently for colobines, the relative size of the incisors compared to other colobines or cercopithecines, is not a clear indication of the amount of incisal use. Moreover, Kay's (1984) notion that folivorous taxa 'prepare their foods less before mastication', if true, likely varies among colobine taxa. Variation in gut morphology would suggest that indeed, different colobine species have different comparative masticatory needs prior to digestion (Chivers 1994; Caton 1998, 1999). Perhaps the use of the incisors – in some form or fashion, helps to prolong the use of molar morphology. Despite high molar cusps, wear is clearly visible – even among young animals – all develop dentin lakes on the top of each cusp and later in life exhibit heavy wear (Figure 5.8). Such extensive wear of the incisors and molars limited use of specimens within each of the 20 museums accessed during data collection. So despite a large number of specimens available for all taxa, few had teeth that retained a full occlusal surface and could be measured for this analysis

The analyses of molar area, splay, crestedness, and height reveals taxa that appear less folivorous as indicated by relatively large teeth with less cresting and splay. Examples include *Rhinopithecus* and *Semnopithecus*. Both of these taxa have fairly catholic diets relative to other Asian colobines (ESM Table 5.1) and exhibit bunodonty, which reduces dental attrition when including more non-leaf foods such as unripe fruits and seeds. In turn, those genera who are more crested than *Rhinopithecus* and *Semnopithecus*, e.g. *Presbytis*, *Trachypithecus* and *Pygathrix*, still show differences in the amount of cresting they exhibit. In the case of cresting, *Presbytis* exceeds *Trachypithecus*, which exceeds *Pygathrix*. Between the latter two taxa which appear more dedicated to leaf consumption (ESM Table 5.1), only *Pygathrix* exhibits a presaccus (Caton 1998), which may relax selection on the degree to which molars crest and splay.

While it appears that all colobines have the molar morphology necessary to exploit both leaves and tough seeds, there is significant variation in the size, crests and cusp heights among the study genera. The more seed-dependent *Presbytis* have relatively high, splayed crested cusps that may indeed enhance tough seed fracture, while *Rhinopithecus*, which has the least colobine-like diet, has large, low, smooth teeth that may better resist fracture when biting stiff foods. These hypotheses concerning molar function may best be tested by collecting data on the mechanical properties of food items and the associated ingestive behaviour for each of these species.

A central goal of physical anthropology and dental ecology is the identification of the biological role (Bock and von Wahlert 1965) of given morphological features. In this study we have attempted to further our understanding of the biological role of the dentition in an array of Asian colobine genera. Our findings provide some initial information necessary to develop additional dental ecological hypotheses and further define the role of teeth in the lives of these primates. Relating gross molar morphology is only one step in attempting to clarify relationships between diet and evolution in primates. It is apparent from previous research that all components of the ingestive and digestive system must be linked to diet among Asian colobines in to more clearly define the role different tooth morphologies play in food processing. For example, in an analysis of chewing bout lengths and rates at the Endangered Primate Rescue Center (EPRC), Cuc Phuong Vietnam, it was found that *Pygathrix nemaeus* and *P. cenerea*, and *Trachypithecus delacouri* and *T. hatinhensis*, had comparable bout lengths when chewing foods of comparable toughness. But the *Pygathrix* species chewed comparable foods half as fast as *Trachypithecus* species (Wright et al. 2008a). This was argued a consequence of *Pygathrix's* ability to use the presaccus of its stomach for additional comminution of leaves. The clade including *Semnopithecus* spp., *Trachypithecus* spp., and *Presbytis* spp. are known to lack a presaccus, whereas the monophyletic *Rhinopithecus* spp., *Pygathrix* spp., and *Nasalis* spp. have a developed presaccus (Caton 1999, 1998). The presaccus of these odd-nosed taxa is likely to function as a gastric mill, reducing the size of ingesta particles prior to the time they enter the saccus (Caton 1998). Thus, species with a presaccus have an additional processing option, one that takes over the function of the dentition or, at the very least, completes the breakdown of food particles started by the teeth. Wright et al. (2008b) additionally found that *Trachypithecus* spp. have more robust mandibular corpora and symphysis, but also greater relative molar areas. These features add to the hypothesis that *Pygathrix* species rely on their digestive tract for leaf comminution and may be termed 'digestive folivores', whereas the two *Trachypithecus* species rely on more oral comminution and may be termed 'ingestive folivores' (Wright et al. 2008b). Additional findings by Babcock et al. (2009) from the EPRC revealed that the two study species of *Pygathrix* relied more on their anterior dentition when ingesting foods than did the two study species of *Trachypithecus*. These findings emphasize molar processing in *Trachypithecus*, while also suggesting greater reliance by *Pygathrix* on the anterior dentition for both nipping and stripping leaves from petioles and stems. In contrast, geophagy has been observed in taxa that lack a presaccus (e.g. *Trachypithecus* and *Presbytis*), but has not been observed among the odd-nosed colobines that possess this additional processing site (Krishnamani et al. 2000; ESM Table 5.1). This may have implications for interpreting the greater relative incisor row length in *Presbytis* and *Trachypithecus* found in this study, given that geophagy often demands scraping terrestrial substrates with the anterior dentition.

Other types of data that have infrequently been integrated with studies of dental functional morphology, in order to clarify dental ecological relationships, include the onset of dental eruption, which is early in leaf-eating primates (Godfrey et al. 2003) and dental eruption sequence. Including information on dental eruption sequence may provide an additional window through which to assess how the dentition might wear through time and thereby provide insights into ingestive behaviour. Although several studies of Asian colobine dental eruption sequence have been conducted, e.g. Schultz (1958) and Harvati (2000), there are still many species for which we have no data.

Another avenue of inquiry which may help interpretation of the dental patterns outlined here, and add additional weight to the ingestive versus digestive folivore hypothesis (Wright et al. 2008a), is gut passage rate or mean retention time (e.g. Dierenfeld et al. 1992; Edwards and Ullrey 1999; Nijboer et al. 2007). In addition, as noted by Kirkpatrick (1998), colobines potentially adapt to new diets or to seasonal changes in diet by the same method as other foregut fermenters: through rapid changes in proportions of gut micro-organisms (Bauchop 1978). An interspecific comparison of gut flora among species would be a profound contribution to our understanding of dental ecology and other ecomorphological relationships among colobines. Using such digestive data, some colobines, e.g. *Presbytis rubicunda*, *P. melalophus*, *P. hosei*, have been hypothesized to be 'poorly adapted' for a folivorous diet (Davies 1991). Indeed our findings for molar function corroborate these findings, reaffirming *Presbytis*' greater dependence on non-leaf plant parts. Ultimately, no matter what the ingestive/digestive systems are like within colobine species, all have limitations on the kinds of plant fibre they can ingest and digest; consequently, many colobines have succumbed to intestinal obstructions (Nijboer 2006).

As Oates and Davies (1994) described nearly 15 years ago, colobines truly are highly varied in their anatomy, ecology and social behaviour. Initial studies of Asian colobine feeding behaviour, and dental size and shape features, such as those presented here, support the idea of great diversity in this radiation, most especially in Asia. And yet all of the other aspects of anatomy, physiology and behaviour – as they relate to feeding – also illustrate great diversity, and hence multiple feeding strategies, among seven genera and 40+ species. Because interpretive behaviour for fossil species is often predicated on what we know of living taxa, we must begin to assess colobine feeding in a more holistic way – including all aspects of ingestive and digestive morphology and behaviour. Clearly an analysis of dental features by themselves would not provide a complete picture of how colobines in fact process the many tough or hard food items they seem to be capable of consuming or are forced to consume seasonally (Wright et al. 2008a,b). Future research directions parallel much of what Oates and Davies began to outline 25 years ago and, sadly, we have only just begun. Many types of data need to be collected from Asian colobine taxa and nearly all species continue to have no data or limited data in one or more areas related to the ingestion and subsequent digestion of food. These include, but are not limited, to (1) genetic data for species of *Presbytis*, *Rhinopithecus*, and *Simias concolor*; (2) dental eruption analyses for *Rhinopithecus* and *Semnopithecus* including *Semnopithecus johnii* and *S. vetulus*; (3) ingestive feeding studies for all colobine taxa; (4) dental morphometric analysis including species' level analyses with comparisons of sympatric species; (5) mandibular morphometric analyses for all seven genera; (6) gut morphology research for *Simias concolor* and all species of *Presbytis*, *Rhinopithecus*, and *Semnopithecus*; (7) ecological data for *Presbytis frontata*, and *Simias concolor* and (8) studies of mean retention time for species of *Presbytis*, *Rhinopithecus*, *Simias concolor* and *Trachypithecus* species (other than *T. cristata* and *T. obscura*). We hope that our endeavours, and those of national and international students and researchers, will begin to fill in these gaps in our understanding the Asian colobine radiation.

Acknowledgements

We wish to acknowledge the generous support of the entities that made data collection possible: the American Museum of Natural History, the Boise Fund, the National Science Foundation (DBS-9221163), Sigma Xi, Washington University in St. Louis and the Wenner-Gren Foundation for Anthropological Research. Also, this work would not have been accomplished without the generous assistance of curators and staff in each of the 20 museum collections sampled in the USA, Europe and Asia. And a special acknowledgement for the many contributions made to this and other projects by the late Dr Daris Swindler; his passion for all things tooth-related and his love of teaching were unparalleled.

6 Morphology and Physiology of Colobine Digestive Tracts

Ikki Matsuda and Marcus Clauss

Introduction

Colobine monkeys differ from all other primates in having a foregut fermentation system featuring a complex, multi-chambered stomach (Bauchop and Martucci 1968; Chivers 1994). The large capacity of their stomach, comprising about 10%–20% of their total body mass, allows the accumulation of ingesta and slows digesta passage, which is essential for the extensive fermentation of 'difficult' plant materials, including leaves, seeds and unripe fruits (Bauchop 1971; Chivers 1994). Thus, obtaining information on colobine morpho-physiological digestive traits, focusing on their forestomach physiology, is indispensable for understanding their ecology and behaviour. After a comprehensive review of the morpho-physiological digestive traits of colobines by Chivers (1994), reports on their natural diets and, more recently, on the their microbiome have increased. Unfortunately, there has not been much progress in terms of clarifying their anatomical and physiological attributes. In this chapter, we review the recent findings on colobine digestive strategies, focusing on their forestomach.

Forestomach Anatomy: Tri-partite versus Quadri-partite

Colobines have either three ('tri-partite'), or four ('quadri-partite') chambers in their forestomach (Chivers 1994). Quadri-partite stomachs are characterized by an additional blind sac, or pouch, named the praesaccus (Figure 6.1) that represents an additional chamber to the three compartments common to all colobines (Langer 1988). Compilations regarding whether a colobine species has a three- or four-chambered forestomach have been published (Langer 1988; Caton 1998; Langer 2017), but no comprehensive overview of the colobine group exists, and the role of the praesaccus has not been elucidated. The existing evidence does not rule out the existence of variation in this characteristic, even within genera, but the issue has not been resolved. To date, it appears that *Colobus*, *Semnopithecus*, *Trachypithecus* and *Presbytis* are the primary taxa with three-chambered stomachs, whereas *Procolobus*, *Piliocolobus*, *Rhinopithecus*, *Pygathrix* and *Nasalis* comprise taxa with four-chambered stomachs. No information is available on *Simias* (Caton 1998).

Different functions for the praesaccus have been proposed, but to date, little evidence exists to support any individual proposal. In *Nasalis* and *Pygathrix*, the praesaccus is lined with a stratified squamous epithelium, and it has a complete

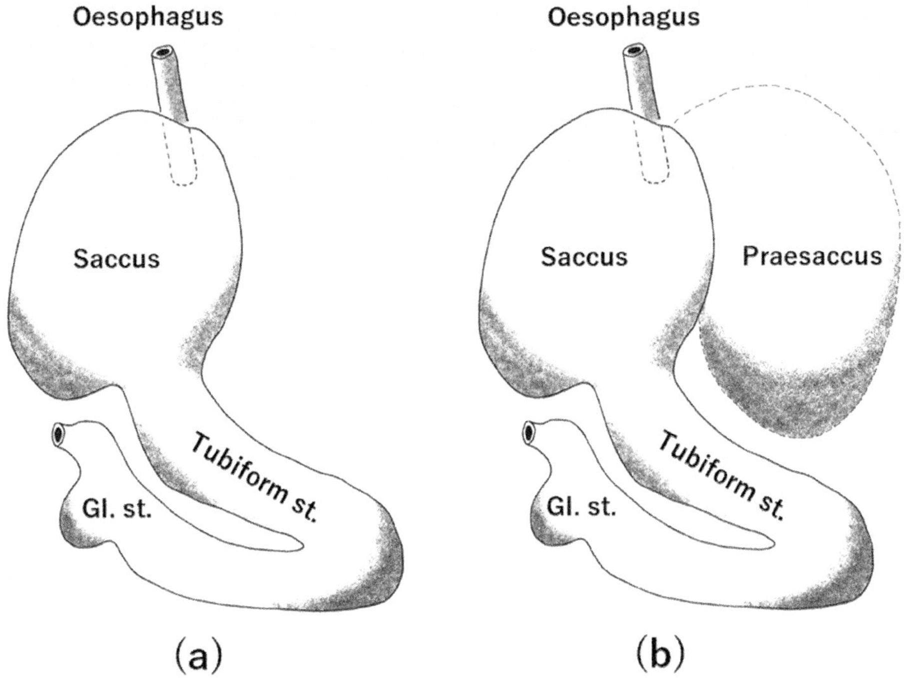

Figure 6.1 Schematic representation of the colobine stomach, illustrating the (a) tri-partite/three-chambered (with the saccus, tubiform, and glandular stomach) and (b) quadri-partite/four-chambered conditions (with an additional praesaccus). Drawn after Langer (1988: 284) for *Procolobus verus*. Note that the volumes and the degree to which the praesaccus can be visually discerned from the saccus may vary between species: Gl. st. = glandular stomach (Matsuda et al. 2019).

longitudinal muscle coat (Hollihn 1971; Caton 1998). Based on its longitudinal muscle cover, squamous epithelium and small size, it has been suggested that the praesaccus may act as a gastric mill in which larger food particles are ground into smaller particles before passing through the rest of the digestive tract (Caton 1998). When *Trachypithecus* was observed to have a higher ingestive chewing rate (in chews/second) than *Pygathrix*, it was suggested that this differences is related to the three-chambered stomach of *Trachypithecus* (which therefore putatively has to comminute food with their teeth by chewing) and the four-chambered stomach in *Pygathrix* (which therefore putatively can rely on the presumed gastric-mill function and does not need to chew as intensively during ingestion) (Wright et al. 2008a). Correspondingly, the terms 'ingestive folivore' for *Trachypithecus* and 'digestive folivore' for *Pygathrix* were coined (Wright et al. 2008b). However, this approach neglects body-size-related variation in chewing rates, from which this difference would be predicted alone (cf. Matsuda et al. 2014), and the overall gastric-mill concept overlooks that, in order to function in this manner, gastroliths would be required (as digesta kneading alone will not achieve particle-size reduction).

Conversely, Chivers (1994) suggested that the additional praesaccus might be an adaptation to seed eating without providing a rationale, or empirical data. By contrast, Langer (2017) considered its development to be an adaptation to folivory, based on the assumption that a diet of low-digestibility items, such as leaves, might be exploited efficiently with a particularly large gastro-intestinal capacity. This hypothetical explanation reverberates the finding of Chivers and Hladik (1980) that folivorous mammals generally have a greater gastro-intestinal surface area in relation to metabolic body size than frugivorous and faunivorous mammals. To clarify the role of the praesaccus in colobines, compiled literature data on the natural diet of colobine species were analysed to compare consumption between three- and four-chambered species (Matsuda et al. 2019a). The results suggest that the praesaccus is an adaptation to a dietary niche featuring a particularly high reliance on leaves (Figure 6.2) as fallback foods in colobine clades with four-chambered stomachs versus a higher reliance on fruits/seeds as foods at times of high fruit availability in clades with three-chambered stomachs, supporting the notion that a large gut capacity is an important characteristic by which herbivores survive on a leafy, high-fibre diets (Müller et al. 2013).

Behavioural Considerations

Rumination Behaviour

Although non-ruminant foregut fermentation, including that found in primates, has been termed 'ruminant-like', and explicitly or implicitly equated with ruminant foregut fermentation (Bauchop and Martucci 1968), functional ruminants (ruminants, camelids) differ fundamentally from non-ruminant foregut fermenters, such as colobines. However, as an exceptional case, in the colobine species *Nasalis larvatus*, observations have been made on the apparent regurgitation and remastication of forestomach contents in 23 wild-living individuals (Figure 6.3), suggestive of a 'rumination' strategy (Matsuda et al. 2011a). In particular, in one male *N. larvatus* specimen that was observed continuously over 169 days, such a rumination strategy was observed on 11 different days, occurring mostly in the morning, and it was associated with significantly higher proportions of daily feeding than on days when it was not observed. This observation is consistent with the concept that intensified mastication permits higher food intake in *N. larvatus* without compromising digestive efficiency. Nonetheless, this behaviour does not appear to be as regular as it is in ruminants, although circumstantial evidence for the regular use of rumination in this species is indicated when measuring their chewing efficiency through their faecal particle size (Matsuda et al. 2014; Thiry et al. 2018).

Posture Constraints in Relation to Forestomach Anatomy

In ruminants, digestive physiology constrains resting positions. The forestomach of both ruminants and camelids is characterized by a sorting mechanism that operates

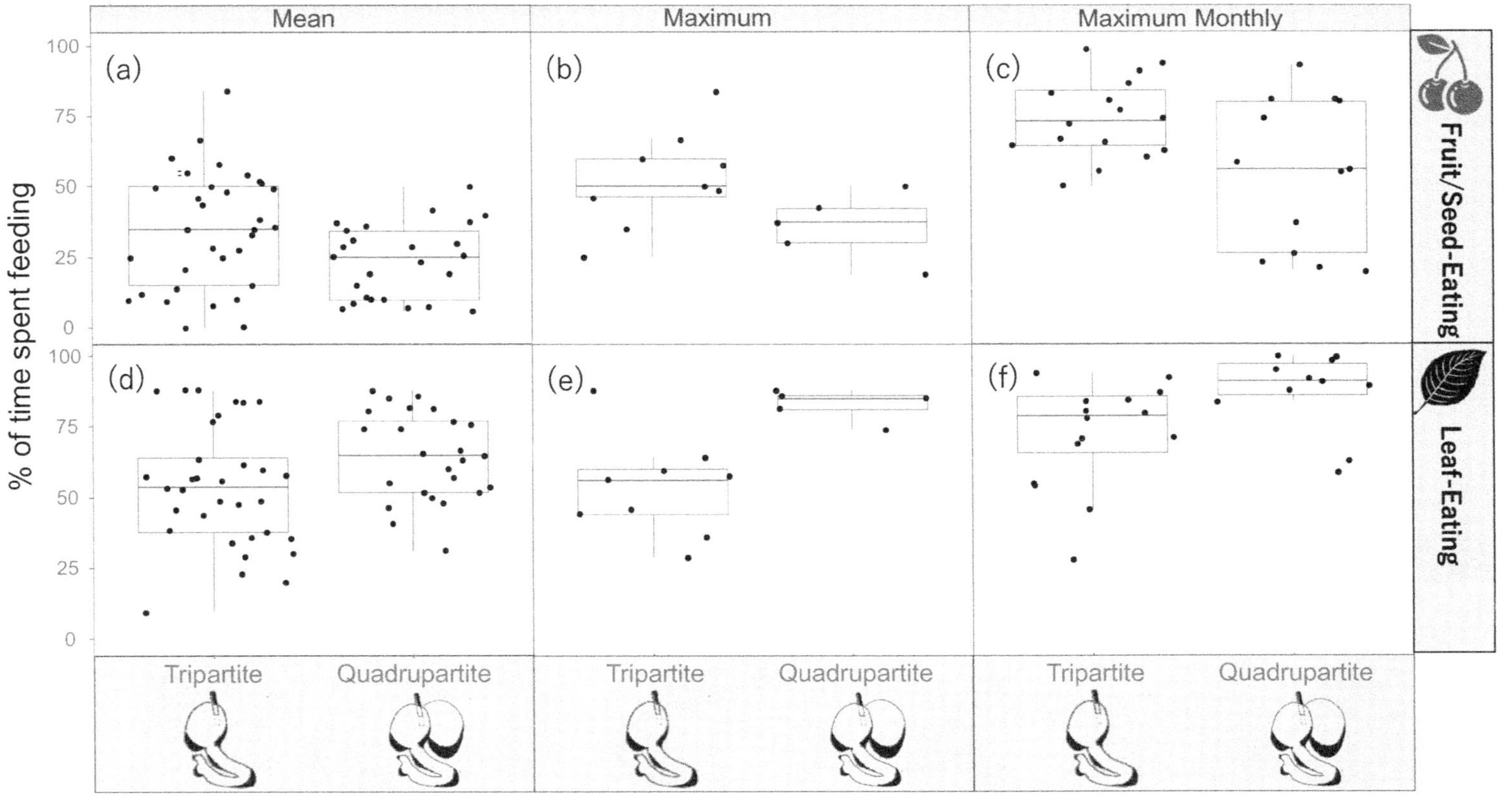

Figure 6.2 Bar graphs illustrating variation of the mean and maximum proportions of fruits and leaves in the natural diet between two groups of colobine monkeys with different forestomach anatomies, i.e. tri-partite/three-chambered vs. quadri-partite/four-chambered. Annual % in each population (a, d), maximum annual % within species (b, e) and monthly maximum % in each population (c, f). The species with three-chambered forestomachs are *Colobus guereza*, *C. polykomos*, *Semnopithecus entellus*, *Trachypithecus vetulus*, *T. obscurus*, *Presbytis thomasi*, *P. femoralis*, *P. rubicunda* and *P. melalophos*. The species with four-chambered forestomachs are *Piliocolobus badius*, *Rhinopithecus roxellana*, *Pygathrix nemaeus* and *Nasalis larvatus*. A clear significant difference only for the maximum proportion of leaves, with species with four-chambered stomachs reaching higher maxima, was determined using both generalized least squares ($P = 0.006$) and phylogenetic generalized least squares ($\lambda = 0.26$, $P = 0.009$). The data are based on Matsuda et al. (2019)

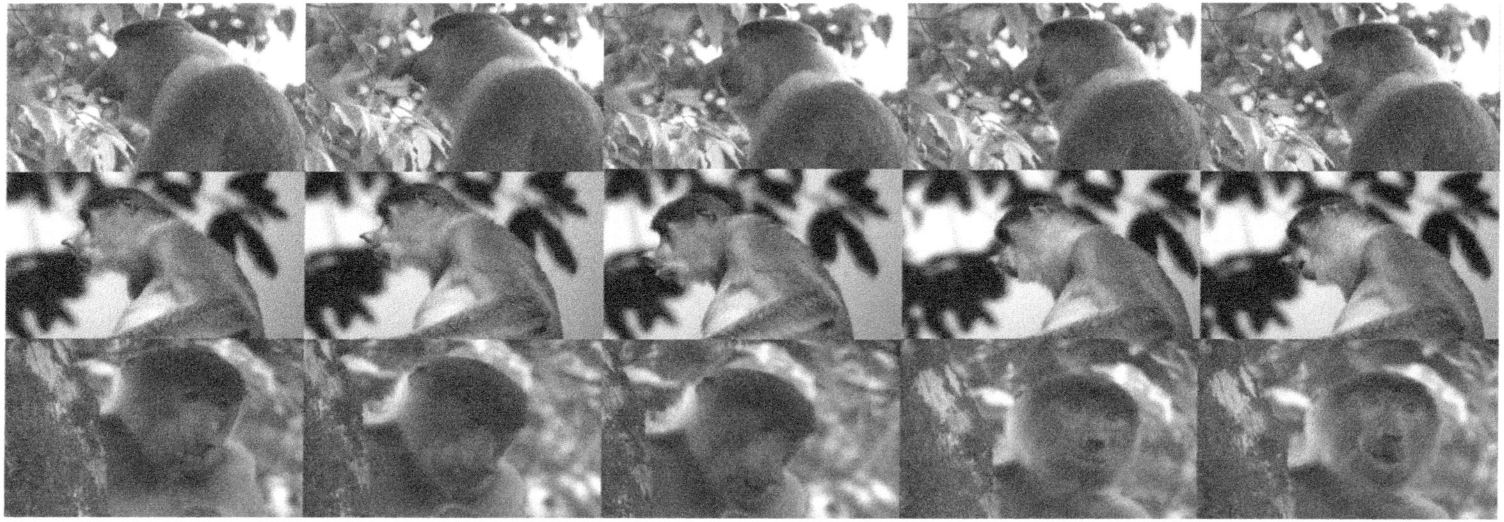

Figure 6.3 Rumination behaviours in proboscis monkeys, including one male (top) and two females (middle and bottom). All individuals display a protruding tongue prior to remastication (Matsuda et al. 2011).

on the density of different-sized particles (Lechner-Doll et al. 1991), with smaller particles generally having a higher density than larger ones (Sutherland 1988; Clauss et al. 2009). Density only operates in relation to gravity, which means the sorting mechanism requires a certain position of the forestomach anatomy in relation to gravity. Thus, both ruminants and camelids typically adopt a sternal resting posture, and they rarely lie on their sides (Balch 1955; Pucora et al. 2019).

For sloths, a group of arboreal, folivorous foregut fermenters, a similar constraint on resting posture was suggested (Clauss 2004), and the predominance of the hypothesized 'sitting' resting posture was later confirmed (Urbani and Bosque 2007), although this may be less related to a density-dependent sorting mechanism and more attributable to the effect of gravity on gas accumulation and eructation.

For colobines, experiments with different-sized digesta markers suggest that there is no particle sorting mechanism in the forestomach (Schwarm et al. 2009; Matsuda et al. 2019b), even for *N. larvatus* despite its reported rumination strategy (Matsuda et al. 2015). Nonetheless, colobines spend significantly more time in the vertical resting posture (73.0 ± 6.0%) than caeco-colic (aka 'hindgut') fermenters (23.2 ± 7.3%) and exhibit a significantly lower postural diversity than caeco-colic-fermenting primates (Matsuda et al. 2017b). Furthermore, in literature data for 31 species of wild-living primates, the mean proportion of time spent sitting was significantly higher in colobines (83.4 ± 9.28%) than in caeco-colic-fermenting primates (69.0 ± 22.1%). These results support the hypothesis that colobines are more constrained in their resting position than primates with other digestive strategies (i.e. caeco-colic-fermenting) and that colobines in particular assume a vertical sitting resting position more often than other primate taxa (Figure 6.4). Again, this may be linked to the necessity of frequently having to eructate digestion gases to avoid pressure on the thorax and respiratory organs.

Digestive Physiology

Forestomach Fermentation

Several functions of forestomachs have been mentioned in the literature. The most considered function is the fermentation of plant fibre, which releases short-chain (or volatile) fatty acids that are absorbed by the host and used as a source of energy (Stevens and Hume 1998). Short-chain fatty acids have been documented in the forestomach of colobines (Drawert et al. 1962; Kuhn 1964; Bauchop and Martucci 1968; Ohwaki et al. 1974; Kay et al. 1976) as well as in their large intestine (Kay et al. 1976). Depending on the fermentability of diet items, the pH in the forestomach will vary. It is normally maintained between 5.0 and 7.0 (Kuhn 1964; Bauchop and Martucci 1968), allowing colobines to actively ferment ingesta using a large microbiome.

The second reason that is traditionally invoked for foregut fermentation is the detoxification of plant secondary compounds by the forestomach microbiome (Kay and Davies 1994). Although individual examples of potentially toxic plant

Figure 6.4 Resting posture in caeco-colic, aka 'hindgut' (above) and foregut (bottom) fermenters. Foregut fermenters (i.e. colobines) are more constrained in their resting position than primates with other digestive strategies. Photos by I. Matsuda

compounds have been mentioned, this concept does not withstand the scrutiny of comparisons with primates that lack a forestomach but still consume plants with plant secondary compounds (Milton 1998). To increase the credibility of the detoxification hypothesis, more research is definitely required.

Another function associated with forestomachs that has received less attention is the use of microbes as both mediators of digestion and sources of nutrients themselves. This is directly linked to the passage of different digesta phases through the forestomach.

Digesta Retention Time and Digesta Flow Patterns

It is generally accepted that the microbial digestion of plant material requires more time than auto-enzymatic digestion. Thus, most herbivores have comparatively long digesta retention times, and herbivorous primates are no exception (Clauss et al. 2008; Müller et al. 2013).

In most mammalian foregut fermenters, solute markers pass through the gastrointestinal tract faster than particulate markers, indicating that fluid moves through the particulate digesta. Notably, this is not related to drinking water intake, but a function of saliva production. This is a basic characteristic of nearly all other mammalian foregut fermenters (Clauss et al. 2004; Schwarm et al. 2009; Dittmann et al. 2015), excluding primates (Müller et al. 2011; Matsuda et al. 2015, 2019b). Washing of forestomach digesta by fluid can be interpreted as a means to harvest the microbiota growing in the forestomach (Müller et al. 2011; Clauss and Hummel 2017). In theory, a restrained degree of forestomach digesta washing could be considered an adaptation to secondary plant compounds. In some browsing ruminants, digesta washing in the forestomach is nearly absent (Dittmann et al. 2015), which might prolong the time soluble toxins are retained in the forestomach for microbial degradation. Nevertheless, other folivores, such as pygmy hippos or sloths, also exhibit distinct digesta washing (Clauss et al. 2004; Vendl et al. 2016), and it is tempting to consider that primates are constrained in this respect. The reason why colobines, even in contrast to arboreal, folivorous sloths, did not evolve higher fluid throughput through their forestomach to intensify the harvest of their forestomach microbes as a source of nutrients remains enigmatic.

One consequence of a low degree of fluid throughput through the forestomach could also be generally low fluid content and hence a lower degree of digesta mixing. Mixing is more probable in the presence of fluid and less probable in a low fluid environment. The degree of digesta mixing is reflected in the excretion patterns of passage markers. An important characteristic of marker excretion curves plotting marker concentrations in outflow (i.e. faeces) over time is the smoothness of the curves. This smoothness reflects a near-complete mixing of the marker with the forestomach contents, and excretion patterns in non-primate mammalian herbivores appear to indicate a high degree of digesta mixing (Figures 6.5a and 6.5b), In a recent study, however, assessing the marker exclusion patterns in 10 foregut-fermenting and 2 caeco-colic-fermenting primate species, it was suggested that these curves display an irregular 'spiky' pattern in primates (Figure 6.5c: Matsuda et al. 2015; Matsuda et al. 2019b). Spiky marker excretion patterns are usually interpreted as coprophagy (Clauss et al. 2007; Espinosa-Gomez et al. 2013), but such behaviour is not typically considered to be a hallmark of primate digestive strategies (although occasional behavioural abnormality is observed in captive primates; e.g. Akers and Schildkraut 1985; Prates and Bicca-Marques 2005; Hopper et al. 2016). Another reason for the spiky pattern could be confusion of samples while collecting faeces, but the large number of findings of spiky patterns across various primate species indicates that this is unlikely. Thus, the most parsimonious explanation for the spiky patterns across primates is the systematic lack of complete digesta mixing in their gastro-intestinal tracts (Matsuda et al. 2019b). Whether incomplete digesta mixing and a lack of a consistently increased fluid throughput in primates represent potential disadvantages remains to be investigated.

Another aspect of forestomach physiology is the additional sorting mechanism documented in the ruminating taxa, the ruminants and the camelids. This sorting mechanism ensures that large particles are selectively retained in the forestomach and subjected to repeated chewing after regurgitation, leading to exceptionally fine particles in the faeces of ruminating herbivores (Clauss et al. 2015). In passage studies, the sorting mechanism leads to a detectable delay of larger particle markers compared with the findings for smaller particle markers (Dittmann et al. 2015), but in

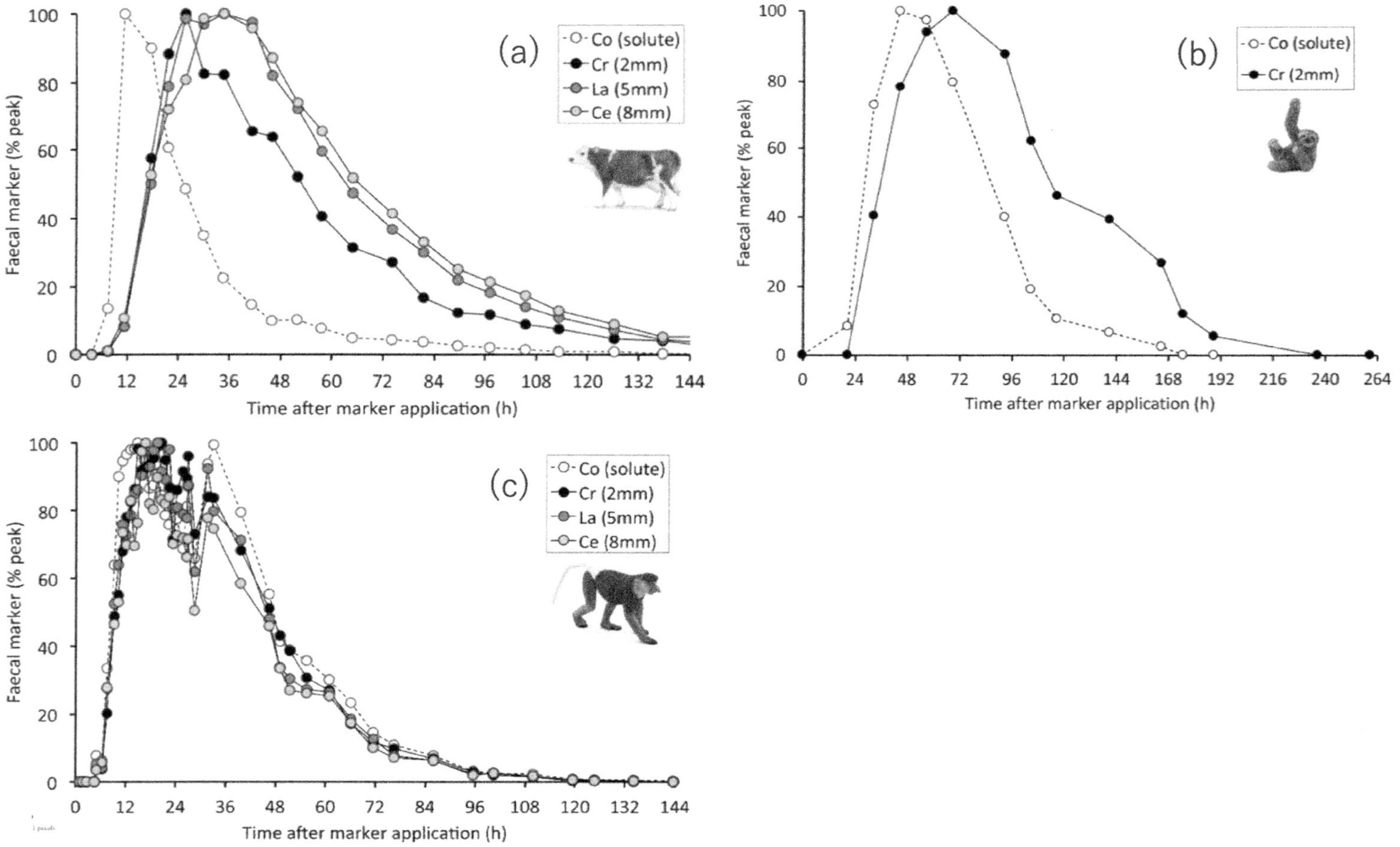

Figure 6.5 Excretion patterns for various passage markers in foregut fermenters, namely (a) domestic cattle, (b) two-toed sloths with relatively smooth curves and (c) proboscis monkeys with spiky curves. The figures are based on Matsuda et al. (2015) and Matsuda et al. (2019)

studies of colobines, even in proboscis monkeys with their occasional ruminant-like behaviour, there was no indication of selective particle retention based on particle size (Schwarm et al. 2009; Matsuda et al. 2015, 2019b). The lack of a sorting mechanism, with a similar retention time for small and large particles will inadvertently lead to either incomplete digestion of the larger particles, or unnecessary time spent retaining the smaller particles.

Faecal Particle Size

Size reduction of the ingested materials is highly relevant for herbivores, as microbial fermentation occurs at a faster rate when the material has smaller particle sizes (Bjorndal et al. 1990). Efficient ingesta particle size reduction, with the associated reduced requirement for extremely long digesta retention, makes the high food intake rates required for homeothermy possible without compromising digestive efficiency (Clauss et al. 2013). Wet-sieving analysis is an established non-invasive approach for measuring faecal particle size to determine the chewing efficiency of mammals (Fritz et al. 2009). Originally applied to captive primates, the method has more recently been used for samples from free-ranging populations (Matsuda et al. 2014; Venkataraman et al. 2014; Weary et al. 2017; Thiry et al. 2018; Schulz-Kornas et al. 2019). Matsuda et al. (2014) compared faecal particle sizes in free-ranging specimens of 12 primate species, including four and eight species of colobines and simple-stomached primates, respectively. The results indicated the possibility previously observed in free-ranging specimens (Matsuda et al. 2011a), that colobines might indeed have adaptations that facilitate a higher degree of ingesta particle-size reduction than observed in simple-stomached primates. In the absence of rumination and selective large-particle retention, this must be due to dental morphology, chewing behaviour or both. In addition, particularly small particles sizes in *N. larvatus* were identified in this study, probably owing to their exceptional strategy of regurgitation and remastication. This might represent an interesting case of convergent physiological adaptation in herbivores, namely colobines and ruminating taxa, which could provide, if rumination of *N. larvatus* is indeed a facultative but not obligatory action, unique insights into the conditions that make this strategy adaptive (Matsuda et al. 2014). While confirming the particularly fine particles in *N. larvatus*, a seasonal influence on chewing efficiency was highlighted in another study, typified by smaller faecal particle size (better chewing efficiency) during the rainy season (Thiry et al. 2018). The mechanisms by which seasonal dietary changes influence colobines' chewing efficiency or faecal particle size are unexplored. Furthermore, the possible effects of dental morphology and stomach anatomy (three- vs. four-chambered) on faecal particle size could be investigated in future studies.

Forestomach Microbiome

Given recent developments in sequencing technology, caeco-colic microbial diversity and community structure based on large amplicon libraries of 16S ribosomal RNA (rRNA) genes, mostly using faecal DNA, have been widely investigated in various vertebrate taxa (Ley et al. 2008; Muegge et al. 2011), including colobines (Chapter 7), but the microbiomes of the foregut have been less studied. This is because, although it is relatively easy to sample faeces from both wild and captive animals, it is difficult to collect pre-gastric contents. To date, in only four studies has it been attempted to characterize the microbiome of the colobine forestomach in *Colobus guereza, C. angolensis, N. larvatus, Pygathrix nemaeus, Rhinopithecus roxellana, Trachypithecus francoisi* and *T.cristatus* in captivity (Zhou et al. 2014; Amato et al. 2016; Hayakawa et al. 2018a; Clayton et al. 2019). A notable exception is a study by Hayakawa et al. (2018a), in which the forestomach microbiomes were compared of free-ranging, semi-free-ranging with supplemental feeding, and captive *N. larvatus*, revealing a decrease in foregut microbial diversity with decreasing habitat diversity (free-ranging > semi-free-ranging > captive). This is consistent with findings of caeco-colic microbial patterns that, compared wild primates with free-ranging conspecifics, captive primates generally have reduced gut microbial diversity, which has been associated with gut dysbiosis (Amato et al. 2013). In addition, echoing the findings of caeco-colic microbial patterns in captive colobines (Amato et al. 2016; Clayton et al. 2016), Hayakawa et al. (2018a) noted that foregut microbiome patterns in *N. larvatus* living in human-related environments are comparable to those in humans, most likely as a consequence of artificial ('Western') diets.

The common phyla in the foregut in free-ranging *N. larvatus* are Bacteroidetes, Firmicutes, Proteobacteria, Actinobacteria and Spirochaetes, indicating that the foregut microbial community does not deviate substantially from that found in captive colobines in general (Zhou et al. 2014; Amato et al. 2016), or even in other foregut-fermenting animals, such as artiodactyls (Samsudin et al. 2011; Dai et al. 2012; Gruninger et al. 2014; Ishaq and Wright 2014; Li et al. 2014; Roggenbuck et al. 2014; Cersosimo et al. 2015; Henderson et al. 2015; Salgado-Flores et al. 2016), rodents (Kohl et al. 2014; Shinohara et al. 2016), sloths (Dill-McFarland et al. 2016), macropods (Pope et al. 2010), and avians (Godoy-Vitorino et al. 2012). Although comparisons of microbial patterns between the foregut and caeco-colon are rare, Clayton et al. (2019) successfully revealed divergent bacterial communities clearly distinguishing the foregut and caeco-colic microbiomes of *P. nemaeus*. Because the forestomach microbiome in colobines has rarely been examined, more metagenomic and functional analyses of foregut microbiome in relation to their living environments might help to elucidate the specialized physiology of colobines.

We note, however, that some caution is necessary. A functional interpretation of findings is increasingly used in molecular studies based on molecular libraries, often without checking for plausibility and mostly without physiological confirmation of the resulting hypotheses. For example, the claim made by Clayton et al. (2019) that methane production in a colobine species should occur in the caeco-colon rather than the forestomach contradicts the finding of methanogenesis in the colobine forestomach (Bauchop and Martucci 1968), which was not discussed by the authors. The claim was also contrary to the general finding that in other foregut fermenters, methanogenesis appears to be more prominent in the forestomach than in the caeco-colon (Immig 1996). The utility of molecular microbiome studies for understanding the physiology of colobines without accompanying physiological measurements, or *in vitro* research on the function of the involved microbes, remains limited.

Colobine Husbandry in Relation to Diets

At present, nearly half of the world's free-ranging primate species are threatened with extinction by habitat destruction and poaching (Estrada et al. 2017), and colobines are no exception (see Chapters 20 and 21). Thus, conservation programmes have become integral aspects of zoological management. Historically, folivorous primates like colobines have often been considered difficult to maintain healthy in captivity, leading to shorter lifespans than free-ranging individuals (Hill 1964; Hollihn 1973; Collins and Roberts 1978). This may be because captive colobines are often fed diets similar to those fed to frugivorous and/or omnivorous primates (Hollihn 1973; Watkins et al. 1985; Edwards et al. 1997), which may lead to gastro-intestinal disorders caused by less fibrous, or excessively well-digestible diets (Hollihn 1971; Nijboer and Clauss 2006; Clauss and Dierenfeld 2008). Commercial fruits typically have a high nutrient density compared with wild fruits (Nijboer and Dierenfeld 1996; NRC 2003; Schwitzer et al. 2009). Incomplete digesta mixing, or a lack of dilution when consuming such well-digestible/high-energy diet items, could explain the particular susceptibility of colobine monkeys to digestive tract problems in captivity because of foregut malfermentation (Clauss and Dierenfeld 2008; Matsuda et al. 2017a). The few available data on forestomach pH in free-ranging and captive colobines also support the concept that diets in captivity may sometimes be too digestible, triggering acidotic forestomach conditions (Nijboer and Clauss 2006). Additionally, genera with a four-chambered stomach, such as *Nasalis*, *Pygathrix* and *Piliocolobus*, are notoriously difficult to maintain and breed, especially in temperate regions (Hollihn 1973; Struhsaker 2010; Matsuda et al. 2017a; Lhota et al. 2019a), compared with the outcomes for species with three-chambered stomachs, i.e. *Colobus*, *Semnopithecus*, *Trachypithecus* and *Presbytis*. This may also be related to the highly digestible diets used in captivity. The higher intake capacity for species with four-chambered stomachs (see the previous section) might be detrimental in the case of more digestible diets in captivity than those in the wild, thereby leading to malfermentation. Conversely, species with three-chambered stomachs might be less susceptible to extreme bouts of malfermentation when fed highly digestible diets, due to their relatively reduced intake capacity. Regardless, modifying captive colobine diets so that the fibre intake is more similar to that of free-ranging individuals would putatively enhance their health and survival in captivity.

To identify an appropriate diet for captive animals, the nutrient composition of the diets of captive and free-ranging individuals is typically compared (NRC 2003; Nijboer et al. 2006; Schwitzer et al. 2009), although this approach requires the sampling and analysis of a large number of food items in the wild coupled with observations of the respective feeding frequency and quantity consumed to determine their overall dietary contribution (Crissey and Pribyl 2007). By contrast, faecal material represents an integrated sample over a certain period of diet intake, it is easier to obtain and it requires fewer samples, but an approach comparing the nutrient composition of faeces in free-ranging and captive individuals is rarely undertaken in colobines. To our knowledge, there have only two attempts to compare faecal nutrients between captive and free-ranging colobines. Chapman et al. (2005a) compared the faecal nitrogen content of free-ranging and captive colobines (*C. angolensis*, *C. guereza* and *Piliocolobus tephrosceles*), finding that quantifying faecal nitrogen levels might be useful for assessing their habitat quality, although they did not differentiate faecal nitrogen derived from indigestible plant protein [neutral detergent fibre (NDF)-bound protein (Rothman et al. 2008a)] and metabolic faecal nitrogen (MFN), a distinction of particular relevance in browsing animals (Steuer et al. 2014). Contrarily, Matsuda et al. (2017a) confirmed that faeces from free-ranging colobines (*N. larvatus*) contained more fibre and less MFN than those from captive specimens, indicating a less digestible diet in the wild. Thus, a comparison of faecal nutrient contents, particularly fibre, may be of immediate relevance to the design of diets than alternative measurements such as microbiome composition or hormone levels (Fujita and Kageyama 2007; Rangel-Negrín et al. 2009; Amato et al. 2016).

To our knowledge, the faecal-fibre (NDF) content of free-ranging colobines such as *N. larvatus* (Matsuda et al. 2017a: 53%–70 %) is much higher than that reported for captive colobines. For captive colobines, values have been reported for *N. larvatus* [42%–64% (Matsuda et al. 2017a); 17% – mean of two different values (Dierenfeld et al. 1992)], *Trachypithecus auratus* [37% – mean of six different values (Nijboer et al. 2006)], *T. françoisi* [31% – mean of three different values (Nijboer et al. 2001) and 28%–44% based on experiments with low-fibre and high-fibre pelleted food (Edwards and Ullrey 1999)], *C. guereza* [28%–51% (Edwards and Ullrey 1999)] and *P. nemaeus* [34%–49% (Edwards and Ullrey 1999)]. The experiments of Edwards and Ullrey (1999) demonstrated that high levels of fibre in pelleted food compounds can contribute to achieving faecal-fibre levels closer to those of free-ranging conditions than traditional, low-fibre primate pellets. Although differences in faecal-fibre levels are likely to occur within species, because of factors related to habitat, season, sex or reproductive status, the general magnitude of differences can serve as a convenient proxy of the appropriateness of any particular diet in captivity. To reduce the occurrence of gastro-intestinal disorders and enhance health and survival, it may be recommendable to alter the diets of captive colobines to replicate the faecal-fibre levels found in free-ranging specimens, although long-term feeding trials will be necessary to test whether more fibrous foods can truly reinforce health and reproductive success. At least, increasing dietary-fibre content leads to more naturally formed faeces in captive colobines (Nijboer et al. 2006).

Conclusions

From the viewpoint of digestive physiology, colobine primates are fascinating, because they illustrate that both caeco-colic and foregut fermentation can evolve within a taxonomic lineage (primates), whereas a whole taxon usually has a consistent digestive anatomy.

It should be remembered that, despite our tendency to think in dichotomies, our propensity to construct obligatory form-function adaptationist scenarios does not necessarily reflect reality. Concerning primates, different morpho-physiological solutions to the challenges of folivory may well exist in parallel, in which a clear advantage of one system over another, such as in caeco-colic versus foregut fermentation, cannot be demonstrated and should not be expected. Recent investigations of the relationships of gastro-intestinal tract dimensions or complexity with diet revealed no clear pattern in primates (Langer and Clauss 2018; McGrosky et al. 2019), suggesting that gastro-intestinal tract morpho-physiology could contain more of a phylogenetic than an ecological signal.

Considering primate chewing efficiency, which generally achieves a lesser degree of particle-size reduction than achieved by other herbivores of similar size (Dunbar and Bose 1991; Fritz et al. 2009; Matsuda et al. 2014), and the low degree of digesta washing and mixing (Matsuda et al. 2019b), it appears that primates, including colobines, are not characterized by high degrees of morpho-physiological adaptations of their digestive tracts relative to other mammals.

Acknowledgements

We thank David J. Chivers and Julie Teichroeb for thoughtful comments on this chapter. IM was supported by the JSPS KAKENHI (#19H03308) while writing this chapter.

7 Colobine Gut Microbiota

New Perspectives on the Nutrition and Health of a Specialized Subfamily of Primates

Katherine R. Amato, Jonathan B. Clayton and Vanessa L. Hale

Introduction

The gut microbiota is a community of bacteria, archaea, microscopic eukaryotes and viruses located in the full gastrointestinal (GI) tract of all mammals (Mackie 2002). For decades, studies have indicated that the gut microbiota in the sacculated colobine foregut plays a critical role in colobine nutrition (Bauchop and Martucci 1968; Kay and Davies 1994). However, until relatively recently, researchers did not have the tools to examine it in detail. The development of affordable, high-throughput DNA sequencing – combined with the identification of microbial DNA barcodes for detecting and quantifying microbial taxa without culturing them – has revolutionized our ability to study microbial communities, including those throughout the GI tract. As a result, we now know that hindgut microbes in most mammals have a variety of influences on host health, ranging from nutrition to immune function to behaviour (Al Nabhani and Eberl 2020; Johnson and Foster 2018; Leshem et al. 2020; Oliphant and Allen-Vercoe 2019; Pronovost and Hsiao 2019; Valdes et al. 2018; Visconti et al. 2019). We also know that shifts in host environmental and lifestyle factors such as diet, social interactions, and stress can alter the hindgut microbiota (Bisanz et al. 2019; David et al. 2014; Hicks et al. 2018; Nagpal et al. 2018; Perofsky et al. 2017; Song et al. 2013; Tung et al. 2015; Vlčková et al. 2017; Wikberg et al. 2020). This information is invaluable for addressing gaps in our understanding of colobine ecology, evolution and health. Nevertheless, the field remains in its relative infancy, and compared to humans, there is a dearth of information describing the colobine fore- and hindgut microbiome.

While gut microbes are important for all non-human primates (hereafter 'primates'), they have long been thought of as essential for leaf-eating primates such as colobines since leaves generally contain high amounts of structural carbohydrates and toxins that can only be processed by microbial enzymes (Davies and Oates 1994; Jablonski 1998a; Milton 1980; Nijboer 2006). For colobines, in particular, the sacculated foregut is believed to be an adaptation to facilitate microbial breakdown of these plant-based compounds. However, our knowledge of the specific microbial taxa that inhabit the fore- and hindguts of colobines and their functions within their hosts is limited. To provide a foundation for continued progress in this area, this chapter assesses current knowledge of the colobine gut microbiome and identifies

This chapter includes Electronic Supplementary Material (ESM) at: www.cambridge.org/colobines

topics for further study. Because there are more published data describing the colobine hindgut microbiome, we focus most of our discussion on this part of the GI tract despite the clear importance of the colobine foregut and its microbiome. We begin by situating colobines in the context of other leaf-eating mammals both within and beyond the primate phylogeny. Subsequently, we address the potential role of the hindgut microbiome in contributing to negative health outcomes in colobines, particularly in captivity. We then explore the impact of habitat degradation on the colobine hindgut microbiome and discuss how these findings can be integrated into evaluations of colobine health in the context of conservation. Finally, we outline some best practices and caveats for future studies of the colobine gut microbiome more generally.

The Gut Microbiome of Leaf-Eating Primates

To some extent, all primates utilize low-quality resources such as woody plants, mature leaves, fungi, unripe fruit and/or plant exudates that are difficult to digest and require greater handling and processing due to mechanical defences, limited nutrient profiles, and high concentrations of indigestible material or toxins (Lambert 2011). However, some taxa rely almost exclusively on these resources either seasonally or year-round. Leaf-eating, in particular, has evolved independently several times throughout the primate phylogeny, and species of strepsirrhines (*Hapalemur* spp., Family: Indriidae), New World monkeys *(Alouatta* spp.*)*, Old World monkeys (Subfamily: Colobinae) and apes (*Gorilla berengei*) are considered leaf-eaters.

Compared to other food resources such as ripe fruit and insects, leaves generally have high amounts of structural carbohydrates and secondary metabolites, which make them hard to digest (Lambert 2011; Matsuda et al. 2017c). Leaf-eating primates exhibit strong food selectivity to reduce intake of these compounds (Chapman and Chapman 2002; Glander 1982; Matsuda et al. 2017c). Both howler monkeys and colobus monkeys, for example, have been shown to target leaves with high protein-to-fibre ratios and appear to moderate intake of food resources containing high levels of secondary metabolites (Chapman and Chapman 2002; Glander 1982; Huffman 1997). Additionally, leaf-eating primates have a digestive anatomy that facilitates microbial processing of a leafy diet by decreasing food particle size and increasing GI volume and retention time, which increases exposure to microbes, as well as increasing GI surface area, which increases absorption of nutrients (Chivers and Hladik 1980, 1984; Hladik 1978; Matsuda et al. 2014). Gorillas have a large overall body size and GI tract while howler monkeys have an enlarged colon; colobines have a sacculated foregut, and sifakas have an enlarged caecum. In these structures, gut microbes ferment otherwise indigestible plant structural carbohydrates into short-chain fatty acids (SCFAs) such as acetate, butyrate and propionate, which can be absorbed by the host and used for energy (Barboza et al. 2009; Mackie 2002; Stevens and Hume 1995). Microbes also regulate xenobiotic metabolism (Bjorkholm et al. 2009), including the breakdown of toxic plant secondary metabolites (Kohl et al. 2014b).

Leaf-eating primates are believed to depend on these microbial functions regardless of the types of plants being consumed. Therefore, a common assumption is that leaf-eating primates possess similar hindgut microbial traits independently of host species and geographical location. Parallel studies in other mammals support this assumption. Plant-eating mammals exhibit similar hindgut microbiomes that are distinct from those of omnivores and carnivores (Muegge et al. 2011), and many ant-eating animals host similar microbial taxa despite being distantly related (Delsuc et al. 2014). Nevertheless, in these studies host diet is confounded with host phylogeny and/or host digestive anatomy, and a recent study of leaf-eating primates suggests that these confounds may be responsible for the reported convergence (Amato et al. 2019). When the hindgut microbiome composition and function of 18 species of wild primates were compared, only 4% of the variation in gut microbiome composition was explained by dietary niche, while 27% was explained by host phylogenetic subgroup (ape, Old World monkey, New World monkey, lemur) (Amato et al. 2019). Similarly, 7% of the variation in hindgut microbiome function was explained by dietary niche while 28% was explained by host phylogenetic subgroup. A handful of microbial taxa and pathways appeared to be enriched in leaf-eating primates compared to non-leaf-eaters, but in most cases the correlations were weak and difficult to interpret.

The results of this study indicate that leaf-eating primates generally do not share hindgut microbial traits and that host phylogeny plays a primary role in shaping the primate hindgut microbiome. In fact, data describing the colobine hindgut microbiome demonstrate that host phylogenetic signals in the primate hindgut microbiome are likely a product of host physiology, including gut anatomy. While geography and phylogeny are confounded for many primate taxa, colobines inhabit both Africa and Asia, where they consume different plant species. Nevertheless, African colobines harbour a hindgut microbiome that is more similar to that of Asian colobines than to those of other primate genera in Africa, such as baboons (Amato et al. 2019).

One notable exception to phylogeny-linked microbiota is a study that examined nine sympatric primates species in Tai National Park, Côte d'Ivoire (Gogarten et al. 2018). This study found that each primate species was associated with a distinct hindgut microbial community despite the shared environment, and that the three colobine species (King colobus – *Colobus plykomos*, Western red colobus – *Procolobus badius*, Olive colobus – *Procolous verus*) had the most similar microbiota. However, microbial composition across the remaining primate species did not reflect the host phylogenetic relationships as the colobines' hindgut microbial communities were more similar to chimpanzees' (Western chimpanzee – *Pan troglodytes verus*) than to the other four more-closely related monkey species (Greater spot-nosed monkey – *Cercopithecus nictitans*, Lesser spot-nosed monkey – *Cercopithesucs petaurista*, Cambell's mona monkey – *Cercopitheus campbelli*, Diana monkey – *Cercopithecus diana*, Sooty mangabey – *Cercocebus atys atys*). The authors speculate that the similarity between colobine and chimpanzee hindgut microbial communities could be linked to chimpanzee hunting and consumption of colobus monkeys – including consumption of colobus intestines.

Aside from circumstances such as predator-prey interactions increasing microbiota similarity between distantly related species, colobines all share a specialized gut anatomy – a foregut composed of either a tripartite stomach (saccus gastricus, tubus gastricus, pars pylorica) or a quadripartite stomach (with an additional compartment, the presaccus), that appears to drive similarities in the hindgut microbiome more than local diet or environmental microbial exposure. Therefore, while hindgut microbes provide critical functions for leaf-eating primates, including colobines, the types of microbes and the functions they provide are constrained by host digestive physiology. This finding is critical for understanding the role of hindgut microbes in facilitating the evolution of specialized diets such as leaf-eating in primates.

The Colobine Gut Microbiome

While the interplay between host physiology and the gut microbiome is critical for facilitating leaf-eating in primates across the phylogeny, the unique colobine foregut increases the effectiveness of the relationship. Compared to the guts of more frugivorous monkeys, the colobine gut has an increased length and volume – providing more time and surface area for microbial fermentation of plant structural carbohydrates into SCFAs as well as detoxification of plant secondary metabolites (Brourton and Perrin 1991; Kay and Davies 1994). Additionally, the colobine foregut allows microbial processes to occur earlier in the GI tract, giving the host access to microbially produced vitamins and detoxified plant secondary compounds that may not be absorbed in the large intestine, where the majority of other primates house their gut microbes. Similarly, microbial communities in the foregut provide hosts with an additional protein source since they are subject to digestion after leaving the foregut (Godoy-Vitorino et al. 2012). As a result, colobines are capable of utilizing less nutrient-dense diets compared to other leaf-eating primates. While many non-colobine leaf-eating primates consume substantial amounts of ripe fruit (*Alouatta*: >50% of diet seasonally, *Propithecus*: 50%–60%, *Gorilla*: 90%), colobines consume more leaves, seeds and unripe fruit (Campbell et al. 2011a), although preferences for ripe fruit have been reported (Danish et al. 2006; Dela 2012; Koenig et al. 1998; Kool 1993; Ruslin et al. 2019).

Given this unique combination of diet and physiology, the colobine fore- and hindgut microbiome is likely to be distinct from that of other primates. Therefore, a better understanding of the colobine gut microbiome depends on comparisons with non-primate mammals. There are a range of mammals including artiodactyls, rodents, sloths and macropods that utilize a foregut fermentation strategy analogous to that of colobines. Ruminants, in particular, represent an interesting comparative system. Despite the fact that most colobines do not actually ruminate (but see Matsuda et al. 2011a), ruminant gut anatomy, physiology and dietary strategy are similar to those of colobines, albeit with grasses as opposed to leaves. Importantly, compared to many other mammalian foregut fermenters, the nutrition, physiology and fore- and hindgut microbiomes of ruminants are well studied. Like the colobine foregut, the rumen allows hosts to maximize foraging potential through the extraction of key nutrients via microbial production of SCFAs, vitamins, and cofactors (Head 1959; Dunlop and Hammond 1965; Lewis 1951). It can also detoxify toxic components in forages (Allison et al. 1990; Krause et al. 2013) and allows hosts to digest the microbial community as a source of protein. Previous studies have shown that colobines and ruminants share convergent endogenous ribonucleases and lysozymes for digesting foregut bacteria (Janiak 2016).

Given the similarities in diet and digestive physiology, we would expect the colobine and ruminant fore- and hindgut microbiomes to be similar. One study of golden snub-nosed monkeys (*Rhinopithecus roxellana*) shows that the hindgut microbiome is enriched in microbial taxa and pathways associated with plant structural carbohydrate breakdown, particularly in females (Liu et al. 2018). Likewise, Xu et al. (2015) demonstrated that the faecal microbiome of *R. bieti* is closely related to that of both the human stomach and the cow rumen, particularly with regard to its glycoside hydrolase profile. However, to date, no study has examined these trends with multiple species of colobines and ruminants.

Here, we capitalize on the growing body of literature describing the hindgut microbiomes of wild animals to systematically compare colobine and ruminant hindgut microbiomes. While comparisons of the foregut are relevant and necessary, data describing the colobine foregut microbiome are scarce (Hayakawa et al. 2018a). Therefore, here we focus on the hindgut. Specifically, we combine and analyse 16S rRNA gene amplicon data generated from faecal samples of 19 species of wild primates, including three species of colobines, and seven species of wild ruminants (order Cetartiodactyla; ESM Table 7.1). As mentioned above, while many other mammalian foregut fermenters exist, we limit our comparison to a single order of ruminants for which we could obtain data from undomesticated, wild individuals. The data we included allowed us to minimize confounds associated with domestication/human contact in ruminants as well as intra-order differences in body size and ecology. After quality filtering (split_library.py, default settings) we used the forward reads from each sample to cluster OTUs at 97% similarity using sortmerna to execute closed-reference OTU-picking against the GreenGenes 13_8 database. Data were rarefied to 3000 reads/sample, and diversity and relative abundance measures were calculated using QIIME (v. 1.9.0, alpha_diversity.py, beta_diversity_through_plots.py, summarize_taxonomy.py).

Our results suggest that, in terms of the presence and absence of microbial taxa, the colobine faecal microbiome is more similar to that of ruminants than to that of other hindgut fermenting primates (Figure 7.1). PERMANOVA reveals that more variation in hindgut microbiome composition is described by the presence or absence of a foregut (Pseudo-$F_{1,175}$ = 21.3, r^2 = 0.11, $p < 0.001$) than by host order (Pseudo-$F_{1,175}$ = 13.0, r^2 = 0.07, $p < 0.001$). When results are weighted using the relative abundances of microbial taxa, the colobine hindgut microbiome is more similar to that of other primates than to that of ruminants (Figure 7.2; gut: Pseudo-$F_{1,175}$ = 14.9, r^2 = 0.08, $p < 0.001$, phylogeny: Pseudo-$F_{1,175}$ = 22.7, r^2 = 0.12, $p < 0.001$). However, more than other primates, colobines possess a hindgut microbiome that is similar to those of ruminants (Figures 7.1 and 7.2),

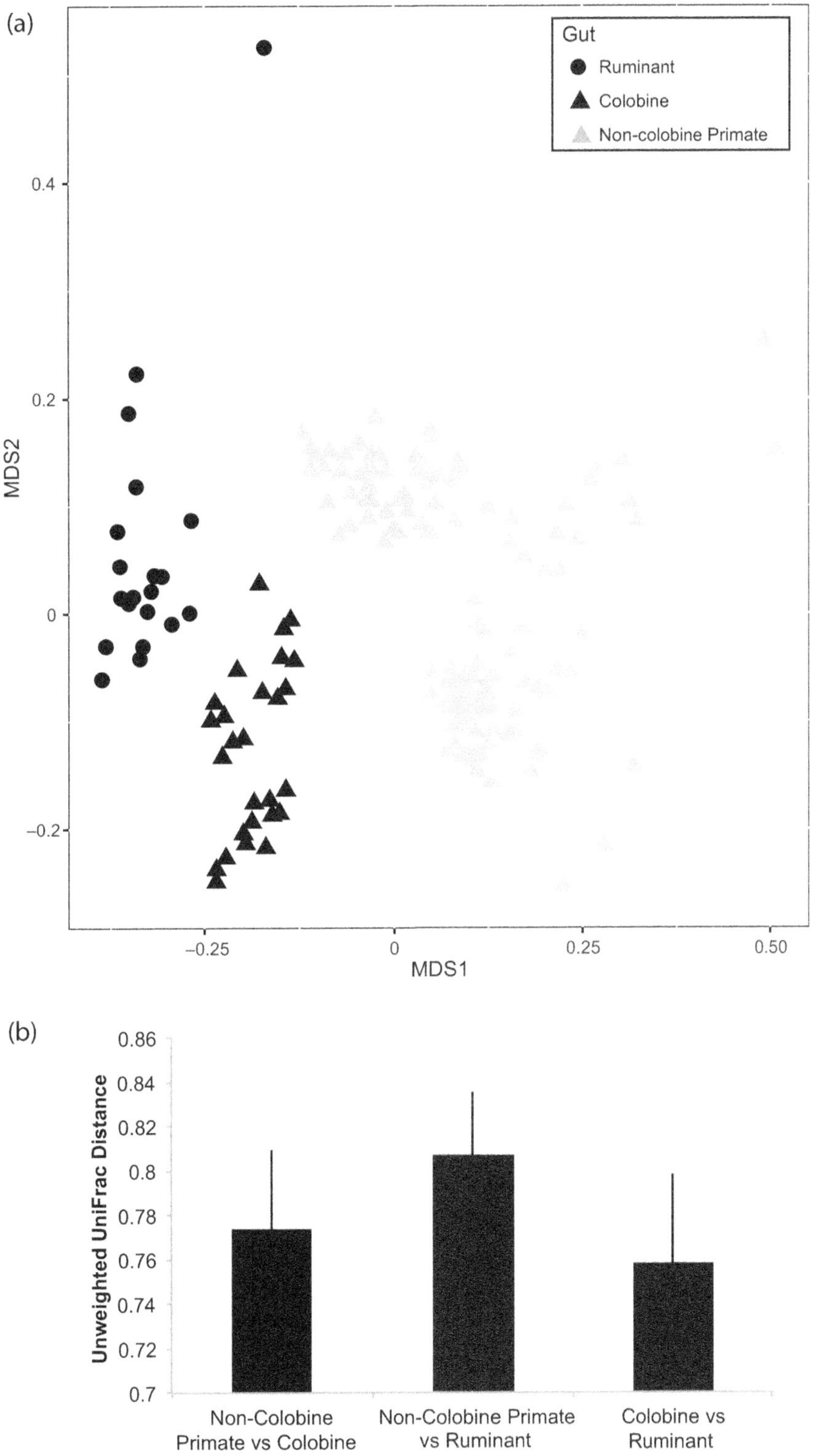

Figure 7.1 (a) Non-metric multidimensional scaling (NMDS) plot comparing the faecal microbiomes of colobines, non-colobine primates and ruminants using unweighted UniFrac distances. (b) Average (±SD) unweighted UniFrac distances among colobines, non-colobine primates and ruminants.

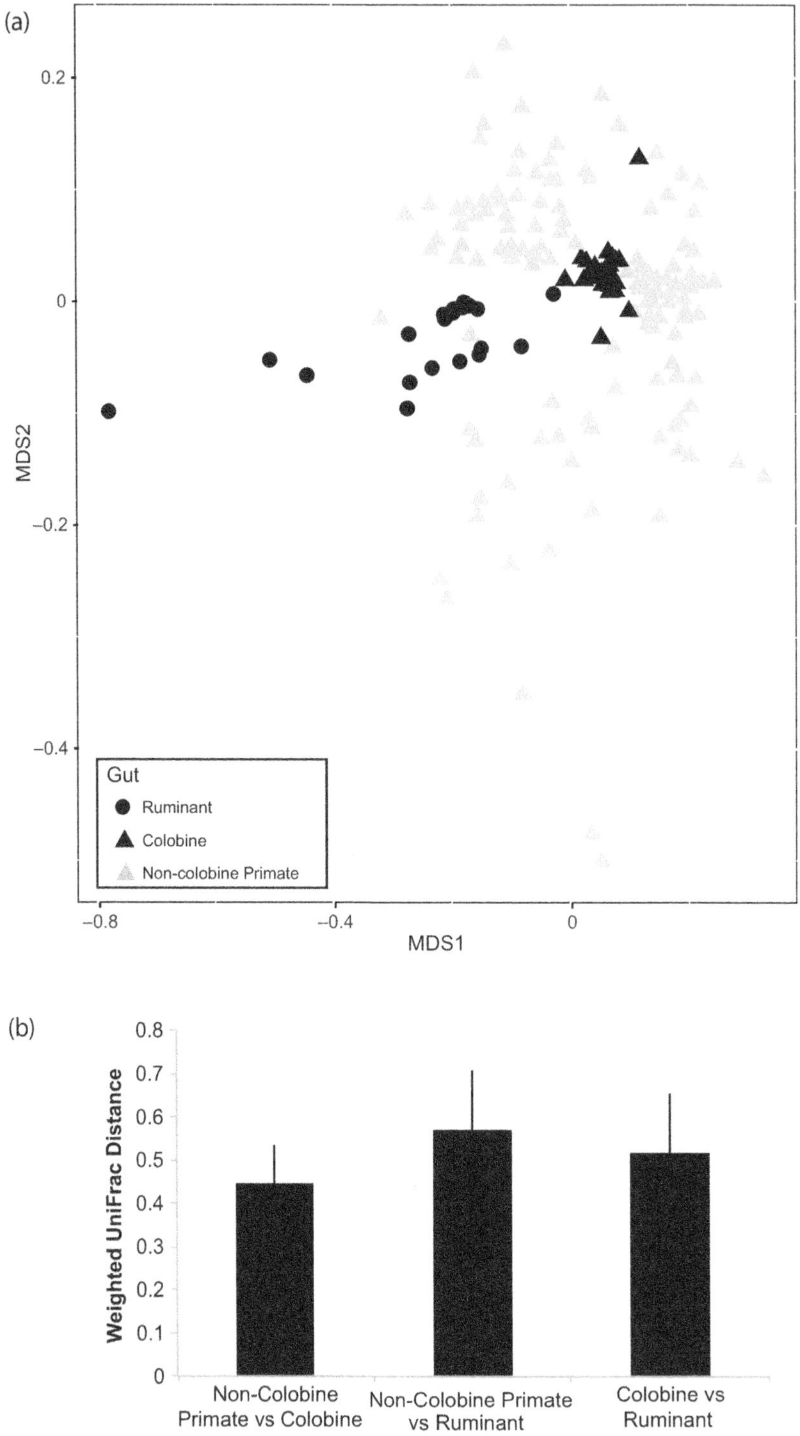

Figure 7.2 (a) Non-metric multidimensional scaling (NMDS) plot comparing the faecal microbiomes of colobines, non-colobine primates and ruminants using weighted UniFrac distances. (b) Average (±SD) weighted UniFrac distances among colobines, non-colobine primates and ruminants.

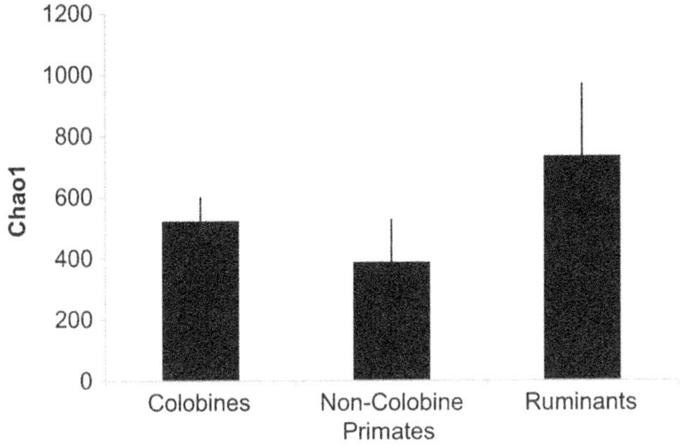

Figure 7.3 Average (±SD) richness of the faecal microbiome of colobines, non-colobine primates and ruminants.

resulting in a microbiome structure that is intermediate between that of a primate and a ruminant.

With a relatively small sample size, it is challenging to pinpoint the hindgut microbiome traits that drive the observed patterns. However, gut microbial diversity appears to be important. Although the colobine faecal microbiome is not as diverse as that of a ruminant, it is generally more diverse than that of other primates (Figure 7.3). Additionally, while colobines share a similar number of microbial taxa with both non-colobine primates and ruminants, none of those taxa are shared among non-colobine primates and ruminants (ESM Table 7.2). Again, this suggests that primate and ruminant hindgut microbiomes are distinct, with colobines representing an intermediate phenotype.

Our findings indicate that the colobine gut is functionally quite similar to that of a ruminant, both in terms of anatomy and gut microbial community structure. While more samples are necessary to examine the impact of factors such as diet across seasons, habitats, and species. These baseline data provide an important foundation for improving our understanding of colobine nutrition and health. Although no microbial OTUs were shared among all of the ruminants and colobines included in our analysis, there is likely to be overlap in microbial functions, perhaps represented by different members of the same genera in colobines and ruminants. Shotgun metagenomic data, which provides information on microbial functional genes and also allows for species-level detection of microbes, will be essential for elucidating these functions and identifying their role in the foregut ecosystem.

Furthermore, despite these interesting patterns, a systematic investigation of the colobine foregut microbiome is necessary to more fully understand its function and potential convergence with the rumen. A dearth of samples currently prohibits extensive analysis. However, three published studies provide preliminary insight. First, at the genus level, the captive snub-nosed monkey foregut microbiome exhibits similarities with the rumen microbiome (Zhou et al. 2014). Together with our analyses, these findings suggest that convergence in the microbiomes of colobines and ruminants occurs in both the foregut and hindgut. Further sampling will allow us to better determine which microbial taxa drive convergence in the foregut and the extent to which relationships vary across host populations and species. Another study analysing the microbiomes of the entire GI tract of captive colobines finds limited differences between the foregut and hindgut (Amato et al. 2016b). However, it is unclear if disease and/or captivity might be driving these patterns. Post-mortem artefactual changes may also have played a role in these results.

In contrast, a separate study on the fore- and hindgut microbiota of captive red-shanked douc langurs (*Pygathrix nemaeus*) found significant differences in microbial diversity and composition between gut sites (Clayton et al. 2019). Hindgut samples had greater microbial diversity, increased Firmicutes to Bacteroidetes ratios (suggesting higher energy harvest capacity), and greater abundances of the taxa *Adlercreutzia, Oscillospira* and *Rosburia.* Foregut samples had greater abundances of *Moryella, Butyrivibrio* and *Lactococcus.* The microbial community differences between gut sites outweighed differences in individual microbial communities, highlighting the remarkable degree to which gut microbial communities can differ based on gut site. Finally, another recent study reported that the diversity of the proboscis monkey foregut microbiome is positively correlated with host dietary diversity across habitats (Hayakawa et al. 2018a). Therefore, we must take these factors into consideration when making generalizations about the composition and function of the colobine foregut microbiome.

Besides host physiology and diet, there are other host-related factors that shape microbial composition within a species or group. One study on wild black-and-white colobus monkeys (*Colobus vellerosus*) in Boabeng-Fiema, Ghana reported that social interactions (i.e. proximity) had a larger influence on the hindgut microbiota than diet or relatedness of the hosts (Wikberg et al. 2020). Amongst the socially transmitted taxa were microbes in the genera *Asteroleplasma, Bacteroides, Desulfovibrio, Eubacterium, Clostridum XIVa, Coprococcus, Lachnospiracea, Desulfurispora, Parabacteroides, Clostridum IV, Flavonifractor, Subdoligranulum. Centipeda* and *Propionispira.* Several of these genera (*Parabacteroides, Coprococcus, Bacterodes, Clostridium, Roseburia*) have been previously associated with sociality in black-and-white colobus (Goodfellow et al. 2019) or howler monkeys (Amato et al. 2017) and play a role in plant digestion. Exactly how these microbes are transmitted (e.g. direct versus indirect contact) and if they provide health benefits or fitness advantages to social interactions within and between hosts are questions yet to be answered. However, another study in the same system demonstrated that social group fission events can also lead to changes in the hindgut microbiome (Goodfellow et al. 2019).

Additionally, a study of Phayre's leaf monkeys (*Trachypithecus crepusculus*) demonstrated that fluctuations in sex hormones predicted female hindgut microbiome composition (Mallott et al. 2020). Specifically, faecal progesterone concentrations were negatively correlated with hindgut microbial diversity and could predict patterns of pairwise sample similarity in overall hindgut microbiome composition. These effects were independent of seasonal changes in rainfall and phytoprogestin consumption. It has been previously suggested that hormone-induced shifts in the gut microbiome that affect microbial functions related to host nutrition could help some wild primates compensate for the nutritional demands of pregnancy and lactation (Amato et al. 2014; Mallott and Amato 2018). These dynamics could be particularly important for leaf-eating primates with clear dietary constraints on intake of energy or select nutrients. More data are necessary to fully explore these hypotheses.

Dysbiosis of the Colobine Gut Microbiome

While gut microbes benefit hosts in many ways, they can also trigger disease in certain circumstances. Many of the health conditions that impact ruminants, such as bloat, nitrite poisoning and acidosis, originate from an imbalance in the microbiome (Krause et al. 2013). For example, gastric acidosis occurs when ruminants that typically utilize a high fibre diet are fed a diet high in simple carbohydrates (Kleen 2003). This change alters the rumen microbiome (Mao et al. 2013). For example, the increased carbohydrate availability stimulates lactic acid fermentation by bacteria such as *Streptococcus bovis* or *Dasytricha* sp., resulting in lower pH levels (Slyter 1976). Lower pH levels inhibit cellulolytic bacterial growth, decreasing fibre digestion and reducing feed efficiency (Russell and Wilson 1996). This process has a number of negative impacts on the health of the host, including damage to the ruminal mucosa, rumen atony, diarrhoea, dehydration, circulatory collapse and even death (Zachary and McGavin 2016).

Similar dynamics have been observed in colobines. Commercially prepared primate diets provided to captive colobines typically have a higher ratio of simple-to-structural carbohydrates compared to wild diets (Matsuda et al. 2017a; Nijboer and Dierenfeld 1996; Oftedal et al. 1991). Although increased amounts of simple carbohydrates increase diet palatability, captive colobines frequently suffer from GI distress, including diarrhoea, vomiting, bloat, and weight loss (Agoramoorthy et al. 2004; Calle et al. 1995; Davies and Oates 1994; Edwards 1997; Ensley et al. 1982; Heldstab 1988; Hill 1964; Hollihn 1973; Janssen 1994; Loomis and Britt 1983; Nijboer and Clauss 2006; Overskei et al. 1992; Shelmidine et al. 2013; Sutherland-Smith et al. 1998; Ullrey 1986). It has long been speculated that the specialized diet and gut physiology of colobines contributes to their susceptibility to these illnesses in captivity (Crissey and Pribyl 2007; Lambert 1998; Ruempler 1998). However, no specific microbial mechanism has been directly identified.

One of the first steps towards understanding the role of gut microbes in captive colobine GI illness is to describe the effect of captivity on the colobine gut microbiome. Several studies of primates more generally have demonstrated a strong impact of captivity on the hindgut microbiome (Amato et al. 2013; Frankel et al. 2019; Greene et al. 2019; Hayakawa et al. 2018b; Lugano et al. 2018; Uenishi et al. 2007), and a few hindgut datasets indicate similar patterns in colobines. For example, red-shanked douc langurs (*Pygathrix nemaeus*) appear to undergo a 'humanization' of the hindgut microbiome as they move from wild to semi-wild to captive environments (Clayton et al. 2016, 2010). This shift includes a reduction in alpha diversity as well as an increase in the relative abundance of microbial taxa such as *Bacteroides*.

Behavioural data combined with an analysis of chloroplast 16S sequences suggest that these changes are a result of altered diets. However, altered environmental exposure to microbes, medical interventions and contact with human caretakers are also likely to have an impact.

Similar patterns are observed when data from wild and captive *P. nemaeus* and *R. roxellana* are compared. In one study, although hindgut bacterial diversity is similar between habitats, wild colobines exhibit higher relative abundances of *Dehalobacterium, Oscillospira, Atopobium, Blautia, Coprobacillus, Desulfotomaculum, Clostridium*, and *Ruminococcus* and lower relative abundances of *Parabacteroides, Prevotella, Epulopiscium, Bacteroides, Desulfovibrio, Butyricimonas, Methanobrevibacter, Phascolarctobacterium*, and *Dialister* (Amato et al. 2016b). Another study, reports reduced hindgut abundances of *Bacteroides vulgatus* in captive compared to provisioned Sichuan snub-nosed monkeys (*Rhinopithecus roxellana*) (Su et al. 2016) while captive Guizhou snub-nosed monkeys (*Rhinopithecus brelichi*) have fewer taxa associated with fibre degradation and more taxa associated with simple sugar degradation as compared to wild *R. brelichi* (Hale et al. 2019). Finally, a single study examines differences in the foregut of wild and captive proboscis monkeys (*Nasalis larvatus*), but patterns are similar to those detected using hindgut data (Hayakawa et al. 2018a). Captive individuals have lower microbial diversity compared to some wild individuals, as well as an increased abundance of potential pathogens, and a decreased abundance of potentially beneficial microbial taxa. Additional samples and data are necessary to determine whether these microbial taxa are universally important for understanding changes in the captive colobine microbiome as well as for pinpointing the health consequences associated with these changes. However, these results provide an important foundation for building future studies and hypotheses.

Finally, one study by Hale et al. (2018) indirectly corroborates that captivity has a disruptive effect on the colobine hindgut microbiome. The data from this study indicate that colobine hindgut microbiomes are strongly influenced by captive institution, suggesting that the strong phylogenetic constraints on the primate hindgut microbiome detected in wild primates are relaxed in captive primates (Hale et al. 2018). The ability of marked environmental shifts associated with captivity, such as diet and microbial exposure, to incite convergence in the hindgut microbiomes of distinct host species may serve as a signal of disruption to the gut microbiome.

Whether or not these disruptions are responsible for GI distress in captive colobines remains unclear. One study examines the potential role of the gut microbiota in driving GI distress in captive *P. nemaeus* at the San Diego Zoo. Here, GI-unhealthy doucs are reported to be enriched for *Succinovibrio, Bulleidia, Pastuerella, Eubacterium, Campylobacter, Megasphaera, Succiniclasticum, Selenomonas, Streptococcus, Acidaminococcus* and *Phascolarctobacterium* throughout different GI sections, compared to GI-healthy doucs (Amato et al. 2016b). In another study, the hindgut microbiota of captive *R. roxellana* with and without diarrhoea were compared. Both groups had similar microbial diversity but distinct composition, and individuals with diarrhoea had higher relative abundances of the genera

Desulfovibrio, *Lactobacillales*, *Planococcaceae*, *Mogibaceriaceae*, *Trichococcus*, *Dorea*, *Methanobrevibacter*, *Christensenellaceae*, *Bacteroidales*, RF39 and *Acinetobacter* (Zhu et al. 2018). Individuals with diarrhoea also had significantly increased gene copy numbers of heat-stable *Escherichia coli* enterotoxins STa and STb present in their stool – suggesting that pathogenic microbes may play a role in captive colobine GI illness. This study also reported significantly altered microbial composition, reduced diversity, and decreased short-chain fatty acid (SCFA) abundances in 'old' monkeys (>6 yo) as compared to 'adult' *R. roxellana* (4–6 yo) – indicating that age, as in humans, may be associated with microbial community changes that can impact health and disease susceptibility (Zapata and Quagliarello 2015).

These small cross-sectional studies leave a number of questions unanswered, however. In addition to having limited power, it is impossible to determine whether the microbial patterns detected are a cause or a symptom of GI distress. Routine sampling of captive colobine gut microbiomes would allow retrospective analyses of samples in cases of illness and death and could begin to allow us to ascertain causation.

Finally, another relevant area of investigation is role of the gut microbiome in determining the extent to which colobine species are differentially affected by captivity. More so than other colobines, *Pygathrix* spp., *Procolobus* spp. and *Nasalis* spp. are reported to frequently develop GI problems of unknown cause in captivity (Gijzen et al. 1966; Janssen 1994; Matsuda et al. 2017a; Ruempler 1998; Struhsaker 2010). These differences in susceptibility are unlikely to be attributable to inter-species variation in diet since the major components of all colobine diets are young and mature leaves, seeds, and in the case of some snub-nosed monkeys (*Rhinopithecus* spp.), lichens (Guo et al. 2007; Harris and Chapman 2007a; Rawson 2006; Ryan et al. 2012; Ulibarri 2013; Workman 2009; Xiang et al. 2007; Zhuo et al. 2006). Furthermore, intra-specific differences in diet composition across time and space are greater than inter-specific differences (Chapman et al. 2002a). Instead sensitivity to GI illness may be related to GI morphology and the associated gut microbiota. Although the signal is weaker in captivity than in the wild, different host species possess different hindgut microbiomes. Without additional sampling, it is effectively impossible to determine how these differences might affect colobine sensitivity to GI distress in captivity. However, since gut anatomy shapes the primate gut microbiome, and species that are difficult to maintain in captivity due to GI distress – such as *Pygathrix* and *Procolobus* (as well as *Rhinopithecus* and *Nasalis*) – have a four-chambered foregut while other species have a three-chambered foregut (*Colobus*, *Semnopithecus*, *Trachypithecus* and *Presbytis*) (Caton 1998), there may be an important link between gut anatomy, the gut microbiome and host sensitivity to GI distress. Indeed, another study indicated that *Procolobus* have a hindgut microbiome that is more distinct than expected from that of black-and-white colobus (*Colobus guereza*) based on phylogenetic relationships, presumably as a result of foregut anatomy (McCord et al. 2013). It has been suggested recently that quadripartite foreguts may have evolved convergently in some African and Asian colobines to facilitate increased seasonal reliance on leaves, since species with quadripartite foreguts appear to consume more leaves than species with tripartite foreguts (Matsuda et al. 2019a). If more stomach chambers are associated with lower diet digestibility and increased microbial fermentation of dietary compounds, it could be that captivity-induced alterations on the hindgut microbiome in species with quadripartite foreguts reflect dysbiosis in the foregut microbiome as a result of higher-quality diets in captivity (i.e. like acidosis in ruminants). This mechanism would also explain the overall greater health consequences of captivity on quadripartite versus tripartite colobines. We do not necessarily see this health disparity in ruminants and other foregut fermenters with four (e.g. cattle, sheep, goats) versus three-chambered (e.g. camels, alpacas, llamas) foreguts; however, many of these animals may have adapted to domestication over the last 4000–10,000 years (Marshall et al. 2014a; Zeder 2008). Additionally, we may be more adept at meeting the nutritional needs of domesticated ruminants due to decades of extensive research and experience optimizing ruminant diets for production and health. As such, the relationship between colobine digestive anatomy, the microbiome, diet and health deserves additional attention as the field progresses.

Conservation Applications

In addition to improving our understanding of colobine health in captivity, research describing the impact of habitat and diet change on the colobine gut microbiome informs conservation efforts. Like most primates, colobines inhabit forests that are subject to a range of anthropogenic disturbances. These disturbances lead to changes in diet, activity budget, social interactions and exposure to humans, all of which can influence the gut microbiome. These factors have been shown to alter the hindgut microbiome in other wild primates (Amato et al. 2013; Bennett et al. 2016; Clayton et al. 2016; Gomez et al. 2015; Perofsky et al. 2017; Tung et al. 2015). Black howler monkeys (*Alouatta pigra*) inhabiting fragmented rainforest have lower hindgut microbial diversity and distinct gut microbiota composition compared to individuals inhabiting continuous rainforest, a pattern that is partly explained by diet (Amato et al. 2013). Furthermore, even absent marked impacts on forest structure, human activity may have effects on the primate gut microbiota. Habituated western lowland gorillas (*Gorilla gorilla*) possess significantly different hindgut bacterial communities compared to unhabituated individuals, likely a result of stress and altered microbial exposure (Gomez et al. 2015).

Like other primates, habitat disturbance appears to have an impact on colobine hindgut microbiomes. Proboscis monkey foregut microbiomes vary with habitat type, forest structure, and provisioning status (Hayakawa et al. 2018a), and the Udzungwa red colobus (*Procolobus gordonorum*) has reduced hindgut microbial diversity in fragmented forest, particularly in the Bacteroidales and Clostridiales clades (Barelli et al. 2015). Red colobus (*Procolobus gordonorum*) in fragmented forest also hosted increased relative abundances of *Faecalibaterium* and reduced relative abundances of

Hallela and *Bacteroides* in the hindgut. However, these findings were not replicated in black-and-white and red colobus (*Colobus guereza, Procolobus rufomitratus*) in Uganda (McCord et al. 2013). Therefore, additional studies are necessary to determine what specific habitat characteristics have an impact on the gut microbiome. Classification of habitats as 'fragmented' or 'unfragmented' is insufficient for predicting gut microbiome alteration, and variables such as fragment size, disturbance type, primate diet, primate social stress and primate exposure to humans must be measured.

It is also important to note that all primate species may not be affected by habitat disturbance in the same way (Amato et al. 2016a; Bennett et al. 2016). Closely related species of howler monkeys (*Alouatta pigra* and *Alouatta palliata*), for example, appear to have hindgut microbiomes with distinct levels of tolerance for habitat fragmentation, and presumably altered diet (Amato et al. 2016a). The same could be true of colobines, particularly given the patterns with health outcomes observed among colobines with distinct foregut morphology. A study comparing the hindgut microbiomes of grey and purple-faced langurs (*Semnopithecus priam* and *S. vetulus*) in Sri Lanka supports this hypothesis (Amato et al. 2020). Compared to purple-faced langurs, grey langurs are habitat generalists and appear to be less perturbed by anthropogenic habitat disturbance. Accordingly, the grey langur hindgut microbiome was more diverse and harboured taxa involved in starch degradation while the purple-faced langur hindgut microbiome harboured more taxa involved in structural carbohydrate degradation. More data to describe these dynamics in multiple species and habitats will be critical for assessing threats to different colobine species as well as suggesting interventions at the microbial level.

Reduced microbial diversity and altered microbial composition in primates facing habitat destruction, fragmentation, increased contact with humans and captivity pose yet unknown health consequences for the host. However, potential influences include reduced digestive efficiency, altered immune function, and increased stress reactivity (Round and Mazmanian 2010; Sonnenburg et al. 2016; Sudo et al. 2004). How quickly these gut microbial shifts occur also remains to be determined with certainty. Preliminary data suggest a period of several weeks is necessary for habitat and/or diet shifts to make an impact on the colobine hindgut microbiome (Clayton et al. 2016; Hale et al. 2019), but additional data from individuals actively experiencing habitat change in the wild as well as individuals moving from wild to captive environments are necessary to better assess these dynamics. Whether changes occur after weeks and months or cumulatively across lifespans, and which GI sections they affect, will dictate the effects on long-term health and fitness. For example, the documented vertical transmission of altered microbial communities across generations (Sonnenburg et al. 2016) may play a more serious role in long-term population health and fitness than acute changes over periods of weeks, and foregut alterations may affect colobine health more than hindgut alterations. Understanding these dynamics will be critical for successful conservation of wild primates, including colobines.

Future Directions and Guidelines for Sampling and Analysis

The microbiome is critical to host health and can also influence fitness (Rosengaus et al. 2011). As sequencing costs continue to decline and new methodologies become available for microbial sampling in captivity and in the wild, more studies may benefit from incorporating an examination of the microbiota (gut, skin, oral, nasal, urogenital) in relation to host health, genetics, feeding ecology, behaviour, evolution and conservation. Many current studies on the primate hindgut microbiome demonstrate intriguing correlations between microbial composition and host phylogeny, diet, habitat and sociality (Amato et al. 2013, 2016a, 2017, 2019; Chen et al. 2020; Clayton et al. 2016; Gogarten et al. 2018; Greene et al. 2018; Hale et al. 2018; Huan et al. 2020; Moeller et al. 2013; Tung et al. 2015; Wikberg et al. 2020). As our understanding of the microbiome continues to grow along with our technologies for examining it – including metagenomics, metabolomics, proteomics, optofluidics, germ-free mouse models, single-cell culture and organoids – future studies will be better equipped to identify the underlying mechanisms driving these correlations.

In ruminants, for example, the growing abundance of metagenomic and transcriptomic data is allowing farmers to identify 'desirable' microbial functions (e.g. decreased methane production, increased feed conversion) and the microbes associated with these functions (Stewart et al. 2018). Detailed genetic and pedigree data in large herds also allows evaluation of how host genes shape the microbiome (Roehe et al. 2016). Together, this information shapes a future vision of microbial engineering or selective breeding to optimize the ruminant microbiome for health and production. In colobines, multi-omic approaches could be used to identify key host-microbe relationships along with microbes or microbial functions critical to wild and captive colobine health. Furthermore, in captive monkeys, microbial transplantation, or the use of prebiotics (substrates that support the growth of select microbes), probiotics (live microbial strains), or synbiotics (a combination of pre- and probiotics) can be evaluated as methods for introducing or engineering 'optimal' microbial communities for colobine health.

Two important challenges for colobine gut microbiome research are the collection of samples that can be used to address questions about microbial mechanisms involved in determining host health, ecology and evolution and the description of the colobine foregut. In the first instance, sample collection should continue to be incorporated into existing studies in both wild and captive settings. Samples from wild primates are of particular importance given their ability to inform our understanding of host-microbe dynamics in selective environments. Many ongoing studies of wild colobines collect the types of behavioural, physiological and environmental data that are most useful for contextualizing microbiome data. Additionally, in many cases faecal samples are being collected for other analyses. Therefore, integrating microbiome analyses into these studies is relatively easy.

Nevertheless, while a unique digestive physiology is likely to benefit colobines nutritionally, it also makes non-invasive studies of the gut microbiota more difficult. Faecal samples are a reasonable proxy for the colonic microbiota, but it is unclear how well they represent the microbial community residing in the foregut. A recent study of captive colobines at the San Diego Zoo reports similar microbial communities along the GI tract of doucs, langurs and black-and-white colobus (*Pygathrix nemaeus, Colobus guereza, Colobus angolensis, Trachypithecus francoisi, Trachypithecus cristatus*) (Amato et al. 2016b), but this pattern may be a symptom of dysbiosis in captivity. Additional data from wild individuals are necessary to corroborate this finding. At present, nearly all studies of the colobine gut microbiota rely on faecal samples. While this practice is ideal for reducing disturbance to wild animals, many of which are endangered, it continues to be unclear whether the resulting data capture the complexities of colobine gut microbiota interactions. Targeted and/or opportunistic collection of foregut samples will be critical for understanding the complete role of gut microbes in determining colobine nutrition and health.

Conclusions

In conclusion, the colobine hindgut microbiome is unique among primates in that it shares many traits with those of ruminants. These same traits make colobines susceptible to GI disease when alterations in diet, such as those associated with captivity, result in shifts in the gut microbiome. It is unclear whether similar changes in diet associated with habitat disturbance also have negative effects on the hindgut microbiome and colobine health in wild populations. Additional data from both captive and wild populations, as well as from the colobine foregut, will help us pinpoint the mechanisms through which host-gut microbe interactions affect colobine health in multiple contexts. These data are not only necessary for improving our understanding of colobine ecology and evolution but will be critical for complementing conservation efforts of some of the world's most vulnerable primates.

8 Colobine Nutritional Ecology

Jessica M. Rothman, Allegra N. DePasquale, Katarina D. Evans and Dominique L. Raboin

Introduction

Colobines are primarily folivores with sacculated stomachs and foregut fermentation. As a consequence, many aspects of their nutritional ecology are unique among primates. Unlike monogastric primates, colobines likely obtain some nutrients through the recycling of urea, microbial digestion, and the production of volatile fatty acids, and this digestive ecology adds further complexity to their diet choices in relation to nutritional ecology.

In the seminal review chapter on colobine diet selection by Waterman and Kool (1994), there are four areas highlighted for future colobine research with respect to nutritional ecology. First, the authors emphasized that more information on intraspecific variability in the nutritional content of food items is needed. Second, they suggested the potential for balancing among different macronutrients and toxins. Third, the authors called for a more comprehensive analysis of the factors affecting food digestion, such as the measurement of fermentation efficiencies and throughput rates of colobines. Fourth, the authors called for more research on the potential digestive adaptations for detoxification of plant secondary metabolites (PSMs). Since the Waterman and Kool (1994) review was published >25 years ago, there has been a dramatic increase in the number of colobus species whose diets and nutrient intakes have been studied and numerous advances in colobus nutrition research. We highlight significant new findings in the areas above, including improvements to nutritional and phytochemical methods. Overall, we aim to expand upon Waterman and Kool's review to increase our understanding of colobine diet and nutritional ecology, as well as the phytochemical basis of colobine food selection. While there are numerous new developments in our understanding of colobine digestion (e.g., Matsuda et al. 2011a, 2019a), since digestive ecology is covered in another chapter (Chapter 6), we will not focus on it here.

What Do Colobines Eat?

Colobines are well known for eating leafy diets and they are able to digest leaves to a larger extent than non-foregut fermenting primates because they are capable of deriving energy from the fibrous plant cell wall using cellulolytic bacteria in their foreguts (Bauchop and Martucci 1968). As a result of these digestive adaptations, their diets tend to be focused on foods that are higher in fibre and protein than diets of other primates, though there is tremendous variation according to species and habitat (Fashing 2007a).

Most colobine diets are primarily made up of leaves (>60% of feeding time in most species), whether from trees, saplings, shrubs or lianas. They almost always include more young than mature leaves in their diets, suggesting a preference for them even when selection is not explicitly measured (e.g., Baranga 1982; Kool 1992; Chapman and Chapman 2002; Zhou Q et al. 2009a; Dunham 2017a; Tsuji et al. 2019). For example, *Piliocolobus tephrosceles* spent 55%–76% of feeding time on young leaves over 4 years (Chapman and Chapman 2002) in Uganda. Young leaves dominate about 75% of feeding observations of *Pygathrix nemaeus* over several years of study in Vietnam (Lippold 1998), similar to *Trachypithecus leucocephalus* in China (Li et al. 2003).

There are some notable exceptions to this pattern: *Trachypithecus pileatus* in Bangladesh ate a diet that comprised a high proportion of mature leaves (42% of feeding records; Stanford 1991b) and *Semnopithecus entellus* consumed more mature than young leaves in their diets in long-term studies (Koenig and Borries 2001). However, as a generality, colobines eat young leaves when they are available (Fashing 2007a). Colobines are often selective in the part of the leaves that they eat; for example, when they eat mature tree leaves, *Procolobus verus* in Sierra Leone usually eat the petioles only leaving the lamina behind (Oates 1988a). Seasonally, leaf petioles are eaten frequently by *Trachypithecus francoisi* and the authors suggest this is because they might provide water during hotter months (Zhou Q et al. 2009a). In a >10 year study of *Piliocolobus tephrosceles* in Uganda, Struhsaker (2010) notes that when feeding on mature leaves the monkeys almost exclusively feed on petioles. Struhsaker notes that for some young leaf species the *P. tephrosceles* ignored the petioles and consumed the lamina, while for other species they did the opposite.

While much of the research on folivory has focused on tree leaves, colobines include lianas and vines to a large extent in their diets. In the forest fragments of Ghana, *Colobus vellerosus* ate leaves from lianas 26% of feeding time (Wong et al. 2006) and in Kenya, *C. angolensis palliatus* also relied heavily on lianas, eating them 21%–38% of feeding time (Dunham 2017a). In Uganda, *C. guereza* fed on vines and lianas about 9% of feeding time (Harris and Chapman 2007a), and in Sierra Leone, lianas accounted for 49% of the *C. polykomos* diet (DaSilva 1993). Liana feeding is also found in Asian colobines; 48% of the diet of *Presbytis pontenziani* was from vines or lianas (Fuentes 1996).

Both African and Asian colobines also regularly consume fruits and seeds, which are high in protein, lipids and non-structural carbohydrates (McKey et al. 1981; Davies 1991; Davies et al. 1999; Fashing 2001b; Dela 2012; Hanya and Bernard 2012; Hanya and Bernard 2015). Thus, colobines are not exclusive folivores. The Indochinese silvered langur (*Trachypithecus germaini*) spent 23% of their time eating fruits (Le et al. 2019) and *Nasalis larvatus* in Malaysia eats a diet of 26% fruit that is mainly unripe (Matsuda et al. 2009a). In Kenya's Kakamega forest, fruits of the Moracae family are important in the diets of *C. guereza* (Fashing 2001b); based on time spent feeding, *C. guereza* spent 44% of their feeding time eating figs. Differences in tree composition might account for the dietary variation and food choices among *C. guereza* in East African forests. For example, in Kakamega, fruits are eaten in relation to their availability (Fashing 2001b), whereas in Kibale, fruits are rarely eaten (Oates 1978).

There are other important food items eaten by colobines, dependent on opportunity or habitat constraints. For example, some populations of *Rhinopithecus bieti* eat lichens year-round as a fallback food as well as dried grass and bark seasonally (Xiang et al. 2007; Grueter et al. 2009b). *S. entellus* consumes scale insects during the monsoon regularly (Srivastava 1991b), and *R. roxellana* consume cicadas occasionally (Yang et al. 2016). Geophagy is infrequent but most species engage in it (Davies and Baillie 1988; Harris and Chapman 2007a; Monaco et al. 2019), and *Piliocolobus kirkii* in Zanzibar, Tanzania eat charcoal, probably to detoxify the toxins in their diets (Struhsaker et al. 1997).

Though some colobines have very diverse diets (e.g., *S. johnii*; Oates et al. 1980; *Presbytis melalophos* Davies et al. 1988; *S. entellus* Sayers and Norconk 2008), it is more typical to see colobines focus on just 1–20 foods for most of their feeding time. For example, *P. rubicunda* in Danum Valley, Sabah of Northern Borneo spent 28% of their feeding time on the young leaves of *Spatholobus macropterus*, which is a leguminous liana (Hanya and Barnard 2012). In Kibale, *C. guereza* ate solely young leaves from one tree species on 27 days of 160 days in a year (Rothman, unpublished data). Fashing (2001b) notes that groups of the same species (*C. guereza*) at Kakamega and Ituri, Democratic Republic of Congo consumed just 28–43 plant species annually. *Trachypithecus delacouri* in the rugged limestone karst mountains depend on just five species for more than 60% of their annual diet (Workman 2010a). While a low dietary diversity implies specialization, it is interesting to consider whether *C. guereza* or colobines generally are adapted to extract nutrients from assorted species and parts, and thus do not need to spend time searching for many different foods, yet they have a digestive ecology that suggests they can digest more fibrous foods. This strategy whereby the acceptable niche is large is very different from a true dietary specialist that only consumes specific plants to fulfil nutrient needs; for example, golden bamboo lemurs (*Hapalemur aureus*) can only live in bamboo forests with specific species of bamboo (Glander et al. 1989). This extreme specialization is certainly not the case for colobines that seem to be able to subsist on a wide variety of different foods. However, from this wide variety, since colobines often specialize on just a few different food species in different habitats, it seems plausible that they can extract nutrients readily from many different food sources. Consequently, it is possible that colobines are able to consume a diet that is much more flexible in macronutrient composition, compared to some of the guenons or macaques, who regulate a balance of protein or total energy, but are dietary generalists (Cui et al. 2018; Takahashi et al. 2019). Nutritional frameworks that include diet and nutrition to describe feeding strategies may prove useful and have not yet been applied to colobines (Raubenheimer et al. 2015; Machovsky-Capuska et al. 2016).

What Are the Nutritional Compositions of Colobine Diets?

Both angiosperm and gymnosperms synthesize two main groups of compounds: primary and secondary metabolites. Primary metabolites are essential to plant function and growth. These include proteins, carbohydrates and lipids (macronutrients) as well as vitamins and minerals (micronutrients). Secondary metabolites are probably inessential to plant functionality but aid in plant defence, whether it be protection from herbivory or sunlight. Plant secondary metabolites (PSMs) are broadly split into three classes: alkaloids, terpenoids and phenolics. While the primary metabolites are essential to the plant, they also form the basis for food nutrients for herbivores. Secondary metabolites can influence dietary strategy by acting as feeding deterrents, reducing plant palatability and digestibility of certain nutrient classes (e.g., binding proteins), or by being toxic to the organism (Freeland and Janzen 1974). As large-bodied folivores, colobines must navigate a complex chemical landscape to meet nutritional needs while coping with the potentially deleterious effects of PSMs.

African Colobines

Although colobus monkeys are distributed across central Africa, much of what we know about the nutritional compositions of their diets emerges from a few key habitats where researchers have studied them. The most detailed nutritional research on wild colobines has taken place in Kibale National Park, Uganda. Two colobines are sympatric in this forest, *Piliocolobus tephrosceles* and *C. guereza*. These two colobines are mainly folivorous and the majority of their diets are made up of young leaves (Struhsaker and Leland 1979; Struhsaker 2010). Their two diets are similar in that they overlap in the foods they eat by 43%, but *C. guereza* eat fewer foods, spend less time feeding and travel less than the *P. tephrosceles* (Chapman and Pavelka 2005). *P. tephrosceles* and *C. guereza* living in the same area of the forest overlap more in their diets than do the different *P. tephrosceles* groups that live in different areas. While both species are likely able to subsist on mature leaves, they almost never do; *P. tephrosceles* rarely eat more than 15% of their diet as mature leaves (Chapman and Pavelka 2005; Struhsaker 2010), though it is apparent that at least *C. guereza* can survive in forest fragments where only mature leaves are available (Preece 2006).

Both the young and mature leaves in Kibale are remarkably high in protein compared to West African forests (Oates et al. 1990; Evans et al. 2021). The young leaves in *P. tephrosceles* diets vary from 12% to 40% crude protein, and the mature leaves vary from 8% to 27%. Fibre in the diet is moderate in young leaves with levels of neutral detergent fibre (NDF) at 21%–63% (Rothman, unpublished data). Notable is the tremendous variability in young leaf quality among and within species (Figure 8.1). There is considerable intra-specific variability in the foods eaten by these colobus; for example, a preferred species of young leaves, *Celtis durandii* (Cannabaceae) varies between 16% and 45% in crude protein (Rothman, unpublished data), suggesting that feeding ecology studies of colobines need to sample the leaves

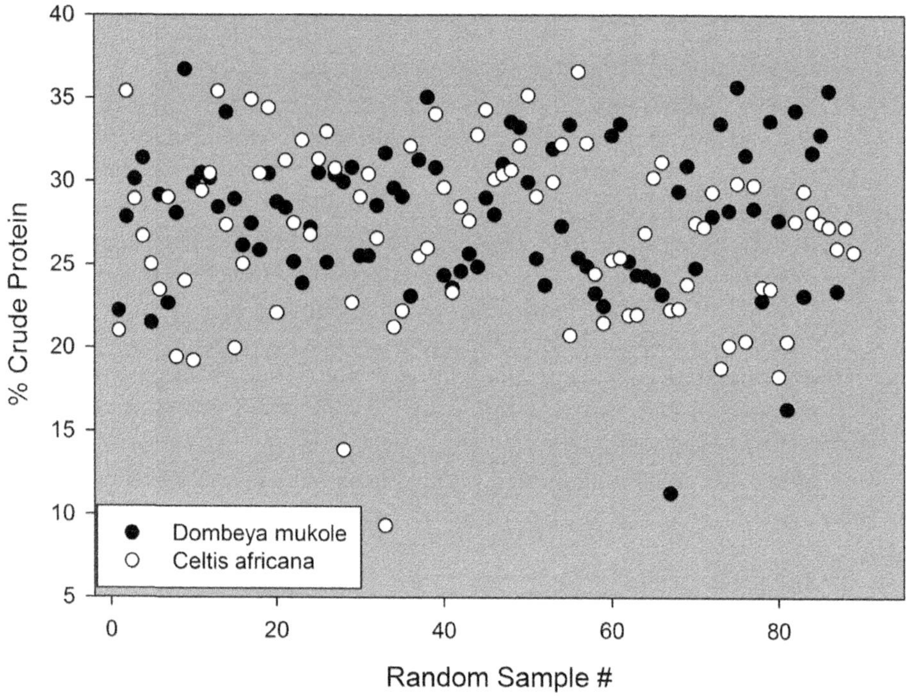

Figure 8.1 Crude protein concentrations of *Celtis africana* and *Dombeya mukole* young leaves in randomly sampled food trees. Both of these young leaf species are eaten by *Colobus guereza* and *Piliocolobus tephroscheles* in Kibale National Park, Uganda.

from the same timepoint and tree for accurate estimations of colobine nutrient intake. This intra-specific variability could be due to season (Baranga 1983) or even the time of day the plant was sampled as young leaves tend to accumulate sugar later in the day (Carlson et al. 2013), but in many cases it is unpredictable (Chapman et al. 2003a). Abiotic factors can also influence plant chemistry, as in a study of leaves in Kibale. In accordance with greenhouse experiments simulating climate change, Kibale young and mature leaves declined in fibre over several decades (Rothman et al. 2005), demonstrating that colobine foods are not static in their chemistry.

In a study of the diets of five groups of Kibale *P. tephrosceles*, the dietary nutritional composition was 38% NDF, 28% acid detergent fibre (ADF) and 16% lignin. The diet was 20% crude protein. Despite dietary differences, the diet nutritional composition was remarkably similar among groups, indicating that the *P. tephrosceles* may balance nutrient intake (Ryan et al. 2012). In fragmented forest surrounding the intact national park, *P. tephrosceles* could subsist on foods that were much lower in protein and higher in fibre than in the intact forest, though these individuals were apparently stressed as measured from higher levels of faecal cortisol (Chapman et al. 2006a).

In Kibale and Kakamega, Kenya, *C. guereza* eat diets with higher concentrations of fibre than *P. tephrosceles*, and similar protein (Fashing et al. 2007a; Curry 2012).

The leaves that form the basis of the *C. guereza* diet in Kenya have a mean composition of 23% crude protein, 48% NDF and 20% lignin (Fashing et al. 2007a). Interestingly, *C. guereza* in Kibale spend more time feeding in trees that have young leaves with a balance of 1.55 non-protein energy to protein, suggesting that they prefer this dietary ratio (Johnson et al. 2017). This relationship was independent of tree size, leaf availability and other social factors. *C. guereza* do experience consequences of food limitation; urinary c-peptide was associated with decreased young leaf availability in Kibale (Harris et al. 2010).

C. angolensis palliatus studied in Diani Forest, Kenya also eat a diet high in young leaves and a large portion of flowers. The metabolizable daily energy intake of females in one study group was about 546–635 kcal/day, and the estimated digestible fibre concentrations in their diet was moderate compared to Kibale colobines at ~38% NDF on a dry matter basis (Dunham and Rodriguez-Saona 2018). The ratio of non-protein energy to protein was 3.5–4.3 (Dunham and Rodriguez-Saona 2018), suggesting that nutrient balancing among colobines may be quite flexible; omnivorous baboons (*Papio ursinus*) have a diet that averages about 5:1 non-protein energy to protein (Johnson et al. 2013), while gorillas (*Gorilla beringei*) are between 4:1–3:1 (Rothman et al. 2011). In preliminary studies of *C. guereza* diets, the ratio of non-protein energy (NPE) to available protein (AP) was 1:1, indicative of the high protein concentrations in Kibale leaves (Rothman et al., unpublished data) and since *C. guereza* stay longer in trees with similar leaf NPE:AP concentrations, there is evidence of balancing. However, *C. guereza* and *Colobus* spp. in general may be quite flexible according to environmental constraints, given that Dunham and Rodriguez-Saona (2018) noted ratios up to 4.3. As well, since the preferred foods of some colobines are energy-rich, it is reasonable to consider that colobines may consume and even prefer much higher ratios under certain circumstances. In fact, it may be that avoidance of PSMs (discussed later) that are typically high in leaves has a stronger influence on colobine food selection than macronutrients.

Piliocolobus preussi in Cameroon similarly eats young leaves (89% of diet) from 17 food species (Usongo and Amubode 2001). These *P. preussi* are faced with much lower protein leaves (range = 8%–15% dry matter). The colobines in Kibale may be eating much more protein than they need in order to balance energy in their diets, similar to *G. beringei* (Rothman et al. 2011), another folivore that lives in a habitat with high environmental protein. While *C. guereza* eats a leafy diet, the colobines in West Africa eat seeds frequently, which tend to be quite fatty though not many quantitative measures have been made (but see: Usongo and Amubode 2001). Seeds are generally higher in lipids and protein and lower in fibre than leaves (Lambert and Rothman 2015), though seeds can also be high in secondary compounds similar to leaves (Janzen 1971). Several authors have suggested that poor soils and tannin-rich leaves contribute to this difference in food choice between East and West African colobines, as well as those in Asia (McKey et al. 1981). For example, the highest proportion of dietary ADF (mature leaves: 64.7%, young leaves: 50.7%) and lowest proportion of crude protein (mature leaves: 7.9%, young leaves: 5.7%, seeds: 9.1%) was found in foods eaten by *C. satanas* in Douala-Edea Forest Reserve,

Cameroon, where soils are known to be acidic, likely affecting leaf nutrient content and, in turn, food selection (Oates et al. 1990).

Asian Colobines

Compiled data on the nutritional compositions of foods for *Semnopithecus johnii* (Oates et al. 1980), *P. rubicunda* (Davies et al. 1988; Hanya and Bernard 2012), *Semnopithecus entellus* (Kar-Gupta and Kumar 1994), *Nasalis larvatus* (Yeager et al. 1997), *Trachypithecus auratus* (Kool 1992) and *Rhinopithecus roxellana* (at Zhouzhi, Hou et al. 2018; at Shennongjia, Liu X. et al. 2013b) reveals that Asian colobine foods are lower in protein and higher in fibre than at African sites. The above Asian colobine foods contain a mean of 13% crude protein and 33% ADF (NDF and other macronutrient data are not available from most sites). As with foods consumed by African colobines, there is a pattern of mature leaves containing more fibre and less protein than young leaves, and seeds being high in all macronutrients aside from fibre. For Asian colobines like *P. rubicunda*, there may be different nutritional roles of young leaves and seeds (Hanya and Bernard 2012). While seeds had more fat than leaves, they contained similar concentrations of protein and thus are not always young leaf replacements for this species as some others have suggested (Davies et al. 1999).

The importance of high protein foods for colobines likely depends on the nutritional quality of the environment and whether environmental protein is limited (McKey et al. 1981). In ecosystems where soils are poor and vegetation is of lower nutritional quality, indicated by lower nitrogen content and higher levels of phenolics and fibre, colobines must be more selective to meet nutritional needs. This was argued by Matsuda et al. (2013) in a comparison between primary forest and secondary riverine forest inhabited by *P. rubicunda* and *N. larvatus*, respectively. In this study, the *P. rubicunda* were more selective in their foods and ate only young leaves compared to the *N. larvatus* that also selected high protein and ate a variety of available foods.

Few studies have estimated the daily nutrient intake of Asian colobines. *R. roxellana* experiences dramatic temperature differences in the temperate forests they inhabit in China (Guo et al. 2017). Based on 55 all day follows with half in each season, *R. roxellana* ate a diet that was much higher in energy in winter (722 kJ/mbm) than spring (339 kJ/mbm). The authors suggested that there were substantial energy costs in winter compared to spring, and the difference in energy intake between the two seasons was remarkably similar to the difference in estimated daily energetic costs of thermoregulation (Guo et al. 2017). When young leaves dominated the diet, they selected those with a high protein-to-fibre ratio, but when young leaves in this temperate forest were absent, the *R. roxellana* switched to high carbohydrate foods such as flower buds and bark (Hou et al. 2018). A homeostatic framework along with nutritional geometry was used for this analysis. These two frameworks are powerful for assessing wild primate diets (Raubenheimer et al. 2015; Hou et al. 2018) and the interaction between primate nutrition and demography (Rothman 2015).

In other habitats, this same species eats about 38% of its diet as lichens; these lichens are higher in sugar and lower in fibre compared to young leaves, bark and flowers (Liu X. et al. 2013b).

How Do Colobus Monkeys Select Dietary Items?

The chemical basis for food selection has been a central question in studies of colobine foraging and nutritional ecology. Researchers seek to understand whether colobines select particular key nutrients, such as protein or energy, or minimize their consumption of feeding deterrents, such as secondary metabolites or fibre. Significant research has been done on both African and Asian taxa to address this question, primarily by assessing levels of macronutrients, micronutrients and secondary compounds in foods consumed compared to those avoided.

Protein-to-Fibre Ratio

Milton (1979; 1980; 1998) proposed that herbivores choose leaves based on their protein and fibre compositions. As Milton notes, consuming excessive fibre is disadvantageous because it occupies space in an animal's stomach and limits protein digestibility. It follows that colobines prefer mature and young leaves with higher protein-to-fibre ratios compared to those leaves less preferred or uneaten. While studies vary in the types of fibre (NDF or ADF) and protein (digestible or crude) that were measured, most studies support that this ratio is a good rough indicator of leaf choice. For example, evidence from studies of *C. guereza* (in Kibale; Chapman et al. 2004, Wasserman and Chapman 2003; in Kakamega, Kenya; Fashing et al. 2007a), *C. satanas* (McKey et al. 1981), *Piliocolobus rufomitratus* (Mowry et al. 1996), *P. tephrosceles* (Chapman and Chapman 2002; Wasserman and Chapman 2003), *Procolobus verus* (Oates 1988a), *Presbytis rubicunda* (at Sepilok, Malaysia; Davies et al. 1988; at Danum Valley, Malaysia; Matsuda et al. 2013), *P. melalophos* (Davies et al. 1988), *S. johnii* (Oates et al. 1980), *S. entellus* (Kar-Gupta and Kumar 1994), *N. larvatus* (at Tanjung Puting, Indonesia; Yeager et al. 1997; at Kinabatangan, Malaysia, Matsuda et al. 2013, 2017), *T. auratus* (Kool 1992) and *R. bieti* (Huang et al. 2010) all demonstrate preferences or selection for high protein-to-fibre leaves. Leaf toughness could be a sensory cue that colobines (*N. larvatus*) use to detect fibre (Matsuda et al. 2017). There are, however, exceptions, including *C. polykomos* (Dasilva 1994), *R. brelichi* (Bleisch et al. 1998), *R. roxellana* (Liu X. et al. 2013b), and *Pygathrix nigripes* (Duc et al. 2009) who do not select based on this ratio. Fashing and colleagues (2007a) noted that macronutrients had a strong effect on the food selection of *C. guereza*, and interestingly, only leaves that were at least 14% crude protein were chosen. In line with this observation, Kibale colobus monkeys preferentially consume leaf buds when they are encountered (Figure 8.2) and these are often 40%–45% crude protein and 30%–35% sugar depending on the tree species, which is incredibly high in both protein and sugar compared to other foods (Rothman, unpublished data).

Figure 8.2 Juvenile *Colobus guereza* eating leaf buds in Kibale National Park, Uganda. Photo by Jessica M. Rothman

Building on this preference, several researchers have noted that the protein-to-fibre ratio of mature leaves often predicts colobine biomass at small and large spatial scales in colobine habitats (Waterman et al. 1988; Oates et al. 1990; Chapman et al. 2002b; Wasserman and Chapman 2003; Chapman et al. 2004; Fashing et al. 2007a). The idea behind the model is that areas that have mature leaves with higher protein-to-fibre ratios can support larger populations of colobines. Though they are not eaten frequently, mature leaves are a well-known colobine fallback food, providing a reliable source of nutrients when preferred foods, primarily young leaves, are unavailable (Waterman et al. 1988). If a site contains more digestible and nutritious leaves, more colobines can thrive in periods when preferred foods are scarce. Consistent with this, Fimbel et al. (2001) notes that the high quality of mature leaves in the Nyungwe Forest, Rwanda, is responsible for its large groups of *C. angolensis ruwenzorii*. Within this forest, the protein-to-fibre ratio is 0.91, considerably higher than at other African sites. Due to the high-quality vegetation that is prevalent in the Nyungwe Forest, Fimbel and colleagues suggest *C. angolensis ruwenzorii* is free from group size constraints caused by feeding competition (Fimbel et al. 2001). While there is support for the protein-to-fibre ratio as both a predictor of food preference and biomass, the model is not without its shortcomings. Protein-to-fibre ratios are typically calculated using crude protein and ADF. Crude protein, however, may not be a biologically relevant measure, as there are several factors that can limit protein availability, such as the presence of tannins (Chapman et al. 2012; Wallis et al. 2012). In addition, crude protein is estimated based on the amount of nitrogen in a plant, but nitrogen is also found in many non-protein plant compounds (Conklin-Brittain et al. 1998; Rothman et al. 2008a). More appropriate chemical and biological assays have been developed in the last decade that could offer more nuanced estimates of protein digestibility. Some of these use combinations of structural and biological assays to discern the types of tannins that may affect primates and their biological activities (DeGabriel et al. 2008; Evans et al. 2021; Matsuda et al. 2017; Marsh et al. 2020). Additionally, ADF is a complex mixture of cellulose and lignin. Cellulose is partially digestible by colobine foregut microbes (Edwards and Ullrey 1998), while lignin is not. Thus, the nutritional mechanism behind the model is poorly understood.

Further evidence against the utility and generality of the protein-to-fibre model comes from Gogarten and colleagues (2012), who sought to determine whether protein-to-fibre ratios in different habitat types in Kibale, namely regenerating versus old growth forest, could predict the number of infants per female in *P. tephrosceles* groups. While there were differences in the protein-to-fibre ratio in the disparate habitat types, they found no corresponding demographic differences. This suggests that the protein-to-fibre ratio does not have an impact on birth rate despite its purported importance for nutrition and biomass. Wallis and colleagues (2012) suggest that the protein-to-fibre ratio correlates with available protein, which leads to the impression of a causative relationship.

Energy

Dasilva (1992, 1994) argued that *C. polykomos* on Tiwai Island, Sierra Leone, foraged according to energy, rather than the protein-to-fibre ratio of foods. These colobines selected seeds and fruits, which are energy-rich. Dasilva argued that *C. polykomos* are not protein limited, as protein is higher than protein requirements in most foods on Tiwai. When protein is abundant, other nutritional aspects, such as energy, are prioritized. Wasserman and Chapman (2003) assessed whether energy content and protein-to-fibre ratios of foods predicts food selection and biomass of colobus monkeys in Kibale. They found no support for Dasilva's claim that colobines are energy-limited. A problem with both studies is the use of gross energy in the analysis. Gross energy does not take into account the digestibility of a food or diet and thus does not portray an accurate assessment of the potential energy that is actually available for digestion (Rothman et al. 2012). However, metabolizable energy was more important in the decision to stay in a patch for *S. entellus* than crude protein in a mosaic habitat that comprises conifers, oak, with smaller trees and shrubs in Nepal (Sayers et al. 2010). It is likely that whatever is environmentally constrained in the habitat might be maximized opportunistically. If leaf protein is high and PSMs are absent, then folivorous colobines will have no problem meeting protein needs. However, if leaves are lignified or high in PSMs, then protein may be selected. Otherwise like mountain gorillas (*G. beringei*), non-protein metabolizable energy may be prioritized since it is likely limited in high fibre leafy diets (Rothman et al. 2011). Despite digestive adaptations to digest fibre in colobines, high lignin and high cellulose foods still present notable constraints as digestive efficiency is low.

Plant Secondary Compounds

Since colobines mainly eat leaves and leaves are typically high in plant secondary metabolites, colobines are faced with having to detoxify, tolerate or avoid these compounds. Oates (1977) examined *C. guereza* food selection in Kibale in relation to secondary metabolites, specifically tannins and alkaloids, and found a strong inverse correlation between food choice and tannins, and no relationship between food choice and alkaloid content. In Kakamega, Fashing et al. (2007a) found that *C. guereza* also avoid foods high in tannins. Similarly, *C. satanas* and *Procolobus verus* select foods low in fibre and tannins (McKey et al. 1981; Oates 1988a). However, results across colobines are inconsistent. Davies et al. (1988) found that neither condensed tannin nor total phenolic content influenced food selection for *Presbytis rubicunda* or *P. melalophos*. The same was found for *R. bieti* (Huang et al. 2010), *R. roxellana* (Liu X. et al. 2013b), and *Piliocolobus rufomitratus* (Mowry et al. 1996). *T. auratus* chose foliage that contained lower levels of tannins and total phenolics, whereas the opposite was found for fruit (Kool 1992). For yet some other studies, results are inconclusive (Kar-Gupta and Kumar 1994).

The inconsistency in results among colobines is unsurprising given the diversity of methods used to measure PSMs. Each class of PSMs contains hundreds if not thousands of individual compounds, each of which may interact differently with each species and specific diet. Some of these may be harmful to colobine gut microflora, others are neutral, and some are beneficial (Freeland and Janzen 1974; Waterman et al. 1980).

Standardized analytical methods are also greatly needed to facilitate comparison of results across studies (Rothman et al. 2012); most studies rely on older chemical assays to estimate tannin contents that use standards that are inappropriate for tropical foods (Rautio et al. 2007; Rothman et al. 2009). As well, the biological as well as structural activity of tannins needs to be considered (Marsh et al. 2020). New assays as well as combinations of different techniques should make it possible to make better estimations of the impact of tannins and perhaps other phenolics have on primate food choice. Thus, the results from previous studies should be interpreted cautiously as unsound methods could encourage incorrect conclusions (Rothman et al. 2009).

Micronutrients: Vitamins and Minerals

Micronutrients, including vitamins and minerals, are critical for maintaining animal health and fitness. Deficiencies in micronutrients can have substantial health costs, including impaired gastrointestinal, cognitive, cardiovascular and immune function, possibly leading to decreased fertility and fecundity, and early mortality. While clearly important for animal homeostasis, plants do not have the same micronutrient requirements, and thus may not be the best sources of vitamins and minerals, particularly sodium, though this varies based on environmental factors, plant part, and species. For herbivores, including colobines, this can be particularly challenging.

Due to their importance, it has been suggested by some authors (Oates 1977; Rode et al. 2003; Harris and Chapman 2007a) that micronutrients influence colobine foraging behaviour and food selection. Yeager (1989) found that plant species in the diet of *N. larvatus* contained relatively more phosphorus and potassium than did non-food plants in the surrounding habitat. Furthermore, young leaves contained higher concentrations of zinc, phosphorus and potassium than did mature leaves. Despite mineral differences in foods versus non-foods, *N. larvatus* does not select foods based on mineral content, likely because these minerals in primate foods greatly exceed mineral requirements (National Research Council 2003). Rode and colleagues (2003) examined mineral intake in *C. guereza* and *P. tephrosceles* in Kibale and found little evidence for selection based on mineral content. However, the authors suggest that sodium might be limiting, as it is low in most foods eaten by colobines. These authors point to certain rare behaviours observed in these colobines, such as urine consumption and drinking from mud puddles, as evidence of sodium-seeking. A later study in Kibale found that *C. guereza* do range in relation to sodium availability, also supporting this hypothesis (Harris and Chapman 2007a). In particular, exotically introduced *Eucalyptus* seems to be a sodium source.

Geophagy, the consumption of earth, has been documented in many colobines [e.g., *Presbytis rubicunda* (Davies and Baillie 1988); *S. johnii* (Oates et al. 1980); *C. guereza* (Oates 1978); *R. bieti* (Li et al. 2014)], among others, and it is hypothesized as a way to meet mineral requirements that are lacking in the diet. Other hypotheses include the adsorption of plant toxins and treatment of gastrointestinal upset. Oates (1978) examined the consumption of soils and water plants by *C. guereza* in relation to micronutrient content and plant toxins and noticed that black and white colobus monkeys in Kibale would regularly descend to the ground to consume plants growing in pools of water, despite the increased predation risk associated with terrestriality. At these pool sites, typically antagonistic *C. guereza* tolerated one another, and often travelled long distances to consume these plants. Oates' study revealed that water plants contained higher levels of minerals compared to dry land plants that *C. guereza* consumed. This was particularly true of sodium, iron, manganese and zinc. Consumed soils contained higher levels of copper, magnesium and iron compared to neighbouring soils, though it is unclear whether these minerals would be bioavailable in soils.

Oates (1978) suggests that *C. guereza* diets may be deficient in sodium and that water plant consumption is a potential strategy for obtaining sufficient sodium and other minerals. He further hypothesized that soil consumption might function to neutralize plant toxins. Because minerals vary in their bioavailability depending on soil composition and other factors, it is hard to know whether colobines consume soils for minerals. In a study of the bioavailability of sodium to chacma baboons, the bioavailability of iron and other minerals was low during digestion simulations, but the adsorptive clay content was high (Pebsworth et al. 2013). While similar simulations have not yet been done on soils eaten by colobines, it is plausible that geophagy's primary function is adsorption of PSMs and/or reducing stomach acidity. We need more sophisticated studies of geophagy similar to Pebsworth and colleagues to unravel this important question. Support for the detoxification function of geophagy was presented by Struhsaker and colleagues (1997), who found that *Piliocolobus kirkii* consumes charcoal primarily to alleviate dietary phenolics, though charcoal is chemically inert and doesn't have any minerals. It is of course likely that geophagy serves multiple functions for colobines in different habitats and with different types of soils/ adsorbent materials.

What Are Future Directions for Colobine Nutritional Ecology Research?

Despite decades of research on colobines, we still do not understand their flexibility in relation to nutritional ecology. While there has been an amazing array of new data emerging on nutrition of different species, we also need systematic studies of the same species in different habitats to investigate nutrient prioritization patterns and understand species' ability to adapt to change. To examine the realized niche of individual species, we need to investigate the nutrients eaten in different habitats by the same species under different ecological and social constraints. In addition, investigating nutritional balance among different macronutrients (balance of protein to non-protein energy, for example; Johnson et al. 2017; Dunham and Rodriguez-Saona 2018), rather than individual nutritional components, may offer greater insights into food selection and preference among the colobines. The use of nutritional geometry may be particularly important to unravel these questions.

While there have been an impressive number of studies on East African and Asian colobines, there have been few studies of the diets of West African colobus monkeys since the original colobine food selection chapter was published (Waterman and Kool 1994). This is likely because it is difficult and perhaps unethical to habituate animals that are subject to the bushmeat trade, which is prevalent in West Africa (Krause et al. 2019). It is hoped that this tragic situation will improve for West African colobines and more research can be carried out, particularly as most species in West Africa are threatened or endangered.

We need information on how PSMs affect food choice using up-to-date methods. Colobine researchers could look to methods in chemical ecology and the animal sciences to address questions related to anti-feedants. Importantly, we need better measures of the PSMs in colobine foods as well as an understanding of how PSMs are distributed in colobine habitats. In addition, we need more information on the physiological strategies that colobines use to cope with PSMs, like salivary proteins, digestive enzymes and microbial detoxification. There has been a focus on tannins, but there are other compounds that may affect food choice. As well, investigating broad spectrums of compounds; i.e., 'total phenolics' and 'tannins' is not very useful since these compounds are incredibly diverse. Collaborations with chemists and chemical ecologists will be important in this respect.

As noted in other chapters in this volume, several colobines are threatened or endangered. Fragmentation of habitat, disease, hunting and climate change all have significant impacts on colobine populations. We need more information on how these various factors impact nutritional ecology. For example, in a study that our research group led, we found that tree leaves in Kibale declined in their protein and increased in fibre over time (Rothman et al. 2015). These findings were in accordance with greenhouse predictions of global climate change (increased rainfall, higher temperatures and higher CO_2). Our results suggest that even when colobines are located in protected areas they are still being affected by humans. Monitoring food availability, nutrient availability and nutritional chemistry over time will provide powerful information on how colobine habitats are changing and how monkeys may adapt. This will guide wildlife managers on the best ways to support colobines faced with human-induced pressures.

Acknowledgements

We are grateful to the editors Ikki Matsuda, Julie Teichroeb and Cyril Grueter for inviting us to contribute to this volume. We thank Colin Chapman, Tom Struhsaker, Joanna Lambert, Bill Foley, John Oates and David Raubenheimer for helpful discussions related to colobine nutrition. JMR's research was supported by NSF 1521528 during the writing of this chapter.

9 Red Colobus Natural History

Amanda H. Korstjens, Alison P. Hillyer and Inza Koné

Introduction

The red colobus, genus *Piliocolobus* (or genus *Procolobus* and subgenus *Piliocolobus*), is a polytypic genus with an unresolved taxonomy. The genus shows wide variation in morphological and behavioural features. The presence of pronounced sexual swellings (which they share with olive colobus), that vary greatly among species, sets this genus apart from sister genus *Colobus*. Red colobus species are wide-spread across sub-Saharan Africa but their distribution is closely linked to the presence of forests because of their largely arboreal lifestyle, and they do not often adapt well to human-dominated landscapes (except *P. kirkii*). The genus *Piliocolobus* is rare among colobines for typically living in large multi-female multi-male social groups with female-biased dispersal and male philopatry. However, several exceptions to this pattern suggest a flexible social system. Red colobus species are Vulnerable to Critically Endangered with the main threats being hunting and forest destruction by human activities.

Taxonomy

Red colobus is considered a monophyletic clade (Wang et al. 2012). The taxonomy is disputed but typically has 18 recognized taxonomic groups put into 17–18 species by Mittermeier et al. (2013) (ESM Table 9.1). The difficulty in settling on a taxonomic categorization is likely related to the fact that the taxa occur allo-patrically, with a possible hybrid zone in the Eastern central range (Colyn 1993; Struhsaker 2010) (Figure 9.1). The Western clade is considered a relatively ancient radiation (Grubb et al. 2003; Ting 2008a) and consists of a large central range for *P. badius* with closely related species *P. temminckii* to the North-West and the most likely extinct *P. waldroni* to the direct East. West-central Africa has the closely related but isolated species *P. pennantii*, *P. epieni* and *P. preussi*. In East Africa three isolated species occur: *P. kirkii* on Unguja Island, Zanzibar; *P. gordonorum* in the Udzungwa mountain range and *P. rufomitratus* in the Tana River area. *P. tephrosceles* occurs in several isolated populations along the rift valley. A large central African forest area harbours the most taxonomic variation, probably due to contracting and expanding forests in the Pleistocene, it contains: *P. tholloni*, *P. oustaleti*, *P. parmienteri*, *P. foai*, *P. semlikiensis*, *P. ellioti*, *P. bouvieri*, *P. langi* and undefined species/subspecies *P. lulindicus*.

This chapter includes Electronic Supplementary Material (ESM) at: www.cambridge.org/colobines

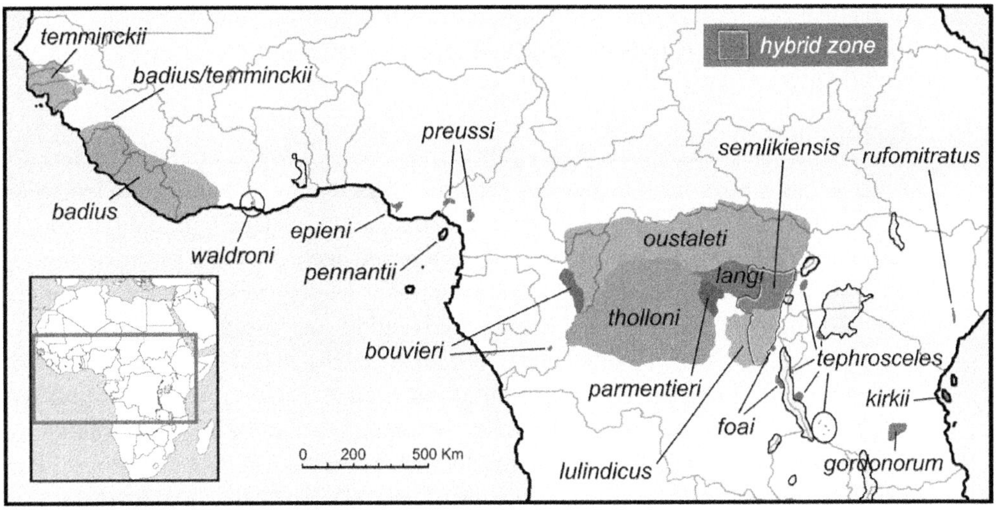

Figure 9.1 Distribution map of red colobus species from the Red Colobus Action Plan (Linder et al. 2021). Printed with permission of Drew Cronin (see also Cronin et al. 2018)

Oates and Ting (2015) argue that the taxonomic confusion may have had implications for the conservation status and protection of different red colobus taxa.

Morphological Features

Variation in the typically red and black pelage, vocalizations, female sexual swellings, body size (ESM Table 9.2) and cranial morphology is extensive (Butynski et al. 2013; Groves 2007; Grubb et al. 2013a; Struhsaker 2010). There is distinct sexual dimorphism in crania (males having a sagittal crest and robust orbital ridges) across red colobus taxa but male and female body-size differences vary and are less than those among genus *Colobus* (Struhsaker 2010). Cardini and Elton (2009a) show that red colobus cranial shape is more driven by phylogeny while size is more sensitive to recent adaptations. They suggest a link between body size and forest productivity as measured by rainfall, but also that smaller size evolved in the more isolated populations (e.g. *P. kirkii* and *P. rufomitratus*). Scapular and forelimb morphology indicates that red colobus have more flexibility in the shoulder to facilitate greater arm flexion, abduction and elevation than genus *Colobus* (Dunham et al. 2015, 2017). Taï red colobus (*P. badius*) most commonly use quadrupedal walking (53%), leaping (17.8%) and climbing (17%) when they move but also use arm swing in 3.7% of observations (unlike the other sympatric monkeys), and are mostly found in the upper canopy (McGraw 1998a).

Variation in sexual swelling size does not appear to reflect variation in sex ratio in the group and shows an inconsistent relationship with sexual size dimorphism but may be mostly following a phylogenetic signal (ESM Table 9.2; Korstjens unpublished; Struhsaker 2010). Two interesting but unstudied features restricted to a few species are the small perineal swelling in young males, which resembles the swelling of the females but is made up of adipose tissue (Kuhn 1972), and the presence of an exaggerated female clitoris (Struhsaker 2010; pers. obs.).

Distribution

Piliocolobus species occur across sub-Saharan Africa (Figure 9.1) but have a less wide distribution than the closely related genus *Colobus* (Korstjens and Dunbar 2007). Current distribution and inter-specific variations are likely the result of the combined effects of allopatric speciation, human disturbance leading to severe fragmentation and isolation of populations, human persecution for meat, competition with cercopithecines (which are often better at travelling across fragmented habitats), and climate change (Burgess et al. 1998; Cardini and Elton 2009a; Delson 1994; Struhsaker 2010; Ting 2008a). Most populations are becoming ever more isolated, leading to further morphological and behavioural differences between taxonomic groups. For example, Cardini and Elton (2011) show that *P. eliotti* has a distinct cranial shape and suggest it has had limited genetic influxes in the recent past. Still, more research on these central African species is needed as this species is also considered to grade into *P. langi* and shows variable pelage coloration (Grubb et al. 2003; Kaisala et al. 2020) Cranial analyses showed that island species *P. kirkii*, has undergone morphologic evolutionary acceleration leading to adaptations to their island habitat (in Zanzibar) with less sexual dimorphism and smaller crania than the nearest continental red colobus species (Nowak et al. 2008). Small, fragmented populations could hold valuable representatives of this vulnerable example of primate radiation.

Habitat and Climate

Red colobus are arboreal, forest-dependent species occurring in highest densities in minimally disturbed forest habitats with high levels of tree coverage; while riparian forests or forest fragments are also important (e.g. Gautier-Hion and Brugière 2005). Zanzibar red colobus (*P. kirkii*) around Jozani inhabits mostly forested land (85.5% of observations, primary, secondary, forest edge, thickets), but is also found in fields with agricultural tree crops (called shambas in the local area and publications; 4.5%), and mangroves (4.5%; Davenport et al. 2019). *P. badius* does not use secondary forest as much as other primates in Tiwai island (Fimbel 1994). Likewise, Udzungwa red colobus, *P. gordonorum*, abundance increases in large blocks of mature semi-deciduous and evergreen forest at relatively low elevation with large basal area of trees, abundance of climbers and limited human disturbance (Cavada et al. 2019). Higher densities at lower altitudes have been linked to the higher abundance of young leaves (Rovero and Struhsaker 2007; Rovero et al. 2009), but *P. gordonorum* has been recorded at up to 2200 m above sea level (asl; Dinesen et al. 2001).

In many areas, climate change (especially reduced rainfall and increased heat in West Africa), human expansion and persecution force the red colobus into forest refuges that are used less by humans e.g.: swamps in the Niger Delta, *P. epieni*: (Grubb and Powell 1999; Luiselli et al. 2015); Senegal's mangroves (Galat-Luong and Galat 2005); Gambian coastal forests (pers. obs.; Mayhew et al. 2020); and Zanzibar

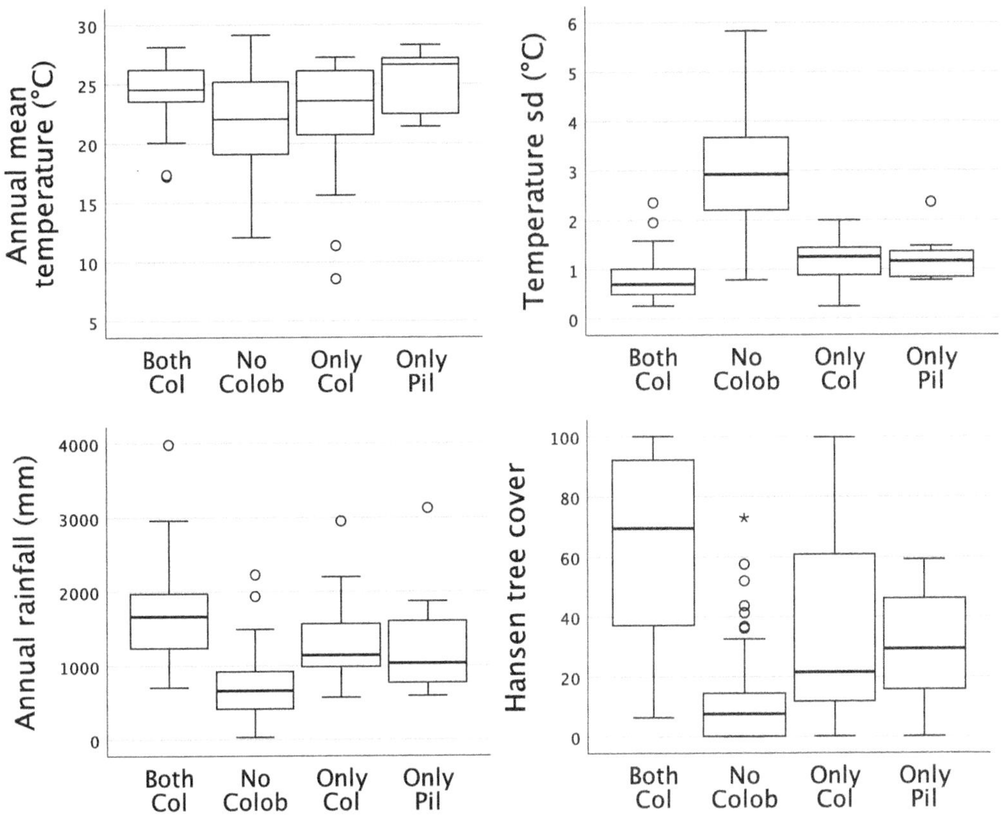

Figure 9.2 Comparison of mean annual temperature (in °C), mean temperature variation across months (in standard deviation across monthly averages), mean annual rainfall (mm) and Hansen's tree cover value (percentage of woody cover) for locations with *Piliocolobus* and *Colobus* present (Both Col: $N = 41$), with only *Colobus* present (Only Col: $N = 51$), with only *Piliocolobus* present (Only Pil: $N = 7$) and without colobines (No Colob: Absent $N = 103$). All sites contained at least one species of diurnal primate, and most are based on protected area location data or study site locations with a minimum distance of 1 degree latitude or longitude separation between sites; data set by Korstjens, Lehmann and Dunbar, e.g. see Korstjens and Dunbar (2007). The Hansen tree cover measurement, which is based on remote sensing data and not actual tree height data, gives a good indication of percentage vegetation cover of approximately >5 m height but should not be considered as an absolute value of forest cover. Box plots show median, quartiles, minimum and maximum (within 1.5 * IQR) and outliers.

mangroves and marsh lands (Nowak and Lee 2013). Most red colobus populations occur in regions experiencing 22°–26°C mean annual temperature and limited temperature variation across months (standard deviations 1.21°–3.26°C), with high levels of rainfall (576–1242 mm per year) and good tree cover (30%–95%; Figure 9.2).

Research Efforts

Most recent red colobus research focuses on conservation status, demography, parasites, diseases and response to fragmentation. The focus on conservation is likely due to the raising of subspecies to species level, a renewed appreciation of the critical status of many red colobus species, and the difficulty of running long-term resource-intensive behavioural studies. A red colobus action plan has brought many red colobus researchers together (see https://portals.iucn.org/library/node/49478) to promote more research and conservation to save red colobus species across Africa. There is a distinct lack of red colobus publications dealing with their natural history (demography, group size, diet, behaviour) outside the most intensely studied sites of: Kibale National Park (NP) in Uganda (*P. tephrosceles*; sites Kanyawara, Ngogo and several forest fragments near the park), Taï NP in Ivory Coast (*P. badius*), Tana river delta in Kenya (*P. rufomitratus*), Zanzibar archipelago Tanzania (*P. kirkii*), and Abuko NP in The Gambia (*P. temminckii*) and many of these studies are not recent (ESM Tables 9.2–9.6). Long-term population trends are available for most of these but also additional sites, including the Udzungwa region in Tanzania (*P. gordonorum*), Korup NP Cameroon (*P. preusii*), Fathala Senegal (*P. temminckii*), and Bioko Island, Equatorial Guinea (*P. pennantii*). There are still many gaps in our knowledge of red colobus biology and the variation across the taxon in their behaviours, demography and even morphology, especially for the variable central African species-complex.

Feeding Ecology

The most consumed dietary items by red colobus are leaves, fruits and flowers, with leaf material (including petioles and leaf buds) typically dominating the diet but there is wide variation among sites and months within sites, which is likely the result of fluctuating availability (ESM Table 9.3). Bark is a common food item in Kibale (0.3%–4.5% of annual diet) but less reported elsewhere (Chapman et al. 2002a). Some geophagy also occurs, mostly from termite mounds, the forest floor and soil from fallen rocks (Pebsworth et al. 2019). Diets vary greatly between months (e.g. Tiwai: Davies et al. 1999; Taï: Korstjens et al. 2007a) and between groups occupying different forest areas within the same general region, showing the importance of long-term and multi-group studies (Kibale NP: Chapman et al. 2002a; Chapman and Chapman 1999).

Red colobus density has been linked to density of food trees and leaf quality, in particular a positive relationship to the protein to fibre ratio in leaves (Chapman and Chapman 2000a; Chapman et al. 2002b; Oates et al. 1990; but for a critique and reanalyses, see Gogarten et al. 2012). Red colobus actively select food on the basis of protein to fibre ratio and general digestability, whilst energy content is not selected for (Wasserman and Chapman 2003); but nutrient content and sugar content can also be relatively high (Danish et al. 2006). Consumption of low-quality food in one month leads to increased gluco-corticoid (stress) levels in the subsequent month (Chapman et al. 2015). Food selection also allows red colobus to buffer against seasonal fluctuations in mineral content within their environment, leading to a relatively stable nutrient intake but a potential shortage of sodium content (Rode et al. 2003). Similarly, despite differences in food items and species selection, protein to fibre ratios of consumed food were very similar across seven Kibale area groups (Ryan et al. 2012). Red colobus diets may include various food items with high levels of oestrogenic compounds which correlated positively with levels of aggression and sexual behaviour but negatively with frequency of grooming in Kibale red colobus (Wasserman et al. 2012). In Zanzibar, charcoal eating (incl. from human kilns) helps red colobus with detoxification of secondary compounds from the Indian almond and mango leaves that they consume in the agricultural mosaics near villages (Cooney and Struhsaker 1997; Struhsaker et al. 1997).

New non-invasive methods help us gain greater understanding of food selection and health. Chapman et al. (2005a) showed that faecal nitrogen levels can be used to determine the levels of protein in the diet, and thus habitat quality for colobines, with less need for measuring the nitrogen in the trees that the primates feed from. Measuring physical traits and condition of animals using parallel lasers along with photographs also has great potential for many unanswered questions on temporal and taxonomic variation in physical traits (Rothman et al. 2008b).

The facio-cranial adaptations of *P. badius* show a relatively limited bite force compared to that of the genus *Colobus*, which supports the observations that *Colobus* more commonly feed on seeds encased within hard (wooded) husks (Koyabu and Endo 2009), but bite force is still more than expected for a species consuming mostly soft food items (Daegling and McGraw 2001; McGraw et al. 2016).

Leaf quality can vary greatly, not only among species but also among individual trees and among sites, although temporal variation in quality was minimal in Kibale (Chapman et al. 2003a). In Kibale, over a 25-year period (see some variation for that area in ESM Table 9.3), leaf quality went down for those trees that had been monitored in this time. However, overall food availability and the average quality of leaves across trees in the forest went up because the availability of high quality trees in the forest had increased (Chapman et al. 2015). Red colobus' over-consumption of leaves and flowers can result in reduced recruitment and fruiting ability in preferred tree species (Kibale, *Markhamia lutea* (Bignoniaceae): Chapman et al. 2013a; Zanzibar, Siex 2005). Likewise, they may also have a role as seed dispersers (Koné et al. 2008). Red colobus get most of their fluids from their diet and water from arboreal water-reservoirs (leaves, tree holes) but have been observed drinking water more extensively in dry regions or periods (e.g. The Gambia, Hillyer et al. 2015; mangrove forests in Zanzibar, Nowak 2008).

Activity Patterns

Red colobus activity budgets vary across species, sites and time periods (ESM Table 9.4). Although data on time budgets is scarce, Korstjens and Dunbar (2007) found that moving time correlated positively with group biomass and negatively with rainfall, while feeding time correlated positively with group size and rainfall variability. The resulting time-budget based models were able to predict distribution patterns of red colobus monkeys as reliable as did standard niche models. Overall, roughly 30%–58% of the time is spent resting, 20%–46% feeding, 5%–22% moving and 2%–12% socializing. Red colobus in an unprotected forest rested more and ate more mature leaves (Chapman et al. 2007), consumed food from more plant species and spent more time feeding (Milich et al. 2014b) than those in undisturbed forest in and near Kibale NP. Steel (2012) found that *P. gordonorum* fed more and rested less in the dry compared to the wet season.

Range Use

Red colobus home ranges vary widely from about 5.5 to 100 ha and daily travel distance from 310 to 1040 m (ESM Table 9.5). Home range size and day journey length variation over different spatial and temporal scales are at best weakly positively correlated to group size (data in ESM Table 9.5), but sometimes this expected relationship is only apparent when food availability is considered (Gogarten et al. 2014; Isbell 2012). Predation patterns can also affect ranging; for example, Ngogo red colobus decreased group size (Stanford 1995) but increased home range area from 93 ha in 1976–1983 to 257–360 ha in 2001–2002, possibly to reduce encounter rates and predictability in response to chimpanzee hunting (Lwanga et al. 2011). In marginal habitats, small red colobus groups may have correspondingly small home ranges as a result of fragmentation and poor food availability (e.g. Zanzibar red colobus in suboptimal habitats had ranges of only 5.5–8.8 ha, Nowak and Lee 2011). Red colobus appear to cross their home range in a way that suggests that their food is not patchily distributed. This is also confirmed by studies showing that they select relatively abundant food sources (Isbell 2012; Korstjens et al. 2007a; Siex and Struhsaker 1999a). Kibale red colobus ranging follows Brownian motion patterns (associated with uniform food distribution) only in the dry season (Reyna-Hurtado et al. 2018). Bonnell et al. (2013) used an individual-based model to show that red colobus use a landmark-based memory and follow the leader foraging strategy.

Predation

Red colobus monkeys' main natural predators are African crowned eagles (*Stephanoaetus coronatus* [Accipitridae]), chimpanzees (*Pan troglodytes*) and leopards (*Panthera pardus* [Felidae]), but they are also hunted by golden cats (*Caracal aurata* (Felidae); Bahaa-el-din et al. 2015), hyenas [Hyaenidae], crocodiles [Crocoddylidae] and large snakes. Royal pythons (*Python regius* [Pythonidae]) and crocodiles preyed on *P. temminckii* in Abuko Nature Reserve, The Gambia in the 1970s–1980s (Starin 1991). Pythons are no longer common in Abuko (APH, pers. obs.; Hillyer 2013). Hyenas and dogs (*Canis lupus familiaris* [Canidae]) hunt *P. temminckii* in Fathala, Senegal (Galat-Luong and Galat 2005). Overall predation rates on arboreal primates at Taï (by leopards, chimpanzees and crowned eagles) are positively correlated with group density and negatively with group size, putting predation rates on red colobus at an intermediate rate compared to sympatric primates (Shultz et al. 2004).

Where leopards occur, they are considered important red colobus predators (Hoppe-Dominik 1984; Struhsaker 2010; Zuberbühler and Jenny 2002). Leopard predation positively correlates with prey population density and body size (Zuberbühler and Jenny 2002). The African crowned eagle is another predator that takes red colobus monkeys of all age-sex classes where it occurs (Mcgraw et al. 2006; Mitani et al. 2001; Pobiner et al. 2007; Struhsaker and Leakey 1990). But, where all three main predators occur, chimpanzees tend to cause the highest mortality (Shultz et al. 2004).

Red colobus are often considered preferred prey of chimpanzees (80% of prey in Taï: Boesch 1994a; 83% of kills in Ngogo: Watts and Amsler 2013; 83% of prey in Mahale: Hosaka et al. 2020). In Taï, chimpanzee hunts occur weekly throughout the year, and even daily in the hunting season (September through November), and individuals of all age-sex classes are killed (Boesch and Boesch-Achermann 2000). In Mahale, red colobus formed 16% of chimpanzee prey before 1976, but this suddenly increased in the 1980s to 83% in the 1990s and 2000s (i.e. >13 kg colobus meat consumed per chimpanzee per year), whilst population density of colobus, group hunting, and female chimpanzee participation in hunting increased (all factors reviewed in Hosaka et al. 2020). Chimpanzee hunting is less frequent in Gombe and Kanyawara in Kibale NP, but it still affects red colobus population structure and survival (Struhsaker 2010). Attack rates in Gombe reach an average of one every 66–80 days (Stanford 1998a).

The highest chimpanzee predation rates occur in Ngogo, where chimpanzees killed around 167 red colobus per year from 1995–1998 and around 322 in 2002, representing 15%–53% of the red colobus population (Teelen 2007b, 2008), resulting in an 89% red colobus population decline between 1975 and 2007 (Lwanga et al. 2011; Mitani et al. 2000; Teelen 2007a). Since 1999, this is the largest known chimpanzee community (total number = 145–205 members, including 24–35 adult males and *ca.* 42–63 adult females), with a 75% success rate per hunting attempt; killing as many as 13 individuals in a single attack (8 of which were infants; Watts and Mitani 2002, 2015). Chimpanzees are more likely to initiate a hunt when encountering red colobus where the forest is more open and trees are shorter (Watts and Mitani 2002), making the colobus more vulnerable. As chimpanzee encounter rates with red colobus are declining, the chimpanzees are hunting other prey more often, although hunting frequency upon encounter with red colobus has remained the same (Watts and Mitani 2015). High cortisol levels in Ngogo colobus may be the result of this intense hunting pressure (Aronsen et al. 2015). At nearby Kanyawara, where chimpanzees hunt less, red colobus had elevated cortisol concentrations for up to two days after a chimpanzee attack (Wasserman et al. 2013).

Anti-predation Strategies

Red colobus anti-predation strategies vary among sites and depend on the predator-prey relationships. Strategies and adaptations include: large group size, arboreality, alarm-calling, poly-specific associations and cooperative defence by males. Red colobus high alarm-calling response is adapted to the hunting strategy of the predators with more calls given to ambush hunters like leopards, who depend on diurnal and crepuscular surprise attacks by hiding and waiting for opportunities in forest areas that primates use frequently (Jenny and Zuberbühler 2005; Zuberbühler et al. 1999), than to pursuit hunters like chimpanzees. In Taï, red colobus will fall silent when chimpanzees are detected at distance and will approach Diana monkey groups if nearby; still, the loud red colobus female copulation calls can often be heard when the rest of the primates in the forest remain silent (pers. obs.; McGraw and Zuberbühler 2008). Similarly, while Diana monkeys adapt their anti-predator behaviour to human hunting strategies (Bshary 2001), red colobus monkey do not (Koné and Refisch 2007).

Red colobus at Gombe and Kibale do not flee like sympatric monkeys when chimpanzees approach, possibly because attack success increases when fleeing is attempted in the relatively open and low forests where attacks are most common (Stanford 1998a). In Kibale and Gombe, group cohesion and vigilance increase when chimpanzees are near (Stanford 1998a p127; Treves 1999). On chimpanzee approach, red colobus re-position whilst alarm calling. The calls change as individuals ascend higher into the canopy. The group will typically fall silent once the chimpanzees are close. If the chimpanzees decide to attack, the colobus initiate alarm calling again. In Gombe, juveniles were the most vulnerable members of the group and alarm call rate increased with the number of immatures present in the group (Stanford 1998a). The sometimes-prolonged attacks influence group repositioning and affect activity budgets. Gombe adult and subadult male colobus counterattack chimpanzees; clustering and alarm calling, leaping and biting, commonly wounding chimpanzee hands, arms, back and scrotum. They will even jump onto the chimpanzees, sometimes managing to drive the chimpanzees away. More red colobus attacking chimpanzees in unison are better at thwarting an attack (Stanford 1998b). Females will attempt to escape with infants or even try to get them back after they are captured despite the risks to themselves (Stanford 1998a). Counter-attacks by male colobus also occur at Kanyawara, Kibale (A. Georgiev. pers. comm.). In contrast, at Ngogo and Taï, subadults and adults are most commonly killed (Boesch 1994a; Teelen 2008). Consequently, all red colobus individuals in a group will seek higher positions in the canopy and will try to escape when under attack.

Red colobus are regularly found in poly-specific associations with cercopithecines, often more than expected by chance (Fathala: Galat-Luong and Galat 2005; Kibale: Chapman and Chapman 2000b; Korup: Astaras et al. 2008; Zanzibar: Struhsaker 1999, 2000a; Taï: Holenweg et al. 1996; Wachter et al. 1997). Typically, a long-term partnership among specific guenon and red colobus groups forms (probably due to home range overlap) (Höner et al. 1997). Poly-specific associations with cercopithecines are considered an anti-predation strategy of red colobus against ground predators, in particular chimpanzees, as cercopithecines typically detect ground predators quicker than do colobus (Bshary and Noë 1997a). Support for this suggestion comes from studies showing that red colobus will initiate associations after hearing a chimpanzee vocalization (Taï: McGraw and Zuberbühler 2008); and association rates are higher for populations with higher chimpanzee densities and during times when there are more infants in a group (Kibale: Chapman and Chapman 2000b). These associations may have some ecological costs but these are likely low, as dietary overlap is minimal between the species (Wachter et al. 1997); but red colobus travel farther when in association with red tail monkeys in Kibale (Chapman and Chapman 2000b). Red colobus in Taï are more likely to come to the ground or lower strata while they are mingling with a terrestrial sooty mangabey group (McGraw and Bshary 2002); and most observations of ground activity of Temminck's red colobus occur when green monkeys are present (Galat-Luong 1988; Galat-Luong and Galat 2005).

The arboreal guenons (*Cercopithecus* spp.; the most common preferred association partner of red colobus) are considered to benefit from poly-specific association because red colobus are typically found in the upper strata where they provide a sentinel function and protective layer for the smaller guenons that are more often prey of crowned eagles (Mitani et al. 2001; Schultz et al. 2004; Struhsaker and Leakey 1990). Kane and McGraw (2018) showed that Diana monkeys do not adjust their behaviour much as a result of these associations although synergistic effects of association and a chimpanzee hunting season resulted in expanded use of the main canopy (versus lower strata), decreased fruit and increased invertebrate consumption. In Kibale, Kanyawara and Ngogo, red-tailed monkeys (*Cercopithecus ascanius*) appear to be mostly responsible for initiating interactions with red colobus (Chapman and Chapman 2000b; Teelen 2007a). *P. badius* in Tiwai (Oates and Whitesides 1990) and *P. tephrosceles* in Gombe (Stanford 1998a) do not associate with cercopithecines more than expected by chance, probably because prey-predator dynamics are different from those elsewhere. In Tiwai, hunting pressure by chimpanzees and eagle attacks are low (Whitesides 1989). In Gombe, the open woodland allows red colobus to hear and see the relatively noisy approach of chimpanzee hunting parties without the sentinel role of guenons (Stanford 1998a, 2002). The difference in chimpanzee-red colobus predator-prey relationships are thought to be the result of three major differences between Taï and Gombe (Bshary and Noë 1997a): (1) Gombe forests are lower and more open, allowing easier detection of predators and prey and less escape opportunities for red colobus; (2) red colobus/chimpanzee body-size ratio is more equal in Gombe than in Taï, making a red colobus male counter-attack more likely to result in injury to the chimpanzee and (3) chimpanzees in Taï use complex cooperative hunting strategies to pursue the prey whilst Gombe chimpanzees may attack simultaneously but do not have differentiated hunting roles. Stern and Goldstone (2005) suggested that red colobus would hesitate longer before leaping than other primates in Kibale, possibly making them an easier prey for chimpanzees.

At most sites where red colobus intermingle with guenons, individuals of both species groom or play with each other.

Social Organization

Red colobus group sizes range from 3 to over 100 and vary among sites, groups at the same sites, and study periods. Most populations have relatively large groups with multiple males and multiple females with their offspring (ESM Table 9.6) and female-biased dispersal from the natal group (see also Chapter 17). Smaller groups are commonly found in the more degraded, disturbed or marginal sites and are considered a response to ecological constraints (Gorgarten et al. 2015; Nowak and Lee 2011; Struhsaker 2010). One-male groups were reported in the early studies of Tana River red colobus (Marsh 1979) where now, female to male sex ratios appear to have decreased, but male numbers per group are still low (ESM Table 9.6) (Karere et al. 2004). A recent survey showed that group sizes for *P. kirkii* were greater in protected areas (20.6) than in unprotected areas (12.8), with a lower female to male ratio outside protected areas (ESM Table 9.6) (Davenport et al. 2019). In Kibale NP, the 'small camp group' at Kanyawara increased from 59 in 2006 to 104 in 2011 (and it is still growing; C. Chapman, pers. comm., 2019), at the very upper level of group sizes in the park but following the park-wide trend of an increase in mean group size (from 28 to 47 in that period) but not density (ESM Table 9.6) (Gogarten et al. 2015). The group size increase may be related to overall increased food availability and quality (Chapman et al. 2015), although protein to fibre ratio of specific individual trees decreased between the 1970s to 2000s (Rothman et al. 2015). Very large groups are expected to split up as group size exceeds a habitat-specific threshold. In Taï, two study groups (Bad1 and Bad2) each contained around 90 individuals in 1997 but they were regularly splitting into sister fractions from 1994–1998, before they split up permanently. During and after the splitting process sister-groups shared the original home range and partner Diana monkey group before slowly separating (Bshary 1995; van Oirschot 2000). In 1999, based on individual recognition of the majority of individuals, Bad1A and B contained 41 and 64 and Bad2A and B 60 and 44 individuals respectively (ESM Table 9.6) (Korstjens et al. 2007).

Red colobus individuals are observed solitary or as a pair external to established bisexual groups in many locations. Decker (1994) also saw small groups of >2 young male *P. rufomitratus*. Typically these pairs or solitary individuals are associated with either cercopithecine or black-and-white colobus groups, during the transitory period between emigration and immigration but often are only observed for a few days (e.g. Taï: pers. obs.; Abuko: pers obs. and Starin 1991; Tiwai: Fimbel 1994; Zanzibar: Davenport and Machaga 2007; Tana River: Karere et al. 2004; Udzungwa: Marshall et al. 2005; fragments near Kibale: Onderdonk and Chapman 2000).

Female dispersal is reported for all study sites but the presence of solitary males and some observations of male immigrations into study groups suggests that males are not always philopatric in all populations. The Zanzibar red colobus groups living in human-dominated landscapes, the Jozani shambas subpopulation, showed dispersal of both sexes (including evidence of immigration by males). This fit the pattern of affiliative bonds among females who actively defended their group at the more intense inter-group interactions in this densely populated subpopulation (Siex 2003; Siex and Struhsaker 1999a). Dispersal by both sexes was also common in the *P. temminckii*'s population in Abuko, possibly due to the degraded condition of this small forest fragment in relatively dry habitat (Starin 1994). Whilst a genetic signal supports female dispersal and male philopatry in the same species in Guinea Bissau's

Cantanhez NP (Minhós et al. 2015). Male takeovers sometimes accompanied by suspected infanticide were recorded in Tana River red colobus (Decker 1994a; Marsh 1978, 1979b).

In Taï *P. badius*, of 12 individually followed (for at least a few days) solitary individuals, 3 were subadult females, 8 were subadult males and 1 was an adult male (sexing young individuals in this population is difficult because of the lack of clitoris in females and still undescended testicles in most solitary males). Another juvenile male (with deformity) spent 9 months in exile of the study group before re-integrating into his natal group as a subadult. At least five study males matured and stayed in their natal group, and one adult male from a neighbouring group successfully joined a study group. Extra-group females were never observed for more than a week in the area whilst such males were observed for months. Dispersal was still considered to be female-biased based on the short time that females would be solitary, the appearance of shy females in study groups, and disappearance of all recognized subadult females after their first swelling period (reviewed in Korstjens et al. 2007a).

In Kibale, female relatedness within the group was higher for the small group than for the large group (Miyamoto et al. 2013), suggesting an effect of competition on female dispersal that had not been detected based on behavioural observations. Detailed monitoring of group membership is greatly hindered in large red colobus groups because females are difficult to recognize individually and many immigrants can be relatively young (probably no red colobus researchers have managed 100% recognition of immatures in focal groups of considerable size).

Red colobus at several study sites show fission-fusion tendencies in which groups split up into smaller units from time to time, either in response to food availability or because the group as a whole is getting relatively large and fluid fission-fusion patterns precede a more permanent group split (Korstjens 2001; Nowak and Lee 2011; Oates 1994; Siex and Struhsaker 1999a; Starin 1994; Struhsaker et al. 2004; van Oirschot 1999).

Inter-group Relationships

Inter-group relationships vary across red colobus populations and taxa, but typically range from neutral to agonistic, involving some threat displays or even chasing; and home ranges tend to overlap at least a little. *P. tephrosceles* in Kibale have few agonistic encounters (6.5%–36% of encounters; Isbell 1983; Struhsaker 2010). In Taï, *P. badius*, overlap between home ranges is small, 30%–50% of encounters include agonistic acts of males only (mostly threats and some chases), and encounters occurred only once per 21–30 full observation days (Korstjens et al. 2002, 2007a). In Zanzibar, males were the main aggressors in encounters in the forest subpopulation whilst all individuals engaged in inter-group aggression in the shamba populations (Siex 2003). Similarly, in Abuko, females and males both engaged in inter-group aggression (Starin 1991, 1994).

Intra-group Aggression and Affiliation

Food competition is not directly evident in red colobus monkeys as most of their food does not seem to be contestable and is considered abundant. However, scramble competition is detectable in Kibale NP (Snaith and Chapman 2005, 2008) and larger groups have higher stress levels (Chapman et al. 2015). Larger group size resulted in higher dietary diversity, more time travelling and less time feeding and socializing (Gorgarten et al. 2014). Typically, most aggressive interactions in red colobus occur among adult males or from males to females with minimal aggression among females. But young subadult males may suffer intense aggression by males as they mature (pers. obs. in Taï). As a result of the males' greater involvement in within- and between-group fights and squabbles and predator defence, red colobus males tend to have more 'healed' fractures than females (*P. preusii* in Cameroon: Chapman and Legge 2009; and *P. tephrosceles* in Kibale: Arlet et al. 2009).

Notable here is that aggression rates observed in the Zanzibar shamba population outside Jozani NP, are greater than those observed in the Jozani forest groups (2.48 versus 0.25 observations/hour), stylized male-male presents were seven times higher and wounds were also more frequent (Siex 2003). In *P. tephrosceles*, the frequency of agonistic interactions was 0.12 events/hour (Struhsaker and Leland 1979). Aggressive interactions commonly involved physical contact in Siex's study (13% and 24% of observed events in Jozani forest and shambas respectively), whilst Struhsaker reports only 15 events with physical contact over 1112 hours. Most aggressive interactions in Siex's study occurred among adult males but in the shamba group, juveniles were also often involved in aggression. Werre (2000) reports only two cases of aggressive physical contact in a 12 months study on *P. epieni*, with other agonistic encounters involving mostly males chasing males or sometimes females. Korstjens et al. (2007) report 0.19 agonistic interactions among females, 0.42 among males, and 0.41 from males towards females per focal follow hour. Only one intra-group agonistic support among females and 13 among males were recorded over 76 observation days (Korstjens 2001; Korstjens et al. 2002; Korstjens et al. 2007a).

Cohesiveness and Bonding

Typically, red colobus groups are widely dispersed throughout the canopy but grooming and close proximity are common during resting. Habitat structure and exposure to anthropogenic disturbance (e.g. proximity to people and habitations) may also affect cohesiveness. For example, in Zanzibar, shamba groups were more cohesive than Jozani forest groups (Siex 2003). The importance and strength of male-male bonds varies among populations and is sometimes expressed through grooming and ritualized male-male presents and hugs. Male-male grooming was common in Struhsaker and Leland's (1979) study at Kibale Kanyawara, while other studies recorded very few grooming bouts among males: in Taï (Korstjens 2001), Zanzibar (Siex 2003) and Guinea Bissau (Minhós et al. 2015). Males in Taï spent more time with neighbours nearby than did females but did not spent more time with males than females and did not groom either sex very often (Korstjens 2001). Females in Taï spent as much time sitting next to or grooming males as females, but if corrected for sex ratio, females showed a preference in grooming and proximity for males (Korstjens et al. 2002). In *P. epieni*, most grooming bouts were among males or from female to male with very little male to female grooming (Werre 2000). Female-female bonds, expressed by grooming, were stronger than those among other age-sex classes in Guinea Bissau (Minhós et al. 2015), Abuko (Starin 1994) and the Zanzibar shambas population (Siex 2003). Interestingly, the pattern observed by Siex (2003) in Zanzibar's shambas groups may be an adaptation to the increased population density and disturbance levels in those areas, as an earlier study in 1980–1981 reported strong male-male bonds and stable male group membership in the same shamba group (Mturi 1991). Abuko is also heavily disturbed and isolated, with frequent male and female migration among only five residential groups, and female involvement in inter-group aggression. In Abuko, the population size and isolation may have resulted in relatively closely related females who had typically more stable group membership than males (who had higher death rates and migrated) (Starin 1994). Coalitions in intra-group encounters in Abuko were rare but occurred in interactions with extra-group males or inter-group encounters and involved most often female-male coalitions (Starin 1994).

Mating Systems, Reproduction and Sexual Behaviour

Detailed information on birth rates, receptive periods, mating strategies and sexual behaviour require long-term studies on recognized individuals, something that is difficult with red colobus. Instead, birth rates can be estimated from female to infant or juvenile ratios in groups (ESM Table 9.6). This ratio shows variation across populations and tends to show the expected trend of less infants per female (i.e. lower reproductive rate) in more degraded habitats. In the Udzungwa mountain range, natality and infant survival appears positively related to forest quality (Struhsaker et al. 2004).

Sexual interactions are probably far more common in red colobus than other colobines due to the long receptive period and sexual swellings of females and the large multi-male groups with strong male sperm competition (Struhsaker 2010). Both females and males initiate sexual interactions but males do so more than females. Females often solicit or accept matings even while they are pregnant. Females tended to solicit interactions and mate more promiscuously when pregnant than during the earlier swelling periods; while males were less interested in females with post-conception swellings than pre-conception swellings (Beziers et al. 2009; Hobeika et al. 2009; Korstjens et al. 2008; Piachaud et al. 2009) Females may refuse or flee to avoid copulating with particular males, who then typically threaten and chase them. Male mate-guarding was observed at Taï (AHK pers. obs.) and consortships were observed in the Tana River area (Mbora and McGrew 2002).

Males are considered multiple-mounters and sperm coagulates to form a sperm plug that subsequent males regularly try to remove before mating (AHK pers. obs.). Multiple males will mate with a female in quick succession, often pushing the preceding male off the female during a copulation (AHK pers. obs.). Although variable among species, males sometimes have their feet on the female's ankles during copulation and the female sometimes turns around and grasps or touches the male (Struhsaker 2010; AHK pers. obs.). Infants are regularly observed to pull or jump on the males during copulation. Starin (2001) observed *P. temminckii* mothers preventing their daughters from mating in some cases, whilst an orphaned subadult female faced no restraints. Most copulations occur while females have a sexual swelling (Struhsaker 2010). In *P. badius*, 90%–95% of 287 copulations recorded occurred while the female had a swelling (AHK unpubl.).

In *P. badius*, *P. temminckii* and *P. preussi*, females produce copulation calls during or sometimes before or after the male mounts her (up to 79% of sexual interactions included a female copulation call in Taï; AHK unpubl.). In *P. temminckii*, females advertise their receptivity through jumping and receptivity quavers but seem to stay silent during copulation (Galat-Luong and Galat 2005; Starin 1991; Struhsaker 1975). Starin (1991, 1994, 2001) reported that turnover of the breeding male was so regular in Abuko, that this male was often not present for much of the lactation period of infants conceived during his tenure. The elaborate displays of the females there may promote extra-group copulations, which were observed in this population (Starin 1991, 1994, 2001), but not in the nearby Taï population of *P. badius* (Korstjens pers. obs.). Infanticide by males has been recorded but appears rare and requires further study (Decker 1994a; Marsh 1978, 1979b; Nowak 2007).

Mating and births are seasonal in some but not all locations and seasons are often not very tightly defined. Taï females had most births at the end of the wet season (75% of observed births occurred from November to January; AHK unpubl.), which coincides with the end of the intense chimpanzee hunting season. Most sexual interactions occurred between January and June (copulation call rates fell from 4–7 calls per hour to 0.5–2 calls per hour in July–December). Up to half the females (12 of 24) in the study group were seen to mate on a single day during the mating season, while outside of this season only two females were receptive on any given day at Taï (AHK unpubl.). Zanzibar colobus in marginal habitats had slightly more births in one group in the first wet and in another group in the first dry season (Nowak and Lee 2011); slightly more births occurred in Abuko in the dry season but births were most constrained by strong intra-group synchrony which may be a side effect of the regular changes in dominant males (Starin 1988, 1991); very weak seasonality is suggested for Kibale, and most other locations (Struhsaker 2010).

Inter-birth interval is unknown for most species. *P. badius* at Taï had mean inter-birth intervals of 15.6 months for 12 identified females (18.8 for 8 surviving infants and 8.0 for 4 infants that disappeared before the age of 10 months). This is short compared to those at other sites: Gombe, 19.2–24.2 months (Stanford

1998a); Abuko 29.4 (Starin 1988, 1991); and Kibale 24.4 (Struhsaker 2010). *P. kirkii* appears to have the slowest reproductive rate recorded based on infants per adult female ratios (ESM Table 9.6). Sexual swelling periods can last from one to 2 weeks (AHK unpubl.; Milich et al. 2014a; Struhsaker 2010). Females in disturbed forests had shorter periods of swelling tumescence, restricted mating more to maximum tumescence, and copulated less than those in old-growth forest in Kibale (Milich et al. 2014a).

Allomothering

Red colobus have very low frequencies of allomothering, but infants sometimes play on other females' laps in Taï (usually, with females that are close associates of the mother) and some allomothering was observed in Zanzibar in the shamba population (Siex 2003). Old juvenile or subadult males have been observed to suckle from females in several species (Struhsaker 2010).

Diseases and Parasites

Understanding the potential for zoonotic and anthropozoonotic disease transfer is increasingly important due to increased risks of human-wildlife pathogen transmission as forests are degraded and hunting of red colobus is common. Gastrointestinal parasites are common and diverse (e.g. Taï: Kouassi et al. 2015). The red colobus-specific version of SIV_{wrc} (Liégeois et al. 2009) and herpes are common in *P. badius* in Taï (Leendertz et al. 2011; Locatelli et al. 2008b) but they are not being transmitted to the chimpanzees, despite regular consumption of red colobus by chimpanzees (Leendertz et al. 2011; Murthy et al. 2013). Two other retroviruses, STLV-1wrc and SFVwrc, on the other hand have been transmitted to the chimpanzees (reviewed in Leendertz et al. 2011). Whilst an anthrax-like virus regularly kills red colobus in Taï, with very few individuals showing an immune response, suggesting high virulence (Zimmermann et al. 2017). A SIV_{wrc} strain found in Temminck's red colobus in Abuko was closely related but distinct from that in Taï (Locatelli et al. 2008a). Logging and an increase in the proportion of forest edge led to higher parasite/disease prevalence in Kibale red colobus. Parasite and food abundance synergistically limited population density around Kibale NP where the reduction of food sources in already fragmented forests directly led to reduced population density, whilst parasite prevalence increased with population density (review in Chapman et al. 2013b). Parasite richness and prevalence are greater in Tana River red colobus living outside compared to inside the National Park and correlate positively with colobus density. Colobus parasite prevalence and richness were lower than those for the more terrestrial mangabeys that live in larger groups and range further (Mbora and McPeek 2009).

Increased contact between primates and humans is leading to increased risks of disease and parasite transmission (Paige et al. 2014) and the risk of emergent strains of some very dangerous viruses (e.g. simian haemorrhagic fever virus Bailey et al.

2014). *Treponema pallidum* infections, the cause of human yaws have been observed in red colobus in West Africa (Fribourg-Blanc and Mollaret 1969; Gogarten et al. 2016; Mayhew et al. 2020). Few studies look at the effect of diseases or parasites on red colobus behavioural ecology. Parasite and disease pressures can drive selection for variable MHC in Kibale red colobus (Simons et al. 2017). Red colobus, at this site also alter their behaviour when infected with whip worms. Infected colobus rest more but move, groom and copulate less, and feed more on bark from species with known medicinal properties (Ghai et al. 2015).

Conservation

Red colobus throughout their range show a declining population trend due to habitat reduction (leading to fragmentation, increased parasite/disease transmission and vulnerability, stress, reduced food availability, and increased exposure to climatic extremes and change) and overhunting (IUCN 2020). In the longer-term, isolated populations can go extinct through stochastic processes. The most threatened members of the radiation include: *P. waldroni, P. pennantii, P. rufomitratus, P. epieni* and *P. preussii* (Cronin et al. 2018). There have recently been some hopeful sightings of species thought to have been locally extirpated, including *P. waldroni* in the Ivory Coast (Bitty et al. 2015; McGraw 2005; Oates et al. 2000a) and *P. bouvieri* in The Republic of Congo (Devreese 2015). In Zanzibar archipelago, there appears to be a good-sized *P. kirkii* population but recruitment is low with only 0.3 infants and 0.25 juveniles/subadults per adult female, supporting the IUCN status of Endangered (Davenport et al. 2019; ESM Table 9.6). This species is under serious threat from forest destruction. At least one translocation of a large group of colobus has proven successful as a way of relocating threatened groups (Struhsaker and Siex 1998). Road kill and feral dogs also threaten this population (Georgiev et al. 2019; Olgun et al. 2020).

Temminck's colobus is under serious threat from forest destruction, hunting, human encroachment, increasing temperatures and drought in West Africa (Galat et al. 2009; Hillyer et al. 2015; Mayhew et al. 2020). In Fathala, human encroachment, increased hunting by dogs and increased drought have led to a reduction in suitable habitat. *P. temminckii* has adapted by (1) consuming more fruit and using new foods (e.g. grasses, herbs, seeds); (2) more terrestrial locomotion (facilitated by associating with terrestrial cercopithecines); (3) increased time in poly-specific associations; (4) using open habitats more than before and (5) using mangrove swamps for resting and feeding (Galat-Luong and Galat 2005). Throughout Guinea Bissau there are significant conservation concerns as red colobus are absent in forests with heavy human disturbance and in decline overall, there is a clear genetic signal for a recent bottleneck and restricted female dispersal (Minhós et al. 2016).

P. rufomitratus saw a 5% decline between 1994 and 2001 at Tana River due to habitat loss (Karere et al. 2004). Anthropogenic and some natural causes resulted in a 34.5% reduction in forest cover in lower Tana River with areas inside the National Park being affected a little less than those outside the park (38% versus 29%

reduction) (Moinde-Fockler et al. 2007; Wahungu et al. 2005). High genetic diversity was found within and between small populations in those fragmented forests, suggesting that the meta-population was large and fragmentation still recent relative to red colobus generation times; a Pliocene-Pleistocene interval bottleneck signature was also detected (Mbora and McPeek 2010). Group size has decreased significantly in Tana River red colobus since 1978 from around 20 to only 9 outside and 12 individuals per group inside the park in 1988, whilst in 2000, group size outside the park increased to 11 and that inside reduced to 10 individuals per group. The number of immatures per adult female did not change but the number of females per male decreased significantly in this time period, suggesting that females suffered greater survival stresses than males (Mbora and Meikle 2004).

Kibale NP has seen a 3.9% annual increase in red colobus populations since the 1970s due to their colonizing of regenerating plantations (Chapman et al. 2018a).

While only two viable populations of *P. epieni* were left in the Niger Delta in 2013, where habitat destruction and lack of protection are driving the species to extinction (Ikemeh 2015).

Fragmentation often leads to crop-foraging which can result in retaliatory killing (e.g. *P. tephrosceles* in Tanzania: Kibaja 2014; *P. temminckii* in The Gambia; Mayhew 2020). The multilevel effects of fragmentation on red colobus populations near Kibale National Park included increased transmission of parasites between humans and primates, severe forest degradation leading to reduction in food trees, increased physiological stress levels in red colobus, increased parasite load and eventually a strong reduction in population size (83% between 2000 and 2010) (reviewed in: Chapman et al. 2013b, 2006a). Individual-based models can be used to help predict the effects of habitat fragmentation, climate change and parasite pressures under varying scenarios (Bonnell et al. 2016, 2018). Over 28 years, in Kibale forest areas, low-intensity logging had limited impact on red colobus populations but high-intensity logging led to reduced population densities and a slow recovery rate (Chapman et al. 2000).

The Udzungwa red colobus is facing severe threats throughout their range, including the impacts of human-induced fires, fragmentation and hunting (Cavada et al. 2019; Dinesen et al. 2001). Using a novel landscape genetics approach, Ruiz-Lopez et al. (2016) showed that Udzungwa red colobus genetic diversity was still similar across isolated forest blocks, but there was very limited gene flow among the blocks, showing recent gene flow being affected by the frequency of human-induced fires and the fragmentation of the area by human activities. They recommend establishment of corridors between the forest fragments to conserve the genetic diversity in the population. Human activities lead to smaller group sizes, while abundance is lower and parasite diversity is higher at higher elevation in the Udzungwa region (Barelli et al. 2019; Marshall et al. 2005). Abundance is linked to the mean basal area of large trees (>20 cm Diameter at Breast Height) and species richness of their food trees (Rovero and Struhsaker 2007). In the same area, red colobus in only recently isolated forest fragments, surrounded by human landscapes, showed lower diversity in gut microbiome than those in less disturbed forest, indicative of a less varied diet. Importantly, they had lost some micro-organisms used for detoxification of plant compounds, which has important implications for translocation, as these individuals would struggle more with the plants in mature forest that contain more toxic compounds (Barelli et al. 2015, 2020). In contrast, microbiome did not differ between red colobus from Kibale National Park and those from surrounding forest fragments (Mccord et al. 2013).

Hunting by humans is a particularly great threat to West and Central African red colobus, where they are among the first to disappear from forests (Covey and McGraw 2014; Gonedelé Bi et al. 2014; Kaisala et al. 2020; Koné and Refisch 2007; Oates 1996b; Refisch and Koné 2005a), but hunting also occurs in more Eastern populations (e.g. Udzungwa: Rovero et al. 2015). In Sierra Leone, red colobus is the preferred primate meat for market because it dries well and they are often hunted to extinction locally, but primate meat is not considered a delicacy and hunting is driven by economic conditions (Davies et al. 2007). Likewise, in Ivory Coast, they are the primates most likely to be extirpated, affected more than other monkeys by hunting and the ones benefitting most from reduced hunting near research or tourism camps (Bi et al. 2014; Campbell et al. 2011b; Gonedelé N'Goran et al. 2012; Refisch and Koné 2005a). Hunting and illegal cocoa farming inside protected areas in Ivory Coast led to the absence of red colobus in all 23 protected areas surveyed in 2010–2013 (excluding Taï NP) (Bitty et al. 2015). One of the most extensive long-term studies on bushmeat has been done on Bioko Island where the Critically Endangered *P. pennantii* is considered the primate species least tolerant to hunting and without stronger intervention it is likely to go extinct (Cronin et al. 2015, 2016, 2017). The little-studied central African species, *P. ellioti* and *P. langi*, are threatened heavily by forest destruction, hunting and mining, but have also suffered periodic fatal epidemics (Kaisala et al. 2020).

Poaching can also be the result of vengeful pursuit due to perceived or real threat of crop-raiding in agricultural plots. *P. kirkii* are considered a pest due to their coconut consumption, but their feeding leads to increased crop yield due to a pruning effect (Siex and Struhsaker 1999b). Poaching of colobus has been suspected in Pirang Community Forest, The Gambia (APH and Roy Armstrong, pers. obs.). Children throw items at colobus on the boundaries of protected land (APH pers. obs.). Free-ranging domestic dogs are an added threat as a result of human encroachment on reserves (e.g. P. Temminck's colobus in Fathala Forest, Senegal: Galat-Luong and Galat 2005; Abuko Nature Reserve: APH, pers. obs.; Bijilo Forest Park, The Gambia: Roy Armstrong, pers. comm.; *P. kirkii*: Georgiev et al. 2019).

Serious declines of *P. preussi* due to overhunting in Korup NP have been reported repeatedly, leading to a lower contribution of red colobus to bushmeat due to their rarity (Bobo et al. 2017; Hofner et al. 2018; Linder and Oates 2011; Waltert et al. 2002). Bobo et al. (2017) report hunting, habitat destruction and disease as the main causes of the decline of up to 80% of red colobus in Korup between 2000 and 2011; they are also hunted as a pet and for local rituals or medicine (Bobo et al. 2012; Fonkwo et al. 2018). Village abandonment can, however, help populations recover (Baya and Storch 2010; Korup 2007–2008).

Increased protection of Jozani forest in Zanzibar appears to have benefitted red colobus but the evident resentment of local people regarding their exclusion from the forest shows the complexities of trying to conserve primates (Salum 2009). This and previously mentioned studies identify the importance of understanding the complex relationship between humans and red colobus monkeys if we are to be successful in saving these primates.

Conservation concerns are also raised in relation to the presence of researchers who may bring diseases and parasites, or may increase the risk of the animals being shot by hunters as habituated groups do not flee from humans. Passive Acoustic Monitoring (PAM) and landscape genetic analysis may reduce these risks as they do not require habituation of animals and researchers are not close to the animals. PAM, may be less effective, however, for the short, low sound intensity calls of red colobus which lacks discrete loud calls, e.g. in Taï N. P., recall rates were lower for *P. badius* than for cercopithecines and *Colobus polykomos* (Heinicke et al. 2015). A novel landscape genetic approach found fire and proximity to villages to be the most important drivers with regard to genetic differentiation in *P. gordonorum* in Udzungwa (Ruiz-Lopez et al. 2016). Microbiome of the gut and vagina may also reveal new understanding of the phylogenetic relatedness among species and the influence of diet and recent environmental changes on populations (Yildirim et al. 2010, 2014).

Conclusion

This review shows the wide variation in red colobus natural history patterns but also highlights a lack of work on central African populations and a lack of recent studies on behaviour and ecology. Red colobus are also notable among the colobines for showing relatively great variation in group size, inter-group and intra-group relationships and dispersal patterns that suggest extreme flexibility in social systems in response to ecological pressures. Unfortunately, red colobus are threatened throughout their range and some of the observed flexibility is the direct result of populations trying to survive in greatly degraded and fragmented populations that are unlikely to be resilient against further degradation and the synergistic effects between habitat degradation, greater human-wildlife interactions and climate change.

Acknowledgements

We thank the editors for inviting us to write this chapter, their patience and reviews of earlier drafts. We thank Alex Georgiev for his constructive review of our draft. We thank Tom Struhsaker for his immense contribution to red colobus conservation and research. We thank the Red Colobus Conservation Network for their work on conserving red colobus and Drew Cronin for permission to use the red colobus range map. AHK and IK thank the Office Ivoirien des Parcs et Réserves (OIPR); the Taï Monkey Project, especially the field assistants who have taught us all about red colobus fieldwork; and the CSRS for support in Ivory Coast. APH and AHK thank the Department of Parks and Wildlife Management, The Gambia and Roy Armstrong for support in The Gambia and highlighting Gambian research.

10 Natural History of Black-and-White Colobus Monkeys

Peter J. Fashing

Introduction

The black-and-white colobus monkeys consist of five arboreal species classified in the genus *Colobus* (*C. angolensis*, *C. guereza*, *C. polykomos*, *C. satanas*, and *C. vellerosus*). Because of the sonorous early morning loud calls given by males and their often striking pelages (Oates and Trocco 1983; Oates et al. 1994), black-and-white colobus are among the most conspicuous primates in the forests they inhabit across equatorial and West Africa. At the same time, they are also generally shy and sedentary monkeys, rendering them challenging study subjects (Fashing 2011). All five species have long been targets of human hunters, for food or for their pelts (Bocian and Anderson 2013; Grubb et al. 1998; McGraw 2007; Mora et al. 2009; Oates 1977b), and habitat loss is a major threat to black-and-white colobus as well (Anderson et al. 2007a; de Jong et al. 2019; Matsuda Goodwin et al. 2019; Oates 1977b, 1996b). While the IUCN Red List classifies *C. guereza* as a species of Least Concern (de Jong et al. 2019), the other black-and-white colobus are regarded as being at greater risk of extinction (*C. angolensis* Vulnerable: de Jong et al. 2020; *C. satanas* Vulnerable: Maisels and Cronin 2020a; *C. polykomos* Endangered: Gonedelé Bi et al. 2020), especially *C. vellerosus* which was recently elevated to Critically Endangered status (Matsuda Goodwin et al. 2020).

Although, like all colobines, black-and-white colobus possess an unusual sacculated stomach well adapted to a folivorous diet (Chivers 1994), their diets often vary seasonally as well as across species and sites (Fashing 2011). Their patterns of activity, range use, and social organization also vary substantially between and within species (Fashing 2011). Here, I set out to summarize what is known about the natural history of *Colobus* as well as identify important areas for further research on this intriguing genus of monkeys.

Taxonomy and Distribution

The five *Colobus* species can be easily distinguished from one another by differences in their pelage (Figure 10.1; Oates et al. 1994). Four of the five species feature differing black-and-white pelage patterns while *C. satanas*, commonly known as the 'black colobus', is entirely black. *C. angolensis* or the 'Angolan colobus' occurs from coastal Kenya and Tanzania in the east to western DR Congo and Angola in the

This chapter includes Electronic Supplementary Material (ESM) at: www.cambridge.org/colobines

Figure 10.1 The five species of black-and-white colobus monkeys: (a) *Colobus angolensis*, (b) *C. guereza*, (c) *C. polykomos*, (d) *C. satanas* and (e) *C. vellerosus*. Photos (a), (c) and (d) by Noel B. Rowe; photo (b) by Yvonne A. de Jong and Tom M. Butynski; photo (e) by Lori-Ann Shibish.

west (ESM Table 10.1) though their distribution is disjunct with large gaps in much of Kenya and Uganda (Fashing 2016a). Because of the evolutionary divergence that has occurred between the many long isolated populations, seven subspecies are recognized today (*C. a. angolensis, C. a cordieri, C. a. cottoni, C. a palliatus, C. a. prigoginei, C. a. ruwenzorii, C. a. sharpei*) (Mittermeier et al. 2013). *C. guereza* or the 'guereza' has the widest distribution of the *Colobus* spp. occurring from Ethiopia, Kenya and Tanzania in the east to Nigeria, Cameroon and Gabon in the west (Fashing 2016b). Gaps also occur in *C. guereza*'s range in parts of East Africa, some of which are thought to have resulted from past intensive hunting practices for their especially beautiful pelts (Oates 1977b). Eight subspecies are presently recognized (*C. g. caudatus, C. g. dodingae, C. g. gallarum, C. g. guereza, C. g. kikuyuensis, C. g. matschiei, C. g. occidentalis, C. g. percivali*) (Mittermeier et al. 2013), though Butynski and de Jong (2018) recently suggested that *C. g. caudatus*, endemic to several forests in northern Tanzania and southern Kenya, warrants elevation to species status as *C. caudatus* due to its geographic isolation and phenotypic distinctiveness. *C. guereza* and *C. angolensis* are known to be sympatric in only one location, Ituri Forest, D.R. Congo (Bocian and Anderson 2013).

The ranges of the other three *Colobus* spp. are narrower, occurring largely in West Africa. *C. satanas* occurs only in Equatorial Guinea (including on the island of Bioko), Gabon and Rep. of Congo (Hearn and Butynski 2016). Two morphologically similar subspecies are recognized (*C. s. anthracinus* and *C. s. satanas*) (Mittermeier et al. 2013). It has long been posited that *C. satanas* and *C. guereza* are sympatric in southeastern Cameroon and northwestern Rep. of Congo, though this overlap has never been confirmed (Mitani 1990; Oates 1994). *C. polykomos* or the 'King colobus' occurs from southwestern Ivory Coast in the east to Guinea Bissau in the west (McGraw 2016). *C. vellerosus* or the 'white-thighed colobus' is distributed from southwestern Nigeria in the east to eastern Ivory Coast in the west (Saj and Sicotte 2016). Although no subspecies are recognized for either *C. polykomos* or *C. vellerosus*, *C. polykomos* × *C. vellerosus* hybrids, commonly referred to as

'Dollman's colobus' and bearing greater morphological similarity to *C. vellerosus* (Groves et al. 1993), occur in southwest-central Ivory Coast (Sery et al. 2006).

Research Efforts

Efforts to study black-and-white colobus natural history began more than a half century ago. Wolfgang Ullrich (1961) spent several months between 1955–1957 in the forests on the slopes of Mount Meru, Tanzania, gathering the first descriptive data on wild *C. guereza*. Other short studies of East African *C. guereza* populations followed, including those by Rudolph Schenkel and Lotte Schenkel-Hulliger (1967) in fragmented highland forest at Limuru, Kenya, Andrea Leskes and N. Acheson (1971) in gallery forest at Chobe, Uganda, Tim Clutton-Brock (1975a) in rain forest at Kibale, Uganda, Robin and Patsy Dunbar (1974, 1976) in gallery forests in northern and central Ethiopia, and Akira Suzuki (1979) in rain forest at Budongo, Uganda. One additional short study by Colin Groves (1973) focused on *C. guereza* in forest fragments in northern Tanzania as well as nearby but non-sympatric populations of *C. angolensis*. Though preliminary and confined to East Africa, these studies provided the first insights into black-and-white colobus behaviour, social organization and diet.

John Oates (1974, 1977a, 1977b, 1977c; Oates et al. 1977) carried out the first intensive ecological study of black-and-white colobus, collecting detailed dietary, ranging and behavioural data on *C. guereza* at Kanyawara study site in Kibale Forest, Uganda over a contiguous 17-month period in the early 1970s for his dissertation research (Figure 10.2). Over the next several decades, Oates's seminal work would inspire and provide a template for all other researchers studying black-and-white colobus, including many PhD students. Subsequent PhD research of comparable length on *C. guereza* was carried out by Carolyn Bocian on niche separation with

Figure 10.2 John Oates (left), seminal black-and-white colobus monkey researcher, in the field with blue monkey expert Rudy Rudran at Kibale Forest, Uganda in 1974. Photo by Peter Waser

sympatric *C. angolensis* in lowland rain forest at Ituri, D.R. Congo (Bocian 1997), Peter Fashing on inter-group relationships, diet and range use in mid-elevation rain forest at Kakamega, Kenya (Fashing 1999, 2001a,b,c), Tara Harris on male loud calls, inter-group relationships and reproduction in mid-elevation rain forest at Kibale, Uganda (Harris 2005, 2006a,b; Harris and Monfort 2006), Anne Marie Schel on male loud calls and other anti-predator behaviour in lowland rain forest at Budongo, Uganda (Schel 2009; Schel and Zuberbühler 2009, 2012a,b), and Dereje Yazezew (2018) and Dereje Tesfaye (2021, in press) on the impacts of planted forest, habitat fragmentation and other anthropogenic disturbance on feeding and ranging ecology in the highland rain forests of central and southern Ethiopia, respectively. During this period, Colin Chapman also led longitudinal work on nutritional and disease ecology in *C. guereza* populations in Kibale Forest (Chapman et al. 2003a; Hodder and Chapman 2012), as well as in fragments of varying sizes near Kibale (Chapman et al. 2007, 2013b; Onderdonk and Chapman 2000). Also recently, Ikki Matsuda and colleagues carried out a study of feeding ecology in a *Colobus guereza* group at Kalinzu Forest, Uganda (Matsuda et al. 2020a). Despite the many intensive research efforts on *C. guereza* in East Africa, the species remains unstudied in the western half of its distribution.

Following Groves's early observations of the species in northern Tanzania, Geraldine Moreno-Black carried out preliminary research on the habitat utilization and nutritional ecology of *C. angolensis* in lowland coastal forest at Diani, Kenya (Moreno-Black and Bent 1982; Moreno-Black and Maples 1977). In the early 1980s, Amy Vedder conducted the first intensive study of *C. angolensis*, focusing on the annual diet of a group of more than 300 individuals in montane rainforest at Nyungwe Forest, Rwanda (Vedder and Fashing 2002). In 1991, Fiona Maisels and colleagues completed an 8-month dietary study of *C. angolensis* in lowland rain forest at Salonga, D.R. Congo (Maisels et al. 1994). Carolyn Bocian's (1997) study of niche separation among sympatric *C. angolensis* and *C. guereza* at Ituri Forest in the mid-1990s was the first PhD study involving *C. angolensis*. Two follow-up studies to Vedder's work on *C. angolensis* at Nyungwe were published in the 2000s, another dietary study led by Cheryl Fimbel (Fimbel et al. 2001) and an activity and range use study led by Peter Fashing (Fashing et al. 2007b). During the same decade, Julie Anderson completed a PhD study of the ecology and conservation biology of *C. angolensis* in forest fragments and their surrounding matrix in the lowland coastal forests of southeastern Kenya (Anderson 2005; Anderson et al. 2007a,b,c).

In the mid-2010s, Noah Dunham carried out dissertation research on diet, habitat use and positional behaviour in *C. angolensis* in a fragment of lowland coastal forest at Diani, Kenya (Dunham 2017a,b; Dunham and Rodriguez-Saona 2018). Concurrently, in a lowland rainforest fragment at Nabugabo, Uganda, Julie Teichroeb began studying a group of 135 individually recognized monkeys belonging to the same subspecies (*C. angolensis ruwenzorii*) that forms the enormous groups at Nyungwe. Because no other *C. angolensis* subspecies is known to form semi-permanent groups of more than 20 individuals, *C. a. ruwenzorii* appears to be unusual. Teichroeb's longitudinal study with her students has to date focused on documenting the social organization (Stead and Teichroeb 2019), habitat use (Adams and Teichroeb 2020), and social bonding patterns of the colobus at Nabugabo (Arseneau-Robar et al. 2018) as well as the immediate impacts of selective logging on their behaviour and ecology (Teichroeb et al. 2019). Lastly, 2016–2017, Alex Miller carried out the first PhD study of the *C. angolensis* population at Nyungwe, Rwanda, focusing on unravelling the social organization of a 500-member study group and examining the selective pressures causing them to form such large groups at this site (Miller 2019; Miller et al. 2020a,b,c).

The first study of *C. vellerosus* was conducted by Dana Olson in the late 1970s in lowland rain forest at Bia, Ghana (Olson 1980, 1986). In 2000, Pascale Sicotte began a still-ongoing project on *C. vellerosus* in a lowland forest fragment at Boabeng-Fiema, Ghana, that is remarkable for being the first to longitudinally track individually recognized African colobines. Unusually detailed studies of dispersal, infanticide, natal attraction and many other topics have been explored in this population by Sicotte and her students (e.g. Bădescu et al. 2015; Sicotte and MacIntosh 2004; Teichroeb and Sicotte 2008a; Teichroeb et al. 2009a, 2011).

C. satanas was first studied briefly by J. Sabater Pí (1973) in Rio Muni, mainland Equatorial Guinea in the late 1960s. Doyle McKey carried out the first detailed work on the socioecology of the species for his PhD research in lowland rain forest at Douala-Edea, Cameroon (McKey 1979; McKey and Waterman 1982; McKey et al. 1981). Subsequent research on *C. satanas* diet and ranging was completed in lowland rain forest at Lopé, Gabon in the mid-1980s by Michael Harrison (Harrison 1986; Harrison and Hladik 1986) and in lowland rain forest at Fôret des Abeilles, Gabon in the mid-1990s by Annie Gautier-Hion (Gautier-Hion et al. 1997) and Marie-Claire Fleury (Fleury 1999; Fleury and Gautier-Hion 1999). Since the late 1980s, intermittent surveys for *C. satanas* and other primates have been carried out repeatedly by Tom Butynski and others in the lowland and montane forests on Bioko Island, Equatorial Guinea (Butynski and Koster 1994; Forrest et al. 2017).

C. polykomos is arguably the least studied black-and-white colobus, though two detailed PhD studies of its ecology have been completed by Georgina Dasilva in lowland rain forest on Tiwai Island, Sierra Leone (Dasilva 1989, 1992, 1993, 1994) and Amanda Korstjens in lowland rain forest at Taï, Ivory Coast (Korstjens 2001; Korstjens et al. 2002, 2005).

Habitat and Climate

All species of black-and-white colobus occur in both primary and secondary lowland rain forests, as well as fragmented forests and gallery forests (ESM Table 10.1). While the other species are believed to be better adapted to undisturbed habitats, *C. guereza* is exceptional in that it achieves much higher densities in forest fragments, gallery forests, and continuous secondary forests than in primary forests (Bocian 1997; Dunbar 1987; Fashing and Cords 2000; Oates 1977a). *C. guereza* is also unique among black-and-white colobus in having been reported to occur in planted forest, though it fares less well in such habitat than in nearby continuous secondary forest

(Fashing et al. 2012). All black-and-white colobus species also inhabit some form of lowland dry forest (ESM Table 10.1). In the cases of *C. angolensis*, *C. polykomos* and *C. satanas*, these dry forests are sometimes in coastal areas, including the unique coral rag and mangrove forests occupied by *C. angolensis* in southeastern Kenya (Bocian and Anderson 2013; Dunham 2017a). Swamp forests also provide rare habitat for *C. guereza*, *C. polykomos* and *C. satanas*, and at Kibale contain sodium-rich swamp plants coveted by *C. guereza* (Oates 1978). Lastly, *C. guereza*, *C. angolensis* and *C. satanas* all also inhabit montane forests, reaching elevations as high as 3300 m (Oates 1977b), 2415 m (Fashing et al. 2007b) and 3000 m (Butynski and Koster 1994), respectively (ESM Table 10.1).

Rainfall is seasonal in African tropical forests, though at least some rain falls each month at most locations where black-and-white colobus have been studied (Oates 1994). Annual rainfall of between 1370 and 3750 mm is typical, with populations in West Africa generally experiencing more rainfall than those in East Africa (e.g. Kalinzu: 1370 mm, Matsuda et al. 2020a; Kibale: 1485 mm, Oates 1994; Diani: 1550 mm, Dunham 2017a; Fôret des Abeilles: 1721 mm, Fleury and Gautier-Hion 1999; Ituri: 1729 mm, Bocian 1997; Nyungwe: 1867 mm, Nyirambangutse et al. 2017; Kakamega: 2220 mm, Cords 1987; Tiwai: 2857 mm, Dasilva 1989; Douala-Edea: 3750 mm, McKey 1979). *C. satanas* in southern Bioko are unusual in that they experience a remarkable >10,000 mm of rain each year (Butynski and Koster 1994; Juste and Fa 1994). Conversely, much lower rainfall of only 700–1200 mm annually is typical of the driest forest sites where black-and-white colobus occur (Fashing and Oates 2013; Fay 1985).

Diet

Of the African colobines, black-and-white colobus exhibit the greatest dietary variability (Fashing 2011). Although most black-and-white colobus eat mostly leaves, substantial dietary variation has been documented between species, between populations within species, and even within single populations over time (ESM Table 10.2).

C. satanas is the only species of black-and-white colobus that cannot be classified as mostly folivorous. At all three sites where they have been studied (Douala-Edea, Lopé and Fôret des Abeilles), their annual diet consists of more fruit (50%–64%), primarily seeds, than leaves (26%–39%) (Fleury and Gautier-Hion 1999; Gautier-Hion et al. 1997; Harrison in Oates 1994; McKey 1978b; McKey et al. 1981). The unusually granivorous diet of *C. satanas* is also more species-rich (mean = 86 species, range 65–109) than the diets of the other more folivorous black-and-white colobus (mean = 46 species, range 27–73) (ESM Table 10.2). Studies of *C. polykomos* have included both a population in Taï Forest that was found to consume fruit (48%) and leaves (48%) at equivalent levels (Korstjens et al. 2007b) and another on Tiwai Island that ate more leaves (58%) than fruit (35%), though fruit (mostly seeds) accounted for up to 75% of the monthly diet on Tiwai when abundant (Dasilva 1994). *C. vellerosus* appears to be the most strongly folivorous (79%) of the West African black-and-white colobus species based on research at a single site, Boabeng-Fiema (Saj and Sicotte 2007a).

The diets of the two most studied species, *C. angolensis* and *C. guereza*, vary widely over time and space (ESM Table 10.2). Studies of *C. angolensis* supergroups (>300->500 individuals) at Nyungwe carried out in 1987–1988 and 2016–2017 revealed a heavy dependence on lichen (21%–32% of annual diet), with lichen accounting for >50% of the diet in months when preferred food items were scarce (Miller et al. 2020a; Vedder and Fashing 2002). This intensive lichen consumption by colobus at Nyungwe is unique among African colobines though has parallels among several Chinese snub-nosed monkeys that also form enormous groups (e.g. *Rhinopithecus bieti, R. roxellana*) (Guo et al. 2007; Kirkpatrick et al. 1998; Chapter 12). Intriguingly, a third dietary study carried out on a *C. angolensis* supergroup at Nyungwe in 1993 (believed to be the same group studied by Miller and colleagues 23 years later: Miller et al. 2020a) found that the monkeys consumed only 5% lichen and that an unusually large proportion (72%) of their annual diet consisted of leaves (Fimbel et al. 2001). This result indicates that the potential for inter-annual variation in diet among *C. angolensis* at Nyungwe is substantial. Miller et al. (2020a) suggest that differences in lichen consumption between the three dietary studies of *C. angolensis* at Nyungwe may be linked to differences in preferred food availability across study periods with 1993 likely having been a banner year for preferred food abundance. Dietary variability is also wide between populations of *C. angolensis*. A population at Ituri ate 50% leaves and 28% fruit (Bocian 1997) while another at Diani was more folivorous at 71% leaves and 14% fruit (Dunham 2017a).

C. guereza exhibits a similar pattern of dietary variability across sites. Multiple studies have been carried out at Kibale and all have found *C. guereza* there to be extremely folivorous (≥80% leaves) (Clutton-Brock 1975a; Harris and Chapman 2007; Oates 1977a; Wasserman and Chapman 2003). Similarly, a recent study of *C. guereza* at Kalinzu revealed that their diet consisted of 87% leaves (Matsuda et al. 2020a). However, at Budongo, Ituri and Kakamega, *C. guereza* ate only 51%–63% leaves overall, with their diets shifting towards being dominated by fruit during months when fruit was most available (Bocian 1997; Fashing 2001b; Plumptre 2006). For example, at Kakamega, during the six months of greatest fruit availability, monthly fruit consumption averaged 50% and reached as high as 81% in November (Fashing 2001b).

Across species and study sites, black-and-white colobus exhibit a tendency to choose young leaves over mature leaves when both are widely available (Dasilva 1994; McKey et al. 1981; Oates 1977a; Tesfaye et al. 2021). This pattern can be explained by the greater nutritional value (higher protein, lower fibre) of young leaves relative to mature leaves (Chapman et al. 2004; Fashing et al. 2007a). Still, the specialized colobine digestive anatomy enables black-and-white colobus to fall back on mature leaves when young leaves are scarce (Dasilva 1994; Fashing 2001, 2004; McKey et al. 1981; Oates 1977a). Occasionally, the nutritional quality of mature leaves in a forest is unusually high, enabling colobus to eat them in large quantities throughout the year. This was the case for *C. angolensis* in Nyungwe Forest during

Fimbel et al.'s (2001) study when mature leaves comprised 40% of the diet (versus 32% young and unidentified leaves) and were of greater nutritional quality than even young leaves at some other colobine study sites.

Recent nutritional studies have moved beyond assessing whether *Colobus* select for high protein content (*C. angolensis* at Salonga: Maisels et al. 1994; *C. guereza* at Ituri: Bocian 1997), low fibre content (*C. angolensis* at Ituri: Bocian 1997), or both (*C. guereza* at Kibale: Chapman et al. 2004; *C. guereza* at Kakamega: Fashing et al. 2007a; *C. satanas* at Douala-Edea: McKey et al. 1981), emphasizing the role of nutrient balancing in the diet. Studies of *C. guereza* at Kibale (Johnson et al. 2017) and *C. angolensis* at Diani (Dunham and Rodriguez-Saona 2018) found that both species exhibit consistent nutrient balancing strategies, though the average daily intake ratios of non-protein energy to available protein differed greatly between them (*C. guereza*, 3.9:1 vs. *C. angolensis*, 1.5:1). Determining whether these differences in nutrient balancing behaviour are related to phylogenetic differences or are simply site-specific will require further study.

Relatively few studies have examined the impacts of selective logging, forest fragmentation and other forms of anthropogenic disturbance on *Colobus* diets. Only two studies, both on *C. guereza* populations (Budongo and Kibale) in western Uganda, have compared *Colobus* diets in selectively logged versus in unlogged forests. Both studies revealed higher levels of fruit consumption by *C. guereza* in logged forest areas (Wasserman and Chapman 2003; Plumptre et al. 2006). The study at Budongo also examined dietary species richness and found values to be almost identical in each forest type (Plumptre et al. 2006).

Studies in southern Ethiopia and at Kibale comparing the diets of *C. guereza* in fragments versus in relatively undisturbed continuous forest both found that groups in fragments consumed more fruits but fewer leaves than those in continuous forest (Tesfaye et al. 2021; Wasserman and Chapman 2003). The study in southern Ethiopia also found that *C. guereza* dietary species richness was higher in fragmented forest (Tesfaye et al. 2021). Similarly, dietary species richness values were higher for *C. angolensis* in forest fragments at Diani (n = 70–73 species; Dunham 2017a) than for conspecifics in continuous forests at Ituri (n = 37 species; Bocian 1997) and Nyungwe (n = 45–67 species; Fimbel et al. 2001; Miller et al. 2020a; Vedder and Fashing 2002). An unusually high reliance on exotic species by *Colobus* in fragments at both Diani and in southern Ethiopia accounts for some of the dietary differences identified between populations in fragments and those in less disturbed continuous forest (Dunham 2017a; Tesfaye et al., 2021).

The diet of *C. vellerosus* has been studied intensively in fragmented forest at Boabeng-Fiema (Saj and Sicotte 2007a; Wong and Sicotte 2006) but nothing has been published on the diet of this species in continuous forest for comparative purposes. Conversely, the diets of both *C. polykomos* and *C. satanas* have been well documented in continuous forest (Dasilva 1994; Fleury and Gautier-Hion 1999; Gautier-Hion et al. 1997; Harrison in Oates 1994; Korstjens et al. 2007b; McKey et al. 1981) but have not yet been studied in fragmented forest.

Activity Patterns

Black-and-white colobus are unusually sedentary monkeys (ESM Table 10.3), rivalled by few other primates for their levels of inactivity (Campbell et al. 2011a). Indeed, black-and-white colobus are markedly less active (mean = 54% time spent resting per day, n = 10 populations; ESM Table 10.3) than the other African colobines (red colobus mean = 47%, n = 10 populations; olive colobus = 40%, n = 1 population; Fashing 2011). This result has been attributed to the greater average intake of mature leaves by black-and-white colobus and their concomitant greater reliance on foregut fermentation, which requires long periods of rest to facilitate digestion (Fashing 2011). Of the field studies of black-and-white colobus, Dasilva's (1992, 1993) research on *C. polykomos* on Tiwai Island explored activity strategies in the greatest detail. She provided compelling evidence that the low activity levels of this population were part of a behavioural, rather than physiological, strategy of conserving energy (Dasilva 1992, 1993). *C. polykomos*'s strategy of behavioural thermoregulation involves actions like reducing energy expenditure at times of preferred food scarcity and adopting hunched positions during rainstorms and when the temperature is low (Dasilva 1992, 1993).

Among the 10 black-and-white colobus populations studied to date, two *C. angolensis* populations are unusual in that they spend less than half of their time resting (ESM Table 10.3; Nyungwe 32%: Fashing et al. 2007b; Ituri 43%: Bocian 1997). *C. angolensis* at Nyungwe are by far the most active *Colobus* population, devoting 42% of their time to feeding and an additional 20% to moving. The unusual activity levels of *C. angolensis* at Nyungwe may be associated with life in large, crowded supergroups and the resulting feeding competition over young leaves and other preferred resources at this site (Fashing et al. 2007b; Miller et al. 2020b). The high activity levels of the 19-member *C. angolensis* group studied at Ituri are more challenging to explain, though may relate in part to the low density of food species at this site (Bocian 1997). The more '*Colobus* typical' activity budget of a third *C. angolensis* study population at Diani (Dunham 2015) suggests that the high activity levels at Nyungwe and Ituri are not the result of phylogenetic differences among *Colobus* at the species level.

Range Use

Mirroring their low activity levels, black-and-white colobus also generally occupy small home ranges and travel short distances each day. However, while mean daily path lengths of black-and-white colobus are consistently low (range = 307–983 m, n = 12 studies; ESM Table 10.4) relative to most other primates (Campbell et al. 2011a), home range size is much more variable (ESM Table 10.4). Groups of *C. angolensis* in Nyungwe Forest and *C. satanas* in Fôret des Abeilles, for example, are unusual in that they adopt semi-nomadic lifestyles involving the occupation of very large ranges that continue to expand in size even after years of study (Fashing et al. 2007b; Fleury and Gautier-Hion 1999). In fact, *C. angolensis*'s home range of

2440 ha at Nyungwe is among the largest home ranges ever recorded for a forest-dwelling primate, and as with so much of their ecology, is probably linked to their enormous group size (Fashing et al. 2007b). Curiously, a 19-member group of *C. angolensis* at Ituri also occupied an unusually large, though still much smaller, home range of 371 ha, thought to be explained by the low density of food species at this site (Bocian 1997). Conversely, three small groups in fragmented forest at Diani survived in home ranges of only 6, 9 and 11 ha, respectively, revealing that *C. angolensis* possesses impressive flexibility in habitat use patterns when faced with habitat fragmentation and disturbance (Dunham 2017a).

Among *C. satanas*, only the group studied at Fôret des Abeilles has been described as semi-nomadic covering a range of 573 ha (Fleury and Gautier-Hion 1999), though groups at the two other *C. satanas* study sites also have larger than typical home ranges for black-and-white colobus (Lopé: 184 ha, Harrison in Oates 1994; Douala-Edea: 60 ha, McKey et al. 1982). These relatively large ranges are probably associated with the foraging challenges posed by the patchy spatial and temporal distribution of *C. satanas*'s primary food item, seeds (McKey et al. 1982). Home range size for *C. polykomos* has been documented at two sites, Tiwai (24 ha: Dasilva 1989) and Taï (77 ha: Korstjens 2001). Home range size for *C. vellerosus* has also been reported for two sites, one a continuous forest (Bia) and one a forest fragment (Boabeng-Fiema). The study group in the continuous forest occupied a home range (48 ha) more than four times the size of the mean home range for five study groups in the fragment (11 ha) (Olson 1986; Teichroeb and Sicotte 2009).

C. guereza usually occupies small home ranges of 8–33 ha in continuous forests, though the group studied at Ituri represents an exception in that it exploited a 100 ha range (ESM Table 10.4). Like for *C. angolensis* at this site, the large range of *C. guereza* may be linked to the low density of food species at Ituri (Bocian 1997). Short studies in fragments indicate that like *C. angolensis*, *C. guereza* can survive in very small ranges where necessary (2.0 ha: Schenkel and Schenkel-Hulliger 1967; 1.5 ha: Leskes and Acheson 1971; 2.1 ha: Dunbar 1987; 3.7 ha: Kruger et al. 1998; 4.8 ha: Rose 1978). However, subsequent longer studies near Kibale have shown that fragmented populations are highly vulnerable to extirpation over time at sites where habitat degradation is severe (Chapman et al. 2007, 2013b).

Like many other primates, most black-and-white colobus exhibit seasonal variation in ranging patterns corresponding with changes in food availability and/or consumption of major dietary items (e.g. young leaves: *C. angolensis* at Ituri, Bocian 1997; seeds: *C. polykomos* at Tiwai, Dasilva 1989; *C. satanas* at Fôret des Abeilles, Lopé and Douala-Edea, Fleury et al. 1999; Harrison in Oates 1994; McKey and Waterman 1982). However, among *C. guereza* at both Kibale and Kakamega, variability in ranging patterns over time appears to be more related to the distribution of infrequently eaten food items that are spatially rare yet nutritionally important, like sodium-rich swamp plants or *Eucalyptus* (Myrtaceae) bark (Fashing 2001a, 2007; Harris and Chapman 2007a; Oates 1978). At Kakamega, for example, although on most days they travelled less than 600 m, groups of *C. guereza* periodically ventured far beyond the 'normal' boundaries of their home range on excursions through intensely defended areas of the ranges of other groups to reach a grove of exotic *Eucalyptus* on the edge of the forest from which they stripped and ate the bark (Fashing 2001a; Fashing et al. 2007a). Total daily path lengths in such instances could exceed mean daily path lengths by over 200% (Fashing 2001a). Thus, *C. guereza* appears to differ from other black-and-white colobus in that variability in its ranging patterns over time may be driven more by rare but nutritionally unique items than by major food items (Fashing et al. 2007a).

Predation

Known natural predators of black-and-white colobus include crowned-hawk eagles (*Stephanoaetus coronatus*), chimpanzees (*Pan troglodytes*), leopards (*Panthera pardus*) and lions (*Panthera leo*). For *C. guereza*, the primary predator appears to be crowned-hawk eagles. Studies in two nearby forest compartments at Kanyawara (Kibale Forest, Uganda) found that *C. guereza* accounted for 39% and 10%, respectively, of the prey of crowned-hawk eagles (Skorupa 1987; Struhsaker and Leakey 1990). In comparison, the rate of chimpanzee predation on *C. guereza* at another Kibale site (Ngogo) proved to be quite low, with the species accounting for only 4% of the chimpanzee's mammalian prey items (Watts and Mitani 2002). Leopards prey on black-and-white colobus at several sites. *C. angolensis* and *C. guereza* combined accounted for 1% of prey items in leopard scats at Ituri Forest (Hart et al. 1996), *C. polykomos* remains were found in 2%–8% of leopard scats at Taï Forest, Ivory Coast (Hoppe-Dominik 1984, Zuberbühler and Jenny 2002), and *C. vellerosus* accounted for up to 10% of the prey items found in leopard scats at Comoé National Park, Ivory Coast (Bodendorfer et al. 2006). *C. vellerosus* are also eaten by lions at Comoé accounting for 5% of the prey items in lion scats at this site (Bodendorfer et al. 2006).

The impact of predation by eagles and leopards on black-and-white colobus evolution is evident in their alarm calling system. Black-and-white colobus often engage in spontaneous early morning loud call choruses referred to as 'roars', and these roars are also sometimes given in response to the sight or sound of predators (Harris et al. 2006; Marler 1969, 1972; Oates et al. 2000b; Poirier-Poulin and Teichroeb 2020). A comparative playback study of *C. guereza* at Budongo Forest and *C. polykomos* at Taï Forest found that for both species leopard vocalizations elicited alarm call responses typically consisting of a snort followed by a few roaring phrases while eagle vocalizations elicited calls generally consisting of no snort and many phrases (Schel et al. 2009). An additional study focusing solely on *C. guereza* at Budongo found that following playback of their roaring utterances denoting leopards, monkeys scanned the area beneath them, while following playback of roaring utterances indicating eagles, monkeys scanned the sky above them (Schel et al. 2010). Thus, black-and-white colobus are obviously closely attuned to the vocalizations of predators and have a sophisticated system for communicating their presence to conspecifics.

Social Organization

The social organizations of black-and-white colobus are diverse (ESM Table 10.5). Some species, like *C. guereza*, nearly always form small groups, typically averaging 7–11 individuals and never exceeding 23 individuals (ESM Table 10.5). Others like *C. polykomos*, *C. satanas* and *C. vellerosus* average ~15 individuals per group, with maximum observed group sizes of 19, 25 and 38, respectively (ESM Table 10.5). *C. angolensis* group sizes are less consistent, ranging from as small as 2–9 individuals per group in northeastern Tanzania to more than 300–500 individuals in some groups of *C. a. ruwenzorii* at Nyungwe (ESM Table 10.5). Multiple *C. a. ruwenzorii* groups have also been reported to form temporary to semi-permanent associations with one another in two forests in southern Uganda, resulting in aggregations of as many as 51 individuals (Sango Bay: Oates 1974, 1994) and 135 individuals (Nabugabo: Stead and Teichroeb 2019), respectively. Recent longitudinal research on recognized individuals revealed that the large group at Nabugabo reflects a multilevel society consisting of many core units each containing multiple females and their offspring and one or more males (Stead and Teichroeb 2019). Another recent study employing social network analysis of clusters of individuals identified to age/sex class during progressions concluded that a >500 member supergroup at Nyungwe represents a complex multilevel society as well (Miller et al. 2020c). These exciting new studies suggest that multilevel social organizations may be typical of *C. a. ruwenzorii.* Curiously, observations of two or more groups coalescing peacefully – though for much shorter periods than in *C. a. ruwenzorii* – have been reported in *C. a. palliata* at Diani (Moreno-Black and Bent 1982) and in *C. a cottoni* at Ituri (Bocian 1997).

Habitat type, logging history, predation risk, dietary choices, feeding competition and infanticide risk all appear to influence black-and-white colobus group sizes. For example, among *C. guereza* populations across East Africa, mean group size tends to be lower in gallery or scrub forest than in rain forest (Dunbar 1987). Evidence that logging history influences group size comes from Kibale, where *C. guereza* groups in lightly logged forest are 25% smaller than those in unlogged forest (Struhsaker 1997). The influence of predation risk on group size can be inferred by comparing black-and-white colobus group sizes at locations with and without certain predators. Struhsaker (2000a) has shown that on Bioko, where crowned-hawk eagles are absent, groups of *C. satanas* are distinctly smaller than in forests on the African mainland, where crowned-hawk eagles occur.

Dietary choices and their interaction with digestive physiology may also influence black-and-white colobus group size. Korstjens and Dunbar (2007) used a systems model incorporating data on ecology and climate to predict that median group size for *Colobus* spp. should be 19, only slightly higher than the actual values in nature. They contend that most black-and-white colobus populations are constrained to small groups for primates because of the low digestibility of their food sources resulting from a reliance on mature leaves as fallback foods, requiring them to devote more time to resting than most other primates (Korstjens and Dunbar 2007).

Furthermore, a field study by Teichroeb and Sicotte (2009) provided evidence consistent with the hypothesis that feeding competition sets the upper limits of group size for *C. vellerosus* at Boabeng-Fiema. Conversely, Chapman and Pavelka (2005) found that it is not ecological variables, but rather infanticide risk [which increases with increasing group size in some primates (Crockett and Janson 2000)], that appears to limit group size for *C. guereza* at Kibale.

Groups of all black-and-white colobus species nearly always include multiple adult females and most, aside from *C. guereza* and a few populations of *C. angolensis*, also usually contain multiple males (ESM Table 10.5). Single male groups are typical in *C. guereza*, though even in this species multi-male groups are not particularly uncommon. Dunbar and Dunbar (1976) suggested the multi-male condition is temporary and unstable for *C. guereza*, though multi-male groups are common at Kakamega and the male composition of these groups can remain consistent for many years (Fashing and Oates 2013).

Like for most primates, the mating systems of black-and-white colobus are related to group composition. Where one-male groups occur, mating is typically polygynous, in which the group male generally monopolizes copulations with females in his group (e.g. *C. guereza*: Bocian 1997, Fashing 2001c). The seasonal multi-male influxes that typify some guenons (*Cercopithecus* spp.) often occupying the same forests as colobines (Cords 1984; Cords et al. 1986) do not occur among black-and-white colobus. Multi-male groups of black-and-white colobus are characterized by promiscuous mating (e.g. *C. angolensis*: Bocian 1997; *C. polykomos*: Dasilva 1989; *C. vellerosus*: Teichroeb and Sicotte 2008b).

Dispersal patterns have been studied in detail only in *C. guereza* and *C. vellerosus*, though preliminary data on the topic are available for *C. polykomos*, *C. satanas* and *C. angolensis* as well. Among *C. guereza* at Kibale, only males have been observed dispersing from their natal groups (Harris et al. 2009; Oates 1977c). The results of subsequent genetic research are also consistent with male-biased dispersal, though suggest that females occasionally disperse too at this site (Harris et al. 2009). More limited observational data on *C. guereza* at Kakamega match up with the genetic results from Kibale, with males being the primary dispersers and females dispersing infrequently as well (Fashing and Oates 2013). *C. vellerosus* at Boabeng-Fiema also exhibit a pattern of male-biased dispersal, though female dispersal is not uncommon (Teichroeb et al. 2009a, 2011). Male *C. vellerosus* most often disperse to groups with lower adult male: adult female ratios or to groups in which they can obtain higher ranks, both strategies probably resulting in improved mating prospects for the transferring male (Teichroeb et al. 2011). Patterns of female dispersal in *C. vellerosus* suggest that they are attracted to groups with 'high quality' males, and that dispersal may help females to reduce their vulnerability to infanticide and improve their access to food (Sicotte et al. 2017; Teichroeb et al. 2009a). Among *C. polykomos* and *C. satanas*, observational research suggests that both sexes disperse, with males appearing to do so more consistently (Dasilva 1989; Fleury 1999; Fleury and Brugière 2013; M. Harrison in Oates 1994; Korstjens et al. 2005; Korstjens and Galat-Luong 2013; Nijssen 1999). Among *C. angolensis* at

Nabugabo, preliminary observations suggest that males and females disperse at equal rates (Arseneau-Robar et al. 2018).

Sexual Behaviour and Reproduction

The sexual behaviour and reproductive parameters are not well known for most species of black-and-white colobus though some scattered information is available (ESM Table 10.6). Copulatory behaviour has been described in one or more populations of all five species. Both sexes solicit copulations among *C. guereza* at Kakamega (Fashing 2011) and Kibale (Harris and Monfort 2006; Oates 1977c) and among *C. vellerosus* at Boabeng-Fiema (Saj and Sicotte 2016). Only males solicit copulations in *C. polykomos* at Tiwai (Dasilva 1989) and *C. angolensis* at Ituri (Bocian 1997), while among *C. angolensis* at Diani and *C. satanas* at Fôret des Abeilles (Fleury 1999), it is only females who solicit copulations (Bocian and Anderson 2013). Copulation calls are not given in any species of black-and-white colobus. Harassment of mating pairs by juveniles is common in *C. guereza* at Kibale (Harris and Monfort 2003; Oates 1977c) and Kakamega (Fashing, pers. observ.) and in *C. vellerosus* at Boabeng-Fiema (Teichroeb, pers. comm.), but has not been reported for other species. Sexual consortships, where pairs separate from their group to mate, are not known to occur in any black-and-white colobus. Females of *C. satanas* and at least one subspecies of *C. angolensis* (*C. a cottoni*) exhibit slight perineal swellings for several days per month when cycling, and in the case of *C. satanas*, also around the time of giving birth (Bocian 1997; Fleury and Brugière 2013).

Age at first pregnancy is known only for *C. vellerosus* at Boabeng-Fiema where it averages 5.82 years (n = 8; Vayro et al. 2016). Hormonal monitoring of two female *C. vellerosus* at Boabeng-Fiema and four female *C. guereza* at Kibale revealed mean gestation lengths of 155 days (Vayro et al. 2016) and 158 days (Harris and Monfort 2006), respectively. Interbirth interval tends to be shorter in *C. guereza* (Kakamega: 17 months, Fashing 2002; Kibale: 21.5 months, Harris and Monfort 2006) and *C. vellerosus* (Boabeng-Fiema: 17.8 months, Vayro et al. 2016) than in *C. satanas* (Fôret des Abeilles: 24 months, Fleury 1999) and *C. polykomos* (Tiwai: 24 months, Dasilva 1989; Taï: 26 months, Korstjens and Galat-Luong 2013). Dunbar (1987, 2018) inferred that *C. guereza* interbirth intervals are significantly longer in multi-male groups than in one-male groups, arguing that the stress created by competition among males in multi-male groups results in reproductive suppression among the females in these groups.

Birth seasonality is absent in most populations of black-and-white colobus [*C. angolensis* at Diani (Anderson 2005), Ituri (Bocian 1997), and Nyungwe (Fimbel et al. 2001); *C. guereza* at Kakamega (Fashing 1999, 2002) and Kibale (Oates 1977c); *C. polykomos* at Taï (Korstjens and Galat-Luong 2013); *C. vellerosus* at Boabeng-Fiema (Saj and Sicotte 2013)]. Curiously, however, *C. polykomos* at Tiwai do display strict birth seasonality, giving birth only between December–February (Dasilva 1989). Furthermore, preliminary evidence suggests *C. satanas* at both Douala-Edea (McKey 1979) and Fôret des Abeilles (Fleury 1999) exhibit some degree of birth seasonality as well. It should also be noted that two of the aseasonally breeding *Colobus* spp., *C. guereza* and *C. vellerosus*, do exhibit considerable synchrony in birth timing among females within groups (Fashing 2002; Oates 1977c; Teichroeb and Sicotte 2008b). Among *C. vellerosus*, this intra-group synchrony can be attributed to new males frequently killing the existing dependent infants following group take-overs and all females subsequently coming into oestrus again concurrently (Teichroeb and Sicotte 2008b; Teichroeb, pers. comm.).

Infants of all black-and-white colobus species except *C. satanas* are born with entirely white coats which contrast strikingly with those of adults (Oates 1994). During the first few months of life, when black-and-white colobus infants remain flamboyantly coloured, they are very attractive to, and are often held by, females other than their mothers (Bădescu et al. 2015; Brent et al. 2008; Dasilva 1989; Dunham and Opere 2016; Horwich and Manski 1975; Korstjens 2001; Oates 1977c). Black-and-white colobus males almost never interact affiliatively with infants, though there are a few notable exceptions to this pattern. In a recent comparative study of *C. angolensis ruwenzorii* at Nabugabo and *C. vellerosus* at Boabeng-Fiema, males of both taxa sometimes handled infants, though rates of infant handling were far higher in the *C. a. ruwenzorii* population (Stead et al. 2021). Intriguingly, males have also been reported to carry infants in the large groups of *C. a. ruwenzorii* at Nyungwe (Fashing 2011), suggesting frequent male care of infants may be yet another behaviour that makes this subspecies unusual among black-and-white colobus.

Key Directions for Future Research on Black-and-White Colobus Monkey Natural History

After more than a half century of field research, much is now known about the natural history of black-and-white colobus monkeys. However, it also readily apparent that many gaps in our understanding still exist and, in this section, I set out to identify and briefly explore some of the most interesting or pressing research avenues remaining to be pursued in *Colobus* natural history. These are, of course, but a fraction of the potential projects that could be carried out on these beautiful and fascinating monkeys.

While most black-and-white colobus form small to medium sized groups that are largely mutually intolerant of one another (*C. guereza*: Fashing 2001c; Harris 2006a, 2010; *C. polykomos*: Korstjens et al. 2005; *C. vellerosus*: Sicotte and MacIntosh 2004), some *C. angolensis* are now known to offer a marked exception to this pattern. The Central African subspecies, *C. a. ruwenzorii*, is particularly notable for the large, complex multilevel societies it forms at Nyungwe and Nabugabo, sites where intensive research is ongoing and revealing novel insights into the benefits and costs of living in such large groups (Miller et al. 2020b,c; Stead and Teichroeb 2019). Curiously, though they form much smaller groups, two other subspecies, *C. a. cottoni* at Ituri and *C. a. palliata* at Diani, have also been described as having relaxed inter-group relations and forming multi-group aggregations, albeit much more transient aggregations than in *C. a. ruwenzorii* (Bocian 1997; Moreno-Black and Bent 1982). The possibility that multilevel social organizations – some more dispersed than others – exist across many or even all *C. angolensis* subspecies warrants investigation and provides strong justification for intensive future research focus on this species across its geographic distribution. Furthermore, *C. angolensis* has the potential to offer an unusual colobine model for human evolution, given that hominin societies have also come to be recognized as multilevel in nature (Chapais 2008; Grueter et al. 2012a, 2020; Stead and Teichroeb 2019). Lastly, investigating why multilevel societies are unique to *C. angolensis* among the African colobines is also a promising avenue for research.

As is readily apparent from this review, *C. guereza* has been studied at many more sites than any other black-and-white colobus monkey. Yet, the vast majority of these studies have been conducted in Uganda and Kenya, especially the most intensive projects (e.g. Chapman et al. 2013b; Fashing 1999; Harris 2005; Oates 1974; Schel 2009). Even in Kenya, an endangered subspecies, *C. g. percivali*, endemic to the Mathews Range in the remote northwest of the country, has been largely ignored, and deserves urgent survey work and ecological study given its dire conservation status (de Jong and Butynski 2012; Mwenja 2009). After decades of taxonomic uncertainty (Fashing and Oates 2013; Yalden et al. 1977), recent genetic research suggests that the two *C. guereza* subspecies endemic to Ethiopia are unequally distributed, with *C. g. guereza* much more widespread and *C. g. gallarum* limited to a small section of eastern Ethiopia (Zinner et al. 2019). While *C. g. guereza* has been the subject of preliminary study in the early 1970s (Dunbar 1987; Dunbar and Dunbar 1974, 1976) as well as of two intensive recent PhD projects (Yazezew 2018; Tesfaye 2021, in press), *C. g. gallarum* has never been studied. Like for *C. g. percivali*, urgent survey and ecological work are needed for *C. g. gallarum* given its limited geographic distribution and the high rate of ongoing forest clearance in Ethiopia (Global Forest Watch 2019). Lastly, although *C. guereza*'s range extends as far west as eastern Nigeria, the species has never been studied west of eastern D.R. Congo. Potential for remedying this gap in our knowledge of the natural history of this widely distributed species exists at sites like Gashaka-Gumti National Park, Nigeria and Dzanga-Sangha National Park, Central African Republic where protected western populations of the species occur.

Bocian's (1997) thesis work on niche separation between sympatric *C. angolensis* and *C. guereza* at Ituri, D.R. Congo remains exceptional among studies of black-and-white colobus monkeys to date. The only other likely area of sympatry between black-and-white colobus species has long been rumoured to be in southeastern Cameroon and northwestern Rep. of Congo (Mitani 1990; Oates 1994). More detailed surveys in this region are needed, and if sympatry is confirmed as expected, a detailed study of niche separation between *C. guereza* and *C. satanas* must be a priority. The considerable dietary differences already documented between non-sympatric populations of these species (ESM Table 10.2) are likely to be magnified in areas of sympatry.

Several studies of the impacts of forest fragmentation on the ecology of *C. angolensis* and *C. guereza* have been carried out to date (Anderson 2005;

Anderson et al. 2007a,b; Chapman et al. 2006b, 2007, 2013b; Dunham 2017a,b; Dunham and Lambert 2016; Dunham and Rodriguez-Saona 2018; Onderdonk and Chapman 2000; Tesfaye et al. 2021; Wasserman and Chapman 2003; Yazezew, n.d.). Both species have the flexibility to cope with life in fragments (Anderson 2005; Dunham 2017a; Fashing and Oates 2013; Tesfaye et al. 2021), with *C. guereza* especially well adapted to fragmentation of its habitat (Fashing and Oates 2013), at least up to a certain threshold of severe degradation (Chapman et al. 2007, 2013b). The ecology of *C. vellerosus* in forest fragments is also well documented (e.g. Teichroeb et al. 2003; Wong and Sicotte 2006, 2007) though comparative data on the species in continuous forests remains largely absent from the literature (though Olson 1986 and Oates 1994 offer a few details). Given that the species is among the 25 most endangered primates on Earth (Schwitzer et al. 2019) and it has already been more than two decades since Oates (1999) raised the alarm about the increasingly empty forests of Ghana and nearby nations, there is considerable urgency to study and protect remaining *C. vellerosus* populations in continuous forest habitat before it becomes no longer possible to do so (Matsuda Goodwin et al. 2020). Conversely, *C. polykomos* and *C. satanas* are well known in continuous forest (Dasilva 1989; Fleury 1999; Korstjens 2001; McKey 1979) but no populations of either species have been studied in fragmented forest. Given the rather limited geographic range of these species and their vulnerability to the bushmeat trade (Cronin et al. 2015; Morra et al. 2009; Refisch and Koné 2005a,b), surveys and ecological studies of each in fragmented habitats must be considered another research priority.

One additional project of great promise relating to black-and-white colobus in West Africa would be to compare the ecology of *C. satanas* populations in the northern and southern sectors of the island of Bioko. The northern population around Pico Basilé receives 2000 mm of rainfall annually while the southern population receives an extraordinary >10,000 mm of rainfall annually, resulting in markedly different ecological conditions over a small geographic area (Butynski and Koster 1994; Juste and Fa 1994). Exploring the impacts of this wide variability in rainfall on the ecology of *C. satanas* on Bioko would yield fascinating insights into the adaptability of this species.

Conclusions

After more than a half century of field research, much is now known about the natural history of the black-and-white colobus monkeys, *C. angolensis*, *C. guereza*, *C. polykomos*, *C. satanas* and *C. vellerosus*. Though long ago regarded as monotonous leaf-eaters, the dietary variation now known to exist both between and within species is considerable. *C. satanas* and one population of *C. polykomos* eat as much or more fruit (mostly seeds) than leaves, and fruit is seasonally foremost in the diet of several otherwise mostly folivorous populations of *C. guereza*. The *C. angolensis* inhabiting Nyungwe Forest, where group size sometimes exceeds 500 individuals, rely almost entirely on leaves in some years, while in others there are several months where the monkeys rely more on lichen than leaves. One dietary pattern that is generally consistent across black-and-white colobus is that they tend to choose young leaves over mature leaves wherever possible due to the greater nutritional value of the former. Recent nutritional studies also suggest that dietary choices by *C. angolensis* and *C. guereza* reflect consistent nutrient balancing strategies.

Most black-and-white colobus are sedentary monkeys, spending >50% of their time inactive because of their need to rest while engaging in foregut fermentation. On a related note, all black-and-white colobus have relatively short daily path lengths and most occupy small home ranges as well. The enormous groups of *C. angolensis* at Nyungwe and the mostly seed-eating *C. satanas*, provide interesting exceptions, occupying large home ranges which they cover slowly through a semi-nomadic lifestyle. In fragmented forests, *C. guereza* have the ability to compress their home ranges into very small areas and to live at extraordinarily high densities. In fact, much evidence points to *C. guereza* being the black-and-white colobus species most adapted to life in disturbed and otherwise marginal habitats.

Black-and-white colobus are susceptible to both aerial and terrestrial predators and typically utter roaring alarm calls when predators are detected. These calls vary in structure depending on the type of predator. Aside from *C. angolensis* at Nyungwe and Nabugabo which form large, complex multilevel groups, black-and-white colobus live in small to medium sized groups that rarely exceed 20 individuals. Habitat type, logging history, predation risk, dietary choices, feeding competition and infanticide risk all appear to influence black-and-white colobus group sizes. Male-biased dispersal is typical, though a lesser rate of female dispersal occurs as well. Black-and-white colobus reproduction is still rather poorly understood. Mating patterns vary across and even within species. Birth seasonality is uncommon though some species exhibit birth synchrony among females within groups. Infants are born all white in all species except *C. satanas* and elicit frequent allomothering behaviour by females, while males usually show little interest in infants.

While much has been learned through field studies of black-and-white colobus over the past half century, there are still many outstanding questions to be answered about the natural history of this interesting genus of monkeys. I have suggested some of the most intriguing or pressing future studies here. Continued support for field studies, including more funding and support for African scientists and students (Atickem et al. 2019), will ensure that exciting new insights into the natural history of black-and-white colobus will continue to be generated over the next half century.

Acknowledgements

I thank the editors for inviting me to write about black-and-white colobus monkey natural history for this volume and Tom Butynski, Cyril Grueter, Alex Miller, Nga Nguyen, Julie Teichroeb and an anonymous reviewer for their valuable feedback on earlier drafts of this chapter. I am also grateful to California State University, Fullerton, the University of Oslo, the US–Norway Fulbright Foundation and San Diego Zoo for their financial and logistical support during the preparation of this chapter.

11 Behaviour and Ecology of Olive Colobus

Julie A. Teichroeb and Amanda H. Korstjens

Introduction

The olive colobus monkey, *Procolobus verus* (van Beneden 1838) is a unique primate in many respects. It is monotypic and early studies showed it to be the smallest of the colobines; a drab-coloured, 'thicket-haunter' that often associates with guenon species, with the distinctive behaviour (among anthropoids) of mothers carrying infants in their mouths (Booth, 1956, 1957). Though these early observations were accurate, more recent research has revealed new information about the ecology, behaviour and social organization of this species. One of the most important features of olive colobus natural history is their habit of following and remaining in association with large groups of guenons (Oates and Whitesides 1990), which influences their behaviour and ranging significantly. Our objective is to review what is currently known about olive colobus behaviour, morphology and ecology to help stimulate further research on this fascinating species.

Morphological Features

The olive colobus is named for its relatively drab coloration, an olive-brown on the back and the tops of the limbs, with a lighter grey on the underside (Hill 1952). The flat face is black and there is a small crest of hair on the crown in both males and females. The tail is slender, untufted and olive-brown. Olive colobus are the smallest of the colobines, showing little sexual dimorphism, with males weighing an average of 4.6 kg (n = 22) and females weighing an average of 4.1 kg (n = 17) (Oates 1988a). Like all colobines, the thumbs are reduced to a tubercle and the back limbs are longer than the fore limbs (Hill 1952). The neonatal coat in olive colobus is not as pronounced as it is in most colobines, with infants being only slightly darker than their mother (Oates 1994).

Adult male olive colobus are notable for having relatively large testes to body size compared to other African colobus monkeys and for having horny spicules on the glans penis (Hill 1952). Sexual swellings occur several times in the life cycle of olive colobus monkeys. Newborn infants have been reported to have swelling of the perineal region. Females have perineal swellings that develop before sexual maturation and then fluctuate in tumescence with female reproductive cycles (Korstjens and Noë 2004). Oates (1994) reports female swellings to be pink or greyish-pink with a width of approximately 6 cm and length of about 5 cm. Relative to body size, they are as large as those of *Piliocolobus badius* and larger than those of many other *Piliocolobus* species (e.g. *P. tephrosceles*; pers. obs.). Prior to attaining sexual maturity, juvenile males actually resemble females in having an undescended penis and testes, an imperforate depression where a female's vaginal opening would be, and a perineal swelling mimicking a female's (Hill 1952). These features suggest that young males may have been selected for female mimicry to allow them to potentially mate when young but avoid direct, aggressive competition with adult males (i.e. the female mimicry hypothesis, Rohwer et al. 1980). Alternatively, young males may be providing a reliable signal of their low status to older, larger males (i.e. the status-signalling hypothesis, Rohwer et al. 1983; Lyon and Montgomerie 1986).

The teeth of olive colobus show adaptations for folivory having the thinnest enamel and relatively the highest second-molar shearing cusps of any Old World anthropoid (Kay 1981). The lower third molar is notable for having six cusps (Napier and Napier 1985). Surprising given the small degree of sexual dimorphism in body size, olive colobus have the greatest sexual dimorphism in canine size (breadth and length) in the African colobines. However, in the other teeth, they show few sex differences in mean values (Hayes et al. 1996). Research has shown that body mass and canine size are under different selective pressures (Plavcan 2004) and that canine size dimorphism in the primates is strongly determined by the frequency and intensity of male-male competition (Plavcan and van Schaik 1992; Plavcan 2004). These results, along with large male testes size, the presence of penile spines and the occurrence of sexual swellings, suggest that sexual selection has played an important role in shaping the morphology of olive colobus.

As in other colobines, the digestive system is set up for foregut fermentation of leaves, allowing olive colobus monkeys to eat a high proportion of this hard to digest food source. The genus *Procolobus* shows a four chambered stomach, with the first two chambers acting as expanding fermenting chambers, the third chamber producing hydrochloric acid to break down the material coming in, before it moves to the fourth chamber, which functions like the stomach in other non-colobine primates (Ankel-Simons 2007). Another unique feature of olive colobus is that the fundus of the stomach and the rectum are sacculated (Hill 1952).

Virological Studies

Research has shown that, like most African primate species, olive colobus are naturally infected with Simian Immunodeficiency Viruses (SIV) (Courgnaud et al. 2003). The newly discovered SIV carried by olive colobus (SIVolc) was found to be most closely related to, and derived from, the SIV carried by western red colobus (*Piliocolobus badius*) labelled SIVwrc (Courgnaud et al. 2003; Liégeois et al. 2009). The SIVs of these two colobus monkeys are most closely related to those found in L'Hoest (*Cercopithecus l'hoesti*) and suntailed monkeys (*C. solatus*) based on full-length genome sequences (SIVlho/sun, Liégeois et al. 2009).

Figure 11.1 Distribution of olive colobus monkeys in West Africa. Data from Rowe and Myers (2016)

Geographic Distribution and Habitat

Olive colobus are located in the Upper Guinea forest block of West Africa, extending from the coastal forests of Sierra Leone in the west all the way to Nigeria in the east, occurring just east of the Niger River (Figure 11.1; Oates 1981; Grubb et al. 1998). This species does not show any evidence of subspecific variation despite being distributed across both the Niger River and the Dahomey Gap, two important zoogeographic barriers (Menzies 1970; Oates 1981; Campbell et al. 2008). The distribution of olive colobus is now highly fragmented and the IUCN currently lists them as Vulnerable, with a decreasing population trend due mostly to habitat loss (Oates et al. 2020a). The species is thought to have declined more than 20% since 1980, especially in the eastern part of its range (Oates et al. 2008).

Olive colobus are diurnal and arboreal, inhabiting the middle and lower strata of the forest where there is dense vegetation (McGraw 1998a). They are commonly found in lowland moist forest along riverbanks and near swamps or in secondary forests (Booth, 1956, 1957; Galat and Galat-Luong 1985; Oates 1988a). They are reported to be most abundant in riverine forest but can also occur in gallery forest in the dry forest zone (Oates 1981). Olive colobus tend to use larger boughs to travel on but forage on fine branches and twigs (McGraw 1998a). In general, smaller branches are used by olive colobus compared to other larger colobus monkeys, due to their preferred strata of the canopy (McGraw 1998b).

Field Studies

There are no ongoing field studies of olive colobus monkeys, but three long-term studies have been conducted in the past and shorter observations of unhabituated groups have been done. The earliest observations were unsystematic and were conducted on unhabituated groups (Booth, 1956, 1957; Kuhn 1964), yet Booth (1956, 1957) especially was able to record some accurate information on olive colobus natural history. In the late 1970s and early 1980s, Galat and Galat-Luong collected data on some primates found in Taï National Park, Ivory Coast, including olive colobus (Galat-Luong and Galat 1978; Galat-Luong 1983; Galat and Galat-Luong 1985).

The first long-term study conducted on a habituated group was carried out by John Oates at Tiwai, Sierra Leone over a total of 21 months spread between June 1982 and January 1987 (Oates, 1988a; 1994). Subsequently, Ronald Noë supervised various student MSc projects and AHK's PhD project in Taï National Park that monitored and collected data on four groups of olive colobus between 1994 and 1999 (Korstjens and Schippers 2003; Korstjens and Noë 2004; Korstjens et al. 2007a). Two habituated groups of olive colobus were again followed at Taï National Park from June 2001 to February 2002 by Jean-Claude Koffi Bene for his PhD dissertation (Bene et al. 2012). Unhabituated groups have also been followed for short periods at two sites in Benin, the continuous Lama Forest and forest fragments around the Community Forest of Domè, by research teams supervised by Brice Sinsin (Djego-Djossou et al. 2018).

Social Organization and Dispersal Patterns

Olive colobus form relatively small groups that have one to three adult males and one to six adult females with immatures. At Tiwai, the average group size was 8.5 (range: 3–11, n = 1), while at Taï it was 7.1 individuals (range: 2–12, n = 10) (reviewed in Fashing 2011).

Monitoring of olive colobus groups at Taï over 5 years, showed that both sexes commonly disperse but that female dispersal is relatively more frequent than male dispersal (Korstjens and Schippers 2003). Their relatively high dispersal rates in comparison to other primates may be due to their associations with guenon species. An individual may not experience increased predation risk while transferring between olive colobus groups if it associates with guenons during this time (Korstjens and Schippers 2003). For instance, Korstjens and Schippers (2003) observed both solitary males and solitary females on occasion and these individuals were always associated with a partner Diana monkey group.

Females at Taï dispersed preferentially to smaller groups that had a single adult male (Korstjens and Schippers 2003), despite the observation that multi-male groups had better immature to female ratios, suggesting that male defence against predators and other groups is beneficial to infant survival (Korstjens and Noë 2004). Dispersal of a female with a young infant has been observed (Korstjens and Schippers 2003), implying that infanticide by males may not be a risk in olive colobus (Korstjens and Noë 2004). Females transferred between groups frequently without a sexual swelling but usually became sexually receptive and developed a swelling upon entering a new group.

The occurrence of male dispersal was linked to a high male/female ratio in the group of origin and thus likely occurred to increase a male's access to mates (Korstjens and Schippers 2003). Males had several options upon dispersal, solitary males were observed attracting females to form a group, males could take over a group of females by ousting the previously resident male, or males could join an existing uni-male, multi-female group to form a multi-male, multi-female group (Korstjens and Schippers 2003).

Juvenile sex could not be determined but juveniles were five times more likely than adults to disappear or emigrate. Juvenile dispersal was not clearly linked with group size and occurred before sexual maturity, so did not seem to be explained by access to mates or avoidance of inbreeding. In terms of the timing of juvenile dispersal, Korstjens and Schippers (2003) note that in four cases, the juvenile's mother had given birth to a new offspring within a month of the dispersal event, suggesting the potential role of parent-offspring conflict or avoidance of competition with kin. Nonetheless, parallel dispersal was also observed frequently at Taï, where colobus transferred into nearby groups together or joined groups with familiar individuals (cf. van Hooff 2000) suggesting that animals may have been able to maintain some kin relationships despite frequent dispersal (Korstjens and Schippers 2003).

Diet

Olive colobus spend most of their feeding time in the middle canopy, dispersed in dense growth and liana tangles and are rarely observed high in emergent trees (Galat and Galat-Luong 1985; Oates 1988a). At both sites where long-term data have been collected, this species has been reported to eat primarily young leaves (Table 11.1). While Oates (1988a) reported that seeds were the second most common food item at Tiwai and were particularly important in the dry season (Davies et al. 1999), Korstjens and colleagues (2007a) did not see seed-eating at Taï and report that fruit was the second most common food item (Table 11.1). In Benin, young leaves were also eaten most often (51%) but dietary diversity was lower in forest fragments (25 species) compared to continuous forest (32 species) (Djego-Djossou et al. 2018).

Olive colobus are reported to be highly selective feeders, ignoring most mature foliage and selecting young leaves. In Tiwai, they selected trees that were not very

Table 11.1. Plant parts (%) in the annual diet of olive colobus at two study sites

Site	Mature leaves	Young leaves	Leaves (unknown age)	Petioles	Fruit	Seeds	Flowers	Other	Source
Tiwai	2	59	4	9	5	14	7	0	a
Taï	1	83	1	0	8	0	4	3	b

[a] Oates (1988).
[b] Korstjens et al. (2007).

common, whilst in Taï, the biomass of the preferred feeding trees was similar to the biomass of trees preferred by red and black-and-white colobus (Korstjens et al. 2007). The young leaves of lianas appear to be particularly important; these made up at least 13% of the diet at Tiwai (Oates, 1988a, 1994). This preference for young foliage likely allows olive colobus to avoid leaves high in secondary compounds (Oates 1988a). If other plant parts besides leaves are considered, lianas were found to make up about 27% of the diet of olive colobus in Tiwai, and 13% in Taï (Korstjens 2001, chapter 6). When fruit is eaten by olive colobus, it tends to be unripe with either dry flesh or very little flesh (Davies et al. 1999).

Activity Patterns and Behaviour

Olive colobus monkeys are notoriously difficult to observe; their coloration and behaviour has evolved for crypticity, they tend to disperse in the dense lower layer of the canopy, making few loud vocalizations, and they can be inactive for long periods (Oates 1988a). The activity patterns of this species appear to be greatly influenced by the guenon groups that they associate with (Oates and Whitesides 1990) and show much less resting and more moving than the typical colobine. At Tiwai and Taï (Oates and Korstjens 2013), activity budgets of 28% and 16% feeding, 39% and 50% resting, 26% and 30% moving, 7% and 4% social respectively are shown. Travel is primarily quadrupedal and olive colobus are noted to leap more than larger colobus monkeys (McGraw 1998a).

Female olive colobus show very little affiliation and coalition formation among females has never been observed (Korstjens et al. 2007a). Co-resident adult males are tolerant of one another and have been seen to form alliances, though only towards extra-group individuals. Co-resident males will jointly threaten and chase individuals from other groups during inter-group encounters (Korstjens and Noë 2004; McGraw and Zuberbühler 2008). Natal attraction and infant handling by individuals other than the mother in olive colobus has not been observed (Oates 1994; AHK, pers. obs.).

Association with Other Species

Olive colobus are notable for their adaptation of living in polyspecific associations with guenon species (Oates and Whitesides 1990). Early observations of this species showed that it is almost always in close proximity to some guenon species, including Campbell's mona monkeys (*Cercopithecus campbelli*), mona monkeys (*C. mona*), spot-nosed monkeys (*C. petaurista*), putty-nosed monkeys (*C. nictitans*) and Diana monkeys (*C. diana*) (Booth 1957; Rucks 1976; Galat-Luong and Galat 1978; Oates 1982). At the two sites where longer-duration studies on olive colobus have been conducted (Tiwai and Taï), Diana monkeys (*C. diana*) are the species most frequently associated with by the colobus, though other guenon species are present (Oates and Whitesides 1990; Korstjens 2001). Diana monkeys are excellent sentinels, often detecting predators before other primate species do (Bshary 2007). Although olive colobus have been observed to switch associations between guenon species in a single day, at Tiwai and Taï, certain olive colobus groups were associated with a partner Diana monkey group and these relationships were long-lasting. At Tiwai, Oates and Whitesides (1990) report that one olive colobus group associated with the same Diana monkey group for at least three years. Individuals from these groups were within 50 m of one another on at least 83% of scan samples and it was the olive colobus that appeared to be maintaining the association by following the Diana monkey group when it moved (Oates and Whitesides 1990). At Taï, olive colobus study groups spent 90%–100% of their time within 50 m of their partner Diana monkey group (Korstjens and Schippers 2003). Interactions between the species, both aggressive and affiliative, have been reported to occur rarely (Oates and Whitesides 1990), with play between juveniles being the most common interaction (Whitesides 1989). While in association with another species, it has been noted that olive colobus tend to adopt the behaviour of that species to some extent (i.e. being more conspicuous when with Diana monkeys but more cryptic when with spot-nosed monkeys) (Galat and Galat-Luong 1985; Oates and Whitesides 1990).

The polyspecific associations formed by olive colobus seem to be part of an evolved, predation avoidance strategy. Although this species lives in small groups and forages cryptically in the low-canopy, it can still gain the advantages of large group size, such as detection and dilution, by staying in close proximity to a guenon group (Oates and Whitesides 1990; Oates 1994). Olive colobus respond to the alarm calls of other species and forming associations with guenons allows them to largely avoid food competition due to differing diets while functionally increasing the size of groups (Oates and Whitesides 1990). In addition, Korstjens and Noë (2004) have argued that Diana monkeys are an important mate-finding resource for olive colobus in Taï, with solitary individuals following Diana groups and using them to find conspecifics and attract mates.

Infant-Carrying

Booth (1957) suggested that a combination of factors led to olive colobus being the only anthropoid to carry their infants in their mouths: the short adult coat, the absence of a thumb and the dense nature of the preferred low-canopy habitat. Early descriptions of this behaviour stated that only young infants were carried in the mouth and later these infants could cling to the mother's ventrum (Booth 1957) or around her neck (Galat-Luong and Galat 1978). Oates (1994) notes that in Tiwai, infants were only ever carried in the mouth. The mother would grasp the infants flank, tucking the belly of the infant into her neck and the infant's tail would wind around the mother's neck and upper back. Figure 11.2 provides a photo of this behaviour and a video is also available at: https://talk.chimpandsee.org/#/subjects/ACP0004hm8. Tiwai mothers were only seen to carry infants when the group moved and infants were put down whenever the mother was stationary. Infant-carrying got less frequent as infants aged, though Oates (1994) observed a large infant of about 10-months old being carried in the mouth.

Figure 11.2 An olive colobus monkey carrying an infant in its mouth. Photo courtesy of W. Scott McGraw

Reproductive Behaviour

The reproduction of olive colobus is moderately seasonal. Oates (1994) reports that most copulations at Tiwai were seen between March and August and the majority of swollen females were observed between April and August (though observations were not taken in the month of September). Young infants were only observed November through April, months that coincided with the dry season. Similarly, Korstjens and Noë (2004) report that at Taï, births occurred from October to April. The timing of mating and the subsequent appearance of infants suggests a typical colobine gestation time of six months (Oates 1994). Korstjens and Schippers (2003) report that at Taï, interbirth intervals showed a mean of 1.6 ($\pm$0.3) years (range: 1.2–2 years, $n = 6$) and females nursed each infant for an average of 12 months.

About half of olive colobus groups contain more than one male and in multi-male groups, both males have been observed to mate, though the alpha male mates much more frequently than the subordinate (Oates 1994; Korstjens and Noë 2004). Females solicit copulations slightly more than males (Korstjens and Noë 2004). At Tiwai, males closely followed and appeared to form consortships with, females that had maximally tumescent swellings, mating with them many times over a few days. These consortships may be mate guarding, as the dispersed feeding pattern of olive colobus in dense vegetation make extra-group copulations likely (Oates 1994). Indeed, at Taï, Korstjens and Schippers (2003) report that adult females often visited neighbouring groups and solitary males while they had a swelling to engage in mating. Copulations and copulation attempts have also been observed during inter-group encounters (Korstjens and Noë 2004). These female strategies to confuse paternity likely contribute to the seeming lack of infanticide by males in olive colobus.

Oates (1994) observed copulations by both males in his Tiwai study group with a single female in close succession without any overt aggression between the males. This behaviour along with the large testes size, spicules on the glans penis (Hill 1952) and coagulating sperm (Korstjens and Noë 2004) are strongly suggestive of sperm competition in olive colobus (Møller 1988). Oates (1994) notes that on a day when the two males in his study group were mating with four different females, one male copulated at least 46 times and the other copulated at least eight times.

The vast majority of copulations that have been observed have been between males and females with a sexual swelling, though rarely, copulations by females with no swelling have been observed (Oates 1994; Korstjens and Noë 2004). At Taï, female sexual swellings last about 17 days (range: 14–20 days, $n = 6$ females) and the time between the onset of two consecutive swellings for two females was 27 and 29 days. Females experience two to eight cycles in their interbirth interval and data indicate that some swellings were non-conceptive because females gave birth not long after their last swelling. A median time of 3.8 months (range: 2.5–5.5 months, $n = 6$) was observed between the last swelling and birth (Korstjens and Noë 2004). Within the same group, females sometimes overlapped in receptivity, but more than one maximally swollen female at a time was not observed. Though males attempted to mate guard maximally swollen females (Oates 1994), the ability of males to monopolize females in olive colobus is greatly hampered by the long duration of female swellings (Korstjens and Noë 2004).

Range Size and Defence

At the two main study sites, the home ranges of olive colobus monkeys have been found to be large for a colobine of such small body and group size. This appears to be largely due to their habitual association with Diana monkey groups (Oates 1994) and perhaps their low population densities. At Tiwai, Oates and Whitesides (1990) reported a home range size of 28 ha for their study group. At Taï, Korstjens (2001) reported a mean home range of 56 ha for the two study groups, with an approximate overlap of 14% with other groups. Groups also had long daily paths for a colobine with a mean of 1212 m travelled per day (range: 482–2105 m). The home range of each olive colobus study group overlapped completely with the range of the Diana monkey group it was associated with (Korstjens and Noë 2004).

Vocalizations

In keeping with its cryptic nature, most calls used by olive colobus are soft and infrequent (Oates and Korstjens 2013). Males are reported to do the majority of vocalizing (Bene et al. 2012) and the most obvious call, which researchers have referred to as the loud call, is given in response to calls by other primate species and during inter-group encounters (Oates and Whitesides 1990). Hill and Booth (1957) termed this a 'laughing call' and described it as rising in pitch to the penultimate syllable 'hoo hoo hoo hoo yow yow wee wee yow', dying away at the last syllable.

Bene et al. (2007) describe eight different call types made by olive colobus during four different contexts, alarm, conflict, peaceful and during inter-group encounters. Three of these call types are used most frequently, the 'Zih', 'Hoo' and 'Zuk', and five others are produced less often, the 'Tr', 'ZZ', 'Whi', 'Ha' and 'Thio'. Bene and colleagues (2012) report that these call types are combined in several ways into different contextual sequences. These authors were able to distinguish nine additional calls that consisted of combinations of the eight call types, showing that olive colobus have a very diverse and potentially powerful communication system.

Inter-group Interactions

Korstjens and Noë (2004) report that groups of olive colobus often exchange loud calls when they come into proximity (0–150 m) and that calls are certain to occur once the groups are within 50 m. Males are the primary vocalizers in these instances, though females will also emit shorter, quieter calls. About half of interactions between groups are reported to include threats (e.g. moving the head and shoulders side to side with an open mouth) and 8% of those recorded at Taï (n = 50) included chasing between groups. Though copulations may occur during inter-group encounters, the presence of swollen female(s) does not appear to influence the amount of aggression that occurs (Korstjens and Noë 2004).

Conclusions

As this summary of olive colobus natural history demonstrates, this monotypic species is unique in many respects. Though it is found in several protected areas, the threat of bushmeat hunting throughout its range is extreme. Renewed research effort with individual recognition is needed to expand our knowledge of this exceptional animal.

Acknowledgements

The authors thank Ikki Mastuda and one anonymous reviewer for their comments on this manuscript.

12 Ecology and Behaviour of Odd-Nosed Colobines

Cyril C. Grueter, Wendy M. Erb, Larry R. Ulibarri and Ikki Matsuda

Introduction

The odd-nosed monkeys represent a monophyletic group of relatively large and phenotypically unique primates. They include five species of snub-nosed monkeys (golden snub-nosed monkey *Rhinopithecus roxellana*, Yunnan snub-nosed monkey *R. bieti*, Guizhou snub-nosed monkey *R. brelichi*, Tonkin snub-nosed monkey *R. avunculus* and Myanmar snub-nosed monkey *R. strykeri*), three species of doucs (red-shanked douc *Pygathrix nemaeus*, black-shanked douc *P. nigripes* and grey-shanked douc *P. cinerea*) as well as simakobu (*Simias concolor*) and the proboscis monkey (*Nasalis larvatus*). These species are ecologically diverse and inhabit a gradient of environments in China and Southeast Asia, from wet equatorial forests in Indonesia to alpine forests at the edge of the Tibetan Plateau. Odd-nosed monkeys tend to be shy and difficult to habituate, and often range over relatively large areas. Many are also renowned for inhabiting remote areas with rugged terrain (e.g. limestone forests, subalpine and swamp forests) and inclement climatic conditions. It is thus not surprising that, until fairly recently, they were among the least studied and most enigmatic extant diurnal primates. However, since the beginning of the new millennium, an expanse of new and exciting research has been conducted on these colobines, which can be attributed to dedicated efforts by a combination of range-country and foreign primatologists. In this chapter, we provide an overview of the current knowledge of the ecology and behaviour of odd-nosed monkeys and analyse some of their key behavioural traits and ecological adaptations in light of what is known about other colobines and primates as a whole.

Distribution

Among the five species of *Rhinopithecus*, three are endemic to China (*R. bieti, R. brelichi, R. roxellana*), one is endemic to Vietnam (*R. avunculus*) and one is found on both sides of the Myanmar/China border (*R. strykeri*). *R. bieti* occupies patches of forest along a narrow band stretching across the Yunling Mountains in northwest Yunnan and southeast Autonomous Prefecture of Xizang/Tibet (Long et al. 1994). The native range of *R. roxellana* extends across several mountain ranges in west/central China (Qionglai Mountains of Sichuan, Min Mountains of Sichuan and Gansu,

This chapter includes Electronic Supplementary Material (ESM) at: www.cambridge.org/colobines

Qinling Mountains of Shaanxi and Daba Mountains of Hubei) (Hu 1998). *Rhinopithecus brelichi* is confined to a small region centering on Mt. Fanjing in the Wuling Mountains of Guizhou Province (Bleisch et al. 1993). *Rhinopithecus avunculus* occurs in pockets of suitable habitat in a small area in northern Vietnam (Ha Giang, Tuyen Quang provinces). The northernmost population in Ha Giang Province lives within a few kilometres off the Chinese border, and it is unknown whether this species' range extends across the border into China's Yunnan Province (Le and Covert 2010). *Rhinopithecus strykeri* was unknown to science until 2010 when it was discovered in northeastern Kachin state, northeastern Myanmar (Geissmann et al. 2011). Following its initial discovery in Myanmar, this species has also been confirmed to occur in the Gaoligong Mountain Range in the Nujiang region of Yunnan Province in China (Long et al. 2012). Among the three species of *Pygathrix*, two are distributed throughout parts of Southeast Asia (*P. nemaeus, P. nigripes*), and one is endemic to Vietnam (*P. cinerea*). *Pygathrix* species were previously known only from isolated forest patches in Vietnam, but since the turn of the millennium, additional populations along the Annamite Range in southeastern Laos extending into northeastern Cambodia have been confirmed (Clements et al. 2008; Nadler et al. 2003; Rawson and Roos 2008; Timmins and Duckworth 1999). *Pygathrix nemaeus* is located in patches throughout central and north-central Vietnam, southeastern Laos and northeastern Cambodia, *P. nigripes* is found in northeastern Cambodia and southern Vietnam, and *P. cinerea* is endemic to south-central Vietnam (Coudrat et al. 2012; Nadler and Brockman 2014). Species distributions overlap in parts of Vietnam and Cambodia. *Simias concolor* is endemic to the Mentawai Islands of Indonesia off the coast of west Sumatra and inhabits all of the major islands (Siberut, Sipora, North Pagai and South Pagai) as well as some minor islets (Tenaza and Fuentes 1995; Whittaker 2006). *Nasalis larvatus* is found only on the island of Borneo.

Research Efforts

The Yunnan or black-and-white snub-nosed monkey (*R. bieti*) received its initial scientific description by Milne-Edwards in 1897 (Milne-Edwards and de Pousargues 1898). Using both indirect methods and direct observations, Wu Baoqi conducted a pilot study on this species in the mid-to-late 1980s in the Yeri district in northwest Yunnan (Wu 1993; Wu et al. 1988). Around the same time, censuses by Long Yongcheng established the species' distributional range and population size (Long et al. 1994, 1996). With the help of Long Yongcheng and two local Tibetans (Zhongtai and Xiaolin), Craig Kirkpatrick undertook his doctoral research on the ecology and social organization of a group of *R. bieti* in the early 1990s at Wuyapiya in the northern part of Baimaxueshan National Nature Reserve (Kirkpatrick 1996). Since then, several unhabituated or semi-habituated groups of *R. bieti* have been the focus of medium- to long-term research, including Cyril Grueter and Li Dayong's study in the Samage Forest (Grueter 2009) and Xiang Zuofu's study in the Honglaxueshan National Nature Reserve in Tibet (Xiang et al. 2007) (ESM Table 12.1). In-depth ongoing research on one habituated group of *R. bieti* at Xiangguqing started in 2008 (e.g. Li Yanhong et al. 2014); this group was 'created' through human-led herding of a sizeable number of individuals away from a natural group and is currently kept within a relatively small delineated patch of its former range and provisioned regularly.

The Sichuan or golden snub-nosed monkey (*R. roxellana*) was first described by Milne-Edwards in 1870, based on specimens obtained from western Sichuan (Allen 1938). The first information on the species' biology came from an early study in the late 1950s in the Qinling Mountains (Liu 1959). Li Baoguo and colleagues established a field site in the Qinling Mountains approximately a quarter century ago; this long-term research has produced detailed analyses of individual life histories and generated novel insights into the complexities of this species' social organization (Qi et al. 2014; Zhao and Li 2009a). The late Ren Renmei and colleagues initiated a research programme at Shennongjia National Nature Reserve (now Shennongjia National Park) in western Hubei Province in 1991 with a particular focus on describing the multi-tiered social organization (see below) of *R. roxellana* (Ren et al. 2000). *Rhinopithecus roxellana* was the first species of *Rhinopithecus* to be habituated and provisioned, first at Zhouzhi in the Qinling Mountains and subsequently at Shennongjia. It has become the most intensely studied *Rhinopithecus* species and arguably the most studied of all odd-nosed monkeys.

The Guizhou or grey snub-nosed monkey (*R. brelichi*) was discovered at the beginning of the twentieth century (Thomas 1903). William (Bill) Bleisch and colleagues conducted the first comprehensive field study on aspects of their positional behaviour, resource requirements and social organization in Fanjingshan National Nature Reserve (Bleisch and Xie 1998; Bleisch et al. 1993). Yang Yeqin and colleagues of the Fanjingshan Nature Reserve stepped in to continue monitoring this species in the mid-1990s (Yang Yeqin et al. 2002). More recently, researchers at the Zoological Society of San Diego Institute for Conservation Research and San Diego State University have become involved in projects revolving around the behavioural ecology and conservation biology of *R. brelichi*.

The Tonkin snub-nosed monkey (*R. avunculus*) was named by Dollman (1912). Mittermeier and Cheney (1987) assumed that this species had already become extinct by the mid-1980s; however, it was rediscovered in 1989. The first preliminary data on the ecology of this species were generated by Ramesh Boonratana and Le Xuanh Canh at Na Hang (Boonratana and Le 1998). Later on, two groups embarked on more systematic studies of this species in Khau Ca, albeit under very difficult field conditions (Dong 2011; Le 2014).

The Myanmar or black snub-nosed monkey (*R. strykeri*) became known to the scientific community in 2010 (Geissmann et al. 2011). Studying these critically endangered primates in the wild is very difficult due to long rainy seasons and very rugged precipitous terrain; however, some preliminary data on the natural history of this species have recently become available through dedicated efforts by researchers, students and staff at Gaoligongshan National Nature Reserve and Fauna and Flora International (FFI) Myanmar (Chen et al. 2015; Meyer et al. 2017). Survey efforts aimed at finding a potentially undescribed species of *Rhinopithecus* in an area between the Salween and Mekong rivers in Yunnan have thus far proven unsuccessful.

The red-shanked douc (*P. nemaeus*) was the first odd-nosed colobine to be scientifically described and classified (Buffon 1776, Linnaeus 1771). Initial data on this species' ecology were gathered by Lois Lippold (1977), with further studies conducted in both captive and wild settings (Lippold 1998; Otto 2005; Pham 1993a). Longer-term studies were conducted by Camille Coudrat and Phaivanh Phiapalath in Hin Namno National Protected Area, Laos (Coudrat et al. 2014; Phiapalath 2009; Phiapalath et al. 2011), and by Katie Bailey and Larry Ulibarri focusing on a population in Son Tra Nature Reserve, Vietnam (Bailey et al. 2018; Ulibarri 2013). Captive studies continue at the Endangered Primate Rescue Center, Vietnam (Bailey et al. 2017; Byron et al. 2017; Pate et al. 2018; Rudolph and Fichtel 2017).

The black-shanked douc (*P. nigripes*) was described as a species by Milne-Edwards (1871), although many researchers considered this a subspecies of *P. nemaeus* until genetic analyses suggested division at the species level (Groves 2001; Roos and Nadler 2001). The first long-term field study on this species was conducted in Nui Chua and Phuoc Binh National Parks, Vietnam by Hoang Minh Duc, followed by Ben Rawson focusing on the population in Mondulkiri Province, Cambodia and Jonathan O'Brian in Cat Tien National Park, Vietnam (Hoang 2007; O'Brian 2014; Rawson 2009).

The grey-shanked douc (*P. cinerea*) was first identified by Nadler (1997) as a subspecies of *P. nemaeus*, and later divided at the species level (Roos and Nadler 2001). Ha Thang Long and colleagues in Kon Ka Kinh National Park, Vietnam are the first and only scientists to conduct long-term research on this species (Ha 2007; 2009; Nguyen et al. 2012). Their project represents the only stable ongoing wild-based research efforts on any *Pygathrix* species.

The simakobu monkey (*S. concolor*) was first described by Miller in 1903, based on specimens collected by W.L. Abbot in South Pagai (Miller 1903). The first natural history study of simakobu was conducted by Ronald Tilson, in central Siberut between 1972 and 1974 (Erb 2012; Tilson 1977). Between 1974 and 1978, Kunio Watanabe observed several groups of simakobu on Siberut at the Sarabua and Grukna study sites (Watanabe 1981). Simakobu research was extended further south to the Pagai Islands by Richard Tenaza in the late 1980s (Erb 2012; Tenaza 1987; Tenaza 1989a,b; Tenaza and Fuentes 1995) and Agustin Fuentes, who made observations of seven simakobu groups for seven months in 1992 on North Pagai Island (Fuentes 1995; Tenaza and Fuentes 1995). Lisa Paciulli continued research on North Pagai in 1996, when she became the first observer to habituate simakobu (Miller and Paciulli 2002). Finally, Susilo Hadi and Wendy Erb initiated dissertation studies at the Pungut study site in northern Siberut in 2005. During Erb's 24-month dissertation research in 2007–2008, she conducted a detailed behavioural study of four habituated groups (Erb 2012).

The proboscis monkey was first described by van Wurmb in 1781 as *Cercopithecus* (now *Nasalis*) *larvatus*. Riverine refuging behaviour by *N. larvatus* is a hallmark on which most research on the species has been based. Owing to the swampy habitats proboscis monkeys live in, much research has been conducted using boats during the hours they are found at their sleeping sites along the river's edge. Early research helped to draw attention to the species but was based mainly on short-term studies from boats that focused on a basic understanding of their social organization and habitat utilization (Bismark 1981; Jeffrey 1979; Kawabe and Mano 1972; Kren 1964; Macdonald 1982; Salter et al. 1985). In the late 1980s, longer-term studies pioneered by Carey Yeager, Elizabeth Bennett and Ramesh Boonratana were conducted (e.g. Bennett and Sebastian 1988; Boonratana 2000; Yeager 1989). These studies revealed that – contrary to earlier assumptions that they mostly eat leaves in mangroves – proboscis monkeys consume high proportions of fruits and/or seeds in response to local phenological conditions, which in turn influence their ranging patterns. These authors also described the proboscis monkeys' social system, which can consist of multilevel associations among adjacent groups. By the 2000s, the attention raised for these unique monkeys had attracted academic pursuits exploring the species' socioecology via observations and genetic analyses (e.g. Feilen and Marshall 2014; Murai et al. 2007; Matsuda et al. 2010a; Munshi-South and Bernard 2011; Roper et al. 2014; Salgado-Lynn 2010; Thiry et al. 2016), and novel topics such as their digestive capabilities and sexual selection of their enlarged noses (e.g. Hayakawa et al. 2018; Koda et al. 2018; Matsuda et al. 2011, 2014, 2015; Thiry et al. 2018). Researchers also began considering conservation issues and the impacts of human activities such as tourism (Leasor and Macgregor 2014), intestinal helminth infections (Klaus et al. 2017, 2018) and landscape changes (Matsuda et al. 2020b; Stark et al. 2012, 2017a).

Habitat and Climate

Odd-nosed monkeys show a wide spectrum of habitat association in Southeast Asia and Indochina, from lowland rain forests in the tropics to subalpine forests of the temperate zone (ESM Table 12.2). The Chinese snub-nosed monkeys live in environments that can be considered extreme compared to other non-human primates: they have colonized high-altitude forests, with *R. bieti* reaching the highest altitude of any non-human primate (4700 m!) (Long et al. 1996). Absolute temperature minima at some sites can reach −15°C (Xiang et al. 2007) and even −30°C (Su et al. 1998). The historical distribution of snub-nosed monkeys in China, however, seems to have extended into climatologically less harsh areas at lower altitudes (Li et al. 2003). Mean annual temperatures at sites where Chinese snub-nosed monkeys occur range from 1 to 17°C, while at the tropical sites of *R. avunculus*, the average temperature is above 20°C (ESM Table 12.3). Annual precipitation at Chinese *Rhinopithecus* sites can be well below 1000 mm, but there are wetter sites such as Khau Ca in Vietnam and Pianma in Yunnan with annual rainfall often exceeding 2000 mm (ESM Table 12.2).

Rhinopithecus roxellana is found mostly in mixed deciduous broadleaf/conifer forest (Kirkpatrick et al. 1999; Li Yiming et al. 2002) and *R. brelichi* inhabits subtropical-temperate mixed deciduous and evergreen broadleaf forest (Bleisch et al. 1993; Wu et al. 2004; Yang Yeqin et al. 2002). Although frequently claimed that 'dark coniferous forest' (i.e. fir forest reaching up to the edge of the tree line) constitutes the optimal habitat for *R. bieti* (e.g. Clauzel et al. 2015), there is substantial variation in habitat association patterns among sites, with fir forest being more frequently used by populations living at high-altitude/high-latitude sites characterized by low plant diversity. At several other sites, mixed deciduous broadleaf and conifer (spruce, hemlock etc.) forests represent the species' preferred habitat type (Grueter 2015a; Huo 2005; Li et al. 2008). At Samage, for example, where there is marked altitudinal zonation of vegetation types, the monkeys utilize mixed forest most frequently, followed by pine forest, sclerophyllous oak forest, and evergreen broadleaf forest (Li et al. 2008). *Rhinopithecus avunculus* is the only species of *Rhinopithecus* associated exclusively with subtropical forest on steep karst limestone (Boonratana and Le 1998). Though little is known about habitat use in *R. strykeri*, interviewees in Yunnan report that *R. strykeri* mainly uses conifer, broadleaf and mixed forest (Ma et al. 2014). A recent study by Chen et al. (2015) has shown that the altitudinal range of these primates extends from 2400 to 3300 m. The main forest types found at these altitudes, in ascending order, are: mid-mountain moist evergreen broadleaf forest, Yunnan hemlock forest and mixed bamboo-conifer forest.

Pygathrix species are found from 0 to 1500 m in a variety of forest types and subtypes. *Pygathrix nemaeus* inhabits secondary moist and dry evergreen broadleaf and mixed deciduous forests in Vietnam and Laos (Phiapalath 2009; Van Peenen et al. 1971). Primary/secondary evergreen broadleaf forests, and mixed conifer forests are habitats occupied by *P. cinerea* (Ha 2009). *Pygathrix nigripes* is found in mixed broadleaf evergreen and conifer forests, submontane evergreen broadleaf forests and deciduous forests, depending on location (Hoang 2007). Mean annual temperatures are typically around 25°C at all *Pygathrix* research sites, and mean annual precipitation ranges from ~700 to over 2700 mm, with most sites averaging more than 1500 mm annually (Hoang 2007; Rawson 2009). Monthly precipitation can vary greatly, with most sites reporting one or more dry season months characterized by little to no rain, and wet season months with over 800 mm (Rawson 2009; Ulibarri 2013).

Simias concolor inhabits a range of habitats in the Mentawai Islands, including primary lowland mixed and dipterocarp forests, mangroves and peat swamps, as well as selectively logged forests and human gardens (Quinten et al. 2010; Tilson 1977; Tenaza and Fuentes 1995; Watanabe 1981). The Mentawai climate is equatorial, exhibiting nearly constant warm and wet climatic conditions throughout the year. Daytime temperatures are usually between 25°C and 32°C (Watanabe 1981). Erb et al. (2012a) documented high mean annual rainfall of 3601 mm in Siberut. The wettest period occurs between September and December; even in the driest month (May), mean precipitation exceeded 200 mm (Erb et al. 2012a), with rain falling on at least 50% of days each month (McNeely et al. 1980).

Early work on *N. larvatus* suggested that they are dependent primarily on mangrove forests for food and cover, but more recent studies revealed that proboscis monkeys also extensively use riverine and other swamp habitats including peat and freshwater swamps (Sha et al. 2008). *Nasalis larvatus* is seldom found in extensive stands of nipah forest, but habitat mosaics of mangrove and nipah can support relatively high densities of proboscis monkeys (Nowak et al. 2019). Mean annual temperatures and precipitation at *N. larvatus* research sites range from 26 to 29 °C and 2500 to 3500 mm, respectively (ESM Table 12.2).

Diet

Rhinopithecus bieti is unusual among primates in their reliance on lichens as a food source. While lichens are consumed throughout the year, their proportional representation in the diet varies with the availability of plant foods. Lichens become a vital fallback food in winter when there is critical lack of alternatives (Grueter et al. 2009b; Kirkpatrick 1996), contributing up to 95% of the diet at one site (Xiang et al. 2007). Lichens have relatively low protein, fibre and deterrent (tannins and phenols) contents, but are enriched in non-structural carbohydrates (Guo et al. 2016; Kirkpatrick 1996; Kirkpatrick et al. 2001; Liu et al. 2013b). The relatively low content of antifeedants and the high amount of digestible energy make lichens a comparatively attractive food resource (Kirkpatrick 1996). Lichens are seasonally supplemented with angiosperm fruits and mature leaves in the fall, young leaves in spring and bamboo shoots in summer (Ding and Zhao 2004; Grueter et al. 2009b, 2010b; Kirkpatrick 1996; Li et al. 2011; Xiang et al. 2007). The shift from a lichen-based diet in winter to a young leaf-based diet can be quite dramatic, with young leaves comprising more than two-thirds of the diet of a group at Samage during peaks of flushing (Grueter et al. 2009b, 2010b). Studies on the nutritional factors influencing choice of foods in *R. bieti* have yielded mixed results. High protein content does not seem to explain food choice, and the effects of fibre on dietary choice remains equivocal (Huang et al. 2010; Kirkpatrick 1996). *Rhinopithecus bieti* also exploit subterranean resources such as plant underground storage organs (Grueter et al. 2009a; Ren et al. 2008).

The diet of *R. roxellana* at most study sites also includes lichens (Guo et al. 2007; Kirkpatrick et al. 1999; Li Yiming 2006; Liu et al. 2013b; Zhao et al. 2020), though this has not been reported for a population living at a relatively low altitude (Li Yankuo et al. 2010). The seasonal variation in food use by this species at high-altitude sites largely matches the one shown by *R. bieti*: lichens are heavily exploited in winter, young leaves become an important dietary constituent in spring, mature leaves are harvested in summer, and fruits/seeds are the most heavily exploited foods in late summer/fall (Guo et al. 2007; Kirkpatrick et al. 1999; Li Yiming 2001, 2006; Li Yankuo et al. 2010; Liu et al. 2013b). In contrast to *R. bieti*, *R. roxellana* seems to make use of a larger variety of fallback foods including leaves, buds, bark and seeds (*ibid.*; see also Hou et al. 2018; Zhao et al. 2020). In one study, *R. roxellana* selected leaves on the basis of crude fibre and non-structural carbohydrate content, and leaves high in carbohydrates and low in fibre were overrepresented in the diet (Liu et al. 2013b). In another study, monkeys selected leaves of species with more protein and lower lignin than non-consumed ones (Hou et al. 2018). Guo S et al. (2018) have shown that *R. roxellana* alters their intake of carbohydrates and fat to compensate for seasonal changes in thermogenic requirements.

The annual diet of *R. brelichi* is composed of 47% leaves, 15% buds, 22% fruits and 9% flowers, but is characterized by pronounced seasonal changes (Guo Y et al. 2018; Xiang et al. 2012) (ESM Table 12.3). Dormant leaf buds are the predominant winter food (Bleisch and Xie 1998; Guo Y et al. 2018; Nie et al. 2009; Xiang et al. 2012). Available protein was significantly higher in leaves of species selected by the monkeys compared with those rejected (Bleisch et al. 1998).

The feeding ecology of *R. avunculus* at Khau Ca has been described in two studies: Dong (2011) recorded a higher proportion of young leaves (46%) than fruits/seeds (32%) in the diet, whereas Le et al. (2007) found that overall, fruits (both ripe and unripe as well as seeds) were the most frequently consumed food items (53%), followed by petioles and immature leaves (33%). Flowers and mature leaves were less important in terms of their contribution to the diet. Food item selection was generally tied to their phenological availability, and the monkeys expressed strong dietary selectivity for certain plant species (Dong 2008). Preferred leaves are low in secondary metabolites and fibre and high in lipids and protein (Lan Anh et al. 2014).

The information that is available on the dietary profile of *R. strykeri* is limited but preliminary data (mainly based on food choice experiments with two captive, wild caught[1] individuals) indicate a large repertoire of plant food species (>170) as well as consumption of lichens (Yang Yin et al. 2018, 2019). Based on preliminary analyses of feeding remains, mature leaves of evergreen trees feature prominently in the diet of this species. Bamboo shoots are also harvested by the monkeys when they are available (Yang Yin et al. 2019; see also Geissmann et al. 2011).

Diets of *Pygathrix nemaeus* in Vietnam consist of predominately leaves (62%–87%), of which most are young leaves, followed by fruits/seeds (10%–37%) (Lippold 1977; Ulibarri 2013). Flowers contribute relatively little in terms of dietary percentage. At one study site the selection of young leaves, fruit and seeds remained high despite changes in phenology, suggesting this species has preferred foods that are selected irrespective of availability (Ulibarri 2013). Dietary seasonality is not the only response to fluctuations in the availability of preferred foods, as seasonal breeding and movements may alleviate dietary stresses (van Schaik et al. 1993). Additionally, there were no significant differences in the fibre or protein content of selected young and mature leaves. Therefore, even though mature leaves are a seasonal fallback resource, their quality is comparable to young leaves in both protein and fibre (Ulibarri 2013). Alternatively, in Laos there was a marked seasonal shift in diet between wet and dry seasons, with leaves comprising 80% of the seasonal diet in the dry season, but only between 21%–39% in the wet season, which was dominated by fruit consumption (54%–57%) (Phiapalath et al. 2011). In these studies, the most important plant families to douc diet were Sapindaceae (Laos) and Dipterocarpaceae (Vietnam).

The annual diet of *P. nigripes* in Vietnam consists of leaves (54%), fruit (19%), seeds (10%), and flowers (15%), with young leaves preferred over mature leaves

[1] The individuals were apparently rescued from poachers (Yang Yin, pers. comm.).

(Hoang 2007). Diet was seasonal, with leaves comprising between 23% of the dietary profile in the wet season when fruit and seeds were more important, to 70% in the dry season. There were no significant differences in fibre or protein content of selected and non-selected foods (Hoang 2007; Hoang et al. 2009; Hoang et al. 2011). In contrast, additional chemical analysis on a different population in Vietnam revealed significant differences in selected versus non-selected foods, with selected foods being enriched in both protein and fibre content (O'Brien 2014). Annual diets of *P. nigripes* in Cambodia were reported as dominated equally by seeds (40%), and leaves (40%), with fruit and flowers providing seasonal contributions to the annual diet (Rawson 2009). The wet season was characterized by increased consumption of seeds (48%), and the dry season by increased leaf consumption (42%). In these studies, several plant families were identified as being important to douc diets, with Fabaceae being among the most important.

The annual diet of *P. cinerea* has been reported as predominately leaves (59%), of which most were young leaves, followed by fruit and seeds (41%) (Ha 2009). Selection of young leaves and fruit correlated with availability. The dry season was characterized by increased consumption of young leaves (82%), and the wet season by increased consumption of fruit and seeds (69%). There were no significant differences in fibre or protein content of selected young and mature leaves, as found in other *Pygthrix* studies (Nguyen et al. 2012). Sapindaceae was considered the most important plant family to the diet of *P. cinerea.*

The diet of *Simias concolor* has been systematically studied at only one site, Pungut, in northern Siberut (Hadi et al. 2012; Erb et al. 2012a; Lestari & Erb 2011). Erb and colleagues documented feeding times on differet food items throughout the year as well as on a monthly basis. Leaves were the most commonly consumed food, comprising 51% of the annual diet (monthly range: 25%–68%), with young leaves and buds contributing 79% of leaf-feeding time. Flowers and fruits comprised 26% and 17% of annual feeding time, respectively, but these values varied greatly across study months (range: flowers = 0%–60%, fruits = 5%–42%), with unripe fruits contributing 71% of fruit-feeding time. Simakobu included other foods, such as insects, fungus and moss in their diet, though these accounted for just 1% of overall feeding time (monthly range: 0%–3%). All told, simakobu fed on 116 different plant species at Pungut over the course of 2 years (Lestari and Erb 2011). Although Hadi and colleagues reported rates, rather than proportions, of simakobu feeding, they found a similar pattern: simakobu ate leaves most frequently (15.8 events/hr) followed by fruits (6.3 events/hr), flowers (4.9 events/hr), and other food items. Interestingly, Paciulli (2011) noted that, during the Indonesian drought of 1997, simakobu in North Pagai spent nearly 80% of their feeding time consuming dipterocarp flowers, leading her to hypothesize that flowers may be an important fallback food for this species, at least at that site (Paciulli, pers. comm.). No nutritional analyses of the simakobu diet have been conducted to date.

Nasalis larvatus is the only colobine species in which an apparent rumination of stomach contents has been observed under free-range conditions (Matsuda et al. 2011a). Proboscis monkeys' natural diet consists of varying proportions of leaves

(38%–73%), fruits (11%–50%) and flowers (3%–12%) (Bennett and Sebastian 1988; Boonratana 2003; Feilen and Marshall 2020; Matsuda et al. 2009; Yeager 1989). *Nasalis larvatus* is characterized by great dietary diversity. They show a high level of fruit/seed eating in fruit seasons and a preference for fruits/seed, instead of leaves, when both are available (Matsuda et al. 2009a; Yeager 1989). However, in most months, consumption of young leaves predominates and there is no significant correlation between monthly young leaf availability and time allocated to eating young leaves (Matsuda et al. 2009a). The dietary choices of *N. larvatus* when consuming young leaves are influenced by their chemical properties and abundance but also by their toughness and in vitro digestibility. Preferred young leaves contain more protein and less fibre than those of the common plant species which are not consumed by *N. larvatus* (Boonratana 2003; Matsuda et al. 2014; Yeager et al. 1997), and preferred leaves are less tough and more digestible than those of the common plants (Matsuda et al. 2017c). In addition, *N. larvatus* foods have higher concentrations of phosphorus and potassium, whereas non-foods have higher concentrations of calcium and manganese (Yeager 1997). Of the preferred species, beyond the advantage in terms of chemical properties, mechanical toughness and digestibility, more abundant plant species are chosen, probably to maximize energy gain per unit time (Matsuda et al. 2018).

Odd-nosed monkeys have also been seen complementing their plant-based diet with invertebrates (*R. bieti*: Xiang et al. 2007; *R. roxellana*: Hou et al. 2018, Yang et al. 2016; *R. brelichi*: Xiang et al. 2013a; *R. strykeri*: Yang Yin et al. 2019; *N. larvatus*: Matsuda, pers. obs.; *S. concolor*: Erb et al. 2012a) and vertebrates [birds, flying squirrels etc.: *R. bieti* (Grueter et al. 2009a); *R. roxellana* (Zhu et al. 2019)], the latter of which can be obtained through hunting or scavenging [*R. bieti* (Ren B et al. 2010); *R. roxellana* (Zhao et al. 2008b)]. Consumption of soil rich in minerals such as calcium, copper, zinc, iron, manganese and sodium has also been recorded (Li D et al. 2014; Rawson and Luu 2011), indicating mineral consumption, pH balancing, toxin buffering or a combination of these influencing factors.

Activity Patterns

Snub-nosed monkeys are principally active during the day, but activities resulting in spatial displacement at night have also been recorded with the aid of camera traps (Tan et al. 2012). Time budgets of snub-nosed monkeys in temperate environments vary significantly among seasons, but not all populations exhibit the same seasonal adjustments. Several populations adopt an energy-economizing foraging strategy in winter when confronted with climatic challenges and dietary stress; they reduce time spent in energetically costly travel and/or increase time spent acquiring food (Ding and Zhao 2004; Grueter et al. 2013; Guo et al. 2007; Ha 2009; Hoang 2007; Li D et al. 2013b; Li Yiming 2009; Rawson 2009; Xiang et al. 2010a). In *R. roxellana* and *R. bieti*, increased feeding effort in winter is the result of a reliance on food resources with relatively low nutrient acquisition rates. The time snub-nosed monkeys commence their daily activities can vary substantially among seasons. For instance, in

R. bieti the average sleeping time per night was 11.5 hrs, but sleeping time ranged from 10.1 hrs in summer to 13.0 hrs in winter (Li D et al. 2010a). Activity budgets have also been shown to vary among age-sex classes. The research of Li Yanhong et al. (2014) has revealed that adult female *R. bieti* spent more time feeding (45%) than adult males (40%). This difference – if biologically significant – may be related to adult females' higher reproductive investment associated with gestation and lactation which demands greater or higher quality food intake, although time spent feeding is not necessarily an accurate reflection of food and energy intake (e.g. Aristizabal et al. 2017).

In *Pygathrix nemaeus* increased travel and vigilant behaviours are seen in more disturbed forests compared to forests with less hunting (Phiapalath and Suwanwaree 2010). *Pygathrix nemaeus* is significantly more inactive when units are fused as a band; and move, vocalize, feed and are vigilant significantly more often when units are fissioned (Ulibarri 2013; Ulibarri et al. 2015). These patterns suggest bands fission into foraging units daily, and vocalizations may be important in coordinating activities between dispersed foraging units. Correlations in daily activity budgets and fission-fusion are likely an adaptation to avoiding scramble competition. Similar to snub-nosed monkeys, although statistically insignificant, adult females spent more time feeding than males in both *P. cinerea* and *P. nemaeus* (Ha 2009; Ha et al. 2010; Ulibarri 2013).

Foraging effort also appears to be a direct consequence of habitat productivity: a population of *R. bieti* living in ecologically depauperate habitats at the northern edge of the species' distribution spent more time feeding and less time resting compared to a population inhabiting a more productive and botanically diverse forest at a lower latitude and altitude (Ding and Zhao 2004; Xiang et al. 2010a) (ESM Table 12.4). Feeding time is further reduced in the tropical-living *R. avunculus* (Dong 2007). A similar pattern can be found among *Pygathrix*, in which populations of *P. nemaeus* and *P. cinerea* inhabiting evergreen forests have a reduced feeding time (Ha 2009; Phiapalath and Suwanwaree 2010; Ulibarri 2013) compared to populations of *P. nigripes* inhabiting more mixed and deciduous forests (Hoang 2007; Rawson 2009). Detailed behavioural studies of simakobu have only been conducted at one site, so comparisons of feeding and diet across habitats are not available for this species.

Like most colobines, *Simias concolor* devotes most of its daily activity budget to resting (49.8 events/hr), while social behaviours sit at the other end of the spectrum (2.1 events/hr: Hadi et al. 2012). Annual variation in *S. concolor* activity budgets has not been published, though a strong seasonal pattern would not be expected, given the overall lack of seasonality in their habitats (Erb et al. 2012a). A brief (7 mos) study found that age-sex classes showed similar activity budgets with the exception of social behaviour: adult females spent a greater proportion of time being social than adult males (Erb 2008).

Resting is the dominant behaviour in *N. larvatus* throughout the year (51%–76%: Matsuda et al. 2009a; Salter et al. 1985). *Nasalis larvatus* is characterized by minimal monthly variation in percentage of time devoted to moving, but time spent feeding shows marked seasonal fluctuations. A significant positive relationship between monthly fruit availability and monthly feeding activity was reported (Matsuda et al. 2009a). In *N. larvatus*, there are sex-related differences in time spent feeding, moving and other social behaviours (Matusda et al. 2009a). Males spend more time feeding and moving than females. Females spend more time grooming than adult males.

Range Use

Snub-nosed monkeys, doucs and most simakobu live at relatively low population densities, with an average of 11 individuals per km^2 for *R. bieti*, 8 for *R. roxellana*, 6 for *P. nigripes* and 20 for *N. larvatus*. Densities for *S. concolor* in Siberut are much higher, up to 220 individuals per km^2 (ESM Table 12.5).

Daily travel distances average 1100 m for *R. bieti*, 1400 m for *R. roxellana*, 900 m for *R. brelichi*, 1100 m for *R. avunculus*, 900–1000 m for *P. nigripes*, 1100 m for *P. cinerea*, 500 m for *P. nemaeus* and 855 m for *N. larvatus* (ESM Table 12.5). Home range sizes average around 18 km^2 for *R. bieti*, 22 km^2 for *R. roxellana*, 35 km^2 for *R. brelichi*, 11 km^2 for *R. avunculus*, and are estimated to be around 17 km^2 for *R. strykeri*, 2 to 5 km^2 for *P. nigripes*, 10 km^2 for *P. cinerea*, and between >0.5 and 3 km^2 for *P. nemaeus*; in *S. concolor*, home range size rarely exceeds 20 ha and in *N. larvatus* it is around 180 ha (ESM Table 12.5). The spatial requirements of snub-nosed monkeys – especially the ones inhabiting relatively unproductive temperate forests – are unusually large by colobine standards. There is also considerable inter-population variation in home range size in snub-nosed monkeys which is attributable to variation in group size and to a lesser degree habitat productivity (Grueter et al. 2008). In contrast to the large flexible home ranges of snub-nosed monkeys, one-male groups of *S. concolor* in northern Siberut ranged over an average area of 7.6 ha and all-male groups occupied small home ranges (mean 6.1 ha) that remained stable over periods of at least two years (Erb 2012). In Erb's study, home range size was not well predicted by group size; although the smallest simakobu group had the smallest home range, the largest group did not have the largest area. Core areas (50% kernel) for one-male groups were 2.2 ha on average, and 1.3 ha for the all-male group. The home ranges of one-male, multi-female groups in *N. larvatus* overlap by an average of >95% (Yeager 1989), and this species is considered non-territorial (Boonratana 2000; Matsuda et al. 2009b). The home range sizes of *N. larvatus* differ among habitats: values were 315 ha (22 ha/individual) in mangrove forest at Abai (Boonratana 1993), 900 ha (56 ha/individual) in mixed mangrove and lowland forests at Samunsam (Bennett and Sebastian 1988), 137 ha (13 ha/individual) in peat swamp forest at Natai Lengkus (Yeager 1989), and 221/138 ha (11.0/9 ha/individual) in a riverine forest at Sukau (Boonratana 2000; Matsuda et al. 2009b). However, other than the figure of 221/138 ha, all of the home range sizes are estimates of river length used by one-male, multi-female groups. Using GPS collars, more comprehensive home range estimates in a riverine forest (range 24–165 ha, mean 81 ha) were obtained for 10 one-male, multi-female groups (Stark et al. 2017b). The variation among habitats in *N. larvatus* may be explained by food availability, though it is difficult to directly compare the available data as the methods used to measure home range and food availability differ across studies.

Among odd-nosed monkeys, certain parts of their home range – presumably areas rich in food resources[2] and areas of relatively low predation threat – are used more frequently than others and some peripheral areas are only visited rarely, perhaps related to forays (Grueter et al. 2008; Hoang 2007; Kirkpatrick et al. 1998; Liu Zehua et al. 2004; Matsuda et al. 2009b; Ulibarri 2013). Daily path lengths are also not consistent across days; patterns of concentrated use of areas with relatively short daily path lengths are followed by long-distance trips to new foraging grounds (Grueter et al. 2008; Kirkpatrick et al. 1998; Ren et al. 2009b). Large-scale home range shifts in response to anthropogenic disturbance have also been reported, and severity of habitat disturbances appears to impact home range size (Grueter et al. 2008; Kirkpatrick et al. 1998; Li et al. 1999).

Patterns of range use are influenced by seasonality and associated environmental variables. Temperate *Rhinopithecus* species typically exhibit shorter daily path lengths in winter or in the dry season, possibly because the energetic costs in the cold season would be prohibitive of extensive travel (Grueter et al. 2013; Tan et al. 2007; Xiang et al. 2013b). While home ranges vary (sometimes dramatically) from season to season, there is no consensus as to what drives this variation. Relationships between phenology of food plants and ranging vary in relation to habitat characteristics and resource distribution. *Rhinopithecus roxellana* at Zhouzhi and *R. bieti* at Samage were found to range within a smaller area in the fall when they foraged for spatially clumped fruit (Grueter et al. 2008; Tan et al. 2007). However, an increase in range size in fall was documented for a group of *R. bieti* at Laojunshan (Ren et al. 2009b) and a group of *R. roxellana* at Shennongjia (Fan et al. 2018); in the latter case, this was attributed to the monkeys' search for fruits and seeds from scattered pine trees. Similar patterns were reported among *Pygathrix* species, with one population of *P. nemaeus* decreasing home range use during the wet fruiting season, but other populations of *P. nemaeus* and *P. nigripes* increasing range use during the wet fruiting season (Hoang 2007; Phiapalath 2009; Ulibarri 2013). Seasonal variation in daily path length has also been shown to be associated with human disturbance: *R. bieti* at Xiaochangdu travelled further in the summer months when local people scoured the forest for mushrooms and medicinal plants (Xiang et al. 2013b). In *N. larvatus*, daily path length of one-male, multi-female groups was shorter on days when the diet included a higher proportion of fruits/seeds (Boonratana 2000; Matsuda et al. 2009b). This appeared to be due to a preference for the fruits/seeds of dominant plant species for which the distance between patches may be shorter. Conversely, these monkeys travelled farther when there were more young leaves than fruits/seeds in their diet (Boonratana 2000; Matsuda et al. 2009a). During the period when the amount of young leaves eaten increased, the monkeys' dietary diversity also increased, indicating that their daily path length increased as they explored and

[2] More quantitative evidence is needed to substantiate this presumption.

fed on a variety of food items (Matsuda et al. 2009b). Boonratana (2000) did not find a significant correlation between the daily path length of *N. larvatus* and the amount of rainfall, whereas Matsuda et al. (2009b) found a significant but a weak negative correlation, suggesting that although the impact of rainfall on ranging is low, weather may also affect their ranging behaviour (Matsuda et al. 2009b).

Little is known about the degree of exclusivity of home ranges of odd-nosed monkeys. Two bands of *R. roxellana* at Shennongjia showed extensive home range and core area overlap (>90%), but they tended to use the overlapping zone at different times, especially in winter (Fan et al. 2018; Liu 2012). To the contrary, at Zhouzhi home range overlap between two neighbouring bands was limited, but they did congregate seasonally in the overlapping zone (Qi et al. 2014). Among *Pygathrix*, it has been reported that home range overlap is minimal, possibly suggesting a degree of territoriality (Hoang 2007; Pham 1993b; Ulibarri 2013 but see Ulibarri and Gartlan 2021a). However, resource defence among colobines is unlikely in areas where density is below carrying capacity (Yeager and Kool 2000). In these *Pygathrix* studies, inhabited areas are small and disturbed, and reduced range overlap may reflect patterns of density and resource availability. In *S. concolor*, home range overlap between neighbouring groups was 12%–13% in Erb's (2012) study and 5% in Hadi et al.'s (2012) study.

Due to the montane-dwelling nature of all snub-nosed monkeys, the factors underlying seasonal variation in altitude use have received considerable interest from primatologists studying several species. Most studies conclude that food availability drives altitudinal ranging (Li et al. 2008; Tan et al. 2007; but see Quan et al. 2011). For example, *R. bieti* at Samage was found to descend to lower altitudes in spring to graze on young foliage and remained at high altitudes in winter to exploit lichen, their winter staple, which is found in higher density in that elevational zone (Grueter et al. 2012b; Li et al. 2008). Temperate snub-nosed monkeys do not move to lower altitudes in winter (Kirkpatrick and Long 1994; Li et al. 2008; Niu et al. 2010; Quan et al. 2011; Tan et al. 2007; Zhong et al. 2008); however, temporary 'shelter seeking' nearer to foothills in the face of deep freeze and heavy snowfalls has been reported (Li et al. 2008; Niu et al. 2010).

The location of sleeping sites in relation to foraging sites varies in snub-nosed monkeys. *Rhinopithecus bieti* at Samage tended to roost in close proximity to feeding sites (Li D et al. 2013a), whereas a group of *R. brelichi* retreated to areas at lower elevations for sleeping (Niu et al. 2010). Groups of *R. bieti* typically use large and well-insulated conifer trees with wide crowns as sleeping trees (Chu et al. 2018; Cui et al. 2006a; Li D et al. 2006; Liu Zehua and Zhao 2004). Among *Pygathrix* species, they appear to roost in proximity of or within feeding trees (Ha 2009; Hoang 2007; O'Brien 2014; Ulibarri 2013). The ranging patterns of *N. larvatus* are affected by the position of sleeping sites because they typically return to trees on the riverbank to sleep. Their core areas are located where the group often establishes sleeping sites or crosses the river (Matsuda et al. 2008a, 2009b). Although several environmental factors such as food availability and air temperature affect riverine refuging of *N. larvatus*, these may not be fundamental factors in their preference for riverine habitat (Matsuda et al. 2011b). One study showed a possible effect of avoidance of biting insects on riverine refuging (Feilen and Marshall 2017). The selection of particular sleeping tree features is likely to be related to risks of predation, though other factors, e.g. injury from falling, ease of social interaction, efficiency of locomotion and decreasing molestation by mosquitoes, also play a role (Bernard et al. 2011; Feilen and Marshall 2014; Thiry et al. 2016).

At many sites odd-nosed monkeys live sympatrically with other primates, but little attention has been directed to investigating how interspecies associations are facilitated. At Samage, niche divergence is evident at the scale of macrohabitat selection, with *R. bieti* preferentially using mixed deciduous conifer forest and rhesus macaques (*Macaca mulatta*) being more associated with evergreen broadleaf forest at lower altitudes (Grueter et al. 2010a). Interspecific associations between *M. mulatta* and *P. nemaeus*, and between common muntjacs (*Muntiacus muntjak*) and *P. nemaeus* appear to be driven by seasonal patterns of flowering and fruiting (Ulibarri 2013). *S. concolor* lives sympatrically with another colobine, the Mentawai langur (*Presbytis potenziani*). These ecologically similar taxa exhibit 60% overalap in food species, but differ in their diets: whereas Mentawai langurs feed most often on fruits, simakobu most often eat leaves (Hadi et al. 2012). Presumably enabled by their low dietary niche overlap, these species exhibit complete overlap in their home ranges.

Predation

Potential terrestrial predators such as wolves, dholes, leopards and lynxes still exist within the distribution range of *R. bieti* (Buzzard et al. 2017; Grueter, pers. obs.; Xiang 2005). Birds of prey have been seen attacking young snub-nosed monkeys (Cui 2003; Li Yiming 2007; Xiang et al. 2009a), and in *R. roxellana* predation of a juvenile monkey by a goshawk was described by Zhang et al. (1999a). It has also been suggested that leopards, dholes, golden cats and wolves prey on *R. roxellana* (Hu et al. 1980; Li Yiming 2007; see also Chu et al. 2018). There is one report of a wolf attack (Yan et al. 1995) and two reports by local field staff of leopards killing *R. roxellana* (Li Yiming 2007; see also Johnson et al. 1993). Various felids, reptiles and birds of prey exist within the distribution ranges of *Pygathrix*, but non-human predation has not been reported in any *Pygathrix* study. *Simias concolor* are the favoured prey of Mentawai's indigenous hunters (Mitchell and Tilson 1986; Tilson 1977; Yanuar et al. 1998). Pythons are the only non-human predators of adult primates in the Mentawai Islands as there are no felids or large raptors present (Tenaza and Tilson 1985). As a result, simakobu showed strong flee responses to playbacks of human voices, but did not differentiate the calls of felid predators from other novel sounds (Yorzinski et al. 2007). *Nasalis larvatus* is at risk of predation by false gavials while swimming across rivers (Yeager 1991a). They are also at risk of predation in trees by predators such as clouded leopards. To reduce the threat of predation by leopards, proboscis monkeys typically sleep in riverside trees where predators can only approach them from the land side (Matsuda et al. 2008b). Indeed, *N. larvatus* remained in inland forest on flooded days because of the reduced predation threat, as terrestrial predators are prevented from hunting due to the deep water covering the forest floor (Matsuda et al. 2010b).

Social System

Social Organization

All snub-nosed monkey species, at least two of the douc species and most likely also proboscis monkeys are organized into multilevel societies with at least two social tiers: the band and the one-male, multi-female unit (OMU) (Grueter 2017; Hoang 2007; Kirkpatrick and Grueter 2010; Kirkpatrick et al. 1998; Li G et al. 2014; Ulibarri 2013; Zhang et al. 2006). A detailed portrayal of the multilevel society of snub-nosed monkeys and other colobines is presented in Chapter 18. Bands of temperate snub-nosed monkeys tend to be very large, typically well above 100 individuals with the largest estimate being 600 (Hu et al. 1980), but smaller bands with less than 100 members also exist (ESM Table 12.6). A group of *R. strykeri* captured on video consisted of approximately 100 individuals (Li G et al. 2014). Band sizes in *R. avunculus* are smaller (80–90) than in other *Rhinopithecus* species which may be related to their more tropical habitat with patchier resource distribution, but could also be the result of habitat constriction.

Band sizes in *Pygathrix* are smaller with most reports ranging between 20 and 51 individuals, and one report on *P. cinerea* at 88 individuals (Dinh et al. 2010; Ha 2009; Hoang 2007; Lippold 1998; Pham 1993b; Phiapalath et al. 2011; Ratajszczak et al. 1990; Rawson 2009; Ulibarri 2013). However, reports do not distinguish between band and unit levels of organization, with two exceptions (Hoang 2007; Ulibarri and Gartland 2021b).

The first account of the social organization of *Simias concolor* reported bachelor males and mixed-sex groups comprising adult male-female pairs that ranged from 2–5 individuals (Erb 2012; Tilson 1977). Although other researchers confirmed these early observations in other populations, Watanabe (1981) was the first to document larger groups of up to 20 individuals, including four adult females, at Grukna in northern Siberut, and multi-female groups with up to nine individuals were counted in Pagai (Tenaza and Fuentes 1995). Multi-male groups – one mixed-sex and one same-sex – were first reported in Pagai (Tenaza and Fuentes 1995). Erb and colleagues tested the hypothesis that preponderance of small groups at some sites was due to human disturbance affecting group composition by compiling data on group composition, hunting rates and habitat disturbance from eight populations (Erb et al. 2012b). They found that the adult sex ratio was negatively impacted by hunting (i.e. groups had fewer females where hunting rates were higher), but habitat disturbance did not affect group composition.

Some *N. larvatus* OMUs appear to actively associate with each other (Boonratana 2000), and it has been suggested that they may create a multilevel society in which specific groups associate at their sleeping sites into separate bands in a manner similar to the fission-fusion patterns among social units observed in the multilevel social systems of other odd-nosed monkeys (Murai 2004b; Yeager 1991b). However, one study examined the hypothesis that the change in local density (defined as the number of other groups within 500 m of the focal group) of OMUs and all-male units is affected by environmental factors such as food availability and by temporal autocorrelation (Matsuda et al. 2010a). The findings suggest the possibility that the local density of monkey groups increases as a result of sleeping sites that are better protected from predators and closer to clumped food sources. This does not exclude the idea that the social system of *N. larvatus* is multilevel, i.e. they may incur benefits from aggregation such as less predation, less harassment/infanticide by all-male groups etc., although the model does not require any social interactions between groups that increase spatial clumping. Additional studies are needed to confirm whether or not *N. larvatus* form multilevel societies.

Subunits within multilevel societies, i.e. the minimum reproductive units, contain a single adult male, one to several adult females and their dependent offspring as well as juveniles (ESM Table 12.6). Multi-male units ('MMUs') have also been documented (Cui et al. 2008; Hoang 2007; Huang et al. 2017a; Kirkpatrick et al. 1999; Liu Zehua et al. 2007b; Matsuda et al. 2020b; Ren et al. 2000; Ulibarri 2013; Yeager 1990a) but they are somewhat unusual and, in some cases, could be an artefact of observational constraints. While OMUs appear to show rather exclusive association with a single band over extended time periods, whole OMUs have been seen moving between bands (Qi et al. 2009, 2014).

Another key element of odd-nosed monkey societies are all-male units (AMUs) (Grueter 2017; Ha 2009; Kirkpatrick et al. 1998; Liu Zehua et al. 2007; Nie et al. 2009; Ren et al. 2000; Ulibarri 2013), which comprise both pre-prime (juvenile, subadult, adult) and post-prime adult males (Qi et al. 2014; Yao et al. 2011). In *Rhinopithecus*, AMUs often show close spatial association with the reproductive units (Qi et al. 2014). Adult and pre-adult individual bachelor males in *Pygathrix* have been observed in several studies (Ha 2009; Hoang 2007; Lippold 1977; Rawson 2009) as have AMUs (Ulibarri 2013). In *N. larvatus*, there are also all-male groups, and males are sometimes found on their own (Murai 2004a).

In *R. bieti* and *R. roxellana* bands are rather cohesive entities, but recurrent fission-fusion has been reported (Grueter et al. 2017a; Kirkpatrick et al. 1999; Ren et al. 2012b; Zhang et al. 2006). In *R. brelichi*, bands appear to be semi-cohesive, exhibiting a seasonal pattern of fission-fusion (Nie et al. 2009; Xiang et al. 2009a; Yang al. 2009). In *R. avunculus*, the current evidence points to a fluid system in which different OMUs are not constantly united in bands (Boonratana and Le 1998; Dong 2011). Seasonal patterns of increased band cohesion are reported in all *Pygathrix* species. In studies on *P. cinerea* and *P. nemaeus*, seasonal patterns of increased band cohesion coincided with increased leaf flush (Ha 2009; Ulibarri 2013). Alternatively, in other studies on *P. nemaeus* and *P. nigripes*, increased band cohesion occurred during the wet season relating to increased fruit abundance (Phiapalath et al. 2011; Rawson 2009). Several studies report recurrent and daily fission-fusion patterns in *Pygathrix* species (Dinh et al. 2010; Ha 2009; Hoang 2007; Ulibarri and Gartland 2021b). In one study on *P. nemaeus*, the daily pattern of fission-fusion was significantly correlated with daily activity patterns, and appears to be an adaptation to reducing the negative effects of scramble competition (Ulibarri et al. 2015).

Between-Group Interactions

Inter-band encounters in snub-nosed monkeys are characterized by lack of aggression (Chen et al. 1989; Ren et al. 2000), and bands have also been seen fusing together on such occasions (Bleisch and Xie 1998; Qi et al. 2014). It has recently even been argued that social tiers exist above the band level, i.e. that bands are linked with each other as part of a larger community ('troop') (Qi et al. 2014; Ulibarri 2013). The occurrence of inter-band encounters in *P. nemaeus* may be related to peaks in fruiting and leaf flush, and were observed to occur when both home range use and seasonal band cohesion were greatest (Ulibarri 2013).

Three studies have described simakobu inter-group encounters in unhabituated populations (Tenaza and Fuentes 1995; Tilson 1977; Watanabe 1981). These encounters involved adult males only, but varied widely in their nature, ranging from mutual retreat, vocal exchanges, vigorous jumping displays and/or aggressive chases and fights. In addition, several researchers noted that adult males produced loud inter-group vocalizations (loud calls) during encounters, following tree falls or thunder, and in pre-dawn choruses (Erb et al. 2016; Kawamura and Megantara 1986; Tenaza 1989a; Tilson 1977, Watanabe 1981). Erb (2012) studied inter-group interactions for two years in habituated groups in Pungut, northern Siberut. She documented 0.25 encounters/day, or one encounter every 4.0 days. As in previous studies, these interactions were variable, though most (83%) involved some degree of aggression; whereas 68% of aggressive encounters involved chasing or fighting, the remaining 32% involved physical or vocal displays only. For one-male groups, encounters occurred in edge or interior areas but never in the core, but for all-male groups, encounters were most frequent in core areas. Based on these observations, Erb hypothesized that males in one-male groups use aggressive encounters and loud calls to monopolize females and maintain exclusive use of core areas.

Dispersal

Available observational and genetic evidence on the most thoroughly studied snub-nosed monkey species (*R. roxellana*) indicate a dispersal system in which males are obligate dispersers, although females regularly emigrate from their natal social units (Chang et al. 2014; Guo et al. 2015; Huang et al. 2017a; Zhao et al. 2008a). Males typically become marginalized during their adolescence, eventually resulting in natal dispersal at ca 3–4 yrs of age and immigration into an AMU (Huang et al. 2017a; Yao et al. 2011; but see Fang et al. 2019). Young pre-prime males can establish their own OMUs either in their natal band or in a new band (Huang et al. 2017a). In *R. roxellana*, females (adults and subadults) often change residency between units within the band, and less often have been observed to leave their natal band altogether and join neighbouring bands (Guo et al. 2015; Qi et al. 2009;

Zhao et al. 2008a). Dispersal of females can be triggered by resident male replacements, but has also been documented during the tenure of their current leader male (Guo et al. 2015). Female *R. roxellana* show a tendency to transfer into social units which contain female relatives (Guo et al. 2015) and smaller units with relatively few females (Zhao et al. 2008a). In *R. bieti*, the likelihood of a female leaving her natal OMU was positively influenced by her residence time in the OMU and negatively influenced by the availability of female relatives; OMUs chosen for immigration contained a higher number of female relatives, fewer fertile feamles (mating competitors) as well as younger leader males with shorter tenure lengths (Xia et al. 2020b). Dispersal has been reported in a number of *Pygathrix* studies, suggesting that both sexes disperse, with males more frequently observed dispersing (Ha 2009; Hoang 2007; Lippold 1977; Rawson 2009; Ulibarri 2013). In one study, *P. nemaeus* bachelor males were classified as either elder males that remained along home range peripheries, pre-adults and pre-prime adults in the process of dispersal, or prime adults that shadowed resident units or bands (Ulibarri 2013).

Only one study has documented long-term changes in *S. concolor* groups, including immigration and emigration patterns. Erb and colleagues (2012b) observed 10 groups during a 24-month study at Pungut in northern Siberut. In 5.1 group-years, they observed six dispersal events (1.2 events/group-year) including five immigrations (one adult and two juvenile females joined a one-male group and one juvenile male and one juvenile female joined an all-male group) and one emigration (one juvenile female left an all-male group to join an adjacent group). They also observed six temporary presences (1.2 events/group-year), during which adult and juvenile females visited one-male and all-male groups for less than two months. Overall, male and female juveniles dispersed at a higher rate than adults. Whereas juvenile females dispersed into both one-male and all-male groups, juvenile males dispersed only into all-male groups, and adult females only into one-male groups. Although two subadult males matured into adults in an all-male group, adult males did not disperse among groups during this study, and this aspect of group formation remains unknown. Although observations of male emigration were one reason Yeager (1990) regarded *N. larvatus* as a female-bonded species, there are also reports of females immigrating into OMUs (Bennett and Sebastian 1988; Matsuda et al. 2012a; Murai et al. 2007; Yeager 1990a). Additionally, AMUs are occasionally joined by females (Boonratana 2002; Yeager and Kool 2000).

Social Interactions and Social Dynamics

Affiliative social interactions in snub-nosed monkeys are largely restricted to individuals belonging to the same OMU. As a result of this, units are more tightly knit whereas the band is more loosely bonded (Grueter 2009; Kirkpatrick et al. 1998; Yan 2012; Zhang et al. 2006). However, interactions creating linkages across units such as infant handling, collective defence and extra-unit mating have been reported (Huang et al. 2017a; Ulibarri 2013; Wada et al. 2015; Xiang et al. 2014; Zhao et al. 2005). Unit leaders are often in a state of mutual tolerance, but do not engage in affiliative behaviour, and aggression ensues when they approach each other too closely or contestable resources are at stake (Dong 2011; Grueter 2009; Kirkpatrick 1996; Zhang et al. 2006; Zhao Qing and Tan 2010). Contestable resources include estrous females (e.g. Zhao et al. 2013) and possibly high-quality food patches such as fruit trees (Grueter et al. 2009a). The establishment of a dominance hierarchy among units as described for *R. roxellana* (Wang et al. 2007; Zhang et al. 2008b) may help curtail frequent aggressive escalations. Relations between OMU and AMU males are universally antagonistic in snub-nosed monkeys (Grueter 2009; Ren et al. 2007, 2010; Zhao and Li 2009b; Zhao et al. 2013). In *N. larvatus*, physical antagonistic interactions between males are rare, and there is evidence that their noses reliably signal status and competitive ability, thereby obviating the need for escalated fights (Koda et al. 2018).

Male mate acquisition strategies in snub-nosed monkeys have been most thoroughly studied in *R. roxellana*, with some data on *R. bieti* recently made available. OMU leaders can be replaced during an invasion of solitary males or males of an AMU (Qi et al. 2009; Ren et al. 2011; Yao et al. 2011; Zhu et al. 2016). After a takeover event, former unit holders generally leave the reproductive unit and become members of an AMU (Qi et al. 2014; Ren et al. 2011; Yao et al. 2016), but some manage to establish new OMUs in their natal band or another band following a takeover (Huang et al. 2017a). After a change in leadership, former unit members usually stay with the new male (Wang et al. 2004; Zhu et al. 2016), but sometimes females emigrate from their natal or resident OMU after the replacement of a leader male (Guo et al. 2015). Males can also secure mates and establish their own breeding unit by luring females into their OMUs (Qi et al. 2009; Yao et al. 2011). Median tenure length in *R. roxellana* at Shennongjia has been reported to be close to 3 years (Yao et al. 2011). In Zhouzhi, males held the alpha position for an average of 2.9 years (Fang et al. 2019). In the wake of unit takeovers, infants can become the victims of infanticidal attacks by new leader males. Two incidents of infanticide have been documented for wild *R. bieti* at two study sites (Ren et al. 2011; Xiang and Grueter 2007), and unequivocal evidence of infanticide has been obtained for *R. roxellana* at Shennongjia (Yao et al. 2016).

In wild *R. bieti*, *R. roxellana*, *P. nigripes* and *P. nemaeus*, allogrooming was observed both between males and females and between females, and there is no consensus as to whether cross-sex bonds are more prominent than same-sex bonds (Grueter 2017; Hoang 2007; Kirkpatrick et al. 1998; Phiapalath 2009; Rawson 2009; Ren et al. 2000; Ulibarri 2013; Wang et al. 2013; Wei et al. 2012; Zhang et al. 2006, 2008a, 2012). Grooming between females is mediated by close kinship ties (Guo et al. 2015). Allocation of social investment within units is partially influenced by seasonality, with more female-female grooming in the birth season which may help nonmothers to gain access to infants, and more female-male grooming in the mating season which may facilitate mating (Wei et al. 2012; Yu et al. 2013). Males do not seem to engage in coercive behaviours to gain (mating) access to females or to keep them in the unit (Qi et al. 2009; Ren B et al. 2003; Zhang et al. 2008a), but males do interfere with females trying to mate with extra-unit males (Qi et al. 2011). There are no published studies of within-group social relationships among *S. concolor*. OMUs in *N. larvatus* are reported to be female-bonded, because the social behaviour of females (which included agonism and grooming) is directed primarily towards their offspring and other adult females (Yeager 1990a). One study of *N. larvatus* focused on inter-individual relationships of identified adult members within OMUs, revealing a bisexual dispersal pattern with few hierarchical relationships (Murai et al. 2004, 2007) and only weakly differentiated grooming patterns among group members (Matsuda et al. 2012a). In addition, the OMU male appears to be socially peripheral compared to the females (Matsuda et al. 2012b).

Agonistic interactions between females are infrequent in snub-nosed monkeys (Cui et al. 2014; Zhang et al. 2010), and females show a high tendency to reconcile after outbursts of aggression (Grueter 2004; Ren et al. 1991; Zhang et al. 2010). Males often bring inter-female conflicts to a halt through policing behaviours (Grueter 2004; Ren et al. 1991). Intra-unit contest competition for food seems to be weakly expressed (e.g. Zhang et al. 2008a), but there are indicators that females may compete over access to the resident male, as shown for example by sexual interference during mating from coresident females (Li and Zhao 2007; Qi et al. 2011; Ren R et al. 1995; Ulibarri 2013; but see Ren B et al. 2003). Females in an OMU can be ranked hierarchically, but consistency and stability of dominant-subordinate relationships and the effect of rank on the tenor of social interactions vary (Cui et al. 2014; He et al. 2013; Li B et al. 2006; Qi et al. 2004; Wei et al. 2012; Zhang et al. 2008a) and require further study. There is also some evidence that higher-ranking females have greater access to mating partners than lower-ranking ones (He et al. 2013).

In snub-nosed monkeys, members of AMUS often form social and sociosexual bonds among each other (Fang et al. 2018a; Lu et al. 2007; Ren et al. 2010), and these bonds are based on kinship (Qi et al. 2017). However, the strength of affiliation among bachelor males can change in relation to the availability of reproductive opportunities: both the distance to the band and the time of year (mating vs. non-mating season) have been shown to influence the degree of social cohesion seen in the bachelor groups (Qi et al. 2017; Zhu et al. 2018).

Reproduction and Sexual Behaviour

Gestation length in odd-nosed colobines ranges from 166 to 210 days and cycle duration is 24–30 days (reviewed in Grueter 2013). The gestation length of simakobu has not yet been determined, but based on published body mass values, Erb and colleagues (2012a) extrapolated a value of 201 days (6.6 months) using the fitted function between body mass and gestation length in wild Asian colobines. Sex ratio at birth in *R. roxellana* can range from male-biased (1.7:1) (Qi et al. 2006, 2008) to slightly female-biased (1:1.1) (Chang et al. 2012). Interbirth interval in all species averages two years, with the exception of *R. brelichi* whose interbirth interval is three years. Infant mortality was 22% in wild *R. roxellana* (Qi et al. 2008). Kirkpatrick and colleagues (1998) estimated infant mortality in wild *R. bieti* to be 55%–60%. In contrast, Li J and colleagues (2014) reported a significantly lower value (7%) for the population at Lasha (for data on a provisioned group, see Xia et al. 2020a). If an individual loses an infant prior to weaning, the subsequent interbirth interval will be shortened (Cui et al. 2006b; Qi et al. 2008; Xia et al. 2020a; Yang et al. 2009). The weaning process in *Rhinopithecus* can commence when infants are 5–7 months old (Cui et al. 2006b; Li Yinhua et al. 2005; Qi et al. 2008); however, Li J et al. (2014) report that weaning began at 13–14 months and ended at 18 months (see also Huang et al. 2012 and Li T et al. 2013). Among *Pygathrix* weaning commences between 12 and 15 months, and although weaning can end as early as 16 months, bouts of suckling have been reported in individuals two years of age (Bett 2011; Lippold 1995; Ruempler 1998; Yeong et al. 2010). Age at sexual maturity in odd-nosed monkeys is earlier in females (3–7 years) than in males (4–8 years; reviewed in Grueter 2013).

Strong reproductive seasonality characterizes the *Rhinopithecus* taxa, both in the wild and in captivity. In *R. brelichi*, births are restricted to a period lasting from the end of March to the end of April (Yang et al. 2009; see also Bleisch et al. 1993; Yang Yeqin et al. 2002), in *R. avunculus* from March to May (Dong 2011), in *R. roxellana* from March to June (Qi et al. 2008; Ren R et al. 1995; Shi et al. 1982; Xiang et al. 2017; Zhang et al. 2000), and in *R. bieti* from February to June (Bai et al. 1987; Cui et al. 2006b; Grueter 2009; Huang et al. 2012; Ji et al. 1998; Li J et al. 2014; Wang S et al. 2012; Xia et al. 2020a; Xiang and Sayers 2009). The reproductive schedule of temperate-living snub-nosed monkeys with birth peaks clustered around the end of winter and early spring is likely an adaptation to periods of increasing or high availability of protein-rich young leaves for lactating mothers; this timing also ensures that infants have sufficient time and energy to mature before the beginning of winter (Huang et al. 2012; Li J et al. 2014; Qi et al. 2008; Xiang and Sayers 2009) and that weaning falls into the spring of the following year when there is adequate nutrient supply (Li J et al. 2014; Xiang et al. 2017). A birth season at the beginning of spring would also correspond to a conception period in the previous fall when energy-rich resources (fruits) are available, which can facilitate ovarian cycling and energetically costly mating activities (Grueter and Zinner 2004; Huang et al. 2012; Li J et al. 2014; Qi et al. 2008; see also Koenig et al. 1997). Among *P. nemaeus*, biannual birth peaks have been reported in February–May and September–October (Kulcharoen and Utara 2010; Lippold 1997; Ruempler 1998; Ulibarri 2013), although several researchers noted that birthing can occur throughout the year. These birthing peaks likely have adaptive significance similar to the phenological timing described among *Rhinopithecus* species.

S. concolor habitats are characterized by relatively constant environmental conditions with limited seasonal variation in climate and phenology, so it is expected that simakobu breeding is not strictly seasonal (Erb et al. 2012a). Although births occur throughout the year, 55% of births occurred during the wettest months, approximately six months after a peak in fruit availability. This pattern suggests that *S. concolor* may be capital breeders with conceptions flexibly timed to female energy reserves, an idea supported by data on female physical condition, where females appear to be in their best physical condition before and at conception, but decline to poor condition after birth. However, it is unclear whether this seasonal clustering of births in *S. concolor* is a result of small sample sizes or some unique features of the Mentawai Islands' ecology (e.g. higher rainfall, less fertile soils). In *N. larvatus*, there is no obvious birth seasonality, although there appear to be more births during the wet season (Boonratana 2011).

Female *Rhinopithecus* display no sexual swellings or any other external morphological signs of reproductive condition (Ren R et al. 1995; Yan and Jiang 2006). In contrast, *Pygathrix* oestrus is accompanied by reddening of the skin on the rump and inguinal area (Lippold 1977; Ruempler 1998). Sexual swellings are exhibited by both juvenile and adult female *S. concolor* (Tenaza 1989b). Female *N. larvatus* also exhibit sexual swelling and their external genitalia become conspicuously pink (Murai 2006). Sexual activities in *R. roxellana* are most frequent during the mating season (Kim et al. 2013; Qi et al. 2011). However, sexual behaviour is not confined to the mating season (Tan et al. 2004), and even pregnant and lactating females have been observed soliciting copulations among *R. roxellana* (Ren B et al. 2003; Yan and Jiang 2006). Similar solicitations have been reported among *P. nemaeus* (Ruempler 1998). Copulations are typically initiated by females in all species of *Rhinopithecus* and *Pygathix* for which data are available (Cui and Xiao 2004; Dong 2011; Guo et al. 2010; Li and Zhao 2007; Ogden et al. 1991; Qi et al. 2011; Ren B et al. 2003; Ren R et al. 1995; Ulibarri 2013; Xiang and Sayers 2009; but see Wang S et al. 2012).

Given the limited reproductive synchrony, *S. concolor* males are likely able to monopolize females and concentrate paternity (Erb 2012). Yet, the presence of sexual swellings could increase within-group synchrony, even in the absence of seasonal reproduction, and facilitate extra-group mating opportunities (Nunn 1999; van Schaik et al. 2001). Detailed studies of female receptivity and mating together with paternity analyses to test the function of sexual swellings in this species and their role in male reproductive monopolization are lacking. In *N. larvatus*, mating is initiated by solicitation from either males or females (Murai 2006; but see Yeager 1990b); both would solicit a female/male with a pouted face, but only females sometimes shake their heads from side to side.

Alloparenting or infant handling in the form of holding, carrying or grooming infants by non-mother caretakers (females, juveniles) is part of the behavioural repertoire of *R. roxellana* (Li Yinhua et al. 2005; Wada et al. 2015; Xi et al. 2008), *R. bieti* (Grueter 2009; Kirkpatrick et al. 1998), *R. avunculus* (Dong 2011), *P. nemaeus* (Lippold 1977), *S. concolor* (Erb, unpubl. data) and *N. larvatus* (Gorzitze 1996; Matsuda et al. 2012b). There are also reports of allonursing in both *R. bieti* (Ren et al. 2012a) and *R. roxellana* (Xiang et al. 2019); at the Shennongjia study site, the majority of young infants are intermittently nursed by females other than their mothers (Xiang et al. 2019). Snub-nosed monkey males can be highly tolerant of immatures (Grueter 2009; Kirkpatrick et al. 1998; Ruempler 1998), and on some rare occasions even actively partake in infant care (Wang S et al. 2012; Xiang et al. 2009b); variation in male interest in infants may partly reflect personality differences among males (Grueter, pers. obs.). Allomothering seems to be facilitated by the egalitarian dominance relationships and relaxed or well-mediated intra-group competition in these colobine societies (Maestripieri 1994; McKenna 1979), as well as the presence of related females in an OMU (Guo et al. 2015; Xiang et al. 2019). This behaviour may be particularly adaptive in ecologically demanding environments such as those inhabited by the temperate snub-nosed monkeys (Xiang et al. 2019) and can confer fitness benefits to the receiver of allocare; the mother. Benefits include increasing time for foraging and grooming and reducing energetic costs associated with infant care (Xi et al. 2008).

Discussion

In many aspects of morphology and behaviour, odd-nosed monkeys are typical colobines. They have morphological and physiological adaptations for leaf-eating (Chapters 5–7). They endure seasonal shortages of preferred foods (Chapters 9–11 and 13–15). One-male units and allomothering are defining elements of their social organization (Chapters 10, 11 and 13–15). Yet in many ways, odd-nosed monkeys deviate strikingly from other colobines. The secondary sexual characteristics of males can be uncommonly distinctive (see Chapter 18). Thriving in habitats from conifer forests to mangrove swamps, these monkeys inhabit some of the least hospitable environments of any extant non-human primate. In particular, the colonization of subalpine forests in temperate China has led to an array of adaptations to chronic and severe climatic extremes, and patchily distributed and exceptionally seasonal resources. The multilevel social organization found in many odd-nosed taxa may represent a unique adaptation that combines the colobine hallmark of OMUs into larger groups able to defend against conspecific males attempting takeovers.

Despite being touted as 'leaf monkeys', odd-nosed monkeys are not obligate folivores; fruits and seeds constitute an essential part of the annual diet of all odd-nosed monkeys except the predominantly lichenivorous populations of *R. bieti* inhabiting ecologically extreme temperate montane environments. This high reliance on lichen is unusual among primates[3] and is a result of seasonality and resource stress. Research has shown that lichens are a moderately high-quality fallback food as they contain considerable amounts of digestible carbohydrates, but are relatively protein deficient (Kirkpatrick 1996). Animals subsisting on lichens are liable to be in negative nitrogen balance (Dubay et al. 2008), so it is plausible that *R. bieti* that fall back almost entirely on lichens in winter are in or near negative nitrogen balance (Bissell 2014). Additional research focusing on how nutrient balancing is achieved in winter would offer novel insights into this species' adaptability, e.g. through applying the Geometric Framework of Nutrition (Simpson and Raubenheimer 2012).[4]

[3] But see Ménard and Vallet (1997) for Barbary macaques (*Macaca sylvanus*) and Vedder and Fashing (2002) and Miller et al. (2020a) for Adolf Friedrich's Angolan colobus monkey (*Colobus angolensis ruwenzorii*)

[4] A recent study using this framework has shown that *R. roxellana* dynamically alter their patterns of nutrient selection to compensate for seasonal changes in thermogenic requirements (Guo et al. 2018).

Taxa with specialized diets may face greater risks due to changing environments and climate change. Given the high importance of lichen in the diet of some snub-nosed monkey populations, the slow regeneration time of this resource (Grueter et al. 2009b; Keon and Muir 2002; Kirkpatrick 1996) and the general susceptibility of lichens to environmental changes such as air pollution and climate change (Aptroot 2009; Seaward 1987; Wang et al. 2020), these ecological features raise concern about the long-term survival of these species. It is not only lichens that are vulnerable, but also host trees such as firs are predicted to decline significantly in the coming decades (Wong et al. 2010). Similarly, some populations of *P. nemaeus* have a predominant dietary reliance on a single species of Dipterocarp tree, *Parashorea stellata* (Ulibarri 2013), which are becoming extirpated throughout their distribution range due to anthropogenic impacts and climate change (Ashton 1988; Corlett and La Frankie 1998; Lippold and Vu 2008; Nguyen et al. 1996). Although feeding primarily on leaves, *N. larvatus* exploits ubiquitous food sources that may make them somehow resilient to small forest losses and fragmentation (Matsuda et al. 2020b).

Odd-nosed monkeys occupy habitats ranging from tropical peat swamp forests at sea level to high-altitude temperate forests dominated by fir trees. This wide spectrum in habitat association is responsible for the variation in dietary richness, ranging from a diet composed of <30 plant species in *R. bieti* at Xiaochangdu to a diet composed of 188 species in *N. larvatus*. While the diet of all colobines shows variation across seasons (Chapters 9–11 and 13–15), seasonality in resource use is particularly pronounced in the temperate-dwelling odd-nosed monkeys which experience more resource stress and temporal dietary restrictions (Hanya et al. 2013; Ting S et al. 2008). The high predictability of fruiting and flushing in temperate forests (Hanya et al. 2013) could encourage a strategy whereby these primates generate fat deposits by feasting on fruit in the fall (see Zhao Qikun 1994) and partially relying on those deposits to afford metabolic costs during the nutritionally stressed winter, thereby increasing their survival prospects. However, seasonal changes in body mass have not yet been recorded for wild odd-nosed colobines.

A combination of ecological and social factors is likely responsible for the expansive nature of many odd-nosed monkeys' home ranges. For snub-nosed monkeys, low habitat productivity, pronounced habitat heterogeneity with resource-rich patches separated by impoverished areas, slow post-harvest renewal rates of foods, and remarkably large group sizes create a unique suite of pressures that largely explain their exceptionally large ranging areas (Grueter et al. 2008; Kirkpatrick et al. 1998; Li D et al. 2010b). In areas where *Pygathrix* live in remnant forest patches, their decreased home range is likely related to increased habitat productivity and the high quality of mature leaves (Hoang 2007; Hoang et al. 2011; Ulibarri 2013).

Social organization of odd-nosed colobines appears to be broadly similar, although detailed data on some species (most notably *Pygathrix*, *R. avunculus* and *R. strykeri*) are missing. Most share the tendency to form band-level societies which seem to vary in cohesiveness/fission-fusion tendencies in to relation habitat productivity and food distribution, with more tropical species exhibiting greater fluidity in grouping than more temperate species (Kirkpatrick 1998; Kirkpatrick and Grueter 2010). Nonetheless, the penchant for modularity in the odd-nosed monkeys is likely to be at least partly phylogenetically inert.

The finer social dynamics within and between different tiers of snub-nosed monkey multilevel societies have only recently been studied in some species. An individual's decision to invest in a particular partner appears affected by the fitness benefits (i.e. perceived mating or infant care value) that partner can provide at a given time, e.g. coresident females are preferred partners for interaction during the birth season (especially when they have infants), whereas males become targets of female attention in the mating season (Wei et al. 2012; Yu et al. 2013). The nature of male-male relations in band societies for most odd-nosed monkeys remains somewhat enigmatic, but several factors indicate a system heavily influenced by competition, including substantial dimorphism, maintenance of distance among leaders, complete lack of affiliation and outbreaks of ritualized or actual fighting under crowded conditions. However, a recent study by Xiang et al. (2014) documented collective action involving OMU leader males. Interestingly, this collective action does not seem to be based on inclusive fitness benefits considering males were not related. Mutualism, whereby males derive immediate direct benefits, provides a better explanatory framework for these events. Vocalizations were more common among male *P. nemaeus* compared to females, and more common when bands were fissioned into units, suggesting that vocalizations may be part of the competitive repertoire between males (in advertising mate quality or resource defence; see also Koda et al. 2018 for *N. larvatus*), and to coordinate distance and activities between males of dispersed foraging units (Ulibarri et al. 2015).

Female dispersal in odd-nosed monkeys implies that either the benefits of dispersal are substantial or the costs are low, depending on the species in question. Indeed, three patterns are consistent with the notion of relatively low costs inherent in changing group residency for females in these taxa. First, the relatively high abundance of food resources leading to low levels of contest competition results in reduced reluctance among colobine females to emigrate (Murai et al. 2007; Zhang et al. 2008a; van Schaik 1989; Wrangham 1987). Second, relatively low predation pressure (as in snub-nosed monkeys) reduces the risk of emigrating and being temporarily disassociated with a group (Kirkpatrick 2011). Third, colobines residing in multilevel societies in which target social units are often part of the same band and are thus both familiar to prospective dispersers and in close spatial proximity, are likely to experience smooth transfers (Kirkpatrick 2011; Zhang et al. 2008a). Inbreeding avoidance is thought to be an important driver of natal female dispersal, at least in *R. roxellana* (Qi et al. 2009; Zhao et al. 2008a). The observation that adult female *R. roxellana* tended to transfer into units with fewer females is indicative of a strategy of avoiding mating competition (Zhao et al. 2008a). However, variables driving dispersal may no longer be fully adaptive in areas of high human-caused habitat fragmentation, in which dispersal opportunities may be limited and the choice of target groups constrained.

A universal cost of forming large groups such as those typically displayed by odd-nosed monkeys is intensified resource competition, which can negatively affect energy budgets, development and reproductive performance and ultimately limit group size (Altmann and Alberts 2005; Dunbar 1988; Janson and Goldsmith 1995; Markham and Gesquiere 2017; Terborgh and Janson 1986; van Schaik 1983). Both males and females compete over food, but while male lifetime reproductive success is ultimately contingent on the availability of females and successful insemination, female reproductive success is limited more by procurement of food than by access to mating partners (Bradbury and Vehrencamp 1977; Brockelman 2009; Trivers 1972). Resource competition can manifest in two ways: scramble and contest (Isbell and Young 2002; Janson 1988; Sterck et al. 1997). Contest competition is expected to prevail where food occurs in defensible clumps, which can result in animals competing aggressively over access to resources, giving rise to stable and linear dominance hierarchies of females, coalitions and female philopatry. Differential intake rates of dominant and subordinate females may translate into higher fitness and reproductive output of dominants (e.g. Pusey et al. 1997; van Noordwijk and van Schaik 1999). Alternatively, under a within-group scramble competition scenario food is dispersed or found in large patches, and the net amount of food available per individual decreases with increasing group size, which may negatively affect reproductive success of all individuals in a group (Hill et al. 2000; Koenig 2002; Snaith and Chapman 2008). Under such a situation, females will gain little by forming dominance relationships or alliances, or by being philopatric.

Knowledge of the levels and intricacies of competition influencing odd-nosed monkey ecology has increased in recent years, but an understanding of how feeding competition impacts female-female relations remains largely unexplored. *Inter-band* competition is unlikely to be of significant importance in these taxa for two reasons. First, inter-band encounters appear to be rare (Kirkpatrick et al. 1998; Zhang et al. 2006; but see Liu 2012), and when they happen bands sometimes seem to intermix (Bleisch and Xie 1998; Qi et al. 2014). *Intra-band* scramble competition, i.e. increased foraging effort necessitated by an increase in group members, appears to be present, yet somewhat weak, in Chinese/temperate *Rhinopithecus* (Grueter and van Schaik 2010; Grueter et al. 2008; see also Chapter 18, but see Liu et al. 2013a; Fan et al. 2018). However, intra-band scramble competition may be driving daily patterns of fission-fusion among units in *P. nemaeus*. In one study, these odd-nosed colobines exhibited a daily fission-fusion pattern between units that correlated to daily activity budgets; units rested significantly more when fused as bands, and moved, fed and vocalized significantly more when fissioned into units, possibly as an adaptation to avoiding intra-band scramble competition (Ulibarri 2013; Ulibarri et al. 2015). *Inter-unit* contest competition may be operating in these societies regarding access to food or mates, and monopolization of valued patches by dominant units is a real possibility. Grueter et al. (2009a) noted that the low density and clumped distribution of preferred resources, e.g. fruiting trees, can be conducive to the occurrence of contest competition in *R. bieti*. They observed two events that can be interpreted as manifestations of contest over access to resources: 'In May 2006, large, dominant OMUs appeared to defend leafing trees (rare *Pterocarya* trees) from other nearby units. The lower-ranking units appeared to wait in nearby conifer trees eating lichens until the more dominant units left the leafing trees. In January 2007, one unit chased away another unit from an *Acanthopanax* tree that still bore fruits' (620). Last, *intra-unit* contest competition for food tends to be unimportant, as evidenced by low rates of agonistic interactions among females in core units (Cui et al. 2014; Zhang et al. 2010).

As a result of low levels of intra-unit feeding competition, relationships among females are relatively relaxed (Yeager and Kirkpatrick 1998). Following Sterck et al. (1997), most odd-nosed monkeys could be classified as 'dispersal-egalitarian', i.e. they have weakly developed, unstable dominance hierarchies, rare or absent coalitions and female transfer. However, there are observations that may run counter to this argument which may be symptomatic of inherent weaknesses in the model (see Koenig and Borries 2009; Korstjens et al. 2002). Linear dominance hierarchies have been reported for *R. bieti* females (Cui et al. 2014) but these were not very stable and tend to be individualistic. Moreover, these data are from captive females which may have experienced heightened competition. Female 'exogamy' also seems to be in conflict with the strong affiliative bonds seen in at least some species, e.g. *R. roxellana* in which females frequently participate in sociopositive interactions (Ren et al. 2000; Zhang et al. 2006), form coalitions against males (Ren et al. 2000, 2011; Zhang et al. 2006), and stick together after male takeovers (Zhang et al. 2008a). Female relationships are likely to provide different kinds of benefits, such as ensuring access to alloparents, which can relieve maternal burden and free up time for the mother to engage in subsistence and hygienic activities (Stanford 1992; Xi et al. 2008). Larger groups of cooperating females may also be more effective at reducing infanticide (Saj et al. 2007).

Infanticide has been observed in two species of snub-nosed monkeys and in proboscis monkeys, although some cases are from semi-free ranging groups. Critical information to assess the functional basis of infanticide is not available for all the documented incidents of infanticide, but the majority of cases conform to predictions of the sexual selection hypothesis. This hypothesis posits that infanticide has evolved as a reproductive strategy for males: upon taking over a social unit, males kill unrelated, unweaned infants to shorten the inter-birth interval of the mother and improve their chances of siring her next infant (Hrdy 1974; van Schaik 2000a). The relative paucity of infanticidal records in *Rhinopithecus* and the absence of records for *Pygathrix* in captivity or the wild[5] may be related to their multilevel social system. Several mechanisms for this putative lowered risk of infanticide are conceivable. First, in a multilevel social system in which possible target units for dispersing females are never far away, females can transfer at relatively low cost and risk. Thus, females have the option of leaving aggressive and potentially infanticidal

[5] Caution is advised against interpreting a lack of infanticide observations given the relatively low observation hours for some *Rhinopithecus* species and all *Pygathrix* species.

males (Teichroeb et al. 2009a). Second, female extra-unit matings are facilitated by close inter-unit proximity. Extra-unit copulations and paternity have been confirmed for *R. roxellana* (Guo et al. 2010; Qi et al. 2020; Zhao et al. 2005), and the resulting paternity dilution represents an additional counter-strategy to infanticide as males are expected to abstain from killing infants that they may have sired (Hrdy 1979; Qi et al. 2020; van Schaik 2000b). Third, collective action among OMU males in response to imminent external threats emanating from bachelor males reduces the frequency of takeovers and associated infant killings (Xiang et al. 2014). Last, abortion may represent another counter-strategy employed by females to avoid infanticide (Ren et al. 2011).

A Precis on the Conservation Status of Odd-Nosed Colobines

Odd-nosed monkeys are restricted to Asia, where 73% of primate species are threatened with extinction (Estrada et al. 2017). The numbers are even worse for odd-nosed monkeys, as 100% of the species in this taxon are listed as either Endangered (*Rhinopithecus bieti, R. brelichi, R. roxellana, Pygathrix nemaeus, P. nigripes, Nasalis larvatus*) or Critically Endangered (*Rhinopithecus avunculus, R. strykeri, Pygathrix cenerea, Simias concolor*) by the IUCN (2019). Odd-nosed monkeys face numerous survival threats (Chapter 20; Li et al. 2018). As relatively large-bodied and slow-moving animals, hunting represents the greatest threat for most odd-nosed species, as monkeys are hunted and trapped for body parts, often for medicinal purposes or consumed as bushmeat. For instance, proboscis monkeys are often hunted for bezoar stones, an intestinal secretion used in traditional Chinese medicine (Meijaard and Nijman 2000), and doucs are hunted for food, wine, and are used to create a variety of medical tonics and balms (Ha 2007; Lippold and Vu 2008). In the Mentawai Islands, simakobu monkeys are the favoured prey of indigenous people, and hunting has caused a rapid decline in their population numbers throughout the archipelago, and affected their social organization (Erb et al. 2012b; Fuentes and Ray 1996). Forest clearing, logging and conversion are major threats for all species, particularly those with large populations outside of protected areas. Roads, dams and mining represent secondary threats to many species, and development associated with tourism are concerns for several snub-nosed monkey populations in China. The widespread forest fires experienced in the peatlands of Borneo have destroyed a significant proportion of proboscis monkey habitat, and represent a major ongoing threat to this species (Meijaard et al. 2008). To halt or reverse the impending extinction of some of these odd-nosed colobines, effective scientific, political and management decisions need to be implemented immediately. These conservation measures must balance the ever-increasing needs of human populations with biodiversity protection and 'address the social, cultural, economic, and ecological interdependencies that are the basis of primate conservation' (Estrada et al. 2017: 11; Chapter 20).

Conclusion

The past two decades have seen impressive growth in the depth and breadth of research on odd-nosed monkeys, most of it conducted in the field. No doubt, the future will hold new discoveries and present new challenges. Much of our increased understanding will certainly come from applied conservation research on responses to habitat fragmentation, with spatial models covering entire landscapes, and through comparative studies of disturbed and undisturbed populations. Continued and refined applications of a variety of methodological tools such as social network analyses, GPS loggers and nutritional, microbial, and endocrinological assays will further improve our understanding of how these primates interact with their social and ecological environment. The wealth of knowledge we now have about odd-nosed monkeys, and their continued survival, is a tribute to the hard work of the current generation of researchers and conservationists, highlighted through contributions to this edited volume. These scientists continue to both advance the frontiers of knowledge and ensure that these monkeys survive into the future.

Acknowledgements

We thank Yang Yin, Julie Teichroeb and one anonymous reviewer for comments on this text.

13 Ecology of *Semnopithecus*

Ken Sayers

Introduction

The Asian colobine genus *Semnopithecus* is among the most phenotypically pliable of all primate genera. This is reflected in their expansive geographical distribution, their impressive ability to colonize and persist in novel habitats, and considerable between-troop ecological and social variation.

Distribution

The present chapter recognizes three species in the genus *Semnopithecus*: the grey langur (aka Hanuman or sacred langur, *S. entellus*), the Nilgiri langur (*S. johnii*) and the purple-faced langur (*S. vetulus*). Recommendations to elevate former subspecies to full species (valuable contributions by Groves 2001; Roos et al. 2014; Chapter 2) based on the taxonomic and/or phylogenetic species concepts (reviewed in Wilkins 2009) are not followed. This conservative stance is preferable because even subspecies distinctions remain provisional due to limited information on within-group, between-group and population-level variation – ecological, morphological, behavioural – across the *Semnopithecus* range (Oppenheimer 1977; Sayers et al. 2008; Nag et al. 2011). In general, the taxonomy in this chapter is modified from Roos et al. (2014; Chapter 2) to consider their species as subspecies which, while in flux, will be mentioned at the outset for reference.[1]

Grey langurs – known for their dusky white coats, dark faces, long tails and importance in Hindu folklore – are sexually dimorphic monkeys found over much of the Indian subcontinent. Historical treatments that recognized 15 or more subspecies (Ellerman and Morrison-Scott 1951) have been reduced to more modest numbers (e.g. Brandon-Jones 2004).

This chapter includes Electronic Supplementary Material (ESM) at: www.cambridge.org/colobines

[1] Until relatively recently many treatments did not recognize *Semnopithecus*, and placed Asian colobines, excepting the odd-nosed forms, into the genus *Presbytis* (e.g. Napier and Napier 1985/1994). While this classification has it merits, it has been largely supplanted with a tripartite arrangement of these primates – *Presbytis*, *Semnopithecus*, *Trachypithecus* – with *Semnopithecus* generally considered a monotypic genus inhabited by *Semnopithecus entellus* (e.g. Oates et al. 1994). Mounting molecular evidence allies the purple-faced and Nilgiri langurs more closely with *Semnopithecus* than *Trachypithecus*, where they traditionally have been housed (Perelman et al. 2011; Wang et al. 2012; Chapters 2 and 15).

The populations can conveniently be divided in two latitudinal groups based on the normal disposition of the caudal appendage. In those with 'southern carriage' the tail loops away from the body and towards the ground (Jay 1965; Roonwal 1979, 1981b; Groves 2001). These include the tufted grey langur (*Semnopithecus entellus priam*), the southernmost variety usually recognized, which occurs in south India and the dry zone of Sri Lanka (Roos et al. 2014). Being the smallest of grey langurs, adult females average around 7 kg and adult males around 10. Also with southern carriage is the Malabar grey langur (*S. e. hypoleucos*) which ranges along the Indian southwest coast, extending east into the south central portion of the subcontinent.

Other grey langur populations exhibit 'northern carriage' where the tail loops forward. The northern plains grey langur (*Semnopithecus entellus entellus*) has an extremely wide distribution across central India; it is supplanted in the plains and foothills of north India and southern Nepal by the terai grey langur (*S.e. hector*). Himalayan grey langurs (*S.e. schistaceus*) follow Bergmann's Rule in their especially large size (Adult ♂♂ > 20 kg; adult ♀♀ > 15 kg) and are found to over 4000 m elevation from possibly Afghanistan in the west to Bhutan in the east.[2]

Other members of the genus have a more limited distribution. Nilgiri langurs (*Semnopithecus johnii*) are found in the Western Ghats, which includes the namesake Nilgiri Hills, of southern India. They are medium to large colobines (adult ♂♂ ~ 13 kg; adult ♀♀ ~ 11 kg) with black coats and substantial napes and crowns of brown (Rowe 1996). Possible hybridization between grey and Nilgiri langurs in the wild has been reported (Hohmann 1988; Nag et al. 2011).

The exclusively Sri Lankan purple-faced langur (*Semnopithecus vetulus*) is found in wet zone rain forests, the dry zone of the east and north, and in the central highland up to 2000 m elevation (Groves 2001). They are diminutive colobines (adult ♂♂ ~ 7 kg; adult ♀♀ ~ 5 kg) with silvered black coats, brownish heads and white mandibular hairs. Proposed subspecies include southern (*S. v. vetulus*) and northern (*S.v. nestor*) wet zone forms, a dry zone variety (*S.v. philbricki*) and a montane dweller (*S.v. monticola*) (Groves 2001).

Research Efforts

There has been considerable investigation of *Semnopithecus*, but this statement must immediately be tempered with the observation that truly long-term field studies remain a rarity. As with other colobines, relatively little research has been conducted

[2] Most classifications recognize two subspecies or species of Himalayan grey langur, differentiated most strongly by the color of the forearms. These are the pale-armed (*S.e. schistaceus*) and dark-armed (*S.e. ajax*) Himalayan langur. The dark-armed variety is reported from Himachal Pradesh and Jammu and Kashmir. Considerable variation in forearm coloration within single troops, and the finding that pelage coloration in living animals does not seem to reflect that described from museum specimens, indicate there is much to learn about the relationships of these animals. See Sayers and Norconk 2008.

in laboratories or zoos.[3] Representative, but not exhaustive, historical listings of field research are given in ESM Tables 13.1–13.3.

Semnopithecus entellus

The grey langur (*Semnopithecus entellus*) is perhaps the most intensively investigated colobine monkey (ESM Table 13.1). Beyond taxonomic studies, early work on this species was primarily of the 'interesting notes' variety (reviewed in Forbes 1894; McCann 1928) but also included pioneering, targeted field observations by naturalist Charles McCann, Assistant Curator with the Bombay Natural History Society, in the 1920s and 1930s (McCann 1933).

Studies of longer duration began in the late 1950s at Jaipur, India by the zoologist Ishwar Prakesh, and at Orcha and Kaukori, India by the anthropologist Phyllis Jay (later Dolhinow). They were followed shortly by the Japan-India Joint Project in Primates Investigation, spearheaded by Yukimaru Sugiyama, which investigated grey langurs at multiple sites from 1961 into the 1970s. Collectively these studies were influential, particularly Jay's descriptions of social organization and age-sex categorization, and Sugiyama's observations (and theoretical treatment) of group male membership changes, troop takeovers and the subsequent fate of infants. Grey langurs studies have continued more-or-less unabated to the present day, slowly chipping away at new habitats within their expansive geographical range. Most have lasted from only several months to several years in duration.

Only two grey langur projects can be considered unequivocally long-term. Observations on the outskirts of Jodhpur, India commenced in the late 1960s, initially under the direction of Surendra Mohnot, and have continued sporadically over the ensuing five decades. Although much of the work at Jodhpur has focused on social organization, reproductive behaviour and the issue of infanticide, studies of diet and other stereotypically 'ecological' topics have also been undertaken. Additionally, grey langurs at Ramnagar in the terai of southern Nepal were under observation for much of the 1990s. With a research programme initiated by Paul Winkler and outlined by Andreas Koenig, Carola Borries and Mukesh Chalise, data collection at Ramnagar was probably the most even-handed of any grey langur site, with detailed treatments of diet, ranging, and social organization and theoretically driven considerations of competition, socioecology and group dynamics.

The history of grey langur field studies can thus be succinctly summarized. The first decade (1955–1964) was largely devoted to the establishment of basic sociological and reproductive parameters. The second decade (1965–1974) witnessed increased focus on diet and ranging, with other studies beginning to utilize the grey langur as a 'model species' to examine specific questions of theoretical interest. Most famously this included infanticide, but also communication and Suzanne Ripley's (1967b) treatment of grey langur locomotion and posture, arguably the most

[3] The most notable exceptions come from colonies previously kept at the University of California, Berkeley and the California (National) Primate Research Center (e.g. Dolhinow 1980; Curtin 1981).

influential article ever published on this species in the domain of physical anthropology. From the third decade on (1975-present) topical foci have continued to broaden, with the 'model species' imperative continuing. The grey langur has proven a lynchpin for investigation of such disparate topics as sexual selection, the socio-ecological model for primate grouping, handedness or lack thereof, temperament, human-animal interactions, optimal foraging theory and movement ecology.

Semnopithecus johnii

Perhaps due to their comparatively restricted geographical distribution, the literature on Nilgiri langurs is much less voluminous than that for grey langurs. Following numerous morphological investigations, natural history notes, and some field observations by McCann (1933), studies of the Nilgiri langur began in earnest in the mid-1960s with the anthropologist Frank Poirier (ESM Table 13.2). His one-year study in Nilgiri District, Madras State, India was focused primarily on basic social organization, but also included preliminary dietary data and a detailed description of auditory and visual communication (Poirier 1970a, 1970b). Shortly thereafter zoologist and conservationist Robert Horwich – working at Periyar Sanctuary after some exploratory investigation by Jiro Tanaka (1965) – added some short-term, but ingenious and theoretically driven, studies of behavioural rhythms (Horwich 1976, 1980).

Among the most influential Nilgiri langur studies was that conducted at Kakachi by John Oates and colleagues (1980) on nutritional chemistry; it has served as a template for similar investigations across the primate order. A moderate number of additional studies, by other research teams, have added further data on Nilgiri langur diet and social organization; topical work has included investigations of niche partitioning and infanticide.

Semnopithecus vetulus

The purple-faced langur is perhaps the least-studied member of the genus (ESM Table 13.3). The dubious value ascribed to ecological and behavioural observation in the early twentieth century is well illustrated by W. C. Osman Hill's 1934 monograph on the species. Based largely on study of dead skeletons and equally dead skins, it is almost wholly morphological and taxonomic, and while showing typical Hill astuteness in these regards, provides little information on the living animals that resided not far from his medical college in Colombo, Sri Lanka. That this general perspective would change is reflected in Hill's laudable *Primates: Comparative Anatomy and Taxonomy* book series which commenced in the 1950s.[4]

Nonetheless, truncated accounts of purple-faced langurs (see also Pocock 1939) were not substantially improved upon until the late 1960s with investigations of

[4] These volumes included very useful reviews of psychological, behavioural and ecological work. Unfortunately, Osman Hill died before the publication of volumes which were to be dedicated to colobine monkeys and apes.

basic social and ecological parameters by Rasanayagam Rudram and G.H. Manley at the Horton Plains, a cloud forest, and Polonnaruwa, an archaeological reserve. The latter site received additional attention near this time, resulting in numerous publications. Two of the most striking were comparative: Theodore Grand's (1976) investigation of the relationship between movement speed and psychosocial factors in langurs (*Semnopithecus entellus* and *S. vetulus*) and toque macaques (*Macaca sinica*) and C.M. Hladik's (1977) investigations of the dietary strategies of grey and purple-faced langurs.

Research on purpled-faced langurs has continued sporadically, mostly in the context of broad survey work (Nijman 2012). Beyond that, of note are Jinie Dela's (2007) intensive study of diet at Panadura and Piliyandala, Eschmann and colleagues' (2008) work on communication (Eschmann et al. 2008) and Rajnish Vandercone and colleagues' comparative analysis of random walk models (*Semnopithecus entellus* and *S. vetulus*, Vandercone et al. 2013).

Habitat and Climate

Categorizations of *Semnopithecus* habitats, as described by field researchers for individual study sites, are given in ESM Tables 13.1–13.3. The grey langur (*S. entellus*) is on the short list of non-human primates inhabiting the widest range of environs, from arid regions and villages, where they are often provisioned, to dry or moist deciduous, evergreen or mixed subtropical forest, to the temperate woodland and scrubby alpine of the Himalayas. Nilgiri langurs (*S. johnii*) of the Western Ghats inhabit areas known locally as shola, which are patches of low-canopy montane forest interspersed by swaths of grassland, and are also found in areas of relatively continuous subtropical or montane tree cover. Purple-faced langurs (*S. vetulus*) are habitat generalists and can be found on rubber plantations, in home gardens, and in dry or wet forests, including montane tropical forest.

Climate varies considerably based on locale, but a unifying feature across most of the *Semnopithecus* range is the alternating monsoon season. The Southwest Monsoon lasts from roughly June to September and provides much of the annual rain for a good portion of the subcontinent, excepting Southeast India and Northeast Sri Lanka, where the most noted precipitation occurs with the Northeast Monsoon from November to March (Hawkins et al. 1986). The most striking climatic extremes occur for *Semnopithecus entellus*. Jodhpur, India is a semi-arid hot zone for much of the year, for example, while at Junbesi, Nepal, a Himalayan site, below-freezing temperatures and snowfall are common from late November to early April.

Diet and Feeding Ecology

As with all colobines, members of *Semnopithecus* exhibit shearing dentitions, multi-chambered stomachs and abundant, symbiotic gut microbes that allow appreciable utilization, when necessary, of high-fibre or otherwise challenging foods (Bauchop and Martucci 1968; Kay and Davies 1994; Lucas and Teaford 1994). These can be viewed as features that can aid in expanding the dietary niche, as opposed to only constricting it (Robinson and Wilson 1998; Sayers 2013, 2017).

Semnopithecus dietary composition by study site is given in ESM Table 13.4. Grey langurs (*S. entellus*) live up to their reputation as 'eclectic feeders' (Ripley 1970: 486) and this has undoubtedly contributed to their demographic success. While leaves make up the plurality or majority of diet at most study sites, stereotypically high-fibre foods, such as mature leaves, are generally of lower preference than young leaves and other items when available synchronously (Kar-Gupta and Kumar 1994; Koenig and Borries 2001). Select fruits and seeds are highly sought-after at most study sites. Additionally, grey langurs exhibit tremendous diversity in supplemental foods; for example, at some lowland sites they are among the most insectivorous of colobine monkeys, while in the Himalayas they frequently extract underground storage organs (USOs) from the ground. Comparative study, while limited, suggests that grey langurs can easily coexist with closely related potential feeding competitors. This is likely due, in part, to both their dietary flexibility (Hladik 1977) and the less-appreciated flexibility of other colobines (Vandercone et al. 2012).

The foraging decisions of grey langurs at Langtang National Park in the Nepal Himalaya have been analysed in context of the optimal diet model from classical foraging theory (Sayers et al. 2010). As predicted, foods of high profitability (metabolizable energy divided by handling time) were preferred and generally taken at the rate they were encountered. The most profitable food in the annual diet was cultivated potato; interestingly, this ephemeral resource was associated with high degrees of active displacements during feeding (Sayers 2013). Other resources were treated differently. Non-seasonal foods of low profitability and high fibre content – evergreen mature leaves and certain species of woody roots and bark – were ignored until the barren winter, when little else was available, at which time they were consumed regularly. Subsistence in such seasonal and marginal habitats provides interesting comparative data when evaluating questions of niche breadth and range expansion in primate and human evolution (Sayers 2014).

Only a small number of dietary investigations have been conducted with the Nilgiri langur (*Semnopithecus johnii*), so generalizations concerning gross plant part exploitation, even if deemed instructive, are not possible. The study by Oates and colleagues (1980), however, established the Kakachi langurs as selective feeders. Few plant species were exploited, and the most heavily exploited items were characterized, most strikingly, by low fibre content. Additional characteristics associated with select staple foods included relatively high protein and water content, low condensed tannins and high pepsin/cellulose digestibility.

Dietary work with purple-faced langurs (*Semnopithecus vetulus*) in some ways presents a microcosm of changing perspectives on colobine monkeys generally. Early work by Hladik (1977) found that purple-faced langurs exploited more leaves and less fruit than sympatric grey langurs, and had an overall diet of comparatively meagre nutritional content. Thus, the purple-faced langur could be considered a textbook colobine monkey as considered at the time, specialized and strongly folivorous, as opposed to the atypical grey langur. Later work in home gardens and cultivated lands would illustrate just how flexible this animal could be, and at two sites (Panadura and Piliyandala) has been shown to be predominately fruit-eating, with a secondary penchant for young leaves (Dela 2007). Criticisms of this work for being conducted in altered environments (Nijman 2012) largely misses the point; the purple-faced langur has a much broader fundamental dietary niche than this species, and colobines in general, have historically been given credit for (reviewed in Sayers 2013). Work at Kaludiyapokuna Forest Reserve has added another population with a strong predilection for immature leaves, a heavy reliance on seasonal resources, and greater exploitation of fruits than mature leaves (Vandercone et al. 2012).

Activity Patterns

Diurnal activity patterns for *Semnopithecus* are given in ESM Table 13.5. Feeding or resting invariably constitute the plurality of the time budget; it should be noted that these activity patterns show partial overlap with more stereotypically frugivorous primates possessing comparable group and body sizes (see Sayers 2013).

The activity of an individual monkey, let alone an entire troop, is influenced by innumerable ecological, social, psychological and physiological factors. It is fair to say that this topic has, for the most part, been addressed at only a very general level. For *Semnopithecus entellus* at Kanha Tiger Reserve, India, for example, females spent more time engaged in social behaviours than males, and the aggregate troop fed more in winter (Newton 1992). Similarly, for grey langurs at Langtang National Park in the Nepal Himalaya, there was a negative correlation between overall vegetation abundance and time devoted to feeding (Sayers and Norconk 2008) although this result was not found at Machiara National Park in the Pakistani Himalaya (Minhas et al. 2013). Additionally, increasing habitat quality has been linked with increasing play behaviour in Indian grey langurs (Sommer and Mendoza-Granados 1995).

Activity research in Nilgiri and purple-faced langurs has stressed detailed description and theory over general quantification. Poirier's (e.g. 1970) classic study of *Semnopithecus johnii*, for example, included an evaluation of infant (age 10–112 days) play behaviour following five ontogenetic stages determined from studies of laboratory rhesus monkeys, in addition to, for all age-sex classes, evaluations of other major activity categories. Horwich (1980), utilizing continuous day-long observations of Nilgiri langurs, noted positive relationships between feeding and movement, movement and group dispersion, movement and auditory or visual displays, play and grooming and rest and social contact. This study was intended to open avenues for assessing the functions and motivations behind activity.

Similar remarks could be made about Suzanne Ripley (1967) and Theodore Grand's (1976) analysis of posture and travel in *Semnopithecus vetulus* – also *S. entellus* and *Macaca sinica* – at Polonnaruwa, Sri Lanka. Ripley provided nothing less than a foundation for a holistic study of bodily attitude incorporating ecology, social behaviour and anatomy. Grand, for his part, found that speed and other aspects of movement more closely reflected troop organization, substrate and individual psychological attitude than osteological differences between the forms. In other words, movement in itself could be considered a form or reflection of 'social behaviour'. Such work illustrates the nuanced insight that be gleaned from outside-the-box studies of activity pattern.

Range Use

Details on *Semnopithecus* ranging are given in ESM Table 13.6. As with activity patterns, range use can be influenced by myriad factors, and it is likely that many of these have yet to be identified.

Semnopithecus entellus offers a relatively large data set. Habitat utilization estimates vary considerably across sites: home ranges from less than 10 to well over 1000 ha, and daily paths averaging from 300 to nearly 2000 m. Differences in methodology across studies may contribute to this variation, but some general comments can nonetheless be made. For those grey langurs living in heterosexual troops, the smallest home ranges tend to occur in areas with greatest population density. This does not seem to apply, however, to all-male bands, which can range over incredible distances even in areas teeming with langurs (Dolhinow 1972a). These results underscore the importance of social and reproductive factors in movement.

On the more ecological side, food availability and dispersion have long been considered paramount with respect to travel patterns. In the Himalayas, where home ranges are comparatively enormous, daily path lengths are generally longest in winter, when food is scarce and highly dispersed (Sayers and Norconk 2008; Minhas et al. 2013) and similar associations have been found at lowland sites (e.g. Newton 1992). Another potential strategy for dealing with food scarcity is to reduce activity and travel, although this does not appear to be modus operandi for the grey langur.

Data from Nilgiri and purple-faced langurs does not, at present, differentiate them from grey langurs living under similar conditions. Nevertheless, some studies of *Semnopithecus johnii* and *S. vetulus* (Horwich 1980; Vandercone et al. 2013) again demonstrate how ranging could be investigated at finer levels, and/or with more attention to underlying mechanisms. Vandercone and colleagues (2013), for example, compared several random walk models to detailed movement and resource data from purple-faced and grey langur troops. The results illuminated those factors of memory, territoriality, tree distribution and feeding patterns that most likely underlie ranging behaviour. A next step would be to utilize such variables to develop realistic ecological and psychological models predicting where an individual or group will likely travel next (see Sayers and Menzel 2012).

Predation

Definitions of predation vary from 'when one organism kills another for food' (classical predation) to the much broader notion of 'any ecological process in which energy and matter flow from one species to another' (Taylor 1984: 3–4).

The treatment here trends towards the latter and will include situations where the exploited species does not necessary die (e.g. parasitism).

As predators, *Semnopithecus* exploit a large number of plants and, in select populations, invertebrates and the occasional fungus.[5] Predation on other vertebrates is essentially non-existent.

Reported predators and parasites of *Semnopithecus* are given on ESM Table 13.7.[6] In a broad review of classical predation, Hart (2007) found that Asian primates are most often reported being killed by felids, with additional persecution from canids, reptiles and raptors. This does not necessarily equate with actual predation danger; an episode where a Bengal tiger majestically dispatches a langur is probably more likely to reach the literature than a case where a deranged, semi-feral dog is implicated. Such danger will also be site-specific, with habitat features and alternative prey as key variables influencing how many monkeys end up on the menu (Seidensticker 1983). For example, although all *Semnopithecus* species spend some time on the ground, especially in disturbed habitats (Poirier 1969a), grey langurs are essentially half-terrestrial, presumably exposing them to a greater number of ground-moving and aerial predators.

Anti-predator behaviour in *Semnopithecus* – which includes considerable vigilance and mobbing activities – is generally considered sufficient evidence for the strong selective pressure exerted by classical predation (e.g. Srivastava 1991a). This is borne out by some direct data; in the most extreme case, Nilgiri langurs were found to make up 81% of leopard (*Panthera pardus*) diet over a three-year period at Periyar Sanctuary, India (reviewed in Hart 2007).

Viral, bacterial, protozoan and metazoan infection is common in wild and laboratory primates; severity of effects varies widely based on host species, host phenotype, parasite type and parasite load (Strait et al. 2012). Colobine monkeys tend to be underrepresented in this literature, and *Semnopithecus* is no exception. Nonetheless, recorded parasites (ESM Table 13.7) include the whipworm (*Trichuris* sp.) in Sri Lankan *Semnopithecus entellus* and *S. vetulus*; *Rotavirus* sp., a pathogen implicated in potentially fatal enteritis, in Indian *S. entellus*; and *Oesophagostomum* spp., a nematode also linked with gastrointestinal distress, in Himalayan *S. entellus*. All are widespread in non-human primates; additional data are required to tease apart their socioecological correlates (e.g. seasonality, relationship with population density) or

[5] This is in addition to invertebrates and fungi that are ingested incidentally while eating targeted plant foods.

[6] Reports of predation are widely scattered in the literature and difficult to document exhaustively. In addition, final tallies will be strongly influenced by research effort. For example, Nancy Muckenhirn (1973) is one of the few *Semnopithecus* workers to have performed a study explicitly investigating predation – in this case, of *S. entellus* and their leopard enemies on Sri Lanka. Studies focusing on the predators themselves are especially valuable, but these are equally, if not more greatly, scattered in the literature. The data on figure 7 in Muckenhirn (1973) can be considered a general outline of the types of predators that *Semnopithecus* face, but needs to be fleshed out with much added research. As far as parasitism goes, Nunn and Altizer (2005) have aided immensely by creating a repository of data with reference to primates. Due largely to religious stricture, *Semnopithecus* are only rarely killed purposefully by humans.

fitness consequences in *Semnopithecus*, although data from other genera provide some clear directional predictions (Nunn and Altizer 2006).

The occurrence of ectoparasites is combatted by individual and social grooming, often thought to be a predominate hygienic function of the behaviour. Nevertheless, while little studied in the genus, ectoparasite prevalence can range from abundance on virtually every monkey (ticks, *S. entellus*, Trapido et al. 1964) to non-existent (all ectoparasites, *S. entellus*, Mitchell 1977). Repercussions can be considerable: the tick-borne illness Kyasanur Forest Disease, transmitted by a flavivirus of that name, causes fatigue and frequent death in South Indian *Semnopithecus entellus*, and also presents a significant human health risk (Holbrook 2012). That parasites have played an important role in primate evolution is without question, although its effects at a broad ecological level have only infrequently been outlined (cf. Freeland 1976).

Social Organization and Behaviour

Social structure and organization as reported from various *Semnopithecus* sites are given in ESM Table 13.8.[7] As in most colobines, the one-male unit is common in reproductive groupings of *Semnopithecus*. In *Semnopithecus johnii* and *S. vetulus*, which possess comparatively small group sizes, it is the predominate form of social organization. In *Semnopithecus entellus*, where group sizes often exceed 20 individuals, multi-male, multi-female troops are increasingly common and indeed modal at many sites. It is generally thought that this is largely a practical repercussion of the number of females that a single male can successfully monopolize under various constraints including population density and breeding seasonality (Newton 1988; Koenig and Borries 2001).

Life history data provides variation on typical Old World monkey themes (see Chapter 16). Single births are generally spaced 1–3 years apart, with increased provisioning, food availability, or infant mortality (e.g. infanticide) known or suspected to reduce age at weaning and/or interbirth interval (*Semnopithecus entellus*, reviewed in Sterck 2012). Males generally disperse at or near puberty either voluntarily or through coercion; female dispersal occurs at low rates – generally less than 5% of females per year – in all three species, at least at select sites (Sterck 1998).

Female dominance hierarchies vary based on species and population. For *Semnopithecus entellus*, perhaps the most common variant involves a well-defined, age-inverse ranking where females are at their zenith early in their reproductive careers (e.g. Abu, Jodhpur and Ramnagar, reviewed in Koenig and Borries 2001).

[7] Numerous investigators have developed and/or refined environmentally-driven models to predict patterns of female primate social organization, and *Semnopithecus* has been a major player in this work. The 'socioecological model' approach has met with mixed success, and for very apparent reasons – phylogeny, physiology and psychology are referenced minimally in these models, and any treatment of grouping that marginalizes entire age-sex classes (such as adult males) in treatments of social dynamics will be incomplete (see, e.g., Zuckerman 1932; Carpenter 1934; Mendoza et al. 2002). A balanced incorporation of all relevant factors is essential. See also Chapter 16 for a detailed evaluation of evidence in Asian colobines.

Workers at other grey langur sites (e.g. Orcha, Kanha) have reported more amorphous and nuanced relationships. Much less has been written about other members of the genus. Poirier (1970b) described Nigiri langur female hierarchies as well defined, albeit subtler than that between males, and illustrated mainly by access to food patches – a result that would later be described for grey langur females at Ramnagar. Purple-faced langurs have been reported to have subtle to indeterminate dominance relationships (Manley, in Roonwal and Mohnot 1977: 308), although it should be noted that this was also the view of grey langurs in the 1960s.

As in primates generally, males in *Semnopithecus* multi-male, multi-female troops can be expected to exhibit a fairly straightforward, albeit temporally shifting, pecking order. Dominant *Semnopithecus entellus* males in multi-male, multi-female troops at Ramnagar, Nepal sire over half of the infants in a troop on average; their long-term reproductive success, however, is considerably lower than for harem males (Launhardt et al. 2001). Males outside of reproductive units occur as solitaries, in pairs or in all-male bands. While all-male bands have been reported in all three species, and are common at some sites, they are not universally characteristic. In Nepal Himalaya *Semnopithecus entellus*, for example, extra-troop males generally occur as solitaries or ephemeral pairs (Bishop 1979). The lowland site of Ramnagar, Nepal, evinces something similar (Koenig and Borries 2001) while at the Pakistani Himalayan site of Machiara National Park, surprisingly, very large all-male bands have been reported (Minhas et al. 2010b). Potential contributors to whether all-male bands form, while not well elucidated, include male tenure in reproductive troops and population density (e.g. Rajpurohit and Mohnot 1988; Koenig and Borries 2001).

Male troop takeovers have been reported in all *Semnopithecus* species, as has infanticide by males, which sometimes occurs in this context (*S. johnii*, Kavana et al. 2014; *S. vetulus*, Rudran 1973a). Most information comes from *Semnopithecus entellus*, where the interpretation of the reasons behind 'infanticide' or 'infant killing' became perhaps the most divisive polemic of twentieth-century primatology. It began in 1965, when Yukimaru Sugiyama reported a troop takeover, precipitated by an all-male band, at Dharwar, India. One of the attackers took over as resident male, and subsequently attacked multiple troop members, including all resident infants, who were seriously injured, and several mothers, who were not. All infants were abandoned.[8] Sugiyama (1965: 413–414) explored several reasons for the new male's behaviour, including a probable reduction in interbirth interval via the females becoming sexually receptive soon after the cessation of lactogenic suckling, and the likelihood that the male was targeting unrelated infants. Sarah Hrdy (1974, 1977b) later incorporated and generalized these ideas into an evolutionary, sexual selection-based hypothesis after making similar observations at Mount Abu. In short, the sexual selection hypothesis views infanticide (of the kind described) as a genetically based, biological trait that enhances reproductive fitness. The hypothesis would

[8] Sugiyama (1966) later experimentally removed an adult male from a harem. All four infants died after bites from an extratroop male, who divided time between his new troop and his old one, also a reproductive unit, until settling back into the latter after 'sexual activity . . . became dull' (p. 63).

be extended to account for infanticide in numerable primate and non-primate taxa (e.g. van Schaik and Janson 2000).

A full examination of the subsequent debate would require a separate book. But suffice it to say that the scenario described by Sugiyama has played out many other times, at many sites, including some with minimal human disturbance, such as Kanha, India (Newton 1986) and Ramnagar, Nepal (Borries et al. 1999a). This would seem to run counter to the opposing social pathology hypothesis (Curtin and Dolhinow 1978) which posits that the single male troop structure most conducive to – but not required by – the 'stereotypical infanticide scenario' is largely a byproduct of abnormal, anthropogenic environments. Nevertheless, criticisms of the sexual selection hypothesis remain constructive; among the most pertinent questions is the unknown target of selection (the definition of the 'trait', e.g. the genetic underpinnings of aggression generally, or infanticide in particular) and the comparative selective importance of the phenomena (e.g. Boggess 1984; Sussman et al. 1994; counterpoints in Sommer 2000; Koenig and Borries 2001).

Less bloody, but possibly more vital, is the habit of allomothering or aunting, where infants are transferred to non-mother females (adults or older immatures) who carry them for a time, and may nurse if lactating. Among Old World anthropoids, it is particularly marked in colobine monkeys (McKenna 1979) and is a common occurrence in all *Semnopithecus* species (e.g. *Semnopithecus entellus*: Jay 1965; *S. johnii*: Poirier 1970b; *S. vetulus*: Rudran 1973a). Functional hypotheses, not mutually exclusive, include increased feeding rates for unencumbered mothers, experience in infant handling for young females, and, potentially, speedier growth and reduced interbirth intervals (Kohda 1985; van Noordwijk 2012). Allomothering and other forms of cooperative care, stemming partially from observations in *Semnopithecus*, have been incorporated into general models of human evolution (e.g. Hrdy 2001).

Discussion

Members of *Semnopithecus*, in the nineteenth century, were known primarily for their complex and in some ways ruminant-like digestive system (Darwin 1871/1981: 197) and in the twentieth century for unsettling occurrences of male troop takeover and infanticide. These characteristics, of course, are not unique to the genus, and should not be relied upon too heavily to characterize why *Semnopithecus* should be of continuing interest to the zoologist, psychologist, or anthropologist (Stanford 1996a).

For one, they are exceedingly flexible primates, with a range equalled by few other genera. Much of this is due to the ubiquitous grey langur, but even more limited study of Nilgiri and purple-faced langurs has illustrated notable phenotypic plasticity in relation to habitat, diet and/or social organization. From the perspective of workers interested in exploring the primate roots of the human condition – a condition primarily characterized by a striking generalism – the ongoing investigation of such animals, and the underpinnings of their behavioural variation, will provide valuable comparative data.

It is useful to identify several areas, by no means exhaustive, that are in great need of further research. Obviously, this includes new investigations of any kind on *Semnopithecus johnii* and *S. vetulus*. While the work performed to date has been insightful, it is fair to say that our knowledge of these species is, by comparison, not much beyond that which was known about grey langurs some four decades ago, due to the sheer volume of studies.

Interestingly, of broad general topics, perhaps the least investigated in *Semnopithecus* is predation. Given that predation danger has historically been considered of paramount importance in animal grouping and behaviour, and that its repercussions on primate evolution has recently been reevaluated (Hart and Sussman 2005), this is hoped to change.

The vast majority of *Semnopithecus* studies have been approached from the angles of evolutionary theory, anthropology and conservation. While these are all very good angles, others, while presenting challenges, could profitably be incorporated. Only a limited number of studies, for example, have dealt with the proximate (genetic, physiological, neurological) mechanisms of behaviour. As with other colobines, psychological studies, including those in sensory ecology, are exceedingly rare. There have yet to be, for example, any detailed studies of how perception, categorization, memory or other cognitive processes are utilized in foraging, social interactions or movement. Ontogenetic studies remain a rarity, as are those that link individual behaviour with group-level phenomena.

These admonitions should not be taken as criticisms. Rather, they are tantalizing opportunities for the intrepid investigator to advance our knowledge of not only of this remarkable genus, but of primate biology generally.

Conclusion

Semnopithecus is a demographically successful, behaviourally and ecologically flexible genus of Asian colobine. Its study has played a major role in the development and study of topics as narrow as digestive physiology, and as broad as natural selection, sexual selection and the ecological niche. Future work will undoubtedly continue to highlight *Semnopithecus* taxa as ideal model organisms to address key questions from numerous academic disciplines.

Acknowledgements

I thank the editors for entrusting me with the chapter on this incredible primate genus. Thanks also to Cyril Grueter and an anonymous reviewer for helpful comments on an earlier version. Work at Langtang National Park, Nepal was supported by the L. S. B. Leakey Foundation and Kent State University and conducted in cooperation with Nepal's Department of National Parks and Wildlife Conservation and Ministry of Forests and Soil Conservation. Support for the writing of this chapter was provided by National Institutes of Health grant P51OD01133 to the Southwest National Primate Research Center and Texas Biomedical Research Institute.

14 Ecology of Sympatric and Allopatric *Presbytis* and *Trachypithecus* Langurs in Sundaland

Vincent Nijman

Introduction

In large parts of the distribution range of colobines only a single species is present or at most two or three species of different genera live sympatrically (Davies and Oates 1994). In western Africa we can find *Colobus*, *Piliocolobus* and *Procolobus*, in central Africa *Colobus* and *Procolobus*, in Myanmar and southern China *Rhinopithecus* and *Trachypithecus*, and in Indochina *Trachypithecus* and *Pygathrix*. In India's western Ghats and on northern Sri Lanka we find two species of the same genus living in sympatry, i.e. *Semnopithecus hypoleucos* and *S. johnii* in India (Hohmann 1988, 1989a) and *S. vetulus* and *S. priam* on Sri Lanka (Hladik 1977). In parts of Myanmar / northeastern India and northern Vietnam two species of *Trachypithecus* occur sympatrically (Choudhury 2014; Fooden 1996).

Sundaland, the area encompassing the Thai-Malay Peninsula, Sumatra, Borneo, Java and smaller surrounding islands is decidedly different. Here we find a mosaic of distribution patterns, with in some areas just one species present, in others two or three species of the same genus, or two or three species of different genera living in sympatry. For example, the silvered langur *Trachypithecus cristatus* lives without any other colobine on the islands of Bangka and Belitung, it lives sympatrically with one *Presbytis* langur throughout most of Sumatra, and possibly with two *Presbytis* langurs in northwestern Sumatra (Vermeer 1998). It lives sympatrically with proboscis monkeys *Nasalis larvatus* along Borneo's coastline, and it lives sympatrically with up to three species of *Presbytis* langurs in other parts of Borneo (Brandon-Jones 1996a,b; Meijaard and Nijman 2003). In various parts of Borneo two or three species of *Presbytis* langur live sympatrically, and globally the most diverse area for colobines is eastern Borneo where we find *T. cristatus*, three species of *Presbytis* langur and the proboscis monkey (D'Agostino et al. 2016; Meijaard and Nijman 2003).

These unique distribution patterns, especially where they pertain to ecologically similar *Trachypithecus* and *Presbytis* langurs, allow for an exploration of the effects of living in sympatry with potential ecological competitors. Morphologically, *Trachypithecus* and *Presbytis* langurs are similar enough for competition to be marked (Davies and Oates 1994). Both langurs have a body mass of between 5.5 and 7.5 kg, with males being slightly larger and heavier than females. Compared to *Trachypithecus*, *Presbytis* langurs have relatively longer hindlimbs, leap more and

This chapter includes Electronic Supplementary Material (ESM) at: www.cambridge.org/colobines

use quadrupedalism less (Fleagle 1977). The stomachs of *Presbytis* langurs are relatively smaller than those of *Trachypithecus* langurs, and dimorphism in body size in *Presbytis* is even less than in *Trachypithecus* (Caton 1999; Chivers 1994). Unfortunately, very few long-term studies (i.e. 12 months or more continuously, or several shorter stints) have been conducted on two species of these two genera in the same area at the same time. McClure (1964) observed groups of pale-thighed langur *P. siamensis* and dusky langur *T. obscurus* over a period of 33 months from a high platform in the forest canopy on the Thai-Malay Peninsula (but unfortunately for the purpose of this chapter mainly *T. obscurus* was observed). Bernstein (1967) also studied these two species for a year, alongside three other primates, and reported on their interactions. Curtin (1980) and MacKinnon and MacKinnon (1980) studied groups of *P. siamensis* and *T. obscurus* in Kuala Lompat on the Thai-Malay Peninsula, while a few years later Hardy (1988) studied *T. obscurus* and Bennett (1983) studied *P. siamensis*, both in Kuala Lompat. Nijman (2001; Nijman and Nekaris 2012) studied sympatric maroon langur *P. rubicunda* and white-fronted langur *P. frontata* in Sungai Wain in east Borneo (see ESM Table 14.2), and Nijman (2001; Nijman and van Balen 1998) also studied sympatric grizzled langurs *P. comata* and eastern ebony langurs *T. auratus* in Mts Dieng, central Java. Beckwith (1995) studied *T. auratus* on Mt Gede-Pangrango in west Java, but not the sympatric *P. comata*. Fortunately, Sujatnika (1992), a few years earlier, working in the same area, did exactly the reverse. Rodman (1973) studied Miller's langur *P. canicrus* in Kutai, eastern Borneo and while *P. frontata* was present, they were so rare that merely their occurrence was recorded. In other long-term study areas only one species of the two genera is present, e.g. Thomas langur *P. thomasi* in Ketambe and Bungana (Gurmaya 1989; Steenbeek and van Schaik 2001; Sterck 1995, 2012; Sterck et al. 2005; Wich et al. 2007); *P. rubicunda* in Gunung Palung, Tanjung Puting and Sebangau (Cheyne et al. 2018; Clink et al. 2017; Ehlers-Smith et al. 2013a,b; Marshall et al. 2014b; Supriatna et al. 1989); *P. comata* in Kamojang (Ruhiyat 1983, 1991); *T. auratus* in Pangandaran and Bali Barat (Brotoisworo 1983; Kool 1989, 1992, 1993; Tsuji et al. 2013a, 2013b, 2015, 2016, 2017; Vogt 2003); Selangor langur *T. selangorensis* in Kuala Selangor (Bernstein 1968; Furuya 1961).

Distribution

The genus *Presbytis* is confined to Sundaland (Figure 14.1). The species with the northernmost distribution, banded langur *P. femoralis*, ranges into southern Myanmar and Thailand, just north of the Istmus of Kra, the area that separates Sundaland from mainland Southeast Asia. The majority of species occur on the islands of Sumatra (seven species, living largely allopatrically) and Borneo (six species, living allopatrically and in sympatry depending on which part of the island we are). One species, the Siberut langur *P. siberu*, lives on the island of Siberut, off the west coast of Sumatra, and another species, the Mentawai langur *P. potenziani* lives on the islands of Sipora, North and South Pagai, just south of Siberut. *Presbytis comata* is found on the western half of Java, and the Natuna langur *P. natunae* lives on the island of Bunguran, midway between Borneo and the Thai-Malay Peninsula.

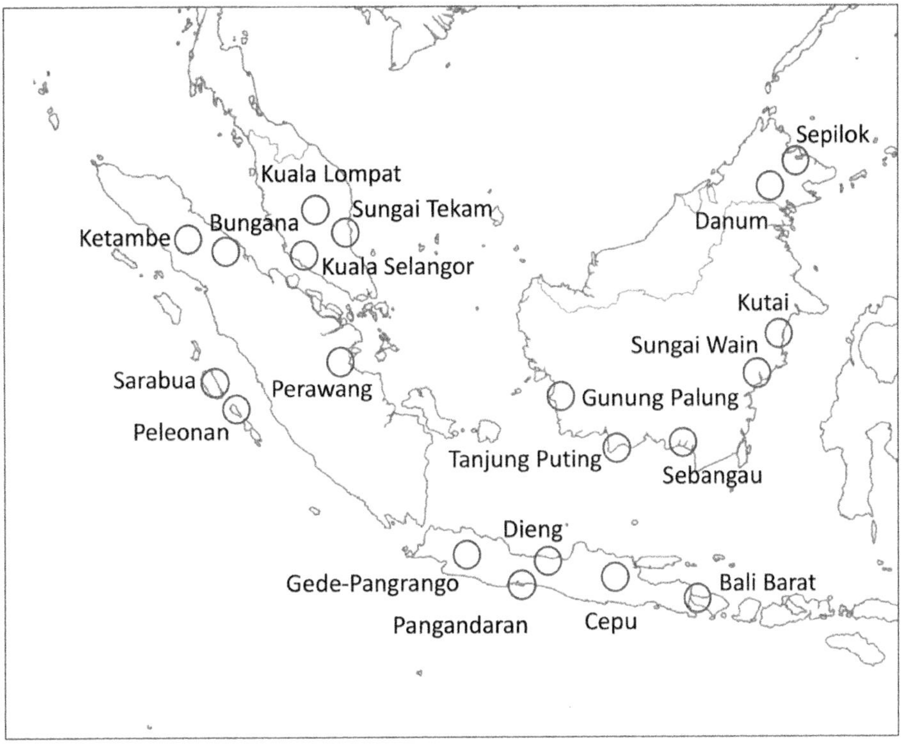

Figure 14.1 Selected study sites in Sundaland where *Presbytis* and/or *Trachypithecus* langurs have been studied.

Presbytis femoralis has a tripartite distribution, with populations on Sumatra, southern Thai-Malay Peninsula and Singapore, and the northern part of the Thai-Malay Peninsula; the central part of the peninsula is occupied by the white-thighed langur *P. siamensis*. Abdul-Latiff et al. (2018) found some support for recognizing the population in the southern Thai-Malay Peninsula as a separate species, Schlegel's langur *P. neglectus*, leaving the disjunct populations on Sumatra and the northern Thai-Malay Peninsula as *P. femoralis*. This suggestion is not followed here (see below under taxonomic and phylogenetic issues).

The species with the smallest geographic ranges are *P. natunae* (1600 km^2) and *P. siberu* (4000 km^2), and the one with the largest is *P. rubicunda* (300,000 km^2). Many of the *Presbytis* langurs are confined to lowland and hill forests below 1000 m asl, or occasionally into the lower montane zone, up to 1500 m asl; and indeed, in much of eastern Sumatra, the Thai-Malay Peninsula and Borneo, few mountain ranges are higher than this. Hose's langur *P. hosei* and Sabah langur *P. sabana* in northern Borneo are found up to 1600 m asl (Goodman 1989; Nijman 2010). On Java, *P. comata*, ranges from sea level far into the montane zone, with resident populations above 2500 m asl (Nijman 2017). Small island endemics, such as *P. natunae*, *P. siberu* and *P. potenziani*, range over the entire elevation range, but this is largely limited to the lowland zone (e.g. the highest point on Bunguran is 1035 m asl, on Siberut it is 384 m asl and on South Pagai it is 275 m asl).

Following Roos (Chapter 2), five species of *Trachypithecus* langur occur within this same region. *Trachypithecus obscurus* from the Thai-Malay Peninsula is largely sympatric with the *P. femoralis* or *P. siamensis*, and with *T. selangorensis*, which is confined to a narrow strip of coastal land in West Malaysia. In the northernmost part of its range in southern Thailand and Myanmar *T. obscurus* may be sympatric with the Tenarassim lutung *T. barbei* (Geissmann et al. 2004). *Trachypithecus cristatus* is found throughout Sumatra, Bangka, Belitung and Borneo. *Trachypithecus auratus*, despite one of its English common names the east Javan ebony langur, is found on throughout the island of Java (including the far west), but also on the islands of Bali and Lombok. The west Javan ebony langur *T. mauritius*, is found in the westernmost part of Java, where it is found in the lowland and hill forests along the north coast and the south coast, with *T. auratus* occurring in the mountains in between (Brandon-Jones 1995b). The recently described golden-crowned langur *P. johnaspinalli*, known only from an animal market in East Java, and presumably originating from Java or other parts of Indonesia (Nardelli 2015), refers almost certainly to partially and selectively bleached *T. auratus* (Nijman 2015).

Different than the *Presbytis* langurs in this region, the *Trachypithecus* langurs are found on a large number of smaller islands in the Indian Ocean (e.g. Langkawi, Penang and Mergui archipelago for *T. obscurus*, Peucang, Sempu and Nusa Barung for *T. auratus*), the Java Sea (e.g. Riau archipelago for *T. cristatus*) and the South China Sea (e.g. Serasan for *T. cristatus*, Perhentian for *T. obscurus*). Many of these islands are situated close to the Southeast Asian mainland or some of the larger islands in the region and would have been connected to these larger landmasses during glacial periods when sea levels were lower than at present.

The species with the smallest geographic ranges are *T. mauritius* (~10,000 km^2) and *T. selangorensis* (~20,000 km^2) and the one with largest is *T. cristatus* (~1,000,000 km^2), noting that many parts within these ranges are not, or no longer, occupied by the respective species. In terms of altitudinal distribution, *T. mauritius* is confined to the lowlands, mostly below 800 m asl, with one record from 1200 m asl (Brandon-Jones 1995b). While they have access to forest at higher elevations these are occupied by *T. auratus* with no evidence of the two species showing an overlap in their distribution. Likewise, *T. cristatus* and *T. selangorensis* are both largely confined to the lowlands, with the highest elevational records for the former being 1200 m asl (Wilson and Wilson 1977) and around 500 m asl for the latter (Southwick and Fedigan 1972). Within the distribution range of *T. cristatus* there are numerous mountain ranges but the species does not seem to enter these higher regions, whereas the distribution range of *T. selangorensis* comprises mainly lowland and hill forests. *Trachypithecus obscurus* is found up to 1800 m asl in the Thai-Malay Peninsula's central highlands. *Trachypithecus auratus* has the largest altitudinal range from sea level to >3500 m asl (Nijman 2014). In western Java, where the highest mountains are typically below 3000 m asl, the species occurs permanently in the upper montane forests just below the peaks, whereas in eastern Java, where several mountains are between 3000 and 3700 m asl, *T. auratus* also occurs in these upper regions (Docters van Leeuwen 1933; Kohlbrugge 1896; Nijman 2014).

Taxonomic and Phylogenetic Issues

Molecular techniques in the research of langurs thus far have been confined largely to taxonomy and phylogenetics. Taxonomies based largely on pelage and/or cranial characters resulted in a limited number of langur species being recognized in Sundaland (Groves 1970; Pocock 1935). Oates et al. (1994) listed seven *Presbytis* species, including *P. melalophos* from the Thai-Malay Peninsula, Sumatra, Bunguran and Borneo, and three species of *Trachypithecus*. Current taxonomies list a larger number of species (Chapter 2). This increase in species number is partially due to a different insight of what constitutes a species and partially due to a better understanding of the variation present in these species. The latter has been greatly aided by several molecular phylogenetic studies (although different studies may have showed different results leading to sometimes conflicting conclusions). While considerable efforts have been made to collect samples from the wild (e.g. Meyer et al. 2011), or to sample specimens from known localities, many molecular phylogenetic studies rely heavily on individuals sampled in zoos or private collections (Rosenblum et al. 1997; Vun et al. 2011; Md-Zain 2001). Furthermore, with notable exceptions (e.g. Meyer et al. 2011; Vun et al. 2011), mostly single mitochondrial markers have been used to infer phylogenetic relationships.

In researching *P. femoralis*, Abdul-Latiff et al. (2018) relied on 501 bp of the hyper-variable region of the mtDNA d-loop to infer the three population's evolutionary history. Unfortunately, individuals of the crucial population in Singapore, the type locality of the species, were not included in their analysis despite being available on GenBank (Ang et al. 2012), nor were samples from Sumatran *P. femoralis* populations included. In the absence of these data, Abdul-Latiff et al.'s (2018) taxonomic conclusion to treat the southern Thai-Malay Peninsula population as a single species, *P. neglectus*, and leaving the other populations within *P. femoralis* seem premature (Nijman 2019).

Issues related to the validity of *T. selangorensis* and *T. mauritius* based on analysis of molecular markers remain unresolved. While Roos et al. (2008) showed strong bootstrap support for a split between *T. selangorensis* and *T. cristatus*, Vun et al. (2011) showed these taxa to be paraphyletic, with one *T. selangorensis* being more closely related to a Bornean *T. cristatus* than to another *T. selangorensis*. Similar lack of support for the recognition of *T. selangorensis* as being distinct from *T. cristatus* was reported by Rosenblum et al. (1997). Morphologically, *T. selangorensis* seems to differ consistently from *T. cristatus* only in the shape of their whiskers (Roos et al. 2008). Support for a clade attributed to *T. mauritius* was supported by low bootstrap values (Roos et al. 2008), and crucially, the location from where they were sampled, Mt. Salak, is clearly outside the range of *T. mauritius* but within that of *T. auratus* (Brandon-Jones 1995b). This may explain that the smallest difference between *T. auratus* and *T. mauritius* (1.9%) is less than the largest within-species difference in *T. cristatus* (2.1%) (Tan et al. 2008). Furthermore, none of the seven 'diagnostic characters' that differentiate the *T. mauritius* specimens from Mt. Salak (sampled within the range of *T. auratus*) from other *T. auratus* individuals, i.e. differences in nucleotides, translate themselves into difference in amino acids (Tan et al. 2008). Morphologically, the only character that separates *T. mauritius* from *T. auratus* is the absence of light-tipped hair that may be present to a varying degree in *T. auratus* (Brandon-Jones 1995b).

Limited progress has been made on the population genetics of *Presbytis* or *Trachypithecus* langurs in Sundaland. This can be partially explained by the lack of proper facilities in the region combined with challenges in exporting primate samples from Indonesia. Thus, so far, the only population level molecular study conducted on these langurs is on a small population of *P. femoralis* in Singapore. Ang et al. (2012), based on variation in the mtDNA d-loop, showed that there was a low level of genetic variation within this isolated population. Singapore is also at the forefront of langur metagenomics, thus providing new and exciting insights into the diet, host genetics and parasite infestations of *P. femoralis* (Srivathsan 2014; Srivathsan et al. 2016).

Research Efforts

Analyses of over 150 papers and reports indexed on Google Scholar in December 2018 dealing with *Presbytis* or *Trachypithecus* langurs from Sundaland (many of which are cited in this and other chapters) shows that the most popular topics for study are (1) ecology, including ranging, feeding, social interactions (*Presbytis* 56 studies; *Trachypithecus* 28 studies), (2) taxonomy and phylogenetics (*Presbytis* 12; *Trachypithecus* 14), (3) diseases and veterinary medicine (*Presbytis* 4, *Trachypithecus* 14), (4) morphology including karyotyping (*Presbytis* 6; *Trachypithecus* 10) and (5) conservation (*Presbytis* 9; *Trachypithecus* 3). This suggests clear differences, with more ecological studies having been conducted on *Presbytis* and more veterinary and morphological studies having been conducted on *Trachypithecus*. This can be explained on the one hand by having many more species of *Presbytis* present in Sundaland with several of them studied at least once in their forest habitat, and some of them, such as *P. thomasi*, over a long period of time, and on the other hand by having more individuals of *Trachypithecus* langurs present in captive populations with some species being used as models to study various human diseases (e.g. Walker et al. 1973). The slightly higher number of conservation studies that have been conducted on the *Presbytis* langurs compared to *Trachypithecus* langurs is easily explained by the larger number of the former that are considered globally threatened.

While many species have been studied for at least one year (ESM Table 14.1), there are several species that only have been recorded during general surveys or that have been studied for shorter periods only. These include Sarawak langur *P. chrysomelas*, *P. frontata*, *P. canicrus*, bicolored langur *P. bicolor*, *P. natunae* and *T. mauritius*. *Trachypithus cristatus*, despite its wide distribution range has been included in many (multispecies) surveys but its ecology has not been studied in detail. Species that have been studied for multiple years at one or two nearby sites include *T. obscurus*, *P. siamensis* and *P. siberu*. Finally a number of species have been studied at multiple sites, for multiple years. These include *P. rubicunda*, *P. thomasi* and *T. auratus* (ESM Table 14.1).

Unfortunately, most field studies on langurs in Sundaland have been conducted in areas where just one species occurs, a smaller number were in areas where two species of different genera occur sympatrically (e.g. *T. obscurus* and *P. siamensis* in the Thai-Malay Peninsula; *T. auratus* and *P. comata* in western Java; ESM Table 14.1), but very few in area where two or three species of the same genus occur in sympatry (e.g. *T. obscurus* and *T. selangorensis* on the west coast of the Thai-Malay Peninsula or different *Presbytis* langurs in various parts of Borneo). Furthermore, even in areas where two or more langurs live sympatrically, studies often focus on just one of the species that is present and do not give details on the other species (this may have to do with the fact that where two or more langurs live sympatrically, often one is common and the other(s) are rare, see below).

Camera traps are currently also employed to gain insight in behaviours that are otherwise difficult to collect, including for instance terrestrially or visits to mineral-rich sources (Cheyne et al. 2018; Matsubayashi et al. 2007; Samejima et al. 2012). Indeed Pebsworth and LaFleur (2014) commented that camera traps do provide a viable data collection alternative, in situations where animal follows and habituation are not advisable. With respect to studying primate behaviour, the camera traps' ability to monitor fixed locations where a specific behaviour or resource use occurs, as well as interactions among and between species visiting these sites, important information has been collected on aspects that would have remained largely hidden from view if not for these camera traps.

Climate and Habitat

Sundaland historically has been covered in rainforest, rainforest and more rainforest (apart from small areas, mainly in the easternmost part of Sundaland, with a longer dry season and where deciduous forest grows). In terms of habitat and climate, then, it appears that the *Presbytis* and *Trachypithecus* langurs occur in wet and forested environments. While their geographic distribution range falls within a narrow latitudinal limit, i.e. between 11°N on the Thai-Malay Peninsula and 9°S on southern Lombok, especially the effects of the monsoons and topography result in a relative large amount of climatic variation. This expresses itself in differences in, amongst others, (1) mean annual temperature, (2) monthly temperature variation, (3) absolute amounts of rainfall and (4) variation in rainfall. Some areas with langurs experience long dry periods (i.e. months during which evaporation exceeds precipitation) whereas others are perhumid when precipitation exceeds 100 mm mo^{-1}.

Daylight length varies little over the region. In the northern Thai-Malay Peninsula it is light for 12:45 hrs during June–July and 11:30 hrs during December–January, and in southern Lombok it is reversed, with 12:35 hrs during December–January and 11:35 hrs during June–July.

Figure 14.2 gives an overview of the variation in climate in areas where *Presbytis* and *Trachypithcus* langurs occur. In terms of precipitation areas with the least

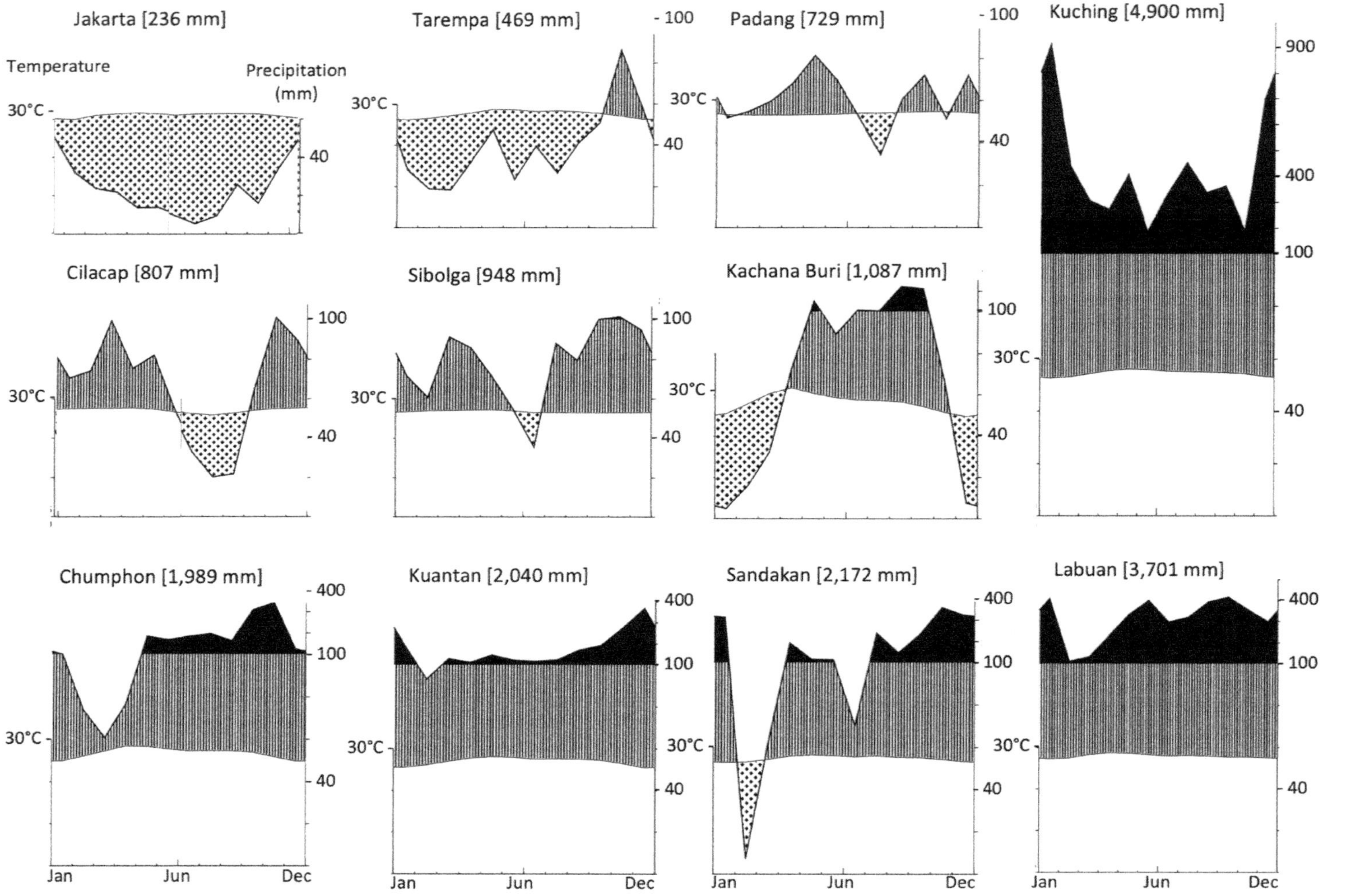

Figure 14.2 Climate diagrams from sites close to sea level with either *Trachypithecus* langurs, *Presbytis* langurs or both, ordered from the lowest amount of annual rainfall to the highest, displaying monthly average temperatures and precipitation. Stippled areas indicate months during which evaporation

amount of rainfall are the north coast of Java (Jakarta meteorological station), with *T. auratus* present, with 236 mm of rainfall, thus experiencing a permanent dry climate (in every month evaporation exceeds precipitation). The Riau Archipelago (Tarempa), where *T. cristatus* occurs, receives 489 mm of annual rainfall and a brief one- or two-month moist period at the end of the year. In southern Thailand [Kachana Buri], where *T. obscurus* is found, rainfall is a relatively high 1087 mm, but with a large variation between months. This reflects itself in a clear dry period in December to February with less than 40 mm monthly rainfall, but a perhumid period in July to September with average monthly rainfall of around 200 mm. The wettest places are indeed the lowland rainforests of Borneo and Java. In Kuching (4900 mm), where *T. cristatus, P. chrysomelas* and *P. rubicunda* are found and in Labuan (3701 mm), where *T. cristatus, P. rubicunda* and *P. hosei* are present, each and every month is perhumid with, on average, more than 200 mm of rainfall. The same is true for parts of central Java where *T. auratus* and *P. comata* live sympatrically, with averages of 3635 mm of rainfall and a perhumid climate.

In the lowlands of Sundaland the variation in monthly average temperatures is minimal. For the meteorological stations mentioned above they all average between 27°C and 29°C, with the largest differences in monthly temperatures for Kachana Buri, i.e. 25°C in December–January and 30°C in April–May.

However, as indicated before not all species of langurs only occur in the lowlands. Temperature variation in the mountains is much more pronounced. The langur with the largest altitudinal range in Sundaland is *T. auratus*. Populations are found in the coastal mangroves but also between 2500 and 3500 m asl on some of Java's highest mountains. The uniformity of the temperature conditions in Java and indeed other parts of Sundaland makes the differences between the climate of the higher regions and that of the low plains prominent (Nijman 2014). In addition to the decrease of temperature of about 0.6°C for each rise of 100 m, heat is more quickly lost from high altitudes at night, and therefore the daily temperature fluctuations are greater in the mountains than in the lowlands, viz ~15°–20°C compared to ~5°–8°C. This means that in areas above 2500 m asl the average monthly temperature is in the low teens. Night-time temperatures, especially in the dry season with clear skies, are in single digits. Depending on the local topography, temperatures can be markedly lower, especially at

Figure 14.2 (*cont.*) exceeds precipitation (i.e. a dry period); the area is hatched when the precipitation curve supersedes the temperature curve (indicating moist periods), and in black are perhumid periods when precipitation exceeds 100 mm mo^{-1}. From top left, listing the langur species present in the area: Jakarta, northcoast of Java, *T. auratus*; Tarempa, Riau Archipelago, *T. cristatus*; Padang, west coast of Sumatra, *P. melalophos* and *T. cristatus*; Kuching, northwestern Borneo, *T. cristatus, P. chrysomelas* and *P. rubicunda*; Cilacap, southcoast of Java, *T. auratus* and *P. comata*; Sibolga, coast of Sumatra, *T. cristatus* and *P. melalophos*; Kanchana Buri, southern Thailand, *T. obscurus*; Chumphon, northern Thai-Malay Peninsula, *T. obscurus* and *P. femoralis*; Kuantan, east coast of Peninsular Malaysia, *T. obscurus* and *P. siamensis*; Sandakan, east coast of Borneo, *T. cristatus, P. rubicunda* and *P. sabana*; Labuan, north coast Borneo, *T. cristatus, P. rubicunda* and *P. hosei*.

night. Since cool air is heavier than warm air, when air cools down at night, it naturally will flow down slopes. If, however, there is no slope down which it can flow, for example in hollows, valleys or plateaus, the air will get progressively colder. This can lead to frost on the ground and night-time temperatures of as low as −10°C have been recorded in areas where *T. auratus* and *P. comata* occurs (Van Steenis 1972).

Presbytis langurs are mostly confined to forest; this includes rainforest, freshwater swamps and peat swamp forests, and secondary forests of various types, but also established rubber plantations and mixed forest gardens. Some species such as *P. comata* occur in high altitude forest where forests are dwarfed. *Trachypithecus* langurs occur in most forests where *Presbytis* langurs occur, but tend to be less frequently found in the interior of certain forests. In addition, they occur in mangroves or beach forests, freshwater swamp forest, in open deciduous forests, teak plantations or in highly disturbed forests. *Trachypithecus cristatus* and possibly *T. selangorensis* appears to be more confined to riverine and coastal forest than the other *Trachypithecus* langurs in Sundaland.

Diet and Feeding Ecology

Presbytis and *Trachypithecus* langurs are traditionally seen to be eating large amounts of leaves, with the remainder of the diet being made up of unripe fruits and/or seeds (Tsuji et al. 2013b). When comparing species from the two genera *Trachypithecus* is the one that is more folivorous and feeds on a larger proportion of mature leaves. Increasingly it has become clear that this is too simplistic a picture, especially when considering data from multiple studies. All studies on *Trachypithecus* langurs in the Sunda region confirm that indeed, on an annual basis, more than half the feeding time is spent on eating leaves (ESM Table 14.1). However, the variation between studies can be considerable. Thus, the diet of *T. auratus* has been studied in a wide range of forests and the level of folivory differs greatly. In mangroves and beach forest it ranges between 56% and 59% (Kartikasari 1986; Supriatna et al. 1989), in deciduous and everwet lowland forest it ranges between 46% and 58% (Kool 1989; Vogt 2003), in montane rainforest it averages 64% (Beckwith 1995), but in teak forests leaves comprise 86% of the langur's diet (Djuwantoko et al. 1994). Not only does the proportion of leaves differ between studies and habitats, also the diversity of plant species that are used for feeding varies up to an order of magnitude (Figure 14.3). In mangroves, *T. auratus* fed on merely 9 species of, by and large, abundant mangrove species (Supriatna et al. 1989), and in beach forest this was only slightly higher, at 14 species. In deciduous forest this increased to 49 species, in lowland forest it was 88 and in the montane rainforest *T. auratus* were recorded feeding on 92 species (Beckwith 1995; Kool 1989; Vogt 2003). Kool (1989) reports high dietary diversity even within a single month, when even the most commonly used food plant contributes less than 15% of that month's diet.

Presbytis langurs equally show a large amount of variability in their diet. Overall, they are less folivorous than *Trachypithecus* langurs. *Presbytis comata* is often seen as the most folivorous of the *Presbytis* langurs based on a study conducted by

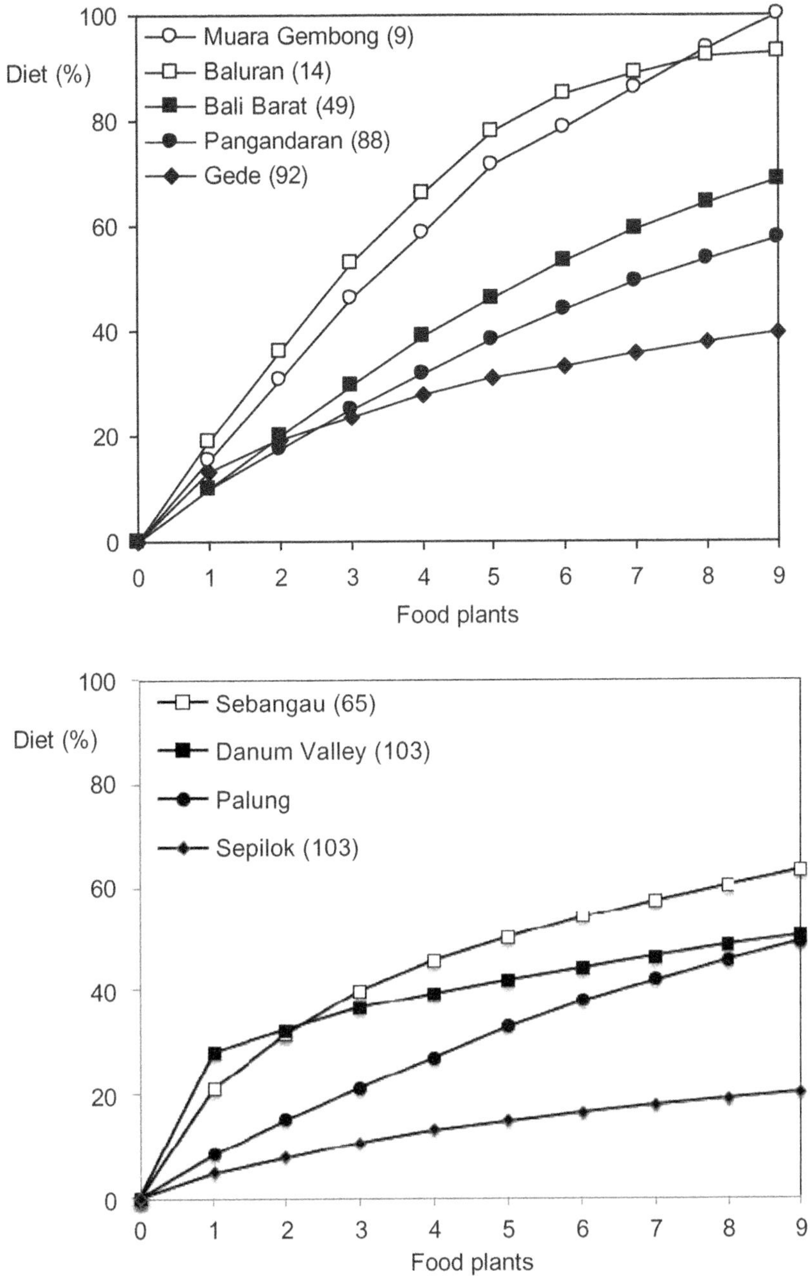

Figure 14.3 Contribution of food plants to the diet of ebony langurs *Trachypithecus auratus* (top) and maroon langurs *Presbytis rubicunda* (bottom) showing the percentage of the diet that is made up of the top nine food plants. Data are from five study areas in Java and Bali and four sites from Borneo. Wetland sites (Muara Gembong, mangroves, Baluran, beach forest, Sebangau, peatswamp forest) are indicated in open symbols. Numbers in brackets indicate the total number of food plants used (for Palung, only information on genera is available). Data for Muara Gembong are from Supriatna et al. (1989); Baluran from Kartikasari (1986); Bali Barat from Vogt (2003); Pangandaran from Kool (1989); Gede from Beckwith (1995); Sebangau from Ehlers-Smith et al. (2013a); Danum Valley from Hanya and Bernard (2012); Palung from Clink et al. (2017); Sepilok from Davies (1984)

Ruhiyat (1983, 1991). Two other studies showed that this may have been an artefact of Ruhiyat's study site having been in montane forests, as at other sites fruit forms a larger part of their diet similar to that seen in other *Presbytis* langurs (Nijman 2017). *Presbytis rubicunda* stands out from the other *Presbytis* langurs in that its diet comprises a large amount of seeds (Clink et al. 2017; Davies 1991; Ehlers-Smith et al. 2013a,b; Hanya and Bernard 2012) such that it can be best described as a granivore rather than a folivore or frugivore. *Presbytis* species that have been studied at various sites clear differences can be seen in their annual diet, albeit it perhaps less varied as seen in *T. auratus* indicated above. In terms of feeding time, the top nine plant species fed on by *Presbytis rubicunda* make up 50% or less of the diet at three lowland forest sites, but they contribute almost two-third of the diet in a peat swamp forest (Figure 14.3). The number of food plants in the diet of this species reaches more than a hundred in Gunung Palung and Sepilok (Clink et al. 2017; Davies 1984) but only 65 in Sebangau (Ehlers-Smith et al. 2013a,b).

Range Use

The mean home range size of a *Presbytis* langur is in the order of 35 hectares, but there is significant within and between species variation (ESM Table 14.1). The species with the largest variation, which is also the species with the largest geographic range, is *P. rubicunda*. In the rainforest of northern Borneo, home range sizes are around 20 hectares, but in the peat swamp forests of southern Borneo they are five times larger. *Presbytis comata, P. thomasi* and *P. sabana* all have home ranges in the order of 15–45 hectares; where the species has been studied at multiple sites there is a three to four-fold difference between the largest and the smallest home range.

Overall, it seems that *Trachypithecus* have a home range in the order of 20 hectares, but differently from the *Presbytis* langurs, some have much smaller ranges; however, there is a reasonable amount of within-species variation (ESM Table 14.1). For *T. auratus*, home ranges are small – three to eight hectares – in the teak forests of Pangandaran (Brotoisworo 1983; Kool 1989) but much larger in the teak forests of Cepu (43 hectares; Djuwantoko 1991). Home ranges in other habitat types vary between 10 and 20 hectares. In the mangroves and coastal forest of the Thai-Malay Peninsula, the range of *Trachypithecus selangorensis* likewise is in the order of 20 hectares. The three studies of *T. obscurus* in Kuala Lompat show that home ranges are in the order of 20–30 hectares, but groups in Teluk Bahan and Bangi live in (much) smaller home ranges, i.e. 13 and 2 hectares, respectively.

The maximum day range of *Presbytis* langurs is in the order of one kilometre, and almost never less than 500 metres. The one species that does stand out, because of its larger day range, is *P. rubicunda*; in several studies it has been recorded to have a day range of over two kilometres (Davies 1984; Ehlers-Smith et al. 2013a; Hanya and Bernard 2012). The maximum day range of *Trachypithecus* langurs in Sundaland appears to be smaller than that of the *Presbytis* langurs and falls within a fairly narrow range of between 500 and 1500 m, but mostly less than one kilometre (ESM Table 14.1). The maximum day range of langur groups may be more in the open

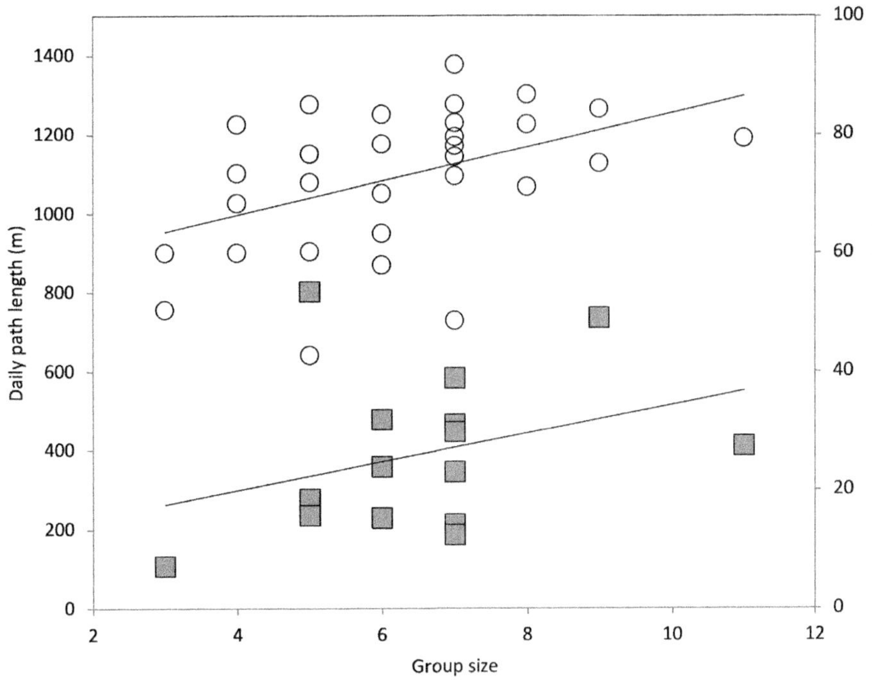

Figure 14.4 Relationship between group size and mean daily path length (open circles, data from 18 groups) and home range size (filled squares, data from 16 groups) in Thomas langurs *Presbytis thomasi*. From Sterck (1995), Steenbeek and van Schaik (2001) and Gurmaya (1989)

forest types (teak, deciduous forest) than in dense rainforest (cf. Djuwantoko 1991; Vogt 2003). For *Presbytis* langurs there does not appear to be a positive relationship between home range size and maximum day range (ESM Table 14.1), but for the *Trachypithecus* langurs there is a positive relationship, albeit it weak one. Within species, however, there does appear to be a positive relationship between home range size and daily path length, as found in *P. thomasi* (Gurmaya 1989; Steenbeek and van Schaik 2001; Sterck 1995), but this is confounded by the fact that group size is both positively correlated with home range size and daily path length. Thus, larger groups have larger home ranges and individuals in larger groups have longer mean daily path lengths than ones living in smaller groups (Figure 14.4).

Mitani and Rodman (1979) devised a defensibility index (D) for primate groups. This value describes the likelihood that a group will encounter its own home range boundary as it moves within it on an average day: $D = d/d'$, where d is equal to the mean daily path length and d' is equal to the diameter of a circle with the area equal to that of the observed home range. A D-index of >1 allows a species to cross the full width of its home range during an average day of travel (Mitani and Rodman 1979). Mitani and Rodman (1979) suggested that this allowed a species to be territorial. Expanding this concept but taking not mean but maximum daily path length into account, allows to establish whether or not a group of primates has to potential to cross its home range within any given day and patrol its entire perimeter. Most

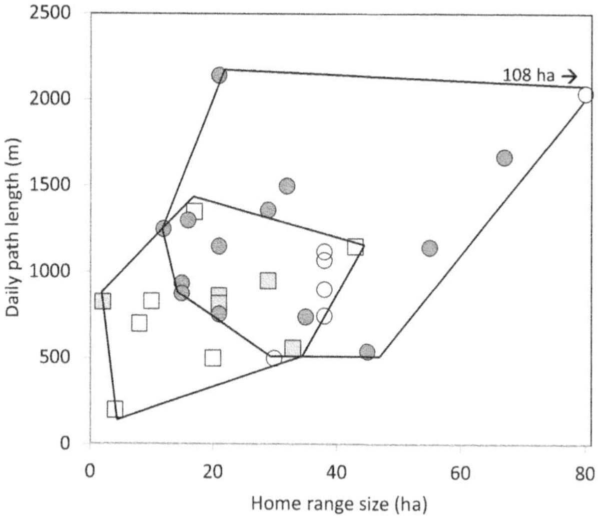

Figure 14.5 Relationship between maximum daily path length in metres and home range size in hectares for three species of *Trachypithecus* langurs (squares) and eight species of *Presbytis* langurs (circles) showing generally larger home ranges and longer daily path lengths in *Presbytis*. *Presbytis rubicunda* in Sebangau has a home range size of 108 hectares. Closed symbols are from study sites where *Presbytis* and *Trachypithecus* langurs live sympatrically; open symbols are from study sites where only one of the two genera is present. Data are from ESM Table 14.1

Trachypithecus groups that have been studied in Sundaland have a D_{max} index of >1, with the exception of *T. selangorensis*. Most groups need two full days or more to patrol the periphery of their home range, apart from *T. auratus* in Pangandaran (Brotoisworo 1983; Kool 1992) and *T. obscurus* in Bangi (Ruslin et al. 2014) who are capable of doing this within one day. Likewise, most *Presbytis* langur groups have a D_{max} index of >1, with the exception of a *P. sabana* group in Silabukan (Mitchell 1994) and a *P. siberu* group in Pungut (Rahayuni 2007). *Presbytis thomasi* in Bukit Lawang and Bungara and *P. rubicunda* in Danum Valley had small home ranges relative to their maximum daily path length (Gurmaya 1989; Hanya and Bernard 2012) and have the potential to move along the entire periphery of their home range within a single day. Other *Presbytis* groups typically have to take at least twice as long (ESM Table 14.1; Figure 14.5).

Habitat use and densities of two sympatric langurs (*P. rubicunda* and *P. frontata*) in Sungai Wain forest, eastern Borneo show how these two ecologically similar species co-exist (ESM Table 14.2). The strongest contrasts in habitat use are seen in swamp forest, as this is used much more relative to its availability by *P. frontata* but not by *P. rubicunda*. Conversely, ridge forest is used more than expected on the basis of its availability by *P. rubicunda* but not by *P. frontata*. Both species use forest on slopes less than its availability would suggest, and both use forest on flat land more than expected on the basis of its availability. In terms of abundance both species also show clear differences. *Presbytis rubicunda* in Sungai Wain occurs at densities of 3.3 ± 0.7 groups/km^2 (with a range 2.5–4.0 groups/km^2) and group sizes average

9.0 ± 2.2 individuals (range 5–13 individuals), resulting in an overall density of around 30 individuals/km^2. In contrast *P. frontata* occurs at lower group densities, i.e. 1.1 ± 1.2 groups/km^2 (range 2.5–4.0 groups/km^2) and groups are smaller (2.7 ± 1.2 individuals, with a range 1–4 individuals). Hence the overall density of *P. frontata* at three individuals/km^2 is about a tenth of that of *P. rubicunda*. Rodman (1973) found a similar difference in densities between *P. frontata* and its sympatric congener, in this case *P. canicrus*. Over a 17-month study he and his team had multiple contacts with *P. canicrus* groups a day, but the encounters with *P. frontata* were so infrequent that they did not warrant analysis (comparison with the species with the smallest dataset that was included in the analysis, the pig-tailed macaque *Macaca nemestrina*, suggests that Rodman and his team had fewer than two encounters a month with *P. frontata* groups).

While *P. rubicunda* consumes a large proportion of seeds, the diet of *P. frontata* has hitherto not been studied. *Presbytis rubicunda* lives sympatrically with *P. sabana* and *P. canicrus*, two species for which leaves comprises a large proportion of their diet (Mitchell 1994; Rodman 1973). It is quite likely that the diet of *P. frontata* likewise differs substantially from that of *P. rubicunda* as to reduce potential between species competition for food.

Activity Patterns and Vocal Behaviour

Both *Presbytis* and *Trachypithecus* langurs are mostly arboreal, but the former more so than the latter. In particular, the *Trachypithecus* langurs living in more deciduous forest types, and both types of langurs living in more disturbed habitats, spent more time on the ground than the ones living in pristine rainforests with a continuous canopy (Cheyne et al. 2018). Both type of langurs occasionally come down to the ground to drink water or to visit mineral sources (salt licks, termite mounts) to engage in geophagy (*P. thomasi*: Sterck 1995; *P. femoralis*: Megantara 1989a; *P. siamensis*: Bennett 1983; *P. hosei*: Nijman 2005; *T. selangorensis*: Bernstein 1968; *T. auratus*: Vogt 2003). Often several individuals from the same group descend to the ground to travel, engage in social activities, or feed on fungi (Cheyne et al. 2018). Most commonly, however, they come down to the ground to feed on the mineral-rich soils (Davies and Baillie 1988; Ruhiyat 1983), either to provide mineral supplementation or for the adsorption of toxins present in their diet.

In terms of activity budgets, *Presbytis* langurs spend about 33% of their time feeding, 55% resting and some 10% moving (ESM Table 14.3). This is very similar to the *Trachypithecus* langurs, other than that *Presbytis* langurs appear to rest less and move more. Time spent being social (grooming, playing etc.) for most species is less than 5%.

In *Presbytis* and *Trachypithecus* langurs loud calls are mainly produced by adult males (Assink and van Dijk 1990; Bennett 1983; Curtin 1980; Fuentes 1994; Kool 1989; Megantara 1989a; Ruhiyat 1983; Vogt 2003) and carry over roughly 500–1000 m. Group encounters in *P. siberu* may include an exchange of male-female loud calls, which have been termed duets, although more than two individuals may contribute (Tilson and Tenaza 1976). In addition, solo loud calls of males and of females have been recorded (Sangchantr 2004). Loud calls are often contagious whereby calling by one male stimulates other males to counter-call. Because of the loud calls' loudness, it is generally assumed that loud calls are directed at other groups and serve extra-group communication among males, particularly in the maintenance of territorial inter-group-spacing and mate defence (van Schaik et al. 1992; Wich 2002; Wich and Nunn 2002). Other frequently cited functions of loud calls include: attracting mates (Bennett 1983; Vogt 2003), defending resources (van Schaik et al. 1992), increasing group cohesion during movement (Bennett 1983), and notifying predators that they have been detected (Wich and Sterck 2003). In most species, loud calls consist of several notes and their presentation is often accompanied by relatively stereotyped positional and locomotor displays, including jumping with stiff legs, and branch shaking (*Presbytis*; Assink and van Dijk 1990; Bennett, 1983, 1994; Megantara 1989a; Ruhiyat 1983; Tilson and Tenaza 1976; *Trachypithecus*: Vogt 2003). *Presbytis* langurs preferentially call during the morning or late afternoon when groups are near their sleeping places (Bennett 1983; Curtin 1980; Fuentes 1994; Gurmaya 1989; Megantara 1989a); males of some species engage in nocturnal calling rounds (*P. siamensis*: Bennett 1983; *P. potenziani*: Fuentes 1994; *P. frontata*: Nijman and Nekaris 2012). Apart from loud calls *Presbytis* and *Trachypithecus* langurs also produce other loud vocalizations; these are less exclusively produced by top ranking males but may occur in similar contexts, e.g. in response to potential predators, or as part of vocal exchanges between adult males of different groups (*Presbytis*: Curtin 1980; *Trachypithecus*: Kool 1989).

In the *Presbytis* langurs loud calls are highly species-specific (T. Geissmann, V. Nijman, J. Vermeer, unpubl. data; Meyer et al. 2011). The majority of the calls consist of tchiks only, and are preceded by purrs in some species. Grunts and woops occur in the loud calls of *P. thomasi* and *P. potenziani.* In all *Presbytis* loud calls except those of *P. potenziani* and *P. hosei*, the duration of note intervals increases from the beginning to at least the middle of the call. The *Trachypithecus* langurs produce a grunt call consisting of a number of exhalation notes produced in alternation with inhalation notes. Inhalations are shorter and less tonal than the exhalation notes and somewhat resemble a hiccup sound. Typically the dominant frequency typically drops across successive exhalations.

Social Behaviour and Organization

For most *Presbytis* langur species, groups contain one adult male and several adult females. In some of the species where larger group sizes, i.e. over 12–15 individuals, are recorded regularly, such as *P. siamensis* and *P. femoralis*, a small number of groups contain two adult males. *Presbytis potenziani, P. siberu* and possibly *P. natunae* live mostly or exclusively in single adult male and single adult female groups (Fuentes 1994; Lammertink et al. 2003; Rahayuni 2007; Watanabe 1981) and may be monogamous. *Presbytis frontata* likewise may be monogamous in those areas where group sizes are consistently small (Nijman and Nekaris 2012). Species with small group sizes, such as *P. natunae, P. frontata, P. siberu* and *P. potenziani*, are regularly recorded in groups containing one adult male and one adult female (Lammertink et al. 2003; Nijman and Nekaris 2012). Three of these species occur on small islands with reduced predation pressure. *Presbytis frontata* seems to occur in one-adult-male, one-adult-female groups in most areas, but in one-male, multi-female groups elsewhere. A similar pattern, but less pronounced and reversed, is seen in *P. comata*. In most areas it occurs in one-male, multi-female groups, and even occasionally in two-male, multi-female groups, but in certain montane areas it is consistently found in one-male, one-female groups as well as one-male, multi-female groups (Nijman 2017). Upon becoming adult, male dispersal is common in *Presbytis*, as is attested by the presence of mostly just one adult male in bisexual groups. Emigrating males can live single, in pairs with another male, or in all-male groups. All-male groups, typically containing fewer individuals than bisexual groups, have been recorded in *P. siamensis, P. rubicunda, P. femoralis, P. comata, P. sabana* and *P. thomasi*.

The *Trachypithecus* langurs in Sundaland occur in one-male, multi-female groups, but a significant proportion of groups contain two or more adult males. Furuya's (1961) *T. selangorensis* study group in Rantau Panjang contained two adult males. One out of six groups of *T. selangorensis* studied by Bernstein (1968) contained two adult males and four out of seven *T. auratus* groups studied by Brotoisworo (1983) contained two or more males, with four adult males in the largest group of 33 individuals. All-male groups have been recorded in *T. autatus* and *T. selangorensis*.

Group sizes in *Presbytis* langurs typically range from three to five (*P. siberu, P. potenziani, P. frontata, P. natunae*), six to eight (*P. thomasi, P. comata, P. sabana, P. canicrus*), and nine to 15 or more (*P. rubicunda, P. femoralis, P. melalophis, P. siamensis*) (Nijman and Nekaris 2012). But within-species variation can be significant. *Presbytis rubicunda* groups that have been studied in various parts of Borneo vary in size from six or seven (Davies 1984; Ehlers-Smith et al. 2013a,b) to 11 or 12 (D'Agostino et al. 2016; Hanya and Bernard 2012), without any apparent difference in the type of habitat in which they were studied (i.e. peat swamp, lowland rainforest, lower montane forest etc.). Figure 14.4 shows the distribution of group sizes for 125 groups of *P. comata*, showing that the largest group on record was three times larger than the mean. About half the groups recorded are within a relatively narrow range of between four and eight individuals (see also Nijman 2017).

Variation in group sizes in *Trachypithecus* langurs is larger than in *Presbytis* langurs, and for all species group sizes of over 20 or even over 25 individuals have been recorded (Bernstein 1968; Brotoisworo 1983; Curtin 1980; Furuya 1961; Ruslin et al. 2018; Vogt 2003). For *T. auratus* and perhaps also other *Trachypithecus* langurs group sizes can be explained in part by the presence of sympatric langurs and/or the presence of predators (Figure 14.6; data from Nijman 1997, 2000, 2017 and references therein). In areas where *P. comata* and *T. auratus* are sympatric, and where a whole suite of predators can be found, *P. comata* has a group size of around six individuals and *T. auratus* of around eight individuals (Figures 14.6a and 14.6d). In areas where *P. comata* is no longer present, but which lie within the historic range of this species, *T. auratus* langurs live in larger groups of around 13 individuals (Figure 14.6c), viz. almost the same size as *P. comata* and *T. auratus* combined in

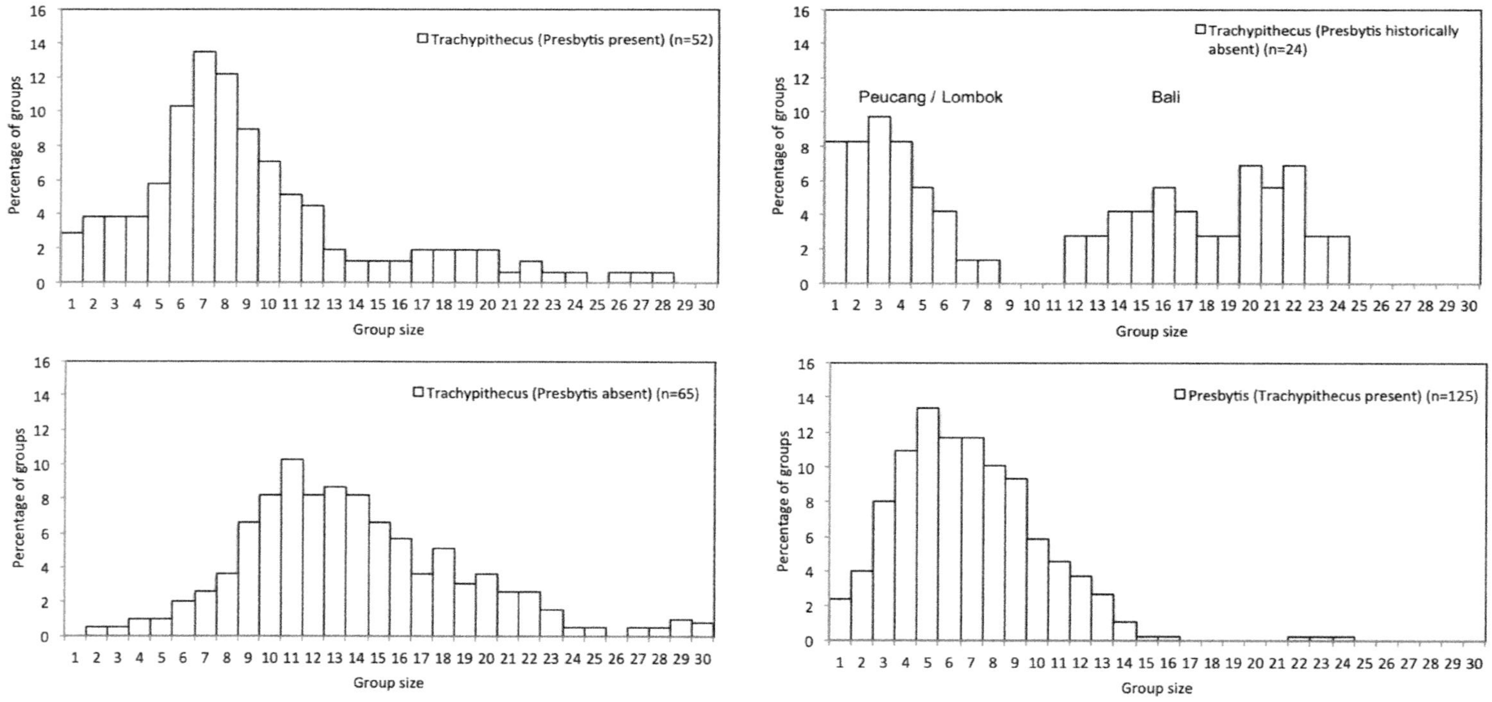

Figure 14.6 Group sizes of ebony langur *Trachypithecus auratus* and grizzled langur *Presbytis comata*, in areas where they occur in sympatry [(a) median group size is 8 and (d) median group size is 6], in areas within the historical range of *P. comata* where *P. comata* is no longer present [(c) median groups size is 13] and on islands where *T. auratus* is present but where *P. comata* probably never was present [(b) median group size 13]. The bimodal distribution in (b) is due to groups on Peucang, Lombok and Sempu Islands (median group size is 3) being markedly smaller than those on Bali Island (median group size is 18). Data are from Nijman (1997, 2000, 2104, 2017, and references therein).

areas where they are sympatric. This may be the result of reduced feeding competition following the extirpation of *P. comata*. A similar pattern is seen on Bali. *Presbytis comata* never occurred there, but the island has (or had until recently) a complete set of predators, similar to Java. On Bali *T. auratus* lives in groups of around 18, thus similar to areas where *P. comata* is no longer present (Figure 14.6b). Finally on islands with a reduced predator presence, such as Lombok, Peucang and Sempu, a different picture emerges, as there is no need for the langurs to live in large groups to increase predator detection. Group sizes of *T. auratus* are drastically smaller, around three to four individuals (Figure 14.6b), which may be a strategy to avoid within-species feeding competition.

Intra-group social interactions in both *Presbytis* and *Trachypithecus* langurs appear to be relatively inconspicuous, relaxed and benign (Chapter 16). In captive *T. obscurus*, Arnold and Barton (2001) found low levels of aggression and absence of severe aggression, and rates of reconciliation were high. These are all characteristics of tolerant species. Among females, interactions are subtle and egalitarian, possibly linked to a general abundance of food sources and low levels of within-group feeding interference (Yeager and Kool 2000). This low level of competition obviates the need for strong hierarchical dominance structures amongst females, and the frequent transfer of females between groups furthermore supports a lack of importance of kin-relationships and kin-related dominance hierarchies.

Gurmaya (1989) reported that in an all-male *P. thomasi* group of 10 individuals, embracing, mounting and grooming was observed frequently (i.e. more than in the one-male, multi-female groups). Mostly these interactions were initiated by the subordinate males, and in about half of the observations the embrace was followed by mounting and in a quarter of the time by grooming. All in all this gave the impression of a relaxed and tolerant group.

A crucial component of the social organization of *Trachypithecus* and *Presbytis* langurs is related to the dispersing sex. In populations (or species) where female dispersal is absent or rare, group composition changes due to male takeovers (i.e. the adult male is replaced by an immigrating adult male). In populations (or species) where female dispersal is common, one or more adult females may immigrate into an existing bisexual group (split-merger), they may join an all-male band or group (usually followed by the eviction of all but one of the adult males), or they may pair up with a solitary male thus forming a new group (Sterck 1995). Both types of dispersal, male and female (nulliparous and parous), occur in *Trachypithecus* (Bernstein 1968; Brotoisworo 1983; Djuwantoko 1992; Hardy 1988; Kool 1992) and *Presbytis* (Ehlers-Smith et al. 2013a,b; Megantara 1989a; Ruhiyat 1983; Sterck 1995). For *T. selangorensis*, Wolf and Fleagle (1977) described that the resident adult male of a large group (19 individuals, including three infants) was replaced by an immigrant male; within three months the three infants disappeared, presumably through infanticide. Almost four months after the take over the deposed adult male re-joined the group but remained subordinate to the new male and appeared peripheral to the group. Davies (1987) described the formation of a new group of *P. rubicunda*, by splitting of a larger group into two smaller ones, following an attack of an immigrating male. Two older females with infants remained with the deposed male but moved their home range whereas the younger nulliparous females remained in the original home range and were joined by the new male. Male takeovers can be relatively benign but Gurmaya (1989) described a case in *P. thomasi* where the ousted male was killed.

A long-term study of *P. thomasi* by Sterck et al. (2005) showed that over a 12.5 year observation period, 12 new langur groups were formed: six through female split-merger, four by aggressive male takeovers and two through the association of a male with a group that had recently lost its resident male by unknown causes. Female transfer involved mainly parous (70%; of these only 15% carried infants), nulliparous (22%) and less frequently juvenile (8%) females. When females emigrate, it is frequently the ones with the oldest offspring that leave first, and when there is a choice between two or more adult males, they will join the group with the youngest male (Sterck et al. 2005).

Data on female dispersal compiled by Sterck (1995) showed that the proportion of females that dispersed in *Trachypithecus* langurs was in the order of 0.14 (*T. auratus*) to 0.19 (*T. selangorensis*) females per year, and in *Presbytis* langurs 0.04 (*P. siamensis*), 0.12 (*P. femoralis*) and 0.28 (*P. thomasi*). Thus, a typical female dispersed roughly once every four to seven years, meaning that over their lifetime they will be part of several groups, with different adult males.

Reproduction and Sexual Behaviour

Based on the long-term presence of single adult male and single adult female groups some populations *P. comata* are thought to be monandrous, i.e. the population comprises a mixture of monogamous groups and groups with one or rarely two adult males (Nijman 2017). *Trachypithecus* langurs appear to live mostly in single adult male and multiple adult female groups (Beckwith 1995; Djuwantoko 1991; Hardy 1988; Vogt 2003), but different from *Presbytis* langurs, two or more adult male in these groups are common (Brotoisworo 1983; Curtin 1980; Furuya 1961). The possible exception to this rule may be *T. auratus* on the island of Lombok (and perhaps other small islands). On Lombok small group sizes, possibly comprising one-male, one-female groups, are the norm (V. Nijman, unpubl. data; see Figure 14.3).

Presbytis and *Trachypithecus* females solicit copulations, and have no or insignificant sexual swellings (Harding 2010; Sjahfirdi et al. 2015; Shelmidine et al. 2007; Tsuji et al. 2013a). The rare occurrence of sexual swellings in colobines is linked to the consistent presence of multiple adult males in these species (Newton and Dunbar 1994). Newborn *Presbytis* and *Trachypithecus* langurs have coat colour that starkly contrasts with that of the adults. In the largely grey and black *Trachypithecus* langurs infants are bright yellow or orange, and even in the erythristic (red) morph of the otherwise black *T. auratus*, the colour of the infants (bright light yellow) stands out from the much darker orange, reddish pelage of the adults. Within the genus *Presbytis*, and within some species more than in others, there is a large amount of variation in pelage coloration (bright yellow, red, to black and earthy colours), and contrast (lighter ventrally and darker dorsally), head coloration (contrasting with the body, longitudinal stripes, naked patches) and face coloration (contrasting overall colour or eye rings) (Nijman and Nekaris 2012). Despite this variation, in all species, newborn infants contrast starkly with adults, making their presence clear to both the mother and other group members. These flamboyant colours furthermore facilitate handling of the infants by other group members, allowing the mother more time to feed (Alley 1980; Ang et al. 2010; Md-Zain et al. 2012; Treves 1997).

The species for which the most complete life history dataset is available is *P. thomasi*: in this species the age at first reproduction is 5.4 years and the mean inter-birth interval after surviving infants is 27 months. When infants do not survive the inter-birth interval is shortened to 18 months (Wich et al. 2007). Comparable data for *Trachypithecus* langurs from Sundaland are not available from wild populations but data from a captive population of *T. selangorensis* are 2.9 years for age at first reproduction and an inter-birth interval after surviving infants of 15 months (Shelmidine et al. 2009). Captivity may have led to faster life histories as data from wild Indochinese grey langur *T. crepusculus* suggest an age at first reproduction of 5.3 years and an interbirth interval of 22 months (Borries et al. 2011).

As noted by Strier (1994), the extent of reproductive seasonality in primates may be correlated with ecological, demographic and social variables, and can have strong effects on the dynamics of social and mating systems. Strict seasonality and synchronicity in reproduction makes it more difficult for individual males to monopolize females and thus will affect the level of actual or potential male-male competition. Conversely, when females can reproduce in any month of the year, individual females become potentially defensible resources; males can have greater confidence about their paternity thus creating opportunities for increased male infant care. There seem to be conflicting reports on whether or not *Presbytis* langurs are seasonal breeders. For some species in some areas it is clear that births occur only during certain months of the year; for instance in *P. femoralis* in Singapore births have only been recorded in June and July (Ang 2010; Ang et al. 2010), but *P. siamensis* living a few 100 km north gives birth throughout the year (Bennett 1983). Likewise, *P. thomasi* in Sumatra, gives birth during all months of the year (Gurmaya 1989). Females mostly give birth to single offspring but cases of twins have been recorded in *P. siamensis* (e.g. Bennett 1988).

Likewise, data from *Trachypithecus* langurs do indicate that there are either differences in reproductive strategies and birth seasonality between species or differences between areas. *Trachypithecus auratus* has a birthing peak in April–June in the montane rainforest (Beckwith 1995; Sujatnika 1992) but births are recorded throughout the year in the more seasonal teak and deciduous forests (Brotoisworo 1983; Djuwantoko 1994; Vogt 2003). There is no indication that there are marked between-year differences. Medway (1970) based on repeat observations of infants and juveniles notes that there was no birth season in *T. selangorensis*. For *T. obscurus* Burton (1984) showed through examination of testicular histologies that males were capable of siring offspring in each month of the year. Chivers and Raemaekers (1980), basing their conclusions on six years of data, noted that for *T. obscurus* births can occur in every month (with their data showing some evidence of higher births in January–February and fewer births in August–September). However, there was large variation between years, including a gap of 12 months during which no births were recorded. They concluded that 'there are indications that mating coincides with the peaks in rainfall that may or may not follow prolonged droughts, which are followed by great abundance of fruit' (Chivers and Raemaekers 1980: 250). Females give birth to one infant, and there do not appear to be any records of twins in *T. obscurus*, *T. auratus*, *T. cristatus* or *T. selangorensis*.

Predation and Anti-predator Behaviour

Predation pressure differs greatly between the different parts of Sundaland where langurs live. Known predators include terrestrial ones, such as canids (dhole *Cuon alpinus* in the Thai-Malay Peninsula, Sumatra and Java, golden jackal *Canis aureus* in the north of the Thai-Malay Peninsula and domestic dogs *Canis familiaris* throughout the region), felids (e.g. tigers *Panthera tigris* in the Thai-Malay Peninsula and Sumatra, and formerly in Java and Bali; leopards *P. pardus* in the Thai-Malay Peninsula and Java and clouded leopards *Neofelis diardi* and *N. nebulosa* on the Thai-Malay Peninsula, Sumatra and Borneo) and arboreal ones such as diurnal raptors (various hawk-eagles of the genus *Nisaetus* and *Aquilla* eagles in the northern part of the region; a crested serpent-eagle *Spilornis cheela* killed an infant *T. obscurus*: Hardy 1988) and perhaps some of the largest owls (e.g. barred eagle-owl *Bubo sumatranus*). Predation on primates by raptors in Asia is far less common that in Africa (including Madagascar) and South America (Fam and Nijman 2011). The highest levels of predation are expected in those areas with a larger range of predators such as the Thai-Malay Peninsula and Sumatra. The lowest levels of predation occurs there where langurs are found on islands with a depauperate set of predators. For the *Presbytis* langurs this includes Singapore (as most large predators have become extinct over the last 150 years), Bunguran (isolated in the South China Sea), and the Mentawai Islands, and for the *Trachypithecus* langurs this includes Lombok (situated east of Wallace's line leading to an absence of felids and canids, although domestic dogs and the large Flores hawk-eagle *N. floris* do pose a risk), Bangka, Belitung and many smaller island scattered throughout the region.

Quantitative studies on predation on langurs are rare, and all come from studies of the predators rather than the prey. In southern Thailand, Steinmetz et al. (2013) assessed the dietary preference of tigers, leopards and dhole based on scats, and found that the two species of langur (*P. femoralis* and *T. obscurus*) were eaten mainly by leopards but not by tigers or dhole. On the Thai-Malay Peninsula, Kawanishi and Sunquist (2008) reported that 1/15 Asiatic golden cat *Catopuma temminckii* and 1/40 dhole scats contained the remains of *T. obscurus*. For East Java, Seidensticker and Suyono (1980) reported that 23/51 leopard scats, 1/2 dhole scats and 0/3 tiger scats contained *T. auratus* remains.

Humans have probably always been amongst the most important predator for langurs. Archaeological evidence from Niah Cave in Northern Borneo and Braholo

Cave in Central Java point at langurs being one of the most important prey items of early humans. For the period 33,000–1200 YBP in Niah Cave Piper and Rabett (2009) noted that 16% of identifiable prey items were of langurs (*Presbytis hosei, P. rubicunda, P. chrysomelas* and/or *P. frontata,* and *T. cristatus*). Remains of *Presbytis* langurs were about twice as common as those of *T. cristatus* (Harrison 1996). For the period 14,000–3000 YBP Amano et al. (2015) reported that *T. auratus* was the most common identifiable prey item in Braholo Cave in central Java, representing some 15% of the total. *Presbytis comata* was recorded as well, but in much smaller numbers. The hunted langurs of both genera were mainly adults (74%) and juveniles (13%), and fewer subadults (6%) and old individuals (7%). In traditional hunter-gatherer societies in the region, langurs continue to be an important prey item. Kuchikura (1988) reported on the hunting efficiency of 15 aboriginal Semaq Beri families living in an 80 km^2 area on the Thai-Malay Peninsula, for whom *T. obscurus* and *P. femoralis* ranked as their most hunted prey. Over the course of a year 136 *T. obscura* and 30 *P. femoralis* were killed, mostly by blowpipe. *Presbytis frontata* and *P. chrysomelas* made up 6% and 3% of mammals killed by Iban hunter-farmers in western Borneo, mostly by shotguns (Wadley et al. 1997). Quinten et al. (2014) estimated that between 1680 and 3360 *Presbytis siberu* were killed annually by aboriginal hunters on the 6000 km^2 large island of Siberut.

Group size and social organization are influenced by predation pressure, such that, large groups are favoured under heavy predation pressure, as greater numbers improve early detection, deterrence and dilution of risk (van Schaik et al. 1983); conversely, small, inconspicuous groups improve predator avoidance (Watanabe 1981). We see a relatively wide range of group sizes in langurs, ranging from 3 or 4 in e.g. *P. siberu* and *P. potenziani* to 17 or 18 in *P. siamensis* and 4 or 5 in *T. auratus* on small islands to over 25 or 30 in *T. auratus* and *T. selangorensis* (ESM Table 14.1 and Figure 14.6). The responses to potential predators differ remarkably between the various species of *Presbytis* and *Trachypithecus* langurs (Nijman and Nekaris 2012). A common response to terrestrial predators, including humans, is for the langurs, and especially the male, to give alarm calls. These alarm calls may function in intraspecific communication, e.g. to warn other members of the group about the presence and location of a predator and to allow synchronization of flight, or by informing the predator that it has been detected and thus advertising perception and unprofitability to predators that depend on unprepared prey. Indeed, Tilson and Tenaza (1976), for *P. siberu*, and Curtin (1980) for *P. siamensis*, noted that adult males would perform distraction displays (loud vocalizations, branch shaking, running through the canopy) when they detected humans (including hunters). During these distraction displays, the adult females and younger group members would hide silently and remained motionless in the canopy. Tenaza and Tilson (1976) added that solitary males or males that were away from their group would flee through the canopy without giving alarm calls, thus indeed suggesting that alarm calls are there to inform other group members as well as the predator. The latter was confirmed experimentally by Wich and Sterck (2003); when presenting a tiger model to *P. thomasi*, males would call when other group members were present but they would remain largely silent when they were on their own.

A very different anti-predator strategy is employed by *P. frontata* (Nijman and Nekaris 2012). Upon detecting the human observer, the group, including the adult male, would mostly remain silent and would gently retreat into the foliage, and then escape along the ground or the forest's undergrowth. Rarely would the adult male produce loud calls, and if he did, these were, in comparison with the other members of the genus, short in duration and function probably just to inform the other group members rather than the predator. Alternatively, upon detection, the group members would hide silently and remain motionless for up to an hour before moving slowly away or fleeing.

Davis (1962: 62) described a more commonly deployed method of fleeing: 'when alarmed they [*P. sabana*] make off through the tree tops in a series of spectacular crashing leaps. The arms and legs are spread-eagled, and the animal throws itself into the foliage without aiming at a particular branch'. Fleeing is mostly through the upper layer of the canopy (e.g. *P. melalophos*, *P. rubicunda*), but some species and especially the ones that are less vibrant in colour such as *P. frontata* and *P. comata*, may flee along the ground or through the lower levels of the forest (Nijman and Nekaris 2012). Irrespective of tactics used, fleeing almost invariably is a synchronized activity, with all group members moving in the same general direction.

The anti-predator behaviours of the various *Trachypithecus* species are similar to that of those *Presbytis* species that live in large groups, i.e. males alarm call when potential predators are detected, and fleeing is noisily and is mainly through the upper canopy. In areas where *Trachypithecus* langurs are more terrestrial (e.g. in mangroves or deciduous forests and open woodlands), the langurs flee into the trees when terrestrial predators are encountered (Bernstein 1968). Mobbing behaviour, whereby group members collectively or in quick succession attack the predator, have been rarely reported in *Presbytis* or *Trachypithecus* langurs, but Tsuji et al. (2016) reported it for *T. auratus*. Upon detection of a 2-m long reticulated python (*Malayopython reticulatus*), three individuals (one adult male, one adult female, one subadult female) of a group of 11 mobbed the snake for about 40 minutes, which resulted in the python rolling itself into a ball thus removing all threats of predation.

Sleep site selection in *Presbytis* and *Trachypithecus* langurs also seems to aid to minimize the risk of predation. While the number of sleeping sites within a home range is often limited, only few studies indicate explicitly that whether or not the same sleeping tree is used on consecutive nights. Ruhiyat (1983) found that one *P. comata* group used 27 different sleep sites over 30 nights, and 23 of these were situated >100 m from each other, whereas for *P. rubicunda* Ehlers-Smith et al. (2013a,b) found 47 different sleeping sites over 96 nights for one group and 30 different sleeping sites over 41 nights for another group. Using different sleeping sites on consective nights and maximizing distances between sleeping sites makes it more challenging for potential predators to predict where langur groups will retreat for the night, thus lowering predation pressure for the langurs. More often than not, the tallest trees in a home range are selected as sleep sites (Davies 1984; Kool 1989; Megantara 1989a; Ruhiyat 1983; Tilson and Tenaza 1982). For instance, while two groups of *T. obscurus* spent very little time at heights above 40 m during the day, both groups used tall emergent trees over 50 m in height to sleep in (Hardy 1988). If the terrain allows, sleeping trees may be situated on ridges or other elevated positions, as for instance found by Ruhiyat (1983) for *P. comata* where 22/27 sleep sites were on ridges.

Discussion

Compared to a quarter century ago when the last compendium on colobine monkeys was published (Davies and Oates 1994) progress has been made on the study of *Presbytis* and *Trachypitecus* langurs within Sundaland. This has been most pronounced for *P. thomasi, P. rubicunda* and *T. auratus*. In 1994 *P. thomasi* was largely known from one excellent >2-year behavioural ecological study in North Sumatra's Bohorok district by Gurmaya (1989), but data collection at another site, Ketambe, was well under way. This now has resulted in a very solid long-term dataset and one of the few that gives us insight into the demography and life histories of *Presbytis* langurs (Steenbeek and van Schaik 2001; Sterck et al. 2005; Wich et al. 2007). *Presbytis rubicunda* was mostly known from two 1-year studies in Sepilok and Tanjung Putting (Davies 1984; Supriatna et al. 1986); this species has now been studied in detail at at least five additional sites, including three (Danum Valley, Sebangau and Gunung Palung) where groups were under observation for more than three years (Cheyne et al. 2018; Clink et al. 2017; Ehlers-Smith et al. 2013ab; Hanya and Bernard 2012; Marshall et al. 2014b). Finally, for *T. auratus* Davies and Oates (1994) relied mostly on one 1.5-year study conducted at Pangandaran (Kool 1989, 1992). Since then the langurs have intermittently been studied in Pangandaran (Mitani and Watanabe 2009; Nijman 2000; Tsuji et al. 2013a, 2016; Watanabe et al. 1996), and combined with data collected in the 1970s and 1980s (Brotoisworo 1983; Brotoisworo and Dirgayusa 1991) we now have a longer-term perspective of this population. More importantly, following the publication of Davies and Oates (1994) *T. auratus* has been studied for a year or more at four distinctly different sites (montane rainforest: Beckwith 1995; teak forest: Djuwantoko 1991; monsoon forest: Friis Hansen et al. 2019; Vogt 2003).

While the aim of this chapter was to explore sympatric *Presbytis* and *Trachypithecus* langurs, it is clear that most studies focus on single species only, sometimes because indeed at the study site only one species is present or because the other is ignored. Little progress has been made since studies on sympatric *P. siamensis* and *T. obscurus* in the Thai-Malay Peninsula in the 1960s and 1970s (Bernstein 1967; Curtin 1980; MacKinnon and MacKinnon 1980; McClure 1964). Studies of two or even three sympatric *Presbytis* langurs are rare – opportunities to study this is best in eastern and northern Borneo – and studies of two sympatric *Trachypithecus* langurs, i.e. *T. selangorensis* and *T. obscurus*, and possibly *T. obscurus* and *T. barbei* in the northernmost part of the distribution range of *T. obscurus* have yet to be conducted.

Overall then it can be concluded that *Presbytis* langurs show a considerable amount of diversity both within and between species in terms of social organization, diet, ranging behaviour and habitat use, but this variation, again both within and between species, is more marked in *Trachypithecus* langurs.

15 Ecology of *Trachypithecus* spp. in the Indo-Burmese Region

Alison M. Behie, Kirrily Apthorp, Rebecca Hendershott and Kayla Ruskin

Introduction

As part of the colobinae subfamily, the genus *Trachypithecus* includes primates that are anatomically specialized to ingest a diet made up primarily of hard to digest leaves, which is then associated with characteristics of their social organization and activity pattern. Colobines as a group are distributed across Africa and Asia. Asian colobines are commonly referred to as langurs/leaf monkeys. They include seven genera: *Pygathrix, Trachypithecus, Semnopithecus, Rhinopithecus, Presbytis, Nasalis* and *Simias*. The focus of this chapter is to describe the behaviour and ecology of Asian colobines within the genus *Trachypithecus* located in the Indo-Burmese region to gain a better picture of the variation that exists within this group and how this is related to their habitat and conservation.

The Indo-Burmese region includes the countries of India, Myanmar, Laos, Cambodia, Vietnam, Thailand and Southern China. It is a key area for primate conservation as it is in the Indo-Burmese Biological Hotspot, which is one of the most biologically important regions globally due to its high levels of species diversity and endemism (Mittermeier et al. 2004). While the biodiversity importance of the region extends well beyond forested areas, it is the forests that are the most biodiverse ecosystems; forests which range from evergreen to mixed deciduous to deciduous dipterocarp and limestone karst. There is also strong seasonality with large variations in rainfall both between coastal and inland areas as well as between seasons within the same habitat. These factors create extreme diversity in the quality of available habitat and the food species available to the animals that live in the region (Mittermeier et al. 2004), and has implications for group size and sociality (Chapter 16).

The Indo-Burmese Hotspot boasts more than 400 species of mammals including a high number of threatened primates (Mittermeier et al. 2004). Of the 20 primates that are endemic to the region seven are from the *Trachypithecus* genus [*Trachypithecus delacouri* (Delacour's langur); *T. francoisi* (Francois langur); *T. poliocephalus* (Cat Ba langur); *T. laotum* (Laotian langur); *T. hatinhensis* (Hatinh langur); *T. germaini* (Indochinese lutung) and *T. shortridgei* (Shortridge's langur)]. This list, however, is unlikely to be accurate due to unresolved taxonomy within the genus in the Indo-Burmese region. In addition to the endemic *Trachypithecus* species, there are other species whose distribution crosses into the Indo-Burmese region including: *T. geei*

This chapter includes Electronic Supplementary Material (ESM) at: www.cambridge.org/colobines

(Gee's golden langur), *T. pileatus* (capped langur), *T. barbei (*Tenaserrim lutung), *T. phayrei (*Phayre's langur), *T. crepusculus (*Indochinese grey langur) and *T. ebenus* (Indochinese black langur). Combined with the endemic species, this makes a total of 15 *Trachypithecus* species found within the area, all of which are in decline and of conservation concern. Specifically, two species are listed as Vulnerable by the IUCN Redlist (*T. laotum, T. pileatus*), seven are listed as Endangered (*T. ebenus, T. francoisi, T. geei, T. germaini, T. hatinhensis, T. phayrei* and *T. shortridgei*), two are listed as Critically Endangered (*T. delacouri* and *T. poliocephalus*) and one as Data Deficient (*T. barbei*). While the IUCN has not evaluated *T. crepusculus, T. margarita* or *T. leucocephalus* as their own species, the latter is listed as Critically Endangered under *T. poliocephalus leucocephalus.*

This high rate of decline amongst *Trachypithecus* species in the region is largely due to high human population pressure that has created rapid economic development, and an overall increased alteration of natural landscapes into agriculture and modified habitat. Past and present forest degradation from logging, exploitation of forest resources, and conversion to agriculture are all common threats facing the habitats of these species (Mazumder 2014; Nadler et al. 2003, 2007; Nadler and Streicher 2004; Schrudde et al. 2010) as are the effects of political unrest (Huang et al. 2008a; Srivastava et al. 2001). Despite efforts from conservation groups, poaching remains a serious threat to these populations in many areas; *T. poliocephalus* has been poached to near extinction on Cat Ba Island in Vietnam for use in monkey balms and wines thought to increase virility and cure ailments (Nadler and Long 2000). Similar fates have been reported for *T. delacouri, T. hatinhensis* and *T. leucocephalus* (Nadler et al. 2003). The rising popularity and economic importance of tourism throughout Asia (Twining-Ward et al. 2018) is also an increasing threat as developments increase and begin to encroach upon the habitats of some of these species. As these pressures continue to impact and fragment the habitats of these species, it is essential that further research is carried out in order to offset and prevent these threats from driving these species, and their habitats, beyond the point of no return and to produce meaningful and long-term conservation.

In this chapter, we outline what is currently known about the behaviour and ecology of these 15 *Trachypithecus* species in the hopes of highlighting areas lacking in our knowledge that may assist in more scientific research and better-informed conservation planning.

Distribution and Habitat

The distribution of many species within the *Trachypithecus* genus is not completely resolved, in part due to uncertainty regarding the taxonomic status and relationships of several of the species. Such taxonomic confusion coupled with a lack of detailed study on the ecology of many of the Indo-Burmese *Trachypithecus* species makes it difficult to accurately identify their entire distribution and habitat preferences, which has serious implications for their ongoing conservation.

Perhaps adding to the confusion regarding their taxonomic relationships is the vastness of the geographic distribution of *Trachypithecus*, ranging from Bangladesh, Bhutan and India, to southern China, across Lao PDR, Cambodia, Vietnam and down into Thailand (ESM Table 15.1) (Groves 2001). This wide distribution has led to the recognition of 15 species in this region that rarely occur sympatrically as they are often separated by geographical features such as rivers.

Based on these challenges, specific distributions for most species remain unclear due to inaccurate historical descriptions of each species, or misidentification by locals and researchers alike. For instance, *Macaca* can often be mistaken for langurs and vice versa, adding to the confusion regarding the exact distribution of these species (Nadler et al. 2003). Furthermore, historical sightings are often unable to be verified, either due to the terrain, or the possibility that the species is now extinct in that location, if it ever truly existed there at all (Nadler et al. 2003; Timmins et al. 2013). To add to the difficulties, a lack of common names for the species can often confuse identification, for example, Timmins et al. (2013), describes the confusion surrounding the identification of *T. germaini* in Lao PDR, where the local name of 'taloung' is used in other areas of the country to simply refer to langurs in general.

Regardless, it is possible to provide general distributions and habitat descriptions for these species (Figure 15.1). While some species have been studied in more detail than others, this has not made their distribution easier to describe. This is because they tend to be studied at specific study sites, restricting our ability to gain a complete picture of the full distribution and habitat of the species within the region. Of *Trachypithecus* in the Indo-Burmese region, one particular group has been more thoroughly mapped than others: the limestone langurs, named due to their restriction to the limestone karst that they inhabit (Groves 2001). These species include *T. delacouri, T. ebenus, T. francoisi, T. hatinhensis, T. laotum, T. leucocephalus* and *T. poliocephalus*, and are found east of the Mekong River in tropical forest covering limestone formations found in Vietnam, Southern China and parts of Lao PDR (González-Monge 2016; Nadler et al. 2003; Workman 2004). They are restricted to limestone karst, which is characterized by collapsed valleys and steep, jagged peaks (which can include elevations up to 200–600 m) that are covered in degraded limestone tropical forest (Harding 2009; Li D et al. 2011; Li and Rogers 2005a; Nguyen et al. 2010; Steinmetz et al. 2011; Zhou Q et al. 2007). Limestone karst forests have distinct vegetation zones, with generally patchy, scrub-like vegetation on summits and cliff faces, thicker vegetation on hill slopes, and higher-quality vegetation with established trees and vegetation layers remaining in unfarmed valleys and flatter regions of the karst (Kim and Thin 1998).

It is uncertain whether or not this limestone karst forest is the preferred or refuge habitat for this group (Li Z and Rogers 2005a,b). Due to the porous nature of the limestone, there is little standing water available, and soil collects in the valleys and base of the high peaks (Li Z and Rogers 2005a; Nguyen et al. 2010). As a result, the valleys, which may offer the most important areas for langurs in terms of foraging, are often converted to agriculture by surrounding villages (Hendershott et al. 2018; Huang et al. 2008a,b; Zhou Q et al. 2013b). Conversion of valleys to farmland and

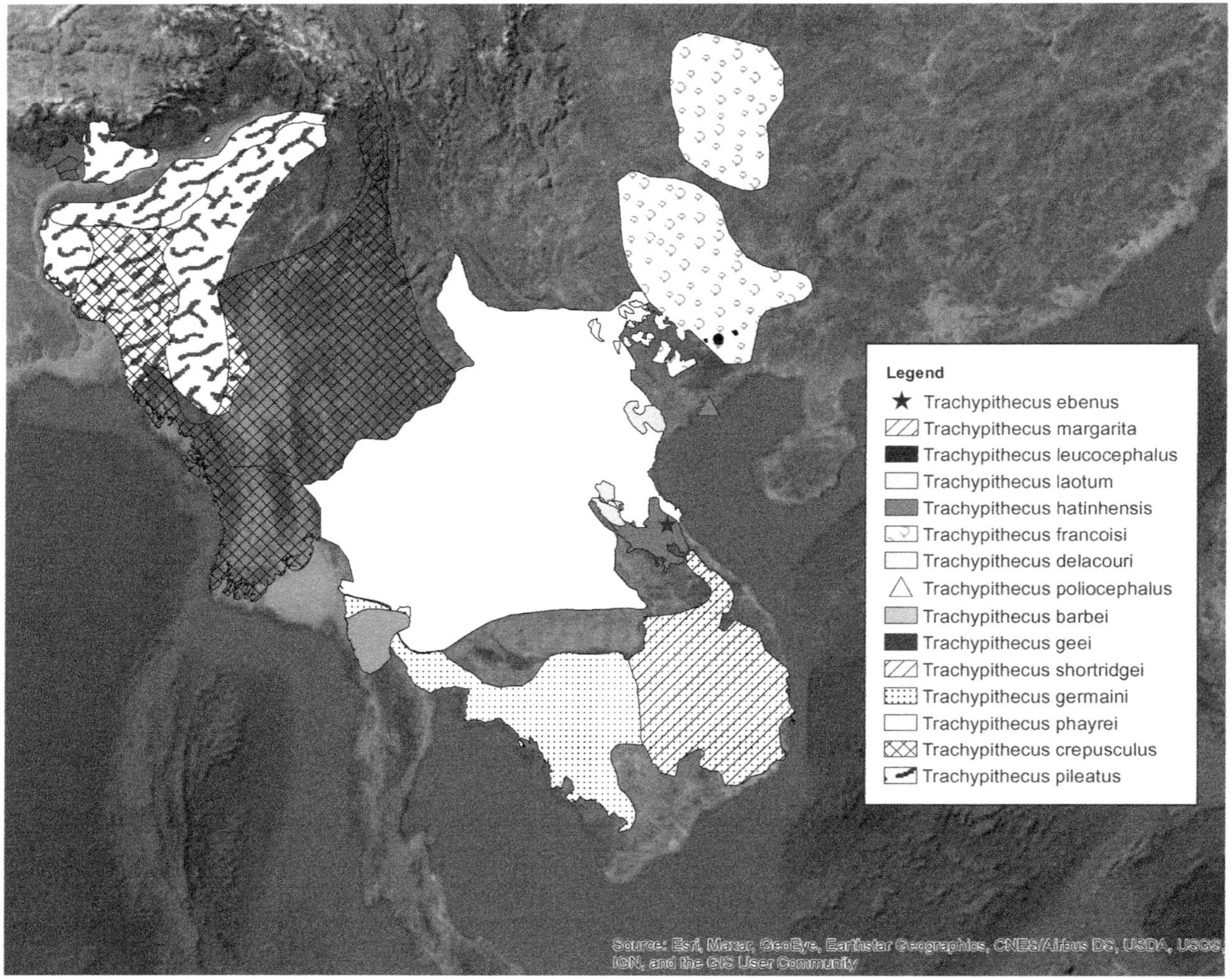

Figure 15.1 Distribution of the 15 Trachypithecus spp. found in the Indoburmese region.

exploitation of the surrounding forest has left many patches of limestone karst forest inhabited by these langurs degraded. For some species such as *T. poliocephalus*, there are no other options for suitable habitat. However, for others, such as *T. laotum*, limestone karst appears to be a preference, as there remains apparently suitable forest surrounding their current distribution (Duckworth et al. 2010).

Very few detailed ecological studies have been carried out on the habitats of non-limestone langurs, and variation reported in their habitats varies from site to site, even within species with small distributions such as *T. shortridgei*. In general, these habitats tend to have more closed canopies, often with distinct upper and lower canopy layers and denser vegetation than that found in limestone karst forests (Srivastava et al. 2001; Wayre 1968). For *T. germaini*, *T. margarita*, and some groups of *T. pileatus* their habitat varies from broadleaf evergreen or semievergreen, to moist deciduous forest (Adimallaiah et al. 2014; Carl 2009; Fan et al. 2015; Gibson and Koenig 2012; González-Monge 2016; Nadler et al. 2003; Pages 2005; Srivastava 2006; Wayre 1968). These habitats can also include bamboo forests, as reported for *T. phayrei*, *T. pileatus* and *T. shortridgei* (Cui et al. 2016; Mazumder 2014), as well as sub-alpine forests and even patches of grasslands and scrub as reported for *T. geei* (Chetry et al. 2010; Mukherjee and Saha 1974). A large part of the variation seen in the habitats of these groups is due to the wide range of elevations they exploit: anywhere from sea level to mountain summits. Of all the langurs, *T. crepusculus* is reported to inhabit the highest elevations of 1700 m–2700 m, resulting in much lower dry season temperatures than for other species (Ma et al. 2015).

While the structure of their habitats may vary, *Trachypithecus* are rarely reported in primary forest, rather they are mainly found in disturbed primary or secondary forest either recovering from, or experiencing, ongoing logging (Fan et al. 2015; Mazumder 2014). Despite this, some species appear to prefer, or have adapted to, secondary and disturbed forest, perhaps due to a shift in the distribution of preferred diet species (Li D et al. 2016; Srivastava 2006; Srivastava et al. 2001).

Such variation in forest type and resultant habitat quality has also been reported to impact population densities among these species with some species being found in larger groups in undisturbed habitat. Groups of *T. laotum* living in remote areas protected from hunting live in larger groups and are less wary of humans than groups in areas more heavily trafficked by humans (Steinmetz et al. 2011). This suggests that these larger sizes in undisturbed habitat are the more 'natural' group size for this species. Similarly, *T. leucocephalus* groups are reportedly larger in higher-quality habitat (Li Z and Rogers 2005b). Conversely, some studies report significantly larger groups in disturbed habitat. For example, *T. geeii* have an average group size of 8.5 individuals in disturbed habitat, but only 6.7 individuals in undisturbed habitat (Lhendup et al. 2018), and there is a negative correlation between habitat quality and group and individual densities in this species (Srivastava 2006), meaning that there are more groups in deteriorated habitat (Srivastava et al. 2001). These variable results may reflect the type of habitat disturbance: habitat fragmentation may lead to higher group and species densities since the same population is being forced to live in less forested areas. Recent isolation means that high population densities may not have stabilized to carrying capacity (Decker 1994a; Dunbar 1987) and crowding through high population density has been known to limit colobine populations (Davies 1994). In contrast, hunting can lead to decreased densities as the number of individuals has been reduced within the same amount of habitat (as seen in *Presbytis hosei*: Nijman 2005). Poor habitat quality can mean that each individual needs more space (for lower quality resources) to sustain themselves (Li Z and Rogers 2005b; Hu 2007). All of these factors are at play for many Critically Endangered species with extremely small population numbers from hunting as well as fragmentation and habitat degradation, as has seen in *T. poliocephalus* (Nadler and Long 2000).

Climate

Based on their distribution, *Trachypithecus* in the Indo-Burmese region experience a tropical monsoon climate, with two main seasons (ESM Table 15.2) (Mukherjee and Saha 1974; Nadler and Long 2000; Schneider et al. 2010). A humid wet season, lasting generally from May to October, delivers 80%–90% of the rainfall for the year, and can include typhoons, which may impact the habitat of some species (Hendershott 2017; Nguyen et al. 2010; Zhou Q et al. 2007). Temperatures tend to peak during this season around July and August (Zhou Q et al. 2007). The dry season then lasts from November to March and brings colder weather to the region, which may drop close to freezing in the high altitude range of some species, such as *T. crepusculus* (Fan et al. 2015).

Climate change is a continuing threat to *Trachypithecus* species in this region, as changes to the length and severity of climatic events are expected to impact their habitats. For example, a species distribution model of *T. francoisi* under current and future climate predictions found that with climate change animals will need to move further North and West to find adequate habitat as the amount of habitat rated as very good or excellent will decrease (Van et al. 2012). Similar changes to habitat are expected across the region, which will exacerbate risks to these species as they already show characteristics associated with high vulnerability to extinction including a large body size, diurnality and a restricted geographic range (Estrada et al. 2017). On a more local scale, as forests are degraded and fragmented they are likely to experience increased light and humidity, changing the localized climate and impacting the distribution of species and their ranging behaviours (Srivastava 2006).

Diet and Feeding Ecology

To cope with their highly folivorous diet, colobines have developed specialized gut and teeth morphology. For teeth, this includes higher, sharper molar cusps with more defined shearing blades and relatively large premolar rows compared to the palate size, which is thought to increase the efficiency of mastication (Kay and Hylander 1978; Oates and Davies 1994b; Scott et al. 2018). This is particularly important for *Trachypithecus* species as this genus tends to rely more on ingestion as a means to assist with leaf digestion through the fast chewing and breaking down of leaves into smaller pieces prior to swallowing to increase the surface area for gut microbe activity (Wright et al. 2008). The morphology and size of the teeth are also thought to be well adapted to consuming seeds with thin, flexible testas, which would be more common in unripe fruit, as seeds tend to increase their mechanical protection during the final stages of development (Davies 1991; Lucas and Teaford 1994). Colobines are also thought to produce large amounts of saliva due to their enlarged salivary glands, which may play a role in the fermentation process and the neutralization of tannins in foods by keeping the pH of the forestomach fluid within an acceptable range to permit active fermentation and producing proline-rich proteins that can bind with tannins and prevent them from interfering with the digestion process (Bauchop 1978; Kay and Davies 1994; Waterman and Kool 1994).

The gastrointestinal tracts of colobines are made up of a capacious multi-chambered stomach, an elongated small intestine that is sacculated throughout its length, and a large, densely haustrated colon (Caton 1999; Chivers 1994; Chivers and Hladik 1980). This overall morphology indicates that there are two areas where fermentation takes place; a feature which would markedly improve their ability to process the fermentable components of their plant-based diets (Caton 1999). The first area is in the stomach, which contains a large sacculated fermenting chamber in the forestomach where the digesta is mixed with a large number of cellulose-digesting bacteria that can produce enzymes to degrade the structural polysaccharides cellulose and hemicelluloses in the plant cell wall and create volatile fatty acids (VFAs) and microbial cell materials, which can be utilized by the host animal (Bauchop 1978; Caton 1999; Chivers and Hladik 1980; Kay and Davies 1994). Forestomach fermentation is also thought to play a role in the breakdown of certain plant toxins, such as alkaloids, amines and organic acids, before the individual absorbs them, which would allow the monkeys to ingest these harmful compounds without experiencing any ill-effects (Kay and Davies 1994). The second area where fermentation takes place is in the colon, which is thought to act in a similar fashion to the forestomach to retain and ferment the undigested residues from the small intestines (Caton 1999; Chivers 1994; Chivers and Hladik 1980). In addition, a number of studies have demonstrated that colobines have reduced rates of passage and prolonged retention of digesta, which aids in the digestion of cell wall material and improves the rate of nutrient extraction (Caton 1999; Dierenfeld et al. 1992; Edwards and Ullrey 1999). Such adaptations of the GI tract may also make colobines well suited for seed digestion, as starch is generally the main storage carbohydrate in seeds, which can be more thoroughly broken down by the forestomach than the small intestines of primates with a simple stomach (Kay and Davies 1994).

The diets of most *Trachypithecus* species in the Indo-Burmese region are primarily made up of leaves, with smaller amounts of fruit, seeds and flowers (ESM Table 15.3). The limestone langurs in particular seem to have the most folivorous diets among these species as many studies have found that they typically spend more than 70% of their time consuming leaves (Hendershott et al. 2017; Huang et al. 2008b; Li Y et al. 2009, 2015, 2016; Li Z and Rogers 2006; Workman 2010a; Yin et al. 2011;

Zhou Q et al. 2013a). Notably, studies on *T. francoisi* and *T. leucocephalus* in Fusui Nature Reserve (China) indicate groups can spend more than 90% of their time feeding on leaves (Huang et al. 2008b; Zhou Q et al. 2013a). However, such high levels of leaf consumption are not found in all populations of limestone langurs as one group of *T. francoisi* in the Nonggang Nature Reserve (China) and multiple groups from the Mayanghe Nature Reserve (China) were found to spend only 53% and 64% of their time on leaves, respectively (Hu 2011; Zhou Q et al. 2006). Of the non-limestone langur species, many have been observed to spend between 50% and 70% of their time consuming leaves, including *T. crepusculus* (Fan et al. 2015), *T. pileatus* (Islam and Husain 1982; Solanki et al. 2008; Stanford 1991b), *T. geei* (Das et al. 2013; Lhendup et al. 2018) and *T. germaini* (Le et al. 2015), while *T. phayrei* and *T. crepusculus* generally spent just under 50% of their time on leaves (Aziz and Feeroz 2009; Gupta and Kumar 1994; Ma et al. 2017; Suarez 2013). When differentiated, most species consumed young leaves more often than mature leaves (Fan et al. 2015; Gupta and Kumar 1994; Hu 2011; Le et al. 2015; Li Y et al. 2015b, 2016; Li Z and Rogers 2006; Ma et al. 2017; Solanki et al. 2008; Suarez 2013; Workman 2010a; Yin et al. 2011; Zhou Q et al. 2006), with the exception of a population of *T. pileatus* in Madhupur National Park (Bangladesh), who spent 42% of their time eating mature leaves compared to only 11% of their time eating young leaves (Stanford 1991b).

Much like between species, there also exists variation between populations of the same species with regard to their consumption of leaves and fruit annually. The most variation within leaf consumption occurs between populations of *T. francoisi* at different study sites that range from 53% to 81% while the least occurs in *T. phayrei* where different populations consume between 45% and 53% leaves (ESM Table 15.3). There is much less variation within species in terms of overall annual fruit consumption that varies from 4% to 17% in *T. leucocephalus*, 9% to 26% in *T. francoisi* and 7% to 22% in *T. phayrei* (ESM Table 15.3). This variation between sites is most likely due to differences in habitat quality and productivity between specific study sites.

In the opposite pattern, fruit and/or seeds are generally consumed for a quarter or a third of the time for most non-limestone species, whereas the limestone langurs can spend less than 10% of their time on these items (ESM Table 15.3). However, this is not always the case as some groups of *T. francoisi* spend approximately 30% of their time ingesting seeds and fruit (Hu 2011; Zhou Q et al. 2006), while some groups of *T. phayrei* and *T. pileatus* spend less than 20% of their time on these same items (Aziz and Feeroz 2009; Solanki et al. 2008). Strikingly, a study on *T. margarita* in the Veun Sai Siem Pang Conservation Area (Cambodia) found that the monkeys spend nearly 90% of their time on fruit and seeds and only 8% of their time on leaves (González-Monge 2016).

Flowers are reported to be eaten by all species studied, although they are generally consumed for less than 10% of feeding time (ESM Table 15.3). In addition to leaves, fruits, seeds and flowers, *Trachypithecus* are also known to eat petioles, stems, roots, bark, wood, gums and pith (Aziz and Feeroz 2009; Biswas et al. 2009; Choudhury

1989; Fan et al. 2015; Gupta and Kumar 1994; Hu 2011; Huang et al. 2008b; Lhendup et al. 2018; Li Y et al. 2015b, 2016, Ma et al. 2017; Solanki et al. 2008; Suarez 2013; Zhou Q et al. 2006, 2009a). Some species may also consume animal matter, including *T. pileatus* in Madhupur National Park (Bangladesh) and *T. crepusculus* in Phu Khieo Wildlife Sanctuary (Thailand), that consume unknown species of caterpillars (Stanford 1991b; Suarez 2013). In the case of *T. crepusculus*, the insects made up a quarter of the diet during the month that they ate them (Suarez 2013) while for *T. pileatus* they only accounted for approximately 1% of the diet (Standford 1991b).

Many of these species also display seasonal differences in their diets – and thus, food factors may limit group size (Chapter 16) – due to variations in the availability of food items. For example, *T. francoisi* in Fusui Nature Reserve (China) consume significantly more leaves and significantly less fruit in the wet season compared to the dry season (Huang et al. 2008b), while *T. phayrei* in Guchengshan (China) spend up to 87% of their time consuming seeds at the start of the dry season but were not observed to consume them at all between April and June, the peak of the wet season (Ma et al. 2017). Such changes in the consumption of certain plant parts is often related to availability, for example in *T. leucocephalus* (Li et al. 2016; Li Z and Rogers 2006), *T. phayrei* (Gupta and Kumar 1994; Ma et al. 2017), *T. francoisi* (Zhou Q et al. 2006) and *T. pileatus* (Stanford 1991b) young leaves and fruit in the diet are correlated with their production in the environment. In addition, low availability of these preferred plant parts can then lead to increased consumption of less-preferred items, such as mature leaves, stems or petioles that are all eaten more frequently by *T. francoisi* when young leaf availability decreases (Zhou Q et al. 2006). These associations between consumption and availability often explain seasonal variation in diet as animals change dietary patterns based on what is produced in different months of the year.

Few studies have explored the nutritional content of foods consumed by *Trachypithecus* in the Indo-Burmese region. One such study on *T. delacouri* revealed the protein-to-fibre ratio was significantly higher in eaten food items compared to available items that were not eaten. No differences were found in any nutritional variable between mature and young leaves (Workman and Van 2009). Similarly, no differences were found between water, protein or fibre between food items for *T. leucocephalus* (Zhou Q et al. 2013a) and nutritional studies in *T. francoisi* found no significant differences in tannin contents of the most and least preferred food items, which may be because this species can tolerate high levels of tannins (Li Y et al. 2015b).

Despite these studies, it is known that leaves across many study sites are not equal in terms of nutrient quality and a number of colobines are documented to experience food limitations and selectivity as well as scramble and contest competition (Borries et al. 2008; Harris et al. 2009; Koenig 2000; Li et al. 2003; Snaith and Chapman 2005; Snaith and Chapman 2008; Chapter 16). For example, female-female agonism among *T. crepusculus* typically occurs around food (Koenig et al. 2004), and pregnant females that require more resources are more likely to show aggression towards or displace other females (Lu et al. 2016). This aggression often decreases when preferred food items peak in availability. Groups of *T. pileatus*, for example, feed in the same tree when the trees are flush with new leaves (Stanford 1991b).

While rare, some *Trachypithecus* species in the region have been observed to occasionally drink water. For example, *T. delacouri* occasionally drink water from both karst bowls and the surrounding wetlands (Workman 2010a), *T. poliocephalus* drink from karst bowls and the surrounding ocean (Hendershott et al. 2017), *T. leucocephalus* drink from karst bowls and small ponds in addition to licking the early morning dew off leaves (Huang and Li 2005; Li Z 2000; Zhou Q et al. 2011b), *T. crepusculus* drink from creeks and standing water (Suarez 2013), and *T. geei* drink from rivers (Mukherjee 1978). Drinking, however, generally accounts for less than 1% of the dietary budget for each species (Hendershott et al. 2017; Ma et al. 2017; Suarez 2013).

Another rare feeding behaviour in *Trachypithecus* is geophagy. *T. phayrei* can spend 0.5% of their time consuming soil (Suarez 2013), while *T. crepusculus* can spend 5.7% of their time engaging in the same behaviour (Fan et al. 2015). Similarly, *T. pileatus* and *T. geei* have also been observed to spend small amounts of time consuming soil (Mukherjee 1978; Solanki et al. 2008), whereas *T. margarita* has been recorded by camera-traps using salt licks (soils with high concentrations of sodium) in the Veun Sai Siem Pang Conservation Area (Cambodia) quite frequently (González-Monge 2016; King et al. 2016; Rawson and Tuong 2011). Additionally, *T. phayrei* increase their daily path length and travel speed on the days that they visit salt licks within their habitat, suggesting that soil is an important component of the diet (Ma et al. 2017). In addition to soil eating, *T. phayrei, T. pileatus, T. leucocephalus* and *T. francoisi* have all been observed to lick the surface of rocks, which may be an important source of minerals for the monkeys (Hendershott et al. 2017; Li et al. 2003; Ma et al. 2017; Zhou Q et al. 2006).

Activity Patterns

Activity budgets in primates vary in accordance with seasonality as well as the quality of the habitat in which they are found, both of which occur in response to changes in availability and location of food resources. Colobines, including the genus *Trachypithecus*, typically spend the majority of their time inactive, largely due to their highly folivorous diet that is high in indigestible fibre, and requires a significant portion of time be dedicated to digestion (Dasilva 1992; Edwards and Ullrey 1999; Kirkpatrick 2007; Oates and Davies 1994b; Stanford 1991a). This diet high in leafy matter also results in the next most common behaviour in this group to be feeding, as it can take time to process bulky leaf matter that is lower in immediate nutritional value than easy-to-digest high-sugar fruit (Clutton-Brock and Harvey 1977; Decker 1994a). Perhaps to compensate for the time they spend resting and feeding, and possibly in response to the lack of aggressive competition needed to maintain a leafy diet, colobines show low rates of social behaviour (Newton and Dunbar 1994) – although see Chapter 16 about this being an oversimplification.

When focusing in on the *Trachypithecus* species in the Indo-Burmese region, animals show the typical colobine activity pattern with the majority of time (21%–75%) inactive on an annual basis. This is followed by time spent feeding (13%–35%), travelling (2%–32%) and then in social behaviours (<1%–30%) (see ESM Table 15.4 for detailed activity budgets of each species). There appears to be an outlier in activity budget in one *T. phayrei* study where animals only spend 21% of time inactive yet engage in social behaviour for 30% of the time. If this study was removed from the table (ESM Table 15.4) above, then the mean time spent inactive on an annual basis would be 34%–75% with social time reduced to <1%–12%, which is more like other colobine species. It should be noted, however, that we could only find studies on the activity budget of seven of the 15 species within this region.

As outlined in the distribution and habitat section of this chapter, habitat quality varies between species and this variation is known to contribute to variation in activity budget both within and between species. For example, *T. leucocephalus* groups in high-quality habitat spend less time feeding and more time playing than groups in low-quality habitat (Li and Rogers 2006). Similar results were found for *T. francoisi* where groups in disturbed forest spend more time travelling and less time resting, likely in response to the lower food availability in the disturbed areas (Zhou Q et al. 2010). Levels of human activity in disturbed forests can also influence time engaged in social behaviour for *T. francoisi* where animals huddle more when human presence is higher. As a result, animals then spend less time resting and feeding (Yang et al. 2007).

Like habitat quality, seasonality also impacts activity budgets with most species showing variation in activity patterns between seasons. In *T. phayrei* in India animals spend significantly more time feeding and less time inactive in winter than in summer or monsoon seasons (Gupta and Kumar 1994). In *T. leucocephalus* animals significantly reduce inactivity time (from 84% in summer-autumn to 57% in winter), which may be due to an increase in sunbathing activity (categorized as separate to inactive in this study) that occurs in the cold winter months to assist animals in thermoregulation (Huang et al. 2003). While *T. francoisi* spend more time feeding and less time resting and grooming in the dry season compared to the wet season, they also show two significant feeding peaks in the dry season, compared to only one in the wet season (Zhou Q et al. 2007). Similarly, the closely related *T. poliocephalus* increases foraging time in the dry season (Hendershott et al. 2017). These last two results suggest that *Trachypithecus* adopt an energy maximizing strategy where animals increase travelling time in response to the low food availability of the dry season, rather than spending more time resting as a response, which would be an energy minimizing strategy. No literature reports energy minimizing as a strategy for *Trachypithecus* species in the Indo-Burmese region.

Like with most primates, *Trachypithecus* species in the Indo-Burmese region show variation in activity patterns between age and sex classes. With respect to age categories, immatures often spend more time playing while adults spend more time resting, feeding and grooming (Zhou Q et al. 2007). However, the opposite pattern has been seen in *T. poliocephalus* where adults spend more time engaged in social behaviour and inactivity than sub-adults and juveniles (Hendershott et al. 2017). However, this difference may be due to social behaviour in this study included grooming, social play, vocalizing, same- and opposite-sex mounting, embracing, young transferring, presenting, harassing a mounting pair, submission, displacement and aggression. Agmen (2014) on the other hand, found no differences in the activity pattern of immatures compared to the adults of wild *T. delacouri*. In terms of sex, studies in both *T. delacouri* and *T. poliocephalus* found females spend more time socializing and less time inactive than males (Hendershott et al. 2017; Workman 2010b). Female *T. delacouri* also spend more time feeding than males (Workman 2010b), although this has not been reported in other species.

The increased social behaviour seen in females in some *Trachypithecus* species may reflect the fact that female langurs are generally more interested in newborn group members, which may facilitate much of their social interactions. High rates of grooming of infants (Hu 2007) and the fact that the majority of social affiliation occurs between mother-infant dyads (Stanford 1991a) supports this view. It is also obvious in the high rates of infant handling/transfer and allomothering seen among langurs, which can start within hours of birth (Jin et al. 2015; Kumar et al. 2005; Kumar and Solanki 2014; Stanford 1992; Yao et al. 2012) (although note that for some groups, allomothering does not start until the infant is a few weeks old: Hu 2007). Given the lack of a strong dominance hierarchy, langur mothers are more permissive with allowing their infants to be handled by others than species with stricter dominance hierarchies (Maestripieri 1994; McKenna 1979; Thierry 2007).

Range Use

As discussed previously, detailed ecological studies on the habitats and distribution of *Trachypithecus* species in the Indo-Burmese region are limited. While species such as *T. francoisi* have been more widely studied than others, our understanding of many of these species' habitats is restricted to specific pockets due to widespread fragmentation of *Trachypithecus* populations. Fragmentation of populations and their habitats has been shown to reduce home ranges and often results in higher densities of groups (Huang et al. 2017c; Srivastava 2006). Most, if not all, of the species under consideration here are experiencing population fragmentation, with groups separated from one another at distances of 2 km–100 km (Huang et al. 2008a), preventing dispersal between areas. For *T. delacouri*, four protected regions in northern Vietnam are home to 40% of the total population, while the remaining 60% are in fragmented pockets (Harding 2009; Nadler et al. 2003). The nature of these isolated habitats means that the use of home ranges by *Trachypithecus* can vary within and between species depending on the circumstances of their habitats.

Folivores are generally not thought to be territorial (Carl 2009), and observations of inter- and intra-species' interactions in some species, such as *T. geei*, appear to support this (Mukherjee and Saha 1974). For other species, such as *T. leucocephalus* and *T. poliocephalus*, distinct ranges and territories have been observed, and aggressive displays and interactions do occasionally occur (Li D et al. 2011). It is possible that this variation in territorial behaviour may be a result of the large differences in home range size (ESM Table 15.5) reported for these species: the largest home range size for *T. geei* is 430 ha (Srivastava 2006), while for *T. leucocephalus* and *T. poliocephalus*, the largest home ranges reported are 52 ha (Huang et al. 2002) and 50 ha (Hendershott et al. 2018), respectively. For these species, the differences in their behaviours may be a result of the quality and degree of habitat fragmentation that they experience, which in turn may impact the density of groups within their habitats. In a study on *T. geei*, Srivastava (2006), showed that the home ranges of groups in disturbed forest (120 ha) were smaller and population densities higher than those in undisturbed forest (430 ha). Thus, for species such as *T. leucocephalus* and *T. poliocephalus*, responses to incursions by conspecifics may be heightened due to limited space and resources, compared to species with larger home ranges (González-Monge 2016). While home range size may influence the behaviour of primates, the size of home ranges do not remain static; the size of a group's home range may fluctuate, as will their behaviour within it, depending on the time of year, past and present climate conditions, food availability and even the way in which home range is measured between studies (Gibson and Koenig 2012; Hendershott et al. 2018; Huang et al. 2017c).

Food availability is an important factor in home range use by non-human primates. The limestone langur group has been found to forage in trees on slopes, exposed rock and particularly in valleys, which often provide the most fertile areas in their habitat (Burton et al.1995; Hendershott et al. 2018; Huang et al. 2002; Li Z *and* Rogers 2006; Nguyen 2006). Members of the limestone langurs have been observed to use almost every strata of their habitat for feeding, socializing, locomoting and sleeping (Burton et al. 1995; Hendershott 2017; Hendershott et al. 2018; Huang and Li 2005; Xiong et al. 2009; Zhou Q et al. 2013b). In contrast, other members of *Trachypithecus* are mainly arboreal, eating and sleeping in tall trees (González-Monge 2016; Mazumder 2014; Mukherjee 1982; Mukherjee and Saha 1974; Wayre 1968). In the case of *T. pileatus*, groups have been observed to spend less than 1% of their time on the ground (Stanford 1991a). Instead, these species rely on tall canopies, sleeping and eating in tree layers from 5m to 50m (González-Monge 2016; Mukherjee and Saha 1974).

While food availability is recognized as a critical factor in determining primate distributions and range size and use, other factors such as densities of conspecifics, terrain types, human presence, presence of human structures such as roads, and the presence of predators also play an important role in distributions (Carl 2009; Schneider et al. 2010). In particular, availability of sleeping sites may be a significant factor in non-human primate distribution (Huang et al. 2000). Rather than sleeping in trees like other *Trachypithecus*, the limestone langur group's preferences for sleeping in caves and rock ledges on cliff faces has been well documented (Grueter and Ding 2006; Harding 2009; Li D et al. 2011; Nadler and Long 2000). The reason for this adaptation is unclear, though it has been variously theorized that it could be in response to thermoregulation or predation avoidance (Duckworth et al. 2010; Huang et al. 2003). However, it is unclear why these species require specialized thermoregulation, particularly when other species with similar ranges are not affected, and *T. crepusculus*, a species that can experience particularly cold winters at high altitudes, is not reported to use sleeping caves (Duckworth et al. 2010; Ma et al. 2015). It is also uncertain that this behaviour is a result of predation avoidance as some sleeping sites appear to be little more than cliff ledges offering no protection, and *Trachypithecus* are not known to have many predators throughout their ranges (Harding 2009; Huang et al. 2003; Li D et al. 2011; Nadler et al. 2003, 2004); despite low predation rates by non-humans, the effect of human predation should not be discounted (Chapter 14). In fact, limestone langur choice of sleeping site makes them easier targets for poachers, as they use a limited number of sleeping sites throughout their home ranges at heights of 20 m–50 m, which are often marked by distinctive stains on the rock below, making them easily identifiable (Nadler and Long 2000; Nguyen 2006; Stenke and Xuan 2004; Workman 2004). Further study is necessary to understand this preference, as it does appear to be an adaptation in response to some factor, as *T. laotum* is observed to use sleeping caves despite the presence of tall trees in forest surrounding the karst formations (Duckworth et al. 2010; Steinmetz et al. 2011).

Predation

Compared to African and Central American primate species, Asian primates appear to have much lower predation and estimated predation rates (Hart 2007). Moreover, an almost complete lack of polyspecific associations in Asian primates supports the idea that there is reduced predation pressure in this area (Stanford 2002; see Chapter 14). While there are many potential predators of primates in Asia, many *Trachypithecus* species in the Indo-Burmese region now live in areas that have few natural predators left. In many cases the only predators are raptors, martens, small felids and viverrids, such as leopards, tigers. This is because large viverrids are locally extinct or occur in such small numbers they are rarely seen in most places (Fan et al. 2015; Green 1981; Hendershott 2017; Jin et al. 2009a; Li D et al. 2011; Wang et al. 2011; Zhou Q et al. 2009b).

While some researchers have never observed any natural predators at all during their studies (Huang et al. 2003; Li Y et al. 2015a), there have been few direct observations of predation events on these species. While studying *T. pileatus* in Bangladesh, Stanford (1989) observed one unsuccessful and one successful predation event by groups of *Canis aureus* (jackals). The unsuccessful incident involved two *C. aureus* chasing and attempting to grab a three month old infant who was crossing the 5m of forest floor between the small sapling she was taking refuge on (after presumable falling from the sleeping tree that the other group members were leaving), while the second successful incident involved a larger group of *C. aureus* who attacked and killed an adult female who was moving around on the forest floor before dragging her body away. Similarly, Borries et al. (2014b) observed a possible predation attempt by *Pardofelis marmorata* (marbled cat) when studying *T. crepusculus* in Thailand. The group of monkeys being observing began emitting alarm calls just prior to the researchers discovering a male juvenile member on the ground underneath a *P. marmorata* that appeared to be chewing on his neck. While the monkey managed to escape briefly and climb up a nearby tree after the cat was startled by the observers and ran away, he soon fell back to the ground and was never seen again.

Along with natural predators, populations living close to or within human-populated areas risk predation from domesticated animals, with Medhi et al. (2004) reporting the deaths of two adult *T. geei* in India due to attacks by *Canis lupus familiaris* (domestic dogs) in 2002 and Chetry et al. (2010) reported the deaths of seven individuals in the same area between 2005 and 2006. In addition to these observed events, Nguyen (2006) reported information from a hunter who killed a *Martes flavigula* (yellow-throated marten) that was found feeding on a female *T. hatinhensis* it had presumably killed, while Hendershott (2017) mentioned reports from ex-poachers who described python (*Python molurus*) predation on *T. poliocephalus*. One example includes a python that had been cut open with *T. poliocephalus* inside, while another was a python seen falling out of a sleeping cave while wrapped around a langur.

Aside from direct observations of predation events, researchers have also obtained information by studying potential predators themselves. The scat of *Panthera tigris* (tigers), *Panthera pardus* (leopards) and *Cuon alpinus* (dholes) in the Pakke Tiger Reserve in India have been studied and showed that while *T. pileatus* made up 1.33% of the diet of *P. pardus*, monkeys did not feature in the diets of either *P. tigris* or *C. alpinus* (Lyngdoh et al. 2014). These Indian *T. pileatus* were also found to make up a small percentage of the diet of both *P. pardus* and *P. tigris* in the areas surrounding the Pakke Tiger reserve (Lyngdoh et al. 2014). Similarly, an analysis of the scat of *P. tigris* and *P. pardus* in the Huai Kha Khaeng Wildlife Sanctuary in Thailand found that *T. crepusculus* made up approximately 0.1% and 3% of the diet of each species respectively (Simcharoen et al. 2018), while the scat of the *Panthera pardus delacouri* (Indochinese leopard) in the Srepok Wildlife Sanctuary in Cambodia indicated that *T. germaini* could make up as much as 1.9% of the diet (Rostro-García et al. 2018). However, some or all of the lutung remains found in the scat may have belonged to a different colobine species that also inhabited the habitat.

In the absence of much direct evidence, indirect evidence, such as the reactions of the monkeys to certain animals can also give an indication of predation risks in these colobines. Lloyd et al. (2006) described an incident of a group of *T. crepusculus* mobbing a *Neofelis nebulosa* (clouded leopard) in Phu Khieo Wildlife Sanctuary in Thailand. Mobbing is a term used to describe a set of actions that the prey species uses to harass a potential predator if they get too close or attack a group member, and can include close approach, vocalizations, lunging, threatening behaviour, shaking and/or breaking branches, pursuing and attacking (Crofoot 2012). As soon as *N. nebulosa* was detected climbing a tree towards members of the group, all individuals moved at least 20 m away, with four individuals remaining relatively close for 20 minutes and rapidly moving back and forth while vocalizing (Lloyd et al. 2006). The authors noted that the same group was observed engaging in the same behaviour towards two *N. nebulosa* two years later, suggesting that this species is perceived as a threat by that particular group.

Vigilance, cowering and vocalizations are also known indications of predation threat. All of these behaviours have been observed by *T. francoisi* (Zhou Q et al. 2009b), *T. pileatus* (Green 1981; Stanford 1989), *T. crepusculus* (Fan et al. 2015), *T. margarita* (González-Monge 2016) and *T. poliocephalus* (Ruskin unpublished data) in response to birds of prey, such as *Spilornis cheela* (crested serpent eagles), *Nisaetus nipalensis* (mountain hawk eagles) and *Ictinaetus malaiensis* (black eagles). These behaviours are particularly prevalent when infants are present, who are retrieved and held by their mothers whenever the birds are present. Alarm calls are also emitted by *T. crepusculus* in the presence of felids or large snakes (Borries et al. 2014a) and young *T. poliocephalus* have been observed vocalizing and pointing at snakes (Ruskin, pers. obs.). In addition to this, a number of researchers have suggested that predation pressure may be an important reason for some species choosing to use caves and ledges on cliffs as sleeping sites (Hendershott 2017; Huang et al. 2003; Li D et al. 2011; Wang et al. 2011; Zhou Q et al. 2009b).

Social Organization

Trachypithecus groups in the Indo-Burmese region typically live in three social groupings: unimale-multifemale, multimale-multifemale and all-male ('bachelor groups'), although this is based on just five species for which there was available published data (ESM Table 15.6). Unimale groups that are reproductively advantageous for males (as it allows them to monopolize access to females) are the most common group type in some species. Among *T. leucocephalus*, it is proposed that the small number of females in unimale groups are what make them monopolizable (Jin et al. 2009a), suggesting that the number of males is relative to the number of females. Interestingly, however, the number of males in groups of *T. crepusculus* do not appear to be regulated by the number of adult females that can be monopolized, and this species is reported to have almost as many multimale-multifemale groups as unimale-multifemale groups (Koenig and Borries 2012).

Mulitmale groups may form in *Trachypithecus* species for a variety of reasons. It has been suggested that as sons get older they may not be immediately evicted, leading to groups having multiple males in an age-graded multimale structure (Hu 2007). These males are unlikely to be sexual competitors as they are likely related to the group females (given maternal relatedness: Liu Z et al. 2013b) and even if they did breed, the resident male (i.e. the sire) will still benefit through kin selection. These multimale groups have been reported to fission in a number of *Trachypithecus* species, possibly to get back to the preferable unimale organization (Jin et al. 2009a). Multimale groups of *T. leucocephalus* are considered to be unstable as a 'temporary adaptive strategy' in response to demographic changes (births, deaths, immigration, emigration) (Jin et al. 2009a). Similarly, multimale groups have been reported to form in the midst of a takeover (Liu Z et al. 2013b), which is then followed by group fissioning (Hu 2007). It thus seems that *Trachypithecus* groups go through cycles of being unimale to being multimale to returning to unimale. Similarly, other Asian colobines regularly split and merge, with groups of both single and multiple adult male residents (Chapter 14).

Bachelor groups occur in some species and it is estimated that 22% of adult male *T. leucocephalus* (Jin et al. 2009a) and 33% of adult (8%) and subadult (25%) male *T. poliocephalus* (Lees et al. 2014) live in non-reproductive groups. These males are most likely waiting until there is a situation that allows them to take over an existing unimale group as a means to acquire and monopolize females and become the resident male of that reproductive group. Alternatively, these groups may contain former resident-males who have had their group taken over.

Group sizes vary based on the type of social organization (ESM Table 15.7), which, ultimately, depends on a complex calculation of infanticide, predation, and food competition risks (Chapter 16). While unimale groups range in size from 3 to 33, multimale groups include anywhere from five to over 90 group members (ESM Table 15.7). Unimale groups include anywhere from 1 to 14 adult females (most groups have 3–9) and 0–22 immature individuals, while multimale groups generally have 2–3 adult males (although there can be over 10), 1–8 adult females (although there can be over 30), and 1–10 immature (although there can be up to 50). In contrast, all-male/male and immature groups have 3–13 group members, with 0–8 adult males (generally 1–6), 0–2 subadult males, and possibly immature offspring that left with the adult male upon a takeover (Jin et al. 2009a; Zhao Q and Pan 2006).

Evidence for dispersal in *Trachypithecus* in the Indo-Burmese region is not consistent with some studies pointing to male dispersal and female philopatry and some pointing to dual dispersal. Male dispersal is supported in *T. francoisi*, where groups are described as living in matrilineal female-philopatric societies, with all emigrants being subadult males less than five years old (Hu 2007). Similarly, *T. leucocephalus* genetic results show males are unrelated to group females, while females are stable group members and genetic relatives (Liu Z et al. 2013b). Dual dispersal, on the other hand, is supported by relatively common observations of both solitary males and females, Suggesting that both sexes migrate into new groups (Duy et al. 2014; González-Monge 2016; Hu et al. 2004; Huang et al. 2002; Jin et al. 2009a; Lees et al. 2014; Nadler 2009; Workman 2010b). Behavioural evidence of *T. leucocephalus* suggests females leave their natal groups (Jin et al. 2009a) and gradually transfer between groups (Li Z and Rogers 2004a). This is not incongruent with the genetic study that indicates females within a group are related (Liu Z et al. 2013b), as there is a possibility that females do migrate, but into groups with known/related female kin or even simultaneous migration with kin, as this helps reduce dispersal risks (Chapter 16). At least one species, *T. crepusculus*, regularly exhibits both male and female dispersal (Borries et al. 2004; Koenig and Borries 2012), which may be driven by infanticide avoidance (Yin et al. 2013), inbreeding avoidance and/or female-female competition (Larney 2013).

Colobines are assumed to be relatively egalitarian due to the non-aggressive nature of scramble competition over widely distributed leaves. This is supported by the low rates of aggression and the lack of a strict hierarchy reported for some

Trachypithecus species. For example, less than 1% of social behaviour recorded in scans for *T. poliocephalus* are agonistic (Hendershott 2017) and *T. pileatus* are described as not having a detectable hierarchy (Stanford 1992). However, it is possible that hierarchies are simply too subtle to immediately identify, as described elsewhere in this volume (Chapters 13 and 16). For example, *T. leucocephalus* are described as having low aggression and no strict dominance (Li Z and Rogers 2004a; Zhao Q et al. 2009), although other researchers have constructed a female dominance hierarchy based on subtle agonistic behaviours despite almost a third of agonistic relationships within the hierarchy being bidirectional (i.e. displacement) (Jin et al. 2015). For those studies that have been able to identify a female dominance hierarchy (e.g. *T. crepusculus* and *T. leucocephalus*), it appears to be linear and age-inversed (Zhao Q et al. 2009).

Unsurprising for a taxon that is predominated by unimale-multifemale grouping, females (both adults and all age-classes) outnumber males anywhere from 150 to 500% (ESM Table 15.8). Adult females may be outnumbered by juveniles, infants and immature group members, indicating the likelihood that offspring are born into a group with older siblings (as each adult female is probably the mother to multiple concurrent group members) and the implication that the population is growing. However, some populations report there to be fewer juvenile, infant and immature group members than adult females, which probably indicates a stagnant or declining population. Similarly, the ratio of adult-to-immature members include both more and less adults per immature individuals, indicating that in some populations the sexually mature adults are not being sufficiently replaced. This may have to do with habitat quality, as some species are reported to reproduce at higher rates in high-quality habitat (Li Z and Rogers 2004a; Srivastava 2006). Alternatively, there may be particularly high infant mortality for some species due to differences in vulnerability to predators, infanticide and malnutrition.

Reproduction and Sexual Behaviour

Individuals within *Trachypithecus* species in the Indo-Burmese region tend to reach sexual maturity between 3 and 5 years of age. For example, *T. leucocephalus* males are sexually mature in the third to fourth year of life, with earlier maturation for females (Tan 1985). Similarly, *T. franoisi, T. delacouri* and *T. hatinhensis* males mature at about five years of age and females at four years of age (unpublished data cited in Nadler et al. 2003). For *T. crepusculus*, females are an average of 5.3 years old (range: 4.8–6.2) when they first give birth (Borries et al. 2011), while *T. leucocephalus* are 5–6 years old (Jin et al. 2009b). Given the gestation length of 6–7 months (Kumar et al. 2005; Lu et al. 2010 as cited in Borries et al. 2011; Lu et al. 2016; Solanki et al. 2007), this means that females typically first conceive around 4–5 years old. Female *T. crepusculus* have a mean cycle length of 28.4 days, and they undergo an average of 3.57 cycles until conception (Lu et al. 2010). It is possible that some *Trachypithecus* species experience menopause or reproductive cessation (Borries and Koenig 2008; Roberts 2015), although whether this specifically applies to wild counterparts of the species discussed in this chapter remains to be clarified.

Overall, sexual behaviour is uncommon among *Trachypithecus* living in the Indo-Burmese region, although there are periods in which it is more common. Sexual behaviour represents just 0.4% of *T. leucocephalus* activity budgets (Burton et al. 1995) and was only seen 10 times in 15 months of fieldwork of *T. francoisi* (Hu 2007). Similarly, it comprises only 2% of *T. poliocephalus* social budgets (Hendershott 2017). This may be due to the unimale-multifemale social structure, which implies that male competition for fertile females occurs primarily in the context of group formation and defence, rather than through sperm competition (supported by the relatively small testes of langurs: Møller 1988), which would require higher rates of copulations. The possibility of limited sperm being an issue for *Trachypithecus* species is supported by the fact that females are typically the initiators of matings; most copulations are preceded by adult female solicitation, although not all solicitations lead to copulations (Hu 2007; Solanki et al. 2007). As further evidence for females competing over limited sperm supplies, females often harass mounts of the resident male with other group females (Hendershott unpublished data; Stanford 1991a). Interestingly, however, and counter to the assumption of limited sperm, masturbation has been observed in a number of male *Trachypithecus* species (Hendershott 2017; Hu 2007). Additionally, this focus on sperm competition and male monopolization of females ignores the element of female choice in mating partners. A genetic analysis of *T. leucocephalus* found that although the resident male has priority of access, non-resident males can surreptitiously breed and sire infants (Liu Z et al. 2013b).

Solicitation takes the form of head-shaking and sexual prostration or grooming (Huang et al. 2015) and is typically less than 10 seconds long (Hu 2007). Among *T. francoisi*, mounts last an average of 7.5 seconds (range 5–12, $n = 10$) (Hu 2007), while *T. pileatus* mounts are 12 seconds (although this increases to about 22 seconds if only successful mounts are considered, and mounts during the peak mating season are longer than mounts in other months) (Solanki et al. 2007). *T. pileatus* can be described as using both single and multiple mounts prior to ejaculation (Stanford 1991a). After copulating, males and females act affiliative towards one another, by grooming, feeding and resting together (Hu 2007; Huang et al. 2015; Solanki et al. 2007). This is unequally distributed between the sexes: males are groomed longer and rest more than the females do (Solanki et al. 2007).

Not all mounts are reproductive in nature. Same-sex mounts (female-female and male-male) and mounts between immature (or adults with immature) individuals have been reported for *T. francoisi* (Hu 2007; Huang et al. 2015), *T. poliocephalus* (Hendershott 2017), and *T. delacouri* (Agmen, pers. comm.). Same-sex and immature mounts may make up over half of all mounts (Hendershott 2017; Huang et al. 2015). These mounts may not typically be preceded by a solicitation among *T. francoisi* (Hu 2007), although solicitations of the subadults (male and female) by an adult female has been reported in this species (Huang et al. 2015). These non-reproductive mounts are relatively short; they only last 2–15 seconds (Hu 2007; Huang et al. 2015).

Although it is not clear what purpose these mounts serve, it is likely they are sociosexual in nature. Huang et al. (2015) assumed that the mounts between an adult female and male and female immature was due to the unusual group structure (there was no adult male) and were therefore acting as 'training' for the immature group members, although this fails to explain why these mounts are seen in 'typical' unimale-multifemale groups. In contrast, the high rate of grooming between non-conceptive mount partners (Huang et al. 2015) suggests there is some social benefit at play. For example, given the high rate of females with clinging infants taking place in same-sex mounts among adults and the subsequent transfer of the infant between individuals (Hendershott unpublished data), it is possible that the mounts are being used to gain access to infants.

Although some langurs do not seem to have strict mating or birth seasons, there are generally peaks (ESM Table 15.9), which may be tied to resource availability and, thus, limits on group size (Chapter 16). Matings and conceptions occur during the dry season for *T. pileatus* (Solanki et al. 2007), while they occur during the wet season for *T. leucocephalus* and *T. crepusculus* (Jin et al. 2009b; Lu et al. 2011), which is the season when young leaves and fruit are most abundant (Jin et al. 2009b). Birth peaks for many species occur in the dry and cold seasons (roughly November–April, although there is regional variation): *T. leucocephalus* (Jin et al. 2009b), *T. poliocephalus* (Leonard et al. 2016), *T. pileatus* (Solanki et al. 2007; Stanford 1992), *T. phayrei* (Adimallaiah et al. 2014) and some others having birth peaks during the transition from the end of the dry season to the beginning of the wet season: *T. leucocephalus* (Tan 1985), *T. francoisi* (Hu 2007), *T. shortridgei* (Li Y et al. 2015a) and *T. crepusculus* (Lu et al. 2016). Beyond an annual seasonal cycle to births, there may be interannual cycles. For example, the Critically Endangered *T. poliocephalus* appear to have flushes of infants every few years (Leonard et al. 2016).

This seasonality to mating/conception and birth/lactation may be an evolved strategy by timing period of high energy demands (gestation and lactation) with resource availability. For example, for *T. crepusculus*, plant parts may increase progestin levels, and given that conception is more likely during periods of high progestin, there may be a direct link between food availability and hormonal effects on conception (Lu et al. 2011). Additionally, lush wet seasons may be the period during which females are able to bank sufficient fat reserves necessary for the gestation process (Jin et al. 2009b). Alternatively, the postbirth season may be timed so that it coincides with the period of ample young leaf and fruit availability in the wet season, which will help energetically sustain females during the extreme caloric draining caused by lactation.

The interbirth interval (IBI) for *Trachypithecus* species living in the Indo-Burmese region is roughly two years (21–26 months) (Borries et al. 2008, 2011; Hu 2007; Jin et al. 2009b; Li Y et al. 2015a; Solanki et al. 2007), which is also reflected in reproductive rates of roughly 0.3–0.6 infants/adult female/year (Jin et al. 2009b; Li Y et al. 2015a; Solanki et al. 2007; Srivastava 2006). Among *T. crepusculus*, females begin ovulating 11.5 months, and conceive 15.6 months, after their last birth with a surviving infant (Borries et al. 2008). This seems to hold true regardless of the sex of the offspring showing no sex-biased maternal investment, as IBIs for sons (26.4 months) are similar to those for daughters (24.1 months) for *T. leucocephalus* (Zhao Q et al. 2009).

This interval between births is shorter if an infant is lost before it is weaned. When females are confronted with a takeover (and thus potential infanticide), their IBI depends on their infants' age and their decision to either leave the group with the previous resident male or to stay with the new male. For *T. leucocephalus* females with older infants at the time of the takeover or females with young, dependent infants who leave with the previous resident male, have IBIs similar to females who do not experience a takeover (roughly 24–25 months) (Zhao Q et al. 2011). Females with young, dependent infants who stay with the new male or who leave and then rejoin the new male, or females who were pregnant at the time of the takeover, have an IBI of 31–34 months; there are significantly longer IBIs during takeovers than during stable tenures (Zhao Q et al. 2011). In contrast, another study of the same species found that females who lose an infant during a takeover have an IBI of 10 months, which is much shorter than the 25 month IBI documented during a stable male tenure (Yin et al. 2013), and male takeovers are reported to speed up a females' return to oestrus in *T. francoisi* (Hu 2007). Similarly, another study of *T. leucocephalus* found that females have an IBI of 12.7 months when they lose an infant, which is roughly half as long as if the infant had survived (23–27 months) (Jin et al. 2009b; Zhao Q et al. 2011).

IBI may also be impacted by access to resources. For example, females in larger groups of *T. crepusculus* have longer IBIs (24.5 months in large group of 25.8 individuals, 22.8 months in medium group of 18.3 individuals, and 21.3 months in small group of 11.4 individuals) and their infants take longer to mature and develop (loss of natal pelage, age at weaning), than females in smaller groups, possibly due to increased resource competition (Borries et al. 2008). Habitat quality also plays a role as it affects resource availability. Among *T. leucocephalus*, only groups in high-quality habitat have infants (Li Z and Rogers 2004a), and smaller groups have higher reproductive rates (unpublished data cited in Zhao Q et al. 2009). Among *T. geeii*, female reproductive rates are higher in less-disturbed forests (Srivastava 2006), suggesting that reproductive capacity is limited for females in poor-quality habitat or larger groups are limited in their acquisition of high-quality food resources.

Weaning occurs at 18–21 months for *Trachypithecus* species living in the Indo-Burmese region (Borries et al. 2011, 2014b; Zhao Q et al. 2008, 2009, 2011), although weaning at 12–14 months is reported for *T. francoisi* (Hu 2007). Like with IBIs, weaning age seems to be associated with takeovers, with females initiating early weaning if a strange male takes over the group. For *T. leucocephalus* living in groups with stable male tenure, weaning occurs at 20.3 months of age, but for those living with a male takeover weaning takes place at 17.7 months (Zhao Q et al. 2011). Interestingly, however, female *T. crepusculus* do not appear to experience severe lactational amenorrhea (a key driver for infanticide as a reproductive tactic); they wean infants almost four months into their next pregnancy (roughly three months before giving birth), and weaning may even occur after the next birth, with the result that mothers can be nursing two infants at once (Borries et al. 2014b).

Infant mortality is influenced by a multitude of factors, such as malnutrition (due to inefficient foraging but higher nutritional requirements), predation (due to lack of vigilance and developed coordination), and infanticide (for unweaned infants in unimale-multifemale groups). Infant mortality for *T. poliocephalus* is 10.6% (2007–2016), although more consistent records (from 2014 to 2016) show a rate as high as 25% (Leonard et al. 2016). Infants of the closely related *T. leucocephalus* have a 6.8% mortality rate in the first month of life, and a 15.8% mortality rate for those under 20 months of age (Jin et al. 2009b).

Research Efforts

As is obvious from reading this chapter, the amount of research done on each species of *Trachyipithecus* in the Indo-Burmese region is far from equal. This may, in part, stem from the taxonomic inconsistencies which have plagued the taxon for years. For example, *T. margarita* is still listed as a subspecies of *T. germaini* by the IUCN just as *T. leucocephalus* is listed as a subspecies of *T. poliocephalus*. Such differences between the way the IUCN classifies species versus the way that many researchers classify species make it difficult to understand where species are located, and which study sites contain the same species. This then makes it difficult to try to collate data from across research sites to gain an overall picture of species behaviour. These taxonomic uncertainties have likely had the biggest implications for *T. crepusculus* and *T. phayrei* as until 2014 *T. crepusculus* was described as a subspecies of *T. phayrei*, thus all studies from Phu Kieo Wildlife Sanctuary in Thailand were reported as *T. phayrei* or *T. phayrei crepusculus*. In 2014, *T. crepusculus* was given species status, thus the animals at this site were now part of this new species making previous papers actually on *T. crepusculus* rather than *T. phayrei*, causing obvious confusion for those studying these species and dilemmas for those trying to coordinate research material across sites. While such issues are not unique to *Trachypithecus* in this region, it does seem to be one of the reasons behind the inequal distribution in research between species.

Of the 138 papers included in our chapter specific to these species, the number specific to each species ranged from a maximum of 33 for *T. leucocephalus* to a low of only one for *T. ebenus* and *T. hantinhensis* (ESM Table 15.10). The vast majority of studies come from the limestone langur group representing 78 of the 138 studies; although of these 54 come from just two species (*T. leucocephalus* and *T. franciosi*). Even these large numbers, however, are deceptive as they often represent numerous papers by the same research time at no more than a few research sites. For example, for the most commonly studied *T. leucocephalus* nearly every published study comes from either Fusui or Nongguan, both part of the karst habitat in Guangxi Province in China. This is also where the majority of studies on *T. francoisi* are done; with no behavioural studies on either species being done on Vietnamese populations, which may reflect difficulty in accessing habitat or the overall limited number of behavioural studies on *Trachypithecus* done at Vietnamese sites. Similarly, 55% of studies on *T. crepusculus* have been done on the population at Phu Khieo Wildlife Sanctuary in Thailand by Andreas Koening, Carola Borries and their team of students and researchers; however, due to a lack of funding this long-term study was shut down in 2014. Of the 13 studies published for *T. poliocephalus* four are by our own research team and represent the first long term (more than 12 month) behavioural study on this species that cover just one of the two reproductive populations in existence. The other eight papers have primarily been written by members of the Cat Ba Langur Conservation Project and focus on threats, status and conservation.

Overall, the majority of studies done on the *Trachypithecus* species of the Indo-Burmese region cover topics of population status and description (23 studies) or distribution and habitat use (24 studies). This likely speaks to the difficulty in studying some of these species in difficult, hard to navigate karst habitat. It may also be due to the taxonomic issues and the recent recognition of some as species. Given the fact that the majority of studies are coming from a limited number of research teams in an even more limited number of study sites, it is not surprising the areas of research cover also vary between species. *T. crepusculus*, for example, has a larger proportion of studies done on reproduction than other *Trachypithecus* species in the region due to the focus on reproduction by Carola Borries and Amy Lu. Catherine Workman's focus on the diet and nutrition of *T. delacouri* explains why 40% of published studies on that species are in the area of feeding and nutritional ecology.

It is also worth noting that due to specific information on social organization only being published on five species, we could not list information on group composition or organization for most species. This is followed up by only seven species on which detailed activity budgets could be obtained, which is fewer than the 10 on which diet budgets were determined. This again, is likely due to the difficulty in working in some of these areas and/or issues in obtaining funding.

Conclusion

As colobines, all *Trachypithecus* species share similar morphology and anatomy to allow them to rely on a diet of hard to digest leafy matter supplemented to different degrees with flowers, fruits, seeds and invertebrates (Oates and Davies 1994b). The species in the Indo-Burmese region are no exception with the diets of these species including 50%–70% leaves, all of which vary seasonally with habitat type and food availability. Despite these similarities in diet, *Trachypithecus* species in this region show a marked diversity of habitats, ranging from harsh limestone karst hills to broadleaf evergreen or semi evergreen forest, to moist deciduous and bamboo forest to sub-alpine or grassland shrubs. Like diet, however, differences in habitat type and elevation do not result in vast differences to overall activity patterns with all populations included in this study showing a typical activity pattern of the majority of time spent inactive followed by feeding, travelling and finally engaging in social behaviours. This is expected for species who need to dedicate a significant amount of their time to ingest and digest a diet of highly fibrous leaves, which may have the associated cost of reducing social behaviour.

When looking at behaviours that are less constrained by dietary adaptations, we still found quite a bit of similarity among the behaviours of *Trachypithecus* in the Indo-Burmese region. For example, when considering social organization and social behaviour, very few differences were found with all species (for which information was available) organizing themselves in unimale, multimale or male only groups with most species showing some combination of all three. This pattern suggests that the baseline social organization is likely unimale, as it offers males the best reproductive opportunities, but that under certain conditions (i.e. high population density) it may make more sense to adopt a multimale group organization where males can work with relatives to monopolize females to ensure they still see either direct or indirect fitness gains. Either way, any society with a prevalence of unimale groups is expected to also feature bachelor groups and have a high incidence of group takeover attempts, infanticide and allomaternal care, all of which feature within the published studies for Indo-Burmese *Trachypithecus* species. Similarly, life history variables and social behaviour are also similar among species, with sexual maturity and interbirth intervals all falling within the range expected for colobines. This suggests that there may be phylogenetic constraint on these reproductive variables as none of them are varying significantly between species living in different environment types with different food availabilities.

These overall similarities in behaviour and reproduction could reflect that fact that while habitat types are diverse, no species of *Trachypithecus* in the Indo-Burmese region are living in pristine or primary habitat. In fact, the majority of species are living in modified and disturbed habitats that are highly fragmented. Possibly the most extreme example of this is *T. poliocephalus* for which there are only two reproductive populations in existence, each of which contain less than 30 individuals and are completely isolated from one another (Lees et al. 2014; Leonard et al. 2016). Similarly, *T. delacouri* is thought to exist in 10 isolated subpopulations, with the population at Van Long Nature Reserve containing half of the 200-individual population (Ebenau et al. 2011). These sorts of fragmented populations are not surprising given the history of deforestation in the region. From 1990 to 1995, the Indo-Burmese region lost an average of 1.76% of forest per annum, second only to the Amazon (Brooks et al. 2002). With the ever-growing human population in the region, coupled with a desire to grow economically, deforestation has not slowed down, causing further isolation of populations and further marginalization to less-preferred habitats.

These deforestation rates are exacerbated throughout Indo-Burma by the high rates of poaching for primates that still occur in some areas, primarily for traditional medicine. This means that many of these species are facing double jeopardy in terms of extinction risk; something that becomes more alarming by the fact that all species, save for one that we do not know enough about, are in some level of decline with three being Critically Endangered. What this review chapter highlights is that we do not know enough about habitat and resource use in most species; this information is essential to best identify the characteristics of high-quality versus low-quality habitat. Results of this kind can then be used to try to reverse the impact of current population fragmentation either by finding suitable areas that can be used to join isolated populations or to set up new, larger areas to combine small populations. This review also points to the fact that the majority of what we know is based on studies from few species, at even fewer specific locations within their range. While this is not ideal, given the struggle to find funding to set up new sites or often to continue long-term sites, our review does showcase the similarity between populations and species, suggesting that results from a few key areas may be transferable to other key populations or species, which is hopeful.

Regardless, moving forward to help curb the tragic loss of any of these species, researchers should be focusing on how their work can be used in an applied conservation context. This is best done through the involvement of both local researchers and local NGOs that can take research results and formulate long-term conservation action plans based in species biology and ecology. This should all be done with an increased focus on ethnoprimatology and how the needs of local people can be built into conservation planning to ensure the long-term co-existence of both humans and non-human primates in the region.

16 Socioecology of Asian Colobines

Elisabeth H. M. Sterck and Tom S. Roth

Introduction

Many diurnal non-human primates live in groups (Sterck et al. 1997), yet these groups show a wide diversity in social organization, mating systems and social structure (Schuelke and Ostner 2012). Socioecological models explain this social diversity using ecological factors (van Schaik 1983, 1989; Sterck et al. 1997; Wrangham 1980; but see Clutton-Brock and Janson 2012), where food competition among females is central. The type of food competition has been linked to female social characteristics (van Schaik 1989; Sterck et al. 1997; Wrangham 1980) and is expected to limit group size (Koenig 2002). However, how folivorous primates like Asian colobines fit in these models has been debated. Several propositions have been made, which will be discussed in detail here. First, in some models folivorous primates are expected to experience only scramble competition (see below; e.g. van Schaik 1989; Sterck et al. 1997), yet this proposition does not fit Nepal sacred langurs (*Semnopithecus schistaceus*: Koenig 2000; Koenig and Borries 2001) and Bengal sacred langurs (*S. entellus*: Borries 1993). Second, folivores are proposed to show no food competition at all (e.g. Isbell 1991; Yeager and Kirkpatrick 1998). Third, the small group sizes often found in folivores are surprising and factors other than food may limit folivores' group size. This has been called the 'Folivore Paradox' (Janson and Goldsmith 1995; Steenbeek and van Schaik 2001). These three propositions lead to different predictions concerning the relationship between female competitive regimes, social relationships and dispersal patterns in the Asian colobines.

First, socioecological models propose a link between ecological factors and female social behaviour. Primates benefit from living in groups since it reduces the risk of predation (Dunbar et al. 2018; Fichtel 2012; van Schaik 1983, 1989) and infanticide (van Schaik and Kappeler 1997; Sterck et al. 1997; Wrangham 1979), but have to balance this with the costs of competition for food. The type of competition depends on the distribution of food sources, where clumped defendable food sources can lead to monopolization within the group or between groups, resulting respectively in contest competition within (within-group contest: WGC) and between (between-group contest: BGC) groups. In addition, scramble competition is found when individuals interfere with the amount group members can eat, yet food sources are not monopolizable. This results in within-group scramble competition (WGS). It has been

This chapter includes Electronic Supplementary Material (ESM) at: www.cambridge.org/colobines

proposed that folivore diets, with their high proportion of leaves, are not monopolizable (Isbell 1991; van Schaik 1983; Wrangham 1980) and will result in WGS (van Schaik 1989; Sterck et al. 1997). The different competition types will affect female social behaviour (van Schaik 1989; Sterck et al. 1997). In folivores, due to a lack of WGC, females are expected to show individual and egalitarian dominance relationships and the ability to disperse between groups. WGC, expected in frugivores, leads to despotic, nepotistic dominance hierarchies where female kin support each other and form coalitions to maintain their rank. BGC is expected to reduce the degree of despotism, because females require their female group members in between-group conflicts. This model has been applied with positive results (e.g. squirrel monkeys, *Saimiri oerstedi and S. sciureus*: Mitchell et al. 1991), but has also been criticized (Clutton-Brock and Janson 2012; Koenig 2002; Thierry 2008). Important counterexamples concern the folivorous Nepal (Koenig 2002) and Bengal sacred langurs (Borries 1993), where the despotic dominance hierarchy has reproductive effects and indicates WGC, without the predicted nepotism. Moreover, female dispersal can occur in species with a despotic dominance hierarchy, contradicting the original prediction (Koenig and Borries 2001).

Second, some researchers propose that folivores have abundant food sources since leaves are omnipresent. They predict that folivores will experience no competition for food (Isbell 1991; Yeager and Kirkpatrick 1998; reviewed in Snaith and Chapman 2007). Any evidence of food competition, either scramble or contest, contrasts with the proposition that folivores lack food competition.

Third, folivores may indeed experience little or no food competition, yet this is a consequence of their relatively small group sizes (Janson and Goldsmith 1995), while the ubiquity of their folivore food would predict relatively large groups (Schuelke and Ostner 2012). This mismatch between expected and observed group sizes has been called the Folivore Paradox (Janson and Goldsmith 1995; Steenbeek and van Schaik 2001). Two solutions have been proposed for the Folivore Paradox. First, the scramble food competition may be underestimated and ecology actually does limit group size (Snaith and Chapman 2005, 2007). This, in principle, proposes that the behaviour of colobines converges with the socioecological model. Second, group size may be limited by infanticide risk since this risk is highest in larger groups (Crockett and Janson 2000; Steenbeek and van Schaik 2001). This second proposition predicts that infanticide risk, and not food competition, has the strongest link with group size effects on female fitness indicators.

Altogether, the relationship between ecology, conspecific threats and female social behaviour in Asian colobines needs further scrutiny. Koenig and Borries (2009) argue that to understand Asian colobine socioecology four questions need to be answered: (1) do Asian colobine females experience food competition and what type (WGC; WGS, BGC); (2) if there is WGC, why are dominance relationships not nepotistic and are female-female coalitions absent; (3) if there is WGC (i.e. a linear dominance hierarchy), why do females disperse and (4) what causes the Folivore Paradox, i.e. why do folivores live in such small groups.

In this chapter, we first describe patterns in female aggression, dominance and dispersal in Asian colobines. Next, we explore the type of food competition experienced by females and link this with measures of food distribution. We contrast these with alternative factors, such as infanticide risk, that may limit group size. For only a few sites and species data are available that link female social behaviour, food competition and food distribution. Therefore, we detail these species and evaluate whether the more limited data on other species yield a general pattern. The taxonomy follows Roos (Chapter 2) and field sites have been assigned to a particular species on the basis of Rowe and Myers (2016). We consider the *Semnopithecus* spp. formerly referred to as grey langurs (formerly *S. entellus*; Brandon-Jones 2004) as one taxonomic group that we label 'sacred langurs'.

Diet and Food Distribution

Colobines are foregut fermenters (Chapter 6) and this allows them to consume considerable amounts of leaves in their diet (Chapter 8). It was expected that mature leaves would form an important part of their diet, which led to the suggestion that colobine food sources are abundant (Wrangham 1980; Yeager and Kirkpatrick 1998; Yeager and Kool 2000). However, the notion of colobines not being limited by food has been criticized (e.g. Snaith and Chapman 2007; Sayers 2013).

The first indication that food does limit colobines regards findings that colobine densities depend on the quality of their diet, measured by the ratio of protein to fibre in mature leaves. Though primarily assessed in African colobus monkeys, colobine population densities are higher when food quality is better (Davies 1994; Chapman et al. 2004; Fashing et al. 2007a). Therefore, food is limiting colobines, which may lead to food competition.

Second, it has become clear that many colobines do not depend on mature leaves but eat a varied diet that contains a large portion of young leaves and fruits (Sterck 2012; Chapter 8). Young leaves and fruits are often seasonal and their availability may be limited. Moreover, colobines can be selective feeders that prefer to consume specific food items (Grueter et al. 2009a; Kirkpatrick 2007; Sayers 2013; Snaith and Chapman 2007). In addition, folivores can deplete food patches (Grueter et al. 2009a; Snaith and Chapman 2005), indicating that WGC exists (Snaith and Chapman 2007) and suggesting that monopolization of these patches may be beneficial. Therefore, folivores may experience competition for food.

Food competition may also depend on the temporal distribution of food (van Schaik 1989), which may be more continuous for colobines than that for frugivorous species. Frugivorous species are strongly dependent on periods in which ripe fruit is available and this is often seasonal (van Schaik et al. 1993; van Schaik and Pfannes 2005). Folivorous colobines, however, may be buffered against strong seasonal variation in food availability. First, because they are more flexible in their diet, they can replace fruits with leaves (e.g. maroon langur, *Presbytis rubicunda*: Clink et al. 2017) or other food (e.g. lichens: golden snub-nosed monkey, *Rhinopithecus roxellana*: Liu et al. 2013b; Yunnan snub-nosed monkey, *R. bieti*: Huang et al. 2017b), allowing them to switch primary food sources (see Chapter 12). Second, colobines prefer unripe fruit and do not often consume ripe fruit (but see Dela 2012). Unripe

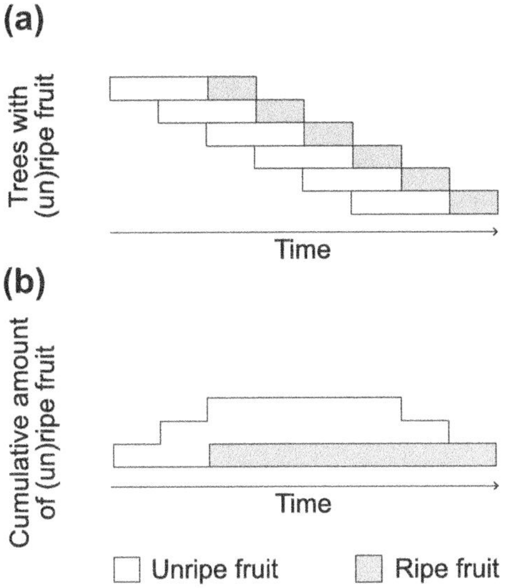

Figure 16.1 Unripe fruit will be less seasonal and be available more often than ripe fruit. Fruit will typically be longer unripe than ripe (here 2:1). (a) Six trees that fruit after one another and that contain two time periods unripe and one time period ripe fruits. (b) Cumulative amount of fruit available: the amount of time that unripe fruit is available is most often longer than when ripe fruit is available.

fruit is available for a longer period than ripe fruit (Yamagiwa et al. 2005; Janmaat et al. 2016), increasing the amount of food present at one moment of time and simultaneously reducing seasonality in food availability (Figure 16.1). Therefore, unripe fruit is more ubiquitous and less likely to incur contest competition than ripe fruit (Sterck 1995). However, some habitats are clearly seasonal, such as the habitat of naturally feeding Nepal sacred langurs (Koenig and Borries 2001) and snub-nosed monkeys in China (Grueter et al. 2009b). In such species or locations, stronger effects of food competition may be found. Indeed, in the Nepal sacred langurs of Ramnagar, a seasonal forest in the Himalayan foothills, a clear seasonal effect of food competition is found (Koenig 2000). Data on seasonality in food competition are lacking for the snub-nosed monkeys.

Altogether, the notion that the preferred foods of folivores are ubiquitous is an oversimplification. The distribution of colobine food sources shows that there is potential for food competition, especially in seasonal habitats. This may be reflected in female social behaviour.

Asian Colobine Female Social Behaviour

If female colobines lack WGC and BGC, it is expected that dominance hierarchies are egalitarian and individualistic and that female dispersal is possible (van Schaik 1989; Sterck et al. 1997). Here we explore whether this is indeed found.

Female Aggression and Dominance

Aggression among Asian colobine females has been reported in several species. A recent cross-taxon analysis indicates that published rates of overall female-female agonism do not differ much between folivore colobines and frugivore cercopithecines (Wheeler et al. 2013). This suggests that colobine females may form despotic and linear dominance hierarchies.

With the current taxonomy (Chapter 2), different species have to be distinguished within the sacred (or grey or Hanuman) langurs. In the Malabar sacred langur, no clear dominance ranks are found among females (*Semnopithecus hypoleucos*; Dharwar: Sugiyama 1965, 1967; Yoshiba 1968).

Two other sacred species are well studied, the Bengal and the Nepal sacred langurs. At several sites, Bengal sacred langur females show aggressive interactions and form linear, i.e. despotic, dominance hierarchies (Abu: Hrdy and Hrdy 1976; Jodhpur: Borries et al. 1991; Lu et al. 2008). These hierarchies are unstable (Jodhpur: Lu et al. 2008). In addition, the dominance hierarchies are age-inversed, since nulliparous females become dominant without forming coalitions, and female dominance rank drops with age (Abu: Hrdy and Hrdy 1976; Jodhpur: Borries et al. 1991). In contrast, at other study sites females may form dominance categories, but dominance within a category is not well defined (Orcha and Kaukori: Jay 1965), or female dominance hierarchies are not important (Kanha Meadows: Newton, pers. comm. in Newton and Dunbar 1994) and the rate of female-female aggression is low. However, these latter studies do not provide behavioural data, hampering the comparison. Altogether, different populations seem to differ in the linearity of the dominance hierarchy.

In Nepal sacred langurs at Ramnagar, females show aggressive interactions and form linear dominance hierarchies (Koenig 2000; Koenig et al. 1998) but these hierarchies are unstable (Koenig 2000) and age-inversed (Koenig 2000; Lu et al. 2013). Notwithstanding this, Nepal sacred langur females at another site show bidirectional aggression (Junbesi: Boggess 1980) indicating that the hierarchies are non-linear. Again, different populations seem to differ in the linearity of the dominance hierarchy.

Altogether, female dominance relationships in these two species of sacred langurs differ between populations (see also Chapter 13). It is possible that populations with an age-inversed linear female dominance hierarchy may represent only some of the ecological settings where these species are found. However, data do not support this proposition. Bengal sacred langurs that live near towns in highly disturbed habitats may either form linear (Abu; Jodhpur) or non-linear (Orcha) dominance hierarchies, whereas populations at undisturbed sites form non-linear hierarchies (Kaukori; Kanha). Nepal sacred langurs that live in a relatively undisturbed but highly seasonal mountain forest (Ramnagar) have a linear dominance hierarchy, while at another site (Junbasi) dominance is not linear. Note that the reports of non-linear dominance hierarchies are based on descriptive data. Therefore, whether the suggested between-population variation in female despotism is linked to food competition remains to be established.

Indications for a linear and age-inversed female dominance hierarchy are also found in Phayre's langur (*Trachypithecus phayrei*, Koenig et al. 2004; but see Lu et al. 2016). Captive red-shanked douc (*Pygathrix nemaeus*: Kavanagh 1978) and Yunnan snub-nosed monkeys (Cui et al. 2014) also have a linear hierarchy, although the rate of aggression is low. In proboscis monkeys (*Nasalis larvatus*) aggression is rare, yet females have conflicts for sleeping sites and, while quantitative data are not available, they are suggested to be hierarchical (Abai and Sukau: Boonratana 1993).

In contrast, dominance hierarchies of other Asian colobine species that have been investigated are not linear and therefore these species may be egalitarian. Female aggression is found in Thomas's langurs (*Presbytis thomasi*), and the rate is similar to that of frugivorous long-tailed macaques (*Macaca fascicularis*: Sterck and Steenbeek 1997). Although in several dyads aggression was unidirectional, no clear dominance hierarchies were found (Sterck and Steenbeek 1997). Also, in Thomas's langurs one nulliparous female rose in rank, consistent with age-inversed dominance. In Nilgiri langurs (*Trachypithecus johnii*), the data on dominance interactions indicate a non-linear dominance hierarchy (Poirier 1970b, table II; note that this contrasts with the [mistaken] conclusion arguing for a linear hierarchy in the original text). Similarly, aggression is rare in capped langurs (*T. pileatus*; Stanford 1991a) and pale thighed langurs (*Presbytis siamensis*: Bennett 1983) and no female dominance hierarchy is discernible. In captive Yunnan snub-nosed monkeys, a linear dominance hierarchy was found (see above), but the rate of female aggression was low (0.13 interactions per hour) and directional inconsistency relatively high (Cui et al. 2014). Another study at the same institute reports that aggression rates are low, aggression is not severe, and high rates of reconciliation are seen (Grueter 2004, who uses the term 'tolerant'). Altogether, this indicates that they can be considered rather egalitarian. In golden snub-nosed monkeys, aggression is bidirectional (Zhang et al. 2008a) and there are high rates of reconciliation (Ren R et al. 1991), suggesting that they are also egalitarian (Zhang et al. 2008a, who uses the term 'relaxed'; see also Chapter 12). This suggests that in many Asian colobines the rate of female-female aggression is low, the age-inverted dominance indicates individualistic hierarchies, and dominance relationships are egalitarian.

Female nepotism is found when related females form coalitions against other females (Sterck et al. 1997). However, in Asian colobines, female coalitions against other females in their own group are not often reported. Accordingly, no indications of nepotism are found in some populations of sacred langurs (Malabar sacred langur, Dharwar: Yoshiba 1968; Nepal sacred langur, Ramnagar: Lu et al. 2013). In contrast, at Orcha and Kaukori such coalitions have been observed (Bengal sacred langur: Jay 1965), yet their effect on female dominance was not established. Nilgiri langur females rarely formed coalitions (Poirier 1970b). In other Asian colobines, female-female coalitions against other females are not reported. Therefore, dominance hierarchies in all these species appear to be individualistic. However, females do have the capacity to form coalitions, since they are formed against infanticidal males (Bengal sacred langurs: Hrdy 1977a; golden snub-nosed monkeys: Zhang et al. 1999b; review: Palombit 2012), including in species with a despotic dominance hierarchy. Therefore, the lack of nepotism in the colobine species with linear female dominance hierarchies and where female relatives are available, such as some well-studied sacred langur populations, is puzzling.

In summary, the combined evidence on aggression for Asian colobine females indicates that rates of aggression among females may vary from low (see above) to similar to cercopithecines females (Wheeler et al. 2013). However, crucial quantitative data on the rates of aggression are especially lacking where verbal accounts indicate low aggression rates. Dominance hierarchies vary in their linearity, ranging from egalitarian to despotic. However, dominance hierarchies do not appear nepotistic, since female-female coalitions against other females are not reported in connection with despotic dominance hierarchies. Also, evidence for age-inversed dominance, meaning that nulliparous females obtain a high rank, is consistent with the proposition that dominance hierarchies are individualistic.

Notwithstanding this general pattern, for many Asian colobine species quantitative data on the rate and direction of aggression are lacking. This may be due to a lack of detailed observations, a lack of individual recognition, or potentially that low rates of female-female aggression remain unpublished. Therefore, publications should report quantified data on female aggression and dominance relationships.

Female Dispersal

The socioecological model predicts that female dispersal may be found when dominance relations are egalitarian and will be absent when they are despotic. Asian colobines show two different dispersal patterns: dispersal by both sexes or dispersal by males with female philopatry. These two dispersal patterns may actually form two ends of a graded scale, where female dispersal may vary from all females to none, while in all species males disperse. Despite this variation in female dispersal, overall colobines are characterized by a relatively high incidence of female dispersal (Sterck 2012).

There is no equivocal evidence that females disperse to avoid food competition. In Thomas's langurs, females emigrate from groups that are larger than the groups they immigrate into, but this is only due to the number of immatures and not the number of adults in the group (Sterck 1997). In addition, females do not disperse when food demands are highest, e.g. when pregnant or lactating or in lean seasons. Therefore, female dispersal as a response to food competition seems to be absent.

Female dispersal may have a function depending on the type of dispersal: primary and secondary dispersal. Primary dispersal concerns nulliparous females that leave their natal group. This is found in several species (ESM Table 16.1). Dispersal of nulliparous females may function to avoid inbreeding. Indeed, primary dispersal is found when male tenure exceeds female age at menarche (Sterck and Korstjens 2000). In Thomas's langurs, nulliparous females disperse when the father of the nulliparous female still remained in the group (Sterck et al. 2005). Also, in golden snub-nosed monkeys, nulliparous females disperse to avoid inbreeding (Qi et al. 2009).

In addition, parous females may disperse after their natal dispersal, which is called secondary dispersal. Secondary dispersal may concern female mate choice. Indeed, in Thomas's langurs parous females disperse to better mating partners, because they often immigrate to new, young males who provide better protection against infanticide after dispersal (Sterck 1997; Sterck et al. 2005). In addition, Nilgiri langur females may disperse after losing an infant to infanticide (1 case: Kavana et al. 2014). In golden snub-nosed monkeys, parous females may also disperse to acquire a better mate (Qi et al. 2009). Additionally, in white-headed langurs (*Trachypithecus leucocephalus*), females with young infants may temporarily disperse together with the old male after a group takeover, likely to avoid infanticide (Zhao Q et al. 2011a).

Overall, female dispersal in Asian colobines fits the pattern predicted by the dominance hierarchy. For instance, in several Asian colobine species (ESM Table 16.1), including one Bengal sacred langur population (at Kanha), the dominance hierarchy is egalitarian and female dispersal is found. In addition, female dispersal is rare or absent in several sacred langur populations with despotic dominance hierarchies (ESM Table 16.1). Therefore, the interaction between female dispersal and linear dominance hierarchies fits the expected pattern (see also Koenig and Borries 2001). One exception is the Phayre's langur, where the dominance hierarchy is despotic yet females regularly disperse. However, the kinship pattern in a group, irrespective of female dispersal, may explain this exception (see below).

The socioecological model (van Schaik 1989; Sterck et al. 1997) proposes that females in species with a nepotistic dominance hierarchy cannot disperse, because dispersal without (related) coalition partners would lead to a low dominance position in the new group where females are not related to the immigrant. This will be especially detrimental when the dominance hierarchy is nepotistic. The setting may be different in Asian colobines, since female dispersal may not disrupt female kinships patterns. Data on Thomas's langurs indicate that females disperse to a new protector male, but females tend to choose the same male as the other females of their group. Therefore, although females may range separately for several months to a year, they know the females in the group of immigration and the kinship patterns in groups are stable in the long run (Figure 16.2; Sterck 1997; Wich and Sterck 2010). Similarly, recent evidence shows that golden snub-nosed monkey females tend to disperse into groups with female kin, or disperse to a new group together (Guo et al. 2015). Unfortunately, no such information is available for other colobine species with female dispersal. However, if this pattern is also present in the Phayre's langur, it may explain their unexpected combination of female dispersal and a linear dominance hierarchy.

Altogether, most data support that notion that female dispersal is found when the dominance hierarchy is egalitarian and it is absent when it is despotic. Therefore, this fits with the patterns proposed by the socioecological model.

Asian Colobine Competition for Food

The proposition that colobine food is ubiquitous (Isbell 1991; Yeager and Kirkpatrick 1998; Yeager and Kool 2000) has led to the suggestion that these primates do not

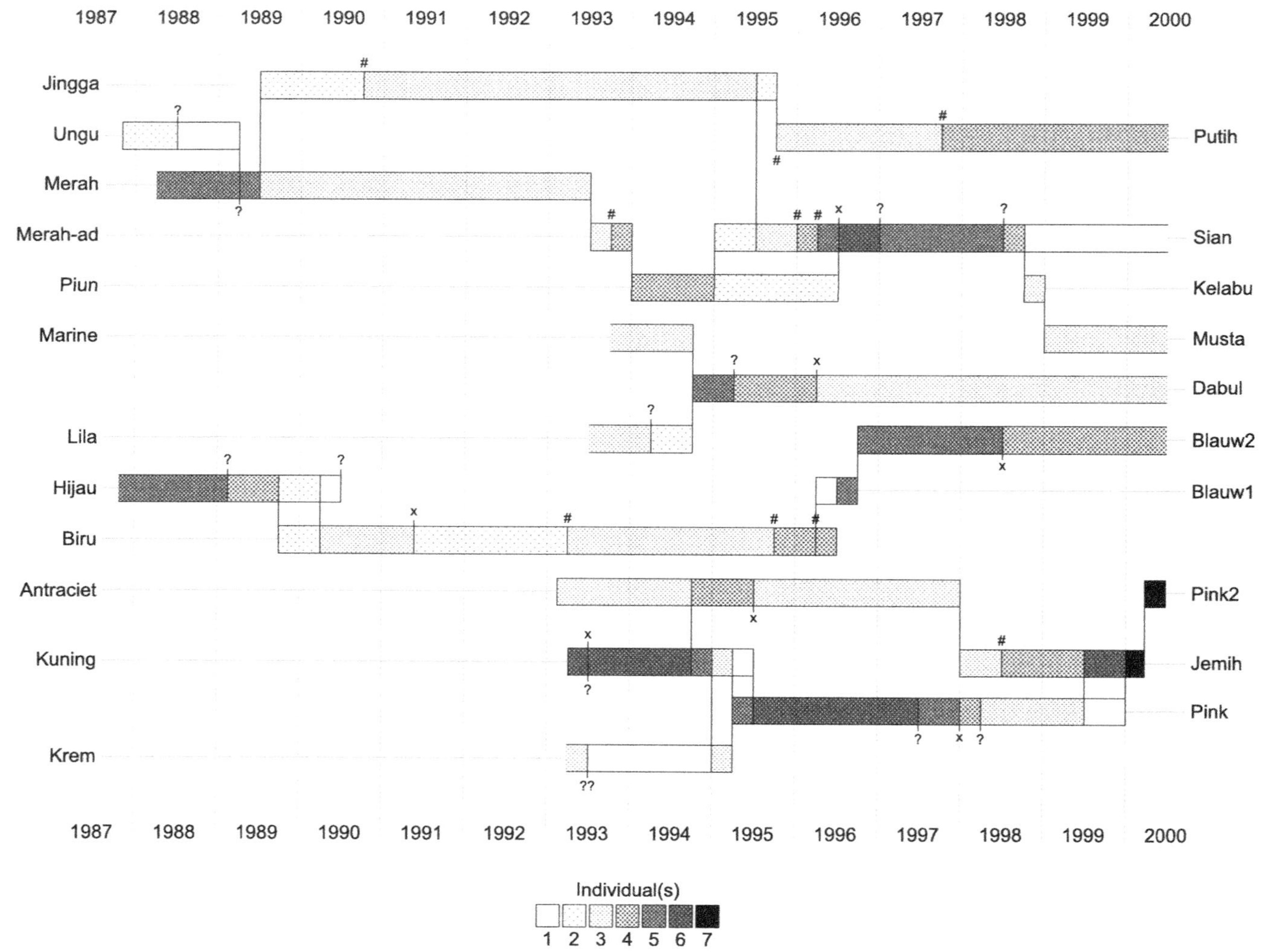

Figure 16.2 Female group membership (depicted in $N = 1–7$ females per group) and female dispersal in the Thomas langurs from Ketambe, Indonesia (after Wich and Sterck 2010, figure 17.9). Each horizontal bar represents a group; the name of the group is shown to the left or right. Vertical lines indicate dispersal events (of one or more females). When a female matures (i.e. 65 months after her birth date) is indicated with #, and this is when she is counted as a new adult female; ?

experience food competition. Similarly, the Folivore Paradox, the phenomenon that folivore primate group sizes are smaller than expected (Janson and Goldsmith 1995), has been interpreted to mean that colobines do not experience competition for food. This may concern a lack of within-group scramble (WGS) or contest competition (WGC). Alternatively, no (net) competition is found because between-group contest competition (BGC) compensates for WGS. WGS and BGC are both group size effects that respectively increase or decrease the amount of food available for the whole group, so success in BGC may increase the availability of food for larger groups, compensating for the costs of WGS. No competition for food implies that colobine monkeys are not food limited. However, population densities depend on the productivity of the habitat (Chapman et al. 2004; Korstjens and Dunbar 2007; Wasserman and Chapman 2003), indicating that food is limiting for colobines. Below, we explore evidence for the different types of food competition on foraging effort or fitness indicators.

Within-Group Contest

WGC is expected when food may be acquired though aggression, measured as aggression, submission and displacements. It is known that rates of female-female agonism do not differ much between colobines and cercopithecines (Wheeler et al. 2013), indicating that colobine foods may also be contestable. Indeed, consistent with the notion that contest competition for food exists, Asian colobine females can be aggressive over food (Thomas's langur: Sterck and Steenbeek 1997; Bengal sacred langur: Borries et al. 1991; Nepal sacred langur: Koenig 2000; capped langurs: Stanford 1991a; Phayre's langur: Koenig et al. 2004). Such aggressive competition can be found for both fruit and leaf sources (Sterck and Steenbeek 1997). Therefore, all types of food may cause aggression (Sterck and Steenbeek 1997; Koenig et al. 1998) and colobine species have the potential to experience WGC.

However, while the potential for food competition is present, in several species it is relatively rarely expressed. Indeed, the rate of aggression is low in capped langurs (Stanford 1991a) and Phayre's langurs (Koenig et al. 2004). In contrast, Thomas's langur females have similar rates of aggression inside food patches as long-tailed macaques (Sterck and Steenbeek 1997), a species with WGC (van Schaik and van Noordwijk 1988; van Noordwijk and van Schaik 1999). Yet they show more aggressive interactions in small food patches that only represent a minor part of their diet (Sterck and Steenbeek 1997). In addition, female dominance does not affect feeding time (Sterck 1995). This contrasts with sacred langurs, where high-ranking females feed in larger feeding parties (Nepal sacred langur, Ramnagar: Koenig et al. 1998) and have a higher food intake (Bengal sacred langur, Jodhpur: Borries 1993).

For an effect of WGC, a differential effect of female dominance on foraging effort should be reflected in female fitness parameters. Accordingly, in Ramnagar Nepal sacred langurs, high-ranking females have better body condition (Koenig 2000) and females in better condition are more likely to conceive (Koenig et al. 1997). In addition, low-ranking females have a lower birth rate than middle- or high-ranking females and infants of low-ranking females have a lower survival rate (but these results may be confounded by age; de Vries et al. 2016). Similarly, in Jodhpur Bengal sacred langurs, low-ranking females have lower birth rates than other females (Borries et al. 1991). In contrast, in Thomas's langurs no rank effects on female reproductive rate are found (Sterck 1995; Sterck et al. 1997). This suggests that for the three best studied species, WGC does occur in the Bengal and Nepal sacred langurs, while it is absent in Thomas's langurs. Unfortunately, for most colobine species no data on female dominance rank or its effect on foraging effort or fitness indicators exist. Therefore, it is not possible to propose what a general Asian colobine pattern of WGC may be. However, the opposing evidence from sacred and Thomas's langurs suggests that variation in the strength of WGC exists.

The effect of female dominance on fitness in sacred langurs has been attributed to WGC, but alternatively may be explained by the age-inversed dominance hierarchy where high-ranking individuals are relatively young. When young females have relatively good body condition, this may cause them to be both high-ranking and have a relatively high reproductive output (Borries et al. 1991; Hrdy and Hrdy 1976; de Vries et al. 2016). However, the suggestion that young females have more offspring is contradicted in another colobine species, where the inter-birth interval of primiparous females is relatively long (silvered langur, *Trachypithecus cristatus*: Shelmidine et al. 2009; primates: Pusey 2012). This suggests that in Bengal sacred langurs it may not be the young age, but rather high dominance that explains high female reproductive output.

Within-Group Scramble

It has been hypothesized by the socioecological model that colobines experience WGS (van Schaik 1989; Sterck et al. 1997), while others suggested that colobines do not experience any form of feeding competition due to the ubiquity of leaves (Isbell 1991; Yeager and Kirkpatrick 1998). This can be tested by determining the relationship of group size with indicators of WGS (ESM Table 16.2). These indicators are either related to foraging effort (e.g. day range, home range size) or fitness indicators (e.g. reproductive rate, inter-birth interval: Snaith and Chapman 2007).

WGS is present when foraging costs increase with group size (ESM Table 16.2). Accordingly, colobines living in larger groups have larger home range sizes (Phayre's langurs: Koenig et al. 2013; capped langurs: Stanford 1991a; Chamba sacred langur, *Semnopithecus ajax*: Minhas et al. 2013; Yunnan snub-nosed monkey: Grueter et al. 2008) and a longer day range (Thomas's langurs: Steenbeek and van Schaik 2001; Yunnan snub-nosed monkey: Grueter and van Schaik 2010; Chamba sacred langur: Minhas et al. 2013). In addition, in larger groups animals spend more time moving and less time resting than in smaller groups (golden snub-nosed monkeys: Liu et al. 2013a). In another species, the diet was lower quality in larger groups, containing more leaves and less fruit (Thomas's langurs: Sterck 1995). In some species, group size becomes smaller in periods with less food (red-shanked doucs: Phiapalath et al. 2011; black-shanked doucs, *Pygathrix nigripes*: Rawson 2009, but see Hoang Minh

Duc 2007). Therefore, the limited evidence indicates that all Asian colobines species with data on the relationship between group size and foraging effort show effects of WGS. This supports the socioecological model and counters that colobines do not experience food competition.

The effect of group size should also be measured on female fitness indicators (ESM Table 16.2). Consistent with WGS, Phayre's langur females in larger groups have lower reproductive rates and infant development is slower (Borries et al. 2008). In Bengal sacred langurs, the inter-birth interval is longer in larger groups (Jodhpur: Sommer and Rajpurohit 1989). In these species a larger group size leads to lower female reproductive output. In contrast, the birth rate is not lower in Thomas's langurs, while infant survival is higher in larger groups (Steenbeek and van Schaik 2001). Nepal sacred langurs in intermediate-sized groups have the best bodily condition and the highest reproductive output (Ramnagar: Koenig 2000), although in the lean season, females in small groups have the best body condition. In Kanha's Bengal sacred langurs, the number of infants per female is higher in larger groups, indicating a higher reproductive rate (Newton and Dunbar 1994). Therefore, the evidence for WGS on female fitness is mixed and effects of BGC may be found.

In the golden snub-nosed monkeys, living in layered societies, a lower birth rate was found in larger one-male units (OMU's), yet no unit size effect on inter-birth intervals and infant survival was present (Zhao D et al. 2011b). However, in species with a layered society, not the measured OMU size, but band size may determine WGS. Since no data on the effect of band size on female fitness are available, we cannot judge fitness effects of WGS.

Altogether, living in a larger group results in a larger foraging effort in all studied species of Asian colobines, indicating that all studied species experience scramble food competition. This greater foraging effort seems to result in a WGS effect on female fitness in several species (Phayre's langurs; Jodhpur's Bengal sacred langurs; possibly golden snub-nosed monkeys), consistent with the socioecological model. However, no negative effect is found in some other species (Thomas's langurs; Ramnagar's Nepal sacred langurs; Kanha's Bengal sacred langurs). Clearly, in these latter species scramble food competition does not limit group size and fitness. This may be due to BGC, which favours larger groups, or to the influence of other limiting factors, such as infanticide risk.

Between-Group Contest

BGC can be expressed in female between-group aggression (ESM Table 16.1). Female between-group aggression has been reported for sacred langurs (Nepal sacred langur; Ramnagar: Koenig 2000; Bengal sacred langur; Abu: Hrdy 1977b; Jodhpur: Borries 1993; Kanha: Newton 1987; Malabar sacred langur; Dharwar: Yoshiba 1968). It is rare in Nilgiri langurs (Poirier 1970b) and golden snub-nosed monkeys (Zhao D et al. 2013), and absent in many other Asian colobine species (reviewed in van Schaik et al. 1992; Sterck 1998).

Female between-group aggression may result in benefits for larger groups. In Ramnagar's Nepal sacred langurs, females in the intermediate-sized group fared better than females in the small and in the large group, indicating a trade-off between BGC and WGS. However, whether this is linked to female between-group aggression is not clear (Koenig 2000). In golden snub-nosed monkeys, female participation in between-group conflicts is highest during the winter, when food availability is relatively low, indicating that females defended access to food during lean periods (Zhao D et al. 2013). The number of participating individuals, and not group size, determines who wins a between-group conflict (Zhao Q and Tan 2010). In addition, in this species larger OMU's have a higher rank and the benefits of this higher rank may explain why OMU's merge (Zhang et al. 2008b). However, it is not clear whether this translates in effects of BGC on female fitness. Therefore, while in several species, female between-group aggression is lacking and no signs of BGC are found, in other species, females aggress females of other groups and in Ramnagar's Nepal sacred langurs indications of BGC are present in reproductive output (Koenig 2000).

In Asian colobines, male between-group aggression is often found and reflects male defence of females (Sterck 2012). Still, when males defend locations with food this may also provide ecological benefits to females. When the sexes are sexually dimorphic and males are larger and/or have long canines, only males and not females may take part in between-group aggressive encounters (Willems et al. 2013). Indeed, many colobines are characterized by sexual dimorphism (Grueter and van Schaik 2009). Moreover, when only one individual of a sex is present, collective action problems between individuals over who should bear the costs of between-group aggression and who derives benefits without participating are absent (Nunn 2000). Therefore, males in one-male groups may be important resource defenders (Willems et al. 2015). Indeed, Asian colobine groups often contain only one male (Sterck 2012) and such a male may perform the defender role. In short, it is possible that BGC takes place in the form of aggressive interactions between males, an effect that has been seen in two species of African colobus monkeys (Chapter 17), but this proposition remains to be tested.

Other Limitations of Group Size

The Folivore Paradox – that in folivores food competition seems absent yet group size is small – may apply when factors other than food competition limit group size. Infanticide has been proposed as an alternative factor limiting group size (Crockett and Janson 2000). In addition, time constraints may provide an alternative explanation (Korstjens and Dunbar 2007).

The sacred langurs are the classic example of a taxon experiencing male infanticide. The Malabar sacred langur was the first species where male infanticide was systematically observed and studied (Sugiyama 1965, 1966). The proposal that male infanticide is a male sexual strategy (Bengal sacred langur: Hrdy 1977a) that has selected for female counterstrategies (cf. Hrdy 1979) has yielded wide support

(Nepal sacred langur: Borries et al. 1999a; primates: Palombit 2012; van Schaik and Janson 2000). The risk of infanticide is pervasive in primates because infant care lasts longer than a pregnancy (van Schaik 2000a) and males are present in bisexual groups to protect their offspring against infanticidal males (van Schaik and Kappeler 1997; Wrangham 1979). Infanticide has been reported in several Asian colobine species (Palombit 2012; van Schaik 2000a; Sterck 1998).

Female anti-infanticidal strategies depend on the number of males in the group. When groups contain one male, females may associate with a male protector as a female counterstrategy against infanticide (Sterck et al. 1997; Wrangham 1979). This counterstrategy is associated with small group size, since only groups with relatively few females will have one resident male (Nunn 1999; Schuelke and Ostner 2012; Srivastava and Dunbar 1996; Treves and Chapman 1996). In addition, females should have the option to change males, which has been confirmed in Asian colobines with female dispersal (see above). Indeed, the adult male protects against infanticide, since the disappearance of the resident male (experimental: Sugiyama 1966; natural: reviewed in Steenbeek 1996; reviewed by Palombit 2012) leads to infanticidal attacks by extra-group males. When groups contain several males, females will mate promiscuously (Hrdy 1979) and female dispersal is not required. Indeed, in Nepal sacred langurs living in multi-male groups, males defend infants against male attacks (Borries et al. 1999b). Therefore, males in both single and multi-male groups provide safety against infanticide by conspecific males.

The risk of infanticide can limit group size when the risk of infanticide increases with group size (Crockett and Janson 2000). Indeed, in a comparison of sacred langur populations, those with a high risk of male takeover, measured as the number of extra-group males, also had larger groups containing more females (Treves and Chapman 1996). However, this evidence is indirect and may be spurious, since populations with more females per group will also result in a larger number of extra-group males. More direct evidence for a higher risk of infanticide is found in Thomas's langurs, where infanticidal attacks tended to occur more often at larger group sizes (Steenbeek and van Schaik 2001). Additionally, in Nepal sacred langurs male immigration was more common in the larger group, and consequently infant mortality as result of infanticide was higher than in the intermediate-sized group (Borries 1997). Unfortunately, no data of infanticide risk are available for other species. However, in Thomas's langurs and possibly in sacred langurs infanticide risk may limit group size.

Alternatively, group size may also be limited by time constraints (baboons: Dunbar 1992; African colobines: Korstjens and Dunbar 2007; Asian colobines: Kavana et al. 2015b). Diurnal primates have about 12 hours per day to obtain sufficient food. In baboons, resting time is considered exchangeable for feeding and travelling time. This adjustment of time budget may be less flexible in colobines, since fore-stomach fermentation may require resting time (Dunbar 1988). Accordingly, the amount of resting time in Malabar sacred langurs and Nilgiri langurs is linked to the proportion of leaves in their diet (Kavana et al. 2015b) and group sizes of Nilgiri langurs are smaller than of Malabar sacred langurs, because their diet requires more resting time.

This would predict that food competition is present and that WGS is expected (cf. Snaith and Chapman 2005, 2007), even though group sizes are relatively small. This converges with the socioecological model.

Evidence for Colobine Food Competition/Folivore Paradox

Altogether, the data clearly show that colobines can experience food competition. Different species, and possibly different populations of the same species, can experience different combinations of costs and benefits of group living. In three different species this has been studied in multiple aspects, in the Ramnagar Nepal sacred langur, the Jodhpur Bengal sacred langur and the Ketambe Thomas's langurs.

Three Well-Studied Species

Nepal sacred langurs at Ramnagar experience WGS, WGC and BGC (Koenig 2000). Groups of intermediate size had the highest female body condition (Koenig 2000), which was linked to female reproductive output (Koenig et al. 1997). Group size effects show that females in the intermediate-sized group fared better than females in the small and large group. The females in the small group have a lower bodily condition than females in the intermediate-sized group because they cannot exert sufficient BGC, while the large group females have a lower bodily condition than females in the intermediate-sized group because of WGS. This indicates that WGS and BGC food competition balance group size. On top of group size effects, female dominance rank is despotic (Lu et al. 2008) and effects of female dominance rank on body condition and reproductive success are found, indicating WGC. As predicted with WGC, female dispersal is rare (Borries 1997; Borries and Koenig 2000). However, nepotism and alliance formation are absent and this is inconsistent with the predictions of the socioecological model (Koenig 2000). Moreover, there is some evidence that infanticide risk, as predicted by the Folivore Paradox, may limit group size at Ramnagar since the infanticide rate in the large group was higher than in the intermediate-sized group (Borries 1997). Simultaneously, the evidence indicates that in the Ramnagar Nepal sacred langurs food competition limits group size (Koenig 2000), and although an additional cost to a large group size may be a high infanticide rate, this seemingly does not lead to relatively small groups. So, it seems that the Folivore Paradox does not apply to this population.

While the findings of the Ramnagar population indicate that all three types of food competition are important (Koenig 2000), it is not clear whether this is a taxon-specific pattern. At Jodhpur, Bengal sacred langur females also experience WGS (Borries 1993; Sommer and Rajpurohit 1989), have a despotic dominance hierarchy suggesting WGC (Borries et al. 1991) and experience female aggression between groups suggesting the potential for BGC (Borries 1993). Therefore, also at Jodhpur all three types of competition may be present. In contrast, other sacred langur populations may show patterns consistent with the Folivore Paradox. A comparative analysis of sacred langur populations indicated that populations with high infanticide risk also have larger groups (Treves and Chapman 1996). However, for the Folivore Paradox to operate, the relation between infanticide risk and group size should be established within a population. Only descriptive data on two groups of Nepal sacred langurs have been reported (Borries 1997). Moreover, group sizes in sacred langurs are not always small and regularly multiple males are present. Therefore, direct evidence for a larger risk of infanticide for females in the larger groups of a population is largely lacking. Thus far, the only convincing evidence suggests that, in this taxon, group size is limited by food competition.

Thomas's langurs at Ketambe experience WGS in foraging effort, but no WGC or BGC (Steenbeek and van Schaik 2001; Sterck 1995; Sterck et al. 1997). The birth rate of females is not affected by group size, indicating that group size effects on foraging (WGS) are not large enough to limit the birth rate. In larger groups immature survival tended to be higher, similarly suggesting that group size effects on foraging (WGS) do not limit immature survival. Larger groups may more effectively protect infants against outside threats, such as predators or infanticidal males. This contrasts with the finding that male takeovers are more prevalent in larger groups, which has been interpreted as a higher risk of infanticide (Steenbeek and van Schaik 2001). Thus, although food competition is present, it does not limit group size since female fitness is not reduced. This finding is consistent with the idea that other factors, e.g. infanticide risk, can limit groups size. However, evidence for a higher risk of infanticide in large groups is mixed: while larger groups may be taken over more often, immature survival is higher (Steenbeek and van Schaik 2001). Altogether, Thomas's langurs fit the Folivore Paradox, but evidence that infanticide risk is the limiting factor is mixed.

Thus, while Ramnagar Nepal sacred langurs experience three types food competition (WGS, BGC and WGC) and Jodhpur Bengal sacred langurs experience WGC that affects female fitness, in Thomas's langurs the WGS effect on foraging effort does not translate into an impact on female reproductive success. This indicates that, with the available data, no general Asian colobine pattern exists. Simultaneously, this variation within Asian colobines opens the possibility of investigating female socioecology.

General Asian Colobine Pattern

For other Asian colobine species a less complete picture exists and few data are available. In all investigated species, indications for a WGS effect on foraging effort are found. However, data of its effect on female reproductive success indicate that living in a large group is in some species disadvantageous, while in others it is advantageous. This suggests that some species may be limited by food competition and the socioecological model may apply, while other species may be limited by other factors, such as infanticide.

Much less attention has been given to BGC and, especially, WGC. Given that females can be aggressive over food sources, it remains surprising that this is often neglected. The characteristics of female relationships, i.e. low intensities of aggression and lacking female-female coalitions, suggests WGC may often be unimportant, but why Asian colobines do not experience WGC more often remains to be determined. Altogether, a lack of data is the main reason we do not fully understand the socioecology of Asian colobines.

The Folivore Paradox Revisited

The few available data indicate that while some Asian colobines are limited by food competition, others are limited by an alternative factor. The best candidate for this alternative factor is that infanticide risk increases with group size (Crockett and Janson 2000). This implies that this male sexual strategy is crucial to understanding female social organization. Still, it begs the question of why there is a Folivore Paradox but not a Frugivore Paradox. In other words, why are frugivorous primates not found in unexpectedly small groups? We propose that an explanation should be sought in the causes and consequences of living in one-male groups, as often found in Asian colobines.

The number of males in a group depends on the number of females and on the seasonality of their fertility (general: Emlen and Oring 1977; primates: Nunn 1999; Srivastava and Dunbar 1996). In species that are relatively a-seasonal, one male can monopolize more females than in highly seasonal species (Figure 16.3a). Folivores are relatively a-seasonal in their food intake (see above), consequently they also have relatively a-seasonal births (Nunn 1999: ESM Table 16.2) and relatively many females associate with one male. Living in one-male groups has consequences for female anti-infanticidal strategies (cf. Palombit 2012). While in multi-male groups females reduce the risk of infanticide by promiscuous mating and spreading the chance of paternity, in one-male groups females depend on the resident male's defending capacities. In multi-male groups the infanticide risk will be higher after a new male has become dominant, but he may be less likely to kill infants of females that he mated with, reducing the overall infanticide risk. In one-male groups, the new dominant male will always be an outsider and pose a risk for all females with infants. Therefore, in one-male groups the infanticide risk will usually be higher than in multi-male groups (but see Teichroeb et al. 2012). This argues that ecology, i.e. low seasonality in food, resulting low birth seasonality is translated into one male groups with many females and a high risk of infanticide.

The relatively skewed sex ratio in these groups, with one male and quite a large number of females, also results in many extra-group males (Figure 16.3b; cf. Treves and Chapman 1996). These extra-group males will aim to take over groups. Since only one male is present, whether a takeover attempt is successful will crucially depend on the relative strengths of the resident and extra-group male(s). The number of females in a group will not determine whether an extra-group male or all-male band succeeds in replacing the resident male. Extra-group males may therefore target in particular groups with many females, since this will maximize their fitness. Therefore, the risk of takeover and infanticide will increase with the number of females in a group. Females may reduce their risk of infanticide by shifting group

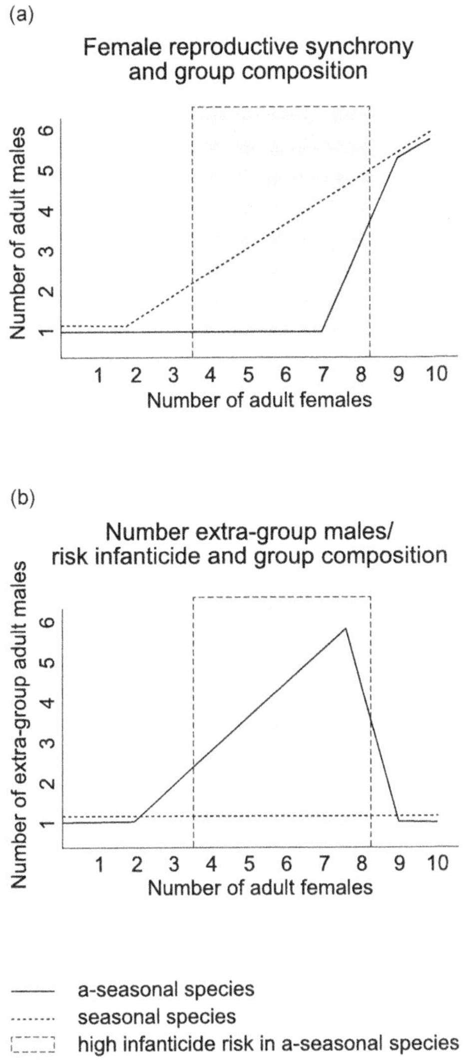

Figure 16.3 The seasonality of food and female reproduction will affect the number of males in a group and as a result determine the risk of infanticide. (a) In seasonal species, one-male groups are replaced by multi-male groups at a lower number of females than in a-seasonal species. (b) A-seasonal populations with one-male groups that contain relatively many females will have relatively more extra-group males. In seasonal species, the number of extra-group males will be low. Extra-group males may form a risk of infanticide (grey box). A high number of extra-group males will lead to more frequent takeovers and a higher risk of infanticide (cf. Treves and Chapman 1996). Note that we aim to illustrate the relationship between the number of females and males. The depicted number of females and males is not based on actual calculations.

membership, either by migration or the group may be temporarily split between some females that reside with the old male and others that reside with a new male (cf. Zhao Q et al. 2011a). In this scenario, the risk of infanticide will be especially strong in large groups with only one male. Since such one-male groups are found in many folivores, this may explain the Folivore Paradox. However, some frugivorous primates that live in one-male groups, e.g. guenons, may also fit the 'Folivore Paradox' and be limited in their group sizes by infanticide risk. Although guenons may breed seasonally, the number of simultaneously fertile females seems relatively low (Nunn 1999). In addition, while groups can temporarily experience multi-male influxes, especially when multiple fertile females are present (Mugatha et al. 2007), they typically contain one adult male (Cords 2000) and experience infanticide (Cords and Fuller 2010). Accordingly, the assertion that guenon populations are limited by food quality, but that group sizes are smaller than expected on the basis of food competition (Korstjens et al. 2018) hints that there may also be a thus far unnoticed 'Frugivore Paradox'.

This proposition also indicates that the Folivore Paradox will not be found in clearly seasonal species, with high reproductive overlap. Indeed, in the Ramnagar Nepal and Jodhpur Bengal sacred langurs not infanticide risk, but food competition is limiting group size. In contrast, infanticide risk is limiting (Steenbeek and van Schaik 2001) for the a-seasonal Thomas's langurs (Sterck and van Hooff 2000).

Discussion

We tested three hypotheses proposed to explain Asian colobine socioecology: (1) the socioecological model that proposes mainly WGS; (2) no food competition due to abundant food and (3) the Folivore Paradox, i.e. infanticide limits group size. When testing these proposals, Koenig and Borries (2009) argued that four questions need to be answered: (1) do Asian colobine females experience food competition and what type (WGC; WGS, BGC); (2) if there is WGC, why are dominance relationships not nepotistic and are female-female coalitions absent; (3) if there is WGC (i.e. a linear dominance hierarchy), why do females disperse and (4) what causes the Folivore Paradox, i.e. why do folivores live in unexpectedly small groups. After our review, we can partially answer these questions.

First, it should be mentioned that very few relevant data are available. Therefore, the answers are based on often scant data from a few species. However, it is clear that all species with relevant data experience WGS effects on their foraging effort (ESM Table 16.2; part of question 1), thereby rejecting proposal 2: Asian colobines do experience food competition. This is consistent with general evidence indicating that folivores actually do experience competition for food (e.g. Majolo et al. 2008; Snaith and Chapman 2007), and that the notion of their preferred foods being ubiquitous is an oversimplification (e.g. Sayers 2013).

Whether food competition is expressed in female reproductive output differs between species, in some it seems limiting, in others not. In the species where no group size effects on female reproductive output is found, either infanticide risk may limit group size, or BGC may counter WGS, consistent with the socioecological model. The Thomas's langurs may be an example of the first scenario (Steenbeek and van Schaik 2001), the Ramnagar Nepal sacred langur of the latter (Koenig 2000). Therefore (part of question 1), BGC is evident in one population, in others it has not been conclusively established.

The presence of WGC has been measured in three species (part of question 1); it is absent in Thomas's langurs and present in Nepal and Bengal sacred langurs (Ramnagar and Jodhpur). In other Bengal sacred langurs (at Abu), the Phayre's langur (Koenig et al. 2004) and the red-shanked douc langurs (Kavanagh 1978) the despotic female dominance hierarchy indicates WGC, yet female rank effects on foraging effort and fitness indicators have not been tested. However, the behaviour of these langurs does not fit the socioecological model in one important aspect: females do not form coalitions and are not nepotistic (Koenig 2000; Koenig et al. 2004). We found no answer to this discrepancy (question 2). One solution may be to argue that despotism need not be accompanied by nepotism. This still leaves open the question of when selection pressures result in nepotism. Alternatively, Asian colobines may only have experienced WGC recently, due to human changes of the environment (cf. Koenig 2000; Sterck 1998, 1999), and may not have yet evolved the optimal evolutionary strategy. To summarize, WGC can be present or absent, females may form despotic dominance hierarchies, yet nepotism is not found. Altogether, Asian langurs can experience different forms of food competition (question 1), yet what species and populations experience which type of food competition and whether food competition limits group size remains to be established for most species.

We offer an explanation for the presence of female dispersal in despotic species (question 3): female dispersal may be easy and not costly when females disperse to a group with previously known female group members, and not to a group with unknown females. The Thomas's langur dispersal pattern (Figure 16.2) suggests that in the long run females stay together with their female group members, even when some have already migrated to a new male while others still remain with the previous one. Similar patterns have been found for female golden snub-nosed monkeys (Guo et al. 2015). The temporary group splitting in other species indicate that this relative flexibility in female grouping may be a general pattern (Sterck and Korstjens 2000; Zhao Q et al. 2011a). However, whether indeed females typically immigrate into groups with previous female associates remains to be tested.

The Folivore Paradox begs for an explanation for why colobines live in relatively small groups. This may result from strong WGS (Snaith and Chapman 2005) of from infanticide risk (Janson and Goldsmith 1995; Steenbeek and van Schaik 2001). In some Asian colobine species, females in larger group have a greater foraging effort and suffer reduced fitness. In these species, group size may be limited by food competition. Also, the suggestion that diet limits the time budget, predicts an effect of food competition. Both of these explanations converge with the socioecological model (Sterck et al. 1997). Alternatively, not food competition but infanticide risk may limit group size. This would be a truly alternative scenario, where a social factor, i.e. a male sexual strategy, limits female group size. There is evidence, albeit mixed, for infanticide limiting group size in Thomas's langurs (Steenbeek and van Schaik 2001). Unfortunately, the relationship between infanticide risk and group size has received little attention in other Asian colobine species. Therefore, it is not clear whether this can explain in general the relatively small group sizes often found.

We also offer a related explanation for the Folivore Paradox (Question 4). Due to their diet folivores may experience relatively little seasonality in food availability. This translates into one male groups with relatively many females, thereby increasing the risk of takeover and/or infanticide by extra-group males. When these males preferentially target groups with many females, group size may be limited by infanticide risk, not by food competition. Thus, the low seasonality in fertility is pivotal for the Folivore Paradox. This suggests that infanticide could limit group size in a-seasonal frugivores as well. In addition, this would predict that the Folivore Paradox does not apply to seasonal folivores. This is consistent with the findings for the Ramnagar Nepal sacred langurs, but whether this also applies to seasonal odd-nosed monkeys remains to be tested.

Conclusion

In conclusion, the selection pressures on female Asian langurs are diverse and they may experience strong selection from food competition and/or from male sexual strategies, in particular infanticide. These patterns are also evident when the socio-ecology of African colobus monkeys is examined (Chapter 17). The balance between these forces will determine whether the enhanced foraging effort with group size is translated in an effect of food competition on female reproductive success. We propose that in more seasonal species, food competition will play a more important role, while in a-seasonal ones this will be male infanticide. How this applies to the seasonal odd-nosed colobines living in layered societies remains to be established (Chapter 18). One puzzling pattern in female social behaviour may have been solved: females in despotic species may disperse when they enter a group with previous female group members. However, the other puzzle, namely the lack of nepotism in species with despotic dominance hierarchy, remains unsolved.

Altogether, the predictions of the socioecological model and the Folivore Paradox can be brought together when the consequences of the low seasonality in folivores are taken into account. This indicates that Asian colobines are not exempt from an effect of ecology on female social organization, but that male sexual strategies can have an exceptionally large impact of female group size and grouping patterns in specific Asian colobine species.

Acknowledgements

We thank the editors Ikki Matsuda, Julie Teichroeb and Cyril Grueter for inviting us to contribute to this volume. Furthermore, we thank Cyril Grueter and Julie Teichroeb for their constructive comments on an earlier version of this chapter.

17 Socioecology of African Colobines

Julie A. Teichroeb

Introduction

Primatologists have used socioecological models for almost four decades to try to explain the wide variability displayed in primate social organization and structure. These models differ in specific predictions but generally agree that differences in the quality and distribution of fitness-limiting resources greatly influence group size, dispersal patterns and social relationships. Though not without controversy and exceptions (Clutton-Brock and Janson 2012; Koenig 2002; Thierry 2008), many of the predictions of socioecological models are upheld for species in the Order Primates (Koenig and Borries 2009).

According to socioecological models (e.g. Table 17.1), for females, who are limited in their reproductive output by food resources (Trivers 1972), the quality and distribution of food is thought to determine the competitive regime both within and between groups and to result in specific female social relationships (Isbell 1991, 2004; Isbell and Pruetz 1998; Isbell and van Vuren 1996; Isbell et al. 1998; van Schaik 1989; Sterck et al. 1997; Wrangham 1980). Food resources that are clumped and worth defending (i.e. high quality) will cause direct and aggressive contest competition (Nicholson 1954), both within and between groups. Within-group contest (WGC) competition will lead to the formation of female dominance hierarchies to decrease the amount of aggression experienced (Maynard Smith and Price 1973) and to female coalition formation. Kin are typically the most reliable allies so WGC leads to female philopatry and despotic, nepotistic dominance hierarchies (van Schaik 1989; Wrangham 1980). Females also benefit by remaining with kin in between-group contest (BGC) competition although the ability to win in inter-group encounters may depend on support from subordinates, which can relax female hierarchies (van Schaik 1989; Sterck et al. 1997). Larger group sizes are also beneficial in winning in BGC (Cheney 1987; Crofoot and Wrangham 2010).

When food resources are lower-quality and distributed more evenly, they are not defensible or worth defending, so little contest competition occurs and kin are not selected to form strong bonds (van Hooff and van Schaik 1994; Sterck et al. 1997; Wrangham 1980). In these situations, within-group scramble (WGS) competition for food may be predominant, leading to a group size effect on feeding efficiency (Chapman et al. 1995; Nicholson 1954) and more food searching for groups of larger

This chapter includes Electronic Supplementary Material (ESM) at: www.cambridge.org/colobines

Table 17.1. Summary of the basic predictions of the socioecological model presented by van Schaik (1989) and Sterck et al. (1997)

Food quality/distribution	Population density[a]	Competitive regime	Social outcomes for females: Dispersal	Social outcomes for females: Dominance
a. Low quality, highly dispersed or large patches	Low	WGS	Yes	Egalitarian and individualistic
b. High quality, large patches (> group size)	High	WGS, BGC	No	Egalitarian and individualistic
OR				
High quality, scattered patches (> group size)	Low			
c. High quality, small patches (< group size)	Low	WGC	No	Nepotistic and despotic
d. Likely high quality, clumped	High (potentially)	WGC, BGC	No	Nepotistic but tolerant

[a] Relative to carrying capacity.

size in similar home ranges (Chapman and Chapman 2000c), which can ultimately limit group size (Koenig 2002). Since female dispersal is often common in species primarily affected by scramble competition (Table 17.1), females may choose to leave their current group for one with fewer individuals or choose a group based on some other important factor like the risk of predation, the quality of males, or the risk of infanticide (Crockett and Janson 2000; Isbell and van Vuren 1996; Sicotte et al. 2017; Steenbeek and van Schaik 2001; Sterck et al. 2005; Teichroeb et al. 2009a).

Folivore group sizes are often much smaller than one would predict on the basis of the food competition that their diets generate, a phenomenon termed the 'folivore paradox' (Janson and Goldsmith 1995; Steenbeek and van Schaik 2001). If folivores are affected by only WGS or no competition at all, they are expected to form large groups. However, many species form very small groups that appear to be far below the threshold where WGS would be experienced. Male reproductive strategies, in particular infanticide by males, may provide an explanation for the folivore paradox (Crockett and Janson 2000), and I will discuss the details of how male and female reproductive strategies interact later in this chapter.

Male reproductive success is predominantly limited by the number of fertilizations they can acquire (Trivers 1972), thus female distribution on the landscape and their patterns of temporal availability are thought to determine male strategies to access and monopolize females (Altmann 1990; Clutton-Brock 1989; Emlen and Oring 1977). The number of males in primate groups is generally determined by the number of females (Altmann 1990; Mitani et al. 1996; Ridley 1986) and when females mate more synchronously, there are usually relatively more males in the group (Nunn 1999). Female driven social evolution in primates is supported by phylogenetic analyses showing that changes in male group size evolutionarily lag behind changes in female group size (Lindenfors et al. 2004). Since females typically distribute themselves according to the available food resources and males defend groups of females (Koenig et al. 2013), this suggests that the mating system that is most prevalent for primate species is female defence polygyny (Emlen and Oring 1977).

In this chapter, I will review what is currently known about the socioecology of colobus monkeys. There are still biases in the data available on primate behaviour towards species that are easy to observe or more closely related to humans (Ramsay and Teichroeb 2019). This means that largely arboreal colobus monkeys that are hard to observe and difficult to identify individually have been neglected to some extent. Nevertheless, data have accumulated for some species showing interesting trends in the socioecology of colobus monkeys.

For the black-and-white colobus, good behavioural data are still lacking for *Colobus satanas* and most *C. angolensis* subspecies, while other species have been studied more intensively (*C. guereza*, *C. vellerosus*, *C. polykomos*) and data are accumulating for Rwenzori Angolan colobus (*C. a. ruwenzorii*). The black-and-white colobus are an excellent group to test predictions of socioecological models because they show the most varied diets of the colobus monkeys (Fashing 2011; Chapter 10) and thus food distribution and social responses should be different as well. Olive colobus (*Procolobus verus*) have been the subject of two longer-duration studies (Korstjens 2001; Oates 1988a) that examined their feeding and associated behaviour, though food competition has not been specifically addressed. Many red colobus species have not been studied in detail due partly to their distribution in areas that have not been politically stable for long periods (taxonomy following Chapter 2). Other issues with collecting detailed behavioural data are the fact that large, arboreal red colobus groups make individual identification very challenging. Some behavioural data are discussed below for *Pilicolobus badius* (Upper Guinea red colobus, located from Côte d'Ivoire to Sierra Leone), *P. rufomitratus* (Tana River red colobus), *P. temminckii* (Temminck's red colobus) and *P. tephrosceles* (ashy red colobus). Unfortunately, little to no detailed behavioural data are available for *P. bouvieri* (Bouvier's red colobus), *P. epieni* (Niger Delta red colobus), *P. foai* (Foa's red colobus), *P. gordonorum* (Udzungwa red colobus), *P. kirkii* (Zanzibar red colobus), *P. langi* (Lang's red colobus), *P. oustaleti* (Oustalet's red colobus), *P. parmentieri* (Lomami red colobus), *P. pennantii* (Pennant's red colobus), *P. preussi* (Preuss's red colobus), *P. semlikiensis* (Semliki red colobus), *P. tholloni* (Tshuapa red colobus) or *P. waldronae* (Miss Waldron's red colobus), which is likely extinct (McGraw 2005).

Diets and Food Distribution

Colobus monkeys are foregut fermenters (Chapter 6) and were originally assumed to eat a large proportion of mature leaves and this, along with inaccurate assessments of scramble competition (see below), led to the supposition that they experience little to no food competition (Isbell 1991; Yeager and Kirkpatrick 1998). However, with greater research effort on different African colobine populations, the dietary flexibility and selective feeding of this group has become obvious. Most African colobines actually eat a diet low in mature foliage and prefer instead young leaves, fruit and/or seeds (reviewed in: Fashing 2011; Chapter 10). For instance, the annual diet of black colobus monkeys (*C. satanas*) contains relatively large amounts of seeds. The lowest proportion of seeds reported in their annual diets was 41% from the Fôret des Abeilles in Gabon (Fleury and Gautier-Hion 1999) and the highest proportion was 60% in Lopé, Gabon (Harrison 1986; Oates 1994). Fruit can also make up a large portion of colobus monkey diets (Arseneau-Robar et al. 2021; Fashing 2001b). These types of foods tend to be distributed in clumps (van Schaik 1989; Strier et al. 1997) and are easy to digest, being low in fibre, and high in sugar in the case of fruit, and high in protein in the case of seeds (Dasilva 1994; Milton 1999; Waterman 1984). When foliage does make up a large proportion of colobus monkey diets, the focus tends to be on easier to digest young leaves. Red colobus provide a powerful example of this. All but one red colobus populations studied have a diet higher in young leaves than mature leaves (20 populations, reviewed in: Fashing 2011), with the exception of ashy red colobus at Gombe National Park, Tanzania where mature foliage was reported to be 44% of the diet (Clutton-Brock 1975a).

In addition, the flexibility of colobus monkey diets is remarkable. It is not uncommon for the same species to have different food preferences at different field sites. For instance, guerezas at Kakamega in Kenya are mostly frugivorous for half the year (Fashing 2001b), while at Kibale National Park in Uganda, they are consistently folivorous (Harris and Chapman 2007a). Similarly, the Rwenzori subspecies of Angolan colobus (*C. a. ruwenzorii*) have the highest mature leaf consumption (40% of the diet) of all the black-and-white colobus monkeys at the high altitude Nyungwe site in Rwanda (Fimbel et al. 2001) and they also feed on lichen, which can make up more than 50% of the diet some months (Miller et al. 2020a; Vedder and Fashing 2002), while in the mid-altitude forest at Lake Nabugabo, Uganda this subspecies feeds primarily on young leaves (65%) and fruit (31%) (Adams and Teichroeb 2020; Arseneau-Robar et al. 2021). Even within small geographical areas, research has shown that different colobus groups can have quite varied diets depending on their home range and the food species available (e.g. Ashy red colobus in and around Kibale National Park, Chapman and Chapman 1999; *C. a. palliatus* at Diani Beach, Dunham 2017a; guerezas at Kibale, Harris and Chapman 2007a).

Large seasonal variation has also been reported in most African colobine diets. Typically, when the preferred food sources of young leaves, fruit or seeds are not available, mature leaves are eaten more often (e.g., McKey et al. 1981; Oates 1977a; Saj and Sicotte 2007a; Struhsaker 1975). Lianas provide an important staple source of leaves for many colobus, and are often relied on heavily in seasons when other foods are rare (e.g. Dasilva 1992; Preece 2006). In terms of seasonal variation in the diet, the olive colobus stands out as an exception as this species manages to maintain a fairly high-quality diet year-round, which may be due to lower tolerance for mature leaves (Oates 1988a; Chapter 11).

This research demonstrates that, even though colobus monkeys are physiologically equipped to feed on mature leaves, they may only do so when other preferred foods are not available. The diets of most colobus species contain a large percentage of young leaves, fruit or seeds and because these higher-quality foods tend to be more patchily distributed, this may result in food competition among females. Foregut fermentation also limits the amount of acidic, juicy, ripe fruit that colobines can digest, which may explain why, when fruit is fed upon, it is often unripe or leathery (Davies et al. 1999; Kay and Davies 2004). This point could have a large impact on the degree of competition that female colobus actually experience when feeding on fruit (see Chapter 16 for potential social consequences of this type of fruit-eating). It is also important to note that gross categories, like the amount of leaves or fruit in the diet, may not be very good predictors of the level of female agonism that will be seen. In a review of rates of female agonism in the primates, Wheeler and colleagues (2013) found that the proportion of leaves in the diet did not predict low rates of agonism, and indeed folivores and frugivores showed similar aggression rates among females. However, it is important to note that these comparisons did not control for the quality of the home range. Below, evidence for food competition in African colobines is detailed.

Food Competition

Within-Group Scramble Effects on Foraging Effort

A major reason why colobines were thought to be exempt from food competition for so long was inaccurate assessments of the occurrence of WGS. With this type of competition, group size affects food intake because a larger number of individuals deplete patches more quickly and search fields overlap (Chapman and Chapman 2000c; Janson and Goldsmith 1995). Thus, initially researchers compared colobine groups of different size, often in neighbouring home ranges, to see if larger groups ranged further as a test of WGS competition (reviewed in: Snaith and Chapman 2007). However, these comparisons were erroneous without controlling for the quality of the home range. Larger groups may not need to range further than smaller groups if they occupy better quality habitat. This important link was brought to the attention of researchers with the Ecological Constraints Model (Chapman and Chapman 2000c; Wrangham et al. 1993). Another issue with measuring WGS correctly is that animals can use several behavioural modifications (or adjustments) to compensate beyond just ranging further to search for food (Borries et al. 2008; Teichroeb and Sicotte 2009; Wrangham et al. 1993); they may also feed and move for longer durations, eat different foods, eat faster, move faster or undergo fission (reviewed in: Teichroeb and Sicotte 2018).

A better understanding of how to measure WGS has led to research confirming that several African colobine populations are affected by this type of food competition (ESM Table 17.2). The white-thighed colobus (aka ursine colobus or Geoffroy's pied colobus, *C. vellerosus*) are an excellent example. This species forms groups with an average of 15 individuals (Oates 1994; Wong and Sicotte 2006) and consumes a high proportion of foliage (74% of the annual diet, Saj and Sicotte 2007a).

Nonetheless, WGS has been confirmed for this species (Saj and Sicotte 2007b; Teichroeb and Sicotte 2009; Teichroeb et al. 2003). Data collected over an annual cycle on four groups of different size with similar home range quality, showed that larger groups ranged farther (larger home ranges, longer daily paths and larger group spread) and spent more time feeding per day (Teichroeb and Sicotte 2009). Later analyses confirmed that WGS competition was present for these groups in both the lean and abundant seasons, however behavioural compensation strategies occurred more often in the lean season for all groups, demonstrating that WGS intensifies seasonally (Teichroeb and Sicotte 2018). The costs of WGS competition in larger groups may explain why female white-thighed colobus tend to disperse from larger groups towards smaller groups (Teichroeb et al. 2009a), although infanticide pressure appears to be a more over-riding reason for this trend (see below).

Gillespie and Chapman (2001) also compared the behavioural manifestations of WGS in two differently sized ashy red colobus groups at Kibale NP, Uganda while controlling for food availability between the groups' ranges. They found that the larger group had longer day ranges, a larger home range and moved significantly faster than the smaller group, showing evidence of WGS. An extension of this work to nine groups, showed in addition increased group spread, reiterating the costs of being in a larger group (Snaith and Chapman 2008). Furthermore, ashy red colobus deplete their food patches. As patch occupancy increased, food intake rates decreased and movement rates within the patch increased, indicating more searching for food. Patch occupancy was also longer in larger groups (Snaith and Chapman 2005).

Even within the smallest groups of colobus monkeys there is evidence for the effects of WGS. Guerezas form groups with an average of nine individuals (range: 2–23, $N = 13$ research sites) and their diets are typically quite folivorous (range: 53%–86% of the annual diet, reviewed in: Fashing 2011). Theoretically, within-group food competition in guerezas should be minimal since they usually reside in such small groups and can feed on foliage (Isbell 1991). This appears to be borne out by some data. For instance, at Kibale, where guerezas feed mostly on young leaves, no evidence of food depletion in a patch over time was found (Tombak et al. 2012). However, also at Kibale, other indicators have shown that guerezas can suffer from food depletion. During a four-month period, when the availability of their top two food sources decreased sharply, two guereza groups were found to increase their day range, visit more patches per day, have larger group spread while feeding, spend more time feeding, and have greater dietary diversity (Harris et al. 2010). Similarly, in the Kakamega Forest, Kenya, where guerezas have been reported to eat a high amount of fruit (Fashing 2001b), an indication of WGS competition for food was present in the largest study group, which had the longest daily path length (Fashing 2001a).

The Rwenzori subspecies of Angolan colobus (*C. a. ruwenzorii*) is a clear outlier in terms of group size and social organization in the colobus monkeys. Relatively cohesive groups of >300 individuals have been reported in the montane area of Nyungwe National Park, Rwanda (Fashing et al. 2007b; Fimbel et al. 2001) and more recently, Miller and colleagues (2020c) counted over 500 animals moving together at the same site. At lower altitude sites, large groups also form but these appear to be more flexible in terms of group size, showing fissions and fusions daily to form subgroups of variable size (Oates 1974; Teichroeb et al. 2019). Research at both Nyungwe and the lower land site of Lake Nabugabo, Uganda has shown that *C. a. ruwnenzorii* are forming a multilevel society, the first found in an African colobine (Miller et al. 2020c; Stead and Teichroeb 2019). There does appear to be a cost in terms of WGS to these large aggregations. In the montane forests of Nyungwe, these very large aggregations of colobus appear to be possible because the animals feed on a fairly high proportion of mature leaves (40% of the annual diet) and large amounts of lichens seasonally (Miller et al. 2020a). Mature leaves at Nyungwe have been found to be higher quality (higher in protein and lower in fibre) than is typical of mature leaves at other sites, and this, along with the wide availability of lichens, appears to allow the colobus to aggregate (Fimbel et al. 2001). Even given this, these large colobus societies have very large home ranges, which is indicative of WGS (Fashing et al. 2007b). Miller and colleagues (2020b) also found that *C. a. ruwenzorii* deplete food patches, particularly when feeding on young leaves, leading to intake rates decreasing and movement rates increasing over time in a patch. At the mid-altitude site at Lake Nabugabo, the diet of *C. a. ruwenzorii* has been found to be much different (high in fruit and young leaves, Arseneau-Robar et al. 2021), and the food competition caused by these more patchy resources may explain why there is frequent fission among core units and the maximum number of colobus that have been reported together is just over 200 individuals (Stead and Teichroeb 2019). Feeding on these patchy and higher-quality food resources may be limiting the size of aggregations possible for *C. a. ruwenzorii* in lower altitude areas (Arseneau-Robar et al. 2021). Indeed, analyses of the numbers of core units clustered together through time has shown that the greatest aggregations occur at Nabugabo in seasons with the greatest fruit availability (Adams et al. 2021).

Fitness Costs of Within-Group Scramble

While indicators of WGS food competition have been found in every colobus species where this question has been assessed, it is still not entirely clear how severely this may influence female reproductive rates. Based on socioecological models, it would be expected that females in larger groups would suffer fitness effects of WGS competition and show decreased energy balance, longer inter-birth intervals or slower infant development (Borries et al. 2008; Koenig 2002; Koenig and Borries 2009). Dunbar (1987) compared reproductive rates in different-sized groups of guerezas in Ethiopia and found that larger, multi-male groups had lower reproductive rates. This result could have been due to WGS competition for food; however, Dunbar (1987) attributed it to the stress females were under due to living with several competing males. Negative physiological effects of limited food availability were found for guerezas in Kibale, in that lactating females had decreased energy balance and two of three females suffered increased parasitism during the time when less food was available (Harris et al. 2010). In their comparison of nine groups of ashy red colobus at Kibale, Snaith and Chapman (2008) found fewer offspring per adult female in larger groups, which suggests that WGS may have had a cost in terms of slower reproductive rates in these groups. These studies are the only ones available that demonstrate fitness costs to WGS in the colobus monkeys. An additional study in white-thighed colobus that used natal coat colour transitions as a proxy for infant development found contrasting evidence. Bădescu and colleagues (2016) found that, even though WGS competition occurs in the population (Teichroeb and Sicotte 2009, 2018), group size did not affect infant development rates. When controlling for group size, it was rather infants that were at greater risk of infanticide (i.e. males, Teichroeb and Sicotte 2008a, and those in multi-male groups, Teichroeb et al. 2012) that transitioned out of their natal coats faster (Bădescu et al. 2016).

Within-Group Contest and Female Dominance Hierarchies

The preferred diet of many colobus species often encompass clumped food sources that have the potential to cause WGC competition, yet the actual outcomes of aggressive interactions between females have been investigated relatively rarely (ESM Table 17.3). Among red colobus females, Struhsaker (1975) reports that weakly expressed dominance hierarchies are present in ashy red colobus at Kibale. Accordingly, aggression amongst females was rare and not often observed in feeding contexts, appearing to be primarily used by females to restrict access to their infants (Struhsaker and Leland 1979). At Abuko Nature Reserve in The Gambia, female Temminck's red colobus were also aggressive primarily over infant access but females in this population are reported to form linear dominance hierarchies (Starin 1991). Nonetheless, fitness benefits from high rank have not been documented for Temminck's red colobus females as age at first parturition, birth rate and number of surviving offspring were not found to correlate with rank (Starin 1991). Only Korstjens and colleagues (2002) report that aggression between females in a red colobus species (Upper Guinea red colobus at Taï) was primarily over food but they did not see sufficient interactions to calculate a dominance hierarchy among females.

Black-and-white colobus provide more data on the occurrence and effects of WGC competition in African colobines (ESM Table 17.3). For example, king or western black-and-white colobus (*C. polykomos*) form mid-sized groups (Tiwai, Sierra Leone, range 9–11 individuals, Dasilva 1989; Taï National Park, Côte d'Ivoire, range 14–19 individuals, Korstjens 2001), that eat a fairly high proportion of plant reproductive parts (35%–48% fruit and seed eating, Dasilva 1989; Korstjens et al. 2007a). Given this, one would expect WGC feeding competition in king colobus (Cheney 1987; van Schaik 1989; Wrangham 1980), which is indeed what has been found. Agonistic interactions among females were relatively common at Taï and these typically took place when the animals were foraging. The frequency of agonism was particularly high when food items had a long handling time (i.e. *Pentaclethra marcophylla* seeds) because females could monopolize these resources and exclude other females (Korstjens et al. 2002). Due to this agonism, Korstjens, Sterck and Noë (2002) were able to construct an individualistic, linear female dominance hierarchy for their study group of king colobus, where four mother-daughter pairs did not occupy adjacent ranks. However, they did not detect an effect of dominance rank on female reproductive success.

In other black-and-white colobus, Harris (2005) reported low rates of agonism between female guerezas but nonetheless, these interactions were directionally consistent, suggesting that a dominance hierarchy among females was present. WGC competition for food also occurs in white-thighed colobus (Wikberg et al. 2013). Agonistic interactions between females primarily occur over food and even occasional foraging on contestable food was sufficient for females to form individualistic dominance relationships that were intermediate in strength (Wikberg et al. 2013). The seasonally available seeds of *Parkia bicolor* and palm nuts of *Borassus aethiopum*, especially caused dominance interactions among females. Wikberg and colleagues (2013) examined female hierarchies in eight groups and these varied in how linear the hierarchy was and the amount of observation required to detect it. Young females began to challenge older females as they matured, so hierarchies were generally predicted by age, while kinship between females was not a factor despite some female philopatry (Wikberg et al. 2013). Although kin did not rank near one another in the female hierarchy in white-thighed colobus, some nepotism was seen in coalition formation. In two groups where females had access to kin as coalition partners, relatedness significantly predicted coalitionary support in one of them and appeared to influence support in the other even though these related females did not necessarily rank closely. This kin support was primary used to direct aggression at males but also at extra-group females (Wikberg et al. 2014).

These studies show that when individuals are recognized and female relationships are studied in colobus monkeys, linear dominance hierarchies may exist, even when only a small portion of the diet is contestable. In addition, even if kin do not rank closely in these hierarchies, which may be individualistic and age-inversed, related females may still provide coalitionary support to one another. The level of WGC competition experienced by colobus monkeys may be set by only a few, monopolizable food items that may be seasonally available. This means that female dominance hierarchies only become important at certain times of the year. Thus, a female colobus monkey's need for coalitionary partners to defend food resources is relatively minimal, leading to lower levels of female bonding than is seen in a typical matrilineal cercopithecine, and allowing female dispersal to take place. More detailed research on a greater number of species is needed to determine if this is a ubiquitous pattern in the African colobines. In addition, there are little data available to examine whether the female dominance hierarchies that exist in colobus monkeys lead to rank-effects on female energy intake or reproductive rates (but see Korstjens et al. 2002), which are important for fully testing socioecological models (Koenig and Borries 2009).

Between-Group Contest

There is good evidence of the effect of BGC feeding competition in a few colobus monkey species (e.g. Fashing 2001; Harris 2005; Korstjens et al. 2005; Miller et al. 2020b; Teichroeb and Sicotte 2018) but participation in encounters varies from high female involvement to almost entirely male involvement. For instance, research at Taï on king colobus found that though males participated in all encounters, the same foods that elicited WGC were important determinants of the level of female involvement in BGC competition. Korstjens (2001) observed total home range overlap (100%) for her study groups at Taï and found that females were involved in 77% ($N = 52$) of between-group conflicts, a high percentage compared to 43.5% ($N = 62$) for female white-thighed colobus (Teichroeb and Sicotte 2018) and 15.2% ($N = 122$) for female guerezas (Fashing 2001c). Korstjens and colleagues (2005) found that females were aggressive in more encounters that occurred in quadrats where a lot of feeding occurred that month (71%) compared to those where food was not at stake (47%) and that their aggressiveness during encounters was seasonal. Females were most intensely aggressive in the two months where fruits of *P. macrophylla*, an important food source with long handling times (Korstjens et al. 2002), were just becoming abundant.

At Kibale, resource quality within guereza home ranges was heterogeneous and groups aggressively defended the core area of their home range, which contained the best resources. Between-group encounters were frequent, leading to a dominance hierarchy between groups, where the highest-ranking groups had higher resource quantity and quality in their core areas (Harris 2006a). Male guerezas in Kibale were more likely to initiate high-level aggression against other groups in areas with valuable food resources (Harris 2010). Smaller groups with a single male of large body size were more likely to win in between-group conflict than larger, multi-male groups (Harris 2010), suggesting that collective action problems were an issue in multi-male groups (Nunn 2000; Willems et al. 2013). Indeed, research at both Kakamega and Kibale has shown that males are the primary participants in between-group conflict in guerezas and that they appear to be defending resources for females (Fashing 2001c; Harris 2005, 2010). Male resource defence may occur indirectly when males drive away reproductive competitors in other groups (i.e. the hired gun strategy, Rubenstein 1986; Wrangham and Rubenstein 1986), however at Kakamega and Kibale, male resource defence appears to be direct (Fashing 2001c; Harris 2005, 2006a, 2010).

The evidence for defence of resources by males in guerezas was the first in the non-human primates and was followed by evidence from chimpanzees (Williams et al. 2004), suggesting that resource defence polygyny (Emlen and Oring 1977) may be more common in the Order Primates than previously thought. Most primate species are still assumed to show female defence polygyny (Altmann 1990); however, more recently evidence has accumulated for resource defence polygyny in all major primate radiations (Koenig et al. 2013). Even when females are typically philopatric, as in guerezas, and are not specifically choosing males based on the home range they defend, male resource defence may evolve because it is beneficial to males to defend food if the females associated with them can reproduce faster with better resource access. There is a high likelihood that male resource defence led to a positive effect on female fitness in guerezas, since Harris (2006a) found that group dominance rank was directly related to the quantity and quality of the food in the core area. Indeed, she collected two-years of preliminary data that suggested that female reproductive success was better in higher-ranked groups.

Besides guerezas (Fashing 2001c; Harris 2005, 2006a, 2010), male defence of resources during BGC competition in colobus monkeys has also been found in white-thighed colobus (Sicotte and MacIntosh 2004; Teichroeb and Sicotte 2018; see also below 'one well-studied species'). Males in this species participated in all aggressive between-group encounters, while female participation occurred in less than half of encounters (Sicotte and MacIntosh 2004; Teichroeb and Sicotte 2018). Even though very large groups could sometimes win in between-group contests by over-whelming smaller groups, as in guerezas, small, uni-male groups of white-thighed colobus tended to win against larger, multi-male groups (Teichroeb et al. 2012; Teichroeb and Sicotte 2018). Direct food defence by males was most obvious in the lean season when WGS intensified and all groups were trying to expand their ranges into areas occupied by neighbouring groups to get enough food (Teichroeb and Sicotte 2018). In this season, all study groups had to range further, leading to an increase in contact with other groups. But by winning in between-group contests against other groups, small, uni-male groups were found to be able to expand their range into already occupied areas. All the losses suffered by the largest study group that contained a range of 7–10 adult males in the lean season were to small, one-male groups. Mid-sized, multi-male groups had the poorest performance during between-group contests. They could not win encounters through large group size or with large, competitive males and they appeared to suffer the most in the lean season. When forced to range further due to WGS, these groups had to move into suboptimal areas near the edge of the forest and avoid other groups (Teichroeb and Sicotte 2018).

Thus, resource defence mediated by males may be an important way through which male strategies are impacting female strategies and affecting the fit of colobus monkeys to the socioecological model. More investigation is needed to understand if this strategy is used widely by males in African colobines. For instance, for king colobus where females were involved in many between-group encounters, males still participated in all encounters (Korstjens 2001), so male resource defence may be occurring. Males are also the primary participants in between-group encounters in both red colobus (Korstjens 2001; Struhsaker 1975) and olive colobus (Korstjens and Noë 2004) but they may be defending females rather than food. For example, comparison of two populations of Zanzibar red colobus (*P. kirkii*), one living in a protected area and one living at high population density in an agricultural area, showed important effects of BGC competition on social structure and implicate female defence of food rather than male defence. Siex (2003) found that, relative to groups in the more forested area, groups in degraded areas showed more cohesion, more female philopatry, and more grooming among females and she related this to the high level of BGC seen in the dense colobus population in degraded areas. For Temminck's red colobus, Starin (1994) reports that females frequently participated in and even started between-group encounters. However, it is worth noting that this species was also studied in a forest fragment with a high population density.

Female Dispersal and Affiliation

The ability to rely on mature foliage as a resource in times of food scarcity and perhaps a reliance on males, rather than female kin, to defend food resources, opens up flexibility in the social responses of female colobus leading to more choice of groups and males, compared to a typical cercopithecine. In the black-and-white colobus dispersal is male-biased. The most female philopatric species is the guereza, for whom female dispersal is rare and all males disperse (Harris et al. 2009a). White-thighed colobus show a pattern of all males dispersing and some females dispersing and parallel transfers involving same-sexed individuals occur often (Teichroeb et al. 2009a, 2011). In king colobus, male and female dispersal have been observed, but the overall pattern appears to be male-biased (Korstjens et al. 2002, 2005). Grooming relationships and strong bonds often occur among the philopatric sex (Wrangham 1980), and going along with these more male-biased dispersal patterns in these species of black-and-white colobus, grooming interactions in guerezas, white-thighed colobus, and king colobus are typically seen among females (Oates 1977c; Korstjens et al. 2002; Saj et al. 2007; Wikberg et al. 2012). Indeed, in white-thighed colobus kinship was important in structuring female social relationships in groups where females resided with kin, but long-term residency status was important in groups where few female relatives were available (Wikberg et al. 2014). Though little is known about social behaviour in *C. satanas*, observations of a new male entering a research group in Gabon suggested that dispersal may be male-biased in this species as well (Fleury and Gautier-Hion 1999). Dispersal in most *C. angolensis* subspecies is unstudied as well, but grooming patterns in *C. a. ruwenzorii* differ from the other black-and-white colobus in being predominantly between males and females (Arseneau-Robar et al. 2018), leading to the prediction that dispersal occurs evenly for both sexes, which is indeed what data are showing (Stead and Teichroeb 2019). At Nabugabo, Uganda both sexes disperse from the natal core unit but males appear to stay within larger band of units that cluster together, while most female dispersal has been to other bands (Adams et al. 2021; Stead and Teichroeb 2019; Teichroeb, unpub. data).

Red colobus are generally described as having female-biased dispersal patterns, with male dispersal to a smaller extent (Marsh 1979b; Starin 1994; Struhsaker 1975; Chapter 9). At Kibale, ashy red colobus males are often in proximity to one another, supporting each other in inter-group contests, and grooming one another more often than expected by chance (Struhsaker 1980; Struhsaker and Leland 1979). Similarly, Werre (2000) describes most grooming as occurring among males in Niger Delta red colobus (*P. epieni*) at Gbanraun in Nigeria. At Taï, Upper Guinea red colobus grooming interactions were primarily observed between males and females, with males receiving most of the grooming (Korstjens 2001). For Temminck's red colobus at the Abuko Nature Reserve, The Gambia, Starin (1994) reports that dispersal occurred for both sexes with females dispersing voluntarily and males often being evicted as subadults and then re-entering their natal group as adults after a period of being solitary. Grooming interactions were primarily seen amongst females despite frequent female dispersal, which was likely due to a high rate of parallel transfer for females (Starin 1994). Coalition formation in Temminck's red colobus occurred primarily between the sexes, however. Only Zanzibar red colobus in degraded areas buck the typical red colobus dispersal pattern by showing male-biased dispersal patterns and despite this, most grooming occurs between the sexes, with females grooming males often. Siex (2003) suggests that females may be more philopatric in this area because of the aforementioned intense between-group conflict they experience.

Olive colobus monkeys also show the dispersal of both sexes and research done at Taï over 5-years indicates that female dispersal is more frequent than male dispersal (Korstjens and Schippers 2003). In agreement with these observations, olive colobus females show very little affiliation and coalitions among females have not been observed (Korstjens et al. 2007a). Grooming among adult males has not been noted in publications but males within the same group appear tolerant of one another and have been seen to form coalitions during inter-group encounters (Korstjens and Noë 2004; McGraw and Zuberbühler 2008).

To summarize this section, female dispersal occurs in all species of African colobine where dispersal patterns have been assessed, although the degree to which females transfer differs (ESM Table 17.3). Males also appear to disperse in all colobus species though again the degree to which this occurs depends on the species. Grooming and proximity among individuals in colobus groups tend to be as expected, given the dispersal patterns that have been observed. Males appear to often be more philopatric in red colobus and to a lesser extent in olive colobus, so female dispersal in these species may be at least partly explained by inbreeding avoidance. In black-and-white colobus, data thus far suggests that all males disperse, so female dispersal in this taxon may require additional explanation. For white-thighed colobus, there are several indications that females disperse to avoid infanticide and not because of food competition and this is discussed below (Sicotte et al. 2017; Teichroeb et al. 2009a) (see 'One Well-Studied Species').

Social Factors Constraining Group Size in African Colobines

The long-held belief that folivores were not affected by food competition (reviewed in Snaith and Chapman 2007), led researchers to wonder why many species of leaf-eaters do not form large groups, a phenomena termed the 'folivore paradox' (Janson and Goldsmith 1995; Steenbeek and van Schaik 2001). Given that large groups provide effective protection from predation (Hamilton 1971) and folivore group sizes were not thought to be constrained by WGS food competition, they were expected to live in large groups. One solution to the folivore paradox is that WGS feeding competition is occurring (as demonstrated above) and that its effect has been underestimated, so that actually it can lead to groups being capped at relatively small sizes (Snaith and Chapman 2005, 2007). This may well be the best solution to the folivore paradox, since even guerezas, that form the smallest groups in the colobus monkeys have shown negative effects of food depletion (Fashing 2001a; Harris et al. 2010). In addition, as demonstrated above, relatively little research has controlled for all of the ways that animals may compensate for the occurrence of WGS. Given this, does the 'paradox' still remain? Do many folivores form groups far below the threshold at which WGS competition for food appears to occur? Perhaps not. However, the social solution to the folivore paradox, which suggests that the threat of infanticide is constraining group size in folivores, does have some merit (Crockett and Janson 2000; Steenbeek and van Schaik 2001). This hypothesis proposes that since larger female groups are more often a target for immigrating males, which may increase infanticide rates, females may try to maintain smaller group sizes through several methods including, dispersing from large to small groups, evicting other females, resisting the immigration of new females or by group fission (Crockett and Janson 2000).

It is difficult to evaluate the contribution of the risk of infanticide by males to constraining group size with the current data available for colobus monkeys but black-and-white colobus provide some support for this hypothesis. Infanticide by males has only been observed in two species of black-and-white colobus (i.e. guerezas at Kibale, Onderdonk 2000; Harris and Monfort 2003; Chapman and Pavelka 2005; white-thighed colobus at Boabeng-Fiema, Teichroeb and Sicotte 2008a; Teichroeb et al. 2012) and one species of red colobus (ashy red colobus at Kibale, Struhsaker and Leland 1985). Infanticide risk has been implicated in constraining group sizes in guerezas, because they show much smaller group sizes than sympatric red colobus at Kibale but are ecologically very similar (Chapman and Pavelka 2005). Red colobus groups at Kibale, where infanticide by males appears to be rare (Chapman and Pavelka 2005; Struhsaker and Leland 1985), are not small and have been growing over time (Gogarten et al. 2014), which suggests that this social pressure is not negatively impacting group size. Rather, high predation risk for red colobus (Teelen 2008; Watts and Amsler 2013), may be driving large, multi-male groups (van Schaik and Hörstermann 1994) since male primates tend to be more vigilant than females (Cheney and Wrangham 1987) and they also engage in direct counter-attacks towards predators (e.g. Boesch 1994a; Stanford 1995, 1998a). At Boabeng-Fiema in Ghana, where infanticide by males in white-thighed colobus is relatively frequent (Teichroeb and Sicotte 2008a), it does appear to play a role in constraining group size (Teichroeb et al. 2012), though not below the size at which WGS occurs (see below). Thus, with the data available, the folivore paradox does not seem to be explained by infanticide risk in the colobus. Indeed, it is unclear whether or not there truly is a paradox because even small groups are affected by WGS. The occurrence of small groups in the colobines is likely a reflection of several costs to group living, which include both WGS and, in some species, infanticide by males. The next section, on white-thighed colobus, provides a good example as to how these differing constraints can play out.

One Well-Studied Species

So, how does infanticide risk affect social organization in folivores where scramble competition for food is known to limit group size? White-thighed colobus, which have now been studied at the Boabeng-Fiema Monkey Sanctuary (BFMS) in Ghana under the supervision of Pascale Sicotte (University of Calgary) for 20 years are an excellent case study for understanding the interaction of the constraints imposed by WGS food competition and infanticide risk. WGC and BGC competition for food also occur for this species and their contributions to the social organization and structure are informative.

At BFMS, about one quarter of groups are uni-male/multi-female and three quarters are multi-male/multi-female. Dispersal is male-biased with all males leaving their natal group, most before sexual maturity and dispersing secondarily throughout their lives (Teichroeb et al. 2011). Female dispersal is facultative, with some females dispersing and some remaining in their natal group and female dispersal occurs secondarily though less often than for males (Teichroeb et al. 2009a). All-male bands (AMBs) occur in the population but are not permanent. Dispersing males form groups (range: 2–7) that sometimes associate for a few months before they choose a bisexual group to attack and attempt immigration into (Saj and Sicotte 2005; Saj et al. 2005; Teichroeb and Sicotte 2008a; Teichroeb et al. 2011). These takeovers are typically successful but slow (mean duration: 7 months) with males from the AMB attempting to evict resident males and then one another. In contrast, group takeovers also occur by single adult males and these are usually quick and decisive (mean duration: 1 month) (Sicotte et al. 2017).

Infanticide by males appears to have a major influence on white-thighed colobus grouping patterns, which also affects how females experience food competition. At BFMS, 38.5% of infant mortality has been attributed to infanticide by males (Teichroeb and Sicotte 2008a). In all observed cases, the perpetrator has been a new immigrant male who became the alpha male, although attacks between groups also occur (Teichroeb et al. 2012). Infanticide is equally likely after fast takeovers by single males and after slow takeovers by AMB males (Sicotte et al. 2017). The sexual selection hypothesis for infanticide (Hrdy 1977b, 1979) has been supported in all observed cases at BFMS. Infanticidal males improve their chances of siring a female's next infant when they kill her current infant because female interbirth intervals are shortened and males have the opportunity to mate with the mother after her infant dies (Teichroeb and Sicotte 2008a; Teichroeb et al. 2012).

Immigrant males in white-thighed colobus are more attracted to larger female groups, which increases infanticide risk in larger groups (Teichroeb et al. 2011, 2012), a common finding in gregarious mammals (e.g. *Alouatta seniculus*, Crockett and Janson 2000; *Theropithecus gelada*, Dunbar 1984; *Panthera leo*, Packer et al. 1988). However, an investigation into group composition and infanticide risk in white-thighed colobus showed that, even when controlling for female group size, groups with relatively more males had significantly more male immigration and higher infanticide rates (Teichroeb et al. 2012). In this respect, white-thighed colobus differ from several other species where multi-male groups have lower rates of infanticide by males (e.g. *G. b. beringei*, Robbins 1995; *Semnopithecus sp.*, Newton 1986; but see Borries 1997). In white-thighed colobus, males in uni-male groups that are able to keep out immigrant males and successfully defend infants show several additional indicators of having better competitive ability compared to males in multi-male groups (i.e. performing longer displays and often winning in between-group encounters against larger, multi-male groups, Teichroeb and Sicotte 2010, 2018; Teichroeb et al. 2012).

The severe effect that infanticide by males has on female and sire reproductive success has led to the evolution of several counter-strategies in white-thighed colobus (Bădescu et al. 2016; Sicotte et al. 2017; Teichroeb and Sicotte 2008a; Teichroeb et al. 2009a; 2012). The most relevant of which, to socioecological theory, are evidence of a female preference for smaller, uni-male groups that tend to have high-quality resident males(s) (Teichroeb et al. 2012). Females demonstrate this preference in several ways. First, they tend to emigrate from larger groups and immigrate into smaller groups. Attempted transfers are also usually to smaller, uni-male groups if the resident male often wins in inter-group encounters against the male(s) in the female's own group. Second, mature, breeding females will force the emigration of young females that have just reached reproductive age in larger groups (13/23 cases of dispersal documented, 56.5%) (Teichroeb et al. 2009a). These young females may attempt to join a nearby group or may form their own group. Third, resident females will aggressively prevent new female immigration into their group, especially in large groups. Additionally, female white-thighed colobus voluntarily emigrate from groups where the male hierarchy is unstable (Sicotte et al. 2017; Teichroeb et al. 2009a). Furthermore, male takeovers in this species are often followed closely by female dispersal if the group is taken over by an AMB that has undecided dominance relationships. However, fast takeovers by single males have never been seen to be followed by female dispersal (Sicotte et al. 2017). Thus, in support of the social solution to the folivore paradox (Crockett and Janson 2000), larger multi-male groups in white-thighed colobus do have greater infanticide risk and are avoided by females. So, infanticide risk is constraining group size but importantly, so is WGS food competition (Teichroeb and Sicotte 2009; Teichroeb et al. 2012). Large groups may persist in the population because of predation risk or because food is patchy to some degree and better home ranges attract more females, but this remains to be substantiated.

Infanticide risk seems to play a prominent role in female preference for smaller groups with higher-quality males in white-thighed colobus, however these strategies have benefits for reducing WGS and WGC food competition, as well as improving competitive ability in BGC competition. First, individuals in smaller groups suffer less from WGS (Chapman and Chapman 2000c; Janson and Goldsmith 1995; Teichroeb and Sicotte 2009). Second, WGC competition for food would also be decreased in white-thighed colobus when breeding females force the emigration of young adult females (Teichroeb et al. 2009a). Wikberg and colleagues (2013) found that maturing females begin to challenge older females in the dominance hierarchy when they become full body size, leading to older females dropping in rank over time. Forcing these young females out of the group before this occurs, allows older females to avoid a drop in rank. Third, recall that in white-thighed colobus smaller, uni-male groups are better at defeating other groups in between-group encounters allowing a range expansion in lean seasons (Teichroeb and Sicotte 2018). Therefore, group size in white-thighed colobus appears to be constrained by several interacting pressures. While there is some support for the social solution to the folivore paradox (Crockett and Janson 2000), the situation is much more complicated than a single blanket solution allows.

Discussion

This overview of our understanding of the socioecology of African colobines demonstrates that the, often surprising, ecological flexibility of this group of animals makes it difficult to predict their social responses to food competition. Five key findings are evident. First, despite early assumptions, the diets of colobus monkeys are variable and mature leaves are often avoided (reviewed in Fashing 2011). This means that colobus do feed on food items that tend to be high quality (low in fibre and high in protein) and have clumped distributions, and which therefore cause competition. Second, when researchers actually look for WGS competition while controlling for differences in range quality for different-sized groups (Chapman and Chapman 2000c), evidence that colobus monkey foraging efficiency is negatively affected by large group size emerges (Gillespie and Chapman 2001; Harris et al. 2010; Snaith and Chapman 2007, 2008; Teichroeb and Sicotte 2009, 2018). What is not clear yet in most populations, however, is whether the intensity of WGS is enough to lead to a negative effect on female reproductive rates (ESM Table 17.2) and most species remain to be studied in regard to the occurrence and effects of WGS. Third, WGC competition is evident for a few species where it has been looked for and even if food is only contestable for brief periods at certain times of year, this appears to be enough to lead to female dominance hierarchies (Korstjens 2001; Wikberg et al. 2013). These dominance hierarchies tend to be individualistic and co-occur with female dispersal, which is also the case in several Asian colobines (Chapter 16). Fourth, BGC competition is also evident in several populations of colobus monkeys that have been studied, however again the social response appears to differ from what is typically seen in cercopithecines. Rather than matrilineal groups becoming ubiquitous to defend the range against other groups (Wrangham 1980), males may be more commonly involved in resource defence in colobus monkeys (Fashing 2001c; Harris 2005, 2006a, 2010; Sicotte and MacIntosh 2004; Teichroeb and Sicotte 2018). Finally, the fifth thing that became clear during this review is that there is not much support for the social solution to the folivore paradox thus far in the colobus monkeys. Many species actually form quite large groups with multiple males, which may be due to predation risk in Africa (van Schaik and Hörstermann 1994), and the effects of food depletion are seen in even the smallest groups (i.e. guerezas, Harris et al. 2010). Thus, it seems more likely that the costs of WGS and its occurrence have been underestimated (Snaith and Chapman 2005, 2007). Infanticide risk does play a part in limiting group size in white-thighed colobus but groups do get large enough to be affected by WGS (Teichroeb et al. 2012; Teichroeb and Sicotte 2018). In other colobus monkeys, there is almost no evidence for the occurrence of infanticide on a regular basis and red colobus form such large groups that the folivore paradox does not seem to really apply to them. Our overall picture of all that constrains colobus monkeys is still skewed however, due to the lack of data on so many species.

How Do African Colobines Fit Current Socioecological Models?

Given the evidence for different types of food competition in African colobines, as well as patterns of dispersal and female dominance relationships, it seems that this group of animals does not fit well into any of the four social categories presented by Sterck et al. (1997): Dispersal Egalitarian, Resident Egalitarian, Resident Nepotistic or Resident Nepotistic Tolerant (Table 17.1). Rather, the picture that emerges from the species of colobus monkeys for which we have data is WGS food competition, at least seasonal WGC and fairly high BGC (likely depending on population density), co-occurring with female dispersal, linear, individualistic female dominance hierarchies and fairly weak affiliative relationships between females. This suggests that the African colobine pattern may be best described by the intermediate situation between WGS and WGC that Sterck and colleagues describe (1997, page 295); where 'food distribution is such that contest occurs, but the benefits are too small to lead to predictable kin support and consistent philopatry (which have costs). Females are thus still likely to disperse despite their forming decided dominance relations' (Figure 17.1). In the two colobus species where we understand the form that female dominance hierarchies take, king colobus and white-thighed colobus, this intermediate situation seems to be occurring. In both species, we see linear female dominance hierarchies that co-occur with female dispersal (Korstjens et al. 2002; Wikberg et al. 2013). The individualistic nature of these hierarchies means that it is possible for transferring females to enter groups without related allies and fight their way up the hierarchy in the new group. There is also evidence in white-thighed colobus that these hierarchies are age-inversed, such that younger, stronger females can attain higher ranks (Wikberg et al. 2013).

It appears that the seasonal nature of WGC competition that these folivores experience does not strongly select for kin-based coalitions to defend food, which would lead to nepotistic female hierarchies. Since this competition is transitory in nature compared to the WGC experienced by species with nepotistic female hierarchies, female dominance hierarchies become important for controlling aggression only at certain times of the year. In addition, the evolutionary benefits of female dispersal can be great and outweigh the benefits of kin-based coalitions to defend food sporadically. In species that usually show female philopatry, it can be extremely costly for females to transfer between groups, leading to them experiencing intense aggression from coalitions of females that can even be fatal (Hammond et al. 2006; Jack and Fedigan 2009; Miller 1998; Payne et al. 2003). Indeed, female philopatry tends to be strongly conserved in evolution (Di Fiore and Rendall 1994), suggesting

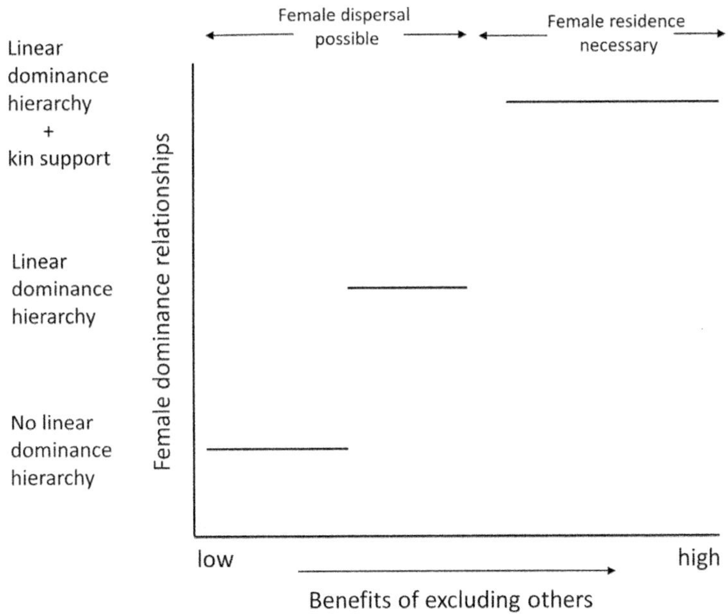

Figure 17.1 Replication of Sterck et al. (1997, figure 5) showing predicted relationships between the reproductive benefits of excluding other females from resources and the impacts on female dominance relationships and dispersal patterns. Reproduced with permission from Springer

that once female dispersal is lost in a lineage it is difficult to get back. Females can benefit in many ways by being able to disperse. They can disperse to smaller groups or those with a better home range to decrease WGS feeding competition (Sterck 1997). It is also the best way for females to practice mate choice since most primates live in bisexual groups and only have within-group males as options for mates unless they disperse (Fedigan 1992; Sterck 1997). Perhaps most important though, female dispersal can lead to several powerful counter-strategies to infanticide by males (van Schaik 1996; Sterck and Korstjens 2000), including choosing the best sire/protector, dispersing with deposed males, and avoiding risky factors like unstable male dominance hierarchies (reviewed in Palombit 2015; Sicotte et al. 2017). Some degree of female dispersal is seen in all the colobus monkey species where it has been investigated, suggesting that all of these benefits outweigh kin-based coalitions to defend food sources which are only defensible sometimes.

The social response to BGC competition in colobus monkeys may more commonly involve male resource defence than in other primate taxa (Fashing 2001c; Harris 2005, 2006, 2010; Sicotte and MacIntosh 2004; Teichroeb and Sicotte 2018). This has been shown in black-and-white colobus monkeys, and the potential for male resource defence in red and olive colobus deserves further investigation. This strategy by males may have also evolved due to the importance of female dispersal for colobus monkeys because it gives males an opportunity to demonstrate their mate quality to females.

So, given the predictions of socioecological models, what effects could the male strategy of defending resources for females in BGC have on female social behaviour and dispersal patterns? And how could this be expressed given that female colobus monkeys appear to also be experiencing a mixture of WGS with seasonal impacts of BGC competition? In Figure 17.2, I present two flow charts to summarize how these pressures may work to shape African colobine societies. I predict that the differences in group size, dispersal patterns and male strategies that we observe between black-and-white (Figure 17.2a) and red colobus (Figure 17.2b) are due to differences in predation risk, ultimately, which has cascading effects on other social strategies. I do not present a scenario for olive colobus since they are so unique and the most important resource for them may be their partner guenon group (Chapter 11).

For both red and black-and-white colobus monkeys, WGS competition for food may occur throughout the year and likely becomes greater in lean seasons (e.g. Teichroeb and Sicotte 2018), which makes small groups beneficial because there are fewer mouths to feed (Chapman and Chapman 2000c). However, if BGC competition is also occurring throughout the year and intensifies when resources are rare, this would select for larger group size, since larger groups tend to win in between-group contests by overwhelming their competitors (Crofoot and Wrangham 2010). If males take on the defence of the range for females though, contests between groups become more about the quality of males and how well they work together, than about group size per se. In black-and-white colobus, the differences in male quality may be large (Teichroeb et al. 2012) or collective action problems are serious enough in multi-male groups, that one-male groups tend to do better in resource defence (at least in guerezas and white-thighed colobus) (Harris 2006, 2010; Teichroeb et al. 2012; Teichroeb and Sicotte 2018). This also makes small groups more advantageous because one male is able to monopolize them. Smaller female groups also have the advantage of being less of a target to infanticidal immigrant males, which is an additional important advantage for females (Figure 17.2a). These factors may explain the smaller group sizes that we see in the black-and-white colobus relative to red colobus.

For red colobus, predation risk is much higher than for black-and-white colobus, at least in forests where they co-occur with chimpanzees. The reasons for this are debated but researchers have hypothesized that red colobus suffer more predation due to their conspicuousness (i.e. noisy groups) and relative ease of capture compared to black-and-white colobus (Mitani and Watts 1999), leading to chimpanzees in particular having evolved a preference for red colobus as prey (Stanford 1998a). The fact that predation pressure is so high (van Schaik and Höstermann 1994; Teelen 2008; Watts and Amsler 2013) means that large groups remain advantageous for dilution and detection (Hamilton 1971), and multiple males become an asset to defend the group from predators (Boesch 1994a; Stanford 1995, 1998a; Struhsaker 2000b) but perhaps also to defend resources. To decrease collection action problems, it then becomes beneficial for males to be closely related when working together to defend the group (Stanford 1998a). Male kinship and the ability for females to confuse paternity in multi-male groups may be what keeps infanticide rates low in red colobus (Figure 17.2b).

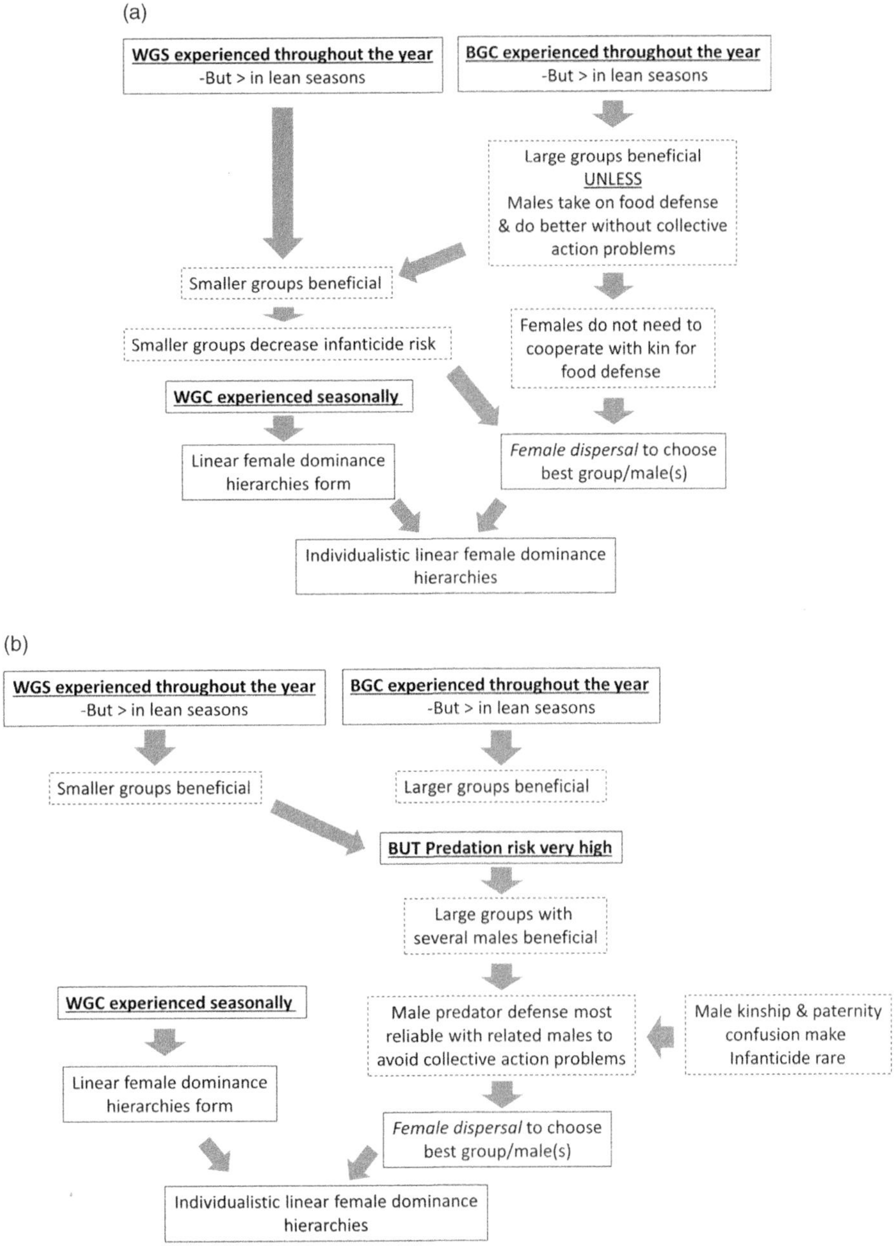

Figure 17.2 Summary of the ways that (a) black-and-white colobus and (b) red colobus may be reacting to a competitive regime with WGS, seasonal WGC and BGC. Solid boxes represent ecological effects and their ultimate outcomes, while ticked boxes represent resulting social strategies. The main difference between the groups is the greater predation risk for red colobus, which leads to different group size requirements and different strategies by males, which in turn influence infanticide risk.

In both scenarios, for black-and-white and red colobus, since females do not have to stay in their natal groups and bond with other females to defend resources, they can disperse allowing them to choose the best situation for them in terms of group size, male quality and male number. In addition, since males take on resource defence, females do not have to appease other females to acquire their help in defence of the home range, so they can form linear dominance hierarchies to deal with the seasonal impact of WGC competition.

Summary and Conclusions

Research over the last 20 years has greatly increased our understanding of the socioecology of the colobus monkeys. However, there are still large gaps in our knowledge because many species have not been studied at all and those that have been studied have often not been examined intensively or with individual recognition. For many of the species where research has been done, we now know their diets and activity budgets and have some understanding of their natural history, however we do not yet fully understand how these ecological factors are shaping competitive regimes and female social relationships. It appears that African colobines do not fit the four social categories normally linked to the socioecological model but rather are falling somewhere in between WGS and WGC. This appears to give rise to very specific male strategies, like male defence of food resources for females, which alters female social strategies in interesting ways and changes how the sexes affect one another. More research on a greater number of colobus species is urgently needed given the state of primate conservation (Estrada et al. 2017). There is a very real possibility that we will lose more colobus monkey species to extinction without there ever being any research on them, as we likely already have with Miss Waldron's red colobus (McGraw 2005).

Acknowledgements

I thank Cyril Grueter, Alexandra Miller and especially Liesbeth Sterck, whose comments improved this chapter.

18 Causes and Consequences of the Formation of Multilevel Societies in Colobines

Cyril C. Grueter

Introduction

Colobines display an array of different types of social organization (Chapters 9–17), with social organization meaning 'group composition and spatio-temporal cohesion' (Kappeler and van Schaik 2002). Various langurs live in uni-male groups with high degrees of territoriality or largely non-overlapping home ranges [e.g. Hose's langur *Presbytis hosei* (Mitchell 1994); purple-faced langur *Semnopithecus vetulus* (Rudran 1973a); and Cat Ba langur *T. poliocephalus* (Hendershott et al. 2016)]. Olive and black-and-white colobus (genera *Colobus* and *Procolobus*) are generally found in small groups with one or more males and several females with their offspring, and groups tend to have overlapping home ranges (Fashing 2011). When social units contain one or two additional males, as seen for example in some langurs (dusky langur, *Trachypithecus obscurus*; Curtin 1980); Indochinese grey langur (*Trachypithecus crepusculus*; Koenig and Borries 2012), then they are essentially multimale-multifemale groups. Much larger multi-male groups are known from a few species/populations of Hanuman langurs (*Semnopithecus* spp.) (e.g. Borries 2000; Newton 1988) and red colobus (*Piliocolobus* spp.) (Struhsaker 2010). Simakobu (*Simias concolor*) were assigned to a monogamous system by early authors (Tilson 1977), but single-male, single-female groups are likely the result of excessive hunting and habitat disturbance reducing group size (Erb et al. 2012b; Watanabe 1981). Finally, in some Asian colobines (most prominently the snub-nosed monkeys, *Rhinopithecus* spp.) and one subspecies of African colobine, social organization assumes a modular form, i.e. social units are characterized by a complete absence of exclusive territories, occupy wholly shared ranges and are nested within a larger, bounded social matrix (Grueter and van Schaik 2010; Kirkpatrick 2011; Kirkpatrick and Grueter 2010; Miller et al. 2020b,c; Yeager and Kirkpatrick 1998) (Figure 18.1).[1]

Multilevel societies (alternatively known as modular societies) encompass two or more nested grouping levels and represent 'social arrangements in which regular or constant proximity as well as coordinated activity among [socio-spatially distinct]

[1] The distinction between modular and non-modular groups is not totally clear-cut. In some taxa of colobines, uni- or multi-male groups have partly overlapping ranges and sometimes peacefully feed together in the same patch and roost at the same site, e.g. capped langurs (*Trachypithecus pileatus*) (Stanford 1991a), golden langurs (*T. geei*) (Mukherjee and Saha 1974), and black colobus (*Colobus satanas*) (Fleury and Gautier-Hion 1999).

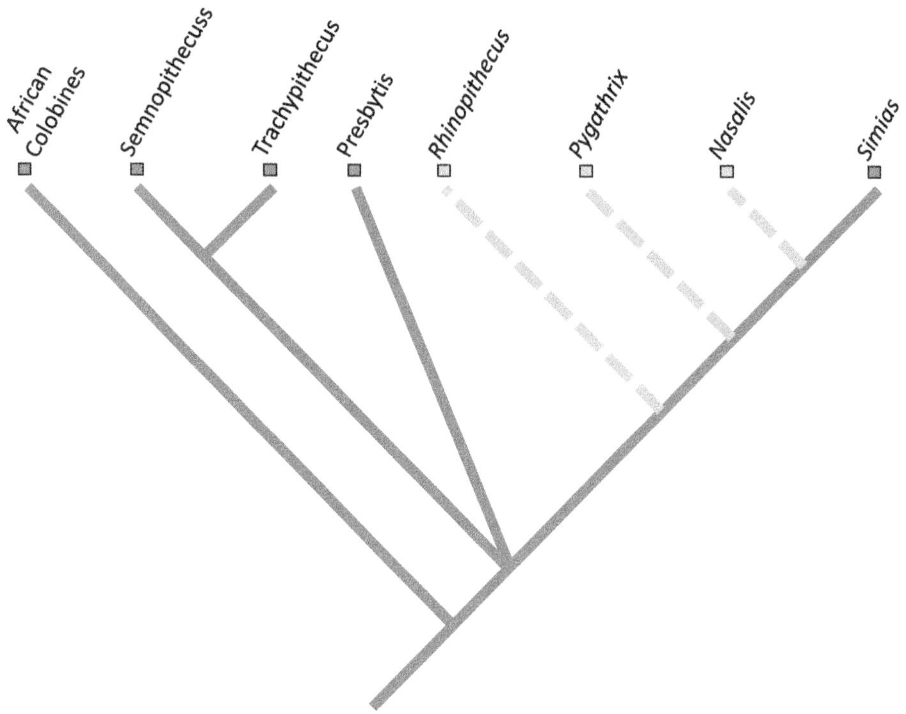

Figure 18.1 Phylogram showing the distribution of modular vs. non-modular social systems in (Asian) colobines. The unbroken lines correspond to non-modular taxa, whereas the dashed lines correspond to modular taxa. African colobines as a whole are classified as 'non-modular', although one species of *Colobus* has recently been described as exhibiting a multilevel system. Phylogenies are based on Perelman et al. (2011) and Roos et al. (2011)

subunits is the norm' (Grueter et al. 2012c: 993–994). The basal unit is typically a spatio-temporally cohesive one-male unit (OMU) or 'harem' with one adult male and one to several females.[2] By coalescing at varying temporal scales and foraging, resting and travelling together, these core units form one or more grouping levels such as bands, herds and troops (Dunbar and Dunbar 1975a; Grueter et al. 2012a, 2017b; Grueter and Zinner 2004; Kummer 1968; Qi et al. 2004; Stammbach 1987; Zhang et al. 2006). Social interactions among individuals occur both within and between the social layers, but affiliative behaviour is clearly more frequently seen within the core unit tier, and core units also tend to represent the reproductive units (Grueter et al. 2017a; Patzelt et al. 2014; Snyder-Mackler et al. 2012; Stammbach 1987; Yeager and Kirkpatrick 1998; Zhang et al. 2012). The nature of intra-unit relationships and the intricacies of the social network differ among species with multilevel societies and depend – among others – on patterns of philopatry and

[2] Occasionally subadult males are also associated with OMUs, e.g. Huang Z et al. (2017a, table 1) and Guo et al. (2017, table 2).

phylogeny (Matsuda et al. 2012b). Non-reproductive males usually form all-male units (AMUs) that are often loosely attached to the bands (Ren et al. 2000; Swedell 2011).

A member of a multilevel society lives simultaneously in both the core unit tier and the higher level (e.g. band) tier, and hence can reap the benefits (and suffer the consequences) that both the core grouping and the band-level grouping offer; examples of the former include social support (e.g. Silk et al. 2009) and access to reproductive partners (e.g. Kawai et al. 1983), and examples of the latter include collective defence or safety in numbers (Grueter and van Schaik 2010; Lehmann et al. 2014; see below).

Virtually all odd-nosed monkeys except simakobu[3] are nowadays generally classified as having a multilevel organization, although the existing evidence is inconclusive for the grey-shanked douc langur (*Pygathrix cinerea*). It was predicted that supergroups of Adolf Friedrichs's Angolan colobus (also known as Rwenzori black-and-white colobus) (*Colobus angolensis ruwenzorii*) in montane Nyungwe National Park, Rwanda, may exhibit a multilevel structure due to similarities in socioecological parameters shared with snub-nosed monkeys (Fashing et al. 2007b) (Figure 18.2). This species does not seem to have a modal social organization, as it exhibits broad intraspecific variation in social organization, likely in response to habitat variation. Group size ranges from <10 in coastal *C. a. palliatus* (Dunham 2017a; Lowe and Sturrock 1998; Moreno-Black and Maples 1977) to over 500 at Nyungwe (Miller et al. 2020b, c). In addition to the large supergroup formation observed in Nyungwe, there are anecdotal accounts of smaller *C. angolensis* groups temporarily fusing to form groups of 30–50 individuals in Uganda (Oates 1974) and Kenya (Moreno-Black and Bent 1982). Recent research at two different sites has attempted to dissect the 'anatomy' of these supergroups. Preliminary data corroborate the existence of subgroups within the larger group. These subgroups are predominatly multi-male at Nyungwe (Miller et al. 2020b, c) and a mix of multi-male and one-male units at Lake Nabugabo Uganda (Stead and Teichroeb 2019). It was suggested by Fashing et al. (2007b) that these supergroups are made possible by the unusually high quality and abundance of mature leaves and widespread availability of lichens in the habitat (Fimbel et al. 2001). Lichens constitute a seasonally important food resource for these colobus (Miller et al. 2020a; Vedder and Fashing 2002). This is supported by the fact that, at a lower altitude field site (Lake Nabugabo) where lichens are largely unavailable and the diet is made up of mostly young leaves and fruit, *C. a. ruwenzorii* show high fission-fusion dynamics among core units (Stead and Teichroeb 2019). Predation from chimpanzees may also contribute to large groups (Fashing et al. 2007b); however, a convergence with snub-nosed monkeys would suggest that conspecific threat also influences aggregations (see below).

Besides colobines, multilevel societies have also evolved in the papionin and hominin lineage (Grueter et al. 2012a). Geladas (*Theropithecus gelada*), hamadryas

[3] The loss of a multilevel system is likely a derived feature in simakobu.

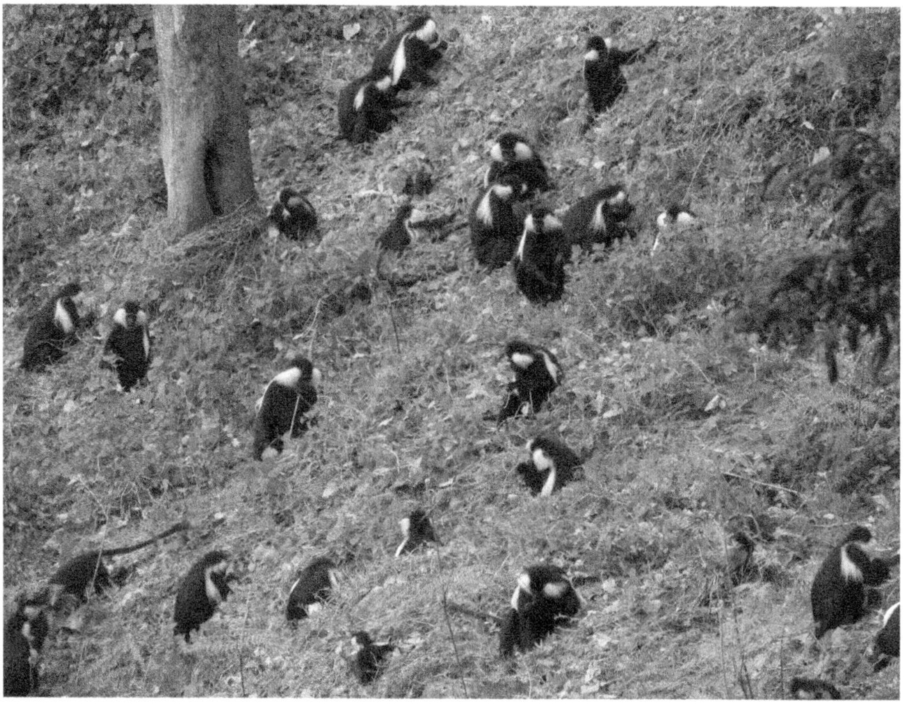

Figure 18.2 Adolf Friedrichs's Angolan colobus foraging for Sericostachys vines and ground herbs in Nyungwe, Rwanda. Photo by Alexandra Miller

baboons (*Papio hamadryas*), Guinea baboons (*Papio papio*) (Grueter 2014; Patzelt et al. 2014), and also the overwhelming majority of human societies form multilevel (multifamily) groups (Chapais 2013; Grueter et al. 2012a; Grueter and White 2014; Rodseth et al. 1991).

Key Features of Multilevel Societies in Snub-Nosed Monkeys and Other Asian Colobines

Social Organization and Social Structure

Until relatively recently, the social organization and structure of snub-nosed monkeys was rather enigmatic due to the virtually insurmountable obstacles of following these extremely large, wide-ranging and elusive bands through their rugged montane terrain. However, a few studies have managed to yield preliminary data on social organization without individual identification, i.e. by relying on data of distances between individuals of different age/sex classes, nearest neighbours and grooming behaviour (Grueter et al. 2017a; Kirkpatrick et al. 1998). Habituation efforts in combination with limited provisioning at a few sites in China have opened up possibilities for individual recognition and studies of social dynamics in as yet unprecedented detail[4] (e.g. Huang Z et al. 2017a; Xiang et al. 2014; Zhu et al. 2016; Figure 18.3).

A modular group differs from a multimale-multifemale group in that females tend to cluster around a single male, thus forming distinct OMUs which are not isolated entities but are part of a larger band (Grueter et al. 2017a; Kirkpatrick et al. 1998; Yeager 1990a; Zhang et al. 2006). Therefore, a good criterion for identifying multilevel societies is a much greater likelihood of an adult male having a female as nearest neighbour than another male (although this obviously does not apply to bachelor groupings) (Grueter et al. 2017a). OMUs can be defined by proximity maintenance among members and significantly higher frequencies of affiliative social exchange with members of their own unit than with other units (Grueter et al. 2017a; Qi et al. 2004; Zhang et al. 2006). Social interactions within core OMUs were shown to be far more close-knit than within the next higher level they are embedded in, i.e. the band (Yan 2012; Zhang et al. 2006). The number of OMUs per band correlates with band size, but few accurate data exist on the number of OMUs in wild groups which would require individual or unit identification, although proxies have been used to distinguish between units such as time intervals between passing individuals in group progressions (Grueter et al. 2017a; Liu Zehua et al. 2007) and proximity patterns when resting in the canopy.

The importance of cross-sex bonds versus female-female bonds in forming the 'glue' keeping an OMU together appears to vary among species and sometimes changes between the mating and birth season (Arseneau-Robar et al. 2018; Grueter 2009; Wang et al. 2013; Wei et al. 2012; Yu et al. 2013; Zhang et al. 2006). Contrary to hamadryas baboons, where males engage in active herding to keep females from straying (Kummer 1968; Swedell and Schreier 2009), herding is not used by odd-nosed colobine males (e.g. proboscis monkey, *Nasalis larvatus*) (Yeager 1991b). Males enforce cohesiveness via more subtle means, e.g. policing behaviour without the use of overt aggression in response to conflicts between females (Grueter 2004; Ren et al. 1991).

In multilevel colobines, behavioural interactions among units are generally neutral (e.g. Yeager 1992), but aggression can ensue (e.g. Zhang et al. 2008b). Males and females that have stayed together in the same unit for some time frequently aid each other in inter-unit aggressive interactions (Zhang et al. 2008b). Zhao et al. (2013), however, report that adult males are the primary participants in inter-unit conflicts, with females taking part in them only sporadically. It has also become known that there are cross-cutting interconnections among OMUs that take various forms, e.g. mergers of OMUs (i.e. females of different OMUs start associating as a single OMU and the surplus male vanishes) (Zhang et al. 2008a), the occasional expression of affiliative behaviours including grooming between females (Zhang et al. 2008a), playing among juveniles (Ren et al. 2000), allomaternal assistance/infant handling

[4] Provisioning may affect group dynamics and social interactions.

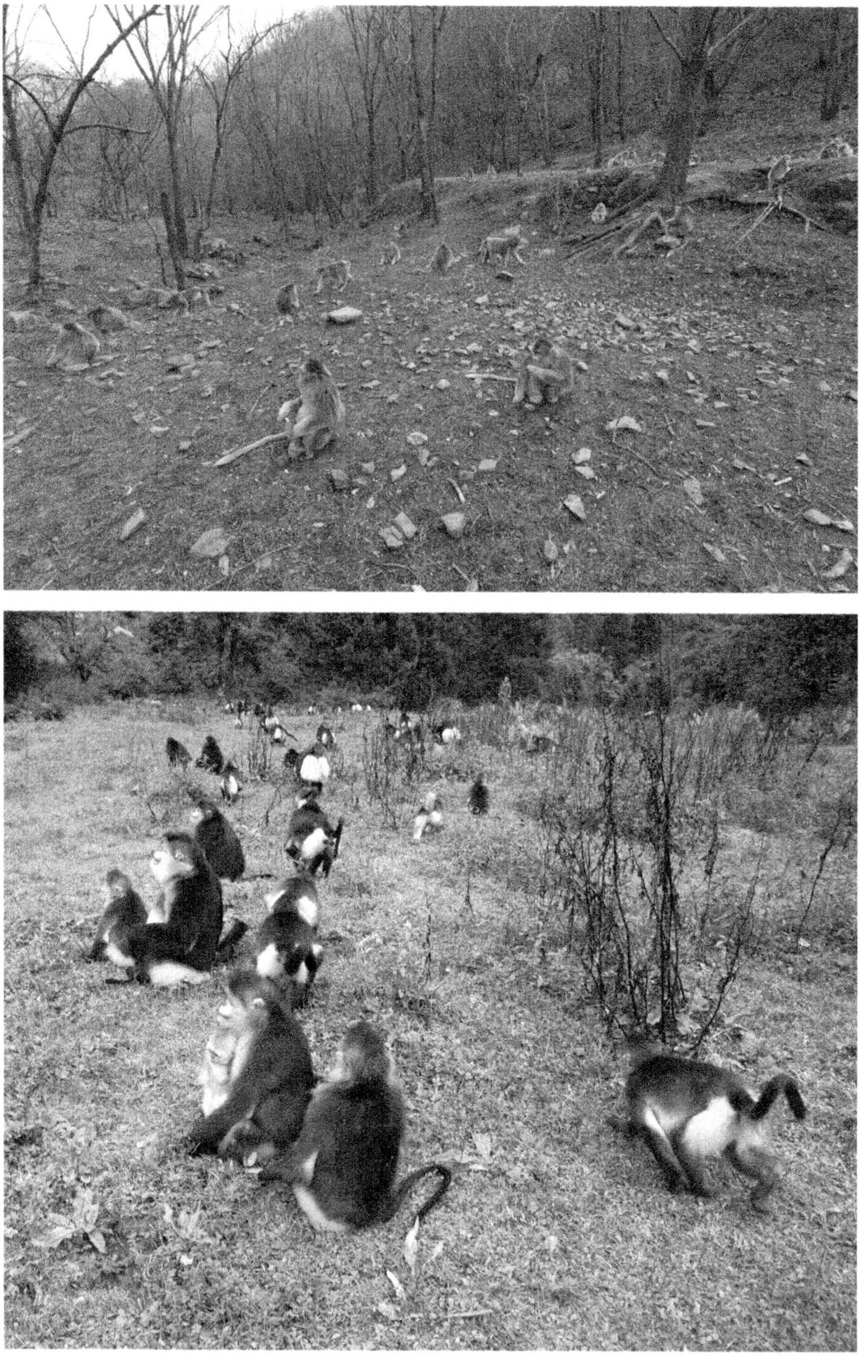

Figure 18.3 Habituated snub-nosed monkey groups: (a) golden snub-nosed monkey (*Rhinopithecus roxellana*) at the Zhouzhi/Yuhuangmiao field site in Shaanxi Province (photo by Xiaoguang Qi); (b) black-and-white snub-nosed monkey (*Rhinopithecus bieti*) at the Xiangguqing/Tacheng field site in Yunnan Province (photo by Pingfen Zhu). The terrestrial habitus depicted in these photos is partly influenced by artificial provisioning (although these colobines are semi-terrestrial under completely wild conditions).

(Ren et al. 2012a; Zhang et al. 2012), extra-unit copulations and paternities (Guo et al. 2010; Qi et al. 2020; Zhao et al. 2005), as well as collective action involving males of separate OMUs for mutualistic benefits (Xiang et al. 2014).

Males typically emigrate from their natal unit when reaching adolescence, but female dispersal has been documented in several multilevel colobines as well (Chang et al. 2014; Guo et al. 2015; Zhao et al. 2008a). Emigrating males typically join an AMU (Murai 2004a; Yao et al. 2011), but sometimes succeed in establishing a new OMU in their natal band or another band (Huang Z et al. 2017a). Females directly transfer into another OMU. In golden snub-nosed monkeys, females (adults and subadults) often change residency between OMUs within the band, and less often also leave their natal band altogether and immigrate into a neighbouring band (Guo et al. 2015; Qi et al. 2009; Zhao et al. 2008a). Female golden snub-nosed monkeys have a propensity for transferring into social units which contain female relatives (Guo et al. 2015). Female dispersal within bands likely contributes to inter-unit tolerance and sporadic affiliation among females and thereby fortifies the maintenance of the multilevel society.

Little is known about how neighbouring bands partition the landscape and whether inter-band relations are best characterized by attraction or repulsion, and how all-male units and single males move in relation to each other and reproductive bands. Cursory anecdotal evidence indicates tolerance at the band level. Bleisch and Xie (1998) for instance found that bands of grey snub-nosed monkeys (*Rhinopithecus brelichi*) at Fanjingshan did not compete when they encountered each other, but rather fused together. When bands of golden snub-nosed monkeys in the Qinling region encountered each other at some feeding sites, they exhibited little aggression (Chen et al. 1989; Ren et al. 2000).

It has recently been argued that there may be social tiers above the band level in snub-nosed monkeys, i.e. that breeding bands (as well as all-male groupings and solitary males) are linked with each other as part of a larger community ('troop') (Qi et al. 2014). This assumption is based on the observation that two bands at Zhouzhi spent some time in a state of close proximity or 'fusion'[5] (ibid.) and also that entire OMUs switched residency in bands (Qi et al. 2009, 2014). Moreover, Qi and colleagues (2014) make the distinction between 'bands' which contain a set of reproductive units only and 'herds' which also contain non-reproductive units[6] (see also Huang Z et al. 2017a).

[5] Existing data on spatial association patterns need to be complemented with field-based observational data on individual interactions among different tiers to validate the proposed supra-band structure of the golden snub-nosed monkeys multilevel society.

[6] The 'herd' level is based on observations of bachelor groups interacting with bisexual group. In many other primate species, bachelor groups are part of the social landscape, but their proximity to reproductive group does not merit the proclamation of a multilevel system. It is therefore unclear if the proposed 'herd' level is biologically meaningful.

Fission-Fusion in Multilevel Societies

While fission-fusion dynamics, i.e. spatio-temporal variation in cohesion of group members and subgroup size/composition (Aureli and Schaffner 2017; Aureli et al. 2008), are typically associated with species living in multimale-multifemale groups such as spider monkeys (*Ateles* spp.) (e.g. Symington 1990), and chimpanzees (e.g. Goodall 1968), they also characterize multilevel colobines to varying degrees (see also Chapter 12). In the context of multilevel societies, fission-fusion occurs along 'predefined societal seams' such as those between OMUs (Couzin and Laidre 2009: R634; Grueter et al. 2012a). It is useful to distinguish between short and long-term patterns of fission, which can coexist in a single taxon. In black-and-white snub-nosed monkeys for example, short-term fission-fusion usually occurs over the course of a foraging day and as a result of logistics of travel, food distribution or human disturbance (Grueter et al. 2017a; Kirkpatrick 1996); longer-term fissioning lasting several days or weeks has been interpreted as a response to a dwindling availability of preferred food resources (Ren et al. 2012b).

In the case of grey snub-nosed monkeys, fission-fusion seems to take place on an even larger timescale: in some months of spring-summer and autumn large groupings of sometimes over 400 animals are seen, but in winter they split up temporarily into several smaller groups with 50–200 animals (Guo et al. 2017; Nie et al. 2009). Whether these larger groupings constitute a higher-order level in the grey snub-nosed monkey multilevel system (similar to the troops proposed for golden snub-nosed monkeys) or are analogous to bands in other snub-nosed monkey species is uncertain. Fission-fusion dynamics also characterize Adolf Friedrichs's Angolan colobus; at Lake Nabugabo, core units fission and fuse with one another throughout the day. In 12 months of follows of one core unit per day (150 days) within a band of 12 units, core units had an average of 2.75 other core units within 50 m and were only alone 23% of the time (Stead and Teichroeb 2019). Hierarchical cluster analysis showed preferential associations of core units indicating a clan level of organization within the band. Thus, at least three tiers of social organization are present: the core unit, clan and band (Stead and Teichroeb 2019). In Nyungwe, band size was significantly larger in months when new leaves were in higher abundance. Moreover, the larger group was sometimes seen to break up in response to attacks by chimpanzees (Miller et al. 2020c).

Evolution of Multilevel Societies in Colobines

Essentially two major evolutionary pathways producing multilevel systems in primates have been identified. In papionins (gelada, hamadryas baboon) and hominins, reconstructions point to a pattern whereby ancestrally mixed-sex groups underwent permanent internal fission (Barton 2000; Grueter et al. 2012a; Swedell and Plummer 2012).[7] In Asian colobines, on the other hand, amalgamation of ancestrally

[7] For a partly alternative model (the 'Large Fission-Fusion Society Model'), see van Schaik (2016) (pp. 306–308).

autonomous units into band-like clusters appears phylogenetically more parsimonious (Grueter et al. 2012a). The multilevel society based on multi-male units observed in Adolf Friedrichs's Angolan colobus may also have originated through the merger of ancestrally solitary units; extant, closely related species of African colobines [black colobus (*Colobus satanus*), guereza (*C. guereza*)] have been seen to form multi-male units with sometimes greatly overlapping home ranges (Fleury and Gautier-Hion 1999; von Hippel 1996), so it is likely that extensive home range overlap among multi-male units paved the way for the fusion of multi-male units into a multilevel society (Miller et al. 2020b,c; Stead and Teichroeb 2019).

The Permissive Basis and Adaptive Significance of Multilevel Societies

Primate social systems, i.e. the spatio-temporal organization of primate females (and indirectly also of males) and their social relationships, result from the combined interactions of individuals (Hinde 1976), which themselves are shaped by ecological factors such as distribution of resources and predation threat (Alexander 1974; Clutton-Brock 2016; van Schaik 1983; Schülke and Ostner 2012; Sterck et al. 1997; Terborgh and Janson 1986), and social factors such as sexual conflict, moulded by life history (Clutton-Brock and Parker 1995; van Schaik 1996; van Schaik and Kappeler 1997). Social organization may also partially be accounted for by phylogenetic inertia (Di Fiore and Rendall 1994) and thus, limited social plasticity and/or by factors correlated with phylogeny, such as life history. Since the precursors to modularity in Asian colobines seem to have been autonomous OMUs, the question arises as to what causal factors prompted existing OMUs to coalesce into bands and what ecological preconditions need to be in place for such supergroups to form.

Higher-level social associations such as module-based bands are expected to be more likely to become established when ecological conditions are such that they do not have a constraining effect on grouping (within certain margins). Without a sufficiently abundant resource base, the prerequisite for the evolution of supergroups is not met (see Rodman 1988). The staple foods of many multilevel colobines appear to be fairly abundant (e.g. lichens in black-and-white snub-nosed monkeys (Grueter et al. 2009b; Kirkpatrick et al. 1998), non-ephemeral young leaves in proboscis monkeys (Boonratana 1993; Matsuda et al. 2009a) and lichens and mature foliage in Adolf Friedrichs's Angolan colobus (Fimbel et al. 2001; Miller et al. 2020a), so the foraging or ranging costs imposed by coalescing into bands are most likely relatively low in these taxa (Grueter and van Schaik 2010).[8] Ulibarri (2013) showed for red-shanked doucs (*Pygathrix nemaeus*) that greater young leaf availability (indicating relaxed ecological constraints) permits greater fusion through less competition. Similarly, in proboscis monkeys, the local density of social units has been shown

[8] Nevertheless, temporary fissioning can occur, presumably due to increased competition for food; e.g. in black-and-white snub-nosed monkeys a decrease in the availability of bamboo shoots appeared to trigger subgrouping behaviour, which suggests that fissions were a response to increasing levels of food competition (Ren et al. 2012b).

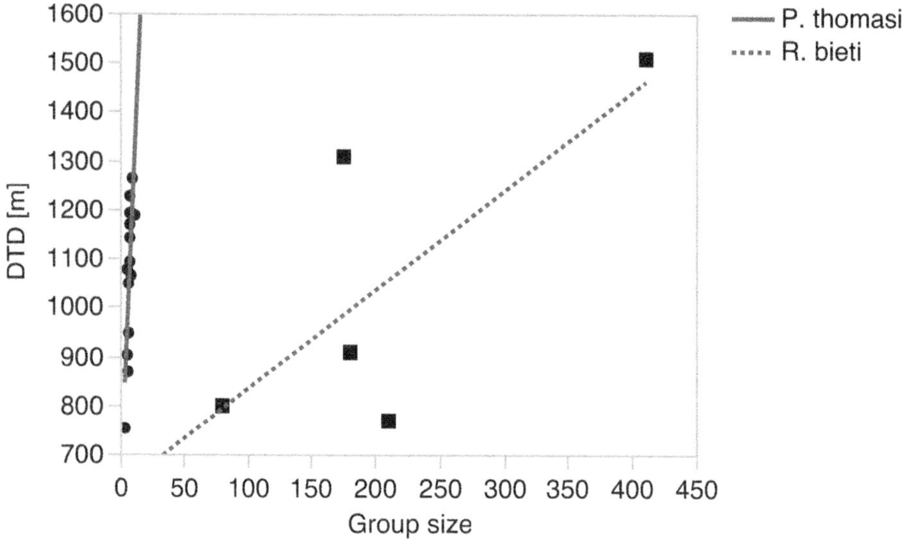

Figure 18.4 Regressions of group size against daily travel distance (DTD) for several groups of temperate-living and modular black-and-white snub-nosed monkeys and tropical-living and non-modular Thomas langurs (*Presbytis thomasi*). Group size refers to band size in black-and-white snub-nosed monkeys. The squares designate black-and-white snub-nosed monkeys, the circles Thomas langurs. Slopes in the non-modular species are steeper by a factor of 30, indicating significant foraging costs (scramble competition) that prevent higher-level groupings.

to be influenced by temporal changes in food availability (Matsuda et al. 2010a). That band size is constrained by the availability of resources and patch sizes is indicated by the fact that Asian colobine bands are larger in more temperate forests where foods seem to occur in larger patches (Grueter et al. 2012c).

A commonly applied operational definition for within-group scramble competition is a positive association between group size and home range size or day journey length (Chapman and Chapman 2000c; Janson and Goldsmith 1995; Takasaki 1981). Such a relationship is expected since larger groups deplete patches more quickly, and in order to avoid food deficiency, they need to expand their search efforts (Janson and van Schaik 1988; van Schaik and van Noordwijk 1988). Other behavioural indicators of scramble competition are time engaged in travelling (Gogarten et al. 2014; Isbell and Young 1993) or feeding (Saj and Sicotte 2007b; Snaith and Chapman 2007). By regressing daily path length and home range size against group size in black-and-white snub-nosed monkeys, the existence of scramble competition within bands could be inferred, but the magnitude of the increase in foraging effort with band size is modest (Grueter et al. 2008; Grueter and van Schaik 2010) (Figure 18.4). There is also limited evidence for scramble feeding competition in a population of golden snub-nosed monkeys at Shennongjia: while adult females in the larger group spent more time moving than those in the smaller group (which is indicative of scramble competition), time spent feeding was not different

(Liu X 2012; Liu X et al. 2013a). And a comparison of the size of both the annual and sesaonal home ranges between these two groups inhabiting the same general area showed hat the larer group consistently occupied a larger home range (Fan P et al. 2018).

Another way of determining the effects of scramble competition is to measure individual energy expenditure and average intake rate in relation to group size (e.g. Grueter et al. 2018; Kurihara and Hanya 2017; Stacey 1986). Data on patch depletion, i.e. how patch occupancy time (feeding time in a single patch) is influenced by feeding group size and patch size and how food intake and movement rates change during patch occupancy, can also reveal whether within-group scramble competition is operative in a given socioecological setting (Snaith and Chapman 2005; see also Tombak et al. 2012). The benefit of this method is that it does not require complicated ecological controls across different conditions of food availability (Snaith and Chapman 2005). An application of this method to Adolf Friedrichs's Angolan colobus in Nyungwe National Park revealed that the subjects deplete food patches when feeding on young leaves, as indicated by decreasing gains (intake rate) despite increasing effort (distance moved whilst feeding). However, intake rates of mature leaves increased during feeding events, suggesting that as preferred food items (new leaves, fruits) are depleted monkeys switch to less favourable foods (mature leaves) (Miller et al. 2020c).

Sufficient food availability may not be the only prerequisite that has to be met for supergroups to form. Another factor that could have facilitated living in near constant close proximity to other social units is low pathogen prevalence. If disease risk is higher in larger groups (although there is little support for this, see, e.g., Nunn 2012), very large band sizes are more likely to prevail in environs with reduced diversity/prevalence of pathogens such as seasonally cold temperate forests (parasite species richness is higher closer to the equator for protozoan parasites; Nunn et al. 2005). Furthermore, the limited physical interaction among individuals of different subunits in a structurally subdivided system (modular system) may limit the prevalence and spread of infections (Nunn et al. 2015; but see Sah et al. 2017).

It could also be argued that ecological conditions are not merely permissive, but actually drive modularity of colobines (Matsuda et al. 2010a). A preliminary review (Grueter and van Schaik 2010) found no evidence for this; however, it may be premature to discard the effect of ecology on modularity. One model may have some power in accounting for the variation in social organization among Asian colobines residing in environments that differ in degree of resource heterogeneity. This *heterogeneity hypothesis* postulates that the necessity to safeguard year-round access to spatially and temporally heterogeneous resources could have created incentives for banding in colobines. In essence, the more heterogeneous the environment becomes (mosaic of distinct habitat types), the larger the area an initial unit needs to cover to have year-round access to resources in all the different habitat types and the higher the chance that it will encounter other units who have the same spatial and dietary needs. As a result of this, units become more tolerant of each other, which could facilitate band formation.[9] This argument is reminiscent of the resource dispersion hypothesis which was initially advanced to explain group formation for solitary foragers (Carr and Macdonald 1986) but has not been applied to supergroup/band formation for multilevel species.

Another 'ecological hypothesis', The *Cody/Altmann hypothesis* (Altmann 1974; Cody 1971; Kirkpatrick et al. 1998) holds that for primates, feeding in a group rather than independently, maximizes per capita food intake by minimizing returns to exhausted patches. Modified for multilevel societies, the hypothesis would predict that bands form because foraging in larger groups reduces the chance of futile visits to depleted areas. However, the very large groups of associated subunits found in multilevel colobines would likely increase the chance of individuals or subunits crossing each other's feeding paths and thereby offset the proposed benefit of preventing visits to depleted patches (*sensu* Harcourt and Stewart 2007). Subordinate units may thus well be able to harvest resources more efficiently when foraging independently. Moreover, applied to colobines, this hypothesis would predict modularity to occur only in areas where resources regrow slowly and are subjected to depletion (e.g. lichens; see Kirkpatrick et al. 1998); however, band formation is a hallmark of a number of Asian colobines inhabiting a variety of environments.

Recently, Amato (2016), in her treatise on the role the gut microbiota in primate ecology and evolution, alluded to the intriguing scenario whereby the increased social contact resulting from multilevel society formation may expose individuals to a larger pool or higher diversity of gut microbial communities with its protective effects such as improving disease resistance or boosting immune response. However, no empirical data are available to validate this claim. Moreover, if it is otherwise hard to get the microbes needed, then why don't many more or even all colobines live in multilevel societies?

The hypothesis that predation has fuelled the formation of super-bands in colobines is probably less tenable;[10] while the dilution effect can clearly explain grouping, the marginal gains of increasing group size are subject to diminishing returns once a certian threshold has been reached (Hamilton 1971; Pulliam 1973). If predation was the main ecological benefit these colobines derive from group-living, we woud not necessarily expect groups of several hundred members, as commonly seen in snub-nosed monkeys (see also Grueter and van Schaik 2010). Besides, giant groups are easier to detect for predators because of their conspicuousness (Vine 1973) and thus not ideal from a predation avoidance perspective.

[9] Whether this elevated tolerance can pave the way to band-level organization in the absence of other selective pressures or behavioural advantages to grouping is not clear.

[10] A notable exception is a study of proboscis monkeys by Matsuda et al. (2010a) which showed that the local density of social units along the river is influenced by spatial heterogeneity, e.g. river width, which enables effective predation avoidance. Moreover, in the case of Adolf Friedrichs's Angolan colobus in Nyungwe, higher-than-normal predation pressure by chimpanzees may be an evolutionary motivation for core groups to coalesce into supergroups (Miller et al. 2020c).

A 'non-ecological' hypothesis that has gained momentum is the *bachelor threat hypothesis* according to which OMUs can better withstand attacks and takeover attempts by encroaching bachelors by congregating into bands. OMU leader males can reduce their likelihood of being targeted by bachelors either through joint defence or safety in numbers (Bleisch and Xie 1998; Grueter and van Schaik 2010; Rubenstein and Hack 2004; Wrangham 1976). Females would also indirectly benefit from a reduced takeover probability, as this would lower the risk of their infants succumbing to infanticide. Rubenstein and Hack (2004) showed for plains zebra (*Equus burchelli*) multilevel societies that as the chance of being harassed by bachelor males increases, stallions exhibit a higher propensity to associate with other stallions to thwart these extra-group hazards.

The salience of bachelor threat in Asian[11] colobine multilevel settings is evidenced by observations showing that bachelor males are not spatially segregated from OMUs but peripherally attached to the band (Grueter et al. 2017a; Hoang 2007; Kirkpatrick 1998; Qi et al. 2017; Yeager 1990), the frequency of male aggression rises when bachelors are nearby (Grueter et al. 2017a), males direct more intense aggression towards bachelor males than towards other resident males (Zhao et al. 2013), and replacements of resident OMU holders can be followed by infanticidal attacks (Agoramoorthy and Hsu 2005; Ren et al. 2011; Yao et al. 2016; see also Xiang and Grueter 2007). Additional support for the hypothesis that bachelor threat shapes modularity/aggregation tendencies comes from a comparative analysis on Asian colobines which showed that where the expected number of non-group males is high, social units have high home range overlap, exhibit a higher association degree and have a higher tendency to form bands (Grueter and van Schaik 2010). Observations that can be interpreted as collective action such as joint patrolling and vigilance among OMU males and joint aggression against intruders have recently been recorded in some populations of golden snub-nosed monkeys (Huang Z et al. 2017a; Krzton 2011; Qi et al. 2014; Xiang et al. 2014; Yao et al. 2016; Zhao and Li 2009b) but thus far not in black-and-white snub-nosed monkeys (Zhu et al. 2016). It is unclear whether this joint collective action represents genuine cooperation among unit leaders, or if males independently respond to threat stimuli in the same manner. Prelimary genetic analyses have shown that inclusive fitness benefits are unlikely to underlie male–male collective action in golden snub-nosed monkeys (Xiang et al. 2014). Instead, by participating in collective action, unit leaders are likely to be more efficient and successful at fending off incursions by extra-group males than by acting without conspecific support.

Consequences of Living in Multilevel Societies

Socially modular primates boast a number of morphological and behavioural peculiarities that seem to be a direct consequence of their crowded and competitive social

[11] In Adolf Friedrichs's Angolan colobus in Nyungwe, few bachelor groups were observed and they were not as large as those observed in snub-nosed monkeys (Miller et al. 2020c).

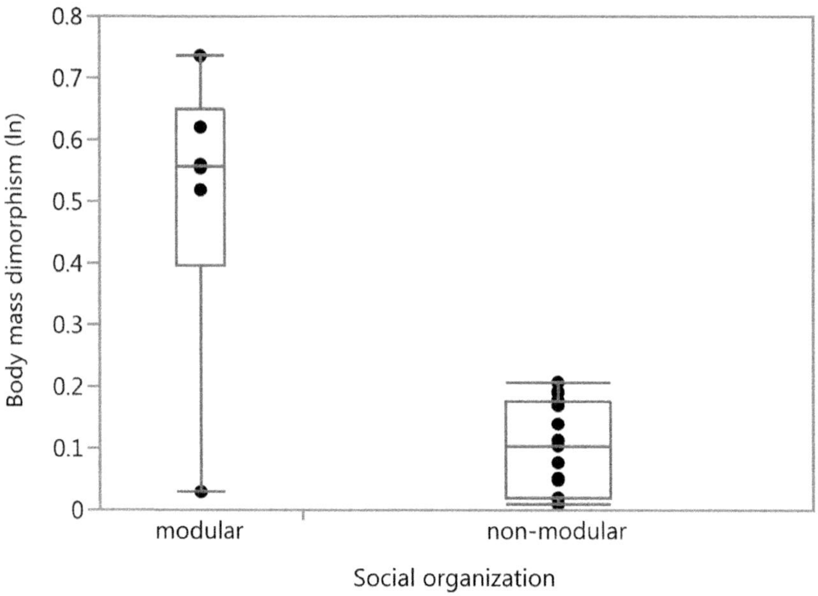

Figure 18.5 Box plots illustrating differences in sexual dimorphism in body mass between Asian colobine species with modular and non-modular social organization ($n_{\mathrm{modular}} = 6$; $n_{\mathrm{non\text{-}modular}} = 15$). Filled circles represent species; species with the same values occupy the same space. Horizontal lines indicate median value, boxes indicate the observations between the twenty-fifth and seventy-fifth percentile and whiskers connect the highest and lowest scores.

environment and the ease at which individuals can interact socially and sexually with members of other social units.

Living in a modular society appears to be associated with heightened levels of mate competition because social units are in regular proximity to one another and thus experience frequent and intense competition over mating access to females. The OMUs are also shadowed by bachelor groups, which also compete with the resident males over access to females. In a phylogenetically controlled comparative analysis, it was shown that sexual dimorphism in body weight differed significantly between modular and non-modular Asian colobines and that social organization was the only variable among a number of other predictors that exerted a significant effect upon sexual dimorphism (Figure 18.5) (Grueter and van Schaik 2009).

Comparative research has also shown that primates in multilevel systems and in large social groups score higher on a Likert scale of dimorphism in ornamentation than species in other types of social system and in smaller groups (Grueter et al. 2015a) (Figure 18.6). Individuals in larger groups are not only confronted with a larger pool of potential competitors but also live in a potentially more anonymous social environment where individual recognition may be limited. As noted above, the conflict potential in a multilevel society is expected to be higher than in other types of social organization due to the close proximity among social units. Ornaments or phenotypic accoutrements are clearly handy in such a setting as they offer reliable

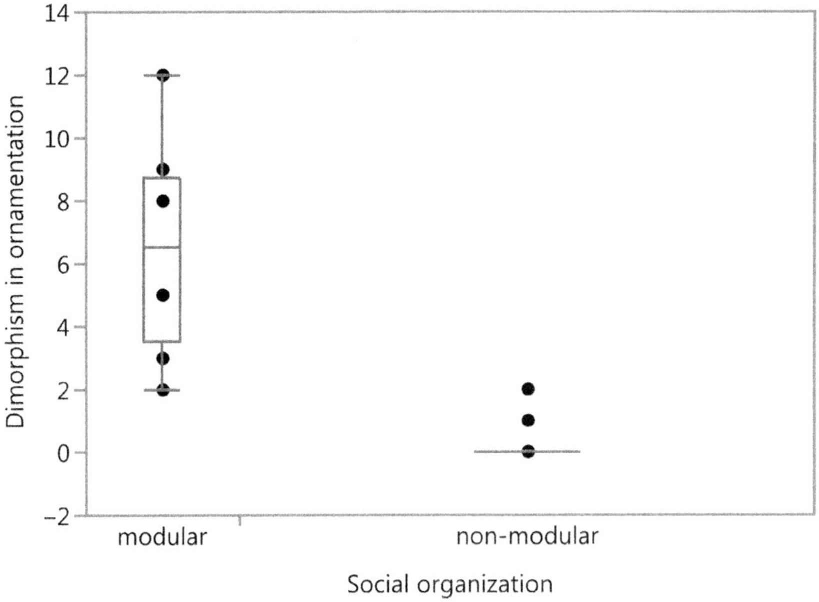

Figure 18.6 Box plots illustrating differences in sexual dimorphism in levels of ornamentation between Asian colobine species with modular and non-modular social organization ($n_{\text{modular}} = 8$; $n_{\text{non-modular}} = 30$). Ornaments were scored on a scale from 0 to 5; the sum of these scores for different trait categories (e.g. capes, ruffs or different fleshy or brightly coloured traits) formed a species-specific total ornamentation value.

at-a-distance assessment of male quality (to females) and fighting ability (to other males). In sum, the covariation of showy ornaments with group size and social organization in primates appears to reflect selection for amplified signals of individual identity, competitive ability or attractiveness in situations of greater anonymity and conflict potential.

Grueter et al. (2015b) examined correlates of facial coloration in one of the more brightly coloured colobines with a multilevel system, the black-and-white snub-nosed monkey. The results of an analysis of lip redness in a sample of bachelor males and 'harem' leaders indicated that lip coloration is a badge of (group-holding) status during the mating season. However, the data were agnostic on whether the mechanisms of selection are likely to revolve around male–male competition, female mate choice or both. Behavioural data are needed to distinguish between these potential mechanisms. The proboscis monkey is another prime example of a colobine that lives in an extremely competitive environment in which potential competitor males sleep in close proximity to each other and females can relatively easily switch residency. It is therefore not surprising that males have developed conspicuous adornments, i.e. enlarged noses. A recent study on proboscis monkeys showed that there are significant positive correlations among nose size, body size and testis size as well as a clear link between nose size and both nasalized acoustic signals and the number of females in OMUs, indicating that males use their noses to audiovisually advertise their competitive ability and quality to conspecifics (Koda et al. 2018). Interestingly, nose size and testis volume are positively correlated in this species, indicating that both pre- and post-copulatory traits were under intense selective pressure. Given that male expenditure on *both* ornaments and ejaculates is costly (Lüpold et al. 2019), the lack of an allocation trade-off between secondary sexual traits and ejaculates is indicative of very high levels of competition.[12]

One by-product of being a member of a cohesive multilevel society based on polygynous reproductive units is that infanticide risk can be reduced. In multilevel systems without male herding and with female choice, females can relatively easily achieve extra-pair copulations, which causes paternity confusion. Qi et al. (2020) have shown that female golden snub-nosed monkeys strategically mate with males outside their OMU to reduce the risk of infanticide should one of those males subsequently become the leader of their OMU. In colobines where OMUs do not assemble into multilevel societies, such a paternity confusion strategy is much less of an option for females and therefore infanticide is a relatively common phenomenon (for a review, see Palombit 2012). Another route through which infanticide can be reduced in multilevel societies is the relative ease at which individuals can transfer to another unit (without incurring risks associated with transferring into an unfamiliar social unit or area). If female dispersal occus in direct response to aggressive behaviour of new males (e.g. Sicotte et al. 2017), it may effectively lower the risk of infanticide.

The cognitive consequences of living in multilevel societies are largely unexplored. One would expect significant cognitive capital to navigate such a complex and presumably cognitively demanding social landscape. According to the social intelligence hypothesis, cognitive capacity emerges out of a need to manage the intricacies of social life (Byrne and Whiten 1988; Dunbar 1993; Humphrey 1976). This hypothesis posits that increased sociality is correlated with increased brain size (e.g. Barton 1996). Snub-nosed monkeys, which live in putatively cognitively challenging multilevel societies, possess the largest brains of all colobines (even after controlling for body size) (van Woerden et al. 2012) and live in the largest groups (Figure 18.7). However, whether this correlative association between brain size and group size suggests coevolution of these two traits is unclear. Very little is known about colobine social cognition. A recent study on captive golden snub-nosed monkeys has shown that they were more sensitive to the gaze of a human experimenter than were François's langurs (*Trachypithecus francoisi*). These findings are consistent with the prediction that golden snub-nosed monkeys, which form large, complex and dynamic multilevel societies, should have stronger

[12] Unexpectedly, a negative correlation between body and canine sizes was found in proboscis monkeys, which could be explained by an interaction between sexual and natural selection, i.e. larger noses in males may interfere with the use of canines, thereby reducing their effectiveness as weapons (Matsuda et al. 2020c).

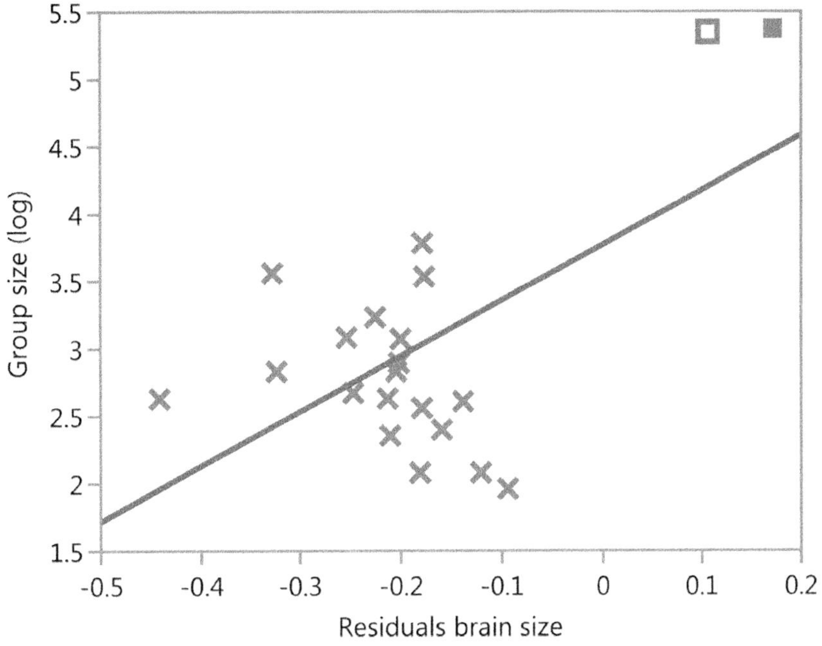

Figure 18.7 The relationship between brain size and group size for all colobines for which respective data are available. The filled square is the data point for golden snub-nosed monkeys; the unfilled square is the data point for black-and-white snub-nosed monkeys. Data are from Isler et al. (2008) and Grueter (2015)

sociocognitive abilities than François's langurs which form uni-male units (Chen et al. 2017). However, an earlier study by Tan et al. (2014) reported that there is no evidence that golden snub-nosed monkeys use others' social cues to locate hidden food in a cooperative task or to steal food in a competitive task. Limited cognitive capacities in a social context (if supported in subsequent studies) could be related to the fact that social interactions in colobine multilevel societies are concentrated within small core social units and the wider social sphere (bands with fission dynamics) has not been a sufficiently strong selective pressure for the evolution of elaborate social cognition (Tan et al. 2014). Alternatively, to quote DeCasien et al. (2017), 'the premise that social complexity necessarily requires cognitive complexity may not always hold, as social living challenges might not require flexible cognitive solutions in real-time, but could be solved using simpler evolved rules-of-thumb (Barrett et al. 2007)'. From a comparative perspective, primates with larger home range overlap – which encompasses the multilevel ones – possess larger endocranial volumes (Grueter 2015b), but whether this link reflects social or socio-spatial intelligence is unclear.

Prima facie, complex social organization is assumed to translate into a necessity for more elaborate social knowledge. The capacity for individual recognition of conspecifics and classifying individuals according to their attributes is fundamental to the evolution of animal sociality as it endows individuals with the ability to manage cooperative and competitive relationships (Seyfarth and Cheney 2012). Whether colobines living in extremely large multilevel societies possess such recognition abilities has not yet been addressed experimentally. In gelada multilevel societies, playback experiments have shown that there is limited vocal recognition among males (Bergman 2010). Also in Guinea baboons, males are more attuned to calls from familiar individuals in their own social unit and either unmotivated or unable to monitor the identities and actions of individuals outside their own social unit (Maciej et al. 2013b).

Given that multilevel societies offer a platform for complex interindividual relationships to emerge that span multiple levels, one would expect a concomitant increase in vocal complexity. Vocal complexity can be quantified in terms of repertoire size (McComb and Semple 2005) or degree of individuality within discrete calls (Pollard and Blumstein 2011). Maciej et al. (2013a) failed to find support for the prediction that the vocal repertoire of modular Guinea baboons is more complex than that of other baboon taxa with less complex social organization. This may be because social organization per se may not reflect the differentiation and diversity of social relationships that individuals exhibit, so multilevel societies may actually not be more socially complex in relation to social cognition (Bergman and Beehner 2015). This link between social and vocal complexity has been virtually unexplored in multilevel colobines. However, one recent study attempted to assess the degree of individuality in the so-called 'coo calls' of adult male golden snub-nosed monkeys and found high levels of differentiation between individuals in these vocalizations which may provide cues for individual recognition in complex multilevel systems (Fan P et al. 2019).

Conclusions

Multilevel societies in colobines seem to have arisen where the ecological costs of grouping are not excessive and the amalgamation of multiple social levels offered additional benefits. Conspecific threat originating from all-male units at the margin of the group may be a potentially important selective force in the evolution of multilevel societies from ancestrally autonomous units. Once in place, multilevel societies can 'simultaneously reap the benefits of various grouping levels and thereby avoid the optimization problem that a one-size fits-all group may face' (Grueter et al. 2017b) (p. R984). We have have made significant strides in recent years towards describing the structure of multilevel systems in snub-nosed monkeys and deciphering their evolution and functional significance but the structure and function of multilevel systems in colobines other than snub-nosed monkeys remain insufficiently known. In addition, topics such as group coordination, communication, decision making and disease transmission in multilevel organizations have received very little if any attention. The social dynamics among males in this complex social setting are also poorly understood, and how males maintain tolerance in spite of competition over limited mating partners remains enigmatic. Multilevel systems in colobines are a treasure trove of interesting research avenues and studies of these intriguing systems promise to yield novel insights that may influence our understanding of primate socioecology in a transformative way.

Acknowledgements

I thank Larry Ulibarri, Alexandra Miller, Julie Teichroeb, Ikki Matsuda and Carel van Schaik for thoughtful comments on this chapter.

19 Colobine Population Ecology

What Limits Population Size

Colin A. Chapman, Amélie Corriveau, Kim Valenta, Fabiola Espinosa-Gómez and Valérie A. M. Schoof

Introduction

A fundamental issue in ecology is determining factors that influence animal abundance. The importance of this theoretical issue has taken on new significance with the need to develop informed management plans for endangered and threatened species. This need is driven by the rapidly rising rate of biodiversity loss; the current extinction rate is approximately 1000 times higher than background rates (Pimm et al. 2014) and estimates suggest that at least 322 vertebrate species have gone extinct since 1500 and that surviving vertebrate species have declined in abundance by 25% since 1970 (Dirzo et al. 2014). Overall, 60% of all primate species are currently threatened with extinction (Estrada et al. 2017) and while it remains to be confirmed, it seems almost a certainty that with the disappearance of Miss Waldron's red colobus (*Procolobus waldronae*) in West Africa (Oates et al. 2016), we have lost the first primate in the last century.

Although the threats to primates are numerous, habitat loss is thought to be the most significant. Global forest loss between 2000 and 2012 was estimated at 2.3 million km^2, with an increase of 2101 km^2 every year in the tropics (Hansen et al. 2013). To put this in perspective, an area approximately the size of the Democratic Republic of Congo was lost in 12 years. This forest loss is primarily driven by increasing human populations and high consumption rates (Crist et al. 2017; Kalbitzer and Chapman 2018). The world's population is expected to rise from 7 billion in 2011 to almost 10 billion in 2050 (United Nations 2009). Globally, agricultural lands expanded by 48,000 km^2 between 1999 and 2008 (Phalan et al. 2013) – an area slightly less than the size of Costa Rica.

If this was not enough, many primate populations, if not the majority, are severely reduced by hunting. Global evaluations of wildlife exploitation are extremely poor; however, in the Congo Basin alone, four million tons of bushmeat are estimated to be harvested each year (equivalent to approximately 4,500,000 cows, or 80 million small (5 kg) monkeys, of course not all bushmeat is primate, Fa and Brown 2009). Primates are also threatened by the changing climate that human actions have caused (Chapman et al. 2020). Temperatures are predicted to increase by 1.5°C by the end of the twenty-first century (IPCC 2014) and researchers have projected that by 2100 75% of all tropical forests present in 2000 will experience temperatures that are higher than

This chapter includes Electronic Supplementary Material (ESM) at: www.cambridge.org/colobines

the temperatures presently supporting closed canopy forests (Wright et al. 2009; Peres et al. 2016). Addressing how to respond to these risks is one of the fundamental questions of both applied conservation and primate population ecology.

Population ecology is the study of the factors affecting population size and structure, and how and why a population changes over time. The theoretical framework of the field is grounded in questions dealing with population growth, regulation, dynamics and demography. The theory has been developed with studies of a variety of organisms including humans, mammals, birds, disease organisms and microorganisms and it has been applied to issues such as wild-harvested fish stocks and dynamics of logged forest stands (Holmes 1995; Sinclair 2003). Ideally, studies quantify change in populations over time and identify the drivers of that change either through experimentation or by identifying factors that change in unison with the population change (Krebs et al. 1995). Because of the slow life histories of primates (Van Allen et al. 2012) quantifying their population changes through long-term studies can rarely be achieved (Chapman et al. 2017). Thus, static approaches are more common, such as comparisons across populations experiencing different ecological conditions, not the fluctuations in population size or composition over time.

The overall goal of our work it to explore the relative importance of potential drivers of colobine population change with the aim of providing information for future conservation efforts. To meet this goal, our first objective is to describe variables influencing colobine population ecology in both Asian and African colobines. Our second objective is to describe small-scale temporal and spatial variation in colobine populations and ecology in Kibale National Park, Uganda (hereafter Kibale), where CAC has conduct long-term research. We summarize our Kibale findings to understand the magnitude of the variation that can occur on small spatial and temporal scales where ecological variables (e.g. forest composition, predator populations) remain more similar than on larger scales (e.g. comparisons among regions). Our final objective is to use this information to ask the fundamental question: What limits colobine population size? Here, we place an emphasis on illustrating where high-quality data are available and where knowledge gaps exist. We emphasize these gaps in the hope of motivating researchers to gather new data aimed at answering these fundamental questions more accurately and providing better information to conservationists trying to apply this knowledge.

Colobine Diet and Population Characteristics

Over 40 African and Asian colobine species have been studied at more than 75 sites, with some sites being studied across multiple years (ESM Table 19.1). As a whole, these data highlight the tremendous diversity of colobine social organization, ranging behaviour and diet. Population density and mean group size are variable in both African colobines and Asian ones (Figure 19.1). Population density ranges from 3 ind/km^2 (*Colobus angolensis*; Ituri, DRC) to 784 ind/km^2 (*Procolobus kirkii;* Jozani – cultivated land, regenerating forest) in African colobines and from ~2 ind/km^2 (*Semnopithecus schistaceus*; Junbesi, Nepal) to 220 ind/km^2 in an

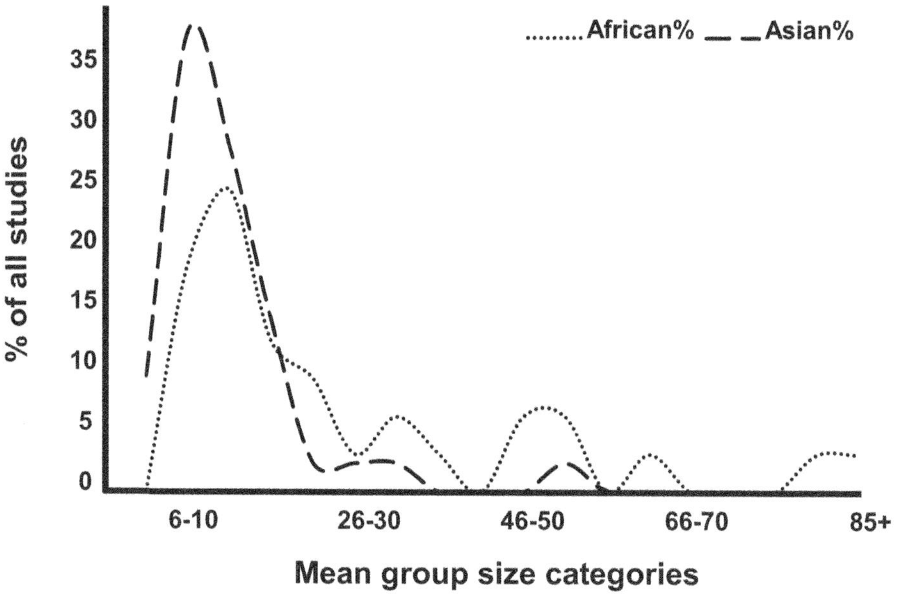

Figure 19.1 Mean group size of African and Asian colobines. Data from ESM Table 19.1 and for presentation groups were placed into bins of five, and a smoothing curve was applied to visualize intermediate group sizes.

Asian colobine, *Simas concolor.* The majority of Asian colobines studied (25/33) had a density of 50 or fewer ind/km^2, while a little more than half (13/25) of African colobine groups had between 50 and 300 ind/km^2. Similarly, while most groups studied had a mean group size of 25 or fewer individuals (22/35 African; 38/41 Asian), group size ranged from 6 individuals in *Colobus guereza* in a fragment at Kibale, Uganda to more than 300 individuals in *Colobus angolensis* at Nyungwe, Rwanda (Figure 19.1). In comparison, Asian colobines mean group size ranged from 3 individuals in *Presbytis potenziani* and *Semnopithecus concolor* (both at Sarabua, Indonesia) to 54 individuals in *Semnopithecus dussumieri* at Kaukori, India. Although the range in mean group size is smaller for Asian than African colobines, some Asian species do associate in large bands ranging from 175 to 450 individuals (e.g. *Rhinopithecus* spp.).

While more than half of the species studied have home ranges of 100 ha or smaller (25/30 of African colobines; 23/35 of Asian colobines), African colobine home range size varies from 0.5 to 1.2 ha in *Procolobus kirkii* in the mature and regenerating forest of Kiwengwa, Zanzibar, to 2440 ha in *Colobus angolensis* in Nyungwe, Rwanda. In Asian colobines, home range variation is even greater, ranging from 2 ha in *Semnopithecus vetulus* at Polonnaruwa, Sri Lanka, to 3500 ha in *Rhinopithecus brelichi* at Fanjingshan, China. Variation in day range is also extensive, varying from 310 m in *P. kirkii* at Jozani, Zanzibar (cultivated land, regenerating forest) to 1212 m in *Procolobus verus* at Taï National, Ivory Coast.

In addition to interspecific variation, there is also a high degree of intraspecific variation in colobine home range use and population density. For instance, the African *Colobus guereza* has a home range of 100 ha and a density of 17 ind/km^2 in Ituri, DRC, but a home range of 28 ha and a density of 100 ind/km^2 in Kibale (Kanyawara; 1971–72), Uganda. Similarly, *Procolobus kirkii* has a home range of 13 ha, a density of 784 ind/km^2 and a day range of 310 m at one site of cultivated land and regenerating forest in Jozani (1999), and a home range of 60 ha, density of 100 ind/km^2 and day range of 1044 m at another forested site in Jozani (1980–81). Similarly, in India, the *Semnopithecus dussumieri* home range is 20 ha and density 121 ind/km^2 in Gir, but home range is ~775 ha and density 3 ind/km^2 in Kaukori.

Just as colobine group sizes and ranging are highly variable, colobine diets are also variable. More than 50% of the diet of most African colobines (38/53) and half of the Asian colobines is composed of leaves, highlighting the highly folivorous nature of the colobine clade. Overall, most colobine diets were composed of less than 20% of mature leaves (African 43/51; Asian 18/27) and between 26% and 75% of young leaves (African 37/51; Asian 18/29). Seeds and fruits accounted for less than half (<50%) of the diet of both African (50/53) and Asian (30/37) colobine species. In most cases (African 42/53; Asian 27/34), flowers accounted for less than 10% of the diet. Despite a generalized dietary reliance on leaves, some colobine species rely heavily on entirely different food sources. For *Rhinopithecus bieti* at three study sites (Wuyapiya, Samage-Baimaxueshan, Tacheng-Yunnan; China), between 60 and 94% of the diet was composed of 'other', a food category principally represented by lichens.

There can also be extensive variation in these parameters at the same location among groups or within the same population over time (ESM Table 19.2). For example, within Kibale there is extensive variation in population characters in red colobus (*Piliocolobus tephrosceles*) and black-and-white colobus (*Colobus guereza*), with red colobus exhibiting more variation than black-and-white colobus. Group size in black-and-white colobus has been reported to range from 4 to 11 individuals, while the group size of red colobus ranges from 14 to 152 individuals (Chapman et al. 2002a; higher value CAC, pers. obs.). Similarly, diet was highly variable. Young leaf consumption in red colobus in Kibale ranged among groups from 14.8% to 84.9% of time spent feeding, while young leaf consumption only ranged from 45.1% to 89.7% among black-and-white colobus groups. The cause of the greater variation in the diets of red colobus is not known, but it may relate to larger group sizes in red colobus resulting in greater variation in the range of individual feeding decisions.

Food Resources

Protein-to-Fibre Model

By far the most commonly tested and best supported model for predicting colobine biomass is the 'protein-to-fibre model'. Based on observations of Central American howler monkeys (*Alouatta palliata*), Milton (1979) proposed that an important criteria in leaf selection was the protein-to-fibre ratio, with leaves with higher protein-to-fibre ratios being selected over those with lower ratios (see Matsuda et al. 2013 for data on selection by two Bornean colobines). Because the digestion of fibre requires fermentation by symbiotic microbes, fibre is often considered an antifeedant as this process is slow, with insoluble fibre (cellulose, hemicellulose and lignin) being only partially digestible (Cancelliere et al. 2018; McNab 2002; Rothman et al. 2012, 2015). Furthermore, nitrogen is a limiting nutrient in many environmental systems. Since nitrogen is predominantly found in protein, herbivores should compensate for this limitation by choosing foods high in protein (White 1993). Waterman et al. (1988) suggested that the biomass of folivorous colobines could be predicted by the weighted contributions of the protein-to-fibre ratio of mature leaves of the most abundant trees in a particular habitat. Subsequently, this index of dietary quality has been successfully applied to predict the biomass of small-bodied folivorous monkeys at local (Chapman et al. 2002b; Ganzhorn 2002) and regional scales (Chapman et al. 2004; Davies 1994; Fashing et al. 2007a; Oates et al. 1990; Waterman et al. 1988) (Figure 19.2).

The mechanism by which this index operates to determine folivore biomass is not clearly understood. Davies (1994) suggested that colobines fed on mature leaves with high protein levels and little fibre when other preferred foods were unavailable, and thus reliance on mature leaves could support high population densities that would otherwise be limited by periods of food scarcity. However, some colobines (e.g. *Piliocolobus tephrosceles*) rarely consume mature leaves because young leaves are always available, yet this index is still a good predictor of their biomass (Chapman et al. 2004). One potential explanation is that the protein-to-fibre ratio of mature leaves in an area is correlated with the protein-to-fibre ratio of foods in general. This idea is supported by data from Kibale, where the protein-to-fibre ratios of mature and young leaves are strongly correlated ($r = 0.837$, $P < 0.001$) (Chapman et al. 2004).

While these studies suggest that the protein-to-fibre ratio of leaves is a critical factor limiting folivorous primate population sizes, there are reasons to be cautious and to avoid premature implementation of this idea into management plans. This scepticism is based on four main factors. First, studies attempting to empirically verify the protein-to-fibre model are correlative, and it is quite possible that this ratio is related to another, as of yet undetermined factor (Chapman et al. 2010a,b; Wallis et al. 2012). Second, protein concentrations of ingested leaves are higher than species' estimated requirements (Oftedal 1991; Rothman et al. 2011). Third, we should use available nitrogen to evaluate this nutritional model. However, studies typically measure total nitrogen, which may be problematic since tannins and fibre-bound nitrogen likely reduce the availability of nitrogen in most folivore foods in unpredictable ways (Rothman et al. 2008a, 2012; Wallis et al. 2012). Finally, new empirical data call into question the generality of this model. For example, in spite of changes in the protein-to-fibre ratio of mature leaves resulting from changes in forest composition (i.e. changes in density of specific species), there were no

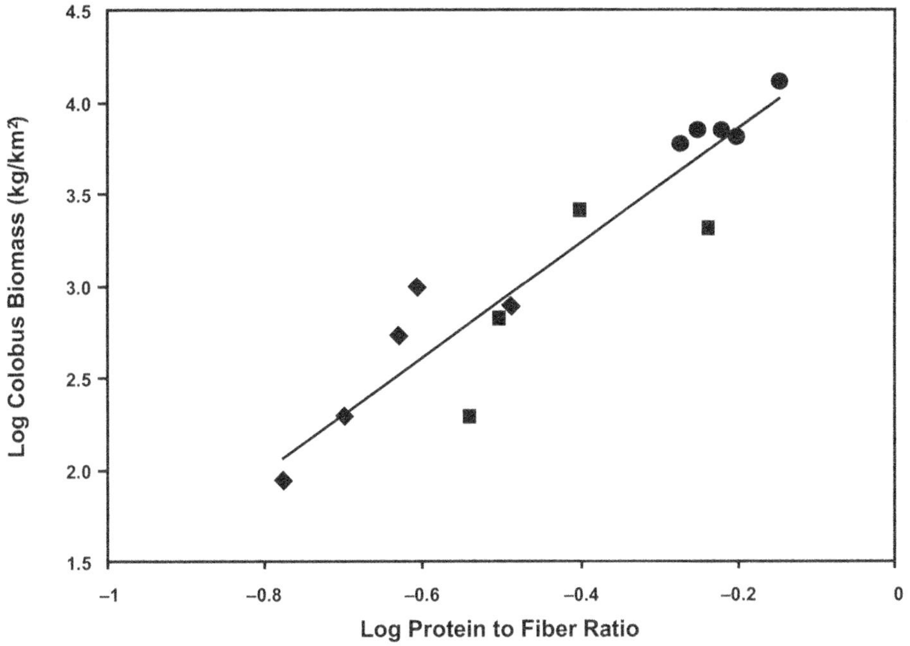

Figure 19.2 The relationship between mature leaf chemistry and colobine biomass at rainforest sites in Africa and Asia. Chemical values are weighted mean percentages of dry mass, standardized to the species basal area to account for different proportions of the flora being sampled at each site. The weighted values were calculated from $\Sigma (P_i + X_i)/\Sigma P_i$, where P_i is the proportion of the basal area contributed by species i and X_i is the chemical measure for species i. This figure is standardized to 100%. Diamonds are sites from around the world (Oates et al. 1990); squares are forest sites within Kibale National Park, Uganda (Chapman et al. 2002b); and open circles are the forest fragments studied from Kibale National Park, Uganda.

detectable changes in the population size of red colobus in Kibale (Chapman et al. 2010a,b). Another example that is inconsistent with model predictions focuses on populations living in regenerating habitats, where leaves have higher protein-to-fibre ratios and lower levels of secondary compounds than old-growth forest trees (Coley 1983). The model predicts that regenerating forests should support increased female fecundity, as evidenced by populations with a greater number of infants per female than populations in old-growth forest. A study in Kibale reports that leaves have higher protein-to-fibre ratios in regenerating habitat, but there was no corresponding difference in the demographic structure of red colobus groups in regenerating versus old-growth forest (Gogarten et al. 2012).

These methodological issues, combined with limited empirical support in the recent studies discussed above, raise doubt as to the general applicability of this model. Further studies are needed to examine under what conditions the model applies and when it does not.

Composition of the Forest

Leguminous trees are an important food source for Southeast Asian colobines. A comparison across nine sites throughout much of Southeast Asia revealed a correlation between the abundance of leguminous trees and colobine biomass in the region (Davies 1994), which could be because of the high protein content typically associated with this type of tree. Alternatively, since there is a negative relationship between the abundance of leguminous versus Dipterocarp trees, it may be that without Dipterocarps the forests are richer and this is what drives the increase in colobine abundance (Davis 1994). However, an analysis of the relationship between African colobine abundance and leguminous trees is not significant (Davies 1994), despite a demonstrated preference for seeds and young leaves of species in this taxonomic group (Maisels et al. 1994; McKey 1978c).

The relationship between leguminous trees and Asian colobine biomass is similar to that found for some frugivores with respect to figs. For example, fig density correlates with the density of orangutans (*Pongo abilii*) and gibbons (*Hylobates* spp.) (Marshall and Leighton 2006; Wich et al. 2004). This positive relationship might be expected because figs contain many essential nutrients and minerals (O'Brien et al. 1998), thereby providing a nutritionally balanced staple food in some areas (Felton et al. 2009, 2013). But as with leguminous trees, the relationship between figs and frugivorous primate density is mired in controversy. Stevenson (2001) assembled data on fruit production and primate abundance from 30 neotropical sites and found no relationship between fig abundance and primate biomass.

Environmental Disaster Causing Food Shortages

Colobine populations could be limited by environmental disasters or unusual environmental events causing dramatic reductions in the food supply. Dittus (1985a) described the effect of a cyclone that cut across the island of Sri Lanka on 23 November 1978. Overall, 46% of all of emergent and upper canopy trees were killed, as were 29% of understory trees. The two colobines found in the area (*Semnopithecus entellus* and *Trachypithecus vetulus*) subsequently over-browsed a number of the remaining trees, resulting in additional tree mortality (Dittus 1985b). The short-term impact of the resulting decrease in food supply was smaller than one might expect, with population declines of only 5% for *S. entellus* and 5%–10% for *T. vetulus* within one month after the cyclone.

Some of the best long-term data on folivore populations are those on the howler monkeys (*Alouatta palliata*) on Barro Colorado Island (BCI), Panama. It should be noted that while howlers have anatomical adaptations for eating leaves, they are heavily reliant on, and appear to prefer, fruit (Pavelka and Knopff 2004). On BCI, fruiting, flowering and leaf set can be disrupted if the rains deviate from their typical seasonal pattern, which has happened five times between 1929 and 1979 (Foster 1982). Following an unusual rainfall event that caused severe fruit crop failures in 1970, howler monkey mortality increased. Despite this there is no evidence that this led to any long-term population crash (Milton 1982; Milton et al. 2005). Another long-term dataset on the population dynamics exists for red colobus and black-and-white colobus in the old-growth forest of Kibale. Over 45 years, during which no ecological disasters occurred, the populations of both species appear stable or gradually increasing (Struhsaker 1997; Chapman et al. 2010b, 2015, 2018a,b).

For natural disasters to limit populations, they would have to occur at a frequency greater than the population's ability to recover. Possibly the most frequent type of natural disaster affecting many forests are hurricanes or cyclones. Hurricane activity varies geographically. For example, between 1920 and 1972, Madagascar was hit by 362 hurricanes (7.0/year) (Ganzhorn 1995). Between 1871 and 1964, an average of 4.6 hurricanes affected the Caribbean each year (Walker et al. 1991). In contrast, mainland Africa is infrequently affected by hurricanes (Chapman et al. 1999). When Hurricane Joan touched land in Nicaragua, 80% of the trees were felled (see also Boucher 1990; Pavelka and Behie 2005), thus the effect of hurricanes on forest systems can be dramatic. However, the probability of a hurricane or cyclone influencing the same population on a frequent basis is unlikely. For example, for the whole island of Puerto Rico, which is in an area of high hurricane activity, the return time is 21 years, thus the chances of a single population being affected twice in a short period of time is low (Dittus 1985a). Given that, where data are available, colobine diets seem quite flexible – possibly mitigating their ability to survive brief ecological crunch periods – and that the probability of a natural disaster hitting the same population multiple times at relatively short intervals is quite small, it seems unlikely that these events limit colobine population size.

Intraspecific Competition

Research on primates have made significant advances with respect to understanding how competition with and between groups of the same species shape a population's behavioural patterns and social organization (Sterck et al. 1997; Wrangham 1980) and recent research on colobines have led to new insights (Koenig and Borries 2006; Snaith and Chapman 2007). This research has taken on a very behavioural flavour examining variables like within-group aggression and day length as a function of group size or food availability (Snaith and Chapman 2008; Teichroeb and Sicotte 2018). As such this body of research has typically supported the importance of food availability as a determinant of population size, which we have previously discussed. For example, folivores have been demonstrated to deplete the resources within a single tree (patch) through their feeding and the speed of patch depletion is a function of patch size and the number of feeding individuals (Chapman 1988; Tombak et al. 2012). Similarly, colobus monkeys have been shown to compete more over food (within-group scramble and between-group competition) when food is scarce (Teichroeb and Sicotte 2018).

Interspecific Competition

Two or more colobine species are found at a number of field sites and at some sites there is considerable dietary overlap between the species (e.g. Kibale – *Colobus guereza* and *Piliocolobus tephrosceles*; Chapman et al. 2002a), while sympatric species at other sites have markedly different diets (e.g. Kuala Lompat – *Presbytis melalophus* and *Trachypithecus obscurus*; Davies 1994). In most situations, it is unlikely that colobines will overlap significantly in diet with cercopithecine monkeys or apes, although at some Asian sites they share some fruit resources (Davies 1991). In Africa, overlap is typically much less. For example, the diet of redtail monkeys and red colobus of Kibale overlapped by only 19.2% of their foraging time despite spending a great deal of time in mixed-species groups (Chapman and Chapman 1996, 2000b). These results suggest that interspecific food competition is low among African colobine and cercopithecine primates.

However, there are a number of reasons to be sceptical about drawing interpretations about competition from these data. First, it could be that competition is only significant during periods of food shortages, such that the available data may be inadequate for detecting competition. Since periods of food scarcity can be decades apart, interspecific competition can be an important, undetected, selective pressure on population dynamics, foraging strategies, digestive physiology and anatomy. Second, there can be a large amount of spatial and temporal variation in diet and this can greatly influence measures of dietary overlap used to evaluate the potential for competition. For example, Struhsaker and Oates (1975) studied red colobus and a black-and-white colobus groups with adjacent home ranges and found dietary overlap to be 7.1%. A similar study by Chapman et al. (2002a) calculated dietary overlap for the two neighbouring groups of red colobus to be 37.3%, while that between red and a black-and-white colobus group was 43.2%, when the black-and-white colobus group's home range fell entirely within the home range of the red colobus group – the scale at which competition actually occurs. These values suggest that we should re-evaluate interpretations from studies of dietary overlap that involve interspecific contrasts of groups that occupy different areas or groups of different species studied at different times. Third, competition can only occur if the resource is limiting. While there are studies showing patch depletion in colobines (Snaith and Chapman 2005; Tombak et al. 2012), there is no study to our knowledge that clearly demonstrates that a population is limited by the availability of a particular resource. Given the scientific evidence needed to demonstrate competition (Connell 1980), it is the authors opinion that the scientific community has not obtained conclusive evidence for the role of competition in limiting colobine populations. However, there is one study in cercopithecines that is suggestive of competition (Houle et al. 2006). Houle et al. (2006) demonstrated that socially dominant primate species could exclude subordinate species from resources, such that the subordinate species tended to feed in the tree after the dominant one had left resulting in lower feeding returns for the subordinate species (higher give-up-times). However, the smaller subordinate species often found fruiting trees before the dominant species did, a mechanism that may enable coexistence. But the potential for competition for fruit might be very different from that for leaves.

Predation

While there are a number of anecdotal descriptions of predation on colobines in both Africa and Asia (reviewed by Davies 1994), only a handful of studies report long-term data on colobine predation rates. In Africa and Asia there are large eagles that are known to prey on primates. In Kibale, three studies have examined the impact of crown-hawk eagles on colobine predation (*Stephanoaetus coronatus*; see also anecdotal reports in (Cordeiro 1992; Gautier-Hion and Tutin 1988; Maisels et al. 1993; Shultz 2002; Shultz et al. 2004) in areas where the colobine density was known. In an 11-month study, Skorupa (1989) found the bones of five black-and-white colobus and three red colobus below the nest of a pair of eagles. In a 39-month study of a single nesting pair, Struhsaker and Leakey (1990) estimated that the minimum percentage killed per year for red colobus males was 0 and 0.047 for females, and <1.08 for male and 0.047 for female black-and-white colobus. Finally, in a 37-month study of the remains under two nests, Mitani et al. (2001) found evidence of four black-and-white colobus and nine red colobus. It is difficult to know the impact of crown-hawk eagles in general since the territories of the birds are not known [estimates range from 3.8 km^2 (Mitani et al. 2001) to 10 km^2 (Struhsaker and Leakey 1990)]; however, given the density of the colobines, their potential reproductive rates, and the pressure exerted by other predators in Kibale (e.g. chimpanzees), it seems unlikely that crown-hawk eagle predation is a limiting factor for these colobine populations. A study of 16 nests in Taï Forest, Ivory Coast, monitored over different periods of time found the remains of 31 *Piliocolobus badius*, nine *Procolobus verus*, and nine *Colobus polykomos* (McGraw et al. 2006), but the time frame over which these animal's remains were deposited was unknown.

In many locations where primates are studied, large felid predators have been hunted to local extinction or their numbers are dramatically reduced; however, there is some interesting data on felid predation from Taï National Park, Ivory Coast. Two studies have conducted faecal analyses and have found colobine remains in leopard (*Panthera pardus*) dung (ESM Table 19.3) (Hoppe-Dominik 1984; Zuberbuhler and Jenny 2002). Interpreting these data is not straightforward and determining actual rates of predation is not possible. Nonetheless, these data suggest that colobines may be frequently preyed upon, indicating that more information is needed on predation by felids at natural densities to understand their impact on colobine populations.

Despite the lack of conclusive evidence that avian or felid predators limit colobine populations, there is clear evidence for the importance of predation by chimpanzees (*Pan troglodytes*) at some, but not all, locations. Davies (1994) presents an excellent review of the early studies of chimpanzee predation of red colobus (Boesch 1994a; Takahata et al. 1984; Uehara 1977), showing that chimpanzees kill a large proportion of the population at some sites, but not at other sites. A 40 month study from Gombe reported that chimpanzees killed between 20% and 40% of the population (Wrangham and Bergmann-Riss 1990). One would imagine that such high predation rates would drive the red colobus to extinction, but it has not.

More recent studies indicate that chimpanzee predation on red colobus correlates with changing red colobus population density at Ngogo field site in Kibale. The very large chimpanzee community there preys heavily on red colobus (Mitani and Watts 1999; Mitani et al. 2002). The high level of predation corresponded with a steep decline in red colobus numbers as indicated by census data (Lwanga et al. 2011; Teelen 2007b). Fortunately for the endangered red colobus population of Kibale, large new areas have become available through forest restoration that are suitable for red colobus (Omeja et al. 2012). Thus, the red colobus population throughout the park is increasing (Adamescu et al. 2018; Chapman et al. 2018a,b)

Disease

Disease can clearly cause short-term reductions in primate population size (Collias and Southwick 1952; Milton 1996; Work et al. 1957). For example, a 50% decline in the howler monkey (*Alouatta palliata*) population on BCI occurred between 1933 and 1951 and was attributed to yellow fever (Collias and Southwick 1952). Over 5000 gorillas are thought to have died from Ebola during a single outbreak (Bermejo et al. 2006). In the Namib desert, heavy tick infestations (*Rhipicephalus* spp.) were speculated as the cause of infant mortality for more than half (n = 18) of recorded chacma baboon deaths (*Papio ursinus*) (Brian and Bohrman 1992). Rudran and Fernandez-Duque (2003) quantified demographic changes in a population of red howler monkeys (*Alouatta seniculus*) over 30 years and reported a 74% population decline that they attributed to disease.

Given the high number of studies on colobines, it is surprising that we know of no case of disease causing dramatic mortality in a population, though some deaths have been attributed to illness. Struhsaker (2010) describes a disease that causes ulcers on the face, scrotum, penis and perineum of red colobus in Kibale, which is suspected as the cause of the death for at least 10 of the 17 adult males in one group. At the Kanyawara site, this disease was first described in 1972 (Struhsaker 2010), but was not observed again until approximately 2012 (Chapman and Goldberg unpublished data). Recently there have been a number of viruses described in red colobus (Goldberg et al. 2008a, 2009; Lauck et al. 2011; Lauck et al. 2013a,b), but there is no indication of these viruses leading to acute mortality. Until data to the contrary are available, disease should not be considered as a major factor influencing colobine populations.

Conclusions

Despite attempts to better understand the factors affecting colobine population dynamics, empirical data on the effects of food quality and availability, competition for food resources, predation and disease remain limited. Given the extent of deforestation and the occurrence of bushmeat hunting, it is imperative that we establish more protected areas that effectively restore critical habitats, as well as reducing deforestation and bushmeat hunting in general (Chapman et al. 2018). However, our ability to do this is currently very limited. Food quality, particularly its protein-to fibre ratio, warrants further research as a parameter that may limit colobine populations, but there are a number of reasons to doubt the generalizability of this model. The composition of forests (i.e. relative abundance of leguminous trees), and the food they contain, may also be a promising means to elucidate colobine population limits in Southeast Asia, but this does not generalize to Africa. There is no evidence that natural disasters occur with sufficient frequently to limit colobine numbers, particularly with their dietary flexibility. Given the difficulty of determining niche overlap and competition, no conclusion can be made regarding the role of interspecific competition in limiting colobine abundance. Predation of both African and Asian colobines occurs, and despite the high rate of predation by chimpanzees in some areas leading to declines in local populations of colobines, predation does not seem to be a general limiting factor. Finally, there is no evidence that disease limits colobine populations, despite its importance in some other monkeys and apes.

Interestingly, we have reached many of the same conclusions regarding factors influencing colobine populations as did Davies (1994) over 20 years ago, despite having added new data and additional examples to this important discussion. It seems most likely that colobines are limited by food availability, but the exact nature of that limitation remains unclear. It is interesting to ask why few advances have been made, but is clear that plenty of opportunities exist to conduct more thorough and detailed research into the question of what limits colobine populations. Areas that we view as especially promising are (1) the nutritional quality of colobine foods with respect to protein, fibre and other parameters like energy, minerals etc.; (2) the importance of disease (e.g. while disease may not cause direct mortality, it may decrease fitness and limit longevity); and finally, (3) the quantification of interspecific competition, such as the study conducted by Houle and colleagues (2006) on cercopithecines. This is especially important given that global deforestation rates in tropical regions are expected to rise as the need to feed the earth's growing population increasingly requires more land for agriculture.

Acknowledgements

Funding was provided by Canada Research Chairs Program, Wildlife Conservation Society, Natural Science and Engineering Research Council of Canada, National Geographic and Fonds Québécois de la Recherche sur la Nature et les Technologies for the research in Kibale. CC thanks the Humboldt Foundation for providing the time to develop some of these ideas and the IDRC grant 'Climate Change and Increasing Human–Wildlife Conflict'. We extend a special thanks to Julian Parada for helpful comments on the research.

20 State of Asian Colobines and Their Conservation Needs

John Sha, Ikki Matsuda, Qihai Zhou, Andie Ang and Tilo Nadler

Introduction

Asian colobines represent 75% of the colobine subfamily of Afroeurasian monkeys and make up close to half of all non-human primate species found in Asia (Groves 2001; Mittermeier et al. 2013). These monkeys are specialized for leaf-eating: multi-chambered stomachs with enlarged foregut and microflora to process plant material (Chapter 6; Chivers 1994; Kay and Davies 1994) and molars with well-developed shear crests adapted for shearing tough food items such as leaves (Chapter 5; Fleagle 2013; Lucas and Teaford 1994; Swindler 2002). Colobines have wide variations in social structures that can consist of one-male multi-female groups, all-male groups and multilevel societies (Grueter and van Schaik 2010; Newton and Dunbar 1994). They are also found in a wide range of habitats (e.g. tropical rainforests, subtropical mountain forests and dry forests), at different latitudinal and altitudinal zones, with elevations ranging from sea level to more than 4000 m asl (Kirkpatrick 2011; Nijman 2014). Owing to the diverse ecological needs of Asian colobines, the successful long-term conservation of these species would require a multitude of strategies to ensure that species-specific protection needs are met, as well as more holistic collaborative approaches to ensure better protection of threatened species across their distribution ranges. For this chapter, we follow the taxonomic classification in Roos et al. (2014) and the IUCN Red List of Threatened Species 2008 (www.iucnredlist.org/) to present an overview of the state of 55* species (87 subspecies) of Asian colobines and discuss the conservation measures and needs for the better protection of these species.

Conservation Status

Across geographical regions and countries in Asia, the number of colobine species and subspecies that are considered threatened ('Critically Endangered', 'Endangered' and 'Vulnerable') are highest in Sundaland (21) and Indo-Burma (20), followed by the Indian sub-continent (12) and China (11) (Figure 20.1). At the taxon level, 14 of 28 *Presbytis*, 23 of 31 *Trachypithecus*, 8 of 15 *Semnopithecus*, all seven *Rhinopithecus*, all three *Pygathrix*, both *Simias* and the only *Nasalis* are threatened (Figure 20.2).

This chapter includes Electronic Supplementary Material (ESM) at: www.cambridge.org/colobines
*Updates to the taxonomy of Asian colobines added new species – *Trachypithecus popa* and elevated subspecies *Trachypithecus phayrei shanicus* to *Trachypithecus melamera* (Roos et al. 2020); subspecies of *Presbytis femoralis* to *P. femoralis*, *P. percura* and *P. robinsonii* (Ang et al. 2020). See ESM Appendix 20.1 for details.

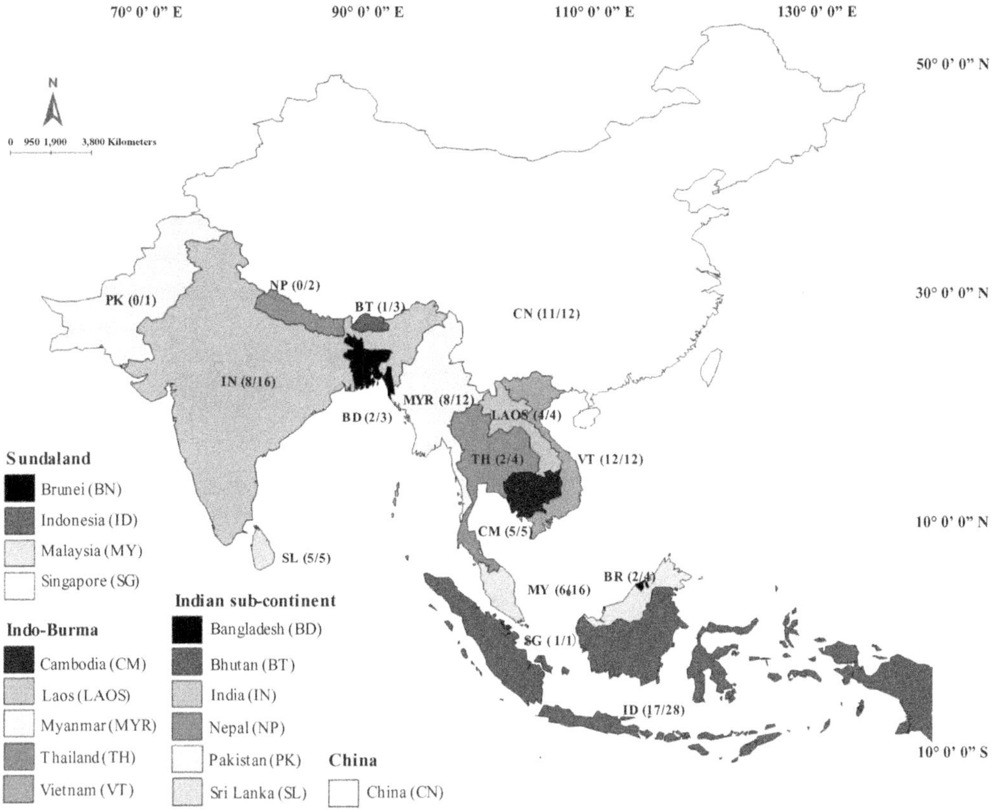

Figure 20.1 Conservation status of Asian colobines classified by broad geographical regions and countries denoted on map by country abbreviation (number of threatened taxa/total). We used the following classification for regions: 'Sundaland' as a subset of the Southeast Asian political region, excluding countries in the gulf of Thailand, i.e. Cambodia, Thailand and Vietnam, which is classified under Indo-Burma, and excluded portions of eastern India and southern China that are classified under 'Indian sub-continent' and 'China', respectively.

The Sundaland region is home to 41 colobine taxa, with the largest number of threatened taxa found in Indonesia (17). Two subspecies of Bornean banded langur (*Presbytis chrysomelas chrysomelas*) in north-western Borneo and *P. c. cruciger* in north-western Borneo and Brunei), two subspecies of simakobu (*Simias concolor concolor* and *S. c. siberu*), Mentawai langur (*Presbytis potenziani*) from Mentawai Islands off the western coast of Sumatra, and the silvered lutung (*Trachypithecus cristatus vigilans*) of Natuna Islands are 'Critically Endangered'. Indo-Burma harbours 24 taxa of colobines, with main distribution ranges within the countries of Vietnam and Myanmar. Here, 20 taxa are threatened and have populations fewer than 1000 individuals. The Myanmar snub-nosed monkey (*R. strykeri*) in Myanmar (also found in China) (Meyer 2017), the Tonkin snub-nosed monkey (*R. avunculus*), grey-shanked douc (*Pygathrix cinerea*), Cat Ba langur (*Trachypithecus poliocephalus*) and Delacour's langur (*T. delacouri*) in Vietnam are 'Critically Endangered'. On the Indian sub-continent, there are 20 taxa of colobines which occur mainly in India and

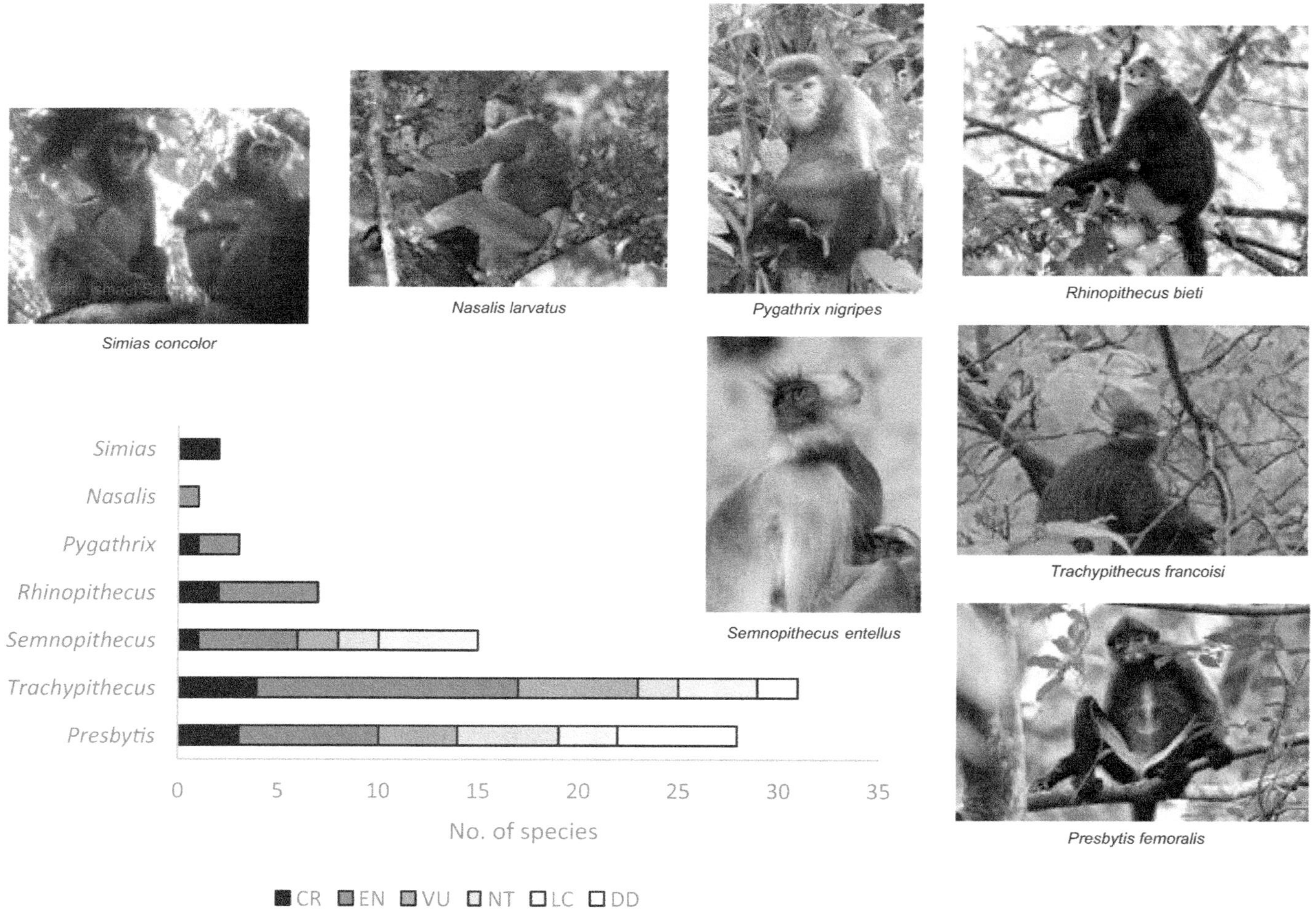

Figure 20.2 Conservation status of Asian colobines (IUCN 2008). Updates to their threat status (IUCN 2020/21) elevated several taxa to threatened status - *Presbytis* (+11) and *Trachypithecus* (+6) (see ESM Appendix 20.1). *Pygathrix nigripes* and *Pygathrix nemaeus* were elevated from EN to CR.

Sri Lanka. The western purple-faced langur (*Semnopithecus vetulus nestor*) is 'Critically Endangered' with no reliable estimates of its population size (Schwitzer et al. 2017) and high likelihood of numerous local extinctions (Rudran 2007). In China, where 12 colobine taxa (with the possible addition of another species, *T. pileatus*) occur, more than three-quarters show trends of decreasing population sizes of fewer than 3000 individuals, and most species are distributed in small and isolated subpopulations across different provinces and counties (Li B et al. 2018; Zhao X et al. 2019a). The white-headed langur (*T. leucocephalus*) is 'Critically Endangered' and likely locally extinct in many areas within its limited range in Guangxi province (Wang et al. 2005). About two-thirds of Asian colobines (*51* taxa) are endemic to only one country and a third (*26* taxa) show distribution ranges across multiple countries (ESM Appendix 20.1).

Status of Colobine Habitats

Asian colobines occur in a wide range of habitats which continue to be lost at alarming rates within Asia. From 2000 to 2014, range countries lost between 2.0% and 12.5% of forest cover, with highest losses in the Sundaland region in Indonesia and Malaysia; and in Cambodia in the Indo-Burma region (UNEP-WCMC and IUCN 2017). India has lost the majority of its moist deciduous forests in the last century, with native vegetation shrunken and restricted to small protected areas (Bajpai et al. 2012). Virtually all of what remains of dry forests in Asia are now concentrated mostly in Myanmar (Miles et al. 2006). The east Deccan Plateau in Sri Lanka has lost most of its evergreen dry forests (Wikramanayake et al. 2002). Coastal wetlands have also been lost or severely degraded throughout Asia (Lee et al. 2006; Zhao S et al. 2006), with estimated losses in China, India and various Asian countries at up to 60% within the past 50 years (Gopal et al. 2013). The limestone hill forests in China have been badly degraded. Many flat lands among hilly terrain have been cultivated and are devoid of natural vegetation (Huang C et al. 2002; Li Y et al. 2007; Zhou et al. 2007).

We used a broad classification of ecological zones following Global Forest Resources Assessment (FAO 2001) to assess habitat use by Asian colobines (Figure 20.3).

Subtropical Humid and Mountain Forests

Subtropical humid forest covers an ecological zone with main distribution south of the Yangtze River in China. *Trachypithecus leucocephalus*, *T. francoisi* and *Rhinopithecus* spp. are found in Guangxi province, the Sichuan basin and Yungui Plateau (Yunnan-Guizhou regions) in southern and southwestern China. Vegetation in this zone consists of pine forest, deciduous forest mixed with evergreen species, and mixed and deciduous evergreen forest. Subtropical mountain systems cover extensive areas of Asia from Turkey to the eastern reaches of the Himalayas in southern China. Three subspecies of golden snub-nosed monkeys (*R. roxellana*) occur within this zone in China's subtropical central and southwestern highlands, where alpine conifer forest is the dominant forest type.

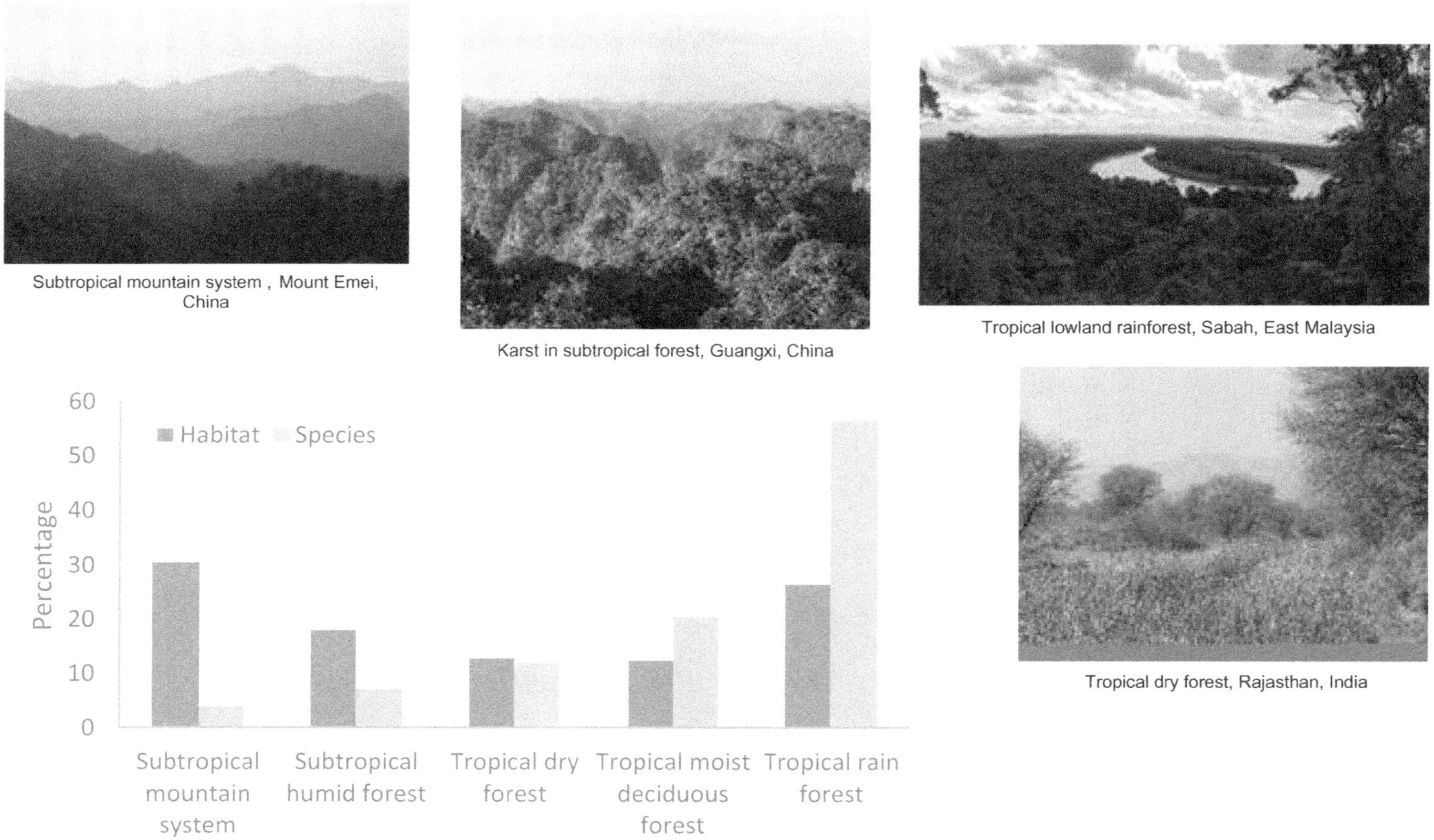

Figure 20.3 Percentage of Asian colobines found in different ecological zones. Species found in more than one zone are included in species counts of the respective zones.

Tropical Dry and Moist Deciduous Forests

Tropical dry forests are found on the coastal plains along the Gulf of Bengal and the north-eastern part of the Deccan Plateau in India and Sri Lanka, dominated by evergreen forest. It also covers parts of the Indo-Burmese region in river basins in Myanmar, Thailand, Cambodia and Vietnam, where dry deciduous dipterocarp forest and mixed deciduous woodland, teak and pine dominate the forest landscape. Colobines that use this zone are mainly found on the Indian sub-continent, with several species of *Semnopithecus* and *Trachypithecus* in India and Sri Lanka, including the 'Critically Endangered' *S. vetulus nestor*. Within the Indo-Burmese region, *T. pileatus* also occurs in these forests.

The moist deciduous zone includes the lowlands of Sri Lanka, much of peninsular India, most of Myanmar and the valleys, lower foothills and low plateaus of Vietnam, Laos and Cambodia. The natural vegetation is mostly deciduous or semi-deciduous forest, commonly known as monsoon forest. Bamboo forests are common in India and Myanmar. Extensive deciduous forests remain on hilly parts of Myanmar and some patches in southern Vietnam. Other parts of the Indo-Burmese region are widely covered with deciduous dipterocarp and teak forest. *Semnopithecus* spp. occur mainly on the Indian subcontinent while in the Indo-Burmese region, species of *Trachypithecus* and *Pyathrix*, and *R. strykeri*

Tropical Rainforests

Tropical rainforest covers large areas of lowland habitats in the Malay Archipelago of Southeast Asia, some parts of India and Sri Lanka on the southwestern coasts, parts of Myanmar and the eastern Himalayan foothills. The lushest rainforests are found in the Malay Archipelago, harbouring rich flora, with Dipterocarpaceae dominating areas west of the Wallace Line. Most of the colobine species in Asia (56 species) can be found within this ecological zone.

Specific Habitats

Karst Limestone Forest

In Southeast Asia, karsts of monsoonal zones of the tropics are found most extensively in Indonesia, Thailand, Laos and Vietnam. Subtropical karsts of South China are found mostly in the southwest of the country with continuous distributions mainly in the three provinces of Guizhou, Guangxi, Yunnan, westward to the Tibetan Plateau and southward to Myanmar, Laos and Vietnam (Jiang et al. 2014). Karst is a unique habitat type that is used by many species of colobines, most of which are threatened. These include the *T. francoisi*-group characterized as 'limestone langurs' (Groves 2004; Zhou et al. 2011b, 2013), and also *R. avunculus*, the Phayre's langur (*T. phayrei*) and the red-shanked douc (*Pygathrix nemaeus*) which occur occasionally in karst habitat.

Flooded Forest

Flooded forest represents another unique set of habitats across Southeast Asia and the Indian sub-continent. Flooded forest habitats that are found in this region include mainly freshwater flooded peat swamp and mangrove forests with over two-thirds of Southeast Asian primates known to use these forest types at least to a certain extent (Sha et al. 2018). These include colobine species like *N. larvatus*, banded langur (*Presbytis femoralis*) and *S. concolor*. On the Indian subcontinent, the black-foots grey langur (*S. hypoleucos*) and one of the rarest primate species in India, the golden langur (*T. geei*) is known to use flooded forests. In the Indo-Burmese region, *T. germaini* uses this forest type to some extent in Thailand, Myanmar and Cambodia.

Highland Forest

Asian colobines are mostly found in lowland forests at low elevations, with only a handful of species found at minimum elevation ranges of above 1000 m asl. These include *Rhinopithecus* spp. in China and Myanmar that inhabit high altitude deciduous broadleaf and conifer evergreen forests between 1000 and 4500 m (Li B et al. 2000; Grueter 2013; Chapter 12; Kirkpatrick and Grueter 2010); and the Nepal grey langur (*S. schistaceus*) and Kashmir grey langur (*S. ajax*) on the Indian sub-continent. Several species can also be found at wide distribution ranges from near sea level to 3000 m asl., for example, *T. auratus* in Indonesia, capped langur (*T. pileatus*) in Bangladesh, Nepal, Bhutan, China, India and Myanmar; and *T. geei* in India (Chapter 15).

Conservation Threats

We assessed specific threats to Asian colobines using the IUCN Threats Classification Scheme (www.iucnredlist.org/resources/threat-classification-scheme). This classification is based on threats to individual taxa, with 12 broad categories of threats, including (1) residential and commercial development; (2) agriculture and aquaculture; (3) energy production and mining; (4) transportation and service corridors; (5) biological resource use; (6) human intrusions and disturbance; (7) natural system modifications; (8) invasive and other problematic species, genes and diseases; (9) pollution; (10) geological events; (11) climate change and severe weather and (12) others. Only eight of these threats had data relevant to Asian colobines, with the exclusion of threats 8, 10, 11 and 12. We present the summarized threats to Asian colobines in Figure 20.4.

Asian colobine taxa are most threatened by biological resource uses like hunting and harvesting (82) and agriculture and aquaculture that result in habitat loss, fragmentation and degradation (81), followed by housing, industry and recreation (58); effects of natural ecosystem modifications from fires and dams (29); transportation and service corridors with building of roads, utility lines and transport lines (25); energy production through hydropower dam construction, oil and gas drilling,

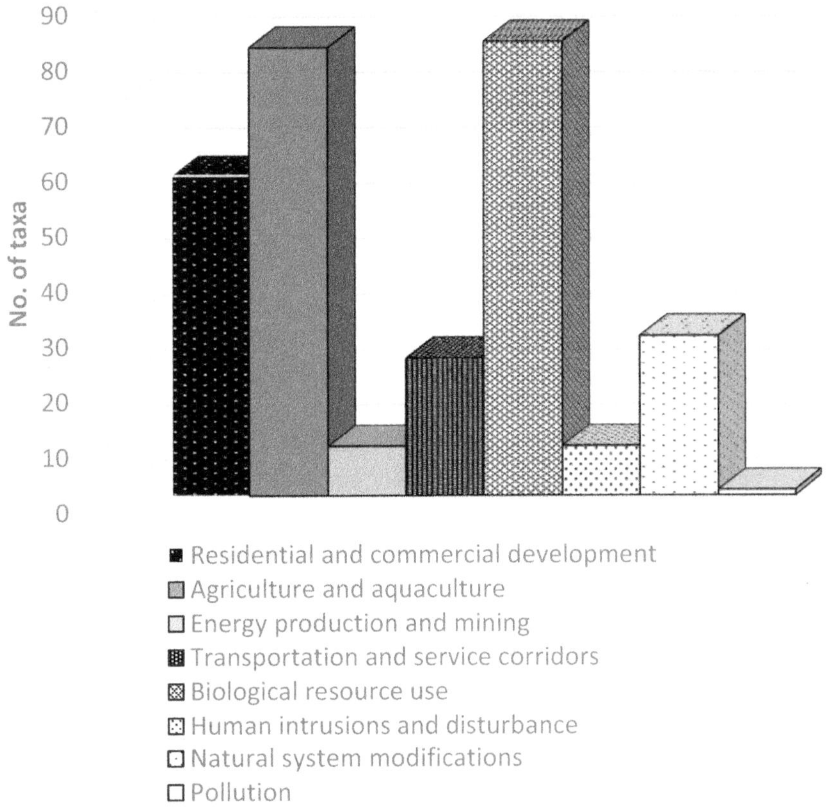

Figure 20.4 Threats to colobine species (IUCN Threats Classification Scheme, www.iucnredlist.org/resources/threat-classification-scheme).

mining and quarrying (9), human intrusions and disturbance through recreation activities and conflicts (9); and pollution (1).

Biological Resource Use

Biological resource use of primate species through illegal hunting for food; sale of body parts used in traditional medicine; zoo and pet trade; biomedical research; and production of ornaments are widespread throughout Asia (Covert et al. 2017; Nijman et al. 2011; Selvan et al. 2013).

The illegal hunting of langurs in Indo-Burma and China remains a significant threat to their survival. During a three-year period, 267 criminal cases with live primates in the illegal trade were recorded in Vietnam, with 41 langur cases representing 16% of recorded cases, and undiscovered or unregistered cases undoubtedly much higher (Tran Thu Hang 2010). During another six-year period (2008–2013), 2916 primate were registered in the illegal trade, an average of 486 primates per year including about 80 colobines (Nadler and Roos 2017). Together with undocumented cases, it is estimated that a minimum of two colobines end up in the illegal trade every week. The 'Critically Endangered' Delacour's langur that is endemic to Vietnam lost, in one decade, between 1990 and 2000 more than 300 individuals or an average of 30 individuals per year – which reduced the total population to about 50% (Nadler 2015). During a decade from 2000 to 2010, 10 out of 19 subpopulations (which were present in the 1990s) were eradicated. The 'Critically Endangered' and also endemic Cat Ba langur had an estimated population in the 1960s of 2400–2700 individuals. During 1970 and 1980, about 500 individuals were killed for the production of traditional medicine. A comprehensive survey in 1999/2000 estimated only 104–135 individuals (Nadler and Ha Thang Long 2000), and the population dropped to the current only 60 individuals (Nadler 2013). The langur populations (*T. leucocephalus* and *T. francoisi*) in Guangxi has similarly decreased dramatically due to hunting (Huang C et al. 2002; Li Y et al. 2007). For example, *T. francoisi*, populations declined by 90% between the early 1980s and early 2000s primarily due to hunting (Li Y et al. 2007). Approximately 100 Critically Endangered *R. strykeri* were hunted in Myanmar and China over the past 20–30 years (Meyer et al. 2017), which is significant given their low population numbers.

In Indonesia, it was shown that even subsistence hunting can have major effects on colobine populations already decimated by land conversion and habitat loss, for example, *S. concolor*, *P. potenziani*; and populations of *Trachypithecus* spp. and *Presbytis* spp. (Estrada et al. 2018; Fuentes 2002). In several langur species, bezoar stones are found in their digestive organs, and were considered as medicine (Meijaard and Nijman 2000). The hunting for these stones dramatically reduced the population of the four grey langur species in Indonesia (*P. frontata*, *hosei*, *sabana* and *canicrus*), because these stones can only be found in only about 5% of individuals; with the collapse of the Hose's langur (*P. hosei*) population through such causes of poaching (Nijman 2005).

Other biological resource uses that pose threats to colobines include subsistence and commercial logging that can negatively impact habitats and food resources. Demand for wood products has also seen ever-expanding worldwide demand since the 1980s, with Southeast Asia accounting for 10% of mahogany exports in 2010, from 2000 to 2010, some 3000 km^2 of mostly lowland forest in Indonesia was lost to logging (Abood et al. 2015; Estrada 2013; Gaveau et al. 2014). In Indonesia, logging activities had documented impacts on several endemic langur species (Supriatna and Mariati 2014). *Presbytis* spp. habitats on Borneo are highly threatened by logging concessions (Smith 2014). On the island of Banguran, Indonesia, *P. natunae* survives in habitats covered with 70% logged forest (Lammertink 2003). In China, the expansion of the timber industry in recent past decades, in addition to illegal logging has led to the loss of 1.5 million ha of forest in many areas that coincide with zones of high primate diversity (Liu XN et al. 2013; Sun et al. 2005). Other habitats used by colobine species like fragile karst landscapes are highly exploited for a variety of products and services, as building and construction material, for cement production and also for decoration, including stones for bonsai (Clements et al. 2006; Nadler and Roos 2017).

Agriculture and Aquaculture

Expansion of agriculture and aquaculture are key drivers affecting trends in habitat loss, fragmentation and degradation of primate habitats. The demand for liquid biofuels energy, particularly ethanol and biodiesel made from corn, sugarcane, soybeans, oil palm etc. is driving large-scaled habitat conversion to cropland (Estrada 2013; Koh and Ghazoul 2008). The expansion of oil palm plantations, and increasingly, soybeans are a major threat to forest loss in Southeast Asia, with Indonesia and Malaysia accounting for 80% of the world's oil palm production (Casson 2003; Estrada 2013; Koh and Ghazoul 2010). Between 1990 and 2010, agricultural expansion in primate range regions resulted in forest cover loss in 68% of the area currently used by primates; and is predicted to lead to unsustainable spatial conflict for 75% of primate species (Estrada et al. 2017). In Indonesia, one of the most important range countries for colobines, the estimated increase of agricultural land from 2001 to 2015 was about 5%, resulting in primate range contraction of 72% (Estrada et al. 2018). Subtropical mountain rainforest and evergreen broadleaf forest are threatened by conversion to arable lands and shrublands, and expansion of rubber plantations (below 500–800 m asl) (Li Y et al. 2007). Prior to logging bans in the late 1990s, highland areas in China were heavily deforested (Zhao Q 1988), and recent studies are showing similar trends in Southeast Asia (Nadler and Roos 2017; Zeng et al. 2018).

Aquaculture in the East Asian region has also seen annual average growth rates in output from 2000 to 2006 more than double those from 1990 to 2000 (Hishamunda et al. 2009); and its contribution to global seafood production now surpasses that of wild-caught fisheries (Froehlich et al. 2018). Conversion of riparian habitats to fish and shrimp farms has severely impacted coastal forests, with the east coast of India witnessing a loss of 2606 ha mangrove area as a result of a 3657 ha increase in aquaculture area was from 1973 to 2006 (Pattanaik and Prasad 2011). Flooded forests are being lost at a very high rate, with peat flooded forest loss of 19.7% and mangrove forest loss of 12.5% between 2000 and 2010 (Miettinen et al. 2011). Several colobine species that are found almost exclusively in these forest types are therefore particularly threatened.

In Sumatra, populations of Thomas' langur (*P. thomasi*), black-and-white langur (*P. bicolor*), black-crested Sumatran langur (*P. melalophos*) and *P. femoralis* have lost up to 82% of their original habitats (Supriatna et al. 2017). Loss of flooded forests in Borneo has resulted in severe fragmentation of *N. larvatus* habitats (Lhota et al. 2019a; Matsuda et al. 2020b; Sha et al. 2008) and the Riau pale-thighed langur (*P. siamensis cana*) in Sumatra (Supriatna and Mariati 2014). The once common Hose's langur has seen a 50%–80% decline in population (Nijman 2005). In India, the expansion of rubber plantations has severely affected many primate species, including *T. phayrei* (Mazumder 2014; Mukajee 2018). In China, gene flow of *Rhinopithecus* spp. appeared to be strongly impeded by agricultural landscapes (Liu Z et al. 2015). The *T. leucocephalus* and *T. francoisi* populations in Guangxi province are completely fragmented by agricultural landscapes and it is impossible for gene exchange among these populations (Huang C et al. 2008a; Li Y et al. 2007). Although some primate species can survive temporarily in fragmented and degraded forests, they are multiple negative effects to food resources, resting sites, predation, conflict with humans, genetic viability and zoonotic disease transmission (reviewed in Estrada et al. 2017; Laurance et al. 2014; Supriatna et al. 2017).

Residential and Commercial Development

Urban landscapes are expanding with urban populations and it is estimated that 60% of the world's population will be totally urbanized by 2030 (Seto et al. 2012) with 90% of the increase concentrated in Asia and Africa (United Nations 2014). In 2012, China's urban population had exceeded its rural population for the first time, with 51.3% of an entire population of nearly 1.35 billion living in cities (Deng et al. 2015). The effects of urbanization are self-explanatory, with urbanized land areas developed at the expense of natural habitats. However, other mixed effects could surface, for example, rural depopulation resulting from human movements to urban areas can sometimes be beneficial for wildlife and protection of reserve areas (Chapman 2018; Li B et al. 2018). Tourism activities, if not well managed, can also result in disturbance of naturally shy colobine species, for example, *N. larvatus* (Lhota et al. 2019b).

Natural Systems Modifications

The rapid proliferation of dams in Asia has caused widespread hydrologic alteration of freshwater ecosystems, especially those of riparian floodplains and wetlands (Gopal et al. 2013; Zhao S et al. 2006; Zhao Q et al. 2012). Tropical peat swamps and mangroves are particularly vulnerable to such effects which can be exacerbated by droughts that cause fires. The El Niño events of 1997–1998 resulted in devastating losses of habitats for flooded forest specialist like the *N. larvatus* in Borneo (Yeager and Frederiksson 1998).

Transportation and Service Corridors

The expansion of trade increases the need for accessibility through more efficient transportation networks. The expansion of industrialized agriculture, logging, mining, oil/gas extraction, and the building of dams and power-line corridors in tropical forest areas is expected to increase human transportation road networks by some 25 million km by 2050 (Estrada et al. 2017). In Indonesia, thousands of logging roads now penetrate deep into protected forests and national parks (Alamgir et al. 2017; Rainer et al. 2018; Supriatna et al. 2017). In Kalimantan, white-fronted langur (*Presbytis frontata*) habitats within protected reserves have been severely fragmented by road networks (Lhota et al. 2019a). Accessibility of a forest is often the most important factor leading to deforestation and other escalating effects like logging, increased bushmeat hunting, and the illegal wildlife trade (reviewed in Clements et al. 2014; Estrada et al. 2017, 2018; Laurance et al. 2009).

Energy Production and Mining

By 2035, global demand for oil and natural gas is projected to increase in primate-rich areas (e.g. by more than 50% in Borneo), and to adversely affect primates (Butt et al. 2013; Estrada et al. 2018). The construction of dams for generating electricity is increasing in the world's most biodiverse river basins including the Mekong River and in China (Winemiller et al. 2016; Zhao S et al. 2006). In Indo-Burma are 70–80 hydropower dams in planning which would partly affect the habitat of colobines (Rainer et al. 2018; Zarfl et al. 2015). Mining concessions are also increasingly threatening primate habitats (Abood et al. 2015). In Kalimantan, Indonesia, gold mining was shown as a major threat to *N. larvatus* (Meijaard and Nijman 2000). On the islands of Sumatra and Borneo, gold mining and limestone karst mining activities have directly impeded conservation efforts to protect many arboreal primates like *Presbytis* spp. and *Trachypithecus* spp. (Supriatna et al. 2017).

Human Intrusions and Disturbance

Some primates are more behaviourally and ecologically resilient than others in the face of anthropogenic disturbance; and depending on the level of human cultural-religious tolerance, this interaction can promote crop raiding and resultant conflict issues (Paterson et al. 2005). The only well-documented species of colobine that is highly adaptable to urban areas is *S. ajax* (Pirta 1997); but other colobines have been documented to use plantation areas, for example, in rubber plantations: *N. larvatus* (Soendjoto 2003), *Trachypithecus* spp. and *Presbytis* spp. (Supriatna et al. 2017). Civil unrest has also affected colobine populations. For example, in Cambodia, armed conflicts have severely affected populations of the black-shanked doucs (*P. nigripes*) through intensification of military-related resource use (Loucks et al. 2009). Ethnic violence that broke out in 1989 in the range of *T. geei* resulted in considerable loss of their forests (Srivastava 2006).

Pollution

The negative effects of pollution on colobine or primate species, for that matter, are not well documented and in the IUCN threats classification, only one species, *R. bieti* is considered to be under threat from 'agricultural and forestry effluents'. Some important food resources for *R. bieti* have been shown to be highly susceptible to environmental changes such as air pollution and climate change (Chapter 12). *R. roxellana* is also exposed to the effects of heavy metal pollution in China (Liu Q et al. 2015). The threat of pollution from mining can contribute to poisoning and pollution of soil and water (Alvarez-Berrıos and Aide 2015), which may lead to longer term negative effects.

Climate Change

Although the IUCN Threats Classification Scheme did not consider any colobines to be threatened by climate change, numerous primates are expected to experience changing climatic conditions. East and Southeast Asia are considered hotspots of primate vulnerability resulting from climate change-induced range contraction (Carvalho et al. 2019; Estrada et al. 2017, 2018; Graham et al. 2016). Predictive models on the effects of changing climates on temperate forest species have shown historical range contraction and fragmentation due to changes in temperature and precipitation (Nüchel et al. 2018; Zhao X et al. 2019b). Changes in ambient temperature can affect forest productivity (Del Grosso et al. 2008), and a decline in colobine abundance may also be explained by environmental change-induced decrease in protein-to-fibre ratio of food plants over the past 30 years (Rothman and Bryer 2019; Rothman et al. 2015). Climate change effects can exacerbate natural systems modifications through increased wildfires, land desiccation and drought, for example, increase forest fires of degraded peatlands in Sumatra and Kalimantan, Indonesia due to El Niño (Laurance et al. 2014); and severe droughts negatively impacting forest areas in China (Qiu 2010).

Conservation Measures and Needs

Protected Areas Management

Forest protection forms one of the main approaches to conserving wild habitats and species (Wich and Marshall 2016), with primates in unprotected areas showing more rapid population declines (Rovero et al. 2015). Protected areas are positively associated with primate occurrence, for example, in India and Vietnam, where many primates are naturally restricted to less than 5% of total land area, and protected areas are their last refuge (e.g. *S. johnii*, *T. geei*, *T. pileatus* and *T. phayrei*, *T. delacouri*, *T. poliocephalus*, *R. avunculus*) (Karanth et al. 2010; Nadler 2015; Nadler and Ha Thang Long 2000; Nadler and Brockman 2014). In Sumatra, protected areas have been shown to be effective in minimizing population decline of *P. siamensis* (Beaudrot et al. 2016); and from 1990 to 2000, protected areas in Sumatra experienced lower deforestation rates than nearby unprotected areas (Gaveau et al. 2009, 2016). Unfortunately, a large percentage of primates remain outside of protected areas, for example, only 17% of primates in Indonesia exist within protected areas (Estrada 2013; Meijaard and Nijman 2003). The Critically Endangered *Presbytis potenziani* is not represented in any protected area or national park system. *P. femoralis* is found only in Tesso Nilo National Park and *P. siberu and S. concolor* are only in Siberut National Park (Supriatna et al. 2017). In India, over 60% of the closed forests in the northeast remain without any kind of legal or community protection (Srivastava 2006) and protected areas are extremely small in size, highly fragmented and surrounded by high human population densities

(Karanth et al. 2010). In China, population growth of *T. francoisi* over three decades have been constrained by the small size of protected areas (Deng et al. 2019).

In recent years, many primate range countries have increased the extent of protected areas (e.g. in SE Asia) but due to competing needs for industrialization, and a significant number of protected areas in Asia are experiencing substantial deforestation (Estrada et al. 2017; Spracklen et al. 2015). Even where areas are strictly protected, these areas may not represent optimal habitats for certain species, for example, the tree cover in protected areas in Vietnam make up only about 80%, while the remaining 20% is composed of shrub, grassland and bare land (Forest Science Institute of Vietnam 2009). In other cases, species of interest may not be found within park boundaries (Chape et al. 2005) or protected area networks may be located in ecological zones that have low value or are located away from biodiversity rich areas (Joppa and Pfaff 2009), while primate-rich lowland forests that are more suited for industrial and agricultural exploitation are not protected (Venter et al. 2014). In Sumatra, many protected areas are in regions with extremely rugged terrain, or with slopes or elevations unsuitable for agriculture. Most Sumatran primates occur in lowland forest or forests of lower slopes, which are not well represented in protected areas (Supriatna et al. 2017). In China, land ownership is often unclear in and around reserve areas and encroachment into reserves for crop cultivation is common. For protected areas to be effective, they need to adequately cover the habitat needs of species, particularly for colobines with specialized habitat and dietary requirements.

Improved connectivity between protected networks is also needed to link fragmented habitats (Anand et al. 2010; Sanderson et al. 2003), across protected areas in each country and across distribution range countries (De Fries et al. 2007). This is important for connecting subpopulations of individual species (e.g. the highly fragmented populations of *Rhinopithecus* and *Trachypithecus* in China (Li B et al. 2018) and grey-shanked douc in Vietnam (Ha Thang Long 2004).

Reforestation and Restoration

An estimated 350–500 million hectares of former tropical forestlands around the world have been deforested or degraded (ITTO 2002). Reforestation and restoration of these lands can thus provide viable solutions for increasing forest cover for sustaining biodiversity (Lamb 2010). In Asia, reforestation efforts at some regional scales had increased forested land area, for example, Asia had a net gain of some 2% forest from 2000 to 2010 (World Bank 2014). In China, substantial investments in reforestation and tree planting efforts since the turn of the century have resulted in slowing deforestation rates and in slight increases in forest cover, with expected positive gains for primate species (Chapman 2018; Li B et al. 2018; Zhao XM et al. 2018). To counteract deforestation, the government of Vietnam implemented several reforestation programmes and Vietnam's forest has increased continuously since 1965 through forest plantation establishment and natural forest rehabilitation

(Luong Thi Hoan 2014). However, these increases in forest area can be partially explained by increased plantations, monocrops of non-native species and the natural regeneration of forests, and also due to the re-categorization and inclusion of previously excluded limestone forest in the broader category of forest (Li B et al. 2018; Pham Thu Thuy et al. 2012). In contrast, the total area of natural primary forest continuously declined and lowland natural forest is almost entirely gone. Although reforestation can result in increased forest area, most of these areas can consist of monoculture plantations, and forest fragmentation and degradation of natural forests continues (Mayfroidt and Lambin 2008). Values of forest coverage, forest growth and loss can also differ according to sources because there is no conformity of definition to the terms primary forest, natural forest, regenerated forest and plantation (Nadler and Roos 2017). Wetland restoration programmes have been increasingly implemented in recent years, but with much criticism about their actual effectiveness (Kodikara et al. 2017; Lhota et al. 2019a). The direct benefits of wetland restoration to Asian colobine species remain unclear and few studies on the effects of restoration projects and their successful contribution to primate conservation are available (Chapman 2018; Estrada et al. 2017).

Enforcement and Enactment of Protection Laws

Although various national and local laws to protect wildlife and their habitats are available within the range countries of Asian colobines, increased enforcement and enactment of better protection laws that are targeted at specific issues are pertinent. The widespread illegal hunting and sale of primates, despite legal protection is a recurrent problem highlighted throughout Asia (Indonesia: Supriatna et al. 2017); India: Karanth et al. 2010; Vietnam: Nadler and Roos 2017; China: Li B et al. 2018). Laws related to protected areas and land uses are also often not well enforced, for example, illegal logging as well as abuse of selective logging concessions (Gaveau et al. 2009); conflicting land tenure claims and imprecise boundaries due to conflicts between traditional law and government law (Riggs et al. 2016) are widespread in Indonesia. In China, protection laws are mainly restricted to the protection of wildlife species per se and reserve staff do not have the authority to enforce encroachment into reserve areas. Contributing factors to these problems are complex and multi-fold, including, for example, limited enforcement powers, lack of funding for infra-structure, training, incentives and local community support (Supriatna et al. 2002; Nadler and Roos 2017). Stronger political will is generally required across Asia and for governments and management agencies to adequately recognize the most important issues related to wildlife and habitat protection laws and improving specific policies that can be practically implemented and enforced on the ground level. In cases where existing wildlife laws are inadequate, prompt revisions are required to better target specific taxa or issues, for example, India's Wildlife (Protection) Amendment Act of 2002 was updated in 2006 to better combat wildlife crimes on endangered species.

Education and Awareness

With widespread anthropogenic activities severely impacting wildlife populations, better conservation of colobines must be enabled through improving public education and political awareness. Sustainable programmes to provide for human needs that have least impacts on wildlife; conservation efforts that promote widespread systemic changes in human behaviour and decision makers and community-based programmes have seen increasing adoption throughout Asian primate range countries in recent years (e.g. Indonesia: Supriatna and Aro 2015; Nekaris et al. 2018; Vietnam: Prosser and Nadler 2017; China: Ellwanger et al. 2015; Niu et al. 2019; India: Srivastava et al. 2006). Such efforts have focused on multiple aspects, from basic conservation awareness for children in rural communities to public participation in enforcement of illegal activities like logging and poaching, to community-oriented initiatives for forest management. The increasing occurrence of primate species in landscape mosaics has also been leveraged by new conservation approaches such as community managed forests of agroecosystems of small-yield agriculture, for example, shade-grown coffee (*Coffea* spp.) and other mixed plantations that can provide connectivity, habitat and food resources for some primate species (Estrada et al. 2012; McLennan et al. 2017). As most colobines are not known to develop crop-raiding behaviour and some species have been shown to be able to survive in marginal habitats, such approaches can provide suitable tools for their conservation, and can be further extended to mitigate commercial-level activities, for conserving high conservation-value species and habitats within oil palm landscapes (Lhota et al. 2019a; Persey et al. 2011) and within logging concessions (Johns and Johns 1995). Many colobine species are highly charismatic, for example, the snub-nosed monkeys, proboscis monkeys and doucs, and can be used as flagship species for wider environmental protection causes. Eco-tourism activities involving primate species are increasingly popular and can be used to effectively promote conservation efforts (Russon and Wallis 2014), but possible negative impacts must be properly managed to avoid disturbance to sensitive colobine species (Lhota et al. 2019b).

Conservation Planning

With inevitable expanding human populations and the need to consume natural resources, sustainable land-use planning is required to ensure the coexistence between economic development and functional natural ecosystems (Estrada et al. 2018). Much of the problems related to, for example, the effectiveness of protected areas and large-scale impacts of industrial exploitation could be largely attributed to a lack of sound conservation planning. In Sumatra, Indonesia, massive forest losses in recent decades was due to a system of decentralizing decisions on forest use from ministry to district levels, which allowed the free and uncoordinated issue of logging and oil palm licences without appropriate planning and without an understanding of forest ecology (Supriatna et al. 2017). In Vietnam, the lack of prospective land-use planning has restricted the potential to extend existing protected areas for securing the long-term viability of the 'Critically Endangered' Delacour's langur (Nadler and Roos 2017).

Such issues highlight the importance of conservation planning which has in part been recognized by some governments in colobine range countries, for example, the announcement, in late 2017, of an emergency action plan by the government of Vietnam: 'Urgent Conservation Action Plan for Primates in Vietnam to 2025 with a vision to 2030' to better protect primate species. In 2017, the Guangxi Forest Bureau and Fauna and Flora International (FFI) announced 'The Conservation Action Plan of François' langurs in Guangxi (2016–2020)'. A 10-year 'State Wildlife Species Action Plan' for three endangered species in Sabah, which includes the proboscis monkeys is also currently pending cabinet approval. Such action plans are needed on different scales, from specific taxa-based targets to state-wide and national-level initiatives, and should be ideally extended across borders to better target the conservation of colobines and their habitats, given that almost a third of colobines have distribution ranges across country borders in Asia. For example, a trans-boundary agreement was reached between China and Myanmar in 2015 to reduce illegal trans-boundary wildlife trade and illegal logging and to protect the Myanmar snub-nosed monkey across its distribution range.

Reintroduction and Captive Management

Where primate species are locally extirpated, reintroductions may be a feasible conservation strategy. Such efforts require for genetically viable reassurance colonies but colobines are known to be difficult species to keep in captivity, especially outside their range habitats. In Vietnam, the Endangered Primate Rescue Center have been conducting reintroduction programmes for Delacour's langurs and Hatinh langurs (Elser et al. 2015; Haus 2009b; Nadler 2012; Nadler and Streicher 2003). A 'Species Action Plan for the Conservation of Raffles' Banded Langur in Malaysia and Singapore' (Ang et al. 2016) also aims at supplementing the small Singapore langur population with new genetic stock. For many threatened species in China, reintroductions are also being considered as a conservation strategy but viable captive populations as a source for reintroductions are currently still limited and effective captive-breeding programmes are not well organized (Li B et al. 2018). The exception is for François' langurs in Guangxi province where there is the largest captive-breeding population of François' langurs and the Guangxi Forestry Bureau launched a long-term François' langur reintroduction project in 2012. With fast dwindling populations of many colobine species, such approaches may become increasingly important, given the right conditions of long-term protection of habitats and monitoring programmes.

Conclusions

The Asian colobine clade is represented by various unique and highly threatened species. Many species having specialized dietary and habitat requirements. Asia, being one of the most densely populated and rapidly urbanizing regions in the world, provides genuine challenges for effective conservation of colobines in this region. To achieve the goal of long-term sustainability of wild habitats and species, conservation measures must balance the ever-increasing needs of human populations with natural resource and biodiversity protection, which are more often than not, in direct conflict with one another. Conservation efforts must thus appropriately consider the mobilization of collective efforts of the global citizenry and conservation awareness of decision makers as crucial enabling factors.

From a scientific point of view, further improvements to knowledge gathering and sharing are needed, e.g. utilizing new technologies for monitoring and analysis, especially for species that are difficult to study, and improving baseline data collection to aid in long-term conservation planning. Finally, the intensification of collaborative efforts can better synergize research and conservation activities on species and habitat protection that will contribute to better conservation of threatened Asian colobines across its distribution range.

Acknowledgements

The authors thank the respective organizations for their support in the writing of this chapter: JS (Sun Yat-sen University), IM (Chubu University), ZQH (Guangxi Normal University), AA (Raffles' Banded Langur Working Group, Singapore) and TN (Vietnam Primate Conservation Program, Vietnam). We also thank the editors of this volume for inviting us to contribute to this important effort and reviewers for their valuable comments to improve this chapter.

21 Conservation of Africa's Colobine Monkeys (Cercopithecidae, Colobinae) with Taxonomic and Biogeographic Considerations

Thomas M. Butynski and Yvonne A. de Jong

Introduction

Among the world's mammals, it is the members of the order Primates that are most threatened by extinction (Schipper et al. 2008). Within Primates, the colobus monkeys of Africa represent one of the most threatened groups (Butynski et al. 2013c; IUCN 2019/2020; Linder et al. 2021; Oates 2011; Struhsaker 2010). Colobines (family Cercopithecidae, subfamily Colobinae) are thumbless, medium-sized, arboreal, folivorous, forest-dependent primates with a complex three- or four-chambered stomach and forelimbs that are shorter than the hindlimbs (Kingdon and Groves 2013; Oates 1977b, 1994, 2011; Oates and Davies 1994b; Struhsaker 2010). This chapter presents an overview of the current taxonomy, biogeography, conservation status and threats for Africa's colobines, as well as recommendations for research and conservation actions. We hope that this chapter will help bring heightened awareness to the present plight of the African colobines and encourage a major increase in research and conservation action for this subfamily of primates. This is urgent. If this does not happen soon, it is likely that it is from within the Colobinae that the first primate species extinctions in at least 11,700 years (i.e. Holocene) will be recorded for mainland Africa (Turvey et al. 2018).

Current Taxonomy of Africa's Colobines

The taxonomy of the African colobines remains far from resolved, having been widely debated and in flux for more than 100 years (e.g. Allen 1939; Butynski et al. 2013c; Colyn 1991; Dandelot 1974; Elliot 1913; Gautier-Hion et al. 1999; Groves 1993, 2001, 2005, 2007; Groves and Ting 2013; Grubb 2002; Grubb and Groves 2013; Grubb et al. 1998, 2003, 2013a,b; Hull 1979; Kingdon 1997, 2015; Linder et al. 2021; Napier 1985; Oates 1986, 2011; Oates and Ting 2015; Oates and Trocco 1983; Oates et al. 1994; Rahm 1970; Schwarz 1928, 1929; Struhsaker 1981, 2010; Struhsaker and Grubb 2013; Thorington and Groves 1970; Ting 2008a,b). The instability of the taxonomy of the African colobines has been identified as one of the causes of inadequate attention given to the conservation of this group, particularly the red colobus monkeys *Piliocolobus* (Cardini and Elton 2009b; Oates and Ting

This chapter includes Electronic Supplementary Material (ESM) at: www.cambridge.org/colobines

2015). One result may be the extirpation of some distinctive populations and near extinction of several species and subspecies.

The taxonomy applied here for Africa's colobines is that derived from the 'IUCN/ SSC African Primate Red List Assessment Workshop' (Rome, April 2016), with the exception that Mount Kilimanjaro guereza *Colobus guereza caudatus* has since been elevated back to species level as *C. caudatus* (Butynski and De Jong 2018). This taxonomy is the one adopted by *The IUCN Red List of Threatened Species 2019/ 2020* (IUCN 2019/2020) and, for *Piliocolobus*, also by the *Red Colobus* (Piliocolobus) *Conservation Action Plan, 2021–2026* (Linder et al. 2021). This taxonomy recognizes three genera: black-and-white colobus monkeys *Colobus* Illiger, 1811, olive colobus monkey *Procolobus* Rochebrune, 1887, and red colobus monkeys *Piliocolobus* (Groves and Ting 2013; Grubb and Groves 2013; Grubb et al. 2013a,b; Kingdon and Groves 2013). All three genera are endemic to Africa. *Colobus* comprises six species and 17 subspecies, *Procolobus* comprises one species, and *Piliocolobus* comprises 17 species and two subspecies. Together, these three genera hold 24 species and 19 subspecies, or a total of 39 taxa. This taxonomy is presented in ESM Table 21.1, together with the current *IUCN Red List* 'category of threat' (IUCN 2019/2020) and some taxonomic notes (see also Chapter 2). Other chapters in this book apply the taxonomy of Groves and Ting (2013). As noted in ESM Table 21.1, these two taxonomies differ for five taxa.

The present taxonomy for Africa's non-human primates stands at 26 genera, 107 species and 192 taxa. Of these, the African colobines comprise 12% of the genera, 22% of the species, and 20% of the taxa. The present taxonomy for Africa's monkeys (Family Cercopithecidae) stands at 16 genera, 79 species and 143 taxa. Of these, the African colobines comprise 19% of the genera, 30% of the species, and 27% of the taxa. Kapale's colobus, recently discovered in Lomami NP, central DRC (J. Hart pers. comm.), is not included in any of the calculations in this chapter.

Below we use the standard abbreviations applied by the *IUCN Red List Categories and Criteria Version 3.1* (IUCN 2012) for designating 'risk of extinction' for species and subspecies. These are: CR: Critically Endangered; EN: Endangered; VU: Vulnerable; NT: Near Threatened; LC: Least Concern; DD: Data Deficient; NE: Not Evaluated. 'Threatened taxa' are defined by IUCN as those that are CR, EN or VU. In order to help keep the reader readily informed of the risk of extinction for each taxon of African colobine while reading this chapter, the category of threat is typically given after the taxon is mentioned for the first time in each paragraph.

Biogeography of Africa's Colobines

All three genera of African colobine occur in primary and secondary forest, swamp forest, riparian forest, gallery forest, lowland forest and dense woodland. *Colobus* and *Piliocolobus* also live in mid-altitude (=transitional) forest and montane forest. In addition, king colobus *Colobus polykomos* (EN), Peters's Angola colobus *Colobus angolensis palliatus* (VU), olive colobus *Procolobus verus* (VU), Temminck's red colobus *Piliocolobus badius temminckii* (EN), Niger Delta red colobus *Piliocolobus epieni* (CR) and Zanzibar red colobus *Piliocolobus kirkii* (EN) use mangrove, while several subspecies of *Colobus* live in bamboo forest (Butynski et al. 2013c; Davies and Oates 1994; Galat-Luong and Galat 2005; Galat-Luong et al. Groves and Ting 2013; Linder et al. 2021; Oates 2011; IUCN 2019/2020; Struhsaker 2010).

Colobines are widespread in tropical Africa, ranging from Senegal and Gambia in the northwest, down the Atlantic Ocean coast to Bioko Island (Equatorial Guinea), Gabon and Angola, then broadly eastwards through the forest belt to Ethiopia and the Indian Ocean coasts of Kenya, Tanzania and Zanzibar Island (Tanzania) (Figures 21.1–21.6). The northwest-most colobine is *P. b. temminckii* (EN) in Forêt Classée de Sangako, west Senegal (13°47′N; 16°25′W; Figure 21.5) (Galat et al. 2009). The northeast-most colobine is Omo River guereza *Colobus guereza guereza* (LC) in northwest Ethiopia (13°12′N; 39°14′E; Figure 21.1). The geographic range of this subspecies once extended into central Eritrea (15°41′N; 38°09′E) but was probably extirpated from Eritrea more than a century ago (Heuglin 1877 cited in Yalden et al. 1977; Yalden et al. 1977; T. Butynski pers. obs.). The southeast-most colobine is Sharpe's Angola colobus *Colobus angolensis sharpei* (VU) in extreme south Tanzania (10°07′S; 34°38′E; Figure 21.2). The southwest-most colobine is Sclater's Angola colobus *Colobus angolensis angolensis* (VU) in central Angola (11°39′S; 16°42′E; Figure 21.2).

Polytypic *Colobus* and polytypic *Piliocolobus* are broadly distributed across tropical Africa from the Atlantic Ocean to the Indian Ocean, whereas monotypic *Procolobus* is confined to West Africa. Africa's colobines occur in 28 countries; *Colobus* in 27 countries, *Procolobus* in 8 countries and *Piliocolobus* in 17 countries (Figures 21.1–21.6; ESM Table 21.2). The only country where *Piliocolobus* occurs where *Colobus* is absent is Gambia. Away from the north half of West Africa, many of the countries in which *Colobus* is present but where *Piliocolobus* is absent, are those latitudinally farthest from the extensive moist forests associated with the equator (e.g. Angola, Chad, Ethiopia, Zambia), or in the vicinity of, and within, the semi-arid Dahomey Gap (i.e. Benin, Togo; Oates 2011) where white-thighed colobus *Colobus vellerosus* (CR) and *P. verus* (VU) are the only colobines. Overall, *Colobus* and *Procolobus* are more arid-adapted than *Piliocolobus*. They may be better able to move across more arid landscapes and survive in smaller forests than *Piliocolobus* and/or able to out-compete *Piliocolobus* under dryer, more seasonal, conditions.

For the purposes of this chapter we use the following definitions for the three African 'regions' in which colobines live (Figures 21.1–21.6):

- 'West Africa': Senegal southeastwards to Bioko Island and Cameroon, inclusive.
- 'Central Africa': Central African Republic (CAR), Equatorial Guinea (exclusive of Bioko Island), Gabon, Congo and Angola eastwards to South Sudan, Democratic Republic of Congo (DRC), and Zambia, inclusive.
- 'East Africa': Ethiopia, Uganda, Rwanda, Burundi, Kenya and Tanzania.

There are 9 species, 5 subspecies, and 11 taxa of colobines in West Africa, 12 species, 8 subspecies, and 18 taxa in Central Africa, and 8 species, 10 subspecies, and 16 taxa in East Africa (Figures 21.1–21.6; ESM Table 21.1). Guereza colobus *Colobus*

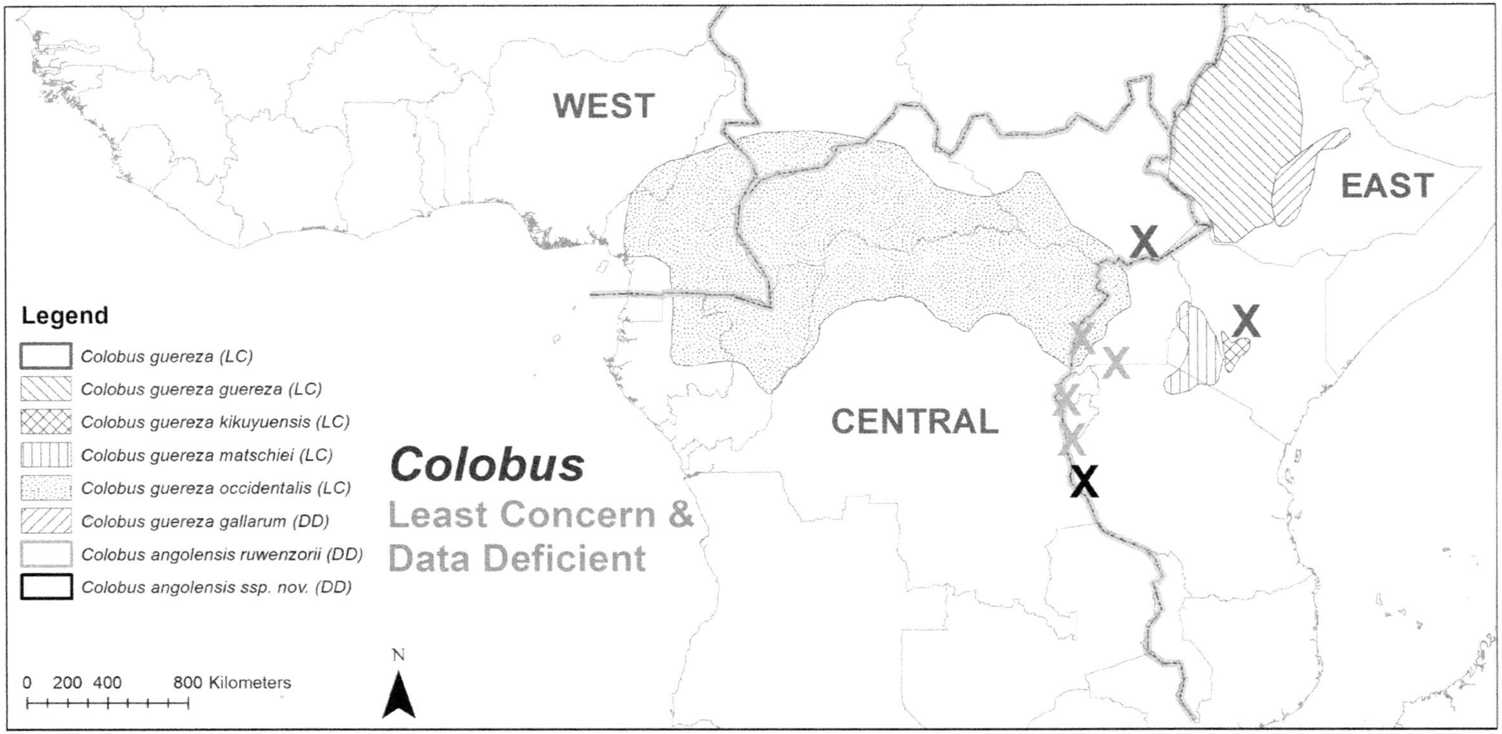

Figure 21.1 Geographic ranges for the 'Least Concern' and 'Data Deficient' taxa of *Colobus* (IUCN 2019/2020).

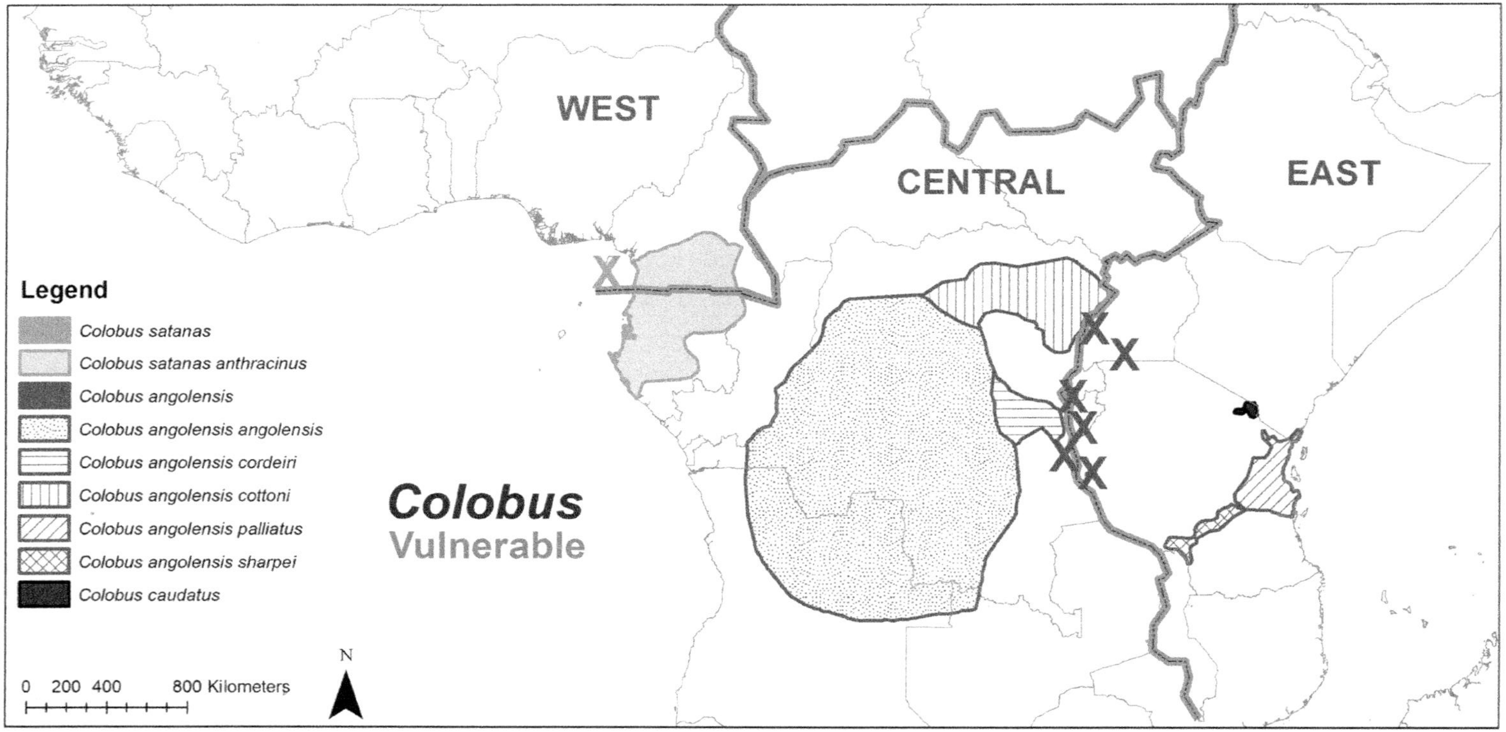

Figure 21.2 Geographic ranges for the 'Vulnerable' taxa of *Colobus* (IUCN 2019/2020).

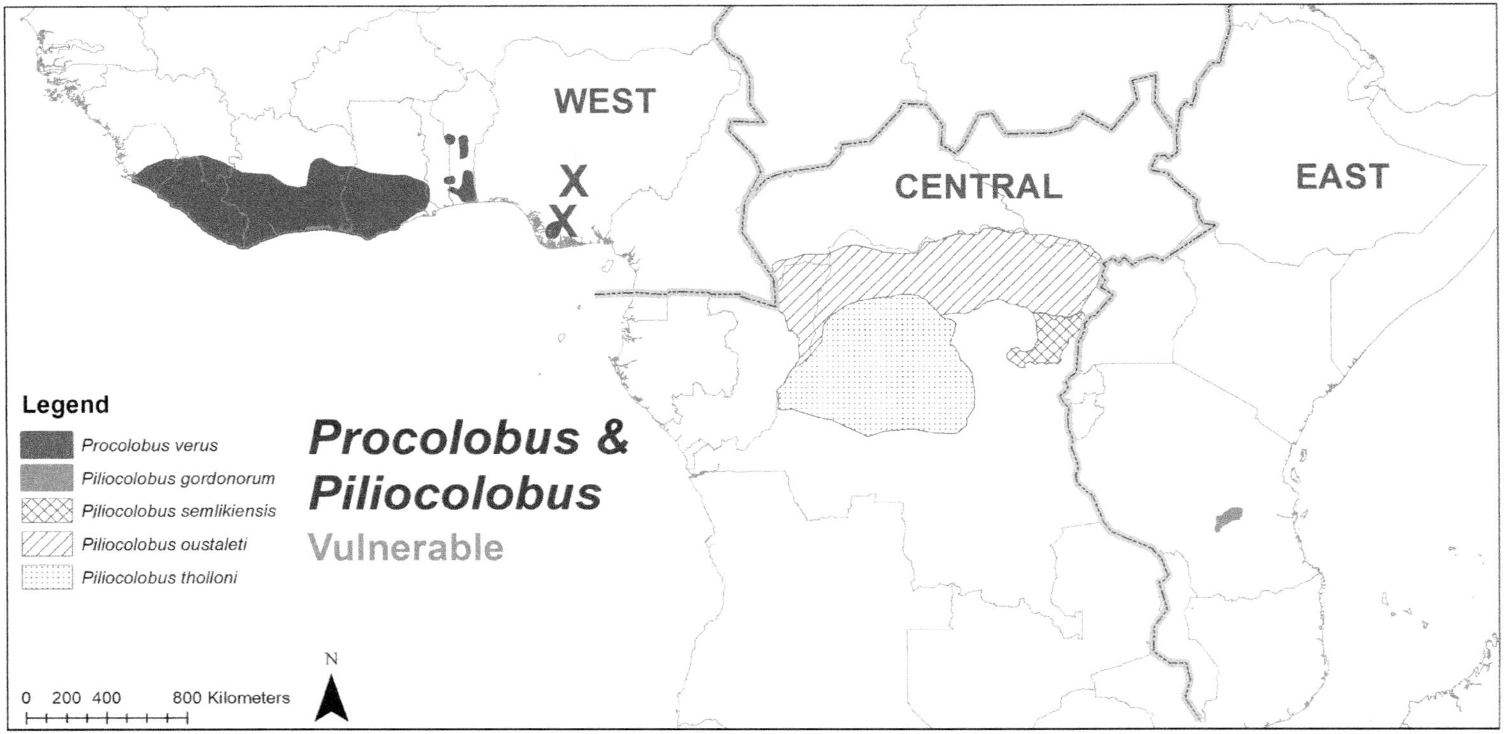

Figure 21.3 Geographic ranges for the 'Vulnerable' *Procolobus verus* and taxa of *Piliocolobus* (IUCN 2019/2020).

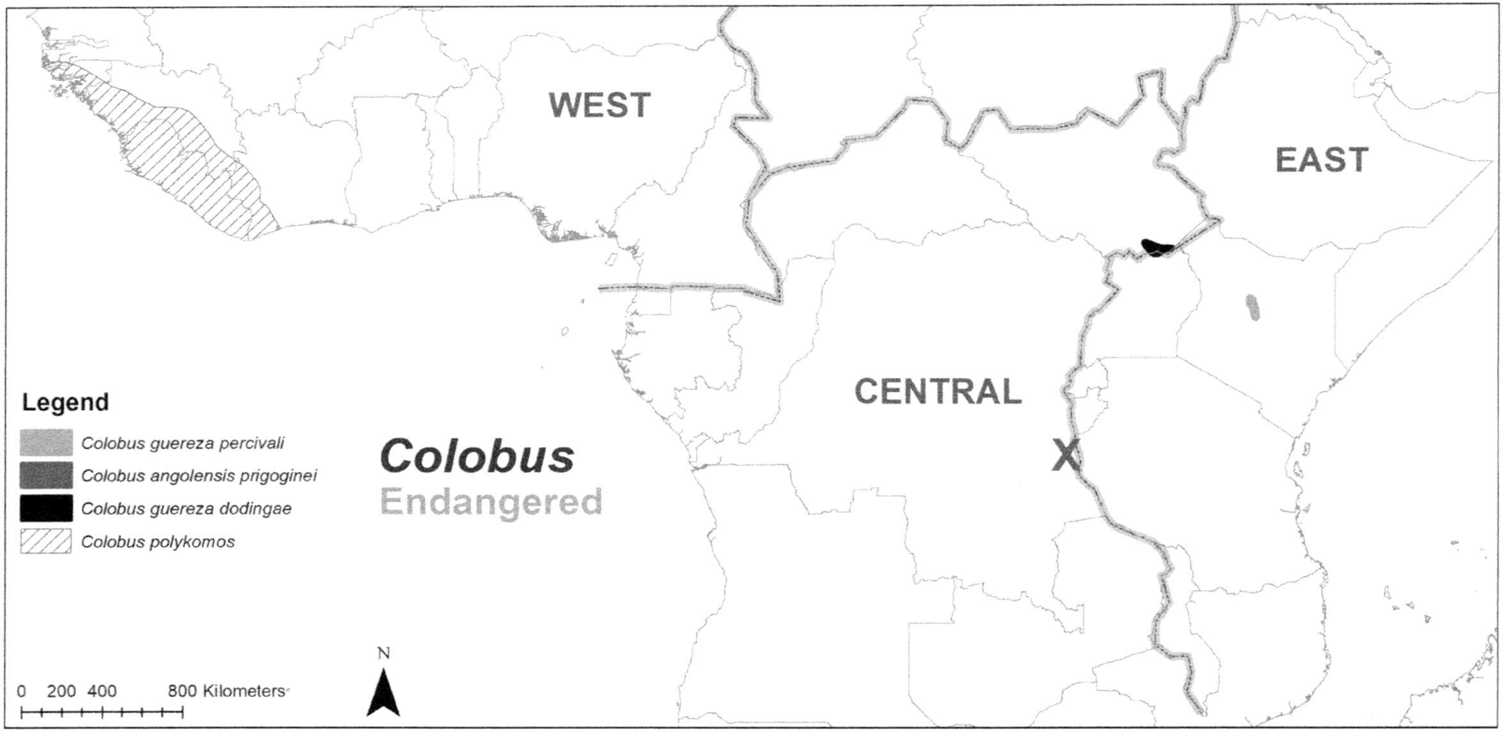

Figure 21.4 Geographic ranges for the 'Endangered' taxa of *Colobus* (IUCN 2019/2020).

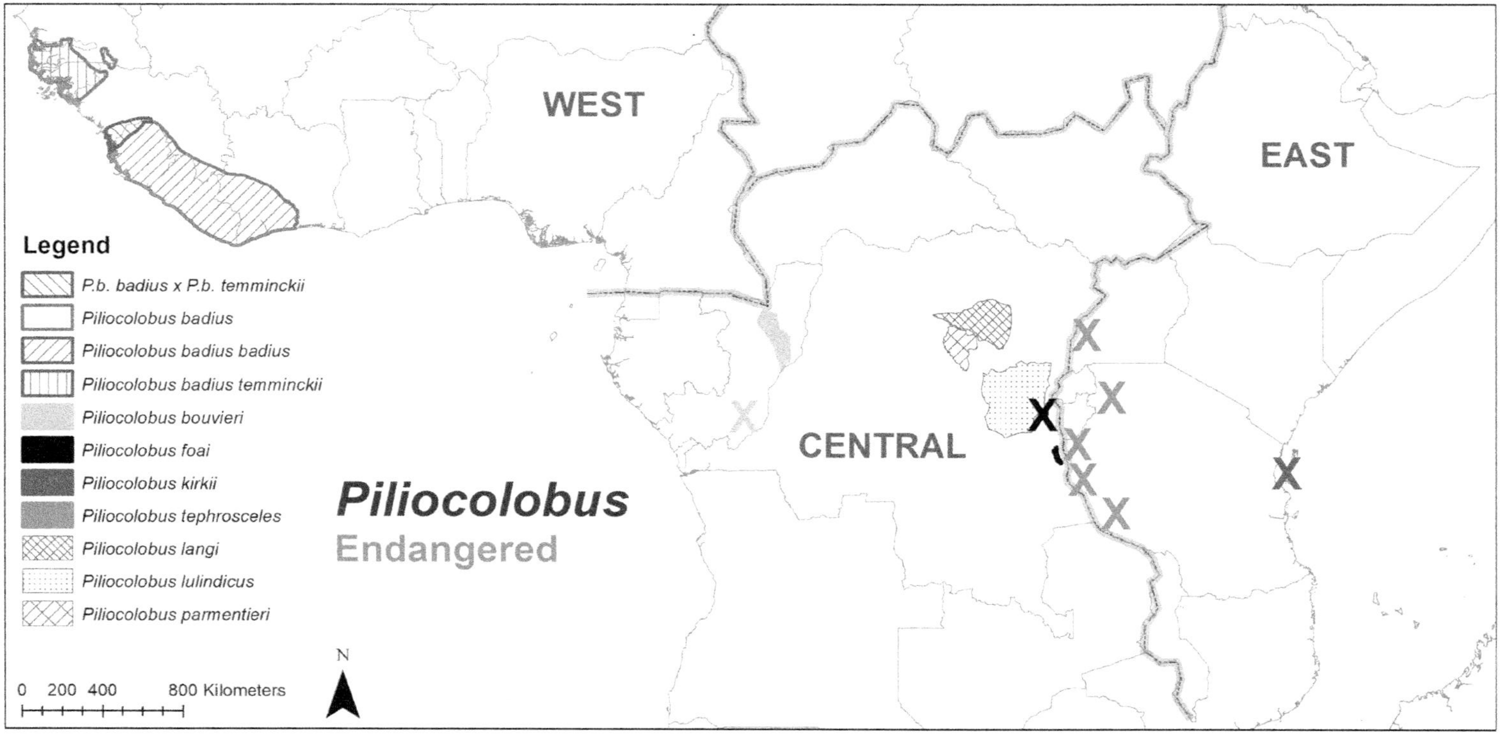

Figure 21.5 Geographic ranges for the 'Endangered' taxa of *Piliocolobus* (IUCN 2019/2020).

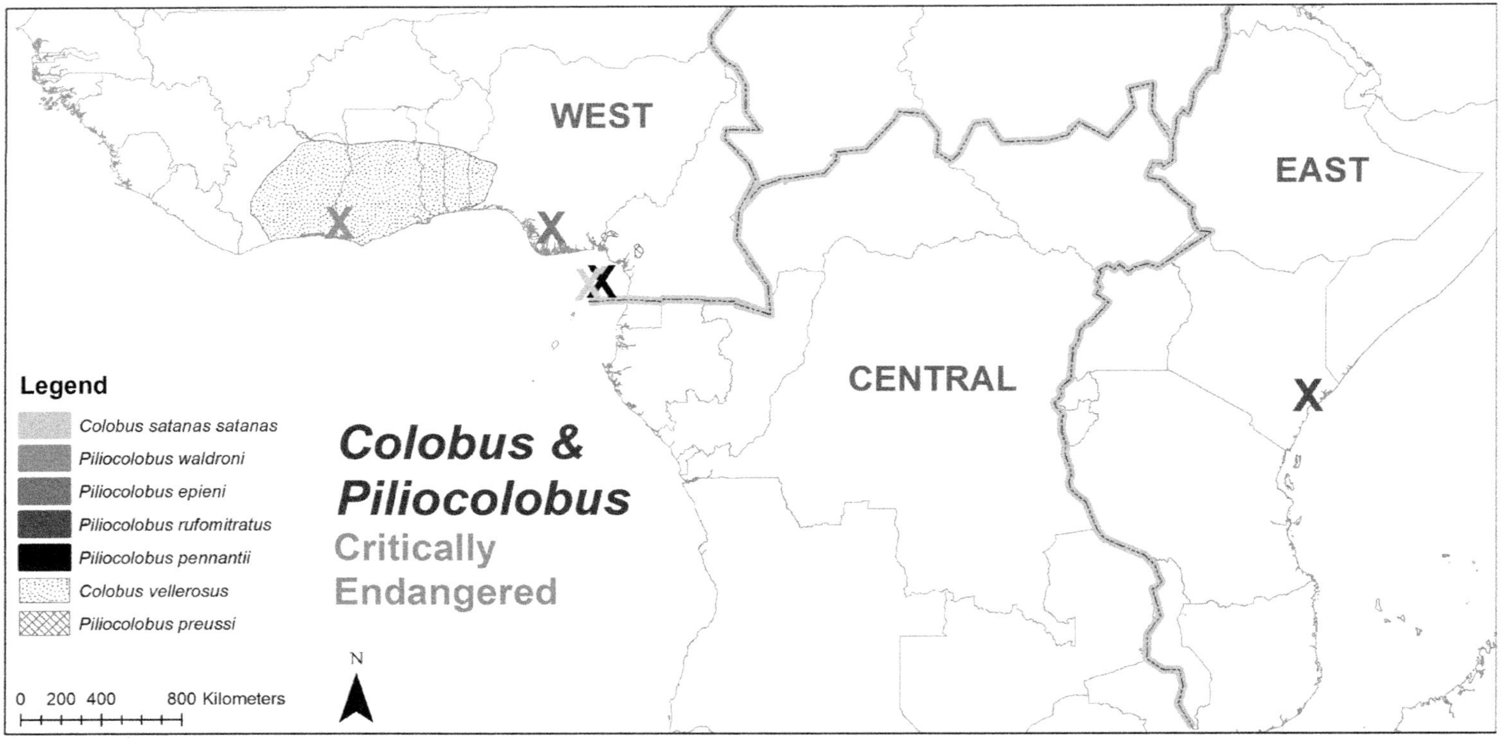

Figure 21.6 Geographic ranges for the 'Critically Endangered' taxa of *Colobus* and *Piliocolobus* (IUCN 2019/2020).

guereza (LC) occurs in all three regions while Angola colobus *Colobus angolensis* (VU), black colobus *Colobus satanas* (VU), and Semliki red colobus *Piliocolobus semlikiensis* (VU) each occur in two regions. Of the subspecies, western guereza *Colobus guereza occidentalis* (LC) occurs in all three regions, while Gabon black colobus *Colobus satanas anthracinus* (VU), Dodinga Hills guereza *Colobus guereza dodingae* (EN), and Rwenzori Angola colobus *Colobus angolensis ruwenzorii* (DD) each occur in two regions.

Countries with the most taxa of colobines are, not surprisingly, typically the largest countries that are on, or close to, the equator (Figures 21.1–21.6; ESM Table 21.2). There are nine species, six subspecies, and 13 taxa in DRC (2,267,050 km^2), of which seven are species of *Piliocolobus* and five are subspecies of *C. angolensis* (VU). DRC holds one-third of Africa's colobine taxa, of which five species, three subspecies and eight taxa are endemic. Tanzania (885,800 km^2) is the next most diverse country in terms of colobines with six species, five subspecies and nine taxa. For their size, Kenya (569,140 km^2) and, especially, Uganda (199,810 km^2), are relatively rich in colobines, each with four species, four subspecies and six taxa. Together, these three East African countries support eight species, nine subspecies, and 15 taxa, or 38% of Africa's colobine taxa. These include four subspecies of *C. angolensis*, five subspecies of *C. guereza* (LC), and five species of *Piliocolobus*. Five of the species, five of the subspecies and 10 of the taxa are endemic to these three countries.

Many forests hold two sympatric genera of colobines, while some have up to three genera, or at least three species. Taï National Park (NP; 3300 km^2), southwest Côte d'Ivoire, Sapo NP (1804 km^2) and Grebo-Krahn NP (971 km^2), southeast Liberia, Gola Forest NP (980 km^2), northeast Liberia, and Tiwai Island Wildlife Sanctuary (12 km^2) and Gola Rainforest NP (711 km^2), southeast Sierra Leone, all have *C. polykomos* (EN), *P. verus* (VU), and Upper Guinea red colobus *Piliocolobus badius badius* (EN) (McGraw and Zuberbühler 2007; Oates 2011). Ituri Forest (62,900 km^2), northeast Democratic Republic of Congo (DRC), has Powell-Cotton's Angola colobus *Colobus angolensis cottoni* (VU), *C. g. occidentalis* (LC), and Oustalet's red colobus *Piliocolobus oustaleti* (VU) (Bocian and Anderson 2013; Colyn 1991; Hart et al. 1986; Thomas 1991). The vast region over which *C. a. cottoni* and *C. g. occidentalis* are sympatric continues southeastwards where they attain sympatry with Kisangani red colobus *Piliocolobus langi* (EN) Hart et al. 2020b) and, even farther to the southeast, with *P. semlikiensis* (VU) in the foothills of the Rwenzori Mountains, central east DRC (Kingdon 1971; Oates 1977b). Lomami NP (8879 km^2), central DRC, has *C. a. angolensis* (VU), Lomami red colobus *Piliocolobus parmentieri* (EN), Tshuapa red colobus *Piliocolobus tholloni* (VU), and the yet to be described Kapale's colobus (J. Hart pers. comm.), although, perhaps, not all four occur in sympatry. Ankasa Conservation Area (524 km^2), southwest Ghana, and Tanoé Forêt Classée (120 km^2), southeast Côte d'Ivoire, both once supported three genera of colobines [*C. vellerosus* (CR), *P. verus*, Miss Waldron's red colobus *Piliocolobus waldroni* (CR)], but *P. waldroni* likely no longer occurs in either area (Oates 2011).

No forest north of Sierra Leone, north of DRC, south of the Congo Basin, or east of the Western (Albertine) Rift Valley supports more than two species of colobine, and most have only one species. We suspect, however, that *C. a. ruwenzorii* (DD), *C. g. occidentalis* (LC), and ashy red colobus *Piliocolobus tephrosceles* (EN) were sympatric on the lower eastern slope of the Rwenzori Mountains prior to the massive destruction of forest in this region. Some large forests east of the Eastern (Gregory) Rift Valley have no colobines, such as those in the Lake Manyara NP-Ngorongoro Crater Conservation Area complex (8960 km^2), north central Tanzania and the Boni-Dodori Forest complex (4000 km^2) and Arabuko-Sokoke Forest Reserve (FR; 416 km^2), north coast of Kenya (T. Butynski and Y. de Jong pers. obs.). Some of these forests, particularly those on the north coast of Kenya between Mombasa and the Tana R. (e.g. Arabuko-Sokoke FR; Anderson 2005, Anderson et al. 2007a), and those in southeast Tanzania between the Rufiji R. and Ruvuma R. (e.g. Rondo Forest, Lindi Forests; Rodgers 1981) seem to have lost their populations of *C. a. palliatus* (VU) during the early 1900s as a result of forest loss and over-hunting.

With the exception of Ituri Forest, where *C. g. occidentalis* (LC) is sympatric with *C. a. cottoni* (VU) (Bocian and Anderson 2013; Colyn 1991; Hart et al. 1986; Thomas 1991), and southeast Cameroon, north Gabon and extreme northwest Congo, where *C. s. anthracinus* (VU) is sympatric with *C. g. occidentalis* (Blom et al. 1992; Colyn 1991; Mitani 1990; Oates 1994), all species within *Colobus* are allopatric. All species within *Piliocolobus* are also allopatric (Figures 21.1–21.6). Two species and one subspecies of colobine are island endemics; *P. kirkii* (EN) on Zanzibar Island, and Bioko red colobus *Piliocolobus pennantii* (CR) and Bioko black colobus *Colobus satanas satanas* (CR) on Bioko Island.

The altitudinal range for *Colobus* is 0–3400 m above sea level (asl; ESM Table 21.2). *Colobus satanas* (VU), *C. vellerosus* (CR), *C. polykomos* (EN) and *C. angolensis* (VU) all occur at sea level. *Colobus guereza* (LC) does not reach sea level, the lowest record being 170 m asl for *C. g. occidentalis* (LC) in central west Gabon (Oates et al. 2019). *Colobus guereza* does, however, reach higher altitudes than other *Colobus* with Djaffa Mountains guereza *Colobus guereza gallarum* (DD) present at 3400 m asl in the Bale Mountains, central Ethiopia (S. Williams pers. comm.). In general, *C. guereza* is the higher altitude species, but there are exceptions at the subspecies level (ESM Table 21.2). *Colobus s. satanas* (CR), on Bioko Island, has the greatest altitudinal gradient of any *Colobus* subspecies (0–3010 m asl; Butynski and Koster 1994).

Procolobus verus (VU) is restricted to lowland forest at 0–200 m asl. The altitudinal range for *Piliocolobus* is 0–2420 m asl (ESM Table 21.2). Of the 17 species of *Piliocolobus*, five occur at sea level while 13 do not occur above 400 m asl. Of the *Piliocolobus*, *P. tephrosceles* (EN) achieves the highest altitude at 2420 m asl (Mbizi FR, southwest Tanzania; T. Davenport pers. comm.). Udzungwa red colobus *Piliocolobus gordonorum* (VU), with an altitudinal range of 250–2200 m asl in the Udzungwa Mountains, central south Tanzania, has the greatest altitudinal gradient (1950 m).

Africa's colobines live under a wide range of rainfall and temperature regimes. For the 24 species, range in mean annual rainfall is 50–1100 cm (ESM Table 21.2).

Seventeen species (71%) have populations where mean minimum annual rainfall is 50–100 cm and 16 species (67%) have populations where mean maximum annual rainfall is 150–250 cm. Thirteen species (54%) live within the mean annual rainfall range of 75–250 cm. This particularly applies to *Piliocolobus* where 11 of the 17 species (65%) live within this range. All three genera have populations living where mean annual rainfall is <75 cm. Those populations living under low rainfall are in riparian forest along perennial rivers. *Colobus s. satanas* (CR) and *P. pennantii* (CR) on Bioko Island experience a mean annual rainfall of 1100 cm at sea level (highest rainfall in Africa). *Colobus satanas* (VU) has the greatest mean annual rainfall gradient at 1000 cm (100–1100 cm), while Tana River red colobus *Piliocolobus rufomitratus* (CR) has the smallest mean annual rainfall gradient at 25 cm (50–75 cm) and is the only species of African colobine that is totally dependent upon riparian forest as all of the other 23 species have populations living where mean annual rainfall is 200 cm or higher.

At 3010 m asl, *C. s. satanas* (CR) endures temperatures near freezing on Pico Basilé, Bioko Island. Mount Kenya guereza *Colobus guereza kikuyuensis* (LC), on Mount Kenya, lives at 3100 m asl where temperatures are sometimes <4°C. *Colobus g. gallarum* (DD) at 3400 m asl in Bale Mountains NP, central Ethiopia, must cope with temperatures <−7°C (S. Williams, pers. com.). *Colobus a. palliatus* (VU) and *P. rufomitratus* (CR), on Kenya's coastal plain, live where temperatures are sometimes >37°C. In Abuko Nature Reserve, west Gambia, *P. badius temminckii* (EN) tolerates temperatures >41°C (Galat et al. 2009). Similarly, *P. oustaleti* (VU) experiences temperatures >41°C in Bangangai Game Reserve (GR), central south South Sudan (Hillman 1983). Of the three genera of African colobines, *Colobus* lives under the greatest ranges of altitude, rainfall and temperature and, therefore, habitats. This particularly applies to *C. s. satanas*. This should serve this genus well in terms of adapting to climate change.

The size of the current geographic range for each of the three genera of African colobine, as measured from the shapefiles for the *IUCN Red List's* range maps (IUCN 2019/2020; Figures 21.1–21.6; ESM Table 21.2), is as follows: *Colobus* = 6,070,000 km^2; *Procolobus* = 420,000 km^2; *Piliocolobus* = 1,550,000 km^2. These values need to be used with great caution, however, as a large portion of these areas comprises non-forest habitat that is unsuitable for colobines; some of the regions included are too arid to support forest and/or big tracts of forest have been lost to agriculture and other human activities. In addition, the limits of the geographic range of most taxa are poorly understood and large areas hold few or no colobines as a result of hunting by humans. These constraints to assessing actual range size are less severe in the more remote, wetter, regions where vast forests still exist and where forest loss to agriculture and colobine loss to hunting do not yet have much impact (e.g. parts of CAR, Congo, DRC, Gabon). It may be that <10% of the area depicted on most of the *IUCN Red List's* African colobine maps is today occupied by colobines, and for some taxa, much less than 10% [e.g. *C. polykomos* (EN), *C. vellerosus* (CR), *P. verus* (VU), western red colobus *Piliocolobus badius* (EN), *P. epieni* (CR)]. Information on current 'area of occupancy' (IUCN 2012: 12) would be far more useful but this information is not available except for some of the most threatened taxa that have tiny geographic ranges and are relatively well surveyed [e.g. *C. s. satanas* (CR; 400 km^2); *P. kirkii* (EN; 1600 km^2); *P. pennantii* (CR; 160 km^2); *P. rufomitratus* (CR; 200 km^2)], or that occur over most of the area of relatively well-studied, well-protected regions [e.g. *C. g. kikuyuensis* (LC; 15,400 km^2); *C. caudatus* (VU; 4000 km^2), *P. gordonorum* (VU; 1700 km^2)]. Accurate information on area of occupancy for several taxa with small ranges is urgently required. For example, while the geographic ranges of Prigogine's Angola colobus *Colobus angolensis prigoginei* (EN) and Mahale Mountains Angola colobus *Colobus angolensis* ssp. nov. (DD) are likely <600 km^2, neither has been the focus of a survey to determine range limits or area of occupancy.

Taking the above-mentioned constraints into consideration, it remains that there are enormous differences in sizes of geographic ranges among genera and species of African colobines (Figures 21.1–21.6; ESM Table 21.2). The *Colobus* with, by far, the largest range is *C. guereza* (LC; 2750,000 km^2), with *C. g. occidentalis* (LC) alone accounting for 2,100,000 km^2. *Colobus caudatus* (VU; 4000 km^2) has, by far, the smallest range. For *Piliocolobus*, *P. oustaleti* (VU; 430,000 km^2) and *P. tholloni* (VU; 500,000 km^2) have the largest ranges, while *P. pennantii* (CR; 160 km^2) and *P. rufomitratus* (CR; 200 km^2) have the smallest ranges.

As indicated above, *Colobus* exhibits much broader environmental limits than either *Procolobus* or *Piliocolobus*, living over a considerably wider range of altitude, rainfall, temperature and habitat types (including small, degraded, habitats) (ESM Table 21.2). One result is that *Colobus* has a geographic range that is more than 14-fold larger than *Procolobus* and about 4-fold larger than *Piliocolobus*.

Conservation Status of Africa's Colobines

The IUCN Red List of Threatened Species 2019–2020

The current category of threat for each of the 24 species and 19 subspecies of African colobine is presented in ESM Table 21.1. ESM Table 21.3 presents a summary of trends for IUCN's category of threat between 2008 and 2019/2020 for the species and subspecies of African colobines. Here are six of the more important conclusions to be drawn from the information in these two tables:

1. The vast majority of African colobines are 'threatened with extinction' (i.e. assessed as VU, EN or CR) (IUCN 2012, 2019/2020); 96% of the 24 species, 68% of the 19 subspecies, and 82% of the 39 taxa. In addition, one or more of the three 'Data Deficient' (DD) subspecies of *Colobus* are likely to be assessed as threatened once the required data become available. For comparison, about 60% of the world's species of primate are threatened (Estrada et al. 2017).
2. The 'most threatened' (i.e. CR) species are *C. vellerosus*, *P. epieni*, *P. pennantii*, Preuss's red colobus *Piliocolobus preussi*, *P. rufomitratus* and *P. waldroni*. The one CR subspecies is *C. s. satanas*. Of the seven CR taxa, six are in West Africa and one is in East Africa (*P. rufomitratus*). These seven taxa are 'considered to be facing a very high risk of extinction in the wild'. (IUCN 2012: 14).

3. *Colobus* is the least threatened of the three genera. The only 'Least Concern' species of African colobine is *C. guereza*, although two of its subspecies are 'Endangered' (*C. g. dodingae* and Mount Uarages guereza *Colobus guereza percivali*). All four of the 'Least Concern' subspecies of African colobine are within *C. guereza*: *C. g. guereza*, *C. g. kikuyuensis*, Mau Forest guereza *Colobus guereza matschiei*, *C. g. occidentalis*.
4. All three 'Data Deficient' taxa are subspecies of *Colobus*: *C. a. ruwenzorii*, *C. a.* ssp. nov., *C. g. gallarum*.
5. All *Piliocolobus* (17 species, 2 subspecies, 18 taxa) are threatened, with all but four of the 18 taxa being EN or CR.
6. In 2008, the category of threat for 37 African colobine species and subspecies was published on the *IUCN Red List*, compared to 43 species and subspecies in 2019/2020. Of the 32 taxa assessed both during 2008 and 2019/2020, eight species were assessed as more threatened, eight remained unchanged and two were assessed as less threatened. Three species moved up two categories of threat [*C. vellerosus* (CR), *C. angolensis* (VU), *P. oustaleti* (VU)]. During this same 11-year period, six subspecies were assessed as more threatened and eight remained unchanged. Four subspecies moved up two categories of threat [*C. a. angolensis* (VU), Cordier's Angola colobus *Colobus angolensis cordieri* (VU), *C. a. cottoni* (VU), *C. caudatus* (VU)].

Since 2009, six issues of *Primates in Peril: The World's 25 Most Endangered Primates* have been published (Mittermeier et al. 2009, 2012; Schwitzer et al. 2014, 2015, 2017, 2019). In these six issues, African colobines have been profiled 13 times: *P. rufomitratus* four times, *P. epieni* four times, *P. pennantii* twice, *C. vellerosus* twice, *P. preussi* once. All five of these species are currently assessed as 'Critically Endangered'.

The colobines represent the most threatened group of primates in Africa, with the species and subspecies within *Piliocolobus* being particularly threatened (IUCN 2019/2020; Linder et al. 2021).

Morphology, Ecology and Behaviour of Africa's Colobines: Predictors of Extinction Risk

While knowledge of morphology, physiology, demographics, ecology and behaviour is important for understanding African colobine biogeography, abundance, conservation status and threats and for finding solutions to counter the threats, these topics are largely beyond the scope of this chapter and will not be reviewed here. This information can be found among the many books and articles cited in this chapter, particularly in Butynski et al. (2013c), Davies (1994), Davies and Oates (1994), Groves and Ting (2013), Linder et al. (2021), Oates (2011) and Struhsaker (1975, 2010), as well as in the current *IUCN Red List* assessments (IUCN 2019/2020). In addition, chapters in this volume by Amato et al. (Chapter 7), Chapman et al. (Chapter 19), Fashing (Chapter 10), Korstjens et al. (Chapter 9), Matsuda and Clauss (Chapter 6),

Rothman et al. (Chapter 8), Teichroeb (Chapter 17) and Teichroeb and Korstjens (Chapter 11) provide some of the most current information available on many aspects of the ecology and behaviour of Africa's colobines.

Due to differences in their biology, colobines vary in their vulnerability and responses to the threats that represent risks of extinction. Here, we limit mention of the morphology, ecology and behaviour of African colobines to those aspects that relate to risks of extinction in response to forest loss and human hunting, the two primary proximate threats. Anderson et al. (2007a), Chapman et al. (2000, 2003b, 2005, 2006d, 2007), Cowlishaw and Dunbar (2000), Fa et al. (2005), Fashing (2011), Isaac and Cowlishaw (2004), Johns and Skorupa (1987), Kamilar and Paciulli (2008), Kümpel et al. (2008), Linder and Oates (2011), Linder et al. (2021), McGraw (2007), Oates (1977b, 1994, 1996b, 2011), Oates and Davies (1994a), Oates et al. (1990), Onderdonk and Chapman (2000), Rovero et al. (2012), Shultz et al. (2004) and Struhsaker (1997, 1999, 2005, 2010) mention morphological, ecological and behavioural traits that make colobines particularly susceptible to extinction through forest loss and human hunting. Several of the biological traits that these authors put forth as predictors for risk of extinction due to forest loss and human hunting are summarized here.

Susceptibility to Forest Degradation, Loss and Fragmentation

Diversity of the Diet

It appears that *Piliocolobus* is less able to adapt to the foods that degraded forests offer than are *Colobus* or *Procolobus*. *Piliocolobus* has been described as 'specialized', 'ecologically sensitive' and 'ecologically fragile'. Dependence on a highly diverse diet makes *Piliocolobus* more susceptible to nutritional stress when habitats are degraded and fragmented, and when the density and diversity of the high canopy trees are reduced. *Colobus* and *Procolobus*, with their less diverse diets, survive better than *Piliocolobus* in disturbed forests, including those affected by selective logging and shifting (= slash-and-burn) agriculture. This is reflected in the fact that, unlike for *Colobus*, no *Piliocolobus* diet has been successfully replicated in captivity and, as such, there is not a single captive population of *Piliocolobus*.

Percentage Mature Leaves in the Diet

Percentage of mature leaves in the diet varies considerably among colobines. Mature leaves are a bigger part of the diet of *Colobus* than of *Procolobus* or *Piliocolobus*. When preferred foods become scarce, the major 'fall-back' food for *Colobus* and *Piliocolobus* is mature leaves. Unlike *Piliocolobus*, however, *Colobus* can digest large quantities of mature leaves and survive on a low-quality diet of mature leaves for long periods. This puts *Colobus*, with its greater dietary flexibility, at an advantage in habitats where plant diversity is relatively low, such as in secondary forest and in relatively dry seasonal forest.

Group Size

Large groups require more food and, therefore, are under greater threat when forest is degraded or lost and sources of food are destroyed. *Colobus* groups typically comprise 5–20 individuals (range 2–38; Butynski et al. 2013c; Fashing 2011; Fashing et al. 2007b; Oates 1994, 2011; von Hippel et al. 2000; Chapters 10 and 19). A major exception is *C. a. ruwenzorii* (DD). In Manwa FR, Lake Nabugabo, southwest Uganda, this subspecies occurs in 'supergroups' (or 'aggregations') of >200 individuals (Chapter 17) and, at Nyungwe NP, southwest Rwanda, supergroups of 300 to >500 individuals are present (Fashing et al. 2007b; Fimbel et al. 2001; Miller et al. 2020a,c). *Procolobus verus* (VU) live in groups of 2–15 individuals (Oates and Korstjens 2013; Chapter 11), while *Piliocolobus* live in groups that typically comprise 15–70 individuals (range 4–152; Fashing 2011; Oates 2011; Struhsaker 2010; Chapters 9 and 19). With the exception of *C. a. ruwenzorii*, group size predicts that, all things being equal, *Piliocolobus* is more vulnerable than *Colobus* or *Procolobus* to forest degradation, loss and fragmentation.

Home Range Size

Colobines with large home ranges are expected to be more susceptible to extinction from forest degradation and fragmentation since large home ranges generally indicate high demand for resources. *Colobus* home ranges are typically 10–70 ha (range 2–100 ha; Fashing 2011; Oates 1994, 2011; Chapters 10 and 19), with the exception of three outlier taxa. The one supergroup of >300 *C. a. ruwenzorii* (DD) studied in Nyungwe NP had a home range of >2650 ha (Fashing et al. 2007b). A group of 19 *C. a. cottoni* (VU) in Ituri Forest had a home range >371 ha (Bocian 1997). A group of 9–14 *C. s. anthracinus* (VU) at Lopé, central Gabon, had a home range >184 ha (Harrison 1986), while one group of 7–15 individuals at Forêt des Abeilles, central Gabon, had a home range >224 ha and a second group of 16–19 individuals had a home range >573 ha (Fleury and Gautier-Hion 1999). These five groups of three taxa of *Colobus* with exceptionally big home ranges demonstrate (1) extreme flexibility in home range size, (2) highly variable diets and (3) that at least some taxa within this genus have the capacity to be semi-nomadic. These three biological traits may be a response to high spatio-temporal variation in the availability of patchy foods (Fleury and Gautier-Hion 1999), and/or long food renewal times (Fashing et al. 2007b; Chapter 10). *Procolobus* and *Piliocolobus* have yet to demonstrate these three capabilities.

Procolobus home ranges are 28–58 ha (Oates and Korstjens 2013; Chapter 11), while *Piliocolobus* home ranges are typically 10–70 ha (range 5–114 ha; Fashing 2011; Oates 1994, 2011; Struhsaker 2010; Chapters 9 and 19). It appears that the typical home range size for most *Colobus*, and for *Procolobus* and *Piliocolobus*, are similar at 10–70 ha. There are, however, important differences among these three genera that must be taken into consideration when assessing how home range size might predict risk of extinction, perhaps particularly diet, group size, home range overlap, territorial behaviour and predation rates (Oates 2011; Struhsaker 2010; Chapters 9, 10 and 19). It is unclear, therefore, whether home range size alone can be applied as a predictor of the risk of extinction for these three genera when forest is degraded and lost.

Geographic Range Size, Ecological Flexibility and Number of Habitat Types

Colobus lives over a much bigger area (6,070,000 km^2; Figures 21.1–21.6; ESM Table 21.2) and, therefore, over a greater latitudinal range and in more habitat types than do *Procolobus* (420,000 km^2) or *Piliocolobus* (1,550,000 km^2). This means that *Colobus* has greater ecological flexibility/adaptability and habitat (niche) breadth than either *Procolobus* or *Piliocolobus*. This trait is predicted to make *Colobus* less sensitive and more resilient to forest degradation, loss and fragmentation than *Procolobus* or *Piliocolobus*. The exceptions appear to be *C. satanas* (VU) and *C. polykomos* (EN; see below).

Susceptibility to Hunting by Humans

Body Size

The smaller the body the less likely a taxon will be hunted. *Procolobus*, with an adult male body weight of 4 kg (Oates and Korstjens 2013), is a less preferred target for hunters than are the more 'profitable' *Colobus* and *Piliocolobus*, where the adult male body weight is typically 7–11 kg (Butynski et al. 2013c; Chapter 9). Beyond this, large-bodied primates are indirectly more vulnerable to extinction through hunting because they have slower life-histories (including long maturation times and lower reproductive rates), are diurnal and slower-moving and, typically, occur at lower intrinsic abundance.

Group Size

Big groups are more readily located by hunters due to larger group spread, more noise and stronger odour. In addition, there are more targets from which to select the most vulnerable individuals.

Home Range Size

Colobines with small home ranges are more susceptible to hunting since restricted ranges make movement more predictable to the hunter and restrict the size of the prey search area.

Smell and Taste of the Meat

Some taxa, notably *P. verus* (VU), apparently have a bad smell and taste and, therefore, are not preferred prey (Oates 2011; Oates and Korstjens 2013).

Colobus satanas (VU) is said to have meat that is bitter and dry (Brugière 1998; Sabater-Pi and Groves 1972).

Cryptic Appearance

Pelage coloration and pattern of *Procolobus* is more cryptic than that of *Piliocolobus* and, particularly, *Colobus*. This, together with its cryptic behaviour and small group size, make *Procolobus* the most difficult of the African colobines to detect.

Cryptic Behaviour

Hunters in forest mainly rely on acoustic cues (i.e. monkey vocalizations and foliage noise as monkeys move) to detect primates. Species that live in small groups and spend much time resting and foraging in dense foliage (e.g. *Procolobus*) are more difficult for hunters to detect than those that live in noisy large groups, and rest and forage in more open situations (e.g. *Piliocolobus*). *Piliocolobus*, in particular, is a 'noisy-mover' as many individuals leap ('crash') through the foliage. In addition, the fresh faeces of *Piliocolobus* have a strong ammonia-like odour that persists for several hours after defecation and that humans can readily detect when within 50 m. Groups of *Piliocolobus*, even when silent and well hidden, can be detected by this odour (T. Butynski pers. obs.). Colobines that have a far-carrying loud call that is frequently given (e.g. *Colobus*) are more readily detected than those that lack a loud call (e.g. *Procolobus*, *Piliocolobus*). The 'roar' of *Colobus* can readily be heard well beyond 1 km. Under ideal circumstances, the roar of *C. guereza* (LC) can be heard for more than 2 km.

Behavioural Flexibility

Compared to other African monkeys, it seems that colobines are not well adapted to detecting and eluding hunters, nor able to learn how to effectively detect and elude hunters. There is some evidence, although inconclusive, that, unlike some other genera of African monkeys (e.g. guenons *Cercopithecus*), *Piliocolobus* is not as able to effectively alter its behaviour in order to enhance avoidance of human hunters (Koné and Refisch 2007). Of Africa's monkeys, *Piliocolobus* appears to be the easiest to hunt. As stated by Struhsaker (1999: 291), 'red colobus seem poorly adapted to human hunting pressure and unable to modify their behaviour accordingly'. Red colobus have the reputation of being the easiest monkeys that a hunter can pursue. They are poorly adapted to the pressure human hunters are able to exert. Due to their susceptibility, red colobus are typically the first primate species to go extinct in areas where they are hunted (Linder et al. 2021). Although it has yet to be demonstrated, it may be that *Colobus*, which has greater ecological flexibility/adaptability than *Piliocolobus*, also has somewhat greater behavioural flexibility. If so, this trait might reduce vulnerability to hunting (e.g. by reducing group size, switching diet, changing range size and ranging pattern, increasing vigilance).

Predicting Extinctions for Africa's Colobines

Africa's colobines are facing an extinction crisis at this time (IUCN 2019/2020; Linder et al. 2021). Chapman et al. (2006d), McGraw (2007), Oates (1996, 2011), Oates and Davies (1994) and Struhsaker (1999, 2010) have put forth predictors of risk of extinction for the colobines, seven of which are listed here. A taxon is at increased risk of extinction when it:

- Is dependent on high canopy, old growth forest.
- Has a large body size (>5 kg) and is relatively loud and conspicuous.
- Occurs where there is much forest loss, and forest loss continues at a high rate (ESM Table 21.4).
- Occurs where there is a high and rapidly increasing human population density (ESM Table 21.5).
- Occurs where human hunting pressure is high and likely to continue to be high.
- Occurs where law enforcement is absent or ineffective.
- Is 'neglected', receiving little or no conservation attention on the ground. The governments responsible exhibit insufficient political will and/or capacity to conserve the taxon.

Not surprisingly, there is much inter-dependency among these seven predictors for colobine extinction, as well as considerable overlap and interplay among them and the traits that make a taxon vulnerable to forest loss and human hunting, the two main proximate threats (see below). It is also not surprising that these predictors are among the criteria applied during the category of threat assessments for the *IUCN Red List* (IUCN 2012).

As indicated in ESM Table 21.1, there are six species and one subspecies of African colobine that are currently assessed at 'Critically Endangered' (IUCN 2019/2020): *C. s. satanas, C. vellerosus, P. epieni, P. pennantii, P. preussi, P. rufomitratus* and *P. waldroni*. It is from among these seven taxa that the first wave of extinctions of the African colobines is expected to emerge. This is expected to be led by *P. waldroni*, a species last observed 20 years ago (Linder et al. 2021; McGraw 2005; Oates et al. 2000a, 2020b). Those colobines with fewer than 1300 individuals remaining, and whose numbers continue to be in steep decline, may not be far behind *P. waldroni* (i.e. *C. s. satanas, P. epieni, P. pennantii, P. rufomitratus*). These are expected to be the first of the contributions by Africa's colobines to the current 'Sixth Mass Extinction' (Ceballos et al. 2020; Turvey et al. 2018).

Threats to Africa's Colobines

In this section, we present the more important threats for African's colobines and provide a few examples of the impact of each threat. These, and other, threats frequently operate in complicated synergies that vary spatially and temporally. The two primary proximate threats to Africa's colobines are forest loss as a result of anthropogenic activities and hunting by humans (ESM Table 21.2). The ultimate threat is humans and their widespread over-exploitation of natural resources in colobine habitats ... including the consumption of colobines (Butynski 2002; Cowlishaw and Dunbar 2000; Davies 1994; Fa et al. 2005; Fashing 2011; Linder and Oates 2011; Linder et al. 2019, 2021; McGraw 2007; N'Goran et al. 2012; Oates 1994, 1996b, 1999, 2011; Oates and Davies 1994a; Rovero et al. 2012; Struhsaker 1997, 2005, 2010).

Growth of the Human Population

The present scale of the human population (7.8 billion people) and its exponential growth, together with excessive consumption, are substantial contributors to the degradation of the natural world, including the escalating loss of biodiversity (Crist et al. 2017). In 2019, the 'rate of natural increase' (i.e. birth rate minus death rate) of the world's human population (including Africa) was 1.1%, while that of Africa was 2.5% (ESM Table 21.5). Rate of natural increase among the 28 countries with colobines was lowest in Gabon and Sierra Leone at 2.0%, and highest in Angola at 3.5%. Rate of natural increase in colobine-rich DRC was 3.2%. During the 58 years between 1960 and 2018, the increase in the human populations of the 28 African countries with colobines ranged from 2.0-fold in Guinea-Bissau and 2.1-fold in CAR, to 5.3-fold both in Uganda and Kenya, to 6.2-fold in Côte d'Ivoire (compared to 0.1-fold in Germany, 0.8-fold in the USA and 1.1-fold in Canada). The human population density in countries with colobines in 2018 ranged from 8 people/km^2 in CAR and Gabon to 435 people/km^2 in Burundi and 499 people/km^2 in Rwanda (compared to 4 people/km^2 in Canada, 36 people/km^2 in the USA and 237 people/km^2 in Germany). The number of people in African countries with colobines is expected to double within the coming 30 years (PRB 2019).

Africa's burgeoning human population growth cannot continue, particularly given that natural resources, including water, soil, forest and wildlife, are being unsustainably used in some regions. This indicates that, under present circumstances, human carrying capacity in these regions has been reached. Ever increasing numbers of people are looking to ever decreasing forest to exploit, forest land to farm on, and wildlife to eat. The vicious cycle now in place has cascading effects as natural resources become scarce, natural productivity declines, ecosystems collapse and humans, as well as wildlife, are increasingly exposed to zoonotic diseases, leading people deeper into poverty with reduced opportunities for food security, good health, education and sustainable development. This, in turn, sparks rises in emigration, immigration and conflict. This problem, the most serious facing Africa, has been largely ignored. We will not say more about this crisis, the damage being done, and the repercussions, as many articles and books have been written on this subject. Ceballos et al. (2020) and Crist et al. (2017) provide recent overviews of the growth of the world's human population as the major driver of biodiversity loss and the related collapse of ecosystems, and suggest solutions to this problem. More specifically, as concerns the future for Africa's forests and primates under the present and growing human population, good coverage of this problem is provided by Cleaver et al. (1992), McGraw (2007), Oates (1999) and Struhsaker (1997, 2010).

Forest Loss

Forest loss is the leading proximate threat for the majority of colobine taxa in Africa (ESM Table 21.2). Forest loss is predominantly the result of agricultural expansion and logging. Other activities that lead to forest loss include fire, mining, fossil fuel extraction, livestock browsing, grazing and trampling, introduction of invasive plants, taking of forest products (e.g. fuelwood, charcoal, poles), and establishment of settlements, roads, railroads, power-lines, dams and plantations of exotic trees (ESM Table 21.2). In many places, forest loss forces colobines to live in human-altered habitats—although they typically do not survive long-term in these often small, fragmented, degraded and ever-dwindling habitats. Here, colobines are at increased exposure to parasites, disease, hunting and starvation. They may also be at risk of the effects of a critically low diversity of gut microbes (Barelli et al. 2015, 2020; Chapter 7).

Information on 'natural forest cover' as of 2010 is available for 27 of the 28 countries with colobines. The exception is South Sudan, which, in any case, has relatively little closed canopy forest (ESM Table 21.4). We suspect that the quality of the data varies greatly from country to country, as does the interpretation of what constitutes 'natural forest'. The definitions that FAO applies for 'natural forest' differ slightly between FAO (1995) and FAO (FRA 2012), but both agree that 'natural forest' is an ecosystem with a minimum of 10% crown cover of indigenous trees and/or bamboo. A 10% crown cover means that very large areas of woodland are included in FAO's estimates for area of natural forest. Forest with <60% crown cover is not typically good habitat for Africa's colobines, especially for *Piliocolobus*. Some populations of colobine, particularly *Colobus* and *Procolobus*, survive in dense woodland and secondary forest where crown cover is somewhat less than 60% (perhaps 40%–60%). *Colobus satanas* (VU) and *Piliocolobus* reach highest abundance in closed canopy forest. FAO defines 'closed canopy forest' as forest with a >60% canopy cover.

The forest cover presented in ESM Table 21.4 for the 27 countries totals *ca.* 4,770,000 km^2. A large but unknown portion of this, however, comprises open woodland to medium dense woodland that does not support colobines. This particularly applies to Angola (584,800 km^2 forest cover), Chad (115,250 km^2), Tanzania (334,280 km^2) and Zambia (494,680 km^2), large countries where only a small portion of the natural forest is closed canopy forest or dense woodland capable of supporting colobines. The amount of closed canopy forest and dense woodland in Africa at this time is not known but is unlikely to be more than 1,700,000 km^2 (see below). Not withstanding the problems with the data for forest cover, it is certain that DRC (1,541,350 km^2 forest cover) holds, by far, the most habitat for African colobines, probably followed by Congo (224,110 km^2), Gabon (220,000 km^2) and Cameroon (199,160 km^2). In 2010, percentage forest cover in these five countries ranged from 36% (Cameroon) to 85% (Gabon), with DRC at 68%.

What appears to be the best set of data for the extent of 'moist forest' in Africa is summarized in Sayer (1992, table 10.1). Moist forest is typically closed canopy forest and, therefore, highly suitable habitat for colobines. Three colobine range countries are not addressed in Sayer (1992), but all three (Burkina Faso, Chad, Zambia) are relatively arid nations with little moist forest and with but one species of colobine, each present on the edge of its range. Unfortunately, most of the data for the area of moist forest are for the 1980s – about 37 years ago. In the 1980s, West Africa (as defined in this chapter), held *ca.* 300,000 km^2 of moist forest, and Central Africa (as defined in this chapter) held *ca.* 1,700,000 km^2 of moist forest (ESM Table 21.4). The countries with the largest area of moist forest were DRC (1,190,000 km^2), Gabon (228,000 km^2), Congo (213,000 km^2), and Cameroon (155,000 km^2). East Africa (as defined in this chapter) had *ca.* 60,000 km^2 of moist forest in the 1980s. In total, the 28 countries with colobines had roughly 2,060,000 km^2 of moist forest during the 1980s (ESM Table 21.4). This is about 16% of the land area of these 28 countries. With a continuing annual deforestation rate in Africa of 1% (FAO 1990), the area of moist forest remaining at this time is *ca.* 1,340,000 km^2, covering about 10% of the land area of the 28 countries with colobines.

Sayer (1992) provides estimates, based on the maps of White (1983), of the original coverage of moist forest for 25 of the 28 countries where colobines occur (ESM Table 21.4). Since the earliest forest clearance of significance did not commence before 5000 years ago (Hamilton 1982), we take 'original' to mean forest cover 5000 years ago. The original extent of moist forest in West Africa was *ca.* 1,630,000 km^2. By the 1990s, *ca.* 82% of this forest has been lost, or roughly 1,330,000 km^2. The original extent of moist forest in Central Africa was *ca.* 3,000,000 km^2. By the 1990s, *ca.* 50% of this forest had been lost, or roughly 1,500,000 km^2. The original extent of moist forest in East Africa was *ca.* 680,000 km^2. By the 1990s, *ca.* 92% of this forest had been lost, or roughly 625,000 km^2. In summary, of the original *ca.* 5,300,000 km^2 of moist forest in these 28 countries, *ca.* 3,450,000 km^2 (65%) has been destroyed, leaving *ca.* 1,855,000 km^2 as of about 1990. Originally, *ca.* 40% of the land area of these 28 countries was covered by moist forest, whereas in 1990 the coverage was about 14%. With a continuing annual deforestation rate in Africa of 1% (FAO 1990), the area of moist forest remaining at this time is *ca.* 1,300,000 km^2, covering about 10% of the land area of the 28 countries with colobines. These values are almost identical with those given at the end of the preceding paragraph. Most of the loss of moist forest in Africa has occurred over the past 100 years, concomitant with the rapidly growing human population (ESM Table 21.5). Given that the main habitat for African colobines is moist forest, 1,300,000 km^2 is likely a reasonable estimate of the amount of colobine habitat remaining at this time. Much of the moist forest that remains is degraded to various degrees as a result of selective logging or shifting agriculture, and much is in fragments that are no longer connected to, or even near, the major blocks of forest. Nonetheless, this forest remains valuable habitat for colobines, at least in the short-term.

As of about 1990, the countries with the highest proportion of original moist forest remaining (ESM Table 21.4) were Congo (62%), Equatorial Guinea (65%), DRC (67%), and Gabon (88%). Of the 25 countries with colobines for which Sayer (1992) provides data on the original area of moist forest, 15 retained <15% of their original forest and three countries retained <5% of their original forest (Burundi 4%, Guinea 4%, Benin 2%).

Although forest loss is most often directly caused by humans, sometimes forest loss is indirectly caused by humans. In Murchison Falls NP, northwest Uganda, for example, increased densities of savanna elephant *Loxodonta africana* Blumenbach, 1797, as well as greater incidence of fire, caused massive tree mortality that led to the conversion of forest to grassland. Elephant abundance increased as a result of reduced hunting and population compression related to the growing human population (Buechner and Dawkins 1961). This loss of forest would have negatively impacted *C. g. occidentalis* (LC). A similar situation exists at this time for riparian forests on the Laikipia Plateau, central Kenya. Here, trees on which *C. g. kikuyuensis* (LC) rely are being killed by elephants, the density of which has dramatically increased over the past 30 years (T. Butynski and Y. de Jong pers. obs.).

Extensive anthropogenic activities within forest influences the ecology, behaviour and carrying capacity of colobines (e.g. Fashing 2007b; Oates 1996b, 1999, 2011; Rovero et al. 2012; Struhsaker 1997, 2005). Since colobines have a long maturation time, reproduce slowly, and are long-lived, the impacts of forest degradation and fragmentation can be greatly delayed, resulting in an 'extinction debt' (Chapman 2006d, et al. 2007; Cowlishaw 1999; McGraw 2007; Struhsaker 1997; von Hippel et al. 2000). Forest fragments are the last refuge for many populations of African colobine, yet they are typically heavily used by people, degraded, not formally protected, and under great threat (Anderson et al. 2007a; Chapman et al. 2007; Estrada et al. 2017; Kitegile et al. 2021; Onderdonk and Chapman 2000). If forest fragments are to be of long-term value for the conservation of colobines, they need to be connected by forest corridors. In reality, given all of the human pressure and the enormous constraints facing conservation in tropical Africa, it appears that few forest fragments outside of protected areas, or their dependent colobines, will survive even in the short-term.

Some Impacts of Forest Loss on *Colobus*

Probably more than any other African colobine, *C. guereza* (LC) does well in secondary forest and on forest edge (Butynski1984; Fashing and Oates 2013; Oates 1977b; Struhsaker 1972, 1975). Moderate levels of logging (i.e. 'selective logging') in Kibale NP (766 km^2) resulted in an increase in abundance of *C. g. occidentalis* (LC) (Chapman et al. 2000; Johns and Skorupa 1987; Skorupa 1986; Struhsaker 1997, 2010). This increased abundance may be due, at least in part, to dietary and behavioural flexibility/adaptability, and to the greater availability of fast-growing, high-protein/lower-fibre colonizing plants that occur in disturbed habitats and that are preferred by *C. guereza* (Oates 1996b; Oates et al. 1990; Onderdonk and Chapman 2000).

Teichroeb et al. (2019) examined the immediate effects of small-scale, selective logging in Manwa FR, southwest Uganda, on *C. a. ruwenzorii* (DD); even a brief period of selective logging was associated with a decrease in fruit in the diet and an increase in young leaves, leaf buds and mature leaves, less movement and foraging, and more resting and social behaviour. There was, however, no immediate effect on the number of *C. a. ruwenzorii* or subgroup size. Similarly, other subspecies of *C. angolensis* (VU) (Bocian and Anderson 2013; De Jong et al. 2020b), *C. guereza* (LC) (De Jong et al. 2019; Fashing and Oates 2013), *C. vellerosus* (CR) (Saj and Sicotte 2013) and *C. caudatus* (VU) (Butynski and De Jong 2018), are also able to survive in forest with low levels of logging, as well as in fragments of secondary forest.

Unlike other *Colobus*, *C. satanas* (VU) (Fleury and Brugière 2013; Maisels and Cronin 2020b; Oates 1977b) and *C. polykomos* (EN) (Gonedelé et al. 2020) prefer pristine forest and old secondary forest and are seldom found in degraded forest. In Lopé Reserve, central Gabon, however, there was no significant difference between densities of *C. s. anthracinus* (VU) in lightly logged and unlogged forests (Brugière 1998). It seems that the low rate of timber extraction (1–2 trees/ha) did not result in a major change in forest composition or structure.

Some Impacts of Forest Loss on *Piliocolobus*

Piliocolobus tephrosceles (EN) has an extremely fragmented geographic range in southwest Uganda and west Tanzania as a result of logging and conversion of forest to agriculture (Figure 21.5) (Chapman et al. 2013b; Davenport et al. 2007; Kitegile et al. 2021; Struhsaker 2010). More than 28 years after selective logging in Kibale NP, *P. tephrosceles* densities in selectively logged forests were lower than in unlogged forests (Chapman et al. 2000). This species responded differently to forest loss than did sympatric *C. g. occidentalis* (LC) (see first paragraph of the previous section). In light to heavily logged forest, *P. tephrosceles* densities declined (Chapman and Chapman 2002; Chapman et al. 2005b, 2007; Oates 1977b, 1996b, Onderdonk and Chapman 2000; Skorupa 1986; Struhsaker 2010). This species appears to lack the dietary flexibility present in *C. g. occidentalis.*

Piliocolobus epieni (CR) is now restricted to a small area of freshwater swamp forest in central Niger Delta (Ikemeh et al. 2019; Oates and Werre 2009). The Niger Delta (Africa's largest delta; 46,420 km^2) holds two colobines, *P. epieni* and *P. verus* (VU) (Baker and Oates 2019; Butynski and De Jong 2019b). Forest loss as a result of farming, logging, oil exploitation, and human hunting, are all serious threats. In 1996, the population of *P. epieni* was $>$10,000 individuals and the geographic range was *ca.* 1500–2000 km^2 (Grubb and Powell 1999; Oates and Werre 2009; Werre 2001). In 2013, 17 years later, the population comprised $<$1000 individuals and the geographic range was *ca.* 78 km^2 (Ikemeh 2015; Ikemeh and Oates 2017). This decline continues and the rate of decline may have accelerated (Ikemeh 2014; Ikemeh et al. 2019). Despite the abundance of forest, fish and oil in the Niger Delta, the region is one of extreme poverty (Moffat and Lindén 1995; UNDP 2011) and one of the world's five most severely oil-affected ecosystems (Butynski and De Jong 2019b). There are no legally protected areas in the Niger Delta (Baker and Oates 2019).

Piliocolobus rufomitratus (CR), is sympatric with the Tana River mangabey *Cercocebus galeritus* Peters, 1879 (CR). These two species are endemic to the highly fragmented riparian and flood-plain forests along a 60-km stretch of the lower Tana River on the north coast of Kenya. Both also have small populations in the upper Tana Delta. *Piliocolobus rufomitratus* occupies about 34 forests that range in size from 1 ha to 500 ha (Butynski and Mwangi 1994, 1995). The area of occupancy is extremely small (<10 km^2) and fewer than 1000 individuals remain (Butynski and Hamerlynck 2016; Butynski et al. 2020). Forests of the lower Tana River face many conservation challenges one of which is the rapid expansion of mesquite *Prosopis juliflora*, an invasive shrub that displaces native plant species, particularly in areas abandoned after clearance of forest for agriculture (CABI 2019; Witt 2017), thereby hampering regeneration of forest on which *P. rufomitratus* and *C. galeritus* depend. For example, in Ndera Community Conservancy, forest cover declined 35% during 2010–2018 while the area covered by *P. juliflora* increased 12-fold. This was due to conversion of forest to agriculture, logging, droughts, drying of the forest, lack of forest regeneration related to a change in the river's course, and change in seasonal flood dynamics as a result of the up-stream dams (Kuraru and King 2019). Invasive species are predicted to become an increasing problem for the forests and primates of the lower Tana River as climate change occurs (Kaeslin et al. 2012). A 1°–2°C rise in global air temperature, together with a 10% reduction in rainfall, is expected to cause a 40%–70% drop in mean annual river run-offs in some areas (IPCC 1992). Should this happen to the rivers of tropical Africa, the extent of riparian forest, a major habitat for many colobine taxa, would be greatly reduced. Since *P. rufomitratus* is completely reliant upon riparian forest, this impact would be particularly severe for this species.

Hunting by Humans

As indicated above, human predation ranks second only to forest loss as an overall proximate threat for Africa's colobines. For several taxa, however, it is unclear as to which of these two threats is more important at this time, as both are prevalent. In addition, both threats often vary spatially and temporally for those taxa with the larger geographic ranges. For some poorly known taxa, there is not enough information by which to judge which of these two threats is the more important [e.g. *C. a. prigoginei* (EN), Foa's red colobus *Piliocolobus foai* (EN)]. A review of the current *IUCN Red List* assessments (IUCN 2019/2020), the *Red Colobus* (Piliocolobus) *Conservation Action Plan, 2021–2026* (Linder et al. 2021), and the literature, indicates, however, that hunting by humans is currently an overall greater threat for the survival of the following colobines than is forest loss: *C. s. anthracinus* (VU), *C. s. satanas* (CR), *C. vellerosus* (CR), *C. polykomos* (EN), *C. g. occidentalis* (LC), *P. b. badius* (EN), Bouvier's red colobus *Piliocolobus bouvieri* (EN), *P. epieni* (CR), *P. gordonorum* (VU), *P. langi* (EN), Lulindi River red colobus *Piliocolobus lulindicus* (EN), *P. oustaleti* (VU), *P. parmentieri* (EN), *P. pennantii* (CR), *P. preussi* (CR), *P. tholloni* (VU), *P. waldroni* (CR). For those species that inhabit mangrove and swamp forest (i.e. *C. vellerosus, C. g. occidentalis, P. bouvieri, P. epieni, P. oustaleti, P. tholloni*), hunting is the greater threat because hunters can, to at least some extent, penetrate these difficult of access habitats while loggers and farmers cannot. Large areas of mangrove and swamp forest provide considerable natural protection even against hunters due to their relative inaccessibility (Galat-Luong et al. 2019; Nowak et al. 2019).

Colobines east of the Albertine Rift (East Region; Figures 21.1–21.6; ESM Table 21.2) generally have small geographic ranges and the vast majority of people in this region consider primates to be unfit for human consumption. Here, most colobines are more threatened by forest loss than by hunting. Several taxa of colobine west of the Albertine Rift (Central Region), in the Congo Basin, have big geographic ranges and, therefore, tend to be more threatened by hunting than by forest loss (Hart et al. 2020a). Most West African (West Region) colobines are highly threatened both by hunting and loss of forest (Linder and Oates 2011; Linder et al. 2021; McGraw 2007; Oates 1996b, 2011).

Primates, including colobines, are hunted for meat for subsistence and sale, as well as for their pelts. With the rapid growth of the human population in Africa, and the related loss of forest and other natural resources, the demand for bushmeat has rapidly increased and has been unsustainably high over large areas for several decades. Access to once remote areas has increased for hunters and traders due to road construction, particularly for timber extraction (Milner-Gulland et al. 2003). In addition, modern hunting technologies (e.g. wire snares, headlamps and shotguns), loss of traditional hunting controls and taboos, and commercialization of bushmeat, have all contributed to increased hunting of primates (Bennett and Robinson 2000; Fitzgibbon et al. 2000; Refisch and Koné 2005b; Rose et al. 2003), and what Crist et al. (2017) refer to as an 'epidemic'. Oates (1996b: 1) states, 'an analysis of survey data suggests that human predation tends to have a greater negative impact on primate populations than does selective logging or low-intensity bush-fallow agriculture'. The demand for primate bushmeat is highest in the forests of West Africa and Central Africa (Abernethy et al. 2013; McGraw 2007; Milner-Gulland et al. 2003), less so in East Africa (Oates 1977b, 1996b; T. Butynski and Y. de Jong pers. obs.). The 'empty forest syndrome' (Harrison 2011b; Redford 1992) is widespread and frequently encountered in West Africa and Central Africa (McGraw 2007; Oates 1999, 2011; Struhsaker 2010).

Both subspecies of *C. satanas* (VU) are threatened, primarily by human hunting (Butynski and Koster 1994; Cronin 2020; Fleury and Brugière 2013; Kümpel et al. 2008; Oates 2011; Maisels and Cronin 2020b). The number of *C. s. satanas* (CR) has declined >80% over the last 30 years (Cronin 2019; Linder et al. 2021), while *C. s. anthracinus* (VU) numbers have declined >30% over the last 20 years (Maisels and Cronin 2020a).

Piliocolobus are the first, or among the first, primates to be severely affected, if not locally extirpated, by hunting. *Piliocolobus* comprises the taxonomic group of primates in Africa most threatened by hunting (Linder et al. 2021; McGraw 2007; Oates 2011; Rovero et al. 2012; Struhsaker 2005, 2010). While the colobines are the African primates most vulnerable to hunting, *Piliocolobus* are particularly sensitive. This makes the members of this genus especially useful as indicators of over-hunting of primates in a region.

Piliocolobus preussi (CR) is widely hunted, including in Ebo Forest (2000 km^2) and Korup NP (1260 km^2), southwest Cameroon (Diaw et al. 2003; Oates 2011; Waltert et al. 2002). All populations are in rapid decline (>80% over the last 30 years), mainly as a result of hunting (Linder et al. 2019, 2021). A large percentage of the hunters in Korup NP do not, themselves, eat *P. preussi* due to the bad odour, tough meat and resemblance to humans (Fonkwo et al. 2018; Hofner 2016). More than 10% of hunters in Korup NP obtain *P. preussi* to keep as pets and to sell when mature. Most immature individuals, however, die in captivity (Fonkwo et al. 2018), as do other *Piliocolobus*.

The situation on Bioko Island (2017 km^2) deserves special mention as the small populations of the island's two endemic colobines, *C. s. satanas* (CR) and *P. pennantii* (CR), are under severe pressure from hunting and, as a result, are on the verge of extinction (Butynski and Koster 1994; Cronin 2019; Cronin et al. 2010, 2015, 2016, 2017, 2020; Hearn et al. 2006). Bioko Island harbours 11 species of primate, including eight genera, one endemic species and six endemic subspecies. Nine of these taxa are threatened (IUCN 2019/2020). For its size, there is probably no site in the world with more taxa of threatened primates (Butynski et al. 2009, 2013c). *Piliocolobus pennantii* (CR) is the most vulnerable primate species to hunting with a geographic range of only about 160 km^2 and population of <1200 individuals after a decline of >80% over the 30 years during 1986–2016 (Cronin 2019; Cronin et al. 2017, 2020). This precipitous decline is almost solely due to hunting with >2433 carcasses appearing in the Malabo bushmeat market during 1997–2018 (Linder et al. 2021). An adult *P. pennantii* carcass fetched US$50 in 2008. *Colobus s. satanas* is the second most vulnerable primate species to hunting with a geographic range of about 465 km^2 and population of <1250 individuals after a decline of >80% over the 30 years during 1986–2016 (Cronin 2020; Cronin et al. 2017). This steep decline is almost solely due to hunting with >5122 carcasses appearing in the Malabo bushmeat market during 1997–2010 (Cronin et al. 2015). Cronin et al. (2015: 17) state, 'Under pressure from human population growth and increasing development, demand for and access to bushmeat will continue to rise, and populations of many game species on Bioko, especially primates, will likely collapse in the face of increasing offtake levels'. These two colobines, and other monkeys endemic to Bioko, are rapidly drifting towards extinction. This catastrophe is happening in a country with Africa's highest per capita income (PCI ranged from US$10,602 to US$20,513 during 2005–2018; Trading Economics 2020), where there is ample food (including readily available fish, chicken, beef and pork at much lower prices than bushmeat), where there is a law banning the hunting of primates, where government has absolute control over the activities of its citizens (including gun-carrying and hunting), and where the leadership could not be more aware of the great negative impact of hunting on its highly unique primate diversity. On Bioko Island, as documented for elsewhere in Africa (McGraw 2007; Oates 1999; Struhsaker 2019), increased prosperity has not translated into the sustainable use of natural resources such as bushmeat, rather it has served to increased demand to the point where several primate taxa are now on the verge of extinction.

Although hunting is most damaging to colobine populations in West Africa and Central Africa, it does impact some colobines in East Africa in the relatively few regions where people eat monkeys. Perhaps most notable is the situation in the Udzungwa Mountains where hunting is a serious threat for all of the diurnal primates, especially the two colobines; *C. a. sharpei* (VU) and the endemic *P. gordonorum* (VU) (Dinesen et al. 2001; Linder et al. 2021; Rovero et al. 2012, 2015, 2019).

While, by far, the primary reason that colobines are hunted in Africa today is for meat, by-products include pelts, pets and various body parts that are used for sale and to satisfy cultural, spiritual and medicinal needs (Fonkwo et al. 2018; Mwenja 2007, 2019). Bobo et al. (2012, 2014) found that *P. preussi* (CR) is not only hunted for meat, but also for medicinal and cultural purposes; pelts are used for making drums and treating burns and coughs, the skull is used to treat coughs/tuberculosis, the tail serves as decoration, and the bones are thought to make a man strong and active.

There was high international demand for *Colobus* pelts, mostly *C. polykomos* (EN), from about the 1850s until about the 1930s for the fashion industry in Europe and America (Oates 1977b). Between 1871 and 1891, 1,750,000 pelts were auctioned in London, the centre of the world's fur trade at that time. In 1889, 223,599 *Colobus* pelts were auctioned in London (Brass 1925 cited in Oates 1977b). According to Sanderson (1957), in 1892, 175,000 *Colobus* pelts were auctioned in London and, by 1902, two million pelts had been exported to Europe. Grubb et al. (1998) estimate that nearly 190,000 *C. vellerosus* (CR) pelts were exported annually from Ghana during the 1890s, and that the mean annual export between 1917 and 1922 was 17,000 pelts. Dunbar and Dunbar (1975) estimate that the number of *C. guereza* (LC) pelts for sale in Ethiopia at any one time during the early 1970s was >200,000, and that at least 40,000 monkeys were killed each year for the pelt trade in but two provinces (Kaffa and Illubabor). The international trade in *Colobus* pelts continued into the 1970s (Oates 1977b) but seems to have largely ended during that decade. The impact of the national and international *Colobus* pelt trade on populations is not known, but must have been considerable, probably causing the extirpation of many local populations (Oates 1977b). While the international trade in *Colobus* pelts has been largely stopped, use within Africa remains.

Hunting by Chimpanzees

The robust chimpanzee *Pan troglodytes* (EN) (Blumenbach 1775) is broadly sympatric with colobines (except south of the Congo R. and east of the Nile R.), with as many as three species of colobine present in some regions of sympatry (Figures 21.1–21.6). *Piliocolobus* dominates the mammalian prey diet of chimpanzees at all four of the long-term chimpanzee study sites where *Piliocolobus* is present, even when other species of monkey, including *Colobus*, are more abundant (Boesch 1994b; Boesch and

Boesch 1989; Boesch and Boesch-Achermann 2000; Bugir et al. 2021; Goodall 1986; Hosaka et al. 2001, 2020; Mitani and Watts 1999; Newton-Fisher 2014; Nishida 2012; Stanford 1998a; Stanford et al. 1994; Uehara 1997, 2003; Watts and Amsler 2013; Watts and Mitani 2002, 2015; Wrangham and Bergman Riss 1990). *Colobus* and *Procolobus* are also hunted by chimpanzees, but *Piliocolobus* is the preferred prey. In general, communities of chimpanzee with a relatively large number of adult and subadult males hunt colobines more, and attain higher hunting success, than communities with relatively few adult and subadult males (Hosaka et al. 2020; Mitani and Watts 2001; Watts and Amsler 2013; Watts and Mitani 2002).

At Ngogo, Kibale NP, the chimpanzee community is exceptionally large (145–205 individuals, including 24–35 adult males; Watts and Mitani 2015). During 2001–2003, this community had a territory of 25 km^2 (Mitani and Watts 1999; Teelen 2008) that expanded to 35 km^2 in 2009 (Watts and Amsler 2013). During 1995–2014, *P. tephrosceles* (EN) was the target during 356 (64%) of observed hunts of vertebrates of which 85% resulted in a least one *P. tephrosceles* being killed. During this period, *P. tephrosceles* accounted for 83% of chimpanzee vertebrate prey with 912 kills, 2.6 kills per *P. tephrosceles* hunt, and 3.0 kills per successful hunt (Watts and Mitani 2015). Between 53% and 75% of the kills were infants and juveniles (Mitani and Watts 1999; Watts and Mitani 2002). This local population declined about 89% during 1975–2007 (Lwanga et al. 2011; Teelen 2008). Watts and Mitani (2002) estimate that chimpanzees killed 6%–12% of the *P. tephrosceles* annually during 1995–1999. A more recent study estimates that 15%–53% were killed each year during 2001–2002, and that this level of harvest is not sustainable (Teelen 2008). This local population had not begun to recover as of 2014 (Watts and Amsler 2013; Watts and Mitani 2015). *Colobus g. occidentalis* (LC) was the second most often hunted prey of chimpanzees at Ngogo during 1995–2014, accounting for 6% of kills. During 64 observed hunts of *C. g. occidentalis*, 62 were killed. Number killed per successful hunt was 1.3 individuals (mostly infants and juveniles). This level of hunting may also be unsustainable (Watts and Mitani 2015).

The community of chimpanzees studied in Gombe NP (35 km^2), northwest Tanzania, comprised 42 individuals in 1991, including eight adult males and four subadult males. During 1974–1991, chimpanzees were observed to kill 744 mammals, of which 553 (74%) were *P. tephrosceles* (EN). Of the 429 kills observed during 1982–1991, 350 (82%) were *P. tephrosceles*, 75% of which were infants and juveniles (Stanford et al. 1994). During one 5-year period, chimpanzees killed 50% of the infants. At one time, only 20% of females survived to maturity (Stanford 1998). During 1982–1991, of 414 hunts of *P. tephrosceles*, 251 (52%) were successful. Mean number of colobus kill per successful hunt was 1.6, with up to seven killed during some hunts (Stanford et al. 1994). Estimates of the annual predation rate for *P. tephrosceles* by chimpanzees within their 18 km^2 home range vary from 16%–32% (Stanford 1996b) to 16%–40% (Uehara 2003) to 42% (Wrangham and Bergman Riss 1990). Mean size of *P. tephrosceles* groups in the late 1960s was 55 individuals (Clutton-Brock 1975b), but this declined to a mean group size of 22 as of 1991 (Stanford et al. 1994).

For chimpanzees in Mahale Mountains NP (1613 km^2), central west Tanzania, *P. tephrosceles* (EN) was the target prey during 78% of 939 observed hunts of primates and ungulates during 1965–2010. During these hunts, 528 *P. tephrosceles* were killed, comprising 76% of the primate and ungulate prey. During 1990–1995, 81% of the 155 *P. tephrosceles* killed were immature. The number of *P. tephrosceles* killed per successful hunt was 1.4. Almost all of the observed kills were by M Community, the size of which varied from about 45 individuals to 101 individuals, and typically included about nine adult and eight subadult males (Hosaka et al. 2001, 2020). During 1981–1995, the annual predation rate of M Community on *P. tephrosceles* within its 30 km^2 home range was 1–4% (Boesch et al. 2002; Uehara 2003).

In Taï NP, the chimpanzee community under study comprised 79 individuals in 1989, of which nine were adult males. During 1979–1986, of the 81 mammals observed to be killed by chimpanzees, 93% were accounted for by the three species of colobines, *P. b. badius* (EN) 77%, *C. polykomos* (EN) 14%, and *P. verus* (VU) 2%. Here, 0.6 *P. b. badius* were captured per hunt (n = 110 hunts), 0.7 *C. polykomos* were captured per hunt (n = 16), and 1.2 *P. verus* (n = 2) were captured per hunt. For *P. b. badius*, 58% of the kills (n = 58) were infants or juveniles (Boesch and Boesch 1989). The number of *P. b. badius* in Taï NP in 2006–2008 was about 97,500 (Shultz et al. 2004). Within the home range of this community, 3%–8% of the *P. b. badius* were killed each year by chimpanzees (Boesch and Boesch-Achermann 2000).

In Kyambura Gorge (8 km^2), Queen Elizabeth NP, southwest Uganda, there are two communities of chimpanzee. *Piliocolobus tephrosceles* (EN) is present but very rare (1 group encountered once in 58 hours of research). A brief study that focused on *C. g. occidentalis* (LC) found that density was higher outside of the chimpanzee activity centres (525 individuals/km^2) than inside of the chimpanzee activity centres (186 individuals/km^2). Groups of *C. g. occidentalis* outside of the chimpanzee activity centres were larger (nine vs. six individuals) and comprised more immature individuals (32% vs. 13%) than groups inside the chimpanzee activity centres (Krüger et al. 1998). The authors surmise that hunting by chimpanzees is likely responsible for these differences.

In summary, the hunting of colobines by chimpanzees is widespread and the impacts on colobine population abundance, demography and behaviour can be substantial. *Piliocolobus* is the most often hunted and captured prey, if not the preferred prey, of chimpanzees. Chimpanzees annually kill 1%–53% of the *Piliocolobus* population within their home ranges at the four study sites mentioned above. Where the annual rate of predation on *Piliocolobus* is low, such as in Mahale (1%–4%) and Taï (3%–8%), this harvest appears to be sustainable. Where the annual rate of predation is high, such as at Ngogo (15%–53%) and Gombe (16%–42%), the impact on the local population of *Piliocolobus* is severe, resulting in a reduction in numbers of groups, group size and abundance and, perhaps, eventual extirpation of the local population (Mitani and Watts 1999; Stanford 1998a; Stanford et al. 1994; Teelen 2008; Watts and Amsler 2013; Watts and Mitani 2002, 2015). The set of biological traits that make *Colobus* and *Piliocolobus* susceptible to hunting by humans (see above) are probably the same as those that make them susceptible to hunting by chimpanzees.

The hunting of colobines by chimpanzees at some sites is not unlike the impacts that unsustainable levels of human hunting have on populations of colobines (see above). We suspect, however, that, unlike human hunting, the situations where there is a high rate of predation on colobines by chimpanzees are ephemeral, and that these populations will eventually recover to former abundance. This is particularly likely to be the case where forests are large (e.g. Kibale, Mahale, Taï) and colobines from the periphery can immigrate to the site of the reduced or extirpated local population. It seems that large communities of chimpanzees, with their many adult and subadult males, are unlikely to significantly reduce their impacts on colobine populations until the size of these chimpanzee communities is considerably reduced. What factors will come into play to bring about these reductions are yet to be observed.

Hunting by Crowned Eagles and Leopards

The other two major predators of African colobines are crowned eagle *Stephanoaetus coronatus* (Linnaeus, 1766; McGraw et al. 2006; Mitani et al. 2001; Shultz and Thomsett 2007; Struhsaker 2010; Struhsaker and Leakey 1990) and leopard *Panthera pardus* (Linneaeus, 1758) (Hart et al. 1996; Hoppe-Dominik 1984; Zuberbühler and Jenny 2007). All but three taxa of African colobine are sympatric both with crowned eagle and leopard; neither predator occurs on Bioko Island where *C. s. satanas* (CR) and *P. pennantii* (CR) are endemic, while leopard, but not crowned eagle, occur on Zanzibar Island where *P. kirkii* (EN) is endemic. Although both of these predators are believed to have important effects on the ecology and behaviour of colobines, their impacts on colobine abundance are typically not nearly as severe as those of humans or chimpanzees (Davies 1994; Struhsaker 2010; Chapter 19). It appears that neither crowned eagles nor leopards remove >3% from colobine populations each year (Struhsaker 2010; Zuberbühler and Jenny 2007), with 1%–3% annual removal probably being typical. That humans and chimpanzees are the more important predators of colobines should not be surprising given that their densities and biomass are generally far higher than those of either crowned eagle or leopard.

Climate Change

As a result of anthropogenic-driven climate change, the Earth is set to become warmer than at any time in the past 1–40 million years. One result of this warming will be the mass extinction of plants and animals during this century. Concerning terrestrial species, Thomas et al. (2004: 146) estimate that, 'for scenarios of maximum expected climate change, 33 percent (with dispersal) and 58 percent (without dispersal) of species are expected to become extinct. For mid-range climate change scenarios, 19 percent or 45 percent (with or without dispersal) of species are expected to become extinct, and for minimum expected climate change 11 percent or 34 percent of species (again, with or without dispersal) are projected to become extinct'.

Thomas et al. (2004) believed that anthropogenic climate change is likely to be the greatest threat to biodiversity in many terrestrial regions, particularly when interactions with other threats are considered. They further state that 'the ability of species to reach new climatically suitable areas will be hampered by habitat loss and fragmentation, and their ability to persist in appropriate climates is likely to be affected by new invasive species' (147).

With Africa's rapidly growing human population, forest loss will not come to a halt. The effects of forest degradation and loss are expected to speed up climate change and climate change is expected to speed up forest degradation and loss (Meijaard 2016; Sheil and Murdiyarso 2009). Nearly all of Africa has experienced increased aridity over the past 200 years, but especially since the 1980s (Nicholson 2001). It is predicted that Africa is the continent most vulnerable to the effects of climate change with a temperature increase this century of as much as 5.8°C, changing rainfall patterns, and more extreme, irregular and frequent climate events (Chapman et al. 2006d; De Jong & Butynski 2021; Houghton et al. 2001; Niang et al. 2014). As mentioned above, it is further predicted that a rise in global air temperature of 1°–2°C, accompanied by a 10% reduction in rainfall, will cause a 40%–70% drop in mean annual river run-offs (IPCC 1992). These changes will have profound and permanent effects on African ecosystems and the biodiversity they support (Kaeslin et al. 2012), including the already threatened colobines.

The prognosis for Africa's forests, and for the forest-dependent primates they support, of the forthcoming climate change is extremely negative, particularly for the colobines, as this crisis will have its greatest impact on those species that are already most threatened with extinction. Climate change will exacerbate the other threats to Africa's colobines, particularly forest loss and human hunting, but also disease and invasive species. The impacts of climate change on Africa's colobines are, however, not going to be equal. The biological traits that make some colobines more susceptible than others to forest loss (see above) are the same traits that affect their vulnerability to climate change. This is because the main impacts of climate change for colobines will be indirect, occurring through the negative effects on forest degradation, loss and fragmentation. This predicts that specialized colobines, namely *Piliocolobus*, with small geographic ranges, small altitudinal gradients, narrow ecological niches and relatively low ecological and behavioural flexibility, will be more negatively affected than the more widespread, altitudinally diverse, generalized, relatively flexible, and resilient, *Colobus*.

There is another likely problem for colobines that climate change is expected to enhance, the impact of which will also vary among taxa. Increased temperature and/or reduced rainfall can lead to lower digestibility of leaves, lower quality leaves (i.e. more fibre, less protein, lower protein-to-fibre ratio) and, perhaps, higher concentrations of plant secondary compounds in leaves (Rothman et al. 2015). This predicts that *Piliocolobus*, the most folivorous of the African colobines, will be affected by this constraint more than *Colobus*.

Shifting ranges, as climate change proceeds, to sites with more tolerable environmental conditions is not likely to be an option for many of Africa's colobines. This is because suitable range will often not exist, is already at carrying capacity for the species, is unprotected from hunting and other threats, or cannot be reached due to various barriers across former dispersal routes, particularly those related to habitat fragmentation.

Colobines are already being affected by climate change. Here are a few cases. According to Nicholson (2001), the most significant change in climate over the past 200 years occurred in the semi-arid regions of West Africa where the 30-year mean annual rainfall declined 20%–40% between 1931–1960 and 1968–1997. *Piliocolobus b. temminckii* (EN), the most northern *Piliocolobus*, has undergone a >50% decline in abundance over the last 30 years (Minhós et al. 2020). This subspecies occurs in almost two dozen protected areas, but most are small (<6 km^2), isolated, and under threat (Linder et al. 2021; Mayhew et al. 2020). Even in the largest protected area, Niokolo-Koba NP (9130 km^2), southeast Senegal, the 300 *P. b. temminckii* are restricted to small patches of forest (Linder et al. 2021). Forests in Gambia and Senegal are drying-up and being lost due to a decline in rainfall that is related to a combination of climate change and increased anthropogenic activities, particularly deforestation. Rainfall in Gambia declined 30% during the 50 years from 1950 to 2000. Mean annual rainfall is projected to be 80 cm in 2020 but <50 cm by 2100 (Urquhart 2016). Mean minimum monthly temperature increased *ca.* 0.5°C per decade from 1970 to 2006, or *ca.* 3.5°C in only 36 years (GoTG 2007). The 2016 annual mean temperature of *ca.* 28°C is projected to increase to 31°–32°C by 2100 (Urquhart 2016). Annual rainfall dropped 24% in Senegal between 1931–1960 and 1961–1985, and this trend has continued. One result is that the north and east limits of the geographic range of *P. b. temminckii* have retreated and the range has become more fragmented (Galat-Luong and Galat 2005; Galat et al. 2009). Annual rainfall in Fathala Forest (76 km^2), Delta du Saloum NP, west Senegal, declined 30% (30 cm) between 1950–1970 and 1987–1997. At present, Fathala Forest holds one of the northern-most populations of *P. b. temminckii.* The area of gallery forest, the habitat used by *P. b. temminckii*, decreased 75% between 1972 and 2002. Between 1973 and 1996–2002, the number of *P. b. temminckii* dropped about 17% to approximately 500 individuals, and mean group size declined from 29 individuals to 16 individuals (Galat-Luong and Galat 2005). Galat-Luong and Galat (2005) observed five adaptations that *P. b. temminckii* made to the advancing arid conditions in Fathala Forest: (1) increased proportions of fruits, grasses, herbs and seeds in the diet, with new species of plants added to the diet; (2) increased terrestrial locomotion; (3) increased time in polyspecific associations, particularly with green monkeys *Chlorocebus sabaeus* (Linnaeus, 1766); (4) increased time in more open habitats; (5) increased time resting and foraging in mangrove swamps. While *P. b. temminckii* appears to have adapted somewhat to climate change, it seems likely that most, if not all, populations of *P. b. temminckii* will perish under the highly unfavourable climate and anthropogenic changes that are expected to occur over all of its geographic range over the next 80 years.

Mount Kilimanjaro, northeast Tanzania, where *C. caudatus* (VU) is endemic, has lost more than one-third of its forest over the last 70 years. This is the result of clearing forest for agriculture on the lower slopes and of fire related to climate change in the 'cloud zone' (i.e. upper montane forest and subalpine forest). During the 82 years from 1922 to 2004, annual rainfall declined 986 mm (39%; Hemp 2009). Off the north slope of Kilimanjaro, in the Amboseli Basin, daily maximum temperature increased >5.2°C in a mere 25 years (1976–2000; Altmann et al. 2002). These climatic changes, together with enhanced solar radiation, have severely diminished cloud cover. This has promoted more frequent, intense and devastating fires that have impacted not only the forest of the cloud zone, but the entire ecosystem. These climate change-induced fires destroyed 150 km^2 of cloud zone forest during 1976–2000, changed the structure and species composition of this zone, and led to a down-slope shift of the upper forest line by 800 m. Climate change-related fires not only rapidly transformed the vegetation cover in the cloud zone, they maintain the newly established bush habitat (Hemp 2009). Although the impacts of these recent climate changes on *C. caudatus* have not been documented, given the loss of 150 km^2 of habitat as of 2000, they are, undoubtedly, highly negative for this endemic, forest-dependent, species.

A similar situation exists on Mount Kenya and Aberdare Range, central Kenya, the two strong-holds of the Kenya endemic *C. g. kikuyuensis* (LC), as well as for the Mathews Range and Ndoto Range, central Kenya, where the endemic *C. g. percivali* (EN) occurs. During the 50-year 1960–2009 era, annual rainfall in this region declined 10 cm. The observed-projected decline for annual rainfall during 1975–2025 is 15 cm, while this will be exacerbated by the observed-projected increase for temperature during this period of 0.9°C (Funk et al. 2010). As Mount Kenya, Aberdare Range and Mathews Range become increasingly hot and dry, one result will be fires that are more frequent and damaging. Burns of 30–70 km^2 are now frequent. Most fires are within montane forest (Henry et al. 2019), the habitat on which both of these *C. guereza* (LC) subspecies rely. This loss of forest must be negative for *C. g. kikuyuensis* and *C. g. percivali*, but to what extent is not known.

Agroecosystems: Forest Loss and Hunting

In tropical Africa, agroecosystems often derive from conversion of moist forest and riparian forest. Agroecosystems are generally under rapid change, have much human activity, and often border protected areas, while the forest that remains is typically degraded, fragmented and heavily used by people (Estrada et al. 2012; Kitegile et al. 2021). With the rapidly growing human population in Africa, and resultant extensive loss of forest, Africa's colobines increasingly rely on agroecosystems where indigenous plants and animals are partially or almost completely replaced with crops, invasive plants and livestock. The extensive agroecosystem of the Laikipia Plateau and Mount Kenya has reduced and fragmented the population of *C. g. kikuyuensis* (LC), causing some individuals to frequently move from natural forest into contiguous plantations of exotic trees to forage (Butynski and De Jong 2014). Similarly, *C. g. occidentalis* (LC) and *P. tephrosceles* (EN) in Kibale NP often forage in exotic tree plantations that are contiguous with the natural forest (Harris and Chapman 2007a; Struhsaker 1975, 2010). *Piliocolobus b. temminckii* (EN) in Senegal and Gambia have begun to eat groundnuts *Arachis hypogaea* as their habitat is converted to agriculture (Galat et al. 2009; Mayhew et al. 2020).

Although many species of African primate raid crops, colobines, being arboreal folivores, typically do not severely damage crops. Some colobines are killed in response to damage to crops and, allegedly, to exotic tree plantations (Oates 1977b). Protecting crops involves costs that are both obvious and not so obvious. Among the less obvious costs to farm families are the increased exposure to zoonotic disease and loss of school days as children remain home to protect crops (Chapman et al. 2005; Humle and Hill 2016).

Colobus g. occidentalis (LC) damage crops at the forest-agriculture interface around Budongo FR, northwest Uganda, accounting for 3% of crop-raids by five species of monkey (Wallace and Hill 2012). Around Kibale NP, primates accounted for 71% of crop damage events by mammals, and 48% of the damage. Of 2461 crop damage events, *C. g occidentalis* was involved in only 11 (0.004%) while none involved *P. tephrosceles* (EN) (Naughton-Treves 1998). There are reports of *C. a. palliatus* (VU) occasionally eating skins of mangoes *Mangifera indica* and oranges *Citrus aurantuim* and *Citrus sinensis*, and leaves of cassava *Manihot esculenta*, sweet potato *Ipomoea batatas* and cow peas *Vigna unguiculata*, on the south coast of Kenya, but the level of damage seems inadequate to cause farmers to retaliate (Anderson et al. 2007a). *Piliocolobus tephrosceles* sometimes raid crops of beans *Phaseolus vulgaris* in the forest-farm mosaic of Mbuzi Forest, southwest Tanzania. Here, farmers' dogs are known to kill *P. tephrosceles* (Kibaja 2014). Along the lower Tana R., *P. rufomitratus* (CR) is occasionally persecuted due to its association with primates that are crop pests, such as olive baboon *Papio anubis* (Lesson, 1827), vervet monkey *Chlorocebus pygerythrus* (F. Cuvier, 1821), and gentle monkey *Cercopithecus mitis* Wolf, 1822 (Linder et al. 2021; T. Butynski, pers. obs.). The same holds true for *P. b. temminckii* (EN) in Gambia (Mayhew et al. 2020).

Human-colobine interactions are not always negative. On Zanzibar Island, for example, *P. kirkii* (EN) eats damaged and immature coconuts. Rather than reducing the coconut harvest, this feeding promotes coconut palm production, probably through pruning. Nonetheless, *P. kirkii* is considered a pest by coconut farmers rather than an asset (Krain et al. 1993 in Siex and Struhsaker 1999a).

It appears that African colobines are increasingly involved in crop raiding and/or food-snatching [e.g. *C. g. kikuyuensis* (LC) at restaurants on Mount Kenya] as they adapt their ecology and diet to cope with human-modified habitats and increased sympatry with humans (Y. de Jong and T. Butynski pers. obs.). Understanding the importance of agroecosystems for Africa's colobines is becoming increasingly essential for colobine management and conservation, as well as for an improved understanding and monitoring of zoonotic diseases.

Diseases and Parasites

Humans and non-human primates, including colobines, are in increasing contact through crop raiding, gathering of forest products, logging, tourism, research and the hunting, butchering and consumption of bushmeat. This enhanced contact translates into a heightened risk of bi-directional transmission between humans, non-human primates and other animals, of viruses, bacteria, endo-parasites and ecto-parasites (Butynski 2001; Butynski and Kalina 1998; Goldberg et al. 2008; Paige et al. 2017; Woodford et al. 2002; Chapter 19). As a result of this increased contact, some of these may become emerging infectious diseases (Chapman et al. 2005b; Estrada et al. 2012, 2017; Kaeslin 2010; Patz et al. 2004). Phylogenetic distance, anthropogenic disturbance (particularly forest degradation, loss and fragmentation), habitat type, environment, ecology, behaviour, demography, population density and stress, are among the many factors that interact in complex ways to influence disease transmission, susceptibility and maintenance, as well as levels of morbidity and mortality (Alexander et al. 2015; Chapman et al. 2005b, 2006e; Ghai et al. 2015; Gillespie and Chapman 2006; Gillespie et al. 2005a,b; Goldberg et al. 2008b; Patz et al. 2004; Teichroeb et al. 2009b).

A wide range of viruses have been identified in African colobines, including *C. s. satanas* (CR), *C. g. matschiei* (LC), *C. g. occidentalis* (LC), *P. verus* (VU), *P. b. badius* (EN), *P. b. temminckii* (EN), *P. kirkii* (EN), *P. preussi* (CR), *P. tephrosceles* (EN) and *P. tholloni* (VU). These include retroviruses (e.g. SIV), orthopoxviruses (e.g. monkeypox), arteriviruses, hepaciviruses, pegiviruses, jingmenviruses and haemorrhagic fever (Bailey et al. 2016; Courgnaud et al. 2003; Goldberg et al. 2008a, 2009; Jezek et al. 1986; Ladner et al. 2016; Lauck et al. 2011, 2013b,c; Leendertz et al. 2010; Liegeois et al. 2009; Locatelli et al. 2008a,b; Sibley et al. 2014). Prevalence of one or more of these viruses in colobine populations is high. While none of these viruses has been linked to mortality, or even morbidity, in colobines, it seems certain that at least some have the potential to cause widespread epidemics with high mortality (Hart et al. 2020a), as well as for cross-species transmission, including to humans.

A disease, described as 'herpes-like', that causes inflammation, blisters and scabs on the face, and inflammation on the genitals, perineum and inguinum of *P. tephrosceles* (EN) in Kibale NP, is implicated in the deaths of at least 10 of 17 adult males in one group (Struhsaker 2000b, 2010). This disease may be caused by a poxvirus (Goldberg et al. 2008a).

Hunting of colobines by chimpanzees may lead to cross-species transmission of diseases. In Taï NP, the hunting and shared consumption of two *P. b. badius* (EN) is associated with two outbreaks of Ebola among chimpanzees (Alexander et al. 2015; Formenty et al. 1999).

Zimmermann et al. (2017) studied *Bacillus cereus* biovar *anthracis* (*Bcbva*) in Taï NP during 2001–2015. *Bcbva* causes an anthrax-like disease in a broad range of mammalian hosts, including *P. b. badius* (EN) and *C. polykomos* (EN). *Bcbva* persisted in Taï NP throughout this 15-year study. These authors conclude that the combination of high mortality and low antibody detection rates indicates that *Bcbva* is of high virulence and is a major cause of death for *P. b. badius* and *C. polykomos* in Taï NP. *Bcbva* poses a threat for *Piliocolobus* and *Colobus* in the several other moist forests where it is known to occur.

During a 2019 survey of *P. langi* (EN) that covered 50,000 km^2 east of Kisangani, northeast DRC, many of the people interviewed reported widespread periodic epidemic die-offs of *P. langi* in the southeast part of the survey area. According to Hart et al. (2020a: p. 10), 'Interview respondents in 16 localities, representing 6 polygons citied episodes of epidemic die-offs of red colobus from 2004 through 2017 (Figure 7). The area affected covered approximately 5000 km^2. All respondents reported finding dead animals in the forest. One hunter stated that he found 50 dead red colobus over the course of a few days. One locality reported that a major die off occurred between 2004 and 2007 and was followed by a minor die off, with fewer dead animals found, in 2017, 10 years later. Many respondents mentioned that the epidemic did not appear to affect other primates. No carcasses of sick animals other than red colobus were found'. Unfortunately, these authors were unable to provide information on the appearance of the dead *P. langi* or on the identity of the disease. They go on to say, 'The epidemic outbreak in the Kisangani red colobus range represents potentially one of the largest areas affected by a primate epidemic accompanied by mass mortality reported to date' (13).

Teichroeb et al. (2009b) conducted a survey of the richness and prevalence of gastrointestinal parasites in *C. vellerosus* (CR) in Boabeng-Fiema Monkey Sanctuary (5 km^2 with a 1.9 km^2 core area), central Ghana. Among 109 faecal samples from males, they identified 11 species: one protistan, four protozoans, five nematodes and one trematode. Among 278 faecal samples from 19 groups of *P. rufomitratus* (CR) in 17 forests at Tana R., Mbora and McPeek (2009) recorded 13 species of helminth and four species of protozoan parasites. Barelli et al. (2019) found five species of parasitic helminths in 251 faecal samples obtained from 25 groups of *P. gordonorum* (EN) in four forest blocks in the Udzungwa Mountains.

Gillespie et al. (2005b) surveyed the richness and prevalence of gastrointestinal parasites in three colobines in southwest Uganda. They recorded five species of gastrointestinal parasites in *C. a. ruwenzorii* (DD; n = 19 faecal samples), 10 in *C. g. occidentalis* (LC; n = 476), and 12 in *P. tephrosceles* (EN; n = 1608).

Of the 15 gastrointestinal parasite species known for the non-human primates and humans of Kibale NP and vicinity, at least eight occur in *P. tephrosceles* (EN), of which at least seven also occur in humans, while at least seven occur in *C. g. occidentalis* (LC), of which at least six also occur in humans. *Ascaris* and *Giardia* are present in *P. tephrosceles* in forest fragments and are common in humans near these fragments. Both parasite genera were absent from pristine areas where interactions between non-human primates and humans were less frequent (Chapman et al. 2005b).

In a second study of gastrointestinal parasites in Kibale NP and vicinity, of 35 *P. tephrosceles* (EN) sampled in forest fragments, 6% were infected with *Giardia* and 14% with *Cryptosporidium*. None of the 25 *C. g. occidentalis* (LC) sampled in forest fragments had either of these two parasites. Neither colobine harboured either of these parasites in the undisturbed forest (Salzer et al. 2007).

Hemoparasites also occur among the colobines of Kibale NP. Twenty-two per cent of nine *C. g. occidentalis* (LC) and 89% of 46 *P. tephrosceles* (EN) were hosts to *Hepatocystis* spp. (Thurber et al. 2013). Although hemoparasites are close relatives of *Plasmodium*, they are not known to cause malaria (Aunin et al. 2020).

It is important to note that for none of the many above-mentioned gastrointestinal and blood parasites is there evidence that they cause mortality in colobines, although there is some evidence for morbidity (Ghai et al. 2015). In humans, some of these parasites have impacts that range from diarrhoea to death. Despite the accumulation of considerable information on disease-causing organisms in Africa's colobines, there are few records of animals with overt clinical symptoms and even fewer records for colobines dying of disease (Davis 1994; Ghai et al. 2015; Chapter 19). It would be surprising, however, if diseases do not, from time-to-time, severely impact populations of colobus, just as they do humans, other non-human primates and probably all mammals. Indeed, the recent findings mentioned above by Zimmermann et al. (2017) and Hart et al. (2020a) indicate that this is the case and that major die-offs of colobines will be documented.

Fire

Grass-bush-forest mosaics occur over large parts of the geographic range of Africa's colobines. In tropical Africa, fires are mainly set by people, often annually, to remove the dense bush and tall (2–3 m) rank grass in order to maintain grasslands, facilitate clearing prior to planting crops, promote a flush of green grass for livestock and wildlife, improve visibility for hunters, kill disease-bearing ticks, and make movement by people and livestock much easier. These fires typically spread to the edges of forest and often into forest, killing seeds, seedlings, saplings and mature trees. Fire, particularly damaging to riparian and gallery forests, not only inhibits forest regeneration, it can create major barriers to dispersal of forest-dependent species, including colobines. Forest cover over vast parts of Africa is in rapid decline as a result of the combination of fire and clearance for agriculture.

Being arboreal and forest-dependent, Africa's colobines are particularly susceptible to fire, both directly through death by fire/smoke, and indirectly through the negative impacts of fire on forest. The habitats of all of Africa's colobines are probably negatively affected to some extent by fire, but those taxa in the hotter, lower rainfall areas, as found around the periphery of the geographic range, are most severely affected (ESM Table 21.2). As indicated in the 'Climate Change' section, the lower rainfall and higher temperatures brought on by climate change will further promote fire and enhance the damage through bigger, hotter and more frequent burns.

Colobus g. dodingae (EN) is endemic to the Dodinga Hills and Imatong Mountains of extreme south South Sudan and extreme central north Uganda, where mean annual rainfall is 50–200 cm. The forests on which this subspecies depends have been, and continue to be, reduced and fragmented by frequent human-caused fire and conversion to agriculture (Butynski and De Jong 2020a; De Jong and Butynski 2015). *Piliocolobus rufomitratus* (CR) of the small and highly fragmented forests of the lower Tana R., where mean annual rainfall is only 50–75 cm, face a similar, although more serious, situation (Butynski et al. 2020; Kivai 2019, 2020).

Annual fire is a major threat to the forests of the Udzungwa Mountains (Dinesen et al. 2001; Linder et al. 2021; Marshall 2007; Rovero et al. 2019; Ruiz-Lopez 2016) where the endemic *P. gordonorum* (VU) occurs and that are a strong-hold for *C. a. sharpei* (VU). Among priority conservation actions for the Udzungwa Mountains is the prevention of fire in order to establish corridors among forest blocks, thereby facilitating the dispersal and increase of forest-dependent species, including *P. gordonorum.*

During fires in Fathala Forest, *P. b. temminckii* (EN) does not typically flee on the ground but seeks refuge in trees. The trees here are, however, not tall enough for colobus to escape from fire. A fire in 1972 killed at least 11 individuals. These fires also make *P. b. temminckii* more vulnerable to predators (Galat-Luong and Galat 2005).

Conservation of Africa's Colobines

To some degree, each taxon of African colobine faces a unique set of threats and conservation challenges. Tailor-made conservation solutions are, therefore, required for all of the 35 threatened and three Data Deficient taxa. Science, education, technology, protection, legislation, partnerships and local capacity building for conservation should all be applied to secure the long-term survival of Africa's colobines. ESM Table 21.2 provides a summary of the main conservation actions needed to reduce the threats to each taxon of African colobine. In this section, we mention the main conservation actions that are being employed to help minimize the threats to Africa's colobines and present a few examples of these actions.

In undertaking the task of minimizing the loss of diversity among Africa's colobines, and for securing the money and other support necessary for this work, it is important to keep in mind (1) that all of Africa's forest-dependent species of primate are at least partly sympatric with one or more species of colobine and that (2) many of Africa's colobines occur in the biologically richest regions of tropical Africa. This means that by conserving colobines and their habits, countless other species that coexist with them will be saved. It also means that colobines can act as conservation's 'flagship species' for some forests (Chapman et al. 2020; Fashing 2011). This is already the case for the following species and forests: *C. vellerosus* (CR) for Boabeng-Fiema Monkey Sanctuary, *C. a. palliatus* (VU) for southeast Kenya, *C. a. ruwenzorii* (DD) for Nyungwe NP, *P. b. temminckii* (EN) for Abuko Nature Reserve and Fathala Forest, *P. epieni* (CR) for the Niger Delta, *P. gordonorum* (VU) for the Udzungwa Mountains, *P. kirkii* (EN) for Zanzibar Island, *P. preussi* (CR) for Korup NP, *P. rufomitratus* (CR) for the lower Tana R. and Tana Delta, *P. tephrosceles* (EN) for Kibale NP. There are several other important forests in Africa where colobines could serve as the flagship species for conservation and as the focus for attracting tourists. These include *C. g. dodingae* (EN) for the Imatong Mountains, *C. g. percivali* (EN) for the Mathews Range and Ndoto Range, *C. caudatus* (VU) for Mount Kilimanjaro and Mount Meru, and *P. pennantii* (CR) for Bioko Island.

Protected Areas

Establishment of protected areas (e.g. national parks, game reserves, forest reserves) are often regarded by governments, natural resource management agencies, conservation NGOs and other institutions, as the best single strategy for conserving natural habitats, their ecological services and biodiversity. Protected areas are perceived as the cornerstones of biodiversity conservation worldwide. Big, well-connected and well-managed protected areas offer the best single conservation tool for African colobines. ESM Table 21.2 provides a list of some of the main protected areas for the conservation of each taxon of African colobine.

Protected areas in all African countries face many challenges and do not always provide a safe refuge for primates, including colobines. Protected areas typically suffer from a combination of insufficient resources, suitably trained, equipped and supported management, security, education and research personnel, corruption, mismanagement, paucity of community and government support, and high levels of illegal activities (ESM Table 21.2). In addition, protected areas are increasingly fragmented and isolated, lacking connectivity with other protected areas or suitable private lands (e.g. ranches, conservancies). Connectivity is essential for gene-flow, migration and species range shifts, particularly in this time of rapid climate change (Saura et al. 2018).

Korup NP is where *P. preussi* (CR) reaches its highest densities. This monkey acted as the flagship species for the creation and expansion of Korup NP and continues in that role (Siewe et al. 2017). Although Korup NP is the strong-hold for *P. preussi*, this population declined 80% during 1990–2016 (Linder et al. 2019). The human population around this park is quickly expanding. Hunting is the main threat, followed by forest loss (Bobo et al. 2017; Diaw et al. 2003; Linder and Oates 2011; Linder et al. 2021). Of great concern is the expansion of oil palm plantations adjacent to Korup NP as well as the proposed pineapple plantations inside the Oban Division of Cross River NP (Linder et al. 2019). The long-term survival of *P. preussi* depends on many factors including those related to improved law enforcement effectiveness, improved local community support for and participation in conservation, and developing economic alternatives to hunting (Linder et al. 2021). Korup NP has recently become even more critical for the survival of *P. preussi* with the declaration by the Government of Cameroon that Ebo Forest, rather than being gazetted as a national park as expected, will be put into two long-term logging concessions totalling 1334 km^2 (B. Morgan, pers. comm.).

There are three species of colobine in Taï NP, all of which are threatened: *C. polykomos* (EN), *P. verus* (VU), *P. b. badius* (EN). In terms of its conservation, however, Taï NP faces much the same situation as Korup NP. The human population has grown dramatically around the park, and with this has come a big increase in hunting. *Colobus polykomos* and *P. b. badius*, the two most vulnerable primates in Taï NP, have been particularly affected by hunting and are now absent from parts of the park (Koné and Refisch 2007; McGraw 2007; McGraw and Zuberbühler 2007; McGraw et al. 2020a, 2020b; Oates 2011). Other problems include illegal logging, agricultural encroachment and weak law enforcement. In addition, rapid clearance of forest surrounding Taï NP is putting more pressure on the park's forest and primates (McGraw 2007). Presence of an anthrax-like disease, *Bcbva*, is also thought to be a major cause of mortality both for *C. polykomos* and *P. b. badius* (see above; Zimmermann et al. 2017).

Unfortunately, many important populations of colobines are outside protected areas. The Niger Delta, for example, has a high primate diversity including the endemic *P. epieni* (CR), yet the Delta lacks effectively protected areas (Baker and Oates 2019; Butynski and De Jong 2019b; Linder et al. 2021). The same is true for *P. rufomitratus* (CR) and sympatric *C. galeritus* (CR), endemic to the lower Tana R. and Tana Delta. Although the Tana River Primate National Reserve (NR; 171 km^2) was created to protect the biodiversity of part of the lower Tana River Ecosystem, a court case to degazette the only protected area within the geographic range of the *P. rufomitratus* and *C. galeritus*, the Tana River Primate NR, was won by the local community. In 2007, the High Court of Kenya ordered the annulment of the reserve, citing lack of proper involvement of the local people during its gazettement. This area is now treated as public land with no formal protection (see below; Butynski and De Jong 2019b; Butynski and Hamerlynck 2016; Butynski et al. 2020; Kivai et al. 2019, 2020). To secure the long-term survival of *P. rufomitratus* and *C. galeritus* under present circumstances, initiatives that enable local people to conserve the forests, rehabilitate degraded areas, manage growth of the human population, and establish sustainable income generating projects (e.g. ecotourism), are required (Butynski and De Jong 2019b). A few conservation initiatives have started in the region, including Ndera Community Conservancy. Rehabilitation of the once flourishing Mchelelo Research Camp and initiation of the Ngwano Community Conservancy and other community forest associations have been proposed (Butynski et al. 2020; Kivai 2019, 2020; Kuraru and King 2019; Linder et al. 2021; Mbora and Allen 2011).

Some populations of colobines occur where forest persists within agroecosystems and on private lands (e.g. ranches, conservancies, hotel compounds, botanical gardens, sacred forests/sacred groves). Most of these forests and their populations of colobines are, however, small, severely fragmented and remain under considerable threat from further degradation and loss. As such, they are unlikely to persist over the long-term without considerable management and financial inputs, and local community support.

Conservation by Tradition

Cultural and religious traditions, including taboos, sometimes assist the conservation of primates in Africa, including colobines. This appears to apply more to East Africa than to West Africa or Central Africa. For example, over most of Ethiopia, cultural and religious traditions prohibit the killing and eating of monkeys, with the penalty of social exclusion (Erena et al. 2020).

The abundance of *C. vellerosus* (CR) has rapidly declined as a result of hunting and forest loss (Gonedelé Bi et al. 2010; Oates 2011; Saj and Sicotte 2013). In Boabeng-Fiema Monkey Sanctuary, central Ghana, there is a taboo on the hunting of *C. vellerosus* that is said to date back to the 1830s when a local oracle instructed the villagers to *care for the monkeys*. People here consider *C. vellerosus* to be 'the children of the gods who protect the villages' (Saj et al. 2006: 286). The number of *C. vellerosus* in and around Boabeng-Fiema Monkey Sanctuary increased from 128 in 1990 (Fargey 1991) to 365 in 2007 (Saj and Sicotte 2013; Wong and Sicotte 2006). This is now one of the largest populations of *C. vellerosus* anywhere (Gonedelé Bi et al. 2010; Matsuda Goodwin et al. 2019). Although *C. vellerosus* is not hunted in this area, the amount of 'good forest' around the periphery of the sanctuary declined by 55% in only 10 years (1990–2000), while within the sanctuary, outside of the 1.9 km^2 core area, 'good forest' declined 52% during this period and land under agriculture increased 118%. This is a direct result of the rapidly growing human population in this area (Saj et al. 2006).

Colobus vellerosus (CR) has fared less well in Côte d'Ivoire where it appears to now be absent from the country's national parks and forest reserves. Here *C. vellerosus* remains only in difficult-to-access swamp forest, such as Tanoé-Ehy Swamp Forest, and in the Dinaoudi Sacred Grove (3 ha), northeast Côte d'Ivoire. Only about 30 individuals remained in Dinaoudi Sacred Grove in 2010. Traditionally, people near Soko Sacred Grove, northeast Côte d'Ivoire, considered *C. vellerosus* as their 'relative', and refrained from hunting it. Not all people new to the area, however, respected this tradition nor this sacred grove. The result is that *C. vellerosus* has been extirpated from Soko Sacred Grove and the forest destroyed (Gonedelé Bi et al. 2010).

There are over 50 'kayas' (= sacred forests) on the coast of Kenya. These range in size from about 3 ha to 300 ha (UNESCO 2008) and hold high biodiversity (Burgess et al. 1998; Githitho 2003). In and around kayas, social taboos, rather than government laws, impact human activities (Colding and Folke 2001). In kayas, taking of natural resources is regulated by traditional knowledge and practices. Some communities still use kayas as ceremonial and/or burial grounds and taboos prohibit use by livestock and removal of forest products. Due to the rapid increase in the human population on Kenya's coast over the last 50 years, however, the size of kayas has dramatically declined and some have been lost, including kayas on the south coast. Some of this loss is due to immigrants who do not always respect traditional customs. This has negatively affected *C. a. palliatus* (VU) (Anderson 2005; Anderson et al. 2007a; Cunneyworth et al. 2020; Swart 2010). In 2008, the Sacred Kaya Mijikenda Forests (10 forests totalling 15.4 km^2) became a UNESCO World Heritage Site (UNESCO 2008).

Sacred forests that have been protected for centuries (or perhaps longer) for their cultural and religious significance are everywhere under severe threat, while many have already been destroyed along with all of their benefits (Anderson et al. 2005; Cowlishaw and Dunbar 2000; Gonedelé Bi et al. 2010; McGraw 2007; Oates 2011; Saj et al. 2006). Sacred forests are typically remnants of much larger forests. Their small size and the many threats posed by the high-density human populations that surround them, mean that these fragments, and their colobines, are highly vulnerable. As with other forest fragments, the long-term survival of sacred forests will require constant vigilance, effective protection and management and, most importantly, ample support from the local community.

Conservation Education

Engagement of local people who rely on forest resources is an essential part of the conservation of Africa's colobines. This makes conservation education and outreach programmes important tools for the conservation of colobines. Effective conservation education programmes must be 'tailor-made' as no community or colobine taxon is the same. Cultural sensitivity and relevant ethnographic insights need to be considered in order to design effective conservation messages. Materials used in a conservation education campaign for *P. preussi* (CR), for example, were the result of ethnographic research. Focusing on communication and outreach, social media accounts were used to both help track the effectiveness of this programme and communicate current information concerning *P. preussi* (Hofner et al. 2019).

Colobus Conservation, an initiative at Diani, south coast of Kenya, is mainly concerned with the conservation of *C. a. palliatus* (VU), the five other species of primate in this area, and the indigenous forest. The primary targets are school children, local people, tourists, and hotel owners and staff, using *C. a. palliatus* as the flagship species. Colobus Conservation also treats and rehabilitates injured primates. Vehicles on the major road through Diani killed or injured 518 primates during 1999–2012 (3% of the primate population; Donaldson and Cunneyworth 2015). Colobus Conservation installed 28 canopy bridges, called 'colobridges'. These were partly funded by the local community. *Colobus a. palliatus*, Hilgert's vervet monkeys *Chlorocebus pygerythrus hilgerti* (Neumann, 1902), and Zanzibar Sykes's monkeys *Cercopithecus mitis albogularis* (Sykes, 1831) now cross these bridges almost 300,000 times each year (Colobus Conservation 2020). Besides greatly reducing road fatalities, colobridges are also a tool for conservation education.

One objective of the *Red Colobus* (Piliocolobus) *Conservation Action Plan, 2021–2026* (Linder et al. 2021) is to engage local communities and integrate them into actions designed to conserve *Piliocolobus*. To prevent forest loss and hunting requires the cooperation of the local communities and local governments. To do this successfully, ample information, advice, trust and alternative sources of income are needed. In addition, conservation education programmes can promote efficient and clean house-hold energy (reducing reliance on wood) and improve collaboration among government agencies, local communities, family planning organizations, conservation NGOs and others.

Translocation

Translocation, as a conservation and animal welfare tool, has been successfully applied in several cases to African colobines, both to help resolve human-colobine conflict and/or as (re)introductions to bolster conservation of the taxon. Translocation of African colobines is, however, seldom possible due to the scarcity of suitable protected habitat, high costs and other factors. Translocation can be an effective conservation tool in certain circumstances, but great care is required, and the IUCN *Guidelines for Reintroduction and other Conservation Translocations* (IUCN/SSC 2013) should always be fully applied.

In Karura Forest, Nairobi, central south Kenya, 137 *C. g. kikuyuensis* (LC) from 23 groups were reintroduced during May 2014–March 2016 from unprotected forest fragments in the nearby Aberdare Range. This new population comprised 160 individuals in December 2019 (P. Fundi pers. comm.). Similarly, 14 *C. g. kikuyuensis* were transferred from the Aberdare Range to Soysambu Conservancy, southwest Kenya, in 1999 (King 1999), and 62 individuals from seven groups during May 2018–March 2019. This population now stands at 80 individuals (Fundi et al. 2020).

In 1973, 15 *P. kirkii* (EN) were introduced to Ngezi-Vumawimbi Nature FR, northwest Pemba Island, Tanzania, in order to establish a second population of this Zanzibar Island endemic. Thirty-five years later, in 2011, there were about 35 individuals in this population (Butynski and De Jong 2011).

Captive Breeding

Considering their threatened status, African colobines might benefit from captive breeding programmes. Although *Colobus* are relatively easy to maintain and breed in captivity, all attempts to maintain *Piliocolobus* in captivity have failed (Amato et al. 2016b; Collins and Roberts 1978; Oates and Davies 1994; Oates and Ting 2015; Struhsaker 2010; Chapter 6). While it appears to not be particularly difficult to translocate wild-caught *Colobus* and *Piliocolobus* from one natural habitat to another (see below), it is not known how challenging it is to successfully translocate captive-bred colobines to natural habitats. What is known, however, is that captive breeding of colobines, and successful translocation of captive-bred colobines to natural forest, will require much expertise, time and money. Maintaining *in situ* wild populations is, by far, the better option, with translocation of wild-caught individuals the next best option.

Research on Africa's Colobines

Research and monitoring are essential tools for the conservation of Africa's colobines. The main research actions required for each taxon are presented in ESM Table 21.2. These research actions were compiled from several sources but especially from the current *IUCN Red List* (IUCN 2019/2020) and the *Red Colobus* (Piliocolobus) *Conservation Action Plan, 2021–2026* (Linder et al. 2021). For the most part, these actions are similar among taxa.

Researchers studying African colobines have played a major role in the conservation of Africa's primates and forests (Fashing 2007b). Some of the earliest and longest contributions have been made by Tom Struhsaker (1975, 1997, 2005, 2010) and John Oates (1977b, 1996a, 1999, 2011), both of whom remain active in colobine research and conservation today, contributing to several 2019/2020 colobine *IUCN Red List* assessments and to the *Red Colobus* (Piliocolobus) *Conservation Action Plan, 2021–2026*.

Although the natural history of some African colobines is well known at several sites, the natural history of most taxa remains largely unstudied and there are vast parts of Africa where no detailed research on any colobine has been undertaken (e.g. Lower Congo Basin, Upper Zambezi Basin). Of particular concern is the near absence of natural history, abundance and detailed biogeographic information for many of the most threatened taxa, including *C. s. satanas* (CR), *C. a. prigoginei* (EN), *C. g. dodingae* (EN), *C. g. percivali* (EN), *P. bouvieri* (EN), *P. epieni* (CR), *P. foai* (EN), *P. langi* (EN), *P. lulindicus* (EN), *P. parmentieri* (EN), *P. pennantii* (CR) and *P. waldroni* (CR). These knowledge gaps are due to a large number of variables, including paucity of field primatologists, unstable taxonomies, remoteness of sites and the related risks, costs and logistic challenges, insecurity, corruption, and expensive and difficult to obtain research and specimen export permits.

The paucity of data for many taxa of African colobine means that conservationists and managers are forced to recommend conservation actions and make other decisions about highly threatened taxa based on insufficient information (Fashing 2007b; Linder et al. 2021; Oates 1996a). Insight into the taxonomy, natural history, abundance and biogeography of the African colobines, as well as the dynamics of meta-populations, dispersal (including gene-flow), habitat ecology, effects of climate change, impact and extent of human activities on colobines and their habitats, and conservation threats, are needed to design effective management strategies for all of the threatened African colobines.

How big the knowledge gaps are is illustrated by the fact that there are three African colobines listed as 'Data Deficient' on the current *IUCN Red List* (ESM Table 21.1; IUCN 2019/2020), by the recent discovery of Kapale's colobus (J. Hart pers. comm.), and by discoveries over the past decade that extend the known geographic ranges of several taxa. These include the following:

- *Colobus polykomos* (EN) in the Fouta Djallon Mountains, west central Guinea, 125 km northeast of the nearest known population (Figure 21.4; Alonso et al. 2018).
- *Colobus g. dodingae* (EN) in the Imatong Mountains of central north Uganda (Figure 21.4; De Jong and Butynski 2015). Previously believed to be endemic to south South Sudan. Now recognized as one of Uganda's most threatened primates.
- *Colobus g. occidentalis* (LC) in the Otzi FR (188 km^2), northwest Uganda (Figure 21.1; Butynski and De Jong 2017). This is a range extension of 120 km to the northeast.
- *Colobus caudatus* (VU) on the lower slopes of Mount Kilimanjaro, central south Kenya (Figure 21.2; Butynski and De Jong 2015, 2018). Previously believed to be

endemic to central north Tanzania. Now recognized as one of Kenya's most threatened primates.
- *Piliocolobus parmentieri* (EN) in Lomami NP (8879 km^2), northeast DRC (Figure 21.5; Hart and Detwiler 2020). This is a range extension of 80 kms to the south.
- *Piliocolobus rufomitratus* (CR) found at Onkolde, Tana Delta, north coast of Kenya (Hamerlynck et al. 2012). This is a small, 7 km, range extension, but an important one for this 'Critically Endangered' species.

Unfortunately, other surveys have found many major range contractions for Africa's colobines over the past century as a result of ever increasing and expanding anthropogenic activities, especially hunting and forest degradation, loss and fragmentation. This is highlighted by the probable national extirpation of the following taxa:

- *Colobus vellerosus* (CR) from Burkina Faso and Nigeria
- *Colobus a. angolensis* (VU) from Zambia
- *Colobus a. prigoginei* (EN) or *C. a. sharpei* (VU) from Zambia
- *Colobus g. occidentalis* (LC) from Rwanda
- *Piliocolobus tephrosceles* (EN) from Burundi and Rwanda
- *Piliocolobus waldroni* (CR) from Côte d'Ivoire and Ghana

The above indicates that Rwanda has lost two of its three species of colobines, and that Zambia has lost both of its species of colobines. Kenya is on the verge of losing *C. caudatus* (VU) while Uganda could soon lose *C. g. dodingae* (EN).

Other recent studies, however, confirm the continued existence of populations that were feared extirpated. Here are six examples:

- *Colobus polykomos* (EN) and *P. b. temminckii* (EN) confirmed present north of the Corubal R. in Dulombi-Boe NP 1 (1770 km^2), central south Guinea-Bissau, for the first time in two decades (Bersacola et al. 2018).
- *Colobus a. ruwenzorii* (DD) last reported in the forests of Sango Bay (151 km^2), southwest Uganda, in 1972 (Oates 1977b, 1994). In 2019, the continued existence of this population was confirmed (Y. de Jong and T. Butynski pers. obs.).
- *Colobus g. matschiei* (LC) found on Mt. Kadam, central east Uganda, in 1972 (Oates 1977b). That this small population, located 40 km north of Mt. Elgon, survives was confirmed in 2019, although much threatened by frequent fire and felling of forest for agriculture (Y. de Jong and T. Butynski pers. obs.).
- *Piliocolobus bouvieri* (EN) found at several sites in Congo in 2007, 2014, 2015, 2016, and 2021, including Ntokou-Pikounda NP (4572 km^2), north central Congo, and Lesio-Louna Reserve (440 km^2), south central Gabon (Figure 21.5; Maisels and Devreese 2020). These are the first records for this species since the 1970s.
- *Piliocolobus langi* (EN) became absent from the bushmeat markets of Kisangani, northeast DRC, in the early 2000s and not recorded in the field after 2012. A survey in search of this species in 2019 found that *P. langi* is still present at a

number of sites over its 69,000 km^2 geographic range (Figure 21.5; Hart et al. 2020a, 2020b). This survey also found, however, that abundance has been greatly reduced and that some populations have been extirpated.
- In 2015, *P. oustaleti* (VU) found to still be present, although uncommon, at the north extreme of its range at several sites in Bangangai GR (171 km^2) and Bire Kpatuos GR (70 km^2), southwest South Sudan. *Colobus g. occidentalis* (LC) is common in both reserves (D. Reeder pers. comm.; Zooniverse 2020). These are the first records of these two colobines for South Sudan since about 1982 (Hillman 1983).

Priority research on African colobines includes the following:

- Additional molecular, morphological and behavioural studies to stabilize the taxonomy, particularly for *Piliocolobus*.
- Improve our understanding of the biogeography of all taxa. The present distribution maps remain crude and, for the more widespread species, often include large areas of obviously unsuitable habitat that should be deleted from future maps. Follow this exercise with ground surveys to at least determine presence or likely absence from areas of probable suitable habitat. The objective is to move towards much-improved estimates of 'Extent of Occurrence' and, eventually, to a good understanding of 'Area of Occupancy' (IUCN 2012) for each taxon. These will allow for the much-improved monitoring of the conservation status of colobines and identify priority regions for conservation actions.

Priority field research projects that can probably be completed in 1–3 months of intensive field work include determining whether:

- *Colobus s. anthracinus* (VU) still occurs in Dja Faunal Reserve (5266 km^2), central south Cameroon.
- *Colobus s. satanas* (CR) and *P. pennantii* (CR) still occur on Pico Basilé (330 km^2), Bioko Island, Equatorial Guinea.
- *Colobus vellerosus* (CR) still occurs in Nigeria and Burkina Faso.
- *Colobus polykomos* (EN) still occurs in Nigeria.
- *Colobus a. angolensis* (VU) still occurs in Zambia.
- *Colobus g. dodingae* (EN) still occurs in the Dodinga Hills, South Sudan, and in Kidepo NP (1344 km^2), Uganda.
- *Piliocolobus semlikiensis* (VU) still occurs in Uganda.
- *Piliocolobus tephrosceles* (EN) still occurs in DRC, Burundi and/or Rwanda.
- *Colobus a. prigoginei* (EN) occurs in Zambia.
- *Colobus a. sharpei* (VU) occurs in Mozambique, Malawi and/or Zambia.
- *Colobus g. percivali* (EN) occurs on Mt. Nyiru, Mt. Kulal and/or Kirisia Hills, Kenya.
- *Colobus g. guereza* (LC) occurs in South Sudan.
- *Procolobus verus* (VU) occurs in Togo.
- *Piliocolobus badius badius* (EN) occurs in Cavally Classified Forest and/or Tonkpi region, southwest Côte d'Ivoire.
- *Piliocolobus waldroni* (CR) is extinct.

Once presence has been established for any of the taxa in the above list, a second phase of research should be undertaken to determine geographic limits, population size, threats and conservation status.

Priority field research projects that can probably be completed in 3–4 months of intensive field work include detailed surveys to determine geographic limits, population size, threats and conservation status of *C. a. ruwenzorii* (DD) in the four forest reserves at Sango Bay, southwest Uganda, and in the contiguous Minziro Nature FR (311 km^2) in northwest Tanzania. These forests may hold the largest, or second largest, population of *C. a. ruwenzorii*. Priority field research projects that can probably be completed in less than 1 year of intensive field work include assessing the geographic range, abundance, threats and conservation status for each of the following particularly poorly known taxa: *C. a. cordieri* (VU), *C. a. prigoginei* (EN), *C. a. ruwenzorii* (DD), *C. a.* ssp. nov. (DD), *C. g. dodingae* (EN), *C. g. guereza* (LC), *C. g. gallarum* (DD), *P. foai* (EN).

Actions for the Conservation of Africa's Colobines

The following are among the actions frequently proposed as necessary for attaining the long-term survival of Africa's primates including the colobines (ESM Table 21.2; Butynski 2002; IUCN 2019/2020; Linder et al. 2021; McGraw 2007; Oates 1996a, 1999, 2011; Struhsaker 1997, 2005, 2010).

- Improve the management and effectiveness of protected areas, establish new protected areas at key colobine sites, and reestablish biological corridors among protected areas.
- Improve understanding of taxon-specific colobine geographic range, abundance, ecology, behaviour, threats and conservation status, and establish long-term colobine population monitoring programmes.
- Make what is known about African colobines readily and freely available on-line to all stakeholders. This involves the digitizing of all older published literature and grey-literature that holds information about colobines and the forests they inhabit. For example, the Tana River Primate Resource Platform (De Jong and Butynski 2020b) aims to provide a complete list of literature and maps related to *P. rufomitratus* (CR), *C. galeritus*, and the forests and ecology of the lower Tana R. and Tana Delta Ecosystem (www.wildsolutions.nl/tana-primates/).
- Increase awareness among people, governments and institutions, locally, regionally and nationally, across tropical Africa, of the importance of forest and biodiversity conservation, with an emphasis on colobine conservation. Use colobines as flagship species.
- Secure the support of local people for colobine conservation, and motivate and enable them to be players in the implementation of colobine conservation activities.
- Enhance, through conservation education, training, information and finance, the capacity of individuals, governments and institutions across tropical Africa to contribute to the conservation of colobines.

- Enhance capacity for law enforcement through training, equipment and financial support, particularly for enforcing laws related to hunting, logging and agricultural encroachment within sites that support colobines.
- Increase awareness among people, institutions and governments across tropical Africa of the relationships between human population density and growth, the demand for limited (or insufficient) natural resources, and poverty, disease, malnourishment, longevity and illiteracy. A first step in confronting this enormous problem would be for all governments in tropical Africa to establish a national population policy, and for the major international donors to support those policies that hold promise. Initiatives that promote conservation education, family planning, availability of contraceptives, and women's reproductive rights should be greatly expanded and given adequate technical and financial support by donor countries.

Africa's Colobine Conservation Successes

ESM Table 21.2 lists some of the most important protected areas for the conservation of African colobines. Many of them, however, are not today effectively conserving their populations of colobines. To end this chapter on a positive note, here is a partial list of the more successful protected areas for the conservation of populations of colobines, although some of these populations are small. Populations of colobines in these protected areas appear poised to survive for at least the next 30 years. Many of these protected areas have large buffer zones, such as the forest reserves around Mt. Kenya NP, Aberdare NP and Mt. Elgon NP, Kenya.

- *Colobus s. anthracinus* (VU): Douala Edéa NP (2715 km^2), Cameroon. Monte Alén NP (1600 km^2), Equatorial Guinea. Birougou NP (688 km^2), Ivindo NP (2967 km^2), Lopé NP (4910 km^2), Minkébé NP (7557 km^2), Monts de Cristal NP (1192 km^2), Waka NP (1061 km^2), Gabon.
- *Colobus vellerosus* (CR): Comoé NP (11,488 km^2), Côte d'Ivoire. Boabeng-Fiema Monkey Sanctuary (5 km^2), Kakum Conservation Area (360 km^2), Mole NP (4576 km^2), Ghana.
- *Colobus polykomos* (EN): Taï NP (3300 km^2), Côte d'Ivoire. Haut Niger NP (6470 km^2), Guinea. Cantanhez Forest NP (1058 km^2), Guinea-Bissau. Gola Forest NP (980 km^2), Grebo-Krahn NP (971 km^2), Sapo NP (1804 km^2), Liberia. Gola Rainforest NP (711 km^2), Loma Mountains NP (332 km^2), Tiwai Island Wildlife Sanctuary (12 km^2), Sierra Leone.
- *Colobus a. angolensis* (VU): Lomami NP (8879 km^2), Salonga NP (36,000 km^2), DRC.
- *Colobus a. cottoni* (VU): Okapi Wildlife R (13,726 km^2), DRC.
- *Colobus a. palliatus* (VU): Shimba Hills NR (192 km^2), Kenya. Saadani NP (1062 km^2), Tanzania.
- *Colobus a. ruwenzorii* (DD): Virunga NP (7769 km^2), DRC. Nyungwe NP (1020 km^2), Rwanda. Rwenzori Mountains NP (996 km^2), Uganda.

- *Colobus a. sharpie* (VU): Udzungwa Mountains NP (2089 km^2), Tanzania.
- *Colobus g. gallarum* (DD): Bale Mountains NP (2308 km^2), Ethiopia.
- *Colobus g. guereza* (LC): Borena-Sayint NP (153 km^2), Chebera Churchura NP (1250 km^2), Omo NP (3895 km^2), Simien Mountains NP (232 km^2), Ethiopia.
- *Colobus g. kikuyuensis* (LC): Aberdare NP (766 km^2), Mount Kenya NP (715 km^2), Kenya.
- *Colobus g. matschiei* (LC): Kakamega FR (198 km^2), Mount Elgon NP (169 km^2), Mount Elgon FR (731 km^2), Southwest Mau FR (600 km^2), Kenya. Mount Elgon NP (1110 km^2), Uganda.
- *Colobus g. occidentalis* (LC): Boumba-Bek NP (2362 km^2), Dja Faunal R (5266 km^2), Lobéké NP (2153 km^2), Mbam and Djerem NP (4291 km^2), Nki NP (3130 km^2), Cameroon. Dzanga-Ndoki NP (1143 km^2), Dzanga-Sangha Special R (6865 km^2), Mbaéré-Bodingué NP (872 km^2), CAR. Nouabalé-Ndoki NP (4150 km^2), Ntokou-Pikounda NP (4572 km^2), Odzala-Kokoua NP (13,546 km^2), Congo. Okapi Wildlife R (13,726 km^2), Virunga NP (7769 km^2), DRC. Ivindo NP (2967 km^2), Minkébé NP (7557 km^2), Mwagna NP (1167 km^2), Gabon. Gashaka Gumti NP (6730 km^2), Nigeria. Bwindi Impenetrable NP (320 km^2), Kibale NP (766 km^2), Queen Elizabeth NP (2056 km^2), Uganda.
- *Colobus caudatus* (VU): Arusha NP (112 km^2), Mount Kilimanjaro NP (1832 km^2), Tanzania.
- Kapale's colobus (undescribed): Lomami NP (8879 km^2), DRC.
- *Procolobus verus* (VU): Comoé NP (11,488 km^2), Taï Forest NP (3300 km^2), Côte d'Ivoire. Ankasa Conservation Area (524 km^2), Bia Conservation Area (361 km^2), Kakum Conservation Area (360 km^2), Ghana. Gola Forest NP (980 km^2), Grebo-Krahn NP (971 km^2), Sapo NP (1804 km^2), Liberia. Gola Rainforest NP (711 km^2), Tiwai Island Wildlife Sanctuary (12 km^2), Sierra Leone.
- *Piliocolobus b. badius* (EN): Taï Forest NP (3300 km^2), Côte d'Ivoire. Gola Forest NP (980 km^2), Grebo-Krahn NP (971 km^2), Sapo NP (1804 km^2), Liberia. Gola Rainforest NP (711 km^2), Tiwai Island Wildlife Sanctuary (12 km^2), Sierra Leone.
- *Piliocolobus b. temminckii* (EN): River Gambia National Park (6 km^2), Gambia. Cantanhez Forest NP (1058 km^2), Guinea-Bissau. Fathala Forest (76 km^2) in Delta du Saloum NP (599 km^2), Niokolo-Koba NP (9130 km^2), Senegal.
- *Piliocolobus gordonorum* (VU): Udzungwa Mountains NP (2089 km^2), Tanzania.
- *Piliocolobus kirkii* (EN): Jozani-Chwaka Bay NP (50 km^2), Ngezi-Vumawimbi Nature FR (20 km^2), Tanzania.
- *Piliocolobus oustaleti* (VU): Dzanga-Ndoki NP (1143 km^2), Dzanga-Sangha Special R (6865 km^2), Mbaéré-Bodingué NP (872 km^2), CAR. Nouabalé-Ndoki NP (4150 km^2), Congo. Okapi Wildlife R (13,726 km^2), DRC.
- *Piliocolobus parmentieri* (EN): Lomami NP (8879 km^2), DRC.
- *Piliocolobus preussi* (CR): Korup NP (1260 km^2), Cameroon. Cross River NP, Oban Division (3000 km^2), Nigeria.
- *Piliocolobus semlikiensis* (VU): Maiko NP (10,885 km^2), Virunga NP (7769 km^2), DRC.

- *Piliocolobus tephrosceles* (EN): Kibale NP (766 km^2), Uganda. Mahale Mountains NP (1613 km^2), Tanzania.
- *Piliocolobus tholloni* (VU): Lomami NP (8879 km^2), Salonga NP (36,000 km^2), DRC.

Summary

- There are 16 genera, 79 species and 143 taxa of African monkey. Of these, the colobines comprise 19% of the genera, 30% of the species, and 27% of the taxa.
- Colobines occur broadly across tropical Africa, from the Atlantic Ocean to the Indian Ocean, and from sea level to 3400 m asl. Africa's colobines live over considerable gradients of temperature (−7°–41°C) and mean annual rainfall (50–1100 cm).
- Size of the geographic ranges for species of African colobines vary greatly, from 160 km^2 to 2,750,000 km^2.
- The vast majority of Africa's colobines are threatened with extinction; 96% of the 24 species, 68% of the 19 subspecies and 82% of the 39 taxa. The six 'Critically Endangered' species are *C. vellerosus, P. epieni, P. pennantii, P. preussi, P. rufomitratus* and *P. waldroni*. All but four of the 18 taxa of *Piliocolobus* are either 'Critically Endangered' or 'Endangered'.
- The two primary proximate threats to Africa's colobines are forest loss as a result of anthropogenic activities and hunting by humans, while the ultimate threat is humans and their widespread over-exploitation of natural resources.
- It is predicted that *P. waldroni* will be the first extinct colobine in Africa, and that *C. s. satanas, P. epieni, P. pennantii* and *P. rufomitratus* will be among those species that follow.
- This chapter reviews (1) the biological traits that make Africa's colobines especially susceptible to extinction through forest loss and human hunting, (2) the threats they face and (3) the impacts of the major threats.
- Finally, this chapter provides an overview of the primary conservation actions that Africa's colobines require, presents priorities for research that will aid the conservation of Africa's colobines, and lists some of the protected areas where colobines are expected to persist for at least the coming 30 years.

Acknowledgements

We thank the editors, Julie Teichroeb, Ikki Matsuda and Cyril Grueter, for inviting us to contribute to this volume. We acknowledge and thank the following people for their unpublished information and/or assistance with this chapter: Neil Baker, Jess Berndt, David Brugière, Colin Chapman, Federica Chiozza, Kathryn Combes, Sam Cotton, Drew Cronin, Pamela Cunneyworth, Tim Davenport, Jean-Pierre Dekker, Jessica Donovan, Bob Dowsett, Peter Fashing, Peter Fundi, Gérard Galat, Anh Galat-Luong, Inza Kone, Reiko Matsuda Goodwin, David Happold, John Hart, Terese Hart, Annika Hillers, Juliet King, Inza Kone, Rebecca Kormos, Joshua

Linder, Boo Maisels, Naomi Matthews, Scott McGraw, Mary Molokwu, Bethan Morgan, Simon Musila, Andy Plumptre, Anne Powys, DeeAnn Reeder, Kim Reuter, Francesco Rovero, Anthony Rylands, Tom Struhsaker, Chris Stuart, Mathilde Stuart, Nelson Ting, Nicolas Tubbs, John Weller, Edward Wiafe, Frank Willems, Stuart Williams and Liz Williamson. We especially thank Lorna Depew and Carly Butynski for reviewing the draft manuscript and Thomas Gillespie, Tony Goldberg, John Mitani and John Oates for reviewing sections of the draft manuscript. We acknowledge, with thanks, the financial support provided by Zoo Atlanta, Margot Marsh Biodiversity Foundation, Primate Action Fund, Critical Ecosystem Partnership Fund, Conservation International, Zoological Society for the Conservation of Species and Populations, Zoo New England, Northern Rangeland Trust, National Geographic Society, and Primate Conservation Inc. Fauna and Flora International kindly provided information on colobines in South Sudan. We are grateful to the Institute of Primate Research, National Museums of Kenya, and Kenya Wildlife Service for serving as our research affiliates in Kenya. We dedicate this chapter to Tom Struhsaker and John Oates in gratitude for the 50 years that each has devoted to research on, and conservation of, Africa's colobines and forests.

22 Directions for Future Research

Julie A. Teichroeb, Cyril C. Grueter and Ikki Matsuda

This comprehensive overview of the behavioural and ecological diversity of the colobines shows that we have greatly expanded our understanding of the taxonomy, phylogeny, morphology, natural history, behaviour and conservation status of this subfamily since Glyn Davies and John Oates (1994) published the first book on them. Nonetheless, there remain many gaps in our knowledge. In Chapter 2, Roos highlights that our current understanding of the taxonomy of colobines should be considered preliminary because classifications are still largely based on phenotypic differences between museum specimens. Changes will likely need to be implemented as data become available on ecology, behaviour, morphology and especially genetics of many species and subspecies. Roos also notes that relative to the cercopithecines, colobines are neglected in study effort and thus new findings have the potential to expand our understanding of their taxonomic diversity, especially in genera such as *Piliocolobus, Colobus, Presbytis, Trachypithecus* and *Semnopithecus* that are found over large geographic areas and are species-rich. In particular, additional molecular, morphological and behavioural data are needed to stabilize the taxonomy of *Piliocolobus* and *Trachypithecus*, which would aid in current conservation and research efforts (Chapters 15 and 21).

It should not come as surprise to anyone that more fossil specimens of colobines are needed. In Chapter 3, Frost, Gilbert and Nakatsukasa note that the fossil record of colobines from the middle Miocene of Africa has greatly expanded from what it was in the early 1990s. This means that, although we have a better understanding of colobine evolution, estimates of the split between the Cercopithecinae and Colobinae typically suggest an early Miocene divergence, leaving the first 5–7 million years of colobine evolution undocumented. The phylogenetic relationships among fossil taxa are also lacking due to few craniodental features that allow one to distinguish different clades. Roos and Zinner further highlight in Chapter 4 that the phylogenetic relationships among extant taxa are also unclear in many respects.

In Chapter 5, Wright and Willis further discuss how a lack of longitudinal studies, life history information, and dental casts in the Asian and African colobines are problematic for understanding how diet links to specific dental patterns. What has become clear over the last 25 years are that colobines contain species with varied diets, including frugivory and granivory, which should lead to variation in dental morphology. For many species, however, dental morphometrics have not been studied at all or not examined in depth. In addition, Wright and Willis layout a list of genera where data on dental eruption, ecology, ingestive feeding, mandibular morphology, gut morphology and retention times are lacking.

In Chapter 6, Matsuda and Clauss highlight that the difficulty in keeping many species of colobines in captivity is due to our lack of understanding of their digestive physiology. The function of the praesaccus is still unknown for those species that have a quadripartite stomach arrangement. Indeed, for *Simias*, no information on the number of chambers in the stomach is even available. It is still unknown why colobines have a low degree of fluid throughput through the forestomach relative to other folivores. For most taxa, the foregut microbiome has not been characterized and related metagenomic and function analyses in relation to the environment have not been done. Amato, Clayton, and Hale (Chapter 7) reiterate this point and discuss how knowledge of specific microbial taxa and their functions in both the fore- and hindguts of colobines is in its infancy, though more is known regarding the hindgut microbiome. Captive colobines that show gastrointestinal distress often have microbiome differences compared to their healthy counterparts but it is not known if this is a cause or a symptom of the distress. Amato and colleagues suggest that routine sampling of captive colobine gut microbiomes would be very helpful in elucidating these issues and preventing the death of captive colobines. Greater understanding of the gut microbiota, diets and morphology across the subfamily may also explain why different colobine taxa show variability in gastrointestinal problems in captivity.

Rothman, DePasquale, Evans and Raboin discuss colobine nutritional ecology in Chapter 8. The authors postulate that, given their digestive anatomy, colobines seem to be able to extract nutrients from many different foods (i.e. they have a wide acceptable niche), yet they often rely on diets containing relatively few species. This suggests that the application of nutritional frameworks to colobine feeding strategies could be very informative. Many more studies are needed on the daily nutrient intake of both Asian and African colobines from a wide variety of sites. It is also still unclear how colobines select dietary items and the criteria proposed, namely the protein-to-fibre model and selection based on energy content, were both difficult to test given the previous analytical techniques. Rothman and colleagues suggest that new methods will help clarify selection criteria, and that colobines at different locations may opportunistically maximize the nutrients that are environmentally constrained whenever they become available. Due to the extreme diversity of plant secondary metabolites (i.e. tannins and phenolics), standardized analytical methods are also desperately needed to determine the actual presence of these in colobine foods and how different species cope with these. The role of micronutrients (i.e. vitamins and minerals) and the degree of their consumption is also unknown for many colobine species. Sodium-seeking has been noted in some studies and geophagy may be a common way for colobines to find micronutrients. Rothman and colleagues stress that monitoring food (and nutrient) availability over time along with nutritional chemistry would provide an ideal way to determine how colobines select plant parts and deal with changing conditions.

The taxon-specific chapters of the book demonstrate the great amount of information that we still do not know about the colobine monkeys. In the red colobus natural history chapter (Chapter 9), Korstjens, Hillyer and Koné highlight the unresolved taxonomy and the lack of basic natural history information for species and populations outside of a few intensively studied field sites. The difficulty of recognizing individuals in large red colobus groups makes collection of data on social relationships, sexual behaviour, mating strategies, receptive periods, birth rates and reproductive success challenging. Although some work has looked at the pathogens present in red colobus populations, few have linked these to their behavioural ecology. The lack of data for so many red colobus taxa is an urgent issue given how vulnerable populations can be to extirpation with increasing human habitat destruction and persecution. The natural history of the black-and-white colobus is a fraction more complete than for the red colobus but as Fashing notes in Chapter 10, there are still relatively large gaps. For instance, *C. guereza*, arguably the best studied of the black-and-white colobus is still unstudied in the western half of its distribution and even in East Africa there are isolated, genetically distinct subspecies and populations where no data are available. The important and fascinating avenues for further research that Fashing suggests are (1) a better understanding of why *C. angolensis* groups are so tolerant of one another relative to other black-and-white colobus; (2) confirmation of sympatry among some black-and-white colobus populations and studies of niche separation; (3) protection and study of remaining critically endangered *C. vellerosus* populations in continuous forest; (4) an assessment of how *C. polykomos* and *C. satanas* deal with forest fragmentation and (5) comparisons of ecology between the northern and southern populations of *C. satanas* on Bioko Island, where rainfall varies 5-fold. In the chapter on olive colobus natural history (Chapter 11), Teichroeb and Korstjens suggest several studies that would fill information gaps for this unique, monotypic species. These include a better understanding of mating strategies to determine the function of large sexual dimorphism in canine size, the presence of some features related to sperm competition, and female-mimicry in young males prior to sexual maturation. Studies that include individual recognition would be very beneficial for expanding our understanding of the enigmatic olive colobus.

Our understanding of the ecology and behaviour of the odd-nosed colobines has increased dramatically since the first book on colobines ~25 years ago; however, Grueter, Erb, Ulibarri and Matsuda emphasize several important areas where data are lacking. With the exception of golden snub-nosed monkeys, our understanding of many aspects of the social system (group stability/fluidity, dispersal patterns, group coordination, between-group interactions, social preferences and competitive regimes) of odd-nosed colobines is still rudimentary. Moreover, because of the logistical challenges of data collection in the field, the natural history of some species (in particular the critically endangered black snub-nosed monkey), is still largely unknown. In Chapter 13, Sayers points out that although grey langurs are arguably the best studied colobine monkeys, this is not true throughout their wide range and there is a dearth of long-term field research on other *Semnopithecus* taxa.

Specifically, Sayers proposes that studies on the impact of predation on grouping and behaviour, the proximate mechanisms of behaviour (e.g. genetics, physiology), ontogeny, sensory ecology and cognition are needed in this genus. In Chapter 14, Nijman underscores the need for research on several species of *Presbytis* and *Trachypithecus* for which very little natural history information is known. He also stresses that niche separation studies in areas where two or more colobines are sympatric are important, given how ecological similarity could lead to competition. Behie, Apthorp, Hendershott and Ruskin (Chapter 15) further note that *Trachypithecus* species in the Indo-Burmese region are almost all under intense pressure from high human populations that are converting habitat to agriculture and hunting. More general ecology studies have been done on the *Trachypithecus* inhabiting limestone karst forests than those in closed canopy forests. However, confusion regarding geographic distributions and taxonomy have hindered both conservation and research efforts. For several species basic data on activity budgets, ranging patterns, social organization and dispersal are still lacking and long-term studies on any species in this genus are rare.

Overviews of the socioecology of the Asian and African colobines by Sterck and Roth (Chapter 16) and Teichroeb (Chapter 17) respectively, show that early assumptions about the lack of food competition in this subfamily are not upheld. Colobine females face both scramble and contest competition for resources to variable degrees, which does lead to dominance hierarchies, albeit often subtle ones that are difficult to detect. However, the number of species for which behavioural data on individually recognized females are available is still small, making it difficult to determine the types and severity of competition experienced, or the types of hierarchies that females show and whether nepotism is occurring. In addition, often absent is an understanding of how food competition and greater foraging effort actually affects female reproductive success in the long-term. The impact of male reproductive strategies (e.g. infanticide, food defence) on females and social organization is also great in the colobines, which impacts how they fit (or do not fit) into current socioecological models. The influence that males can have on social structure and organization also makes colobines extremely interesting for future studies that could expand socioecological models.

In Chapter 18, Grueter discusses multilevel societies in the colobines and highlights that a combination of relaxed ecological constraints and social selective pressures may have played a role in the evolutionary coalescence of nuclear units into higher-tier entities. However, the multilevel systems of several taxa (three species of snub-nosed monkeys and the doucs) are insufficiently known, and many topics such as group coordination, communication, decision making, social cognition and disease transmission have received very little, if any, attention.

It is becoming critical to understand the factors determining colobine abundance given current population declines. In Chapter 19, Chapman, Corriveau, Valenta, Espinosa-Gómez and Schoof indicate that few advances in our understanding of the determinants of colobine population dynamics have been made since the Davies and Oates (1994) volume. They impart this to limited data on the effects of food quality, availability and competition, as well as predation and disease on colobine population dynamics. The authors also emphasize how these data deficiencies hamper our ability to predict and mitigate population declines. The conservation chapters in this book reiterate some of these points. Sha, Matsuda, Zhou, Ang and Nadler state in Chapter 20 that many species of Asian colobines are highly threatened. Their specialized ecological requirements render them vulnerable to environmental changes that are occurring at an increasing rate throughout their distribution range. Biological resource use, expansion of agriculture, aquaculture and land conversions associated with other anthropogenic activities are particularly threatening colobine habitats. The conservation of Asian colobines must focus on more effective conservation planning, including more comprehensive protected areas management, reforestation and restoration, enforcement and enactment of protection laws, sound reintroduction, captive management, education and awareness programmes aimed at long-term sustainability of wild habitats and species. In Chapter 21, Butynski and De Jong stress the number of species and subspecies of African colobines where geographic ranges are not confirmed, stating that this information, along with current population numbers, is urgent for taxa with limited distributions to fully understand their conservation status. They provide a list very useful targeted project ideas for particular areas where colobine occurrence data are lacking. Butynski and De Jong also emphasize that since most colobus monkey taxa are threatened with extinction, there is a great need for more data on their reactions to emerging threats like climate change, shifts in infectious disease prevalence, forest fragmentation and the increasing encroachment of humans. This is especially challenging given the lack of research on many African colobines including some of the most threatened. Basic natural history and abundance data are missing for colobines in large swaths of central Africa due to the many challenges of working in these often-unstable areas. This lack of knowledge greatly hampers the creation of effective conservation actions and management strategies.

We have learned a great deal about colobines in the 25 years since the first *Colobine Monkeys* book was published, but as this review shows there are still many gaps in our knowledge. Besides all those topics listed above, it is notable that when we first prepared the proposal for this book, we included a chapter on cognition in colobines. However, this chapter was not even possible to write due to the almost complete absence of data in this area. We also do not provide a chapter on colobine community ecology and their role in processes such as seed dispersal, predation and pollination because of the dearth of information on these topics. Our work on this book demonstrated that, as for most topics, the more we learn, the more obvious it is how much we do not yet know. It is thus our hope that this book informs and inspires future generations of scientists to work on this extraordinary group of animals.

References

Abdul-Latiff, M. A. B., Baharuddin, H., Abdul-Patah, P. & Md-Zain, B. M. 2019. Is Malaysia's banded langur, *Presbytis femoralis femoralis*, actually *Presbytis neglectus neglectus*? Taxonomic revision with new insights on the radiation history of the *Presbytis* species group in Southeast Asia. *Primates* **60**: 63–79.

Abernethy, K. A., Coad, L., Taylor, G., Lee, M. E. & Maisels, F. 2013. Extent and ecological consequences of hunting in Central African rainforests in the twenty-first century. *Philosophical Transactions of the Royal Society B: Biological Sciences* **368**: 20130494.

Abood, S. A., Lee, J. S. H., Burivalova, Z., Garcia-Ulloa, J. & Koh, L. P. 2015. Relative contributions of the logging, fiber, oil palm, and mining industries to forest loss in Indonesia. *Conservation Letters* **8**: 58–67.

Adamescu, G. S., Plumptre, A. J., Abernethy, K. A. et al. 2018. Annual cycles are the most common reproductive strategy in African tropical tree communities. *Biotropica* **50**: 418–430.

Adams, F. V. & Teichroeb, J. A. 2020. Microhabitat use in Rwenzori Angolan colobus monkeys at Nabugabo, Uganda demonstrates intraspecific variability. *International Journal of Primatology* **41**: 24–44.

Adams, F. V., Arseneau-Robar, T. J. M., Bonnell, T. R., Stead, S. M. & Teichroeb, J. A. 2021. Temporal patterns in the social network of core units in Rwenzori Angolan colobus monkeys: Effects of food availability and interunit dispersal. *Ecology and Evolution* **11**: 3251–3263.

Adhikaree, S. & Shrestha, T. K. 2011. Food item selection of Hanuman langur (*Presbytes entellus*) in different season in Char-Koshe jungle of eastern terai, Nepal. *Nepalese Journal of Biosciences* **1**: 96–103.

Adimallaiah, D., Thiyagesan, K. & Gupta, A. K. 2014. Population status of Phayre's langur *Trachypithecus phayrei* in Sepahijala Wildlife Sanctuary, Tripura, northeast India. *Primate Conservation* **28**: 159–163.

Agmen, F. 2014. *Conservation strategies for Delacour's langur (*Trachypithecus delacouri*) in Vietnam: Behavioural comparisons and reviewing a release.* PhD thesis, Australian National University, Canberra.

Agoramoorthy, G. & Hsu, M. 2005. Occurrence of infanticide among wild proboscis monkeys (*Nasalis larvatus*) in Sabah. *Northern Borneo Folia Primatologica* **76**: 177–179.

Agoramoorthy, G., Alagappasamy, C. & Hsu, M. J. 2004. Can proboscis monkeys be successfully maintained in captivity? A case of swings and roundabouts. *Zoo Biology* **23**: 433–544.

Ahamed, R. & Dharmaretnam, M. 2003. Ranging pattern, feeding and time budget of langurs (*Semnopithecus entellus*) in a recently established home range at Eastern University campus, Batticaloa, Sri Lanka. *Journal of Science* **3**: 1–10.

Ahamed, R. & Dharmaretnam, M. 2015. Hand preference in wild Hanuman langurs (*Presbytis entellus*). *International Journal of Biological and Pharmaceutical Sciences* **2**: 40–46.

Aimi, M. & Bakar, A. 1992. Taxonomy and distribution of *Presbytis melalophos* group in Sumatera, Indonesia. *Primates* **33**: 191–206.

Aimi, M. & Bakar, A. 1996. Distribution and deployment of *Presbytis melalophos* group in Sumatera, Indonesia. *Primates* **37**: 399–409.

Akbar, M. A., Rizaldi, Novarino, W., Perwitasari-Farajallah, D. & Tsuji, Y. 2019. Activity budget and diet in silvery lutung *Trachypithecus cristatus* at Gunung Padang, West Sumatra, Indonesia. *Biodiversitas* **20**: 719–724.

Akers, J. S. & Schildkraut, D. S. 1985. Regurgitation/reingestion and coprophagy in captive gorillas. *Zoo Biology* **4**: 99–109.

Al Nabhani, Z. & Eberl, G. 2020. Imprinting of the immune system by the microbiota early in life. *Mucosal Immunology* **13**: 183–189.

Alam, M. M., Jaman, M. F., Hasan, M. M. et al. 2014. Social interactions of Hanuman langur (*Semnopithecus entellus*) at Keshabpur and Manirampur of Jessore district of Bangladesh. *Bangladesh Journal of Zoology* **42**: 217–225.

Alamgir, M., Campbell, M. J., Sloan, S. et al. 2017. Economic, socio-political and environmental risks of road development in the tropics. *Current Biology* **27**: R1130.

Alba, D. M., Delson, E., Carnevale, G. et al. 2014. First joint record of *Mesopithecus* and cf. Macaca in the Miocene of Europe. *Journal of Human Evolution* **67**: 1–18.

Alba, D. M., Montoya, P., Pina, M. et al. 2015. First record of *Mesopithecus* (Cercopithecidae, Colobinae) from the Miocene of the Iberian Peninsula. *Journal of Human Evolution* 88: 1–14.

Alexander, K. A., Sanderson, C. E., Marathe, M. et al. 2015. What factors might have led to the emergence of Ebola in West Africa? *PLOS Neglected Tropical Diseases* 9: e0003652.

Allen, G. M. 1938. *The Mammals of China and Mongolia (Part I).* New York: American Museum of Natural History.

Allen, G. M. 1939. A checklist of African mammals. *Bulletin of the Museum of Comparative Zoology* 83: 1–763.

Alley, T. R. 1980. Infantile colouration as an elicitor of caretaking behaviour in Old World primates. *Primates* 21: 416–429.

Alonso, C., Hernansaiz, A. S., Fernández-Garcia, J. M. et al. 2018. Range extension of the king colobus *Colobus polykomos* (Zimmermann, 1780) in North Fouta Djallon (Guinea). *African Primates* 13: 1–8.

Altmann, J. 1990. Primate males go where the females are. *Animal Behaviour* 39: 193–195.

Altmann, J. & Alberts, S. C. 2005. Growth rates in a wild primate population: ecological influences and maternal effects. *Behavioral Ecology and Sociobiology* 57: 490–501.

Altmann, J., Alberts, S. C., Altmann, S. A. & Roy, S. B. 2002. Dramatic change in local climate patterns in the Amboseli basin, Kenya. *African Journal of Ecology* 40: 248–251.

Altmann, S. A. 1974. Baboons, space, time, and energy. *American Zoologist* 14: 221–248.

Alvarez-Berríos, N. L. & Aide, T. M. 2015. Global demand for gold is another threat for tropical forests. *Environmental Research Letters* 10: e014006.

Amano, N., Moigne, A. M., Ingicco, T. et al. 2016. Subsistence strategies and environment in Late Pleistocene-Early Holocene Eastern Java: evidence from Braholo Cave. *Quaternary International* 416: 46–63.

Amato, K. R. 2016. Incorporating the gut microbiota into models of human and non-human primate ecology and evolution. *American Journal of Physical Anthropology* 159: 196–215.

Amato, K. R., Kuthyar, S., Ekanayake-Weber, M. et al. 2020. Gut microbiome, diet, and conservation of endangered langurs in Sri Lanka. *Biotropica* 52: 981–990.

Amato, K. R., Leigh, S. R., Kent, A. et al. 2014. The role of gut microbes in satisfying the demands of adult female and juvenile wild, black howler monkeys (*Alouatta pigra*). *American Journal of Physical Anthropology* 155: 652–664.

Amato, K. R., Martinez-Mota, R., Righini, N. et al. 2016a. Phylogenetic and ecological factors impact the gut microbiota of neotropical primate species. *Oecologia* 180: 717–733.

Amato, K. R., Metcalf, J. L., Song, S. J. et al. 2016b. Using the gut microbiota as a novel tool for examining colobine primate GI health. *Global Ecology and Conservation* 7: 225–237.

Amato, K. R., Sanders, J., Song, S. J. et al. 2019. Evolutionary trends in host physiology outweigh dietary niche in structuring primate gut microbiomes. *ISME Journal* 13: 576–587.

Amato, K. R., van Belle, S., Di Fiore, A. et al. 2017. Patterns in gut microbiota similarity associated with degree of sociality among sex classes of a Neotropical primate. *Microbial Ecology* 74: 250–258.

Amato, K. R., Yeoman, C. J., Kent, A. et al. 2013. Habitat degradation impacts black howler monkey (*Alouatta pigra*) gastrointestinal microbiomes. *ISME Journal* 7: 1344–1353.

Amerasinghe, F. P., Vancuylenberg, B. W. B. & Hladik, C. M. 1971. Comparative histology of the alimentary tract of Ceylon primates in correlation with the diet. *The Ceylon Journal of Science, Biological Sciences* 9: 75–87.

An, Z., Kutzbach, J. E., Prell, W. L. & Porter, S. C. 2001. Evolution of Asian monsoons and phased uplift of the Himalaya-Tibetan plateau since Late Miocene times. *Nature* 411: 62–66.

Anand, M. O., Krishnaswamy, J., Kumar, A., & Bali, A. 2010. Sustaining biodiversity conservation in human-modified landscapes in the Western Ghats: remnant forests matter. *Biological Conservation* 143: 2363–2374.

Ancrenaz, M., Calaque, R. & Lackman-Ancrenaz, I. 2004 Orangutan nesting behavior in disturbed forest of Sabah, Malaysia: implications for nest census. *International Journal of Primatology* 25: 983–1000.

Anderson, J. 2005. *Habitat fragmentation and metapopulation dynamics of the Angola black-and-white colobus (*Colobus angolensis palliatus*) in coastal Kenya.* PhD thesis, University College, London.

Anderson, J., Cowlishaw, G. & Rowcliffe, J. M. 2007a. Effects of forest fragmentation on the abundance of *Colobus angolensis palliatus* in Kenya's coastal forests. *International Journal of Primatology* 28: 637–655.

Anderson, J., Rowcliffe, J. M. & Cowlishaw, G. 2007b. The Angola black-and-white colobus (*Colobus angolensis palliatus*) in Kenya: historical range contraction and current conservation status. *American Journal of Primatology* 69: 664–680.

Anderson, J., Rowcliffe, J. M. & Cowlishaw, G. 2007c. Does the matrix matter? A forest primate in a complex agricultural landscape. *Biological Conservation* 135: 212–222.

Anderson, L. K. 2001. Captive population analysis and group management methods of *Colobus angolensis palliatus* at the San Diego Zoo. *Association of Zoos & Aquariums Annual Conference Proceedings*: 397–403.

Anderson, M. 2019. *Functional morphology, variation, and niche Separation in the large-bodied fossil colobines*. PhD thesis, University of Oregon, Eugene.

Anderson, M., Frost, S. R., Gilbert, C. C. & Delson, E. 2014. A reassessment of dental variation in the genus *Cercopithecoides* and its implications for species diversity [Abstract]. *American Journal of Physical Anthropology* S58: 67.

Anderson, M., Frost, S. R., Gilbert, C. C. & Delson, E. 2015. Cranial shape and intrageneric diversity in the genus *Cercopithecoides* [Abstract]. *American Journal of Physical Anthropology* S60: 69.

Andrews, P., Harrison, T., Delson, E., Bernor, R. L. & Martin, L. 1996. Distribution and biochronology of European and Southwest Asian Miocene catarrhines. In Bernor, R. L., Fahlbush, V. & Mittmann, H.-W. (Eds.), *The Evolution of Western Eurasian Neogene Mammal Faunas*. New York: Columbia University Press. Pp. 168–207.

Ang A. 2010. *Banded leaf monkeys in Singapore preliminary data on taxonomy, feeding, ecology, reproduction and population size*. PhD thesis, National University of Singapore, Singapore.

Ang, A., D'Rozario, V., Jayasri, S. L. et al. 2016. Species Action Plan for the Conservation of Raffles' Banded Langur (*Presbytis femoralis femoralis*) in Malaysia and Singapore. Apple Valley, MN: IUCN SSC Conservation Breeding Specialist Group.

Ang, A., Ismail, M. R. B. & Meier, R. 2010. Reproduction and infant pelage colouration of the banded leaf monkey (Mammalia: Primates: Cercopithecidae) in Singapore. *Raffles Bulletin of Zoology* 52: 5.

Ang, A., Srivasthan, A., Md-Zain, B. M., Ismail, M. R. B. & Meier, R. 2012. Low genetic variability in the recovering urban banded leaf monkey population of Singapore. *Raffles Bulletin of Zoology* 60: 589–594.

Ang, A., Roesma, D. I., Nijman, V., Meier, R. & Srivathsan, A. 2020. Faecal DNA to the rescue: Shotgun sequencing of non-invasive samples reveals two subspecies of Southeast Asian primates to be Critically Endangered species. *Scientific reports* 10(1): 1–16.

Ankel-Simons, F. 2007. *Primate Anatomy*, 3rd ed. Burlington, VT: Academic Press.

Aptroot, A. 2009. Lichens as an indicator of climate and global change. In Letcher, T. M. (Ed.), *Climate Change: Observed Impacts on Plant Earth*. Amsterdam: Elsevier. Pp. 401–408.

Arambourg, C. 1959. Vertébratés Continentaux du Miocene Supérieur de l'Afrique du Nord. Publications du Service de la Carte Geologique de L'Algerie (ns) Paléontologie. *Memoire* 4: 5–159.

Aristizabal, J. F., Rothman, J. M., García-Feria, L. M. & Serio-Silva, J. C. 2017. Contrasting time-based and weight-based estimates of protein and energy intake of black howler monkeys (*Alouatta pigra*). *American Journal of Primatology* 79: 1–8.

Arlet, M. E., Carey, J. R. & Molleman, F. 2009. Species, age and sex differences in type and frequencies of injuries and impairments among four arboreal primate species in Kibale National Park, Uganda. *Primates* 50: 65–73.

Arnold, K. & Barton, R. A. 2001. Postconflict behavior of spectacled leaf monkeys (*Trachypithecus obscurus*). I. Reconciliation. *International Journal of Primatology* 22: 243–266.

Aronsen, G. P., Beuerlein, M. M., Watts, D. P. & Bribiescas, R. G. 2015. Redtail and red colobus monkeys show intersite urinary cortisol concentration variation in Kibale National Park, Uganda. *Conservation Physiology* 3: cov006.

Arseneau-Robar, T. J. M., Changasi, A. H., Turner, E. & Teichroeb, J. A. 2021. Diet and activity budget in Colobus angolensis ruwenzorii at Nabugabo, Uganda: are they energy maximizers? *Folia Primatologica* 92: 35–48.

Arseneau-Robar, T. J. M., Joyce, M. M., Stead, S. M. & Teichroeb, J. A. 2018. Proximity and grooming patterns reveal opposite-sex bonding in Rwenzori Angolan colobus monkeys (*Colobus angolensis ruwenzorii*). *Primates* 59: 267–279.

Ashalakshmi, N. C., Nag, K. S. C. & Karanth, K. P. 2015. Molecules support morphology: species status of South Indian populations of the widely distributed Hanuman langur. *Conservation Genetics* 16: 43–58.

Ashton, P. S. 1988. Dipterocarp biology as a window to the understanding of tropical forest structure. *Annual Review of Ecology and Systematics* 19: 347–370.

Assink, P. R. & Van Dijk, I. F. 1990. *Social organization, ranging and density of* Presbytis thomasi *at Ketambe (Sumatra), and a comparison with other* Presbytis *species at several Southeast Asian locations.* MSc thesis, University of Utrecht, Utrecht, The Netherlands.

Astaras, C., Mühlenberg, M. & Waltert, M. 2008. Note on drill (*Mandrillus leucophaeus*) ecology and conservation status in korup National Park, southwest cameroon. *American Journal of Primatology* **70**: 306–310.

Atickem, A., Stenseth, N. C., Fashing, P. J. et al. 2019. Build science in Africa. *Nature* **570**: 297–300.

Aunin, E., Böhme, U., Sanderson, T. et al. 2020. Genomic and transcriptomic evidence for descent from *Plasmodium* and loss of blood schizogony in *Hepatocystis* parasites from naturally infected red colobus monkeys. *PLOS Pathogens* **16**: e1008717.

Aureli, F. & Schaffner, C. M. 2017. Fission–fusion. In *The International Encyclopedia of Primatology.*

Aureli, F., Schaffner, C. M., Boesch, C. et al. 2008. Fission-fusion dynamics: new research frameworks. *Current Anthropology* **49**: 627–654.

Aziz, M. & Feeroz, M. 2009. Utilization of forest flora by Phayre's leaf-monkey *Trachypithecus phayrei* (Primates: Cercopithecidae) in semi-evergreen forests of Bangladesh. *Journal of Threatened Taxa* **1**: 257–262.

Babcock, M., Wright, B. W., Wright, K. A., O'Brien, J., Ulibarri, L. & Nadler, T. 2009. Chew before you swallow? Ingestive versus digestive folivory among species of *Pygathrix* and *Trachypithecus. American Journal of Physical Anthropology* **S49**: 85.

Bădescu, I., Sicotte, P., Ting, N. & Wikberg, E. C. 2015. Female parity, maternal kinship, infant age and sex influence natal attraction and infant handling in a wild colobine (*Colobus vellerosus*). *American Journal of Primatology* **77**: 376–387.

Bădescu, I., Wikberg, E. C., MacDonald, L. J. et al. 2016. Infanticide pressure accelerates infant development in a wild primate. *Animal Behaviour* **114**: 231–239.

Bahaa-el-din, L., Henschel, P., Butynski, T. M. et al. 2015. The African golden cat *Caracal aurata*: Africa's least-known felid. *Mammal Review* **45**: 63–77.

Bai, S., Zou, S., Lin, S., Tuo, D., Tu, Z. & Zhong, T. 1987. A preliminary observation on distribution, number and population structure of *Rhinopithecus bieti* in the Baima Xueshan Natural Reserve, Yunnan, China. *Zoological Research* **8**: 413–419 (in Chinese with English abstract).

Bailey, A. L., Lauck, M., Ghai, R. R. et al. 2016. Arteriviruses, pegiviruses, and lentiviruses are common among wild African monkeys. *Journal of Virology* **90**: 6724–6737.

Bailey, A. L., Lauck, M., Weiler, A. et al. 2014. High genetic diversity and adaptive potential of two simian hemorrhagic fever viruses in a wild primate population. *PLOS ONE* **9** 0090714.

Bailey, K. E., Carlson, D. L., Tran, V. B. & Ha, T. L. 2018. Arm-swinging in the red-shanked douc (*Pygathrix nemaeus*) in the Son Tra Nature Reserve, Vietnam. *American Journal of Physical Anthropology*, Congress Supplement **165**: 16–17.

Bailey, K. E., Lad, S. E. & Pampush, J. D. 2017. Functional morphology of the douc langur (*Pygathrix* spp.) scapula. *American Journal of Primatology* **79**: e22646.

Bajpai, O., Kumar, A., Mishra, A. K., Sahu, N., Behera, S. K. & Chaudhary, L. B. 2012. Phenological study of two dominant tree species in tropical moist deciduous forest from the Northern India. *International Journal of Botany* **8**: 66–67.

Baker, L. R. & Oates, J. F. 2019. Diversity and conservation of primates in the flooded forests of southern Nigeria. In Barnett, A. A., Matsuda, I. & Nowak, K. (Eds.), *Primates in Flooded Habitats: Ecology and Conservation.* Cambridge: Cambridge University Press. Pp. 315–325.

Balch, C. C. 1955. Sleep in ruminants. *Nature* **175**: 940–941.

Baranga, D. 1982. Nutrient composition and food preferences of colobus monkeys in Kibale Forest, Uganda. *African Journal of Ecology* **20**: 113–121.

Baranga, D. 1983. Changes in chemical composition of food parts in the diet of colobus monkeys. *Ecology* **64**: 668–673.

Barboza, P. S., Parker, K. L. & Hume, I. D. 2009. *Integrative Wildlife Nutrition.* Springer-Verlag: Berlin Heidelberg.

Barelli, C., Albanese, D., Donati, C. et al. 2015. Habitat fragmentation is associated to gut microbiota diversity of an endangered primate: implications for conservation. *Scientific Reports* **5**: 14862.

Barelli, C., Gonzalez-Astudillo, V., Mundry, R. et al. 2019. Altitude and human disturbance are associated with helminth diversity in an endangered primate, *Procolobus gordonorum. PLOS ONE* **14**: e0225142.

Barelli, C., Pafčo, B., Manica, M. et al. 2020. Loss of protozoan and metazoan intestinal symbiont biodiversity in wild primates living in unprotected forests. *Science Reports* **10**: 10917.

Barrett, L., Henzi, P. & Rendall, D. 2007. Social brains, simple minds: does social complexity really require cognitive complexity? *Philosophical Transactions of the Royal Society of London B* **362**: 561–575.

Barton, R. A. 1996. Neocortex size and behavioral ecology in primates. *Proceedings of the Royal Society B* **263**: 173–177.

Barton, R. A. 2000. Socioecology of baboons: the interaction of male and female strategies. In Kappeler, P. (Ed.), *Primate Males: Causes and Consequences of Variation in Group Composition.* Cambridge: Cambridge University Press. Pp. 97–107.

Bauchop, T. & Martucci, R. W. 1968. Ruminant-like digestion of the langur monkey. *Science* **161**: 698–700.

Bauchop, T. 1971. Stomach microbiology of primates. *Annual Review of Microbiology* **25**: 429–436.

Bauchop, T. 1978. Digestion of leaves in vertebrate arboreal folivores In Montgomery, G. G. (Ed.), *The ecology of arboreal folivores.* Washington, DC: Smithsonian Institution Press. Pp. 193–204.

Baya, L. & Storch, I. 2010. Status of diurnal primate populations at the former settlement of a displaced village in cameroon. *American Journal of Primatology* **72**: 645–652.

Beaudrot, L., Ahumada, J. A., O'Brien, T. et al. 2016. Standardized assessment of biodiversity trends in tropical forest protected areas: the end is not in sight. *PLOS Biology* **14**: e1002357.

Beck, B. B. & Tuttle, R. 1972. The behavior of gray langurs at a Ceylonese waterhole. In Tuttle, R. (Ed.), *The Functional and Evolutionary Biology of Primates.* Chicago: Aldine-Atherton. Pp. 351–377.

Beckwith, R. S. 1995. *The ecology and behaviour of the Javan black langur, in a lower montane rain forest, West Java.* PhD thesis, University of Cambridge, Cambridge.

Bene, J. C. K., Ouattara, K., Bitty, E. A. & Inza, Koné. 2012. Combination calls in olive colobus monkeys (*Procolobus verus*) in Taï National Park, Côte d'Ivoire. *Journal of Asian Scientific Research* **2**: 466.

Bene, K. J., Kone, I. & Zuberbuhler, K. 2007. Répertoire et contextes sociaux des cris unitaires du colobe vert (procolobus verus) dans le Parc National de Taï (PNT), Côte d'Ivoire. *Sciences & Nature* **4**: 137–147.

Benefit, B. R. 1987. *The molar morphology, natural history, and phylogenetic position of the Middle Miocene monkey Victoriapithecus.* PhD thesis, New York University, New York.

Benefit, B. R. 1999. *Victoriapithecus*: the key to Old World monkey and catarrhine origins. *Evolutionary Anthropology* **7**: 155–174.

Benefit, B. R. 2000. Old World monkey origins and diversification: an evolutionary study of diet and dentition. In Whitehead, P. F. & Jolly, C. (Eds.), *Old World Monkeys.* Cambridge: Cambridge University Press. Pp. 133–179.

Benefit, B. R. 2008. The biostratigraphy and palaeontology of fossil cercopithecoids from eastern Libya. *Geology of East Libya* **3**: 247–266.

Benefit, B. R. & Pickford, M. 1986. Miocene fossil cercopithecoids from Kenya. *American Journal of Physical Anthropology* **69**: 441–464.

Benefit, B. R., McCrossin, M., Boaz, N. T. & Pavlakis, P. 2008. New fossil cercopithecoids from the late miocene of as Sahabi, Libya. *Garyounis Scientific Bulletin* **5**: 265–282.

Bennett, E. L. 1983. *The banded langur: Ecology of a colobine in a West Malaysian rain-forest.* PhD thesis, University of Cambridge, Cambridge.

Bennett, E. L. & Davies, A. G. 1994. The ecology of Asian colobines. In Davies, A. G. & Oates, J. F. (Eds.), *Colobine Monkeys: Their Ecology, Behaviour and Evolution.* Cambridge: Cambridge University Press. Pp. 129–171.

Bennett, E. L. & Robinson, J. G. 2000. Hunting of wildlife in tropical forests. Implications for biodiversity and forest peoples. *The World Bank, Environment Department Papers* **76**. P. 44.

Bennett, E. L. & Sebastian, A. C. 1988. Social organization and ecology of proboscis monkeys (*Nasalis larvatus*) in mixed coastal forest in Sarawak. *International Journal of Primatology* **9**: 233–255.

Bennett, E. L. 1988. The occurrence of twins and accompanying behavioural changes in the banded langur, *Presbytis melalophos. Primates* **29**: 557–563.

Bennett, G., Malone, M., Sauther, M. L. et al. 2016. Host age, social group, and habitat type influence the gut microbiota of wild ring-tailed lemurs (*Lemur catta*). *American Journal of Primatology* **78**: 883–892.

Bergman, T. J. 2010. Experimental evidence for limited vocal recognition in a wild primate: implications for the social complexity hypothesis. *Proceedings of the Royal Society B* **277**: 3045–3053.

Bergman, T. J. & Beehner, J. C. 2015. Measuring social complexity. *Animal Behaviour* **103**: 203–209.

Bermejo, M., Rodriguez-Teijeiro, J. D., Illera, G. et al. 2006. Ebola outbreak killed 5000 gorillas. *Science* **314**: 1564–1564.

Bernard, H., Matsuda, I., Hanya, G. & Ahmad, A. H. 2011. Characteristics of night sleeping trees of proboscis monkeys (*Nasalis larvatus*) in Sabah, Malaysia. *International Journal of Primatology* 32: 259–267.

Bernard, H., Matsuda, I., Hanya, G. et al. 2019. Feeding ecology of the proboscis monkey in Sabah, Malaysia, with special reference to plant species-poor forests. In Barnett, A. A., Nowak, K. & Matsuda, I. (Eds.), *Primates in Flooded Habitats: Ecology and Conservation*. Cambridge: Cambridge University Press. Pp. 89–98.

Bernstein, I. S. 1967. Intertaxa interactions in a Malayan primate community. *Folia Primatologica* 7: 198–207.

Bernstein, I. S. 1968. The lutong of Kuala Selangor. *Behaviour* 32: 1–16.

Bersacola, E., Bessa, J., Frazão-Moreira, A., Biro, D., Sousa, C. & Hockings, K. J. 2018. Primate occurrence across a human impacted landscape in Guinea-Bissau and neighbouring regions in West Africa: using a systematic literature review to highlight the next conservation steps. *PeerJ* 6: e4847.

Bett, N. N. 2011. Mother-infant relationships and infant development in captive grey-shanked douc langurs. *Vietnamese Journal of Primatology* 1: 17–28.

Beziers, P., Hobeika, S. & Korstjens, A. H. 2009. Are dominant males more successful reproductively? *Folia Primatologica* 80: 151–152.

Bigoni, F., Stanyon, R., Wimmer, R. & Schempp, W. 2003. Chromosome painting shows that the proboscis monkey (*Nasalis larvatus*) has a derived karyotype and is phylogenetically nested within asian colobines. *American Journal of Primatology* 60: 85–93.

Bigoni, F., Stone, G., Perelman, P. & Stanyon R. 2006. Cytotaxonomy of Colobinae primates with reference to reciprocal chromosome painting of Colobus guereza and humans. In Sineo, L. & Stanyon, R. (Eds.), *Primate Cytogenetics and Comparative Genomics*. Florence: Firenze University Press.

Birchette, M. G. 1982. *The postcranial skeleton of* Paracolobus chemeroni. PhD thesis, Harvard University.

Birdlife. 2004. *Cat Tien National Park. Sourcebook of Existing and Proposed Protected Areas in Vietnam*, 2nd ed. Hanoi: Birdlife International Vietnam Programme and the Forest Inventory and Planning Institute.

Bisanz, J. E., Upadhyay, V., Turnbaugh, J. A., Ly, K. & Turnbaugh, P. 2019. Diet induces reproducible alterations in the mouse and human gut microbiome. *Available at SSRN 3330558*.

Bishop, J. M. & Bishop, N. H. 1978. *An Ever-Changing Place*. New York: Simon and Shuster.

Bishop, N. H. 1975. *Social behavior of langur monkeys (*Presbytis entellus*) in a high altitude environment*. PhD thesis, University of California, Berkeley.

Bishop, N. H. 1979. Himalayan langurs: temperate colobines. *Journal of Human Evolution* 8: 251–281.

Bismark, M. 1981. Preliminary survey of the proboscis monkey at Tanjung Putting Reserve, Kalimantan. *Tigerpaper* 8: 26.

Bissell, H. 2014. *The nutritional ecology of the black-and-white snub-nosed monkey*. PhD thesis, University of Wisconsin-Madison.

Biswas, J., Das, N., Borah, D., Sangma, A., Ray, P. & Das, J. 2009. Status and distribution of least known primate species: *Slow loris* and capped langur in the Protected Areas of Assam, India and its feeding ecology. Final Report of Primate Research Centre NE India, Wildlife Information Liaison Development, Zoo Outreach Organization and Margot Marsh Biodiversity Foundation Collaborative Project No PRCNE/Tecr-7:1–39.

Bitty, E. A., Gonedelé Bi, S., Bené, J. C. K., Kouassi, P. K. & McGraw, W. S. 2015. Cocoa farming and primate extirpation inside cote d'Ivoire's protected areas. *Tropical Conservation Science* 8: 95–113.

Bjorkholm, B., Bok, C. M., Lundin, A., Rafter, J., Hibberd, M. L. & Pettersson, S. 2009. Intestinal microbiota regulate xenobiotic metabolism in the liver. *PLOS ONE* 4: e6958.

Bjorndal, K. A., Bolten, A. B. & Moore, J. E. 1990. Digestive fermentation in herbivores: effect of food particle size. *Physiological Zoology* 63: 710–721.

Bleisch, W. V. & Xie, J. 1998. Ecology and behavior of the Guizhou snub-nosed langur (*Rhinopithecus brelichi*). In Jablonski, N. (Ed.), *The Natural History of the Doucs and Snub-Nosed Monkeys*. Singapore: World Scientific Press. Pp. 217–241.

Bleisch, W. V., Cheng, A., Ren, X. & Xie, J. 1993. Preliminary results from a field study of wild Guizhou snub-nosed monkeys (*Rhinopithecus brelichi*). *Folia Primatologica* 60: 72–82.

Bleisch, W. V., Liu, Z. M., Dierenfeld, E. S. & Xie, J. H. 1998. Selected nutrient analysis of plants in the diet of the Guizhou snub-nosed monkey (*Rhinopithecus* [Rhinopithecus] *brelichi*). In *The Natural History of the Doucs and Snub-Nosed Monkeys*: World Scientific. Pp. 241–254.

Blom, A., Alers, M. P. T., Feistner, A. T. C., Barnes, R. F. W. & Barnes, K. L. 1992. Primates in Gabon – current status and distribution. *Oryx* **26**: 223–234.

Boaz, N. T. 2008. A view to the south: Eo-Sahabi palaeoenvironments compared and implications for hominid origins in Neogene north Africa. *Garyounis Scientific Bulletin* **5**: 291–308.

Boaz, N. T. & Meikle, W. E. 1982. Fossil remains of Primates (Cercopithecoidea and Hominoidea) from the Sahabi Formation. *Garyounis Scientific Bulletin, Special Issue* **4**: 41–48.

Bobo, K. S., Aghomo, F. F. & Ntumwel, B. C. 2014. Wildlife use and the role of taboos in the conservation of wildlife around the Nkwende Hills Forest Reserve; South-west Cameroon. *Journal of Ethnobiology and Ethnomedicine* **11**: 1–23.

Bobo, K. S., Ntumwel, C. B., Aghomo, F. F. & Ayemele, K. G. A. 2017. The conservation status of two threatened primates in the Korup Region, southwest Cameroon. *Primate Conservation* **31**: 1–12.

Bobo, K. S., Ntumwel, C. B., Aghomo, F. F. & Dschang, C. 2012. Hunter's perception on uses of Preuss's red colobus *Procolobus preussi* and red-capped mangabey *Cercocebus torquatus*, and related conservation issues, in the Nkwende Hills area, southwest Cameroon. *Life Sciences Leaflets* **8**: 28–34.

Bocian, C. M. 1997. *Niche separation of black-and-white colobus monkeys (*Colobus angolensis *and* C. guereza*) in the Ituri Forest.* PhD thesis, City University of New York, New York.

Bocian, C. M. & Anderson, J. 2013. *Colobus angolensis.* In Butynski, T. M., Kingdon, J. & Kalina, J. (Eds.), *Mammals of Africa: Vol. 2. Primates.* London: Bloomsbury. Pp. 103–108.

Bock, W. J. & von Wahlert, G. 1965. Adaptation and the form-function complex. *Evolution* **19**: 269–299.

Bodendorfer, T., Hoppe-Dominik, B., Fischer, F. & Linsenmair, K. E. 2006. Prey of the leopard (*Panthera pardus*) and the lion (*Panthera leo*) in the Comoé and Marahoué National Parks, Côte d'Ivoire, West Africa. *Mammalia* **70**: 231–246.

Boesch, C. 1994a. Chimpanzee-red colobus monkeys: a predator-prey system. *Animal Behaviour* **47**: 1135–1148.

Boesch, C. 1994b. Cooperative hunting in wild chimpanzees. *Animal Behaviour* **48**: 653–667.

Boesch, C. & Boesch, H. 1989. Hunting behavior of wild chimpanzees in the Taï National Park. *American Journal of Physical Anthropology* **78**: 547–573.

Boesch, C. & Boesch-Achermann, H. 2000. *The Chimpanzees of the Taï Forest: Behavioural Ecology and Evolution.* Oxford: Oxford University Press.

Boesch, C., Uehara, S. & Ihobe, H. 2002. Variations in chimpanzee-red colobus interactions. In Boesch, C., Hohmann, G. & Marchant, L. F. (Eds.), *Behavioural Diversity in Chimpanzees and Bonobos.* Cambridge: Cambridge University Press. Pp. 221–230.

Boggess, J. 1980. Intermale relations and troop male membership changes in langurs (*Presbytis entellus*) in Nepal. *International Journal of Primatology* **1**: 233–274.

Boggess, J. 1984. Infant killing and male reproductive strategies in langurs (*Presbytis entellus*). In Hausfater, G. & Hrdy, S. B. (Eds.), *Infanticide: Comparative and Evolutionary Perspectives.* New York: Aldine. Pp. 283–310.

Bonnell, T. R., Campennì, M., Chapman, C. A. et al. 2013. Emergent group level navigation: an agent-based evaluation of movement patterns in a folivorous primate. *PLOS ONE* **8**.

Bonnell, T. R., Ghai, R. R., Goldberg, T. L., Sengupta, R. & Chapman, C. A. 2016. Spatial patterns of persistence for environmentally transmitted parasites: effects of regional climate and local landscape. *Ecological Modelling* **338**: 78–89.

Bonnell, T. R., Ghai, R. R., Goldberg, T. L., Sengupta, R. & Chapman, C. A. 2018. Spatial configuration becomes more important with increasing habitat loss: a simulation study of environmentally-transmitted parasites. *Landscape Ecology* **33**: 1259–1272.

Boonratana, R. 1993. *The Ecology and behaviour of the proboscis monkey (*Nasalis larvatus*) in the Lower Kinabatangan, Sabah.* PhD thesis, Faculty of Graduate Studies, Mahidol University, Bangkok, Thailand.

Boonratana, R. 2000. Ranging behavior of proboscis monkeys (*Nasalis larvatus*) in the lower Kinabatangan, Northern Borneo. *International Journal of Primatology* **21**: 497–518.

Boonratana, R. 2002. Social organisation of proboscis monkeys (*Nasalis larvatus*) in the Lower Kinabatangan, Sabah, Malaysia. *Malayan Nature Journal* **56**: 57–75.

Boonratana, R. 2003. Feeding ecology of proboscis monkeys (*Nasalis larvatus*) in the Lower Kinabatangan, Sabah, Malaysia. *Sabah Parks Nature Journal* **6**: 1–6.

Boonratana, R. 2011. Observations on the sexual behaviour and birth seasonality of proboscis monkey (*Nasalis larvatus*) along the Lower Kinabatangan River, northern Borneo. *Asian Primates Journal* **2**: 2–7.

Boonratana, R. & Le, X. C. 1998. Preliminary observations of the ecology and behavior of the Tonkin snub-nosed monkey (*Rhinopithecus avunculus*) in Northern Vietnam. In Jablonski, N. G. (Ed.), *The Natural History of the Doucs and Snub-Nosed Monkeys*. Singapore: World Scientific Press. Pp. 207–217.

Booth, A. H. 1956. The distribution of primates in the Gold Coast. *Journal of the West African Science Association* 2: 122–133.

Booth, A. H. 1957. Observations on the natural history of the olive colobus monkey, *Procolobus verus* (van Beneden). *Journal of Zoology* 129: 421–430.

Borisoglebskaya, M. B. 1981. A new species of monkey (Mammalia, Primates) from the Pliocene of Northern Mongolia. *Trudy Sovmestnoj Sovetsko-Mongol'skoj Paleontologicekoj Ekspedicii* 15: 95–108, 125 (in Russian with English summary).

Borries, C. 1993. Ecology of female social relationships: Hanuman langurs (*Presbytis entellus*) and the van Schaik Model. *Folia Primatologica* 61: 21–30.

Borries, C. 1997. Infanticide in seasonally breeding multimale groups of Hanuman langurs (*Presbytis entellus*) in Ramnagar (South Nepal). *Behavioral Ecology and Sociobiology* 41: 139–150.

Borries, C. 2000. Male dispersal and mating season influxes in Hanuman langurs living in multi-male groups. In Kappeler, P. M. (Ed.), *Primate Males: Causes and Consequences of Variation in Group Composition*. Cambridge: Cambridge University Press. Pp. 146–158.

Borries, C. & Koenig, A. 2000. Hanuman langurs: infanticide in multimale groups. In Van Schaik, C. P. & Janson, C. H. (Eds.), *Infanticide by Males and Its Implications*. Cambridge: Cambridge University Press. Pp. 99–122.

Borries, C. & Koenig, A. 2008. Reproductive and behavioral characteristics of aging in female Asian colobines. In Atsalis, S., Margulis, S. W. & Hof, P. R. (Eds.), *Primate Reproductive Aging*. Switzerland: Karger. Pp. 80–102.

Borries, C., Koenig, A. & Winkler, P. 2001. Variation in life history traits and mating patterns in female langur monkeys (*Semnopithecus entellus*). *Behavioral Ecology and Sociobiology* 50: 391–402.

Borries, C., Larney, E., Derby, M. & Koenig, A. 2004. Temporary absence and dispersal in Phayre's leaf monkeys (*Trachypithecus phayrei*). *Folia Primatologica* 75: 27–30.

Borries, C., Larney, E., Lu, A., Ossi-Lupo, K. & Koenig, A. 2008. Costs of group size: lower developmental and reproductive rates in larger groups of leaf monkeys. *Behavioral Ecology* 19: 1186–1191.

Borries, C., Launhardt, K., Epplen, C., Epplen, J. T. & Winkler, P. 1999a. DNA analyses support the hypothesis that infanticide is adaptive in langur monkeys. *Proceedings of the Royal Society of London B: Biological Sciences* 266: 901–904.

Borries, C., Launhardt, K., Epplen, C., Epplen, J. T. & Winkler, P. 1999b. Males as infant protectors in Hanuman langurs (*Presbytis entellus*) living in multimale groups – defence pattern, paternity and sexual behaviour. *Behavioral Ecology and Sociobiology* 46: 350–356.

Borries, C., Lu, A., Ossi-Lupo, K., Larney, E. & Koenig, A. 2011. Primate life histories and dietary adaptations: a comparison of Asian colobines and macaques. *American Journal of Physical Anthropology* 144: 286–299.

Borries, C., Lu, A., Ossi-Lupo, K., Larney, E. & Koenig, A. 2014b. The meaning of weaning in wild Phayre's leaf monkeys: last nipple contact, survival, and independence. *American Journal of Physical Anthropology* 154: 291–301.

Borries, C., Primeau, Z. M., Ossi-Lupo, K., Dtubpraserit, S. & Koenig, A. 2014a. Possible predation attempt by a marbled cat on a juvenile Phayre's leaf monkey. *Raffles Bulletin of Zoology* 62: 561–565.

Borries, C., Sommer, V. & Srivastava, A. 1991. Dominance, age, and reproductive success in free-ranging female hanuman langurs (*Presbytis entellus*). *International Journal of Primatology* 12: 231–257.

Borries, C., Sommer, V. & Srivastava, A. 1994. Weaving a tight social net: allogrooming in free-ranging female langurs (*Presbytis entellus*). *International Journal of Primatology* 15: 421–443.

Boucher, D. H. 1990. Growing back after hurricanes: catastrophes may be critical to rain forest dynamics. *Bioscience* 40: 163–166.

Bouckaert, R., Heled, J., Kühnert, D. et al. 2014. BEAST 2: a software platform for Bayesian evolutionary analysis. *PLOS Computational Biology* 10: e1003537.

Bradbury, J. W. & Vehrencamp, S. L. 1977. Social organization and foraging in emballonurid bats: III. Mating systems. *Behavioral Ecology and Sociobiology* 2: 1–17.

Brandon-Jones, D. 1984a. Colobus and leaf monkeys. In MacDonald, I. D. (Ed.), *Encyclopedia of Mammals*. London: George Allen and Unwin. Pp. 398–410.

Brandon-Jones, D. 1984b. *All the World's Animals: Primates*. New York: Torstar Books, Inc.

Brandon-Jones, D. 1993. The taxonomic affinities of the Mentawai Islands sureli, *Presbytis potenziani* (Bonaparte, 1856) (Mammalia: Primates: Cercopithecidae). *The Raffles Bulletin of Zoology* **41**: 331–357.

Brandon-Jones, D. 1995a. *Presbytis fredericae* (Sody, 1930), an endangered colobine species endemic to Central Java. *Primate Conservation* **16**: 68–70.

Brandon-Jones, D. 1995b. A revision of the Asian pied leaf monkeys (Mammalia: Cercopithecidae: superspecies *Semnopithecus auratus*), with a description of a new species. *The Raffles Bulletion of Zoology* **43**: 3–43.

Brandon-Jones, D. 1996a. *Presbytis* species sympatry in Borneo versus allopatry in Sumatera: an interpretation. In Edwards, D. S., Booth, W. E. & Choy S. C. (Eds.), *Tropical Rainforest Research – Current Issues*. Dordrecht, The Netherlands: Kluwer. Pp. 71–76.

Brandon-Jones, D. 1996b. The Asian Colobinae as indicators of Quaternary climatic change. *Biological Journal of the Linnean Society* **59**: 327–350.

Brandon-Jones, D., 2004. A taxonomic revision of the langurs and leaf monkeys (Primates: Colobinae) of South Asia. *Zoos' Print Journal* **19**: 1552–1594.

Brandon-Jones, D., Duckworth, J. W., Jenkins, P. D. et al. 2007. The genitive of species-group scientific names formed from personal names. *Zootaxa* **1541**: 41–48.

Brandon-Jones, D., Eudey, A. A., Geissmann, T. et al. 2004. Asian primate classification. *International Journal of Primatology* **25**: 97–164.

Brass, E. 1925. *Aus dem Reiche der Pelze*. Berlin, Germany: Neuen Pelzwaren-Zeitung und Kürschner-Zeitung. 709 pp.

Brent, L. J. N., Teichroeb, J. A. & Sicotte, P. 2008. Preliminary assessment of natal attraction and infant handling in wild *Colobus vellerosus*. *American Journal of Primatology* **70**: 101–105.

Brian, C. & Bohrman, R. 1992. Tick infestation of baboons (*Papio ursinus*) in the Namib Desert. *Journal of Wildlife Diseases* **28**: 188–191.

Brockelman, W. Y. 2009. Ecology and the social system of gibbons. In Lappan, S. & Whittaker, D. J. (Eds.), *The Gibbons*. New York: Springer. Pp. 211–239.

Brooks, T. M., Mittermeier, R. A., Mittermeier, C. G. et al. 2002. Habitat loss and extinction in the hotspots of biodiversity. *Conservation Biology* **16**: 909–923.

Broom, R. & Robinson, J. T. 1950. A new sub-fossil baboon from Kromdraai, Transvaal. *Annals of the Transvaal Museum* **21**: 242–245.

Brotoisworo, E. 1983. Population dynamic of lutung (*Presbytis cristata*) in Pananjung-Pangandaran nature reserve, West Java. In *Training Course on Wildlife Ecology, May 5–June 15, 1983*. Bogor: Biotrop. Pp. 1–24.

Brotoisworo, E. & Dirgayusa, I. W. 1991. Ranging and feeding behavior of *Presbytis cristata* in the Pangadaran Nature Reserve, West Java, Indonesia. In Ehara, A., Kimura, T., Takenaka, O. & Iwamonto, M. (Eds.), *Primatology Today*. Amsterdam: Elsevier Science.

Brourton, M. R. & Perrin, M. R. 1991. Comparative gut morphmetrics of vervet (*Cecopithecus aethiops*) and Samango (*C. mitis erytharchus*) monkeys. *Zeitschrift für Säugetierkunde* **56**: 65–71.

Brugière, D. 1998. Population size of the black colobus monkey *Colobus satanas* and the impact of logging in the Lopé Reserve, central Gabon. *Biological Conservation* **86**: 15–20.

Brugière, D., Gautier, J.-P., Moungazi, A. & Gautier-Hion, A. 2002. Primate diet and biomass in relation to vegetation composition and fruiting phenology in a rain forest in Gabon. *International Journal of Primatology* **23**: 999–1024.

Bshary, R. 1995. *Rote Stummelaffen, Colobus badius, und Dianameerkatzen, Cercopithecus diana, im Taï-Nationalpark, Elfenbeinküste: Wozu assoziieren sie?*, Ludwig-Maximilian-Unviersität München, München.

Bshary, R. 2001. Diana monkeys, cercopithecus diana, adjust their anti-predator response behaviour to human hunting strategies. *Behavioral Ecology and Sociobiology* **50**: 251–256.

Bshary, R. 2007. Interactions between red colobus monkeys and chimpanzees. *Cambridge Studies in Biological and Evolutionary Anthropology* **1**: 155–170.

Bshary, R. & Noë, R. 1997a. Anti-predation behaviour of red colobus monkeys in the presence of chimpanzees. *Behavioral Ecology and Sociobiology* **41**: 321–333.

Bshary, R. & Noë, R. 1997b. Red colobus and diana monkeys provide mutual protection against predators. *Animal Behaviour* **54**: 1461–1474.

Buechner, H. K. & Dawkins, H. C. 1961. Vegetation change induced by elephants and fire in Murchison Falls National Park, Uganda. *Ecology* **42**: 752–766.

Buffon, Compte de GLL. 1766. *Historie naturelle, générale et particulière, avec la description du cabinet du roi.* Tome Quatorzième: Paris. Pp. 298–303.

Bugir, C. K., Butynski, T. M. & Hayward, M. W. 2021. Prey preferences of the chimpanzee (*Pan troglodytes*). *Ecology and Evolution* 11: 7138–7146.

Burgess, N. D., Clarke, G. P., Hermitage, T. et al. 1998. Coastal forests of eastern Africa: status, endemism patterns and their potential causes. *Biological Journal of the Linnean Society* 64: 337–367.

Burton, F. D., Snarr, K. A. & Harrison, S. E. 1995. Preliminary report on *Presbytis francoisi leucocephalus*. *International Journal of Primatology* 16: 311–327.

Burton, G. J. 1984. Testicular histology of the dusky leaf monkey (*Presbytis obscura*) as it relates to birth pattern in peninsular Malaysia. *International Journal of Primatology* 5: 183–195.

Butt, N., Beyer, H. L., Bennett, J. R. et al. 2013. Biodiversity risks from fossil fuel extraction. *Science* 342: 425–426.

Butynski, T. M. 1984. Ecological Survey of the Impenetrable (Bwindi) Forest, Uganda, and Recommendations for its Conservation and Management. Unpublished report to the Uganda Government and Wildlife Conservation International, New York. 68 pp. www.wildsolutions.nl.

Butynski, T. M. 1995. Primates and hydropower. *Swara* 18: 28–30.

Butynski, T. M. 2001. Africa's great apes. In Beck, B. B., Stoinski, T. S., Hutchins, M. et al. (Eds.), *Great Apes & Humans: The Ethics of Coexistence*. Washington, DC: Smithsonian Institution Press. Pp. 3–56.

Butynski, T. M. 2002. Conservation of the guenons: an overview of status, threats, and recommendations. In Glenn, M. E. & Cords, M. (Eds.), *The Guenons: Diversity and Adaptation in African Monkeys*. New York: Kluwer Academic/Plenum. Pp. 411–424.

Butynski, T. M. & De Jong, Y. A. 2011. Zanzibar red colobus on Pemba Island, Tanzania: population status 38 years post-introduction. In Soorae, P. S. (Ed.), *Global Re-introduction Perspectives: 2011*. Abu Dhabi, UAE: IUCN/SSC Re-introduction Specialist Group. Pp. 168–174.

Butynski, T. M. & De Jong, Y. A. 2014. Primate conservation in the rangeland agroecosystem of Laikipia County, Central Kenya. *Primate Conservation* 28: 117–128.

Butynski, T. M. & De Jong, Y. A. 2015. Distribution and conservation status of the Mount Kilimanjaro guereza *Colobus guereza caudatus* Thomas, 1885. *Primate Conservation* 29: 107–113.

Butynski, T. M. & De Jong, Y. A. 2017. Biogeography, Taxonomy, Abundance, and Conservation Status of the Primates of Northeast Uganda and West Kenya. Unpublished report to the National Geographic Society, Washington, DC. 88 pp. www.wildsolutions.nl.

Butynski, T. M. & De Jong, Y. A. 2018. Geographic range, taxonomy, and conservation of the Mount Kilimanjaro guereza colobus monkey (Primates: Cercopithecidae: *Colobus*). *Hystrix: Italian Journal of Mammalogy* 29: 81–85.

Butynski, T. M. & De Jong, Y. A. 2019a. *Colobus guereza* ssp. *matschiei*. *The IUCN Red List of Threatened Species 2019*: e.T136846A17983227. www.iucnredlist.org.

Butynski, T. M. & De Jong, Y. A. 2019b. Primates of Africa's coastal deltas and their conservation. In Barnett, A. A., Nowak, K. & Matsuda, I. (Eds.), *Primates in Flooded Habitats: Ecology and Conservation*. Cambridge: Cambridge University Press. Pp. 244–258.

Butynski, T. M. & De Jong, Y. A. 2020a. *Colobus guereza* ssp. *dodingae*. *The IUCN Red List of Threatened Species 2020*. www.iucnredlist.org/.

Butynski, T. M. & De Jong, Y. A. 2020b. *Colobus angolensis* ssp. nov. *The IUCN Red List of Threatened Species 2020*. www.iucnredlist.org/.

Butynski, T. M. & De Jong, Y. A. 2020c. *Colobus angolensis* ssp. *ruwenzorii*. *The IUCN Red List of Threatened Species 2020*. www.iucnredlist.org/.

Butynski, T. M. & Hamerlynck, O. 2016. Tana River red colobus *Piliocolobus rufomitratus* (Peters, 1879). In Schwitzer, C., Mittermeier, R. A., Rylands, A. B. et al. (Eds.), *Primates in Peril: The World's 25 Most Endangered Primates 2014–2016*. Arlington, VA: IUCN/SSC Primate Specialist Group. Pp. 20–22. www.primate-sg.org/storage/pdf/PrimatesInPeril2014-2016.pdf.

Butynski, T. M. & Kalina, J. 1998. Gorilla tourism: a critical look. In Milner-Gulland, E. J. & Mace, R. (Eds.), *Conservation of Biological Resources*. Oxford: Blackwell Science. Pp. 294–313.

Butynski, T. M. & Kingdon, J. 2013. *Procolobus preussi* Preuss's red colobus. In Butynski, T. M., Kingdon, J. & Kalina, J. (Eds.), *Mammals of Africa: Vol. 2. Primates*. London: Bloomsbury. Pp. 134–136.

Butynski, T. M. & Koster, S. H. 1994. Distribution and conservation status of primates in Bioko Island, Equatorial Guinea. *Biodiversity and Conservation* 3: 893–909.

Butynski, T. M. & Mwangi, G. 1994. Conservation Status and Distribution of the Tana River Red Colobus and Crested Mangabey. Unpublished report to the Kenya Wildlife Service and Zoo Atlanta, Nairobi, Kenya. 68 pp. www.wildsolutions.nl.

Butynski, T. M. & Mwangi, G. 1995. Census of Kenya's endangered red colobus and crested mangabey. *African Primates* 1: 8–10.

Butynski, T. M., De Jong, Y. A. & Hearn, G. W. 2009. Body measurements for the monkeys of Bioko Island, Equatorial Guinea. *Primate Conservation* 24: 99–105.

Butynski, T. M., Grubb, P. & Kingdon, J. 2013a. *Procolobus badius*: western red colobus. In Butynski, T. M., Kingdon, J. & Kalina, J. (Eds.), *Mammals of Africa*. London: Bloomsbury. Pp. 128–134.

Butynski, T. M., Grubb, P. & Kingdon, J. 2013b. *Procolobus pennantii* Pennant's red colobus (Bioko red colobus). In Butynski, T. M., Kingdon, J. & Kalina, J. (Eds.), *Mammals of Africa: Vol. 2. Primates*. London: Bloomsbury. Pp. 137–141.

Butynski, T. M., Kingdon, J. & Kalina, J. 2013c. *Mammals of Africa: Vol. 2. Primates*, London: Bloomsbury.

Butynski, T. M., Kingdon, J. & Kalina, J. (Eds.). 2013d. *Procolobus gordonorum* Udzungwa red colobus (Iringa / Uhehe / Gordon's red colobus). In *Mammals of Africa: Vol. 2. Primates*. London: Bloomsbury. Pp. 148–151.

Buzzard, P., Li, X. & Bleisch, W. 2017. The status of snow leopards Panthera uncia, and high altitude use by common leopards P. pardus, in north-west Yunnan, China. *Oryx* 51: 587–589.

Byrne, R. & Whiten, A. 1988. *Machiavellian Intelligence: Social Expertise and the Evolution of Intellect in Monkeys, Apes and Humans*. Oxford: Oxford University Press.

Byron, C. D., Granatosky, M. C. & Covert, H. H. 2017. An anatomical and mechanical analysis of the douc monkey (genus *Pygathrix*), and its role in understanding the evolution of brachiation. *American Journal of Physical Anthropology* 164: 801–820.

CABI. 2019. *Prosopis juliflora* (mesquite). www.cabi.org/isc/datasheet/43942.

Calle, P., Raphael, B., Stetter, M. et al. 1995. Gastrointestinal linear foreign bodies in silver leaf langurs: *Trachypithecus cristatus ultimus*. *Journal of Zoo and Wildlife Medicine* 26: 87–97.

Campbell, C., Fuentes, A., MacKinnon, K., Bearder, S. & Stumpf, R. 2011a. *Primates in Perspective*, 2nd ed. New York: Oxford University Press.

Campbell, G., Kuehl, H., Diarrassouba, A., Goran, P. K. N. & Boesch, C. 2011b. Long-term research sites as refugia for threatened and over-harvested species. *Biology Letters* 7: 723–726.

Campbell, G., Teichroeb, J. A. & Paterson, J. D. 2008. Distribution of diurnal primate species in Togo and Bénin. *Folia Primatologica* 79: 15–30.

Cancelliere, E. C., Chapman, C. A., Twinomugisha, D. & Rothman, J. M. 2018. The nutritional value of feeding on crops: diets of vervet monkeys in a humanized landscape. *African Journal of Ecology* 56: 160–167.

Cardini, A. & Elton, S. 2009a. Geographical and taxonomic influences on cranial variation in red colobus monkeys (Primates, Colobinae): introducing a new approach to 'morph' monkeys. *Global Ecology and Biogeography* 18: 248–263.

Cardini, A. & Elton, S. 2009b. The radiation of red colobus monkeys (Primates, Colobinae): morphological evolution in a clade of endangered African primates. *Zoological Journal of the Linnean Society* 157: 197–224.

Cardini, A. & Elton, S. 2011. GeMBiD, a geometric morphometric approach to the study of biological diversity: an example study of the red colobus (*Procolobus* [*Piliocolobus*]) species complex. *International Journal of Primatology* 32: 377–389.

Carl, K. M. 2009. *Home range size, daily path length, and territoriality in Phayre's leaf monkeys (*Trachypithecus phayrei*)*. MSc thesis, Stony Brook University, Stony Brook, NY.

Carlson, B. A., Rothman, J. M. & Mitani, J. C. 2013. Diurnal variation in nutrients and chimpanzee foraging behavior. *American Journal of Primatology* 75: 342–349.

Carpenter, C. R. 1934. A field study of the behavior and social relations of howling monkeys. *Comparative Psychology Monographs* 10: 1–168.

Carr, G. M. & Macdonald, D. W. 1986. The sociality of solitary foragers: a model based on resource dispersion. *Animal Behaviour* 34: 1540–1549.

Carvalho, J. S., Graham, B., Rebelo, H. et al. 2019. A global risk assessment of primates under climate and land use/cover scenarios. *Global Change Biology* 25: 3163–3178.

Casson, A. 2003. *Oil Palm, Soybeans & Critical Habitat Loss*. Gland, Switzerland: World Wide Fund for Nature.

Caton, J. M. 1998. The morphology of the gastrointestinal tract of *Pygathrix nemaeus*. In Jablonski, N. G. (Ed.), *Natural History of the Doucs and Snub-nosed Monkeys*. Singapore: World Scientific. Pp. 129–149.

Caton, J. M. 1999. Digestive strategy of the asian colobine genus *Trachypithecus*. *Primates* **40**: 311–325.

Cavada, N., Tenan, S., Barelli, C. & Rovero, F. 2019. Effects of anthropogenic disturbance on primate density at the landscape scale. *Conservation Biology* **33**: 873–882.

Ceballos, G., Ehrlich, P. R. & Raven, P. H. 2020. Vertebrates on the brink as indicators of biological annihilation and the sixth mass extinction. *Proceedings of the National Academy of Sciences of the United States of America* **117**: 13569–13602.

Cerling, T. E., Ehleringer, J. R. & Harris, J. M. 1998. Carbon dioxide starvation, the development of C_4 ecosystems, and mammalian evolution. *Philosophical Transactions of the Royal Society of London B* **353**: 159–171.

Cersosimo, L. M., Lachance, H., St-Pierre, B., van Hoven, W. & Wright, A. D. 2015. Examination of the rumen bacteria and methanogenic archaea of wild impalas (*Aepyceros melampus melampus*) from Pongola, South Africa. *Microbial Ecology* **69**: 577–585.

Chalise, M. K. 1995. *Comparative study of feeding ecology and behaviour of male and female langurs* (Presbytis entellus). PhD thesis, Tribhuvan University, Kathmandu.

Chang, C.-H., Takai, M. & Ogino, S. 2012. First discovery of colobine fossils from the early to middle Pleistocene of southern Taiwan. *Journal of Human Evolution* **63**: 439–451.

Chang, Z., Liu, Z., Yang, J., Li, M. & Vigilant, L. 2012. Noninvasive genetic assessment of the population trend and sex ratio of the Shennongjia population of Sichuan snub-nosed monkeys (*Rhinopithecus roxellana*). *Chinese Science Bulletin* **57**: 1135–1141.

Chang, Z., Yang, B., Vigilant, L. et al. 2014. Evidence of male-biased dispersal in the endangered Sichuan snub-nosed monkey (*Rhinopithexus roxellana*). *American Journal of Primatology* **76**: 72–83.

Chapais, B. 2008. *Primeval Kinship: How Pair-Bonding Gave Birth to Human Society*. Cambridge, MA: Harvard University Press. 368 pp.

Chapais, B. 2013. Monogamy, strongly bonded groups, and the evolution of human social structure. *Evolutionary Anthropology* **22**: 52–65.

Chape, S., Harrison, J., Spalding, M. & Lysenko, I. 2005. Measuring the extent and effectiveness of protected areas as an indicator for meeting global biodiversity targets. *Philosophical Transactions of the Royal Society of London B: Biological Sciences* **360**: 443–455.

Chapman, C. A. 1988. Patch use and patch depletion by the spider and howling monkeys of Santa Rosa National Park, Costa Rica. *Behaviour* **105**: 99–116.

Chapman, C. A. 2018. A road for a promising future for China's primates: the potential for restoration. *Zoological Research* **39**: 244–248.

Chapman, C. A. & Chapman, L. J. 1996. Mixed-species primate groups in the Kibale Forest: Ecological constraints on association. *International Journal of Primatology* **17**: 31–50.

Chapman, C. A. & Chapman, L. J. 1999. Implications of small scale variation in ecological conditions for the diet and density of red colobus monkeys. *Primates* **40**: 215–231.

Chapman, C. A. & Chapman, L. J. 2000a. Constraints on group size in red colobus and red-tailed guenons: examining the generality of the ecological constraints model. *International Journal of Primatology* **21**: 565–585.

Chapman, C. A. & Chapman, L. J. 2000b. Interdemic variation in mixed-species association patterns: common diurnal primates of Kibale National Park, Uganda. *Behavioral Ecology and Sociobiology* **47**: 129–139.

Chapman, C. A. & Chapman, L. J. 2000c. Determinants of group size in social primates: the importance of travel costs. In Boinski, S. & Garber, P. A. (Eds.), *Group movement in social primates and other animals: patterns, processes and cognitive implications*. Chicago: University of Chicago Press. Pp. 24–42.

Chapman, C. A. & Chapman, L. J. 2002. Foraging challenges of red colobus monkeys: influence of nutrients and secondary compounds. *Comparative Biochemistry and Physiology Part A: Molecular & Integrative Physiology* **133**: 861–875.

Chapman, C. A. & Pavelka, M. S. 2005. Group size in folivorous primates: ecological constraints and the possible influence of social factors. *Primates* **46**: 1–9.

Chapman, C. A., Balcomb, S. R., Gillespie, T. R., Skorupa, J. P. & Struhsaker, T. T. 2000. Long-term effects of logging on African primate communities: a 28-year comparison from Kibale National Park, Uganda. *Conservation Biology* **14**: 207–217.

Chapman, C. A., Bicca-Marques, J. C., Dunham, A. E., Fan, P., Fashing, P. J., Gogarten, J. F., Guo, S., Huffman, M. A., Kalbitzer, U., Li, B., Ma, C., Matsuda, I., Omeja, P. A., Sarkar, D., Sengupta, R., Serio-Silva, J. C., Tsuji, Y. & Stenseth, N. C. 2020. Primates can be a rallying symbol to promote tropical forest restoration. *Folia Primatologica* **91**: 1–19.

Chapman, C. A., Bonnell, T. R., Sengupta, R., Goldberg, T. L. & Rothman, J. M. 2013a. Is *Markhamia lutea*'s abundance determined by animal foraging? *Forest Ecology and Management* **308**: 62–66.

Chapman, C. A., Bortolamiol, S., Matsuda, I. et al. 2018a. Primate population dynamics: variation in abundance over space and time. *Biodiversity and Conservation* **27**: 1221–1238.

Chapman, C. A., Chapman, L. J. & Gillespie, T. R. 2002a. Scale issues in the study of primate foraging: red colobus of Kibale National Park. *American Journal of Physical Anthropology* **117**: 349–363.

Chapman, C. A., Chapman, L. J., Bjorndal, K. A. & Onderdonk, D. A. 2002b. Application of protein-to-fiber ratios to predict colobine abundance on different spatial scales. *International Journal of Primatology* **23**: 283–310.

Chapman, C. A., Chapman, L. J., Jacob, A. L. et al. 2010a. Tropical tree community shifts: implications for wildlife conservation. *Biological Conservation* **143**: 366–374.

Chapman, C. A., Chapman, L. J., Kaufman, L. & Zanne, A. E. 1999. Potential causes of arrested succession in Kibale National Park, Uganda: growth and mortality of seedlings. *African Journal of Ecology* **37**: 81–92.

Chapman, C. A., Chapman, L. J., Naughton-Treves, L., Lawes, M. J. & Mcdowell, L. R. 2004. Predicting folivorous primate abundance: validation of a nutritional model. *American Journal of Primatology* **62**: 55–69.

Chapman, C. A., Chapman, L. J., Rode, K. D., Hauck, E. M. & McDowell, L. R. 2003a. Variation in the nutritional value of primate foods: among trees, time periods, and areas. *International Journal of Primatology* **24**: 317–333.

Chapman, C. A., Corriveau, A., Schoof, V. A. M., Twinomugisha, D. & Valenta, K. 2017. Long-term primate research and its significance for developing theory and conservation plans. *Journal of Mammalogy* **98**: 652–660.

Chapman, C. A., Ghai, R. R., Jacob, A. L. et al. 2013b. Going, going, gone: a 15-year history of the decline in abundance of primates in forest fragments. In Marsh, L. K. & Chapman, C. A. (Eds.), *Primates in Fragments: Complexity and Resilience*. Springer Press. Pp. 89–100.

Chapman, C. A., Gillespie, T. R. & Goldberg, T. L. 2005b. Primates and the ecology of their infectious diseases: how will anthropogenic change affect host-parasite interactions? *Evolutionary Anthropology* **14**: 134–144.

Chapman, C. A., Hou, R. & Kalbitzer, U. 2018. What will climate change mean for primates? In *Primatology, Bio-cultural Diversity and Sustainable Development in Tropical Forests: A Global Perspective*. UNESCO, Mexico City, Mexico.

Chapman, C. A., Lawes, M. J. & Eeley, H. A. C. 2006d. What hope for African primate diversity? *African Journal of Ecology* **44**: 116–133.

Chapman, C. A., Lawes, M. J., Naughton-Treves, L. & Gillespie, T. 2003b. Primate survival in community-owned forest fragments: are metapopulation models useful amidst intensive use? In Marsh, L. K. (Ed.), *Primates in Fragments: Ecology and Conservation*. Boston: Kluwer Academic/Plenum. Pp. 63–78.

Chapman, C. A., Naughton-Treves, L., Lawes, M. J., Wasserman, M. D. & Gillespie, T. R. 2007. Population declines of colobus in western Uganda and conservation value of forest fragments. *International Journal of Primatology* **28**: 513–528.

Chapman, C. A., Omeja, P. A., Kalbitzer, U., Fan, P. & Lawes, M. J. 2018b. Restoration provides hope for faunal recovery: changes in primate abundance over 45 years in Kibale National Park, Uganda. *Tropical Conservation Science*. **11**.

Chapman, C. A., Rothman, J. M. & Lambert, J. E. 2012. Primate foraging strategies and nutrition: behavioral and evolutionary implications. In John C. Mitani, Josep Call, Peter M. Kappeler, Ryne A. Palombit & Joan B. Silk (Eds.), *The Evolution of Primate Societies*. Chicago: University of Chicago Press. Pp. 145–167.

Chapman, C. A., Schoof, V. A. M., Bonnell, T. R., Gogarten, J. F. & Calme, S. 2015. Competing pressures on populations: long-term dynamics of food availability, food quality, disease, stress and animal abundance. *Philosophical Transactions of the Royal Society B: Biological Sciences* **370**.

Chapman, C. A., Speirs, M. L., Gillespie, T. R., Holland, T. & Austad, K. M. 2006b. Life on the edge: gastrointestinal parasites from the forest edge and interior primate groups. *American Journal of Primatology* **68**: 397–409.

Chapman, C. A., Struhsaker, T. T., Skorupa, J. P., Snaith, T. V. & Rothman, J. M. 2010b. Understanding long-term primate community dynamics: implications of forest change. *Ecological Applications* **20**: 179–191.

Chapman, C. A., Wasserman, M. D. & Gillespie, T. R. 2006c. Behavioural patterns of colobus in logged and unlogged forests: the conservation value of harvested forests. In Newton-Fisher, N., Notman, H., Reynolds, V. et al. (Eds.), *Primates of Western Uganda*. New York: Springer. Pp. 373–390.

Chapman, C. A., Wasserman, M. D., Gillespie, T. R. et al. 2006a. Do food availability, parasitism, and stress have synergistic effects on red colobus populations living in forest fragments? *American Journal of Physical Anthropology* 131: 525–534.

Chapman, C. A., Wasserman, M. D., Gillespie, T. R. et al. 2006e. Do food availability, parasitism, and stress have synergistic effects on red colobus populations living in forest fragments? *American Journal of Physical Anthropology* 131: 525–534.

Chapman, C. A., Webb, T., Fronstin, R., Wasserman, M. D. & Santamaria, A. M. 2005a. Assessing dietary protein of colobus monkeys through faecal sample analysis: a tool to evaluate habitat quality. *African Journal of Ecology* 43: 276–278.

Chapman, C. A., Wrangham, R. W. & Chapman, L. J. 1995. Ecological constraints on group size: an analysis of spider monkey and chimpanzee subgroups. *Behavioural Ecology and Sociobiology* 36: 59–70.

Chapman, T. J. & Legge, S. S. 2009. The dangers of multi-male groupings: trauma and healing in cercopithecoid monkeys from cameroon. *American Journal of Primatology* 71: 567–573.

Chasen, F. N. 1940. A handlist of Malaysian mammals. A systematic list of the mammals of the Malay Peninsula, Sumatra, Borneo and Java, including the adjacent small islands. *Bulletin of the Raffles Museum, Singapore, Strait Settlements* 15: 1–209.

Chen, F., Min, Z., Luo, S. & Xie, W. 1989. An observation of the behavior and some ecological habits of the golden monkey (*Rhinopithecus roxellana*) in Qing Mountains. In Chen, F. (Ed.), *Progress in the Studies of Golden Monkeys*. Xian: Northwest University Press. Pp. 237–242.

Chen, T., Gao, J., Tan, J., Tao, R. & Su, Y. 2017. Variation in gaze-following between two Asian colobine monkeys. *Primates* 58: 525–534.

Chen, T., Li, Y., Liang, J., Li, Y. & Huang, Z. 2020. Variations in the gut microbiota of sympatric François' langurs and rhesus macaques living in limestone forests in southwest Guangxi, China. *Global Ecology and Conservation* 22: e00929.

Chen, Y., Xiang, Z., Wang, X. et al. 2015. Preliminary study of the newly discovered primate species *Rhinopithecus strykeri* at Pianma, Yunnan, China using infrared camera traps. *International Journal of Primatology* 36: 679–690.

Cheney, D. L. 1987. Interactions and relationships between groups. In Smuts, B. B., Cheney, D. L., Seyfarth, R. M. et al. (Eds.), *Primate Societies*. Chicago: University of Chicago Press. Pp. 267–281.

Cheney, D. L. & Wrangham, R. W. 1987. Predation. In Smuts, B. B., Cheney, D. L., Seyfarth, R. M. et al. (Eds.), *Primate Societies*. Chicago: University of Chicago Press. Pp. 227–239.

Chetry, D., Chetry, R., Ghosh, K. & Bhattacharjee, P. C. 2010. Status and conservation of Golden langur in Chakrashila Wildlife Sanctuary, Assam, India. *Primate Conservation* 25: 81–86.

Cheyne, S. M., Neale, C. J., Thompson, C., Wilcox, C. H., Smith, Y. C. E. & Smith, D. A. E. 2018. Down from the treetops: red langur (*Presbytis rubicunda*) terrestrial behavior. *Primates* 59: 437–448.

Chhangani, A. K. 2002. Group composition and sex ratio in Hanuman langurs (*Semnopithecus entellus*) in the Aravali Hills of Rajasthan, India. *Zoos' Print Journal* 17: 848–852.

Chhangani, A. K. & Mohnot, S. M. 2006. Ranging behaviour of Hanuman langurs (*Semnopithecus entellus*) in three different habitats. *Primate Conservation*:171–177.

Chivers, D. 1994. Functional anatomy of the gastrointestinal tract. In Davies, A. G. & Oates, J. F. (Eds.), *Colobine Monkeys: Their Ecology, Behaviour and Evolution*. Cambridge: Cambridge University Press. Pp. 205–227.

Chivers, D. J. & Hladik, C. M. 1980. Morphology of the gastrointestinal tract in primates: comparisons with other mammals in relation to diet. *Journal of Morphology* 166: 337–386.

Chivers, D. J. & Hladik, C. M. 1984. Diet and gut morphology in primates. In David J. Chivers, Bernard A. Wood & Alan Bilsborough (Eds.) *Food Acquisition and Processing in Primates*. New York: Springer. Pp. 213–230.

Chivers, D. J. & Raemaekers, J. J. 1980. Long-term changes in behaviour. In Chivers, D. J. (Ed.), *Malayan Forest Primates: 10 Years of Study in Tropical Rainforest*. New York: Plenum Press. Pp. 209–260.

Choudhury, A. 1989. Ecology of the Capped langur (*Presbytis pileatus*) in Assam, India. *Folia Primatologica* 52: 88–92.

Choudhury, A. 2014. Distribution and current status of the capped langur *Trachypithecus pileatus* in India, and a review of geographic variation in its subspecies. *Primate Conservation* 28: 143–157.

Chu, Y., Sha, J. C. M., Kawazoe, T. & Dong, X. 2018. Sleeping site and tree selection by Sichuan snub-nosed monkeys (*Rhinopithecus roxellana*) in Baihe Nature Reserve, Sichuan, China. *American Journal of Primatology* 80: e22936.

Clarke, P., Pradhan, G. & van Schaik, C. P. 2009. Intersexual conflict in primates: infanticide, paternity allocation, and the role of coercion. In

Muller, M. N. & Wrangham, R. W. (Eds.), *Sexual Coercion in Primates and Humans: An Evolutionary Perspective on Male Aggression against Females*. Cambridge, MA: Harvard University Press. Pp. 42–77.

Clauss, M. 2004. The potential interplay of posture, digestive anatomy, density of ingesta and gravity in mammalian herbivores: why sloths do not rest upside down. *Mammal Review* **34**: 241–245.

Clauss, M. & Dierenfeld, E. S. 2008. The nutrition of browsers. In Fowler, M. E. & Miller, R. E. (Eds.), *Zoo and Wild Animal Medicine: Current Therapy*. St. Louis: Saunders Elsevier. Pp. 444–454.

Clauss, M. & Hummel, J. 2017. Physiological adaptations of ruminants and their potential relevance for production systems. *Revista Brasileira de Zootecnia* **46**: 606–613.

Clauss, M., Besselmann, D., Schwarm, A., Ortmann, S. & Hatt, J. M. 2007. Demonstrating coprophagy with passage markers? The example of the plains viscacha (*Lagostomus maximus*). *Comparative Biochemistry and Physiology A: Molecular & Integrative Physiology* **147**: 453–459.

Clauss, M., Fritz, J., Bayer, D. et al. 2009. Physical characteristics of rumen contents in four large ruminants of different feeding type, the addax (*Addax nasomaculatus*), bison (*Bison bison*), red deer (*Cervus elaphus*) and moose (*Alces alces*). *Comparative Biochemistry and Physiology A* **152**: 398–406.

Clauss, M., Schwarm, A., Ortmann, S. et al. 2004. Intake, ingesta retention, particle size distribution and digestibility in the hippopotamidae. *Comparative Biochemistry and Physiology A: Molecular & Integrative Physiology* **139**: 449–459.

Clauss, M., Steuer, P., Erlinghagen-Lückerath, K. et al. 2015. Faecal particle size: digestive physiology meets herbivore diversity. *Comparative Biochemistry and Physiology A* **179**: 182–191.

Clauss, M., Steuer, P., Müller, D. W. H., Codron, D. & Hummel, J. 2013. Herbivory and body size: allometries of diet quality and gastrointestinal physiology, and implications for herbivore ecology and dinosaur gigantism. *PLOS ONE* **8**: e68714.

Clauss, M., Streich, W. J., Nunn, C. L. et al. 2008. The influence of natural diet composition, food intake level, and body size on ingesta passage in primates. *Comparative Biochemistry and Physiology A* **150**: 274–281.

Clauzel, C., Deng, X., Wu, G., Giraudoux, P. & Li, L. 2015. Assessing the impact of road developments on connectivity across multiple scales: application to Yunnan snub-nosed monkey conservation. *Biological Conservation* **192**: 207–217.

Clayton, J. B., Vangay, P., Huang, H. et al. 2016. Captivity humanizes the primate microbiome. *Proceedings of the National Academy of Sciences* **113**: 10376–10381.

Clayton, J. B., Al-Ghalith, G. A., Long, H. T. et al. 2018. Associations between nutrition, gut microbiome, and health in a novel nonhuman primate model. *Scientific Reports* **8**.

Clayton, J. B., Shields-Cutler, R. R., Hoops, S. L. et al. 2019. Bacterial community structure and function distinguish gut sites in captive red-shanked doucs (*Pygathrix nemaeus*). *American Journal of Primatology* e22977.

Cleaver, K., Schreiber, G. & Ryden, P. 1992. Population, environment and griculture. In Sayer, J. A., Harcourt, C. S. & Collins, N. M. (Eds.), *The Conservation Atlas of Tropical Forests. Africa*. Hants: Macmillan. Pp. 49–55.

Clements, G. R., Antony, J., Lynam, A. J. et al. 2014. Where and how are roads endangering mammals in South-east Asia's forests? *PLOS ONE* **9**: e115376.

Clements, R., Sodhi, N. S., Schilthuizen, M. & Ng, P. K. 2006. Limestone karsts of Southeast Asia: imperiled arks of biodiversity. *AIBS Bulletin* **56**: 733–742.

Clements, T., Rawson, B., Pollard, E., O'Kelly, H. & Hor, N. M. 2008. Conservation status and monitoring of black-shanked douc, *Pygathrix nigripes* and yellow-cheeked crested gibbon *Nomascus gabriellae* in the Seima Biodiversity Conservation Area, Cambodia. Abstracts of the 'Conservation of Primates in Indochina' symposium. Cuc Phuong, Vietnam. P. 18.

Clink, D. J., Dillis, C., Feilen, K. L., Beaudrot, L. & Marshall, A. J. 2017. Dietary diversity, feeding selectivity, and responses to fruit scarcity of two sympatric Bornean primates (*Hylobates albibarbis* and *Presbytis rubicunda rubida*). *PLOS ONE* **12**: e0173369.

Clutton-Brock, T. H. 1974. Activity patterns of red colobus (colobus *badius tephrosceles*). *Folia Primatologica* **21**: 161–187.

Clutton-Brock, T. H. 1975a. Feeding behaviour of red colobus and black and white colobus in east Africa. *Folia Primatologica* **23**: 165–207.

Clutton-Brock, T. H. 1975b. Ranging behaviour of red colobus (colobus *badius tephrosceles*) in the gombe National Park. *Animal Behaviour* **23**: 706–722.

Clutton-Brock, T. H. 1989. Mammalian mating systems. *Proceedings of the Royal Society London B* **236**: 339–372.

Clutton-Brock, T. & Janson, C. H. 2012. Primate socioecology at the crossroads: past, present, and future. *Evolutionary Anthropology* **21**: 136–150.

Clutton-Brock, T. H. & Harvey, P. H. 1977. Species differences in feeding and ranging behaviour in primates. In Clutton-Brock, T. H. (Ed.), *Primate Ecology: Studies of Feeding and Foraging Behaviour in Lemurs, Monkeys, and Apes*. London: Academic Press. Pp. 557–584.

Codron, D., Luyt, J., Lee-Thorpe, J. A., Sponheimer, M., de Ruiter, D. & Codron, J. 2005. Utilization of savanna-based resources by Plio-Pleistocene baboons. *South African Journal of Science* **101**: 245–248.

Cody, M. L. 1971. Finch flocks in the Mojave Desert. *Theoretical Population Biology* **2**: 142–158.

Coley, P. 1983. Herbivory and defensive characteristics of tree species in a lowland tropical forest. *Ecological Monographs* **53**: 209–233.

Collias, N. & Southwick, C. 1952. A field study of population density and social organization in howling monkeys. *Proceedings of the National Academy of Sciences* **96**: 143–156.

Collins, L. & Roberts, M. 1978. Arboreal folivores in captivity – maintenance of a delicate minority. In Montgomery, G. G. (Ed.), *The Ecology of Arboreal Folivores*. Washington, DC: Smithsonian Institution Press. Pp. 5–12.

Collins, L. & Roberts, M. 1978. Arboreal folivores in captivity – maintmanoe of a delicate minority. In G. G. Montgomery, ed., *The Ecology of Arboreal Folivores*. Washington, DC: Smithsonian Institution Press. Pp. 5–12.

Colobus Conservation. 2020. *Canopy Bridges for Primate Conservation*. www.colobusconservation.org.

Colyn, M. 1991. L'importance zoogéograpique du Bassin du Fleuve Zaire pour la speciation: le cas des Primates simiens. *Annales Sciences Zoologiques Musée Royal de l'Afrique Centrale, Tervuren, Belgique* **264**: 1–250.

Colyn, M. 1993. Coat colour polymorphism of red colobus monkeys (*Colobus badius*, primates, colobinae) in eastern zaire: taxonomic and biogeographic implications. *Journal of African Zoology* **107**: 301–320.

Conklin-Brittain, N. L., Dierenfeld, E. S., Wrangham, R. W., Norconk, M. & Silver, S. C. 1999. Chemical protein analysis: a comparison of Kjeldahl crude protein and total ninhydrin protein from wild, tropical vegetation. *Journal of Chemical Ecology* **25**: 2601–2622.

Connell, J. H. 1980. Diversity and coevolution of competitiors or the ghost of competition past. *Oikos* **35**: 131–138.

Conroy, G. C., Senut, B., Gommery, D., Pickford, M. & Mein, P. 1996. New primate remanins from the Miocene of Namibia, Southern Africa. *American Journal of Physical Anthropology* **99**: 487–492.

Constantino, P. J., Lucas, P. W., Lee, J.-W. & Lawn, B. R. 2009. The influence of fallback foods on great ape tooth enamel. *American Journal of Physical Anthropology* **4**: 653–660.

Cooney, D. O. & Struhsaker, T. T. 1997. Adsorptive capacity of charcoals eaten by Zanzibar red colobus monkeys: implications for reducing dietary toxins. *International Journal of Primatology* **18**: 235–246.

Cordeiro, N. 1992. Behaviour of blue monkeys (*Cercopithecus mitis*) in the presence of crowned hawk eagles (*Stephanoaetus coronatus*). *Folia Primatol* **59**: 203–207.

Cords, M. 1984. Mating patterns and social structure in redtail monkeys (*Cercopithecus ascanius*). *Zeitschrift für Tierpsychologie* **64**: 313–339.

Cords, M. 1987. Mixed-species association of *Cercopithecus* monkeys in the Kakamega Forest, Kenya. *University of California Publications in Zoology* **117**: 1–109.

Cords, M. 2000. The number of males in guenon groups. In Kappeler, P. M. (Ed.), *Primate Males*. Cambridge: Cambridge University Press. Pp. 84–96.

Cords, M. & Fuller, J. L. 2010. Infanticide in *Cercopithecus mitis stuhlmanni* in the Kakamega Forest, Kenya: variation in the occurrence of an adaptive behavior. *International Journal of Primatology* **31**: 409–431.

Cords, M., Mitchell, B. J., Tsingalia, H. M. & Rowell, T. E. 1986. Promiscuous mating among blue monkeys in the Kakamega Forest, Kenya. *Ethology* **72**: 214–226.

Corlett, R. T. & La Frankie, J. V., Jr. 1998. Potential impacts of climate change on tropical Asian forests through an influence of phenology. *Climate Change* **39**: 439–453.

Coudrat, C. N. Z., Duckworth, J. W. & Timmins, R. J. 2012. Distribution and conservation status of the red-shanked douc (*Pygathrix nemaeus*) in Lao PDR: an update. *American Journal of Primatology* **74**: 874–889.

Coudrat, C. N. Z., Nanthavong, C. & Nekaris, K. A. I. 2014. Conservation of the red-shanked douc

Pygathrix nemaeus in Lao People's Democratic Republic: density estimates based on distance sampling and habitat suitability modelling. *Oryx* **48**: 540–547.

Courgnaud, V., Formenty, P., Akoua-Koffi, C. et al. 2003. Partial molecular characterization of two simian immunodeficiency viruses (SIV) from African colobids: SIVwrc from Western red colobus (*Piliocolobus badius*) and SIVolc from olive colobus (*Procolobus verus*). *Journal of Virology* **77**: 744–748.

Couzin, I. D. & Laidre, M. E. 2009. Fission–fusion populations. *Current Biology* **19**: R633–R635.

Covert, H. H., Duc, H. M., Quyet, L. K., Ang, A., Harrison-Levine, A. & Van Bang, T. 2017. Primates of Vietnam: conservation in a rapidly developing country. *Anthropology Now* **9**: 27–44.

Covey, R. & McGraw, W. S. 2014. Monkeys in a west African bushmeat market: implications for cercopithecid conservation in eastern liberia. *Tropical Conservation Science* **7**: 115–125.

Cowlishaw, G. 1999. Predicting the pattern of decline of African primate diversity: an extinction debt from historical deforestation. *Conservation Biology* **14**: 1183–1193.

Cowlishaw, G. & Dunbar, R. I. 2000. *Primate Conservation Biology*. Chicago: University of Chicago Press.

Cracraft, J. 1983. Species concepts and speciation analysis. In Johnston, R. F. & Power, D. M. (Eds.), *Current Ornithology*. New York: Plenum Press. Pp. 159–187.

Crissey, S. D. & Pribyl, L. S. 2007. Utilizing wild foraging ecology information to provide captive primates with an appropriate diet. *Proceedings of the Nutrition Society* **56**: 1083–1094.

Crist, E., Mora, C. & Engelman, R. 2017. The interaction of human population, food production, and biodiversity protection. *Science* **356**: 260–264.

Crockett, C. M. & Janson, C. H. 2000. Infanticide in red howlers: female group size, male membership and a possible link to folivory. In van Schaik, C. & Janson, C. (Eds.), *Infanticide by Males and Its Implications*. Cambridge: Cambridge University Press. Pp. 75–98.

Crofoot, M. C. 2012. Why mob? Reassessing the costs and benefits of primate predator harassment. *Folia Primatologica* **83**: 252–273.

Crofoot M. C. & Wrangham, R. W. 2010. Intergroup aggression in primates and humans: the case for a unified theory. In Kappeler P. M. & Silk, J. B. (Eds.), *Mind the Gap: Tracing the Origins of Human Universals*. Heidelberg: Springer. Pp. 171–196.

Cronin, D. T. 2019. *Piliocolobus pennantii. The IUCN Red List of Threatened Species 2019*: e. T41025A92653653. www.iucnredlist.org/.

Cronin, D. T. 2020. *Colobus satanas* ssp. *satanas*. *The IUCN Red List of Threatened Species 2020*. www .iucnredlist.org/.

Cronin, D. T., Bocuma Meñe, D., Butynski, T. M. et al. 2010. Opportunities Lost: The Rapidly Deteriorating Conservation Status of the Monkeys on Bioko Island, Equatorial Guinea (2010). Unpublished report by the Bioko Biodiversity Protection Program, Drexel University, to the Government of Equatorial Guinea, Malabo, Equatorial Guinea. 39 pp.

Cronin, D. T., Linder, J., Ting, N. & Ekwoge, A. 2018. Coordinators of the Red Colobus Conservation Action Plan. Blog post for National Geographic. https://blog.nationalgeographic.org/2018/05/29/saving-Africas-most-threatened-primate-group-from-extinction/.

Cronin, D. T., Riaco, C., Linder, J. M. et al. 2016. Impact of gun-hunting on monkey species and implications for primate conservation on Bioko island, Equatorial Guinea. *Biological Conservation* **197**: 180–189.

Cronin, D. T., Sesink Clee, P. R., Mitchell, M. W. et al. 2017. Conservation strategies for understanding and combating the primate bushmeat trade on Bioko island, Equatorial Guinea. *American Journal of Primatology* **79**: e22663.

Cronin, D. T., Woloszynek, S., Morra, W. A. et al. 2015. Long-term urban market dynamics reveal increased bushmeat carcass volume despite economic growth and proactive environmental legislation on Bioko Island, Equatorial Guinea. *PLOS ONE* **10**: e0137470.

Cui, L. 2003. A note on an interaction between *Rhinopithecus bieti* and a buzzard at Baima Snow Mountain. *Folia Primatologica* **74**: 51–53.

Cui, L., Huo, S., Zhong, T., Xiang, Z., Xiao, W. & Quan, R. 2008. Social organization of black-and-white snub-nosed monkeys (*Rhinopithecus bieti*) at Deqin, China. *American Journal of Primatology* **70**: 169–174.

Cui, L., Quan, R. & Xiao, W. 2006a. Sleeping sites of black-and-white snub-nosed monkeys (*Rhinopithecus bieti*) at Baima Snow Mountain, China. *Journal of Zoology* **270**: 192–198.

Cui, L., Sheng, A., He, S. & Xiao, W. 2006b. Birth seasonality and interbirth interval of captive *Rhinopithecus bieti*. *American Journal of Primatology* **68**: 457–463.

Cui, L., Sun, Q. & Li B. 2014. Dominance hierarchy and social relationships in a group of captive black-and-white snub-nosed monkeys (*Rhinopithecus bieti*). *Zoological Research* 35: 204–213.

Cui, L. & Xiao, W. 2004. Sexual behavior in a one-male unit of *Rhinopithecus bieti* in captivity. *Zoo Biology* 23: 545–550.

Cui, L. W., Li, Y. C., Ma, C. et al. 2016. Distribution and conservation status of Shortridge's capped langurs *Trachypithecus shortridgei* in China. *Oryx* 50: 732–741.

Cui, Z. W., Wang, Z. L., Shao, Q., Raubenheimer, D. & Lu, J. Q. 2018. Macronutrient signature of dietary generalism in an ecologically diverse primate in the wild. *Behavioral Ecology* 29: 804–813.

Cunneyworth, P., De Jong, Y. A., Butynski, T. M. & Perkin, A. W. 2020. *Colobus angolensis* ssp. *palliatus*. *The IUCN Red List of Threatened Species 2020*. www.iucnredlist.org/.

Curry, J. 2012. *Sex differences in the diet of* Colobus guereza. MSc thesis, Hunter College, New York.

Curtin, R. & Dolhinow, P. 1978. Primate social behavior in a changing world. *American Scientist* 66: 468–475.

Curtin, R. A. 1975. *The socio-ecology of the common langur,* Presbytis entellus, *in the Nepal Himalaya.* PhD thesis, University of California, Berkeley.

Curtin, R. A. 1981. Strategy and tactics in male gray langur competition. *Journal of Human Evolution* 10: 245–253.

Curtin, R. A. 1982. Range use of gray langurs in highland Nepal. *Folia Primatologica* 38: 1–18.

Curtin, S. H. & Chivers, D. J. 1978. Leaf-eating primates of peninsular Malaysia: the siamang and the dusky leaf monkey. In Montgomery, G. G. (Ed.), *The Ecology of Arboreal Folivores.* Washington, DC: Smithsonian Institution Press. Pp. 441–464.

Curtin, S. H. 1976. Niche separation in sympatric Malaysian leaf-monkeys (*Presbytis obscura* and *Presbytis melalophos*). *Yearbook Physical Anthropology* 20: 421–439.

Curtin, S. H. 1980. Dusky and banded leaf monkeys. In Chivers, D. J. (Ed.), *Malayan Forest Primates: Ten Years' Study in Tropical Rain Forest.* New York: Plenum Press. Pp. 107–145.

D'Agostino, J., Spehar, S. N. & Delgado, R. 2016. The behavioural contexts of red langur (*Presbytis rubicunda*) loud calls in the Wehea Forest, East Kalimantan, Indonesia. *Folia Primatologica* 87: 1–10.

Daegling, D. J. & McGraw, W. S. 2001. Feeding, diet, and jaw form in west African colobus and procolocus. *International Journal of Primatology* 22: 1033–1055.

Dai, X., Zhu, Y., Luo, Y. et al. 2012. Metagenomic insights into the fibrolytic microbiome in yak rumen. *PLOS ONE* 7: e40430.

Dandelot, P. 1971. Order Primates, suborder Anthropoidea. In Meester, J. & Setzer, H. W. (Eds.), *The Mammals of Africa: An Identification Manual.* Washington, DC: Smithsonian Institution Press. Pp. 1–43.

Danish, L., Chapman, C. A., Hall, M. B., Rode, K. D. & Worman, C. O. D. 2006. The role of sugar in diet selection in redtail and red colobus monkeys. In Hohmann, G., Robbins, M. M. & Boesch, C. (Eds.), *Feeding Ecology in Apes and Other Primates.* Cambridge: Cambridge University Press. Pp. 473–487.

Darwin, C. 1871/1981. *The Descent of Man, and Selection in Relation to Sex.* Princeton: Princeton University Press.

Das, R., Singha, H., Sahu, H. & Choudhury, K. 2013. Golden langur *Trachypithecus geei* (Khajuria, 1956) feeding on *Cryptocoryne retrospiralis* (Roxb.) Kunth (Family: Araceae): a rare feeding observation in Chirang Reserve Forest, Assam, India. *Journal of Threatened Taxa* 5: 5013–5015.

Dasilva, G. L. 1989. *The ecology of the western black and white colobus (*Colobus polykomos polykomos *Zimmerman 1780) on a riverine island in south-eastern Sierra Leone.* PhD thesis, University of Oxford, Oxford.

Dasilva, G. L. 1992. The western black-and-white colobus as a low-energy strategist: activity budgets, energy expenditure and energy intake. *Journal of Animal Ecology* 61: 79.

Dasilva, G. L. 1993. Postural changes and behavioural thermoregulation in *Colobus polykomos*: the effect of climate and diet. *African Journal of Ecology* 31: 226–241.

Dasilva, G. L. 1994. Diet of *Colobus polykomos* on Tiwai Island: selection of food in relation to its seasonal abundance and nutritional quality. *International Journal of Primatology* 15: 655–680.

Davenport N. E. & Machaga, S. J. 2007. Census and conservation assessment of the red colobus (*Procolobus rufomitratus tephrosceles*) on the Ufipa Plateau, southwest Tanzania: newly-discovered, threatened and extinct populations. *Primate Conservation* 22: 97–105.

Davenport, T. R. B. 2019. *Piliocolobus kirkii* (errata version published in 2020). *The IUCN Red List of Threatened Species 2019*: e.T39992A168568335. www.iucnredlist.org/.

Davenport, T. R. B., Fakih, S. A., Kimiti, S. P. et al. 2019. Zanzibar's endemic red colobus *Piliocolobus kirkii*: first systematic and total assessment of population, demography and distribution. *Oryx* 53: 36–44.

David, L. A., Maurice, C. F., Carmody, R. N. et al. 2014. Diet rapidly and reproducibly alters the human gut microbiome. *Nature* 505: 559–566.

Davies, A. G. 1984. *An ecological study of the red leaf monkey (*Presbytis rubicunda*) in the dipterocarp forest of northern Borneo.* PhD thesis, University of Cambridge, Cambridge.

Davies, A. G. 1987. Adult male replacement and group formation in *Presbytis rubicunda. Folia Primatologica* 49: 111–114.

Davies, A. G. 1991. Seed-eating by red leaf monkeys (*Presbytis rubicunda*) in dipterocarp forest of Northern Borneo. *International Journal of Primatology* 12: 119–144.

Davies, A. G. 1994. Colobine populations. In Davies, A. G. & Oates, J. F. (Eds.), *Colobine Monkeys: Their Ecology, Behaviour and Evolution.* New York: Cambridge University Press. Pp. 285–310.

Davies, A. G. & Baillie, I. C. 1988. Soil-eating by red leaf monkeys (*Presbytis rubicunda*) in Sabah, Northern Borneo. *Biotropica* 20: 252–258.

Davies, A. G. & Oates, J. F. 1994. *Colobine Monkeys: Their Ecology, Behaviour and Evolution.* Cambridge: Cambridge University Press. 415 pp.

Davies, A. G., Bennett, E. L. & Waterman, P. G. 1988. Food selection by two South-east Asian colobine monkeys (*Presbytis rubicunda* and *Presbytis melalophos*) in relation to plant chemistry. *Biological Journal of the Linnean Society* 34: 33–56.

Davies, A. G., Oates, J. F. & Dasilva, G. L. 1999. Patterns of frugivory in three West African colobine monkeys. *International Journal of Primatology* 20: 327–357.

Davies, A. G., Schulte-Herbrüggen, B., Kümpel, N. F. & Mendelson, S. 2007. Hunting and trapping in gola forests, south-eastern sierra leone: bushmeat from farm, fallow and forest. In Glyn Davies & David Brown (Eds.), *Bushmeat and Livelihoods: Wildlife Management and Poverty Reduction.* London: Blackwell. Pp. 15–31.

Davis, D. D. 1962. Mammals of the lowland rain-forest of north Borneo. *Bulletin of the National Museum of Singapore* 31: 5–129.

De Fries, R., Hansen, A., Turner, B. L., Reid, R. & Liu, J. 2007. Land use change around protected areas: management to balance human needs and ecological function. *Ecological Applications* 17: 1031–1038.

de Jong, Y. A. & Butynski, T. M. 2012. The primates of East Africa: country lists and conservation priorities. *African Primates* 7: 135–155.

de Jong, Y. A. & Butynski, T. M. 2015. Finding a New Monkey for East Africa. National Geographic Society Newsroom. https://blog.nationalgeographic.org/2015/02/05/finding-a-new-monkey-for-east-africa/.

de Jong, Y. A. & Butynski, T. M. 2018. *Primates of East Africa: Pocket Identification Guide.* Austin: Global Wildlife Conservation, Tropical Pocket Guide Series. www.wildsolutions.nl.

de Jong, Y. A. & Butynski, T. M. 2020a. *Colobus angolensis* ssp. *prigoginei*. *The IUCN Red List of Threatened Species 2020.* www.iucnredlist.org/.

de Jong, Y. A. & Butynski, T. M. 2020b. Tana River Primate Resource Platform. www.wildsolutions.nl/tana-primates/.

De Jong, Y. A., & Butynski, T. M. 2021. Is the southern patas monkey *Erythrocebus baumstarki* Africa's next primate extinction? Reassessing taxonomy, distribution, abundance, and conservation. *American Journal of Primatology* 83. e23316. doi.org/10.1002/ajp.23316.

de Jong, Y. A., Butynski, T. M. & Oates, J. F. 2019. *Colobus guereza. The IUCN Red List of Threatened Species 2019*: e.T5143A17944705. www.iucnredlist.org/.

de Jong, Y. A., Cunneyworth, P., Butynski, T. M., Maisels, F., Hart, J. A. & Rovero, F. 2020. *Colobus angolensis. The IUCN Red List of Threatened Species 2020*: e.T5142A17945007.

de Vries, D., Koenig, A. & Borries, C. 2016. Female reproductive success in a species with an age-inversed hierarchy. *Integrative Zoology* 11: 433–446.

DeCasien, A. R., Williams, S. A. & Higham, J. P. 2017. Primate brain size is predicted by diet but not sociality. *Nature Ecology & Evolution* 1: 0112.

Decker, B. S. 1994a. Effects of habitat disturbance on the behavioral ecology and demographics of the tana river red colobus (*Colobus badius ruformitratus*). *International Journal of Primatology* 15: 703–737.

Decker, B. S. 1994b. Endangered primates in the selous game reserve and an imminent threat to their habitat. *Oryx* 28: 183–190.

Deino, A. L., Tauxe, L., Monaghan, M. & Hill, A. 2002. 40Ar/39Ar geochronology and paleomagnetic stratigraphy of the Lukeino and lower Chemeron Formations at Tabarin and Kapcheberek, Tugen Hills, Kenya. *Journal of Human Evolution* 42: 117–140.

Del Grosso, S., Parton, W., Stohlgren, T. et al. 2008. Global potential net primary production predicted from vegetation class, precipitation, and temperature. *Ecology* 89: 2117–2126.

Dela, J. 2007. Seasonal food use strategies of *Semnopithecus vetulus nestor* at Panadura and Piliyandala, Sri Lanka. *International Journal of Primatology* 28: 607–626.

Dela, J. D. 2012. Western purple-faced langurs (*Semnopithecus vetulus nestor*) feed on ripe and ripening fruits in human-modified environments in Sri Lanka. *International Journal of Primatology* 33: 40–72.

Delson, E. 1973. *Fossil colobine monkeys of the circum-Mediterranean region and the evolutionary history of the Cercopithecidae (*Primates, Mammalia*)*. PhD thesis, Columbia University, New York.

Delson, E. 1975. Evolutionary history of the Cercopithecidae. In Szalay, F. S. (Ed.), *Approaches to Primate Paleobiology; Contributions to Primatology*, vol. 5. Basel: S. Karger. Pp. 167–217.

Delson, E. 1984. Cercopithecid biochronology of the African Plio-Pleistocene: correlation among eastern and southern hominid-bearing localities. *Courier Forschungsinstitut Senckenberg* 69: 199–218.

Delson, E. 1994. Evolutionary history of the colobine monkeys in paleoenvironmental perspective. In Davies, A. G. & Oates, J. F. (Eds.), *Colobine Monkeys: Their Ecology, Behaviour and Evolution*. Cambridge: Cambridge University Press. Pp. 11–43.

Delson, E., Groves, C. P., Grubb, P., Miu, C. A. & Wang, S. 1982. Family Cercopithecidae. In Honacki, J. H., Kinman, K. E. & Koeppl, J. W. (Eds.), *Mammal Species of the World*. Lawrence, KS: Association of Systematics Collections. Pp. 230–242.

Delson, E., Terranova, C. J., Jungers, W. L. et al. 2000. Body mass in Cercopithecidae (Primates, Mammalia): estimation and scaling in extinct and extant taxa. *Anthropological Papers of the American Museum* 83: 1–159.

Delsuc, F., Metcalf, J. L., Parfrey, L. W. et al. 2014. Convergence of gut microbiomes in myrmecophagous mammals. *Molecular Ecology* 23: 1301–1317.

Deng, H., Cui, H., Zhao, Q. et al. 2019. Constrained François' Langur (*Trachypithecus francoisi*) in Yezhong nature reserve, Guizhou, China. *Global Ecology and Conservation* 19: e00672.

Deng, X., Huang, J., Rozelle, S., Zhang, J. & Li, Z. 2015. Impact of urbanization on cultivated land changes in China. *Land Use Policy* 45: 1–7.

Deshcherevskaya, O. A., Avilov, V. K., Ba, D. D., Cong, H. T. & Kurbatova, J. A. 2013. Modern climate of the Cat Tien National Park (South Vietnam): climatological data for ecological studies. *Atmospheric and Oceanic Physics* 49: 819–838.

Detwiler, K. M., Hart, J. A., Maisels, F., Thompson, J., Reinartz, G. & Struhsaker, T. T. 2020. *Piliocolobus tholloni* (amended version of 2019 assessment). *The IUCN Red List of Threatened Species 2020*: e.T18257A166598109. www.iucnredlist.org/.

Devreese, L. 2015. World's first photo of monkey thought extinct in Congo. www.cercocebus.be/press/.

Dewit, I., Dittus, W. P. J., Vercruysse, J., Harris, E. A. & Gibson, D. I. 1991. Gastro-intestinal helminths in a natural population of *Macaca sinica* and *Presbytis* spp. at Polonnaruwa, Sri Lanka. *Primates* 32: 391–395.

Di Fiore, A. & Rendall, D. 1994. Evolution of social organization: a reappraisal for primates by using phylogenetic methods. *Proceedings of the National Academy of Sciences* 91: 9941–9945.

Diaw, M. C., Tiani, A. M., Jum, C. N., Milol, A. & Wandji, D. N. 2003. Assessing Long-term Management Options for the Villages in the Korup National Park: An Evaluation of All Options. Bogor, Indonesia: Center for International Forestry Research (CIFOR). 69 pp. www.cifor.org/knowledge/publication/1398.

Dierenfeld, E., Koontz, F. & Goldstein, R. 1992. Feed intake, digestion and passage of the proboscis monkey (*Nasalis larvatus*) in captivity. *Primates* 33: 399–405.

Dill-McFarland, K. A., Weimer, P. J., Pauli, J. N., Peery, M. Z. & Suen, G. 2016. Diet specialization selects for an unusual and simplified gut microbiota in two- and three-toed sloths. *Environmental Microbiology* 18: 1391–1402.

Dinesen, L., Lehmberg, T., Rahner, M. C. & Fjeldsa, J. 2001. Conservation priorities for the forests of the Udzungwa mountains, Tanzania, based on primates, duikers and birds. *Biological Conservation* 99: 223–236.

Ding, W. & Zhao, Q. 2004. Rhinopithecus bieti at Tacheng, Yunnan: Diet and daytime activities. *International Journal of Primatology* 25: 583–598.

Dinh, T. P. A., Nguyen, D. H. C. & Huynh, T. N. H. 2010. Status and distribution of red-shanked douc langurs (*Pygathrix nemaeus*) and threats to their population at Son Tra Nature Reserve, Danang City. In Nadler, T., Rawson, B. M. & Van, N. T. (Eds.), *Conservation of Primates in Indochina*. Frankfurt Zoological Society and Conservation International: Hanoi. Pp. 71–78.

Diouck, D. 1999. *Adaptations aux modifications du milieu des Colobes bais (*Colobus badius temmincki*) de la Fôret de Fathala, Parc National du Delta du Saloum, Sénégal.* Thesis, Cheikh-Anta-Diop University, Dakar.

Dirzo, R., Young, H. S., Galetti, M., Ceballos, G., Isaac, N. J. B. & Collen, B. 2014. Defaunation in the Anthropocene. *Science* 345: 401–406.

Dittmann, M. T., Runge, U., Ortmann, S. et al. 2015. Digesta retention patterns of solute and different-sized particles in camelids compared with ruminants and other foregut fermenters. *Journal of Comparative Physiology B* 185: 559–573.

Dittus, W. P. J. 1985a. The influence of cyclones on the dry evergreen forest of Sri Lanka. *Biotropica* 17: 1–14.

Dittus, W. P. J. 1985b. The influence of leaf-monkeys on their feeding trees in a cyclone-disturbed environment. *Biotropica* 17: 100–106.

Djego-Djossou, S., Wiafe, E., Hakizamana, D., Mensah, G. A. & Sinsin, B. A. 2018. Comparative feeding ecology and dietary between olive colobus monkey (*Procolobus verus*) groups in forest fragments and continuous forest, Benin. *Journal of Entomology and Zoology Studies* 6: 287–291.

Djuwantoko, S. A., Yuliani, U. & Komarudin, H. 1994. Diet and feeding behaviour of Silvered langurs in Teak plantation forest. *Kongres I Apapi dan Seminar Nasional Primata III. Depok 13–14 May 1994.* Depok: Pusat Studi Biodiversitas Universitas Indonesia.

Djuwantoko. 1991. *Habitat use of silver leaf monkey (*Semnopithecus auratus *E. Geoffroy, 1812) in teak (*Tectona grandis *Linneaus F.) plantation of Cepu, Central Java, Indonesia.* PhD thesis, University of the Philippines, Los Banos, Philippines.

Docters van Leeuwen, W. 1933. Biology of plants and animals in the higher parts of Mount Pangerango-Gedeh in West Java. *Verhandelingen Koninklijke Akademie van Wetenschappen* 31: 1–278.

Dolhinow, P. 1972a. The North Indian langur. In Dolhinow, P. (Ed.), *Primate Patterns*. New York: Holt, Rinehart and Winston. Pp. 181–238.

Dolhinow, P. 1980. An experimental study of mother loss in the Indian langur monkey (*Presbytis entellus*). *Folia Primatologica* 33: 77–128.

Dolhinow, P. J. 1972b. Primate patterns. In Dolhinow, P. J. (Ed.), *Primate Patterns*. New York: Holt, Rinehart and Winston. Pp. 352–392.

Dollman, G. 1912. A new snub-nosed monkey. *Proceedings of the Zoological Society of London* 106: 503–504.

Donaldson, A. & Cunneyworth, P. 2015. Case study: canopy bridges for primate conservation. In Van der Ree, R., Smith, D. J. & Grilo, C. (Eds.), *Handbook of Road Ecology*. Hoboken, NJ: John Wiley. Pp. 341–343.

Dong, T. H. 2007. *Behavioural ecology and conservation of* Rhinopithecus avunculus *in Vietnam.* MSc thesis, Australian National University, Canberra.

Dong, T. H. 2010. Social organization and range use size in Tonkin snub-nosed (*Rhinopithecus avunculus*) monkey in Khau Species and Habitat Conservation Area. *Primate Research* 26 (Suppl.): Abstract #660.

Dong, T. H. 2011. *Ecology, Behavior and Conservation of the Tonkin Snub-nosed Monkey (*Rhinopithecus avunculus*) in Vietnam.* PhD thesis, Australian National University, Canberra.

Drawert, F., Kuhn, H. J. & Rapp, A. 1962. Reaktions-Gaschromatographie, III. Gaschromatographische Bestimmung der niederflüchtigen Fettsäuren im Magen von Schlankaffen (Colobinae). *Hoppe-Seyler's Zeitschrift für physiologische Chemie* 329: 84–89.

Dubay, S., Hayward, G. & Martínez, C. 2008. Nutritional value and diet preference of arboreal lichens and hypogeous fungi for small mammals in the Rocky Mountains. *Canadian Journal of Zoology* 86: 851–862.

Duc, H. M., Baxter, G. S. & Page, M. J. 2009. Diet of *Pygathrix nigripes* in Southern Vietnam. *International Journal of Primatology* 30: 15–28.

Duckworth, J. W., Boonratana, R., Robichaud, W. G. & Timmins, R. J. 2010. A review of François' leaf monkey *Trachypithecus francoisi* (sensu lato) in Lao PDR. *Primate Conservation* 25: 61–79.

Dunbar, R. I. M. 1984. *Reproductive Decisions: An Economic Analysis of Gelada Baboon Social Strategies*. Princeton, NJ: Princeton University Press. 258 pp.

Dunbar, R. I. M. 1987. Habitat quality, population dynamics, and group composition in a colobus monkey (*Colobus guereza*). *International Journal of Primatology* 8: 299–329.

Dunbar, R. I. M. 1988. *Primate Social Systems*. Ithaca, NY: Cornell University Press.

Dunbar, R. I. M. 1992. Time: a hidden constraint on the behavioural ecology of baboons. *Behavioral Ecology and Sociobiology* 31: 35–49.

Dunbar, R. I. M. 2018. Social structure as a strategy to mitigate the costs of group living: a comparison of gelada and guereza monkeys. *Animal Behaviour* 136: 53–64.

Dunbar, R. I. M. & Bose, U. 1991. Adaptation to grass-eating in gelada baboons. *Primates* 32: 1–7.

Dunbar, R. I. M. & Dunbar, E. P. 1974. Ecology and population dynamics of *Colobus guereza* in Ethiopia. *Folia Primatologica* 21: 188–208.

Dunbar, R. I. M. & Dunbar, E. P. 1975a. *Social Dynamics of Gelada Baboons*. Basel, Switzerland: Karger.

Dunbar, R. I. M. & Dunbar, E. P. 1976. Contrasts in social structure among black-and-white colobus monkey groups. *Animal Behaviour* 24: 84–92.

Dunbar, R. I. M. & Dunbar, P. 1975b. Guereza monkeys: will they become extinct in Ethiopia? *Walia* 6: 14–15.

Dunbar, R. I. M., MacCarron, P. & Robertson, C. 2018. Trade-off between fertility and predation risk drives a geometric sequence in the pattern of group sizes in baboons. *Biology Letters* 14: 20170700.

Dunham, N. T. 2015. Ontogeny of positional behavior and support use among *Colobus angolensis palliates* of the Diani Forest, Kenya. *Primates* 56: 183–192.

Dunham, N. T. 2017a. Feeding ecology and dietary flexibility of *Colobus angolensis palliatus* in relation to habitat disturbance. *International Journal of Primatology* 38: 553–571.

Dunham, N. T. 2017b. *Feeding ecology of black and white colobus monkeys from south coastal Kenya: the influence of spatial availability, nutritional composition, and mechanical properties*. PhD thesis, Ohio State University, Columbus.

Dunham, N. T. & Lambert, A. L. 2016. The role of leaf toughness on foraging efficiency in Angola black and white colobus monkeys (*Colobus angolensis palliatus*). *American Journal of Physical Anthropology* 161: 343–354.

Dunham, N. T. & Opere, P. O. 2016. A unique case of extra-group infant adoption in free-ranging Angola black and white colobus monkeys (*Colobus angolensis palliatus*). *Primates* 57: 187–194.

Dunham, N. T. & Rodriguez-Saona, L. E. 2018. Nutrient intake and balancing among female *Colobus angolensis palliatus* inhabiting structurally distinct forest areas: effects of group, season, and reproductive state. *American Journal of Primatology* 80: e22878.

Dunham, N. T., Kane, E. E. & McGraw, W. S. 2015. Scapular morphology and forelimb use during foraging in four sympatric cercopithecids. *Folia Primatologica* 86: 474–489.

Duy, T. P., Bosch, O. J. H., Nguyen, N. C. & Tuyen, L. T. 2014. Dynamics and viability of the Critically Endangered Cat Ba langur: a new perspective for conservation actions. Proceedings of the 57th Annual Meeting of the ISSS-2013 HaiPhong, Vietnam.

Ebenau, A., Nadler, T., Zinner, D. & Roos, C. 2011. Genetic population structure of the Critically Endangered Delacour's langur (*Trachypithcus delacouri*) in Van Long Nature Reserve in Vietnam. *Vietnamese Journal of Primatology* 5: 1–15.

Edwards, M. 1997. *Leaf eating primates' nutrition and dietary husbandry*. Nutrition Advisory Group.

Edwards, M. S. & Ullrey, D. E. 1999. Effect of dietary fiber concentration on apparent digestibility and digesta passage in non-human Primates II. Hindgut and foregut-fermenting folivores. *Zoo Biology* 18: 537–549.

Egi, N., Nakatsukasa, M., Kalmykov, N. P., Maschenko, E. N. & Takai, M. 2007. Distal humerus and ulna of *Parapresbytis* (Colobinae) from the Pliocene of Russia and Mongolia: phylogenetic and ecological implications based on elbow morphology. *Anthropological Science* 115: 107–117.

Ehlers-Smith, D. A., Ehlers-Smith, Y. C. & Cheyne, S. M. 2013a. Home-range use and activity patterns of the red langur (*Presbytis rubicunda*) in Sabangau tropical peat-swamp forest, central Kalimantan Indonesian Borneo. *International Journal of Primatology* 34: 957–972.

Ehlers-Smith, D. A., Husson, S. J., Ehlers-Smith, Y. C. & Harrison, M. E. 2013b. Feeding ecology of red langurs in Sabangau tropical peat-swamp forest, Indonesian Borneo: extreme granivory in a non-masting forest. *American Journal of Primatology* 75: 848–859.

Ellermann, J. R. & Morrison-Scott, T. C. S. 1951. *Checklist of Palaeartic and Indian Mammals 1758 to 1946*. London: British Museum (Natural History). 810 pp.

Elliot, D. G. 1913. *A Review of the Primates: Vol. 3. Anthropoidea (Miopithecus to Pan)*. Monograph Series. New York: American Museum of Natural History.

Ellwanger, A., Riley, R. P., Niu, K. & Tan, C. 2015. Local people's knowledge and attitudes matter for the future conservation of the endangered Guizhou snub-nosed monkey (*Rhinopithecus brelichi*) in Fanjingshan National Nature Reserve, China. *International Journal of Primatology* 36: 33–54.

Elser, S. K., Nguyen, H. C. & Brühl, C. A. 2015. Reintroduction of the 'critically endangered' Delacour's langur (*Trachypithecus delacouri*) into Van Long Nature Reserve, Ninh Binh Province, Vietnam. *Vietnamese Journal of Primatology* 2: 1–13.

El-Zaatari, S., Grine, F. E., Teaford, M. F. & Smith, H. F. 2005. Molar microwear and dietary reconstructions of fossil cercopithecoidea from Plio-Pleistocene deposits of South Africa. *Journal of Human Evolution* 49: 180–205.

Ensley, P., Rost, T., Anderson, M. et al. 1982. Intestinal obstruction and perforation caused by undigested *Acacia* sp. leaves in langur monkeys. *Journal of the American Veterinary Medical Assocation* 181: 1351–1354.

Erb, W. M. 2008. Conservation small grant award report: Behavioral ecology of simakobu monkeys (*Simias concolor*) in northern Siberut, Indonesia. *American Society of Primatologists (ASP) Bulletin* 32: 8–10.

Erb, W. M. 2012. *Male-male competition and loud calls in one-male groups of simakobu (*Simias concolor*)*. PhD thesis, State University of New York, Stony Brook, NY.

Erb, W. M., Borries, C., Lestari, N. S. & Hodges, J. K. 2012a. Annual variation in ecology and reproduction of wild simakobu (*Simias concolor*). *International Journal of Primatology* 33: 1406–1419.

Erb, W. M., Borries, C., Lestari, N. S. & Ziegler, T. 2012b. Demography of simakobu (*Simias concolor*) and the impact of human disturbance. *American Journal of Primatology* 74: 580–590.

Erb, W. M., Ziegler, T., Lestari, N. S. & Hammerschmidt, K. 2016. Are simakobu (*Simias concolor*) loud calls energetically costly signals? *American Journal of Physical Anthropology* 161: 44–52.

Erena, M. G., Bekele, A. & Debella, H. J. 2020. Bushmeat hunting practices in Jorgo-Wato Protected Forest, western Ethiopia. *International Journal of Ecology and Environmental Sciences* 46: 61–72.

Eschmann, C., Moore, R. & Nekaris, K. A. I. 2008. Calling patterns of Western purple-faced langurs (Mammalia: Primates: Cercopithecidea: *Trachypithecus vetulus nestor*) in a degraded human landscape in Sri Lanka. *Contributions to Zoology* 77: 57–65.

Espinosa-Gomez, F., Gomez-Rosales, S., Wallis, I. R., Canales-Espinosa, D. & Hernandez-Salazar, L. 2013. Digestive strategies and food choice in mantled howler monkeys Alouatta palliata mexicana: bases of their dietary flexibility. *Journal of Comparative Physiology B* 183: 1089–1100.

Estrada, A. 2013. Socioeconomic contexts of primate conservation: population, poverty, global economic demands, and sustainable land use. *American Journal of Primatology* 75: 30–45.

Estrada, A., Garber, P. A., Mittermeier, R. A. et al. 2018. Primates in peril: the significance of Brazil, Madagascar, Indonesia and the Democratic Republic of the Congo for global primate conservation. *PeerJ* 6: e4869.

Estrada, A., Garber, P. A., Rylands, A. B. et al. 2017. Impending extinction crisis of the world's primates: Why primates matter. *Science Advances* 3: e1600946.

Estrada, A., Raboy, B. E. & Oliveira, L. C. 2012. Agroecosystems and primate conservation in the tropics: a review. *American Journal of Primatology* 74: 696–711.

Evans, K. D., Foley, W. J., Chapman, C. A. & Rothman, J. M. 2021. Deconstructing Protein in the Diet and Biomass of Colobine Primates. *International Journal of Primatology* 42(2): 283–300.

Fa, J. E. & Brown, D. 2009. Impacts of hunting on mammals in African tropical moist forests: a review and synthesis. *Mammal Review* 39: 231–264.

Fa, J. E., Ryan, S. F. & Bell, D. J. 2005. Hunting vulnerability, ecological characteristics and harvest rates of bushmeat species in afrotropical forests. *Biological Conservation* 121: 167–176.

Fam, S. D. & Nijman, V. 2011. *Spizaetus* hawk-eagles as predators of arboreal colobines. *Primates* 52: 105–110.

Fan, P., Garber, P., Chi, M. et al. 2015. High dietary diversity supports large group size in Indo-Chinese gray langurs in Wuliangshan, Yunnan, China. *American Journal of Primatology* 77: 479–491.

Fan, P., Li, Y., Stanford, C. B. et al. 2018. Home range variation of two different-sized groups of golden snub-nosed monkeys (*Rhinopithecus roxellana*) in Shennongjia, China: implications for feeding competition. *Zoological Research* 39: 1–8.

Fan, P., Liu, R., Grueter, C. C. et al. 2019. Individuality in coo calls of adult male golden snub-nosed monkeys (*Rhinopithecus roxellana*) living in a multilevel society. *Animal Cognition* 22: 71–79.

Fang, G., Dixson, A. F., Qi, X. & Li, B. 2018a. Male-male mounting behaviour in free-ranging golden snub-nosed monkeys (*Rhinopithecus roxellana*). *Folia Primatologica* 89: 150–156.

Fang, G., Gao, X., Zhang, D. et al. 2019. Lengthy leader male tenure delays male offspring dispersal in a primate multilevel society. *Behaviour* **156**: 1371–1391.

Fang, G., Li, M., Liu, X. et al. 2018b. Preliminary report on Sichuan golden snub-nosed monkeys (*Rhinopithecus roxellana roxellana*) at Laohegou Nature Reserve, Sichuan, China. *Scientific Reports* **8**: 16183.

FAO. 1988. *An Interim Report on the State of Forest Resources in the Developing Countries*. Rome, Italy: Food and Agriculture Organization of the United Nations. 18 pp.

FAO. 1990. *The State of Food and Agriculture 1990*. Rome, Italy: Food and Agriculture Organization of the United Nations. 225 pp.

FAO. 1995. *State of the World's Forests*. Rome, Italy: Food and Agriculture Organization of the United Nations. www.fao.org/3/X6953E/X6953E00.htm#TOC.

Fargey, A. 1991. Assessment of the Conservation Status of the Boabeng-Fiema Monkey Sanctuary. Unpublished report to the Flora and Fauna Preservation Society, Kumasi, Ghana.

Fashing, P. J. 2001a. Activity and ranging patterns of guerezas in the Kakamega Forest: intergroup variation and implications for intragroup feeding competition. *International Journal of Primatology* **22**: 549–577.

Fashing, P. J. 2001b. Feeding ecology of guerezas in the Kakamega Forest, Kenya: the importance of Moraceae fruit in their diet. *International Journal of Primatology* **22**: 579–609.

Fashing, P. J. 2001c. Male and female strategies during intergroup encounters in guerezas (*Colobus guereza*): evidence for resource defense mediated through males and a comparison with other primates. *Behavioral Ecology and Sociobiology* **50**: 219–230.

Fashing, P. J. 2002. Population status of black and white colobus monkeys (*Colobus guereza*) in the Kakamega Forest, Kenya: are they really on the decline? *African Zoology* **37**: 119–126.

Fashing, P. J. 2004. Mortality trends in the African cherry (*Prunus africana*) and the implications for colobus monkeys (*Colobus guereza*) in Kakamega Forest, Kenya. *Biological Conservation* **120**: 449–459.

Fashing, P. J. 2007a. African colobine monkeys: Patterns of between-group interaction. In Campbell, C., Fuentes, A., MacKinnon, K. et al. (Eds.), *Primates in Perspective*, 1st ed. Oxford: Oxford University Press. Pp. 201–224.

Fashing, P. J. 2007b. Behavior, ecology, and conservation of colobine monkeys: an introduction. *International Journal of Primatology* **28**: 507–511.

Fashing, P. J. 2011. African colobine monkeys: their behavior, ecology, and conservation. In Campbell, C. J., Fuentes, A., MacKinnon, K. C. et al. (Eds.), *Primates in Perspective*, 2nd ed. New York: Oxford University Press. Pp. 203–229.

Fashing, P. J. 2016a. Angolan colobus, *Colobus angolensis*. In Rowe, N. & Myers, M. (Eds.), *All the World's Primates*. Charlestown, RI: Pogonias Press. Pp. 522–523.

Fashing, P. J. 2016b. Guereza, *Colobus guereza*. In Rowe, N. & Myers, M. (Eds.), *All the World's Primates*. Charlestown, RI: Pogonias Press. Pp. 524–526.

Fashing, P. J. & Cords, M. 2000. Diurnal primate densities and biomass in the Kakamega Forest: an evaluation of census methods and a comparison with other forests. *American Journal of Primatology* **50**: 139–152.

Fashing, P. J. & Oates, J. F. 2013. *Colobus guereza*. In Butynski, T. M., Kingdon, J. & Kalina, J. (Eds.), *Mammals of Africa: Vol. 2. Primates*. London: Bloomsbury. Pp. 111–119.

Fashing, P. J. & Oates, J. F. 2019. *Colobus guereza* ssp. *gallarum*. *The IUCN Red List of Threatened Species 2019*: e.T5150A17983175. www.iucnredlist.org/.

Fashing, P. J., Dierenfeld, E. S. & Mowry, C. B. 2007a. Influence of plant and soil chemistry on food selection, ranging patterns, and biomass of *Colobus guereza* in Kakamega Forest, Kenya. *International Journal of Primatology* **28**: 673–703.

Fashing, P. J., Mulindahabi, F., Gakima, J.-B. et al. 2007b. Activity and ranging patterns of Angolan black-and-white colobus (*Colobus angolensis ruwenzorii*) in Nyungwe Forest, Rwanda: possible costs of large group size. *International Journal of Primatology* **28**: 529–550.

Fashing, P. J., Nguyen, N., Luteshi, P., Opondo, W., Cash, J. F. & Cords, M. 2012. Evaluating the suitability of planted forests for African forest monkeys: a case study from Kakamega Forest, Kenya. *American Journal of Primatology* **74**: 77–90.

Fashing, P. J., Tesfaye, T., Yazezew, D. & Oates, J. F. 2019. *Colobus guereza* ssp. *guereza*. *The IUCN Red List of Threatened Species 2019*: e.T136896A17983254. www.iucnredlist.org/.

Fay, J. M. 1985. Range extensions of four *Cercopithecus* species in the Central African Republic. *Primate Conservation* **6**: 63–68.

Fedigan, L. M. 1992. *Primate Paradigms: Sex Roles and Social Bonds*. Chicago: University of Chicago Press.

Feilen, K. L. & Marshall, A. J. 2014. Sleeping site selection by proboscis monkeys (*Nasalis larvatus*) in

West Kalimantan, Indonesia. *American Journal of Primatology* **76**: 1127–1139.

Feilen, K. L. & Marshall, A. J. 2017. Multiple ecological factors influence the location of proboscis monkey (*Nasalis larvatus*) sleeping sites in West Kalimantan, Indonesia. *International Journal of Primatology* **38**: 448–465.

Feilen, K. L. & Marshall, A. J. 2020. Responses to spatial and temporal variation in food availability on the feeding ecology of proboscis monkeys (*Nasalis larvatus*) in West Kalimantan, *Indonesia. Folia Primatologica.* **91**: 399–416.

Felton, A. M., Felton, A., Rumiz, D. I. et al. 2013. Commercial harvesting of Ficus timber – an emerging threat to frugivorous wildlife and sustainable forestry. *Biological Conservation* **159**: 96–100.

Felton, A. M., Felton, A., Wood, J. T. et al. 2009. Nutritional ecology of spider monkeys (*Ateles chamek*) in lowland Bolivia: how macro-nutrient balancing influence food choices. *International Journal of Primatology* **30**: 675–696.

Fichtel, C. 2012. Predation. In Mitani, J. C., Call, J., Kappeler, P. M. et al. (Eds.), *The Evolution of Primate Societies*. Chicago: The University of Chicago Press. Pp. 169–194.

Fimbel, C. 1994. The relative use of abandoned farm clearings and old forest habitats by primates and a forest antelope at tiwai, sierra leone, west Africa. *Biological Conservation* **70**: 277–286.

Fimbel, C., Vedder, A., Dierenfeld, E. & Mulindahabi, F. 2001. An ecological basis for large group size in *Colobus angolensis* in the Nyungwe Forest, Rwanda. *African Journal of Ecology* **10**: 83–92.

Finstermeier, K., Zinner, D., Brameier, M. et al. 2013. A mitogenomic phylogeny of living primates. *PLOS ONE* **8**: e69504.

Fiore, R. R. (2015). *A survey of Indochinese silvered langurs* (Trachypithecus germaini) *in Phu Quoc National park, Vietnam*. MSc thesis, University of Colorado, Boulder.

Fitri, R. & Novarino, W. 2013. Kepadatan populasi dan struktur kelompok Simpai (*Presbytis melalophos*) serta jenis tumbuhan makanannya di hutan pendidikan dan penelitian biologi (HPPB) Universitas Andalas. *Jurnal Biologi Universitas Andalas* **2**: 25–30.

Fitzgibbon, C. D., Mogaka, H. & Fanshawe, J. H. 2000. Threatened mammals, subsistence harvesting and high human population densities: a recipe for disaster? In Robinson, J. G. & Bennett, E. L. (Eds.), *Hunting for Sustainability in Tropical Forests*. New York: Columbia University Press. Pp. 154–167.

Fleagle, J. G. 1977. Locomotor behavior and muscular anatomy of sympatric Malaysian leaf-monkeys (*Presbytis obscura* and *Presbytis melalophos*). *American Journal of Physical Anthropology* **46**: 297–307.

Fleagle, J. G. 2013. *Primate Adaptation and Evolution*. 3rd ed. New York, NY: Academic Press

Fleury, M. C. 1999. *Ecologie et organisation sociale du colobe satan Colobus satanas*. PhD thesis, Université de Rennes I, Rennes, France.

Fleury, M. C. & Brugière, D. 2013. *Colobus satanas*. In Butynski, T. M., Kingdon, J. & Kalina, J. (Eds.), *Mammals of Africa: Vol. 2. Primates*. London: Bloomsbury. Pp. 97–100.

Fleury, M. C. & Gautier-Hion, A. 1999. Seminomadic ranging in a population of black colobus (*Colobus satanas*) in Gabon and its ecological correlates. *International Journal of Primatology* **20**: 491–509.

Fonkwo, S. N., Mbida, M., Angwafo, T. E. & Ebua, V. B. 2018. Hunting of Preuss's red colobus (*Procolobus preussi*) in Korup National Park, Cameroon. *International Journal of Biodiversity and Conservation* **10**: 100–105.

Fonkwo, S. N., Mbida, M., Angwafor, T. E. & Ebua, V. B. 2015. Activity budget of preuss's red colobus (*Procolobus preussi*) in korup National Park, south-west region, Cameroon. *International Journal of Biological and Chemical Sciences* **9**: 1799–1808.

Fooden, J. 1996. Zoogeography of Vietnamese primates. *International Journal of Primatology* **17**: 845–899.

Forbes, H. O. 1894. *A Hand-book to the Primates*. London: W. H. Allen.

Forest Science Institute of Vietnam. 2009. *Vietnam Forestry Outlook Study*. Food and Agriculture Organization of the United Nations Regional Office for Asia and the Pacific, Bangkok.

Formenty, P., Boesch, C., Wyers, M. et al. 1999. Ebola virus outbreak among wild chimpanzees living in a rain forest of Côte d'Ivoire. *Journal of Infectious Diseases* **179**: S120–S126.

Forrest, D. L., Muatiche, F., Riaco, C., Gonder, M. K. & Cronin, D. T. 2017. Primate communities along a protected area border: a two-site comparison of abundance and hunting response in Bioko, Equatorial Guinea. *African Primates* **12**: 23–36.

Foster, R. B. 1982. The seasonal rhythm of fruitfall on Barro Colorado Island. In Leigh, E. G., Rand, A. S. & Windsor, D. M. (Eds.), *The Ecology of a Tropical*

Forest. Washington, DC: Smithsonian Institution Press. Pp. 151–172.

Fourie, N. H., Lee-Thorpe, J. A. & Ackermann, R. R. 2008. Biogeochemical and craniometric investigation of dietary ecology, niche separation, and taxonomy of Plio-Pleistocene cercopithecoids from the Makapansgat Limeworks. *American Journal of Physical Anthropology* **135**: 121–135.

FRA. 2012. *Forest Resources Assessment Working Paper 180, Terms and Definitions*. Rome, Italy: FAO Forestry Department. 31 pp. www.fao.org/3/ap862e/ap862e00.pdf.

Frankel, J. S., Mallott, E. K., Hopper, L. M., Ross, S. R. & Amato, K. R. 2019. The effect of captivity on the primate gut microbiome varies with host dietary niche. *American Journal of Primatology* **81**: e23061.

Freedman, L. 1957. The fossil Cercopithecoidea of South Africa. *Annals of the Transvaal Museum* **23**: 121–262.

Freeland, W. J. 1976. Pathogens and the evolution of primate sociality. *Biotropica* **8**: 12–24.

Freeland, W. J. & Janzen, D. H. 1974. Strategies in herbivory by mammals: the role of plant secondary compounds. *The American Naturalist* **108**: 269–289.

Fribourg-Blanc, A. & Mollaret, H. H. 1969. Natural treponematosis of the African primate. *Primates in Medicine* 3: 113.

Fritz, J., Hummel, J., Kienzle, E. et al. 2009. Comparative chewing efficiency in mammalian herbivores. *Oikos* **118**: 1623–1632.

Froehlich, H. E., Runge, C. A., Gentry, R. R., Gaines, S. D. & Halpern, B. S. 2018. Comparative terrestrial feed and land use of an aquaculture-dominant world. *Proceedings of the National Academy of Sciences* 201801692.

Frost, S. R. & Alemseged, Z. 2007. Middle Pleistocene fossil Cercopithecidae from Asbole, Afar Region, Ethiopia. *Journal of Human Evolution* **53**: 227–259.

Frost, S. R. & Delson, E. 2002. Fossil Cercopithecidae from the Hadar Formation and surrounding areas of the Afar Depression, Ethiopia. *Journal of Human Evolution* **43**: 687–748.

Frost, S. R. 2001a. New Early Pliocene Cercopithecidae from Aramis, Middle Awash Valley Ethiopia. *American Museum Novitates* **3350**: 1–36.

Frost, S. R. 2001b. *Fossil Cercopithecidae of the Afar Depression, Ethiopia: species systematics and comparison to the Turkana Basin*. PhD thesis, City University of New York, New York.

Frost, S. R., Gilbert, C. C., Pugh, K. D., Guthrie, E. H. & Delson, E. 2015. The Hand of *Cercopithecoides williamsi* (Mammalia, Primates): earliest evidence for thumb reduction among colobine monkeys. *PLOS ONE* **10**: e0125030.

Frost, S. R., Haile-Selassi, Y. & Hlusko, L. 2009. Cercopithecidae. In Haile-Selassie, Y. & WoldeGabriel, G. (Eds.), *Ardipithecus kadabba: Late Miocene Evidence from the Middle Awash, Ethiopia*. Berkeley: University of California Press. Pp. 135–158.

Frost, S. R., Plummer, T., Bishop, L. C. et al. 2003. Partial cranium of Cercopithecoides kimeui Leakey, 1982 from Rawi Gully, Southwestern Kenya. *American Journal of Physical Anthropology* **122**: 191–199.

Frost, S. R., Simpson, S. W., Levin, N. E. et al. 2020a. Fossil Cercopithecidae from the early Pliocene Sagantole Formation at Gona, Ethiopia. *Journal of Human Evolution* **144**: 102789.

Frost, S. R., Ward, C. V., Manthi, F. K. & Plavcan, J. M. 2020b. Cercopithecid fossils from Kanapoi, West Turkana, Kenya (2007–2015). *Journal of Human Evolution* **140**: 102642.

Fuentes, A. 1994. *The socioecology of the Mentawai island langur (*Presbytis potenziani*)*. PhD thesis, University of California, Berkeley.

Fuentes, A. 1996. Feeding and ranging in the Mentawai Island langur (*Presbytis potenziani*). *International Journal of Primatology* **17**: 525–548.

Fuentes, A. 2002. Monkeys, humans, and politics in the Mentawai islands: no simple solutions in a complex world. In Fuentes, A. & Wolfe, L. D. (Eds.), *Primates Face to Face: The Conservation Implications of Human and Nonhuman Primate Interconnections*. Palo Alto, CA: Cambridge University Press. Pp. 187–207.

Fuentes, A. and Ray, E. 1996. Humans, habitat loss and hunting: the status of the Mentawai Islands primates on Sipora and Pagai Islands. *Asian Primates*, **5**: 5–9.

Fuentes, A. & Tenaza, R. R. 1995. Infant parking in the pig-tailed langur (*Simias concolor*). *Folia Primatologica* **65**: 172–173.

Fujita, S. & Kageyama, T. 2007. Polymerase chain reaction detection of Clostridium perfringens in feces from captive and wild chimpanzees, *Pan troglodytes*. *Journal of Medical Primatology* **36**: 25–32.

Fundi, P., Combes, K. & Omengo, F. 2020. Capture and Release of Mount Kenya Guereza (*Colobus guereza kikuyuensis*) from Kipipiri to Soysambu Conservancy. Unpublished report by the Institute of Primate Research, Nairobi, Kenya. 17 pp.

Funk, C., Eilerts, G., Davenport, F. & Michaelson, J. 2010. A climate trend analysis of Kenya – August 2010. United States Geological Survey Fact Sheet

2010–3074. 4 pp. https://fews.net/sites/default/files/documents/reports/FEWS%20Kenya%20Climate%20Trend%20Analysis.pdf.

Furuya, Y. 1961. The social life of silvered leaf monkeys. *Primates* **3**: 41–60.

Gabis, R. 1960. Les os des membres des singes cymlmorphes. *Mammalia* **24**: 577–602.

Galat, G. & Galat-Luong, A. 1985. La communauté de primates diurnes de la Forêt de Taï, Côte d'Ivoire. *Revue d'Ecologie-La Terre et La Vie* **40**: 3–32.

Galat, G., Galat-Luong, A. & Nizinski, G. 2009. Increasing dryness and regression of the geographical range of temminck's red colobus *Procolobus badius temminckii*: implications for its conservation. *Mammalia: International Journal of the Systematics, Biology & Ecology of Mammals* **73**: 365–368.

Galat-Luong, A. 1983. *Socio-écologie de trois colobes sympatrique,* Colobus badius, C. polykomos, *et* C. verus *du Parc National de Taï, Côte d'Ivoire.* PhD thesis, Université Pierre et Marie Curie, Paris, France.

Galat-Luong, A. 1988. Monkeys in the Pirang forest. Pirang. Ecological Investigations in a Forest Island in the Gambia. *Stiftung Walderhaltung in Afrika, Hamburg, and Bundesforschungsanstalt für Forst- und Holzwirtschaft, Hamburg, Warnke Verlag, Reinbek.*

Galat-Luong, A. & Galat, G. 1978. *Abondance relative et associations plurispécifiques de primates diurnes du Parc National de Taï, Côte d'Ivoire.* Adiopodoumé: ORSTOM.

Galat-Luong, A. & Galat, G. 2005. Conservation and survival adaptations of temminck's red colobus (*Procolobus badius temmincki*), in Senegal. *International Journal of Primatology* **26**: 585–603.

Galat-Luong, A., Galat, G., Coles, R. & Nizinski, J. 2019. African flooded areas as refuge habitats. In Barnett, A. A., Nowak, K. & Matsuda, I. (Eds.), *Primates in Flooded Habitats: Ecology and Conservation.* Cambridge: Cambridge University Press. Pp. 304–314.

Galat-Luong, A., Galat, G., Oates, J. F. et al. 2016. *Piliocolobus temminckii. The IUCN Red List of Threatened Species 2016*: e.T18247A92646945. www.iucnredlist.org/.

Ganzhorn, J. U. 1995. Cyclones over Madagascar: fate or fortune? *Ambio* **24**: 124–125.

Ganzhorn, J. U. 2002. Distribution of a folivorous lemur in relation to seasonally varying food resources: integrating quantitative and qualitative aspects of food characteristics. *Oecologia* **131**: 427–435.

Gatinot, B. L. 1975. *Ecologie d'un Colobe bai (Colobus badius temmincki, Kuhl 1820) dans un milieu marginal au Senégal,* Université de Paris.

Gatinot, B. L. 1977. Le régime alimentaire du colobe bai au sénégal. *Mammalia* **41**: 373–402.

Gatinot, B. L. 1978. Characteristics of the diet of west African red colobus. In D. J. Chivers & J. Herbert (Eds.), *Recent Advances in Primatology: Vol. 1. Behaviour.* New York: Academic Press. Pp. 253–255.

Gautier-Hion, A. & Brugière, D. 2005. Significance of riparian forests for the conservation of central African primates. *International Journal of Primatology* **26**: 515–523.

Gautier-Hion, A. & Tutin, C. E. G. 1988. Simultaneous attack by adult males of a polyspecific troop of monkesy against a crowned hawk eagle. *Folia Primatologica* **51**: 149–151.

Gautier-Hion, A., Colyn, M. & Gautier, J.-P. 1999. *Histoire Naturelle des Primates D'Afrique Centrale.* Libreville, Gabon: ECOFAC. 162 pp.

Gautier-Hion, A., Gautier, J.-P. & Moungazi, A. 1997. Do black colobus in mixed-species groups benefit from increased foraging. *Comptes Rendus de l'Académie des Sciences* **320**: 67–71.

Gaveau, D. L., Epting, J., Lyne, O. et al. 2009. Evaluating whether protected areas reduce tropical deforestation in Sumatra. *Journal of Biogeography* **36**: 2165–2175.

Gaveau, D. L., Sloan, S., Molidena, E. et al. 2014. Four decades of forest persistence, clearance and logging on Borneo. *PLOS ONE.* **9**: e101654.

Gaveau, D., Wich, S. A. & Marshall, A. J. 2016. Are protected areas conserving primate habitat in Indonesia? In Wich, S. A. & Marshall, A. J. (Eds.), *An introduction to primate conservation.* Oxford, UK: Oxford University Press. Pp. 193–204.

Geissmann, T., Groves, C. P. & Roos, C. 2004. The Tenasserim lutung, *Trachypithecus barbei* (Blyth, 1847) (Primates: Cercopithecidae): description, of a live specimen, and a reassessment of phylogenetic affinities, taxonomic history, and distribution. *Contributions to Zoology* **73**: 271–282.

Geissmann, T., Lwin, N., Aung, S. S. et al. 2011. A new species of snub-nosed monkey, genus *Rhinopithecus* Milne-Edwards, 1872 (Primates, Colobinae), from northern Kachin state, northeastern Myanmar. *American Journal of Primatology* **73**: 96–107.

Georgiev, A. V., Melvin, Z. E., Warketin, A. S., Winder, I. C. & Kassim, A. 2019. Two cases of dead-infant carrying by female Zanzibar red colobus

(*Piliocolobus kirkii*) at Jozani-Chwaka Bay National Park, Zanzibar. *African Primates* 13: 57–60.

Gevaerts, H. 1992. Birth seasons of *Cercopithecus, Cercocebus and Colobus* in Zaire. *Folia Primatologica* 59: 105–113.

Ghai, R. R., Fugère, V., Chapman, C. A., Goldberg, T. L. & Davies, T. J. 2015. Sickness behaviour associated with non-lethal infections in wild primates. *Proceedings of the Royal Society B: Biological Sciences* 282: 20151436.

Gibson, L. & Koenig, A. 2012. Neighboring groups and habitat edges modulate range use in Phayre's leaf monkeys (*Trachypithecus phayrei crepusculus*). *Behavioral Ecology and Sociobiology* 66: 633–643.

Gijzen, A., Mortelmans, J. & Vercruysse, J. 1966. Notes on the Zanzibar red colobus at Antwerp Zoo. *International Zoo Yearbookd* 6.

Gilbert, C. C., Goble, E. & Hill, A. 2010. Miocene Cercopithecoidea from the Tugen Hills, Kenya. *Journal of Human Evolution* 59: 465–483.

Gilbert, W. H. & Frost, S. R. 2008. Cercopithecidae. In Gilbert, W. H. & Asfaw, B. (Eds.), *Homo erectus: Pleistocene Evidence from the Middle Awash, Ethiopia.* Berkeley: University of California Press. Pp. 115–132.

Gillespie, T. R. & Chapman, C. A. 2001. Determinants of group size in the red colobus monkey (*Procolobus badius*): an evaluation of the generality of the ecological-constraints model. *Behavioral Ecology and Sociobiology* 50: 329–338.

Gillespie, T. R. & Chapman, C. A. 2006. Prediction of parasite infection dynamics in primate metapopulations based on attributes of forest fragmentation. *Conservation Biology* 20: 441–448.

Gillespie, T. R., Chapman, C. A. & Greiner, E. C. 2005a. Effects of logging on gastrointestinal parasite infections and infection risk in African primates. *Journal of Applied Ecology* 42: 699–707.

Gillespie, T. R., Greiner, E. C. & Chapman, C. A. 2005b. Gastrointestinal parasites of the colobus monkeys of Uganda. *Journal of Parasitology* 91: 569–573.

Githitho, A. 2003. The Sacred Mijikenda Kaya Forests of coastal Kenya and biodiversity conservation. In Lee, C. & Schaaf, T. (Eds.), *The Importance of Sacred Natural Sites for Biodiversity Conservation.* Paris, France: UNESCO. Pp. 27–35.

Glander, K. 1982. The impact of plant secondary compounds on primate feeding behavior. *Yearbook of Physical Anthropology* 25: 1–18.

Glander, K. E., Wright, P. C., Seigler, D. S., Randrianasolo, V. & Randrianasolo, B. 1989. Consumption of cyanogenic bamboo by a newly discovered species of bamboo lemur. *American Journal of Primatology* 19: 119–124.

Global Forest Resources Assessment. 2000. Main Report (FAO, Rome, 2001).

Global Forest Watch (GFW). 2020. Forest Management Designed for Action. www.globalforestwatch.org/.

Global Forest Watch. 2019. Ethiopia. www.globalforestwatch.org/dashboards/country/ETH.

Gochfeld, M. 1974. Douc langurs. *Nature* 247: 167.

Godfrey, L. R., Samonds, K. E., Jungers, W. L. & Sutherland, M. R. 2003. Dental development and Primate life histories. In Kappeler, P. M. & Pereira, M. E. (Eds.), *Primate Life Histories and Socioecology.* Chicago: University of Chicago Press.

Godoy-Vitorino, F., Goldfarb, K. C., Karaoz, U. et al. 2012. Comparative analyses of foregut and hindgut bacterial communities in hoatzins and cows. *ISME Journal,* 6: 531–541.

Gogarten, J. F., Bonnell, T. R., Brown, L. M. 2014. Increasing group size alters behavior of a folivorous primate. *International Journal of Primatology* 35: 590–608.

Gogarten, J. F., Davies, T. J., Benjamino, J. et al. 2018. Factors influencing bacterial microbiome composition in a wild non-human primate community in Taï National Park, Côte d'Ivoire. *ISME Journal* 12: 2559–2574.

Gogarten, J. F., Düx, A., Schuenemann, V. J. et al. 2016. Tools for opening new chapters in the book of Treponema pallidum evolutionary history. *Clinical Microbiology and Infection* 22: 916–921.

Gogarten, J. F., Guzman, M., Chapman, C. A. 2012. What is the predictive power of the colobine protein-to-fiber model and its conservation value? *Tropical Conservation Science* 5: 381–393.

Gogarten, J. F., Jacob, A. L., Ghai, R. R. et al. 2015. Group size dynamics over 15+ years in an African forest primate community. *Biotropica* 47: 101–112.

Goldberg, T. L., Chapman, C. A., Cameron, K. et al. 2008a. Serologic evidence for a novel poxvirus in endangered red colobus monkeys. *Emerging Infectious Diseases* 14: 801–803.

Goldberg, T. L., Gillespie, T. R., Rwego, I. B., Estoff, E. L. & Chapman, C. A. 2008b. Forest fragmentation as cause of bacterial transmission among nonhuman primates, humans, and livestock, Uganda. *Emerging Infectious Diseases* 14: 1375–1382.

Goldberg, T. L., Sintasath, D. M., Chapman, C. A. et al. 2009. Co-infection of Ugandan red colobus (*Procolobus [Piliocolobus] rufomitratus tephrosceles*) with novel, divergent delta-, lenti- and spuma- retroviruses. *Journal of Virology* 83: 11318–11329.

Gomez, A., Petrzelkova, K. J., Yeoman, C. J. et al. 2015. Gut microbiome composition and metabolomic profiles of wild western lowland gorillas (*Gorilla gorilla gorilla*) reflect host ecology. *Molecular Ecology* 24: 2551–2565.

Gonedelé Bi, S., Bitty, A., Gnangbé, F. et al. 2010. Conservation status of Geoffroy's pied colobus monkey *Colobus vellerosus* Geoffroy, 1834 has dramatically declined in Côte D'Ivoire. *African Primates* 7: 19–26.

Gonedelé Bi, S., Bitty, A., Ouatara, K. & McGraw, W. S. 2014. Primate surveys in Côte D'ivoire's sassandra-bandama interfluvial region with notes on a remnant population of black-and-white colobus. *African Journal of Ecology* 52: 491–498.

Gonedelé Bi, S., Koné, I., Matsuda Goodwin, R. et al. 2020. *Colobus polykomos. The IUCN Red List of Threatened Species 2020.* www.iucnredlist.org/.

González-Monge, A. 2016. *The socioecology, and the effects of human activity on it, of the Annamese silvered langur* (Trachypithecus margarita) *in northeastern Cambodia.* PhD thesis, Australian National University, Canberra.

González-Monge, A. & Behie, A. M. 2019. The effects of selective logging on the habitat use of the Annamese silvered langur (*Trachypithecus margarita*) in northeast Cambodia. In Behie, A. M., Teichroeb, J. & Malone, N. (Eds.), *Primate Research and Conservation in the Anthropocene.* Cambridge: Cambridge University Press. Pp. 101–119.

Goodall, J. 1968. The behaviour of free-living chimpanzees in the Gombe Stream Reserve. *Animal Behaviour Monographs* 1: 165–311.

Goodall, J. 1986. *The Chimpanzees of Gombe: Patterns of Behavior.* Cambridge, MA: Harvard University Press. 673 pp.

Goodfellow, C. K., Whitney, T., Christie, D. M. et al. 2019. Divergence in gut microbial communities mirrors a social group fission event in a black-and-white colobus monkey (*Colobus vellerosus*). *American Journal of Primatology* 81: e22966.

Goodman, S. M. 1989. Predation by the grey leaf monkey (*Presbytis hosei*) on the contents of a bird's nest at Mt. Kinabalu Park, Sabah. *Primates* 30: 127–128.

Goodman, M., Porter, C. A., Czelusniak, J. et al. 1998. Toward a phylogenetic classification of primates based on DNA evidence complemented by fossil evidence. *Molecular Phylogenetics and Evolution* 9: 585–598.

Gorzitze, A. B. 1996. Birth-related behaviors in wild proboscis monkeys (*Nasalis larvatus*). *Primates* 37: 75–78.

GoTG. 2007. The Gambia National Adaptation Programme of Action (NAPA) on Climate Change. Department of State for Forestry & the Environment, Banjul, The Gambia. 97 pp. https://unfccc.int/resource/docs/napa/gmb01.pdf.

Graham, T. L., Matthews, H. D. & Turner, S. E. 2016. A global-scale evaluation of primate exposure and vulnerability to climate change. *International Journal of Primatology* 37: 158–174.

Grand, T. I. 1976. Differences in terrestrial velocity in *Macaca* and *Presbytis*. *American Journal of Physical Anthropology* 45: 101–108.

Green, K. M. 1981. Preliminary observations on the ecology and behavior of the capped langur, *Presbytis pileatus*, in the Madhupur forest of Bangladesh. *International Journal of Primatology* 2: 131–151.

Greene, L. K., Bornbusch, S. L., McKenney, E. A. et al. 2019. The importance of scale in comparative microbiome research: new insights from the gut and glands of captive and wild lemurs. *American Journal of Primatology* 81: e22974.

Greene, L. K., McKenney, E. A., O'Connell, T. M. & Drea, C. M. 2018. The critical role of dietary foliage in maintaining the gut microbiome and metabolome of folivorous sifakas. *Scientific Reports* 8: 14482.

Grimes, K. H. 2000. *Guereza dietary and behavioural patterns at the Entebbe Botanical Gardens.* MA thesis, University of Calgary, Calgary, AB.

Groves, C. 2012. Species concepts in primates. *American Journal of Primatology* 74: 687–691.

Groves, C. P. 1970. The forgotten leaf-eaters, and the evolution of of the Colobinae. In Napier, J. R. & Napier, P. H. (Eds.), *Old World Monkeys: Ecology, Systematics and Behavior.* New York: Academic Press. Pp. 555–587.

Groves, C. P. 1973. Notes on the ecology and behaviour of the Angola colobus (*Colobus angolensis* P. L. Sclater 1860) in N. E. Tanzania. *Folia Primatologica* 20: 12–26.

Groves, C. P. 1989. *A Theory of Human and Primate Evolution.* Oxford: Clarendon Press. 375 pp.

Groves, C. P. 1993. Order Primates. In Wilson, D. E. & Reeder, D. M. (Eds.), *Mammal Species of the World: A Taxonomic and Geographic Reference*, 2nd ed.

Washington, DC: Smithsonian Institution Press. Pp. 243–277.

Groves, C. P. 2000. The phylogeny of the Cercopithecoidea. In Whitehead, P. F. & Jolly, C. J. (Eds.), *Old World Monkeys*. Cambridge: Cambridge University Press. Pp. 77–98.

Groves, C. P. 2001. *Primate Taxonomy*. Washington, DC: Smithsonian Institution Press. 350 pp.

Groves, C. P. 2004. Taxonomy and biogeography of primates in Vietnam and neighbouring regions. In Nadler, T., Streicher, U. & Long, H. T. (Eds.), *Conservation of Primates in Vietnam*. Hanoi: Frankfurt Zoological Society. Pp. 15–22.

Groves, C. P. 2005. Order Primates. In Wilson, D. E. & Reeder, D. M. (Eds.), *Mammal Species of the Word: A Taxonomic and Geographic Reference*, 3rd ed. Baltimore, MD: Johns Hopkins University Press. Pp. 111–184.

Groves, C. P. 2007. The taxonomic diversity of the colobinae of Africa. *Journal of Anthropological Sciences* **85**: 7–34.

Groves, C. P. & Ting, N. 2013. Subfamily Colobinae, Tribe Colobini. In Mittermeier, R. A., Rylands, A. B. & Wilson, D. E. (Eds.), *Handbook of the Mammals of the World: Vol. 3. Primates*. Barcelona, Spain: Lynx Edicions. Pp. 698–712.

Groves, C. P., Angst, R. & Westwood, C. 1993. The status of *Colobus polykomos dollmani* Schwarz. *International Journal of Primatology* **14**: 573–586.

Groves, C. P., Cotterill, F. P. D., Gippoliti, S. et al. 2017. Species definitions and conservation: a review and case studies. *Conservation Genetics* **18**: 1247–1256.

Grubb, P. 2002. Red Colobus (Subgenus *Piliocolobus*) Systematics. Unpublished draft manuscript. 23 pp. www.wildsolutions.nl/grubb_2002.

Grubb, P. & Groves, C. P. 2013. Subgenus *Procolobus*. In Butynski, T. M., Kingdon, J. & Kalina, J. (Eds.), *Mammals of Africa: Vol. 2. Primates*. London: Bloomsbury. P. 121.

Grubb, P. & Powell, C. B. 1999. Discovery of red colobus monkeys (*Procolobus badius*) in the niger delta with the description of a new and geographically isolated subspecies. *Journal of Zoology* **248**: 67–73.

Grubb, P., Butynski, T. M., Oates, J. F. et al. 2003. Assessment of the diversity of African primates. *International Journal of Primatology* **24**: 1301–1357.

Grubb, P., Struhsaker, T. & Siex, K. S. 2013a. Subgenus *Piliocolobus*. In Butynski, T. M., Kingdon, J. & Kalina, J. (Eds.), *Mammals of Africa: Vol. 2. Primates*. London: Bloomsbury. Pp. 125–128.

Grubb, P., Struhsaker, T. & Siex, K. S. 2013b. Genus *Procolobus*. In Butynski, T. M., Kingdon, J. & Kalina, J. (Eds.), *Mammals of Africa: Vol. 2. Primates*. London: Bloomsbury. P. 120.

Grubb, P. J., Jones, T. S., Davies, A. G. et al. 1998. *Mammals of Ghana, Sierra Leone, and The Gambia*. Saint Ives: The Trenedine Press.

Grueter, C. C. 2004. Conflict and postconflict behavior in captive black-and-white snub-nosed monkeys (*Rhinopithecus bieti*). *Primates* **45**: 197–200.

Grueter, C. C. 2009. *Determinants of modular societies in snub-nosed monkeys (*Rhinopithecus bieti*) and other colobines*. PhD thesis, University of Zurich, Zurich, Switzerland.

Grueter, C. C. 2013. *The Biology of the Snub-nosed Monkeys, Douc Langurs, Proboscis Monkeys and Simakobu*. Hauppauge, NY: Nova Science. 149 pp.

Grueter, C. C. 2014. Primate model offers insights into male bonding in complex societies. *Proceedings of the National Academy of Sciences* **111**: 14645–14646.

Grueter, C. C. 2015a. *Field Guide to the Flora and Fauna of the Golden Monkey National Park/Baimaxueshan Nature Reserve, Yunnan, China*. Manchester, UK: Siri Scientific Press.

Grueter, C. C. 2015b. Home range overlap as a driver of intelligence in primates. *American Journal of Primatology* **77**: 418–424.

Grueter, C. C. & Ding, W. 2006. An observation of Francois' langurs using caves at Mayanghe National Nature Reserve, Guizhou, China. *Zoological Research* **27**: 558–560.

Grueter, C. C. & van Schaik, C. P. 2009. Sexual size dimorphism in Asian colobines revisited. *American Journal of Primatology* **71**: 609–616.

Grueter, C. C. & van Schaik, C. P. 2010. Evolutionary determinants of modular societies in colobines. *Behavioral Ecology* **21**: 63–71.

Grueter, C. C. & White, D. R. 2014. On the emergence of large-scale human social integration and its antecedents in primates. *Structure and Dynamics* **7**: 1–27.

Grueter, C. C. & Zinner, D. 2004. Nested societies: convergent adaptations of baboons and snub-nosed monkeys? *Primate Report* **70**: 1–98.

Grueter, C. C., Chapais, B. & Zinner, D. 2012a. Evolution of multilevel social systems in nonhuman primates and humans. *International Journal of Primatology* **33**: 1002–1037.

Grueter, C. C., Isler, K. & Dixson, B. J. 2015a. Are badges of status adaptive in large complex primate groups? *Evolution and Human Behavior* 36: 398–406.

Grueter, C. C., Li, D., Feng, S. & Ren, B. 2010a. Niche partitioning between sympatric rhesus macaques and Yunnan snub-nosed monkeys at Baimaxueshan Nature Reserve, China. *Zoological Research* 31: 516–522.

Grueter, C. C., Li, D., Ren, B. & Li, M. 2013. Overwintering strategy of Yunnan snub-nosed monkeys: adjustments in activity scheduling and foraging patterns. *Primates* 54: 125–135.

Grueter, C. C., Li, D., Ren, B. & Wei, F. 2010b. Feeding ecology of *Rhinopithecus* bieti in the Samage Forest, Baimaxueshan Nature Reserve, China. In Nadler, T., Rawson, B. M. & Van, N. T. (Eds.), *Conservation of Primates in Indochina.* Hanoi: Frankfurt Zoological Society and Conservation International. Pp. 157–169.

Grueter, C. C., Li, D., Ren, B., Wei, F. & Li, M. 2017a. Deciphering the social organization and structure of wild Yunnan snub-nosed monkeys (*Rhinopithecus bieti*). *Folia Primatologica* 88: 358–383.

Grueter, C. C., Li, D., Ren, B., Wei, F. & van Schaik, C. P. 2009a. Dietary profile of *Rhinopithecus bieti* and its socioecological implications. *International Journal of Primatology* 30: 601–624.

Grueter, C. C., Li, D., Ren, B. et al. 2009b. Fallback foods of temperate-living primates: a case study on snub-nosed monkeys. *American Journal of Physical Anthropology* 140: 700–715.

Grueter, C. C., Li, D., Ren, B., Xiang, Z. & Li, M. 2012b. Food abundance is the main determinant of high-altitude range use in snub-nosed monkeys. *International Journal of Zoology* 2012: 739419.

Grueter, C. C., Li, D., van Schaik, C. P. et al. 2008. Ranging of *Rhinopithecus* bieti in the Samage Forest, China. I. Characteristics of range use. *International Journal of Primatology* 29: 1121–1145.

Grueter, C. C., Matsuda, I., Zhang, P. & Zinner, D. 2012c. Multilevel societies in primates and other mammals: introduction to the special issue. *International Journal of Primatology* 33: 993–1001.

Grueter, C. C., Qi, X., Li, B. & Li, M. 2017b. Multilevel societies. *Current Biology* 27: R984–986.

Grueter, C. C., Qi, X., Zinner, D. et al. 2020. Multilevel organisation of animal sociality. *Trends in Ecology and Evolution* 35: 834–847.

Grueter, C. C., Robbins, A. M., Abavandimwe, D. et al. 2018. Quadratic relationships between group size and foraging efficiency in a herbivorous primate. *Scientific Reports* 8: 16718.

Grueter, C. C., Zhu, P., Allen, W. L. et al. 2015b. Sexually selected lip colour indicates male group-holding status in the mating season in a multi-level primate society. *Royal Society Open Science* 2: 150490.

Gruninger, R. J., Sensen, C. W., McAllister, T. A. & Forster, R. J. 2014. Diversity of rumen bacteria in Canadian cervids. *PLoS ONE* 9: e89682.

Gunderson, V. 1977. Some observations on the ecology of colobus *badius* temmincki, abuko nature reserve, the gambia, west Africa. *Primates* 18: 305–314.

Guo, A., Dang, X., Chen, F. et al. 2016. Condensed tannins contents of foods of *Rhinopithecus bieti* in Mt Lasha, Yunnan, China. *Acta Theriologica Sinica* 36: 388–396 (in Chinese with English abstract).

Guo, S., Hou, R., Garber, P. A. et al. 2018. Nutrient-specific compensation for seasonal cold stress in a free-ranging temperate colobine monkey. *Functional Ecology* 32: 2170–2180.

Guo, S., Huang, K., Ji, W., Garber, P. A. & Li, B. 2015. The role of kinship in the formation of a primate multilevel society. *American Journal of Physical Anthropology* 156: 606–613.

Guo, S., Ji, W., Li, M., Chang, H. & Li, B. 2010. The mating system of the Sichuan snub-nosed monkey (*Rhinopithecus roxellana*). *American Journal of Primatology* 72: 25–32.

Guo, S., Li, B. & Watanabe, K. 2007. Diet and activity budget of *Rhinopithecus roxellana* in the Qinling Mountains, China. *Primates* 48: 268–276.

Guo, Y., Zhou, J., Song, X., Deng, H., Qiu, Y., Shi, L. & Zhou, J. 2017. The population of *Rhinopithecus brelichi* in Fanjingshan National Nature Reserve, Guizhou, China. *Acta Theriologica Sinica* 37: 104–108.

Guo, Y., Zhou, J., Xie, J. et al. 2018. Altitudinal ranging of the Guizhou golden monkey (*Rhinopithecus brelichi*): patterns of habitat selection and habitat use. *Global Ecology and Conservation* 16: e00473.

Gupta, A. K. & Chivers, D. J. 2000. Feeding ecology and conservation of the Golden langur (*Trachypithecus geei* Khajuria) in Tripura, Northeast India. *Journal of the Bombay Natural History Society* 97: 349–362.

Gupta, A. K. & Kumar, A. 1994. Feeding ecology and conservation of the Phayre's leaf monkey *Presbytis phayrei* in Northeast India. *Biological Conservation* 69: 301–306.

Gurmaya, K. J. 1986. Ecology and behavior of *Presbytis thomasi* in Northern Sumatra. *Primates* 27: 151–172.

Gurmaya, K. J. 1989. Ecology, behavior and sociality of Thomas' leaf monkey in North Sumatra. In Ehara, A.

& Kawamura, S. (Eds.), *Comparative Primate Monographs* No. 2. Institute of Ecology, University of Padjadjaran.

Ha, T. L. 2004. Distribution and ststus of the grey-shanked douc langur (Pygathrix cinerea) in Vietnam. In Nadler, T., Streicher, U. & Long, H. T. (Eds.), *Conservation of Primates in Vietnam*. Hanoi: Frankfurt Zoological Society. Pp. 52–57.

Ha, T. L. 2007. Distribution, population and conservation status of the grey-shanked douc (*Pygathrix cinerea*) in Gia Lai Province, central highlands of Vietnam. *Vietnamese Journal of Primatology* **1**: 55–60.

Ha, T. L. 2009. *Behavioural ecology of grey-shanked douc monkey in Vietnam*. PhD thesis, University of Cambridge, Cambridge.

Ha, T. L., Nguyen, T. T., Tran, H. V. & Ho, T. M. 2010. Activity budget of grey-shanked douc langurs (*Pygathrix cinerea*) in Kon Ka Kinh National Park, Vietnam. *Vietnamese Journal of Primatology* **1**: 27–40.

Ha, Nguyen Hai, Dinh Huy Tri, Nguyen Xuan Dang, Bui Ngoc Thanh, and Tran Dinh Anh. "Photo evidence for the occurrence of the black 'ebenus' morph of the Hatinhlangur (*Trachypithecus hatinhensis*) in the Phong Nha-Ke Bang National Park and comments on this morph." *Vietnamese Journal of Primatology* 3, no. 2 (2020): 49–52.

Hadi, S. 2012. *Niche differentiation of two sympatric colobines,* Simias concolor *and* Presbytis potenziani *on the Mentawai Island of Siberut, Indonesia*. PhD thesis, Georg-August University Göttingen, Göttingen, Germany.

Hadi, S., Ziegler, T. & Hodges, J. K. 2009. Group structure and physical characteristics of simakobu monkeys (*Simias concolor*) on the Mentawai Island of Siberut, Indonesia. *Folia Primatologica* **80**: 74–82.

Hadi, S., Ziegler, T., Waltert, M. et al. 2012. Habitat use and trophic niche overlap of two sympatric colobines, *Presbytis potenziani* and *Simias concolor*, on Siberut Island, Indonesia. *International Journal of Primatology* **33**: 218–232.

Hale, V. L., Tan, C., Niu, K. et al. 2018. Diet versus phylogeny: a comparison of gut microbiota in captive colobine monkey species. *Microbial Ecology* **75**: 515–527.

Hale, V. L., Tan, C., Niu, K. et al. 2019. Gut microbes in wild and captive Guizhou snub-nosed monkeys, *Rhinopithecus brelichi*. *American Journal of Primatology*: e22989.

Hall, J. S., White, L., Williamson, E. A., Inogwabini, B.-I. & Ilambu, O. 2003. Distribution, abundance, and biomass estimates for primates within kahuzi-biega lowlands and adjacent forest in eastern drc. *African Primates* **6**: 35–42.

Hallet, B. & Molnar, P. 2001. Distorted drainage basins as markers of crustal strain east of the Himalayas. *Journal of Geophysical Research* **106**: 13697–13709.

Hamerlynck, O., Luke, Q., Nyange, T. M., Duvail, S. & Leauthaud, C. 2012. Range extension, imminent threats and conservation options for two endangered primates: the Tana River red colobus *Procolobus rufomitratus rufomitratus* (Peters, 1879) and the Tana River mangabey *Cercocebus galeritus* (Peters, 1879) in the Lower Tana Floodplain and Delta, Kenya. *African Primates* **7**: 211–217.

Hamilton, A. C. 1982. *Environmental History of East Africa: A Study of the Quaternary*. London: Academic Press. 328 pp.

Hamilton, W. D. 1971. Geometry for the selfish herd. *Journal of Theoretical Biology* **31**: 295–311.

Hammond, R. L., Lawson Handley, L. J., Winney, B. J., Bruford, M. W. & Perrin, N. 2006. Genetic evidence for female-biased dispersal and gene flow in a polygynous primates. *Proceedings of the Royal Society London B* **273**: 479–484.

Hansen, M. F., Nawangsari, V. A., van Beest, F. M., Schmidt, N. M., Stelvig, M., Dabelsteen, T., Nijman, V. 2020. Habitat suitability analysis reveals high ecological flexibility in a "strict" forest primate. *Front Zool* **17**: 6. doi: 10.1186/s12983-020-00352-2

Hanya, G. & Bernard, H. 2012. Fallback foods of red leaf monkeys (*Presbytis rubicunda*) in Danum Valley, Borneo. *International Journal of Primatology* **33**: 322–337.

Hanya, G. & Bernard, H. 2015. Different roles of seeds and young leaves in the diet of red leaf monkeys (*Presbytis rubicunda*): comparisons of availability, nutritional properties, and associated feeding behavior. *International Journal of Primatology* **36**: 177–193.

Hanya, G., Tsuji, Y. & Grueter, C. C. 2013. Fruiting and flushing phenology in Asian tropical and temperate forests: implications for primate ecology. *Primates* **54**: 101–110.

Harcourt, A. H. & Stewart, K. J. 2007. *Gorilla Society: Conflict, Compromise, and Cooperation Between the Sexes*. Chicago: University of Chicago Press.

Harding, L. E. 2009. *Trachypithecus delacouri* (Primates: Cercopithecidae). *Mammalian Species* **43**: 118–128.

Harding, L. E. 2010. *Trachypithecus cristatus* (Primates: Cercopithecidae). *Mammalian Species* **42**: 149–165.

Hardy, G. M. 1988. *Comparative socio-ecology of dusky langurs at Kuala Lompat West Malaysia*. PhD thesis, Cambridge Universtity, Cambridge.

Harjenti, T. D. 1996. *Perilaku Makan dan Jenis Makanan Surili (*Presbytis comata *Desmarest 1922) di Hutan Brussel, Gunung Patuha, Cidewey, Jawa Barat*. BSc thesis, Universitas Padjadjaran, Bandung, Indonesia.

Harris, J. M., Brown, F. H. & Leakey, M. G. 1988. Stratigraphy and paleontology of Pliocene and Pleistocene localities west of Lake Turkana, Kenya. *Contributions in Science, Natural History Museum of Los Angeles County* **399**: 1–128.

Harris, J. M., Leakey, M. G. & Cerling, T. E. 2003. Early Pliocene tetrapod remains from Kanapoi, Lake Turkana Basin, Kenya. *Contributions in Science, Natural History Museum of Los Angeles County* **468**: 39–112.

Harris, T. R. 2005. *Roaring, intergroup aggression, and feeding competition in black and white colobus monkeys (*Colobus guereza*) at Kanyawara, Kibale National Park, Uganda*. PhD thesis, Yale University, New Haven, CT.

Harris, T. R. 2006a. Between-group contest competition for food in a highly folivorous population of black and white colobus monkeys (*Colobus guereza*). *Behavioral Ecology and Sociobiology* **61**: 317–329.

Harris, T. R. 2006b. Within- and among-male variation in roaring by black and white colobus monkeys (*Colobus guereza*): what does it reveal about function? *Behaviour* **143**: 197–218.

Harris, T. R. 2010. Multiple resource values and fighting ability measures influence intergroup conflict in guerezas (*Colobus guereza*). *Animal Behaviour* **79**: 89–98.

Harris, T. R. & Chapman, C. A. 2007a. Variation in diet and ranging of black and white colobus monkeys in Kibale National Park, Uganda. *Primates* **48**: 208–221.

Harris, T. R. & Chapman, C. A. 2007b. Variation in the diet and ranging behavior of black-and-white colobus monkeys: implications for theory and conservation. *Primates* **28**: 208–221.

Harris, T. R. & Monfort, S. L. 2003. Behavioral and endocrine dynamics associated with infanticide in a black and white colobus monkey (*Colobus guereza*). *American Journal of Primatology* **61**: 135–142.

Harris, T. R. & Monfort, S. L. 2006. Mating behavior and endocrine profiles of wild black and white colobus monkeys (*Colobus guereza*): toward an understanding of their life history and mating system. *American Journal of Primatology* **68**: 383–396.

Harris, T. R., Caillaud, D., Chapman, C. A. & Vigilant, L. 2009a. Neither genetic nor observational data, alone, are sufficient for understanding sex-biased dispersal in a social, group-living species. *Molecular Ecology* **18**: 1777–1790.

Harris, T. R., Chapman, C. A. & Monfort, S. L. 2010. Small folivorous primate groups exhibit behavioral and physiological effects of food scarcity. *Behavioral Ecology* **21**: 46–56.

Harris, T. R., Fitch, W. T., Goldstein, L. M. & Fashing, P. J. 2006. Black and white colobus monkey (*Colobus guereza*) roars as a source of both honest and exaggerated information about body mass. *Ethology* **112**: 911–920.

Harrison, M. J. S. 1986. Feeding ecology of black colobus, *Colobus satanas*, in central Gabon. In Else, J. G. & Lee, P. C. (Eds.), *Primate Ecology and Conservation*. Cambridge: Cambridge University Press. Pp. 31–37.

Harrison, M. J. S. & Hladik, C. M. 1986. Un primate granivore: le colobe noir dans la forêt du Gabon; potentialité d'évolution du comportement alimentaire. *Revue d'Ecologie (La Terre et la Vie)* **41**: 281–298.

Harrison, R. D. 2011b. Emptying the forest: hunting and the extirpation of wildlife from tropical nature reserves. *BioScience* **61**: 919–924.

Harrison, T. 1996. The palaeoecological context at Niah Cave, Sarawak: evidence from the primate fauna. *Bulletin of the Indo-Pacific Prehistory Association* **14**: 90–100.

Harrison, T. 2011a. Cercopithecids (Cercopithecidae, Primates). In Harrison, T. (Ed.), *Paleontology and Geology of Laetoli: Human Evolution in Context, Fossil Hominins and the Associated Fauna*, vol. 2. Dordrecht, The Netherlands: Springer. Pp. 83–139.

Harrison, T. & Delson, E. 2007. *Mesopithecus sivalensis* from the Late Miocene of the Siwaliks [Abstract]. *American Journal of Physical Anthropology* **132**: 126.

Harrison, T. & Harris, E. E. 1996. Plio-Pleistocene cercopithecids from Kanam East, western Kenya. *Journal of Human Evolution* **30**: 539–561.

Hart, D. 2007. Predation on primates: a biogeographical analysis. In Gursky, S. & Nekaris, K. A. I. (Eds.), *Primate Anti-Predator Strategies*. New York: Springer. Pp. 27–59.

Hart, D. & Sussman, R. W. 2005. *Man the Hunted: Primates, Predators, and Human Evolution*. New York: Westview Press.

Hart, J. A., Laudisoit, A., Struhsaker, T. T. & Oates, J. F. 2020b. *Piliocolobus langi* (amended version of 2019 assessment). *The IUCN Red List of Threatened Species 2020*: e.T18261A166605018. www.iucnredlist.org/.

Hart, J. A., Maisels, F., Oates, J. F. et al. 2020c. *Piliocolobus oustaleti* (amended version of 2019 assessment). *The IUCN Red List of Threatened Species 2020*: e.T18255A166598553. www.iucnredlist.org/.

Hart, J. A., Maisels, F. & Ting, N. 2020d. *Piliocolobus lulindicus. The IUCN Red List of Threatened Species 2020*: e.T18262A96192471. www.iucnredlist.org/.

Hart, J. A., Ting, N. & Maisels, F. 2020e. *Piliocolobus foai. The IUCN Red List of Threatened Species 2020*: e.T18252A92659769. www.iucnredlist.org/.

Harvati, K. 2000. Dental eruption sequence among colobine primates. *American Journal of Physical Anthropology* 112: 69–85.

Haus, T., Vogt, M. & Forster, B. 2009b. Observations on the Hatinh langur (*Trachypithecus hatinhensis*) during point and line transect sampling in the PhongNha-Ke Bang National Park, Central Vietnam. *Vietnamese Journal of Primatology* 3: 17–27.

Haus, T., Vogt, M., Forster, B., Vu, N. T. & Ziegler, T. 2009a. Distribution and population densities of diurnal primates in the karst forests of Phong Nha-Ke Bang National Park, Quang Binh Province, central Vietnam. *International Journal of Primatology* 30: 301–312.

Hawkins, R. E., Norden, D. & Sahgal B. 1986. *Encyclopedia of Indian Natural History: Centenary Publication of the Bombay Natural History Society 1883–1983*. Delhi: Oxford University Press.

Hayakawa, T., Nathan, S., Stark, D. J. et al. 2018a. First report of foregut microbial community in proboscis monkeys: are diverse forests a reservoir for diverse microbiomes? *Environmental Microbiology Reports* 10: 655–662.

Hayakawa, T., Sawada, A., Tanabe, A. S. et al. 2018b. Improving the standards for gut microbiome analysis of fecal samples: insights from the field biology of Japanese macaques on Yakushima Island. *Primates* 59: 423–436.

Hayes, V. J., Freedman, L. & Oxnard, C. E. 1996. Dental sexual dimorphism and morphology in African colobus monkeys as related to diet. *International Journal of Primatology* 17: 725–757.

He, H., Zhao, H., Qi, X. et al. 2013. Dominance rank of adult females and mating competition in Sichuan snub-nosed monkeys (*Rhinopithecus roxellana*) in the Qinling Mountains, China. *Chinese Science Bulletin* 58: 2205–2211.

He, K., Hu, N., Orkin, J. D. et al. 2012. Molecular phylogeny and divergence time of *Trachypithecus*: with implications for the taxonomy of *T. phayrei*. *Zoological Research* 33: E104-E110.

Hearn, G. W. & Butynski, T. M. 2016. Black colobus, *Colobus satanas*. In Rowe, N. & Myers, M. (Eds.), *All the World's Primates*. Charlestown, RI: Pogonias Press. Pp. 528–529.

Hearn, G., Morra, W. A. & Butynski, T. M. 2006. Monkeys in Trouble: The Rapidly Deteriorating Conservation Status of the Monkeys on Bioko Island, Equatorial Guinea. Unpublished report by the Bioko Biodiversity Protection Program, Drexel University, to the Government of Equatorial Guinea, Malabo, Equatorial Guinea. 27 pp.

Heinicke, S., Kalan, A. K., Wagner, O. J. J. et al. 2015. Assessing the performance of a semi-automated acoustic monitoring system for primates. *Methods in Ecology and Evolution* 6: 753–763.

Heldstab, A. 1988. Management and disease problems in douc langurs at the Basel Zoo. *American Association of Zoo Veterinarians Annual Conference Proceedings (Toronto, Canada)*. Pp. 184–187.

Hemp, A. 2009. Climate change and its impact on the forests of Kilimanjaro. *African Journal of Ecology* 47: 3–10.

Hendershott, R. L. 2017. *Socioecology of Cat Ba langurs (*Trachypithecus poliocephalus*): Implications for conservation*. PhD thesis, Australian National University, Canberra.

Hendershott, R., Behie, A. & Rawson, B. 2016. Seasonal variation in the activity and dietary budgets of Cat Ba langurs (*Trachypithecus poliocephalus*). *International Journal of Primatology* 37: 586–604.

Hendershott, R., Behie, A. & Rawson, B. 2017. Erratum to: seasonal variation in the activity and dietary budgets of Cat Ba langurs (*Trachypithecus poliocephalus*). *International Journal of Primatology* 38: 613–622.

Hendershott, R., Rawson, B. & Behie, A. 2018. Home range size and habitat use by Cat Ba langurs (*Trachypithecus poliocephalus*) in a disturbed and fragmented habitat. *International Journal of Primatology* 39: 547–566.

Henderson, G., Cox, F., Ganesh, S. et al. 2015. Rumen microbial community composition varies with diet and host, but a core microbiome is found across a wide geographical range. *Scientific Reports* 5: 14567.

Henry, M. C., Maingi, J. K. & McCarty, J. 2019. Fire on the water towers: mapping burn scars on Mount

Kenya using satellite data to reconstruct recent fire history. *Remote Sensing* 11: 104.

Herries, A. I. R., Kappen, P., Kegley, A. D. T. et al. 2014. Palaeomagnetic and synchotron analysis of >1.95 Ma fossil-bearing palaeokarst at Haasgat, South Africa. *South African Journal of Science* 110: 1–12.

Heuglin von, T. 1877. *Reise in Nordost-Afrika. Schilderungen aus dem Gebiete der Beni Amer und Habab nebst zoologischen Skizzen und einem Führer für Jagdreisende*, 2 vols. Braunschweig, Germany: George Westermann.

Hicks, A. L., Lee, K. J., Couto-Rodriguez, M. et al. 2018. Gut microbiomes of wild great apes fluctuate seasonally in response to diet. *Nature Communications* 9: 1786.

Hill, A. C., Leakey, M. G., Kingston, J. D. & Ward, S. 2002. New cercopithecoids and a hominoid from 12.5 Ma in the Tugen Hills succession, Kenya. *Journal of Human Evolution* 42: 75–93.

Hill, O. 1964. The maintenance of langurs (Colobidae) in captivity; experiences and some suggestions. *Folia Primatologica* 2: 222–231.

Hill, R. A., Lycett, J. E. & Dunbar, R. I. M. 2000. Ecological and social determinants of birth intervals in baboons. *Behavioral Ecology* 11: 560–564.

Hill, W. C. O. 1934. A monograph on the purple-faced leaf-monkeys (*Pithecus vetulus*). *Ceylon Journal of Science (B)* 9: 23–88.

Hill, W. C. O. 1939. An annotated systematic list of the leaf-monkeys. *Ceylon Journal of Science* 21: 277–305.

Hill, W. C. O. 1952. The external and visceral anatomy of the olive colobus monkey (*Procolobus verus*). *Proceedings of the Zoological Society of London* 122: 127–186.

Hill, W. C. O. & Booth, A. H. 1957. Voice and larynx in African and Asiatic Colobidae. *Journal of the Bombay Natural History Society* 54: 309–321.

Hillman, J. C. 1983. An Ecological Survey and Management Recommendations for Bangangai Game Reserve, South West Sudan, with Special Reference to the Bongo Antelope. Unpublished report to the New York Zoological Society, New York. 93 pp.

Hillyer, A. P., Armstrong, R. & Korstjens, A. H. 2015. Dry season drinking from terrestrial man-made watering holes in arboreal wild Temminck's red colobus, The Gambia. *Primate Biology* 2: 21–24.

Hinde, R. 1976. Interactions, relationships and social structure. *Man* 11: 1–17.

Hishamunda, N., Ridler, N. B., Bueno, P. & Yap, W. G. 2009. Commercial aquaculture in Southeast Asia: some policy lessons. *Food Policy* 34: 102–107.

Hladik, C. M. 1977. A comparative study of the feeding strategies of two sympatric species of leaf monkeys: *Presbytis senex* and *Presbytis entellus*. In Clutton-Brock, T. H. (Ed.), *Primate Ecology: Studies of Feeding and Ranging Behaviour in Lemurs, Monkeys and Apes*. London: Academic Press. Pp. 323–353.

Hladik, C. M. 1978. Adaptive strategies of primates in relation to leaf-eating. In Montgomery, G. G. (Ed.), *The Ecology of Arboreal Folivores*. Washington, DC: Smithsonian Institution Press. Pp. 373–395.

Hlusko, L. J. 2006. A new large Pliocene colobine species (Mammalia: Primates) from Asa Issie, Ethiopia. *Geobios* 39: 57–69.

Hlusko, L. J. 2007. A new Late Miocene species of *Paracolobus* and other cercopithecidae (Mammalia: Primates) fossil from Lemudong'o. *Kenya. Kirtlandia* 56: 72–85.

Hoang, M. D. 2007. *Ecology and conservation status of the black-shanked douc (*Pygathrix nigripes*) in Nui Chua and Phuoc Binh National Parks, Ninh Thuan Province, Vietnam*. PhD thesis, University of Queensland, Brisbane, Australia.

Hoang, M. D., Baxter, G. S. & Page, M. J. 2009. Diet of *Pygathrix nigripes* in southern Vietnam. *International Journal of Primatology* 30: 15–28.

Hoang, M. D., Baxter, G. S. & Page, M. J. 2011. Preliminary results on food selection of the black-shanked douc langurs (*Pygathrix nigripes*) in southern Vietnam. *Vietnamese Journal of Primatology* 1: 29–40.

Hoang, M. D., Ly, N. S. & Pham, V. X. 2004. Present Status of the Black-shanked Douc Langur (*Pygathrix nigripes*) in Nui Chua National Park, Ninh Thuan Province. Unpublished Report to Institute of Tropical Biology and Nui Chua National Park, Vietnam, Ho Chi Minh City.

Hobeika, S., Beziers, P. & Korstjens, A. H. 2009. The accuracy of sexual swellings as indicators for the reproductive status of female red colobus (*Piliocolobus tephrosceles*). *Folia Primatologica* 80: 161–162.

Hodder, S. A. M. & Chapman, C. A. 2012. Do nematode infections of red colobus (*Procolobus rufomitratus*) and black-and-white colobus (*Colobus guereza*) on humanized forest edges differ from those on nonhumanized forest edges? *International Journal of Primatology* 33: 845–859.

Hofner, A. N., Jost Robinson, C. A. & Nekaris, K. A. I. 2018. Preserving preuss's red colobus (*Piliocolobus preussi*): an ethnographic analysis of hunting, conservation, and changing perceptions of primates in ikenge-bakoko, cameroon. *International Journal of Primatology* 39: 895–917.

Hofner, A. N., Robinson, C. A. J., Linder, J. M. & Robinson, O. D. 2019. Partners for red colobus: protecting Preuss's red colobus (*Piliocolobus preussi*) in Cameroon. *African Primates* 13: 68.

Hohmann, G. 1988. Analysis of loud calls provides new evidence for hybridization between two Asian leaf monkeys (*Presbytis johnii, Presbytis entellus*). *Folia Primatologica* 51: 209–213.

Hohmann, G. 1989a. Comparative study of vocal communication in two Asian leaf monkeys, *Presbytis johnii* and *Presbytis entellus*. *Folia Primatologica* 52: 27–57.

Hohmann, G. 1989b. Group fission in Nilgiri langurs (*Presbytis johnii*). *International Journal of Primatology* 10: 441–454.

Hohmann, G. 1990. Loud calls of male purple-faced langurs (*Presbytis senex*). *Folia Primatologica* 55: 200–206.

Holbrook, M. R. 2012. Kyasanur forest disease. *Antiviral Research* 96: 353–362.

Holenweg, A. K., Noë, R. & Schabel, M. 1996. Waser's gas model applied to associations between red colobus and diana monkeys in the Taï National Park, ivory coast. *Folia Primatologica* 67: 125–136.

Hollihn, K. U. 1971. Das Verhalten von Guerezas (*Colobus guereza* und *Colobus polykomos*), Nasenaffen (*Nasalis larvatus*) und Kleideraffen (*Pygathrix nemaeus*) bei der Nahrungsaufnahme und ihre Haltung. *Mammalian Biology* 36: 65–95.

Hollihn, U. W. E. 1973. Remarks on the breeding and maintenance of Colobus monkeys *Colobus guereza*, Proboscis monkeys *Nasalis larvatus* and Douc langurs *Pygathrix nemaeus* in zoos. *International Zoo Yearbook* 13: 185–188.

Holmes, J. C. 1995. Population regulation: a dynamic complex of interactions. *Wildlife Research* 22: 11–20.

Höner, O., Leumann, L. & Noë, R. 1997. Dyadic associations of red colobus and diana monkey groups in the Taï National Park, ivory coast. *Primates* 38: 281–291.

Hoppe-Dominik, B. 1984. Etude du spectre des proies de la panthère, panthera pardus, dans le parc national de Taï en côte d'Ivoire. *Mammalia* 48: 477–487.

Hopper, L. M., Freeman, H. D. & Ross, S. R. 2016. Reconsidering coprophagy as an indicator of negative welfare for captive chimpanzees. *Applied Animal Behaviour Science* 176: 112–119.

Horwich, R. H. 1972. Home range and food habits of the Nilgiri langur, *Presbytis johnii*. *Journal of the Bombay Natural History Society* 69: 1–13.

Horwich, R. H. 1976. The whooping display in Nilgiri langurs: an example of daily fluctuations superimposed on a general trend. *Primates* 17: 419–431.

Horwich, R. H. 1980. Behavioral rhythms in the Nilgiri langur, *Presbytis johnii*. *Primates* 21: 220–229.

Horwich, R. H. & Manski, D. 1975. Maternal care and infant transfer in two species of *Colobus* monkeys. *Primates* 16: 49–73.

Hosaka, K., Nakamura, M. & Takahata, Y. 2020. Longitudinal changes in the targets of chimpanzee (*Pan troglodytes*) hunts at Mahale Mountains National Park: how and why did they begin to intensively hunt red colobus (*Piliocolobus rufomitratus*) in the 1980s? *Primates* 61: 391–401.

Hosaka, K., Toshida, N., Hamai, M., Matsumoto-Oda, A. & Uehara, S. 2001. Predation of mammals by the chimpanzees of the Mahale Mountains, Tanzania. In Galdikas, B. M. F., Briggs, N. E., Sheeran, L. K. et al. (Eds.), *All Apes Great and Small: Vol. 1. African Apes*. New York: Plenum. Pp. 107–130.

Hou, R., He, S., Wu, F. et al. 2018. Seasonal variation in diet and nutrition of the northern-most population of *Rhinopithecus roxellana*. *American Journal of Primatology* 80: e22755.

Houghton, J. T., Ding, Y., Griggs, D. J. et al. 2001. *Climate Change 2001: The Scientific Basis. Contribution of Working Group I to the Third Assessment Report of the Intergovernmental Panel on Climate Change*. Cambridge: Cambridge University Press. 881 pp.

Houle, A., Vickery, W. L. & Chapman, C. A. 2006. Testing mechanisms of coexistence among two species of frugivorous primates. *Journal of Animal Ecology* 75: 1034–1044.

Hrdy, S. B. 1974. Male-male competition and infanticide among the langurs (*Presbytis entellus*) of Abu, Rajasthan. *Folia Primatologica* 22: 19–58.

Hrdy, S. B. 1977a. Infanticide as a primate reproductive strategy. *American Scientist* 65: 40–49.

Hrdy, S. B. 1977b. *The Langurs of Abu: Female and Male Strategies of Reproduction*. Cambridge, MA: Harvard University Press.

Hrdy, S. B. 1979. Infanticide among animals: a review, classification, and examination of the implications for the reproductive strategies of females. *Ethology and Sociobiology* 1: 13–40.

Hrdy, S. B. 2001. Mothers and others. *Natural History* **110**: 50–62.

Hrdy, S. B. & Hrdy, D. B. 1976. Hierarchical relations among female Hanuman langurs (Primates: Colobinae, *Presbytis entellus*). *Science* **193**: 913–915.

Hu, G. 2007. *Socioecology and behavioural flexibility of Francois' langur (*Trachypithecus francoisi*) in Mayanghe Nature Reserve, Southwest China.* PhD thesis, Australian National University, Canberra.

Hu, G. 2011. Dietary breadth and resource use of François' langur in a seasonal and disturbed habitat. *American Journal of Primatology* **73**: 1176–1187.

Hu, G., Dong, X., Wei, Y., Zhu, Y. & Duan, X. 2004. Evidence for a decline of François' langur *Trachypithecus françoisi* in Fusui Nature Reserve, south-west Guangxi, China. *Oryx* **38**: 48–54.

Hu, J. 1998 *Rhinopithecus roxellanae*. In Wang, S. (Ed.), *China Red Data Book of Endangered Animals: Mammalia*. Beijing: Science Press. Pp. 65–68.

Hu, J., Deng, Q., Yu, Z., Zhou, S. & Tian, Z. 1980. Research on the ecology and biology of the giant panda, golden monkey, and other rare species. *Journal of Nanchong Normal College* **2**: 1–39 (in Chinese with English abstract).

Hu, Y. M., Zhou, Z. X., Huang, Z. W. et al. 2017. A new record of the capped langur (*Trachypithecus pileatus*) in China. *Zoological Research* **38**: 203.

Huan, Z., Yao, Y., Yu, J. et al. 2020. Differences in the gut microbiota between Cercopithecinae and Colobinae in captivity. *Journal of Microbiology* **8**: 367–376.

Huang, C. & Li, Y. 2005. How does the white-headed langur (*Trachypithecus leucocephalus*) adapt locomotor behavior to its unique limestone habitat? *Primates* **46**: 261–167.

Huang, C., Li, Y., Zhou, Q. et al. 2008a. Karst habit fragmentation and the conservation of the white-headed langur (*Trachypithecus leucocephalus*) in China. *Primate Conservation* **23**: 133–139.

Huang, C., Wei, F., Li, M. & Li, Y. 2003. Sleeping cave selection, activity pattern and time budget of white-headed langurs. *International Journal of Primatology* **24**: 813–824.

Huang, C., Wei, F., Li, M., Quan, G. & Li, H. 2002. Current status and conservation of white-headed langur (*Trachypithecus leucocephalus*) in China. *Biological Conservation* **104**: 221–225.

Huang, C., Wu, H., Zhou, Q., Li, Y. & Cai, X. 2008b. Feeding strategy of François' langur and white-headed langur at Fusui, China. *American Journal of Primatology* **70**: 320–326.

Huang, C., Xue, Y., Wei, Y. & Li, Y. 2000. Habitat vegetation and selection of white-headed leaf monkey (*Trachypithecus leucocephalus*). *Acta Theriologica Sinica* **20**: 180–185.

Huang, C., Zhou, Q., Li, Y., Cai, X. & Wei, F. 2005. Activity rhythm and diurnal time budget of Francois langur (*Trachypithecus francoisi*) in Guangxi, China. *Acta Theriologica Sinica* **26**: 380–386.

Huang, C., Zhou, Q., Li, Y., Huang, Z. & Wei, X. 2015. Non-conceptive sexual behavior and its function in an unusually composed group of Francois langurs (*Trachypithecus francoisi*) in Guangxi, China. *Vietnamese Journal of Primatology* **2**: 29–38.

Huang, Z., Bian, K., Liu, Y. et al. 2017a. Male dispersal pattern in golden snub-nosed monkey (*Rhinopithecus roxellana*) in Qinling Mountains and its conservation implication. *Scientific Reports* **7**: 46217.

Huang, Z., Cui, L., Scott, M. B., Wang, S. & Xiao, W. 2012. Seasonality of reproduction of wild black-and-white snub-nosed monkeys (*Rhinopithecus bieti*) at Mt. Lasha, Yunnan, China. *Primates* **53**: 237–245.

Huang, Z., Huo, S., Yang, S., Cui, L. & Xiao, W. 2010. Leaf choice in black-and-white snub-nosed monkeys *Rhinopithecus bieti* is related to the physical and chemical properties of leaves. *Current Zoology* **56**: 643–649.

Huang, Z., Qi, X., Garber, P. A. et al. 2014. The use of camera traps to identify the set of scavengers preying on the carcass of a golden snub-nosed monkey (*Rhinopithecus roxellana*). *PLOS ONE* **9**.

Huang, Z., Scott, M. B., Li, Y. et al. 2017b. Black-and-white snub-nosed monkey (*Rhinopithecus bieti*) feeding behavior in a degraded forest fragment: clues to a stressed population. *Primates* **58**: 517–524.

Huang, Z., Yuana, P., Huang, H. et al. 2017c. Effect of habitat fragmentation on ranging behavior of white-headed langurs in limestone forests in Southwest China. *Primates* **58**: 423–434.

Huffman, M. A. 1997. Current evidence for self-medication in primates: a multidisciplinary perspective. *American Journal of Physical Anthropology: The Official Publication of the American Association of Physical Anthropologists* **104**: 171–200.

Hull, D. B. 1979. A craniometric study of the black and white colobus Illiger, 1811 (Primates: Cercopithecoidea). *American Journal of Physical Anthropology* **51**: 163–182.

Humle, T. & Hill, C. M. 2016. People-primate interactions: implications for primate conservation. In Wich, S. A. & Marshall, A. J. (Eds.), *An Introduction to Primate*

Conservation. Oxford: Oxford University Press. Pp. 219–240.

Humphrey, N. K. 1976. The social function of intellect. In Bateson, P. P. G. & Hinde, R. A. (Eds.), *Growing Points in Ethology*. Cambridge: Cambridge University Press. Pp. 303–317.

Huo, S. 2005. *Diet and habitat use of Rhinopithecus bieti at Mt Longma, Yunnan*. PhD thesis, Kunming Institute of Zoology, Kinming, China.

Hylander, W. L. 1975. Incisor size and diet in anthropoids with special reference to Cercopithecidae. *Science* **189**: 1095–1098.

Ikemeh, R., Oates, J. F. & Inaoyom, I. 2019. *Piliocolobus epieni. The IUCN Red List of Threatened Species 2019*: e.T41024A92656391. www.iucnredlist.org/.

Ikemeh, R. A. 2014. *Niger Delta Red Colobus Conservation Project in Bayelsa State: Assessing the Species' Population Status, Current Distribution, and Prevalent Threats in Order to Design an Effective Conservation Plan*. Unpublished report by the SW/ Niger Delta Forest Project, Abuja, Nigeria.

Ikemeh, R. A. 2015. Assessing the population status of the critically endangered niger delta red colobus (*Piliocolobus* epieni). *Primate Conservation* **29**: 87–96.

Ikemeh, R. A. & Oates, J. F. 2017. Niger Delta red colobus monkey, *Piliocolobus epieni* (Grubb and Powell, 1999). In Schwitzer, C., Mittermeier, R. A., Rylands, A. B. et al. (Eds.), *Primates in Peril: The World's 25 Most Endangered Primates 2016–2018*. Arlington, VA: IUCN SSC Primate Specialist Group, International Primatological Society, Conservation International, Bristol Zoological Society.

Immig, I. 1996. The rumen and hindgut as source of ruminant methanogenesis. *Environmental Monitoring and Assessment* **42**: 57–72.

International Tropical Timber Organization (ITTO). 2002. Guidelines for the Restoration, Management and Rehabilitation of Degraded and Secondary Tropical Forests (ITTO), Yokohama, Japan.

IPCC. 1992. *Climate Change: The IPCC 1990 and 1992 Assessments. Intergovernmental Panel on Climate Change*. Nairobi, Kenya: United National Environment Programme. 178 pp. www.ipcc.ch/report/climate-change-the-ipcc-1990-and-1992-assessments/.

IPCC. 2014. Climate Change 2014: Synthesis Report. Contribution of Working Groups I, II and III to the Fifth Assessment Report of the Intergovernmental Panel on Climate Change [Core Writing Team, R. K. Pachauri and L. A. Meyer (Eds.)]. IPPC, Geneva, Switzerland.

Isaac, N. J. B. & Cowlishaw, G. 2004. How species respond to multiple extinction threats. *Proceedings of the Royal Society B: Biological Sciences* **271**: 1135–1141.

Isbell, L. A. 1983. Daily ranging behaviour of red colobus (*Colobus badius tephrosceles*) in kibale forest, Uganda. *Folia Primatology* **41**: 34–48.

Isbell, L. A. 1991. Contest and scramble competition: Patterns of female aggression and ranging behavior among primates. *Behavioral Ecology* **2**: 143–155.

Isbell, L. A. 2004. Is there no place like home? Ecological bases of female dispersal and philopatry and their consequences for the formation of kin groups. In Chapais, B. & Berman, C. M. (Eds.), *Kinship and Behavior in Primates*. Oxford: Oxford University Press. Pp. 71–108.

Isbell, L. A. 2012. Re-evaluating the ecological constraints model with red colobus monkeys (*Procolobus rufomitratus tephrosceles*). *Behaviour* **149**: 493–529.

Isbell, L. A. & Pruetz, J. D. 1998. Differences between vervets (*Cercopithecus aethiops*) and patas monkeys (*Erythrocebus patas*) in agonistic interactions between adult females. *International Journal of Primatology* **19**: 837–855.

Isbell, L. A. & Van Vuren, D. 1996. Differential costs of locational and social dispersal and their consequences for female group-living primates. *Behaviour* **133**: 1–36.

Isbell, L. A. & Young, T. P. 1993. Social and ecological influences on activity budgets of vervet monkeys, and their implications for group living. *Behavioral Ecology and Sociobiology* **32**: 377–385.

Isbell, L. A. & Young, T. P. 2002. Ecological models of female social relationships in primates: similarities, disparities, and some directions for future clarity. *Behaviour* **139**: 177–202.

Isbell, L. A., Pruetz, J. D. & Young, T. P. 1998. Movements of vervets (*Cercopithecus aethiops*) and patas monkeys (*Erythrocebus patas*) as estimators of food resource size, density, and distribution. *Behavioral Ecology and Sociobiology* **42**: 123–133.

Ishaq, S. L. & Wright, A. D. 2014. High-throughput DNA sequencing of the ruminal bacteria from moose (*Alces alces*) in Vermont, Alaska, and Norway. *Microbial Ecology* **68**: 185–195.

Islam, M. A. & Husain, K. Z. 1982. A preliminary study on the ecology of the capped langur. *Folia Primatologica* **39**: 145–159.

Isler, K., Kirk, E. C., Miller, J. M. A. et al. 2008. Endocranial volumes of primate species: scaling analyses using a comprehensive and reliable data set. *Journal of Human Evolution* **55**: 967–978.

IUCN 2019/2020. *The IUCN Red List of Threatened Species. Version 2020-2.* www.iucnredlist.org/.

IUCN. 2012. *IUCN Red List Categories and Criteria: Version 3.1*, 2nd ed. Gland, Switzerland. https://portals.iucn.org/library/sites/library/files/documents/RL-2001-001-2nd.pdf.

IUCN/SSC. 2013. *Guidelines for Reintroductions and other Conservation Translocations.* Version 1.0. Gland, Switzerland: IUCN Species Survival Commission. 57 pp.

Iwamoto, M., Hasegawa, Y. & Koizumi A. 2005. A Pliocene colobine from the Nakatsu Group, Kanagawa, Japan. *Anthropological Science* **113**: 123–127.

Jablonski, N. G. 1998a. *The Natural History of the Doucs and Snub-Nosed Monkeys.* New Jersey: World Scientific. 382 pp.

Jablonski, N. G. 1998b. The evolution of the doucs and snub-nosed monkeys and the question of the phyletic unity of the odd-nosed colobines. In Jablonski, N. G. (Ed.), *The Natural History of the Doucs and Snub-nosed Monkeys.* Singapore: World Scientific. Pp. 13–52.

Jablonski, N. G. 2002. Fossil Old World monkeys: the late Neogene radiation. In Hartwig, W. C. (Ed.), *The Primate Fossil Record.* Cambridge: Cambridge University Press. Pp. 255–299.

Jablonski, N. G. & Frost, S. R. 2010. Chapter 31. Cercopithecoidea. In Werdelin, L. & Sanders W. J. (Eds.), *The Cenozoic Mammals of Africa.* Oakland: University of California Press. Pp. 393–428.

Jablonski, N. G. & Gu, Y. 1991. A reassessment of *Megamacaca lantianensis*, a large monkey from the Pleistocene of north-central China. *Journal of Human Evolution* **20**: 51–66.

Jablonski, N. G. & Peng, Y.-Z. 1993. The phylogenetic relationships and classification of the doucs and snub-nosed monkeys of China and Vietnam. *Folia Primatologica* **60**: 36–55.

Jablonski, N. G., Leakey, M. G., Ward, C. V. & Antón, M. 2008. Systematic paleontology of the large colobines. In Jablonski, N. G. & Leakey, M. G. (Eds.), *Koobi Fora Research Project. The Fossil Monkeys*, vol. 6. San Francisco: California Academy of Sciences. Pp. 31–102.

Jablonski, N. G., Su, D. F., Flynn, L. J. et al. 2014. The site of Shuitangba (Yunnan, China) preserves a unique, terminal Miocene fauna. *Journal of Vertebrate Paleontology.* **34**: 1251–1257.

Jablonski, N., Su, D., Kelly, J., Flynn, L. J. & Ji, X. 2011. The Mio-Pliocene colobine monkey, *Mesopithecus*, in China [Abstract]. *American Journal of Physical Anthropology* **144** (S52): 174.

Jack, K. M. & Fedigan, L. M. 2009. Female dispersal in a female-philopatric species, *Cebus capucinus. Behaviour* **146**: 471–497.

Janiak, M. C. 2016. Digestive enzymes of human and nonhuman primates. *Evolutionary Anthropology* **25**: 253–266.

Janmaat, K. R. L., Boesch, C., Byrne, R. et al. 2016. Spatio-temporal complexity of chimpanzee food: how cognitive adaptations can counteract the ephemeral nature of ripe fruit. *American Journal of Primatology* **78**: 626–645.

Janssen, D. 1994. *Morbidity and mortality of douc langurs (Pygathrix nemaeus) at the San Diego Zoo. AAZV*; Pittsburg, PA.

Janson, C. H. & Goldsmith, M. L. 1995. Predicting group size in primates: foraging costs and predation risks. *Behavioral Ecology* **6**: 326–336.

Janson, C. H. & van Schaik, C. P. 1988. Recognizing the many faces of primate food competition: methods. *Behaviour* **105**: 165–186.

Janson, C. H. & van Schaik, C. P. 2000. The behavioral ecology of infanticide by males. In van Schaik, C. P. & Janson, C. H. (Eds.), *Infanticide by Males and Its Implications.* Cambridge: Cambridge University Press. Pp. 469–494.

Janson, C. H. 1988. Intra-specific food competition and primate social structure: a synthesis. *Behaviour* **105**: 1–17.

Janzen, D. H. 1971. Seed predation by animals. *Annual Review of Ecology and Systematics* **2**: 465–492.

Jay, P. 1963. The Indian langur monkey (*Presbytis entellus*). In Southwick, C. H. (Ed.), *Primate Social Behavior.* Princeton, NJ: D. Van Nostrand. Pp. 114–123.

Jay, P. 1965. The common langur of North India. In DeVore, I. (Ed.), *Primate Behavior: Field Studies of Monkeys and Apes.* New York: Holt, Rinehart and Winston. Pp. 197–249.

Jay, P. C. 1962. Aspects of maternal behavior among langurs. *Annals of the New York Academy of Sciences* **102**: 468–476.

Jeffrey, S. M. 1979. The proboscis monkey: some preliminary observations. *Tigerpaper* **6**: 5–6.

Jenny, D. & Zuberbuhler, K. 2005. Hunting behaviour in west African forest leopards. *African Journal of Ecology* **43**: 197–200.

Jezek, Z., Arita, I., Mutombo, M. et al. 1986. Four generations of probable person-to-person transmission of human monkeypox. *American Journal of Epidemiology* 123: 1004–1012.

Ji, W., Zou, R., Shang, E. et al. 1998. Maintenance and breeding of snub-nosed monkeys (*Rhinopithecus bieti*) In Jablonski, N. (Ed.), *The Natural History of the Doucs and Snub-Nosed Monkeys*. Singapore: World Scientific Press. Pp. 323–335.

Jiang Z, Lian Y & Qin X. 2014. Rocky desertification in Southwest China: impacts, causes, and restoration. *Earth-Science Reviews* 132: 1–2.

Jin, T., Wang, D., Pan, W. & Yao, M. 2015. Nonmaternal infant handling in wild white-headed langurs (*Trachypithecus leucocephalus*). *International Journal of Primatology* 36: 269–287.

Jin, T., Wang, D., Zhao, Q. et al. 2009a. Social organization of white-headed langurs (*Trachypithecus leucocephalus*) in the Nongguan Karst Hills, Guangxi, China. *American Journal of Primatology* 71: 206–213.

Jin, T., Wang, D., Zhao, Q. et al. 2009b. Reproductive parameters of wild *Trachypithecus leucocephalus*: seasonality, infant mortality and interbirth interval. *American Journal of Primatology* 71: 558–566.

Johns, A. D. 1983. *Ecological effects of selective logging in a West Malaysian rainforest*. PhD thesis, University of Cambridge, Cambridge.

Johns, A. D. & Skorupa, J. P. 1987. Responses of rainforest primates to habitat disturbance: a review. *International Journal of Primatology* 8: 157–191.

Johns, A. G. & Johns, B. G. 1995. Tropical forest primates and logging: long-term coexistence?. *Oryx* 29: 205–211.

Johnson, C. A., Raubenheimer, D., Chapman, C. A. et al. 2017. Macronutrient balancing affects patch departure by guerezas (*Colobus guereza*). *American Journal of Primatology* 79: 1–9.

Johnson, C. A., Raubenheimer, D., Rothman, J. M., Clarke, D. & Swedell, L. 2013. 30 days in the life: daily nutrient balancing in a wild chacma baboon. *PLOS ONE* 8.

Johnson, J. 1984. The function of all-male trouping structure in the Nilgiri langur, *Presbytis johnii*. In Roonwal, M. L., Mohonot, S. M. & Rathore, N. S. (Eds.), *Current Primate Researches Jodhpur*. University of Jodhpur. P. 397.

Johnson, K. G., Wang, W., Reid, D. G. & Hu, J. 1993. Food habits of Asiatic leopards (*Panthera pardus fusea*) in Wolong Reserve, Sichuan, China. *Journal of Mammalogy* 74: 646–650.

Johnson, K. V.-A. & Foster, K. R. 2018. Why does the microbiome affect behaviour? *Nature Reviews Microbiology* 16: 647–655.

Jolly, C. J. 1970. The seed-eaters: a new model of hominid differentiation based on a baboon analogy. *Man* 5: 5–26.

Joppa, L. N. & Pfaff, A. 2009. High and far: biases in the location of protected areas. *PLOS ONE* 4: e8273.

Joseph, G. K. & Ramachandran, K. K. 2003. Distribution and demography of the Nilgiri langur (*Trachypithecus johnii*) in Silent Valley National Park and adjacent areas, Kerala, India. *Primate Conservation* 19: 78–82.

Jouffroy, F. K., Godinot, M. & Nakano, Y. 1991. Biometrical characteristics of primate hands. *Human Evolution* 6: 296–306.

Juste, J. B. & Fa, J. E. 1994. Biodiversity conservation in the Gulf of Guinea islands: taking stock and preparing action. *Biodiversity and Conservation* 3: 759–771.

Kaeslin, E., Redmond, I. & Dudley, N. 2012. *Wildlife in a Changing Climate*. FAO Forestry Paper 167. Rome, Italy: Food and Agriculture Organization. 124 pp.

Kaisala, D., Falay, P., Mande, C. et al. 2020. *Rediscovery of the Kisangani Red Colobus*. Report to Global Wildlife Conservation and the Frankfurt Zoological TL2 Project. www.bonoboincongo.com/wp-content/uploads/2020/03/2020-February-Kisangani-Red-Colobus-REPORT.pdf

Kalb, J. E., Jeager, M., Jolly, C. J. & Kana, B. 1982. Preliminary geology, palaeontology and paleoecology of a Sangoan site at Andalee, Middle Awash valley, Ethiopia. *Journal of Archaeological Science* 9: 349–363.

Kalbitzer, U. & Chapman, C. A. 2018. Primate responses to changing environments in the Anthropocene. In Kalbitzer, U. & Jack, K. M. (Eds.), *Primate Life Histories, Sex Roles, and Adaptability – Essays in Honour of Linda M. Fedigan*. New York: Springer.

Kalmykov, N. P. & Maschenko, E. N. 1992. The northernmost early Pliocene Cercopithecidae from Asia. *Paleontological Journal* 26: 178–181.

Kamilar, J. M. & Paciulli, L. 2008. Examining the extinction risk of specialized folivores: a comparative study of colobine monkeys. *American Journal of Primatology* 70: 816–827.

Kane, E. E. & McGraw, W. S. 2018. Effects of chimpanzee (*Pan troglodytes*) hunting seasonality and red colobus (*Piliocolobus badius*) association on diana monkeys (*Cercopithecus diana*) in Taï National Park, Côte d'Ivoire. *International Journal of Primatology* 39: 532–546.

Kankane, P. L. 1984. Studies on the Hanuman langur, *Presbytis entellus*, at the Madhav National Park,

Shivpuri (Madhya Pradesh, India). In Roonwal, M. L., Mohnot, S. M. & Rathore, N. S. (Eds.), *Current Primate Researches*. Jodhpur: University of Jodhpur. Pp. 23–31.

Kankane, P. L. 1988. Environmental factors and reproductive seasonality in the Indian langur, *Presbytis entellus*, on the Indian subcontinent. *Records of the Zoological Survey of India* 85: 19–35.

Kappeler, P. M. & van Schaik, C. P. 2002. Evolution of primate social systems. *International Journal of Primatology* 23: 707–740.

Karanth, K. K., Nichols, J. D. & Hines, J. E. 2010. Occurrence and distribution of Indian primates. *Biological Conservation* 143: 2891–2899.

Karanth, K. P. 2008. Primate numts and reticulate evolution of capped and golden leaf monkeys (Primates: Colobinae). *Journal of Biosciences* 33: 761–770.

Karanth, K. P. 2010. Molecular systematics and conservation of the langurs and leaf monkeys of South Asia. *Journal of Genetics* 89: 393.

Karanth, K. P., Singh, L., Collura, R. V. & Stewart, C.-B. 2008. Molecular phylogeny and biogeography of langurs and leaf monkeys of South Asia (Primates: Colobinae). *Molecular Phylogenetics and Evolution* 46: 683–694.

Karanth, P. K., Singh, L. & Stewart, C.-B. 2010. Mitochondrial and nuclear markers suggest Hanuman langur (Primates: Colobinae) polyphyly: implications for their species status. *Molecular Phylogenetics and Evolution* 54: 627–663.

Karere, G. M., Oguge, N. O., Kirathe, J. et al. 2004. Population sizes and distribution of primates in the lower tana river forests, Kenya. *International Journal of Primatology* 25: 351–365.

Kar-Gupta, K. & Kumar, A. 1994. Leaf chemistry and food selection by common langurs (*Presbytis entellus*) in Rajaji National Park, Uttar Pradesh, India. *International Journal of Primatology* 15: 75–93.

Kartikasari, S. N. 1986. *Studi populasi dan perilaku lutung (*Presbytis cristata, Raffles*) di Taman Nasional Baluran, Jawa Timor.* BSc thesis, Institut Pertanian Bogor, Bogor, Indonesia.

Kasanene, J. M. & Ross, E. A. 2008. Community benefits from long-term research programs: a case study from Kibale National Park, Uganda. In Wrangham, R. & Ross, E. (Eds.), *Science and Conservation in African Forests: The Benefits of Long-Term Research.* Cambridge: Cambridge University Press. Pp. 99–114.

Katoh, S., Beyene, Y., Itaya, T. et al. 2016. New geological and palaeontological age constraint for the gorilla-human lineage split. *Nature* 530: 215–218.

Kavana, T. S., Erinjery, J. J. & Singh, M. 2014. Male takeover and infanticide in Nilgiri langurs *Semnopithecus johnii* in the Western Ghats, India. *Folia Primatologica* 85: 164–177.

Kavana, T. S., Erinjery, J. J. & Singh, M. 2015a. Diet of Nilgiri langur *Semnopithecus johnii* inhabiting tropical montane shola in the Nilgiri Hills, South India. *Asian Primates Journal* 5: 3–11.

Kavana, T. S., Erinjery, J. J. & Singh, M. 2015b. Folivory as a constraint on social behaviour of langurs in South India. *Folia Primatologica* 86: 420–431.

Kavanagh, M. 1978. The social behaviour of doucs (*Pygathrix nemaeus nemaeus*) at San Diego Zoo. *Primates* 19: 101–114.

Kawabe, M. & Mano, T. 1972. Ecology and behavior of the wild proboscis monkey, *Nasalis larvatus* (Wurmb), in Sabah, Malaysia. *Primates* 13: 213–227.

Kawai, M., Dunbar, R. I. M., Ohsawa, H. & Mori, U. 1983. Social organization of gelada baboons: social units and definitions. *Primates* 24: 13–24.

Kawamura, S. & Megantara, E. N. 1986. Observation of primates in logged forest on Sipora Island, Mentawai. *Kyoto University Research Report of Studies on Asian Non-Human Primates* 5: 1–12.

Kawanishi, K. & Sunquist, M. E. 2008. Food habits and activity patterns of the Asiatic golden cat (*Catopuma temminckii*) and dhole (*Cuon alpinus*) in a primary rainforest of Peninsular Malaysia. *Mammal Study* 33: 173–177.

Kay, R. F. 1975. The functional adaptations of primate molar teeth. *American Journal of Physical Anthropology* 43: 195–216.

Kay, R. F. 1978. Molar structure and diet in extant cercopithecidae. In Butler, P. & Joysey, K. (Eds.), *Function and Evolution of Teeth.* New York: Academic Press. Pp. 309–339.

Kay, R. F. 1981. The Nut-Crackers – A New Theory of the Adaptations of the Ramapithecinae. *American Journal of Physical Anthropology* 55: 141–151.

Kay, R. F. & Hylander, W. L. 1978. The dental structure of mammalian folivores with special reference to primates and Phalangeroidea (Marsupialia). In Montgomery, G. G. (Ed.), *The Ecology of Arboreal Folivores.* Washington, DC: Smithsonian Institution Press. Pp. 173–191.

Kay, R. N. B. & Davies, A. G. 1994. Digestive physiology. In Davies, A. G. & Oates, J. F. (Eds.), *Colobine Monkeys: Their Ecology, Behaviour and Evolution.* Cambridge: Cambridge University Press. Pp. 229–249.

Kay, R. N. B., Hoppe, P. & Maloiy, G. M. O. 1976. Fermentative digestion of food in the colobus monkey *Colobus polykomos*. *Experientia* 32: 485–487.

Keon, D. B. & Muir, P. S. 2002. Growth of *Usnea longissima* across a variety of habitats in the Oregon Coast Range. *The Bryologist* 105: 233–242.

Khan, M. A., Kelley, J., Flynn, L. J., Babar, M. A. & Jablosnki, N. G. 2020. New fossils of *Mesopithecus* from Hasnot, Pakistan. *Journal of Human Evolution* 145: 102818.

Khan, M. A. R. 1984. Ecology and conservation of the common langur *Presbytis entellus* in Bangladesh. In Roonwal, M. L., Mohnot, S. M. & Rathore, N. S. (Eds.), *Current Primate Researches*. Jodhpur: University of Jodhpur. Pp. 33–39.

Khatun, U. H., Ahsan, M. F. & Røskaft, E. 2011. Feeding behaviour and ecology of the common langurs (*Semnopithecus entellus*) of Keshabpur in Bangladesh. In Røskaft, E. & Chivers, D. J. (Eds.), *Proceedings of the International Conference on Biodiversity, University of Chittagong*. Chittagong: University of Chittagong. Pp. 21–33.

Kibaja, M. 2014. Diet of the ashy red colobus (*Piliocolobus tephrosceles*) and crop-raiding in a forest-farm mosaic, Mbuzi, Rukwa region, Tanzania. *Primate Conservation* 28: 109–116.

Kim, J. W. & Thin, N. N. 1998. The vegetation of the CatBa National Park in Vietnam. *Korean Journal of Ecology* 21: 139–149.

Kim, Y., Ko, E., Lappan, S. et al. 2013. Changes in fecal estrogen levels and sexual behavior in captive Sichuan snub-nosed monkeys (*Rhinopithecus roxellana*) following a male replacement. *Zoo Biology* 32: 342–346.

King, A., Behie, A. M., Hon, N. & Rawson, B. 2016. Patterns of salt lick use by mammals and birds in northeastern Cambodia. *Cambodian Journal of Natural History* 1: 40–50.

King, J. 1999. Rescue and Translocation of Colobus Guereza Troops from Kipipiri to Elementaita. Unpublished report by Wakuluzu Colobus Trust, Diani, Kenya. 19 pp.

Kingdon, J. 1971. *East African Mammals – An Atlas of Evolution in Africa: Vol. 1. Primates*. London: Academic Press. 446 pp.

Kingdon, J. 1997. *The Kingdon Field Guide to African Mammals*, 1st ed. London: Academic Press.

Kingdon, J. 2015. *The Kingdon Field Guide to African Mammals*, 2nd ed. New York: Academic Press.

Kingdon, J. & Groves, C. P. 2013. Subfamily Colobinae. In Butynski, T. M., Kingdon, J. & Kalina, J. (Eds.), *Mammals of Africa: Vol. 2. Primates*. London: Bloomsbury. Pp. 93–95.

Kingston, J, Jacobs, B. F., Hill, A. & Deino, A. 2002. Stratigraphy, age and environments of the late Miocene Mpesida Beds, Tugen Hills, Kenya. *Journal of Human Evolution* 42: 95–116.

Kinzey, W. G. 1992. Dietary and dental adaptations in the Pitheciinae. *American Journal of Physical Anthropology* 88: 499–514.

Kirkpatrick, R. C. 1996. *Ecology and behavior of the Yunnan snub-nosed langur (*Rhinopithecus bieti*, Colobinae)*. PhD thesis, University of California, Davis.

Kirkpatrick, R. C. 1998. Ecology and behavior in snub-nosed and douc langurs. In Jablonski, N. G. (Ed.), *The Natural History of the Doucs and Snub-nosed Monkeys*. Singapore: World Scientific. Pp. 155–190.

Kirkpatrick, R. C. 1999. Colobine diet and social organization. In Dolhinow, P. & Fuentes, A. (Eds.), *The Nonhuman Primates*. London: Mayfield. Pp. 93–105.

Kirkpatrick, R. C. 2007. The Asian colobines: diversity among leaf-eating monkeys. In Campbell, C. J., Fuentes, A., Mackinnon, K. C. et al. (Eds.), *Primates in Perspective*. Oxford: Oxford University Press. Pp. 186–200.

Kirkpatrick, R. C. 2011. The Asian colobines: diversity among leaf-eating monkeys In Campbell, C. J., Fuentes, A., MacKinnon, K. C. et al. (Eds.), *Primates in Perspective*. New York: Oxford University Press. Pp. 189–202.

Kirkpatrick, R. C. & Grueter, C. C. 2010. Snub-nosed monkeys: multilevel societies across varied environments. *Evolutionary Anthropology* 19: 98–113.

Kirkpatrick, R. C. & Gu, H. J. 1999. Ecology and conservation of golden monkeys *Rhinopithecus roxellana* at Baihe Nature Reserve (Min Mountains, Sichuan). Unpublished Report to Sichuan Department of Forestry and The Zoological Society of San Diego.

Kirkpatrick, R. C. & Long, Y. 1994. Altitudinal ranging and terrestriality in the Yunnan snub-nosed monkey (*Rhinopithecus bieti*). *Folia Primatologica* 63: 102–106.

Kirkpatrick, R. C., Gu, H. & Zhou, X. 1999. A preliminary report on Sichuan snub-nosed monkeys (*Rhinopithecus roxellana*) at Baihe Nature Reserve. *Folia Primatologica* 70: 117–120.

Kirkpatrick, R. C., Long, Y. C., Zhong, T. & Xiao, L. 1998. Social organization and range use in the Yunnan snub-nosed monkey *Rhinopithecus bieti*. *International Journal of Primatology* **19**: 13–51.

Kirkpatrick, R. C., Zou, R., Dierenfeld, E. S. & Zhou, H. 2001. Digestion of selected foods by Yunnan snub-nosed monkey *Rhinopithecus bieti* (Colobinae). *American Journal of Physical Anthropology* **114**: 156–162.

Kitegile, A. S., Mtui, A. S. & Mwamende, K. 2021. Population and conservation status of endangered ashy red colobus in Ufipa Plateau: Updates 10 years after first report. *Tanzania Journal of Forestry and Nature Conservation* **90**: 83–96.

Kivai, S. M., Loyola, L. C., Wieczkowski, J. et al. 2019. Tana River red colobus *Piliocolobus rufomitratus* (Peters, 1879). In Schwitzer, C., Mittermeier, R. A., Rylands, A. B. et al. (Eds.), *Primates in Peril: The World's 25 Most Endangered Primates 2018–2020*. Washington, DC: IUCN/SSC Primate Specialist Group, International Primatological Society, Global Wildlife Conservation, and Bristol Zoological Society. Pp. 43–45. www.globalwildlife.org/wp-content/uploads/2019/10/Primates-in-Peril-2018-2020.pdf.

Klaus, A., Strube, C., Roper, K. M. et al. 2018. Fecal parasite risk in the endangered proboscis monkey is higher in an anthropogenically managed forest environment compared to a riparian rain forest in Sabah, Borneo. *PLoS ONE* **13**: e0195584.

Klaus, A., Zimmermann, E., Röper, K. M. et al. 2017. Co-infection patterns of intestinal parasites in arboreal primates (proboscis monkeys, *Nasalis larvatus*) in Borneo. *International Journal for Parasitology: Parasites and Wildlife* **6**: 320–329.

Knauf, S., Gogarten, J. F., Schuenemann, V. J. et al. 2018. Nonhuman primates across sub-saharan Africa are infected with the yaws bacterium treponema pallidum subsp. pertenue. *Emerging Microbes & Infections* **7**: 1–4.

Koda, H., Murai, T., Tuuga, A. et al. 2018. Nasalization by *Nasalis larvatus*: larger noses audiovisually advertise conspecifics in proboscis monkeys. *Science Advances* **4**: eaaq0250.

Kodikara, K. A., Mukherjee, N., Jayatissa, L. P., Dahdouh-Guebas, F. & Koedam, N. 2017. Have mangrove restoration projects worked? An in-depth study in Sri Lanka. *Restoration Ecology* **25**: 705–716.

Koenig, A. 2000. Competitive regimes in forest-dwelling Hanuman langur females (*Semnopithecus entellus*). *Behavioural Ecology and Sociobiology* **48**: 93–109.

Koenig, A. 2002. Competition for resources and its behavioral consequences among female primates. *International Journal of Primatology* **23**: 759–783.

Koenig, A. & Borries, C. 2001. Socioecology of Hanuman langurs: the story of their success. *Evolutionary Anthropology* **10**: 122–137.

Koenig, A. & Borries, C. 2006. The predictive power of socioecological models: a reconsideration of resource characteristics, agonism and dominance hierarchies. In Hohmann, G., Robbins, M. M. & Boesch, C. (Eds.), *Feeding Ecology in Apes and Other Primates*. Cambridge: Cambridge University Press. Pp. 263–284.

Koenig, A. & Borries, C. 2009. The lost dream of ecological determinism: time to say goodbye? . . . or a White Queen's proposal? *Evolutionary Anhropology* **18**: 166–174.

Koenig, A. & Borries, C. 2012. Social organization and male residence pattern in Phayre's leaf monkeys. In Kappelar, P. M. & Watts, D. (Eds.), *Long-Term Field Studies of Primates*. New York: Springer Press. Pp: 215–236.

Koenig, A., Beise, J., Chalise, M. K. & Ganzhorn, J. U. 1998. When females should contest for food – testing hypotheses about resource density, distribution, size, and quality with Hanuman langurs (*Presbytis entellus*). *Behavioral Ecology and Sociobiology* **42**: 225–237.

Koenig, A., Borries, C., Chalise, M. K. & Winkler, P. 1997. Ecology, nutrition, and timing of reproductive events in an Asian primate, the Hanuman langur (*Presbytis entellus*). *Journal of Zoology* **243**: 215–235.

Koenig, A., Larney, E., Lu, A. & Borries, C. 2004. Agonistic behavior and dominance relationships in female Phayre's leaf monkeys – preliminary results. *American Journal of Primatology* **64**: 351–357.

Koenig, A., Scarry, C. J., Wheeler, B. C. & Borries, C. 2013. Variation in grouping patterns, mating systems and social structure: what socio-ecological models attempt to explain. *Philosophical Transactions of the Royal Society B: Biological Sciences* **368**: 20120348.

Koh, L. P. & Ghazoul, J. 2008. Biofuels, biodiversity, and people: understanding the conflicts and finding opportunities. *Biological Conservation* **141**: 2450–2460.

Koh, L. P. & Ghazoul, J. 2010. Spatially explicit scenario analysis for reconciling agricultural expansion, forest protection, and carbon conservation in Indonesia. *Proceedings of the National Academy of Sciences* **107**: 11140–11144.

Kohda, M. 1985. Allomothering behaviour of New and Old World monkeys. *Primates* 26: 28–44.

Kohl, K. D., Miller, A. W., Marvin, J. E., Mackie, R. & Dearing, M. D. 2014a. Herbivorous rodents (*Neotoma* spp.) harbour abundant and active foregut microbiota. *Environmental Microbiology* 16: 2869–2878.

Kohl, K. D., Weiss, R. B., Cox, J., Dale, C. & Dearing, M. D. 2014b. Gut microbes of mammalian herbivores facilitate intake of plant toxins. *Ecology Letters* 17: 1238–1246.

Kohlbrugge, J. H. F. 1896. Bijdragen tot de natuurlijke geschiedenis van menschen en dieren IV. *Zoogdieren van den Tengger. Natuurkundig Tijdschrift voor Nederlandsch-Indië* 55: 261–298.

Koné, I. & Refisch, J. 2007. Can monkey behavior be used as an indicator for poaching pressure? a case study of the diana guenon (*Cercopithecus diana*) and the western red colobus (*Procolobus badius*) in the Taï National Park, Côte d'Ivoire. In McGraw, W. S., Zuberbühler, K. & Noë, R. (Eds.), *Monkeys of the Taï Forest*. Cambridge: Cambridge University Press. Pp. 257–298.

Koné, I., Lambert, J. E., Refisch, J. & Bakayoko, A. 2008. Primate seed dispersal and its potential role in maintaining useful tree species in the Taï region, Côte-d'Ivoire: implications for the conservation of forest fragments. *Tropical Conservation Science* 1: 293–306.

Kool, K. 1993. The diet and feeding behavior of the silver leaf monkey *Trachypithecus auratus sondaicus* in Indonesia. *International Journal of Primatology* 14: 667–700.

Kool, K. M. 1989. *Behavioural ecology of the silver leaf monkey,* Trachypithecus auratus sondaicus, *in the Pandangaran Nature Reserve, West Java, Indonesia.* PhD thesis, University of New South Wales, Sidney.

Kool, K. M. 1992. Food selection by the silver leaf monkey, *Trachypithecus auratus sondaicus*, in relation to plant chemistry. *Oecologia* 90: 527–533.

Korstjens, A. H. 2001. *The mob, the secret sorority, and the phantoms: an analysis of the socio-ecological strategies of the three colobines of Taï.* PhD thesis, Utrecht University, Utrecht, The Netherlands.

Korstjens, A. H. & Dunbar, R. I. M. 2007. Time constraints limit group sizes and distribution in red and black-and-white colobus monkeys. *International Journal of Primatology* 28: 551–575.

Korstjens, A. H. & Galat-Luong, A. 2013. *Colobus polykomos*. In Butynski, T. M., Kingdon, J. & Kalina, J. (Eds.), *Mammals of Africa: Vol. 2. Primates.* London: Bloomsbury. Pp. 100–103.

Korstjens, A. H. & Noë, R. 2004. Mating system of an exceptional primate, the olive colobus (*Procolobus verus*). *American Journal of Primatology* 62: 261–273.

Korstjens, A. H. & Schippers, E. P. 2003. Dispersal patterns among olive colobus in Tai National Park. *International Journal of Primatology* 24: 515–539.

Korstjens, A. H., Bergmann, K., Deffernez, C. et al. 2007a. How small-scale differences in food competition lead to different social systems in three closely related sympatric colobines. In McGraw, S., Zuberbuhler, K. & Noë, R. (Eds.), *The Monkeys of the Taï Forest, Ivory Coast: An African Primate Community*. Cambridge: Cambridge University Press. Pp. 72–108.

Korstjens, A. H., Hobeika, S., Beziers, P. & Heistermann, M. 2008. What *Procolobus* can tell us about the evolution of female sexual signals. *Primate Eye* 96 (special issue): 19.

Korstjens, A. H., Lehmann, J. & Dunbar, R. I. M. 2018. Time constraints do not limit group size in arboreal guenons but do explain community size and distribution patterns. *International Journal of Primatology* 39: 511–531.

Korstjens, A. H., Nijssen, E. C. & Noë, R. 2005. Intergroup relationships in western black-and-white colobus, *Colobus polykomos polykomos. International Journal of Primatology* 26: 1267–1289.

Korstjens, A. H., Schippers, E. P., Nijssen, E. C. et al. 2007b. The influence of food on the social organisation of three colobine species. In Noë, R., McGraw, S. & Zuberbühler, K. (Eds.), *Monkeys of the Taï Forest: An African Primate Community.* Cambridge: Cambridge University Press. Pp. 72–108.

Korstjens, A. H., Sterck, E. H. M. & Noe, R. 2002. How adaptive or phylogenetically inert is primate social behaviour? a test with two sympatric colobines. *Behaviour* 139: 203–225.

Kouassi, R. Y. W., McGraw, W. S., Yao, P. K. et al. 2015. Diversity and prevalence of gastrointestinal parasites in seven non-human primates of the Taï National Park, Côte d'Ivoire. *Parasite* 22: 1.

Koufos, G. D. 2019. Late Turolian *Mesopithecus* (Mammalia: Cercopithecidae) from Axios Valley (Macedonia, Greece): earliest presence of *M. monspessulanus* in Europe. *Comptes Rendus Palevol* 18: 1057–1072.

Koyabu, D. B. & Endo, H. 2009. Craniofacial variation and dietary adaptations of African colobines. *Journal of Human Evolution* 56: 525–536.

Krause, T., Nielsen, T., Guia-Diaz, L., Lehsten, V., Olsson, O. & Zelli, F. 2019. What future for primates?

Conservation struggles in the forests of Cross River State, Nigeria. *Sustainability Science* **14**: 1515–1529.

Krebs, C. J., Boutin, S., Boonstra, R. et al. 1995. Impact of food and predation on the snowshoe hare cycle. *Science* **269**: 1112–1115.

Kren, J. A. 1964. Observations on the habits of the proboscis monkey, *Nasalis larvatus* (Wurmb.), made in the Brunei Bay area, Borneo. *Zoologica* **49**: 183–192.

Krishnamani, R. & Mahaney, W. C. 2000. Geophagy among primates: adaptive significance and ecological consequences. *Animal Behaviour* **59**: 899–915.

Krüger, O., Affeldt, E., Brackmann, M. & Milhahn, K. 1998. Group size and composition of *Colobus guereza* in Kyambura Gorge, southwest Uganda, in relation to chimpanzee activity. *International Journal of Primatology* **19**: 287–297.

Krzton, A. 2011. Coordinated patrolling behavior of unrelated breeding males in the golden snub-nosed monkey (*Rhinopithecus roxellana*). *American Journal of Physical Anthropology* **144**: 193.

Kuchikura, Y. 1988. Efficiency and focus of blowpipe hunting among Semaq Beri hunter-gatherers of Peninsular Malaysia. *Human Ecology* **16**: 271–305.

Kuhn, H.-J. 1964. Zur Kenntnis Von Bau Und Funktion Des Magens Der Schlankaffen (Colobinae). *Folia Primatologica* **2**: 193–221.

Kuhn, H.-J. 1967. Zur Systematik der Cercopithecidae. In Starck, D., Schneider, R. & Kuhn, H.-J. (Eds.), *Neue Ergebnisse der Primatologie*. Stuttgart: Gustav Fischer. Pp. 25–46.

Kuhn, H.-J. 1972. On the perineal organ of male *Procolobus badius*. *Journal of Human Evolution* **1**: 371–376.

Kulcharoen, N. & Utara, Y. 2010. Reproduction of red-shanked douc langurs (*Pygathrix nemaeus*) at Dusit Zoo, Thailand. In Nadler, T., Rawson, B. M. & Van, N. T. (Eds.), *Conservation of Primates in Indochina*. Frankfurt Zoological Society and Conservation International, Hanoi. Pp. 179–184.

Kumar, A. & Solanki, G. S. 2008. Population status and conservation of capped langurs (*Trachypithecus pileatus*) in and around Pakke Wildlife Sanctuary, Arunachal Pradesh, India. *Primate Conservation* **23**: 97–105.

Kumar, A. & Solanki, G. S. 2014. Role of mother and allomothers in infant independence in capped langur *Trachypithecus pileatus*. *Journal of the Bombay Natural History Society* **111**: 3–9.

Kumar, A., Solanki, G. S. & Sharma, B. K. 2005. Observations on parturition and allomothering in wild capped langur (*Trachypithecus pileatus*). *Primates* **46**: 215–217.

Kumar, B. D., Sankar, M., Kumar, R. et al. 2018. Molecular Identification of Oesophagostomum spp. from Himalayan Grey Langur. *International Journal of Current Microbiology and Applied Sciences* **7**: 146–151.

Kummer, H. 1968. *Social Organization of Hamadryas Baboons: A Field Study*. Chicago: The University of Chicago Press.

Kümpel, N. F., Milner-Gulland, E. J., Rowcliffe, M. & Cowlishaw, G. 2008. Impact of gun-hunting on diurnal primates in continental Equatorial Guinea. *International Journal of Primatology* **29**: 1065–1082.

Kunimatsu, Y., Nakatsukasa, M., Sawada, Y. et al. 2007. A new Late Miocene great ape from Kenya and its implications for the origins of African great apes and humans. *Proceedings of the National Academy of Sciences of the United States of America* **104**: 19220–19225.

Kunimatsu, Y., Nakatsukasa, M., Sawada, Y. et al. 2016. A second hominoid species in the early Late Miocene fauna of Nakali (Kenya). *Anthropological Science* **124**: 75–83.

Kuraru, S. & King, J. 2019. Analysis of Land Cover Change in Ndera Community Conservancy, Tana River County, 2010–2018. Unpublished report by the Northern Rangeland Trust and Ndera Community Conservancy, Isiolo, Kenya. 7 pp.

Kurihara, Y. & Hanya G. 2017. Comparison of energy balance between two different-sized groups of Japanese macaques (*Macaca fuscata yakui*). *Primates* **58**: 413–422.

Ladner, J. T., Wiley, M. R., Beitzel, B. et al. 2016. A multicomponent animal virus isolated from mosquitoes. *Cell Host Microbe* **20**: 357–367.

Lakim, M. H. 2008 *Comparative behavioral ecology of sympatric* Presbytis rubicunda *and* Macaca fascicularis *in Tawau Hills Park, Sabah, Malaysia*. PhD thesis, Universiti Malaysia Sabah, Kota Kinabalu, Malaysia.

Lamb, D. 2010. *Regreening the Bare Hills: Tropical Forest Restoration in the Asia-Pacific Region*. Springer Science & Business Media.

Lambert, J. E. 1998. Primate digestion: interactions among anatomy, physiology, and feeding ecology. *Evolutionary Anthropology* **7**: 8–20.

Lambert, J. E. 2011. Primate nutritional ecology: feeding biology and diet at ecological and evolutionary scales. In Campbell, C., Fuentes, A., MacKinnon, K. C.

et al. (Eds.), *Primates in Perspective*, 2nd ed. New York: Oxford University Press. Pp. 512–522.

Lambert, J. E. & Rothman, J. M. 2015. Fallback foods, optimal diets, and nutritional targets: responses to varying food availability and quality. *Annual Review of Anthropology* **44**: 593–612.

Lammertink, M., Nijman, V. & Setiorini, U. 2003. Population size, Red List status and conservation of the Natuna leaf monkey *Presbytis natunae* endemic to the island of Bunguran, Indonesia. *Oryx* **37**: 472–479.

Lan, A. N. T., Dang, N. X., Huan, N. X. & Duc, N. A. 2014. Food choice of the Tonkin snub-nosed monkey *Rhinopithecus avunculus* (Dollman, 1912) in Khau Ca Species and Habitat Conservation, Ha Giang Province. *Tap Chi Sinh Hoc-Academia Journal of Biology* **36**: 179–188 (in Vietnamese with English abstract).

Langer, P. 1988. *The Mammalian Herbivore Stomach*. Stuttgart/New York: Gustav Fischer Verlag.

Langer, P. 2017. *Comparative Anatomy of the Gastrointestinal Tract in Eutheria: Taxonomy, Biogeography and Food. Vol I: Afrotheria, Xenarthra and Euarchontoglires*. Vol II: Laurasiatheria, general discussion. De Gruyter, Berlin.

Langer, P. & Clauss, M. 2018. Morphological adaptation of the eutherian gastrointestinal tract to diet. *Vertebrate Zoology* **68**: 237–252.

Larney, E. 2013. *The influence of genetic and social structure on reproduction in Phayre's leaf monkeys* (Trachypithecus phayrei crepusculus). PhD thesis, Stony Brook University, Stony Brook, NY.

Lauck, M., Hyeroba, D., Tumukunde, A. et al. 2011. Novel, divergent simian hemorrhagic fever viruses in a wild Ugandan red colobus monkey discovered using direct pyroseqeuncing. *PLOS ONE* **6**: e19056.

Lauck, M., Sibley, S. D., Hyeroba, D. et al. 2013a. Exceptional simian hemorrhagic fever virus diversity in a wild African primate community. *Journal of Virology* **87**: 688–691.

Lauck, M., Switzer, W. M., Sibley, S. D. et al. 2013b. Discovery and full genome characterization of two highly divergent simian simian immunodeficiency viruses infecting black-and-white colobus monkeys (*Colobus guereza*) in Kibale National Park, *Uganda. Retrovirology* **10**: 107.

Lauck, M., Sibley, S. D., Lara, J. et al. 2013c. A novel hepacivirus with an unusually long and intrinsically disordered NS5A protein in a wild Old World primate. *Journal of Virology* **87**: 8971–8981.

Launhardt, K., Borries, C., Hardt, C., Epplen, J. T. & Winkler, P. 2001. Paternity analysis of alternative male reproductive routes among the langurs (*Semnopithecus entellus*) of Ramnagar. *Animal Behaviour* **61**: 53–64.

Laurance, W. F., Goosem, M. & Laurance, S. W. 2009. Impacts of roads and linear clearings on tropical forests. *Trends Ecology & Evolution* **24**: 659–669.

Laurance, W. F., Sayer, J. & Cassman, K. G. 2014. Agricultural expansion and its impacts on tropical nature. *Trends in Ecology and Evolution* **29**: 107–116.

Laws, J. W. & Laws, J. V. H. 1984. Social interactions among adult male langurs (*Presbytis entellus*) at Rajaji Wildlife Sanctuary. *International Journal of Primatology* **5**: 31–49.

Lazaridis, G., Tsoukala, E., Rae, T. C. et al. 2018. *Mesopithecus pentelicus* from the Turolian locality of Kryopigi (Kassandra, Chalkidiki, Greece). *Journal of Human Evolution* **121**: 128–146.

Le, H. T., Hoang, D. M. & Covert, H. H. 2019. Diet of the Indochinese silvered langur (*Trachypithecus germaini*) in Kien Luong Karst area, Kien Giang Province. *American Journal of Primatology* **81**: e23041.

Le, H. T., Hoang, M. D. & Covert, H. 2015. The study in the diet of the Indochinese silvered langur (*Trachypithecus germaini* Milne-Edwards, 1876) in Kien Luong Karst Area, Kiengiang Province. *Journal of Biotechnology* **13**: 1185–1193.

Le, K. Q. 2014. *Positional behavior and support use of the Tonkin snub-nosed monkeys (*Rhinopithecus avunculus*) in Khau Ca Forest, Ha Giang Province, Vietnam*. PhD thesis, University of Colorado, Boulder.

Le, K. Q. & Covert, H. H. 2010. Another population of the Tonkin snub-nosed monkey (*Rhinopithecus avunculus*) discovered in Ha Giang Province, Vietnam. *Vietnamese Journal of Primatology* **4**: 19–25.

Le, K. Q., Covert, H. H. & Wright, B. W. 2006. Status of the critically endangered Tonkin snub-nosed monkey (*Rhinopithecus avunculus*) at Du Gia Nature Reserve, Ha Giang Province, Vietnam. *International Journal of Primatology* **27**(Suppl 1):Abstract #428.

Le, K. Q., Nguyen, A. D., Vu, A. T., Wright, B. W. & Covert, H. H. 2007. Diet of the Tonkin snub-nosed monkey (*Rhinopithecus avunculus*) in the Khau Ca area, Ha Giang Province, Northeastern Vietnam. *Vietnamese Journal of Primatology* **1**: 75–84.

Leakey, M. G. 1982. Extinct large colobines from the Plio-Pleistocene of Africa. *American Journal of Physical Anthropology* **58**: 153–172.

Leakey, M. G. 1987. Colobinae (Mammalia, Primates) from the Omo Valley, Ethiopia. In Les faunas Plio-Pleistocenes de la Basse Vallee de l'Omo (Ethiopie). Tome 3, Cercopithecidae de la Formation de Shungura: 148–169. Cahiers de Paleontologie, Travaux de Paleontologie Est-Africaine. Paris: Editions du CNRS

Leakey, M. G. & Delson, E. 1987. Fossil Cercopithecidae from the Laetolil Beds, Tanzania. In Leakey, M. D. & Harris, J. M. (Eds.), *The Pliocene Site of Laetoli, Northern Tanzania*. Oxford: Oxford University Press. Pp. 91–107.

Leakey, M. G. & Leakey, R. E. F. 1973. New large Pleistocene Colobinae (Mammalia, Primates) from East Africa. *Fossil Vertebrates of Africa* 3: 121–138.

Leakey, M. G., Teaford, M. F. & Ward, C. V. 2003. Cercopithecidae from Lothagam. In Leakey, M. G. & Harris, J. M. (Eds.), *Lothagam: The Dawn of Humanity in East Africa*. New York: Columbia University Press. Pp. 201–248.

Leakey, R. E. F. 1969. New Cercopithecidae from the Chemeron Beds of Lake Baringo, Kenya. *Fossil Vertebrates of Africa* 1: 53–69.

Leasor, H. C. & Macgregor, O. J. 2014. Proboscis monkey tourism: Can we make it 'ecotourism'? In Russon, A. E. & Wallis, J. (Eds.), *Primate Tourism: A Tool for Conservation?* Cambridge: Cambridge University Press. Pp. 56–75.

Lebatard, A., Bourlès, D. L., Duringer, P. et al. 2008. Cosmogenic nuclide dating of *Sahelanthropus tchadensis* and *Australopithecus bahrelghazali*: Mio-Pliocene hominids from Chad. *Proceedings of the National Academy of Sciences* **105**: 3226–3231.

Lebatard, A.-E., Bourlès, D. L., Braucher, R. et al. 2010. Application of the authigenic 10Be/9Be dating method to continental sediments: reconstruction of the Mio-Pleistocene sedimentary sequence in the early hominid fossiliferous areas of the northern Chad Basin. *Earth and Planetary Science Letters* **297**: 57–70.

Lechner-Doll, M., Kaske, M. & Engelhardt, W. V. 1991. Factors affecting the mean retention time of particles in the forestomach of ruminants and camelids. In Tsuda, T., Sasaki, Y. & Kawashima, R. (Eds.), *Physiological Aspects of Digestion and Metabolism in Ruminants*. San Diego, CA: Academic Press. Pp. 455–482.

Lee, S. Y., Dunn, R. J., Young, R. A. et al. 2006. Impact of urbanization on coastal wetland structure and function. *Austral Ecology* **31**: 149–163.

Leen, Y., Ruppert, N. & Resely, N. F. N. 2019. Activities, habitat use and diet of wild dusky langurs. *Journal of Sustainability Science and Management* **14**: 71–85.

Leendertz, S. A. J., Junglen, S., Hedemann, C. 2010. High prevalence, coinfection rate, and genetic diversity of retroviruses in wild red colobus monkeys (*Piliocolobus badius badius*) in Taï National Park, Côte d'Ivoire. *Journal of Virology* **84**: 7427–7436.

Leendertz, S. A. J., Locatelli, S., Boesch, C. et al. 2011. No evidence for transmission of sivwrc from western red colobus monkeys (*Piliocolobus badius badius*) to wild west African chimpanzees (*Pan troglodytes verus*) despite high exposure through hunting. *BMC Microbiology* **11**.

Lees, C., Rawson, B. M., Behie, A. M., Hendershott, R. & Leonard, N. 2014. Preliminary population viability analysis of the Critically Endangered Cat Ba langur (*Trachypithecus poliocephalus*). IUCN SSC Conservation Breeding Specialist Group, Fauna & Flora International, Hanoi.

Lehmann, J., Lee, P. & Dunbar, R. I. M. 2014. Unravelling the function of community-level organization. In Dunbar, R. I. M., Gamble, C. & Gowlett, J. A. J. (Eds.), *Lucy to Language: The Benchmark Papers*. Oxford: Oxford University Press. Pp. 245–276.

Leonard, N., Luan, M. S., Passaro, R. & Raffel, M. 2016. Current status of the Cat Ba Langur population: Numbers, population trend, and birth rates. *Abstracts of the International Primatological Society 2016 Meeting (August 2016, Chicago, IL, USA)*.

Leppä, M. M., Karonen, M., Tähtinen, P., Engström, M. T. & Salminen, J. P. 2018. Isolation of chemically well-defined semipreparative liquid chromatography fractions from complex mixtures of proanthocyanidin oligomers and polymers. *Journal of Chromatography A* **1576**: 67–79.

Leshem, A., Liwinski, T. & Elinav, E. 2020. Immune-microbiota interplay and colonization resistance in infection. *Molecular Cell* **78**: 597–613.

Leskes, A. & Acheson, N. H. 1971. Social organization of a free-ranging troop of black and white colobus monkeys (*Colobus abyssinicus*). In Kummer, H. (Ed.), *Proceedings of the Third International Congress of Primatology, Zurich 1970: Vol. 3. Behavior*. Basel: S. Karger. Pp. 22–31.

Lestari, N. S. & Erb, W. M. 2011. Identification and composition of feeding plants species of simakobu monkeys (*Simias concolor*) in northern Siberut, Mentawai Archipelago. *Widyariset* **14**: 323–332.

Levin, N. E. 2015. Environment and climate of early human evolution. *Annual Review of Earth and Planetary Sciences* **43**: 405–429.

Levin, N. E., Simpson, S. W., Quade, J. et al. in press. The 6-million-year record of ecological and environmental change at Gona, Afar Region, Ethiopia. In Reynolds, S. C. & Bobe, R. (Eds.), *African Paleoecology and Human Evolution*. Cambridge: Cambridge University Press.

Levin, N. E., Simpson, S. W., Quade, J., Cerling, T. E. & Frost, S. R. 2008. Herbivore enamel carbon isotopic composition and the environmental context of *Ardipithecus* at Gona, Ethiopia. In Quade, J. & Wynn, J. G. (Eds.), *The Geology of Early Humans in the Horn of Africa: Geological Society of America Special Paper 446*. Boulder, CO: Geological Society of America. Pp. 215–234.

Ley, R. E., Hamady, M., Lozupone, C. et al. 2008. Evolution of mammals and their gut microbes. *Science* **320**: 1647–1651.

Lhendup, S., Tshering, U. & Tenzin, J. 2018. Population structure and habitat use of golden langur (*Trachypithecus geei*) in Royal Manas National Park, Bhutan. *International Journal of Fauna and Biological Studies* **5**: 97–101.

Lhota, S., Scott, K. S. & Sha, J. C. M. 2019b. Primates in flooded forests of Borneo: opportunities and challenges for ecotourism as a conservation strategy. In Nowak, K., Barnett, A. A. & Matsuda, I. (Eds.), *Primates in Flooded Habitats: Ecology and Conservation*. Cambridge: Cambridge University Press. Pp. 331–339.

Lhota, S., Sha, J. C. M., Bernard, H. & Matsuda, I. 2019a. Proboscis monkey conservation: beyond the science. In Behie, A. M., Teichroeb, J. A. & Malone, N. M. (Eds.), *Primate Research and Conservation in the Anthropocene*. Cambridge: Cambridge University Press. Pp. 182–196.

Li, B. & Zhao, D. 2007. Copulation behavior within one-male groups of wild *Rhinopithecus roxellana* in the Qinling Mountains of China. *Primates* **48**: 190–196.

Li, B., Chen, C., Ji, W. & Ren, B. 2000. Seasonal home range changes of the Sichuan snub-nosed monkey (*Rhinopithecus roxellana*) in the Qinling Mountains of China. *Folia Primatologica* **71**: 375–386.

Li, B., Jia, Z., Pan, R. & Ren, B. 2003. Changes in distribution of the snub-nosed monkey in China. In Marsh, L. (Ed.), *Primates in Fragments: Ecology and Conservation*. New York: Kluwer Academic/Plenum. Pp. 29–51.

Li, B., Li, M., Li, J. et al. 2018. The primate extinction crisis in China: Immediate challenges and a way forward. *Biodiversity and Conservation* **27**: 3301–3327.

Li, B., Ren, B. & Gao, Y. 1999. A change in the summer home range of Sichuan snub-nosed monkeys in Yuhuangmiao, Qinling Mountains. *Folia Primatologica* **70**: 269–273.

Li, B. B., Li, H., Zhao, D., Zhang, Y. & Qi, X. 2006. Study on dominance hierarchy of the Sichuan snub-nosed monkey (*Rhinopithecus roxellana*) in Qinling Mountains. *Acta Theriologica Sinica* **26**: 18–25.

Li, D., Grueter, C. C., Ren, B. et al. 2013a. Distribution of sleeping sites of the Yunnan snub-nosed monkey (*Rhinopithecus bieti*) in the Samage Forest, China. *Integrative Zoology* **8**: 327–334.

Li, D., Grueter, C. C., Ren, B. et al. 2008. Ranging of *Rhinopithecus bieti* in the Samage Forest, *China. II. Use of land cover types and altitudes. International Journal of Primatology* **29**: 1147–1173.

Li, D., Grueter, C., Ren, B. et al. 2006. Characteristics of night-time sleeping places selected by golden monkeys (*Rhinopithecus bieti*) in the Samage Forest, Baima Snow Mountain Nature Reserve, China. *Integrative Zoology* **1**: 141–152.

Li, D., Ren, B., Grueter, C. C., Li, B. & Li, M. 2010a. Nocturnal sleeping habits of the Yunnan snub-nosed monkey in Xiangguqing, China. *American Journal of Primatology* **72**: 1092–1099.

Li, D., Ren, B., He, X. et al. 2011. Diet of *Rhinopithecus bieti* at Xiangguqing in Baimaxueshan National Nature Reserve. *Acta Theriologica Sinica* **31**: 338–346 (in Chinese with English abstract).

Li, D., Ren, B., Hu, J. et al. 2013b. Time budgets of *Rhinopithecus bieti* at Xiangguqing in the Baimaxueshan National Nature Reserve, Northwest Yunnan, China. *Acta Theriologica Sinica* **33**: 223–231.

Li, D., Ren, B., Hu, J. et al. 2014. Geophagy of Yunnan snub-nosed monkeys (*Rhinopithecus bieti*) at Xiangguqing in the Baimaxueshan Nature Reserve, China. *North-Western Journal of Zoology* **10**: 293–299.

Li, D., Ren, B., Li, B. & Li, M. 2010b. Range expansion as a response to incraesing group size in the Yunnan snub-nosed monkey. *Folia Primatologica* **81**: 315–329.

Li, D., Yuan, P., Krzton, A., Huang, C. & Zhou, Q. 2016. Dietary adaptation of white-headed langurs. *Mammalia* **80**: 153–162.

Li, G., Chen, Y., Sun, W. et al. 2014. Preliminary observation of population status and social organization of *Rhinopithecus strykeri* in Pianma

Town, Nujiang County, China. *Acta Theriologica Sinica* 34: 323–328 (in Chinese with English abstract).

Li, J., He, Y., Huang, Z. et al. 2014. Birth seasonality and pattern in black-and-white snub-nosed monkeys (*Rhinopithecus bieti*) at Mt. Lasha, Yunnan. *Zoological Research* 35: 474–484.

Li, T., Ren, B., Li, D., Zhu, P. & Li, M. 2013. Mothering style and infant behavioral development in Yunnan Snub-Nosed monkeys (*Rhinopithecus bieti*) in China. *International Journal of Primatology* 34: 681–695.

Li, Y. B., Huang, C. M., Ding, P., Tang, Z. & Wood C. 2007. Dramatic decline of François' langur *Trachypithecus francoisi* in Guangxi province, China. *Oryx* 41: 38–43.

Li, Yanhong, Li, D., Ren, B. et al. 2014. Differences in the activity budgets of Yunnan snub-nosed monkeys (*Rhinopithecus bieti*) by age-sex class at Xiangguqing in Baimaxueshan Nature Reserve, China. *Folia Primatologica* 85: 335–342.

Li, Yankuo, Jiang, Z. & Miao, T. 2013. Diet and its seasonality of golden snub-nosed monkeys (*Rhinopithecus roxellana*) in Qingmuchuan Nature Reserve, Shaanxi Province, China. *Acta Theriologica Sinica* 33: 246–257.

Li, Yankuo, Jiang, Z., Li, C. & Grueter, C. C. 2010. Effects of seasonal folivory and frugivory on ranging patterns in *Rhinopithecus roxellana*. *International Journal of Primatology* 31: 609–626.

Li, Yiming. 2001. The seasonal diet of the Sichuan snub-nosed monkey (*Rhinopithecus roxellana*) in Shennongjia Nature Reserve, China. *Folia Primatologica* 72: 40–43.

Li, Yiming. 2002. The seasonal daily travel in a group of Sichuan snub-nosed monkey (*Pygathrix roxellana*) in Shennongjia Nature Reserve, China. *Primates* 43: 271–276.

Li, Yiming. 2004. The effect of forest clear-cutting on habitat use in Sichuan snub-nosed monkey (*Rhinopithecus roxellana*) in Shennongjia Nature Reserve, China. *Primates* 45: 69–72.

Li, Yiming. 2006. Seasonal variation of diet and food availability in a group of Sichuan snub-nosed monkeys in Shennongjia Nature Reserve, China. *American Journal of Primatology* 68: 217–233.

Li, Yiming. 2007. Terrestriality and tree stratum use in a group of Sichuan snub-nosed monkeys. *Primates* 48: 197–207.

Li, Yiming. 2009. Activity budgets in a group of Sichuan snub-nosed monkeys in Shennongjia Nature Reserve, China. *Current Zoology* 55: 173–179.

Li, Yiming, Stanford, C. B. & Yang, Y. 2002. Winter feeding tree choice in Sichuan snub-nosed monkeys (*Rhinopithecus roxellanae*) in Shennongjia Nature Reserve, China. *International Journal of Primatology* 23: 657–675.

Li, Ying-Chun, Liu, F., He, X. Y. et al. 2015a. Social organization of Shortridge's capped langur (*Trachypithecus shortridgei*) at the Dulongjiang Valley in Yunnan, China. *Zoological Research* 36: 152–160.

Li, Yinhua, Li, B. & Tan, C. L. 2005. Behavioral development within one-year-old individuals of Sichuan snub-nosed monkeys *Rhinopithecus roxellana* in the Qinling Mountains. *Acta Zoologica Sinica* 51: 953–960.

Li, Youbang, Ding, P., Huang, C. & Lu, S. 2015b. Total tannin content of foods of François' langur in Fusui, Guangxi, China: Preliminary study. *Acta Ecologica Sinica* 35: 16–22.

Li, Youbang, Ding, P., Huang, C., Jiang, P. & Wood, C. 2009. Dietary response of a group of François' langur *Trachypithecus francoisi* in a fragmented habitat in the county of Fusui, China: Implications for conservation. *Wildlife Biology* 15: 137–146.

Li, Z. 2000. *The socioecology of white-headed langurs* (Presbytis leucocephalus) *and its implications for their conservation.* PhD thesis, University of Edinburgh, Edinburgh, UK.

Li, Z. & Rogers, M. E. 2004a. Social organization of white-headed langurs *Trachypithecus leucocephalus* in Fusui, China. *Folia Primatologica* 75: 97–100.

Li, Z. & Rogers, M. E. 2004b. Habitat quality and activity budgets of white-headed langurs in Fusui, China. *International Journal of Primatology* 25: 41–54.

Li, Z. & Rogers, M. E. 2005a. Are limestone hills a refuge or essential habitat for white-headed langurs in Fusui, China? *International Journal of Primatology* 26: 437–452.

Li, Z. & Rogers, M. E. 2005b. Habitat quality and range use of white-headed langurs in Fusui, China. *Folia Primatologica* 76: 185–195.

Li, Z. & Rogers, M. E. 2006. Food items consumed by white-headed langurs in Fusui, China. *International Journal of Primatology* 27: 1551–1567.

Li, Z., Wei, Y. & Rogers, E. 2003. Food choice of white-headed langurs in Fusui, China. *International Journal of Primatology* 24: 1189–1205.

Li, Z., Zhang, Z., Xu, C. et al. 2014. Bacteria and methanogens differ along the gastrointestinal tract of Chinese roe deer (*Capreolus pygargus*). *PLOS ONE* 9: e114513.

Liedigk, R., Thinh, V. N., Nadler, T., Walter, L. & Roos C. 2009. Evolutionary history and phylogenetic position of the Indochinese grey langur (*Trachypithecus crepusculus*). *Vietnamese Journal of Primatology* 1: 1–8.

Liedigk, R., Yang, M., Jablonski, N. G. et al. 2012. Evolutionary history of the odd-nosed monkeys and the phylogenetic position of the newly described Myanmar snub-nosed monkey *Rhinopithecus strykeri*. *PLOS ONE* 7: e37418.

Liégeois, F., Lafay, B., Formenty, P. et al. 2009. Full-length genome characterization of a novel simian immunodeficiency virus lineage (sivolc) from olive colobus (*Procolobus verus*) and new sivwrcpbb strains from western red colobus (*Piliocolobus badius badius*) from the Taï forest in ivory coast. *Journal of Virology* 83: 428–439.

Lindenfors, P., Fröberg, L. & Nunn, C. L. 2004. Females drive primate social evolution. *Proceedings of the Royal Society of London B* 271(Suppl 3): S101-S103.

Linder, J. M. & Oates, J. F. 2011. Differential impact of bushmeat hunting on monkey species and implications for primate conservation in Korup National Park, Cameroon. *Biological Conservation* 144: 738–745.

Linder, J. M., Cronin, D. T., Ting, N. et al. 2021. *Red Colobus (*Piliocolobus*) Conservation Action Plan 2021–2026. Gland, Switzerland*: IUCN.

Linder, J., Morgan, B. J., Abwe, E. E. et al. 2019. *Piliocolobus preussi. The IUCN Red List of Threatened Species* 2019: e.T41026A92633245. www.iucnredlist.org/.

Linnaeus, C. 1771. *Mantissa Plantarum Altera*, 6th ed. Stockholm.

Lippold, L. K. 1977. The douc langur: A time for conservation. In Prince Rainier HSH & Bourne, G. H. (Eds.), *Primate Conservation*. New York: Academic Press. pp. 513–537.

Lippold, L. K. 1998. Natural history of douc langurs. In Jablonski, N. (Ed.), *The Natural History of the Doucs and Snub-nosed Monkeys*. Singapore: World Scientific. Pp. 191–206.

Lippold, L. K. & Vu, N. T. 2008. The time is now: survival of the douc langurs of Son Tra, Vietnam. *Primate Conservation* 23: 1–5.

Liu, J. 2013. Forest sustainability in China and implications for a telecoupled world. *Asia and the Pacific Policy Studies* 1: 230–250.

Liu, Q., Chen, Y.-P., Maltby, L. & Ma, Q.-Y. 2015. Exposure of the endangered golden monkey (*Rhinopithecus roxellana*) to heavy metals: a comparison of wild and captive animals. *Environmental Science and Pollution Research* 22: 6713–6720.

Liu, X. 2012. *Behavioral ecology of the Sichuan snub-nosed monkey (*Rhinopithecus roxellana*) in Shennongjia, China*. PhD thesis, University of Southern California, Los Angeles.

Liu, X. N., Feng, Z. M., Jiang, L. G. et al. 2013. Rubber plantation and its relationship with topographical factors in the border region of China, Laos and Myanmar. *Journal of Geographical Sciences* 23: 1019–1040.

Liu, X., Fan, P., Che, R. et al. 2018. Fecal bacterial diversity of wild Sichuan snub-nosed monkeys (*Rhinopithecus roxellana*). *American Journal of Primatology* 80: e22753.

Liu, X., Stanford, C. B. & Li, Y. 2013a. Effect of group size on time budget of Sichuan snub-nosed monkeys (*Rhinopithecus roxellana*) in Shennongjia National Nature Reserve, China. *International Journal of Primatology* 34: 349–360.

Liu, X., Stanford, C. B., Yang, J., Yao, H. & Li, Y. 2013b. Foods eaten by the Sichuan snub-nosed monkey (*Rhinopithecus roxellana*) in Shennongjia National Nature Reserve, China, in relation to nutritional chemistry: *R. roxellana* diet and nutritional chemistry. *American Journal of Primatology* 75: 860–871.

Liu, Zehua & Zhao, Q. 2004. Sleeping sites of Rhinopithecus bieti at Mt. Fuhe, Yunnan. *Primates* 45: 241–248.

Liu, Zehua, Ding, W. & Grüter, C. C. 2004. Seasonal variation in ranging patterns of Yunnan snub-nosed monkeys *Rhinopithecus bieti* at Mt. Fuhe, China. *Acta Zoologica Sinica* 50: 691–696.

Liu, Zehua, Ding, W. & Grueter, C. C. 2007. Preliminary data on the social organization of black-and-white snub-nosed monkeys (*Rhinopithecus bieti*) at Tacheng, China. *Acta Theriologica Sinica* 27: 120–122.

Liu, Z., Huang, C., Zhou, Q. et al. 2013b. Genetic analysis of group composition and relatedness in white-headed langurs. *Integrative Zoology* 8: 410–416.

Liu, Z., Liu, G., Roos, C. et al. 2015. Implications of genetics and current protected areas for conservation of 5 endangered primates in China. *Conservation biology* 29: 1508–1517.

Liu, Z., Ren, B., Wei, F. et al. 2007. Phylogeography and population structure of the Yunnan snub-nosed monkey (*Rhinopithecus bieti*) inferred from mitochondrial control region DNA sequence analysis. *Molecular Ecology* **16**: 3334–3349.

Liu, Z., Ren, B., Wu, R. et al. 2009. The effect of landscape features on population genetic structure in Yunnan snub-nosed monkeys (*Rhinopithecus bieti*) implies an anthropogenic genetic discontinuity. *Molecular Ecology* **18**: 3831–3846.

Liu, Z., Wang, B., Nadler, T. et al. 2013. Relatively recent evolution of pelage coloration in Colobinae: phylogeny and phylogeography of three closely related langur species. *PLOS ONE* **8**: e61659.

Lloyd, E., Kreetiyutanont, K., Prabnasuk, J., Grassman, L. I., Jr. & Borries, C. 2006. Observation of Phayre's leaf monkeys mobbing a clouded leopard at Phu Khieo Wildlife Sanctuary (Thailand). *Mammalia* **70**: 158–159.

Locatelli, S., Lafay, B., Liegeois, F. et al. 2008a. Full molecular characterization of a simian immunodeficiency virus, sivwrcpbt from Temminck's red colobus (*Piliocolobus badius temminckii*) from Abuko nature reserve, the Gambia. *Virology* **376**: 90–100.

Locatelli, S., Liegeois, F., Lafay, B. et al. 2008b. Prevalence and genetic diversity of simian immunodeficiency virus infection in wild-living red colobus monkeys (*Piliocolobus badius badius*) from the Taï forest, Côte d'Ivoire. sivwrc in wild-living western red colobus monkeys. *Infection, Genetics and Evolution* **8**: 1–14.

Long, Y., Kirkpatrick, R., Zhong, T. & Xiao, L. 1994. Report on the distribution, population, and ecology of the Yunnan snub-nosed monkey (*Rhinopithecus bieti*). *Primates* **35**: 241–250.

Long, Y., Kirkpatrick, C., Zhong, T. & Xiao L. 1996. Status and conservation strategy of the Yunnan snub-nosed monkey. *Chinese Biodiversity* **4**: 145–152.

Long, Y., Momberg, F., Ma, J. et al. 2012. *Rhinopithecus strykeri* found in China! *American Journal of Primatology* **74**: 871–873.

Loomis, M. & Britt, J. 1983. *An Epizootic of Entamoeba Histolytica in Colobus Monkeys. AAZV*; Tampa, FL.

Loucks, C., Mascia, M. B., Maxwell, A. et al. 2009. Wildlife decline in Cambodia, 1953–2005: exploring the legacy of armed conflict. *Conservation Letters* **2**: 82–92.

Lowe, A. J. & Sturrock, G. 1998. Behaviour and diet of *Colobus angolensis palliatus* Peters, 1868, in relation to seasonality in a Tanzanian dry coastal forest. *Folia Primatologica* **69**: 121–128.

Lu, A., Beehner, J. C., Czekala, N. M. et al. 2011. Phytochemicals and reproductive function in wild female Phayre's leaf monkeys (*Trachypithecus phayrei crepusculus*). *Hormones and Behavior* **59**: 28–36.

Lu, A., Borries, C., Gustison, M. L., Larney, E. & Koenig, A. 2016. Age and reproductive status influence dominance in wild female Phayre's leaf monkeys. *Animal Behaviour* **117**: 145–153.

Lu, A., Koenig, A. & Borries, C. 2008. Formal submission, tolerance and socioecological models: a test with female Hanuman langurs. *Animal Behaviour* **76**: 415–428.

Lu, A., Koenig, A., Borries, C. & Caselli, A. 2013. Effects of age, reproductive state, and the number of competitors on the dominance dynamics of wild female Hanuman langurs. *Behaviour* **150**: 485–523.

Lu, J. & Li, B. 2006. Diurnal activity budgets of the Sichuan snub-nosed monkey (*Rhinopithecus roxellana*) in the Qinling Mountains of China. *Acta Theriologica Sinica* **26**: 26–32.

Lu, J., Zhao, D. & Li, B. 2007. Homosexual mounting within one all-male juvenile unit in wild Sichuan snub-nosed monkeys (*Rhinopithecus roxellana*). *Acta Theriologica Sinica* **27**: 14–17.

Lucas, P. W., Constantino, P. J. & Wood, B. A. 2008. Inferences regarding the diet of extinct hominins: structural and functional trends in dental and mandibular morphology within the hominin clade. *Journal of Anatomy* **4**: 486–500.

Lucas, P. W. & Teaford, M. F. 1994. Functional morphology of colobine teeth. In Davies, A. G. & Oates, J. F. (Eds.), *Colobine Monkeys: Their Ecology, Behaviour and Evolution.* Cambridge: Cambridge University Press. Pp. 173–203.

Lugano, S. D., Nyerere, K. A., Kariuki, W. K. et al. 2018. Gastrointestinal microbial flora in wild and captive olive baboons (*Papio anubis*). *American Journal of Infectious Diseases and Microbiology* **6**: 30–37.

Luiselli, L., Amori, G., Akani, G. C. & Eniang, E. A. 2015. Ecological diversity, community structure and conservation of Niger delta mammals. *Biodiversity and Conservation* **24**: 2809–2830.

Luong, T. H. 2014. Forest resources and forestry in Vietnam. *Journal of Vietnamese Environment* **2**: 171–177.

Lüpold, S., Simmons, L. W. & Grueter, C. C. 2019. Sexual ornaments but not weapons trade off against testes size in primates. *Proceedings of the Royal Society B* **286**: 20182542.

Lwanga, J. S., Struhsaker, T. T., Struhsaker, P. J., Butynski, T. M. & Mitani, J. C. 2011. Primate population dynamics over 32.9 years at Ngogo, Kibale National Park, Uganda. *American Journal of Primatology* **73**: 997–1011.

Lyngdoh, S., Gopi, G. V., Selvan, K. M. & Habib, B. 2014. Effect of interactions among ethnic communities, livestock and wild dogs (*Cuon alpinus*) in Arunachal Pradesh, India. *European Journal of Wildlife Research* **60**: 771–780.

Lyon, B. E. & Montgomerie, R. D. 1986. Delayed maturation in passerine birds: reliable signaling by subordinate males? *Evolution* **40**: 605–615.

Ma, C., Fan, P. F., Zhang, Z. Y. et al. 2017. Diet and feeding behavior of a group of 42 Phayre's langurs in a seasonal habitat in Mt. Gaoligong, Yunnan, China. *American Journal of Primatology* **79**: e22695.

Ma, C., Huang, Z., Zhao, X. et al. 2014. Distribution and conservation status of *Rhinopithecus strykeri* in China. *Primates* **55**: 377–382.

Ma, C., Luo, Z., Liu, C. et al. 2015. Population and conservation status of Indochinese gray langurs (*Trachypithecus crepusculus*) in the Wuliang Mountains, Jingdong, Yunnan, China. *International Journal of Primatology* **36**: 749–763.

Macdonald, D. W. 1982. Notes on the size and composition of groups of proboscis monkey, *Nasalis larvatus*. *Folia Primatologica* **37**: 95–98.

Machovsky-Capuska, G. E., Senior, A. M., Simpson, S. J. & Raubenheimer, D. 2016. The multidimensional nutritional niche. *Trends in Ecology & Evolution* **31**: 355–365.

Maciej, P., Ndao, I., Hammerschmidt, K. & Fischer, J. 2013a. Vocal communication in a complex multi-level society: constrained acoustic structure and flexible call usage in Guinea baboons. *Frontiers in Zoology* **10**: 58.

Maciej, P., Patzelt, A., Ndao, I., Hammerschmidt, K. & Fischer, J. 2013b. Social monitoring in a multilevel society: a playback study with male Guinea baboons. *Behavioral Ecology and Sociobiology* **67**: 61–68.

Mackie, R. I. 2002. Mutualistic fermentative digestion in the gastrointestinal tract: diversity and evolution. *Integrative and Comparative Biology* **42**: 319–326.

MacKinnon, J. R. & MacKinnon, K. S. 1980. Niche differentiation in a primate community. In Chivers, D. J. (Ed.), *Malayan Forest Primates: 10 Years of Study in Tropical Rainforest*. New York: Plenum Press. Pp. 167–190.

Maestripieri, D. 1994. Social structure, infant handling, and mothering styles in group-living Old World monkeys. *International Journal of Primatology* **15**: 531–553.

Maisels, F. 2020a. *Colobus angolensis* ssp. *angolensis*. *The IUCN Red List of Threatened Species 2020*. www.iucnredlist.org/.

Maisels, F. 2020b. *Colobus angolensis* ssp. *cordieri*. *The IUCN Red List of Threatened Species 2020*. www.iucnredlist.org/.

Maisels, F. 2020c. *Colobus angolensis* ssp. *cottoni*. *The IUCN Red List of Threatened Species 2020*. www.iucnredlist.org/.

Maisels, F. & Cronin, D. T. 2020b. *Colobus satanas*. *The IUCN Red List of Threatened Species 2020*. www.iucnredlist.org/.

Maisels, F. & Cronin, D. T. 2020a. *Colobus satanas*. *The IUCN Red List of Threatened Species 2020*: e.T5145A17944405.

Maisels, F. & Devreese, L. 2020. *Piliocolobus bouvieri* (amended version of 2019 assessment). *The IUCN Red List of Threatened Species 2020*: e.T18250A166600357. www.iucnredlist.org/.

Maisels, F. & Ting, N. 2020. *Piliocolobus semlikiensis*. *The IUCN Red List of Threatened Species 2020*: e.T92657343A92657454. www.iucnredlist.org/.

Maisels, F., Gauthierhion, A. & Gautier, J. P. 1994. Diets of two sympatric colobines in zaire: more evidence on seed-eating in forests on poor soils. *International Journal of Primatology* **15**: 681–701.

Maisels, F., Gautier, J.-P. & Bosefe, J. 1993. Attacks by crowned heagles (*Stephanoaetus coronatus*) on monkeys in Zaire. *Folia Primatologica* **61**: 157–159.

Majolo, B., de Bortoli Vizioli, A. & Schino, G. 2008. Costs and benefits of group living in primates: group size effects on behaviour and demography. *Animal Behaviour* **76**: 1235–1247.

Majumder, A., Parida, A., Sankar, K. & Qureshi, Q. 2011. Utilization of food plant species and abundance of Hanuman langurs (*Semnopithecus entellus*) in Pench Tiger Reserve, Madhya Pradesh, India. *TAPROBANICA* **2**: 105–108.

Mallott, E. K. & Amato, K. R. 2018. The microbial reproductive ecology of white-faced capuchins (*Cebus capucinus*). *American Journal of Primatology* **80**: e22896.

Mallott, E. K., Borries, C., Koenig, A., Amato, K. R. & Lu, A. 2020. Reproductive hormones mediate changes in the gut microbiome during pregnancy and lactation in phayre's leaf monkeys. *Scientific Reports* **10**: 1–9.

Mao, S. Y., Zhang, R. Y., Wang, D. S. & Zhu, W. Y. 2013. Impact of subactue ruminal acidosis (SARA) adaptation on rumen microbiota in dairy cattle using pyrosequencing. *Anaerobe* **24**: 12–19.

Markham, A. C. & Gesquiere, L. R. 2017. Costs and benefits of group living in primates: an energetic perspective. *Philosophical Transactions of the Royal Society B* **372**: 20160239.

Marler, P. 1969. *Colobus guereza*: territoriality and group composition. *Science* **163**: 93–95.

Marler, P. 1972. Vocalizations of East African monkeys II: black and white colobus. *Behaviour* **42**: 175–197.

Marsh, C. W. 1978. *Ecology and Social Organization of the Tana River Red Colobus, Colobus Badius Ruformitratus*. Bristol University Library.

Marsh, C. W. 1979a. Comparative aspects of social organization in the Tana River red colobus, *Colobus badius ruformitratus*. *Zeitschrift fur Tierpsychologie* **51**: 337–362.

Marsh, C. W. 1979b. Female transference and mate choice among tana river red colobus. *Nature* **281**: 568–569.

Marsh, C. W. 1981a. Ranging behaviour and its relation to diet selection in tana river red colobus (*Colobus badius* rufomitratus). *Journal of Zoology* **195**: 473–492.

Marsh, C. W. 1981b. Time budget of Tana River red colobus. *Folia Primatologica* **35**: 147–178.

Marsh, K. J., Wallis, I. R., Kulheim, C., Clark, R., Nicolle, D., Foley, W. J. & Salminen, J. P. 2020. New approaches to tannin analysis of leaves can be used to explain *in vitro* biological activities associated with herbivore defence. *New Phytologist* **225**: 488–498.

Marshall, A. J., Beaudrot, L. & Wittmer, H. U. 2014b. Responses of primates and other frugivorous vertebrates to plant resource variability over space and time at Gunung Palung National Park. *International Journal of Primatology* **35**: 1178–1201.

Marshall, A. R. 2007. *Disturbance in the Udzungwas: Responses of monkeys and trees to forest degradation*. PhD thesis, University of York, York, UK.

Marshall, A. R. & Leighton, M. 2006. How does food availability limit the population density of white-bearded gibbons? In Hohmann, G., Robbins, M. M. & Boesch, C. (Eds.), *Feeding Ecology in Apes and Other Primates: Ecological, Physical and Behavioral Aspects*. New York: Cambridge University Press. Pp. 313–335.

Marshall, A. R., Topp-Jørgensen, J. E., Brink, H. & Fanning, E. 2005. Monkey abundance and social structure in two high-elevation forest reserves in the Udzungwa mountains of Tanzania. *International Journal of Primatology* **26**: 127–145.

Marshall, F. B., Dobney, K., Denham, T. & Capriles, J. M. 2014a. Evaluating the roles of directed breeding and gene flow in animal domestication. *Proceedings of the National Academy of Sciences* **111**: 6153–6158.

Matsubayashi, H., Lagan, P., Majalap, N. et al. 2007. Importance of natural licks for the mammals in Bornean inland tropical rain forests. *Ecological Research* **22**: 742–748.

Matsuda Goodwin, R., Gonedelé Bi, S., Nobimè, G. et al. 2020. *Colobus vellerosus*. *The IUCN Red List of Threatened Species 2019*: e.T5146A17944551.

Matsuda, I., Abram, N. K., Stark, D. J. et al. 2020b. Population dynamics of the proboscis monkey *Nasalis larvatus* in the Lower Kinabatangan, Sabah, Borneo, Malaysia. *Oryx* **54**: 583–590.

Matsuda, I., Bernard, H., Tuuga, A. et al. 2017a. Fecal nutrients suggest diets of higher fiber levels in free-ranging than in captive proboscis monkeys (*Nasalis larvatus*). *Frontiers of Veterinary Science* **4**: 246.

Matsuda, I., Chapman, C. A. & Clauss, M. 2019a. Colobine forestomach anatomy and diet. *Journal of Morphology* **280**: 1608–1616.

Matsuda, I., Chapman, C. A., Shi Physilia, C. Y., Mun Sha, J. C. & Clauss, M. 2017b. Primate resting postures: constraints by foregut fermentation? *Physiological and Biochemical Zoology* **90**: 383–391.

Matsuda, I., Clauss, M., Tuuga, A., Sugau, J., Hanya, G., Yumoto, T., Bernard, H. & Hummel, J. 2017c. Factors affecting leaf selection by foregut-fermenting proboscis monkeys: new insight from *in vitro* digestibility and toughness of leaves. *Scientific Reports* **7**: 42774.

Matsuda, I., Espinosa-Gomez, F. C., Ortmann, S. et al. 2019b. Retention marker excretion suggests incomplete digesta mixing across the order primates. *Physiology Behaviour* **208**: 112558.

Matsuda, I., Ihobe, H., Tashiro, Y. et al. 2020a. The diet and feeding behavior of the black-and-white colobus (*Colobus guereza*) in the Kalinzu Forest, Uganda. *Primates* **61**: 473–484.

Matsuda, I., Kubo, T., Tuuga, A. & Higashi, S. 2010a. A Bayesian analysis of the temporal change of local density of proboscis monkeys: Implications for environmental effects on a multilevel society. *American Journal of Physical Anthropology* **142**: 235–245.

Matsuda, I., Murai, T., Clauss, M. et al. 2011a. Regurgitation and remastication in the foregut-fermenting proboscis monkey (*Nasalis larvatus*). *Biology Letters* **7**: 786–789.

Matsuda, I., Nakabayashi, M., Otani, Y. et al. 2019c. Comparison of plant diversity and phenology of riverine and mangrove forests with those of the dryland forest in Sabah, Borneo, Malaysia. In Barnett, A. A., Nowak, K. & Matsuda, I. (Eds.), *Primates in Flooded Habitats: Ecology and Conservation*. Cambridge: Cambridge University Press. Pp. 15–28.

Matsuda, I., Sha, J. C., Ortmann, S. et al. 2015. Excretion patterns of solute and different-sized particle passage markers in foregut-fermenting proboscis monkey (*Nasalis larvatus*) do not indicate an adaptation for rumination. *Physiology and Behaviour* **149**: 45–52.

Matsuda, I., Stark, D. J., Saldivar, D. A. R. et al. 2020c. Large male proboscis monkeys have larger noses but smaller canines. *Communications Biology* 3: 1–7.

Matsuda, I., Tuuga, A. & Bernard, H. 2011b. Riverine refuging by proboscis monkeys (*Nasalis larvatus*) and sympatric primates: Implications for adaptive benefits of the riverine habitat. *Mammalian Biology* **76**: 165–171.

Matsuda, I., Tuuga, A. & Higashi, S. 2008b. Clouded leopard (*Neofelis diardi*) predation on proboscis monkeys (*Nasalis larvatus*) in Sabah, Malaysia. *Primates* **49**: 227–231.

Matsuda, I., Tuuga, A. & Higashi, S. 2009a. The feeding ecology and activity budget of proboscis monkeys. *American Journal of Primatology* **71**: 478–492.

Matsuda, I., Tuuga, A. & Higashi, S. 2009b. Ranging behavior of proboscis monkeys in a riverine forest with special reference to ranging in inland forest. *International Journal of Primatology* **30**: 313–325.

Matsuda, I., Tuuga, A. & Higashi, S. 2010b. Effects of water level on sleeping-site selection and inter-group association in proboscis monkeys: why do they sleep alone inland on flooded days? *Ecological Research* **25**: 475–482.

Matsuda, I., Tuuga, A., Akiyama, Y. & Higashi, S. 2008a. Selection of river crossing location and sleeping site by proboscis monkeys (*Nasalis larvatus*) in Sabah, Malaysia. *American Journal of Primatology* **70**: 1097–1101.

Matsuda, I., Tuuga, A., Bernard, H. & Furuichi, T. 2012a. Inter-individual relationships in proboscis monkeys: a preliminary comparison with other non-human primates. *Primates* **53**: 13–23.

Matsuda, I., Tuuga, A., Bernard, H., Sugau, J. & Hanya, G. 2013. Leaf selection by two Bornean colobine monkeys in relation to plant chemistry and abundance. *Scientific Reports* 3: 1–6.

Matsuda, I., Tuuga, A., Hashimoto, C. et al. 2014. Faecal particle size in free-ranging primates supports a 'rumination' strategy in the proboscis monkey (*Nasalis larvatus*). *Oecologia* **174**: 1127–1137.

Matsuda, I., Zhang, P., Swedell, L., Mori, U., Tuuga, A., Bernard, H. & Sueur, C. 2012b. Comparisons of intraunit relationships in nonhuman primates living in multilevel social systems. *International Journal of Primatology* **33**: 1038–1053.

Mayfroidt, P. & Lambin, E. F. 2008. Forest transition in Vietnam and its environmental impact. *Global Change Biology* **14**: 1319–1336.

Mayhew, M., Cramer, J. D., Fenton, L., Dittrich, A. & Armstrong, R. 2020. A new hotspot for Temminck's red colobus (*Piliocolobus badius temminckii*) in The Gambia: the feasibility of a community approach to conservation. *Primate Conservation* **34**: 129–141.

Maynard Smith, J. M. & Price, G. R. 1973. The logic of animal conflict. *Nature* **246**: 15–18.

Mazumder, M. K. 2014. Diversity, habitat preferences, and conservation of the primates of Southern Assam, India: The story of a primate paradise. *Journal of Asia-Pacific Biodiversity* **7**: 347–354.

Mbora, D. N. M. & Allen, L. 2011. The Tana Forests'People for Conservation and Conservation for People's Initiative'. Unpublished report to the Mohamed bin Zayed Species Conservation Fund, Abu Dhabi, UAE.

Mbora, D. N. M. & McGrew, W. C. 2002. Extra-group sexual consortship in the Tana river red colobus (*Procolobus rufomitratus*)? *Folia Primatologica* **73**: 210–213.

Mbora, D. N. M. & McPeek, M. A. 2009. Host density and human activities mediate increased parasite prevalence and richness in primates threatened by habitat loss and fragmentation. *Journal of Animal Ecology* **78**: 210–218.

Mbora, D. N. M. & McPeek, M. A. 2010. Endangered species in small habitat patches can possess high genetic diversity: the case of the Tana River red colobus and mangabey. *Conservation Genetics* **11**: 1725–1735.

Mbora, D. N. M. & Meikle, D. B. 2004. The value of unprotected habitat in conserving the critically endangered tana river red colobus (*Procolobus* rufomitratus). *Biological Conservation* **120**: 91–99.

McCann, C. 1928. Notes on the common Indian langur (*Pithecus entellus*). *Journal of the Bombay Natural History Society* **33**: 192–194.

McCann, C. 1933. Observations on some of the Indian langurs. *Journal of the Bombay Natural History Society* 36: 618–628.

McClure, H. E. 1964. Some observations of primates in climax dipterocarp forest near Kuala Lumpur, Malaya. *Primates* 5: 39–58.

McComb, K. & Semple, S. 2005. Coevolution of vocal communication and sociality in primates. *Biology Letters* 1: 381–385.

McCord, A. I., Chapman, C. A., Weny, G. et al. 2013. Fecal microbiomes of non-human primates in western Uganda reveal species-specific communities largely resistant to habitat perturbation. *American Journal of Primatology* 76: 347–354.

McDougal, I. & Feibel, C. S. 2003. Numberical age control for the Miocene-Pliocene succession at Lothagam, a hominoid-bearing sequence in the northern Kenya Rift. In Leakey, M. G. & Harris, J. M. (Eds.), *Lothagam: The Dawn of Humanity in East Africa*. New York: Columbia University Press. Pp. 43–64.

McGraw, W. S. 1998a. Comparative locomotion and habitat use of six monkeys in the Taï forest, ivory coast. *American Journal of Primatology* 46: 229–250.

McGraw, W. S. 1998b. Posture and support use of Old World monkeys (Cercopithecidae): the influence of foraging strategies, activity patterns, and the spatial distribution of preferred food items. *American Journal of Primatology* 46: 229–250.

McGraw, W. S. 2005. Update on the search for miss Waldron's red colobus monkey. *International Journal of Primatology* 26: 605–619.

McGraw, W. S. 2007. Vulnerability and conservation of the Taï monkey fauna. In Noë, R., McGraw, S. & Zuberbühler, K. (Eds.), *Monkeys of the Taï Forest: An African Primate Community*. Cambridge: Cambridge University Press. Pp. 290–316.

McGraw, W. S. 2016. King colobus, *Colobus polykomos*. In Rowe, N. & Myers, M. (Eds.), *All the World's Primates*. Charlestown, RI: Pogonias Press. Pp. 527–528.

McGraw, W. S. & Bshary, R. 2002. Association of terrestrial mangabeys (*Cercocebus atys*) with arboreal monkeys: experimental evidence for the effects of reduced ground predator pressure on habitat use. *International Journal of Primatology* 23: 311–325.

McGraw, W. S. & Zuberbühler, K. 2007. The monkeys of the Taï Forest: an introduction. In McGraw, W. S., Zuberbühler, K. & Noë, R. (Eds.), *Monkeys of the Taï Forest: An African Primate Community*. Cambridge: Cambridge University Press. Pp. 1–48.

McGraw, W. S. & Zuberbuhler, K. 2008. Socioecology, predation, and cognition in a community of West African monkeys. *Evolutionary Anthropology* 17: 254–266.

McGraw, W. S., Cooke, C. & Shultz, S. 2006. Primate remains from African crowned eagle (*Stephanoaetus coronatus*) nests in Ivory Coast's Taï Forest: implications for primate predation and early hominid taphonomy in south Africa. *American Journal of Physical Anthropology* 131: 151–165.

McGraw, W. S., Gonedelé Bi, S. & Oates, J. F. 2020a. *Piliocolobus badius* ssp. *badius*. *The IUCN Red List of Threatened Species 2020*: e.T40009A92646161. www.iucnredlist.org/.

McGraw, W. S., Minhós, T., Bersacola, E. et al. 2020b. *Piliocolobus badius*. *The IUCN Red List of Threatened Species 2020*: e.T161247840A161259430. www .iucnredlist.org/.

McGraw, W. S., van Casteren, A., Kane, E., Geissler, E., Burrows, B. & Daegling, D. J. 2016. Feeding and oral processing behaviors of two colobine monkeys in Taï Forest, Ivory Coast. *Journal of Human Evolution* 98: 90–102.

McGrosky, A., Meloro, C., Navarrete, A., Heldstab, S. A., Kitchener, A. C., Isler, K. & Clauss, M. 2019. Gross intestinal morphometry and allometry in primates. *American Journal of Primatology* 81: e23035.

McKee, J. K., von Mayer, A. & Kuykendall, K. L. 2011. New species of Cercopithecoides from Haasgat, North West Province, South Africa. *Journal of Human Evolution* 60: 83–93.

McKenna, J. J. 1979. The evolution of allomothering behavior among colobine monkeys: function and opportunism in evolution. *American Anthropologist* 81: 818–840.

McKey, D. B. 1978. Soils, vegetation, and seed-eating by black colobus monkeys. In Montgomery, G. G. (Ed.), *The Ecology of Arboreal Folivores*. Washington, DC: Smithsonian Institution Press. Pp. 423–437.

McKey, D. B. 1979. *Plant chemical defenses and the feeding and ranging behavior of colobus monkeys in African rainforests*. PhD thesis, University of Michigan, Ann Arbor.

McKey, D. B. & Waterman, P. G. 1982. Ranging behavior of a group of black colobus (*Colobus satanas*) in the Douala-Edea Reserve, Cameroon. *Folia Primatologica* 39: 264–304.

McKey, D. B., Gartlan, J. S., Waterman, P. G. & Choo, G. M. 1981. Food selection by black colobus monkeys (*Colobus satanas*) in relation to plant chemistry. *Biological Journal of the Linnean Society* 16: 115–146.

McLennan, M. R., Spagnoletti, N. & Hockings, K. J. 2017. The implications of primate behavioral flexibility for sustainable human-primate coexistence in anthropogenic habitats. *International Journal of Primatology* 38: 105–121.

McNab, B. K. 2002. *The Physiological Ecology of Vertebrates: A View from Energetics*. Ithaca, NY: Cornell University Press.

McNeely, J. A., Whitten, A., Whitten, J. & House, A. 1980. *Saving Siberut: A Conservation Master Plan*. WWF-IUCN Indonesia Programme, Bogor.

Md-Zain, B. M. 2001. *Molecular systematics of the genus* Presbytis. PhD thesis, Columbia University, New York.

Md-Zain, B. M. & Chng, C. E. 2011. The activity patterns of a group of Cantor' dusky leaf monkeys (*Trachypithecus obscurus halonifer*). *International Journal of Zoological Research* 7: 59–67.

Md-Zain, B. M. & Ruslin, F. 2012. Nilai-nilai murni dalam system kekeluargaan lutong kelabu (*Trachypithecus cristatus*). *Jurnal Hadhari* 4: 103–128.

Md-Zain, B. M., Morales, J. C., Hasan, M. N. et al. 2008. Is *Presbytis* a distinct monophyletic genus: inferences from mitochondrial DNA sequences. *Asian Primates Journal* 1: 26–35.

Medhi, R., Chetry, D., Bhattacharjee, P. C. & Patiri, B. N. 2004. Status of *Trachypithecus geei* in a rubber plantation in western Assam, India. *International Journal of Primatology* 25: 1331–1337.

Medway, L. 1970. Breeding of the silvered leaf monkey, *Presbytis cristata*, in Malaya. *Journal of Mammalogy* 51: 630–632.

Meena, A. K., Sharma, G. & Rajpurohit, L. S. 2015. Recent case of resident male replacement followed by infanticide in uni-male bisexual troop of Hanuman langur (*Semnopithecus entellus*) in Jodhpur (India). *Journal of Global Biosciences* 4: 3373–3378.

Megantara, E. N. 1989a. Ecology, behavior and sociality of *Presbytis femoralis* in East Central Sumatra. In Ehara, A. & Kawamura, S. (Eds.), *Comparative Primate Monographs* No. 2. Institute of Ecology, University of Padjadjaran. Pp. 171–301.

Megantara, E. N. 1989b. *Ecology, behavior and sociality of* Presbytis femoralis *in Eastcentral Sumatra*. PhD thesis, University of Padjadjaran, Padjadjaran, Indonesia.

Meijaard, E. 2016. The role of multifunctional landscapes in primate conservation. In Wich, S. A. & Marshall, A. J. (Eds.), *An Introduction to Primate Conservation*. Oxford: Oxford University Press. Pp. 205–218.

Meijaard, E. & Nijman, V. 2000. Distribution and conservation of the proboscis monkey (*Nasalis larvatus*) in Kalimantan, Indonesia. *Biological Conservation* 92: 15–24.

Meijaard, E. & Nijman, V. 2003. Primate hotspots on Borneo: predictive value for general biodiversity and the effects of taxonomy. *Conservation Biology* 17: 725–732.

Meijaard, E., Nijman, V. & Supriatna, J. 2008. *Nasalis larvatus*. The IUCN Red List of Threatened Species *2008*: e.T14352A4434312.

Meikle, W. E. 1987. Fossil Cercopithecidae from the Sahabi Formation. In Boaz, N. T., Arnauti, A. E., Gaziry, A. W. et al. (Eds.), *Neogene Paleontology and Geology of Sahabi*. New York: Alan R. Liss. Pp. 119–127.

Ménard, N. & Vallet, D. 1997. Behavioral responses of Barbary macaques (*Macaca sylvanus*) to variations in environmental conditions in Algeria. *American Journal of Primatology* 43: 285–304.

Mendoza, S. P., Reeder, D. M. & Mason, W. A. 2002. Nature of proximate mechanisms underlying primate social systems: simplicity and redundancy. *Evolutionary Anthropology* 11: 112–116.

Menzies, J. I. 1970. An eastward extension to the known range of the olive colobus monkey (*Colobus verus*, Van Beneden). *Journal of the West African Science Association* 15: 83–84.

Merceron, G., Koufos, G. D. & Valentin, X. 2009. Feeding habits of the first European colobine, *Mesopithecus* (Mammalia, Primates): evidence from a comparative dental microwear analysis with modern cercopithecids. *Geodiversitas* 31: 865–878.

Meyer, D., Momberg, F., Matauschek, C. et al. 2017. Conservation status of the Myanmar or black snub-nosed monkey *Rhinopithecus strykeri*. Fauna & Flora International, Yangon, Myanmar; Institute of Eastern-Himalaya Biodiversity Research, Dali, China; and German Primate Center, Göttingen.

Meyer, D., Rinaldi, I. D., Ramlee, H, Perwitasari-Farajallah, D., Hodges J. K. & Roos, C. 2011. Mitochondrial phylogeny of leaf monkeys (genus *Presbytis*, Eschscholtz, 1821) with implications for taxonomy and conservation. *Molecular Phylogenetics and Evolution* 59: 311.319.

Miettinen, J., Shi, C. & Liew, S. C. 2011. Deforestation rates in insular Southeast Asia between 2000 and 2010. *Global Change Biology* 17: 2261–2270.

Miles, L., Newton, A. C., DeFries, R. S., Ravilious, C., May, I., Blyth, S., Kapos, V. & Gordon, J. E. 2006. A global overview of the conservation status of tropical dry forests. *Journal of Biogeography* 33: 491–505.

Milich, K. M., Bahr, J. M., Stumpf, R. M. & Chapman, C. A. 2014a. Timing is everything: expanding the cost of sexual attraction hypothesis. *Animal Behaviour* 88: 219–224.

Milich, K. M., Stumpf, R. M., Chambers, J. M. & Chapman, C. A. 2014b. Female red colobus monkeys maintain their densities through flexible feeding strategies in logged forests in Kibale National Park, Uganda. *American Journal of Physical Anthropology* 154: 52–60.

Miller, A. 2019. *Social organisation and ecological basis for supergroup formation in Rwenzori colobus.* PhD thesis, The University of Western Australia, Perth.

Miller, A., Judge, D. S., Uwingeneye, G. et al. 2020b. Feeding competition inferred from patch depletion in a supergroup of Rwenzori black-and-white colobus monkeys (*Colobus angolensis ruwenzorii*) in Rwanda. *Behaviour* 157: 731–760.

Miller, A., Judge, D., Uwingeneye, G., Ndayishimiye, D. & Grueter, C. C. 2020a. Diet and use of fallback foods by Rwenzori black-and-white colobus (*Colobus angolensis ruwenzorii*) in Rwanda: implications for Supergroup Formation. *International Journal of Primatology* 41: 434–457.

Miller, A., Uddin, S., Judge, D. S. et al. 2020c. Spatiotemporal association patterns in a supergroup of Rwenzori black-and-white colobus (*Colobus angolensis ruwenzorii*) are consistent with a multilevel society. *American Journal of Primatology* 82: e23127.

Miller, C. T. & Paciulli, L. M. 2002. Patterns of lateralized hand use in an arboreal primate, *Simias concolor. American Journal of Primatology* 56: 231–236.

Miller, E. R., Benefit, B. R., McCrossin, M. L. et al. 2009. Systematics of early and middle Miocene Old World monkeys. *Journal of Human Evolution* 57: 195–211.

Miller, G. S. 1903. Seventy new Malayan mammals. *Smithsonian Miscellaneous Collections* 45: 1–73.

Miller, L. E. 1998. Fatal attack among wedge-capped capuchins. *Folia Primatologica* 69: 89–92.

Milne-Edwards, A. 1871. Note sur une nouvelle espece de semnopitheque provenant de la Cochinchine. *Nouvelles Annales du Muséum d'Histoire Naturelle, Paris* 6: 7–9.

Milne-Edwards, A. & de Pousargues, E. 1898. *Le rhinopithèque de la vallée du haut Mékong* (*Rhinopithecus bieti*, A. M.-E.). Paris: Masson.

Milner-Gulland, E. J. & Bennett, E. L. & SCB. 2003. Wild meat: the bigger picture. *Trends in Ecology and Evolution* 18: 351–357.

Milton, K. 1979. Factors influencing leaf choice by howler monkeys: a test of some hypotheses of food selection by generalist herbivores. *American Naturalist* 114: 362–378.

Milton, K. 1980. The *foraging strategy of howler monkeys.* PhD thesis, Columbia University, New York.

Milton, K. 1982. Dietary quality and demographic regulation in a howler monkey populations. In Leigh, E. G., Rand, A. S. & Windsor, D. M. (Eds.), *The Ecology of a Tropical Forest.* Washington, DC: Smithsonian Institution Press. Pp. 273–289.

Milton, K. 1996. Effects of bot fly (*Alouattamyia baeri*) parasitism on a free-ranging howler (*Alouatta palliata*) population in Panama. *Journal of Zoology* 239: 39–63.

Milton, K. 1998. Physiological ecology of howlers (*Alouatta*): energetic and digestive considerations and comparison with the colobinae. *International Journal of Primatology* 19: 513–548.

Milton, K. 1999. Nutritional characteristics of wild primate foods: do the diets of our closest living relatives have lessons for us?. *Nutrition* 15: 488–498.

Milton, K., Giacalone, J., Wright, S. J. & Stockmayer, G. 2005. Do frugivore population fluctuations reflect fruit production? Evidence from Panama. In *Tropical Fruits and Frugivores.* New York: Springer. Pp. 5–35.

Minhas, R. A., Ahmed, K. B., Awan, M. S. & Dar, N. I. 2010a. Habitat utilization and feeding biology of Himalayan grey langur (*Semnopithecus entellus ajex*) in Machiara National Park, Azad Kashmir, Pakistan. *Zoological Research* 31: 177–188.

Minhas, R. A., Ahmed, K. B., Awan, M. S. & Dar, N. I. 2010b. Social organization and reproductive biology of Himalayan grey langur (*Semnopithecus entellus ajex*) in Machiara National Park, Azad Kashmir (Pakistan). *Pakistan Journal of Zoology* 42: 143–156.

Minhas, R. A., Ali, U., Awan, M. S. et al. 2013. Ranging and foraging of Himalayan grey langurs (*Semnopithecus ajax*) in Machiara National Park, Pakistan. *Primates* 54: 147–152.

Minhós, T., Chikhi, L., Sousa, C., Vicente, L. M., da Silva, M. F., Heller, R., Casanova, C. & Bruford, M. W. 2016. Genetic consequences of human forest exploitation in two colobus monkeys in guinea bissau. *Biological Conservation* 194: 194–208.

Minhós, T., Ferreira da Silva, M. J., Bersacola, E., Galat, G., Galat-Luong, A., Mayhew, M. & Starin, E. D. 2020. *Piliocolobus badius* ssp. *temminckii. The IUCN Red List of Threatened Species 2020*: e. T18247A92648587. www.iucnredlist.org/.

Minhós, T., Sousa, C., Vicente, L. M. & Bruford, M. W. 2015. Kinship and intragroup social dynamics in two sympatric African colobus species. *International Journal of Primatology* 36: 871–886.

Mitani, J. C. & Rodman P. S. 1979. Territoriality: the relation of ranging pattern and home range size to defendability, with an analysis of territoriality among primate species. *Behavioral Ecology and Sociobiology* 5: 241–251.

Mitani, J. C. & Watts, D. P. 1999. Demographic influences on the hunting behaviour of chimpanzees. *American Journal of Physical Anthropology* 109: 439–454.

Mitani, J. C. & Watts, D. P. 1999. Demographic influences on the hunting behavior of chimpanzees. *American Journal of Physical Anthropology* 109: 439–454.

Mitani, J. C. & Watts, D. P. 2001. Why do chimpanzees hunt and share meat? *Animal Behaviour* 61: 915–924.

Mitani, J. C., Gros-Louis, J. & Manson, J. H. 1996. Number of males in primate groups: comparative tests of competing hypotheses. *American Journal of Primatology* 38: 315–332.

Mitani, J. C., Sanders, W. J., Lwanga, J. S. & Windfelder, T. L. 2001. Predatory behavior of crowned hawk-eagles (*Stephanoaetus coronatus*) in Kibale National Park, Uganda. *Behavioral Ecology and Sociobiology* 49: 187–195.

Mitani, J. C., Sanders, W. J., Lwanga, J. S. & Windfelder, T. L. 2001. Predatory behavior of crowned hawk-eagles (*Stephanoaetus coronatus*) in Kibale National Park, Uganda. *Behavioral Ecology and Sociobiology* 49(2): 187–195.

Mitani, J. C., Struhsaker, T. T. & Lwanga, J. S. 2000. Primate community dynamics in old growth forest over 23.5 years at Ngogo, Kibale National Park, Uganda: implications for conservation and census methods. *International Journal of Primatology* 21: 269–286.

Mitani, J. C., Watts, D. P. & Muller, M. N. 2002. Recent developments in the study of wild chimpanzee behaviour. *Evolutionary Anthropology* 11: 9–25.

Mitani, M. & Watanabe, K. 2009. The situation of the Pangandaran Nature Reserve in West Java, Indonesia in 2008, with special reference to vegetation and the population dynamics of primates. *Primate Research* 25: 5–13.

Mitani, M. 1990. A note on the present situation of the primate fauna found from south-eastern Cameroon. *Primates* 30: 307–323.

Mitchell, A. H. 1994. *Ecology of Hose's langur* (Presbytis hosei) *in logged and unlogged dipterocarp forest of northeast Borneo*. PhD thesis, Yale University, New Haven, CT.

Mitchell, C. L., Boinski, S. & van Schaik, C. P. 1991. Competitive regimes and female bonding in two species of squirrel monkeys (*Saimiri oerstedi* and *S. sciureus*). *Behavioral Ecology and Sociobiology* 28: 55–60.

Mitchell, R. M. 1977. *Accounts of Nepalese mammals and analysis of the host-ectoparasite data by computer techniques*. PhD thesis, University of Iowa, Ames.

Mittermeier, R. A. & Cheney, D. L. 1987. Conservation of primates and their habitats. In Cheney, D. L., Seyfarth, R. M., Wrangham, R. W. et al. (Eds.), *Primate Societies Smuts, B.B.* Chicago: University of Chicago Press. Pp. 477–490.

Mittermeier, R. A., Robles-Gil, P., Hoffmann, M. et al. 2004. *Hotspots revisited: Earth's biologically richest and most endangered ecoregions*. CEMEX, Mexico City, Mexico. 390 pp.

Mittermeier, R. A., Rylands, A. B. & Wilson, D. E. 2013. *Handbook of the Mammals of the World: Vol. 3. Primates*. Barcelona: Lynx Edicions. 951 pp.

Mittermeier, R. A., Rylands, A. B., Schwitzer, C. et al. 2012. *Primates in Peril: The World's 25 Most Endangered Primates 2010–2012*. Arlington, VA: IUCN/SSC Primate Specialist Group. 40 pp. www.researchgate.net/publication/312535824_Primates_in_Peril_The_World's_25_Most_Endangered_Primates_2010-2012.

Mittermeier, R. A., Wallis, J., Rylands, A. B. et al. 2009. *Primates in Peril: The World's 25 Most Endangered Primates 2008–2010*. Arlington, VA: IUCN/SSC Primate Specialist Group. 84 pp. https://portals.iucn.org/library/sites/library/files/documents/2009-067.pdf.

Mittra, E. S., Fuentes, A. & McGrew, W. C. 1997. Lack of hand preference in wild Hanuman langurs (*Presbytis entellus*). *American Journal of Physical Anthropology* 103: 455–461.

Miyamoto, M. M., Allen, J. M., Gogarten, J. F. & Chapman, C. A. 2013. Microsatellite DNA suggests that group size affects sex-biased dispersal patterns in red colobus monkeys. *American Journal of Primatology* **75**: 478–490.

Moeller, A. H., Peeters, M., Ndjango, J. B., Li, Y., Hahn, B. H. & Ochman, H. 2013. Sympatric chimpanzees and gorillas harbor convergent gut microbial communities. *Genome Research* **23**: 1715–1720.

Moffat, D. & Lindén, O. 1995. Perception and reality: assessing priorities for sustainable development in the Niger Delta, AMBIO. *Journal of Human Environment* **24**: 527–538.

Mohnot, S. 1971a. Ecology and behaviour of the hanuman langur, *Presbytis entellus* (Primates: Cercopithecidae) invading fields, gardens and orchards around Jodhpur, western India. *Tropical Ecology* **12**: 237–249.

Mohnot, S. M. 1971b. Some aspects of social changes and infant-killing in the Hanuman langur, *Presbytis entellus* (Primates: Cercopithecidae), in western India. *Mammalia* **35**: 175–198.

Moilanen, J., Sinkkonen, J. & Salminen, J. 2013. Characterization of bioactive plant ellagitannins by chromatographic, spectroscopic and mass spectrometric methods. *Chemoecology* **23**: 165–179.

Moinde-Fockler, N. N., Oguge, N. O., Karere, G. M., Otina, D. & Suleman, M. A. 2007. Human and natural impacts on forests along lower tana river, Kenya: implications towards conservation and management of endemic primate species and their habitat. *Biodiversity and Conservation* **16**: 1161–1173.

Møller, A. P. 1988. Ejaculate quality, testes size and sperm competition in primates. *Journal of Human Evolution* **17**: 479–488.

Monaco, E. T., Borries, C., Nikolei, J. et al. 2019. The function of geophagy in Nepal gray langurs: sodium acquisition rather than detoxification or prevention of acidosis. *American Journal of Physical Anthropology* **168**: 170–179.

Mongabay. 2020. *Afrotropical realm: total Africa.* https://rainforests.mongabay.com/deforestation/archive/Total_Africa.htm.

Monge, A. G. 2016. *The socioecology, and the effects of human activity on it, of the Annamese silvered langur (*Trachypithecus margarita*) in Northeastern Cambodia.* PhD thesis, Australian National University, Canberra.

Moore, R. S., Nekaris, K. A. I. & Eschmann, C. 2010. Habitat use by western purple-faced langurs *Trachypithecus vetulus nestor* (Colobinae) in a fragmented suburban landscape. *Endangered Species Research* **12**: 227–234.

Morales, J. D., Disotell, T. R. & Melnick, D. J. 1999. Molecular phylogenetic studies of nonhuman primates. In Dolhinow, P. & Fuentes, A. (Eds.), *The Nonhuman Primates.* London: Mayfield. Pp. 18–28.

Moreno-Black, G. S. & Bent, E. F. 1982. Secondary compounds in the diet of *Colobus angolensis*. *African Journal of Ecology* **20**: 29–36.

Moreno-Black, G. S. & Maples, W. R. 1977. Differential habitat utilization of four Cercopithecidae in a Kenyan forest. *Folia Primatologica* **27**: 85–107.

Morra, W., Hearn, G. & Buck. A. J. 2009. The market for bushmeat: *Colobus satanas* on Bioko Island. *Ecological Economics* **68**: 2619–2626.

Mowry, C. B., Decker, B. S. & Shure, D. J. 1996. The role of phytochemistry in dietary choices of Tana River red colobus monkeys (*Procolobus badius rufomitratus*). *International Journal of Primatology* **17**: 63–84.

Mturi, F. A. 1991. *The feeding ecology and behavior of the red colobus monkey (*Colobus badius kirkii*).* PhD thesis, University of Dar es Salaam, Dar es Salaam, Tanzania.

Mturi, F. A. 1993. Ecology of the Zanzibar red colobus monkey, *Colobus badius kirkii* (Gray, 1968), in comparison with other red colobines. In Lovett, J. C. & Wasser, S. K. (Eds.), *Biogeography and Ecology of the Rain Forests of Eastern Africa.* Cambridge: Cambridge University Press. Pp. 243–266.

Muckenhirn, N. A. 1973. *Leaf-eaters and their predator in Ceylon: ecological roles of gray langurs,* Presbytis entellus, *and leopards.* PhD thesis, University of Maryland, College Park.

Muegge, B. D., Kuczynski, J., Knights, D. et al. 2011. Diet drives convergence in gut microbiome functions across mammalian phylogeny and within humans. *Science* **332**: 970–974.

Mugatha, S. M., Ogutu, J. O., Cords, M. & Maitima, J. M. 2007. Dynamics of male residence and female oestrus during a breeding season of blue monkeys in the Kakamega Forest, Kenya. *African Journal of Ecology* **45**: 49–54.

Mukherjee, R. P. 1978. Further observations on the golden langur (*Presbytis geei* Khajuria, 1956), with a note to capped langur (*Presbytis pileatus* Blyth, 1843) of Assam. *Primates* **19**: 737–747.

Mukherjee, R. P. 1982. Notes on Barbe's leaf monkey *Presbytis barbei* Blyth. *Journal of the Bombay Natural History Society* **79**: 184–185.

Mukherjee, R. P. 2018. Status, conservation and management of non-human primates in India: an overview. *Environment and Sociobiology* **15**: 83–88.

Mukherjee, R. P. & Saha, S. S. 1974. The golden langurs (*Presbytis geei* KHAJURIA, 1956) of Assam. *Primates* **15**: 327–340.

Müller, D. W. H., Caton, J., Codron, D. et al. 2011. Phylogenetic constraints on digesta separation: variation in fluid throughput in the digestive tract in mammalian herbivores. *Comparative Biochemistry and Physiology A* **160**: 207–220.

Müller, D. W., Codron, D., Meloro, C. et al. 2013. Assessing the Jarman-Bell Principle: Scaling of intake, digestibility, retention time and gut fill with body mass in mammalian herbivores. *Comparative Biochemistry and Physiology A: Molecular & Integrative Physiology* **164**: 129–140.

Munshi-South, J. & Bernard, H. 2011. Genetic diversity and distinctiveness of the proboscis monkeys (*Nasalis larvatus*) of the Klias Peninsula, Sabah, Malaysia. *Journal of Heredity* **102**: 342–346.

Murai, T. 2004a. Social behaviors of all-male proboscis monkeys when joined by females. *Ecological Research* **19**: 451–454.

Murai, T. 2004b. *Social structure and mating behavior of proboscis monkey* Nasalis larvatus *(Primates; Colobinae)*. PhD thesis, Hokkaido University, Sapporo, Japan.

Murai, T. 2006. Mating behaviors of the proboscis monkey (*Nasalis larvatus*). *American Journal of Primatology* **68**: 832–837.

Murai, T., Mohamed, M., Bernard, H., Mahedi, P. A., Saburi, R. & Higashi, S. 2007. Female transfer between one-male groups of proboscis monkey (*Nasalis larvatus*). *Primates* **48**: 117–121.

Murthy, S., Couacy-Hymann, E., Metzger, S. et al. 2013. Absence of frequent herpesvirus transmission in a nonhuman primate predator-prey system in the wild. *Journal of Virology* **87**: 10651–10659.

Mwenja, I. 2007. A new population of De Brazza's monkey in Kenya. *Primate Conservation* **22**: 117–122.

Mwenja, I. 2009. *The Distribution of the Endangered Mt. Uarges Guereza, the de Brazza's, the Patas, and the Sykes' monkey, and the Somali and Senegal Lesser Galagos in Samburu, Northern Kenya*. Unpublished survey report, Institute of Primate Research, National Museums of Kenya. Pp. 1–29.

Mwenja, I. 2019. *Colobus guereza* ssp. *percivali*. *The IUCN Red List of Threatened Species 2019*: e.T40007A17983118. www.iucnredlist.org/.

N'Goran, P. K., Boesch, C., Mundry, R. et al. 2012. Hunting, law enforcement, and African primate conservation. *Conservation Biology* **26**: 565–571.

Nadler, T. 1997. A new subspecies of douc langur, *Pygathrix nemaeus cinereus* ssp. nov. *Zoologischer Garten (NF)* **67**: 165–176.

Nadler, T. 2009. Observations of Lao langurs (*Trachypithecus [laotum] laotum*) and black langurs (*Trachypithecus [laotum] hatinhensis morph ebenus*) in Khammouane Province, Laos and Remarks to Their Systematic Position. *Vietnamese Journal of Primatology* **1**: 9–15.

Nadler, T. 2012. Reintroduction of the 'Critically Endangered' Delacours langur (*Trachypithecus delacouri*) – a preliminary report. *Vietnamese Journal of Primatolology* **2**: 67–72.

Nadler, T. 2013. Cat Ba langur. In Mittermeier, R. A., Rylands, A. B. & Wilson, D. E. (Eds.), *Handbook of the Mammals of the World: Vol. 3. Primates*. Barcelona, Spain: Lynx Editions. Pp. 748–749.

Nadler, T. 2015. The critical status of the Delacour's langur (*Trachypithecus delacouri*) and the call for a National Action Plan. *Vietnamese Journal of Primatology* **2**: 1–12.

Nadler, T. & Brockman, D. 2014. *Primates of Vietnam*. Vietnam: Endangered Primate Rescue Center. Pp. 172–295.

Nadler, T. & Long, H. T. 2000. *The Cat Ba Langur: Past, Present and Future – The Definitive Report on Trachypithecus poliocephalus, the World's Rarest Primate*. Hanoi: Frankfurt Zoological Society. 104 pp.

Nadler, T. & Roos, C. 2017. Impending extinction crisis of the world's primates – implications for Vietnam. *Vietnamese Journal of Primatology* **2**: 25–35.

Nadler, T. & Streicher, U. 2003. Re-introduction possibilities for endangered langurs in Vietnam. *Re-introduction NEWS* **23**: 35–37.

Nadler, T. & Streicher, U. 2004. Conservation of primates in Vietnam – an overview. In Nadler, T., Streicher, U. & Long, H. T. (Eds.), *Conservation of primates in Vietnam*. Hanoi: Frankfurt Zoological Society. Pp. 5–14.

Nadler, T., Momberg, F., Dang, N. & Lormee, N. 2003. *Leaf Monkeys. Vietnam Primate Conservation Status Review*. Part 2 Hanoi: Fauna & Flora International.

Nadler, T., Thanh, V. N. & Streicher, U. 2007. Conservation status of Vietnamese primates. *Vietnamese Journal of Primatology* **1**: 7–26.

Nadler, T., Walter, L. & Roos, C. 2005. Molecular evolution, systematics and distribution of the taxa within the silvered langur species group (*Trachypithecus* [*cristatus*]) in Southeast Asia. *Zoologischer Garten (NF)* **75**: 238–247.

Nag, K. S. C., Pramod, P. & Karanth, K. P. 2011. Taxonomic implications of a field study of morphotypes of Hanuman langurs (*Semnopithecus entellus*) in peninsular India. *International Journal of Primatology* 32: 830–848.

Nagpal, R., Shively, C. A., Register, T., Appt, S. A. & Yadav, H. Y. 2018. Gut microbiome composition in non-human primates consuming a Western or Mediterranean diet. *Frontiers in Nutrition* 5: 28.

Nakatsukasa, M., Mbua, E., Sawada, Y. et al. 2010. Earliest colobine skeletons from Nakali, Kenya. *American Journal of Physical Anthropology* 143: 365–382.

Napier, J. R. 1970. Paleoecology and catarrhine evolution. In Napier, J. R. & Napier, P. H. (Eds.), *Old World Monkeys: Ecology, Systematics and Behavior.* New York: Academic Press. Pp. 53–95.

Napier, P. H. 1985. *Catalogue of Primates in the British Museum (Natural History) and Elsewhere in the British Isles. Part 3: Family Cercopithecidae, Subfamily Colobinae.* London: British Museum (Natural History). 111 pp.

Napier, J. R. & Napier, P. H. 1967. *A Handbook of Living Primates.* London: Academic Press. 456 pp.

Napier, J. R. & Napier, P. H. 1985/1994. *The Natural History of the Primates.* Cambridge, MA: The MIT Press.

Napier, J. R. & Napier, P. H. 1994. *The Natural History of the Primates.* London: Academic Press. 200 pp.

Nardelli, F. 2015. A new Colobinae from the Sundiac region: the golden-crowned langur *Presbytis johnaspinalli*, sp. nov. *International Zoo News* 62: 323–336.

National Research Council. 2003. *Nutrient Requirements of Nonhuman Primates*, 2nd rev. ed. Washington, DC: National Academies Press.

Naughton-Treves, L. 1998. Predicting patterns of crop damage by wildlife around Kibale National Park, Uganda. *Conservation Biology* 12: 156–168.

Nekaris, K. A. I., McCabe, S., Spaan, D., Ali, M. I. & Nijman, V. 2018. A novel application of cultural consensus models to evaluate conservation education programs. *Conservation Biology* 32: 466–476.

Newton, P. N. 1985a. The behavioural ecology of forest hanuman langurs. *Tiger Paper* 12: 3–7.

Newton, P. N. 1985b. A note on golden jackals (*Canis aureus*) and their relationship with langurs (*Presbytis entellus*) in Kanha Tiger Reserve. *Journal of the Bombay Natural History Society* 82: 633–634.

Newton, P. N. 1986. Infanticide in an undisturbed forest population of Hanuman langurs, *Presbytis entellus. Animal Behaviour* 34: 785–789.

Newton, P. N. 1987. The social organization of forest Hanuman langurs (*Presbytis entellus*). *International Journal of Primatology* 8: 199–232.

Newton, P. N. 1988. The variable social organization of Hanuman langurs (*Presbytis entellus*), infanticide, and the monopolization of females. *International Journal of Primatology* 9: 59–77.

Newton, P. N. 1992. Feeding and ranging patterns of forest hanuman langurs (*Presbytis entellus*). *International Journal of Primatology* 13: 245–285.

Newton, P. N. 1994. Social stability and change among forest hanuman langurs (*Presbytis entellus*). *Primates* 35: 489–498.

Newton, P. N. & Dunbar, R. I. 1994. Colobine monkey society. In Davies, A. G. & Oates, J. F. (Eds.), *Colobine Monkeys: Their Ecology, Behaviour and Evolution.* Cambridge: Cambridge University Press. Pp. 311–346.

Newton-Fisher, N. E. 2014. The hunting behavior and carnivory in wild chimpanzees. In Henkel, W. & Tattersall, T. (Eds.), *Handbook of Paleoanthropology.* 2nd ed. Berlin, Germany: Springer-Verlag. Pp. 1661–1691.

Nguyen, M. H. 2006. Some observations on the Hatinh langur, *Trachypithecus laotum hatinhensis* (Dao, 1970), in north central Vietnam. *Primate Conservation* 21: 149–154.

Nguyen, L. T., Schmidt, H. A., von Haeseler, A. & Minh, B. Q. 2015. IQ-TREE: a fast and effective stochastic algorithm for estimating Maximum-Likelihood phylogenies. *Molecular Biology and Evolution* 32: 268–274.

Nguyen, N. C., Cao, T. C., Vu, V. C. et al. 1996. *Vietnam Forest Trees. Forest Inventory and Planning Institute.* Hanoi: Agricultural Publishing House. P. 142.

Nguyen, T. T., Ha, T. L., Bui, V. T., Tran, H. V. & Nguyen, A. T. 2012. The feeding behaviour and phytochemical food content of grey-shanked douc langurs (*Pygathrix cinerea*) at Kon Ka Kinh National Park, Vietnam. *Vietnamese Journal of Primatology* 2: 25–35.

Nguyen, V. Q., Tran, D. T. & Dinh, V. H. 2010. Landscapes and ecosystems of tropical limestone: case study of the Cat Ba Islands, Vietnam. *Journal of Ecology and Field Biology* 33: 23–36.

Niang, I., Ruppel, O. C., Abdrabo, M. A. et al. 2014. Africa. In Barros, V. R., Field, C. B., Dokken, D. J. et al. (Eds.), *Contribution of Working Group II to the Fifth Assessment. Report of the Intergovernmental Panel on Climate Change. Climate Change 2014: Impacts, Adaptation, and*

Vulnerability. Part B: Regional Aspects. Cambridge: Cambridge University Press. Pp. 1199–1265.

Nicholson, A. J. 1954. An outline of the dynamics of animal populations. *Australian Journal of Zoology* 2: 9–65.

Nicholson, S. E. 2001. Climatic and environmental change in Africa during the last two centuries. *Climate Research* 17: 123–144.

Nie, S., Xiang, Z. & Li, M. 2009. Preliminary report on the diet and social structure of gray snub-nosed monkeys (*Rhinopithecus brelichi*) at Yangaoping, Guizhou, China. *Acta Theriologica Sinica* 29: 326–331.

Nijboer, J. 2006. *Fibre intake and faeces quality in leaf-eating primates.* PhD thesis, Utrecht University, Utrecht, The Netherlands.

Nijboer, J. & Clauss, M. 2006. The digestive physiology of colobine primates. In Nijboer, J. (Ed.), *Fibre Intake and Faeces Quality in Leaf-Eating Monkeys.* Pp. 9–28.

Nijboer, J. & Dierenfeld, E. S. 1996. Comparison of diets fed to southeast Asian colobines in North American and European zoos, with emphasis on temperate browse composition. *Zoo Biology* 15: 499–507.

Nijboer, J., Becher, F., van der Kuilen, J. & Beynen, A. C. 2001. Chemical analysis and consistency of faeces produced by captive monkeys (*Francois langurs, Trachypithecus francoisi*) fed supplemental fibre. *Veterinary Quarterly* 23: 76–80.

Nijboer, J., Clauss, M., Olsthoorn, M. et al. 2006. Effect of diet on the feces quality in Javan langur (*Trachypithecus auratus auratus*). *Journal of Zoo and Wildlife Medicine* 37: 366–372.

Nijboer, J., Clauss, M., van de Put, K. et al. 2007. Influence of two different diets on fluid and particle retention time Javan langur (*Trachypithecus auratus auratus*). *Der Zoologische Garten* 77: 36–46.

Nijman, V. 1997. On the occurrence and distribution of *Presbytis comata* (Desmarest, 1822). *Contributions to Zoology* 66: 247–256.

Nijman, V. 2000. Geographic distribution of ebony leaf monkey *Trachypithecus auratus. Contributions to Zoology* 69: 157–177.

Nijman, V. 2001. *Forest (and) primates: conservation and ecology of the endemic primates of Java and Borneo.* Wageningen: Tropenbos International.

Nijman, V. 2005. Decline of the endemic Hose's langur *Presbytis hosei* in Kayan Mentarang National Park, east Borneo. *Oryx* 39: 223–226.

Nijman, V. 2010. Ecology and conservation of the Hose's langur group (Colobinae: *Presbytis hosei, P. canicrus, P. sabana*): a review. In Gurskey-Doyen, S. & Supriatna, J. (Eds.), *Indonesian Primates.* New York, NY: Springer. Pp. 269–284.

Nijman, V. 2012. Purple-faced Langurs in human-modified environments feeding on cultivated fruits: a comment to Dela (2007, 2012). *International Journal of Primatology* 33: 743–748.

Nijman, V. 2014. Distribution and ecology of the most tropical of the high-elevation montane colobines: the ebony langur on Java. In Grow, N. B., Gursky-Doyen, S. & Krzton, A. (Eds.), *High Altitude Primates.* New York, NY: Springer. Pp. 115–132.

Nijman, V. 2015. Newly described golden-crowned langurs *Presbytis johnaspinalli* are most likely partially bleached ebony langurs *Trachypithecus auratus. International Zoo News* 62: 403–406.

Nijman, V. 2017. Group composition and monandry in grizzled langurs, *Presbytis comata*, on Java. *Folia Primatologica* 88: 237–254.

Nijman, V. 2019. *Presbytis neglectus* or *P. femoralis*, Colobine molecular phylogenies, and GenBank submission of newly generated DNA sequences. *Folia Primatologica* 91: 228–239.

Nijman, V., Nekaris, K. A., Donati, G., Bruford, M. & Fa, J. 2011. Primate conservation: measuring and mitigating trade in primates. *Endangered Species Research* 13: 159–161.

Nijman, V. & Nekaris, K. A. I. 2012. Loud calls, startle behaviour, social organisation and predator avoidance in arboreal langurs (Cercopithecidae: *Presbytis*). *Folia Primatologica* 83: 274–287.

Nijman, V. & van Balen, S. B. 1998. A faunal survey of the Dieng Mountains, Central Java, Indonesia: distribution and conservation of endemic primate taxa. *Oryx* 32: 145–156.

Nijssen, E. C. 1999. *Female philopatry in* Colobus polykomos polykomos: *Fact or fiction?* MA thesis, Utrecht University, Utrecht, The Netherlands.

Nishida, T. 2012. *Chimpanzees of the Lakeshore.* Cambridge: Cambridge University Press. 320 pp.

Nishimura, T. D., Takai, M., Senut, B. et al. 2012. Reassessment of *Dolichopithecus (Kanagawapithecus) leptopostorbitalis*, a colobine monkey from the Late Pliocene of Japan. *Journal of Human Evolution* 62: 548–561.

Niu, K., Liu, W., Xiao, Z. et al. 2019. Exploring local perceptions of and attitudes toward endangered François' langurs (*Trachypithecus francoisi*) in a human-modified habitat. *International Journal of Primatology* 40: 331–355.

Niu, K., Tan, C. L. & Yang, Y. 2010. Altitudinal movements of Guizhou snub-nosed monkeys (*Rhinopithecus brelichi*) in Fanjingshan National Nature Reserve, China: Implications for conservation management of a flagship species. *Folia Primatologica* **81**: 233–244.

Nowak, K. 2007. *Behavioural flexibility and demography of* Procolobus kirkii *across floristic and disturbance gradients.* PhD thesis, University of Cambridge, Cambridge.

Nowak, K. 2008. Frequent water drinking by Zanzibar red colobus (*Procolobus kirkii*) in a mangrove forest refuge. *American Journal of Primatology* **70**: 1081–1092.

Nowak, K. & Lee, P. C. 2011. Demographic structure of Zanzibar red colobus populations in unprotected coral rag and mangrove forests. *International Journal of Primatology* **32**: 24–45.

Nowak, K. & Lee, P. C. 2013. Status of Zanzibar red colobus and Sykes's monkeys in two coastal forests in 2005. *Primate Conservation* **27**: 65–73.

Nowak, K., Barnett, A. A. & Matsuda, I. 2019. *Primates in Flooded Habitats: Ecology and Conservation.* Cambridge: Cambridge University Press.

Nowak, K., Cardini, A. & Elton, S. 2008. Evolutionary acceleration and divergence in *Procolobus kirkii. International Journal of Primatology* **29**: 1313–1339.

Nowak, K., Maisels, F., Baker, L. R. & Rainey, H. 2019. Conservation value of Africa's flooded habitats to non-human primates. In Barnett, A. A., Matsuda, I. & Nowak, K. (Eds.), *Primates in Flooded Habitats: Ecology and Conservation.* Cambridge: Cambridge University Press. Pp. 341–346.

NRC. 2003. *Nutrient Requirements of Nonhuman Primates*, 2nd rev. ed. Washington, DC: National Academies Press.

Nüchel, J., Bøcher, P. K., Xiao, W., Zhu, A. X. & Svenning, J. C. 2018. Snub-nosed monkeys (*Rhinopithecus*): potential distribution and its implication for conservation. *Biodiversity and Conservation* **27**: 1517–1538.

Nunn, C. L. 1999. The number of males in primate social groups: A comparative test of the socioecological model. *Behavioral Ecology and Sociobiology* **46**: 1–13.

Nunn, C. L. 2000. Collective benefits, free-riders, and male extra-group conflict. In Kappeler, P. M. (Ed.), *Primate Males.* Cambridge: Cambridge University Press. Pp. 192–204.

Nunn, C. L. 2012. Primate disease ecology in comparative and theoretical perspective. *American Journal of Primatology* **74**: 97–509.

Nunn, C. L. & Altizer, S. 2006. *Infectious Diseases in Primates: Behavior, Ecology and Evolution.* Oxford: Oxford University Press.

Nunn, C. L. & Altizer, S. M. 2005. The global mammal parasite database: an online resource for infectious disease records in wild primates. *Evolutionary Anthropology* **14**: 1–2.

Nunn, C. L., Altizer, S. M., Sechrest, W. & Cunningham, A. A. 2005. Latitudinal gradients of parasite species brichness in primates. *Diversity and Distributions* **11**: 249–256.

Nunn, C. L., Jordán, F., McCabe, C. M., Verdolin, J. L. & Fewell, J. H. 2015. Infectious disease and group size: More than just a numbers game. *Philosophical Transactions of the Royal Society B* **370**: 20140111.

Nyirambangutse, B., Zibera, E., Uwizeye, F. K. et al. 2017. Carbon stocks and dynamics at different successional stages in an Afromontane tropical forest. *Biogeosciences* **14**: 1285–1303.

O'Brien, J. A. 2014. *The ecology and conservation of black-shanked doucs (*Pygathrix nigripes*) in Cat Tien National Park, Vietnam.* PhD thesis, University of Colorado, Boulder.

O'Brien, T. G., Kinnaird, M. F., Dierenfeld, E. S., Conklin-Brittain, N. L., Wrangham, R. W. & Silver, S. C. 1998. What's so special about figs? *Science* **392**: 668.

Oates, J. F. 1974. *The ecology and behaviour of the black-and-white colobus monkey (*Colobus guereza *Ruppell) in East Africa.* PhD thesis, University of London, London.

Oates, J. F. 1977a. The guereza and its food. In Clutton-Brock, T. H. (Ed.), *Primate Ecology: Studies of Feeding and Ranging Behavior in Lemurs, Monkeys and Apes.* New York: Academic Press. Pp. 275–321.

Oates, J. F. 1977b. The guereza and man. In Prince Ranier III & Bourne, G. H. (Eds.), *Primate Conservation.* London: Academic Press. Pp. 419–467.

Oates, J. F. 1977c. The social life of a black and white colobus monkey, *Colobus guereza. Zeitschrift für Tierpsychologie* **45**: 1–60.

Oates, J. F. 1978. Water-plant and soil consumption by guereza monkeys (*Colobus guereza*): a relationship with minerals and toxins in the diet? *Biotropica* **10**: 241–253.

Oates, J. F. 1981. Mapping the distribution of West African rain forest monkeys: issues, methods, and preliminary results. *Annals of the New York Academy of Sciences* **376**: 53–63.

Oates, J. F. 1982. In search of rare forest primates in Nigeria. *Oryx* **16**: 431–436.

Oates, J. F. 1986. *Action Plan for African Primate Conservation: 1986–90.* Stony Brook, NY: IUCN/SSC Primate Specialist Group. 80 pp.

Oates, J. F. 1988a. The diet of the olive colobus monkey, *Procolobus verus*, in Sierra Leone. *International Journal of Primatology* 9: 457–478.

Oates, J. F. 1988b. The distribution of *Cercopithecus* monkeys in West African forests. In Gautier-Hion, A., Bourlière, F., Gautier, J. P. et al. (Eds.), *A Primate Radiation: Evolutionary Biology of the African Guenons.* Cambridge: Cambridge University Press. Pp. 79–103.

Oates, J. F. 1994. The natural history of African colobines. In Davies, A. G. & Oates, J. F. (Eds.), *Colobine Monkeys: Their Ecology, Behaviour and Evolution.* Cambridge: Cambridge University Press. Pp. 75–128.

Oates, J. F. 1996a. *African Primates: Status Survey and Conservation Action Plan.* Gland, Switzerland: IUCN/SSC Primate Specialist Group. 80 pp.

Oates, J. F. 1996b. Habitat alteration, hunting and the conservation of folivorous primates in African forests. *Australian Journal of Ecology* 21: 1–9.

Oates, J. F. 1999. *Myth and Reality in the Rain Forest: How Conservation Strategies Are Failing in West Africa.* Berkeley: University of California Press.

Oates, J. F. 2011. *Primates of West Africa: A Field Guide and Natural History.* Arlington, VA: Conservation International. 557 pp.

Oates, J. F. & Trocco, T. F. 1983. Taxonomy and phylogeny of black-and-white colobus monkeys. *Folia Primatologica* 40: 83–113.

Oates, J. F. & Ting, N. 2015. Conservation consequences of unstable taxonomies: the case of the red colobus monkeys. In Behie, A. M. & Oxenham, M. F. (Eds.), *Taxonomic Tapestries.* Canberra, Australia: ANU Press. Pp. 321.

Oates, J. F. & Davies, A. G. 1994a. Conclusions: the past, present and future of the colobines. In Davies, A. G. & Oates, J. F. (Eds.), *Colobine Monkeys: Their Ecology, Behaviour and Evolution.* Cambridge: Cambridge University Press. Pp. 347–358.

Oates, J. F. & Davies, G. 1994b. What are the colobines? In Davies, A. G. & Oates, J. F. (Eds.), *Colobine Monkeys: Their Ecology, Behaviour and Evolution.* Cambridge: Cambridge University Press. Pp. 1–10.

Oates, J. F. & Korstjens, A. H. 2013. *Procolobus verus* olive colobus (Van Beneden's colobus). In Butynski, T. M., Kingdon, J. & Kalina, J. (Eds.), *Mammals of Africa: Vol. 2. Primates.* London: Bloomsbury. Pp. 121–124.

Oates, J. F. & Werre, J. L. 2009. Niger Delta red colobus *Procolobus epieni.* In Mittermeier, R. A., Wallis, J., Rylands, A. B. et al. (Eds.), *Primates in Peril: The World's 25 Most Endangered Primates 2008–2010. Primate Conservation* 24: 1–57. https://portals.iucn.org/library/sites/library/files/documents/2009-067.pdf.

Oates, J. F. & Whitesides, G. H. 1990). Association between olive colobus (*Procolobus* verus), diana guenons (*Cercopithecus diana*), and other forest monkeys in Sierra Leone. *American Journal of Primatology* 21: 129–146.

Oates, J. F., Abedi-Lartey, M., McGraw, W. S., Struhsaker, T. T. & Whitesides, G. H. 2000a. Extinction of a West African red colobus monkey. *Conservation Biology* 14: 1526–1532.

Oates, J. F., Bocian, C. M. & Terranova, C. J. 2000b. The loud calls of black-and-white colobus monkeys: new information and a reappraisal of their phylogenetic and functional significance. In Whitehead, P. F. & Jolly, C. J. (Eds.), *Old World Monkeys.* Cambridge: Cambridge University Press. Pp. 431–452.

Oates, J. F., Davies, A. G. & Delson, E. 1994. The diversity of living colobines. In Davies, A. G. & Oates, J. F. (Eds.), *Colobine Monkeys: Their Ecology, Behaviour and Evolution.* Cambridge: Cambridge University Press. Pp. 45–73.

Oates, J. F., Gippoliti, S. & Groves, C. P. 2008. *Procolobus verus. The IUCN Red List of Threatened Species 2008*: e.T18245A7886880.

Oates, J. F., Gonedelé Bi, S., Ikemeh, R., Koné, I., McGraw, S., Nobimè, G., Osei, D. & Wiafe, E. 2020a. *Procolobus verus* (amended version of 2019 assessment). *The IUCN Red List of Threatened Species* 2020: e.T18245A166610679. www.iucnredlist.org/.

Oates, J. F., Koné, I., McGraw, S. & Osei, D. 2020b. *Piliocolobus waldroni. The IUCN Red List of Threatened Species 2020*: e.T18248A166620835. www.iucnredlist.org/.

Oates, J. F., Struhsaker, T. T., Maisels, F. & Fashing, P. J. 2019. *Colobus guereza* ssp. *occidentalis. The IUCN Red List of Threatened Species 2019*: e.T136891A17983202. www.iucnredlist.org/.

Oates, J. F., Struhsaker, T. T. & McGraw, W. S. 2016. *Piliocolobus waldronae, IUCN Red List of Threatened Species 2016.* International Union for Conservation of Nature and Natural Resources (IUCN).

Oates, J. F., Swain, T. & Zantovska, J. 1977. Secondary compounds and food selection by colobus monkeys. *Biochemical Systematics and Ecology* 5: 317–321.

Oates, J. F., Waterman, P. G. & Choo, G. M. 1980. Food selection in the South Indian leaf-monkey, *Presbytis johnii*, in relation to leaf chemistry. *Oecologia* **45**: 45–56.

Oates, J. F., Whitesides, G. H., Davies, A. G., Waterman, P. G., Green, S. M., Dasilva, G. L. & Mole, S. 1990. Determinants of variation in tropical forest primate biomass: new evidence from west Africa. *Ecology* **71**: 328–343.

Oftedal, O. T., Whiten, A., Southgate, D. A. T. & Van Soest, P. 1991. The nutritional consequences of foraging in primates: the relationship of nutrient intakes to nutrient requirements. *Philisophical Transactions: Biological Sciences* **334**: 161–170.

Ogden, J. J., Olson, T. L. & Miner, V. 1991. Declines in sociosexual behavior in golden monkeys (*Rhinopithecus roxellana*): associated environmental and social variables. *Zoo Biology* **10**: 491–498.

Ohwaki, K., Hungate, R. E., Lotter, L., Hofmann, R. R. & Maloiy, G. 1974. Stomach fermentation in East African colobus monkeys in their natural state. *Applied Microbiology* **27**: 713–723.

Olgun, H., Mohammed, M. K., Mzee, A. J., Green, M. E. L., Davenport, T. R. B. & Georgiev, A. V. 2020. The impact and implications of vehicle collisions on the endangered and endemic Zanzibar red colobus (*Piliocolobus kirkii*). *BioRxiv* 2020.01.17.906909; https://doi.org/10.1101/2020.01.17.906909

Oliphant, K. & Allen-Vercoe, E. 2019. Macronutrient metabolism by the human gut microbiome: major fermentation by-products and their impact on host health. *Microbiome* **7**: 91.

Olson, D. K. 1980. Male interactions and troop split among black-and-white colobus monkeys (*Colobus polykomos vellerosus*). *Paper presented at the Eighth Congress of the International Primatological Society, Florence, Italy.*

Olson, D. K. 1986. Determining range size for arboreal monkeys: methods, assumptions, and accuracy. In Taub, D. M. & King, F. A. (Eds.), *Current Perspectives in Primate Social Dynamics*. New York: Van Nostrand Reinhold. Pp. 212–227.

Onderdonk D. A. 2000. Infanticide of a newborn black-and-white colobus monkey (*Colobus guereza*) in Kibale National Park, Uganda. *Primates* **41**: 209–212.

Onderdonk, D. A. & Chapman, C. A. 2000. Coping with forest fragmentation: the primates of Kibale National Park, Uganda. *International Journal of Primatology* **21**: 587–611.

Oppenheimer, J. R. 1977. *Presbytis entellus*, the Hanuman langur. In Prince Rainier III & Bourne, G. (Eds.), *Primate Conservation*. New York: Academic Press. Pp. 469–512.

Oppenheimer, J. R. 1978. Aspects of the diet of the Hanuman langur. In Chivers, D. J. & Herbert, J. (Eds.), *Recent Advances in Primatology: Vol. 1. Behaviour*. London: Academic Press. Pp. 337–342.

Osterholz, M., Walter, L. & Roos, C. 2008. Phylogenetic position of the langur genera *Semnopithecus* and *Trachypithecus* among Asian colobines, and affiliations of their species groups. *BMC Evolutionary Biology* **8**: 58.

Otto, C. 2005. *Food Intake, Nutrient Intake, and Food Selection in Captive and Semi-free Douc Langurs*. Münster: Schuling Verlag.

Overskei, T., Pirie, G., Vice, C. et al. 1992. *Entamoeba histolytica* infection in Hanuman langurs (*Presbytis entellus*) and purple-faced langurs (*Presbytis senex*). Oakland, CA: AAZV.

Paciulli, L. M. 2004. *The effects of logging, hunting, and vegetation on the densities of the Pagai, Mentawai Island primates*. PhD thesis, State University of New York, Stony Brook.

Paciulli, L. M. 2010. The relationship between nonhuman primate densities and vegetation on the Pagai, Mentawai Islands, Indonesia. In Gursky-Doyen, S. & Supriatna, J. (Eds.), *Indonesian Primates*. New York: Springer. Pp. 199–215.

Paciulli, L. M. 2011. *Simias concolor*. In Rowe, N. & Myers, M. (Eds.), *All the World's Primates*. www.alltheworldsprimates.org. Charlestown, RI: Primate Conservation Inc.

Paciulli, L. M. & Holmes, S. 2008. Activity budget of simakobu monkeys (*Simias concolor*) inhabiting the Mentawai Islands, Indonesia. *Primate Eye* 96: Abstract.

Packer, C., Herbst, L., Pusey, A. E., Bygott, J. D., Hanby, J. P., Cairns, S. J. & Mulder, M. B. 1988. Reproductive success of lions. In Clutton-Brock, T. H. (Ed.), *Reproductive Success of Individual Variation in Contrasting Breeding Systems*. Chicago: University of Chicago Press. Pp. 363–383.

Pages, G., Lloyd, E. & Suarez, S. A. 2005. The impact of geophagy on ranging behavior in Phayre's leaf monkeys (*Trachypithecus phayrei*). *Folia Primatologica* **76**: 342–346.

Paige, S. B., Bleecker, J., Mayer, J. & Goldberg, T. 2017. Spatial overlap between people and non-human primates in a fragmented landscape. *Ecohealth* **14**: 88–99.

Paige, S. B., Frost, S. D. W., Gibson, M. A. et al. 2014. Beyond bushmeat: animal contact, injury, and zoonotic disease risk in western Uganda. *Ecohealth* 11: 534–543.

Pallas, L., Daver, G., McKaye, H. T. et al. 2019. A window into the early evolutionary history of Cercopithecidae: late Miocene evidence from Chad, Central Africa. *Journal of Human Evolution* 132: 61–79.

Palombit, R. A. 2012. Infanticide: male strategies and female counterstrategies. In Mitani, J. C., Call, J., Kappeler, P. M. et al. (Eds.), *The Evolution of Primate Societies*. Chicago: The University of Chicago Press. Pp. 432–468.

Palombit, R. A. 2015. Infanticide as sexual conflict: coevolution of male strategies and female counterstrategies. *Cold Spring Harbor Perspectives in Biology* 7: a017640.

Pan, R., Groves, C. & Oxnard, C. 2004. Relationships between the fossil colobine *Mesopithecus pentelicus* and extant cercopithecoids, based on dental metrics. *American Journal of Primatology* 62: 287–299.

Pate, C., Ulibarri, L., White, F. & Frost, S. 2018. Cranial morphometric analysis on *Pygathrix nemaeus* and *Pygathrix cinerea*. *American Journal of Physical Anthropology* 165: 201.

Paterson, J. D. & Wallis, J. 2005. *Conflict and Commensalism: The Human–Primate Interface.* Norman, OK: American Society of Primatology.

Pattanaik, C. & Prasad, S. N. 2011. Assessment of aquaculture impact on mangroves of Mahanadi delta (Orissa), East coast of India using remote sensing and GIS. *Ocean and Coastal Management* 54:789–795.

Patz, J. A., Daszak, P., Tabor, G. M. et al. 2004. Unhealthy landscapes: policy recommendations on land use change and infectious disease emergence. *Environmental Health Perspectives* 112: 1092–1098.

Patzelt, A., Kopp, G. H., Ndao, I., Kalbitzer, U., Zinner, D & Fischer, J. 2014. Male tolerance and male-male bonds in a multilevel primate society. *Proceedings of the National Academy of Sciences* 111: 14740–14745.

Pavelka, M. S. M. & Behie, A. M. 2005. The effect of Hurricane Iris on the food supply of black howlers (*Alouatta pigra*) in southern Belize. *Biotropica* 37: 102–108.

Pavelka, M. S. M. & Knopff, K. H. 2004. Diet and activity in black howler monkeys (*Alouatta pigra*) in southern Belize: does degree of frugivory influence activity level? *Primates* 45: 105–111.

Payne, H. F. P., Lawes, M. J. & Henzi, P. S. 2003. Fatal attack on an adult female *Cercopithecus mitis erythrarchus*: implications for female dispersal in female-bonded societies. *International Journal of Primatology* 24: 1245–1350.

Pebsworth, P. A. & LaFleur, M. 2014. Advancing primate research and conservation through the use of camera traps: introduction to the special issue. *International Journal of Primatology* 35: 825–840.

Pebsworth, P. A., Huffman, M. A., Lambert, J. E. & Young, S. L. 2019. Geophagy among nonhuman primates: a systematic review of current knowledge and suggestions for future directions. *American Journal of Physical Anthropology* 168: 164–194.

Pebsworth, P. A., Seim, G. L., Huffman, M. A., Glahn, R. P., Tako, E. & Young, S. L. 2013. Soil consumed by chacma baboons is low in bioavailable iron and high in clay. *Journal of Chemical Ecology* 39: 447–449.

Peng, Y. Z., Pan, R. L. & Jablonski, N. G. 1993. Classification and evolution of Asian colobines. *Folia Primatologica* 60: 106–117.

Perelman, P., Johnson, W. E., Roos, C. et al. 2011. A molecular phylogeny of living primates. *PLOS Genetics* 7: e1001342.

Peres, C. A., Emilio, T., Schietti, J., Desmoulière, S. J. & Levi, T. 2016. Dispersal limitation induces long-term biomass collapse in overhunted Amazonian forests. *Proceedings of the National Academy of Sciences* 113: 892–897.

Perofsky, A. C., Lewis, R. J., Abondano, L. A., Di Fiore, A. & Meyers, L. A. 2017. Hierarchical social networks shape gut microbial composition in wild Verreaux's sifaka. *Proceedings of the Royal Society B* 284: 20172274.

Persey, S. & Imanuddin, L. 2011. *A Practical Handbook for Conserving High Conservation Value Species and Habitats within Oil Palm Landscapes.* London: Zoological Society of London.

Phalan, B., Bertzky, M., Butchart, S. H. M. et al. 2013. Crop expansion and conservation priorities in tropical countries. *PLOS ONE* 8: e51759.

Pham, N. 1993a. First results of the diet of the red-shanked douc langur, *Pygathrix nemaeus*. *Australian Primatology* 8: 5–6.

Pham, N. 1993b. The distribution and status of the douc langur (*Pygathrix nemaeus*) in Vietnam. *Asian Primates* 3: 2–3.

Pham, N. 1994. Preliminary results on the diet of the red-shanked douc langur (*Pygathrix nemaeus*). *Asian Primates* 4: 9–11.

Pham, T. T., Moeliono, M., Nguyen, T. H., Nguyen, H. T. & Vu, T. H. 2012. The context of REDD in Vietnam.

Bogor, Indonesia: Center for International Forestry Research, Occasional Paper 75, RECOFT.

Phiapalath, P. 2009. *Distribution, behavior and threat of red-shanked douc* langur Pygathrix nemaeus *in Hin Namno National Protected Area, Khammouane Province, Lao PDR.* PhD thesis, Suranaree University of Technology, Nakhon Ratchasima, Thailand.

Phiapalath, P. & Suwanwaree, P. 2010. Time budget and activity of red-shanked douc langurs (Pygathrix nemaeus) in Hin Namno National Protected Area, Lao PDR. In Nadler, T., Rawson, B. M. & Van, N. T. (Eds.), *Conservation of Primates in Indochina.* Hanio: Frankfurt Zoological Society and Conservation International. Pp. 171–178.

Phiapalath, P., Borries, C. & Suwanwaree, P. 2011. Seasonality of group size, feeding and breeding in wild red-shanked douc langurs (Lao PDR). *American Journal of Primatology* **73**: 1134–1144.

Piachaud, M., Beziers, P., Hobeika, S. & Korstjens, A. H. 2009. What is the best strategy to access females in oestrus? *Folia Primatologica* **80**.

Pickford, M., Senut, B. & Hadoto, D. 1993. *Geology and Paleobiology of the Albertine Rift Valley Uganda-Zaire: Vol. 1. Geology.* Orleans, France: International Center for Training and Exchanges in the Geoscience.

Pimm, S. L., Jenkins, C. N., Abell, R. et al. 2014. The biodiversity of species and their rates of extinction, distribution, and protection. *Science* **344**: 1246752.

Piper, P. J. & Rabett, R. J. 2009. Hunting in a tropical rainforest: evidence from the Terminal Pleistocene at Lobang Hangus, Niah Caves, Sarawak. *International Journal of Osteoarchaeology* **19**: 551–565.

Pirta, R. S., Gadgil, M. & Kharshikar, A. V. 1997. Management of the rhesus monkey *Macaca mulatta* and Hanuman langur *Presbytis entellus* in Himachal Pradesh, India. *Biological Conservation* **79**: 97–106.

Plavcan, J. M. 2004. Sexual selection, measures of sexual selection, and sexual dimorphism in primates. In Kappeler, P. M. & van Schaik, C. P. (Eds.), *Sexual Selection in Primates: New and Comparative Perspectives.* Cambridge: Cambridge University Press. Pp. 230–252.

Plavcan, J. M. & van Schaik, C. P. 1992. Intrasexual competition and canine dimorphism in anthropoid primates. *American Journal of Physical Anthropology* **87**: 461–477.

Plumptre, A. J. 2006. The diets, preferences, and overlap of the primate community in the Budongo Forest Reserve, Uganda: effects of logging on primate diets. In Newton-Fisher, N. E., Notman, H., Paterson, J. D. et al. (Eds.), *Primates of Western Uganda.* New York: Springer. Pp. 345–371.

Plumptre, A. J. & Reynolds, V. 1994. The effect of selective logging on the primate populations in the Budongo forest reserve, Uganda. *Journal of Applied Ecology* **31**: 631–641.

Pobiner, B. L., DeSilva, J., Sanders, W. J. & Mitani, J. C. 2007. Taphonomic analysis of skeletal remains from chimpanzee hunts at Ngogo, Kibale National Park, Uganda. *Journal of Human Evolution* **52**: 614–636.

Pocock, R. I. 1928. The langurs or leaf monkeys of British India. *Journal of the Bombay Natural History Society* **32**: 660–672.

Pocock, R. I. 1935. The monkeys of the genera *Pithecus* (or *Presbytis*) and *Pygathrix* found to the East of the Bay of Bengal. *Proceedings of the Zoological Society of London* **104**: 895–962.

Pocock, R. I. 1939. *The Fauna of British India, including Ceylon and Burma: Mammals. 1. Primates and Carnivores (in part), Families Felidae and Viverridae*, 2nd ed. London: Taylor & Francis. 463 pp.

Podzuweit, D. 1994. *Sozio-Ökologie weiblicher Hanuman languren (*Presbytis entellus*) in Ramnagar, Sudnepal.* PhD thesis. Georg-August-Universität, Göttingen, Germany.

Poirier, F. E. 1969a. Behavioral flexibility and intertroop variation among Nilgiri langurs (*Presbytis johnii*) of South India. *Folia Primatologica* **11**: 119–133.

Poirier, F. E. 1969b. The Nilgiri langur (*Presbytis johnii*) Troop: its composition, structure, function and change. *Folia Primatologica* **10**: 20–47.

Poirier, F. E. 1970a. The communication matrix of the Nilgiri langur (*Presbytis johnii*) of South India. *Folia Primatologica* **13**: 92–136.

Poirier, F. E. 1970b. The Nilgiri langur (*Presbytis johnii*) of South India. In Rosenblum, L. A. (Ed.), *Primate Behaviour: Vol. 1. Developments in Field and Laboratory Research.* New York: Academic Press. Pp. 251–383.

Poirier-Poulin, S. & Teichroeb, J. A. 2020. The vocal repertoire of an African colobine, *Colobus angolensis ruwenzorii*: a multi-level society compared to congeners in stable groups. *Behaviour* **157**: 597–628.

Pollard, E., Clements, T., Nut, M. H., Ko, S. & Rawson, B. 2007. *Status and Conservation of Globally Threatened Primates in the Seima Biodiversity Conservation Area.* Phnom Penh, Cambodia: Wildlife Conservation Society.

Pollard, K. A. & Blumstein, D. T. 2011. Social group size predicts the evolution of individuality. *Current Biology* **21**: 413–417.

Pope, P. B., Denman, S. E., Jones, M. et al. 2010. Adaptation to herbivory by the Tammar wallaby includes bacterial and glycoside hydrolase profiles different from other herbivores. *Proceedings of the National Academy of Sciences* 107: 14793–14798.

Pozzi, L., Hodgson, J. A., Burrell, A. S. et al. 2014. Primate phylogenetic relationships and divergence dates inferred from complete mitochondrial genomes. *Molecular Phylogenetics and Evolution* 75: 165–183.

Prakash, I. 1962. Group organization, sexual behaviour and breeding season of certain Indian monkeys. *Japanese Journal of Ecology* 12: 83–86.

Prates, H. M. & Bicca-Marques, J. C. 2005. Coprophagy in Captive Brown Capuchin Monkeys (*Cebus apella*). *Neotropical Primates* 13: 18–21.

PRB. 2019. *World Population Data 2019, Africa.* Washington, DC: Population Reference Bureau. www.prb.org.

Preece, G. A. 2006. Factors influencing variation in the population densities of *Colobus guereza*, within selectively logged forest at the Budongo Forest Reserve. In Newton-Fisher, N. E., Notman, H., Paterson, J. D. et al. (Eds.), *Primates of Western Uganda.* New York: Springer. Pp. 23–43.

Pronovost, G. N. & Hsiao, E. Y. 2019. Perinatal interactions between the microbiome, immunity, and neurodevelopment. *Immunity* 50: 18–36.

Prosser, S. & Nadler, T. 2017. The Vietnam Primate Conservation Program – Report 2016. *Vietnamese Journal of Primatology* 2: 89–100.

Pucora, E., Schiffmann, C. & Clauss, M. 2019. Resting postures in terrestrial mammalian herbivores. *Journal of Mammalogy* 100: 552–563.

Pulliam, H. R. 1973. On the advantages of flocking. *Journal of Theoretical Biology* 38: 419–422.

Pusey, A. 2012. Magnitude and sources of variation in female reproductive performance. In Mitani, J. C., Call, J., Kappeler, P. M. et al. (Eds.), *The Evolution of Primate Societies.* Chicago: The University of Chicago Press. Pp. 343–366.

Pusey, A., Williams, J. & Goodall, J. 1997. The influence of dominance rank on the reproductive success of female chimpanzees. *Science* 277: 828–831.

Qi, X., Li, B., Garber, P. A., Ji, W., and Watanabe, K.. 2009. Social dynamics of the golden snub-nosed monkey (*Rhinopithecus roxellana*): female transfer and one-male unit succession. *American Journal of Primatology* 71: 670–679.

Qi, X., Garber, P. A., Ji, W. et al. 2014. Satellite telemetry and social modeling offer new insights into the origin of primate multilevel societies. *Nature Communications* 5: 5296.

Qi, X., Grueter, C. C., Fang, G. et al. 2020. Multilevel societies facilitate infanticide avoidance through increased extrapair matings. *Animal Behaviour* 161: 127–137.

Qi, X., Huang, K., Li, Y. et al. 2017. Male cooperation for breeding opportunities contributes to the evolution of multilevel societies. *Proceedings of the Royal Society B* 284: 20171480.

Qi, X., Li, B. & Ji, W. 2008. Reproductive parameters of wild female Rhinopithecus roxellana. *American Journal of Primatology* 70: 311–319.

Qi, X., Li, B. & Li, Y. 2006. Maternal investment and birth sex ratio bias of the golden snub-nosed monkey *Rhinopithecus roxellana* in Qinling Mountains of China. *Acta Zoologica Sinica* 52: 1–10.

Qi, X., Li, B., Tan, C. L. & Gao, Y. F. 2004. Spatial structure in a golden snub-nosed monkey *Rhinopithecus roxellana* group while no-locomotion. *Acta Zoologica Sinica* 50: 697–705.

Qi, X., Yang, B., Garber, P. A., Ji, W., Watanabe, K. & Li, B. 2011. Sexual interference in the golden snub-nosed monkey (*Rhinopithecus roxellana*): A test of the sexual competition hypothesis in a polygynous species. *American Journal of Primatology* 73: 366–377.

Qiu, J. 2010. China drought highlights future climate threats. *Nature* 465: 142–143.

Quan, R., Ren, G., Behm, J. E., Wang, L., Huang, Y., Long, Y. & Zhu, J. 2011. Why does *Rhinopithecus bieti* prefer the highest elevation range in winter? A test of the sunshine hypothesis. *PLOS ONE* 6: e24449.

Quinten, M. C., Waltert, M., Syamsuri, F. & Hodges, J. K. 2010. Peat swamp forest supports high primate densities on Siberut Island, Sumatra, Indonesia. *Oryx* 44: 147–151.

Quinten, M., Stirling, F., Schwarze, S., Dinata, Y. & Hodges, K. 2014. Knowledge, attitudes and practices of local people on Siberut Island (West-Sumatra, Indonesia) towards primate hunting and conservation. *Journal of Threatened Taxa* 6: 6389–6398.

Raaum, R. L., Sterner, K. N., Noviello, C. M., Stewart, C.-B. & Disotell, T. R. 2005. Catarrhine primate divergence dates estimated from complete mitochondrial genomes: concordance with fossil and nuclear DNA evidence. *Journal of Human Evolution* 48: 237–257.

Rae, T. C., Röhrer-Ertl, O., Wallner, C.-P. & Koppe, T. 2007. Paranasal pneumatization of two late Miocene colobines: Mesopithecus and Libypithecus

(Cercopithecidae: Primates). *Journal of Vertebrate Paleontology* **27**: 768–771.

Rahaman, H. 1973. The langurs of the Gir Sanctuary (Gujarat): a preliminary survey. *Journal of the Bombay Natural History Society* **70**: 294–314.

Rahayuni, D. R. 2007. *Studi kohabitasi antara simakobu (*Simias concolor*) dan joja (*Presbytis potenziani*) di area Siberut Conservation Program (SCP), Pulau Siberut, Kepulauan Mentawai, Sumatera Barat.* BSc thesis, Institut Pertanian Bogor, Bogor, Indonesia.

Rahm, U. H. 1970. Ecology, zoogeography and systematics of some African forest monkeys. In Napier, J. R. & Napier, P. H. (Eds.), *Old World Monkeys: Ecology, Systematics and Behavior.* New York: Academic Press. Pp. 589–626.

Rahman, M. M., Jaman, M. F., Khatun, M. T. et al. 2015. Feeding ecology of Northern Plains Sacred langur *Semnopithecus entellus* (Dufresne) in Jessore, Bangladesh: dietary composition, seasonal and age-sex differences. *Asian Primates Journal* **5**: 24–39.

Rainer, H., White, A. & Lanjouw, A. 2018. *State of the Apes – Infrastructure Development and Ape Conservation.* Cambridge: Cambridge University Press.

Rajendran, S., Saseendran, P. C., Subramanian, H., Chitra, R. & Yuvaraj, N. 2004. A survey of gastro-intestinal parasitic infection in Nilgiri langur (*Semnopithecus johnii*) at Kalakkad-Munanthurai Tiger Reserve, Tamil Nadu. *Zoo's Print Journal* **19**: 1454.

Rajpurohit, L. S. & Sommer, V. 1991. Sex differences in mortality among langurs (*Presbytis entellus*) of Jodhpur, Rajasthan. *Folia Primatologica* **56**: 17–27.

Rajpurohit, L. S., Chhangani, A. K., Rajpurohit, R. S. & Mohnot, S. M. 2003. Observation of a sudden resident-male replacement in a unimale bisexual troop of Hanuman langurs, *Semnopithecus entellus*, around Jodhpur (India). *Folia Primatologica* **74**: 85–87.

Rajpurohit, L. S., Mohnot, S. M. & Sommer, V. 1995. Wanderers between harems and bachelor bands: male Hanuman langurs (*Presbytis entellus*) at Jodhpur in Rajasthan. *Behaviour* **132**: 255–299.

Ramachandran, K. & Joseph, G. K. 2001. Feeding ecology of Nilgiri langur (*Trachypithecus johnii*) in Silent Valley National Park, Kerala, India. *Indian Forester* **127**: 1155–1164.

Ramlee, H. 2013. *Distribution, ecology and systematics of* Presbytis hosei *and other leaf monkey species in North Borneo.* PhD thesis, Australian National University, Canberra.

Ramsay, M. S. & Teichroeb, J. A. 2019. Anecdotes in primatology: temporal trends, anthropocentrism, and hierarchies of knowledge. *American Anthropologist* **121**: 680–693.

Rangel-Negrín, A., Alfaro, J. L., Valdez, R. A., Romano, M. C. & Serio-Silva, J. C. 2009. Stress in Yucatan spider monkeys: effects of environmental conditions on fecal cortisol levels in wild and captive populations. *Animal Conservation* **12**: 496–502.

Rasmussen, D. T., Friscia, A. R., Gutierrez, M. et al. 2019. Primitive Old World monkey from the earliest Miocene of Kenya and the evolution of cercopithecoid bilophodonty. *Proceedings of the National Academy of Sciences* **116**: 6051–6056.

Ratajszczak, R., Cox, R. & Ha, D. D. 1990. A preliminary survey of primates in North Viet Nam. Gland: World Wide Fund for Nature.

Raubenheimer, D., Machovsky-Capuska, G. E., Chapman, C. A. & Rothman, J. M. 2015. Geometry of nutrition in field studies: an illustration using wild primates. *Oecologia* **177**: 223–234.

Rautio, P., Bergvall, U. A., Karonen, M. & Salminen, J. P. 2007. Bitter problems in ecological feeding experiments: commercial tannin preparations and common methods for tannin quantifications. *Biochemical Systematics and Ecology* **35**: 257–262.

Ravosa, M. J. & Profant, L. A. 2000. Evolutionary morphology of the skull in Old World monkeys. In Whitehead, P. F. & Jolly, C. (Eds.), *Old World Monkeys.* Cambridge: Cambridge University Press. Pp. 237–268.

Rawson, B. 2006. Activity budget in black-shanked douc langur (*Pygathrix nigripes*). *International Journal of Primatology* **27**: 307.

Rawson B. M. 2009. *The socio-ecology of the black-shanked douc (*Pygathrix nigripes*) in Mondulkiri Province, Cambodia.* PhD thesis, Australian National University, Canberra.

Rawson, B. M. & Luu, T. B. 2011. Preliminary observations of geophagy amongst Cambodia's Colobinae. *Vietnamese Journal of Primatology* **1**: 41–46.

Rawson, B. M. & Roos, C. 2008. A new primate species record for Cambodia: *Pygathrix nemaeus*. *Cambodian Journal of Natural History* **1**: 7–11.

Redford, K. 1992. The empty forest. *Bioscience* **41**: 412–422.

Reena, M. & Ram, M. B. 1992. Rate of takeovers in groups of Hanuman langurs (*Presbytis entellus*) at Jaipur. *Folia Primatologica* **58**: 61–71.

Refisch, J. & Koné, I. 2005a. Impact of commercial hunting on monkey populations in the Taï region, Cote d'Ivoire. *Biotropica* 37: 136–144.

Refisch, J. & Koné, I. 2005b. Market hunting in the Taï Region, Côte d'Ivoire and implications for monkey populations. *International Journal of Primatology* 26: 621–629.

Reichenbach, H. G. L. 1862 [1862–1863]. *Central-Atlas für zoologische Gärten und für Thierfreunde. Die vollständigste Naturgeschichte der Affen.* Dresden, Leipzig: Woldemar Türk's. 204 pp.

Reis, M. D., Gunnell, G. F., Barba-Montoya, J. et al.. 2018. Using phylogenomic data to explore the effects of relaxed clocks and calibration strategies on divergence time estimation: primates as a test case. *Systematic Biology* 67: 594–615.

Ren, B., Li, D., Garber, P. A. & Li, M. 2012a. Evidence of allomaternal nursing across one-male units in the Yunnan snub-nosed monkey (*Rhinopithecus bieti*). *PLOS ONE* 7: e30041.

Ren, B., Li, D., Garber, P. A. & Li, M. 2012b. Fission-fusion behavior in Yunnan snub-nosed monkeys (*Rhinopithecus bieti*) in Yunnan, China. *International Journal of Primatology* 33: 1096–1109.

Ren, B., Li, D., He, X., Qiu, J. & Li, M. 2011. Female resistance to invading males increases infanticide in langurs. *PLOS ONE* 6: e18971.

Ren, B., Li, D., Liu, Z. et al. 2010. First evidence of prey capture and meat eating by wild Yunnan snub-nosed monkeys in Yunnan, China. *Current Zoology* 56: 227–231.

Ren, B., Li, M., Long, Y. & Wei, F. 2009a. Influence of day length, ambient temperature, and seasonality on daily travel distance in the Yunnan snub-nosed monkey at Jinsichang, Yunnan, China. *American Journal of Primatology* 71: 233–241.

Ren, B., Li, M., Long, Y., Wu, R. & Wei, F. 2009b. Home range and seasonality of Yunnan snub-nosed monkeys. *Integrative Zoology* 4: 162–171.

Ren, B., Li, M. & Wei, F. 2008. Preliminary study on digging and eating underground storage plant corms by wild Yunnan snub-nosed monkeys at Tacheng, Yunnan, China. *Acta Theriologica Sinica* 28: 237–241.

Ren, B., Liang, B., Zhang, S., Li, Q. & Grueter, C. C. 2007. Effects of temporary removal and replacement of the alpha male on social behavior of the captive Sichuan snub-nosed monkey *Rhinopithecus roxellana. Acta Zoologica Sinica* 53: 755–762.

Ren, B., Zhang, S., Xia, S. et al. 2003. Annual reproductive behavior of *Rhinopithecus roxellana. International Journal of Primatology* 24: 575–589.

Ren, R., Su, Y., Yan, K. et al. 1998. Preliminary survey of the social organization of *Rhinopithecus roxellana* in Shennongjia National Natural Reserve, Hubei, China. In Jablonski, N. G. (Ed.), *The Natural History of the Doucs and Snub-Nosed Monkeys.* Singapore: World Scientific Press. Pp. 269–279.

Ren, R., Yan, K., Su, Y. et al. 1991. The reconciliation behavior of golden monkeys (*Rhinopithecus roxellanae roxellanae*) in small breeding groups. *Primates* 32: 321–327.

Ren, R., Yan, K., Su, Y. et al. 1995. The reproductive behavior of golden monkeys in captivity (*Rhinopithecus roxellana roxellana*). *Primates* 36: 135–143.

Ren, R., Yan, K., Su, Y. et al. 2010. Social behavior of a captive group of golden snub-nosed langur *Rhinopithecus roxellana. Zoological Studies* 49: 1–8.

Ren, R., Yan, K., Su, Y. et al. 2000. *A Field Study of the Society of Rhinopithecus roxellanae.* Beijing: Beijing University Press (in Chinese with English section).

Reyna-Hurtado, R., Teichroeb, J. A., Bonnell, T. R. et al. 2018. Primates adjust movement strategies due to changing food availability. *Behavioral Ecology* 29: 368–376.

Ridley, M. 1986. The number of males in a primate troop. *Animal Behaviour* 34: 1848–1858.

Riggs, R. A., Sayer, J., Margules, C. et al. 2016. Forest tenure and conflict in Indonesia: contested rights in Rempek Village, Lombok. *Land Use Policy* 57: 241–249.

Ripley, S. 1965. *The ecology and social behavior of the ceylon gray langur,* Presbytis entellus thersites. PhD thesis, University of California, Berkeley.

Ripley, S. 1967a. Intertroop encounters among Ceylon gray langurs (*Presbytis entellus*). In Altmann, S. A. (Ed.), *Social Communication among Primates.* Chicago: The University of Chicago Press. Pp. 237–253.

Ripley, S. 1967b. The leaping of langurs: a problem in the study of locomotor adaptation. *American Journal of Physical Anthropology* 26: 149–170.

Ripley, S. 1970. Leaves and leaf-monkeys: The social organization of foraging in gray langurs *Presbytis entellus thersites.* In Napier, J. R. & Napier, P. H. (Eds.), *Old World Monkeys: Evolution, Systematics, and Behavior.* New York: Academic Press. Pp. 481–509.

Robbins, M. M. 1995. A demographic analysis of male life history and social structure of mountain gorillas. *Behaviour* 132: 21–47.

Roberts, H. 2015. Reproductive *characteristics of captive langurs and gibbons: life history and reproductive senescence*. Honours thesis, Australian National University, Canberra.

Roberts, P., et al. 2014. Continuity of mammalian fauna over the last 200,000 y in the Indian subcontinent. *Proceedings of the National Academy of Sciences of the United States of America* **111**: 5848–5853.

Robinson, B. W. & Wilson, D. S. 1998. Optimal foraging, specialization, and a solution to Liem's paradox. *The American Naturalist* **151**: 223–235.

Rode, K. D., Chapman, C. A., Chapman, L. J. & McDowell, L. R. 2003. Mineral resource availability and consumption by colobus in Kibale National Park, Uganda. *International Journal of Primatology* **33**: 541–573.

Rodgers, W. A. 1981. The distribution and conservation status of colobus monkeys in Tanzania. *Primates* **22**: 33–45.

Rodman, P. S. 1973. Synecology of Bornean primates: I. *A test for interspecific interactions in spatial distribution of five species. American Journal of Physical Anthropology* **38**: 655–659.

Rodman, P. S. 1978. Diets, densities and distributions of Bornean primates. In Montgomery, G. G. (Ed.), *The Ecology of Arboreal Folivores*. Washington, DC: Smithsonian Institution Press. Pp. 465–478.

Rodman, P. S. 1988. Resources and group sizes of primates. In Slobodchikoff, C. N. (Ed.), *The Ecology of Social Behavior*. San Diego, CA: Academic Press. Pp. 83–108.

Rodseth, L., Wrangham, R. W., Harrigan, A. M. & Smuts, B. B. 1991. The human community as a primate society. *Current Anthropology* **32**: 221–254.

Roehe, R., Dewhurst, R. J., Duthie, C.-A. et al. 2016. Bovine host genetic variation influences rumen microbial methane production with best selection criterion for low methane emitting and efficiently feed converting hosts based on metagenomic gene abundance. *PLOS genetics* **12**: e1005846.

Roggenbuck, M., Sauer, C., Poulsen, M., Bertelsen, M. F. & Sorensen, S. J. 2014. The giraffe (*Giraffa camelopardalis*) rumen microbiome. *FEMS Microbiology Ecology* **90**: 237–246.

Rohwer, S., Fretwell, S. D. & Niles, D. M. 1980. Delayed maturation in passerine plumages and the deceptive acquisition of resources. *American Naturalist* **115**: 400–437.

Rohwer, S., Klein, W. P. Jr. & Heard, S. 1983. Delayed plumage maturation and the presumed prealternat molt in American redstarts. *Wilson Bulletin* **95**: 199–208.

Ronquist, F., Teslenko, M., van der Mark, P. et al. 2012. MrBayes 3.2: efficient Bayesian phylogenetic inference and model choice across a large model space. *Systematic Biology* **61**: 539–542.

Roonwal, M. L. & Mohnot, S. M. 1977. *Primates of South Asia: Ecology, Sociobiology, and Behavior*. Cambridge, MA: Harvard University Press. 421 pp.

Roonwal, M. L. 1979. Field study of geographical, subspecific and clinal variations in tail carriage in the Hanuman langur, *Presbytis entellus* (Primates) in South Asia. *Zoologischer Anzeiger* **202**: 235–255.

Roonwal, M. L. 1981a. Intraspecific variation in size, proportion of body parts and weight in the Hanuman langur, *Presbytis entellus* (Primates), in South Asia, with remarks on subspeciation. *Records of the Zoological Survey of India* **79**: 125–158.

Roonwal, M. L. 1981b. New field data on tail carriage in the common South Asian Langur, *Presbytis entellus* (Primates), and its biological and evolutionary significance. *Proceedings of the Indian National Science Academy* **B47**: 26–40.

Roonwal, M. L., Prite, R. S. & Saha, S. S. 1984. Geographical boundary between the northern and southern tail styles in the common South Asian langur, *Presbytis entellus* (Primates). *Journal of the Zoological Society of India* **36**: 15–26.

Roos, C. & Nadler, T. 2001. Molecular evolution of the douc langurs. *Zoologischer Garten (NF)* **71**: 1–6.

Roos, C. 2004. Molecular evolution and systematics of Vietnamese primates. In Nadler, T., Streicher, U. & Long, H. T. (Eds.), *Conservation of Primates in Vietnam*. Hanoi: Haki. Pp. 23–28.

Roos, C., Boonratana, R., Supriantna, J., Fellowes, J. R., Groves, C. P., Nash, S. D., Rylands, A. B. & Mittermeier, R. A. 2014. An updated taxonomy and conservation status review of Asian primates. *Asian Primates Journal* **4**: 2–38.

Roos, C., Liedigk, R., Thinh, V. N., Nadler, T. & Zinner, D. 2019. The hybrid origin of the Indochinese gray langur *Trachypithecus crepusculus*. *International Journal of Primatology* **40**: 9–27.

Roos, C., Nadler, T. & Walter, L. 2008. Mitochondrial phylogeny, taxonomy and biogeography of the silvered langur species group (*Trachypithecus cristatus*). *Molecular Phylogenetics and Evolution* **47**: 629–636.

Roos, C., Thanh, V. N., Walter, L. & Nadler, T. 2007. Molecular systematics of Indochinese primates. *Vietnamese Journal of Primatology* **1**: 41–53.

Roos, C., Zinner, D., Kubatko, L. S. et al. 2011. Nuclear versus mitochondrial DNA: evidence for

hybridization in colobine monkeys. *BMC Evolutionary Biology* **11**: 77.
Roos, C., Helgen, K. H., Portela, Miguez R. et al. 2020. Mitogenomic phylogeny of the Asian colobine genus *Trachypithecus* with special focus on *Trachypithecus phayrei* (Blyth, 1847) and description of a new species. *Zoolgical Research* **41**: 656–669.
Roper, K. M., Scheumann, M., Wiechert, A. B., Nathan, S., Goossens, B., Owren, M. J. & Zimmermann, E. 2014. Vocal acoustics in the endangered proboscis monkey (*Nasalis larvatus*). *American Journal of Primatology* **76**: 192–201.
Rose, A. L., Mittermeier, R. A., Langrand, O. et al. 2003. *Consuming Nature*. Palos Verdes Peninsula, California CA: Altisima Press. 200 pp.
Rose, M. D. 1978. Feeding and associated positional behavior of black and white colobus monkeys (*Colobus guereza*). In Montgomery, C. G. (Ed.), *The Ecology of Arboreal Folivores*. Washington, DC: Smithsonian Institution Press. Pp. 253–262.
Rosenblum, L. L., Supriatna, J., Hasan, M. N. & Melnick, D. J. 1997. High mitochondrial DNA diversity with little structure within and among leaf monkey populations (*Trachypithecus cristatus* and *Trachypithecus auratus*). *International Journal of Primatology* **18**: 1005–1028.
Rosengaus, R. B., Zecher, C. N., Schultheis, K. F., Brucker, R. M. & Bordenstein, S. R. 2011. Disruption of the termite gut microbiota and its prolonged consequences for fitness. *Applied Environmental Microbiology* **77**: 4303–4312.
Ross, C. 1993. Take-over and infanticide in South Indian Hanuman langurs (*Presbytis entellus*). *American Journal of Primatology* **30**: 75–82.
Rossie, J. B., Gilbert, C. C. & Hill, A. 2013. Early cercopithecid monkeys from the Tugen Hills, Kenya. *Proceedings of the National Academy of Sciences* **110**: 5818–5822.
Rostro-García, S., Kamler, J. F., Crouthers, R. et al. 2018. An adaptable but threatened big cat: Density, diet and prey selection of the Indochinese leopard (*Panthera pardus delacouri*) in eastern Cambodia. *Royal Society Open Science* **5**: 171187.
Rothman, J. M. & Bryer, M. A. H. 2019. The effects of humans on the primate nutritional landscape. In Behie, A. M., Teichroeb, J. A. & Malone, N. (Eds.), *Primate Conservation in the Anthropocene*. Cambridge: Cambridge University Press.
Rothman, J. M. 2015. Nutritional geometry provides new insights into the interaction between food quality and demography in endangered wildlife. *Functional Ecology* **29**: 3–4.
Rothman, J. M., Chapman, C. A. & Pell, A. N. 2008a. Fiber-bound nitrogen in gorilla diets: implications for estimating dietary protein intake of primates. *American Journal of Primatology* **70**: 690–694.
Rothman, J. M., Chapman, C. A. & Van Soest, P. J. 2012. Methods in primate nutritional ecology: a user's guide. *International Journal of Primatology* **33**: 542–566.
Rothman, J. M., Chapman, C. A., Struhsaker, T. T. et al. 2015. Long-term declines in nutritional quality of tropical leaves. *Ecology* **96**: 873–878.
Rothman, J. M., Chapman, C. A., Twinomugisha, D. et al. 2008b. Measuring physical traits of primates remotely: the use of parallel lasers. *American Journal of Primatology* **70**: 1191–1195.
Rothman, J. M., Dusinberre, K. & Pell, A. N. 2009. Condensed tannins in the diets of primates: a matter of methods? *American Journal of Primatology* **71**: 70–76.
Rothman, J. M., Raubenheimer, D. & Chapman, C. A. 2011. Nutritional geometry: gorillas prioritize non-protein energy while consuming surplus protein. *Biology Letters* **7**: 847–849.
Round, J. L. & Mazmanian, S. K. 2010. Inducible Fox p3+ regulatory T-cell development by a commensal bacterium of the intestinal microbiota. *Proceedings of the National Academy of Sciences* **107**: 12204–12209.
Rovero, F. & Struhsaker, T. T. 2007. Vegetative predictors of primate abundance: utility and limitations of a fine-scale analysis. *American Journal of Primatology* **69**: 1242–1256.
Rovero, F., Barelli, C., Butynski, T. M., Marshall, A. J. & Struhsaker, T. T. 2019. *Piliocolobus gordonorum. The IUCN Red List of Threatened Species 2019*: e. T40015A92629595. www.iucnredlist.org/.
Rovero, F., Davenport, T. R. B., De Jong, Y. A. & Butynski, T. M. 2020. *Colobus angolensis sharpei. The IUCN Red List of Threatened Species 2020*. www .iucnredlist.org/.
Rovero, F., Marshall, A. R., Jones, T. & Perkin, A. 2009. The primates of the Udzungwa mountains: diversity, ecology and conservation. *Journal of Anthropological Sciences* **87**: 93–126.
Rovero, F., Mtui, A., Kitegile, A., Jacob, P., Araldi, A. & Tenan, S. 2015. Primates decline rapidly in unprotected forests: evidence from a monitoring program with data constraints. *PLOS ONE* **10**: e0118330.

Rowe, N. 1996. *The Pictorial Guide to the Living Primates*. New York: Pogonias Press. 263 pp.

Rowe, N. & Myers, M. 2016. *All the World's Primates*. New York: Pogonias Press. 800 pp.

Rowell, T. E. & Richards, S. M. 1979. Reproductive strategies of some African monkeys. *Journal of Mammalogy* **60**: 58–69.

Rowell, T. E. & Richards, S. M. 1979. Reproductive strategies of some African monkeys. *Journal of Mammalogy* **60**: 58–69.

Roy, D. 2012. Group-size and age-sex composition of Nilgiri langur *Trachypithecus johnii* (Primates: Cercopithecidae) in India. *TAPROBANICA* **4**: 83–87.

Roy, D., Ashokkumar, M. & Desai, A. A. 2012. Foraging Ecology of Nilgiri Langur (*Trachypithecus johnii*) in Parimbikulam Tiger Reserve, Kerala, India. *Asian Journal of Conservation Biology* **1**: 92–102.

Rubenstein, D. I. 1986. Ecology and sociality in horses and zebras. In Rubenstein, D. I. & Wrangham, R. W. (Eds.), *Ecology and Social Evolution: Birds and Mammals*. Princeton, NJ: Princeton University Press. Pp. 282–302.

Rubenstein, D. I. & Hack, M. 2004. Natural and sexual selection and the evolution of multi-level societies: insights from zebras with comparisons to primates. In Kappeler, P. M. & van Schaik, C. P. (Eds.), *Sexual Selection in Primates: New and Comparative Perspectives*. New York: Cambridge University Press. Pp. 266–279.

Rucks, M. 1976. *Notes on the Problems of Primate Conservation in Bia National Park*. Accra, Ghana: Report to the Department of Game and Wildlife.

Rudolph, K. & Fichtel, C. 2017. Inhibitory control in douc langurs (*Pygathrix nemaeus* and *P. cinerea*). *Vietnamese Journal of Primatology* **2**: 73–81.

Rudran, R. 1973a. Adult male replacement in one-male troops of purple-faced langurs (*Presbytis senex senex*) and its effect on population structure. *Folia Primatologica* **19**: 166–192.

Rudran, R. 1973b. The reproductive cycles of two subspecies of purple-faced langurs (*Presbytis senex*) with relation to environmental factors. *Folia Primatologica* **19**: 41–60.

Rudran, R. 2007. A survey of Sri Lanka's endangered and endemic Western purple-faced langur (*Trachypithecus vetulus nestor*). *Primate Conservation* **22**: 139–144.

Rudran, R. & Fernandez-Duque, E. 2003. Demographic changes over thirty years in a red howler population in Venezuela. *International Journal of Primatology* **24**: 925–948.

Rudran, R., Dayananda, H. G. S., Jayamanne, D. D. & Sirimanne, D. G. R. 2013. Food habits and habitat use patterns of Sri Lanka's western purple-faced langur. *Primate Conservation* **27**: 99–108.

Ruempler, U. 1998. Husbandry and breeding of douc langurs (*Pygathrix nemaeus nemaeus*) at Cologne Zoo. *International Zoology Yearbook* **36**: 73–81.

Ruhiyat, Y. 1983. Socio-ecological study of *Presbytis aygula* in West Java. *Primates* **24**: 344–359.

Ruhiyat, Y. 1991. Observations of Presbytis aygula in two localities of Java. *Comparative Primatological Monographs* **3**: 149–191.

Ruiz-Lopez, M. J., Barelli, C., Rovero, F. et al. 2016. A novel landscape genetic approach demonstrates the effects of human disturbance on the Udzungwa red colobus monkey (*Procolobus gordonorum*). *Heredity* **116**: 167–176.

Ruslin, F., Matsuda, I. & Md-Zain, B. M. 2019. The feeding ecology and dietary overlap in two sympatric primate species, the long-tailed macaque (*Macaca fascicularis*) and dusky langur (*Trachypithecus obscurus obscurus*), in Malaysia. *Primates* **60**: 41–50.

Ruslin, F., Yaakop, S. & Zain, B. M. M. 2014. A preliminary study on activity budget, daily travel distance and feeding behaviour of long-tailed macaques and spectacled dusky leaf monkey in Bangi campus of Universiti Kebangsaan Malaysia, Selangor. *AIP Conference Proceedings* **688**: article 5.

Russell, J. B. & Wilson, D. B. 1996. Why are ruminal cellulolytic bacteria unable to digest cellulose at low pH? *Journal of Dairy Science* **79**: 1503–1509.

Russon, A. E. & Wallis, J. 2014. Primate tourism as a conservation tool: a review of the evidence, implications, and recommendations. In Russon, A. E. & Wallis, J. (Eds.), *Primate Tourism: A Tool for Conservation?* Cambridge: Cambridge University Press. Pp. 313–333.

Ryan, A. M., Chapman, C. A. & Rothman, J. M. 2012. How do differences in species and part consumption affect diet nutrient concentrations? A test with red colobus monkeys in Kibale National Park, Uganda. *African Journal of Ecology* **51**: 1–10.

Sabater Pi, J. 1973. Contribution to the ecology of *Colobus polykomos satanas* (Waterhouse 1838) of Rio Muni, Republic of Equatorial Guinea. *Folia Primatologica* **19**: 193–207.

Sabater-Pi, J. & Groves, C. 1972. The importance of higher primates in the diet of the Fang of Río Muni. *Man* **7**: 239–243.

Sah, P., Leu, S. T., Cross, P. C., Hudson, P. J. & Bansal, S. 2017. Unraveling the disease consequences and mechanisms of modular structure in animal social networks. *Proceedings of the National Academy of Sciences* **114**: 4165–4170.

Saj, T. L. & Sicotte, P. 2005. Male takeover in *Colobus vellerosus* at Boabeng-Fiema Monkey Sanctuary, central Ghana. *Primates* **46**: 211–214.

Saj, T. L. & Sicotte, P. 2007a. Predicting the competitive regime of female *Colobus vellerosus* from the distribution of food resources. *International Journal of Primatology* **28**: 315–336.

Saj, T. L. & Sicotte, P. 2007b. Scramble competition among *Colobus vellerosus* at Boabeng-Fiema, Ghana. *International Journal of Primatology* **28**: 337–355.

Saj, T. L. & Sicotte, P. 2013. *Colobus vellerosus*. In Butynski, T. M., Kingdon, J. & Kalina, J. (Eds.), *Mammals of Africa: Vol. 2. Primates*. London: Bloomsbury. Pp. 109–111.

Saj, T. L. & Sicotte, P. 2016. White-thighed Colobus, *Colobus vellerosus*. In Rowe, N. & Myers, M. (Eds.), *All the World's Primates*. Charlestown, RI: Pogonias Press. Pp. 529–530.

Saj, T. L., Marteinson, S., Chapman, C. A. & Sicotte, P. 2007. Controversy over the application of current socioecological models to folivorous primates: *Colobus vellerosus* fits the predictions. *American Journal of Physical Anthropology* **133**: 994–1008.

Saj, T. L., Mather, C. & Sicotte, P. 2006. Traditional taboos in biological conservation: the case of *Colobus vellerosus* at the Boabeng-Fiema Monkey Sanctuary, Central Ghana. *Social Science Information* **45**: 285–310.

Saj, T. L., Teichroeb, J. A. & Sicotte, P. 2005. The population status of the ursine colobus (*Colobus vellerosus*) at Boabeng-Fiema, Ghana. In Paterson J. D. & Wallis J. (Eds.), *Commensalism and Conflict: The Human Primate Interface*. Norman, OK: American Society of Primatologists. Pp. 350–375.

Salgado-Flores, A., Hagen, L. H., Ishaq, S. L. et al. 2016. Rumen and cecum microbiomes in reindeer (*Rangifer tarandus tarandus*) are changed in response to a lichen diet and may affect enteric methane emissions. *PLOS ONE* **11**: e0155213.

Salgado-Lynn, M., Stanton, D. W. G., Sakong, R. et al. 2010. Microsatellite markers for the proboscis monkey (*Nasalis larvatus*). *Conservation Genetics Resources* **2**: 159–163.

Salter, R. E., MacKenzie, N. A., Nightingale, N., Aken, K. M. & Chai P. K. P. 1985. Habitat use, ranging behaviour, and food habits of the proboscis monkey, *Nasalis larvatus* (van Wurmb), in Sarawak. *Primates* **26**: 436–451.

Salum, L. A. 2009. Ecotourism and biodiversity conservation in jozani-chwaka bay National Park, Zanzibar. *African Journal of Ecology* **47**(Suppl. 1): 166–170.

Salzer, J. S., Rwego, I. B., Goldberg, T. L., Kuhlenschmidt, K. S. & Gillespie, T. R. 2007. *Giardia* sp. and *Cryptosporidium* sp. infections in primates in fragmented and undisturbed forest in western Uganda. *Journal of Parasitology* **93**: 439–440.

Samejima, H., Ong, R., Lagan, P. & Kitayama, K. 2012. Camera-trapping rates of mammals and birds in a Bornean tropical rainforest under sustainable forest management. *Forest Ecology and Management* **270**: 248–256.

Samsudin, A. A., Evans, P. N., Wright, A. D. & Al Jassim, R. 2011. Molecular diversity of the foregut bacteria community in the dromedary camel (*Camelus dromedarius*). *Environmental Microbiology* **13**: 3024–3035.

Sanderson, I. T. 1957. *The Monkey Kingdom: An Introduction to the Primates*. New York: Chanticleer Press. 200 pp.

Sanderson, J. K., Alger, G. A. B., da Fonseca, G. et al. 2003. *Biodiversity Conservation Corridors: Planning, Implementing, and Monitoring Sustainable Landscapes*. Washington, DC: Conservation International.

Sangchantr, S. 2004. *Organization and ecology of mentawai leaf monkeys (*Presbytis potenziani*)*. PhD thesis, Columbia University, New York.

Saura, S., Bertzky, B., Bastin, L. et al. 2018. Protected area connectivity: shortfalls in global targets and country-level priorities. *Biological Conservation* **219**: 53–67.

Sayer, J. A. 1992. A future for Africa's tropical forests. In Sayer, J. A., Harcourt, C. S. & Collins, N. M. (Eds.), *The Conservation Atlas of Tropical Forests. Africa*. Hants: Macmillan. Pp. 81–93.

Sayers, K. 2013. On folivory, competition, and intelligence: generalisms, overgeneralizations, and models of primate evolution. *Primates* **54**: 111–124.

Sayers, K. 2014. High altitude primates, extreme primates, and anthropological primatology: or, there is more to human evolution than tool use, culture, or African apes. In Grow, N. B., Gursky-Doyen, S. & Krzton, A. (Eds.), *High Altitude Primates*. New York: Springer. Pp. 325–350.

Sayers, K. 2017. Folivory. In Fuentes, A. (Ed.), *The International Encyclopedia of Primatology*. Chichester, UK: Wiley Blackwell. Pp. 414–418.

Sayers, K. & Menzel, C. R. 2012. Memory and foraging theory: chimpanzee utilization of optimality heuristics in the rank-order recovery of hidden foods. *Animal Behaviour* **84**: 795–803.

Sayers, K. & Norconk, M. 2008. Himalayan *Semnopithecus entellus* at Langtang National Park, Nepal: diet, activity patterns, and resources. *International Journal of Primatology* **29**: 509–530.

Sayers, K., Norconk, M. A. & Conklin-Brittain, N. L. 2010. Optimal foraging on the roof of the world: Himalayan langurs and the classical prey model. *American Journal of Physical Anthropology* **141**: 337–357.

Schel, A. M. 2009. *Anti-predator behaviour of Guereza colobus monkeys (*Colobus guereza*)*. PhD thesis, University of St. Andrews, St. Andrews, UK.

Schel, A. M. & Zuberbühler, K. 2009. Responses to leopards are independent of experience in Guereza colobus monkeys. *Behaviour* **146**: 1709–1737.

Schel, A. M. & Zuberbühler, K. 2012a. Dawn chorusing in guereza colobus monkeys. *Behavioral Ecology and Sociobiology* **66**: 361–373.

Schel, A. M. & Zuberbühler, K. 2012b. Predator and non-predator long-distance calls in Guereza colobus monkeys. *Behavioural Processes* **91**: 41–49.

Schel, A. M., Candiotti, A. & Zuberbühler, K. 2010. Predator-deterring alarm call sequences in Guereza colobus monkeys are meaningful to conspecifics. *Animal Behaviour* **80**: 799–808.

Schel, A. M., Tranquilli, S. & Zuberbühler, K. 2009. The alarm call system of two species of black-and-white colobus monkeys (*Colobus polykomos* and *Colobus guereza*). *Journal of Comparative Psychology* **123**: 136–150.

Schenkel, R. & Schenkel-Hulliger, L. 1967. On the sociology of free-ranging colobus (*Colobus guereza caudatus* Thomas 1885). In Starck, D., Schneider, R. & Kuhn, H. J. (Eds.), *Progress in Primatology*. Basel: Karger. Pp. 185–194.

Schipper, J., Chanson, J. S., Chiozza, F. et al. 2008. The status of the world's land and marine mammals: diversity, threat, and knowledge. *Science* **141**: 67–77.

Schneider, I., Tielen, I. H. M., Rode, J., Levelink, P. & Schrudde, D. 2010. Behavioral observations and notes on the vertical ranging pattern of the Critically Endangered Cat Ba langur (*Trachypithecus poliocephalus poliocephalus*) in Vietnam. *Primate Conservation* **25**: 111–117.

Schrudde, D., Levelink, P. & Raffel, M. 2010. Protection of the Cat Ba langur (Trachypithecus [poliocephalus] poliocephalus) through the 'Cat Ba Langur Conservation Project'. In Nadler, T., Rawson, B. & Ngoc, T. V. (Eds.), *Conservation of Primates in Indochina*. Hanoi: Frankfurt Zoological Society and Conservation International. Pp. 237–243.

Schuelke, O. & Ostner, J. 2012. Ecological and social influcences on sociality. In Mitani, J. C., Call, J., Kappeler, P. M. et al. (Eds.), *The Evolution of Primate Societies*. Chicago: The University of Chicago Press. Pp. 195–219.

Schultz, A. H. 1958. Cranial and dental variability in colobus monkeys. *Proceedings of the Zoological Society of London* **130**: 79–105.

Schultz, S., Noë, R., McGraw, W. S. & Dunbar, R. I. M. 2004. A community-level evaluation of the impact of prey behavioural and ecological characteristics on predator diet composition. *Proceedings of the Royal Society of London Series B-Biological Sciences* **271**: 725–732.

Schulz-Kornas, E., Stuhlträger, J., Clauss, M., Wittig, R. M. & Kupczik, K. 2019. Dust affects chewing efficiency and tooth wear in forest dwelling Western chimpanzees (*Pan troglodytes verus*). *American Journal of Physical Anthropology* **169**: 66–77.

Schwarm, A., Ortmann, S., Wolf, C., Streich, W. J. & Clauss, M. 2009. Passage marker excretion in red kangaroo (*Macropus rufus*), collared peccary (*Pecari tajacu*) and colobine monkeys (*Colobus angolensis, C. polykomos, Trachypithecus johnii*). *Journal of Experimental Zoology. Part A, Ecological Genetics and Physiology* **311**(9): 647–661.

Schwarz, E. 1928. Bemerkungen über die roten stummelaffen. *Zeitschrift für Säugetierkunde* **3**: 92–97.

Schwarz, E. 1929. On the local races and distribution of the black and white colobus monkeys. *Proceedings of the Zoological Society of London* **99**: 585–598.

Schwitzer, C., Mittermeier, R. A., Rylands, A. B. et al. 2014. *Primates in Peril: The World's 25 Most Endangered Primates 2012–2014*. Arlington, VA: IUCN SSC Primate Specialist Group. 87 pp. https://portals.iucn.org/library/sites/library/files/documents/IUCN-2014-018.pdf.

Schwitzer, C., Mittermeier, R. A., Rylands, A. B. et al. 2017. *Primates in Peril: The World's 25 Most Endangered Primates 2016–2018*. Arlington, VA: IUCN SSC Primate Specialist Group. 99 pp.

Schwitzer, C., Mittermeier, R. A., Rylands, A. B. et al. 2019. *Primates in Peril: The World's 25 Most Endangered Primates 2018–2020*. Washington, DC:

IUCN SSC Primate Specialist Group, International Primatological Society, Global Wildlife Conservation & Bristol Zoological Society. 130 pp.

Schwitzer, C., Mittermeier, R. A., Rylands, A. B. et al. 2015. *Primates in Peril: The World's 25 Most Endangered Primates 2014–2016*. Arlington, VA: IUCN SSC Primate Specialist Group. 93 pp.

Schwitzer, C., Polowinsky, S. Y. & Solman, C. 2009. Fruits as foods – common misconceptions about frugivory. In Clauss, M., Fidgett, A. L., Hatt, J. M. et al. (Eds.), *Zoo Animal Nutrition IV*. Fürth: Filander Verlag. Pp. 131–168.

Scott, J. E., Campbell, R. M., Baj, L. M., Burns, M. C., Price, M. S., Sykes, J. D. & Vinyard, C. J. 2018. Dietary signals in the premolar dentition of primates. *Journal of Human Evolution* 121: 221–234.

Seaward, M. R. D. 1987. Effects of quantitative and qualitative changes in air pollution on the ecological and geographical performance of lichens. In Hutchinson, T. & Meema, K. M. (Eds.), *The Effects of Atmospheric Pollutants on Forests, Wetlands and Agricultural Ecosystems*. Berlin: Springer. Pp. 439–450.

Seidensticker, J. 1983. Predation by *Panthera* cats and measures of human influence in habitats of South Asian monkeys. *International Journal of Primatology* 4: 323–326.

Seidensticker, J. & Suyono, I. 1980. *The Javan Tiger and the Meru-Betiri Reserve: A Plan for Management*. Gland: IUCN.

Selby, M. S., Reno P. L., McCollum, M. A. & Lovejoy, C. O. 2005. Thumb reduction in colobines: Adaptation or pleiotropy? *American Journal of Physical Anthropology Suppl* S40: 187.

Selvan, K. M., Gopi, G. V., Habib, B. & Lyngdoh, S. 2013. Losing threatened and rare wildlife to hunting in Zero valley, Arunachal Pradesh, India. *Current Science* 104: 1492–1495.

Semaw, S., Simpson, S. W., Quade, J. et al. 2005. Early Pliocene hominins from Gona, Ethiopia. *Nature* 433: 301–305.

Senut, B. 1994. Cercopitheccoidea Neogenes et Quaternaries du Rift occidental (Ouganda). In Senut, B. & Pickford, M (Eds.), *Geology and Paleontology of the Albertine Rift Valley, Uganda-Zaire Vol II Paleontology*. Orleans: CIFIG. Pp. 195–205.

Serge Bobo, K., Bonito Ntumwel, C., Florence Aghomo, F. & Aurele Ayemele, K. G. 2017. The conservation status of two threatened primates in the korup region, southwest cameroon. *Primate Conservation* 31(1): 37–48.

Sery, G. B., Zinner, D., Koné, Bi, Z. G. et al. 2006. A West African black-and-white colobus monkey, *Colobus polykomos dollmani* Schwarz, 1927, facing extinction. *Primate Conservation* 21: 55–61.

Seto, K. C., Güneralp, B. & Hutyra, L. R. 2012. Global forecasts of urban expansion to 2030 and direct impacts on biodiversity and carbon pools. *Proceedings of the National Academy of Sciences* 109: 16083–16088.

Seyfarth, R. M. & Cheney, D. L. 2012. Knowledge of social relations. In Mitani, J. C., Call, J., Kappeler, P. M., Palombit, R. A. & Silk, J. B. (Eds.), *The Evolution of Primate Societies*. Chicago: The University of Chicago Press. Pp. 628–642.

Sha, C. M., Fam, S. D. & Ang, H. F. 2018. South-east Asian primates in swamp forests. In Nowak, K., Barnett, A. A. & Matsuda, I. (Eds.), *Primates in Flooded Habitats: Ecology and Conservation*. Cambridge: Cambridge University Press.

Sheil, D. & Murdiyarso, D. 2009. How forests attract rain: an examination of a new hypothesis. *BioScience* 59: 341–347.

Shellis, R. P. & Hiiemae, K. M. 1986. Distribution of enamel on the incisors of old world monkeys. *American Journal of Physical Anthropology* 71: 103–113.

Shelmidine, N., Borries, C. & Koenig, A. 2007. Genital swellings in silvered langurs: what do they indicate? *American Journal of Primatology* 69: 519–532.

Shelmidine, N., Borries, C. & McCann C. 2009. Patterns of reproduction in Malayan silvered leaf monkeys at the Bronx Zoo. *American Journal of Primatology* 71: 852–859.

Shelmidine, N., McAloose, D. & McCann, C. 2013. Survival patterns and mortality in the North American population of silvered leaf monkeys (*Trachypithecus cristatus*). *Zoo Biology* 32: 177–188.

Shi, D., Li, G. & Hu, T. 1982. Preliminary studies on the ecology of the golden-haired monkey. *Zoological Research* 3: 105–110.

Shinohara, A., Uchida, E., Shichijo, H., Sakamoto, S. H., Morita, T. & Koshimoto, C. 2016. Microbial diversity in forestomach and caecum contents of the greater long-tailed hamster *Tscherskia triton* (Rodentia: Cricetidae). *Mammalian Biology* 81(1): 46–52.

Shultz, S. & Thomsett, S. 2007. Interactions between African crowned eagles and their prey community. In Noë, R., McGraw, S. & Zuberbühler, K. (Eds.), *Monkeys of the Taï Forest: An African Primate Community*. Cambridge: Cambridge University Press. Pp. 171–193.

Shultz, S. 2002. Population density, breeding chronology and diet of crowned eagles *Stephanoaetus coronatus* in Tai National Park, Ivory Coast. *Ibis* **144**: 135–138.

Shultz, S., Noe, R., McGraw, W. S. & Dunbar, R. I. M. 2004. A community-level evaluation of the impact of prey behavioural and ecological characteristics on predator diet composition. *Proceedings of the Royal Society B-Biological Sciences* **271**(1540): 725–732.

Sibley, S. D., Lauck, M., Bailey, A. L. et al. 2014. Discovery and characterization of distinct simian pegiviruses in three wild African Old World monkey species. *PLOS ONE* **9**: e98569.

Sicotte, P. & MacIntosh, A. J. 2004. Inter-group encounters and male incursions in *Colobus vellerosus* in central Ghana. *Behaviour* **141**: 533–553.

Sicotte, P., Teichroeb, J. A., Vayro, J. V., Fox, S. A., Bădescu, I. & Wikberg, E. C. 2017. The influence of male takeovers on female dispersal in *Colobus vellerosus*. *American Journal of Primatology* **79**: e22436.

Siewe, S., Vadjunec, J. M. & Caniglia, B. 2017. The politics of land use in the Korup National Park. *Land* **6**: 1–22.

Siex, K. S. 2003. *Effects of population compression on the demography, ecology, and behavior of the Zanzibar red colobus monkey* (Procolobus kirkii). PhD thesis, Duke University, Durham, NC.

Siex, K. S. 2005. Habitat destruction, population compression and overbrowsing by the Zanzibar red colobus monkey (*Procolobus kirkii*). In Paterson, J. D. & Wallis, J. (Eds.), *Commensalism and Conflict: The Human-Primate Interface*. Norman, OK: American Journal of Primatology. Pp. 294–337.

Siex, K. S. & Struhsaker, T. T. 1999a. Colobus monkeys and coconuts: a study of perceived human–wildlife conflicts. *Journal of Applied Ecology* **36**: 1009–1020.

Siex, K. S. & Struhsaker, T. T. 1999b. Ecology of the Zanzibar red colobus monkey: demographic variability and habitat stability. *International Journal of Primatology* **20**: 163–192.

Siex, K. S. & Struhsaker, T. T. 2013. *Procolobus kirkii* Zanzibar red colobus (Kirk's red colobus). In Butynski, T. M., Kingdon, J. & Kalina, J. (Eds.), *Mammals of Africa: Vol. 2. Primates*. London: Bloomsbury. Pp. 151–154.

Silk, J. B., Beehner, J. C., Bergman, T. J. et al. 2009. The benefits of social capital: close social bonds among female baboons enhance offspring survival. *Proceedings of the Royal Society of London B* **276** (1670): 3099–3104.

Simcharoen, A., Simcharoen, S., Duangchantrasiri, S., Bump, J. & Smith, J. L. D. 2018. Tiger and leopard diets in western Thailand: evidence for overlap and potential consequences. *Food Webs* **15**: e00085.

Simons, E. L. & Delson, E. 1978. Cercopithecidae and Parapithecide. In Maglio, V. J. & Cooke, H. B. S. (Eds.), *Evolution of African Mammals*. Cambridge, MA: Harvard University Press. Pp. 100–119.

Simons, E. L. 1967. A fossil *Colobus* skull from the Sudan (Primates, Cercopithecidae). *Postilla* **111**: 1–12.

Simons, N. D., Eick, G. N., Ruiz-Lopez, M. J. et al. 2017. Cis-regulatory evolution in a wild primate: infection-associated genetic variation drives differential expression of mhc-dqa1 in vitro. *Molecular Ecology* **26**: 4523–4535.

Simpson, S. J. & Raubenheimer, D. 2012. *The Nature of Nutrition: A Unifying Framework from Animal Adaptation to Human Obesity*. Princeton: Princeton University Press.

Sinclair, A. R. E. 2003. Mammal populations regulation, keystone processes and ecosystem dynamics. *Philosophical Transactions of the Royal Society of London, Series B* **358**: 1729–1740.

Singh, M. E., Singh, M. R., Kumara, H. N., Kumar, M. A. & d'Souza, L. 1997. Inter-and intra-specific associations of non-human primates in Anaimalai Hills, South India. *Mammalia* **61**: 17–28.

Singh, M. R., Singh, M., Ananda Kumar, M., Kumar, H. N., Sharma, A. K. & Sushma, H. S. 2000. Niche separation in sympatric lion-tailed macaques (*Macaca silenus*) and Nilgiri langur (*Presbytis johnii*) in an Indian tropical rain forest. *Primate Report* **58**: 83–95.

Singh, M., Kumara, H. N., Kavana, T. S., Erinjery, J. J. & Kumar, S. 2016. Demography and reproductive output in langurs of the Western Ghats, India. *Primates* **57**: 501–508.

Singh, M., Roy, K. & Singh, M. 2011. Resource partitioning in sympatric langurs and macaques in tropical rainforests of the central Western Ghats, South India. *American Journal of Primatology* **73**: 335–346.

Sjahfirdi, L., Aldi, N., Maheshwari, H. & Astuti, P. 2015. Aplikasi Fourier Transform Infrared (FTIR) dan pengamatan pembengkakan genital pada specsies primate, lutung jawa (*Trachypithecus auratus*) untuk mendeteksi masa subur. *Indonesian Journal of Veterinary Sciences* **9**: 156–160.

Skorupa, J. P. 1986. Responses of rainforest primates to selective logging in Kibale Forest, Uganda: a summary report. In Benirschke, K. (Ed.), *Primates*. New York: Springer-Verlag. Pp. 57–70.

Skorupa, J. P. 1989. Crowned eagles *Stephanoaetus coronatus* in rainforest: observations on breeding chronology and diet at a nest in Uganda. *Ibis* **131**: 294–298.

Slyter, L. L. 1976. Influence of acidosis on rumen function. *Journal of Animal Science* **43**: 910–929.

Smith, D. A. E. 2014. The effects of land-use policies on the conservation of Borneo's endemic Presbytis monkeys. *Biodiversity and Conservation* **23**: 891–908.

Snaith, T. V. & Chapman, C. A. 2007. Primate group size and interpreting socioecological models: do folivores really play by different rules? *Evolutionary Anthropology* **16**: 94–106.

Snaith, T. V. & Chapman, C. A. 2008. Red colobus monkeys display alternative behavioral responses to the costs of scramble competition. *Behavioral Ecology* **19**: 1289–1296.

Snaith, T. V. & Chapman, C. A. 2005. Towards an ecological solution to the folivore paradox: patch depletion as an indicator of within-group scramble competition in red colobus monkeys (*Piliocolobus tephrosceles*). *Behavioral Ecology and Sociobiology* **59**: 185–190.

Snyder-Mackler, N., Beehner, J. C. & Bergman, T. J. 2012. Defining higher levels in a gelada multilevel society. *International Journal of Primatology* **33**: 1054–1068.

Soendjoto, M. A. 2003. Adaptasi bekantan (*Nasalis larvatus*) terhadaphutan karet: Studikasus di Kabupaten Tabalong, Kalimantan Selatan. Usulan Penelitian. Program Pasca Sarjana, Institut Pertanian Bogor.

Solanki, G. S., Kumar, A. & Sharma, B. K. 2007. Reproductive strategies of *Trachypithecus pileatus* in Arunachal Pradesh, India. *International Journal of Primatology* **28**: 1075–1083.

Solanki, G., Kumar, A. & Sharma, B. 2008. Feeding ecology of *Trachypithecus pileatus* in India. *International Journal of Primatology* **29**: 173–182.

Sommer, V. & Mendoza-Granados, D. 1995. Play as indicator of habitat quality: a field study of langur monkeys (*Presbytis entellus*). *Ethology* **99**: 177–192.

Sommer, V. & Mohnot, S. 1985. New observations on infanticides among hanuman langurs (*Presbytis entellus*) near Jodhpur (Rajasthan/India). *Behavioral Ecology and Sociobiology* **16**: 245–248.

Sommer, V. & Rajpurohit, L. S. 1989. Male reproductive success in harem troops of Hanuman langurs (*Presbytis entellus*). *International Journal of Primatology* **10**: 293–317.

Sommer, V. 1985. *Weibliche und Männliche Reproduktionsstrategien der Hanuman Languren (*Presbytis entellus*) von Jodhpur, Rajastan/Indiën.* PhD thesis, Universität Göttingen, Göttingen, Germany.

Sommer, V. 1987. Infanticide among free-ranging langurs (*Presbytis entellus*) at Jodhpur (Rajasthan/India): recent observations and a reconsideration of hypotheses. *Primates* **28**: 163–197.

Sommer, V. 2000. The holy wars about infanticide. Which side are you on? And why? In van Schaik, C. P. & Janson, C. H. (Eds.), *Infanticide by Males and its Implications*. Cambridge: Cambridge University Press. Pp. 9–26.

Sommer, V., Srivastava, A. & Borries, C. 1992. Cycles, sexuality, and conception in free-ranging langurs (*Presbytis entellus*). *American Journal of Primatology* **28**: 1–27.

Song, S. J., Lauber, C., Costello, E. K. et al. 2013. Cohabiting family members share microbiota with one another and with their dogs. *eLife* **2**: e00458.

Sonnenburg, E. D., Smits, S. A., Tikhonov, M. et al. 2016. Diet-induced extinction in the gut microbiota compounds over generations. *Nature* **529**: 212–215.

Southwick, C. H. & Fedigan, F. C. 1972. Population studies of Malaysian primates. *Primates* **13**: 1–18.

Spassov, N. & Geraads, D. 2007. *Dolichopithecus balcanicus* sp. nov., a new Colobinae (Primates, Cercopithecidae) from the early Pliocene of southeastern Europe, with a discussion on the taxonomy of the genus. *Journal of Human Evolution* **52**: 434–442.

Spracklen, B. D., Kalamandeen, M., Galbraith, D., Gloor, E. & Spracklen, D. V. 2015. A global analysis of deforestation in moist tropical forest protected areas. *PLOS ONE* **10**: e0143886.

Springer, M. S., Meredith, R. W., Gatesy, J. et al. 2012. Macroevolutionary dynamics and historical biogeography of primate diversification inferred from a species supermatrix. *PLOS ONE* **7**: e49521.

Srivastava, A. 1989. *Feeding ecology and behaviour of the Hanuman langur,* Presbytis entellus. PhD thesis, University of Jodhpur, Jodhpur.

Srivastava, A. 1991a. Cultural transmission of snake-mobbing in free-ranging Hanuman langurs. *Folia Primatologica* **56**: 117–120.

Srivastava, A. 1991b. Insectivory and its significance to langur diets. *Primates* **32**: 237–241.

Srivastava, A. 1992. Use of resources by free-ranging female langurs (*Presbytis entellus*) during different reproductive phases. *Folia Primatologica* 59: 157–162.

Srivastava, A. 2006a. Conservation of threatened primates of Northeast India. *Primate Conservation* 20: 107–113.

Srivastava, A. 2006b. Ecology and conservation of the golden langur, *Trachypithecus geei*, in Assam, India. *Primate Conservation* 21: 163–170.

Srivastava, A. & Dunbar, R. I. M. 1996. The mating system of Hanuman langurs: a problem in optimal foraging. *Behavioral Ecology and Sociobiology* 39: 219–226.

Srivastava, A., Biswas, J., Das, J. & Bujarbarua, P. 2001. Status and distribution of golden langurs (*Trachypithecus geei*) in Assam, India. *American Journal of Primatology* 55: 15–23.

Srivastava, K. K., Zacharias, V. J., Bhardwaj, A. K., Joseph, P. & Joseph, S. 1996. Some observations on troop structure, activity budget and food habits of the Nilgiri Langur (*Presbytis johnii*) in Periyar during monsoon (June-August). *Indian Forester* 122: 946–950.

Srivathsan, A. 2014. *From barcoding to metagenomics: molecular identification techniques for ecological studies of endangered primates*. PhD thesis, National University of Singapore, Singapore.

Srivathsan, A., Ang, A., Vogler, A. P. & Meier, R. 2016. Fecal metagenomics for the simultaneous assessment of diet, parasites, and population genetics of an understudied primate. *Frontiers in Zoology* 13: 17.

Stacey, P. B. 1986. Group size and foraging efficiency in yellow baboons. *Behavioral Ecology and Sociobiology* 18: 175–187.

Stammbach, E. 1987. Desert, forest and montane baboons: multilevel-societies. In Smuts, B. B., Cheney, D. L., Seyfarth, R. M. et al. (Eds.), *Primate Societies*. Chicago: University of Chicago Press. Pp. 112–120.

Stanford, C. B. 1996b. The hunting ecology of wild chimpanzees: implications for the evolutionary ecology of Pliocene hominoids. *American Journal of Physical Anthropology* 98: 96–113.

Stanford, C. B. 1988. Ecology of the capped langur and Phayre's leaf monkey in Bangladesh. *Primate Conservation* 9: 125–128.

Stanford, C. B. 1989. Predation on capped langurs (*Presbytis pileata*) by cooperatively hunting jackals (*Canis aureus*). *American Journal of Primatology* 19: 53–56.

Stanford, C. B. 1991a. *The Capped Langur in Bangladesh: Behavioural Ecology and Reproductive Tactics*. New York: Karger. 202 pp.

Stanford, C. B. 1991b. The diet of the capped langur (*Presbytis pileata*) in a moist deciduous forest in Bangladesh. *International Journal of Primatology* 12: 199–216.

Stanford, C. B. 1991c. Social dynamics of intergroup encounters in the capped langur (*Presbytis pileata*). *American Journal of Primatology* 25: 35–47.

Stanford, C. B. 1992. Costs and benefits of allomothering in wild capped langurs (*Presbytis pileata*). *Behavioral Ecology and Sociobiology* 30: 29–34.

Stanford, C. B. 1995. The influence of chimpanzee predation on group size and anti-predator behaviour in red colobus monkeys. *Animal Behaviour* 49: 577–587.

Stanford, C. B. 1996a. The colobines: beyond infanticide. *American Journal of Primatology* 38: 187–189.

Stanford, C. B. 1998a. *Chimpanzee and Red Colobus: The Ecology of Predator and Prey*. Cambridge, MA: Harvard University Press.

Stanford, C. B. 1998b. Predation and male bonds in primate societies. *Behaviour* 135: 513–533.

Stanford, C. B. 2002. Avoiding predators: expectations and evidence in primate antipredator behavior. *International Journal of Primatology* 23: 741–757.

Stanford, C. B., Wallis, J., Mpongo, E. & Goodall, J. 1994. Hunting decisions in wild chimpanzees. *Behaviour* 131: 1–18.

Starin, E. D. 1978. A preliminary investigation of home range use in the Gir Forest langur. *Primates* 19: 551–567.

Starin, E. D. 1988. Gestation and birth-related behaviors in Temminck's red colobus. *Folia Primatologica* 51: 161–164.

Starin, E. D. 1991. *Socioecology of the red colobus monkey in The Gambia with particular reference to female-male differences and transfer patterns*. PhD thesis, City University of New York, New York.

Starin, E. D. 1994. Philopatry and affiliation among red colobus. *Behaviour* 130: 253–270.

Starin, E. D. 2001. Patterns of inbreeding avoidance in Temminck's red colobus. *Behaviour* 138: 453–465.

Stark, D. J., Nijman, V., Lhota, S., Robins, J. G. & Goossens, B. 2012. Modeling population viability of local proboscis monkey Nasalis larvatus populations: conservation implications. *Endangered Species Research* 16: 31–43.

Stark, D. J., Vaughan, I. P., Evans, L. J. et al. 2017a. Combining drones and satellite tracking as an effective tool for informing policy change in riparian habitats: a proboscis monkey case study. *Remote Sensing in Ecology and Conservation* 4: 44–52.

Stark, D. J., Vaughan, I. P., Ramirez Saldivar, D. A., Nathan, S. K. & Goossens, B. 2017b. Evaluating methods for estimating home ranges using GPS collars: a comparison using proboscis monkeys (*Nasalis larvatus*). *PLOS ONE* 12: e0174891.

Stead, S. M. & Teichroeb, J. A. 2019. A multi-level society comprised of one-male and multi-male core units in an African colobine (*Colobus angolensis ruwenzorii*). *PLOS ONE* 14: e0217666.

Stead, S. M., Bădescu, I., Raboin, D. L. et al. 2021. High levels of infant handling by adult males in Rwenzori Angolan colobus (*Colobus angolensis ruwenzorii*) compared to two closely related species, *C. guereza* and *C. vellerosus*. *Primates* 62: 637–646.

Steel, I. R. 2012. *The effects of habitat parameters on the behavior, ecology, and conservation of the Udzungwa red colobus monkey (*Procolobus gordonorum*).* PhD thesis, Duke University, Durham, NC.

Steel, R. I. 2014. Using multiple travel paths to estimate daily travel distance in arboreal, group-living primates. *Primates* 56: 71–75.

Steenbeek, R. 1996. What a maleless group can tell us about the constraints on female transfer in Thomas's langurs *Presbytis thomasi*. *Folia Primatologica* 67: 169–181.

Steenbeek, R. 1999. Tenure related changes in wild Thomas's langurs I: between-group interactions. *Behaviour* 136: 595–625.

Steenbeek, R. & van Schaik, C. P. 2001. Competition and group size in Thomas's langurs (*Presbytis thomasi*): the folivore paradox revisited. *Behavioral Ecology and Sociobiology* 49: 100–110.

Steenbeek, R., Sterck, E. H. M., de Vries, H. & van Hooff, J. A. R. A. M. 2000. Costs and benefits of the one-male, age-graded, and all-male phases in in wild Thomas's langur groups. In Kappeler, P. M. (Ed.), *Primate Males*. Cambridge: Cambridge University Press. Pp. 130–145.

Steinmetz, R., Seuaturien, N. & Chutipong, W. 2013. Tigers, leopards, and dholes in a half-empty forest: assessing species interactions in a guild of threatened carnivores. *Biological Conservation* 163: 68–78.

Steinmetz, R., Timmins, R. J. & Duckworth, J. W. 2011. Distribution and conservation status of the Lao leaf monkey (*Trachypithecus (francoisi) laotum*). *International Journal of Primatology* 32: 587–604.

Stenke, R. & Xuan C. C. 2004. The golden-headed langur (*Trachypithecus poliocephalus*) on Cat Ba Island – Status, threat factors amd recovery options. In Nadler, T., Streicher, U. & Long, H. T. (Eds.), *Conservation of primates in Vietnam*. Hanoi: Frankfurt Zoological Society. Pp. 72–77.

Sterck, E. H. M. 1995. *Females, foods and fights*. PhD thesis, University of Utrecht, Utrecht, The Netherlands.

Sterck, E. H. M. 1997. Determinants of female dispersal in Thomas langurs. *American Journal of Primatology* 42: 179–198.

Sterck, E. H. M. 1998. Female dispersal, social organization, and infanticide in langurs: are they linked to human disturbance? *American Journal of Primatology* 44: 235–254.

Sterck, E. H. M. 1999. Variation in langur social organization in relation to the socioecological model, human habitat alteration, and phylogenetic constraints. *Primates* 40: 199–213.

Sterck, E. H. M. 2012. The behavioral ecology of colobine monkeys. In Mitani, J. C., Call, J., Kappeler, P. M. et al. (Eds.), *The Evolution of Primate Societies*. Chicago: The University of Chicago Press. Pp. 65–90.

Sterck, E. H. M., Watts, D. P. & van Schaik, C. P. 1997. The evolution of female social relationships in nonhuman primates. *Behavioral Ecology and Sociobiology* 41: 291–309.

Sterck, E. H. M., Willems, E. P., van Hooff, J. A. & Wich, S. A. 2005. Female dispersal, inbreeding avoidance and mate choice in Thomas langurs (*Presbytis thomasi*). *Behaviour* 142: 845–868.

Sterck, E. H. M. & Korstjens, A. H. 2000. Female dispersal and infanticide avoidance in primates. In van Schaik, C. P. & Janson, C. H. (Eds.), *Infanticide by Males and Its Implications*. Cambridge: Cambridge University Press. Pp. 293–321.

Sterck, E. H. M. & Steenbeek, R. 1997. Female dominance relationships and food competition in the sympatric Thomas langur and long-tailed macaque. *Behaviour* 134: 749–774.

Sterck, E. H. M. & van Hooff, J. A. R. A. M. 2000. The number of males in langur groups: monopolisability of females or demographic processes? In Kappeler, P. M. (Ed.), *Primate Males*. Cambridge: Cambridge University Press. Pp. 120–129.

Stern, M. & Goldstone, R. 2005. Red colobus as prey: the leaping habits of five sympatric old world monkeys. *Folia Primatologica* 76: 100–112.

Sterner, K. N., Raaum, R. L., Zhang, Y. P., Stewart, C. B. & Disotell, T. R. 2006. Mitochondrial data support an odd-nosed colobine clade. *Molecular Phylogenetics and Evolution* 40: 1–7.

Steuer, P., Südekum, K.-H., Tütken, T. et al. (2014). Does body mass convey a digestive advantage for large herbivores? *Functional Ecology* **28**: 1127–1134.

Stevens, C. E. & Hume, I. D. 1995. *Comparative Physiology of the Vertebrate Digestive System*, 2nd ed. New York: Cambridge University Press.

Stevens, C. E. & Hume, I. D. 1998. Contributions of microbes in vertebrate gastrointestinal tract to production and conservation of nutrients. *Physiological Reviews* **78**: 393–427.

Stevens, N. J., Seiffert, E. R., O'Connor, P. M. et al. 2013. Palaeontological evidence for an Oligocene divergence between Old World monkeys and apes. *Nature* **497**: 611–614.

Stevenson, P. R. 2001. The relationship between fruit production and primate abundance in Neotropical communities. *Biological Journal of the Linnean Society* **72**: 161–178.

Stewart, C. B. & Disotell, T. R. 1998. Primate evolution – in and out of Africa. *Current Biology* **8**: R582–88.

Stewart, R. D., Auffret, M. D., Warr, A. et al. 2018. Assembly of 913 microbial genomes from metagenomic sequencing of the cow rumen. *Nature Communications* **9**: 1–11.

Strait, K., Else, J. G. & Eberhard, M. L. 2012. Parasitic diseases of nonhuman primates. In Abee, C. R., Mansfield, K., Tardif, S. et al. (Eds.), *Nonhuman Primates in Biomedical Research: Vol. 2. Diseases*, 2nd ed. London: Elsevier. Pp. 197–297.

Strasser, E. & Delson, E. 1987. Cladistic analysis of cercopithecid relationships. *Journal of Human Evolution* **16**: 81–99.

Strier, K. B. 1994. Myth of the typical primate. *American Journal of Physical Anthropology* **37**: 233–271.

Struhsaker, T. T. 1972. Rain-forest conservation in Africa. *Primates* **13**: 103–109.

Struhsaker, T. T. 1975. *The Red Colobus Monkey.* Chicago: University of Chicago Press.

Struhsaker, T. T. 1978a. Food habits of five monkey species in the Kibale Forest, Uganda. In Chivers, D. J. & Herbert, J. (Eds.), *Recent Advances in Primatology*. London: Academic Press. Pp. 225–248.

Struhsaker, T. T. 1978b. Interrelations of red colobus monkeys and rain-forest trees in the Kibale Forest, Uganda. In Montgomery, G. G. (Ed.), *The Ecology of Arboreal Folivores*. Washington, DC: Smithsonian Institution Press. Pp. 397–422.

Struhsaker, T. T. 1980. Comparison of the behaviour and ecology of red colobus and redtail monkeys in the Kibale Forest, Uganda. *African Journal of Ecology* **18**: 33–51.

Struhsaker, T. T. 1981. Forest and primate conservation in East Africa. *African Journal of Ecology* **19**: 99–114.

Struhsaker, T. T. 1997. *Ecology of an African Rain Forest: Logging in Kibale and the Conflict Between Conservation and Exploitation.* Gainesville: University Press of Florida.

Struhsaker, T. T. 1999. Primate communities in Africa: the consequences of long-term evolution or the artifact of recent hunting. In Fleagle, J. G., Janson, C. & Reed, K. (Eds.), *Primate Communities.* Cambridge: Cambridge University Press. Pp. 289–294.

Struhsaker, T. T. 2000a. The effects of predation and habitat quality on the socioecology of African monkeys: lessons from the islands of Bioko and Zanzibar. In Jolly, C. J. & Whitehead, P. F. (Eds.), *Old World Monkeys.* Cambridge: Cambridge University Press. Pp. 393–430.

Struhsaker, T. T. 2000b. Variation in adult sex ratios of red colobus monkey social groups: implications for interspecific comparisons. In Kappeler, P. (Ed.), *Primate Males.* Cambridge: Cambridge University Press. Pp. 108–119.

Struhsaker, T. T. 2005. Conservation of red colobus and their habitat. *International Journal of Primatology* **26**: 525–538.

Struhsaker, T. T. 2010. *The Red Colobus Monkeys: Variation in Demography, Behavior, and Ecology of Endangered Species.* New York: Oxford University Press.

Struhsaker, T. T. & Grubb, P. 2013. *Procolobus rufomitratus.* In Butynski, T. M., Kingdon, J. & Kalina, J. (Eds.), *Mammals of Africa: Vol. 2. Primates.* London: Bloomsbury. Pp. 142–147.

Struhsaker, T. T. & Leakey, M. 1990. Prey selectivity by crowned hawk-eagles on monkeys in the Kibale forest, Uganda. *Behavioral Ecology and Sociobiology* **26**: 435–443.

Struhsaker, T. T. & Leland, L. 1979. Socioecology of five sympatric monkey species in the Kibale Forest, Uganda. *Advances in the Study of Behavior* **9**: 159–228.

Struhsaker, T. T. & Leland, L. 1985. Infanticide in a patrilineal society of red colobus monkeys. *Zeitschrift für Tierpsychologie* **69**: 89–132.

Struhsaker, T. T. & Leland, L. 1987. Colobines: infanticide by adult males. In Smuts, B., Cheney, D., Seyfarth, R. et al. (Eds.), *Primate Societies.* Chicago: University of Chicago Press. Pp. 83–97.

Struhsaker, T. T. & Siex, K. S. 1998. Translocation and introduction of the Zanzibar red colobus monkey:

success and failure with an endangered island endemic. *Oryx* 32: 277–284.

Struhsaker, T. T. & Ting, N. 2020. *Piliocolobus tephrosceles. The IUCN Red List of Threatened Species 2020*: e.T18256A92661680. www.iucnredlist.org/.

Struhsaker, T. T., Cooney, D. O. & Siex, K. S. 1997. Charcoal consumption by Zanzibar red colobus monkeys: its function and its ecological and demographic consequences. *International Journal of Primatology* 18: 61–72.

Struhsaker, T. T., Grubb, P. & Siex, K. S. 2013. *Procolobus gordonorum* Udzungwa red colobus (Iringa / Uhehe / Gordon's red colobus). In Butynski, T. M., Kingdon, J. & Kalina, J. (Eds.), *Mammals of Africa: Vol. 2. Primates*. London: Bloomsbury. Pp. 148–151.

Struhsaker, T. T., Marshall, A. R., Detwiler, K. et al. 2004. Demographic variation among Udzungwa red colobus in relation to gross ecological and sociological parameters. *International Journal of Primatology* 25: 615–658.

Su, C., Zuo, R., Liu, W. et al. 2016. Fecal bacterial composition of Sichuan snub-nosed monkeys (*Rhinopithecus roxellana*). *International Journal of Primatology* 37: 518–533.

Su, Y., Ren, R., Yan, K. et al. 1998. Preliminary survey of the home range and ranging behavior of golden monkeys (*Rhinopithecus roxellana*) in Shennongjia National Natural Reserve, Hubei, China. In Jablonski, N. G. (Ed.), *The Natural History of the Doucs and Snub-Nosed Monkeys*. Singapore: World Scientific Press. Pp. 255–268.

Suarez, S. A. 2013. Diet of Phayre's leaf-monkey in the Phu Khieo Wildlife Sanctuary, Thailand. *Asian Primates Journal* 3: 2–12.

Sudo, N., Chida, Y., Aiba, Y. et al. 2004. Postnatal microbial colonization programs the hypothalamic-pituitary-adrenal system for stress response in mice. *Journal of Physiology* 558: 263–275.

Sugiyama, Y. 1964. Group composition, population density and some sociological observations of Hanuman langurs (*Presbytis entellus*). *Primates* 5: 7–37.

Sugiyama, Y. 1965. On the social change of Hanuman langurs (*Presbytis entellus*) in their natural condition. *Primates* 6: 381–418.

Sugiyama, Y. 1966. An artificial social change in a Hanuman langur troop (*Presbytis entellus*). *Primates* 7: 41–72.

Sugiyama, Y. 1967. Social organization of Hanuman langurs. In Altmann, S. A. (Ed.), *Social Communication Among Primates*. Chicago: University of Chicago Press. Pp. 221–236.

Sugiyama, Y. 1976. Characteristics of the ecology of the Himalayan langurs. *Journal of Human Evolution* 5: 249–277.

Sugiyama, Y., Yoshiba, K. & Pathasarathy, M. D. 1965. Home range, mating season, male group and inter-troop relations in Hanuman langurs (*Presbytis entellus*). *Primates* 6: 73–106.

Sujana, K. A., Sivaperuman, C. & Anil-Kumar, N. 2012. Lianas as a food resource for nilgiri langur (*Trachypithecus johnii* Fischer 1829) in forest of Wayanad, Western Ghats, India. *International Journal of Plant, Animal and Environmental Sciences* 2: 239–243.

Sujatnika 1992. *Studi Habitat Surili (*Presbytis aygula Linnaeus, 1758*) dan Pola Penggunaanya di Taman Nasional Gunung Gede-Pangrango dan Kawasan Hutan Haurbentes-Jasinga.* BSc thesis, Institut Pertanian, Boror, Indonesia.

Sun, X. F., Wang, L. Q. & Gu, Z. B. 2005. A brief overview of China's timber market system. *International Forestry Review* 6: 221–226.

Sunderraj, S. F. W. 2001. Ecology and conservation of Nilgiri langur (*Trachypithecus johnii*). *Envis Bulletin: Wildlife and Protected Areas* 1: 49–59.

Sunderraj, S. F. W. & Johnsingh, A. J. T. 2001. Impact of biotic disturbances on Nilgiri langur habitat, demography and group dynamics. *Current Science* 80: 428–436.

Supriatna, J. & Ario, A. 2015. Primates as flagships for conserving biodiversity and parks in Indonesia: Lessons learned from West Java and North Sumatra. *Primate Conservation* 29: 123–131.

Supriatna, J. & Mariati, S. 2014. Degradation of primate habitat at TessoNilo Forest with special emphasis on Riau pale-thighed surili (*Presbytis siamensis cana*). *Journal of Environmental Protection* 5: 1145.

Supriatna, J., Adimuntja, C., Mitrasetia, T. et al.. 1989. Chemical analysis of food plant parts of two sympatric monkeys (*Presbytis aurata and Macaca fascicularis*) in the mangrove forests of Muara Gembong, West Java. In Soerianegara, I., Zamora, P. M., Kartawinata, K. et al. (Eds.), *Symposium on mangrove management: its ecological and economical considerations, Bogor 9–11 August 1988*. Bogor: SEAMEO-Biotrop. Pp. 161–169.

Supriatna, J., Dwiyahreni, A. A., Winarni, N., Mariati, S. & Margules, C. 2017. Deforestation of primate habitat on Sumatra and adjacent islands, Indonesia. *Primate Conservation* 31: 71–82.

Supriatna, J., Manullang, B. O. & Soekara, E. 1986. Group composition, home range, and diet of the maroon leaf monkey (*Presbytis rubicunda*) at Tanjung Puting Reserve, Central Kalimantan, Indonesia. *Primates* 27: 185–190.

Supriatna, J., Wijayanto, I., Manullang, B. O., Anggraeni, D. & Wiratno, E. S. 2002. The state of siege for Sumatra's forest and protected areas: stakeholders' views during devolution, and political plus economic crises in Indonesia. In *Proceedings of IUCN/WCPA-East Asia*. Apple Valley, MN: IUCN SSC Conservation Breeding Specialist Group. Pp. 439–456.

Suryana, D. 2010. *Studi Perilaku Makan dan Palatabilitas Rekrekan (*Presbytis fredericae *Sody, 1930) di Kawasan Hutan dan Perkebunan Karet Desa Gutomo Kabupaten Pekalongan Provinsi Jawa Tengah.* BSc thesis, Institut Pertanian Bogor, Bogor, Indonesia.

Sussman, R. W., Cheverud, J. M. & Bartlett, T. Q. 1994. Infant killing as an evolutionary strategy: reality or myth? *Evolutionary Anthropology* 3: 149–151.

Sutherland, T. M. 1988. Particle separation in the forestomach of sheep. In Dobson, A. & Dobson, M. J. (Eds.), *Aspects of Digestive Physiology in Ruminants.* Ithaca, NY: Cornell University Press. Pp. 43–73.

Sutherland-Smith, M., Janssen, D. & Lowenstine, L. 1998. *Gastric analyses of colobine primates.* Omaha, NE: AAZV.

Suwa, G., Asfaw, B., Nakaya, H., Katoh, S. & Beyene, Y. In press. Early Pleistocene fauna and palaeoenvironments at Konso, Ethiopia. In Reynolds, S. & Bobe, R. (Eds.), *African Palaeoecology and Human Evolution.* Cambridge: Cambridge University Press.

Suwa, G., Beyene, Y., Nakaya, H. et al. 2015. Newly discovered cercopithecid, equid and other mammalian fossils from the Chorora Formation, Ethiopia. *Anthropological Science* 123: 19–39.

Suzuki, A. 1979. The variation and adaptation of social groups of chimpanzees and black and white colobus monkeys. In Bernstein, I. S. & Smith, E. O. (Eds.), *Primate Ecology and Human Origins.* New York: Garland STPM Press. Pp. 153–173.

Swart, C. 2010. *Measuring the state of health of sacred forests, Kenya. Using the black-and-white colobus monkey (*Colobus angolensis palliatus*) as an indicator species.* MSc thesis, Imperial College London, London.

Swedell, L. & Plummer, T. 2012. A papionin multi-level society as a model for early hominin evolution. *International Journal of Primatology* 33: 1165–1193.

Swedell, L. & Schreier, A. 2009. Male aggression towards females in hamadryas baboons: conditioning, coercion, and control. In Muller, M. N. & Wrangham, W. R. (Eds.), *Sexual Coercion in Primates and Humans: An Evolutionary Perspective on Male Aggression against Females.* Cambridge, MA: Harvard University Press. Pp. 244–268.

Swindler, D. R. 1976. *Dentition of Living Primates.* New York: Academic Press.

Swindler, D. R. 1979. The incidence of underbite occlusion in leaf-eating monkeys. *Ossa* 6: 261–272.

Swindler, D. R. 1983. Variation and homology of the primate hypoconulid. *Folia Primatologica* 41: 112–123.

Swindler, D. R. 2002. *Primate Dentition: An Introduction to the Teeth of Non-Human Primates.* New York: Cambridge University Press.

Swindler, D. R. & Orlosky, F. J. 1974. Metric and morphological variability in the dentition of colobine monkeys. *Journal of Human Evolution* 3: 135–160.

Swindler, D. R., McCoy, H. A. & Hornbeck, P. V. 1967. The dentition of the baboon (*Papio anubis*). In Vagtborg, H. (Ed.), *The Baboon in Medical Research*, vol. 2. Austin: University of Texas Press. Pp. 133–150.

Symington, M. 1990. Fission-fusion social organization in *Ateles* and *Pan. International Journal of Primatology* 11: 47–61.

Szalay, F. S. & Delson, E. 1979. *Evolutionary History of the Primates.* New York: Academic Press. 550 pp.

Takahashi, M. Q., Rothman, J. M., Raubenheimer, D. & Cords, M. 2019. Dietary generalists and nutritional specialists: feeding strategies of adult female blue monkeys (*Cercopithecus mitis*) in the Kakamega Forest, Kenya. *American Journal of Primatology* 81: e23016.

Takahata, Y. T., Hasegawa, T. & Nishida, T. 1984. Chimpanzee predation in the Mahale Mountains from August 1979 to May 1982. *International Journal of Primatology* 5: 213–233.

Takai, M. & Maschenko, E. N. 2009. *Parapresbytis eohanuman*: the northernmost colobine monkey from the Pliocene of Transbaikalia. *Asian Paleoprimatology* 5: 1–14.

Takai, M., Soe, A. N., Maung, M., Tsubamoto, T., Egi, N., Nishimura, T. D. & Nishioka, Y., 2015. First discovery of colobine fossils from the late Miocene/early Pliocene in central Myanmar. *Journal of Human Evolution* 84: 1–15.

Takasaki, H. 1981. Troop size, habitat quality, and home range area in Japanese macaques. *Behavioral Ecology and Sociobiology* 9: 277–281.

Tan, B. 1985. The status of primates in China. *Primate Conservation* 5: 63–81.

Tan, C. L., Guo, S. & Li, B. 2007. Population structure and ranging patterns of *Rhinopithecus roxellana* in Zhouzhi National Reserve, Shaanxi, China. *International Journal of Primatology* 28: 577–591.

Tan, C. L., Li, B. & Zhao, D. 2004. What's sex got to do with it? A preliminary study on the sexual behavior of Sichuan snub-nosed monkeys (*Rhinopithecus roxellana*) in Qinling, China. *Folia Primatologica* 75(Suppl. 1): 27.

Tan, D. S. H., Ali, F., Kutty, S. N. & Meier, R. 2008. The need for specifying species concepts: How many species of silvered langurs (*Trachypithecus cristatus* group) should be recognized? *Molecular Phylogenetics and Evolution* 49: 688–689.

Tan, J., Tao, R. & Su, Y. 2014. Testing the cognition of the forgotten colobines: a first look at golden snub-nosed monkeys (*Rhinopithecus roxellana*). *International Journal of Primatology* 35: 376–393.

Taylor, R. J. 1984. *Predation*. New York: Chapman and Hill.

Teaford, M. F. 1983. Functional morphology of the underbite in two species of langurs. *Journal of Dental Research* 62: 183.

Teaford, M. F., Kay, R. F. & Ungar, P. S. 2008. Molar shape and molar microwear in the Koobi Fora monkeys: ecomorphological implications. In Jablonski, N. G. & Leakey, M. G. (Eds.), *Koobi Fora Research Project, the Fossil Monkeys*, vol. 6. San Francisco: California Academy of Sciences. Pp. 337–358.

Teelen, S. 2007a. Influence of chimpanzee predation on associations between red colobus and red-tailed monkeys at Ngogo, Kibale National Park, Uganda. *International Journal of Primatology* 28: 593–606.

Teelen, S. 2007b. Primate abundance along five transect lines at ngogo, Kibale National Park, Uganda. *American Journal of Primatology* 69: 1030–1044.

Teelen, S. 2008. Influence of chimpanzee predation on the red colobus population at Ngogo, Kibale National Park, Uganda. *Primates* 49: 41–49.

Teichroeb, J. A. & Sicotte, P. 2008a. Infanticide in ursine colobus monkeys (*Colobus vellerosus*) in Ghana: new cases and a test of the existing hypotheses. *Behaviour* 145: 727–755.

Teichroeb, J. A. & Sicotte, P. 2008b. Social correlates of fecal testosterone in male ursine colobus monkeys (*Colobus vellerosus*): the effect of male reproductive competition in aseasonal breeders. *Hormones and Behaviour* 54: 417–423.

Teichroeb, J. A. & Sicotte, P. 2009. Test of the ecological-constraints model on ursine colobus monkeys (*Colobus vellerosus*) in Ghana. *American Journal of Primatology* 71: 49–59.

Teichroeb, J. A. & Sicotte, P. 2010. The function of male agonistic displays in ursine colobus monkeys (*Colobus vellerosus*): male competition, female mate choice or sexual coercion? *Ethology* 116: 366–380.

Teichroeb, J. A. & Sicotte, P. 2018. Cascading competition: the seasonal strength of scramble influences between-group contest in a folivorous primate. *Behavioral Ecology and Sociobiology* 72: 6.

Teichroeb, J. A., Bridgett, G. R., Corriveau, A. & Twinomugisha, D. 2019. The immediate impact of selective logging on Rwenzori Angolan Colobus (*Colobus angolensis ruwenzorii*) at Lake Nabugabo, Uganda. In Behie, A. M. Teichroeb, J. A. & Malone, N. (Eds.), *Primate Research and Conservation in the Anthropocene*. Cambridge: Cambridge University Press. Pp. 120–140.

Teichroeb, J. A., Kutz, S. J., Parkar, U., Thompson, R. C. A. & Sicotte, P. 2009b. Ecology of the gastrointestinal parasites of *Colobus vellerosus* at Boabeng-Fiema, Ghana: possible anthropozoonotic transmission. *American Journal of Physical Anthropology* 140: 498–507.

Teichroeb, J. A., Saj, T. L., Paterson, J. D. & Sicotte, P. 2003. Effect of group size on activity budgets of *Colobus vellerosus* in Ghana. *International Journal of Primatology* 24: 743–758.

Teichroeb, J. A., Sicotte, P. & Wikberg, E. C. 2011. Dispersal in male ursine colobus monkeys (*Colobus vellerosus*): influence of age, rank and contact with other groups on dispersal decisions. *Behaviour* 148: 765–793.

Teichroeb, J. A., Wikberg, E. C. & Sicotte, P. 2009a. Female dispersal patterns in six groups of ursine colobus (*Colobus vellerosus*): infanticide avoidance is important. *Behaviour* 146: 551–582.

Teichroeb, J. A., Wikberg, E. C., Bădescu, I., Macdonald, L. J. & Sicotte, P. 2012. Infanticide risk and male quality influence optimal group composition for *Colobus vellerosus*. *Behavioral Ecology* 23: 1348–1359.

Tenaza, R. R. 1987. The status of primates and their habitats in the Pagai Islands, Indonesia. *Primate Conservation* 8: 104–110.

Tenaza, R. R. 1989a. Female sexual swellings in the Asian colobine *Simias concolor*. *American Journal of Primatology* **17**: 81–86.

Tenaza, R. R. 1989b. Intergroup calls of male pig-tailed langurs (*Simias concolor*). *Primates* **30**: 199–206.

Tenaza, R. R. & Fuentes, A. 1995. Monandrous social organization of pigtailed langurs (*Simias concolor*) in the Pagai Islands, Indonesia. *International Journal of Primatology* **16**: 295–310.

Tenaza, R. R. & Tilson, R. L. 1985. Human predation and Kloss's gibbon (*Hylobates klossii*) sleeping trees in Siberut Island, Indonesia. *American Journal of Primatology* **8**: 299–308.

Terborgh, J. & Janson, C. H. 1986. The socioecology of primate groups. *Annual Review of Ecology and Systematics* **17**: 111–135.

Tesfaye, D. in press. The Omo River guereza (*Colobus guereza guereza*) in habitats with varying levels of fragmentation and disturbance in the southern Ethiopian Highlands: behavioral ecology and phylogeny. PhD thesis, University of Oslo, Oslo, Norway.

Tesfaye, D., Fashing, P. J., Atickem, A., Bekele, A. & Stenseth, N. C. 2021. Feeding ecology of the Omo River guereza (*Colobus guereza guereza*) in habitats with varying levels of fragmentation and disturbance in the southern Ethiopian Highlands. *International Journal of Primatology* **42**: 64–88.

Thierry, B. 2007. Unity in diversity: lessons from macaque societies. *Evolutionary Anthropology: Issues, News, and Reviews* **16**: 224–238.

Thierry, B. 2008. Primate socioecology, the lost dream of ecological determinism. *Evolutionary Anthropology* **17**: 93–96.

Thinh, V. N., Mootnick, A. R., Geissmann, T. et al. 2010. Mitochondrial evidence for multiple radiations in the evolutionary history of small apes. *BMC Evolutionary Biology* **10**: 74.

Thiry, V., Clauss, M., Stark, D. J. et al. 2018. Faecal particle size in free-ranging Proboscis monkeys, *Nasalis larvatus*: variation between seasons. *Folia Primatologica* **89**: 327–334.

Thiry, V., Stark, D. J., Goossens, B. et al. 2016. Use and selection of sleeping sites by proboscis monkeys, *Nasalis larvatus*, along the Kinabatangan River, Sabah, Malaysia. *Folia Primatologica* **87**: 180–196.

Thomas, C. D., Cameron, A., Green, R. E. et al. 2004. Extinction risk from climate change. *Nature* **427**: 145–148.

Thomas, O. 1903. On a new Chinese monkey. *Processes Zoological Society of London* **1**: 224–226.

Thomas, S. C. 1991. Population-densities and patterns of habitat use among anthropoid primates of the ituri forest, zaire. *Biotropica* **23**: 68–83.

Thorington, R. W. & Groves, C. P. 1970. An annotated classification of the Cercopithecoidea. In Napier, J. R. & Napier, P. H. (Eds.), *Old World Monkeys: Evolution, Systematics, and Behaviour*. London: Academic Press. Pp. 629–647.

Thorndike, R. M. & Dinnel, D. L. 2001. *Basic Statistics for the Behavioral Sciences*. New Jersey: Prentice-Hall.

Thurber, M. I., Ghai, R. R., Hyeroba, D. et al. 2013. Co-infection and cross-species transmission of divergent *Hepatocystis* lineages in a wild African primate community. *International Journal of Parasitology* **43**: 613–619.

Tilson, R. L. 1976. Infant coloration and taxonomic affinity of the Mentawai Islands leaf monkey, *Presbytis potenziani*. *Journal of Mammalogy* **57**: 766–769.

Tilson, R. L. 1977. Social organization of simakobu monkeys (*Nasalis concolor*) in Siberut Island, Indonesia. *Journal of Mammalogy* **58**: 202–212.

Tilson, R. L. & Tenaza, R. R. 1976. Monogamy and duetting in an Old World monkey. *Nature* **263**: 320–321.

Tilson, R. L. & Tenaza, R. R. 1982. Interspecific spacing between gibbons (*Hylobates klossii*) and langurs (*Presbytis potenziani*) on Siberut Island, Indonesia. *American Journal of Primatology* **2**: 355–361.

Timmins, R. J. & Duckworth, J. W. 1999. Status and conservation of douc langurs (*Pygathrix nemaeus*) in Laos. *International Journal of Primatology* **20**: 469–489.

Timmins, R. J. & Evans, T. D. 1996. Wildlife and habitat survey of the Nakai-Nam Theun National Biodiversity Conservation Area. Vientiane: Wildlife Conservation Society.

Timmins, R. J. & Khounboline, K. 1996. A preliminary wildlife and habitat survey of Hin Namno National Biodiversity Conservation Area, Khammouane 156 Province, Lao PDR. Vientiane: Wildlife Conservation Society.

Timmins, R. J., Steinmetz, R., Poulsen, K., Evans, T. D., Duckworth, J. W. & Boonratana, R. 2013. The Indochinese silvered leaf monkey *Trachypithecus germaini* (*sensu lato*) in Lao PDR. *Primate Conservation* **26**: 75–87.

Ting, N. 2001. *The hip and thigh of* Paracolobus mutiwa *and* Paracolobus chemeroni. MA thesis, University of Missouri, Columbia.

Ting, N. 2008a. Mitochondrial relationships and divergence dates of the African colobines: evidence of Miocene origins for the living colobus monkeys. *Journal of Human Evolution* 55: 312–325.

Ting, N. 2008b. *Molecular systematics of red colobus monkeys (*Procolobus [Piliocolobus]*): understanding the evolution of an endangered primate.* PhD thesis, City University of New York, New York.

Ting, N., Tosi, A. J., Li, Y., Zhang, Y. P. & Disotell, T. R. 2008. Phylogenetic incongruence between nuclear and mitochondrial markers in the Asian colobines and the evolution of the langurs and leaf monkeys. *Molecular Phylogenetics and Evolution* 46: 466–474.

Ting, S., Hartley, S. & Burns, K. C. 2008. Global patterns in fruiting seasons. *Global Ecology and Biogeography* 17: 648–657.

Tiwari, S., Reddy, D. M., Pradheeps, M., Sreenivasamurthy, G. S. & Umapathy, G. 2017. Prevalence and co-occurrence of gastrointestinal parasites in Nilgiri Langur (*Trachypithecus johnii*) of fragmented landscape in Anamalai Hills, Western Ghats, India. *Current Science* 113: 2194–2200.

Tombak, K. J., Reid, A. J., Chapman, C. A. et al. 2012. Patch depletion behavior differs between sympatric folivorous primates. *Primates* 53: 57–64.

Trading Economics. 2020. Equatorial Guinea GDP per capita. https://tradingeconomics.com/equatorial-guinea/gdp-per-capita.

Tran, B. V., Nguyen, M. A., Nguyen, D. Q. et al. 2017. Current conservation status of Germain's langur (*Trachypithecus germaini*) in Vietnam. *Primates* 58: 435–440.

Tran, T. H. 2010. Stopping the trade of Vietnams primates: experiences and cases from ENV's Wildlife Crime Unit. In Nadler, T., Rawson, B. M. & Van Ngoc, T. (Eds.), *Conservation of Primates in Indochina.* Frankfurt Zoological Society and Conservation International.

Trapido, H., Goverdhan, M. K., Rajagopalan, P. K. & Rebello, M. 1964. Ticks ectoparasitic on monkeys in the Kyasanur forest disease area of Shimoga district, Mysore State, India. *The American Journal of Tropical Medicine and Hygiene* 13: 763–772.

Treves, A. 1997. Primate natal coats: a preliminary analysis of distribution and function. *American Journal of Physical Anthropology* 104: 47–70.

Treves, A. 1999. Has predation shaped the social systems of arboreal primates? *International Journal of Primatology* 20: 35–67.

Treves, A. & Chapman, C. A. 1996. Conspecific threat, predation avoidance, and resource defense: implications for grouping in langurs. *Behavioral Ecology and Sociobiology* 39: 43–53.

Trivers, R. L. 1972. Parental investment and sexual selection. In Campbell, B. G. (Ed.), *Sexual Selection and the Descent of Man.* Chicago: Aldine. Pp. 136–179.

Tsuji Y., Hanya G. & Grueter C. C. 2013b. Feeding strategies of primates in temperate and alpine forests: a comparison of Asian macaques and colobines. *Primates* 54: 201–215.

Tsuji, Y., Mitani, M., Widayati, K. A., Suryobroto, B. & Watanabe, K. 2019. Dietary habits of wild Javan lutungs (*Trachypithecus auratus*) in a secondary-plantation mixed forest: effects of vegetation composition and phenology. *Mammalian Biology* 98: 80–90.

Tsuji, Y., Ningsih, J. I. D. P., Kitamura, S., Widayati, K. A. & Suryobroto, B. 2017. Neglected seed dispersers: endozoochory by Javan lutungs (*Trachypithecus auratus*) in Indonesia. *Biotropica* 49: 539–545.

Tsuji, Y., Prayitno, B. & Suryobroto, B. 2016. Report on the observed response of Javan lutungs (*Trachypithecus auratus mauritius*) upon encountering a reticulated python (*Python reticulatus*). *Primates* 57: 149–153.

Tsuji, Y., Widayati, K. A., Hadi, I., Suryobroto, B. & Watanabe, K. 2013a. Identification of individual adult female Javan lutungs (*Trachypithecus auratus sondaicus*) by using patterns of dark pigmentation in the pubic area. *Primates* 54: 27–31.

Tsuji, Y., Widayati, K. A., Nila, S., Hadi, I., Suryobroto, B. & Watanabe, K. 2015. 'Deer' friends: feeding associations between colobine monkeys and deer. *Journal of Mammalogy* 96: 1152–1161.

Tung, J., Barreiro, L. B., Burns, M. B. et al. 2015. Social networks predict gut microbiome composition in wild baboons. *eLife* 4: e05224.

Turvey, S. T., Bruun, K., Ortiz, A. et al. 2018. New genus of extinct Holocene gibbon associated with humans in Imperial China. *Science* 360: 1346–1349.

Tutin, C. E. G., Ham, R., White, L. & Harrison, M. J. S. 1997. The primate community of the Lope Reserve, Gabon: diets, responses to fruit scarcity, and effects on biomass. *American Journal of Primatology* 42: 1–24.

Tuttle, R. H. 1975. Parallelism, brachiation, and hominoid phylogeny. In Luckett, W. P. & Szalay, F. S. (Eds.), *Phylogeny of the Primates.* New York: Plenum Press. Pp. 447–480.

Twining-Ward, L., Li, W., Bhammar, H. & Wright, E. 2018. *Supporting sustainable livelihoods through wildlife tourism.* Washington, DC: Tourism for

Development: World Bank, https://openknowledge.worldbank.org/handle/10986/29417 License: CC BY 3.0 IGO.

Uehara, S. 1977. Predation on mammals by the chimpanzee (*Pan troglodyes*). *Primates* 38: 193–214.

Uehara, S. 2003. Population densities of diurnal mammals sympatric with the chimpanzees of the Mahale Mountains, Tanzania: comparison between the census data of 1996 and 2000. *African Study Monographs* 24: 169–179.

Uenishi, G., Fujita, S., Ohashi, G. et al. 2007. Molecular analyses of the intestinal microbiota of chimpanzees in the wild and in captivity. *American Journal of Primatology* 69: 367–376.

Ulibarri, L. R. 2013. *The socioecology of red-shanked doucs (*Pygathrix nemaeus*) in Son Tra Nature Reserve, Vietnam.* PhD thesis, University of Colorado, Boulder.

Ulibarri, L. R. & Gartland, K. N. 2021a. Ranging and territoriality in red-shanked doucs (*Pygathrix nemaeus*) at Son Tra Nature Reserve, Vietnam. *American Journal of Primatology* 83: e23292.

Ulibarri, L. R. & Gartland, K. N. 2021b. Group composition and social structure of red-shanked doucs (*Pygathrix nemaeus*) at Son Tra Nature Reserve, Vietnam. *Folia Primatologica*. https://doi.org/10.1159/000518594.

Ulibarri, L. R., Hoang, B., Nguyen, C. & Streicher, U. 2015. Influences of intragroup scramble competition and intergroup contest competition within the modular society of red-shanked doucs (*Pygathrix nemaeus*) in Son Tra Nature Reserve, Vietnam. Meeting of the American Society of Primatologists. Bend: Oregon. June 17–19.

Ullrey, D. E. 1986. Nutrition of primates in captivity. In Benirschke, K. (Ed.), *Primates*. New York: Springer. Pp. 823–835.

Ullrich, W. 1961. Zur biologie und soziologie der Colobusaffen (*Colobus guereza caudatus Thomas 1885*). *Der Zoologischer Garten* 25: 305–368.

UNDP. 2011. *Human Development Report 2011: Sustainability and Equity – A Better Future for All.* New York: United Nations Development Programme. 179 pp. http://hdr.undp.org/sites/default/files/reports/271/hdr_2011_en_complete.pdf.

UNEP-WCMC & IUCN. 2017. Protected Planet. www.protectedplante.net/c/world-database-on-protected-areas.

UNESCO. 2008. UNESCO Wild Heritage List: Sacred Kaya Mijikenda Forests. https://whc.unesco.org/en/list/1231/.

Ungar, P. S. 1995. Fruit preferences of four sympatric primate species at Ketambe, northern Sumatra, Indonesia. *International Journal of Primatology* 16: 221–245.

Ungar, P. S. 1996. Dental microwear of European Miocene catarrhines: Evidence for diets and tooth use. *Journal of Human Evolution* 31: 355–366.

United Nations. 2009. *World population prospects*. New York: United Nations.

United Nations. 2014. Department of Economic and Social Affairs, Population Division: World Urbanization Prospects, the 2014 revision.

Urbani, B. & Bosque, C. 2007. Feeding ecology and postural behaviour of the three-toed sloth (*Bradypus variegatus flaccidus*) in northern Venezuela. *Mammalian Biology/Zeitschrift für Säugetierkunde* 72: 321–329.

Urquhart, P. 2016. National Climate Change Policy of The Gambia. Banjul, The Gambia: Unpublished report of The Gambia-European Union Cooperation and Department of Water Resources. 63 pp. http://meccnar.gm/sites/default/files/2017_NCCP%20FINAL%20DRAFT.pdf.

Usongo, L. I. & Amubode, F. O. 2001. Nutritional ecology of Preuss's red colobus monkey (*Colobus badius preussi* Rahm 1970) in Korup National Park, Cameroon. *African Journal of Ecology* 39: 121–125.

Valdes, A. M., Walter, J., Segal, E. & Spector, T. D. 2018. Role of the gut microbiota in nutrition and health. *BMJ* 361: k2179.

van Allen, B. G., Dunham, A. E., Asquith, C. M. & Rudolf, V. H. 2012. Life history predicts risk of species decline in a stochastic world. *Proceedings of the Royal Society of London B* 279: 2691–2697.

van Hooff, J. A. R. A. M. 2000. Relationships among non-human primate males: a deductive framework. In Kappeler, P. M. (Ed.), *Primate Males: Causes and Consequences of Variation in Group Composition*. Cambridge: Cambridge University Press. Pp. 183–191.

van Hooff, J. A. R. A. M. & van Schaik, C. P. 1994. Male bonds: affiliative relationships among nonhuman primate males. *Behaviour* 130: 309–337.

van Noordwijk, M. A. 2012. From maternal investment to lifetime maternal care. In Mitani, J. C., Call, J., Kappeler, P. M. et al. (Eds.), *The Evolution of Primate Societies*. Chicago: The University of Chicago Press. Pp. 321–342.

van Noordwijk, M. A. & van Schaik, C. P. 1999. The effects of dominance rank and group size on female lifetime reproductive success in wild long-tailed macaques, *Macaca fascicularis*. *Primates* **40**: 105–130.

van Oirschot, B. 1999. *Group Fission in Western Red Colobus (Procolobus badius) Taï National Park, Côte d'Ivoire*. Leiden: Institute of Evolutionary and Ecological Sciences, Universiteit Leiden.

van Oirschot, B. 2000. Group fission in Taï red colobus (*Procolobus badius*). *Folia Primatologica* **71**: 205.

van Peenen, P. F. D., Light, R. H. & Duncan, J. F. 1971. Observations on mammals of Mt. Son Tra, South Vietnam. *Mammalia* **35**: 126–143.

van Schaik, C. P. 1983. Why are diurnal primates living in groups? *Behaviour* **87**: 120–144.

van Schaik, C. P. 1989. The ecology of social relationships amongst female primates In Standen, V. & Foley, R. A. (Eds.), *Comparative Socioecology*. Oxford: Blackwell. Pp. 195–218.

van Schaik, C. P. 1996. Social evolution in primates: the role of ecological factors and male behaviour. *Proceedings of the British Academy* **88**: 9–32.

van Schaik, C. P. 2000a. Infanticide by male primates: The sexual selection hypothesis revisited. In van Schaik, C. P. & Janson, C. H. (Eds.), *Infanticide by Males and Its Implications*. Cambridge: Cambridge University Press. Pp. 27–60.

van Schaik, C. P. 2000b. Social counterstrategies against infanticide by males in primates and other mammals In Kappeler, P. M. (Ed.), *Primate Males Causes and Consequences of Variation in Group Composition*. Cambridge: Cambridge University Press. Pp. 34–52.

van Schaik, C. P. 2016. *The Primate Origins of Human Nature*. New York: John Wiley & Sons.

van Schaik, C. P. & Hörstermann, M. 1994. Predation risk and the number of adult males in a primate group: a comparative test. *Behavioral Ecology and Sociobiology* **35**: 261–272.

van Schaik, C. P. & Janson, C. H. 2000. *Infanticide by Males and its Implications*. Cambridge: Cambridge University Press.

van Schaik, C. P. & Kappeler, P. M. 1997. Infanticide risk and the evolution of male-female association in primates. *Proceedings of the Royal Society B: Biological Sciences* **264**: 1687–1694.

van Schaik, C. P. & Pfannes, K. R. 2005. Tropical climates and phenology: a primate perspective. In Brockman, D. K. & van Schaik, C. P. (Eds.), *Seasonality in Primates*. Cambridge: Cambridge University Press. Pp. 23–54.

van Schaik, C. P. & van Noordwijk, M. A. 1988. Scramble and contest in feeding competition among female long-tailed macaques (*Macaca fascicularis*). *Behaviour* **105**: 77–98.

van Schaik, C. P., Assink, P. R. & Salafsky, N. 1992. Territorial behavior in Southeast Asian langurs: resource defense or mate defense. *American Journal of Primatology* **26**: 233–242.

van Schaik, C. P., Terborgh, J. W. & Wright, S. J. 1993. The phenology of tropical forests: adaptive significance and consequences for primary consumers. *Annual Review of Ecology and Systematics* **24**: 353–377.

van Schaik, C. P., van Noordwijk, M. A. & Nunn, C. L. 2001. Sex and social evolution in primates. In Lee, P. C. (Ed.), *Comparative Primate Socioecology*. New York: Cambridge University Press. Pp. 204–231.

van Schaik, C. P., Van Noordwijk, M. A., Warsono, B. & Sutriono, E. 1983. Party size and early detection of predators in Sumatran forest primates. *Primates* **24**: 211–221.

van Steenis, C. G. G. J. 1972. *The Mountain Flora of Java*. Leiden: Brill.

van Woerden, J. T., Willems, E. P., van Schaik, C. P. & Isler, K. 2012. Large brains buffer energetic effects of seasonal habitats in catarrhine primates. *Evolution* **66**: 191–199.

Van, V. M., Mai, T. H., Tuyet, L. T. M. & Tan, P. V. 2012. Study on the distribution of Francois langurs (*Trachypithecus francoisi*) in Northern Vietnam under climate change scenario. *EnviroInfo: Part 1 Core Application Areas* 1–10.

Vandercone, R. P., Dinadh, C., Wijethunga, G., Ranawana, K. & Rasmussen, D. T. 2012. Dietary diversity and food selection in Hanuman langurs (*Semnopithecus entellus*) and purple-faced langurs (*Trachypithecus vetulus*) in the Kaludiyapokuna Forest Reserve in the dry zone of Sri Lanka. *International Journal of Primatology* **33**: 1382–1405.

Vandercone, R., Premachandra, K., Wijethunga, G. P. et al. 2013. Random walk analysis of ranging patterns of sympatric langurs in a complex resource landscape. *American Journal of Primatology* **75**: 1209–1219.

Vasudev, D., Kumar, A. & Sinha, A. 2008. Resource distribution and group size in the common langur *Semnopithecus entellus* in southern India. *American Journal of Primatology* **70**: 680–689.

Vayro, J. V., Fedigan, L. M., Ziegler, T. E. et al. 2016. Hormonal correlates of life history characteristics in wild female *Colobus vellerosus*. *Primates* **57**: 509–519.

Vedder, A. & Fashing, P. J. 2002. Diet of a 300-member Angolan colobus monkey (*Colobus angolensis*) supergroup in the Nyungwe Forest, Rwanda. *American Journal of Physical Anthropology* **117** (suppl. 34): 159–160.

Vendl, C., Frei, S., Dittmann, M. T. et al. 2016. Digestive physiology, metabolism and methane production of captive Linne's two-toed sloths (*Choloepus didactylus*). *Journal of Animal Physiology Animal Nutrition* **100**: 552–564.

Venkataraman, V. V., Glowacka, H., Fritz, J. et al. 2014. Effects of dietary fracture toughness and dental wear on chewing efficiency in geladas (*Theropithecus gelada*). *American Journal of Physical Anthropology* **155**: 17–32.

Venter, O., Fuller, R. A., Segan, D. B. et al. 2014. Targeting global protected area expansion for imperiled biodiversity. *PLOS Biology* **12**: e1001891.

Vermeer, J. 1998. New information about the distribution of *Presbytis* on Sumatra. *Asian Primates* **6**: 9–10.

Vignaud, P., Duringer, P., Mackaye, H. T. et al. 2002. Geology and paleontology of the Upper Miocene Toros-Menalla hominid locality, Chad. *Nature* **418**: 152–155.

Vine I. 1973. Detection of prey flocks by predators. *Journal of Theoretical Biology* **40**: 207–210.

Visconti, A., Le Roy, C. I., Rosa, F. et al. 2019. Interplay between the human gut microbiome and host metabolism. *Nature Communications* **10**: 1–10.

Vlčková, K., Shutt-Phillips, K., Heistermann, M. et al. 2017. Impact of stress on the gut microbiome of free-ranging western lowland gorillas. *Microbiology* **164**: 40–44.

Vogel, C. 1966. Morphologishe studien am gesichtsschadel Catarrhiner Primaten. *Bibliotheca Primatologica* **4**: 1–226.

Vogel, C. 1971. Behavioral differences of Presbytis entellus in two different habitats. *Proceedings of the 3rd International Congress of Primatology* 3: 41–47.

Vogt, M. 2003. *Freilanduntersuchungen zur Ökologie und zum Verhalten von* Trachypithecus auratus kohlbruggei *(Haubenlanguren) im West-Bali-Nationalpark, Indonesien.* PhD thesis, Eberhard-Karls-Universität, Tübingen, Germany.

von Hippel, F. A. 1996. Interactions between overlapping multimale groups of black and white colobus monkeys (*Colobus guereza*) in the Kakamega Forest, Kenya. *American Journal of Primatology* **38**: 193–209.

von Hippel, F. A., Frederick, H. & Cleland, E. 2000. Population decline of the black and white colobus monkey (*Colobus guereza*) in the Kakamega Forest, Kenya. *African Zoology* **35**: 69–75.

Vu, N. T., Le, V. K., Le, K. Q. et al. 2007. *Survey results for red-shanked douc langur (Pygathrix nemaeus nemaeus) in Son Tra Nature Reserve, Da Nang City, Central Vietnam.* Technical report. Hanoi: Vietnam National University.

Vun, V. F., Mahani, M. C., Lakim, M., Ampeng, A. & Md-Zain, B. M. 2011. Phylogenetic relationships of leaf monkeys (*Presbytis*; Colobinae) based on cytochrome *b* and 12S rRNA genes. *Genetics and Molecular Research* **10**: 368–381.

Wachter, B., Schabel, M. & Noë, R. 1997. Diet overlap and polyspecific associations of red colobus and diana monkeys in the Taï National Park, ivory coast. *Ethology* **103**: 514–526.

Wada, K., Li, B. & Watanabe, K. 2015. Affiliative interactions between one-male units in a band of Sichuan snub-nosed monkeys (*Rhinopithecus roxellana*) living in the Qinling Mountains, China. *Primates* **56**: 327–337.

Wadley, R. L., Colfer, C. J. P. & Hood, I. G. 1997. Hunting primates and managing forests: the case of Iban forest farmers in Indonesian Borneo. *Human Ecology* **25**: 243–271.

Wahungu, G. M., Muoria, P. K., Moinde, N. N., Oguge, N. O. & Kirathe, J. N. 2005. Changes in forest fragment sizes and primate population trends along the river tana floodplain, Kenya. *African Journal of Ecology* **43**: 81–90.

Walker, J. S., Cadigan, F. C., Vosdingh, R. A. & Chye, C. T. 1973. The silvered leaf-monkey of Malaysia, *Presbytis cristatus*: disease model for human scrub typhus. *Journal of Infectious Diseases* **128**: 223–226.

Wallace, D. E. & Hill, C. M. 2012. Crop damage by primates: quantifying the key parameters of crop-raiding events. *PLOS ONE* **7**: e46636.

Wallis, I. R., Edwards, M. J., Windley, H. et al. 2012. Food for folivores: nutritional explanations linking diets to population density. *Oecologia* **169**: 281–291.

Waltert, M., Lien, Faber, K. & Muhlenberg, M. 2002. Further declines of threatened primates in the korup project area, south-west cameroon. *Oryx* **36**: 257–265.

Wan, Y., Quan, R., Ren, G. et al. 2013. Niche divergence among sex and age classes in black-and-white snub nosed monkeys (*Rhinopithecus bieti*). *International Journal of Primatology* **34**: 946–956.

Wang, B., Zhou, X., Shi, F. et al. 2015. Full-length *numt* analysis provides evidence for hybridization between the Asian colobine genera *Trachypithecus* and *Semnopithecus*. *American Journal of Primatology* **77**: 901–910.

Wang, C., Hou, R., Wang, M. et al. 2020. Effects of wet atmospheric nitrogen deposition on epiphytic lichens in the subtropical forests of Central China: Evaluation of the lichen food supply and quality of two endangered primates. *Ecotoxicology and Environmental Safety* **190**: 110128.

Wang, H., Tan, C., Gao, Y. & Li, B. 2004. A takeover of resident male in the Sichuan snub-nosed monkey *Rhinopithecus roxellanae* in Qinling Mountains. *Acta Zoologica Sinica* **50**: 859–862.

Wang, S., Huang, Z., He, Y. et al. 2012. Mating behavior and birth seasonality of black-and-white snub-nosed monkeys (*Rhinopithecus bieti*) at Mt. Lasha. *Zoological Research* **33**: 241–248.

Wang, S., Luo, Y. & Cui, G. 2011. Sleeping site selection of Francois's langur (*Trachypithecus francoisi*) in two habitats in Mayanghe National Nature Reserve, Guizhou, China. *Primates* **52**: 51–60.

Wang, W., Forstner, M. R. J., Zhang, Y.-P. et al. 1997. A phylogeny of Chinese leaf monkeys using mitochondrial ND3-ND4 gene sequences. *International Journal of Primatology* **18**: 305–320.

Wang, X. P., Yu, L., Roos, C. et al. 2012. Phylogenetic relationships among the colobine monkeys revisited: new insights from analyses of complete mt genomes and 44 nuclear non-coding markers. *PLOS ONE* **7**: e36274.

Wang, X. P., Yu, L., Roos, C. et al. 2012. Phylogenetic relationships among the colobine monkeys revisited: new insights from analyses of complete mitochondrial genomes and forty-four nuclear non-coding markers. *PLOS ONE* **7**: e36274.

Wang, X., Li, B., Wu, X., He, P. & Hu, Y. 2007. Dominance hierarchy of Sichuan snub-nosed monkey (*Rhinopithecus roxellana*) OMUs in Qinling Mountains by feeding superiority. *Acta Theriologica Sinica* **27**: 344–349.

Wang, X., Wang, C., Qi, X. et al. 2013. A newly-found pattern of social relationships among adults within one-male units of golden snub-nosed monkeys (*Rhinopithecus roxellana*) in the Qinling Mountains, China. *Integrative Zoology* **8**: 400–409.

Wangchuk, T. 2005. *The evolution, phylogeography, and conservation of the golden langur (*Trachypithecus geei*) in Bhutan.* PhD thesis, University of Maryland, Baltimore.

Wangchuk, T., Inouye, D. W. & Hare, M. P. 2008. The emergence of an endangered species: evolution and phylogeny of the *Trachypithecus geei* of Bhutan. *International Journal of Primatology* **29**: 565–582.

Wasserman, M. D. & Chapman, C. A. 2003. Determinants of colobine monkey abundance: the importance of food energy, protein and fibre content. *Journal of Animal Ecology* **72**: 650–659.

Wasserman, M. D., Chapman, C. A., Milton, K. et al. 2012. Estrogenic plant consumption predicts red colobus monkey (*Procolobus rufomitratus*) hormonal state and behavior. *Hormones and Behavior* **62**: 553–562.

Wasserman, M. D., Chapman, C. A., Milton, K., Goldberg, T. L. & Ziegler, T. E. 2013. Physiological and behavioral effects of capture darting on red colobus monkeys (*Procolobus rufomitratus*) with a comparison to chimpanzee (*Pan troglodytes*) predation. *International Journal of Primatology* **34**: 1020–1031.

Watanabe, K. 1981. Variations in group composition and population density of the two sympatric Mentawaian leaf-monkeys. *Primates* **22**: 145–160.

Watanabe, K., Mitani, M., Arakane, T. et al. 1996. Population changes of *Presbytis auratus* and *Macaca fascicularis* in the Pangandaran Nature Reserve, West Java, Indonesia. *Primate Research* **12**: 271.

Waterman, P. G. 1984. Food acquisition and processing as a function of plant chemistry. In Chivers, D. J., Wood, B. A. & Bilsborough, A. (Eds.), *Food Acquisition and Processing in Primates*. New York: Plenum Press. Pp. 177–211.

Waterman, P. G. & Kool, K. M. 1994. Colobine food selection and plant chemistry. In Davies, A. G. & Oates, J. F. (Eds.), *Colobine Monkeys: Their Ecology, Behaviour and Evolution*. New York: Cambridge University Press. Pp. 251–284.

Waterman, P. G., Mbi, C. N., McKey, D. B. & Gartlan, J. S. 1980. African rainforest vegetation and rumen microbes: Phenolic compounds and nutrients as correlates of digestibility. *Oecologia* **47**: 22–33.

Waterman, P. G., Ross, J. A. M., Bennett, E. L. & Davies, A. G. 1988. A comparison of the floristics and leaf chemistry of the tree flora in two Malaysian rain forests and the influence of leaf chemistry on populations of colobine monkeys in the Old World. *Biological Journal of the Linnean Society* **34**: 1–32.

Watkins, B. E., Ullrey, D. E. & Whetter, P. A. 1985. Digestibility of a high-fiber biscuit-based diet by black and white colobus (*Colobus guereza*). *American Journal of Primatology* 9: 137–144.

Watts, D. P. & Amsler, S. J. 2013. Chimpanzee-red colobus encounter rates show a red colobus population decline associated with predation by chimpanzees at Ngogo. *American Journal of Primatology* 75: 927–937.

Watts, D. P. & Mitani, J. C. 2002. Hunting behavior of chimpanzees at Ngogo, Kibale National Park, Uganda. *International Journal of Primatology* 23: 1–28.

Watts, D. P. & Mitani, J. C. 2015. Hunting and prey switching by chimpanzees (*Pan troglodytes schweinfurthii*) at Ngogo. *International Journal of Primatology* 36: 728–748.

Wayre, P. 1968. The golden langur and the Manas Sanctuaries. *Oryx* 9: 337–339.

Weary, T., Wrangham, R. & Clauss, M. 2017. Applying wet sieving fecal particle size measurement to frugivores: a case study of the Eastern chimpanzee (*Pan troglodytes schweinfurthii*). *American Journal of Physical Anthropology* 163: 510–518.

Wei, W., Qi, X., Guo, S. et al. 2012. Market powers predict reciprocal grooming in golden snub-nosed monkeys (*Rhinopithecus roxellana*). *PLOS ONE* 7: e36802.

Weitzel, V. & Groves, C. P. 1985. The nomenclature and taxonomy of the colobine monkeys of Java. *International Journal of Primatology* 6: 399–409.

Weitzel, V. 1978. Dental Morphology of Two Broadly Sympatric Subgenera of *Presbytis*. *American Journal of Physical Anthropology* 48: 447.

Werre, J. L. R. 2000. *Ecology and behavior of the Niger Delta red colobus (*Procolobus badius epieni*)*. PhD thesis, City University of New York, New York.

Werre, J. L. R. 2001. Primates of the central Niger Delta, Nigeria. *African Primates* 5: 33–37.

Wheeler, B. C., Scarry, C. J. & Koenig, A. 2013. Rates of agonism among female primates: a cross-taxon perspective. *Behavioral Ecology* 24: 1369–1380.

White, F. 1983. *The Vegetation of Africa: A Descriptive Memoir to Accompany the UNESCO/AETFAT/UNSC Vegetation Map of Africa*. Paris, France: UNESCO. 358 pp.

White, L. J. T. 1994. Biomass of rain forest mammals in the Lopé Reserve, Gabon. *Journal of Animal Ecology* 63: 499–512.

White, T. C. R. 1993. *The Inadequate Environment: Nitrogen and the Abundance of Animals*. Berlin: Springer-Verlag.

White, T. D., Ambrose, S. A., Suwa, G. et al. 2009. Macrovertebrate paleontology and the Pliocene habitat of *Ardipithecus ramidus*. *Science* 326: 87–93.

White, T. D., WoldeGabriel, G., Asfaw, B. et al. 2006. Asa Issie, Aramis and the origin of *Australopithecus*. *Nature* 440: 883–889.

Whitesides, G. H. 1989. Interspecific associations of diana monkeys, *Cercopithecus diana*, in Sierra Leone, West Africa: biological significance or chance? *Animal Behaviour* 37: 760–776.

Whitesides, G. H. 1989. Interspecific associations of Diana monkeys, *Cercopithecus diana*, in Sierra Leone, West Africa: biological significance or chance? *Animal Behaviour* 37: 760–776.

Whitesides, G. H., Oates, J. F., Green, S. M. & Kluberdanz, R. P. 1988. Estimating primate densities from transects in a West African rain forest: a comparison of techniques. *Journal of Animal Ecology* 57: 345–367.

Whittaker, D. J. 2006. A conservation action plan for the Mentawai primates. *Primate Conservation* 20: 95–105.

Whybrow, P. J. 1992. Land movements and species dispersal. In Jones, S., Martin, R., Pilbeam, D. et al. (Eds.), *The Cambridge Encyclopedia of Human Evolution*. Cambridge: Cambridge University Press. Pp. 169–173.

Wich, S. A. & Marshall, A. J. 2016. *An Introduction to Primate Conservation*. New York: Oxford University Press.

Wich, S. A. & Nunn, C. L. 2002. Do male 'long-distance calls' function in mate defense? A comparative study of long-distance calls in primates. *Behavioural Ecology and Sociobiology* 52: 474–484.

Wich, S. A. & Sterck, E. H. M. 2003. Possible audience effect in Thomas langurs (Primates; *Presbytis thomasi*): an experimental study on male loud calls in response to a tiger model. *American Journal of Primatology* 60: 155–159.

Wich, S. A. & Sterck, E. H. M. 2010. Thomas langurs: ecology and sexual conflict between males and females. In Gursky-Doyen, S. & Supriatna, J. (Eds.), *Indonesian Primates*. New York, NY: Springer Science+Business Media. Pp. 285–308.

Wich, S. A. 2002. *The structure and function of male Thomas Langur loud calls*. PhD thesis, Utrecht Universit, Utrecht, The Netherlands.

Wich, S. A., Buij, R. & van Schaik, C. P. 2004. Determinants of orangutan density in the dryland forest of the Leuser ecosystem. *Primates* 45: 177–182.

Wich, S. A., Steenbeek, R., Sterck, E. H. M., Korstjens, A. H., Willems, E. P. & van Schaik, C. P. 2007.

Demography and life history of Thomas Langurs (*Presbytis thomasi*). *American Journal of Physical Anthropology* 69: 641–651.

Wich, S. A., Vogel, E. R., Larsen, M. D. et al. 2011. Forest fruit production is higher on Sumatra than on Borneo. *PLOS ONE* 6: e21278.

Wikberg, E. C., Sicotte, P., Campos, F. A. & Ting, N. 2012. Between-group variation in female dispersal, kin composition of groups, and proximity patterns in a black-and-white colobus monkey (*Colobus vellerosus*). *PLOS ONE* 7: e48740.

Wikberg, E. C., Teichroeb, J. A., Bădescu, I. & Sicotte, P. 2013. Individualistic female dominance hierarchies with varying strength in a highly folivorous population of black-and-white colobus. *Behaviour* 150: 295–320.

Wikberg, E. C., Ting, N. & Sicotte, P. 2014. Kinship and residency status structure female social networks in black-and-white colobus monkeys (*Colobus vellerosus*). *American Journal of Physical Anthropologists* 153: 365–376.

Wikberg, E., Christie, D., Sicotte, P. & Ting, N. 2020. Social interactions across groups of colobus monkeys (*Colobus vellerosus*) explain similarities in their gut microbiomes. *Animal Behaviour* 163: 17–31.

Wikramanayake, E. D., Dinerstein, E. & Loucks, C. J. 2002. *Terrestrial Ecoregions of the Indo-Pacific: a Conservation Assessment*, vol. 3. Washington, DC: Island Press.

Wilkins, J. S. 2009. *Species: A History of the Idea*. Berkeley: University of California Press.

Willems, E. P., Arseneau, T. J. M., Schleuning, X. & van Schaik, C. P. 2015. Communal range defence in primates as a public goods dilemma. *Philosophical Transactions of the Royal Society B: Biological Sciences* 370: 20150003.

Willems, E. P., Hellriegel, B. & van Schaik, C. P. 2013. The collective action problem in primate territory economics. *Proceedings of the Royal Society B: Biological Sciences* 280: 20130081.

Williams, J. M., Oehlert, G. W., Carlis, J. V. & Pusey, A. E. 2004. Why do male chimpanzees defend a group range? *Animal Behaviour* 68: 523–532.

Willis, M. S. 1995. *Dental variation in Asian colobines*. PhD thesis, Washington University, St. Louis, MO.

Willis, M. S. & Hildebolt, C. F. 1991. Review and analysis of colobine dental literature. *American Journal of Physical Anthropology*, Supplement 12: 185.

Willis, M. S. & Swindler, D. R. 2004. Molar size and shape variations among Asian colobines. *American Journal of Physical Anthropology* 125: 51–60.

Wilson, C. C. & Wilson, W. L. 1977. Behavioral and morphological variation among primate populations in Sumatra. *Yearbook of Physical Anthropology* 20: 207–233.

Winemiller, K. O., McIntyre, P. B., Castello, L. et al. 2016. Balancing hydropower and biodiversity in the Amazon, Congo, and Mekong. *Science* 351: 128–299.

Winkler, P. 1988. Feeding behavior of a food-enhanced troop of Hanuman langurs (*Presbytis entellus*) in Jodhpur, India. In Fa, J. E. & Southwick, C. H. (Eds.), *Ecology and Behavior of Food -Enhanced Primate Groups*. New York: Alan R Liss. Pp. 3–24.

Wolf, K. E. 1984. *Reproductive competition among co-resident male silvered leaf monkeys (*Presbytis cristata*)*. PhD thesis, Yale University, New Haven, CT.

Wolf, K. E. & Fleagle J. G. 1977. Adult male replacement in a group of silvered leaf-monkeys (*Presbytis cristata*) at Kuala Selangor, Malaysia. *Primates* 18: 949–955.

Wong, M. H., Duan, C., Long, Y., Luo, Y. & Xie, G. 2010. How will the distribution and size of subalpine Abies georgei forest respond to climate change? A study in northwest Yunnan, China. *Physical Geography* 31: 319–335.

Wong, S. N. P. & Sicotte, P. 2006. Population size and density of *Colobus vellerosus* at the Boabeng-Fiema Monkey Sanctuary and surrounding forest fragments in Ghana. *American Journal of Primatology* 68: 465–476.

Wong, S. N. P. & Sicotte, P. 2007. Activity budget and ranging patterns of *Colobus vellerosus* in forest fragments in central Ghana. *Folia Primatologica* 78: 245–254.

Wong, S. N., Saj, T. L. & Sicotte, P. 2006. Comparison of habitat quality and diet of *Colobus vellerosus* in forest fragments in Ghana. *Primates* 47: 365–373.

Woodford, M. H., Butynski, T. M. & Karesh, W. B. 2002. Habituating the great apes: the disease risk. *Oryx* 36: 153–160.

Work, T. H., Trapido, H., Murthy, D. P. N. et al. 1957. Kyasanur forest disease. III. A preliminary report on the nature of the infection and clinical manifestations in human being. *Indian Journal of Medical Sciences* 11: 619–645.

Workman, C. 2004. Primate conservation in Vietnam: Toward a holistic environmental narrative. *American Anthropologist* 106: 346–352.

Workman, C. 2009. Diet of the Delacour's langur (*Trachypithecus delacouri*) in Van Long Nature

Reserve, Vietnam. *American Journal of Primatology* 72: 317–324.

Workman, C. 2010a. Diet of the Delacour's langur (*Trachypithecus delacouri*) in Van Long Nature Reserve, Vietnam. *American Journal of Primatology* 72: 317–324.

Workman, C. 2010b. *The foraging ecology of the Delacour's langur (*Trachypithecus delacouri*) in Van Long.* PhD thesis, Duke University, Durham, NC.

Workman, C. & Schmitt, D. 2011. Positional behavior of Delacour's langurs (*Trachypithecus delacouri*) in northern Vietnam. *International Journal of Primatology* 33: 19–37.

Workman, C. & Van D. L. 2009. The chemistry of eaten and uneaten leaves by Delacour's langurs (*Trachypithecus delacouri*) in Van Long Nature Reserve, Vietnam. *Vietnamese Journal of Primatology* 3: 29–36.

World Bank. 2014. Agricultural land. Food and Agriculture Organization. http://data.worldbank.org/indicator/AG.LND.AGRI.ZS.

World Bank. 2020. World Bank Open Data. https://data.worldbank.org/.

Worldatlas. 2020. Worldatlas. www.worldatlas.com/.

Wrangham, R. W. & Bergmann-Riss, E. Z. 1990. Rates of predation on mammals by Gombe chimpanzees 1972–1975. *Primates* 31: 157–170.

Wrangham, R. W. 1976. *Aspects of Feeding and Social Behavior in Gelada Baboons.* A Report to the Science Research Council.

Wrangham, R. W. 1979. On the evolution of Ape social systems. *Social Science Information* 18: 336–368.

Wrangham, R. W. 1980. An ecological model of female-bonded primate groups. *Behaviour* 75: 262–300.

Wrangham, R. W. 1987. Evolution of social structure. In Smuts, B. B., Cheney, D. L., Seyfarth, R. M. et al. (Eds.), *Primate Societies.* Chicago: University of Chicago Press. Pp. 282–296.

Wrangham, R. W., Gittleman, J. L. & Chapman, C. A. 1993. Constraints on group size inprimates and carnivores: population density and day-range as assays of exploitation competition. *Behavioral Ecology and Sociobiology* 32: 199–209.

Wrangham, R. W. & Rubenstein, D. I. 1986. Social evolution in birds and mammals. In Rubenstein, D. I. & Wrangham, R. W. (Eds.), *Ecology and Social Evolution: Birds and Mammals.* Princeton, NJ: Princeton University Press. Pp. 452–470.

Wright, B. W., Prodhan, R., Wright, K. & Nadler, T. 2008b. Mandibular morphology as it relates to ingestive and digestive folivory in *Trachypithecus* and *Pygathrix*. *Vietamese Journal of Primatology* 2: 25–32.

Wright, B., Ulibarri, L., O'Brien, J. et al. 2008a. It's tough out there: variation in the toughness of ingested leaves and feeding behavior among four colobinae in Vietnam. *International Journal of Primatology* 29: 1455–1466.

Wright, S. J., Muller-Landau, H. C. & Schipper, J. 2009. The future of tropical species on a warmer planet. *Conservation Biology* 23: 1418–1426.

Wu, B. 1993. Patterns of spatial dispersion, locomotion and foraging behavior in three groups of the Yunnan snub-nosed langur (*Rhinopithecus bieti*). *Folia Primatologica* 60: 63–71.

Wu, B., Zhong, T. & Wu, J. 1988. A preliminary survey of ecology and behavior on a Yunnan snub-nosed monkey (*Rhinopithecus bieti*) group. *Zoological Research* 9: 373–384.

Wu, G., Wang, H. C., Fu, H. W., Zhao, J. Z. & Yang, Y. Q. 2004. Habitat selection of Guizhou golden monkey (*Rhinopithecus roxellanae brelichi*) in Fanjing Mountain Biosphere Reserve, China. *Journal of Forestry Research (Harbin)* 15: 197–202.

Xi, W., Li, B., Zhao, D., Ji, W. & Zhang, P. 2008. Benefits to female helpers in wild *Rhinopithecus roxellana*. *International Journal of Primatology* 29: 593–600.

Xia, W., Ji, S., Ren, B. et al. 2020b. Proximate causes of dispersal for female Yunnan snub-nosed monkeys. *Zoological Research* 41: 78–81.

Xia, W., Ren, B., Zhou, H. et al. 2020a. Reproductive parameters of wild Rhinopithecus bieti. *Folia Primatologica.* 91: 202–218.

Xiang, Z. 2005. *The ecology and behavior of black-and-white snub-nosed monkeys (*Rhinopithecus bieti, Colobinae*) at Xiaochangdu in Honglaxueshan National Nature Reserve, Tibet, China.* PhD thesis, Kunming Institute of Zoology CAS, Kunming, China.

Xiang, Z. & Grueter, C. C. 2007. The first direct evidence of infanticide and cannibalism in wild snub-nosed monkeys (*Rhinopithecus bieti*). *American Journal of Primatology* 69: 249–254.

Xiang, Z. F. & Sayers, K. 2009. Seasonality of mating and birth in wild black-and-white snub-nosed monkeys (*Rhinopithecus bieti*) at Xiaochangdu, Tibet. *Primates* 50: 50–55.

Xiang, Z. F., Huo, S., Xiao, W., Quan, R. C. & Grueter, C. C. 2007. Diet and feeding behavior of *Rhinopithecus bieti* at Xiaochangdu, Tibet: Adaptations to a marginal environment. *American Journal of Primatology* 69: 1141–1158.

Xiang, Z., Fan, P., Chen, H. et al. 2019. Routine allomaternal nursing in a free-ranging Old World monkey. *Science Advances* 5: eaav0499.

Xiang, Z., Huo, S. & Xiao, W. 2010a. Activity budget of *Rhinopithecus bieti* at Tibet: Effects of day length, temperature and food availability. *Current Zoology* 56: 650–659.

Xiang, Z., Huo, S., Xiao, W., Quan, R. & Grueter, C. C. 2009a. Terrestrial behavior and use of forest strata use in a group of black-and-white snub-nosed monkeys *Rhinopithecus bieti* at Xiaochangdu, Tibet. *Current Zoology* 55: 180–187.

Xiang, Z., Liang, W., Nie, S. & Li, M. 2013a. A short note on extractive foraging behavior in gray snub-nosed monkeys. *Integrative Zoology* 8: 389–394.

Xiang, Z., Nie, S., Chang, Z., Wei, F. & Li, M. 2010b. Sleeping sites of *Rhinopithecus brelichi* at Yangaoping, Guizhou. *International Journal of Primatology* 31: 59–71.

Xiang, Z., Sayers, K. & Grueter, C. C. 2009b. Direct paternal care in black-and-white snub-nosed monkeys. *Journal of Zoology* 278: 157–162.

Xiang, Z., Xiao, W., Huo, S. & Li, M. 2013b. Ranging pattern and population composition of *Rhinopithecus bieti* at Xiaochangdu: implications for conservation. *Chinese Science Bulletin* 58: 2212.

Xiang, Z., Yang, B., Yu, Y. et al. 2014. Males collectively defend their one-male units against bachelor males in a multi-level primate society. *American Journal of Primatology* 76: 609–617.

Xiang, Z., Yang, W., Qi, X. et al. 2017. An examination of factors potentially influencing birth distributions in golden snub-nosed monkeys (*Rhinopithecus roxellana*). *PeerJ* 5: e2892.

Xiang, Z.-F., Liang, W.-B., Nie, S.-G. & Li, M. 2012. Diet and feeding behavior of *Rhinopithecus brelichi* at Yangaoping, Guishou. *American Journal of Primatology* 74: 551–560.

Xiong, J., Gong, S., Qiu, C. & Li, Z. 2009. Comparison of locomotor behaviour between white-headed langurs *Trachypithecus leucocephalus* and Francois' langurs *T. francoisi* in Fusui, China. *Current Zoology* 55: 9–19.

Xu, B., Xu, W., Li, J. et al. 2015. Metagenomic analysis of the *Rhinopithecus bieti* fecal microbiome reveals a broad diversity of bacterial and glycoside hydrolase profiles related to lignocellulose degradation. *BMC Genomics* 16: 1–11.

Yalden, D. W., Largen, M. J. & Kock, D. 1977. Catalogue of the mammals of Ethiopia 3. Primates. *Monitore Zoologico Italiano* 9: 1–52.

Yamagiwa, J., Basabose, A. K., Kaleme, K. & Yumoto, T. 2005. Diet of Grauer's gorillas in the Montane Forest of Kahuzi, Democratic Republic of Congo. *International Journal of Primatology* 26: 1345–1373.

Yan, C. 2012. *Social interaction and dispersal patterns of golden snub-nosed monkeys (*Rhinopithecus roxellana*) living in multi-level societies.* PhD thesis, University of Illinois, Urbana.

Yan, K., Su, Y., Li, J. et al. 1995. The guarding behavior of golden monkeys. In Xia, W. & Zhang, R. (Eds.), *Primate Research and Conservation.* Beijing: China Forestry. Pp. 250–255 (in Chinese).

Yang, B., Zhang, P., Garber, P. A., Hedley, R. & Li, B. 2016. Sichuan snub-nosed monkeys (*Rhinopithecus roxellana*) consume cicadas in the Qinling Mountains, China. *Folia Primatologica* 87: 11–16.

Yang, L., Minghai, Z., Jianzhang, M., Ankang, W. & Shusen, Z. 2007. Time budget of daily activity of Francois lanur (*Trachypithecus francoisi francoisi*) in disturbance habitat. *Acta Ecologica Sinica* 27: 1715–1722.

Yang, M., Sun, D. Y., Zinner, D. & Roos, C. 2009. Reproductive parameters in Guizhou snub-nosed monkeys (*Rhinopithecus brelichi*). *American Journal of Primatology* 71: 266–270.

Yang, M., Yang, Y., Cui, D. et al. 2012. Population genetic structure of Guizhou snub-nosed monkeys (*Rhinopithecus brelichi*) as inferred from mitochondrial control region sequences, and comparison with *R. bieti* and *R. roxellana*. *American Journal of Physical Anthropology* 147: 1–10.

Yang, S. 2000. *Habitat, diet, range use and social organization of* Rhinopithecus bieti *at Jinsichang.* PhD thesis, Kunming Institute of Zoology CAS, Kunming, China.

Yang, Y., Groves, C., Garber, P. et al. 2019. First insights into the feeding habits of the Critically Endangered black snub-nosed monkey, *Rhinopithecus strykeri* (Colobinae, Primates). *Primates* 60: 143–153.

Yang, Y., Lei, X. & Yang, C. 2002. *Ecology of the Wild Guizhou Snub-Nosed Monkey.* Guiyang, China: Guizhou (in Chinese with English section).

Yang, Y., Roos, C., Momberg, F., Lwin, N., Huang, Z., Groves, C., Behie, A. & Wen, X. 2018. Current conservation status and study process of the black snub-nosed monkey (*Rhinopithecus strykeri*). 27th International Primatological Society Congress. Nairobi, Kenya. Abstract #13265.

Yanuar, A., Fuentes, A. & Studd, K. 1998. A short report on the current status of the Mentawai snub-nosed langur (*Simias concolor concolor*) on Simalegu Island, South Pagai, Mentawai, Indonesia. *Tropical Biodiversity* 5: 299–305.

Yao, H., Liu, X., Stanford, C. et al. 2011. Male dispersal in a provisioned multilevel group of *Rhinopithecus roxellana* in Shennongjia Nature Reserve, China. *American Journal of Primatology* 73: 1280–1288.

Yao, H., Yu, H., Yang, B. et al. 2016. Male infanticide in the golden snub-nosed monkey (*Rhinopithecus roxellana*), a seasonally breeding primate. *International Journal of Primatology* 37: 175–184.

Yao, M., Yin, L., Zhang, L. et al. 2012. Parturitions in wild white-headed langurs (*Trachypithecus leucocephalus*) in the Nongguan Hills, China. *International Journal of Primatology* 33: 888–904.

Yazezew, D. 2018. Population estimate and behavioural ecology of Omo River guerezas (*Colobus guereza guereza*) from Wof-Washa Natural and Plantation Forest, central highlands, Ethiopia. PhD thesis, Addis Ababa University, Addis Ababa, Ethiopia.

Yeager, C. P. 1989. Feeding behavior and ecology of the proboscis monkey (*Nasalis larvatus*). *International Journal of Primatology* 10: 497–530.

Yeager, C. P. 1990a. Proboscis monkey (*Nasalis larvatus*) social organization: Group structure. *American Journal of Primatology* 20: 95–106.

Yeager, C. P. 1990b. Notes on the sexual behavior of the proboscis monkey (*Nasalis larvatus*). *American Journal of Primatology* 21: 223–227.

Yeager, C. P. 1991a. Possible antipredator behavior associated with river crossings by proboscis monkeys (*Nasalis larvatus*). *American Journal of Primatology* 24: 61–66.

Yeager, C. P. 1991b. Proboscis monkey (*Nasalis larvatus*) social organization: Intergroup patterns of association. *American Journal of Primatology* 23: 73–86.

Yeager, C. P. & Frederiksson, G. 1998. *Fire Impacts on Primates and Other Wildlife in Kalimantan, Indonesia, during 1997/1998*. Jakarta, Indonesia: WWF.

Yeager, C. P. & Kirkpatrick, R. C. 1998. Asian colobine social structure: ecological and evolutionary constraints *Primates* 39: 147–155.

Yeager, C. P. & Kool, K. 2000. The behavioral ecology of Asian colobines. In Whitehead, P. F. & Jolly, C. J. (Eds.), *Old World Monkeys*. Cambridge: Cambridge University Press. Pp. 497–521.

Yeager, C. P., Silver, S. C. & Dierenfeld, E. S. 1997. Mineral and phytochemical influences on foliage selection by the proboscis monkey (*Nasalis larvatus*). *American Journal of Primatology* 41: 117–128.

Yeong, C., Tan, C. & Meijer, L. 2010. Behavioral development in captive red-shanked douc langurs (Pygathrix nemaeus). In Nadler, T., Rawson, B. M. & Van, N. T. (Eds.), *Conservation of Primates in Indochina*. Hanoi: Frankfurt Zoological Society and Conservation International. Pp. 185–196.

Yildirim, S., Yeoman, C. J., Janga, S. C. et al. 2014. Primate vaginal microbiomes exhibit species specificity without universal lactobacillus dominance. *ISME Journal* 8: 2431–2444.

Yildirim, S., Yeoman, C. J., Sipos, M. et al. 2010. Characterization of the fecal microbiome from non-human wild primates reveals species specific microbial communities. *PLOS ONE* 5(11)L e13963.

Yin, L., Jin, T., Watanabe, K. et al. 2013. Male attacks on infants and infant death during male takeovers in wild white-headed langurs (*Trachypithecus leucocephalus*). *Integrative Zoology* 8: 365–377.

Yin, L., Liu, W., Zhao, Q. et al. 2011. A video-aided study of the diet of wild white-headed langurs (*Trachypithecus leucocephalus*). *Folia Primatologica* 82: 33–44.

Yorzinski, J. L. & Ziegler, T. 2007. Do naïve primates recognize the vocalizations of felid predators? *Ethology* 113: 1219–1227.

Yoshiba, K. 1968. Local and intertroop variability in ecology and social behavior of common Indian langurs. In Jay, P. C. (Ed.), *Primates: Studies in Adaptation and Variability*. New York: Holt, Rinehart and Winston. Pp. 217–242.

Youlatos, D. & Koufos, G. D. 2009. Locomotor evolution of *Mesopithecus* (Primates: Colobinae) from Greece: evidence from selected astragalar charactrs. *Primates* 51: 23–35.

Yu, L., Wang, G. D., Ruan, J. et al. 2016. Genomic analysis of snub-nosed monkeys (*Rhinopithecus*) identifies genes and processes related to high-altitude adaptation. *Nature Genetics* 48: 947–952.

Yu, Y., Xiang, Z., Yao, H., Grueter, C. C. & Li, M. 2013. Female snub-nosed monkeys exchange grooming for sex and infant handling. *PLOS ONE* 8: e74822.

Zachary, J. F. & McGavin, M. D. 2016. *Pathologic Basis of Veterinary Disease Expert Consult-E-BOOK*. London: Elsevier Health Sciences.

Zachos, J., Pagani, M., Sloan, L., Thomas, E. & Billups, K. 2001. Trends, rhythms, and aberrations in global climate 65 Ma to the present. *Science* 292: 686–693.

Zain, B. M. M., Morales, J. C., Hasan, M. N., Abdul, J., Lakim, M., Supriatna, J. & Melnick, D. J. 2008. Is

Presbytis a distinct monophyletic genus: inferences from mitochondrial DNA sequences. *Asian Primates Journal* 1: 26–36.

Zapata, H. J. & Quagliarello, V. J. 2015. The microbiota and microbiome in aging: potential implications in health and age-related diseases. *Journal of the American Geriatrics Society* 63: 776–781.

Zapfe, H. 1991. Mesopithecus pentelicus *Wagner aus dem Turolien von Pikermi bei Athen, Odontologie und Osteologie (Eine Dokumentation)*. Ferdinand Berger & Söhne, Vienna-Horn.

Zarfl, C., Lumsdon, A. E., Berlekamp, J., Tydecks, L. & Trockner, K. 2015. A global boom in hydropower dam construction. *Aquatic Sciences* 77: 161–170.

Zeng, Z., Estes, L., Ziegler, A. D. et al. 2018. Highland cropland expansion and forest loss in Southeast Asia in the twenty-first century. *Nature Geoscience* 11: 556.

Zhang, J., Zhao, D. & Li, B. 2010. Postconflict behavior among female Sichuan snub-nosed monkeys *Rhinopithecus roxellana* within one-male units in the Qinling Mountains, China. *Current Zoology* 56: 222–226.

Zhang, L., Hua, N. & Sun, S. 2008. Wildlife trade, consumption and conservation awareness in southwest China. *Biodiversity and Conservation* 17: 1493–1516.

Zhang, P., Li, B., MacIntosh, A. J., Watanabe, K. & Qi, X. 2012. A proximity-based social network of the Sichuan snub-nosed monkey (*Rhinopithecus roxellana*). *International Journal of Primatology* 33: 1081–1095.

Zhang, P., Watanabe, K. & Li, B. 2008a. Female social dynamics in a provisioned free-ranging band of the Sichuan snub-nosed monkey (*Rhinopithecus roxellana*) in the Qinling Mounains, China *American Journal of Primatology* 70: 1013–1022.

Zhang, P., Watanabe, K., Li, B. & Qi, X. 2008b. Dominance relationships among one-male units in a provisioned free-ranging band of the Sichuan snub-nosed monkeys (*Rhinopithecus roxellana*) in the Qinling Mountains, China. *American Journal of Primatology* 70: 634–641.

Zhang, P., Watanabe, K., Li, B. & Tan, C. L. 2006. Social organization of Sichuan snub-nosed monkeys (*Rhinopithecus roxellana*) in the Qinling Mounains, Central China. *Primates* 47: 374–382.

Zhang, S., Liang, B. & Wang, L. 1999b. Infanticide within captive groups of Sichuan golden snub-nosed monkeys (*Rhinopithecus roxellana*). *Folia Primatologica* 70: 274–276.

Zhang, S., Liang, B. & Wang, L. 2000. Seasonality of matings and births in captive Sichuan golden monkeys (*Rhinopithecus roxellana*). *American Journal of Primatology* 51: 265–269.

Zhang, S., Ren, B. & Li, B. 1999a. A juvenile Sichuan golden monkey (*Rhinopithecus roxellana*) predated by a goshawk (*Accipiter gentilis*) in the Qinling Mountains. *Folia Primatologica* 70: 175–176.

Zhang, Y. R. & Wang, S. N. 2018. Top ten conservation projects for Chinese wild animals – maintaining the beauty of the world. China Green Time (in Chinese). 3 April.

Zhang, Y.-P. & Ryder, O. A. 1998. Mitochondrial cytochrome b gene sequences of Old World Monkeys: with special reference on evolution of Asian colobines. *Primates* 39: 39–49.

Zhao, D. & Li, B. 2009a. 23 years research of Sichuan snub-nosed monkeys (*Rhinopithecus roxellana*) in Zhouzhi National Nature Reserve, China. *Asian Primates Journal* 1: 19–23.

Zhao, D. & Li, B. 2009b. Do deposed adult male Sichuan snub-nosed monkeys *Rhinopithecus roxellana* roam as solitary bachelors or continue to interact with former band members? *Current Zoology* 55: 235–237.

Zhao, D., Chen, Z., Li, B. & Romero, T. 2013. Sex-specific participation in inter-group conflicts within a multilevel society: the first evidence at the individual level. *Integrative Zoology* 8: 441–454.

Zhao, D., Ji, W., Li, B. & Watanabe, K. 2008a. Mate competition and reproductive correlates of female dispersal in a polygynous primate species (*Rhinopithecus roxellana*). *Behavioral Processes* 79: 165–170.

Zhao, D., Li, B. & Watanabe, K. 2011. Impact of group size on female reproductive success of free-ranging *Rhinopithecus roxellana* in the Qinling Mountains, China. *Folia Primatologica* 82: 1–12.

Zhao, D., Li, B., Li, Y. & Wada, K. 2005. Extra-unit sexual behaviour among wild Sichuan snub-nosed monkeys (*Rhinopithecus roxellana*) in the Qinling Mountains of China. *Folia Primatologica* 76: 172–176.

Zhao, D., Wang, X., Watanabe, K. & Li, B. 2008b. Eurasian blackbird predated by wild *Rhinopithecus roxellana* in the Qinling Mountains, China. *Integrative Zoology* 3: 176–179.

Zhao, H., Dang, G., Wang, C. et al. 2015. Diet and seasonal changes in Sichuan snub-nosed monkeys (*Rhinopithecus roxellana*) in the southern Qinling

Mountains in China. *Acta Theriologica Sinica* **35**: 130–137.

Zhao, H., Li, J., Wang, X. et al. 2020. Nutrient strategies of the Sichuan snub-nosed monkey (*Rhinopithecus roxellana*) when confronted with a shortage of food resources in the Qinling Mountains, China. *Global Ecology and Conservation* **22**: e00963.

Zhao, Q. 1988. Status of the Yunnan snub-nosed monkey. *Primate Conservation* **9**: 131–134.

Zhao, Q. 1994. Seasonal changes in body weight of *Macaca thibetana* at Mt. Emei, China. *American Journal of Primatology* **32**: 223–226.

Zhao, Q. & Pan, W. 2006. Male–immature interactions seem to depend on group composition in white-headed langur (*Trachypithecus leucocephalus*). *Acta Ethologica* **9**: 91–94.

Zhao, Q. & Tan, C. L. 2010. Inter-unit contests within a provisioned troop of Sichuan snub-nosed monkeys (*Rhinopithecus roxellana*) in the Qinling Mountains, China. *American Journal of Primatology* **73**: 262–269.

Zhao, Q., Borries, C. & Pan, W. 2011. Male takeover, infanticide, and female countertactics in white-headed leaf monkeys (*Trachypithecus leucocephalus*). *Behavioral Ecology and Sociobiology* **65**: 1535–1547.

Zhao, Q., Jin, T., Wang, D. et al. 2009. Lack of sex-biased maternal investment in spite of a skewed birth sex ratio in white-headed langurs (*Trachypithecus leucocephalus*). *Ethology* **115**: 280–286.

Zhao, Q., Liu, S., Deng, L. et al. 2012. The effects of dam construction and precipitation variability on hydrologic alteration in the Lancang River Basin of southwest China. *Stochastic Environmental Research and Risk Assessment* **26**: 993–1011.

Zhao, Q., Tan, C. L. & Pan, W. 2008. Weaning age, infant care, and behavioral development in Trachypithecus leucocephalus. *International Journal of Primatology* **29**: 583–591.

Zhao, S., Peng, C., Jiang, H., Tian, D., Lei, X. & Zhou, X. 2006. Land use change in Asia and the ecological consequences. *Ecological Research* **21**: 890–896.

Zhao, X. M., Ren, B. P., Garber, P. A., Li, X. H. & Li, M. 2018. Impacts of human activities and climate change on the distribution of snub-nosed monkeys in China during the past 2000 Years. *Diversity and Distributions* **24**: 92–102.

Zhao, X., Ren, B., Li, D. et al. 2019b. Climate change, grazing, and collecting accelerate habitat contraction in an endangered primate. *Biological Conservation* **231**: 88–97.

Zhao, X., Ren, B., Li, D. et al. 2019a. Effects of habitat fragmentation and human disturbance on the population dynamics of the Yunnan snub-nosed monkey from 1994 to 2016. *PeerJ* **7**: e6633.

Zhong, T., Xiao, L., Huo, S. et al. 2008. Altitudinal range of black-and-white snub-nosed monkeys (*Rhinopithecus bieti*) at Baima Snow Mountain, China. *Zoological Research* **29**: 181–188.

Zhou, Q., Huang, C., Li, M. & Wei, F. 2009b. Sleeping site use by *Trachypithecus francoisi* at Nonggang Nature Reserve, China. *International Journal of Primatology* **30**: 353–365.

Zhou, Q., Huang, C., Li, M. & Wei, F. 2011a. Ranging behavior of the François' langur (*Trachypithecus francoisi*) in limestone habitats of Nonggang, China. *Integrative Zoology* **6**: 157–164.

Zhou, Q., Huang, C., Li, Y. & Cai, X. 2007. Ranging behavior of the Francois' langur (*Trachypithecus francoisi*) in the Fusui Nature Reserve, China. *Primates* **48**: 320–323.

Zhou, Q., Huang, H., Tang, X. & Huang, C. M. 2010. Seasonal variation in the activity budgets of the white-headed langur. *Acta Theriologica Sinica* **30**: 449–455.

Zhou, Q., Huang, Z., Wei, X., Wei, F. & Huang, C. 2009a. Factors influencing interannual and intersite variability in the diet of Trachypithecus francoisi. *International Journal of Primatology* **30**: 583–599.

Zhou, Q., Luo, B., Wei, F. & Huang, C. 2013b. Habitat use and locomotion of the Francois' langur (*Trachypithecus francoisi*) in limestone habitats of Nonggang, China. *Integrative Zoology* **8**: 346–355.

Zhou, Q., Tang, X., Huang, H. & Huang, C. 2011b. Factors affecting the ranging behavior of whiteheaded langurs (*Trachypithecus leucocephalus*). *International Journal of Primatology* **32**: 511–523.

Zhou, Q., Tang, Z., Li, Y. & Huang, C. 2013a. Food diversity and choice of white-headed langur in fragmented limestone hill habitat in Guangxi, China. *Acta Ecologica Sinica* **33**: 109–113.

Zhou, Q., Wei, F., Li, M., Huang, C. & Luo, B. 2006. Diet and food choice of (*Trachypithecus francoisi*) in the Nonggang Nature Reserve, China. *International Journal of Primatology* **27**: 1441–1460.

Zhou, X., Meng, X., Liu, Z. et al. 2016. Population genomics reveals low genetic diversity and adaptation to hypoxia in snub-nosed monkeys. *Molecular Biology and Evolution* **33**: 2670–2681.

Zhou, X., Wang, B., Pan, Q. et al. 2014. Whole-genome sequencing of the snub-nosed monkey provides insights into folivory and evolutionary history. *Nature Genetics* **46**: 1303–1310.

Zhu, P., Grueter, C. C., Garber, P. A. et al. 2018. Seasonal changes in social cohesion among males in a same-sex primate group. *American Journal of Primatology* **80**: e22914.

Zhu, P., Ren, B., Garber, P. A. et al. 2016. Aiming low: a resident male's rank predicts takeover success by challenging males in Yunnan snub-nosed monkeys. *American Journal of Primatology* **78**: 974–982.

Zhu, Z., Huang, T., Yao, H., Yang, W. & Xiang Z. 2019. Chinese babax (*Babax lanceolatus*) was predated by a wild *Rhinopithecus roxellana* in Shennongjia National Park, China. *Acta Theriologica Sinica* **39**: 585–589.

Zimmermann, F., Köhler, S. M., Nowak, K. et al. 2017. Low antibody prevalence against Bacillus cereus biovar anthracis in Taï National Park, Côte d'ivoire, indicates high rate of lethal infections in wildlife. *PLOS Neglected Tropical Diseases* **11**: e0005960.

Zingeser, M. R. 1970. The morphological basis of the underbite trait in langurs (*P. melalophus* and *T. cristatus*) with an analysis of adaptive and evolutionary implications. *American Journal of Physical Anthropology* **32**: 179–186.

Zinner, D., Arnold, M. L. & Roos, C. 2011. The strange blood: natural hybridization in primates. *Evolutionary Anthropology* **20**: 96–103.

Zinner, D., Tesfaye, D., Stenseth, N. C. et al. 2019. Is *Colobus guereza gallarum* a valid endemic Ethiopian taxon? *Primate Biology* **6**: 7–16.

Zisheng, A., Kutzbach, J. E., Prell, W. L. & Porter, S. C. 2001. Evolution of Asian monsoons and phased uplift of the Himalaya–Tibetan plateau since Late Miocene times. *Nature* **411**: 62.

Zooniverse. 2020. South Sudan Diversity Cam. www.zooniverse.org/projects/southsudanwildlife/south-sudan-diversitycam.

Zuberbühler, K. & Jenny, D. 2007. Interaction between leopard and monkeys. In Noë, R., McGraw, S. & Zuberbühler, K. (Eds.), *Monkeys of the Taï Forest: An African Primate Community*. Cambridge: Cambridge University Press. Pp. 133–154.

Zuberbühler, K., Jenny, D. & Bshary, R. 1999. The predator deterrence function of primate alarm calls. *Ethology* **105**: 477–490.

Zuckerman, S. 1932. *The Social Life of Monkeys and Apes*. London: Kegan Paul, Trench, Trubner.

Index